THE PAPERS OF DANIEL WEBSTER

CHARLES M. WILTSE, EDITOR-IN-CHIEF

SERIES THREE: DIPLOMATIC PAPERS

Daniel Webster, by
George P. A. Healy,
1848. Department of
State, Washington,
D.C.

Lord Ashburton, by
George P. A. Healy,
1843. Department of
State, Washington,
D.C.

The Papers of
Daniel Webster

Diplomatic Papers, Volume 1

1841-1843

KENNETH E. SHEWMAKER, EDITOR

KENNETH R. STEVENS AND ANITA McGURN,

ASSISTANT EDITORS

PUBLISHED FOR

DARTMOUTH COLLEGE BY THE

UNIVERSITY PRESS OF NEW ENGLAND

HANOVER, NEW HAMPSHIRE AND

LONDON, ENGLAND 1983

THE UNIVERSITY PRESS

OF NEW ENGLAND

Sponsoring Institutions

BRANDEIS UNIVERSITY

BROWN UNIVERSITY

CLARK UNIVERSITY

DARTMOUTH COLLEGE

UNIVERSITY OF NEW HAMPSHIRE

UNIVERSITY OF RHODE ISLAND

TUFTS UNIVERSITY

UNIVERSITY OF VERMONT

The edition of the Papers of Daniel Webster, of which this is Volume 1 in the Diplomatic Series, has been made possible through grants from the Program for Editions of the National Endowment for the Humanities, an independent Federal agency; and through the continuing support, both administrative and financial, of the National Historical Publications and Records Commission. The edition is sponsored and published by Dartmouth College.

Foreword

The commercial world and its robust subsidiaries, manufacturing, banking, and transportation, had constituted the setting for Webster's professional life since his admission to the Massachusetts bar in 1805. The buyers and sellers, the shippers and mill owners and bankers were his clients, his constituents, and his friends. Their world was his world, not the less so because he had accepted Harrison's offer to head the cabinet in 1841. The process of fusing the former British colonies into a commercial empire in their own right was begun by John Adams, who led the country through an undeclared war with France in defense of trade. The peace-loving Jefferson had used the Navy rather than the Treasury to ransom American commerce from the Barbary pirates; and Madison had fought with Britain to keep the sea lanes open. Webster, himself a man of world vision, was prepared to use all the resources of his department to extend and enlarge the international trade that constituted for him the sinews of national prosperity.

As Professor Shewmaker ably shows in this first volume of Webster's diplomatic papers, he pursued his goal with single-minded zeal as long as he remained secretary of state. He was responsible for our first mission to China, for bringing the Hawaiian Islands into the American sphere of influence, and for broadening the base of our representation in Latin America. He extended for the first time the protection of the flag to American missionaries abroad; and he joined with Great Britain and other European powers in a concerted attempt to suppress the African slave trade. His every effort was directed toward peace and commerce with all the world.

His mercantile orientation is most clearly shown in his negotiations with Lord Ashburton, which comprise the largest single segment of this book. Reflecting the aspirations and economic faith of a commercial people knocking at the door of world power, he believed that trade between nations was more important than a few square miles of territory. Although for a variety of compelling reasons the United States and Great Britain were drifting perilously close to war, the fact remained that one-third of American imports came from the United Kingdom while almost half of our exports were taken by that country. The continuation of this mutually profitable trade required a settlement of outstanding differences, and settled they were in the Treaty of Washington. Diplomacy for Webster was indeed the handmaiden of commerce.

CHARLES M. WILTSE

Acknowledgments

Many individuals and institutions have assisted in the creation of this volume, and it is a genuine pleasure to be able to acknowledge their contributions. The source of each document printed in *Diplomatic 1* is indicated by a location symbol, and the editors are indebted to the archives, historical societies, individual collectors, and libraries that have made these documents available. In particular, the editors would like to thank Roger A. Bruns, Dianne M. Buncombe, Sara Dunlap Jackson, and Mary A. Giunta of the National Historical Publications and Records Commission. The frequent and cheerful assistance of these able and dedicated professionals made this volume possible. The staff of Baker Library at Dartmouth College, and especially Patricia A. Carter, Virginia Close, Robert D. Jaccaud, and William S. Moran, also provided a continuous support system that was essential to the completion of the *Diplomatic Papers*. Anthony A. Roth of the Historical Society of Pennsylvania and Robert Sparks of the Massachusetts Historical Society rendered valuable aid in the identification of several obscure historical figures. The editors also are grateful to Harvard University Press and to Lois Bannister Merk for permission to reprint the map entitled "Northeastern Boundary Problem 1798–1842" as published in *Fruits of Propaganda in the Tyler Administration* by Frederick Merk, Cambridge, Mass.: Copyright (c) 1971 by the President and Fellows of Harvard College. Peter Kelemen and Mark Sonnenfeld of Dartmouth College not only redrew the "Northeastern Boundary Problem" map for this volume, but they also contributed the excellent maps on the Northwest Boundary and the Oregon Question.

The editors also are profoundly grateful to those who have generously provided the financial support for the *Diplomatic Papers*: Dartmouth College, the National Endowment for the Humanities, the National Historical Publications and Records Commission, and Mr. A. Marvin Braverman, Dartmouth Class of 1929, of Washington, D.C.

In addition to Mr. Braverman, other Dartmouth men and women helped in a variety of ways. Many colleagues in the Department of History took time from busy schedules to share their expertise and to read various parts of the manuscript: Jere R. Daniell (United States), Gene R. Garthwaite (Middle East), Michael D. Green (Native American), P. David Lagomarsino (Spain), John S. Major (China), Marysa Navarro (Latin America), Leo Spitzer (Africa), and Heide Whelan (Russia).

Donald W. McNemar, the Headmaster of Phillips Andover Academy and an authority on international law, also helped to make this a better book than it otherwise would have been. The editors also very much appreciate the encouragement of Presidents John G. Kemeny and David T. McLaughlin, Provost Leonard M. Rieser, and Executive Officer of the Faculty of Arts and Sciences William B. Durant. Mr. Durant, in particular, was unfailingly helpful in dealing with the manifold administrative and financial arrangements involved in the publication of *Diplomatic* 1. Gail M. Patten, the efficient Administrative Assistant of the Department of History, meticulously typed much of the manuscript, which facilitated matters greatly. The large Dartmouth contribution also included the following student research assistants: Alan Berolzheimer, Lisa Campney, John W. Christy, John G. Douglass, Michael R. Elitzer, Robert A. Gagnon, Michael C. Hanson, William J. Lynn, and Scott N. Peters. Finally, Mrs. Lore Spalteholz of Hanover, N.H., and Mr. and Mrs. Wilfred Thuren of Norwich, Vermont were of assistance in translating some documents in German, Norwegian, and Swedish.

A very special word of appreciation goes to the staff of the Webster Papers. Charles M. Wiltse, the Editor-in-Chief, read the entire manuscript and made many thoughtful suggestions. Mary V. Anstruther, Assistant to the Editor-in-Chief, also helped out in a variety of ways. Finally, Harold Moser, now editor of the Papers of Andrew Jackson, contributed not only his special skills as a scholar, but also extended the gift of friendship.

Contents

Maps appear on pages 482, 625, and 827

Introduction

On November 19, 1841, shortly after returning to Washington from a vacation in Massachusetts, Daniel Webster wrote the following note to Charles Henry Thomas, the supervisor of his 1,400-acre estate at Marshfield:[1]

> Here I am, at my table, and my work—in good health, but not feeling so well as when I was in the Boat with Seth, or sitting under the bushes up at 'Island Creek Pond.' . . . I ought to have been a fisherman. But it is too late to change.

Posterity can be glad that Webster persevered at his desk and did not devote his life to catching fish, for as secretary of state he established a distinguished record. In the basic work on the office of secretary of state, Alexander De Conde has ranked Webster among the top ten diplomatists in American history.[2]

In light of that high standing, one might assume that historians have devoted considerable attention to Webster's career at the Department of State. This, however, is not the case. Most of the scholarship on the Republic's first Whig secretary of state has focused on the monumental treaty with Lord Ashburton of 1842, and De Conde's favorable assessment of Webster is based primarily upon the negotiation of that accord. The understandable emphasis of historians on the Treaty of Washington has led to a neglect of other aspects of Webster's record and has made him what might be called a lesser-known great secretary of state.

This is the first of two volumes designed to fill the large gaps in existing accounts of one of America's outstanding secretaries of state. Edward Everett's *The Diplomatic and Official Papers of Daniel Webster while Secretary of State*, published in 1848, is the only edition of Webster's state papers.[3] Everett's authorized work does not approach modern editorial standards. He did not include selections from Webster's private correspondence, he omitted some important documents, he frequently printed extracts instead of the complete text, he did not provide annotations, he "improved" Webster's prose, and, of course, he did not deal with

1. Daniel Webster to Charles Henry Thomas, November 19, 1841, NhD.

2. Alexander De Conde, *The American Secretary of State: An Interpretation* (New York, 1962), p. 172.

3. [Edward Everett, ed.], *The Diplomatic and Official Papers of Daniel Webster while Secretary of State* (New York, 1848).

Webster's second incumbency at the Department of State from 1850 to 1852. In order to remedy these shortcomings and to provide a balanced account of Webster's career, a careful search has been made of the existing primary sources. The official records of the Department of State for the twenty-four countries with which the United States held diplomatic relations from 1841 to 1843 have been read, as has Webster's private correspondence.[4] Other important collections such as correspondence with miscellaneous foreign states, the records of boundary and claims commissions, and special missions have been scrutinized, as have the consular files for Canton, Havana, Honolulu, Montevideo, Shanghai, and Zanzibar. The documents printed below have been selected from this mountain of primary sources. The purpose of this volume is to provide a comprehensive overview of Webster's record in the Department of State from 1841 to 1843 and to illuminate his role in the formulation of American foreign policy.

When Webster became William Henry Harrison's secretary of state on March 6, 1841, he was a vigorous man at the height of his career. He entered office with a towering national and international reputation as an outstanding lawyer, orator, and politician. Since the famous debate with Senator Robert Y. Hayne in 1830, Webster had been a leading spokesman for American nationalism; by 1841 he was widely known as a defender of the Constitution and an upholder of the Union. At the age of fifty-nine, Webster was robust and full of zest for life. A hard worker, he typically rose at four o'clock in the morning, put in a twelve-hour day, and was among the first to arrive at the Department of State and the last to leave.

Physical stamina was not all that qualified Webster for the position of secretary of state. Among the qualities thought desirable for that high office are experience in diplomacy, law, politics, and travel abroad Webster had never held a diplomatic appointment; nor, aside from a smattering of French, did he command any modern foreign language. On the other side, he had become acquainted with many European leaders such as Sir Robert Peel and King Louis Philippe during a six-month visit to England and the Continent in 1839. Webster certainly met the legal and political standards for an ideal secretary of state. As a young man, he studied under an eminent international lawyer, Christopher Gore, and beginning with maritime cases growing out of the War of 1812, Webster gained an extensive knowledge of international law through his own legal practice. This background helps to explain the enduring contribu-

4. From 1841 to 1843 the United States held diplomatic relations with the following countries: Austria, Belgium, Brazil, Chile, Colombia, Denmark, France, Great Britain. Hawaii, Mexico, Morocco, Netherlands, Peru, Portugal, Prussia, Russia, Sardinia, Spain, Sweden and Norway, Texas, Tunis, Turkey (Ottoman Empire), the Two Sicilies, and Venezuela.

tions to international jurisprudence that Webster made while serving as secretary of state, the most noteworthy being the important doctrine of self-defense that he set forth in relation to the *Caroline* and McLeod disputes. As for political qualifications, by 1841 Webster had a total of twenty years of service in Congress, eight as a representative from New Hampshire and Massachusetts and twelve as a senator from Massachusetts.

In addition to legal and political expertise, Webster brought to the office of secretary of state intelligence, the gift of presence, and an ability to get along well with his peers. John Quincy Adams, who tended to assume the worst about Webster, assessed him as an envious man with a "ravenous ambition" and a "rotten heart." But Adams granted that the new secretary of state possessed a "gigantic intellect."[5] Webster's intellectual brilliance is reflected in his state papers, which, for the most part, are thoughtful, tightly reasoned, and clearly written. As for ambition, since 1830 Webster had yearned for the presidency. "At thirty," he once told his friend William Plumer, "Alexander had conquered the world; and I am forty."[6] That driving ambition had not always worked to Webster's advantage. By 1841 he was deeply in debt, and his name was popularly associated with the interests of the financial titans of Boston, Philadelphia, and New York City. A compulsive spender, Webster was renowned for his improvidence with money and an opulent way of life. These shortcomings were counterbalanced, however, by his graciousness, dignified bearing, and courtly manners. Webster was no saint, but he was an impressive and charismatic leader who did everything with style. Lord Ashburton, for example, relished Webster's imported madeira and lively table talk as an escape from the intense pressures of negotiation, and even the puritanical and crotchety Adams invariably found Webster to be an engaging and amiable host.

As the nation's foremost diplomat, Webster's demeanor was important, especially in relating to the presidents under whom he served. The office of secretary of state is an extension of the presidency, and the main responsibility of the secretary of state is to assist the chief executive in formulating, interpreting, and implementing American foreign policy. The key variable in determining a secretary's effectiveness is his relationship with the president. Webster got on well with Harrison, for whom he had campaigned in 1840. On April 4, 1841, however, precisely one month after his inauguration, Harrison became the first president to die in office. For Webster, this meant establishing a rapport with John Tyler, a rigid states' rights Whig and slaveholder from Virginia. It is a tribute to both men that they overcame their many differences and worked together as a smoothly coordinated team. Tyler came to regard Webster

5. Adams, *Memoirs*, 11:20.
6. William Plumer, "Reminiscences

of Daniel Webster," in *W&S*, 17:560.

as a model cabinet officer and "the first among statesmen."[7] In an address titled "The Dead of the Cabinet" delivered by Tyler in 1856, the former president praised his former secretary of state as able, deferential, and firm in upholding the interests of the United States.[8]

Initially, Tyler and Webster were united by their mutual dislike for Henry Clay, the dynamic leader of the Whig party in Congress. Webster had supported Harrison's candidacy in 1840 from a determination that if he could not have the nomination, it would not go to his great rival from Kentucky either. On September 11, 1841, following Tyler's second veto of a national bank bill, Clay engineered a political crisis. The entire Tyler cabinet resigned, with the notable exception of the secretary of state. He remained at his post for several reasons. Webster liked the secretaryship and the prestige that went with being the chief cabinet officer, he shared Tyler's suspicion of Clay's motives, he wanted to advance his presidential aspirations through diplomatic achievement, and he genuinely hoped to resolve the pressing Anglo-American differences that were then in the process of negotiation. The entire Massachusetts congressional delegation backed Webster's decision to remain at his post, Adams basing his support on the belief that Webster's presence "was indispensably necessary to save us from a most disastrous and calamitous war" with England.[9]

Tyler was formally read out of the Whig party on September 13, 1841, and as time passed Webster's position became increasingly awkward. With the ratification of the Treaty of Washington in August 1842, the same Whigs who had urged him to remain as secretary of state a year earlier called upon him to leave office. Supreme Court Justice Joseph Story, a trusted friend, advised Webster to resign with the same pen with which he had signed the agreement with Ashburton. Instead of following what appeared to be sound political logic, Webster persisted in the high-risk decision of remaining with a president without a party. When the Massachusetts Whig state convention declared a final and complete separation from Tyler and endorsed Clay for the presidency in mid-September, Webster responded in character. In a defiant speech to a Whig audience at Faneuil Hall on September 30, he ended any possibility of a graceful exit from the Tyler administration. "I am, Gentlemen," he snapped, "a little hard to coax, but as to being driven, that is out of the question."[10]

Not only was Daniel Webster a stubborn individualist who did not respond mildly to pressure, but he also had never been a strong party man. There was a maverick quality to Webster, and he shared some of

7. Cited in Oliver Perry Chitwood, *John Tyler: Champion of the Old South* (New York and London, 1939), pp. 269–270.

8. *Tylers*, 2:393–394.
9. Adams, *Memoirs*, 11:36.
10. *W & S*, 3:125.

the antiparty sentiments of the Founding Fathers. He believed in government by disinterested gentlemen and found the partisanship of the Age
of Jackson distasteful. Webster's disregard for party regularity in 1842
might have cost him any chance of a presidential nomination, for he
alienated many Whigs. To add insult to injury, he soon discovered that
his days in the Tyler administration were numbered. When the president
moved toward association with loco foco Democrats and the annexation
of slaveholding Texas in the winter of 1842–1843, Webster no longer
had much choice. Tyler needed a secretary of state, his son recalled, willing to "go the full length of the Texas question. Certainly that man was
not Webster."[11] When Webster finally resigned on May 8, 1843, he not
only had lost ground in his intense struggle with Henry Clay for the
leadership of the Whig party but also was bereft of power and influence
even in his home state of Massachusetts. Webster had before him a massive job of political rebuilding, but he left behind an outstanding record
in foreign policy.

International politics were nearly as deranged as American domestic
politics in the early 1840s, and the United States and Great Britain
seemed to be on a collision course toward war. The crisis in Anglo-
American relations was a compound of many elements, but the most
pressing issue when Webster assumed office was the strange case of
Alexander McLeod, which John Quincy Adams aptly summarized as
"that wretched question about the State right of New York to hang Mc-
Leod."[12] On November 12, 1840, McLeod, a Canadian deputy sheriff,
had been arrested in Lewiston, New York and charged with murder and
arson in connection with the *Caroline* incident of 1837. The *Caroline*
was an American steamer engaged in supplying arms and munitions to
Canadian rebels under the leadership of William L. Mackenzie, and the
destruction of that vessel was the most explosive occurrence of the short-
lived Canadian uprising of 1837–1838. On the night of December 29,
Canadian soldiers boarded the *Caroline*, which was moored at Schlosser,
New York. They set the steamer on fire and towed it into the Niagara
River, where it sank just short of the falls. During the fracas, an American named Amos Durfee was killed. Not only had the *Caroline* affair
resulted in the death of an American citizen and the destruction of
American property, but it also constituted a violation of American territorial sovereignty. From the date of the *Caroline* incident onward, the
authorities of the state of New York were on the lookout for any of those
who might have been involved in the events of December 29, 1837. Such
is the background to the arrest and indictment of Alexander McLeod.

With the Van Buren administration taking the position that it could
do nothing to interfere with the legal processes of the sovereign state of

11. *Tylers*, 2:263–264.   12. Adams, *Memoirs*, 11:36.

New York, Lord Palmerston, the fiery British foreign secretary, truculently threatened on February 9, 1841 that "McLeod's execution would produce war; war immediate and frightful in its character, because it would be a war of retaliation and vengeance."[13] The duke of Wellington thought war probable, as did Henry S. Fox, the British minister to the United States. Reports from Lewis Cass and Andrew Stevenson, the American envoys to France and to England, respectively, emphasized the clear and present danger of an Anglo-American conflict. Stevenson was so jittery that he advised Commodore Isaac Hull to move the Mediterranean squadron closer to the United States. On September 30, President Tyler personally intimated to Fox that if McLeod were convicted and executed, he would try to prevent a rupture in Anglo-American relations by denying the British minister his passport. With the advantage of hindsight, some historians have assumed that there was no real possibility of war in 1841, but hindsight was an advantage denied to Webster and Tyler. Like many contemporaries, the new secretary of state believed that the McLeod affair constituted a serious threat to peace, and he acted accordingly.

Webster reversed the policy of his predecessor, John Forsyth, and accepted the British contention that since those involved in the raid upon the *Caroline* were acting under the orders of British authorities in Canada, the issue was properly one between the United States government and that of England, not one between Alexander McLeod and the state of New York. Webster also prepared for the possibility of war with Britain by sending a secret agent, Albert Fitz, on a mission of reconnaissance to the Caribbean. Confidential agents also infiltrated the ranks of the so-called Patriot Hunters. These secret societies of Canadian rebels and American sympathizers were spread across the length of the Canadian-American frontier. With a membership estimated at 40,000 to 50,000, they were formidable enough to be a cause for concern. They tried to embroil the United States and Britain in war by threatening to assassinate McLeod, and they later made several attempts to disrupt the Webster-Ashburton negotiations. In 1841, however, Webster sought above all to avert a conflict for which the United States was ill prepared by securing the release of McLeod from a New York jail.

Webster's effort to secure McLeod's freedom was frustrated by the division of federal and state powers, which prevented the federal government from bringing a case involving international relations under its immediate jurisdiction. Governor William Henry Seward of New York was not eager to risk his political career by releasing McLeod, but Webster was equally determined not to allow events simply to take their course. The result was a spectacular federal-state confrontation with

13. Palmerston to Fox, February 9, 1841, FO 97/19 (PRO).

important constitutional implications. The U.S. government, as Fox wrote to Palmerston on July 27, 1841, found itself "in the embarrassing position of having its interpretation of international law contradicted by an inferior power."[14] The strain in Anglo-American relations eased in September when Sir Robert Peel became prime minister and the conciliatory Lord Aberdeen replaced Palmerston as foreign secretary, but the McLeod case was still unresolved. Unable to halt the proceedings, Webster planned to seek a writ of error from the U.S. Supreme Court in the event of McLeod's conviction. Moreover, the secretary of state, who in private life was one of the most highly regarded lawyers in the United States, confidentially offered legal advice to McLeod's counsel, Joshua A. Spencer, who shortly after taking McLeod's case was appointed U.S. district attorney for the Northern District of New York. When Governor Seward demanded that President Tyler remove Spencer from the case, the correspondence between the two men became so bitter that the president refused to discuss the matter further, and it was Webster who had to maintain communications with Albany. Ironically, when the case finally went to trial in October 1841, it took the jury less than twenty minutes to declare Alexander McLeod, who had an airtight alibi, not guilty.

To his credit, Webster did not simply breathe a sigh of relief at the release of McLeod. In an act of creative statesmanship, he drafted a law that allowed future cases involving persons acting under the authority of a foreign government to be removed from state to federal jurisdiction. On August 29, 1842, Congress passed what might be called the "McLeod law."

In a broader perspective, McLeod's acquittal on October 12, 1841, was a necessary prelude to the resolution of the larger issues that endangered Anglo-American relations. Foremost among those larger issues was the boundary between the United States and British North America. Nearly the entire line from Maine to Oregon was unresolved, but in 1841 the focus of attention was on the tinderbox situation in the Northeast. Webster aptly characterized the northeastern boundary question as "entangled in meshes" of "projects and counterprojects, explorations and arbitrations."[15] The problem dated to the Peace of Paris of 1783, and it involved not only the line between Maine and New Brunswick but also that at the head of the Connecticut River in New Hampshire and that along the forty-fifth parallel in Vermont and New York. The peace commissioners of 1783 had framed articles of settlement based upon imprecise geographical information, and they had failed to attach a map to the Paris accord. Furthermore, in 1818 it was discovered that because

14. Cited in Alastair Watt, "The Case of Alexander McLeod," *Canadian Historical Review*, 12 (June 1931): 155.
15. W & S, 9:87, 97.

of an inaccurate survey of the forty-fifth parallel, the United States had unknowingly constructed a million-dollar fort at Rouses Point that was entirely on British territory. Fort Montgomery, or "Fort Blunder" as it was thereafter known, was regarded by American military experts as the most important strategic installation on the northern frontier, and they wanted to keep it. Even today such communities as Derby Line, Vermont, are divided by a meandering line about a quarter mile too far north of the midline between the North Pole and the equator. Citing records of the liquor consumed, local historians believe that British surveyor John Collins was inebriated on the job in 1774.[16] In 1827 Britain and the United States submitted the northeastern boundary dispute to the king of the Netherlands for arbitration. When that monarch went beyond the protocol of arbitration and suggested a compromise of the issue, however, in 1832 the U.S. Senate voted not to accept the king's decision. The boundary from Lake Superior to the Lake of the Woods also had never been agreed upon. The major dispute involved 12,027 square miles in contention between Maine and New Brunswick, but the entire line from the Saint Croix River to the Lake of the Woods needed pacification.

Not the least of Webster's qualifications for the office of secretary of state was his familiarity with the northeastern boundary controversy. In 1839, he submitted to the Van Buren administration a farsighted proposal for resolving the dispute. The Democrats had not adopted Webster's plan for an informal negotiation looking toward a settlement based upon a conventional line, but as secretary of state Webster had the opportunity to implement his own ideas.[17]

The controversy over the boundary was the most important of a plethora of differences between the United States and Great Britain. Also at issue between the two countries was the still unsettled *Caroline* dispute; the self-proclaimed right of the British to visit and search American vessels on the high seas in order to suppress the African slave trade; the related and historic quarrel over impressment; the question of renewing the extradition provision of the Jay Treaty, which had expired in 1807; and the *Creole* affair, which occurred after Webster became secretary of state and involved the mutiny of American slaves and their escape to British territory. All of these issues were on the agenda when Webster and Ashburton sat down together at the negotiating table in the summer of 1842.

Senator Thomas Hart Benton of Missouri complained that the Webster-Ashburton negotiations had been "tracklessly conducted," and it certainly is one of the least well documented of the major negotiations in American history.[18] Adhering to his plan of an informal approach, Web-

16. See "Partly in Vermont: A Borderline Case," *Time*, August 13, 1979.

17. "Memorandum on the Northeast Boundary Negotiations" *Correspondence*, 4:346–349.

18. *Cong. Globe*, 27th Cong., 3d sess., app., p. 14.

ster studiously avoided protocol and the usual procedures of diplomacy. No minutes were kept and few notes were exchanged. The articles of the treaty and related correspondence dealing with disputes such as that over the *Caroline* were drafted after Webster and Ashburton had reached agreement and were then submitted to Tyler for final review. President Tyler and his secretary of state worked harmoniously together. The former exercised overall supervision and on one occasion rendered valuable assistance by persuading an exhausted British envoy to postpone the fulfillment of a repeatedly expressed desire to escape the intense heat of muggy Washington by returning to the cooler breezes of England. But it was Daniel Webster who hammered out the accord, initialed on August 9. The Treaty of Washington, as it was known at the time, was an achievement in personal diplomacy, a procedure commonplace in our time but one unusual by nineteenth-century standards.

The Webster-Ashburton Treaty also qualifies as one of the most complicated and controversial in American history. In terms of territory, it involved more than seven million acres of land bordering on the four states of Maine, New Hampshire, New York, and Vermont. In terms of participants in the negotiations, it involved the four parties of Great Britain, the United States, and state commissioners from Maine and Massachusetts. In terms of issues, it involved complex boundary disputes, the African slave trade, the right of visit and search, impressment, extradition, and the *Caroline* and *Creole* affairs. In terms of consequences, it fixed the boundary that now exists between Canada and the United States, resolved disputes nearly as old as Daniel Webster himself, left little of a significant nature other than the Oregon question for the United States and Britain to quarrel over, and paved the way for an Anglo-American rapprochement.

With more than a touch of pride, Webster favorably compared his achievement to the labors of Castlereagh, Nesselrode, Metternich, and Talleyrand—a judgment not universally shared by others.[19] Palmerston assessed what he called "Lord Ashburton's capitulation" as an imbecile treaty and one of the worst ever negotiated, and historian Samuel Flagg Bemis has sourly concluded that "Webster achieved a diplomatic triumph —against his own country."[20] The Treaty of Washington is certainly open to criticism, especially in view of its failure to address the Oregon question, but the opinions of Palmerston and Bemis represent untenable extremes. The accord with Ashburton ended a potentially explosive crisis

19. *W & S*, 9:94.

20. Palmerston as cited in Howard Jones, *To the Webster-Ashburton Treaty: A Study in Anglo-American Relations, 1783–1843* (Chapel Hill, N.C., 1977), p. 170, and Herbert

C. F. Bell, *Lord Palmerston* (2 vols., London, New York, and Toronto, 1936), 2:333; Samuel Flagg Bemis, *John Quincy Adams and the Foundations of American Foreign Policy* (New York, 1949), p. 481.

with Britain and brought tranquillity to a Canadian-American frontier that had been chronically troubled since 1837. The joint cruising convention, in which both countries promised to maintain an independent naval force of at least eighty guns off the west coast of Africa to cooperate in suppressing the slave trade, quieted the visit and search controversy. To attain that article of the treaty, Webster had to walk a tightrope between the antislavery inclinations of New England abolitionists and the proslavery inclinations of President Tyler. Both the *Caroline* and *Creole* disputes were finessed in supplemental correspondence accompanying the agreement, and Webster's masterful letter on impressment had the merit of forcefully stating the American position on that irreconcilable subject. The extradition article was more important than has been generally recognized. It helped to put an end to the lawless operations of the Patriot Hunters, and it served as a model for extradition treaties with other countries. As Webster stated, "It has never been complained of by any body, except by murderers, and fugitives, and felons themselves." Webster also judged the retention of Rouses Point to be "forty times" more valuable than any strategic advantages gained by the British.[21] Overall, the Webster-Ashburton Treaty was a reasonable compromise of Anglo-American differences on terms honorable to both sides.

Most of the criticism of the Webster-Ashburton agreement has dealt less with the terms of the treaty itself than with the means employed in obtaining that accord. The controversy over means originated in 1846 when Congressman Charles Jared Ingersoll attempted to impeach Webster retroactively for misconduct while serving as secretary of state. Ingersoll, a Democrat from Pennsylvania and chairman of the House Committee on Foreign Affairs, initially charged Webster with obstructing McLeod's trial, paying Spencer's fee from federal funds, and warning Seward that New York City would be "laid in ashes" unless McLeod were released. These accusations got nowhere, and Webster further humiliated Ingersoll by delivering a punishing speech in which he remarked that his accuser possessed a "grotesque" mind with screws "loose all over." Ingersoll then brought a new set of charges against Webster. The former secretary of state, he said, had unlawfully used the secret contingent fund to corrupt the press in Maine and had left the Department of State with some $1,200 of that fund unaccounted for. After taking testimony from former president Tyler and others, a select committee of the House of Representatives concluded on June 9, 1846, that there was no evidence "to impeach Mr. Webster's integrity or the purity of his motives in the discharge of the duties of his office."[22] Although Webster's name was cleared in 1846, the taint of scandal has lingered. In 1971, Frederick

21. *W & S*, 9:110.
22. Howard Jones, "The Attempt to Impeach Daniel Webster," *Capitol Studies*, 3 (Fall 1975): 31–41. See also *Correspondence* 6.

Merk concluded that Webster had used unworthy means to achieve a worthy end and that he was "undoubtedly guilty of improper use of secret funds."[23]

The question of whether Webster employed unethical means centers on the actions he took in trying to moderate the behavior of the inhabitants of the state of Maine. Since the interest of Massachusetts in the northeastern boundary question was almost purely financial, the main obstacle to a negotiated settlement was the intransigence of Maine. The Maine legislature resolved in 1838 that it would not accept any negotiation by the U.S. government for a compromise line, and two years later it called upon the federal authorities to occupy the area in dispute. To surmount the obstacle of state particularism, Webster adopted a plan set forth by Francis O. J. Smith, a newspaper publisher and former Democratic congressman from Maine. The idea was not to coerce Maine to approve any specific line. Rather, it was to induce the people, politicians, and press of Maine to agree to the appointment of state commissioners authorized to participate in and to consent to a negotiated compromise of the disputed boundary. Webster's new approach, then, was to seek a conventional line with the assent of Maine and Massachusetts. That approach did not involve imposing a settlement on Maine. During the negotiations, for example, Webster was willing to relinquish the Madawaska settlements to England. Because the Maine commissioners proved to be tough bargainers, however, Lord Ashburton ended up conceding the southern Madawaska to the United States. When it came to the northeastern boundary issue, Webster played the role of mediator between the men of Maine and the British envoy.

The ethical problem was that the Smith-Webster plan had involved a $12,000, ten-month sub rosa propaganda campaign in Maine financed out of the secret service fund. That account had been established by Congress in 1810 "for the contingent expenses of intercourse between the United States and foreign nations "[24] The $12,000 was used to plant articles in journals and newspapers, to circulate pacific memorials, and to pay lobbyists such as Smith, Jared Sparks, and Peleg Sprague. Sparks, for example, made a special trip to Augusta in May 1842 to show Governor John Fairfield two maps, one drawn by Sparks himself, indicating that cartographical evidence tended to support the British claim. Webster himself undertook a similar mission to Massachusetts, and he authored unsigned editorials in the Washington, D.C., *National Intelligencer* emphasizing the theme that a negotiated settlement was the only alternative to a calamitous war. The well-orchestrated Smith-Webster campaign culminated in the vote of the Maine legislature on May 26 to ap-

23. Frederick Merk, *Fruits of Propaganda in the Tyler Administration* (Cambridge, Mass., 1971), p. 72.

24. 2 *U.S. Stat.* 608–609.

point four commissioners empowered to accept a conventional line, provided they were unanimous in their decision.

The controversy over means has a sequel, for Webster also sent the famous Sparks map, along with the treaty and other documents, to the U.S. Senate. He never maintained that this dubious piece of cartography was definitive, but he implied that it would work to the disadvantage of the United States in the event that the treaty failed and Britain and America had to engage in another arbitration of the northeastern boundary issue. On August 20, the Senate advised and consented to the Treaty of Washington by an overwhelming vote of 39 to 9. In light of the stormy political atmosphere prevailing at the time, that was a surprisingly large majority. The president had become so unpopular that an influenza epidemic was nicknamed the "Tyler Grippe," and the standing of the secretary of state in the Whig party was doubtful.[25] As Richard N. Current has pointed out, the negotiation and ratification of the Webster-Ashburton Treaty was as much a triumph in "the manipulation of public opinion" as it was an achievement of diplomacy.[26]

The Treaty of Washington is generally regarded as Webster's greatest diplomatic achievement. However controversial the means employed, the agreement did have the merit, as Merk conceded, "of preserving peace."[27] Most scholars do not believe that allowing Britain 893 square miles more than the Netherlands award of 1831 was too great a price to pay for avoiding the possibility of a third Anglo-American war. Charles S. Campbell, for example, has assessed the Webster-Ashburton Treaty as a "monument to British-American good sense."[28]

Webster's reputation as one of America's greatest secretaries of state rests almost solely upon the negotiation of the accord with Lord Ashburton. Scholars have focused so much on that agreement that other aspects of his secretaryship have been underestimated. From most accounts of Webster's first term at the Department of State, one might assume that the only significant event of those years was the treaty of 1842. This, however, is far from being the case. Not only did Webster usher in a new and friendlier era in Anglo-American relations, but he also pioneered in establishing an American foreign policy toward the Pacific and East Asia. Furthermore, he earned the distinction of being the first secretary of state to extend to American missionaries abroad the full diplomatic protection of the United States government.

The so-called Tyler Doctrine ranks as one of Daniel Webster's more

25. Chitwood, *John Tyler*, p. 318.

26. Richard N. Current, "Webster's Propaganda and the Ashburton Treaty," *Mississippi Valley Historical Review*, 34 (September 1947): 187.

27. Merk, *Fruits of Propaganda*, p. 32.

28. Charles S. Campbell, *From Revolution to Rapprochement: The United States and Great Britain, 1783–1900* (New York, 1974), p. 62.

important diplomatic achievements. Contained in President Tyler's special message to Congress of December 30, 1842, it stated emphatically that in regard to Hawaii the United States opposed "any attempt by another power . . . to take possession of the islands, colonize them, and subvert the native Government."[29] Not only had those words been drafted by the secretary of state, but they also were preceded by his December 19 statement to the Hawaiian envoys Timoteo Haalilio and William Richards that the United States was "more interested in the fate of the Islands and of their government, than any other Nation."[30] With the Tyler Doctrine, the United States took the lead in upholding Hawaiian independence. Although the message of 1842 did not specifically invoke the Monroe Doctrine, it was phrased in terms reminiscent of the principles of 1823 and applied some of those maxims to the Sandwich islands. Webster had long been a staunch defender of what he called Monroe's "declaration." In a speech delivered before the House of Representatives on April 14, 1826, Webster called Monroe's "declaration" a national "treasure of reputation" and vowed "to guard it."[31] In addition to drawing upon the principles of the past, the Tyler Doctrine anticipated those of the future. Like the second Open Door Note of 1900, it called for maintaining the territorial integrity of a weak nation threatened by European colonialism.

If the Tyler Doctrine was the first major assertion of an American interest in the Pacific region, the Treaty of Wanghia of 1844 was the second. That important agreement established diplomatic relations between China and the United States and put American trading rights on a legal basis. Caleb Cushing negotiated the Wanghia accord under instructions from Webster dated May 8, 1843, the same day that the secretary of state submitted his resignation.

The Treaty of Washington—the only agreement in American history in which the United States relinquished a substantial amount of territory that it had claimed as its own—suggests that Webster was not much of a territorial expansionist. He was, however, a commercial expansionist who sought to promote American trade. Like most New England Whigs, Webster was port oriented.[32] He initiated the Cushing mission partly in response to the desire of the China-trade merchants to replace an economic relationship based upon Chinese sufferance with one clearly defined by treaty rights. The mission also reflected the influence of Peter Parker, the first American medical missionary to China. At Webster's request, on January 30, 1841, Parker wrote the secretary-designate an important letter outlining his proposals for a treaty negotiation with the Chinese empire. In 1841, as John Quincy Adams expressed it, "The time

29. *Messages and Papers*, 4:212.
30. See pp. 870–871, below.
31. *Works*, 3:200.
32. See Norman A. Graebner, *Empire on the Pacific: A Study in American Continental Expansion* (New York, 1955), p. 70.

had not yet come, either in our own history or in that of China, for a diplomatic mission from the United States to the Celestial Empire."[33] By 1843, however, the Opium War had been terminated by the Treaty of Nanking, which opened four new ports to the British victors. The time was now ripe for a move by the United States.

As in the negotiations over the northeastern boundary, Webster relied on what we today call experts in the formation of a policy toward China. On March 20, 1843, he sought information and opinions from knowledgeable persons by distributing a circular to those involved in the China trade. By April, the secretary of state had a wealth of informed responses at his disposal, and much of the advice was incorporated into the instruction of May 8. Webster even carefully scrutinized a list of gifts to be given to Chinese officials, with an eye toward impressing them with the power and technological sophistication of the United States. Included among the items were a model American steam engine and a global map to enable "the Celestials" to "see they are not the 'Central Kingdom.' "[34] Careful attention to detail also is reflected in the historic instruction of May 8, which constitutes the first comprehensive statement of U.S. foreign policy toward China.

Because he was out of office when America's first treaty with China was signed, Webster's role has often been underestimated. Ironically, he has been as much condemned for allegedly authoring President Tyler's condescending and offensive ceremonial letter of July 12, 1843, to the emperor of China as he has been praised for the dignified and prudent instruction of May 8.[35] Webster drafted the president's letter, but he also complained in 1845 that it had been altered by his successor, Abel P. Upshur. For a time, Webster even contemplated exposing Upshur for a shoddy job of plagiarism.[36] Webster need not have been concerned, for in initiating the Cushing mission and in establishing the goal of acquiring most-favored-nation treatment for American commerce, he had made one of his most enduring contributions to American foreign policy. The instruction of May 8, 1843, formed the basis of U.S. policy toward China until superseded by the Open Door Notes of 1899–1900, of which it, along with the Tyler Doctrine, was the godfather. In 1851, moreover, during his second incumbency at the Department of State, Webster also drafted the original instruction for what eventually became the famous Perry expedition to Japan. Because of his role in formulating the Tyler

33. Adams, *Memoirs*, 10:445.

34. See pp. 907–910, below.

35. See Tyler Dennett, *Americans in Eastern Asia: A Critical Study of the Policy of the United States with Reference to China, Japan and Korea in the 19th Century* (New York, 1922), pp. 139–141, and Kenneth Scott Latourette, *The History of Early Relations between the United States and China, 1784–1844* (New Haven, Conn., 1917), pp. 130–135.

36. See Van Tyne, p. 506.

Doctrine and in initiating the Cushing and Perry missions, Webster should be known as the pioneer in establishing an American foreign policy toward East Asia and the Pacific.

The last of Webster's major initiatives as secretary of state from 1841 to 1843 grew out of the plight of American missionaries in Syria. In 1841, the authorities of the Ottoman Empire sought their removal from the area around Mount Lebanon. Prior to the 1840s, the Department of State tended to look upon missionaries as individuals under their own responsibility, subject to whatever restrictions foreign governments imposed upon them.[37] American treaty rights, moreover, such as those of the Turkish-American Treaty of Commerce and Navigation of 1830, focused on the activities of merchants and said nothing about the evangelical profession. For the most part, the missionaries themselves shied away from seeking the support of the U.S. government.

When Commodore David Porter, the U.S. minister at Constantinople, adopted the usual position that the treaty of 1830 dealt strictly with commercial rights and advised the missionaries not to resist expulsion, their parent organization, the American Board of Commissioners for Foreign Missions, took the unusual position of appealing for assistance over Porter's head to the secretary of state. In a precedent-setting response dated February 2, 1842, Webster directed Porter to extend to American missionaries the same "succor and attentions" that he gave to American merchants.[38] Webster thereby earned the gratitude of the A.B.C.F.M., which made him an honorary member of the organization, and he laid the groundwork for what eventually became a new American foreign policy. Webster's immediate successors at the Department of State from 1843 to 1850 were not sympathetic to the needs of the evangelical profession and reverted to traditional attitudes, but when Webster resumed the secretaryship in 1850 he reasserted his emphatic conviction that the U.S. government had a fundamental responsibility to protect American citizens abroad, regardless of their professions. That position was finally adopted as basic American foreign policy after 1852 by Webster's successors, beginning with his protégé, Edward Everett.

The Treaty of Washington, the Tyler Doctrine, the Cushing mission, and the instruction to Porter are the high points of Webster's first term at the Department of State. There were also low points, however, and Webster suffered disappointments and setbacks while serving as secretary of state. Aside from the agreement with Ashburton, no other major treaty was successfully concluded from 1841 to 1843. A project begun by Webster for an extradition agreement with France modeled on Article 10 of the Treaty of Washington was completed by his successor and

37. See James A. Field, Jr., *America and the Mediterranean World, 1776–1882* (Princeton, N.J., 1969), pp. 285–286.

38. See pp. 280–281, below.

ratified in 1844, but a similar project with Prussia failed to make headway in the 1840s and had to be taken up again by Webster in the 1850s. A treaty of commerce with the Republic of Texas signed on July 30, 1842, was rejected by the Texans because of crippling amendments added by the U.S. Senate.

Texas proved to be a source of much difficulty for Webster, and the triangular relationship between Texas, Mexico, and the United States helps to explain a deterioration in Mexican-American relations. Webster's offers to mediate Texan-Mexican differences were rebuffed, the Santa Fé expedition embittered United States–Mexican affairs, and the Thomas ap Catesby Jones incident destroyed any lingering hope for the implementation of the tripartite plan. In the fall of 1841, Mexican armed forces captured approximately 350 members of an expedition dispatched by President Mirabeau B. Lamar of Texas with the dual purpose of opening trade relations with Santa Fé and of inducing the inhabitants of New Mexico to join hands with Texas in its struggle against Mexico. About 200 of those involved in the ill-fated expedition were U.S. citizens, including prominent Americans such as George Wilkins Kendall of the New Orleans *Picayune*, and to Webster fell the delicate responsibility of trying to secure the release of his countrymen. This was a task that Webster performed admirably. Working through the U.S. ministers at Mexico City, Powhatan Ellis and Waddy Thompson, he secured not only the liberation of the American prisoners but also that of the Texans.

When the negotiations over the Santa Fé prisoners were concluded, Webster instructed Thompson in June 1842 to sound out Mexico about a cession of part of California to the United States. Webster's eye was on the spacious port of San Francisco, which he described to his son in 1845 as "twenty times as valuable to us as all Texas."[39] During the negotiations with Ashburton, Webster had advanced what has been called the "tripartite plan." Finding Ashburton hamstrung by constrictive instructions that bound him to a line at the Columbia River, Webster sought to break the logjam over the Oregon question with a three-pronged proposal. The United States would concede a boundary at the Columbia River if Britain could persuade Mexico to sell San Francisco and a surrounding enclave to the Americans. The British were lukewarm to the idea, and the Mexicans refused even to consider such an arrangement. At this unpromising juncture in the fall of 1842, Commodore Jones, the commander of the Pacific squadron, committed an unbelievable faux pas.

Acting on the basis of unconfirmed rumors of the outbreak of war between Mexico and the United States and fearing that Mexico might cede California to Britain, on October 19, 1842, Jones seized Monterey, the capital of the Mexican province of Upper California. After discovering

39. *PC*, 2:204.

his error, Jones returned his bloodless conquest to the totally surprised Mexican authorities, but the damage had been done. To say the least, the Jones affair stirred up a hornet's nest for the secretary of state. Facing the thankless task of explaining the unexplainable, Webster assessed Jones's behavior as "a freak of his own brain."[40] On January 17, 1843, Webster officially apologized for Jones's unauthorized blunder, but the reaction in Mexico was so violent that the negotiations for the purchase of San Francisco had to be suspended. The Jones incident ended the tripartite plan, which Webster may have promoted in part to distract Tyler from his fixation about annexing Texas to the United States.[41] When Webster left office on May 8, President Tyler was moving toward the acquisition of Texas, and Mexican-American relations were strained to the breaking point. Webster's greatest failures as secretary of state from 1841 to 1843 were his inability to resolve the Oregon question and to improve a relationship with Mexico that was already troubled when he assumed office, though, in both of these matters, he was hampered by circumstances largely beyond his control.

Some of the problems confronted by Webster as secretary of state, such as the Jones incident, were colorful, but a considerable amount of his time was devoted to managing the routine issues that arise in relations among nations. Much of American foreign policy then, as now, revolved around commercial and legal problems such as the interpretation of treaties and the litigation of claims cases. Webster employed his legal expertise to good advantage in dealing with such issues. Knowledge of international law and the ability to frame a cogent argument are not prerequisites to the office of secretary of state, but disputes such as that with Spain over the *Amistad* suggest that perhaps they should be. The controversy over the release of the slaves of the *Amistad* by the U.S. Supreme Court centered on divergent interpretations of the Pinckney Treaty of 1795, and Webster ably defended the position of his "client," the government of the United States. Other disputes, such as that with Britain over the *Creole*, with Denmark over the sound dues, and with Lewis Cass over the Treaty of Washington, suggest that Webster was a model secretary of state when it came to advocating and defending the policies adopted by the Harrison-Tyler administrations.

Webster was a talented advocate who approached the world with a certain set of conservative, legalistic, and nationalistic assumptions. His mind was eminently pragmatic. He left no memoirs, and he did not tend to philosophize about issues. Rather, he dealt with problems as they arose in a prudent fashion. He was inclined, as Richard N. Current wrote, "to think things ought to be kept pretty much as they were."[42]

40. Adams, *Memoirs*, 11:346–347.
41. See Sydney Nathans, *Daniel Webster and Jacksonian Democracy* (Baltimore, 1973), pp. 42–43.
42. Richard N. Current, *Daniel Webster and the Rise of National*

Valuing stability more than change, he responded cautiously to such developments as the request by the self-proclaimed State of the Isthmus for diplomatic recognition as an independent nation. In 1840, the Colombian provinces of Panama and Veraqua had declared themselves independent and had joined together to form a new country; in 1841 they sought to establish international relations with the United States. Their agent, William Radcliff, held out the tempting prospects of canal-route rights and increased trade. Webster's carefully worded response of January 28, 1842, however, adhered to the traditional American policy on recognition. Until fully satisfied that the State of the Isthmus could maintain its sovereignty, the United States would not depart from that "wise yet generous caution" that had characterized "its steps in similar cases."[43] Webster's denial of a grant of immediate recognition proved wise indeed, for it soon was learned that the two rebellious provinces had rejoined the Republic of New Granada.

The letter to Radcliff shows that Webster was well versed in the traditions of American foreign policy. By 1841, the United States had developed a set of policy guidelines. The most important of these grew out of George Washington's Farewell Address of September 17, 1796, Congress's No-Transfer Resolution of January 15, 1811, and James Monroe's message of December 2, 1823. As previously mentioned, Webster was an early defender of Monroe's declaration, and Washington was his boyhood idol. Aided by a remarkable memory, Webster also was fully aware of the no-transfer principle, which he reiterated in 1843 when President Tyler became concerned about possible British intervention in Cuba.[44]

Like Washington, Webster was a staunch nationalist who promoted American economic interests abroad, as in the Treaty of Wanghia. He also took a Hamiltonian view of the constitutional primacy of federal over state power in the realm of foreign policy, as in the case of Alexander McLeod. Webster's nationalism is further reflected in the Treaty of Washington. That accord, he emphasized in 1846 in a two-day speech defending the agreement before the Senate, upheld the honor of the United States. The treaty, he said, helped to suppress crime through the article on extradition, helped to promote legitimate American commerce through the article on the coasting trade, helped to suppress the illegal African slave trade through the joint cruising convention, and helped to advance the cause of world peace through the articles on the northeastern boundary.[45] The Treaty of Washington embodies Webster's conservative and legalistic nationalism.

Daniel Webster was a man of the middle who valued what he called

---

Conservatism (Boston and Toronto, 1955), p. 10.
43. See pp. 355–356, below.
44. See pp. 369–372, below.
45. "Defence of the Treaty of Washington," in W & S, 9:78–150.

"the exercise of calm reason" as the only way by which "truth can be arrived at, in questions of a complicated nature" between states that understood and respected "the intelligence and the power of the other."[46] He looked upon the agreement with Ashburton as being just that—a "treaty of equivalents" based upon concessions by two nations who understood and respected one another.[47] That masterpiece of "calm reason" not only stands as Webster's most important contribution to the history of American foreign policy but also summarizes his world view.

46. See Webster to Everett, January 29, 1842, "The Crisis in Anglo-American Relations," pp. 177–185, below.

47. *W & S,* 9:147.

PLAN OF WORK

This is the first of two volumes on Daniel Webster's career as secretary of state. He served in that capacity under William Henry Harrison and John Tyler from March 6, 1841, to May 8, 1843, and under Millard Fillmore from July 23, 1850, to October 24, 1852. The two volumes of diplomatic papers have been organized to correspond with Webster's two terms as secretary of state.

The *Diplomatic Papers*, which include selections from Webster's private letters and from State Department documents, have been designed as companion volumes to the *Correspondence* series. *Correspondence 5*, which covers the same chronological period as *Diplomatic 1*, calendars the private letters written by Webster while secretary of state under Harrison and Tyler, and cross-references those that are published in this book. The documents included in *Diplomatic 1* have been drawn from the microfilm edition of the Papers of Daniel Webster and from the records of the Department of State, most of which are available on film from the National Archives and Records Service of the General Services Administration. Although the *Guide and Index to the Microfilm Edition of the Papers of Daniel Webster*, edited by Charles M. Wiltse (Ann Arbor, Mich., 1971), conveniently indexes Webster's private papers, there is no similar guide to the thousands of documents relevant to Webster's secretaryships contained in the diplomatic and consular files of the Department of State. In order to use these voluminous records, the researcher must be familiar with the various record groups and select for himself or herself the reels that contain Webster material.

The official records of the Department of State for the nineteenth century are grouped into six basic categories, each of which has been filmed separately: Diplomatic and Consular Instructions, Despatches from United States Ministers and Consuls, Notes to Foreign Legations in the United States, Notes from Foreign Legations in the United States, Miscellaneous Letters, and Domestic Letters. Instructions are the directives from the secretary of state to the ministers and consuls of the United States serving abroad, and they are organized first by country and then by date. Despatches are the communications from those diplomats and consuls, and they are organized in the same manner. Notes to Foreign Legations consists of those letters sent by the Department of State to the representatives of foreign governments residing in the United States. Notes from Foreign Legations contains the messages sent from those envoys to the secretary of state. These documents are also organized by country and chronology. The Miscellaneous file is a large one, containing letters addressed to the Department of State by correspondents other than diplomatic and consular officials. It is organized solely on a chronological basis. Although difficult to use, Miscellaneous Letters is a gold mine of valuable information. Many of the documents published below have been taken from this relatively unused record group. Domestic Letters, the companion file to Miscellaneous Letters, contains the communications written by officials of the Department of State to individuals other than diplomats and consuls. It too is organized only chronologically. In addition, there are a number of other files relevant to Webster's secretaryship, such as Special Missions, but the six categories described above comprise the basic record groups of the Department of State for the nineteenth century. Like the *Correspondence* series, the *Diplomatic Papers* integrates both microfilm and letterpress publication and seeks to provide the scholar and general reader with the essential Webster in annotated form. The *Diplomatic Papers* complement and render more useful the various microfilm collections, but those who wish to undertake in-depth studies will have to consult the microfilm edition of the Papers of Daniel Webster and the records of the Department of State.

The *Diplomatic Papers* have been organized topically, and the selections under the various headings have been made with the view of allowing the documents themselves to set forth the developments in American foreign policy during Webster's secretaryship. As the section entitled "The World and Daniel Webster" suggests, an effort has also been made to avoid the pitfalls of a crisis-oriented approach and to provide a balanced and representative sample of the many issues and problems that Webster confronted in dealing with the twenty-four countries with which the United States held diplomatic relations in 1841–1843. While a topical format has necessitated the occasional printing under one heading of a document that contains remarks about several foreign policy issues, the problem of overlap has been dealt with through "see above" and "see below" annotations. Not only does a topical organization facilitate mastery of the almost unmanageable number of documents in the records of the Department of State, but it also has the advantage of allowing the reader to see the internal and external pressures to which Webster responded in formulating and implementing American foreign policy. Webster's place in the history of international relations is the least well studied aspect of his versatile career. By illustrating in the *Diplomatic Papers* the overall scope of his important contributions to American foreign policy, the editors hope that scholars will be encouraged to undertake further investigations.

EDITORIAL METHOD

Within the topical headings, letters and other documents included in this volume are arranged in chronological sequence, irrespective of whether Webster was the writer or the recipient. The only exception is letters that were sent as enclosures. These have been placed immediately after the document they accompanied. Date and point of origin have been placed at the upper right of each letter. If all or part of this information has been supplied by the editors, the supplied material appears in square brackets, with a question mark if conjecture. Instructions and dispatches were usually numbered, and these numbers have been placed at the upper left of each document. The complimentary close, which in the original manuscripts often takes up three or four lines, has been run continuously with the last line of the text.

All documents are reproduced in full except in those rare instances where the only surviving text is either incomplete or from a printed source that did not reproduce the document in its entirety. Needless to say, texts from printed sources are used only when the original manuscript has not been found but the letter is of sufficient importance to warrant its inclusion. Underscorings, though possibly made in some instances by clerks of the Department of State, have been retained as found in the original documents.

The letters themselves have been reproduced in type as true to the original as possible. Misspellings have been retained without the use of the obtrusive "(*sic*)"; abbreviations and contractions have been allowed to stand unless the editors felt that they would not be readily understood by the reader. In such cases the abbreviation has been expanded, with square brackets enclosing the letters supplied. Punctuation, too, has been left as Webster and his correspondents used it, save those cases where it makes for redundancy in the typed script. For example, when the last word on one page is rendered again at the top of the next, the extra word is silently deleted. The same is done for redundant quotation marks. Dashes clearly intended as periods have been so written. Superscript letters in abbreviations or contractions have been brought down, but a period is supplied only if the last letter of the abbreviation is not the last letter of the word abbreviated. In all other cases, periods, apostrophes, dashes, and other forms of punctuation have been left as Webster and his contemporaries used them. The ampersand, far more frequently used than the spelled-out "and," has been retained, but diacritical marks over contractions have been omitted even where the contraction itself is retained.

Canceled words or passages that are obvious mistakes that were immediately corrected have been left out altogether; those that show some change of thought or attitude or have stylistic or psychological implications have been included between angled brackets. Interlineations by the author have been incorporated into the text, but marginal passages, again if by the author, have been treated as postscripts and placed below the signature.

Foreign words and names have been printed as they appear in the original documents. In those cases where variations in spelling might be confusing to the reader, a modern form of the word or name has been supplied in square brackets. When a diplomat such as Pedro Alcántara de Argaiz, the Spanish minister to the United States, departed from convention by using Argaiz as his surname, he has been indexed under both Alcántara and Argaiz. In transliterating Chinese, both the Wade-Giles and Pinyin systems have been employed.

In order to keep explanatory footnotes to a minimum, general headnotes precede each section of documents. These essays are designed to provide the historical background necessary to understand Webster's actions as secretary of state, to highlight the significance of particular documents, or to explain the sequence of complex diplomatic negotiations. Footnotes are used to identify persons, places, events, issues, or situations related to specific letters and other documents.

Individuals are identified only once, generally the first time they are mentioned. For the convenience of the reader who may have missed this initial reference, the appropriate index entry is printed in boldface type. Well-known individuals—those in the *Dictionary of American Biography* or the *Biographical Directory of the American Congress*—have been identified only in their diplomatic context, using an "at that time" formula. For those in the DAB the index entry is marked with an asterisk; a dagger indicates those found in the BDAC. The extent of footnoting has been reduced by adding given names and initials in square brackets where text references are to surnames only.

Immediately following each document is an unnumbered note providing the provenance of the document. For Department of State materials, the log docketing, if any, is supplied, as are any endorsements on a document made in Webster's hand. If appropriate, identifications of the writer or recipient are placed in these unnumbered notes. The symbols used in the provenance notes are the standard descriptive and location symbols of the Union Catalog Division of the Library of Congress. Those appearing in the present volume have been listed under Abbreviations and Symbols, below.

Webster Chronology, 1840–1843

1840

May 21	Britain proclaimed sovereignty over New Zealand.
November	Harrison and Tyler elected.
November 12	Alexander McLeod arrested in New York state and charged with murder and arson in connection with the *Caroline* incident of 1837.
December 11	Webster accepted Harrison's invitation to become secretary of state.

1841

January 30	In a letter to Webster, Peter Parker proposed a diplomatic mission to China.
January–February	Webster began laying plans for a compromise settlement of the northeastern boundary dispute.
February 9	The British government threatened war over the McLeod affair.
February 22	Webster resigned his Senate seat.
March 4	William Henry Harrison inaugurated.
March 5	Webster unanimously confirmed as secretary of state.
March 6	Webster assumed the duties of office.
March 12	The British minister in Washington demanded the release of Alexander McLeod.
March–October	Webster sought unsuccessfully to persuade Governor Seward of New York to release McLeod.
March 30	The Russian government offered to help resolve the McLeod dispute.
April 4	Harrison died.
April 6	Tyler assumed office as president.

April 24	Webster formulated the doctrine of self-defense.
May 29	The Spanish minister in Washington demanded indemnification in the *Amistad* case.
June 7	Francis O. J. Smith advanced a plan of propaganda to resolve the northeastern boundary dispute.
July 12	The New York Supreme Court remanded McLeod for trial.
July 28	Webster instructed William S. Murphy as special agent to Central America.
August 6	Webster advised Joshua A. Spencer on how to conduct McLeod's defense.
August 16	Tyler vetoed Henry Clay's bill for a national bank.
August 27	Foreign Secretary Palmerston asserted a distinction between "visit" and "search" in order to suppress the slave trade.
August 28	Lord Melbourne resigned, and Sir Robert Peel began forming a new ministry.
September 3	Lord Aberdeen replaced Palmerston as foreign secretary.
September 5	The British minister in Washington protested the action of the New York Supreme Court in the McLeod case.
September 9	Tyler vetoed a second bank bill.
September 10–11	With the exception of Webster, the members of Tyler's cabinet resigned.
September 13	Edward Everett appointed minister to Britain.
September 19	James W. Grogan abducted from Alburg, Vermont, by Canadian soldiers.
September– February 1842	Members of the Santa Fé expedition captured and marched overland to Mexico City.
October 4	The Canadian authorities released Grogan.
October 11	Tyler proposed to Webster the acquisition of Texas by treaty.
November 7	Slaves aboard the *Creole* seized the vessel and sailed it to Nassau, where they were declared free by British authorities.

November 24	King of Hawaii requested that the United States recognize the Sandwich islands as an independent nation.
November 29	Webster remonstrated against British violations of the Rush-Bagot agreement of 1817.
December 7	Tyler delivered his first Annual Message.
December 20	Austria, Britain, France, Prussia and Russia signed the Quintuple Treaty.

1842

January 28	Webster declined to grant diplomatic recognition to the State of the Isthmus.
February 2	Webster extended the official protection of the U.S. government to American missionaries serving in foreign lands.
February 10	Washington Irving appointed minister to Spain.
February 13	Lewis Cass protested against the Quintuple Treaty.
March 2	John Sheridan Hogan released from jail in Lockport, New York, for want of sufficient testimony; after being arrested a second time, he was again released on the same grounds in April in Utica, New York.
April 4	Lord Ashburton arrived in the United States.
April 12	Webster instructed Isaac Rand Jackson to support American missionaries in Denmark.
April 25	In a conversation with Ashburton, Webster intimated a tripartite solution to the Oregon question.
May 14	Jared Sparks sent by Webster on a confidential trip to Maine.
May 26	Maine appointed state commissioners authorized to accept a conventional line.
June 17	Ashburton and Webster commenced negotiations on the northeastern boundary.
June 27	Webster asked the U.S. minister to Mexico to seek the acquisition of San Francisco.
July	The French occupied the Marquesas islands.

July 21	Albert Fitz confidentially reported on British military installations in the West Indies.
July 30	Treaty of commerce between Texas and the United States signed; later rejected by Texas because of amendments by the U.S. Senate.
August 1	Webster issued his letter on the *Creole*.
August 6	Webster issued his letter on the *Caroline*.
August 8	Webster issued his letter on impressment.
August 9	Treaty of Washington signed.
August 11	Treaty of Washington submitted to the Senate.
August 20	Treaty of Washington approved by the Senate.
August 22	Treaty of Washington ratified by the United States.
August 29	Law enacted, drafted by Webster as an outgrowth of the McLeod case, giving federal courts jurisdiction in cases involving aliens charged with crimes committed under the authority of a foreign government.
August 29	Treaty of Nanking signed.
September 11	Mexican forces under General Adrian Woll captured San Antonio.
October 3	Cass resigned as Minister to France.
October 5	Treaty of Washington ratified by Britain.
October 13	Ratifications of the Treaty of Washington exchanged at London.
October 19	Commodore Thomas ap Catesby Jones seized Monterey, California.
November 10	Treaty of Washington proclaimed.
November 15	British minister in Washington proposed a treaty negotiation on Oregon.
December 5	Timoteo Haalilio and William Richards arrived in Washington from Hawaii.
December 19	In a letter to Haalilio and Richards, Webster formulated what came to be known as the "Tyler Doctrine."
December 25	Texans defeated in the battle of Mier.

December 30	In a special message to Congress, the president proclaimed the Tyler Doctrine.

1843

January 14	In an instruction to the U.S. consul at Havana, Webster reiterated the no-transfer policy.
January 17	Webster disavowed Jones's seizure of Monterey.
January 29	Webster transformed the tripartite idea into a plan.
January 30	Claims convention signed in Mexico City; convention proclaimed on March 30.
February 28	House Committee on Foreign Affairs refused to recommend funds for a special mission to Britain.
March 2	Webster commenced negotiations with the Prussian minister in Washington for a convention on extradition.
March 3	Everett confirmed by the Senate as commissioner to China.
March 15	Tyler nominated for the presidency by a group of New York supporters.
March 15	George Brown of Massachusetts sent to Hawaii as the first U.S. commissioner.
March 16	Draft convention on extradition between Prussia and the United States completed.
March 20	Webster issued a circular requesting information about China.
March 21	Webster asked the secretary of the navy to uphold American rights in Oregon by force if necessary.
March 28	In an instruction to Everett, Webster denied any distinction between "visit" and "search."
April 18	Everett declined to accept the mission to China.
April 26	Webster commenced negotiations with the French minister in Washington for a convention on extradition.
May 8	Caleb Cushing accepted the appointment as U.S. commissioner to China.

May 8   Webster issued the instructions to Cushing that formed the basis of the Treaty of Wanghia of July 3, 1844.

May 8   Webster resigned as secretary of state; Hugh Swinton Legaré appointed to the post *ad interim*.

May 15   Webster left Washington for retirement at Marshfield.

Abbreviations and Symbols

DESCRIPTIVE SYMBOLS

AD	Autograph Document
ADS	Autograph Document Signed
AL	Autograph Letter
AL draft	Autograph Letter, draft
ALS	Autograph Letter Signed
ANS	Autograph Note Signed
Copy	Copy, not by writer
LC	Letterbook Copy
LS	Letter Signed

LOCATION SYMBOLS

CtY	Yale University
CtY-M	Yale University, Medical School
DLC	Library of Congress
DNA	United States National Archives, Washington, D.C.
H-Ar	Public Archives, Honolulu, Hawaii
MB	Boston Public Library
MH	Harvard University
MH-H	Harvard University, Houghton Library
MHi	Massachusetts Historical Society, Boston
MdHi	Maryland Historical Society, Baltimore
MiU-C	University of Michigan, William L. Clements Library
MoSHi	Missouri Historical Society, Saint Louis
NRU	University of Rochester
NcD	Duke University
NhD	Dartmouth College
NHi	New-York Historical Society, New York City
NhHi	New Hampshire Historical Society, Concord
NjMoHP	Morristown National Historical Park, Morristown, N.J.
OHi	Ohio Historical Society, Columbus
PHi	Historical Society of Pennsylvania, Philadelphia
PRO	Public Record Office, London, England
TxSjM	San Jacinto Museum of History Association, Deer Park, Tex.
UK	British Library, London, England

SHORT TITLES

Adams, *Memoirs*	Charles Francis Adams, ed., *Memoirs of John Quincy Adams* (12 vols., Philadelphia, 1874–1877).
ASP: FR	Walter Lowrie and Matthew St. Clair, eds., *American State Papers: Foreign Relations* (6 vols., Washington, D.C., 1832–1859).
CR	William R. Manning, ed., *Diplomatic Correspondence of the United States: Canadian Relations* (4 vols., Washington, D.C., 1940–1945).
Cong. Globe	*The Congressional Globe* (46 vols., Washington, D.C., 1833–1873).
Correspondence	Charles M. Wiltse and others, eds., *The Papers of Daniel Webster, Correspondence* (7 vols., Hanover, N.H. and London, 1974–198–).
Curtis	George Ticknor Curtis, *Life of Daniel Webster* (2 vols., New York, 1870).
Diplomatic Papers	Kenneth E. Shewmaker and others, eds., *The Papers of Daniel Webster, Diplomatic Papers* (2 vols., Hanover, N.H. and London, 1982–198–).
Hansard's	*Hansard's Parliamentary Debates*, 3d Series (356 vols., London, 1830–1891).
IAA	William R. Manning, ed., *Diplomatic Correspondence of the United States: Inter-American Affairs* (12 vols., Washington, D.C., 1932–1939).
International Arbitrations	John Bassett Moore, *History and Digest of International Arbitrations* . . . (6 vols., Washington, D.C., 1898).
International Law Digest	John Bassett Moore, *A Digest of International Law* . . . (8 vols., Washington, D.C., 1906).
Legal Papers	Alfred S. Konefsky and Andrew J. King, eds., *The Papers of Daniel Webster, Legal Papers* (3 vols., Hanover, N.H. and London, 1982–198–).
MHi Proc.	*Proceedings of the Massachusetts Historical Society.*
mDW	Microfilm Edition of the Papers of Daniel

	Webster (Ann Arbor, 1971). References followed by frame numbers.
mDWs	Microfilm Edition of the Papers of Daniel Webster, Supplementary Reel.
Messages and Papers	James D. Richardson, ed., *A Compilation of the Messages and Papers of the Presidents . . . 1789–1897* (10 vols., Washington, D.C., 1896–1899).
PC	Fletcher Webster, ed., *The Private Correspondence of Daniel Webster* (2 vols., Boston, 1856).
Treaties	Hunter Miller, ed., *Treaties and Other International Acts of the United States of America* (8 vols., Washington, D.C., 1931–1948).
Tylers	Lyon G. Tyler, *The Letters and Times of the Tylers* (3 vols., Richmond and Williamsburg, 1884–1896).
U.S. Stat.	*United States Statutes at Large.* References are preceded by volume numbers and followed by page numbers.
Van Tyne	Claude H. Van Tyne, ed., *The Letters of Daniel Webster* (New York, 1902).
W & S	James W. McIntyre, ed., *The Writings and Speeches of Daniel Webster* (18 vols., New York, 1903).
Works	Edward Everett, ed., *The Works of Daniel Webster* (6 vols., Boston, 1851).

SERIES THREE: DIPLOMATIC PAPERS

VOLUME ONE: 1841–1843

Daniel Webster's Appointment as Secretary of State

Because of his stature in the Whig party and his national reputation as a guardian of the Constitution and the Union, it was not surprising that Daniel Webster was offered a position in the new administration of William Henry Harrison. Webster, moreover, had been instrumental in helping Harrison secure the Whig nomination in 1840 and had campaigned vigorously for him in the general election. The president-elect offered Webster the secretaryship of either the State Department or the Treasury Department. There were many reasons for accepting the former. Although the office of secretary of state was no longer regarded as the stepping-stone to the presidency, it was still a possible avenue to the White House. As the senior cabinet member holding the highest non-elective office in the Republic, the secretary of state held a position of national power and prestige. As secretary of state, Webster could hope to wield considerable influence and to gain ascendancy over his great political rival, Henry Clay. He also wanted to be able to deal directly with the pressing issues in Anglo-American relations as the country's foremost diplomat.

FROM WILLIAM HENRY HARRISON

Frankfort, Ky, 1st Dec. 1840.

My dear Sir,

I received your kind letter of the 11th Inst.[1] at this place on this day week, just as I was about to set out for Lexington to dine with Mr. [Henry] Clay[2] who had waited on me here and invited me up to dine with some of my old friends. I expected to be absent but three days & left yours & other letters to be answered on my return but I found it impossible to get away or evade the hospitalities of my friends in & about Lexington until this morning & I avail myself of the first moments of being alone to write you.[3]

Since I was first a candidate for the Presidency, I had determined if successful to solicit your able assistance in conducting the Administra-

1. Not found.
2. Clay (1777–1852) was elected U.S. senator from Kentucky in 1836. He resigned from the Senate on March 31, 1842.
3. In Kentucky Harrison met, in addition to Henry Clay, Whig leaders John Jordan Crittenden (1787–1863), Robert Perkins Letcher (1788–1861), and Charles Anderson Wickliffe (1788–1869).

tion & I now ask you to accept the State or Treasury Department. I have myself no preference of either for you, but it may perhaps be more difficult to fill the latter than the former if you should decline it. It was the post designed for you in the supposition that you had given more attention to the subject of the finances than Mr. Clay to whom I intended to have offered the State Department. This as well as any other post in the Cabinet I understood before my arrival here (from an intimate friend of that Gentleman) he would decline. This he has since done personally to me. If you should think it advisable to pursue the same course will you do me the favor to name some one of your *Eastern* friends for the Treasury or some other Department. Would you recommend your Governor Elect for the Treasury if you should determine to decline it?[4]

I shall set out tomorrow for Louisville & shall be at home as soon as your answer can reach Cleves.[5] Do not believe my dear Sir that I mean by what I have said above to restrict your advise as to the formation of the Cabinet to a single individual, give me your advise freely & fully upon that & every other subject & whether you occupy a place in the Cabinet or not, & it will be at all times thankfully received by your friend

W. H. Harrison

Copy. NhHi. Published in *PC*, 2:90–91, and Curtis, 2:48. Original not found. Harrison (1773–1841; Hampden-Sydney College).

TO WILLIAM HENRY HARRISON

My Dear Sir,   Washington Decr. 11. 1840

Having been detained on my way by the late storm, I did not reach this City until the Evening of the 9th, & yesterday morning, the 10th your letter of the 1st inst[1] was delivered to me by Col [William Key] Bond.[2]

It becomes me, in the first place, to acknowledge my grateful sense of the confidence, evinced by your communication, & to assure you how highly I value this proof of your friendship & regard.

The question of accepting a Seat in your Cabinet, should it be tendered to me, has naturally been the subject of my reflections, and of consultation with friends. The result of these reflections & consultations has been, that I should accept the office of Secretary of State, should it be offered to me, under circumstances such as now exist.

I am willing, therefore, to undertake the duties of the office, prepared to give to their faithful discharge my best ability and all my efforts.

You are kind enough to suggest that my acquaintance with the sub-

4. John Davis (1787–1854; Yale 1812) of Massachusetts.

5. Cleves, a small Ohio town near North Bend, was the location of Harrison's home.

1. See above.

2. Bond (1792–1842) served as a Whig representative from Chillicothe, Ohio, 1835–1840.

jects of currency, & finance, might render me useful, as Head of the Treasury. On that subject, my view has been this. I think all important questions of Revenue, Finance, & Currency properly belonging to the Executive, should be *Cabinet* questions; that every member of the Cabinet should give them his best consideration; & especially that the results of these deliberations should receive the sanction of the President. This seems necessary to Union, & efficiency of action. If to these counsels I may be supposed able to contribute any thing useful, I shall withhold myself from no degree of labor, & no just responsibility.

For the daily details of the Treasury, the matters of account, and the supervision of subordinate officers, employed in the collection and disbursement of the public monies, I do not think myself to be particularly well qualified. I take this occasion to say, that I entirely concur in the opinion which has been expressed by you, that on the subjects of finance & revenue, as on other great subjects, the duty of originating important measures properly belongs to Congress.

By accepting now the offer of the Department of State, however, I do not wish to preclude you from again suggesting the Treasury Department to me, if you should find it more easy to fill the former than the latter office satisfactorily, with another person.

You are pleased to ask my opinions in regard to the manner of filling other Departments. On this important & delicate subject, I will write to you, within two days; I now only assure you, that in what I may say, my object will be only to make suggestions for your consideration; as I have confidence in your judgment, & no motive but to see you surrounded by a strong, comprehensive & popular Cabinet, such as shall satisfy the expectation of the Country, & promise success and honor to your Administration.

AL draft. NhHi. Published in *PC*, 2:93–94.

FROM WILLIAM HENRY HARRISON

North Bend
My Dear Sir   Dec. 27th 1840

I duly received your favor announcing your having acceded to my Wish in taking a place in the New Cabinet & I entirely approve of your choice of the two tendered to you.[1]

Your subsequent letter making suggestions as to the filling the other Departments has also been received & I thank you for them.[2] I will come to no definite conclusion as to the Treasury, War & Navy until I reach Washington, which will be about the last of Jany.

I tell you however in confidence that I have positively determined

1. See above.   2. Not found.

against [Thaddeus] Stevens.[3] There is no consideration which would induce me to bring him into the Cabinet. We should have no peace with his intriguing, restless disposition. We will have nobody of that character, & if we do not & can secure men of competent talents & moral worth we can ensure to ourselves a quiet & successful administration. Depend upon it We have the people with us & if We do not depart from our *professions* they will stick to us. I am glad to say that as far as I can learn your call to the State Dept has given universal satisfaction to our political friends.

From the number visitters which I have here I have less leasure than when I am [in] Cincinnati. I am dr sir Most truly yours   W. H. Harrison

ALS. NhHi. Published in *PC*, 2:97.

3. Stevens (1792–1868; Dartmouth 1814), who at that time was practicing private law, had supported Harrison in the elections of 1836 and 1840.

"Dividing the Spoils": Diplomatic Appointments Influenced by Webster

During the campaign of 1840, the Whigs inveighed against the Jacksonian "spoils system" and called for appointments based upon merit rather than politics. Once in office, however, the Whigs behaved like Jacksonians. As the first Whig secretary of state, Webster controlled a number of posts. One of his first appointments was that of his son, Daniel Fletcher Webster, to the important position of chief clerk of the Department of State. The chief clerk superintended the daily business of the department and functioned as acting secretary of state in the secretary's absence. Although Fletcher Webster was a competent individual, he sometimes exasperated such elder statesmen as John Quincy Adams, who complained on one occasion that Fletcher was "bloated with self-sufficiency" (*Memoirs*, 11:249).

Adams also complained when Webster replaced the experienced Samuel D. Heap at the Tunis consulate with William B. Hodgson but neglected to mention Hodgson's knowledge of the languages and culture of the Middle East. Hodgson, in fact, owed his training to Adams, who in 1826 had sent him and a number of other young men of promise to the Barbary consulates so that the United States could develop a corps of trained public servants for that region (*Memoirs*, 7:106–107).

By the middle of the nineteenth century, the United States was the only important Western nation that did not have a career foreign service. Generally, it can be said that the Whigs, like the Democrats before them, tried to make the best appointments possible within the confines of the existing, nonprofessional system. Webster was justly proud of several of his diplomatic officers. Washington Irving, aside from his travels in Spain and his novel *The Alhambra*, was an excellent choice for minister to Spain by virtue of his training in law, fluency in Spanish, and previous experience as secretary of legation in London. It may be that Webster's tangled finances influenced his choice of Isaac Rand Jackson as minister to Denmark, for Jackson loaned the secretary of state money toward the purchase of a home in Washington. Moreover, Edward Everett, who became minister to Great Britain, had helped raise funds to support Webster in the past. Yet both men were good choices, and they served ably at their posts. The appointments influenced by Webster show that the Whig ascendancy did not mean the end of the patronage system, but he did try to see that those Whigs who represented the United States abroad were men of ability and competence.

FROM CHRISTOPHER HUGHES

No. 2
Private,
Sir,   Stockholm, 25th May, 1841
    I enclose, under this cover, a Despatch for the Secretary of the Trea-
sury, containing a rather voluminous work, composed by a very respectable Nobleman and prominent politician of this Country, Count Frölick.[1]
The subject is Banking; the object is to suggest plans & principles for a
National Bank in—and remodelling the Credit System of,—the United
States.
    Count Frölick is an old acquaintance of mine,—a very zealous & in-
defatigable labourer in the study & resea[r]ches of Political economy,—
has often been chosen, by the Dist. President of the Committee for the
management of the National Bank of Sweden and has volunteered this
offering to my Government; which, Mr [Thomas] Ewing[2] may make a
burnt one, if he so deem fit. I transmit it at Count Frölicks request; &
there—my "ministry," no—my *"Charge"*—begins & ends!
    I find it will never do, to make this "a Despatch"; so I will mark it *"pri-
vate"*; which will permit scribbling—& pretermit copying; the hateful
occupation of now 27 years—when "Chargé" I have been; & "yet, no
holiday have seen."
    I have not the advantage or honour to know Mr. [John] Tyler;[3] but I
have long since conceived a most respectful opinion of him, as a public
man; & I may add, as a private one; for my impression is that Mr. Tyler
is a great personal friend of Mr. [Henry] Clay; and *you know*, my affection & devotion for Mr. Clay; and *I know*, that Mr. Clay—nor any of Ye
Great & Powerful Friends of mine—will ever do (or have ever done) any
thing useful or acceptable, to me. The Waters of the Atlantic have a
Lithean—and a pernicious property! & so much the worse *for me*! However, I shall continue to hold up my head & my heart; & to cherish myself, by not abating one atom—or iota—of my own comfortable & com-
placent self-esteem!
    "Before Great Agamemnon reigned,—reigned other Kings as good as
he—and great."
    I have read with great interest and satisfaction, Mr. Tyler's *address**
to the Nation:[4] I have not been more pleased with its positions, princi-

---

    1. This may be a reference to Fritz
Heinrich Frölick (1807–1877), a pioneer banker in Kristiani (Oslo), but
not a nobleman.
    2. Ewing (1789–1871; Ohio Uni-
versity 1815) was secretary of the
Treasury from March to September
of 1841.

    3. Tyler (1790–1862; William and
Mary 1807) became president upon
Harrison's death, taking the oath of
office on April 6, 1841.
    4. President John Tyler's inaugural
address, April 9, 1841. See *Messages
and Papers*, 4:36–39.

ples & purview, than Europe has been pleased, & *surprised*, of its brevity; a precious quality in state papers; & the more so, because *safe*; & especially in *our* Documents; but it is not the *use*, in Terra Jonathanid— *Documentum* ex eliquo capere—"I guess." (Accro! forsooth!)

"*I wonder*" (old Mr. Carroll of Maryland,[5] in whose house & family I was reared—not "*raised*", was always—"*a wondering*"; a *wonderful* fine *old* Gentleman was he; & *young* one—was I, when honoured—at Annapolis—by his notice & hospitality.) Well! "I *wonder*"—if Mr. Tyler knows, that there is such a being living as me! Perhaps—*not*! But you, my dear Sir, may say to him, that no man has served the state, *at home*— with more zeal & fidelity—(& I would fain hope I may add—"I have done the state some service"!) than I have served it *abroad*; & for now Twenty Seven Years!; just *half* my life—bating one year!—for I am 55!—but fresh & effective yet—"I reckon". That, I am known & have friends at every court in Europe, & among the highest & most puissant: & verily believe, that I should be welcome, & might be efficient, at any of them! I have never neglected advancing & promoting—if possible,—& certainly *never* omitted vindicating—a right or interest—of my country & countrymen—when & where I had the means to do so—any & every where in Europe. In short—I might appeal to numbers of my fellow men at home, for the truth of this; as well as to public approbation; from Mr. [James] Madison to Mr. [Martin] V[an] Buren![6] From Zenith to Nadir! and what has it availed me? & what *will* it avail me? "nothing—*so long* as Mordecai"—the mere *party* man sitteth at the Presidents "gate!"[7] And I am now an old Swan—(or, perhaps, an old *Goose*—)singing my own *requiem*; I would rather again call on my old friend, Cicero, & write—"*Requiesco* in aliquo", provided that "*aliquis*" were *You*; or Mr .Tyler! *N'importe*!

In 1823—when I was home & Mr. [James] Monroe was President—He offered me, kindly—& I refused it—partly—a Certificate, in form of a private Letter, of my efficiency, services, & fitness for *any* European Post; any mission!—& actually apologized to me—for the *injustice*, the habits & practice of the Government—guard our diplomacy—forced him to do to me!—that is—the pernicious and unjustifiable habit, of giving away the missions as recompense for party service!—as cups are given at New Market, to Jockies!—in our case—to Riders of men! But—is this never to cease? That same year—Mr. [George] Caning[8]—who had become cured of his errors & prejudices on *our* subject—& partly, cured, by me—for I was honoured with the intimacy and confidence of that Great Man (—by

5. Possibly Charles Carroll (1737–1832; Jesuit College of Bohemia at Hermans Manor, Maryland, College de St. Omer in France) of Maryland.

6. Van Buren (1782–1862).

7. The quotation is from Esther 2:19–23.

8. Canning (1770–1827) was British foreign secretary, 1822–1827.

the way—I doubt *if* Sir R[obert] Peel[9]—whom I know & well—be not as deeply imbued with these errors & prejudices—as any old boy of Geo III's[10] time!)—that very year—Mr. Canning wanted me to be made Minister in London! I told him, that I might as well—ask the Pope for a Cardinal's Hat. a few years after—we *had* a *Swiss*-Cardinal at London![11] & what good did he do us there? I might say—*any where*—in Europe? Ask Mr. Clay that one! A *Swiss* is *never* denationalized or naturalized! But I am getting "lengthy"—& abusive! Well! Here I am—still pretty firm—but looking *down* Hill; now or never; if you dont do something for me—*now*—you can't—nor you sha'n't—soon! I am a plain & open applicant for employment, & *advancement* in what has become my *profession*!. I make no [semblance] nor ceremony in thus explaining my wishes & *claims*, founded on 27 years consecutive, and, I believe, satisfactory service in Europe! and in requesting you, my dear Sir, to make them known to the President. This climate can no longer be borne by me; I have become old & bleached in it; & my health & constitution require a change. The Post I should *prefer* is Vienna, as Minister. That, however, I fear, pressed & surrounded as Genl. [William Henry] Harrison was & as I suppose, the President is, is not to be achieved! But, I should think, that I might be indulged with the Post of Naples, as Chargé d'affaires; and, if *not* Naples, why not allow me to return to my old station of Brussels? where I know every body; & where, I may say, the King[12] has very friendly consideration for me; & where, I am sure, I could be useful.

I wrote with the same plainness my wishes to General Harrison, and, I repeat here, what I wrote then, & have written to you, Sir, that my private affairs,—*in all & every case,*—require my temporary presence at home; and I now request that you would ask the President to grant me leave, to make *a visit* home; and to communicate to me, His pleasure, as soon as you conveniently can;—that I may make the necessary arrangements required by my household concerns *here*. I shall be sincerely obliged to you, my dear Sir, for an early answer, on this,—*to me*—important matter.

You may assure the President that the footing of our concerns & relations with this Government & with the commercial community in Sweden, leaves nothing to be desired; indeed, it cannot be better! and our public interests will suffer, in no respect, by my temporary absence from my post; I can, as formerly, leave the papers & property of the Legation,

9. Peel (1788–1850) served as British prime minister from 1841 to 1846.

10. King George III (1738–1820), ruled 1760–1820.

11. This probably refers to Swiss-born Albert Gallatin (1761–1849; University of Geneva 1779), who replaced the ailing Rufus King (1755–1827; Harvard 1777), minister 1825–1826, as American minister to the Court of St. James, 1826–1827.

12. King Leopold I (1790–1865), ruled 1831–1865.

in the hands of Mr. [Carl D.] Arfwedson,[13] our Consul; who is, in every respect, a most fit and trustworthy person. I repeat, Sir, that I *beseech* you, to communicate to me, as soon as you can, the decision of the President on this, my application for leave; & my hope & confidence, that He will grant me the desired leave.

If, as I really hope may happen, You give me *another* post & a *better* climate; nothing could give *me greater pleasure—nor more secure the public interests of our country*—than appointing, as *my Successor* at Stockholm, Him who was my immediate *Predecessor!* I mean, Mr. [John James] Appleton,[14] of Massachusetts! He was removed most unrighteously & unjustly, in 1830—when I was, with about as much reason, &, perhaps, wisdom, dismissed of my place, at Brussels, & sent to Sweden. It is *impossible* to serve our country more zealously, efficiently, honourably & successfully, than it *was* served, by Mr. Appleton in Sweden; & nothing could be higher, or better, than [the] standing & position, enjoyed by Him at Stockholm; The Court, the Society, and the community esteemed & respected him; and his return to this country would give great & universal satisfaction; & should I succeed, in obtaining the *change* that I desire—*south*—I should really *rejoice*, at Mr. Appleton's being restored to his old post;—as I sincerely lamented at the time, that it fell upon *me*, to be the innocent & reluctant cause of his being removed from a Residence, where he was so highly & so justly valued & esteemed. This has ever been my opinions & feelings as regards Mr. Appleton; and I have often thought of imparting them to You, Sir; as I emphatically *did* to your different predecessors—since 1830!

Perhaps, considering my veteran station in our foreign corps—I may be indulged in saying a word—as it is a conscientious & a favourable one of some of my diplomatic brothers or Colleagues, now in Europe. It shall be brief & emphatic! I think it would be impossible for the U. States to have three more effective & respected & excellent Ministers in Europe than Mr. [Lewis] Cass—Mr. [Henry] Wheaton—& Mr. [Churchill Caldom] Cambreleng![15] I say this, without regarding party points; or *"how"* they *"got there"*; but *there*, they *are*, & from my *own* personal observa-

13. Arfwedson (1806–1855) was a Swedish businessman and writer who served as American consul, 1838–1855. In the antebellum period, those who represented the United States abroad as consuls were often foreign nationals.

14. Appleton (1792–1864) was secretary of the American legation to Portugal, 1819–1822; secretary to the Spanish legation, 1822–1824; chargé d'affaires to the Kingdom of the Two Sicilies, 1825; chargé to Sweden and Norway, 1826–1830. George Washington Lay (1798–1860), not Appleton, received the appointment as Hughes's successor at Stockholm and served 1842–1845.

15. Cass (1782–1866) was minister to France, 1836–1842; Wheaton (1785–1848; Brown 1802) was minister to Prussia, 1837–1846); and Cambreleng (1786–1862) served as minister to Russia, 1840–1841.

tion,—on the spot—& my various means & sources of European information (the fruit of countless connections, & long matured habits) I am warranted in repeating, that the country *cannot* be more effectively served & honourably represented, than it is by the three Gentlemen I have *presumed* to name.

And now, Sir, I have written more, perhaps, than is wise, *in* me—or agreeable, *to* you: but, I write, as I feel, & as I speak; candidly and freely; &, I believe, never offensively. Though it may be, a *little* flippantly! However, I believe, that I am in safe, because just hands; &, I *also* believe, that you have confidence in my candour & honesty.

I shall be—& am now—exceedingly anxious to hear from you! You know the frightful history of my daughter's suffering in the burning ship, Poland, last year;[16] & you may conceive my eager & natural desire, again to embrace my child! Now, *my only child*. For you know, how I have been afflicted; & where (that horrid Florida war)[17] since I saw you in London. Besides this consideration, her solid interests *require* my presence; for the Pennsylvania Bank & the Franklin Bank of Baltimore have included her in the sufferers, they have spread through the land![18] But enough! Only—if the Government *can* & *will* do anything for me—may I pray you, to commune about my interests, with *my friend* Mr. Clay, & you may consult Mr. [John Quincy] Adams,[19] (whose Amistad speech I read, last night!!!)—about my fitness. As to Mr. Clay—*I openly avow* my devotion *to* & admiration and friendship *for* him! And, Minister—Charge—or *Citizen, I will never desert Him.* I learned *to know* & *to value* him, when I was young—at Ghent! &, I repeat, *others* may—I never *will*—give him up! I am quite willing, if you think fit, & *rethink* fit, that this rapid (perhaps *rabid*) scrawl may be read by Mr. Tyler. To whom, I offer my respectful compliments; as I do those of sincere condolence to Mrs. [Caroline Le Roy] Webster[20] & to you, Sir, on the family sorrow that has befallen you![21] In my youth, I here passed happy days, & was intimate,

16. During an Atlantic crossing the *Poland* was struck by lightning and burned at sea. Following a few desperate days, the voyagers were rescued by a passing ship. See *Letter of Miss Margaret Smith Hughes to Her Father, Narrating the Loss of the Packet Ship Poland, on Her Way from New York to Havre, 16 May, 1840* (Baltimore, 1845).

17. The Second Seminole War, 1835–1842.

18. The Franklin Bank of New York failed in 1829, the Bank of Pennsylvania in 1841.

19. Adams (1767–1848; Harvard 1787), who after leaving the presidency served as congressman from Massachusetts from 1831 until his death, was at that time serving as chairman of the House Committee on Foreign Affairs.

20. Mrs. Webster (1797–1882), daughter of New York merchant Herman Le Roy (1758–1841), married DW on December 12, 1829.

21. Caroline Le Roy Webster's father, Herman Le Roy, died March 13, 1841.

with the family of Mr. LeRoy. Truly & respectfully your's

Christopher Hughes.

P.S. You can say to Mr. [Gustavus de] Nordin,[22] that his King[23] is in excellent health & great activity. I met him yesterday; I was on the Box of a 4-in hand & His Majesty saluted me & the Coachmen; & seemed highly pleased at our exaltations: The Coachman was Count [Matusseure?], Russian Minister,[24] one of the [illegible]est men in Europe. The King is now 80. The Diet say: "He must pay his own Debts:" & H.M. is doing so.

*But I here beg leave to enter my solemn and un-"expunge"-able, protest, against the use of the word "ultimate"—as a verb! This violence shall never be borne, or countenanced—by me! You may do as you like! & of course, as usual, will do so. CH.

A L S. DNA, RG 59 (Despatches, Norway and Sweden). Rec'd July 15, 1841. Endorsed: "Leave granted." Hughes (1786–1849; Princeton 1805) began a life-long diplomatic career as secretary to the American commissioners at Ghent in 1814. He was chargé d'affaires to Sweden and Norway at Stockholm in 1819, chargé to the Netherlands in 1825, and chargé at Stockholm again in 1830. In 1842 he returned to the Netherlands as chargé. Hughes was the son-in-law of General Samuel Smith (1752–1839), military hero of the American Revolution and organizer of the defense of Baltimore in the War of 1812. Smith also represented Maryland in one or the other House of the U.S. Congress for forty years.

TO ISAAC RAND JACKSON

Absolutely & strictly confidential
My Dear Sir,   Washington Feb. 12. 1841

I write you on a subject entirely personal & private, & beg of you, as soon as you have read it, to burn this letter. If what I am about to say strikes you as impracticable, take no notice of this—nor make any answer. If otherwise, please write to me that you think the thing can be done—& let me know this, in course of mail.

Well—the case is this. I am going to stay here, probably, & if so, I must have a *House*. I am not in a condition to buy one, so much of my means is vested *Westward*—and I do not find it easy to find one for rent. A good house is to be sold—for about $13.000—& it will require one or two thousand to repair it completely—say 15.000 in all. The House is thought to be fully worth the cost. In that respect, I should follow the best advice.

22. Nordin (1799–1867) served as minister to the United States from Sweden and Norway, 1838–1845.

23. King Charles XIV John (1763–1844) ruled as king of Sweden and Norway from 1818 to 1844.

24. Probably a reference to Count Adam Thaddeus Matuszewicz, the Russian ambassador to Sweden and Norway, 1839–1842.

Now, in the first place, it has occurred to me that you might be inclined to buy it, as an investment, & let me occupy it;

Or, you might incline to enable me to buy it, by furnishing the means to pay for it, to the extent say, of one half—& probably the owner will be willing to take a mortgage for the balance. This last I should prefer.

Now, My Dear Sir, *keeping this religiously private*, do as I have said above—either burn this, & never give it another thought—or answer it, just as strikes you—remembering only that I have a desire to hear from you by return of Post, if convenient. Yours truly   Danl Webster

ALS. MdHi. Jackson (1804–1842), a lawyer of Philadelphia, was commissioned chargé d'affaires to Denmark on May 20, 1841. He died in Copenhagen on July 27, 1842.

FROM ISAAC RAND JACKSON

Dear Sir   Philada Monday Morning 15 Feby 1841.

I have this moment only received your letter of the 12th inst.[1] It shall be immediately destroyed according to your request—but as I value the smallest portion of your regard too highly to run the risk of losing it through any misapprehension of my motives, I cannot refrain from writing in reply to it, though contrary to your directions. I trust you will forgive me.

My pecuniary situation is this. The principal part of my income is derived from real estate which is not entirely within my control. Of the rest of my means, nearly all is now so locked up by the mode of its investment that, though probably safe, it is wholly unavailable for present use.

I have ventured to disobey your directions so far as to write this explanation of my present circumstances, that I may add thereto my sincerest assurance that nothing but utter inability could prevent me from instantly availing myself of the opportunity you offer me. I am, with much respect, Faithfully yours   I R J

ALS copy. MdHi.

FROM ISAAC RAND JACKSON

Dear Sir   Philada 17 March 1841

Sickness in my family will not permit me to go to Washington tomorrow, as I had intended. It may possibly keep me here another week—and as you may have made some arrangements for the use of the two thousand dollars to which I referred when I last had the pleasure of seeing you, I must ask of you the favour to point out some convenient and

1. See above.

proper mode of remitting this sum to you. It is ready and awaits only your order. I have the honour to be With much respect faithfully yours
I.R.J.

ALS copy. MdHi.

TO ISAAC RAND JACKSON

D Sir   [March 19, 1841]
    Please send a check—drawn not by you, but by some Cashier—payable to bearer—on some Bank in Baltimore, Philad[elphi]a—or NY.
    Come here, as soon as you can leave home.

AL. MdHi.

FROM ISAAC RAND JACKSON

Dear Sir   Philada 20 March 1841
    I shall be in Washington on Monday evening if possible, but on Tuesday at the farthest, and, as no time will be lost, I prefer to bring with me those papers rather than to run the risk of transmitting them by mail. I have the honour to be With great respect faithfully yours   I.R.J.

ALS copy. MdHi.

FROM ISAAC RAND JACKSON

Dear Sir   [March 1841]
    Oppressed as the President is by crowds of importunate claimants, I feel some delicacy in Speaking to him in relation to any appointment for myself. I have to-day, however, written a short note on the subject, which I have sent to him enclosed in a letter from Mr [John] Lee of Maryland,[1] and accompanied by one from Governor [Edward Douglass] White of Louisiana.[2] These letters will explain my wishes—and as General [William Henry] Harrison has always evinced the kindest feelings towards me, and is fully aware that I have laboured in his cause ardently and, I believe, not unsuccessfully during the past five years, I think he would willingly accede to any reasonable request on my part.
    But if my wishes are gratified, I am well aware that I shall be much indebted therefore to your own kind offices on my behalf—and I therefore pledge you my honour that, in case I receive either of the appoint-

1. Lee (1788–1871), congressman from Maryland, 1823–1825, and Jackson's brother-in-law.
    2. White (1795–1847; University of Nashville 1815), U.S. congressman from 1829 to 1835, governor of Louisiana from 1835 to 1839, and again a congressman, 1839–1843.

ments I have named,[3] I will return to this country whenever you may think it expedient that I should come, and will devote my time, my labour and my means unshrinkingly and without stint in any way that shall best further your interests. My Southern friends assure me that you are daily gaining strength at the South—and as appearances promise, I should have to console myself for the shortness of my stay abroad, by the pleasure of aiding in another successful presidential election. I have the honour to be With much respect faithfully yours I.R.J.

A L S copy. MdHi.

FROM ISAAC RAND JACKSON

Dear Sir   Philad 8 April 1841.

I take the liberty to send you the enclosed letter[1] to be placed before President Tyler or not, as you may think best.

In several of my late interviews with General [William Henry] Harrison,[2] he had said to me, almost in the same words—"I assure you, Mr. Jackson, that your interests shall be consulted before any thing is done with Naples." This I certainly considered a promise of that mission or an equivalent. And when I last saw him and explained to him my particular reasons for wishing an early action in my case, the only matter in doubt seemed to be the time when my nomination should be made.

If the President be made aware that the mission to Naples was thus virtually disposed of, it might facilitate, and, to avoid the importunities of other applicants, perhaps hasten my appointment. I am especially led to this belief by a conversation I have this day had with my brother-in-law, Mr. John Lee of Maryland, who knows Mr. [John] Tyler intimately—and who says, that from Mr. Tyler's well-known high sense of honour, there can scarcely be a doubt but that he will carry out the intentions of the late president with regard to any appointment, where there is no strong objection to the individual named therefor. And that if it be made known to him that before General Harrison's death it was the understanding that I should go to Naples, the appointment will be made immediately.

I beg you not to think me importunate about this matter, but rather that I do not wish to lose a single point that may promise a more immediate fulfilment of my wishes. Pardon me, too, for saying that I have

3. One of the positions to which Jackson refers was that of chargé d'affaires at Naples.

1. The enclosure to which Jackson refers is also addressed to DW and dated April 8. In it Jackson recounts Harrison's promise to him and reiterates his desire to secure the post at Naples.

2. President Harrison died April 4, 1841.

scarcely ever yet received a favour from any one, that I have not found some mode to repay, fourfold. The knowledge of this, I am well aware, can have no weight with you, still it is a consolation to myself while seeking so great a kindness from another. My heart is set upon this mission absolutely—and I would rather lose half the remainder of my existence than be disappointed. I leave my fate entirely in your hands, and pray you to believe me, with much respect, faithfully yours   (Signed)

I. R. Jackson

ALS copy. MdHi.

FROM ISAAC RAND JACKSON

Dear Sir   Philada 12 June 1841.

It was my intention to have been in Washington before this, or I should sooner have expressed to you my sincere thanks for your kindness in recommending me to the appointment which I now have the honour to hold. I beg you to receive those thanks now, and to believe that I shall ever feel myself deeply indebted to you for the warm interest you have been pleased to take in my appointment. Neither time nor absence can deprive me of this deep sense of your kindness.

Pardon me for saying that I have been exceedingly gratified by your late letter to Mr. [Henry Stephen] Fox.[1] Not because it is an able diplomatic paper—that was a matter of course—but because, in addition to its powerful argument, its tone is so dignified—so proudly national that it has extorted much praise from even your political opponents. They cannot refrain from some exultation that the apparent inclination to arrogance on the part of Mr. Fox should have been so quietly yet pointedly rebuked. The calm logic of this paper will I am sure be well appreciated in England.

I have just been examining, too, your communication in relation to the Sound Dues[2]—& I cannot help thinking that my delay may prove a fortunate circumstance in enabling me to proceed on my mission more fully prepared to attain a result favourable to our commercial interests & satisfactory to our government. I have the honour to be With great respect Yours faithfully   (Signed) I. R. Jackson

ALS copy. MdHi.

1. See DW to Fox, April 24, 1841, "The Crisis in Anglo-American Relations," pp. 58–68, below. Fox (1791–1846) was minister plenipotentiary to the United States from 1835 to 1843.

2. See DW to Tyler, May 24, 1841, *Senate Documents*, 27th Cong., 1st sess., Serial 390, No. 1. On the Danish sound dues controversy, see "The World and Daniel Webster: Denmark," pp. 255–272, below.

TO PETER CHARDON BROOKS

Private & confidential

My Dear Sir   Washington July 8. 1841

We must soon appoint a minister to London. It is a most important place, just now, as well as the most honorable office in the gift of the Govt. If I were not quite so poor, I should be proud of the place myself, if I could get it; but I am too poor to go to London, & too poor, probably, to stay where I am, long. I have more than half an inclination to recommend Mr [Edward] Everetts[1] immediate appointment; but I have no very recent information from him, nor do I know how the climate would suit his wife's health.[2] Somebody must be appointed very soon. I have not made up my mind, conclusively; & if I had, it is not absolutely certain that my recommendation would be followed. I should be glad, however, to hear from you on the subject, who probably know Mr Everett's wishes.

It would be most agreeable, if you could get into the cars, & come here for a day or two. Yrs very truly   Danl Webster

ALS. MHi. Brooks (1767–1849) was a wealthy Boston merchant and the father-in-law of Edward Everett.

FROM [PETER CHARDON BROOKS]

My dear Sir   Boston July. 13. 1841

I am honored with your confidential letter of the 8th instant,[1] and feel exceedingly obliged by the interest you take in Mr. [Edward] Everett. I hear from him often, and in some of his letters, marked private, he makes mention of a possible mission abroad always expressing the utmost reliance on your friendship and influence. My last from him is dated May. 29 received July. 3.

Knowing your kind feelings toward Mr. Everett I may, in confidence, say any thing to you. In one of his late letters after speaking of his wife's improved health—he says "I have reason to think it not unlikely that I may have an appointment abroad. If it is one that I can accept with convenience I shall do so. I cannot go to either of the Northern Courts. If the mission to England France or Vienna should be offered me I should accept it."

I have been very careful to keep to myself all Mr. E[verett] has written to me on this subject.

I should be happy to make a short visit to Washington but if it were otherwise convenient the season of the year would seem to forbid it, unless in cases of necessity. I pray you to make my most respectful compli-

1. Everett (1794–1865; Harvard 1811) was minister to Britain from 1841 to 1845.

2. Charlotte Gray Brooks Everett (1800–1859).
1. See above.

ment to Mrs. [Caroline Le Roy] Webster. I was disappointed in not seeing your son on his return from Europe,[2] but his time here was so short that he was gone before I heard of his arrival. His friends say he is very much improved by being abroad. Mr. Everett & the family speak highly of him & miss him very much.

Speaking of yourself, My dear Sir, how on earth could they do without you at Washington? The country depends upon you & is more indebted to you than to any other man.

A L draft. MHi.

TO HIRAM KETCHUM

Private
Dr Sir   July 22. '41
Will you please tell me all about Mr [Hugh] Maxwell's son.[1] How old is he—what is his Education—what languages, does he write & speak. In short, what is he fit for?

There is such a rush for every thing in my Dept. I have no peace. I should be most happy, indeed, to oblige Mr Maxwell—if I can. Yrs   DW.

A L S. NhD. Ketchum (c. 1792–1870), a lawyer from New York City, was a friend and political supporter of Webster.

TO EDWARD EVERETT

Private
My Dear Sir   Washington July 24. 1841
I have the pleasure to inform you that you are nominated to the Senate, as minister to England; an announcement, which you will not doubt it gives me great pleasure to make. I am in hopes the nomination will be confirmed, so as that I may notify it to you by the same conveyance which takes this, but the Senate is much engaged today, (Saturday) & will probably be so on Monday, so that it may not before Tuesday go into Executive Session, which would be too late, I fear, for this opportunity. No kind of opposition, however, is expected. So far as I hear, the nomination satisfies every body, but a few violent partizans, like the conductors of the Globe.[1]

2. Edward Webster (1820–1848; Dartmouth 1841) traveled and studied in Europe, 1839–1841. He lived for some time with the Everetts in Florence.

1. Maxwell (1787–1873) was a prominent New York City lawyer. His son, John Stevenson Maxwell (d. 1870; Princeton 1836), was appointed secretary of the legation to Russia.

1. On July 23, 1841, the Washington *Daily Globe* criticized the nomination of Everett because he was known to be an opponent of slavery at a time when one of the questions at issue with England was the slave trade.

Mr [Andrew] Stevenson[2] will leave London about the first of September, with Mr [Benjamin] Rush.[3] As nobody but the consul[4] will be left in London, it will be desirable that you repair to your post, (if you accept it) as soon as may be; although it is hardly to be expected that you should be in England, by the time of Mr Stevenson's departure. I trust Mrs [Charlotte Gray Brooks] Everett will not be afraid of this march to the North on her health. If I could have afforded it, I should have put myself in competition with you for this place; but, as I wrote to Mr [Peter Chardon] Brooks[5] the other day, I am too poor even to stay here, & much less am I able to go abroad. You may hear of me soon, for ought I know, at Marshfield, with my friend [Seth] Peterson.[6]

We are in the midst of the Session; & I may say in the crisis of our affairs. If we get along with the Bank Bill, Bankrupt-Bill, Land Bill, & Revenue Bill, all which are on the tapis, we shall stand strong with the public. But some of these measures are of doubtful result. The great difficulty consists in producing & maintaining harmony of action among the Whigs.

I ought to mention, perhaps, while thus writing privately, that the President is of opinion that persons now appointed to missions abroad will not be expected to remain very long, in their situations. Various considerations lead him to this, <abou> in regard to which I can communicate with you hereafter. I give the hint now, only to the end that <if> you may understand that if you <ca> accept the mission, you will not be required to fill it longer than might perhaps be agreeable to you. I am, Dear Sir, Yrs truly   Danl Webster

ALS. MHi. Published in PC, 2:105–106.

TO EDWARD EVERETT

Private

My Dear Sir   Washington Nov. 20. 1841

I hope this will find you in London. When your commission was forwarded, I had no time to write you privately. Your nomination was op-

2. Stevenson (1784–1857; William and Mary c. 1799) served as minister to the Court of St. James from 1836 until replaced by Everett. Stevenson did not leave London until the end of October, and Everett arrived November 18.

3. Rush (1811–1877; Princeton 1829) was secretary of legation for Great Britain and for a time acted as chargé d'affaires, 1837–1841.

4. Thomas Aspinwall (1786–1876;

Harvard 1804) was the American consul at London, 1815–1853.

5. See above, DW to Brooks, July 8, 1841.

6. Peterson (1788–1866), one of Webster's employees at Marshfield, often acted as Webster's boatman and fishing companion. Out of respect for Peterson's knowledge of the sea and of the best fishing grounds, Webster called him "Commodore" Peterson.

posed in the Senate,[1] in a manner, & for reasons quite unexpected. All spoke well of your talents & qualifications, but the objection was, that we were in danger of constant controversies with England, upon the subject of slaves, & that on that point your views were not such as the Southern Gentlemen approved. To your appointment to France or Spain, there would have been no objection. A strong desire was expressed, that the nomination should be withdrawn, & that you should be appointed to some other place. But it appeared to me, that that wd be worse for you than rejection. In the end, the vote was stronger than I had any hopes, & some who voted agt you, would have voted otherwise if necessary. Among them, I believe was Mr [William Campbell] Preston.[2] Mr [Henry] Clay was very strongly in your favor; which I mention the more readily, as his general course, thro the extra session, has not been such as I would cordially approve. Mr [Rufus] Choate's[3] efforts on the occasion were able, & said to have been very effective. We all owe him much. The President was friendly, decided, & immoveable, thro' the whole proceeding.

It was lamentable, indeed to see Northern men, [Levi] Woodbury,[4] [James] Buchanan,[5] &c &c acting such a part as they did act.[6]

You see what convulsions have shaken the Whig party, & how adverse has been the general result of the fall elections. Whether we can recover ourselves, is quite uncertain. There wd appear to be an inevitable breach between the friends of Mr [John] Tyler, & those of Mr Clay. For my part, I shall go with Mr Tyler, certainly, or else leave the Administration. Much as I deplore his vetos, he yet thinks he has been unfairly & unkindly treated. The New Administration come together with good feelings, & harmonious purposes; & I suppose events will teach us, before the end of the ensuing session, what general results we may look for in the future. I wish you would write a kind letter to the President.

Mr. [Andrew] Stevenson is yet in Philadelphia, but expected here to-day.

I have taken the House, that was Mr [Thomas] Swann's, & am getting into it.[7] Mrs [Caroline Le Roy] W[ebster] is now in N.Y. but will be here

1. Southern opposition in the Senate to Everett's appointment arose because of Everett's attitude toward slavery. After heated debate, the nomination was confirmed on September 11, 1841. *Executive Journal, 1837–1841*, p. 438.

2. Preston (1794–1860; South Carolina College 1812) served as U.S. senator from South Carolina from 1833 to 1842.

3. Choate (1799–1859; Dartmouth 1819) was chosen to fill Webster's vacant seat in the Senate when the latter became secretary of state.

4. Woodbury (1789–1851; Dartmouth 1809) served as U.S. senator from New Hampshire, 1841–1845.

5. Buchanan (1791–1868; Dickinson College 1809) was at that time a senator from Pennsylvania, 1834–1845.

6. Both Woodbury and Buchanan voted against Everett's confirmation.

7. Swann (1766–1841) was a prominent lawyer and at one time U.S. district attorney for Washington, D.C.

next week. Edward will be with us, for the winter, & read in some office.

John Watson,[8] of the Brunswick Hotel, has been a sort of Banker of mine. Will you be good enough to send him 100£ on my account, which I will remit to you hereafter. I will thank you to do so. Write me as often as you can. You will hear from me officially, by an early opportunity. Give my best regards to your family. Yrs truly   Danl Webster

A L S . MHi.

FROM SAMUEL DAVIES HEAP

Consulate of the U. States

Sir,   Tunis 17th. Nov. 1841

I have the honor to inform you that by letters just received from my Son[1] at Washington I learn that the President has been pleased to supersede me in this Consulate.[2] This is an event, certainly not anticipated by me, after a faithful service of nearly forty years; eighteen of which, have been devoted to the duties of this consulate, in a manner to meet with the approbation of each succeeding administration.

My Son informs me that he understood it was the intention of the President to offer me the situation of Dragoman or Interpreter to the Legation at Constantinople, I think, however, that he must have been misinformed, as, independent of the circumstance of my being totally unqualified to undertake the duties of that office, it is not probable, that after having served so many years in situations of much higher responsibility, a proposition so mortifying should be made to me. If I have in anyway forfeited the confidence of the government, let it be wholly withdrawn from me, as I cannot consent, whatever inconveniencies may result to me, to serve in any situation subordinate to the one I now hold, or in one, the duties of which, I do not feel myself perfectly competent to discharge.

I have been absent from the U.S. for twenty five years, with the exception of a few months in 1825 and consequently am personally unknown to the government but, Sir, I cannot permit myself to believe, that I am now, in my advanced period of life, to be cast on my own limited resources, with a numerous family dependent on me. No, Sir, I love my country too much, and my confidence in my Government is too great, to allow me for a moment to harbour such an idea.

8. Not identified.

1. It is not known which of Heap's sons (Gwinn Harris, Lawrence, or Samuel D., Jr.) notified his father of his impending replacement.

2. Instead of sending Heap a formal letter of recall, Webster ordered his successor, William Brown Hodgson (1807–1871), dragoman 1831–1833, to deliver to Heap a new commission as dragoman to the legation in Constantinople. See below, DW to Hodgson, September 22, 1841, "The World and Daniel Webster: The 'Barbary Powers,'" pp. 290–292.

I cannot here enter into a detail of the services I have rendered, there are documents however, existing in the Department over which you preside which will satisfy you Sir that I have claims which entitle me to the favorable consideration of my country.

With sentiments of the highest consideration I have the honor to be, very Respectfully Sir, Your Most Obed. Servt.   S. D. Heap

ALS. DNA, RG 59 (Consular Despatches, Tunis). Rec'd March 31, 1842. Heap (1781–1853; Jefferson College of Medicine 1803) left a career as a naval surgeon to serve as chargé d'affaires at Tunis from 1823 to 1824. In 1825 he was appointed consul and served in this capacity until his removal by Webster.

FROM SAMUEL DAVIES HEAP

Sir,   Tunis 17th Feby 1842

I have the honor to inform you that Mr [William Brown] Hodgson,[1] my successor in the Consulate, arrived here on the 11th Inst. No time was lost in obtaining for him an audience with H[is] H[ighness] the Bey,[2] by whom, as well as his ministers and the European Consuls, his Colleagues, he was received in a manner which must have been gratifying to him that is to say his reception was such as was due to the representative of the Government of the U. States, than which, I am proud to say none is more respected here.

Mr. Hodgson on his arrival at the Consulate presented me with a commission of Dragoman to the U. S. Legation near the Sublime Porte, which the President has thought proper to honor me with, for this manifestation of confidence I beg to tender my sincere thanks.

In Nov. last I received a letter from my Son informing me that upon learning that the Government intended to remove me from this Consulate, he had repaired to Washington for the purpose of seeing you on the

1. Hodgson, consular officer and philologist, was sent to Algiers as a language student in 1826 by President John Quincy Adams because the U.S. government was so devoid of expertise about the Middle East that letters received in Arabic could not be translated. After three years in Algiers, Hodgson worked as a clerk-interpreter in the Department of State. In 1831 he became dragoman to the American legation in Constantinople, but he was unceremoniously fired two years later by Commodore David Porter (1780–1843), the ill-tempered retired naval officer whom Andrew Jackson (1767–1845) had appointed to represent the U.S. to the Ottoman Empire. From 1833 to 1840 Hodgson received occasional appointments as a special agent to Egypt, Morocco, Peru, and Prussia. Because of his friendship with Webster, Hodgson in 1841 finally achieved the position he had worked for most of his life when President Tyler appointed him consul to Tunis. See Thomas A. Bryson, *An American Consular Officer in the Middle East in the Jacksonian Era: A Biography of William Brown Hodgson, 1801–1871* (Atlanta, 1979).

2. Ahmad Bey (d. 1855), who ruled 1837–1855, is remembered for his efforts to reorganize Tunisia in Western fashion.

subject, but that he has been deprived of that pleasure in consequence of you[r] absence in Massachusetts, that he had consequently sought and obtained an interview with the President who has kindly informed him that I had not been removed, but transferred to the Legation at Constantinople as Dragoman; on the receipt of this information, I did myself the honor of addressing you disclaiming the qualifications necessary for the performance of the duties of that situation, my acceptance of which would place me in a false position. Of that despatch I have the honor herewith to transmit a duplicate.[3] In a subsequent interview with which my son had been honored by the President, fully aware that I was not acquainted with the Turkish language and apprehensive of the consequences that might result to me from a change to a colder climate, he urged these objections, with perhaps an indiscreet, but I trust a pardonable pertinacity. The President was kind enough to assure him that the arrangement had been made with the best possible feeling toward Com. [David] Porter[4] and myself, that he was aware that I knew nothing of the Turkish language, that Mr. [John Porter] Brown[5] would not suffer by the change, and that I would be perfectly satisfied with my new situation. With these assurances Sir, I cannot hesitate a moment to accept the appointment with which I have been honored, and I trust that by a zealous attention to the interests of the Government, I shall enjoy a continuance of its confidence and consideration.

I shall make my arrangements for embarking for Constantinople without loss of time. With Sentiments of the highest Consideration I have the honor to be Very Respectfully Sir, Your Most Obed. Servt.   S. D. Heap

ALS. DNA, RG 59 (Consular Despatches, Tunis).

FROM WILLIAM BROWN HODGSON

No. 8
Sir,   London, July 3d 1842
I had the honor, in my dispatch No. 7,[1] from Malta, to communicate to you, my absence from Tunis. The ability and gentlemanly character of Mr. [William R. B.] Gale,[2] whom I left in charge of the Consulate, jus-

3. See above.
4. Porter was chargé d'affaires to the Ottoman Empire from 1831 to 1839 and thereafter minister until his death in 1843.
5. John Porter Brown (1814–1872) joined his uncle, David Porter, in Constantinople in 1832 and was appointed dragoman in 1836. He held that and various other positions at

the American legation until his death.
1. DNA, RG 59 (Consular Despatches, Tunis), May 16, 1842.
2. William R. B. Gale, previously a vice consul at Malta, remained acting consul at Tunis until replaced in 1843 by John Howard Payne (1791–1852; Union College), who served until 1845.

tify me in giving every assurance, that the interests of the United States in Tunis, will be preserved.

I have now, Sir, the honor to inform you that unexpected events, have compelled me to come to London from Italy. Those events are connected with my early nuptials with an American Lady.[3] They were to have been solemnized in Switzerland; but as the *Code civil* which rules in the Swiss Confederation, besides other formalities, requires a previous residence of six months, we were compelled to come to London.

I have not been allowed to take this important step in the career of life, without accepting the condition of resigning my present appointment. I, therefore, Sir, very respectfully submit thro' you to the President, my Commission as Consul of the United States for the Kingdom of Tunis; and as this letter of resignation will reach the Department on the 21' day of July, the day of the month, on which my Commission is dated, I shall in my accounts with the United States' Bankers here, consider my resignation as made on that day.

I beg, Sir, that the President and yourself, will be pleased to regard my resignation, as an alternative upon which, I feel, that my happiness depends. It has not been adopted, but with much respectful reference to the obligations which I owe you, for an honorable appointment recently conferred. Nor, can I forget, that I was educated by the Government of my country, for a special service in its foreign relations. If the President should be pleased to call me again to that service, I could not decline the duty and the honor. Until that period may arrive, when I can be restored to my proper career, and I believe that, in the affairs of Government as of individuals, *quisquis* in *arte sua*, is the correct rule, I should be happy to serve my country at this; or a Continental court, as Secretary of Legation.[4]

The objections to my present office, would not apply to that. I have the honor to be, with profound respect, Sir, Your Very Obt Sevt.

Wm. B. Hodgson

ALS. DNA, RG 59 (Consular Despatches, Tunis). Rec'd July 20, 1842.

TO GEORGE TICKNOR

Dr Sir   Feb. 18. '42

The mission to Spain is fixed off, as you wished.[1] Mr [Joseph Green]

3. Hodgson married Margaret Telfair, a wealthy heiress, in London on July 11, 1842. She accepted his proposal of marriage on the condition that he resign from his recent appointment.

4. Hodgson never entered government service again. He spent the rest of his life traveling and pursuing his scholarly interests.

1. Washington Irving (1783–1859) was appointed minister to Spain on February 10, 1842, and served in that capacity until 1846.

Cogswell is nominated for Secretary.[2] I am happy in having had some agency in bringing into the public service Gentlemen of worth & distinction, whose appointment is likely, not only to be useful to the Country, but to gratify a high feeling, by showing a respect to scholars & men of letters. Madrid is likely enough to be an important point, in our foreign relations.

I am not ashamed of London, Madrid, & Copenhagen. [Henry] Wheaton does us honor at Berlin; Mr [Lewis] Cass is respectable, I believe in Paris, & as for the rest—

I will be diplomatic—& speak, if I speak at all—by the card.

Remember me most kindly to Mrs [Anna Eliot] Ticknor.[3] When the Spring comes, come with it, & look at us. And in the mean time, & always, be assured of my attachment & regard.   Danl. Webster

ALS. DLC. Published in W & S, 16:363. Ticknor (1791–1871; Dartmouth 1807).

TO NICHOLAS BIDDLE

Strictly private & confidential
Dear Sir   Mar: 11. 43

I may as well tell you, in the strictest confidence, the whole truth, respecting the state of things here. The President is still resolved to try the chances of an *Election*. This object enters into every thing, & leads, or will lead, to movements in which I cannot concur. He is quite disposed to throw himself altogether into the arms of the loco foco party.[1] This is just enough towards the Whigs—but it is not just to himself, or his own fame & character. He has altogether too high an opinion of the works which can be wrought by giving *offices* to hungry applicants. And he is surrounded by these, from morning to night. Every appointment, therefore, from the highest to the lowest, raises a question of *political effects*. This is terrible; especially in the Department where I am; & I fear the interest of the Country, & the dignity of the Govt may both suffer from it. Before the Whigs quarreled with the President, I had no reason to complain of any want of proper influence, in regard to appointments connected with foreign affairs; altho' the President had quite too many persons on hand to be provided for as chargés. Mr [Edward] Everett, Mr

2. Cogswell (1786–1871; Harvard 1806) refused the appointment as secretary of the legation to Spain. Alexander Hamilton, Jr. (1816–1890; West Point), son of James Alexander Hamilton and grandson of the late secretary of the Treasury, accepted the post and later became chargé d'affaires.

3. Anna Eliot Ticknor (1800–1885) was the youngest daughter of wealthy Boston merchant Samuel Eliot (d. 1820).

1. This refers to a faction of the Democratic party that favored, among other things, hard money and the strict construction of the Constitution.

[Washington] Irving, poor Mr [Isaac Rand] Jackson, &c were persons appointed on my recommendation.

Since the formal abandonment of the President by the Whigs, my position is entirely changed. As I can bring him no support, I can ask him for nothing. Between us, personally, there is entire good will; & if his object now was *only* to get thro his present term with credit, we should agree, in every thing. But I am expecting, every day, measures, which I cannot stand by, & face the Country.[2] I must, therefore, leave my place. It seems inevitable. Who will take it; I know not; or what is to become of us all, I know not. I fear, a confused & unsatisfactory scene is before us.

When you have read this burn it. Yrs truly   D.W.

A L S. DLC. Published with some deletions in Reginald C. McGrane, ed., *The Correspondence of Nicholas Biddle Dealing with National Affairs, 1807–1844* (Boston, 1919), pp. 345–346. Biddle (1786–1844; Princeton 1801), retired president of the Bank of the United States of Pennsylvania, formerly the Bank of the United States.

TO EDWARD EVERETT

Private and Confidential
Dear Sir   May. 12. 184[3]

One word about Genl. Duff Green.[1] He took no letter from me, except one to Mr. Joshua Bates,[2] on his own private affairs. I think the President gave him nothing but the letter to you, which I did not see.

I told him he could do nothing, officially or semi-officially. That any such thing, beside being useless, wd be disrespectful to you. I fear the President's notions are not quite strict enough, on such points; but he has high regard for you, & always speaks of you in the kindest manner. Yourself & [Washington] Irving are the principal monuments of *my* administration of the Department. It is well the appointments were made when they were. We were then all "going," as the phrase is, for honor and renown. Yrs truly   D.W.

I trust they will send you from N.Y. Mr. [Albert] Gallatin's *Lecture on Maps*,[3] by this conveyance.

2. Webster resigned from the cabinet May 8, 1843, over the issue of the annexation of Texas.

1. Green (1791–1875) acted as a personal representative of President Tyler to England and France, 1841–1844. Everett was annoyed by Green's activities, which he perceived as intereference with his responsibilities as minister to Britain.

2. Bates (1788–1864) was born in Massachusetts but spent much of his life in Europe, initially as a general agent for a leading New England shipping merchant, William Gray (1750–1825). He later formed a banking partnership with the House of Baring.

3. Gallatin presented a lecture on the northeastern boundary at a meeting of the New-York Historical Society on April 15, 1843. DW addressed the same meeting.

☞ What a flagellation Ld. B. gave the Genl.[4] At present, the Genl. is firing no guns.

ALS. MHi.

4. Probably a reference to Baron Henry Peter Brougham's (1778–1868) castigation of General Lewis Cass in the House of Lords, April 7, 1843. Brougham claimed that Cass had tried to promote discord between Britain and the United States "by the circulation of arguments upon ques-tions of international law, of even the rudiments of which he had no more conception than he had of the languages spoken in the moon." See *Hansard's*, 68:605–606, and "The Aftermath and Implementation of the Treaty of Washington: The Cass-Webster Debate," pp. 710–775, below.

The Crisis in Anglo-American Relations (1841–1842)

Problems with Great Britain dominated American foreign policy at the beginning of Webster's first term as secretary of state. Upon assuming office, he found himself confronted with a full-blown crisis in Anglo-American relations. The critical components of this crisis were three separate issues, each serious enough to threaten the outbreak of war: the disputed northeastern boundary, the *Caroline* affair and associated McLeod case, and the visit and search controversy.

Difficulties over the boundary dividing British North America and the United States dated back to the Treaty of Paris of 1783. The peace commissioners in Paris had agreed on a line that ran north from the source of the Saint Croix River to the "highlands" that supposedly divided the streams flowing into the Saint Lawrence River from those emptying into the Atlantic Ocean. Implementing this agreement was more difficult than reaching it. The commissioners had used a later edition of a 1755 map drawn by John Mitchell, a physician and botanist who was probably originally from Britain and had returned there from Virginia in 1746. Mitchell's map was a creditable work for its time, but the commissioners had failed to adopt it officially or to attach any map to the treaty itself. Imprecise geographical information compounded the uncertainty.

The peace commissioners had used Mitchell's reference to the Saint Croix River as a departure point for the boundary. But there was no Saint Croix River as described by the words of the treaty of 1783, and the selection of a substitute meant possession of thousands of miles of valuable territory. Secondly, the highlands used as a landmark in the Treaty of Paris could not be identified. In the dispute over what constituted the highlands, the Americans insisted that the term referred to a geographic watershed, and the British maintained that it meant conspicuous elevations. The differences in interpretation again translated into the reality of territory.

Between the end of the American Revolution and Webster's appointment as secretary of state there had been a number of efforts to establish the boundary between the United States and Canada. In 1798 American and British commissioners chosen according to the terms of the Jay Treaty agreed that the Schoodic River best matched the description given of the Saint Croix in the treaty of 1783. After the Treaty of Ghent of 1814, another commission divided the islands of Passamaquoddy Bay between the two countries. The location of the highlands, however, remained in dispute, despite the efforts of several boundary explorations. In accordance with the terms of the Treaty of Ghent, this question had been submitted to the king of the Netherlands, William I, for arbitration. Albert Gallatin prepared the American case with the assistance of William Preble, a judge of the supreme court of Maine. They argued in favor of the long-held American contention that the highlands were the watershed dividing streams flowing into the Saint Lawrence from those flowing into the Atlantic, but the British again insisted that the reference in the treaty of 1783 was to a specific elevation. In his decision of 1831, the king decided that it was impossible to locate the highlands. Although he was supposed to determine which side had the more valid claim, William I ruled that the countries compromise their differences—an idea accepted by the British but rejected by Maine and the U.S. Senate. Since the king had gone beyond his authority as defined in the protocol of arbitration, the United States was within its rights in declining the award, but the issue as a consequence remained unresolved.

The boundary controversy heated up in 1839 in the so-called Aroostook War. Canadian and American settlers had moved into the disputed Aroostook valley, which contained rich tracts of timber. With both sides attempting to control the valley, an explosive situation developed. When Maine introduced an armed posse into the area, the British countered by dispatching regular troops. A military confrontation was averted by President Martin Van Buren with the aid of General Winfield Scott, but as late as June 1841 the Aroostook problem required delicate diplomatic handling by Webster.

The tinderbox situation in the northeast inclined Webster toward compromise, but the politicians of Maine adamantly opposed a settlement on any terms but their own. To surmount this domestic roadblock, Webster accepted the proposal of Francis O. J. Smith that public opinion "be brought into right shape in Maine by enlisting certain leading men *of both political parties*" (Smith to DW, [June 7, 1841], below). Contemporaries raised moral reservations about Webster's use of secret service funds to finance a propaganda campaign in Maine, and the debate continues in our time. In Frederick Merk's opinion, the Webster-Smith effort violated the principles of federal and state relations by subsidizing "underground electioneering to manage the sentiment of a state of the Union" (*Fruits of Propaganda in the Tyler Administration* [Cambridge, Mass., 1971], p. 89). By contrast, Howard Jones believes that Webster did not act illegally and that his actions were justified by the threat to peace posed by the intransigent behavior of Maine (*To the Webster-Ashburton Treaty: A Study in Anglo-American Relations, 1783–1843* [Chapel Hill, N.C., 1977], p. 94).

A similar intermingling of diplomatic and domestic concerns characterized the second great problem in Anglo-American relations, the *Caro-*

line affair and the related case of Alexander McLeod. In the winter of 1837 a band of Canadian rebels and their American supporters occupied Navy Island, a British possession in the Niagara River. When the insurgents, known as Patriot Hunters, chartered the steamboat *Caroline*, apparently for use in an assault upon Canada, British militia took action. During the night of December 29 British irregulars attacked the boat, which was then moored at Fort Schlosser on the American side of the river. In the ensuing struggle one man—an American named Amos Durfee—was killed. The *Caroline* was towed to the middle of the river, burned, and sunk.

After some talk of war in Congress, an exchange of notes between the British and the American governments, and a visit by General Scott to the frontier, the *Caroline* crisis abated. The incident, however, was not settled. In November 1840, just as Webster was about to become secretary of state, a Canadian citizen, Alexander McLeod, was arrested in New York and charged with the murder of the single fatality of the *Caroline*. War seemed imminent. The documents published below on the *Caroline* and the McLeod case show how the new secretary of state handled an important diplomatic-political crisis that soon became deeply embroiled in the constitutional issues of federal-state relations. Governor William Henry Seward of New York and President John Tyler of Virginia engaged in a vituperative correspondence over the federal government's part in the trial of McLeod. Seward became incensed when Tyler appointed McLeod's attorney, Joshua A. Spencer, as the U.S. district attorney for northern New York. Webster, moreover, worked closely with Spencer on the defense. The trial ended well, in the acquittal of McLeod, but Tyler and Webster were not content to let the broader issue rest. In his annual message to Congress of December 7, 1841, Tyler recommended a law permitting the removal of cases that, like McLeod's, involved international relations from the state to the federal courts. The law, passed on August 29, 1842, empowered U.S. district court and Supreme Court justices to issue writs of habeas corpus when foreign nationals were held for acts committed under the explicit authority of their governments (5 *U.S. Stat.* 539–540).

The documents on the crisis in Anglo-American relations suggest that Webster was a skilled negotiator and a creative statesman. Not only did he use the McLeod case to avert future crises arising from instances in which foreign nationals acted under the authority of their governments, but he made an enduring contribution to international law by defining in a letter to Henry S. Fox of April 24, 1841, the conditions that justified an attack in the name of self-defense (see below). In 1945–1946, the Nuremberg Tribunal expressly endorsed Webster's doctrine of self-defense, and as recently as 1976, the Israelis drew upon Webster's views to justify their raid at the Entebbe airport in Uganda. Speaking before the United Nations Security Council on July 9, Ambassador Chaim Herzog characterized Webster's statement to Fox as "the classic formulation" of the right of self-defense. Herzog argued, quoting Webster, that such military actions as that at Entebbe were justified when "there is a 'necessity of self-defence, instant, overwhelming, leaving no choice of means and no moment for deliberation'" (verbatim record of the 1939th meeting of the United Nations Security Council, July 9, 1976). In 1981, when Israel attacked Iraq's nuclear research station at Tuwaitha, Ambassador Otunnu, the representative of Uganda to the Security Council of the United Nations, reminded Israel of Webster's doctrine of self-defense. Speaking on June 15, he concluded that the Israeli raid was "plainly inconsistent with the requirements of self-defence under general international law" as established by Secretary Webster (verbatim record of the 2282nd meeting of the United Nations Security Council, June 15, 1981).

Differences between the United States and Britain over the slave trade raised issues between the countries as complicated as those growing out of the boundary and the *Caroline*-McLeod disputes. From 1839 to 1841, Andrew Stevenson, American minister to the Court of Saint James, had maintained a running feud with the British over the question of the search and seizure of American vessels suspected of being engaged in the slave trade. The American position was consistent with international law: no right of search existed in time of peace. Webster's diplomacy backed that policy.

Like the question of search, the *Creole* case arose from the clash of American and British attitudes toward slavery. The *Creole* was bound from Richmond to New Orleans in October 1841 when 19 of the slaves on board captured the ship and demanded that it be sailed to Nassau, British territory, where slavery was illegal. Upon the ship's arrival, British authorities temporarily held the 19 mutineers but released the other 116 slaves. To Webster fell the responsibility of negotiating the delicate issues growing out of the *Creole* mutiny.

In addition to the major disputes at issue between Britain and the United States, other problems aggravated relations between the two countries. The kidnapping by Canadians of an American citizen named James W. Grogan held the potential of becoming a McLeod case in reverse, but the Grogan incident was ably defused by Fletcher Webster, acting as secretary of state in his father's absence. Difficulties over extradition, the implementation of the Rush-Bagot agreement of 1817, and the continuing attempts of the Patriot Hunters to embroil America and England in a war further contributed to the atmosphere of crisis. Daniel Webster summarized the climate of the times in a letter to Seward dated September 23, 1841, wherein he wrote: "If we cannot repress these lawless acts, we shall ere long be involved in an inglorious border warfare, of incursion and retaliation, ending perhaps in general hostilities" (see below).

The final document in this section is a confidential report by Albert Fitz about British military strength in the Caribbean. In October 1841, Webster selected Fitz as a secret agent to investigate the defenses of the British West Indies because of Fitz's familiarity with those British possessions. Webster's instructions, which probably were oral, have not been found, but their substance is indicated in Fitz's report. In testimonial letters written later, Webster expressed his great satisfaction with the manner in which Fitz had performed his secret and sensitive duties (see Fitz to James Buchanan, August 10, 1845, and the testimonials by DW of February 27, 1844, November 4, 1845, and June 2, 1849, in FO 5/560, PRO). Although tensions between Britain and the United States had lessened considerably by the time Fitz filed the document printed below, the Fitz mission suggests the severity of the crisis in Anglo-American relations in the fall of 1841.

After McLeod's acquittal on October 12, 1841, relations between the United States and Britain began to improve. In the month prior to McLeod's release, Lord Melbourne's ministry had fallen to one formed by Sir Robert Peel. The fiery Lord Palmerston was removed as foreign secretary in favor of the less strident Lord Aberdeen. Late in December, American minister Edward Everett informed Webster that Alexander Baring, Lord Ashburton, would be sent to the United States with full powers to settle all issues between the two countries. A new era in Anglo-American relations was at hand.

TO THEOPHILUS PARSONS

My Dear Sir: Washington, January 28th—1841.
There can be no objection to any temperate, tho' firm, expression of opinion, by our Legislature, on the Boundary question.[1] Yet it behoves us to consider what the present state of the subject is.

By the Treaty of Ghent, it was admitted and acknowledged, that the question of the Northeastern Boundary, was a question, on which the two Governments might not agree; and it was stipulated, in the Treaty, that in that event, the question should be made matter of arbitration, by a friendly Power. An arbitration was had—the arbitrator decided—but his decision satisfied neither party, and both rejected it.[2] The parties, then, as it seemed, were referred back to the stipulation in the Treaty,

1. Massachusetts passed a resolve on the boundary on March 13, 1841. *Acts and Resolves Passed by the Legislature of Massachusetts in the Year 1841* (Boston, 1841), p. 420.

2. This refers to the Netherlands arbitration of 1831. The British government was willing to accept the award, but the United States government refused to do so.

and are to try another arbitration. A negotiation, preparatory to such other arbitration, is now in progress between the two Governments, but has not, as yet, terminated in a Convention. This is the actual state of things.

It might have been better to have avoided the necessity of this second arbitration, and to have proposed a line by compromise. In my opinion, that might well have been thought of. But no such attempt was made, on either side. The negotiation for exploration,[3] arbitration &c., must go on, unless something occurs to break it off, till a Convention shall be concluded.

The real ground of complaint is the dilatoriness of the proceedings, and the consequent postponement of the final adjustment. On this point, a Resolution, in proper terms, but with a firm tone, might be useful, and certainly would be proper.

I do not see, therefore, on the whole, that the proposed Resolutions can do more, than,

    1st To express a strong sense of the right of our side of the Case; and
    2d To complain of delay, and urge the high importance of hastening the negotiation to its close.

I have not yet seen the Governor's Message,[4] but you will perceive, by what I have written, that I concur in the views which you express. We must avoid alarming the country with the fear of rupture, at the same time that we assert our rights firmly, express proper confidence in our own Government—and urge the importance of an early settlement of the dispute. Yours, with great regard.   Danl Webster

L S. MB. Published in Van Tyne, pp. 227–228. (A draft of this letter exists, mDW 17349. AL draft. NhHi.) Parsons (1797–1882; Harvard 1815) was, in 1841, the Boston representative to the Massachusetts Senate.

FROM EDWARD KENT

(*Private*)

Dear Sir,   Augusta Feby 17 1841

In view of the relation, which it is understood you will sustain to the new administration and the position I now occupy, I have taken the liberty at this early day to submit to you & through you to the President elect some considerations, on a subject of great interest & importance to the United States & particularly to Maine. I do not intend to enter into a discussion of the great questions, pending unadjusted between this country

3. Webster's transcriber wrongly substituted "explanation" for "exploration." Webster corrected the error in the final copy, but Van Tyne, working from the draft, repeated the mistake.

4. In a message to the state senate on January 22, Governor John Davis criticized Britain's indisposition to settle the northeastern boundary. The text of the address is in the Boston *Atlas*, January 27, 1841.

& Great Britain, as you understand them and I am well aware feel them, in all their importance & intricacy. One of these questions, *our great question of boundary*, is in a state which requires ability, firmness & prudence in those who are to manage it. Maine feels at this time *peculiarly* sensitive & restless under the arrogant pretensions & hostile movements of our opponents. There will be a strong & earnest appeal for aid & protection, for *direct* & *immediate* action on the part of the General Government. The spirit of our people is *getting up* & it will increase in strength & extent & will not be satisfied unless a course of policy is adopted at Washington at once *firm* & *active*. The long delays in negotiation, the wearisome diplomatic discussions, beginning about nothing and ending where they began, have led us in Maine to lessen very much, if not to give up entirely our faith in this mode of adjustment. If it is the design, as I trust & believe it is, of the new administration, to enter upon this subject, with a directness of purpose and distinctness of language hitherto unknown and to adopt a new mode of treating the question & if it shall be the wish of the administration to *avoid direct collision pending negotiations* and at the same time to satisfy Maine that the question is in progress under favorable auspices for us, I am confident no course could be taken, which would do so much to effect these objects as the *appointment of a Minister to England from this State*, who shall be qualified by his knowledge, experience, general character & firmness to place the question in such a position as may be desired by his government & by the State of Maine. I feel *strongly* that it will be very difficult if not impossible to keep our people from direct collision, if some assurance is not given by the new administration *by its acts* that this question is regarded as of the first importance. If we are to have a Southern man again in that station,[1] after so many years of continued occupancy from that section, the feeling here will be I fear, that the old course is to be resumed and a long & lingering course of diplomatic evasions, changing of front &c &c "point no point" discussions will once more overcloud the prospect of settlement. But if, on the other hand, Maine sees that one of her own citizens is sent as Minister and that a new prospect is opening, I have no doubt that a general expression of satisfaction & gratification will at once be heard and the Administration will gain strength and friends & its course on the question be approved & *acquiesced in*. I am confident that no other course could be taken, which would be so popular in Maine & tend so directly to satisfy & quiet the public mind.

I trust you will pardon my freedom & frankness when I say that it seems to me clear that a Northern man should be selected for this mission & that Maine, before any other State, if she can present a candidate

1. Andrew Stevenson, a Virginian,   1841.
served as minister to Britain, 1836–

qualified, should be gratified. Has she such a man. I think she has, and that *George Evans*[2] is the man. Of his qualifications I need not speak. He is as well known at Washington as at home. I therefore will say nothing more on that point. But I do feel that for the reasons suggested and only hinted at, his selection would be the most popular & useful & in every aspect which can be made. Maine would much regret the loss of Mr. Evans from the Senate, but would yield him readily if he is to stand at the post, where our interests will require a vigilant, talented, & prudent man. I have no right however to say that Maine would be willing to risk the election of a successor by delay beyond the time of adjournment of the Legislature. But this will not occur much, if any before the first of April. With my best wishes for the success of the new administration, I remain very respectfully your most obd sevt   Edward Kent.

A L S. NhD. Published in Curtis, 2:59–60. Kent (1802–1877; Harvard 1821) was governor of Maine in 1841.

TO EDWARD KENT

Private

Dear Sir   Washington Feb. 23. 1841

Mr Randall[1] has handed me your letter.[2] The subject of the North Eastern Boundary will undoubtedly attract the President's attention, among his first duties.

You must be aware of three things.

1st That the two Governments have agreed to settle this question by means of a joint commission, with an ultimate umpirage.

2. That they have agreed, that the negotiation of a Convention, for the completion of this arrangement shall be conducted *in Washington.*

3. That the basis of such Convention is already agreed upon, & that only some matters of detail remain unsettled.

In this state of the case, it will be the duty of the new Administration doubtless to hasten the steps of the parties, in concluding the Convention, as far as may be, consistently with propriety; but I do not see what else is to be done, unless we say at once that we will break off the negotiations & resort to force; a step, I am sure, for which the Country is not prepared.

It is to be recollected, that Maine, constantly declining compromise, has insisted, unwaveringly, on the ascertainment of the absolute right of

2. Evans (1797–1867; Bowdoin 1815), a Maine lawyer, served in the U.S. House of Representatives, 1829–1841, and in the U.S. Senate, 1841–1847.

1. This probably refers to Benjamin Randall (1789–1857; Bowdoin 1809), Whig representative in Congress from Maine, 1839–1843.

2. See above.

the case. To comply, in this respect, with what she has so strongly persisted in, <With this view> the arrangement now in progress was entered into, as being obviously the only mode of ascertaining that right,
& as being, also in strict compliance with the stipulations in the Treaty
of Ghent. Under these circumstances, it seems reasonable that nothing
but unpardonable delay on the other side should induce the Govt of the
United States <to look to any other modes of settlement> to take any
measures, except such as may be calculated to accelerate the completion
of the Convention.

I should be very sorry, & am sure the President, & the whole Administration would be sorry, to see any new excitement getting up, on
this delicate subject. You are aware, that nothing can be more dangerous
than popular excitement, without a definite, as well as a just object. As
things now stand, excitement can have no effect but to create counter
excitement, & probably delay, still further, the object of all parties, that
is a pacific & an immediate adjustment of the controversy.

I beg you to understand, that this letter is written as a private letter,
without consultation with any individual whatever.

The suggestion in your letter which relates to a distinguished public
man & friend of ours shall be respectfully communicated to the President
in due time. I have the honor to be, with great regard, your ob servt

A L draft. DLC. Published in Curtis, 2:60–61.

FROM LEWIS CASS

Private   (Confidential)
Dear Sir: Paris March 5. 1841
The last arrivals from the United States lead to the belief, that you
will be the Secretary of State under the new administration. Under this
presumption I write to you, and even if it is not so, my letter can do no
harm. It will still be in good hands.

I suppose you are aware of the instructions given by the British Ministry to their Minister at Washington [Henry Stephen Fox].[1] The subject is
no secret here and was freely spoken of to me by *one who knew*. If [Alex-
ander] McLeod[2] is executed, the Minister is to leave the United States.
It is the casus belli. But any sentence, short of this, is not to lead to this
result.

The immediate occasion of my writing to you, at this moment, is as
follows. A person, with good means of information called upon me this

1. The British minister to the
United States was instructed by Foreign Secretary Palmerston regarding
the McLeod case on February 9, 1841
(FO 5/358, PRO). Henry John Tem-
ple, Lord Palmerston (1784–1865),
was minister for foreign affairs from
1835 to 1841.
2. McLeod (1796–1871). See below,
passim.

morning, and told me, that orders had been given to a large portion of the British fleet in the Mediterranean, to rendez vous gradually at <Malta> Gibraltar, with the view sending them from there to Halifax. That unusual energy was displayed in the Navy yards, and that fourteen steam frigates would be ready to be upon the coast of the United States, if necessary, in the month of June, and that the first stroke would be at New York. That all this is finally determined, I do not believe, but that the general outline is correct, I doubt not. My informant had *good* means of information.

Of one thing I am sure. There is a bad feeling against us in England, and this feeling is daily and manifestly augmenting. It is not to be misunderstood among the many English, who are at Paris. And the sooner you are prepared for the consequences at home, the wiser you will be. The next war upon the ocean is to see greater changes, than have occurred in naval operations since the invention of gunpowder. The events upon the Syrian coast have opened all eyes here to surpassing effects of steam.[3] What is to prevent a fleet of steam frigates from being, as it were, its own messenger, and entering at once into the Harbour of New York. I shall not speculate upon the consequences, because you can estimate them better than I can. But I cannot but recommend, that every exertion be used to create without delay a steam marine. You want heavy floating batteries in your harbours. Practical men are losing their confidence in permanent fortifications before this new enemy. These heavy pieces, carrying balls weighing from sixty to one hundred throw their missiles with a force and precision, which stone and mortar cannot withstand and they move so rapidly, that they are soon beyond the reach of station[ar]y fortifications.

I won't bore you any more at this moment, but trust that my motives will furnish my excuse for troubling you. I am, Dear Sir, With great regard, Truly yours   Lew Cass

ALS. NhD. Published in Curtis, 2:62–63.

FROM JOHN CANFIELD SPENCER

Dear Sir,   Albany, March 6, 1841.

Gov. [William Henry] Seward,[1] in consequence of his recent domestic affliction,[2] is obliged to be absent from this city for some time, and as the [Alexander] McLeod affair has assumed a new aspect, from the re-

3. The British used steam vessels in naval operations against Syrian towns occupied by Egyptian forces in 1840, culminating in the bombardment and capture of Acre in November.

1. Seward (1801–1872; Union College 1820) served as governor of New York from 1838 to 1842.

2. Seward's elder brother, Benjamin Jennings, died late in February 1841.

cent declarations of the British Ministers in Parliament,[3] I have thought it not improper to address you on the subject. But as I write without any directions from the Governor, this must be deemed merely an individual and unofficial communication. You will have learned from the letter of Gov. Seward to Mr. [John] Forsyth,[4] dated the 27th ult.[5] that the Chief Justice of the [New York] Supreme Court[6] had been requested to preside at the court of Oyer and Terminer to be held at Lockport for the county of Niagara, on the fourth Monday of the present month. He has consented to hold the court, and the Attorney General of this State[7] will appear in behalf of the People. In the ordinary course the Indictment against McLeod would be bro't on for trial at that court. I am sorry to discover in Gov. Seward's letter, a copy of which he sent to me, an error of great importance. He represents the Indictment against McLeod as being for *arson* only; when it is for murder, and in all the seventeen counts he is charged as principal vs. accessory in murder, and the burning of the Caroline is stated only as an incident. The consequences are very different; by our law arson is punishable only by imprisonment in a State Prison, while a conviction for murder must be followed by a sentence of death. If the charge was for arson only, the matter might be differently dealt with.

According to our statutes, the prisoner might apply for a *certiorari* to remove the Indictment to the Supreme Court, who could then order it to be tried in any county where a fair and impartial trial could be secured. The omission by McLeod or his counsel,[8] hitherto, to make such an application,[9] has given rise to apprehensions that for some reason he does

3. On February 8 and 9, in the course of parliamentary debates on the McLeod case, William Lamb, Lord Melbourne (1779–1848), prime minister 1835–1841, avowed that the government would take measures to defend the safety of British subjects and vindicate the national honor. *Hansard's*, 56:364–374, 455–460.

4. Forsyth (1780–1841; Princeton 1799) served as U.S. secretary of state from 1834 to 1841.

5. Seward to Forsyth, February 27, 1841, DNA, RG 59 (Misc. Letters).

6. Samuel Nelson (1792–1873; Middlebury College 1813) was later a justice of the U.S. Supreme Court. When the McLeod trial finally took place in October, it was not at Lockport but at Utica, and the presiding judge was not Nelson but Philo Gridley (1796–1864; Hamilton College

1816) of the fifth judicial circuit. Gridley was later elected to the state supreme court.

7. Willis Hall (1801–1868; Yale 1824) was at that time attorney general of New York.

8. McLeod's Lockport attorneys were Hiram Gardner (1800–1874) and Alvin C. Bradley. McLeod was also represented by Joshua Austin Spencer (1790–1857) of Utica, who was appointed U.S. district attorney for northern New York before the trial was held but remained, nevertheless, as McLeod's counsel. See DW to Joshua A. Spencer, April 19, 1841, below.

9. Affidavits for a change of venue were filed with the New York Supreme Court on March 22. In July the court transferred the trial to Utica, in Oneida County.

not choose to be removed into the interior, and that his reason may be a hope of being forcibly released by British troops. It must be confessed that the situation of the county just within 15 miles of Lake Ontario, offers some temptation for such a movement. The tone of remark indulged by British ministers in the recent debate, of which an account is brought by the Steamer President, is supposed by some to confirm these apprehensions. For myself I can not believe that the British authorities would direct or sanction a step attended with such awful consequences. But the Canadian population along the frontier, are highly exasperated at McLeod's arrest, and would incur any peril for his deliverance. Many of them would delight in any act that would provoke retaliation, and there are unfortunately many more on our side, ready for any pretext for aggression.

The United States have some troops at Fort Niagara, and a greater number at Buffalo. Probably some arrangement of them might be made, under the charge of a high military officer, which would tend much to intimidate from aggression, and which would be eminently serviceable in resisting it, if made. Without undertaking even to advise what would be expedient, when there are others so much more competent to determine, I may at least say that, even the presence of such a man as Gen. [Winfield] Scott would restore confidence and security to the frontier.[10]

In the progress of this very unpleasant affair, it may be desired by you that the trial of McLeod should be delayed. If he should not make any effort for that purpose, it will still be in the power of the Attorney General to postpone it. Should you wish to communicate unofficially, any views on this or any other point connected with this matter, a private intimation to me will receive prompt and cheerful attention.

Should the trial proceed, the question will doubtless be presented how far the orders of his superiors, or the assumption of the whole transaction by the British government, can be a defense in a court of law. For myself, I have been unable to perceive the ground on which it could be admitted. If you can give us any references that will cast any light on the subject, we will be very thankful; and if you have time to give your own views, they will be gratefully received. It should be recollected that the time appointed for holding the court, is the 22nd of the present month of March. With great respect and regard Your obedt. Servt.

John C. Spencer.

ALS. DNA, RG 59 (Misc. Letters). Rec'd March 11, 1841. Spencer (1788–1855; Union College 1806) served as secretary of state of New York, 1839–

10. Secretary of War John Bell (1797–1869; Cumberland College 1814), who served from March to September 1841, ordered Scott to New York in mid-March. Scott (1786–1866; William and Mary) had been instrumental in persuading the two powers to submit the dispute to arbitration in 1839.

1841. President Tyler appointed him secretary of war in October 1841 and he served until March 1843, when he became secretary of the treasury.

TO JOHN CANFIELD SPENCER

                                            Department of State
Dr. Sir,   11 March, 1841.
    I promised to write to Mr [Millard] Fillmore[1] at New York, a letter which he was to deliver to you at Albany, and which letter I ought to have written yesterday, but the great pressure of other business prevented. This morning I have received yours of the 6th[2] relating to the same important subject, upon which it was my purpose to write to Mr Fillmore, and I hasten therefore, to address you directly. The subject has become exceedingly delicate and important. We are expecting every hour a formal demand from Mr [Henry Stephen] Fox to deliver up, or release Mr [Alexander] McLeod. Mean time, the President is exceedingly anxious for McLeod's personal safety and security. We think that steps should be immediately taken to change the venue, to Albany, or some other county remote from the scene of excitement and of possible danger. The utmost care, we think, ought to be used to prevent any attempt either to rescue him by persons from Canada, or to use violence towards him, by persons on our side.
    When we shall have received the formal recognition, by the English Government, of the act for which McLeod is privately prosecuted, as an act of public force, done under its authority I shall have occasion to write you again, and shall make any further answer to your letter, which may appear necessary. The main object of this is to press the high importance of guarding McLeod from all possible danger. Consequences of the most serious nature might follow, if he should become the subject of popular violence, either by his friends or his foes.
    I pray you to speak to Mr Fillmore, if in Albany, and explain to him how this letter comes to be addressed directly to you, instead of himself. I am &c.   Signed—Daniel Webster

LC. DNA, RG 59 (Domestic Letters).

FROM HENRY STEPHEN FOX

                                            Washington
                                            March 12th 1841
    The Undersigned, Her Britannick Majesty's [Queen Victoria][1] Envoy Extraordinary and Minister Plenipotentiary, is instructed by His Govern-

1. Fillmore (1800–1874) served from 1837 to 1843 as a Whig congressman from western New York, the area in which the alleged murder by McLeod took place.
2. See above.
1. Queen Victoria (1819–1901) ruled 1837–1901.

ment to make the following official communication to the Government of the United States

Her Majesty's Government have had under their consideration the correspondence which took place at Washington in December last, between the United States Secretary of State Mr. [John] Forsyth and the Undersigned, comprising two official letters from the Undersigned to Mr Forsyth dated the 13th and 29th of December, and two official letters from Mr Forsyth to the Undersigned dated the 26th and 30th of the same month,[2] upon the subject of the arrest and imprisonment of Mr Alexander McLeod[3] of Upper Canada by the authorities of the State of New York, upon a pretended charge of arson and murder as having been engaged in the capture and destruction of the Steam Boat "Caroline" on the 29th of December 1837.

The Undersigned is directed in the first place to make known to the Government of the United States, that Her Majesty's Government entirely approve of the course pursued by the Undersigned in that correspondence, and of the language adopted by him in the official letters above mentioned.

And The Undersigned is now instructed again to demand from the Government of the United States, formally, in the name of the British Government, the immediate release of Mr Alexander McLeod.

The grounds upon which the British Government make this demand upon the Government of the United States, are these: that the transaction on account of which Mr McLeod has been arrested and is to be put upon his trial, was a transaction of a publick character, planned and executed by persons duly empowered by Her Majesty's Colonial Authorities to take any steps and to do any acts which might be necessary for the defence of Her Majesty's territories, and for the protection of Her Majesty's Subjects; and that consequently those subjects of Her Majesty who engaged in that transaction, were performing an Act of Publick duty for which they cannot be made personally and individually answerable to the Laws and Tribunals of any Foreign Country.

The transaction in question may have been, as Her Majesty's Government are of opinion that it was, a justifiable employment of force for the purpose of defending the British Territory from the unprovoked attack of a Band of British Rebels and American Pirates, who having been permitted to arm and organize themselves within the Territory of the United States, had actually invaded and occupied a portion of the Territory of Her Majesty: or it may have been, as alleged by Mr Forsyth in his Note

2. DNA, RG 59 (Notes from Foreign Legations, Britain; Notes to Foreign Legations, Britain). Forsyth's last letter is dated December 31, 1841, instead of December 30, 1841.

3. McLeod was at the time of his arrest a Canadian deputy sheriff who often entered the United States to obtain evidence.

to the Undersigned of the 26th of December, "a most unjustifiable invasion in time of peace of the territory of the United States." But this is a question essentially of a political and international kind, which can be discussed and settled only between the Two Governments, and which the Courts of Justice of the State of New York cannot by possibility have any means of judging or any right of deciding.

It would be contrary to the universal practice of Civilized Nations to fix individual responsibility upon persons who with the sanction or by the orders of the Constituted Authorities of a State engage in Military or Naval Enterprizes in their Country's cause; and it is obvious that the introduction of such a Principle would aggravate beyond measure the miseries, and would frightfully increase the demoralizing effects of war, by mixing up with national exasperation the ferocity of personal passions, and the cruelty and bitterness of individual Revenge.

Her Majesty's Government cannot believe that the Government of the United States can really intend to set an example so fraught with evil to the community of Nations, and the direct tendency of which must be to bring back into the practice of modern war, atrocities which civilization and Christianity have long since banished.

Neither can Her Majesty's Government admit for a moment the validity of the Doctrine advanced by Mr Forsyth, that the Federal Government of the United States has no power to interfere in the matter in question, and that the decision thereof must rest solely and entirely with the State of New York.

With the particulars of the internal compact which may exist between the several States that compose the Union, Foreign Powers have nothing to do: the Relations of Foreign Powers are with the aggregate Union: that Union is to them represented by the Federal Government; and of that Union the Federal Government is to Them the only organ. Therefore when a Foreign Power has redress to demand for a wrong done to it by any State of the Union, it is to the Federal Government, and not to the separate State, that such Power must look for redress for that wrong. And such Foreign Power cannot admit the plea that the separate State is an independent Body over which the Federal Government has no control. It is obvious that such a Doctrine, if admitted, would at once go to a Dissolution of the Union as far as its Relations with Foreign Powers are concerned; and that Foreign Powers, in such case, instead of accrediting Diplomatick Agents to the Federal Government, would send such Agents not to that Government but to the Government of each Separate State; and would make their Relations of Peace and War with each State depend upon the result of their separate intercourse with such State, without reference to the Relations they might have with the rest.

Her Majesty's Government apprehend that the above is not the conclusion at which the Government of the United States intend to arrive;

yet such is the conclusion to which the arguments that have been advanced by Mr Forsyth necessarily lead.

But be that as it may, Her Majesty's Government formally demand, upon the grounds already stated, the immediate release of Mr McLeod; and Her Majesty's Government entreat the President of the United States to take into his most deliberate consideration the serious nature of the consequences which must ensue from a rejection of this demand.

The United States Government will perceive, that in demanding Mr McLeod's release, Her Majesty's Government argue upon the assumption that he was one of the persons engaged in the capture of the Steam Boat "Caroline": but Her Majesty's Government have the strongest reasons for being convinced that Mr McLeod was not in fact engaged in that transaction: and the Undersigned is hereupon instructed to say, that although the circumstance itself makes no difference in the Political and International Question at issue; and although Her Majesty's Government do not demand Mr McLeod's release upon the ground that he was not concerned in the capture of the "Caroline", but upon the ground that the capture of the "Caroline" was a transaction of a publick character for which the persons engaged in it cannot incur private and personal responsibility; yet the Government of the United States must not disguise from themselves, that the fact that Mr McLeod was not engaged in the transaction, must necessarily tend greatly to inflame that National Resentment which any harm that shall be suffered by Mr McLeod at the hands of the Authorities of the State of New York will infallibly excite throughout the whole of the British Empire.

The Undersigned, in addressing the present Official Communication, by order of His Government, to Mr Webster Secretary of State of the United States, has the honor to offer to him the assurance of his distinguished consideration.   H. S. Fox

DS. DNA, RG 59 (Notes from Foreign Legations, Britain). Rec'd March 13, 1841. Published in CR, 3:616–618.

FROM LEWIS CASS

(Confidential)

Dear Sir;   Paris, le 15 March 1841

I wrote you by the last Steam-Packet,[1] communicating to you some information, I have received respecting the designs of the British government. Since then the state of our affairs with England has been attracting the attention of Europe, and considerable anxiety prevails upon the subject. I saw the King[2] four times last week, and each time he was very

1. See above, Cass to DW, March 5, 1841.

2. Louis Philippe (1773–1850) ruled 1830–1848.

desirous of knowing what would be the result; and last evening I had a long conversation with him, when he entered fully into the whole affair. He deprecates war, and has shown the greatest wisdom and firmness in the support of peace. But he fears that France could not long be kept out of the contest were the United States and England once engaged. First because there is every where here a deep rooted aversion to England, and secondly because a naval warfare would soon excite some of those pretensions, which England arrogates to herself upon the Ocean. I doubt not that Mr [Andrew] Stevenson keeps you well informed of every thing over the channel. But the English publick feeling is as easily ascertained here as in London, for there are many thousands of English, who have established their residence here. It is a remarkable fact, that I have met but one who was not perfectly satisfied of the propriety of the attack upon the Caroline, and as to the boundary, they take it upon trust, and seem to suppose the contested territory as clearly theirs as Middlesex. We must not shut our eyes to the fact, that a war with us would meet with almost universal support in England. One of the bitterest articles against us has just appeared in the Sun,[3] a radical Journal, heretofore very friendly. The fact is the English are the most *credulous* people upon the face of the Earth in all that concerns their own wishes or pretensions. They are always right and every body else wrong. But we have war, they will fight bitterly. They will unite & put forth all their strength [and] tho' this consideration ought not to induce us to give way to arrogance or unjust pretensions, it ought to stimulate us to make immediate, I may almost say immense preparations. Bend all your efforts *to steam*. Equip all the steam vessels you can. Establish the most powerful steam batteries in the exposed ports, and especially in New York. If you depend on Stone walls and fixed fortifications to keep steam vessels out of your harbours, you will, in the hour of trial, be disappointed. This is now the universal sentiment here. I am, Dear Sir, With much regard, Truly yours

Lew Cass

ALS. NhD. Published in Curtis, 2:63–64.

TO JOHN JORDAN CRITTENDEN

Department of State,

Sir,   Washington 15th March 1841.

Alexander McLeod, a Canadian subject of Her Britannick Majesty, is now imprisoned at Lockport, in the State of New York, under an indictment for murder, alleged to have been committed by him, in the attack on, and destruction of, the Steamboat Caroline, at Schlosser, in that

3. The *London Sun*, March 10, 1841, stated that Britain possessed "ample means of terribly avenging any outrage" against the national honor.

State, on the night of the 29th December 1837; and his trial is expected to take place, at Lockport, on the 22nd instant.

You are apprised of the correspondence, which took place between Mr [John] Forsyth, late Secretary of State, and Mr [Henry Stephen] Fox, Her Brittannick Majesty's Minister here, on the subject, in December last.[1]

In his note to Mr Fox of the 26th of that Month, Mr Forsyth says; "if the destruction of the Caroline was a public act, of persons in Her Majesty's service, obeying the order of their superior authorities, this fact has not been before communicated to the Government of the United States, by a person authorised to make the admission, and it will be for the Court which has taken cognizance of the offence, with which Mr McLeod is charged, to decide upon its validity, when legally established before it.

The President deems this to be a proper occasion, to remind the Government of Her Britannick Majesty, that the case of the Caroline has been long since brought, to the attention of Her Majesty's principal Secretary of State for Foreign Affairs [Lord Palmerston], who, up to this day, has not communicated its decision thereupon. It is hoped that the Government of Her Majesty will perceive the importance of no longer leaving the Government of the United States uninformed of its views and intentions, upon a subject which has naturally produced much exasperation, and which has led to such grave consequences."

I have now to inform You, that Mr Fox has addressed a note to this Department, under date of the 12th instant,[2] in which, under the immediate instruction and direction of his Government, he demands, formally and officially, McLeod's immediate release, on the ground, that the transaction, on account of which he has been arrested, and is to be put upon his trial, was of a public character, planned and executed by persons duly empowered, by Her Majesty's Colonial authorities, to take any steps, and to do any acts, which might be necessary for the defence of Her Majesty's Territories, and for the protection of Her Majesty's Subjects; and that consequently those subjects of Her Majesty, who engaged in that transaction, were performing an act of public duty, for which they cannot be made personally and individually answerable to the Laws and Tribunals of any Foreign Country; and that Her Majestys Government, has further directed Mr Fox to make known to the Government of the United States, that Her Majesty's Government entirely approve of the course pursued by Mr Fox, and the language adopted by him in the correspondence above mentioned.

There is, therefore, now, an authentic declaration, on the part of the British Government, that the attack on the Caroline was an act of public

1. See above, Fox to DW, March 12, 1841.   2. See above, Fox to DW, March 12, 1841.

force, done by Military men, under the orders of their superiors, and is recognized, as such, by the Queen's Government. The importance of this declaration is not to be doubted, and The President is of opinion that it calls upon him for the performance of a high duty.

That an Individual forming part of a public force, and acting under the authority of his Government, is not to be held answerable, as a private trespasser or malefactor, is a principle of public Law, sanctioned by the usages of all civilized nations, and which the Government of the United States has no inclination to dispute. This has no connection, whatever, with the question, whether in this case, the attack on the Caroline was, as the British Government think it, a justifiable employment of force for the purpose of defending the British Territory from unprovoked attack, or whether it was a most unjustifiable invasion, in time of peace, of the Territory of the United States, as this Government has regarded it. The two questions are essentially different; and while acknowledging that an Individual may claim immunity from the consequences of acts, done by him, by showing that he acted under National Authority, this Government is not to be understood as changing the opinions which it has heretofore expressed, in regard to the real nature of the transaction which resulted in the destruction of the Caroline. That subject it is not necessary, for any purpose connected with this communication, to discuss. The views of this Government in relation to it, are known to that of England; and we are expecting the answer of that Government to the communication which has been made to it.[3]

All that is intended to be said, at present, is, that since the attack on the Caroline is avowed, as a National act, which may justify reprisals, or even general War, if the Government of the United States, in the judgment which it shall form of the transaction, and of its own duty, should see fit so to decide, yet that it raises a question entirely public and political, a question between independent nations, and that individuals concerned in it, cannot be arrested and tried before the ordinary Tribunals, as for the violation of municipal Law. If the attack on the Caroline was unjustifiable, as this Government has asserted, the law which has been violated is the law of Nations; and the redress, which is to be sought, is the redress authorised, in such cases, by the provisions of that Code.

You are well aware that the President has no power to arrest the proceedings, in the Civil or Criminal Courts of the State of New York. If this Indictment were pending in one of the Courts of the United States, I am directed to say, that the President, upon the receipt of Mr Fox's last communication, would have immediately directed a *nolle prosequi* to be entered.

Whether, in this case, the Governor of New York have that power, or,

3. Stevenson to Palmerston, May 22, 1838, is enclosed with No. 49.

Stevenson to Forsyth, May 24, 1838, DNA, RG 59 (Despatches, Britain).

if he have, whether he would feel it his duty to exercise it, are points upon which we are not informed. It is understood that McLeod is holden also on Civil process, sued out against him by the owner of the Caroline.[4] We suppose it very clear that the Executive of the State cannot interfere with such process; and indeed if such process were pending in the Courts of the United States, the President could not arrest it. In such and many analagous cases, the party prosecuted or sued, must avail himself of his exemption, or defence, by Judicial proceedings, either in the Court into which he is called or in some other Court. But whether the process be criminal or civil, the fact of having acted under public authority, and in obedience to the orders of lawful Superiors, must be regarded as a valid defence; otherwise, individuals would be holden responsible for injuries resulting from the acts of Government, and even from the operations of public War.

You will be furnished with a copy of this instruction, for the use of the Executive of New York [William Henry Seward], and the Attorney General of that State [Willis Hall]. You will carry with You, also, authentic evidence of the recognition by the British Government of the destruction of the Caroline, as an act of public force done by National Authority.

The President is impressed with the propriety of transferring the trial from the scene of the principal excitement to some other and distant County. You will take care that this be suggested to the Prisoners Counsel. The President is gratified to learn that the Governor of New York has already directed that the trial take place, before the Chief Justice of the State [Samuel Nelson].

Having consulted with the Governor, you will proceed to Lockport; or wherever else the trial may be holden, and furnish the Prisoners Counsel, with the evidence of which you will be in possession, material to his defence. You will see that he have skilful and eminent Counsel, if such be not already retained, and although You are not desired to act as Counsel Yourself, You will cause it to be signified to him, and to the Gentleman who may conduct his defence, that it is the wish of this Government, that in case his defence be overruled by the Court in which he shall be tried, proper steps be taken, immediately, for removing the cause, by Writ of Error, to the Supreme Court of the United States.

The President hopes you will use such despatch, as to make your arrival at the place of trial sure, before the trial comes on; and he trusts you will keep him informed of whatever occurs, by means of a correspondence through this Department. I have the honor to be, Mr. Attorney General, Your obedient Servant   Danl Webster

LS. NcD. Published in *W & S*, 9:262–266. Crittenden served from March until September 1841 as attorney general of the United States.

4. William Wells (1806–1885), of Buffalo, New York.

TO WILLIAM HENRY SEWARD

Private   Department of State,
My dear Sir: Washington, March 17th 1841.

The President has learned, not directly, but by means of a letter from a friend,[1] that you had expressed a disposition to direct a *nolle prosequi* in the case of the Indictment against [Alexander] McLeod, on being informed, by this Government, that the British Government had officially avowed the attack on the Caroline, as an act done by its own authority.

The President directs me to express his thanks for the promptitude with which you appear disposed to perform an act, which he supposes proper for the occasion, and which is calculated to relieve this Government from embarrassments and the Country from some dangers of collision with a foreign power.

You will have seen Mr [John Jordan] Crittenden, whom I take this occasion to commend to your kindest regard. I have the honor to be, Very truly, Yours   Danl Webster

LS. NRU. Published in *Works*, 5:134.

FROM ANDREW STEVENSON

No. 119.   Legation of U. States
Sir,   London March 18. 1841

My last dispatch was under date of the 9th instant,[1] by the British Queen. In that, I expressed the opinion, that the Government were not disposed to take measures, that would lead to immediate collision with the United States. I have no reason to change the opinion, unless it is to be found in the military preparations that are making, & the opinions of the Press & the Public. That the Press and the people, are under deep excitement is true. Indeed, the strongest feelings of indignation are entertained and expressed towards the U. States, growing out of the affair of the Caroline, & especially the detention of [Alexander] McLeod; the Boundary Question, and our Banking, and financial matters. This excitement is kept up by the Press, which is here, an Engine of great power, & must always when united (as it now is) affect not only the Public at large, but influence, more or less, the action of the Government. Of the extent to which it has been carried, you will be able to judge from the files of News Papers, which I have collected and have the honor herewith to transmit.[2]

You will not fail to notice the various statements which they contain

1. Webster again referred to Harrison's unidentified friend in his 1846 speech in the Senate defending the Webster-Ashburton Treaty. See *Works*, 5:133.

1. No. 118. Stevenson to DW, March 9, 1841, DNA, RG 59 (Despatches, Britain).
2. Not included in Department of State records.

of preparations making by the Government at most of their Naval and Military Stations. I have reason to believe that they are extensive, & however desirous the Government are for Peace, that the preparations are continued with zeal and activity. What the final destination of the vessels & armaments fitting out may be, is certainly not known (being kept secret as is the custom) but from all I see and learn, I have no doubt they are intended for any emergency that may arise on the American Coasts— Such, is the general opinion. It should also be borne in mind that the settlement of their affairs in the East, & their difficulties with France, will leave them a large disposeable force, both Naval & Military, and with it the means of giving to any war, a character of great activity & extent.

In Parliament, all has been quiet for the last ten days. I mentioned in my last dispatch, that the subject of our pending Relations, would in all probability have been taken up last week in the House of Commons. A notice to that effect was given by Mr [Joseph] Hume,[3] for Thursday last. Nothing however was done. When the time came the subject was suffered to pass, by general consent. All Parties seem disposed to unite in supporting the Government in the measures they may deem it proper to take. Indeed it has been currently reported and believed that the *Conservatives* have determined to forbear from making any attack upon the Ministry until their present difficulties with the U. States are settled. This would seem to be confirmed by a leading editorial article in yesterdays 'Times' in which it is declared, *"That the instructions sent out to Mr. [Henry Stephen] Fox by the President steamer, must already have apprised the American Government, that how much soever the People of England may be divided on questions of Home Policy, their unanimity in determining that McLeod must be either surrendered or avenged—a unanimity alike calm—cordial—& firm—was without a precedent, & was not rashly to be driven to extremities."*

In the Examiner however of Saturday, which I forward, you will see a well written and temperate article, taking our side of the question so far as to show that McLeod, ought not be demanded, or given up by the authorities of New York, until after trial. It was attacked in The Chronicle & Globe of Tuesday, & the views they give may be regarded as demi official. From these articles, and especially that of the Chronicle, many are led to believe who before doubted that the orders sent out to Mr Fox were to demand *the release of McLeod, & if refused to return home.* Such is I think the opinion of the Public, but I understood yesterday from a Distinguished Whig[4] (friendly to the Government) that he believed Mr Fox had not been instructed to return if McLeod was not surrendered. My informant is very intimate with several members of the Government, with one

3. See Stevenson's postscript in No. 118. Stevenson to DW, March 9, 1841, DNA, RG 59 (Despatches, Britain).

Hume (1777–1855) was a leader of the parliamentary radicals.
4. Not identified.

of whom, he had recently conversed on the subject. He said however that nothing transpired as to the nature of the instructions which had been sent out. It is however needless to speculate on the subject, as the instructions have already been made known to our Government, and will reach us in the course of the next two weeks. The Boston steamer of the first arrived on Tuesday night, but brought nothing of importance. All are therefore waiting with anxiety, the news by the steamers of the tenth & the 15th. They will bring the first intelligence of Mr Fox's instructions & the effect produced in the U. States. Until their arrival, no movement on the subject will probably be made in Parliament.

I inclose the official order in council, laid before Parliament, conferring a Pension on Lieut. [Shephard] McCormick for wounds received in the affair of the Caroline.[5] Under existing circumstances, I can only repeat what I said in a former communication, that from all I see & hear, we should lose no time in making the necessary preparations for the defense of the Country.

In relation to my return to the U. States, I beg leave to enquire, whether I shall need a letter from the present President, to enable me to do so. If so, I must ask your attention to the matter, & to the request contained in my despatch of the 3rd instant.[6] As my arrangements were nearly completed for returning in the early part of the year, I shall be forced to renew the contract for my House, or take another, at an increased pecuniary sacrifice, which I may not find it convenient, to make. I have submitted however under a sense of duty, & must therefore ask to be informed as soon as convenient, of the wishes of the Government on the subject. I am Sir, very respectfully Yr. obt servant,   A. Stevenson

LC. DNA, RG 59 (Despatches, Britain). Rec'd April 10, 1841. Published in *CR*, 3:618–620.

COUNT NESSELRODE TO ALEXANDER DE BODISCO

Translation.   [March 18/30, 1841]

Copy of a despatch from the Vice Chancellor Count [Karl Robert] de Nesselrode to M. [Alexander] de Bodisco dated Saint Petersburg 18/30th March 1841.[1]

5. McCormick (b. 1794), of the Royal Navy, received a pension of five shillings a day for life by an order in council of March 5, 1841.

6. No. 117. Stevenson to DW, March 3, 1841, DNA, RG 59 (Despatches, Britain). Stevenson asked to be allowed to return to the United States as soon as possible.

1. Russia did not adopt the Gregorian calendar until 1917, using the Julian system of reckoning until that time.

The news lately received from America, relative to the affair of Mr [Alexander] McLeod, has produced a deep impression upon the mind of the Emperor.[2] It is not without the most acute feelings of regret, that His Majesty sees a cause of new difficulties (*complications*) arise between two nations, the objects of his common esteem, and with which, he maintains relations so amicable and intimate. At the moment when in concert with his ally Great Britain, he has succeeded in extinguishing the last germs of war in the east, and in consolidating that peace in Europe, which has been for 25 years productive of so many advantages in every way to the United States themselves, he would experience a twofold regret, in admitting even the chance of seeing this peace endangered, in another hemisphere, for a question which involves in itself no principle of national right, (*nationalité*) or of policy, and the intrinsic importance of which, what ever may be the considerations attached to it by local feeling, cannot certainly be placed in comparison with the deplorable calamities which would be occasioned by the difficulties raised in opposition to its settlement. Independantly of the strong interest which he takes in the prosperity of the United States, it is difficult for the Emperor to regard with indifference the prospect of a collision, the effects of which would undoubtedly react upon Europe, would interrupt all commercial relations between the two Continents and would thus even affect the particular interests of Russia. Under this last circumstance, His Majesty conceives that he has some right to call on the Government of the United States to reflect on this most serious subject. It does not certainly enter into the idea of our August Sovereign, to express any opinion upon the matter in dispute; and still less to interfere, without being called [*appelé*] to do so, in an affair, which notwithstanding its ulterior consequences, does not concern him directly. If nevertheless, in this state of things the counsels of an impartial friend, may exercise any influence over the decisions of the American Government, His Majesty would be most sincerely rejoiced to see them received with good will, and thus to contribute his part in the honourable settlement of a difference, so much to be regretted by both Governments. He relies with pleasure and confidence on the moderate disposition of the new President. He flatters himself that the first use which the President will make of his power on receiving it, will be to exert his influence over the American Congress, with the view of removing this most difficult question, beyond the reach of party feeling, and of preventing local passions and animosities, from prevailing fatally, over the general interests of the Union. Be so kind Sir as to express to the President the wish and the hope in the name of our August master. The Cabinet of Washington has known the sentiments which His Imperial

2. Nicholas I (1796–1855) ruled 1825–1855.

Majesty has avowed towards it, too long, not to appreciate the motives which have induced him this day, to address to it the words of peace and reconciliation. Receive Sir the assurance &c &c.

Copy. DNA, RG 59 (Notes from Foreign Legations, Russia). Rec'd June 4, 1841. Endorsed: "Informally communicated by Mr de Bodisco." Nesselrode (1780–1862) was the Russian foreign minister from 1822 to 1856. Bodisco (1799–1854) was Russian minister to the United States, 1837–1854.

FROM WILLIAM HENRY SEWARD

Private
My Dear Sir,   Albany, March 22nd 1841
I have just received your letter of the 17th instant[1] in which you say that the President has learned not directly, but by means of a letter from a friend that I had expressed a disposition to enter a nolle prosequi in the case of the indictment against Alexander McLeod, on being informed by the Federal government that the government of Great Britain had officially avowed the attack on the "Caroline" as an act done by its own authority.

Although suffering much from ill health I avail myself of the first moment to request you to state to the President that whoever his correspondent may be, there is an entire misapprehension on his part. I have neither expressed nor entertained the disposition to direct a nolle prosequi in the case of the prisoner. On the contrary, the consideration of the subject and the formation of my opinion in relation to it were reserved until the authentic information now communicated by Mr [John Jordan] Crittenden should be received.[2] That gentleman is fully possessed of all my views. They have been communicated to him with the frankness which the occasion demands, and which it is peculiarly important should exist in regard to the matter in question between the authorities of this state and those at Washington.

Mr Crittenden will I doubt not do full justice to the desire entertained on my part to act in harmony with and in proper deference to the opinions of the President. I am, with the highest respect Your obedient servant
                                    William H. Seward

LS. DLC. Published in Curtis, 2:66.

FROM JACOB MERRITT HOWARD

(*Private and Confidential*)   Detroit April 6. 1841.
Sir—In compliance with your polite request made in a brief interview

1. See above, DW to Seward, March   2. Crittenden met with Seward in
17, 1841.   Albany in March 1841.

last month, I take occasion to inform you that in passing along the Ohio frontier I fell in with a gentleman, an acquaintance of mine, who is a member of a "Patriot Lodge," so called.[1] In the course of a free conversation he communicated the following information; and as it was without injunction of any kind, but entirely voluntary on his part, I feel at liberty to communicate it to you, thinking it may perhaps be of some value, in reference to the ulterior views of the patriots.

Our interview was at Cleaveland, one of the principal seats of patriot operations on the American side & the place where one of their most effective lodges holds its meetings. My informant states that he is a member of this lodge, (he is a gentleman of education and respectable connections at the east); that the several lodges along the frontier are at this time organizing anew and holding secret meetings in anticipation of a war between this country & G. Britain; that such an event is anxiously hoped for by their leaders; that the lodge at Cleaveland held a meeting about the 20th ult. at which Dr. [Charles] Duncombe,[2] a refugee from Chatham, U. C. attended and addressed the meeting.

I am pretty well acquainted with the reputation of Dr. D[uncombe] in Canada. Before the late disturbances he was regarded as a gentleman of respectability—was a man of wealth and had been a member of the Provincial parliament, of honorable standing and extensive popularity. He is a man of talent and sagacity, but, with [William Lyon] McKenzie[3]—a man without a single quality demanded by the occasion—was compelled to fly, and thus incurred the forfeiture of his entire estate.

Dr D[uncombe] informed his audience that there is no use whatever in the Canadian patriots making any further efforts to throw off the British yoke unless war shall take place between the two countries; & to that effect spoke with great feeling and earnestness, urging his friends to lay aside all expectation of succeeding against the Government until that event should transpire, and stating that the same views were entertained by the patriot leaders universally. My informant fully concurred in these views, and further stated that he had been informed by these leaders that in case of a *war* they stand ready to furnish *ten thousand* volunteers

1. Not identified, but perhaps a reference to General Winfield Scott's nephew, Orrin Scott, who organized a number of Patriot Lodges along the Ohio frontier. See Oscar A. Kinchen, *The Rise and Fall of the Patriot Hunters* (New York, 1956), p. 37.

2. Duncombe (1792–1867), a physician of radical views, served in the assembly of Upper Canada before becoming involved in the December 1837 uprising at London, Ontario. He fled to the United States, where he often spoke to patriot societies.

3. Mackenzie (1795–1861), the Canadian leader of the 1837 rebellion, fled to the United States after its failure. He received an eighteen-month prison sentence in 1839 for violating United States neutrality law but was pardoned by President Martin Van Buren in 1840.

along the lines, and that their officers are already appointed & prepared to take the field.

Dr D[uncombe] in his speech expressed the hope of revolutionizing *England*, and spoke of the cessation of commerce between that country and the U. S. as a means of disabling G. Britain from paying the interest on her national debt & thus creating discontent among her capitalists who hold government stocks, and stated that the non-consumption of British manufactures in the U. S. & Ireland, would tend powerfully to produce the same result; that the *temperance* movements in the latter country had the same object in view; that societies were forming there as well as in N. York, Phila &c. among the Irish for the purpose of diminishing the consumption of British goods.

It must be confessed these latter are rather *indirect* modes of conquering Great Britain!

My informant further stated that in case of an invasion of Canada by the U. S. it is the intention of this volunteer force, or rather of the principal leaders, to proclaim the *independence* of the Canadas & establish at the earliest possible moment a provisional government, placing it in the hands of the leading insurgents; but that without a war no such attempt will be made. I inferred very clearly that it is their intention, in case of hostilities, to be taken into the service of, or rather to be called with, the U. States, and to be commanded by their own officers, thus aiming at whatever glory or gain there may be in such an enterprise, but making the U. S. a mere instrument in their hands for conquering the provinces.

I should have taken no notice of this communication, had I not known its author and been satisfied of his sincerity and veracity: *Sit mihi fas audita loqui.*[4] And I send you the statement the more readily that it is substantially confirmed from other sources equally audible. Should we have a war, this force might be made available but it would require great circumspection to secure the benefit of their exertions to the U. S.; & as for an *independent* government in Canada, to pass under the French yoke in a twelvemonth, the U. States will I think be slow to fight for that.

Heaven protect us from a war, at least for the present, while we are defenseless. We have among us some spirits who profess a wish to measure swords with our transatlantic kinsfolk, but they are not numerous. Of one thing however you may be assured, that rather than See G. Britain wrest from us one particle which is our own, or trample upon any of our rights, however inconsiderable, the people on the frontier would rush to arms and fight it out, however severe the contest. In that case, though I deprecate war as the direst of all calamities, I could wish to see the sources of future disputes dried up, by the expulsion of British power

---

4. "What ear has heard let tongue make known," from Vergil's *Aeneid.*

from the Canadas. But at present there is no movement here which threatens the interruption of our pacific relations. Very truly & respectfully yr obt servt   J. M. Howard

A L S . NhD. Howard (1805–1871; Williams College 1830) was at that time a Whig congressman from Michigan.

TO JOHN TYLER

Private
To the President
My Dear Sir   [c. April 1841]

I think I have learned, pretty fully, the real objects & plan of operation, of these "Hunter's Lodges," "Patriotic Societies," &c which are in existence all along the Northern frontier, from Maine to Wisconsin.[1]

1. They are in constant correspondence with the disaffected in Canada; & these disaffected persons come over the line, & harrangue them, in their secret meetings.

2. They do not expect to be able to invade Canada, with any hope of success, unless war break out, *between Canada & the United States*, but they *desire that event, above all things*, & to bring it about will naturally join in any violence, or outbreaks, if they think they can do so, with impunity. They may even attempt violence upon [Alexander] McLeod, should he be discharged by the Courts, or on his way from the Prison to the place where the Court shall be sitting.

The aggregate of the members of all these clubs is probably not less than ten thousand. Cleveland is rather their Headquarters.

3. If war breaks out, these persons do not propose to join the forces of the United States, but to unite themselves to the disaffected in Canada, declare the Provinces free, & set up another Government.

I am told that Regimental officers are already designated, for the command of these volunteers.

That such as above described is the real state of things, there can be no doubt.

It is evidently full of danger, & I am quite surprised at the apparent ignorance, or supineness of the Govt of N.Y. who represent, constantly, that there is no danger of any violence.

Our duty, is, I think, in the first place, to have officers all along the frontier, in whom we have confidence, & to let them understand that there is danger.

In the next place, it becomes us to take all possible care that no personal violence be used on McLeod. If a mob should kill him, war wd be inevitable, in ten days. Of this there is no doubt.

1. Most of the information in this letter is from Jacob Merritt Howard's letter of April 6, 1841, above.

I regret that the Atty Genl. [Willis Hall] did not go on, & confer with McLeod's Counsel, notwithstanding the postponement of the trial. They appear to me to be men of no great force, & who place their main reliance on being able to prove an *alibi* for their clients. But such a defence does not meet the exigency of the case, nor fulfil the duty of this Govt.

I must pray your early consideration of this subject, & shall be glad of an opportunity for consultation, & for taking your direction.

AL draft. NhHi. Published in Van Tyne, pp. 232–233.

TO JOSHUA AUSTIN SPENCER

Private and confidential
Dear Sir: Washington, April 16. 1841
It is said that you are of counsel for [Alexander] McLeod, and upon this suggestion I send you copies of a correspondence which has recently taken place between this Department and Messrs. [Hiram] Gardner and [Alvin C.] Bradley, other counsel for the same party.

Having the pleasure of your acquaintance, but not knowing these gentlemen, I should be glad to carry on with you, directly, any correspondence which may be necessary, if informed by you that what I have heard is true, that you are one of the prisoner's counsel.[1] With true regard, your's   Danl Webster

LS. PHi.

TO JOSHUA AUSTIN SPENCER
(Official and Confidential)   Department of State.
Sir: Washington, 19th April, 1841
I have the pleasure to send you by this day's mail a Commission as District Attorney for the Northern District of New York. Since I wrote you four days ago[1] I have learned from Gen. [Winfield] Scott that you are retained as Counsel for Alexander McLeod. Although you will appear for him, as any other Counsel, and under his own retainer, I yet deem it my duty, since the appointment now announced to you, to communicate to you the views entertained by this Government in regard to McLeod's case, and for that purpose I transmit the copy of an instruction, given from this Department to the Attorney General of the U. States [John Jordan Crittenden], on the 15th March last.[2]

1. On April 21, Spencer informed DW that he was one of McLeod's lawyers. He also wrote that he would "be happy to receive any communication" from DW about the case. Spen-

cer to DW, April 21, 1841, DNA, RG 59 (Misc. Letters).
  1. See above.
  2. See above, DW to Crittenden, March 15, 1841.

You are aware that information of the postponement of the hearing[3] stayed the steps of the Attorney General at Albany [Willis Hall], and that, in the ordinary course of things, it would now be some months before a trial would come on.

We hear that the case has been removed into the Supreme Court of the State,[4] by the common process, and that it is intended by McLeod's Counsel to bring him before that Court for the purpose of being discharged.

It is my duty to say to you, that the President wishes to see an early disposition made of this matter, as he thinks that McLeod's longer imprisonment would be cause of much regret under existing circumstances.

I suppose there is no doubt that the question of his right to be discharged may be raised, on the return of the Habeas Corpus, as well by the principles of general law, as by the statute of New York—the ground relied upon not being in contradiction to any thing in the return.

You will consider the transmission of Mr Crittenden's instructions as confidential, and give them no publicity, and you will please keep this Department advised of every step taken in the case. I have the honor, &c.

D.W.

LC. DNA, RG 59 (Domestic Letters).

TO HENRY STEPHEN FOX

Department of State,
Washington, 24th of April, 1841

The Undersigned, Secretary of State of the United States, has the honor to inform Mr [Henry Stephen] Fox, Envoy Extraordinary and Minister Plenipotentiary of Her Britannic Majesty, that his note of the 12th[1] of March was received and laid before the President.

Circumstances well known to Mr Fox have necessarily delayed, for some days, the consideration of that note.[2]

The Undersigned has the honor now to say, that it has been fully considered, and that he has been directed by the President to address to Mr Fox the following reply.

Mr Fox informs the Government of the United States, that he is instructed to make known to it, that the Government of Her Majesty entirely approve the course pursued by him, in his correspondence with Mr

3. The trial of McLeod was postponed after the court clerk erred in giving only five days' notice of the hearing rather than the six required by the laws of New York. *Documents of the Assembly of the State of New York* (vol. 7), 64th Sess., 1841, No. 292, pp. 23–24.

4. At the arraignment on March 22, 1841, McLeod entered a plea of not guilty and obtained a writ of certiorari removing the record of the case to the state supreme court.

1. See above, Fox to DW, March 12, 1841.

2. President Harrison died April 4, 1841.

[John] Forsyth, in December last,[3] and the language adopted by him on that occasion, and that that Government have instructed him again to demand from the Government of the United States, formally, in the name of the British Government, the immediate release of Mr Alexander Mc-Leod; "that the grounds upon which the British Government make this demand upon the Government of the United States, are these: that the transaction on account of which Mr. McLeod has been arrested and is to be put upon his trial, was a transaction of a public character, planned and executed by persons duly empowered by Her Majesty's Colonial authorities to take any steps and to do any acts which might be necessary for the defence of Her Majesty's territories and for the protection of Her Majesty's subjects; and that consequently those subjects of Her Majesty who engaged in that transaction were performing an act of public duty for which they cannot be made personally and individually answerable to the laws and tribunals of any foreign country."

The President is not certain that he understands, precisely, the meaning intended by Her Majesty's Government to be conveyed, by the foregoing instruction.

This doubt has occasioned, with the President, some hesitation, but he inclines to take it for granted that the main purpose of the instruction was, to cause it to be signified to the Government of the United States, that the attack on the steamboat "Caroline" was an act of public force, done by the British Colonial authorities, and fully recognised by the Queen's Government at home, and that, consequently, no individual concerned in that transaction, can, according to the just principle of the laws of Nations, be held personally answerable in the ordinary courts of law, as for a private offence; and that upon this avowal of Her Majesty's Government Alexander McLeod, now imprisoned, on an indictment for murder, alleged to have been committed in that attack, ought to be released, by such proceedings as are usual and are suitable to the case.

The President adopts the conclusion that nothing more than this could have been intended to be expressed from the consideration, that Her Majesty's Government must be fully aware, that in the United States, as in England, persons confined under judicial process, can be released from that confinement only by judicial process. In neither country, as the Undersigned supposes, can the arm of the Executive power interfere, directly or forcibly, to release or deliver the prisoner. His discharge must be sought in a manner conformable to the principles of law, and the proceedings of Courts of judicature. If an indictment, like that which has been found against Alexander McLeod, and under circumstances like those which belong to his case, were pending against an individual, in one of the courts of England, there is no doubt, that the law officer of the

3. See above, Fox to DW, March 12, 1841.

crown might enter a *nolle prosequi*, or that the prisoner might cause himself to be brought up on *habeas corpus*, and discharged, if his ground of discharge should be adjudged sufficient, or that he might prove the same facts, and insist on the same defence, or exemption, on his trial.

All these are legal modes of proceeding, well known to the laws and practice of both countries. But the Undersigned does not suppose that, if such a case were to arise in England, the power of the Executive Government could be exerted in any more direct manner. Even in the case of Embassadors, and other public Ministers, whose right to exemption from arrest is personal, requiring no fact to be ascertained but the mere fact of diplomatic character, and to arrest whom is sometimes made a highly penal offence, if the arrest be actually made, it must be discharged by application to the courts of law.

It is understood that Alexander McLeod is holden as well on civil as on criminal process, for acts alleged to have been done by him, in the attack on the "Caroline;" and his defence, or ground of acquittal, must be the same in both cases. And this strongly illustrates, as the Undersigned conceives, the propriety of the foregoing observations; since it is quite clear that the Executive Government cannot interfere to arrest a civil suit, between private parties, in any stage of its progress; but that such suit must go on, to its regular judicial termination. If, therefore, any course different from such as have been now mentioned, was in contemplation of Her Majesty's Government, something would seem to have been expected, from the Government of the United States, as little conformable to the laws and usages of the English Government as to those of the United States, and to which this government cannot accede.

The Government of the United States, therefore, acting upon the presumption, which it readily adopted that nothing extraordinary or unusual was expected or requested of it, decided, on the reception of Mr Fox's note, to take such measures as the occasion and its own duty appeared to require.

In his note to Mr Fox of the 26th of December last,[4] Mr Forsyth, the Secretary of State of the United States, observes, that "if the destruction of the "Caroline" was a public act, of persons in Her Majesty's service, obeying the order of their superior authorities, this fact has not been before communicated to the Government of the United States by a person authorized to make the admission; and it will be for the court which has taken cognizance of the offence with which Mr McLeod is charged to decide upon its validity when legally established before it." And adds, "the President deems this to be a proper occasion to remind the Government of her Britannic Majesty, that the case of the "Caroline" has been long since brought to the attention of Her Majesty's Principal Secretary

4. Forsyth to Fox, December 26, 1840, DNA, RG 59 (Notes to Foreign Legations, Britain).

of State for Foreign Affairs [Lord Palmerston], who up to this day, has not communicated its decision thereupon. It is hoped that the Government of Her Majesty will perceive the importance of no longer leaving the Government of the United States uninformed of its views and intentions upon a subject, which has naturally produced much exasperation and which has led to such grave consequences."

The communication of the fact, that the destruction of the "Caroline" was an act of public force, by the British authorities, being formally made————to the Government of the United States, by Mr Fox's note, the case assumes a decided aspect.

The Government of the United States entertains no doubt, that after this avowal of the transaction, as a public transaction, authorized and undertaken by the British authorities, individuals concerned in it ought not, by the principles of public law, and the general usage of civilized States, to be holden personally responsible in the ordinary tribunals of law, for their participation in it. And the President presumes that it can hardly be necessary to say, that the American People, not distrustful of their ability to redress public wrongs, by public means, cannot desire the punishment of individuals, when the act complained of is declared to have been an act of the Government itself.

Soon after the date of Mr Fox's note, an instruction was given to the Attorney General of the United States [John Jordan Crittenden],[5] from this Department, by direction of the President, which fully sets forth the opinions of this Government on the subject of McLeod's imprisonment, a copy of which instruction, the Undersigned has the honor herewith to enclose.

The indictment against McLeod is pending in a State Court, but his rights, whatever they may be, are no less safe, it is to be presumed, than if he were holden to answer in one of the Courts of this Government.

He demands immunity from personal responsibility, by virtue of the law of Nations, and that law, in civilized States, is to be respected in all courts. None is either so high, or so low, as to escape from its authority, in cases to which its rules and principles apply.

This Department has been regularly informed, by His Excellency the Governor of the State of New York [William Henry Seward], that the Chief Justice of that State [Samuel Nelson] was assigned to preside at the hearing and trial of McLeod's case, but that owing to some error or mistake, in the process of summoning the jury, the hearing was necessarily deferred. The President regrets this occurrence, as he has a desire for a speedy disposition of the subject. The counsel of McLeod have requested authentic evidence of the avowal by the British Government of the attack on, and destruction of, the "Caroline" as acts done under its

5. See above, DW to Crittenden, March 15, 1841.

authority and such evidence will be furnished to them by this Department.

It is understood that the indictment has been removed into the Supreme Court of the State by the proper proceeding for that purpose, and that it is now competent for McLeod, by the ordinary process of *habeas corpus*, to bring his case for hearing before that tribunal.

The Undersigned hardly needs to assure Mr Fox, that a tribunal, so eminently distinguished for ability and learning as the Supreme Court of the State of New York, may be safely relied upon, for the just and impartial administration of the law in this, as well as in other cases; and the Undersigned repeats the expression of the desire of this Government that no delay may be suffered to take place in these proceedings, which can be avoided. Of this desire Mr Fox will see evidence in the instructions above referred to.

The Undersigned has now to signify to Mr Fox that the Government of the United States has not changed the opinion which it has heretofore expressed to Her Majesty's Government, of the character of the act of destroying the "Caroline." It does not think that that transaction can be justified by any reasonable application or construction of the right of self-defence under the laws of Nations. It is admitted that a just right of self-defence attaches always to Nations, as well as to individuals, and is equally necessary for the preservation of both. But the extent of this right is a question to be judged of by the circumstances of each particular case; and when its alleged exercise has led to the commission of hostile acts, within the territory of a Power at peace, nothing less than a clear and absolute necessity can afford ground of justification. Not having, up to this time, been made acquainted with the views and reasons, at length, which have led Her Majesty's Government to think the destruction of the "Caroline" justifiable as an act of self-defence, the Undersigned, earnestly reviewing the remonstrance of this Government against the transaction, abstains, for the present, from any extended discussion of the question. But it is deemed proper, nevertheless, not to omit, to take some notice of the general grounds of justification, stated by Her Majesty's Government, in their instruction to Mr Fox.

Her Majesty's Government have instructed Mr Fox to say, that they are of opinion, that the transaction, which terminated in the destruction of the "Caroline," was a justifiable employment of force, for the purpose of defending the British Territory from the unprovoked attack of a band of British rebels and American pirates, who, having been "permitted" to arm and organize themselves within the territory of the United States, had actually invaded a portion of the territory of Her Majesty.

The President cannot suppose that Her Majesty's Government, by the use of these terms, meant to be understood as intimating, that those acts, violating the laws of the United States, and disturbing the peace of the

British Territories, were done under any degree of countenance from this Government, or were regarded by it with indifference; or, that under the circumstances of the case, they could have been prevented, by the ordinary course of proceeding. Although he regrets, that by using the term "permitted," a possible inference of that kind might be raised, yet such an inference, the President, is willing to believe, would be quite unjust to the intentions of the British Government.

That on a line of frontier, such as separates the United States from Her Britannic Majesty's North American Provinces, a line long enough to divide the whole of Europe into halves, irregularities, violences, and conflicts should sometimes occur equally against the will of both Governments, is certainly easily to be supposed. This may be more possible, perhaps, in regard to the United States, without any reproach to their Government, since their institutions entirely discourage the keeping up of large standing armies in time of peace, and their situation happily exempts them from the necessity of maintaining such expensive and dangerous establishments. All that can be expected, from either government, in these cases, is good faith, a sincere desire to preserve peace and do justice, the use of all proper means of prevention, and, that if offences cannot, nevertheless, be always prevented, the offenders shall still be justly punished. In all these respects, this Government acknowledges no delinquency in the performance of its duties.

Her Majesty's Government are pleased, also, to speak of those American citizens, who took part with persons in Canada, engaged in an insurrection against the British Government as "American pirates." The Undersigned does not admit the propriety or justice of this designation. If citizens of the United States fitted out, or were engaged in fitting out, a military expedition from the United States, intended to act against the British Government in Canada, they were clearly violating the laws of their own country, and exposing themselves to the just consequences, which might be inflicted on them, if taken within the British Dominions. But notwithstanding this, they were, certainly, not pirates, nor does the Undersigned think that it can advance the purpose of fair and friendly discussion, or hasten the accommodation of national difficulties so to denominate them. Their offence, whatever it was, had no analogy to cases of piracy. Supposing all that is alleged against them to be true, they were taking a part in what they regarded as a civil war, and they were taking a part on the side of the rebels. Surely, England herself has not regarded persons thus engaged as deserving the appellation which Her Majesty's Government bestows on these citizens of the United States.[6]

It is quite notorious, that for the greater part of the last two centuries, subjects of the British crown have been permitted to engage in foreign

6. In international law, piracy was defined generally as illegal acts for private ends, and insurgents usually were not treated as pirates.

wars, both national and civil, and in the latter in every stage of their progress, and yet it has not been imagined that England has at any time allowed her subjects to turn pirates. Indeed, in our own times, not only have individual subjects of that crown gone abroad to engage in civil wars, but we have seen whole regiments openly recruited, embodied, armed, and disciplined in England, with the avowed purpose of aiding a rebellion against a nation, with which England was at peace; although it is true, that subsequently, an Act of Parliament was passed to prevent transactions so nearly approaching to public war without license from the crown.[7]

It may be said, that there is a difference between the case of a civil war, arising from a disputed succession, or a protracted revolt of a colony against the mother country, and the case of the fresh outbreak, or commencement of a rebellion. The Undersigned does not deny, that such distinction may, for certain purposes, be deemed well founded. He admits, that a Government, called upon to consider its own rights, interests, and duties, when civil wars break out in other countries, may decide on all the circumstances of the particular case, upon its own existing stipulations, on probable results, on what its own security requires, and on many other considerations. It may be already bound to assist one party, or it may become bound, if it so chooses, to assist the other, and to meet the consequences of such assistance. But whether the revolt be recent, or long continued, they who join those concerned in it, whatever may be their offence against their own country, or however they be treated, if taken with arms in their hands, in the territory of the Government, against which the standard of revolt is raised, cannot be denominated Pirates, without departing from all ordinary use of language in the definition of offences. A cause which has so foul an origin as piracy, cannot, in its progress, or by its success, obtain a claim to any degree of respectability, or tolerance, among nations; and civil wars, therefore, are not understood to have such a commencement.

It is well known to Mr Fox, that authorities of the highest eminence in England, living and dead, have maintained, that the general law of Nations does not forbid the citizens or subjects of one Government, from taking part in the civil commotions of another. There is some reason indeed, to think, that such may be the opinion of Her Majesty's Government at the present moment.

The Undersigned has made these remarks, from the conviction that it is important to regard established distinctions, and to view the acts

7. Webster is alluding to the participation of British subjects, including English soldiers and sailors acting without orders, in the Latin American revolutions in the years after 1800. Parliament forbade British participation in these revolutions in the Foreign Enlistment Act of 1819, but the law was not strictly enforced.

and offences of individuals in the exactly proper light. But it is not to be inferred, that there is, on the part of this Government any purpose of extenuating, in the slightest degree, the crimes of those persons, citizens of the United States, who have joined in military expeditions against the British Government in Canada. On the contrary, the President directs the Undersigned to say, that it is his fixed resolution that all such disturbers of the national peace, and violaters of the laws of their country, shall be brought to exemplary punishment. Nor will the fact, that they are instigated and led on to these excesses, by British subjects, refugees from the Provinces, be deemed any excuse or palliation; although it is well worthy of being remembered, that the prime movers of these disturbances on the borders are subjects of the Queen who come within the territories of the Uniietd States, seeking to enlist the sympathies of their citizens, by all the motives which they are able to address to them, on account of grievances, real or imaginary. There is no reason to believe that the design of any hostile movement from the United States against Canada, has commenced with citizens of the United States. The true origin of such purposes and such enterprises is on the other side of the line. But the President's resolution to prevent these transgressions of the laws is not, on that account, the less strong. It is taken, not only in conformity to his duty under the provisions of existing laws,[8] but in full consonance with the established principles and practice of this Government.

The Government of the United States has not, from the first, fallen into the doubts, elsewhere entertained, of the true extent of the duties of neutrality. It has held, that however it may have been in less enlightened ages, the just interpretation of the modern law of Nations is, that neutral States are bound to be strictly neutral; and that it is a manifest and gross impropriety for individuals to engage in the civil conflicts of other States, and thus to be at war, while their government is at peace. War and peace are high national relations, which can properly be established or changed only by nations themselves.

The United States have thought, also, that the salutary doctrine of nonintervention by one Nation with the affairs of others is liable to be essentially impaired, if, while Government refrains from interference, interference is still allowed to its subjects, individually or in masses. It may happen indeed, that persons choose to leave their country, emigrate to other regions, and settle themselves on uncultivated lands, in territories belonging to other States. This cannot be prevented by Governments, which allow the emigration of their subjects and citizens; and such persons, having voluntarily abandoned their own country, have no

8. The primary American neutrality law of 1818 codified previous neutrality acts of 1794 and 1797. In response to the Canadian rebellion of 1837 Congress passed a supplementary act of 1838 designed to curtail military expeditions along the frontier.

longer claims to its protection, nor is it longer responsible for their acts. Such cases, therefore, if they occur, show no abandonment of the duty of neutrality.

The Government of the United States has not considered it as sufficient, to confine the duties of neutrality, and non-interference, to the case of Governments, whose territories lie adjacent to each other. The application of the principle may be more necessary in such cases, but the principle itself, they regard as being the same, if those territories be divided by half the globe. The rule is founded in the impropriety and danger, of allowing individuals to make war on their own authority, or, by mingling themselves in the belligerent operations of other Nations, to run the hazard of counteracting the policy, or embroiling the relations, of their own Government. And the United States have been the first, among civilized Nations, to enforce the observance of this just rule of neutrality and peace, by special and adequate legal enactments. In the infancy of this Government, on the breaking out of the European wars, which had their origin in the French Revolution, Congress passed laws with severe penalties, for preventing the citizens of the United States from taking part in those hostilities.

By these laws, it prescribed to the citizens of the United States what it understood to be their duty, as neutrals, by the law of Nations, and the duty, also, which they owed to the interest and honor of their own country.

At a subsequent period, when the American Colonies of a European Power took up arms against their Sovereign, Congress, not diverted from the established system of the Government, by any temporary considerations, not swerved from its sense of justice and of duty, by any sympathies which it might naturally feel for one of the Parties, did not hesitate, also, to pass acts applicable to the case of Colonial insurrection and civil war. And these provisions of law have been continued, revised, amended, and are in full force at the present moment. Nor have they been a dead letter, as it is well known, that exemplary punishments have been inflicted on those who have transgressed them.[9] It is known, indeed, that heavy penalties have fallen on individuals, citizens of the United States, engaged in this very disturbance in Canada with which the destruction of the "Caroline" was connected. And it is in Mr Fox's knowledge also, that the act of Congress of March 10th 1838, was passed for the precise purpose of more effectually restraining military enterprises, from the United States into the British Provinces, by authorizing the use of the most sure, and decisive preventive means. The Undersigned may add, that it stands on the admission of very high British authority, that during

9. Webster's reference is to the Neutrality Acts of 1817 and 1818, which were enacted in response to the Latin American wars of independence.

the recent Canadian troubles, although bodies of adventurers appeared on the border, making it necessary for the people of Canada to keep themselves in a state prepared for self-defence, yet that these adventurers were acting by no means in accordance with the feeling of the great mass of the American People, or of the Government of the United States.[10]

This Government, therefore, not only holds itself above reproach in every thing respecting the preservation of neutrality, the observance of the principle of non-intervention, and the strictest conformity, in these respects, to the rules of international law, but it doubts not that the world will do it the justice to acknowledge, that it has set an example, not unfit to be followed by others, and that by its steady legislation on this most important subject, it has done something to promote peace and good neighborhood among Nations, and to advance the civilisation of mankind.

The Undersigned trusts, that when Her Britannic Majesty's Government shall present the grounds at length, on which they justify the local authorities of Canada, in attacking and destroying the "Caroline," they will consider, that the laws of the United States are such as the Undersigned has now represented them, and that the Government of the United States has always manifested a sincere disposition to see those laws effectually and impartially administered. If there have been cases in which individuals, justly obnoxious to punishment, have escaped, this is no more than happens in regard to other laws.

Under these circumstances, and under those immediately connected with the transaction itself, it will be for Her Majesty's Government to show, upon what state of facts, and what rules of national law, the destruction of the "Caroline" is to be defended. It will be for that Government to show a necessity of self-defence, instant, overwhelming, leaving no choice of means, and no moment for deliberation. It will be for it to show, also, that the local authorities of Canada,—even supposing the necessity of the moment authorized them to enter the territories of the United States at all,—did nothing unreasonable or excessive; since the act justified by the necessity of self-defence, must be limited by that necessity, and kept clearly within it. It must be shown that admonition or remonstrances to the persons on board the "Caroline" was impracticable, or would have been unavailing; it must be shown that daylight could not be waited for; that there could be no attempt at discrimination, between the innocent and the guilty; that it would not have been enough to seize and detain the vessel; but that there was a necessity, present and inevitable, for attacking her, in the darkness of the night, while moored to the shore, and while unarmed men were asleep on board, killing some and

10. This is perhaps a reference to a statement in Parliament on March 5, 1841, by William Ewart (1798– 1869) that the mass of the American people favored peace with Britain. *Hansard's*, 56:1356.

wound[ing] others, and then drawing her into the current, above the cataract, setting her on fire, and, careless to know whether there might not be in her the innocent with the guilty, or the living with the dead, committing her to a fate, which fills the imagination with horror. A necessity for all this, the Government of the United States cannot believe to have existed.

All will see, that if such things be allowed to occur, they must lead to bloody and exasperated war; and when an individual comes into the United States from Canada, and to the very place, on which this drama was performed, and there chooses to make public and vainglorious boast of the part he acted in it, it is hardly wonderful that great excitement should be created, and some degree of commotion arise.

This Republic does not wish to disturb the tranquillity of the world. Its object is peace, its policy, peace. It seeks no aggrandisement by foreign conquest, because it knows that no foreign acquisitions could augment its power and importance so rapidly as they are already advancing, by its own natural growth, under the propitious circumstances of its situation. But it cannot admit, that its Government has not both the will, and the power to preserve its own neutrality, and to enforce the observance of its own laws upon its own citizens. It is jealous of its rights, and among others, and most especially, of the right of the absolute immunity of its territory, against aggression from abroad; and these rights it is the duty and determination of this Government fully and at all times to maintain; while it will at the same time, as scrupulously, refrain from infringing on the rights of others.

The President instructs the Undersigned to say, in conclusion, that he confidently trusts, that this, and all other questions of difference between the two Governments, will be treated by both, in the full exercise of such a spirit of candor, justice, and mutual respect, as shall give assurance of the long continuance of peace between the two countries.

The Undersigned avails himself of this opportunity to assure Mr Fox of his high consideration.   Danl Webster.

LC. DNA, RG 59 (Notes to Foreign Legations, Britain). Published in *Works*, 6:250–262.

WILLIAM HENRY SEWARD TO JOHN TYLER

Sir,   Albany, May 4. 1841

I have just learned from the public prints that the District Attorney of the United States for the Northern District of New York [Joshua Austin Spencer] is in attendance upon the Supreme Court of this State in behalf of Alexander McLeod who is indicted for murder committed in the destruction of the boat Caroline, and which indictment is pending in the Courts of this State. As the Attorney General of this State [Willis Hall] and the District Attorney of Niagara County[1] have charge of the prosecution in behalf of the People of the State of New York, the unseemly aspect is presented of a conflict between the Federal Government and that of this State, which I respectfully submit to you is not calculated to inspire confidence among the Common Constituents of both, in the harmonious relations and views of the two governments; nor to challenge that respect from Great Britain, to which our institutions are entitled, and which it is so essential to preserve, particularly in the present state of the controversy with her.

I am sure I need do no more than call your attention to the subject, to induce such a disposition of it as will manifest the regard which there can be no doubt of your entertaining for the rights and character of this State in the conduct of a prosecution for an offense against her sovereignty. Very respectfully Your obedient Servant   William H. Seward

L s. DNA, RG 59 (Misc. Letters). Published in George E. Baker, ed., *The Works of William H. Seward* (5 vols., New York, 1853–1854), 2:558–559.

JOHN TYLER TO WILLIAM HENRY SEWARD

Sir: Washington, May 7th 1841
I have the honor to acknowledge the receipt of your Excellency's letter of the 4th instant[1] in which you are pleased to say that you have "just learned from the public prints that the District Attorney of the United States for the Northern District of New York [Joshua Austin Spencer] is in attendance on the Supreme Court of this State (New York) in behalf of Alexander McLeod who is indicted for murder committed in the destruction of the boat Caroline, and which indictment is pending in the Supreme Court of this State," and that "as the Attorney General of this State [Willis Hall] and the District Attorney of Niagara County [Jonathan L. Woods] have charge of the prosecution in behalf of the people of the State of New York, the unseemly aspect is presented of a conflict between the Federal Government and that of this State which I respectfully submit to you is not calculated to inspire confidence among the common constituents of both in the harmonious relations and views of the two Governments; nor to challenge that respect from Great Britain to which our institutions are entitled, and which it is so essential to preserve particularly in the present state of controversy with her."

In reply I have the honor to say that the District Attorney of the United States for the Northern District of New York has received no orders from this Government to appear as Counsel in defence of McLeod, nor can I believe that in the absence of such orders he has under-

1. Jonathan L. Woods (1798–1865)   later served as a county judge.
became district attorney in 1840 and   1. See above.

taken to assume that task in his official character. So far as I am informed Mr Spencer acts entirely in his private capacity as a practising attorney of the State of New York[,] in consequence of a retainer which dates back from a period antecedent to his having had official station conferred on him. I am sure that in this you will see nothing unseemly or calculated either to encourage a belief of the want of harmony in the relations or views of the two Governments or in any way to diminish the respect of any foreign government for our institutions. This government has done no more in reference to the trial to be had before the Supreme Court of New York than to furnish the Counsel for the accused upon their requisition, with such documentary evidence as was to be found in the State Department and which was believed by them to be necessary to be used in this defence.

In giving your Excellency the foregoing explanation I am not to be understood as denying to this Government, in order to the fullfilment of its international duties and obligations, the right to resort to all constitutional and legitimate means within its power. The confidence which I feel in the learning and justice of the Supreme Court of New York, and in the tribunals instituted by her for dispensing full and perfect justice, would cause me to avoid the commission of any act which would bear a doubtful construction.

I pray your Excellency to accept assurances of my high consideration and respect.   John Tyler

LC. DNA, RG 59 (Domestic Letters).

WILLIAM HENRY SEWARD TO JOHN TYLER

State of New York
Executive Department
Sir: Albany, May 10th 1841

I acknowledge sincere pleasure in the confirmation of the belief I have all along entertained that the District Attorney of the United States for the Northern District [Joshua Austin Spencer] in appearing in the Supreme Court of this state as counsel and advocate against the People and for a prisoner indicted for murder and arson, is acting without orders or direction from the President of the United States. I am left to infer, however, that the conduct of the defence of the accused by that officer in his unofficial capacity and in pursuance of a previous retainer is regarded as unobjectionable. Trusting that you may feel at liberty to consider suggestions leading to a different conclusion I beg leave most respectfully to observe that various and conflicting opinions prevail in this state concerning the guilt or innocence of the accused and his personal responsibility for the offense laid to his charge. These opinions are unavoidably affected by feelings and interests growing out of the disturbed relations between this country and Great Britain. There is happily, however, one sentiment in which the People of this state concur, which is, that the question involved in the prosecution of [Alexander] McLeod can be settled no otherwise than justly and honorably to the state and the country if the decision shall be made by the courts of law in the ordinary course of legal proceedings. At the same time this confidence in the decision of the courts could not remain unimpaired if either the Federal or state government were supposed to interfere in any manner with the proceedings of the judicial tribunals.

The apparent want of harmony between the government of the United States and that of this state exhibited by the appearance of the District Attorney of the United States as counsel requires explanation. Fully impressed with the conviction that even an appearance of conflict would be as much regretted by yourself as it could be by the authorities of New York, I beg leave to submit with all respect whether in so delicate a matter that would not be the safer course [which] requires no explanation. The prosecution must at least labor under a disadvantage when it is seen that it is regarded by the Federal government as possessed of so little justice or merit that the legal representative of that government is left at liberty by laying aside his official character to appear against the state in their court. Our citizens will feel that if they cannot have the aid of the Federal government in a prosecution in which the honor and dignity of the state are concerned they have a right at least to expect that that prosecution shall not encounter the opposition of [an] officer of the United States even in his individual and unofficial capacity.

I cannot see that that functionary if required to desist from the further prosecution of duties so incongruous with his official relations would be obliged to make any sacrifice of personal interests and feelings different from that which is expected of every citizen when called to execute a public trust, and whatever his sacrifices might be they would be altogether unworthy of consideration in opposition to the public welfare. I have no doubt that if the District Attorney should withdraw from the case, the court would allow to his client ample time to procure other counsel.

In submitting these views I am very desirous not to be misunderstood. I am governed by no vindictive feelings towards the prisoner. I desire that he may have a legal deliverance if innocent and be convicted if guilty. If the assumption of the responsibility by the British government is a legal defence for him I shall cheerfully submit to the decision of the Court in that respect. But I desire also that the decision, whatever it may be, may not be attended with any circumstance which shall deprive it of its salutary effect or in any degree diminish the confidence which my fellow citizens have hitherto indulged in regard to the principles and patriotism of the government of the United States. Be pleased to accept the assurance of high respect with which I remain your obedient servant

William H. Seward

ALS. DNA, RG 59 (Misc. Letters).

TO DANIEL FLETCHER WEBSTER

My Dear Son   Boston May 10. 1841

I recd this morning your letter of the 7th instant.[1]

[Alexander] McLeod's affair stands well, at present, & I hope the President will be cautious of holding correspondence with the Govr of New York [William Henry Seward], on the subject. If the President will re-peruse my letter to Mr [Henry Stephen] Fox,[2] & the instructions to Mr [John Jordan] Crittenden,[3] & read my letters to Mr Joshua A[ustin] Spencer,[4] he will find, I think, that they are all congruous, & that they leave us exactly right.

McLeod will apply by *his own Counsel*, & we shall do nothing but permit proper Evidence. He is before the New York Court, & that Tribunal must take the responsibility. *We* have nothing to act at N. Y. except that her Courts administer the law, properly, & I do not wish it to appear that any thing is done, on *our* application. It will be made to appear before the Court, that the destruction of the Caroline was a public act of the British Government, fully avowed as such; that it was an Act, agt which the Govt of the U. S. made public remonstrance, & that it now constitutes a natural question, actually under discussion between the two Governments. All this appearing, it will be for the Court of New York, upon its own responsibility, without any asking from us, to apply to the case the general principle of the Law of Nations. Let us, as far as possible, avoid the appearance of any thing's being done, on <our request> any particular request of ours.

I wish you to show this letter to the President, & suggest to him that I shall be in N. York in season to confer with Gentlemen before the 15th[5]— the day fixed for the hearing; & if he has any wishes on the subject, they may be communicated to me, there. And I will be obliged to you to lose no time, in replying to this, under my address to the Astor House.

1. Not found.
2. See above, DW to Fox, April 24, 1841.
3. See above, DW to Crittenden, March 15, 1841.
4. See above, DW to Spencer, April 16 and April 19, 1841.

5. Webster apparently met with Joshua A. Spencer and perhaps with Hiram Gardner and Alvin C. Bradley in New York. See DW to Daniel Fletcher Webster, May 16, 1841, extant in *PC*, 2:104–105.

I am well, notwithstanding the weather, but am excessively busy with daily things. Yours affectionately

AL. MHi. Published in *W & S*, 16:342. Webster (1813–1862; Harvard 1833) was DW's eldest son.

TO FRANCIS CALLEY GRAY

Private & confidential
My Dear Sir,   Boston May 11. 1841.

I wrote you from New York on the 3rd instant,[1] the day of your departure from Boston, expressing the wish, that you would not leave London, until you should hear from me again.

I avail myself of the opportunity of the return of the Britannia to inform you of the purposes of that request.

You are well acquainted with the history, & the merits of the question respecting our North Eastern Boundary, & advised, probably, of the State of the pending negotiation, between the United States & England, on that subject. In this last respect, nothing important has occurred since Mr. [Martin] Van Buren's message to Congress, of last December.[2]

It is much to be desired that this negotiation should be so hastened, as that the Convention, in which it is expected to result, may be laid before the Senate, at the ensuing session of Congress. My purpose is, on my return to Washington, to address Mr. [Henry Stephen] Fox officially, on this part of the subject.

But supposing this to be accomplished, & a joint exploration & survey provided for, with power in the Commissioners to decide the question, & establish the line, or, in case of disagreement, an umpire to be resorted to, whose decision shall be final, it is obvious that much time must be consumed, & great expense incurred, by such a proceeding, with perhaps a doubtful result, at last.

It is therefore, perhaps worth inquiring, whether a shorter way to an amicable & satisfactory adjustment may not be found. Before suggesting my notions on this point, I wish to say that I write now, not only unofficially, but, if I may so express myself, merely experimentally, not intending to bind even myself by any thing I may suggest, & much less others. Indeed, I could not bind others, if I would. The substance of what I wish to say is this. You will of course be more or less in the Court Circles of London, & no doubt this question of the boundary will often be brought into conversation; & I should like that you should lead these conversations, if you can, so as to bring out suggestions from the gentlemen connected with the Government.

1. Not found.
2. Van Buren summarized the boundary controversy in his fourth annual message to Congress of December 5, 1840. See *Messages and Papers*, 3:602–604.

I have some reason to think Lord Palmerston would be glad, if this matter could be settled, without the delay & expense of exploration &c. &c. Possibly there may be some idea of an *exchange* of territory suggested. If you find it convenient, lead those you may meet with to this idea. You know we always thought the monument does not stand on the line of the St. Croix. How would England like to let us go down to the Madawaska, &, in return, let them have the Dutch line, further up? Or what perhaps is still more practicable, let us run from the monument to Eel river & by that river to the St. Johns; & let England go by the Madawaska, & the lakes at its head, & so reach the St. Lawrence at the mouth of the Trois Pistoles?

You know, also, we think Grand Menan should have been assigned to us. Does England attach great value to that Island, or Campo Bello?

In these conversations you will of course not mention my name, or intimate any thing, as being a proposition from this side of the water, official or unofficial; but get what suggestions you can from them.

If they wish nothing but a proper connexion between their two Provinces, it is obvious that the line of the Madawaska gives them that.

You will see Mr. [Nassau William] Senior[3] doubtless, & he is a man of intelligence & life. He will readily create *accidents*, which shall bring you & Mr. [John] Backhouse[4] together, & perhaps throw you in the way of Lord Palmerston. You will doubtless, also, see Mr. Francis T[hornhill] Baring[5] & Mr. [Henry] LaBouchere,[6] & though they hold very high official stations, they are very likely to talk freely upon this subject of the Boundary. If you find Mr. [Samuel] Jaudon[7] still in London, I wish you to show him this letter. He will understand the reason of this request, & explain it to you. But I apprehend he will have sailed for the United States.

I shall hope to hear from you, so soon as you may have anything to communicate. Yours with much true regard,

P.S. Let me again commend to you great caution, & to find out English opinions & feelings on this subject, in good tempered & apparently acci-

3. Senior (1790–1864), the internationally known political economist, was master of the chancery, 1836–1855.

4. Backhouse (1783?–1845) had served as the permanent British undersecretary for foreign affairs since 1817.

5. Baring (1796–1866), nephew of Alexander Baring, Lord Ashburton (1774–1848), was chancellor of the exchequer, 1839–1841, and a member of Parliament, 1826–1865.

6. LaBouchere, Lord Taunton (1798–1869), was active in colonial administration and served as president of the Board of Trade from August 1839 to September 1841.

7. Jaudon (1796–1874; Princeton 1813), formerly cashier of the Bank of the United States under Nicholas Biddle, commenced in 1837 to direct the Bank's agency in London.

dental conversations, rather than by any direct inquiring. If you make the acquaintance of Mr. [Sylvain] Van de Weyer, the Belgian Minister,[8] I think you might converse with him a little confidentially. He is a person of talent, & address, & his dispositions are, I have no doubt, friendly.

Copy. NHi. Published without postscript in PC, 2:102–103. Endorsed by DW: "Copy of my private letter to F. C. Gray." Gray (1790–1856; Harvard 1809), from a wealthy shipping family, had been a state senator in Massachusetts in 1826, 1828, 1829, 1831, and 1843 and was known for his interest in public affairs.

FROM JOHN TYLER

Dear Sir,   Washington May 15. 1841

I have deemed it best to enclose to you the accompanying letter from Govr [William Henry] Seward and also my reply[1]—Please read the reply and if you see nothing to object to give it Gov. Sewards address. His requisition upon me is most extraordinary—and I trust it has been sufficiently answered. We have some matters here awaiting your arrival of which most probably your son has already advised you. With true regard yr sv   John Tyler

ALS. DLC.

WILLIAM HENRY SEWARD TO JOHN TYLER, WITH ENCLOSURES

Executive Department
Albany, May 18th: 1841

I have the honor to transmit a copy of a communication from His Excellency the Governor of the Canadas[1] on the subject of the surrender of Charles F. Mitchell,[2] a fugitive from justice, with a copy of my reply thereto. I am with high respect Your most obedient Servant

William H. Seward

LS. DNA, RG 59 (Misc. Letters).

8. Van de Weyer (c. 1802–1874), son-in-law of Joshua Bates, a prominent banker and American partner of the House of Baring, was Belgian minister to the Court of St. James.

1. See above, Seward to Tyler, May 10, 1841. Tyler's response to Seward of May 15, in which he refuses to remove Spencer from McLeod's case, is printed in Tylers, 2:208–209.

1. Charles Edward Poulett Thom-

son, Lord Sydenham (1799–1841), served as governor of Lower Canada from 1839 to 1841 and as governor-general of British North America from February to September 1841.

2. Mitchell (b. 1808?), from Lockport, New York, was a member of the U.S. House of Representatives, 1837–1841. He fled to Canada in 1841 after being indicted for forging bank notes.

ENCLOSURE: LORD SYDENHAM TO WILLIAM HENRY SEWARD

Government House
Montreal, 14 May 1841

I have the honor to acknowledge the receipt of your Excellency's letter of the 7 instant,[1] requesting the surrender of one Charles F. Mitchell, against whom an indictment has been found for a forgery committed in the State of New York.

The crime charged against Mitchell being an offence against those general laws which prevail in every civilized community I can have no hesitation in delivering him over to be dealt with according to the laws of the country which he is said to have offended. To shelter on our Soil a man charged with an offence of this nature, after he has been demanded by the proper authorities, would be no less at variance with what I concur with your Excellency in thinking to be specially for the interest of two bordering countries, than to detain in custody an individual charged with an offence which has been publicly avowed and justified by his government, is in my opinion repugnant to those principles of justice which ought to regulate the conduct of all states. I have much pleasure, therefore, in complying with your Excellency's requisition and shall take immediate steps for the conveyance of Mitchell in custody to the frontier of Canada, and his delivery there into the custody of the authorities of the State of New York. I have the honor to be, Sir: Your Excellency's most obedient servant   (signed) Sydenham

Copy. DNA, RG 59 (Misc. Letters). Published in *Documents of the Assembly of the State of New York* (vol. 7), 64th Sess., 1841, No. 292, p. 31.

ENCLOSURE: WILLIAM HENRY SEWARD TO LORD SYDENHAM

Sir,   Albany, May 18th 1841

I acknowledge your Excellency's letter of the 14th instant[1] informing me of your decision to surrender Charles F. Mitchell to the agent of this state in compliance with my request. This act of enlightened courtesy is highly appreciated by myself, and I have no doubt will be viewed in the same light by the President of the United States, to whom it shall immediately be made known.

I regret to learn from an allusion in your letter that your Excellency labors under some misapprehension concerning the detention of a British subject in this state. Whatever may have been the character of the original transaction in consequence of which that person was arrested, he had the misfortune before any affirmance of that transaction by the British Government to be indicted in one of our courts, and as is said upon con-

1. Seward to Sydenham, May 7,   1. See above.
1841, DNA, RG 59 (Misc. Letters).

fessions of his own for the crimes of murder and arson committed in this state. His detention is solely to answer that indictment, and your Excellency may be assured not only that he will have a fair and impartial trial, but also that if the assumption of the responsibility of his offence by his government, ought according to the common law or laws of nations to relieve him from personal responsibility he will be acquitted, for that cause alone, even if under other circumstances, he could be convicted of the heinous offenses laid to his charge by the Grand Jury. I am, Sir: with very high respect Your Excellency's obedient servant

(signed) William H. Seward

Copy. DNA, RG 59 (Misc. Letters). Published in *Documents of the Assembly of the State of New York* (vol. 7), 64th Sess., 1841, No. 292, p. 32.

JOHN TYLER TO WILLIAM HENRY SEWARD

Sir—   Washington May 25th 1841

Your letter of the 20th Inst.[1] was received by the mail of monday, and I must be allowed to express my regret that Your Excellency has not been able to see in my last letter[2] sufficient reasons for my declining to deprive a man placed upon trial for his life, of the services of his retained counsel merely because that counsel holds a commission from this Government the nature and character of which in no way conflicts with the engagement he has entered into with the person under trial. I had heretofore supposed that the right of every man to a fair and impartial trial, to be confronted with his accusers, and to be defended by counsel of his own retaining, admitted of no question but was deeply engraven on the hearts of the american people. I must be pardoned for expressing my suprise that Your Excellency speaking in the name of the Great State of New York, should have entered Your dissent to the correctness of propositions which I had hoped would have been recognized as incontestable.

In the first letter with which I was honored, by Your Excellency,[3] You were pleased to call my attention to the information which You had derived from the newspapers that the District Attorney for the U. States for the northern District of New York [Joshua Austin Spencer] was in attendance on the Supreme Court of New York as counsel for [Alexander] McLeod, and expressed your opinion that as the state of New York was represented in the prosecution by the Attorney General of the state [Willis Hall] and District Attorney of Niagara County [Jonathan L. Woods], the matter wore an unseemly aspect &c. To that letter I promptly replied[4] that Mr Spencer appeared in the case under no orders from this

1. Seward to Tyler, May 20, 1841, DNA, RG 59 (Misc. Letters).

2. Tyler to Seward, May 15, 1841, DNA, RG 59 (Misc. Letters).

3. See above, Seward to Tyler, May 4, 1841.

4. See above, Tyler to Seward, May 7, 1841.

Government, or in his character of District Attorney, but simply in his private character as a practising attorney of the state of New York and upon a retainer of a date anterior to the date of his commission as District Attorney. Your letter in reply[5] expressed Your pleasure at the fact thus communicated, but went further and intimated Your desire that Mr Spencer might, under directions to emanate from myself be induced to retire from the case altogether. With this request I respectfully declined a compliance for reasons stated in my letter of the 15th of May,[6] because by the laws of the state of New York Mr Spencer was fully authorized to undertake civil and criminal causes pending in the Courts of New York—that he was the retained counsel of the U. States only in cases in which the U. States was a party on the record, or in which, I will now add, he was particularly desired to appear by this Government, and that to require him to abandon causes to which the U. States were not parties, would subject the U. States to the certain hazard of being unrepresented in the courts. I proceeded from this in substance to state, that notwithstanding it had been the constant practice for the District Attorneys in all the states to appear in all causes in which the U. States had no interest, (meaning clearly no such interest as had been alluded to). Yet that Yours was the first instance in which a requisition of the character of that made by Yourself had been made, I took occasion in both of my letters to guard against the inference of any disclaimer of right on the part of this Government in a case wherein it was esteemed material to protect either its own interests or to enable it to acquit itself of the obligations imposed by the international law, of resorting to all the means in its power to defend the one or to acquit itself of the other, but that my confidence was unqualified in the judicial tribunals of New York, and that in the case of McLeod no cause for interference existed.

Misapprehending, as I am bound to suppose, the true intent and meaning of my letter of the 15th May and detaching a single sentence thereof, Your Exellency has seen cause to ascribe to me an indifference to the rights of New York,[7] which nothing which has occurred can justify and which upon further reflection and with more extended information, You would have been among the last to have made. The attack on the Caroline, when viewed as an act of public force committed by the British Government within the territory of the United States, is undoubtedly a matter in which the Government of the U. States is bound to take an interest,

5. See above, Seward to Tyler, May 10, 1841.

6. See above, Tyler to DW, May 15, 1841, and Tyler to Seward, May 15, 1841, DNA, RG 59 (Misc. Letters).

7. In his letter of May 20 Seward had objected to Tyler's claim that it was customary for United States attorneys to maintain private practices by appearing in cases in which the United States had no interest. Tyler made the assertion in his letter to Seward of May 15. See *Tylers*, 2:208–209.

and to which, I trust, neither my predecessor nor myself have shown any degree of inattention. But when it is viewed as divested of its character as a public transaction, and where those concerned in it are regarded merely as individuals, committing crimes against the laws of New York, then certainly the case requires nothing to be done by this Government, as auxiliary to the power of that state. Nor can this Government have more to do with that trial, than with a trial for any other offence against the laws of the state, unless, indeed, it find itself called upon, for the protection of some interests of the U. States, or by its high duty of preserving the peace of the country and of superintending its foreign relations, to take care, by the exercise of its acknowledged powers, that such interest be guarded, or that no just ground of complaint be furnished to other nations. It was in this sense, and this only, that I spoke of McLeod's trial as one in which the Government of the U. States had no interest, and I repeat my regret that Your Excellency should have thought there was ground for ascribing to me any other meaning. It will suffice for me to say that this Government will take care that no just cause of censure shall be ascribed to it for any indifference to the rights of any one state of this union or to the honor of the country at large. But when Your Excellency has sedulously urged upon me the propriety of non-interference in the trial of McLeod, and when Your wishes have been fully gratified in this aspect, will it not appear somewhat singular that You should nevertheless complain that I do not interfere *against the accused*, by depriving him of his counsel. You ask neutrality in the matter on the part of this Government, and when that neutrality is actually avowed, Your Excellency still remains dissatisfied. I take occasion now to repeat, that Mr Spencer has not appeared in defence of McLeod at the instance of this Government or in his character of District Attorney for the U. States, and that this Government has had no agency in the trial now pending before the Supreme Court of New York other than as I have heretofore stated to You, to furnish the counsel of the accused with such papers and documents as the State Department afforded, and which were regarded by his counsel as necessary for his defence, what right then of New York has been abandoned by this Government or in any way put at hazard? Have the rights of the judiciary been in any way interfered with by this Government? The case of McLeod is in the hands of that very Judiciary for its calm, unbiased and independent decision. If the accused be acquitted it will only be from the conviction of the learned judges that the law, national or municipal, requires his discharge. Will such acquittal release this Government from the obligation of urging upon the British Government remuneration for the wrong done in the destruction of the Caroline under orders avowed to have proceeded from that Government; In what respect is the state of things altered by the discharge of McLeod should such take place, so far as the right of this Government for demand of reparations from Great Britain is concerned. I can well conceive that his condemnation might impair the force of our demands for remuneration by enabling Great Britain to rely upon the fact in exoneration of herself, but in what way his acquittal founded as it most probably will be if it takes place, upon the ground that that Government has assumed the whole responsibility growing out of the transaction, can weaken our claim on her, Your Excellency, will pardon me for saying, surpasses my comprehension.

I am most happy to concur in opinion with Your Excellency that the destruction of the Caroline is a question in which every state of this union is interested equally. The interests of New York are merged in those of the U. States. The question is no longer local but national, and while I shall at all times be pleased to receive suggestions from Your Excellency in regard to it, and shall give to them all the consideration to which they are entitled as emanating from the chief magistrate of an independent state, Yet I shall be equally prepared to receive and maturely to consider similar suggestions from the Governor of any other state.

You are pleased to intimate the belief that Mr Spencer has been retained as counsel for McLeod by the Government of Great Britain. Whether this be so is a matter which may be better known to Your Excellency than to myself. I readily admit that I have not felt it to be my duty to enquire of Mr Spencer in regard to it, and if you shall esteem it to be your duty to enquire of a counsel practising in Your courts as to the quarter from which he obtains his compensation I doubt not but that You will promptly receive a satisfactory answer. Your Excellency must pardon me, however for believing that it is a subject with which I can have nothing to do, not conceiving that either the honor or interests of the Country can be at all involved in it. Surely that honor can never be affected by an appeal on a question of law to the judiciary no matter at whose instance such appeal is made.

In conclusion permit me to hope that our correspondence on this subject may end here, for however much I may feel myself honored and altho' I shall at all times be highly pleased to receive communications from Your Excellency on all matters of public interest, yet I cannot perceive what good is to be atchieved by prolonging *this* correspondence. The Argument in the case of McLeod has terminated for the present at least, and the case now rests in the hands to which it has been committed by the constitution and laws of the state of New York. I can see no practical good as likely to arise from prolonging the discussions which have so unexpectedly to myself arisen between us.

I tender to Your Excellency renewed assurances of my high considerations. John Tyler

LS. DNA, RG 59 (Misc. Letters). Published in part in *Tylers*, 2:210–211.

EDWARD KENT TO JOHN TYLER

State of Maine
Executive Department
Sir,   Augusta, May 25th 1841

In pursuance of the request of the Legislature of this State, I have the honor to enclose to you, herewith, a copy of the Report of the Joint Select Committee upon the North Eastern Boundary, and of the Resolves relating to the North Eastern Boundary, adopted by both Branches of the Legislature.[1] I deem it proper, at the same time, to give you information in a condensed form, of the present condition of the territory belonging to this State and claimed by a foreign power; and to reiterate the requests heretofore made upon the General Government and those set forth in the accompanying Resolves.

It is unnecessary to recapitulate the proceedings of the authorities of this State and of New Brunswick and of the United States and Great Britain, immediately subsequent to the occupation of the territory by the armed civil posse and militia of Maine in eighteen hundred thirty nine. The official documents heretofore communicated, with those on file in the Department of State at Washington, fully explain and set forth the origin, proceedings and grounds which led to the termination of the military movements, and the expressed terms upon which Maine consented to withdraw her military force.[2] I will however call your attention to the precedent declaration of Maj. Gen. Sir John Harvey,[3] then Lieut. Governor of Her Majesty's Province of New Brunswick, "that it is not the intention of the Lieutenant Governor of Her Brittannic Majesty's Province of New Brunswick, under the expected renewal of negotiations between the cabinets of London and Washington, on the subject of said disputed territory, without renewed instructions to that [e]ffect from his government, to seek to take military possession of that territory, or to seek by military force to expel the armed civil *posse* or the troops of Maine."[4]

1. The report of the joint select committee of March 30, 1841, and the Maine Resolves of April 30, 1841, are found in a bound manuscript of the British Foreign Office, "Correspondence Relating to the Boundary between the British Possessions in North America and the United States of America, under the Treaty of 1783," in nine parts (London, 1838–1843). See pt. 6, pp. 96–129.

2. Mutual antagonisms and conflict over the region's timber resources caused the eruption of the "Aroostook War" of 1839 between the troops of New Brunswick and the militia of Maine. A truce was concluded that allowed Maine to keep a "civil posse" under the command of the state land agent in the disputed area.

3. Harvey (1778–1852) served as lieutenant governor of New Brunswick from 1837 until 1841, when he was relieved of his position after Governor-General Sydenham complained to London about his conciliatory actions toward Maine.

4. Winfield Scott to Harvey, March

Immediately after this annunciation the troops of Maine were withdrawn, and a small armed civil force remained at Fort Fairfield, and shortly afterwards a similar force was stationed at Fish river. These two posts are still thus occupied. During the year eighteen hundred thirty-nine a detachment of Her Majesty's troops was ordered to and took post on that part of the territory North of the St. John, and near the North-west head of Lake Temiscouata, at the commencement of the Portage road, so called, where they have erected fortifications and barracks. Military possession was thus taken, as it seems to me, in direct violation of the pledge and understanding of the parties; and, in a short time thereafter, a detachment was sent to occupy a post near the South end of the aforesaid Lake; and within a few months past, a further inroad has been made into the heart of the territory by the location of a military force at and in the vicinity of the mouth of the Madawaska on the St. John river. The General Government was notified of this movement by my predecessor, in his letter to the President of the United States, dated December 15th 1840,[5] enclosing a copy of the letter to him from the Lieut. Governor of New Brunswick.

I have taken pains to ascertain, as nearly as possible, the present location and number of the British troops, stationed on the territory belonging to Maine and in its immediate vicinity. The Land Agency of the State has visited that portion of our State, during the past winter, and from his report and other sources, I am satisfied that there is a force, now upon the territory, of about four hundred men, with a full complement of officers, arms and munitions of war. Two companies of infantry, numbering about sixty five men each, under the command of a Major, are stationed in what is properly called "the Madawaska Settlements," and distributed thus; about one hundred men at "the church," on the North side of the St. John about four miles below the mouth of the Madawaska; about thirty men, under the command of a Lieutenant, on the North side of the St. John river at the mouth of the Madawska; at this point they are erecting fortifications. Mr [Elijah Livermore] Hamlin[6] says, he saw ten or twelve men at work on the top of a hill, about one hundred rods North easterly from the mouth of the Madawaska, blasting

21, 1839 (with Harvey's concurring signature, dated March 23, 1839), in British Foreign Office, "Correspondence Relating to the Boundary," pt. 3, pp. 81–82.

5. John Fairfield to Van Buren, December 15, 1840, DNA, RG 59 (Misc. Letters). Harvey's letter is dated December 10, 1841. In 1838 Fairfield (1797–1847), a Democrat, resigned his seat in the U.S. House of Repre-

sentatives, which he had held since 1835, to accept the governorship of Maine in 1839. He returned in 1843 to the Senate, where he remained until his death.

6. Hamlin (1800–1872; Brown 1819), brother of the future vice president, was active in Maine politics. His report was presented to the Maine House of Representatives on March 15, 1841.

the ledge which crops out at that place; and he was informed that the Engineer had directed it to be lowered twelve feet. Between the hill and the river, another party was engaged in erecting log huts, and another, in the adjacent woods, in cutting and hewing timber.

At the Grand Falls on the St. John, near the Boundary line, but supposed to be within the limits of New Brunswick, a sergeant and sixteen men are stationed, who have charge of a depot of artillery and military stores. At the South end or foot of Temiscouata Lake there are about seventy five men, and at the Portage road, first spoken of, about two hundred men. These statements may not be strictly accurate as to numbers, but I am satisfied that they are substantially correct.

I may here properly allude to a few facts, bearing upon this subject, and indicative of a design on the part of Great Britain to make such a disposition of her forces, and to construct and prepare such facilities for their movements, that, upon very short notice, a large and effective force may be concentrated at any one of various points on the territory. At the River du Loup on the St. Lawrence, at the termination of the Portage road, which connects that point with the lake Temiscouata, about four hundred men were stationed last fall, with a depot of artillery and military stores. I understand that the authorities of Canada have, within the present year, appropriated twenty thousand dollars for completing the said Portage road and also the road down the Madawaska river to its mouth. A bridge across the river Aroostook near its junction with the St. John, within the limits of New Brunswick, is now being erected, at a very considerable expense, by the Government; and a very liberal appropriation has been made, as I understand, by the Assembly of New Brunswick, to be expended on the road between Woodstock and Madawaska. When this bridge and the roads are completed, there will be an uninterrupted line of communication from the St. Lawrence to the City of St. John, on which troops may be readily moved and concentrated.

The allegation, that these military movements are made by the authority of the Governor General of Canada, whilst it relieves the distinguished and honorable officer, late at the head of the Provincial Government of New Brunswick, from any imputations of having been an active and willing agent in the breach of the agreement made by him, is yet entirely unsatisfactory as a justification, or excuse even, for what is so palpably a breach of the spirit and, what appears to me, the plain meaning and extent of the official pledge, which has never been repudiated by the home government. In view of these facts, and the proceedings of the Legislature, I feel bound to say to the President, "that this State is still suffering the extreme unresisted wrong of British invasion, begun in 1839, repeated in 1840, and continued to this time, in violation of solemn and deliberate pledges from abroad, guaranteed by our own Executive Government." And in pursuance of the wishes of the Legislature, as expressed in their solemn and deliberate Resolves, it is my duty respectfully to re-quest and call upon the President of the United States, "to fulfill the obli-gation of the Federal Constitution, by causing the immediate removal or expulsion of the foreign invading force now stationed within the bounds of Maine; and, other methods failing, to cause military possession to be taken of the disputed territory." And I join in "the earnest trust and ex-pectation, that the National Government will not fail speedily to cause our just rights," in reference to the whole question, "too long neglected, to be vindicated and maintained, either by negotiation or by arms."[7] In pursuance of the spirit and manifest intent of that other resolution of the Legislature, which invokes the General Government to provide for our future protection against foreign aggression, by the establishment of military force upon the frontier, and to relieve this State from the present heavy burden of its own needful, unavoidable defence, I had the honor to address the honorable Secretary of War [John Bell], under date of the 15th inst,[8] asking the immediate establishment of two detachments of United States troops on that portion of the territory now in the possession of Maine, one at Fort Fairfield and the other at Fish river, and thus re-lieve the present armed civil force of this State at those posts; leaving Maine to exercise her jurisdiction and protect her citizens and property, by agents and otherwise, as in other parts of her undisturbed territory. I indulge the confident hope, that a movement so justifiable, so necessary and important will not be long delayed. I would beg leave to refer to that letter, for a more full exposition of my views upon this topic.

The other Resolves,[9] containing the declared opinions and wishes of a Sovereign State, on this subject of vital importance to her rights and interests, will, I am sure, be regarded as entitled to careful consideration, and receive that attention and have that weight and influence to which they are justly entitled.

I deem it proper, also, to enclose to you a copy of a letter[10] from Capt. Stover Rines, in charge of the force at Fish river, to the late Land Agent of Maine, in relation to the transactions alluded to in the correspondence in December last, between the Lieut. Governor of New Brunswick and

7. These quotations are from the Maine Resolves enclosed with Kent's letter to Tyler. Since the purport of those resolves is adequately sum-marized by Kent, they have not been printed here.

8. Kent to Bell, May 15, 1841, DNA, RG 107 (Records of the Office of the Secretary of War).

9. The substance of the other re-solves affirmed the resolutions of pre-vious state legislatures in declaring Maine's right to the "whole of its ter-ritory" according to the Treaty of Paris of 1783, offering the state's re-sources to the national government in the cause, and urging that the de-termination of the boundary be com-pleted by the end of the year.

10. Stover Rines to Rufus McIn-tire, January 27, 1841; not included in this publication. Neither Rines nor McIntire, the land agent of Maine, could be further identified.

the Governor of Maine [John Fairfield]. Also a copy of a letter from Francis Rice, Esq., the Magistrate refered to in the correspondence.[11] From these documents it will clearly appear, that the alledged causes, for the recent movement of her Majesty's troops to the Madawaska Settlement, are unfounded in fact, and that Sir John Harvey was misinformed in the premises.

It is clear, that there has never been any foundation for the allegation, that the individuals refered to were abused[,] threatened or insulted, as was represented to Maj. Gen. Sir John Harvey and by him made the excuse for the location of Her Majesty's troops, at the last named station. The assigned causes can no longer be allowed to justify or excuse the act. With the highest respect, I have the honor to be, Your obedient Servant,   Edward Kent

L C . DNA, RG 59 (Misc. Letters).

WILLIAM HENRY SEWARD TO JOHN TYLER

                                   State of New York
                                   Executive Department
Sir,   Albany, June 1st 1841

I acknowledge the receipt of your letter of the 25th of May,[1] in which after reviewing the subject you have done me the honor to discuss in former communications you conclude with the expression of an opinion that a prolongation of the correspondence would be unprofitable, and a desire that it might be regarded as closed.

No one could be more fully convinced than I am of the importance of harmony between the government of the United States and that of this state in regard to questions of deep interest to the latter and affecting the relations of the country with a foreign power. I need not advert to the many and cogent reasons why I must necessarily desire to consider with candor and approve with earnestness the measures and policy adopted by the government of the Union. It was with profound regret I discovered that the correspondence, begun with such a disposition on my part, and having in view only the prevention of an apparent misunderstanding between the government of the United States and this state had from some cause taken such a course as to exhibit in a measure the reality of the misunderstanding the appearance of which was deprecated. Such a

11. Rice to [Stover Rines], January 26, 1841. When a number of American citizens gathered at an inn in Madawaska on November 2, 1840, to vote in the presidential election, they became involved in an altercation with Rice, a Canadian magistrate. Rice declares in this letter that he had not been mistreated by Rines or his men on the night in question. In the letter to McIntire mentioned in note 10, above, Rines stated that his relations with Rice had always been cordial.

1. See above, Tyler to Seward, May 25, 1841.

result was as unlooked for by myself as I am sure it was on your part. Solicitous now that it may be made to disappear I will not go back to inquire when or how the correspondence received so unfortunate a direction, but will cheerfully acknowledge all the responsibility for it that may be supposed to rest upon me. I take the liberty also to say that in addressing you directly during the known absence of the Secretary of State, in consequence of which a previous communication to him on a different subject had failed to receive the notice which I knew you would have accorded to it,[2] it was far from my desire or expectation to engage you in a correspondence the conducting which in person I am well aware must have been very inconvenient. I acknowledge myself obliged by the attention manifested in the course you have taken, and I shall be entirely satisfied with a reference of this communication if it shall be regarded as meriting or requiring any attention, to an appropriate department as indeed I should have been with a similar disposition of the subject at any stage of discussion.

I beg leave to say further that if I had been acting individually I should have deemed it my duty to defer to your opinions and acquiesce in your decisions as soon as they became known to me. With these explanations I trust I may be allowed to observe that the representative character in which I stand enjoins me from leaving the subject without first taking care that the positions which I have deemed it my duty to make plain on behalf of this state be rescued from misapprehension. A similar privilege in what is there claimed has been already exercised as a right on your part. I trust however that in performing a duty which thus seems to remain, I shall not manifest a desire, as I shall endeavor not to furnish occasion for a reply.

Your remark in your last communication[3] that you had heretofore supposed that the right of every man to a fair and impartial trial, to be confronted with his accusers, and to be defended by counsel of his own retaining, admitted of no question, but was deeply engraven on the hearts of the American People, and you are pleased to express surprise that speaking in the name of the State of New York I should have entered my dissent to the correctness of this proposition which you had hoped would have been regarded as incontestable.

Your known respect for justice encourages me to believe that you would not conclude me from observing that the general rights of accused persons have not been understood on my part to be among the subjects discussed. It is not within my recollection that the proposition

2. Seward wrote DW about the Mitchell extradition case on April 28, but learning that DW was not in Washington, he addressed a letter to Tyler on the same subject on May 2, 1841. For both letters, see DNA, RG 59 (Misc. Letters).

3. See above, Tyler to Seward, May 25, 1841.

which you have now stated has been before submitted for my consideration, and it is certain that my supposed dissent from it does not appear on the record.

The correspondence has related to the case of Alexander McLeod, charged under peculiar circumstances with the crime of murder. His particular right under those circumstances to be defended by a counsellor who holds the office of District Attorney of the United States [Joshua Austin Spencer] may, if you deem it material, be admitted to have been involved. Yet your position on that subject, thus most liberally stated, and excluding the peculiar circumstances relied upon on my part, is very different from the proposition you have through misapprehension now stated, and to which you have affixed my dissent. It contains no question concerning the right of that accused person to a fair and impartial trial, and no denial of his right to be confronted with his accusers. In regard to his right to a fair and impartial trial, I beg leave to recal to your recollection that in my first communication to the government of the United States in relation to his case,[4] it was expressly stated that a just regard for the honor of this state as well as a due consideration of the importance of the case to the accused and the possible influence of the result of the proceeding upon the relations existing between this country and Great Britain had seemed to me to require that he should have a fair and impartial trial, and it was announced that to secure that important object the Chief Justice of the Supreme Court, who is the highest judicial officer in the state authorized to try criminal cases, and who does not usually preside on such occasions had been required to hold Court, and that no objection would be raised to the removal of the scene of trial beyond the reach of excitement and of every prejudicial influence. The same determination to afford the accused person a fair and impartial trial has been repeatedly avowed, and nothing inconsistent with it will be found in any of my communications.

Again, so far from the prisoner's right to be confronted with his accusers has been challenged it has been considered a grievance that while a menace from Great Britain is impending over the government of the United States, a person holding the office of District Attorney under the latter government is engaged in an effort to procure the discharge of the prisoner without his being confronted with his accusers. What has been objected to was that the District Attorney of the United States should be acting in conflict (as was assumed) with the authorities of New York in a proceeding deeply interesting to the state, and sanctioned by the President of the United States. The prisoner's right under all the peculiar circumstances of the case to be defended by the District Attorney of the United States because that officer was a counsellor in the courts of this

4. Seward to Forsyth, February 27, 1841, DNA, RG 59 (Misc. Letters).

state has been denied and this it is respectfully submitted is the extent to which I can justly be said to have dissented from the humane and enlightened proposition you have now laid down, and to which as a general rule with some necessary modification, I am happy in being able to declare my free assent.

What has been denied, if my position be stated in the form you have preferred to adopt, is the absoluteness of the right of an accused person to be defended by counsel of his own retaining. If the right be absolute, the accused may disarm public justice by retaining the witness, the prosecuting attorney, or even the judge. You have admitted, however, that the rule is not universal, and you maintain, that the present case is not to be received among admitted exceptions. The converse has been held on my part, and this is the precise point at issue. The proposition being thus accurately presented, and my dissent properly understood, I cheerfully concur in waiving further argument on that question.

The correction thus made renders it almost unnecessary for me to advert to the misapprehension with which your communication opens. I am there represented as having requested you to deprive a man place[d] upon trial for his life of his retained counsel merely because that counsel holds a commission from the government, the nature and character of which in no way conflict with the engagement he has entered into with the person under trial. Certainly no one reading this statement would suppose that a question had been raised at any time, whether, when the circumstances of the case and the nature and character of the office of District Attorney were considered, there was not in fact a conflict between his official duties and character and his engagement as counsel for the accused. And yet that question has been among the chief points in controversy throughout the whole discussion.

Again, the form you have adopted in presenting the suggestion I had the honor to make seems to me not altogether liberal. That suggestion was that the District Attorney of the United States was acting in the proceeding in question in a manner which indicated an apparent conflict between the authorities of the United States and those of this state. The previous retainer of that functionary by the accused was set up on your part as a reason why he ought not to be required to desist from the defence. Even though this might be admitted to be a sufficient reason for declining to deprive the prisoner of his retained counsel, it would by no means follow that there was no other mode of avoiding the conflict deprecated. If it be so certainly wrong to deprive an accused person on trial for his life of retained counsel, because that counsel happens to be the District Attorney of the United States, I trust I may be permitted now to express my regret that if that relation of the counsel was known at the time of his appointment, it could not have been thought important, in view of the peculiar circumstances of the case, to inquire whether it was indispensably necessary to assign the duties of District Attorney to a person lying under such an engagement.

It seems to be regarded by you as a light consideration that an officer holding a commission from the United States may be paid by the government of Great Britain for challenging the jurisdiction of the courts of this state in a cause instituted for the purpose of vindicating the lives and property of its citizens, with the sanction of the President, and when a war between Great Britain and the United States is supposed to depend upon the exercise of the jurisdiction thus challenged. I can only excuse the error which I have committed in dwel[l]ing upon a circumstance which you regard as so unimportant, by pleading the prejudice supposed to be sustained by the history of our own as well as of other countries and even higher authority, which inculcates the danger of entrusting a cause to one who lies under obligations to an adversary.

You are pleased to observe that misapprehending the tenor of your communication and detaching a sentence from its connection, I had made an occasion to ascribe to your indifference to the rights of the State of New York which nothing that has occurred justify. I acknowledge most gratefully the kindness of the succeeding remark, that upon further reflection and with more extended information I would have been among the last to have done you such injustice.

I owe it to myself to state that when writing the communication referred to it did not occur to me that the effect of the sentence to which you have alluded was qualified by the context. I will not recur to the correspondence which has passed either to enquire whether it was not my duty to act upon such information as I possessed, or to ascertain whether the error into which it appears I have fallen might not be defended or executed, but will freely admit that injustice was done in supposing you to have felt any less interest in the rights of the State of New York than that which you have now carefully defined. As this is a subject, however, of deep interest, not only on account of its bearing upon the matter out of which this correspondence has arisen but also because it involves the mutual rights and obligations of this state and of the government of the United States, I shall deem it my duty to state the positions of both parties accurately and shall then be content to leave them without discussion.

Your positions are stated by you as follows. "The attack on the Caroline, when viewed as an act of public force, committed by the British government within the territory of the United States, is undoubtedly a matter in which the government of the United States is bound to take an interest, and to which I trust neither my predecessor nor myself have shown any degree of inattention. But when it is viewed as divested of its character as a public transaction, and when those concerned in it are regarded merely as individuals committing crimes against the laws of

New York, then certainly the case requires nothing to be done by this government as auxiliary to the power of that state. Nor can this government have more to do with that trial than with a trial for any other offence against the laws of the state, unless indeed it find itself called upon for the protection of some interest of the United States, or by its high duty of perserving the peace of the country and of superintending its foreign relations, to take care by the exercise of its acknowledged powers that such interest be guarded, or that no just ground of complaint be furnished to other nations. It was in this sense and in that only that I spoke of McLeod's trial as one in which the government of the United States had no interest, and I repeat my regret that your Excellency should have thought there was ground for ascribing to me any other meaning." Again you declare that you concur with me in opinion that "the destruction of the Caroline is a question in which every State of this Union is interested equally." You observe also that "the interests of New York are merged in those of the United States," that "the question is no longer local but national," and you add "while I shall at all times be pleased to receive suggestions from your Excellency in regard to it, and shall give to them all the consideration to which they are entitled as emanating from the Chief Magistrate of an independent state, yet I shall be equally prepared to receive and maturely to consider similar suggestions from the Governor of any other state."

These are the views of the government of the United States concerning its interest in the subject of the attack upon the Caroline. On my part I declare most cheerfully my concurrence with them so far as they relate to the attack upon the Caroline viewed as an act of public force committed by the British government within the territory of the United States, and directly cognizable by the government of the United States as a national question. I will take leave also to say that I should be especially grieved if my communications had any where manifested the disposition, directly, and, I must be allowed to say, prematurely censured, to obtrude advice in regard to this much of the subject, or to claim any especial attention from you beyond what might be due to the Executive of any other state, or even any other citizen of any one of the United States.

In regard to the same subject viewed in the aspect presented by the prosecution by this state against Alexander McLeod, as a participator in the attack upon the Caroline and the murder of a citizen of this state, the following positions are held by this Department. The offenders in the transaction referred to, if arrested at the time, might unquestionably have been brought to justice by the judicial authorities of this state, and the prisoner's subsequent voluntary entrance within that territory places him in the same situation. There is no principle of international law of reason or justice which entitles such offenders to immunity before the legal tribunals when coming voluntarily within their independent and undoubted jurisdiction, because they acted in obedience to their superior authorities, or because their acts have become the subject of diplomatic discussion between the two governments. The avowal or justification of the outrage by the British authorities so far from in any way entitling the offender or his government to a discontinuance of the prosecution commenced by this state might itself be an additional ground of complaint. The application of the government of the Union to that of Great Britain for the redress of an outrage to the peace, dignity and rights of the United States, cannot deprive the state of New York of her undoubted right of vindicating through the exercise of her judicial power the property and lives of her citizens.[5]

The government of the United States heretofore voluntarily assumed these positions in behalf of the State of New York, and made them known to Great Britain, before either an avowal of the attack upon the Caroline or a formal demand for the release of McLeod without trial was made by the British government, and when both were well anticipated. The government of the United States made known to the authorities of the State of New York the grounds it had thus assumed in her behalf and received their assent. Thus the government of the United States became pledged to maintain and guaranty at all hazards and in every event not only the prosecution it had so solemnly sanctioned in the face of Great Britain and before the world, but also all the principles before defined as those which are maintained by this Department.

The avowal by the British government and the peremptory demand for the release of McLeod, which were anticipated, have now been made, but they cannot affect the rights of this state or the obligations of the United States. The demand for the release of McLeod involves a discontinuance of its proceedings by this state, and a compliance with the demand cannot be made without an abandonment of the ground already put in issue between the government of the United States and that of Great Britain. Notwithstanding the issue was chosen and tendered by itself. The government of the United States now declares that it has no interest in the prosecution carried on by the State of New York, except in contingencies which have not happened and it is not alleged are expected to occur.

It is held by this Department that the State of New York cannot without dishonor, especially under what must be construed as a menace by Great Britain, retire from the prosecution by which she is vindicating the property and lives of her citizens. It is most respectfully held also that the government of the United States cannot, consistently with its solemn

5. In this paragraph Seward paraphrases from Secretary of State Forsyth's note to Henry Stephen Fox of December 26, 1840 (DNA, RG 59, Notes to Foreign Legations, Britain).

sanction and pledge disavow an interest in that proceeding, or withhold from this state countenance and support. It is not neutrality on the part of the government of the United States in regard to the proceeding that has been invoked, as you have assumed. It is the continuance of favor, the redemption of a pledge, the fulfilment of a guaranty. And it was because the action of the District Attorney of the United States to embarrass, thwart, and defeat in an extraordinary manner the prosecution instituted by this state, seemed inconsistent not merely with the favor of the Federal government thus relied upon, but even with neutrality itself, that the subject was respectfully brought to the notice of the President of the United States.

It is felt that it was unjust on the part of the government of the United States, when the representation thus rendered necessary was respectfully made, to answer by pleading the rights of attorneys, and the powers conferred by their licenses, by refining upon the obligations of retainers and the general privileges of accused persons, and by disavowing all obligations, duty, interest, or concern in regard to the proceeding in question, except in remote and unlooked for contingencies.

I am asked what right of this state had been abandoned by the government of the United States, or in any way put at hazard, and whether the rights of her judiciary have been in any way interfered with by that government. Although at the same time invited not to reply to questions so pertinent, and under which silence would be so conclusive of affirmation, I must nevertheless be permitted most respectfully to answer, that the local crime for which this state prosecutes and the public aggression for which the United States demands redress were identical. The same facts and circumstances constitute both. The District Attorney of the United States has heretofore been required, and it is always within his province to ascertain those facts and circumstances for the use of the government in support of its demand for redress, and it is altogether inconsistent with his duty that he should deny their existence or palliate their flagrancy. If there was no assault upon the Caroline and the murder of [Amos] Durfee[6] to be vindicated by the State of New York, then there was no outrage upon the peace, dignity and rights of the United States to be redressed by their government. The defence of the prisoner in the former case involves a denial of all the grounds upon which the latter can be maintained. The District Attorney of the United States, by his retainer in the former, became bound to maintain not only that his client did not participate in the aggression for which the government of the United States demands satisfaction, but also that no such transaction has ever taken place; that if it did take place he is not amenable, although the government of the United States has declared he is so; that if he

6. Durfee (d. 1837), a stage driver from Buffalo, was killed while standing on the dock next to the *Caroline*.

were responsible, still the courts of this state have not the jurisdiction over him which the President of the United States has solemnly affirmed in their behalf; and finally that the transaction was lawful, just and right, notwithstanding the declaration of the government of the Union to the contrary. All these positions have been already maintained by the District Attorney, and so strikingly incongruous are they with his official relations, and with the obligations and duties of the government of the United States, that that government deems it by no means unimportant to affirm and reiterate that he is acting without its authority or direction, although not without its permission. The same functionary informs the court, moreover, with an asseveration of full knowledge of the views and wishes of the government of the United States, but disclaiming its direct authority for the communication, that that government is looking anxiously to that tribunal for a discharge of the prisoner, without confronting him with his accusers and without a trial, and he enforces his appeal for so dishonorable a decision by declaring, but whether upon the authority of the British government, or from his knowledge of the secrets of his own, does not appear, that if the court shall exercise its undoubted jurisdiction our frontier will be lined with British bayonets and our coasts with the navies of the proud adversary who has justified his client's offence, and made his cause her own.

The President of the United States leaves me to suppose that he sees in all this nothing calling for his interposition, unhappily moreover expressly disclaims all interest in the judicial vindication of the lives and property of the citizens of this state, except it shall hereafter become necessary for purposes foreign to the present state of the case, and even dwells upon supposed advantages to be derived from the discharge of the accused without a trial upon the ground of the assumption of his offense by the government of Great Britain.

No right of this state may be lost. The extraordinary proceedings I have described may not have the effect to which they so manifestly tend. I trust it will be so. But it is obvious that the judicial vindication of the lives and property of our citizens has been put at hazard. If it shall happen as you have speculated that the prisoner is discharged and without a trial, it will then be remembered that Great Britain had peremptorily demanded the prisoner's release and that the government of the United States was represented to the Court by a person standing in an intimate relation with the government and enjoying its confidence as earnestly desiring such a result, and the People of this state will be left to the painful consideration how far a conclusion so gratifying to the offending government and so humiliating to themselves was produced by such honest judicial convictions as you rely upon, and how far it was induced by the circumstances against which I have felt myself constrained to present my remonstrance. I earnestly hope that in such an event the confidence of the People of this state in their Judiciary may be found as salutary in healing their discontent as is now anticipated by the government of the United States.

I take leave of the subject with the assurance that none will be more sincerely gratified than myself if the succeeding events shall prove that your views concerning it are, as from habitual deference I can cheerfully admit they may be, as much more just than my own, as the exalted position from which they have been taken is more favorable than the place I occupy to an examination of the whole ground. I have the honor to remain with the highest respect your obedient servant   William H. Seward

LS. DNA, RG 59 (Misc. Letters). Published in George E. Baker, ed., *The Works of William H. Seward* (5 vols., New York, 1853–1854), 2:567–577.

FROM FRANCIS ORMAND JONATHAN SMITH

Private

Mr. Webster—   [June 7, 1841]

I have revolved the boundary question still further in my own mind, with reference to my devoting any services to it—And I am yet of opinion that an Agency instituted upon the plan, and conducted in the spirit, I have hinted at in our conversation,[1] will bring the two people immediately interested in it,[2] to an agreement upon it, rendering other modes of negotiation between the two primary governments of those people, unnecessary, except to execute the agreement of the former—though not designed to supercede its progress in the mean time.

The mistake and inefficiency of all past efforts upon this subject has laid in directing negotiation *at the wrong end of the dispute*. The dispute, in reality, and the interest in reality, has not been so much with the federal government and the British government, as with the people of Maine and the people of the British Provinces. Consequently, semi-official intercourse among the latter parties might have been made long since altogether effectual, as well as direct, while official intercourse, through the studied and shy forms of diplomacy between the former, could hardly fail to be otherwise than indirect and ineffectual, from the very nature of the subject.

Now my plan is, to prepare public sentiment in Maine for a compromise of the matter, through a conventional line, founded partly in consideration of an exchange of territory, and partly in a pecuniary indem-

1. Smith called on DW at his home in Washington in May 1841. For Smith's testimony on his dealings with DW and related documents, see *House Reports*, 29th Cong., 1st sess., Serial 490, No. 684.

2. Probably a reference to DW and British Foreign Minister Lord Aberdeen. George Hamilton-Gordon, Lord Aberdeen (1784–1860), was foreign minister from 1841 to 1846.

nity to Maine and Massachusetts for the difference in the exchange of territory thus made.

The process of exchange of territory & pecuniary indemnity would be a sufficient recognition of the rights of Maine to satisfy her honor and pride—while the latter would appeal to her *interests* and be just towards her rights—and her present pecuniary condition will predispose her people towards it, if it can be made to seem to have its origin with themselves. This, however, is the most delicate part of the enterprise.

But, public sentiment upon this matter can be brought into right shape in Maine, by enlisting certain leading men of both political parties (yet not politically) and through them, at a proper time hereafter, guiding aright the public press.

Having obtained the favorable opinion of the leading political men of Maine, through regular and successive approaches, towards a conventional line, (all of which is feasible by a few months steady and well directed correspondence and the active agency of a very select few) and drawing after this an appropriate expression of the public press, the same work could be accomplished in a much less time among the citizens of the interested provinces—and the whole may be combined into corresponding and reciprocal resolutions of the Legislative assemblies of the two local governments, at their next winter sessions, in ample season for Congress to confirm all at its next regular session.

A few thousand dollars expended upon such an agency will accomplish more than hundreds of thousands expended through the formalities and delays of ordinary diplomatic negotiations & surveys—and more than millions would, if the parties shall be brought into belligerent attitudes on the subject—and, what is more—it would avert all occasion for such a national calamity as the latter event would certainly be, however thrice armed in justice our quarrel might be.

The <pro> whole proceeding must be conducted with system and prudence. I would have it commence with the proper enlistment of the services of a few judicious co-operators at different points in Maine, and extending their circle gradually, without display or the betrayal of official authority as opportunity might be created—drawing silently in the voluntary and patriotic aid of men of influence of both political parties— carefully ripening the whole into a compact before the supposed interests or prejudices of any class should be excited in relation to it on account of the credit it might reflect upon the administration which had accomplished it.

So confident am I that this proceeding would prove effectual and most honorable to all concerned, that I am extremely solicitous for the honor of your own and President Tyler's administration, and for the interest and quiet of Maine, that it should be attempted. In the worst view, the hazard will be of comparatively small amount in expenses before some developments will be made to you of its progress, such as would enable you and the President to judge of the propriety of pursuing it. But the persons immediately engaged in it should feel if it was a subject worthy of their whole time and effort to accomplish it, both in a personal, political and national point of view. And regarding it in this aspect, I have concluded, upon reflection, to say, that if you do not think of one more likely to render the desired service with more efficiency than myself, and I can be furnished with the requisite means to set such co-agencies at work as I may think essential, subject at all times to your cognizance, and accountable at all times for the use of the means wanted and furnished, I will enter upon it without delay.

My own compensation I should expect to be definitively fixed at the rate of $3500 per annum—and my necessary travelling expenses, postage & incidental expenses (all subjected to your revision & approval) paid by the government. And in case of a successful arrangement, it would not be unreasonable to expect the allowance of a liberal commission as disbursing agent, on whatever sums the negotiation might ultimately involve. Success would warrant almost any expenditure.

In case you adopt these views, and decide to make the trial, the sooner I am informed of it the more it will be to my accommodation. And in that event, there is a paper or two, signed by a former delegation from Maine, in Congress, in your department of which I should desire a copy.[3] With the most friendly consideration, I have the honor to be, your Obt Svnt   Francis O. J. Smith

ALS. NhHi. Published in Frederick Merk, *Fruits of Propaganda in the Tyler Administration* (Cambridge, Mass., 1971), pp. 143–145. Smith (1806–1876), an influential lawyer, newspaper publisher, entrepreneur, and politician of Maine, suggested a boundary by compromise as early as 1837 to President Martin Van Buren. For a description of Smith and his relationship with DW, see Merk, *Fruits of Propaganda*, esp. pp. 59–64.

FROM FRANCIS ORMAND JONATHAN SMITH

Private
Dear Sir—   Portland July 2. 1841.
I have by correspondence, and personal intercourse, communicated with leading and influential gentlemen, of both political parties, in five of our principal counties, on the subject of adjusting our N. E. Boundary upon the basis contemplated in our late interviews. And the result is, that I am no less sanguine than heretofore, that the proposition can be made to come before our next Legislature, *from our own people*, in the shape

3. Smith may have had in mind the Maine Joint Select Committee Report of March 1841 and the state legislature's resolves of April 1841. See above, Kent to Tyler, May 25, 1841.

of which I now enclose a copy,[1] unless you discover something objectionable therein.

I learn, that the inhabitants of the Aroostook County, (immediately interested) can be brought very unanimously into it, provided a stipulation can be secured for a limited navigation of the St. John—& hence I present *that* point. Can there be any grave doubt of Gt. Britain's acceding to it in that shape?

To our *maritime* towns & counties, the worth of national peace, for the sake of Commerce, is the inducement suggested.

To our *interior* counties, the payment of our public debt & riddance of taxation, is the moving consideration which the proposition is intended to put forth.

To the *partisans* of [John] Fairfield's late administration, & the defenders of the late military fooleries on the lines, the payment of the expenses incurred by the State, is "a consummation devoutly to be wished" and it is here held out.

After I shall have procured the signatures of certain leading men of both parties in this county, I shall employ the necessary persons to visit every town in the county, & obtain the principal men in each to cooperate, and at once proceed to the execution of a similar operation in each of the other counties.

One friend of great sagacity & influence in Penobscot Co[unt]y.[2] & one intimately acquainted with the people and interests of *Aroostook* County, writes me thus—"If a move is desirable in the premises, I can get the leading locos in Aroostook County committed to the measure, in advance . . . The inhabitants of the Aroostook County, & a good many of the inhabitants of Penobscot, are extremely desirous of extending their enterprise to the territory South of the St. Johns. They are, as a preliminary, desirous of getting the free use of the St. Johns for carrying their timber out. Such a body can be obtained here, in favor of the measure, that no political advantage can be taken of it. And several loco votes in the Legislature can be secured for it. I can so manage it, with certain leading men of the opposition, that they will stand as God fathers to the project and must fight it through. Their interest, their honor, and last tho' not least, their *vanity* will unite in pressing them on."

Such is the character of my encouragements thus far—in confirmation of my original convictions.

1. Smith's enclosed proposal called for a boundary running along "the St. John River, from the outlet of Eel River up to the Madawaska River, thence through the East River and Lake Temiscouata to the highlands." Other terms of Smith's proposal are included in his letter.

2. John Hodgdon (1800–1883) was a Bangor lawyer and land agent of Maine from 1834 to 1838. Smith quotes from a letter from Hodgdon of June 17, 1841, which is published in Merk, *Fruits of Propaganda*, pp. 148–150.

I shall write as matters progress, that you may be minutely informed on it. With great regard, Your Obt Svnt   Francis O. J. Smith

A L S . NhHi. Published with enclosure in Frederick Merk, *Fruits of Propaganda in the Tyler Administration* (Cambridge, Mass., 1971), pp. 150–153.

FROM JOSHUA AUSTIN SPENCER

Private.
Sir,   Utica 12, July 1841
    With the same mail which takes this letter I forward a copy of the opinion of the Court delivered this morning by Judge [Esek] Cowen.[1] Will you allow me to ask of you its early perusal & then to give me your views in relation to future movements.
    One remedy is by writ of Error to our Court for the correction of Errors, & should the Judgt be there affirmed to bring Error to the U.S. Sup. Court at Washington. The other course is to go down to the circuit for trial. The latter is much the shortest way, for we have a Circuit in *Livingston* on the 21. Sept. next, and in Ontario on 27. Nov. We may elect which county. The remedy by writ of Error will require the winter to bring it to a close. [Alexander] McLeod is suffering by confinement and is anxious for a speedy determination of the cause. He has no fear of conviction on a trial at the circuit.
    There will be no embarrassment thrown in the way of either course whichever we may elect to take.
    I shall hope to hear from you at your earliest convenience & before the close of the present term of the Sup. Court. Very respectfully Your obt Servt   J. A. Spencer

A L S . NhHi.

TO JOSHUA AUSTIN SPENCER

(Copy.)
Private.
My Dear Sir: Washington, July 15, 1841
    I have to acknowledge the receipt of your letter of the 12th instant.[1]
    Officially, I have of course no advice to give, on the subject of further proceedings in [Alexander] McLeod's case. But my private opinion is

1. McLeod filed for a writ of habeas corpus arguing that the attack on the *Caroline* was a public act of the British over which the state of New York had no jurisdiction. Cowen (c. 1799–1844), an associate justice of the state supreme court, denied the writ, ruling that murder could not be justified as a public act in the absence of declared war. 25 Wendell's *Reports* 483–603 (1841).
    1. See above.

clear, that the true course is to go to trial, the earliest possible opportunity. Yours with regard,   (Signed) Danl. Webster

Copy. NhHi. Published in Van Tyne, p. 234.

TO JOSEPH STORY

Dr Sir   July 16. [1841][1]
    [Esek] Cowan's opinion you will have read.[2] It is hollow, false, & almost dishonest, from beginning to end. The cause will now go to trial, & as there is little doubt that [Alexander] McLeod will be *acquitted*. The evidence is said to be clear, that he was not engaged in the expedition *at all*.

    The question of law, therefore, will not go further, in all probability; for the sake of truth, however, & national character, this opinion must be *reviewed*, & dealt with as its demerits deserve. *Nobody but yourself can do this*. You must, therefore, laying aside all other things, give a day or two, to the subject.[3] This is indispensable. Send me the matter, which you put together, & I will see it come forth, in some semi-official manner; & I pray you let me have it, within ten days. I will see that the Speeches made on the subject in the Senate & House of Representatives, (such as are good for any thing) be sent you tomorrow. Yrs truly   Danl Webster

ALS. MHi. Published in *W & S*, 16:379–380. Story (1779–1845; Harvard 1798) served in the Massachusetts legislature, 1805–1807, 1811, and as a U.S. congressman, 1808–1809, before President James Madison appointed him to the Supreme Court in 1811. In 1829 Story also accepted a position at Harvard Law School but served on the Supreme Court until his death.

TO HIRAM KETCHUM

My Dear Sir   Sunday Eve' [July 1841]
    There is not a possibility that little [William Henry] Seward can hurt us. He has been treated, according to the dignity of N.Y.—not according to his own merits. He is a contemptible fellow—& that is the end of it. I wish we had no worse difficulties, than with him. If the letters between him & the President[1] be published, he will appear in his true light. *He did not send to the Legislature all the correspondence he had, at the time.*[2]

    1. Incorrectly dated 1842 in *W & S* and in *MHi Proc.*, 14, 2d Series (1900–1901):412.
    2. See above, Spencer to DW, July 12, 1841.
    3. Story did not review Cowen's opinion, but it was criticized at length by Daniel Bryant Tallmadge (1793–1847), a judge of the Superior Court of New York, 1838–1843. 26 Wendell's *Reports* 663–703 (1841).
    1. See above, Seward to Tyler, May 4, 1841; Tyler to Seward, May 7, 1841; Seward to Tyler, May 10, 1841; Seward to Tyler, May 18, 1841; Tyler to Seward, May 25, 1841; Seward to Tyler, June 1, 1841.
    2. Seward submitted his official

We may perhaps yet have a war, on account, or by reason, of, the conduct of this small [illegible] of political character.

My wife is going north; for the residue of the Summer. It is possible, I may go with her to N.Y.—& return next morning. If so, I will see you, for 1/2 a minute.   Yrs. D.W.

ALS. NhD.

TO JOSHUA AUSTIN SPENCER

Department of State

Washington, August 6th 1841

The Governor of New York [William Henry Seward] has communicated to this Department a report made to him by the Attorney General of that State [Willis Hall],[1] communicating the decision of the Supreme Court of New York, upon the application of Alexander McLeod to be discharged from imprisonment.

Entertaining the highest respect for the learning and ability of the Court, the President cannot, nevertheless, but feel the deepest regret, that in a question growing out of the foreign relations of the country, and one which may very seriously affect the national peace, its decision is so directly opposed to the opinions which this Government entertains, and has officially expressed. But as the question is a judicial one, and must ultimately be decided by the Courts of Law, the Government can do no more than to see that it be carried regularly to the tribunals of the last resort. Nor will its sense of the duty which it owes the country suffer it to do less. Thus far I have had no occasion to correspond with you, officially upon the subject except in regard to the furnishing evidence, from this Department,[2] supposed by the prisoner's counsel to be proper and useful for his defence. But the President thinks the time has come when it is proper that you should be written to, as District Attorney of the United States, to the end that you may make the following communication to Alexander McLeod, your client; viz that the President of the United States wishes him to decide for himself, whether he will put himself on trial before the Jury or whether he prefers that a Writ of Error should be sued out and prosecuted on the judgment of the Court already pronounced. If he shall elect the latter course you are hereby directed to aid and assist him in bringing the cause before the Supreme Court of the United States. If he prefer the former course and choose to

correspondence to the New York legislature on May 19, 1841, but did not include either his letter to President Tyler of May 10 or Tyler's response of May 15.

1. Seward to DW, July 26, 1841,

DNA, RG 59 (Misc. Letters), enclosing a copy of Hall to Seward, July 24, 1841.

2. See above, DW to Spencer, April 19, 1841.

go to trial before a Jury, you will of course be present at that trial, being already his own retained Counsel; and the President directs that on such trial you make known to the Court the opinions of this Government as those opinions have been officially promulgated, on the question of McLeods liability to Indictment for any alleged participation in the destruction of the Caroline, and that you state the grounds of National Law, upon which the opinions rest: and that in case of conviction you adopt the proper measures for bringing the cause to the Supreme Court of the United States.

It is with unfeigned regret that the President finds himself obliged to take notice of the proceedings of the State Courts of New York; but the highest considerations of duty influence his conduct in this respect. The care of the foreign relations of the country is confided to the Government of the United States; with that Government, and not with any State Government is trusted the higher power of making peace and making war; and that Government is responsible if anything occur, which it could prevent, furnishing just ground of complaint to other nations. This is a responsibility which the Government of the United States cannot avoid. If the pacific relations now subsisting between the United States and England should be disturbed, by the proceedings in the case of McLeod, the consequences are to fall, not on New York alone, but on the whole union, and the defence of the honor and interest of the country and the safety of its citizens, devolves not on the Government of New York alone, but on the Government of the United States. The President therefore feels himself under obligations of the highest and most sacred character, to do whatever the Constitution and the laws allow, to prevent all just ground of complaint, on the part of other nations, to maintain the high character which the United States now possess for the observance of those rules which govern the intercourse of nations, and to take care that if the calamity of war come upon us, it shall be for a cause in which reason, public law, and the voice of an enlightened age shall declare our side of the controversy to be the just side.   [Daniel Webster]

LC. DNA, RG 59 (Domestic Letters).

TO WILLIAM HENRY SEWARD

Department of State,
Sir—   Washington, 24 Augt 1841.
I have the honor to inform Your Exellency that a letter was yesterday communicated to this Department by Her Britannic Majesty's Minister, Mr. [Henry Stephen] Fox, extracts from which are herewith enclosed.[1]

1. Fox to DW, DNA, RG 59 (Notes from Foreign Legations, Britain). The letter, dated August 8, 1841, from Albany, does not bear a signature. The extracts sent to Seward warn that a group of patriots intend-

The letter was written by a gentleman whose character for respectability and information is known to Mr. Fox, and was addressed, the early part of this month, to the British authorities in Canada.

It is to be hoped that the dangers pointed out in these extracts are not real, or at least that they are exaggerated, but some circumstances, of public notoriety, give too much reason to believe that illegal designs of some sort are on foot. The President directs me, in making this communication to Your Excellency, to express his confidence that the Government of New York, will take proper measures to secure the person of Alexander McLeod, now a prisoner under the protection of the laws of that State, against violence. It is hardly necessary to say, that any such proceeding as it is suggested is now meditated, while it would be an outrage upon all law and justice, would be an occurrence very likely to affect, most seriously, the peace of the country. I am, Sir, respectfully, Your obedient servant,   Danl Webster

L S. NRU.

LORD PALMERSTON TO HENRY STEPHEN FOX

No. 23   Foreign Office,
Sir,   August 24th 1841

Her Majesty's Government received with very great regret the second American Counter Draft of a Convention for determining the Boundary between the United States and the British North American Provinces which you transmitted to me last Autumn in your Despatch No 23,[1] because that Counter Draft contained so many inadmissible Propositions that it plainly shewed, that Her Majesty's Government could entertain no hope of concluding any arrangement on this subject with the Government of Mr [Martin] Van Buren, and that there was no use in taking any further steps in the negotiations, till the new President should come into power.

Her Majesty's Government had certainly persuaded themselves that the Draft which, in pursuance of your Instructions, you presented to Mr [John] Forsyth on the 28th of July 1840,[2] was so fair in its provisions, and so well calculated to bring the differences between the two Governments about the Boundary, to a just and satisfactory conclusion, that it would have been at once accepted by the Government of the United States; or that if the American Government had proposed to make any

---

ed to lynch McLeod and that they had removed seven artillery pieces from state arsenals to carry out their plan.

1. Palmerston meant No. 12, dated August 15, 1840. See DW to Fox,

June 10, 1841, DNA, RG 59 (Notes to Foreign Legations, Britain).

2. Fox to Forsyth, July 28, 1840, DNA, RG 59 (Notes from Foreign Legations, Britain).

alterations in it, those alterations would have related merely to matters of detail, and would not have borne upon any essential points of the arrangement; and Her Majesty's Government were the more confirmed in this hope because almost all the main principles of the arrangement which that Draft was intended to carry into execution had, as Her Majesty's Government conceived, been either suggested by, or agreed to by, the United States' Government itself.

But instead of this, the United States Government proposed a second Counter Draft, differing essentially from the Draft of Her Majesty's Government, and containing several inadmissible propositions. In the first place, the United States' Government proposed to substitute for the Preamble of the British Draft, a Preamble to which Her Majesty's Government can not possibly agree; because it places the whole question at issue, upon a wrong foundation; upon the Treaty of Ghent, instead of upon the Treaty of 1783; and for this reason, besides other objections to the wording of it, Her Majesty's Government can not consent to the Preamble of the last American Draft, but must adhere to the Preamble of the last British Draft presented in July 1840.

The next alteration proposed by the American Counter Draft, is in Article 2 of that Draft, by which it would be stipulated, that the Commissioners of Survey shall meet, in the first instance, at Boston. To this Her Majesty's Government can not consent, because Boston is not a convenient place for the purpose; and because their meeting in a town within the United States, would, in various ways, be inconvenient. Her Majesty's Government must therefore still press Quebec, as the best point to start from; because it is the nearest to the western end of the Disputed Territory, the Point at which Her Majesty's Government propose that the operations of the Commissioners shall begin.

In the 3rd Article of the American Counter Draft, reference is again made, by a Quotation, to the Treaty of Ghent, and to that reference Her Majesty's Government must again object.

In that same 3rd Article a new method is proposed for determining the point at which the Commissioners shall begin their Survey.[3] But Her Majesty's Government are of opinion that there are the strongest reasons for beginning the Survey from the Head of the Connecticut River. For up to a certain distance eastward from that Point, the former Commissioners of the two Governments found Highlands, which they agreed in considering the Highlands of the Treaty;[4] and it is only from a Point some way

3. The American proposal called for the surveyors to begin at a point agreed upon by two of the American and two of the British commissioners.

4. The boundary commissioners appointed according to the terms of the Treaty of Ghent never agreed on the location of the "highlands" referred to in the treaty of 1783. In reports filed in 1821, the Americans claimed that the "highlands" referred to the watershed dividing those rivers

Eastward of the Head of the Connecticut, that the Two Lines of Boundary claimed by the Two Governments respectively, begin to diverge. It seems, therefore natural that the Commissioners should begin their Survey from the Head of the Connecticut; and no good reason has been assigned by the United States' Government for not consenting to such an arrangement. It is obvious moreover that by starting from the Western end of the disputed Boundary Line, much time may by possibility be saved. For, if it should happen that, from the Point where the two Lines of Boundary claimed by the Two Governments respectively, begin to diverge, there should be found by local examination, only one Range of Highlands corresponding with the Words of the Treaty, it is manifest that, whether that Range should be found to trend away in the direction of the Line claimed by Great Britain, or should be ascertained to take a course in conformity with the American Claim, the Commissioners, in either case, would in the outset, find a clue; which might guide them in their further researches. Her Majesty's Government therefore disagree to this third Article as proposed by the United States' Government, and again press the Third Article as it stands in the British Draft of July 1840.

The seventh Article of the American Counter Draft proposes that the Commission which was originally intended as a Commission to explore the Country, should become a Commission to examine Archives. But those different kinds of Duties would in their nature be incompatible with each other. The Commissioners will find that an accurate examination of the Country, will occupy all their time, and will be a work of intense labour; and to impose upon them besides the duty of searching the public Records at Washington and in London, would only impede them in the performance of their proper Duties.

That which the Commissioners are to be appointed to examine, is the face of the Country; and by comparing the Features of the Country, with the description contained in the Treaty of 1783, they are to mark out the

that flowed into the Saint Lawrence River from those that flowed into the Atlantic. The British argued that the "highlands" referred to conspicuous elevations. U.S. Secretary of State Edward Livingston (1764–1836; Princeton 1781), secretary 1831–1833, had been a commissioner in the earlier boundary negotiations between Maine and the federal government. In 1833, he suggested to British minister Charles Richard Vaughan (1774–1849), minister 1825–1835, that, having failed to locate the highlands described as lying due north of the Saint Croix River, the two countries should draw a direct line from the head of the river to whatever highlands existed, even if that moved the boundary line farther west. Because of Livingston's proposal, Palmerston apparently concluded that the United States had agreed that the highlands were west of the Saint Croix. Livingston to Vaughan, May 28, 1833, DNA, RG 59 (Notes to Foreign Legations, Britain).

Boundary on the Ground. If either Government should think that any Documents which may be in Its possession can throw light upon any Questions to be solved by the Commissioners, It can of its own accord lay such Documents before the Commission. But Her Majesty's Government cannot possibly agree that such Documents whether they be Maps, Surveys, or any thing else, shall be deemed by the Commissioners to be other than ex-parte Statements, furnished in order to assist the Commission in its own Investigations; unless such Maps, Surveys or other Documents, shall be acknowledged, and signed by Two Commissioners on each side, as being authentic evidence of the facts upon which they may bear; and Her Majesty's Government must insist upon the Stipulation to this effect which is contained in the British Draft of July 1840. But the wording of this seventh Article of the American Counter Draft is, in this respect, insidious; for under the guise of an engagement that each party shall furnish the other with Documents for mutual Information, it tends to enable the United States' Government to put upon the Records of the Commission, as authentic, any Maps, Surveys, or Documents, which it may think advantageous to the American case, however incorrect such Maps, Surveys, or other Documents may be.

But of all the Propositions made by the American Counter Draft, none can be more inadmissible than that contained in Article 10: For that Article again proposes that [John] Mitchels' Map shall be acknowledged as Evidence, bearing upon the Question to be decided; whereas every body who has paid any attention to these matters, now knows, that Mitchel's Map is full of the grossest inaccuracies as to the Longitude and Latitude of Places; and that it can be admitted as evidence of nothing, but of the deep ignorance of the Person who framed it.[5] Her Majesty's Government can never agree to this Proposal, nor to any modification of it.

To the 16th and 17th Articles of the American Counter Draft, Her Majesty's Government must decidedly object. The 16th Article reproduces in another Form the Association of Maine Commissioners with the Commission of Survey; and to this, in any shape whatever, Her Majesty's Government, for the reasons already assigned, must positively decline to consent.

The 17th Article of the American Counter Draft tends to introduce the State of Maine as a Party to the Negotiation between the Government of

5. Mitchell (d. 1768), probably originally from Britain, became a respected physician and botanist in Virginia prior to his return to England in 1746. His map of North America was published in 1755 and thereafter reissued with many changes. It is certain that a Mitchell's map was used in the peace negotiations at Paris in 1782 and 1783, but which edition is not known. See *Treaties*, 3:328–350.

Great Britain and the Government of the United States. But to this Her Majesty's Government cannot agree. The British Government when negotiating with the United States, negotiates with the Federal Government, and with that Government alone; and the British Government could not enter into negotiation with any of the separate states, of which the Union is composed, unless the Union were to be dissolved, and those states were to become distinct and independent Communities, making Peace and War for themselves.

With the Federal Government Her Majesty's Government would be ready and willing to negotiate for a Conventional Line: Indeed the British Government has more than once proposed to the Federal Government to do so; and whenever the Federal Government shall say, that it is able and prepared to enter into such a Negotiation, Her Majesty's Government will state the arrangement which it may have to propose upon that Principle.

Such being the view which Her Majesty's Government take of the Counter Draft proposed in August of last year by Mr Forsyth, it only remains for me to instruct you to bring under the consideration of Mr Webster the Draft which you presented to Mr Forsyth in July 1840; and to say that Her Majesty's Government would wish to consider Mr Forsyth's Counter Draft as "non avenu," rather than to give it a formal and reasoned rejection, and that Her Majesty's Government would prefer replacing the Negotiation on the ground on which it stood in July of last year, entertaining as they do an ardent hope that the present Government of the United States may, upon a full and fair consideration of the British Draft, find it to be one calculated to lead to a just determination of the Questions at issue between the two Governments. If Mr Webster should agree to this course, and should approve of the Treaty as it stands in the British Draft of July, you are instructed to propose to him The King of Prussia, the King of Sardinia, and The King of Saxony as the Three Sovereigns who should name the three members of the Commission of Arbitration.[6]

It seems desirable to choose Sovereigns who are not likely from their maritime or Commercial Interests, to have feelings of jealousy towards either Great Britain, or the United States: it is desirable to choose Sovereigns in whose Dominions men of Science and of Intelligence are likely to be found; and it seems to Her Majesty's Government that in both these respects, the Three Sovereigns above-mentioned would be a proper Selection. But if Mr Webster should decline acceding to this course, and should think it necessary that he should receive an Official Answer to Mr Forsyth's Counter Draft, you will then present to him a Note drawn

6. Frederick William IV (1795–1861) of Prussia; Charles Albert (1798–1849) of Sardinia; Frederick Augustus (1797–1854) of Saxony.

up in accordance with the Substance of this Despatch. I am with great Truth and Regard, Sir, Your most obedient, humble Servant   Palmerston

L S . DNA, RG 59 (Notes from Foreign Legations, Britain).

FROM ANDREW STEVENSON

No. 131.   Legation of the U. States
Sir,   London August 31 1841.

The "Acadia" Steamer from Boston arrived on Saturday but brought me nothing from your Department. Mr McLeod[1] who called yesterday with a Passport as Bearer of despatches informed me that the Bag which was to have been forwarded to him at Boston, did not reach him <before> in time for the sailing of the Steamer on the morning of the 16th. As I anticipated in my despatch of the 18th instant,[2] the present Ministry have been defeated in both Houses of Parliament, and the conservatives will come into Power. I forward an official Copy of the Queen's Speech,[3] with the Papers containing full accounts of the Proceedings in Parliament. Lord Melbourne[4] and Lord John Russell,[5] gave in their resignations last night, but will remain in Office, until their successors can form a Government and come in. This may be expected tomorrow, or the next day. You will see that the subject of [Alexander] McLeod's continued imprisonment, was taken up last week in the Commons, and an explanation given by Lord Palmerston.[6] It was declared however by Sir Robert Peel, to be neither *full, or satisfactory.* You will perceive that a public meeting was held yesterday at the Colonial Club House in which resolutions were passed censuring McLeod's continued imprisonment, and remonstrating <his> against his trial.[7] This it is supposed, will lead to others.

I received yesterday a communication from Lord Palmerston, under date of the 27 *instant*, in reply to my note of the 22nd of May 1838, on the subject of the destruction of the Caroline.[8] His Lordship has waited until the last moment, to answer my note, and after detailing the whole circumstances connected with the affair, justifies it, as an act of justifiable defence, properly done by the British Colonial authority for the pro-

1. Probably Donald McLeod, the associate editor of the Washington *Madisonian* from May 1840 to March 1841.

2. Stevenson to DW, August 18, 1841, DNA, RG 59 (Despatches, Britain).

3. An address by the queen was read to Parliament on August 24, 1841. *Hansard's*, 59: 13–16.

4. Melbourne formed a Whig gov-

ernment in 1834, which held, with some interruptions, until his resignation in 1841.

5. Russell (1792–1878) served as colonial secretary under Melbourne from 1839 to 1841.

6. *Hansard's*, 59:265–270.

7. London *Times*, August 31, 1841.

8. Enclosed with Stevenson to DW, September 18, 1841, below.

tection of British subjects, and property, and the security of Her Majesty's Territory. He avers moreover that the United States Government were aware before my note of May 1838, was written, of this determination of Her Majesty's Government. I shall acknowledge the receipt of this note to Lord Palmerston before he resigns the Seals of Office, and reply to those parts of it, which demand my immediate notice. His Lordship's [communication] is too long to be copied in time for tomorrow's steamer & I wish moreover, to accompany it with a copy of the reply which I shall endeavor to note today.

I also received yesterday two other notes from Lord Palmerston, on the subject of the African Seizures.[9] Instead of disavowing & making atonement for the injuries done to our Vessels, and Committed by the commandants of their cruisers, they excuse & justify them, and now assert a right of detaining & examining the Papers of all Vessels, sailing under the American Flag, to see if they are genuine and protected with documents entitling them to the protection of the <Flag,> Country, under <which> whose flag they are sailing. In other words, that the British cruisers employed for the purpose of opposing the Slave Trade, still have the right of stopping any American Vessel, on the High seas, and determining whether their Papers be genuine or not. The right asserted in these Acts amounts to that of Search, and detention & in a <way> manner the most offensive and injurious to the Rights & Honor of our Country & the Vessels & property of its Citizens. I shall acknowledge the receipt of these communications as soon as the new Ministry come into Power; and will immediately forward Copies of them, with my answer for the information of the Government. I shall refrain from all further discussions, and content myself with a Protest against <any> the exercize of any such Power as that claimed, and a reiteration of the determination of my Government, that its Flag shall cover all the sails under it. I am Sir, very respectfully, Yr. obt svt   A. Stevenson

ALS. DNA, RG 59 (Despatches, Britain). Rec'd September 20, 1841. Extract published in CR, 3:660–661.

FROM WILLIAM HENRY SEWARD

Sir   Albany September 3d. 1841[1]

I was at Auburn on the 30th of August and received there your communication of the 24th of that month.[2] Two other copies of the same

9. Palmerston to Stevenson, September 2, 1841, enclosed with Stevenson to DW, September 18, 1841, below.

1. Baker incorrectly dates this letter September 23, 1841.
2. See above, DW to Seward, August 24, 1841.

letter have since been received; one of which was delivered to me by Major General [Winfield] Scott, and the other was found at Utica.

By that communication I am informed that it has been represented to you by Her Britannic Majesty's Minister Mr [Henry Stephen] Fox, that he had received information, that a movement relating to Alexander Mc-Leod was contemplated in this State by persons designated "Patriots," and that it had been their intention to assassinate him on his being released from confinement,—that the persons engaged had subsequently resolved to hasten their design so as to anticipate any interference by the United States Government—that to accomplish their object they had determined to force open the State arsenals and remove several pieces of artillery—that this had already been done, and that the "patriots" had in their possession seven field-pieces which were secreted in canal boats —that a person named [John] Rolph,[3] who was their agent in New York, had sent from that city a supply of ammunition, which had been conveyed to the vicinity of Utica—that it was now the intention of the conspirators to assemble at Whitestown (the place where McLeod is confined) and to surround the jail and demand his delivery from the keeper —that in case of a refusal or resistance they would display and threaten to effect their entrance by means of the artillery—that having got McLeod into their power they intended instantly to "lynch" him—that the strongest detachment to be engaged in the enterprize would arrive at Whitestown concealed in canal boats and the other division would assemble in the woods near Utica—that "the notorious [Benjamin] Lett was openly and actively engaged in furthering the designs of his infamous associates—that he had been seen at noonday on Tuesday last in the public Streets of Buffalo, and no efforts were made on the part of the State officers to arrest him."[4]

You observe in your communciation that "it is to be hoped that the dangers thus pointed out in the communication of "Her Britannic Majesty's Minister are not real, or at least that they are exaggerated; yet that some circumstances of public notoriety give too much reason to believe that illegal designs of some sort are on foot." You assure me of the President's confidence that the Government of this State will take measures "to secure the person of Alexander McLeod now a prisoner under the laws of this state against violence." And you very truly remark that any such proceeding as is supposed by Her Britannic Majesty's Minister to

3. Rolph (1793–1870), a physician, served in the Upper Canadian assembly from 1824 to 1837. Implicated in the rebellion of 1837, he fled to the United States, where he was active in Patriot organizations. He practiced medicine in Rochester, New York, but returned to Canada in 1843 after the government issued an amnesty.

4. Lett (c. 1814–1858) was a fugitive involved in a number of border incidents. He was captured in September 1841 and served a term in prison.

be contemplated, while it would be an outrage upon all law and justice, would be an occurrence very likely to affect most seriously the peace of the country.

Immediately upon receiving this communication I proceeded to the vicinity of Whitesboro (called also Whitestown) with a view to adopt such measures as the exigency might require.

In my letter of the 26th of July last[5] I informed the President that the motion of Alexander McLeod to be discharged without a trial was denied by the Supreme Court—that his application for a change of venue had been granted, and that the cause would be tried at a circuit court to be held in the County of Oneida on the 27th day of the present month of September. Upon this decision being made the prisoner was, by order of the court, committed to the custody of the Sheriff of Oneida County,[6] and has since been confined in the jail of that county at Whitesboro distant four miles from the city of Utica.

On the 10th day of August last[7] I apprised the President that two field-pieces, the property of the People of this State, had been abstracted in a very secret manner from their depositories in Cayuga county—that I had made extraordinary efforts to ascertain the place of their concealment, and to discover the offenders, but as yet without success. I mentioned further in the same communication a suspicion that the pieces of ordnance thus removed had been taken with a view to some demonstration upon the Canadian frontier; but I stated that I had no knowledge of any grounds for the suspicion, except the similarity of the movement, to what had happened on the frontier of this State a few years since. I further informed the President that I had taken measures to protect the military property of the State—that I had given notice of the transaction which had occurred to Colonel [James] Bankhead,[8] who then commanded a regiment of United States Artillery at Buffalo, and had requested him to inform me whether any indications of a renewal of the disturbances on the frontier had manifested themselves under his observation. The result of very diligent inquiries is that instead of there being in the possession of the "Patriots" seven field-pieces taken from the State Arsenals, it is quite certain that they have only three pieces. One of these was taken from a gun house at Auburn in the county of Cayuga, another belonging to the State was removed from an open place in the same county, where it had lain a long time exposed, and the third which was similarly ex-

5. Seward to Tyler, July 26, 1841, DNA, RG 59 (Misc. Letters).

6. David Moulton was elected sheriff of Oneida County in 1840 but was removed by Seward in 1842 for official misconduct. See Baker, ed., *Works of Seward*, 2:441–445.

7. Seward wrote to President Tyler about the fieldpieces on August 11, not 10. Seward to Tyler, DNA, RG 59 (Misc. Letters).

8. Bankhead (d. 1856) entered the army in 1809 and rose to the rank of brigadier general in the Mexican War.

posed did not belong to the State and was not taken from any of its depositories.

The Commissary General of this State has in pursuance of my directions been engaged ever since the transaction became known to me, in efforts to find the stolen ordnance, and to discover the persons by whom it was removed.[9] Rewards have been offered for a restoration of the property and arrest of the offenders. Orders have been issued to all the Commandants of Regiments of Artillery, and Keepers of arsenals within the State, directing them to guard the public arms and ordnance with strict care. The Collectors of tolls, and the District Attorneys of the several counties traversed by the Canals have been required, and the Marshall of the United States for the Northern District[10] has been requested, to use all necessary efforts to bring the offenders to punishment, and to guard against such depredations in future. I have occasion to regret that I am deprived of the co-operation of the District Attorney of the United States [Joshua Austin Spencer], for the district where these alarms have arisen—His engagement as counsel for McLeod placed it out of my power to communicate with him upon the subject.

Colonel [Ichabod Bennet] Crane[11] of the United States Army recently informed me that he had reason to believe there was a depository of arms and ordnance kept by "Patriots" at Sandusky or Cleveland; and he suggested that the pieces of cannon stolen from this State, might have been conveyed to such depository. Major General Scott stated to me that he had information which led him to concur in the opinion expressed by Colonel Crane. Major General Scott intends as you are aware to visit Cleveland and Sandusky, and he has engaged to give some information concerning the guns taken from this State, if that supposition should prove to be true.

I have addressed His Excellency the Governor of Ohio,[12] requesting him to ascertain and inform me, whether such a depository has been established in Ohio.

Upon inquiring of the Sheriff and First Judge of Oneida County,[13] I have been informed by them, that some unknown persons with arms have been seen lurking about Whitesboro, under circumstances which in-

9. In his annual report for 1841 the commissary general of New York, Adoniram Chandler, remarked that a diligent investigation failed to locate the missing fieldpieces or identify the culprits. *Documents of the Assembly of the State of New York* (vol. 5), 64th Sess., 1841, No. 80. Chandler served in this capacity from 1841 to 1842.

10. Clark Robinson, not otherwise identified.

11. Crane (d. 1857) had been a career artillery officer since 1809.

12. Thomas Corwin (1794–1865) had been a Whig congressman from 1831 to 1840 before he served a term as governor of Ohio, 1840–1842.

13. Fortune C. White was first judge of Oneida County from 1840 to 1845.

duced the public officers to believe it possible that there might be a design to endanger the person of McLeod.

It is not possible in my judgment that such a plot as Mr Fox mentions can be carried into effect in the county of Oneida. Oneida is one of the most populous and enlightened counties in the State, and any attempt to break the public peace or to produce popular disturbance there, would be instantly put down by the citizens.

It is true that Benjamin Lett is still at large. I was informed moreover by the District Attorney of Erie county,[14] that that notorious offender had recently been in the City of Buffalo, but that he was unknown at the time to the police. It is altogether untrue, if I am correctly informed, that any of the officers of the State have manifested any want of energy in bringing him to punishment, unless it be the Sheriff of Oswego County[15] who was responsible for the delivery of the prisoner at the State Prison. Lett is a British subject. He escaped from Canada, after having committed some atrocious crimes there. The Canadian authorities offered rewards amounting to four thousand dollars for his arrest as I am informed. He was subsequently convicted in Oswego County in this State of arson committed in a fiendlike attempt to burn and destroy a Steamboat filled with human beings, and upon that conviction he was sentenced to be imprisoned in the State Prison at Auburn for seven years. On his way under the care of the Sheriff of Oswego County, to the State Prison, Lett made his escape at the imminent peril of his life, by leaping from a rail road car while it was under full motion I immediately issued a proclamation designed to aid the Sheriff in his efforts to recapture the prisoner, offering a reward which was considered sufficient to secure his arrest, and I despatched special agents in pursuit of the prisoner; but he eluded pursuit and it has been understood that he has lurking places on the frontier, where he is supported and abetted by confederates in contempt of the laws of this State and those of his own country.

Colonel Bankhead of the United States Army recently stationed at Buffalo, informed me last October that he had ascertained the offenders place of retreat, and wanted only my authority to arrest him—this was promptly given. The Colonel however informed me some five weeks since, that Lett was aware of the pursuit and it had not been possible to arrest him.

I some time since gave the police of Rochester and Buffalo to understand that the sum originally offered for the arrest of Lett would be doubled, but public notice to that effect was not given because I feared its effect might be to drive the fugitive out of the country.

14. Henry Smith was district attorney of Erie County from 1838 to 1841, and Henry W. Rogers held that position from 1841 to 1844.

15. Norman Rowe was sheriff of Oswego County from November 1840 to November 1843.

It remains for me to state for the information of the President, what measures have been adopted since the receipt of your communication.

I have instructed the Sheriff of Oneida County to employ a guard of thirty persons to watch and protect the jail until the case of McLeod is decided. I have directed notice to be given to the proper military officers of Oneida County, that they may be in readiness to call out any force necessary to preserve the public peace and secure the safety of the prisoner.

I have directed that a volunteer Artillery company of citizens of Oneida County, to the number of one hundred men, be immediately enlisted, organized, armed, and equipped, supplied with ammunition and held in readiness.

I have by proclamation increased the rewards offered for the recapture of Lett to the sum of nine hundred dollars, which together with the sum of one hundred dollars heretofore offered by the Sheriff of Oswego County will make the sum of One Thousand dollars, which will be paid for the arrest of the offender.

I have further employed a confidential agent to traverse the line of canals and obtain information of the purposes and plans of those who may be engaged in any such design as that mentioned in your communication.

I have called the Sheriff of Oswego County to account for the escape of Lett and his continuing at large.

Copies of various official papers relating to the subject of your communication are herewith transmitted. I trust the President will find in the proceedings taken by this department sufficient grounds to justify him in assuring Her Britannic Majesty's Government that the State of New York is as jealously watching over the personal safety of Alexander McLeod while he is a prisoner under her protection, as she has firmly insisted that he shall answer at her tribunals, for the flagrant violation of her laws of which he stands accused.

And I beg leave to assure the President, that while this State is not to be deterred by any menace which Great Britain may offer, from judicially vindicating the lives and property of her citizens, she is at the same time most careful to prevent any violation of the rights of any subject of the British Government.

I should not perform my whole duty, if I did not state further that the feelings of irritation which have heretofore existed upon the frontier have not altogether subsided—that if I am correctly informed, the challenge of the jurisdiction of this State over Alexander McLeod made by the British Government, has increased that irritation, and that the building two armed vessels at Chippewa[16] to cruise upon the Lakes has an

16. The British maintained two steam warships at Chippewa on Lake Erie, the *Minos* and the *Toronto*. See Kenneth Bourne, *Britain and the*

effect to exasperate many people in this State, who regard with very natural apprehensions the military preparations of our neighbor, in a time when there are so many exaggerated rumors of diplomatic collision between this country and Great Britain.

I am obliged to express my concurrence in the belief, that movements of some sort to disturb the peace between this country and the British provinces, are in contemplation. I am of opinion however, notwithstanding the communication of Her Britannic Majesty's Minister, that the cannon taken from this State, have a destination towards the Lakes, and a contact with the British Steamers building there, rather than a bombardment of the jail of Oneida County.

But I confess my information like that professed by the General Government, quite inconclusive. I shall not fail to communicate all the information which I shall be able to acquire. I have the honor to be with the highest respect, Your obedient servant   William H. Seward

LS. DNA, RG 59 (Misc. Letters). Published in George E. Baker, ed., *The Works of William H. Seward* (5 vols., New York, 1853–1854), 2:578–583.

FROM HENRY STEPHEN FOX

Washington

Sir   September 5th 1841

Her Majesty's Government were officially informed by me of the opinion pronounced at Utica, in the month of July last, by the Supreme Court of the State of New York, in the case of Mr [Alexander] McLeod, a British subject now detained in custody in that State, charged with a pretended crime,—the said Court having refused to order the discharge of Mr McLeod, and having assumed the right of remanding him for trial by the ordinary course of Law.

The decision of the Supreme Court of New York is in direct contradiction to the formal opinion of the Federal Government, as communicated to me in your official letter of the 24th of last April,[1] and as recorded in the instructions addressed by You, by direction of the President, to the Attorney General of the United States [John Jordan Crittenden],[2] which were inclosed and referred to in that letter.

The Principle of International Law, asserted and claimed by Great Britain, as required to be applied to this case, was recognized and affirmed by the Federal Government: namely, that, the act for which Mr McLeod is indicted being the public and avowed act of his Government, it cannot render him amenable to the ordinary Courts of Law, but can only become the subject of national discussion between the Two Govern-

Balance of Power in North America, 1815–1908 (London, 1967), p. 89.
1. See above, DW to Fox, April 24,
1841.
2. See above, DW to Crittenden, March 15, 1841.

ments. But this Principle has been attempted to be set at naught by the aforesaid decision of the Court of New York.

I am directed to state to you that Her Majesty's Government place entire Confidence in the just intentions of the Federal Government in this matter, and they cannot doubt that the President will find the means of speedily giving effect to those Principles of International Law which the Federal Government has Itself acknowledged.

Her Majesty's Government however look with intense anxiety for an early settlement of the affair, because they cannot disguise from Themselves the vast importance of the results which may depend upon the mode of its conclusion.

It would be unbecoming the position of either Government to utter idle threats of war; but it is not undue to the station which both hold in the civilized World; that one, while it declares that it is itself acting in the same pacific spirit, should exhort the other to use its utmost efforts to avert from both Nations the heavy calamity of War.

I avail myself of this occasion to renew to You the assurance of my distinguished consideration   H. S. Fox

L S. DNA, RG 59 (Notes from Foreign Legations, Britain). Published in *CR*, 3:673.

FROM WILLIAM HENRY SEWARD

State of New York
Executive department
Dear Sir: Albany September 6th 1841.

I enclose a copy of a letter from His excellency the Governor General of British North America [Lord Sydenham], soliciting a surrender of John H. DeWitt[1] a fugitive from justice charged with arson.

The President of the United States is aware of the advantages which must result from a reciprocity in the surrender of fugitives between this country, and the British provinces. He is aware also that in a recent instance of much public importance, the case of Charles F. Mitchell,[2] you were authorized by him to obtain and did procure the good offices of Mr. [Henry Stephen] Fox in obtaining a surrender of that person.

The laws of this state authorise me to surrender but since the Vermont case,[3] the better opinion, as I have before had occasion to inform you

1. The enclosure, Lord Sydenham to Seward, August 19, 1841, stated that a witness observed DeWitt committing an act of arson on the Niagara frontier in April 1841. DeWitt then fled to New York.

2. See above, Seward to Tyler, May 18, 1841.

3. A Canadian citizen, George Holmes, committed murder and fled to Vermont. When the Vermont Supreme Court ordered Holmes held for delivery to Canadian authorities, he appealed to the U.S. Supreme Court for a writ of habeas corpus. The Supreme court in *Holmes* v. *Jennison*,

was here believed to be, that the power to demand is national exclusively, and our law cannot be regarded as constitutional unless the Executive acts as an agent of the General Government. I wish especially to [end] all [error] on the subject while I acknowledge the obligation due from this country to the courtesy of the Canadian authorities in that respect. Will you have the goodness to submit this [subject] to the President and state to him that I will make the surrender if he shall see fit to intimate to me that such a proceeding is thought proper or is desired by him. I have the honor to be With the highest respect and esteem Your obedient servant   William H. Seward

A L S . DNA, RG 59 (Misc. Letters). Rec'd September 8, 1841. Endorsed by DW: "The Secretary of State requests the opinion of the Atty Genl. on the subject of this letter. Sept. 9—D.W."

FROM JOHN TYLER

Dr Sir;   [c. September 8, 1841]
    I return you under cover the two notes from Mr [Henry Stephen] Fox of the 5th[1] and 6th[2] Inst. In that of the 5th I am glad to perceive something of a softened tone, and only regret that in the concluding paragraph he should have regarded it as necessary to advert to <serious consequences> important results, which might be regarded as containing a threat. I hope that we may hear no more of *threatened consequences*, which only serve to excite the public mind here by calling into question the good faith of the United States and arousing the pride of their people. Mr Fox has been given fully to understand that the case of [Alexander] McLeod cannot be withdrawn from the courts, but must there abide its final issue. For myself I should have preferred that the case should have been brought up from the Supreme court of New York, to the Supreme court of the U. States, but that matter has been contrould by the decision of the Prisoner himself.
    As to the detachment to be <stationed> substituted in place of the civil *posse* of Maine Mr Fox seems to take a correct view. I should however regret that the British Govt should make that a pretext for throwing, in garrison, troops on the South of the St. John's. The settlements on the Madawaska are more safe with U.S. regular troops in their vicinity, than a mere civil *posse*—and hence the less necessity for introducing an armed force by the British govt. It is therefore both hoped and expected

---

14 *Peters* 540 (1840), could not agree on a decision, but in an opinion Chief Justice Roger B. Taney held that Holmes should be discharged. The Vermont Supreme Court on rehearing followed Taney's lead and or-

dered the prisoner released.
    1. See above, Fox to DW, September 5, 1841.
    2. Fox to DW, September 6, 1841, DNA, RG 59 (Notes from Foreign Legations, Britain).

that until an actual, or at least a threatened necessity shall arise, no such step may be taken by the British govt.

The above are some of the thoughts which occur to me on reading Mr Fox's two notes. Truly Yrs   John Tyler

A L S . NjMoHP. Published in *Tylers*, 2:212–213.

TO WILLIAM HENRY SEWARD

Department of State
Sir: Washington, 9th September, 1841
I have the honor to acknowledge the receipt of Your Excellency's letter of the 3d instant.[1] It has been laid before the President, who directs me to say that it has afforded him much satisfaction, and that he highly approves,[2] so far as he is competent to judge at a distance, of the arrangements adopted by you for the preservation of the safety of Alexander McLeod's person; arrangements which, he trusts, leave few grounds of apprehension.

The Attorney [Joshua Austin Spencer] and Marshal of the United States for the Northern District of New York [Clark Robinson], and all other officers in the service of this government, will be directed to aid the authorities of New York, or act concurrently with them, for the preserving the peace and maintaining the sovereignty of the laws, so far as may be in their power. I have the honor to be, Your Excellency's most obedient servant,   Danl Webster

L S . NRU. Published in *Tylers*, 2:213–214.

TO JOSHUA AUSTIN SPENCER

Department of State
Sir: Washington, 9th September, 1841
This department has recently received information which gives reason to believe that measures are again in agitation by persons within your District, having for their object hostilities against the British authorities in Canada and, possibly, against those of the State of New York, also.[1] The President consequently directs me to apprize you thereof, and to convey to you his wish and expectation that you will, so far as may be in your power, aid the authorities of New York, or act concurrently with them, in preserving the public peace and maintaining the sovereignty of the laws. I am, Sir, your obedient servant,   Danl Webster

L S . NhD.

1. See above, Seward to DW, September 3, 1841.

2. Tyler to DW, September 7, 1841, mDW 20176.

1. Later in September, Patriots attempted to blow up locks on the Welland canal and to attack the British warships *Minos* and *Toronto*.

TO HIRAM KETCHUM

My dear Sir,   September 10, 1841. Friday, three o'clock.

[Thomas] Ewing, [John] Bell, [George Edmund] Badger, and [John Jordan] Crittenden will resign to-morrow.[1] They settled that last evening, at a meeting at which I was not present, and announced it to me to-day. I told them I thought they had acted rashly, and that I should consider of my own course. I shall not act suddenly; it will look too much like a combination between a Whig cabinet and a Whig Senate to bother the President. It will not be expected from me to countenance such a proceeding.

Then, again, I will not throw the great foreign concerns of the country into disorder or danger, by any abrupt party proceeding.

How long I may stay, I know not, but I mean to take time to consider. Yours,   D.W.

Text from PC, 2:110. Original not found.

TO WILLIAM HENRY SEWARD, WITH ENCLOSURE

                                        Department of State
Dear Sir: Washington, 14th September, 1841.

I have the honor to acknowledge the receipt of your letter of the 11th instant.[1]

I am happy to learn that you think no effort will be made to endanger the personal safety of Alexander McLeod. We continue to receive letters holding out fears of some break-out, on the frontiers, but all is so vague and general that it hardly helps to guide the judgment in forming a proper rule of conduct. Enclosed are extracts of a letter addressed to me by an intelligent gentleman of New York.[2] You will estimate their suggestions at their true value, but as you must be better informed than we can be, your opinion that the peace will not be broken by attempts against the person of McLeod, gives great satisfaction.

We learn that the arsenal at Rome, where there are eight or ten thousand muskets with cartridges, &c. is unguarded by any respectable force. It is said, indeed, to be in the keeping of only six or seven laboring people. The President has thought it his duty to guard the security of this property of the United States by ordering a company of Colonel [James]

1. The entire cabinet, except Webster, resigned on September 11, after President Tyler vetoed the Fiscal Corporation Act. Ewing, the secretary of the treasury, helped draft the bill Tyler vetoed. Bell, secretary of war; Badger (1795–1866), secretary of the navy; and Crittenden, attorney general, had all served since March of that year. Postmaster General Francis Granger (1792–1868; Yale 1811) hesitated but also resigned.

1. Seward to DW, September 11, 1841, DNA, RG 59 (Misc. Letters).

2. See enclosure, below.

Bankhead's[3] regiment to be stationed at Rome. I am, with very high respect, Your obedient servant, Danl Webster

LS. NRU.

ENCLOSURE: FROM [WILLIAM LEETE STONE]

New York
Dear Sir.   September 8th 1841
    Having just returned from the Northern portion of the State I lose no time in communicating to you certain information which I obtained, during my absence, from sources of unquestionable authority, relating to the case of Alexander McLeod, and the relations of this country with Great Britain in connexion therewith.
    I have been assured, and with such vouchers for the truth of the information as make it impossible to doubt, that the conviction of McLeod (if he goes to trial) *per fas aut nefas*[1] is a thing determined on.
    That any required amount of evidence can and will be brought forward for this purpose; that secret movements of a most nefarious and mischievous character have been and still are made in the Northern counties, and about Utica pregnant with danger to the safety of McLeod, even in the event of an acquittal; and finally that the present aspect of the case is most alarming, and such as to require the prompt and vigorous interposition of the General Government, if there is any way in which its power can be exerted with good effect.
    I am very well aware, my dear Sir, that information more definite than mine, and quite as reliable, may already have been placed in your possession.
    Nevertheless I have thought it my duty to write, in the hope that the wisdim of the President, and his Cabinet may be able to devise sufficient means for meeting what I cannot but look upon as a most alarming crisis. I am, Sir with great respect Yours

Copy. NRU. DNA, RG 59 (Misc. Letters). Stone (1792–1844) was the prominent publisher of the New York *Commercial Advertiser*. Although Webster forwarded to Seward only extracts of Stone's letter and did not name the source, the letter is printed here in full because of its importance.

FROM WILLIAM HENRY SEWARD

State of New York
Executive Department
Dear Sir.   Albany September 16, 1841.
    I have caused very diligent inquiries to be made throughout the western part of this State with a view to ascertain whether there are any

3. See above, Seward to DW, September 3, 1841.   1. "By fair means or foul."

grounds for supposing that any design is entertained by any persons to molest Alexander McLeod during or after his trial. You are doubtless aware that there are a thousand rumors of that sort abroad.

Thus far I find no cause whatever to believe that such a purpose is in contemplation any where. Nevertheless, aware of the extreme importance of preventing any thing like a disturbance of the peace, and especially any unlawful molestation of the prisoner, I deem it my duty to take efficient measures on the subject: For that purpose, I have availed myself of the President's intimation conveyed in your recent letter[1] to request the Marshall of the United States, for the Northern District [Clark Robinson] to visit me with a view of securing his personal attendance at the trial and afterwards if necessary.

Will you have the goodness to inform me whether such a proceeding will be approved by the President? I have the honor to be, with very high respect Your obedient Servant   William H. Seward

LS. DNA, RG 59 (Misc. Letters). Rec'd September 19, 1841. Endorsed by DW: "Ansr that the President entirely approves that proceeding."

FROM WILLIAM HENRY SEWARD

                                    State of New York
                                    Executive Department
Dear Sir,   Albany September 17, 1841

By an arrangement made between the Government of the United States and that of Great Britain and Ireland in 1817 and promulgated by the President's proclamation on the 28th of April 1818,[1] it was Stipulated that "the naval force to be maintained upon the American Lakes by the respective parties should thereafter be confined to the following vessels on each side: that is—
"On Lake Ontario, to one vessel not exceeding one hundred tons burden, and armed with an eighteen pound cannon. On the Upper Lakes, to two vessels not exceeding like burden each, and armed with like force.
On the waters of Lake Champlain, to one vessel not exceeding like burden, and armed with like force."

It was further agreed that if either party should thereafter be desirous of annulling the said agreement, and should give six months notice to that effect, it should cease to be binding after the expiration of six months from the date of such notice.

I transmit, for the information of the President, a copy of a communication from the Marshall of the United States for the Northern District

1. See above, DW to Seward, September 9, 1841.

1. President James Monroe's announcement of the Rush-Bagot agreement is in *Messages and Papers*, 2: 36. For the text of the agreement, see *Treaties*, 2:645–647.

[Clark Robinson];[2] from which it appears, that Her Britannic Majesty's Government has now at Chippewa on Lake Erie, one steam Ship of war of five hundred tons burden, named the "Minos" prepared for eighteen guns, and having a pivot carriage on deck ready to mount a sixty eight pounder, calculated to be manned with seventy five men, and already furnished with a full complement of Muskets, Hatchets, Boarding pikes, Cutlasses &c. It appears also by the same communication that the British Government has another steam ship of war named the "Toronto" lying in the same port of equal tonnage and capacity for war.

Under the circumstances of the case, it seems my duty to inquire whether the President has received notice of a desire on the part of the British Government to annul the stipulation to which I have referred. The preparations of that Government show very fully that it is not its purpose to continue the stipulation.

While I by no means relinquish the hope that the peace between the two countries may be maintained, I beg leave to suggest most respectfully to the President the inquiry whether an armament of at least corresponding power with that which I have described, ought not to be provided for the defence of the north frontier of this State. I am moved to make this communication not only by the conviction that our northern frontier ought not to be exposed, but by an inquietude on the subject which prevails among the people in the towns situated upon the lakes. That inquietude seems neither unnatural nor unreasonable when the present condition and circumstances of our northern frontier are duly considered. I have the honor to be with the highest respect Your Obedient Servant,

William H. Seward

L S . DNA, RG 59 (Misc. Letters). Rec'd September 19, 1841.

FROM ANDREW STEVENSON, WITH ENCLOSURES

No. 132

Sir,   London Septr 18. 1841

I have now the honor to transmit to you Copies of Lord Palmerston's two Notes on the subject of the Caroline Steamer, with my answers.[1] But for the attempt which his Lordship makes, to throw the responsibility of the delay which had been suffered to take place, in answering my Note of May 1838,[2] upon our Government, I should have confined myself to a simple acknowledgment of the receipt of his first Note, and its transmission to you. The character of his communication however, was such as to make it my duty to notice it. Indeed, to have permitted its state-

2. Clark Robinson to Seward, September 13, 1841, DNA, RG 59 (Misc. Letters).

1. See enclosures, below.

2. See Stevenson to Palmerston, May 22, 1838, enclosed in No. 49. Stevenson to Forsyth, May 24, 1838, DNA, RG 59 (Despatches, Britain).

ments and conclusions to have passed unnoticed, would have been, to have acquiesced in their correctness and justice, and given to them a weight to which they are not entitled. I deemed it my duty therefore, upon public as well as personal considerations, to have the facts distinctly and officially set forth, and the responsibility of the delay placed where it properly belonged. This I flatter myself I have done, and you will perceive in Lord Palmerston's last Note, that he admits there is not essential difference between us as to the facts, however we might differ as to the conclusions and inferences to be drawn from them. No reply was given to my second Note.

I likewise transmit copies of the two communications received from Lord Palmerston, in relation to the African Seizures, referred to in my last despatch, with my answer to them[3]—regarding the right asserted by this Government, as one of a most unwarrantable character, I felt it to be my duty to seize the earliest opportunity of protesting against it in the strongest manner, and stating to Lord Aberdeen, that my Government would not fail to regard such an attempt over the Vessels of the United States on the high seas, as Violating its Rights of Sovereignty and the Honor of its Flag, and affecting most deeply, the Commercial and Navigating Interests of its Citizens. In making my Note however as strong as I could well do, to be respectful, I took care as you will perceive to do it in a manner to leave no doubt of the undiminished desire of the United States to unite in all measures best calculated to preserve the pacific relations of the two Countries, upon the foundations of Justice, friendship and mutual Rights.

I need not say that I have acted in accordance with what I believed to be the wishes of the Government, and shall feel gratified if my course meets the approbation of the President. I have long looked to this subject as one out of which difficulties were likely to arise between the two Governments. This opinion I have more than once expressed in my communications to our Government. The course of this Government has been influenced in a great measure no doubt, by the abolition feeling which is deep and strong here, and the mistaken opinions so generally entertained by the British public, as to the extent and influence of the same feelings, in the United States.

3. In two notes relating to the slave trade dated August 27, 1841, Palmerston said that the British did not pretend that a right to "search" American vessels existed but insisted on a right to "visit" ships suspected of being engaged in the slave trade in order to examine the vessel's papers. In his reply of September 10, directed to Lord Aberdeen, Stevenson retorted that Palmerston's distinction between visit and search was "wholly fictitious." Palmerston's distinction was untenable, for international law sanctioned visit and search only during time of war, unless a mutual search treaty specifically provided for the boarding of vessels during time of peace.

Having failed in getting the American Government to unite in yielding the qualified right of Search, this Government are now disposed to exercise it under another, and more offensive form.[4] Whether the present Ministry will go the full length of the doctrines asserted in Lord Palmerston's Note is to be seen. No answer has yet been given to my Note to Lord Aberdeen. I presume one may soon be expected.

On Monday last the Diplomatique Corps had their first Audience with Lord Aberdeen at the Foreign Office. They were severally introduced, and his Lordship's reception of me, was friendly and conciliatory. In the course of our short interview the existing relations of the two Countries were referred to, and more particularly the case of [Alexander] McLeod. Lord Aberdeen said that it was a subject of much interest and anxiety, and one the importance of which, he felt most sensibly. He hoped there would be no difficulty in McLeod's being released, upon the grounds asserted in your communications to the Attorney General [John Jordan Crittenden],[5] and Mr [Henry Stephen] Fox[6]—and which he said Her Majesty's Government had confidently expected would have been acquiesced in by the Authorities of New York. That this he thought was greatly to be desired by both Governments. He then asked my impressions as to what would be the probable course our Government would take. I stated briefly the substance of the explanation which I had given to Lord Palmerston, and referred to in my Despatch of the 18th of August.[7] That McLeod would certainly be tried by the Authorities of New York—That if he was acquitted, the question so far as it regarded him, would be at an end—That if on the Contrary he was convicted, the Government of the United States would no doubt be prepared to take such steps as it might deem proper under the circumstances—That these questions however of conflicting jurisdiction between the National and State Governments were of a highly delicate and important character, on which different opinions were entertained in the United States—That I could express no opinion as to the course that could, or would be taken on the subject, further than to assure his Lordship, that whatever power the Government of the United States, *could constitutionally and rightfully exercise in the case*, would be exerted whenever it became necessary and proper for it to do so. Lord Aberdeen remarked, that in case of a conviction by the Authorities of New York he presumed no judgment of the Court would be attempted to be carried into effect, until the questions involved

4. The Quintuple Treaty of December 20, 1841, concluded by Britain, Austria, France, Prussia, and Russia, declared the slave trade to be piracy and granted a restricted mutual right of search. France failed to ratify the treaty and as Stevenson's remarks indicate, the United States wholeheartedly opposed the convention.

5. See above, DW to Crittenden, March 15, 1841.

6. See above, DW to Fox, April 24, 1841.

7. Stevenson to DW, August 18, 1841, DNA, RG 59 (Despatches, Britain).

in the case had been finally decided between the National and State Authorities. I replied that I was entirely uninformed on the subject, and could therefore give no opinion. That I presumed however no effort would be made to enforce any sentence of the State Court, pending the decision of the Case in the Court of the United States, if it should be carried there. It is proper also <to say> that I should state that I have avoided as much as possible in the explanations I have given, to speak in a manner to excite or justify any unreasonable expectations on the part of this Government, as to the result of this affair. In my conversations with Lord Palmerston and Lord Aberdeen, I stated expressly that I was not authorized to give any assurances as to what would be done, nor was I prepared to express any opinion on the subject. My object has been to keep things as quiet as I could until some final action should take place, and prevent the Government here from adopting measures calculated to lead to Collision between the two Governments, before the final trial. You will see from the debate in the House of Commons yesterday, that the subject was attended to by Lord John Russell and Sir Robert Peel as one of deep importance.[8]

I enclose a list of the New Cabinet. I have had no opportunity as yet of forming an opinion as to the effect which the change of Administration will have upon the Political relations of the two Countries. In the only interview which I have had with <Lord> the Earl of Aberdeen he impressed me very favorably and seemed to be extremely desirous of preserving our Amicable relations. Such he assured me was his sincere desire, and that of the Government. With the other members of the Cabinet, and especially those who will take a leading share in the New Government, I have had as yet no other intercourse than the interchange of official visits. I see nothing however to justify me in supposing that they are less disposed than their predecessors, to preserve peace between the two Countries.

The series of papers forwarded will give you all the news of Public Interest.

The Boston Steamer of the 1st which arrived in Liverpool on Wednesday last brought me nothing from your Department. I am Sir, very respectfully Your obedient servant   A. Stevenson

ALS. DNA, RG 59 (Despatches, Britain). Rec'd October 9, 1841. Published in part in CR, 3:676–677.

ENCLOSURE: LORD PALMERSTON TO ANDREW STEVENSON

August 27, 1841

The Undersigned, Her Majesty's Principal Secretary of State for For-

8. *Hansard's*, 59:525–526, 540–541.

eign Affairs in proceeding to reply to the Note which Mr [Andrew] Stevenson, Envoy Extraordinary and Minister Plenipotentiary from the United States of America at this Court, addressed to him on the 22nd of May 1838,[1] upon the subject of the Capture and destruction of the Steam Boat "Caroline" by a Detachment of Her Majesty's Forces, on the River Niagara, on the night of the 29th December, 1837, thinks it necessary in the first place to explain the reasons why this reply has not been made sooner.

Mr Stevenson's Note which had been proceded by a Correspondence on this subject between Mr [Henry Stephen] Fox and Mr [John] Forsyth in January 1838,[2] was accompanied by voluminous Documents, purporting to contain statements of facts collected by the Law Officers of the United States Government from a variety of Witnesses whom they had examined for this purpose; and it was absolutely necessary that before Her Majesty's Government could give a full answer to Mr Stevenson's Note, Copies of those Documents should be sent to the Governor General of Canada [Lord Sydenham], in order that he might direct Witnesses on the British side to be examined; and that he might transmit to Her Majesty's Government, correct Accounts of those transactions to which the statements of the American Witnesses related.

The proceedings connected with these inquiries necessarily occupied a considerable portion of time, and it was not till the Spring of the Year 1839 that full information was received.

Other Border conflicts also happened which appeared to Her Majesty's Government to diminish the relative importance of the Affair of the Caroline, and it seemed to Her Majesty's Government, that the Government of the United States, could not but feel that the result of all these events must be, that there was a large account to be settled between the Two Governments, which must be adjusted entirely or not at all; and that it was useless to discuss seperate and particular Incidents, as if they were the only points to be arranged between the Two Countries.

Moreover the Government of the United States was perfectly aware, even before Mr Stevenson's Note of May 1838 was written, that Her Majesty's Government considered the destruction of the Caroline as a justifiable act of self defence, properly done by the local British Authorities, for the protection of British Subjects and their property, and for the Security of Her Majesty's Territories.

This opinion had been made known to the United States Government

1. See Stevenson to Palmerston, May 22, 1838, enclosed in No. 49. Stevenson to Forsyth, May 24, 1838, DNA, RG 59 (Despatches, Britain).
2. Fox to Forsyth, January 4, 1838, DNA, RG 59 (Notes from Foreign Legations, Britain); Forsyth to Fox, January 5 and January 19, 1838, DNA, RG 59 (Notes to Foreign Legations, Britain).

by Mr Fox in an Official Note to Mr Forsyth,[3] and by the Undersigned in more than one Conversation with Mr Stevenson.

Moreover Mr Stevenson, in his Note of May 1838, did not represent the transaction as being the unauthorized enterprize of private Individuals acting upon their own responsibility, and which it was doubtful whether Her Majesty's Government would, or would not consider as being a matter for which the British Government and Nation were answerable. But Mr Stevenson, on the contrary, represented the transaction as one which had been deliberately planned with the knowledge and approbation of the Lieutenant Governor of Upper Canada,[4] and executed by Armed Troops, forming a portion of the British Force stationed at Chippewa; and Mr Stevenson called upon Her Majesty's Government to disavow and disapprove the conduct of the Lieutenant Governor in this respect. But Her Majesty's Government did not after the receipt of Mr Stevenson's Note retract the opinions expressed on this matter by Mr Fox, and by the Undersigned; nor did Her Majesty's Government in any manner disavow or disapprove the Conduct of the Lieutenant Governor of Canada; and therefore both that which Her Majesty's Government had done, and that which Her Majesty's Government abstained from doing, could leave no doubt whatever on the mind of the President, that the British Government intended to decline to comply with the demand contained in Mr Stevenson's Note.

It is to be presumed that it was a conviction to this effect, which induced Mr Stevenson to refrain from pressing for an Answer to his Note, without Special Instructions from his Government to do so; and which also led Mr Forsyth to instruct Mr Stevenson to abstain till further orders,[5] from taking any step in the matter.

The Government of the United States seems, like that of Her Majesty, to have felt that no good could arise from the Communication of a formal Refusal on the part of Great Britain, to comply with a Demand explicitly made by the United States; and that it might be better to let that refusal be inferred from the silence of the British Government.

But as recent Communications received from the United States Government shew, that a formal reply to Mr Stevenson's Note of the 28th of May 1838 is desired by the President, the Undersigned feels that he is bound to give it; and he has, therefore, now again to declare that in the opinion of Her Majesty's Government the Capture and Destruction of the

3. Fox to Forsyth, February 6, 1838, DNA, RG 59 (Notes from Foreign Legations, Britain).

4. Sir Francis Bond Head (1793–1875) held the post from 1836 until 1838. He resigned after receiving severe criticism in Lord Durham's report on Canada.

5. Forsyth to Stevenson, September 11, 1839, DNA, RG 59 (Instructions, Britain).

Caroline was a justifiable act of self defence, and that Her Majesty's Government *far from* disavowing and disapproving the then Lieutenant Governor of Canada who sanctioned; or the officers and Men of Her Majesty's Forces who planned and executed this transaction;—on the Contrary, fully avow *and entirely approve* the Conduct, in this respect, of *all* those persons; that *no redress is due* by Her Majesty's Government on this Account, and that therefore, none can be given.

The grounds upon which this opinion rests will be found in the following Summary of the leading facts of the Case: and Her Majesty's Government cannot but indulge a hope that the Government of the United States will see in this statement and in the proofs by which it is supported, sufficient reason for the Decision of Her Majesty's Government. If a wrong had really been done by Her Majesty's Colonial Authorities, Her Majesty's Government would most readily have given Reparation; but if, on the other hand, it can be shewn that no wrong has been done, and that the transaction in question was in truth a defensive measure on the part of the British Authorities, in North America, the Government of the United States is too just, to press for a reparation which is not due.

In December 1837 no Civil War existed in Canada; there was no party within the British provinces arrayed in Arms against the Queen's Authority; Disturbances had indeed broken out in Lower Canada in the Autumn of the year 1837, but those disturbances had been promptly quelled by the energetic Loyalty of Her Majesty's Canadian Subjects, and by the action of Her Majesty's regular Troops. Those disturbances had ended after a short conflict and with little loss of life on either side. The Leaders of the Insurrection had fled to the United States, and for some time before December 1837 order and tranquility had been restored in the Canadian Provinces.

In this state of things a small Band of Canadian Refugees who had taken shelter in the State of New York, formed a League with a number of Citizens of the United States, for the purpose of invading the British Territory—Not to join a party engaged in Civil War because Civil War at that time in Canada there was none, but in order to commit within the British Territory the Crimes of Robbery, Arson, and Murder; Her Majesty's Government and Her Majesty's Minister at Washington [Henry Stephen Fox] have called these people Pirates; and the American Secretary of State, in a recent Note to Mr Fox,[6] observes that this name cannot properly be applied to them. The undersigned is ready to admit that technically the word "Pirate" is applied to persons, who, without authority or commission, commit upon the high Seas, the Crimes which this Band of offenders determined to commit upon the Land. But if the term is in this

6. DW to Fox, April 18, 1841, DNA, RG 59 (Notes to Foreign Legations, Britain).

case inappropriate, it is so, not on account of the nature of the Acts, which these men were about to perpretrate; but on account of the Element in which these Acts were to be committed.

The intentions of these men were publicly known; but the Government of New York took no effectual steps to prevent them from carrying those Intentions into effect.

By a neglect on the part of that Government, which seems to admit of but one explanation, the Storehouses which contained the Arms and Ammunition of the State were left unguarded; and were consequently broken open by this Gang, who carried off from thence in open day, and in the most public manner, Cannon and other implements of War.

After some days preparation these people proceeded without any interruption from the Government or Authorities of the State of New York, and under the Command of an American Citizen, to invade and occupy Navy Island, a part of the British Territory;[7] and having engaged the Steam Boat Caroline which for their special Service was cut out of the Ice in which she had been inclosed in the Port of Buffalo, they used her for the purpose of bringing over to Navy Island from the United States Territory Men, Arms, Ammunition, Stores, and Provisions.

The preparations made for this Invasion of British Territory by a Band of Men organized, Armed and equipped within the United States, and consisting partly of British Subjects, and partly of American Citizens, had induced the British Authorities to station a Military Force at Chippewa to repel the threatened invasion and to defend her Majesty's Territory.

The Commanders of that Force[8] seeing that the Caroline was used as a means of Supply *and Reinforcement* for the Invaders who had occupied Navy Island, judged that the Capture and Destruction of that Vessel would prevent Supplies and Reinforcements from passing over to the Island and would moreover deprive the Force in the Island of the means of passing over to the British Territory on the Main Land. They therefore determined at once to Capture the Caroline, both for the purpose of impeding the further progress of the Invaders and to hasten their Retreat from Navy Island. The British Commanders having taken this determination; lost no time in carrying it into execution; because every hour's delay would have defeated their purpose; but in order to avoid as much

7. Canadian rebel leader William Lyon Mackenzie appointed Rensselaer Van Rensselaer (1801–1850), of Albany, as commander of the Patriot forces on the island. A son of Solomon Van Rensselaer, who fought in the War of 1812, Van Rensselaer later led an unsuccessful attack on Kingston and was imprisoned for violating American neutrality law.

8. Sir Allan Napier MacNab (1798–1862), Speaker of the Upper Canadian assembly, commanded the militia at Chippewa. MacNab ordered Andrew Drew (1792–1878), a British naval officer, to lead the assault on the Caroline.

as possible loss of life and effusion of blood on either side, in accomplishing their object, they chose to capture the Vessel by a surprize in the night, when the Marauders being assailed unawares, and in the dark, by persons acting upon a concerted plan, would be less able to resist, and would be more easily overcome, than if attacked by daylight, and necessarily warned for defence, by seeing the gradual approach of the British Boats.

Accordingly seven British Boats with an officer and eight Men in each, all of them volunteers from the British Force stationed at Chippewa, started on the night of the 29th of December 1837 from Chippewa to cut out the "Caroline" which they expected to find at Navy Island; but which they discovered lower down the River moored at the wharf at Fort Schlosser. After being challenged by the watch on deck, they boarded the vessel, and after a short but smart resistance during which some of the boarding Party were severely wounded, they carried the Vessel; drove on shore the Crew and the other persons who were on board; cast her off from her mooring, and proceeded to tow her away, intending to carry her over to the British Shore. But they found her too heavy to be towed up against the stream; and therefore after carefully seeing that there was nobody left on board, they set her on fire, and let her drift down to the Falls. Having thus accomplished their object, they returned quickly to Chippewa, without any retaliatory attack upon that portion of the hostile band, who were collected at Fort Schlosser and who intended no doubt to pass over the next day in the Caroline to Navy Island.

In executing this operation the British Party used no greater degree of violence, than was necessary to carry the Vessel. They took with them no fire arms and had nothing but cutlasses and some swords, borrowed for the occasion, from the Cavalry stationed at Chippewa.

Such of the Persons found on board the Caroline, as did not resist, were put on shore uninjured, and as the Vessel was close to the Wharf, the greater part of the persons on board landed without difficulty. It appears that a few were wounded, and Her Majesty's Government very much regret that one American Citizen named [Amos] Durfee lost his life by a shot through the Head. But as it is positively declared by the British Party that they took no fire arms with them and as it is proved that the American Party had fire arms and used them it seems possible to account for the death of Durfee without assuming that he fell by the hands of the British Party.

The Details, of which the foregoing statement is a summary, are given in Inclosures to this Note,[9] and the Undersigned requests that Mr Stevenson will have the goodness to draw the special attention of his Government to the particulars contained in those Inclosures. For an attentive

9. Palmerston's note contained a number of affidavits of British participants in the *Caroline* raid.

perusal of those Inclosures will shew, how erroneous are many of the statements, which have been transmitted to Mr Stevenson, and of which he gave a summary in his note of December 1838.[10] But some other parts of that summary are perfectly consistent with the British statement, and tend to confirm, instead of contradicting it.

Mr Stevenson begins his narrative by stating, that towards the end of December 1837 the Caroline was cleared from the Port of Buffalo, with a view of running between that Port and Schlosser; and for the purpose of carrying Passengers and Freight. But Mr Stevenson omits to state that the Caroline was "cleared" not only from the Custom House, but from the Ice, in which she had been locked up for the Winter; and he has omitted to explain whence and how arose that sudden outburst of traffic on the River between Buffalo and Schlosser, which, in the depth of a North American Winter could render it a profitable undertaking to set on the Caroline as a Passage Vessel, between those two points, between which there is an established railway communication.

Mr Stevenson commences his narrative by stating, that he is about to give a recital of the *"prominent and important facts"* of the case; and yet he omits all mention of the most prominent and most important fact of the whole transaction; of that fact which indeed is the very foundation of the whole proceeding; and in which lies the essence of the whole matter; namely, the then recent invasion of the British Territory at Navy Island, by a Band of British Refugees and American Citizens, com-manded by a Citizen of the Union, organized and equipped under the eyes, and there is too much reason to suspect, with the connivance of the Authorities of New York; and provided with cannon and other arms and warlike stores, which were the public property of that State, and were taken openly and without impediment from the Storehouses of the State.

Mr Stevenson, however, is obliged to admit that the very first thing that was done by this Steam Vessel which had cleared out to carry Pas-sengers and Freight between Buffalo and Fort Schlosser, was to land Passengers and Freight, not at Fort Schlosser at all, but at Navy Island, then occupied by the Hostile Force which had invaded it from the United States.

Mr Stevenson says that the Caroline then went on to Fort Schlosser, but he does not assert that she landed at that place, any Passengers or Freight from Buffalo; but he admits that this Steam Boat, whose pro-fessed employment was to run between Buffalo and Schlosser, having first disembarked her Passengers and Freight from Buffalo, not at Schlosser but at Navy Island; and having arrived subsequently at Schlos-ser returned not to Buffalo, but to Navy Island; and then, not once, but

10. There is no note of December 1838 that summarizes the attack on the *Caroline.* Palmerston probably had Stevenson's note of May 22, 1838, in mind.

twice in the very day on which she arrived at Schlosser, went from Schlosser to Navy Island, and back from Navy Island to Schlosser: And thus it appears even from Mr Stevenson's own statement, that the real purpose for which the Caroline was employed, was not to run with passengers and Freight from Buffalo to Schlosser, and from Schlosser to Buffalo, but to convey Passengers and Freight from Buffalo and from Schlosser to Navy Island; a place not within the United States Territory, but a British Island; to which in ordinary times no man would have thought of carrying either Passengers or Freight because it has scarcely any Inhabitants, and has neither accommodation for Travellers, nor demand for Mercantile Commodities; and is in fact, in consequence of the strength of the current at that point so difficult of access for rowing boats, that on that account the Invaders found a Steam Vessel necessary, as a sure and safe means of communication with the shore.

What then was the reason why in the depth of winter, the "Caroline" carried in one single day, three cargoes of Passengers and Freight, to this usually almost uninhabited Island? Why the answer is plain: these pretended Passengers were reinforcements for the Band of Invaders, who had seized possession of that portion of British Territory; and the Freight consisted of arms and warlike Stores. This fact is perfectly notorious, and has been admitted by Mr [Gilman] Appleby the Master,[11] who in his recent examination in the case of Mr [Alexander] McLeod, confessed that part of this pretended Freight was nothing more or less, than a six pounder.

It is clear therefore from Mr Stevenson's own statement, that the Caroline was not engaged in the innocent occupations of commerce, but was employed to assist the hostile proceedings of the Band, who had invaded the British Territory; that she had three times in one day made landings on British Territory for hostile purposes; that her character was identified with that of the Band on Navy Island; and that the British Authorities were fully justified in treating her as an Enemy's Vessel, and in capturing or destroying her, as such.

Mr Stevenson then goes on to say that the Caroline was moored for the night to the wharf at Fort Schlosser, and that on board of her there were her own officers and Crew, accounting to *ten* in number, and *twenty three* other Individuals, *all Citizens of the United States*, who were unable to procure lodgings at the Inn. That Inn indeed, as is well known— was entirely filled that night, with other Citizens of the United States, who had no doubt repaired thither for the same purpose for which the

11. The *Caroline*, owned by William Wells, was commanded by Gilman Appleby of Buffalo, who was reputed to be a member of the Patriots. Although Palmerston is incorrect in stating that Appleby specifically admitted that there was a cannon on board, there is little question that this was the case. See *Gould's Stenographic Reporter*, 2.

abovementioned Twenty three had come; and Mr Stevenson says that all the Thirty three persons on board the Caroline, retired to rest, *except the night watch.* Now upon this, the Undersigned would beg to remark, in passing, that considering that the Caroline was a small Steamer and pretended to be destined merely as a Passage Vessel in the River between Buffalo and Schlosser, it seems strange that she should have been encumbered with so large a number of Officers and men then; and the fact that the Master deemed it necessary to set a night watch, seems to indicate a consciousness on his part, that he was engaged in an undertaking which might probably expose him to the very danger, which actually came upon him.

Mr Stevenson then states that about midnight the Caroline was boarded by People from four or five Boats, who armed with Pistols, Swords and Cutlasses, began an indiscriminate attack upon the unarmed Crew and Inmates of the Vessel, under the cry of "give no quarter"; that the Steamer was yielded without resistance, and was then set on fire, and sent down the Falls.

Now upon this, the Undersigned would beg to remark that it is stated by the British Witnesses; that the Parties in the Boats took no Fire Arms with them; and there was evidently a good reason for this; because in the darkness of the night they could not have used Fire Arms without danger to each other; for although each might be able to distinguish Friend from Foe, as far as his Sword could reach, he could not possibly tell who might find himself in the way of the range of a Pistol or Musket Bullet; and as the Parties from the different Boats were to board the "Caroline" at different parts, and in opposite directions, they would by using Fire Arms have been as likely to shoot one another, as to shoot any of the Enemy's Party. The strong probability therefore is that the British Statement upon this head is the true one; and as it is proved that the American Party had Fire Arms, it may not unnaturally be supposed, that in the confusion of their surprize, and in the darkness of the night, they may have mistaken the report of the Fire Arms discharged by their own Party, for a report of Fire Arms discharged by the Boarders.

In a similar way it may be possible to account, for the assertion, wholly untrue that the Boarding Party cried out to each other to give no quarter. For it appears that one of the Party desired another to put on Shore unharmed one of the people found in the "Caroline," saying that they wanted the Vessel, but did not want to make *any Prisoners*; and in the hurry and alarm of the surprise, the People on board the Caroline, might have construed that declaration into an instruction to give no Quarter.

If indeed the boarding Party had meant to put the People in the Caroline to death, and if it were true, as stated <by> to Mr Stevenson, and recited in his Note, that a Party of Men from four or five Boats, who could not therefore well have been less than Forty in Number, and who are said to have been armed with Swords and Pistols, boarded by surprise a Vessel containing Thirty three Men, wholly unarmed, mostly asleep at the time, and all of them unresisting, is it possible, that if the intention of such a Boarding Party had been to give us no Quarter, a great portion of the People in the Caroline must not have perished that Night? And yet the only one among the Number who lost his life was Durfee, who probably fell by a shot from his own Friends.

These Facts which are now clearly ascertained, completely vindicate the Boarding Party from the charge of unnecessary violence in performing the Public Service on which they were employed.

Mr Stevenson then proceeds to say, that there was no Fortification of any kind at Schlosser; that hostilities were not commenced on the American Side, and that no shot from Cannon or from other Fire Arms had been discharged from the American Shore on the Morning of the 29th of December, as pretended by one of the British Officers.

As to the last point, the Undersigned requests the particular attention of the United States' Government to the Statements made regarding it, by the British Witnesses, and on the correctness of which, Her Majesty's Government must be permitted to rely. That there was no Fortification at Schlosser her Majesty's Government are ready to admit; for although the place is called Fort Schlosser, Her Majesty's Government believe that no fortified Building at present exists there. It is also perfectly true that no Hostilities had been commenced on the American Side, if by that expression Mr Stevenson means the American side of the River but that Hostilities had been commenced by the Americans is now an Historical Fact; and those Hostilities consisted in an Invasion of British Territory by an armed Force from the State of New York. In fact, the People of New York had begun to make War against Her Majesty's Canadian Provinces. They had done so apparently with the connivance of the Authorities of the State. Not only the New York Territory at Schlosser had lost its Neutral Character, and had become Enemies Land, but other portions of the Territory of that State had assumed the same condition.

One or other of two things must be: either the Government of New York knowingly and intentionally permitted the Band of Invaders to organize and equip themselves within the State, and to arm themselves for War against British Territory, out of the Military Stores of the State; or else the State Government had lost its authority over the Border Districts; and the Districts were for the moment in open defiance of the Power of the State Government as well as at War with the opposite British Province.

In the first case the British Authorities in Canada had a right to retaliate War for War: In the second case, they were no longer bound to respect as Neutral that portion of Territory which by shaking off its obedience to a Neutral Government, had ceased to be Neutral, and could certainly not be entitled to the privilege of protecting Persons, who were actively engaged in making War upon Her Majesty's Territory.

And this is an answer to the objection, if it should be made by the United States' Government, that even admitting that the Caroline was employed in the Service of the Invaders of Navy Island, which it is presumed will no longer be denied; the British Authorities in Canada might have dealt with her as an Enemy if they had found her within the British Limits, but had no right to pursue and Capture her within the Limits of the United States.

The answer to that objection is, that although Schlosser is unquestionably within the Limits of the United States, it had ceased at that time to preserve that Neutral and Peaceful character, which every part of the United States was bound to maintain, even if Civil War had been raging in Canada; but which was, if possible, still more incumbent upon every portion of the Union, at a time when Peace prevailed, not only between the United States and Great Britain, but within the Canadian Provinces themselves.

These then are the grounds upon which Her Majesty's Government conceive that the Government of the United States has no just right to demand Reparation for the Capture and Destruction of the Caroline; and these are the grounds upon which it is impossible for Her Majesty's Government to consent that any such Reparation shall be made.

The undersigned requests Mr Stevenson to accept the Assurances of his high consideration.   (Signed) Palmerston

Copy. DNA, RG 59 (Despatches, Britain). Published in *CR*, 3: 643–660.

ENCLOSURE: ANDREW STEVENSON TO LORD PALMERSTON

                                         32 Upper Grosvenor Street
My Lord,   August 31st 1841

I had the honor to receive yesterday, the Official communication which your Lordship did me the honor to address to me under date of the 27th instant,[1] in reply to my Note of the 22nd of May 1838,[2] relative to the capture & destruction of the Steam Boat "Caroline" in the month of December 1837, by a Party of Her Majesty's Canadian subjects, within the limits and territorial jurisdiction of the United States.

As the representations contained in Your Lordship's Note, touching this proceeding, differ so essentially in point of fact, from those which were made to the Government of the United States, and which I had the honor of communicating to Her Majesty's Government, in my first Note, and may consequently lead to a more thorough investigation of the whole

1. See above.

2. Stevenson to Palmerston, May 22, 1838, enclosed in No. 49. Stevenson to Forsyth, May 24, 1838, DNA, RG 59 (Despatches, Britain).

affair, in order that the material facts of the Case, may be more fully ascertained, and as I am on the eve of returning to the United States, and there is reason to believe that my Successor may soon be expected in England,[3] with instructions from his Government on the subject, I do not feel it necessary, or proper, to embark in the general discussion of the important questions embraced by your Lordship's Note. I shall therefore hasten to transmit a Copy of your Lordship's communication for the information of my Government, and respectfully ask that the Statements and proofs, to which it refers, may be furnished to me at the earliest convenient day, for the purpose of being forwarded with your Lordship's Note.

In the meantime I deem it proper to submit to your Lordship's consideration some observations which have been rendered necessary by certain parts of your Lordship's communication, and which demand my immediate notice.

In accounting for the delay which has taken place in communicating the answer of Her Majesty's Government in the case of the "Caroline," and the incidents arising out of the Border difficulties, on the American and Canadian Frontiers, your Lordship holds the following language— *"The Government of the United States was perfectly aware, even before Mr [Andrew] Stevenson's Note of May 1838 was written, that Her Majesty's Government considered the destruction of the Caroline as a justifiable Act of self defence, properly done by the British Colonial authorities for the protection of British subjects and their property, and for the security of Her Majesty's Territories. This opinion had been made known to the United States Government by Mr. [Henry Stephen] Fox in an Official Note to Mr. [John] Forsyth, and by the undersigned in more than one conversation—with Mr Stevenson."* And again in another part of your Lordship's Note, it is stated—*"That Her Majesty's Government did not after the receipt of Mr Stevenson's Note retract the opinions expressed in the matter by Mr. Fox, and by the undersigned, nor did Her Majesty's Government in any manner disavow or disapprove the conduct of the local Governor of Canada [Sir Francis Bond Head], and therefore both that, which Her Majesty's Government had done, and that which Her Majesty's Government abstained from doing, could leave no doubt whatever on the mind of the President of the United States that the British Government intended to decline to comply with the demand contained in Mr Stevenson's Note."* And again your Lordship further observes—*"It is to be presumed that it was a communication to this effect which induced Mr. Stevenson to refrain from pressing for an answer to his Note without special instructions from His Government to do so, and which*

3. Stevenson left London on October 22, 1841. His successor, Edward Everett, arrived at his post on November 18.

also led Mr Forsyth to instruct him to abstain 'till further orders from taking any step in the matter."

Now if it is intended in these parts of your Lordship's Note, to leave it to be inferred, that the Capture and destruction of the Caroline Steamer, was in the opinion of Her Majesty's Government a justifiable act of self defence by the Colonial Authorities, or that this opinion and avowal had been officially made known by Mr. Fox to the Government of the United States, in his correspondence with the Secretary of State, prior to the arrest of [Alexander] McLeod, or by your Lordship to me, then I take leave to say most distinctly, that any such inference is wholly unwarranted, inasmuch as no such avowal or opinion was either communicated by Mr. Fox to my Government, or by your Lordship to me. That it was not made by Mr. Fox, a brief recapitulation of the facts will shew. In his first Note to Mr. Forsyth, written immediately after the occurrence took place,[4] and to which it is presumed your Lordship refers, Mr Fox confines himself to the expression of *his own opinion*, as to the nature of the transaction, and not that of his *Government*. Indeed, as late as the 23rd of December 1840,[5] in an official Note to the American Government he expressly declared that he had no authority whatever to pronounce the opinion of Her Majesty's Government on the Case, but felt bound to record his own opinion. Besides, how could Mr. Fox in February 1838, be supposed to express the opinion of His Government upon a transaction, the existence of which was then unknown to her Majesty's Government; and to which neither application for redress, or complaint had been made? If Mr. Fox's communication to Mr. Forsyth could have been regarded by the American Government as communicating the avowal, or opinion of Her Majesty's Government, my instructions, and the Note of May 1838, would no doubt have been of a very different character. Whatever opinion therefore might have been entertained and expressed by Mr. Fox, from the circumstances detailed by the Canadian Authorities, it is quite certain that as late as December 1840 he could have made no such communication, to my Government as that which may be inferred from those parts of your Lordship's Note.

That any answer was ever given, or communication made by your Lordship to me subsequent to my Note of 1838, which presented the Case as one for redress, will not it is presumed be pretended. On the contrary, so marked was the delay on the part of your Lordship to answer my Note and make known the decision of Her Majesty's Government, that in September 1839, I drew the special attention of my Government

4. Fox to Forsyth, January 4, 1838, DNA, RG 59 (Notes from Foreign Legations, Britain).

5. The correct reference is to Fox to Forsyth, December 29, 1840, DNA, RG 59 (Notes from Foreign Legations, Britain).

to the subject,[6] and asked to be instructed, whether I was to press for an answer, and if so, the degree of urgency that I was to adopt.

In the answer I received,[7] I was told by Mr. Forsyth, that no further instructions were then required; not however for the reasons which your Lordship, is pleased to assign, but expressly, on the ground, *"that Mr. Forsyth had had frequent conversations with Mr Fox on the subject, and one especially of a very recent date from which the President was led to expect that Her Majesty's Government would answer my Note, without any further delay."* I beg leave to refer your Lordship to the Official correspondence on this part of the subject, which was laid before Congress, and published by their Order.[8] Then at least, the Government of the United States could have had no such official information as to the opinion of Her Majesty's Government, as that which your Lordship's Note would seem to infer. The enquiry then is, was there any communication made by your Lordship prior to my Note of May 1838? Now, it is readily admitted, that I had two conversations with your Lordship on the subject of the "Caroline," to which I presume the allusion in your Note points. Those conversations however it is proper to say were entirely of an *informal and desultory character,* and took place immediately on the arrival of the first intelligence of the Schlosser affair in England, and that through the Public press. It is also admitted, that in these conversations, I did understand your Lordship to intimate distinctly an opinion; that the case might turn out to have been one, which Her Majesty's Government might feel itself bound to justify as one of self defence. No official information however had at the time when these conversations took place, been received by Her Majesty's Government. The substance of these conversations, it is proper also to say, were communicated by me at the time to my Government, and were also made public, and will speak for themselves. Whether conversations of this character, as early as *February 1838* can rightfully be regarded as amounting to an official avowal or approval, by Her Majesty's Government, of a proceeding which had not then been officially made known, or become the subject of complaint, of redress, it is not necessary now, to enquire into, or decide. If therefore it was only intended by your Lordship, (as I flatter myself it was) to represent these conversations as the only grounds upon which the Statements contained in your Lordship's Note, have been made, nothing can be more correct, than that such conversations, (though of an informal and unofficial character) did take place, and that your Lord-

6. Stevenson actually requested instructions in July and received a reply in September. Stevenson to Forsyth, July 2, 1839, DNA, RG 59 (Despatches, Britain).

7. Forsyth to Stevenson, September 11, 1839, DNA, RG 59 (Instructions, Britain).

8. *Executive Documents*, 26th Cong., 2d sess., Serial 383, No. 33.

ship is justly entitled to the full benefit of this admission. All then that I mean to say is, that apart from these conversations, no other communication ever took place between us on the subject, until after the arrest and imprisonment of McLeod, by the Authorities of the State of New York, and which doubtless led to the avowal by Her Majesty's Government, of the original proceeding.

Upon the subject of the delay which was permitted to take place in answering my Note, it is not my duty to enquire. That is a matter for your Lordship and Her Majesty's Government. That delay I had neither the right, nor the power of controlling. It was certainly not produced by me, nor by my Government, and the responsibility must rest where it properly belongs.

I deem it unnecessary to trouble your Lordship with any further observations. I have felt it due to myself and my Government to avail myself of the earliest moment of correcting officially any misapprehension, which the Statements contained in your Lordship's Note might be susceptible of. I accordingly seize an opportunity before Your Lordship's retirement from the Foreign Office to address to you this communication.

I need not assure your Lordship how sincerely I should lament that any misunderstanding should arise between us, in relation to a matter which is so capable of explanation; and that too in a moment, when the Public relations in which we have stood to each other, are about, in all probability to cease for ever; and which have been sustained by those of a personal character, so eminently gratifying and satisfactory.

I beg your Lordship to accept assurances of my high consideration.

(signed) A. Stevenson

Copy. DNA, RG 59 (Despatches, Britain). Published in CR, 3:661–665.

ENCLOSURE: LORD PALMERSTON TO ANDREW STEVENSON

Foreign Office
September 2d 1841

The Undersigned, Her Majesty's Principal Secretary of State for Foreign Affairs, has the honour to acknowledge the receipt of the Note of the 31st ultimo from Mr. [Andrew] Stevenson,[1] Envoy Extraordinary and Minister Plenipotentiary from the United States of America, in reply to the note from the Undersigned, dated the 27th ultimo,[2] upon the subject of the capture and destruction of the Steam Boat "Caroline."

The Undersigned is glad to find that there is no essential difference between Mr Stevenson and the Undersigned as to their impressions with

1. See above.
2. See above, Palmerston to Stevenson, August 27, 1841.

regard to the facts to which Mr Stevenson's note refers; and for greater precision, the Undersigned would beg leave to recapitulate them.

The "Caroline" was captured and destroyed on the night of the 29th of December 1837.

On the 5th of January 1838, Mr [John] Forsyth addressed a note to Mr [Henry Stephen] Fox,[3] accompanied by numerous Affidavits and Documents, setting forth the American version of the capture of the "Caroline" which Mr Forsyth stated would necessarily form the subject of a demand for redress upon Her Majesty's Government.

Mr Fox immediately forwarded Copies of these papers to the Lieutenant Governor of Upper Canada [Sir Francis Bond Head] and reported thereupon to Her Majesty's Government.

On the 6th of February following Mr Fox addressed a Note to Mr Forsyth,[4] in which he transmitted the accounts which he had then received from Sir Francis Head of the circumstances which appeared to justify the act of the Canadian Authorities in the destruction of the "Caroline"; and in this note Mr Fox wrote to Mr Forsyth as follows:

"The piratical character of the Steam Boat 'Caroline' and the necessity of self defense and self preservation, under which Her Majesty's Subjects acted, in destroying that Vessel, would seem to be sufficiently established.

"At the time when the event happened, the ordinary Laws of the United States were not enforced within the frontier district of the State of New York. The authority of the Law was overborne publickly by piratical violence. Through such violence, Her Majesty's subjects in Upper Canada had already suffered; and they were threatened with still further injury and outrage. This extraordinary state of things appears naturally and necessarily to have impelled them to consult their own security, by pursuing and destroying the Vessel of their piratical enemy, wherever they might find her."

Mr Forsyth in his answer dated the 13th of February,[5] observes, that the statement of facts in the papers sent by Mr Fox, is at variance with the information communicated to the United States Government, and repeats the statement of his intention to address a complaint supported by evidence to Her Majesty's government.

He further states; "Even admitting that the documents transmitted with your note contain a correct statement of the occurrence, they furnish no Justification of the aggression committed upon the territory of the United States": and he concludes by a complaint against Sir Francis Head, as having acted on this occasion inconsistently with the declara-

3. See above, Palmerston to Stevenson, August 27, 1841.

4. See above, Palmerston to Stevenson, August 27, 1841.

5. Forsyth to Fox, February 13, 1838. DNA, RG 59 (Notes to Foreign Legations, Britain).

tion which he made in his speech at the opening of the Provincial Parliament, in which he expressed his "confidence in the disposition of the United States Government to restrain its Citizens from taking part in the conflict which was raging in the Province."

To this Mr Fox replied in a note dated the 16th of February,[6] that although he "did not acquiesce in the view which the United States Government are disposed to take of the facts connected with that transaction; yet as the Legation was not the final authority competent to decide the question on the part of Great Britain, and as Mr Forsyth informed him that a Representation would in due time be addressed to Her Majesty's Government in England, he considered it most consistent with his duty to avoid entering at present into any further controversy on the subject."

The account of the transaction reached England on the 2d of February 1838. Between that time and the month of May of that year, the Undersigned has [had] some conversations with Mr Stevenson on the subject.

The Undersigned kept no Memorandum of them and therefore cannot say on what days they took place, nor how many they were; but Mr Stevenson says they were two; and the Undersigned has no doubt that Mr Stevenson is correct. If the Undersigned is not mistaken in his recollection, one, at least, of these conversations was at the Foreign Office; and the Undersigned has an impression that on that occasion he read or shewed to Mr Stevenson some of the statements which Her Majesty's Government had then received of the Transaction from the Government of Canada.

At all events Mr Stevenson's recollection tallies with that of the Undersigned as to the fact, that the Undersigned then intimated to Mr Stevenson distinctly the opinion of Her Majesty's Government, that the act would turn out to have been a Justifiable measure of self defense.

On the 22d of May of that year 1838 Mr Stevenson by Instructions from his Government addressed to the Undersigned an Official note,[7] demanding reparation for the destruction of the Caroline; and stated that <in> the United States' Government considered that transaction as "an outrage upon United States' Citizens, and a violation of United States' Territory, committed by British Troops, from the Province of Upper Canada; and that this outrage was planned and executed with the knowledge and approbation of the Lieutenant Governor of Upper Canada"; and this note was accompanied by inclosures containing full details of the American version of the case.

On the 26th of June the Undersigned acknowledged the receipt of this

6. Fox to Forsyth, February 16, 1838, DNA, RG 59 (Notes from Foreign Legations, Britain).

7. Stevenson to Palmerston, May 22, 1838, enclosed in No. 49. Stevenson to Forsyth, May 24, 1838, DNA, RG 59 (Despatches, Britain).

note,[8] and stated that the attention of the British Government would be given to the matter.

From that time till the early part of the present year when the account of the arrest of Mr [Alexander] McLeod reached this Country it is correctly stated in Mr Stevenson's note, that "no other communication upon the subject of the 'Caroline' ever took place between Mr Stevenson and the Undersigned," with the single exception that the case of the Caroline was incidentally alluded to, but not mentioned by name, in a passage of Mr Stevenson's note of the 26th of September 1839,[9] as a question pending between the two Governments. But during the interval, nearly three years, the case of the "Caroline" was, upon one occasion, the subject of communication between Mr Stevenson and his own Government. For, it appears, that in September 1839 Mr Stevenson not having then received any reply from Her Majesty's Government to the demand for reparation which he had made in May 1838, asked Mr Forsyth whether he should press for an answer;[10] and if so, with what degree of urgency he should do so; and it appears that Mr Forsyth, in reply,[11] informed Mr Stevenson that no further instructions on that matter were required; as, in consequence of some conversations with Mr Fox, the President was led to expect an answer from Her Majesty's Government without any further delay.

No answer however was given by Her Majesty's Government; and yet, until after the arrest of Mr McLeod had happened, which took place on the 12th of November 1840, no further notice was taken of the affair of the "Caroline," either by Mr Stevenson or by the United States Government, in any communication to Her Majesty's Government.

Now from these facts Her Majesty's Government draw the following conclusions

It seems to Her Majesty's Government demonstrable, that even before Mr Stevenson's Note of the 22nd of May 1838 was presented Mr Stevenson and the Government of Washington, were made aware of the opinion of Her Majesty's Government that the destruction of the "Caroline" had been a justifiable act of self defense.

For it cannot be disputed that the Undersigned, as Secretary of State, was fully competent to convey the opinion of Her Majesty's Government, authentically, to the Minister of the United States and that Mr Stevenson so thought, is shown by the fact of his having deemed it right to com-

8. The correct date is June 6, 1838. See Palmerston to Stevenson, June 6, 1838, DNA, RG 59 (Notes from Foreign Legations, Britain).

9. Stevenson to Palmerston, September 26, 1839, DNA, RG 59 (Despatches, Britain).

10. See above. Palmerston repeats the error made by Stevenson in his note, above. Stevenson requested instructions on July 2, 1839.

11. See above.

municate to his own Government the substance and result of his above-mentioned conversations with the Undersigned.

Those conversations were undoubtedly informal, inasmuch as they did not arise in consequence of any communication which Mr Stevenson was instructed by his Government to make to the Undersigned; and they were conversations of that kind which frequently take place between the Minister of a Foreign government and the Secretary of State, with a view to a preliminary undertaking upon matters which are likely to be subjects of formal discussion between their respective Governments, and in order to prepare the way for such future discussions.

It is indeed quite true as observed by Mr Stevenson, that the strong opinion expressed by Mr Fox in January 1838,[12] could not, at that time, have been expressed in consequence of specific instructions from Her Majesty's Government; because there had not been time for him to have received any such instructions; but a Minister Plenipotentiary has a general authority to speak and act on behalf of his Government; and if his words and acts are not disavowed by his Government in due time, the Government by its silence adopts, and becomes responsible for them. But the opinions expressed by Mr Fox in January 1838 upon the subject of the destruction of the Caroline, were not disavowed by Her Majesty's Government, and have never been disavowed by them to this day.

Now the Undersigned does not of course mean to say, that the opinions so expressed by Mr Fox, and by himself, were final and conclusive decisions of Her Majesty's Government in the case, although certainly that given in writing by Mr Fox was as strong and unequivocal as words could well convey, and it is obvious that those opinions having been expressed before the date of Mr Stevenson's Note of May 1838, could not at any rate have been decisions upon the demand made in that note: and as those opinions had been founded upon the information which Her Majesty's Colonial Authorities had then transmitted to Mr Fox, and to Her Majesty's Government, it was possible that Counter Statements founded upon information collected by the United States Government might satisfy Her Majesty's Government that their first view of the case, and their first opinion regarding it, however strong that opinion might have been, were erroneous. The Undersigned, therefore, does not mean to say and never has contended, that either his conversations with Mr Stevenson, or Mr Fox's note to Mr Forsyth, ought to have precluded the demand which was afterwards made by Mr Stevenson's Note of 1838. But the Undersigned contends that that demand was made with a previous knowledge, on the part of the United States' Government, of the views and opinions

12. Fox to Forsyth, January 4, 1838. See above, Palmerston to Stevenson, August 27, 1841, enclosed in Stevenson to DW, September 18, 1841.

of Her Majesty's Government, as to the transactions to which the demand related.

The Undersigned has further to remark that the words of Mr Stevenson's Note of May 1838, distinctly prove that the Government of the United States did not entertain any doubt whatever, whether the capture and destruction of the "Caroline" had been the unauthorized act of Individuals, for which such Individuals were to be made responsible in their private capacity; or whether it had been a public act done by Persons in the Service of the British Government, and obeying superior Authority; and for which, consequently, the British Government was to be responsible. Because the specific complaint of Mr Stevenson was, that the act was committed *"by a portion of the British Forces stationed at Chippewa;"* and that *"it was planned and executed with the knowledge and approbation of the Lieutenant Governor of Upper Canada,"* and that *"it was the Invasion of the Territory and Sovereignity of an Independent nation by the Armed Forces of a friendly Power;"* and the specific demand which Mr Stevenson made was, that "the whole proceeding should be *disavowed and disapproved,* and that such redress as the nature of the case obviously required should be promptly made," by the British Government. The Undersigned therefore maintains that the very contents of Mr Stevenson's note of 1838, preclude the United States' Government from attempting to make Mr McLeod or any other British Subject personally answerable for any share they may be supposed to have had, in the destruction of the *"Caroline;"* and that Mr Forsyth was mistaken in saying, as he did, in his note to Mr Fox of the 26th of December 1840,[13] that, up to that time, the United States Government had had no Authentic Announcement that the destruction of the "Caroline" was a public Act, of Persons in Her Majesty's Service, obeying the Order of Superior Authorities. For Mr Forsyth would have found that authentic announcement, in the Note of his own Plenipotentiary, presented in pursuance of Instructions from himself, so long ago as May 1838. But while, on the one hand, the Undersigned contends that the United States' Government knew in the early part of 1838, that Her Majesty's government thought the destruction of the "Caroline" a justifiable act; on the other hand, the Undersigned begs to state, that, Her Majesty's Government by continuing to give no reply to the demand made in Mr Stevenson's note of May 1838 was in fact, practically declining to comply with that demand; and the only legitimate inference which the United States' Government could draw from that silence, was that Her Majesty's Government adhered to the opinion which it had originally expressed.

13. Forsyth to Fox, December 26, 1840, DNA, RG 59 (Notes to Foreign Legations, Britain).

It appears, then, from Mr Stevenson's Statement, that, for nearly three years, the United States' Government acquiesced in the silence of Her Majesty's Government on this subject; for though in October 1839,[14] Mr Forsyth stated as a reason for not pressing Her Majesty's Government for an Answer, that the President had been led by some conversation of Mr Fox to expect the British Answer without any further delay; yet that reason necessarily ceased with the further lapse of time, and could not be said to have held good, as long as till the beginning of 1840.

Mr Stevenson, moreover, specifically states in his note of the 31st Ultimo, that, during the whole interval between the date of his note of May 1838, and the time when the arrest of Mr McLeod became known in England, in February 1841, no communication ever took place between himself and the Undersigned on the subject of the "Caroline." Now, as neither Mr Stevenson, nor the late President Van Buren, have ever shewn themselves deficient in watchful and active attention to all matters in which the just Rights of the United States have been concerned, the Undersigned conceives that he has not much erred in supposing, as stated by him in his former communication, that this long and intentional silence of the United States' Government, and of its Minister at this Court, upon the subject of the "Caroline," arose from the consideration to which the Undersigned adverted in that Note.

In hazarding that supposition it seems to the Undersigned that he had assumed nothing but what is highly honourable to the Government of the United States, and that he has only imagined that Government to have been guided by the same feelings of <consideration> conciliation when the Undersigned begs to assure Mr Stevenson, have invariably animated the Government of Her Majesty, in all its dealings and intercourse with Mr Stevenson, and with the Government, which Mr Stevenson has so ably and honourably represented at this Court

The Undersigned has the honour to renew to Mr Stevenson the assurance of his highest consideration.   (Signed) Palmerston

Copy. DNA, RG 59 (Despatches, Britain).

TO HENRY STEPHEN FOX

Department of State
Sir: Washington, 20 Sept. 1841.

Your note of the 5th of this month[1] was duly received and laid before the President.

It is true, as you state, that the decision of the Supreme Court of the State of New York, pronounced in the case of Alexander McLeod, is in

14. Palmerston again errs. The correct citation is Forsyth to Stevenson, September 11, 1839, DNA, RG 59

(Instructions, Britain).
1. See above, Fox to DW, September 5, 1841.

contradiction to the opinion of this Government, as communicated to you,[2] and as acted on by itself. But the decision of that court is not final. A writ of error may be prosecuted to remove the question, first to the Court of Errors to the State of New York, and ultimately to the Supreme Court of the United States at Washington.

This Department is informed that it is the wish of McLeod to go to trial at once, before a jury, in the expectation of an acquittal;[3] but reserving nevertheless his right, if his defence should be overruled, and he should be convicted, to prosecute his appeal to the Court of Errors of the State, and the Supreme Court of the United States.

This Government is as anxious as that of Her Majesty can be, for an early settlement of this affair. I quite concur with you, that it would be unbecoming either Government to utter threats of war. Both Governments must be supposed to understand their own rights, duties, and responsibilities; and to act in the full contemplation of results, probable or possible. Allusions to consequences, in diplomatic intercourse, in cases in which both parties are aware of all the facts, can hardly be necessary, if intended merely as admonitory; and if allowed to partake, in any degree, of the tone of menace, they usually very justly defeat their own purposes.

The Government of the United States has given sufficient proof of its disposition to obey and uphold the great principles of international law. While performing its duty in this respect, it does not permit itself to call in doubt the disposition of other Governments to perform their's; and, in the consciousness of the rectitude of its own proceedings, it awaits results, not with indifference, certainly, but with composure.

I avail myself of this occasion to renew to you the assurance of my distinguished consideration.   Danl Webster

L C. DNA, RG 59 (Notes to Foreign Legations, Britain).

FROM ALEXANDER MCLEOD

Whitesboro' Jail Oneida County

Sir,   20 Sept 1841

May I beg you will inform me from what source you obtained your information *that I boasted, on this frontier that I was one of the party employed by the Canadian Government to destroy the "Caroline."*[1] I am Sir Your most obedient Humble Servant   Alexander McLeod

A L S . DNA, RG 59 (Misc. Letters). Endorsed by DW: "I understand it to be in the evidence before the magistrate."

2. See above, DW to Fox, April 24, 1841.

3. See above, Spencer to DW, July 12, 1841.

1. See above, DW to Fox, April 24, 1841.

TO JOSHUA AUSTIN SPENCER

Private

Dear Sir: Washington Septr 21. 1841

It strikes me that the ground of legal defence, in [Alexander] McLeod's case, may be stated in two ways:

1. That the act, for which he is indicted, was Committed by order of superiors, &c. (as stated in my instructions to Mr [John Jordan] Crittenden.)[1]

2. That the attack on the Caroline has been regarded by the Government of the United States as an act of public force of the British Crown, and satisfaction demanded for it of the British Government.

The British Government acknowledges the attack on the Caroline as an act of its own, and holds itself ready to justify it.

It has therefore become a national dispute. It may be settled by negotiation, or treaty, or made the occasion of reprisal, or war, as the Government of the United States may decide; but the question is entirely without, or beyond, the jurisdiction of the municipal courts of New York.

It is a case for appeal, or writ of error, to the Supreme Court of the United States;

Because McLeod sets up an exemption from the municipal laws of New York, under or by virtue of the Constitution of the United States, which invests the Government of the United States with the exclusive control of all questions of war with foreign nations, whether general or partial, and of peace, and all questions of reprisals, or retaliation and with every thing connected with the foreign relations of the Country. And the attack on the Caroline is an incident, or occurrence, arising in the foreign relations of the Country, and affecting its state, as a state of peace or war, the true character of which can only be judged of and decided by the Government of the United States—which Government has pronounced its decision thereupon. Yours truly

(signed) Danl Webster

Copy. PHi.

WINFIELD SCOTT TO JOHN BELL

N. York, Sep 21, 1841.

I came here this morning, having spent four or five days, in visiting the fortifications of this Harbour before proceeding to Washington.[1]

Passing thro' Rome & Utica, I saw Lieut. [Horace] Brooks[2] recently

1. See above, DW to Crittenden, March 15. 1841.

1. Scott became general-in-chief of the army on the death of General Al-

exander Macomb (1782–1841) in June, 1841.

2. Brooks (d. 1894; U.S. Military Academy 1835).

sent up to the former place with a company of the 2d Artillery, & gave him minute instructions from his government in case he should be called upon to support the civil authority; & I also, thro' Mr. J[oshua] A[ustin] Spencer, caused it to be suggested to the Sheriff of that county (Oneida) [David Moulton] that, in case of any unlawful attempt on the jail, or the person of [Alexander] McLeod, (going to & from the court-house) the company would be found a steady & efficient *posse*.

Mr. Spencer had received from Canada many of the depositions to be read in the defense of his client, & was sanguine in the expectation of establishing the *alibi*. I communicated to him my doubts founded on what I had recently heard of the opposing testimony. It is probable that the trial will not be brought on before the first *proximus*, as Mr [Hiram] Gardner had written to Mr S[pencer] that he hardly hoped to be ready at an earlier day.

At Albany, I had, on the same subject, separate & very interesting interviews with the Governor [William Henry Seward] & Secretary of State.[3] The former evidently desires, & confidently expects the acquittal of McLeod. He intends a visit to Mr. Chief Justice [Samuel] Nelson[4] (who, if well enough, will preside at the trial) about the 25th instant;— thence to proceed to Utica or Whitesboro, & there to remain till the jury shall have rendered its verdict. He desires me (& I have complied with his wishes) to instruct Lieut. Brooks to wait upon him as soon as he arrives in the vicinity of the trial, & told me that it was his intention to place McLeod under the safe-conduct of Lieut. Brooks' company for any part of the frontier of the U. States McLeod might designate. I suggested to the Governor (as I had before done to Mr. J. A. Spencer) the route by Lake Champlain, & I have instructed Lieut Brooks to take, for the escort, the whole, or any part of his company, as might be thought best.

In making this arrangement with me, the Governor proceeded upon the supposition that McLeod would be acquitted. He said nothing of a pardon in the other case; but from what he expressly declared at the conference with Mr. [John Jordan] Crittenden, in March,[5] as well as the conversation I had at Auburn in August, with Mr. Seward & [his] father (Judge [Elijah] Miller)[6] I but little doubt that the Governor intends that Lieut. Brooks shall escort McLeod to the frontier immediately after the trial, no matter what may be the verdict of the jury.

I have thought it best to give the foregoing particulars in this hasty

3. Scott refers to the secretary of state of New York, John Canfield Spencer.

4. See above, John Canfield Spencer to DW, March 6, 1841.

5. See above, DW to Crittenden, March 15, 1841, and Seward to DW,

March 22, 1841.

6. Seward was in Auburn during the second week of August 1841. Seward became the junior law partner of Judge Miller of Auburn in January 1823 and his son-in-law in October 1823.

letter at once, as they may be interesting to the President & Department of State. I remain, Sir, With great respect, Yr most ob. Ser.

Winfield Scott

A L S . DNA, RG 59 (Misc. Letters). Rec'd September 26, 1841.

FROM WILLIAM HENRY SEWARD

State of New York.
Executive Department.
Dear Sir   Albany September 22d 1841.

I had occasion some weeks since to communicate for the information of the President an opinion,[1] that the field-pieces unlawfully seized in this state had a destination towards the frontier, and were to be used in aggressions against Canada rather than in an attack upon the jail at Whitesboro.

I have also communicated to the President[2] the facts that the British Authorities had provided two armed steam vessels on the Niagara river, and that this preparation for war produced much inquietude upon the American side of the Lake. I took the liberty at the same time to inquire whether the British Government had given notice to the President of its desire to annul the stipulation between the two countries, by which the naval force to be maintained upon the lakes by the respective parties was limited. I further submitted that it was important to put upon the Lakes an armament at least equal to that established by the British Government.

It is now my duty to offer some further considerations upon the same subject. I mentioned in my letter of the 21st[3] that a magazine at Lockport had been entered, and that a large quantity of gun-powder was removed therefrom. I received information last evening that an attempt had been made, with partial success, to blow up the locks on the Wellands Canal at Allenburgh in Upper Canada.

It was stated in the Buffalo Commercial Advertiser of Saturday last that the British Steam Ships the Minos and Toronto had moved out into the river between Navy Island and the Canada shore, and that during Friday night the vessels were fired upon by persons who had for that purpose taken a field-piece from the American Shore.[4]

By letters just received from the Honorable H[oratio] J. Stow[5] Re-

1. See above, Seward to DW, September 3, 1841.

2. See above, Seward to DW, September 17, 1841.

3. Seward to DW, September 21, 1841, DNA, RG 59 (Misc. Letters).

4. The Washington, D.C., *National Intelligencer*, September 23, 1841, carries an account of these events drawn from the New York *Commercial Advertiser*.

5. Stow (d. 1859) was judge of the Recorder's Court of the city, 1839–1842, and before that a lawyer in Buffalo.

corder of the city of Buffalo, and the Honorable Seth C[otton] Hawley[6] a member of Assembly residing in the same city, I am confirmed in the truth of the representations I have heretofore made concerning the alarmed and excited state of public feeling among the citizens on this side of the frontier.

There are I think sufficient indications of popular discontent in Canada, to warrant a belief that efforts will be made there to overthrow the Government. It cannot be questioned that among the citizens of the frontier counties in this State, and the Western States, there are strong sympathies favoring such a movement. If it be admitted, as I presume to be the case, that the immense military and naval preparation made in Canada have for their object the suppression of intestine commotions and the preservation of tranquility, it is equally manifest that those preparations carried on in full view of the American shore, are regarded by many of our citizens, as having for their design some aggression against this country. It is hardly to be expected that, if a civil war should again break out in Canada, absolute neutrality could be maintained on this side of the frontier under existing laws. And it therefore seems, with all respect, to me to be very important that the Northern frontier be put into a condition of defence. I need not say that its condition now is in no degree secure. The Commerce of Lake Erie is immence—a very considerable trade is carried on also upon Lake Ontario and Lake Champlain. The British Government have now two large Steam ships on the Niagara river above the falls, completely armed and manned, and they are building another, said to be of Nine hundred tons burden at Kingston on Lake Ontario. Probably there are not less than ten thousand regular troops in the Canadas.[7] On our side of the frontier we have not an armed vessel, nor a full regiment of troops. Should hostilities break out, our commerce could be swept from the Lakes, and our towns be destroyed before force could be gathered for their defence.

The troubles to which I have adverted lie much deeper than the prosecution against Alexander McLeod, and although the conviction and execution of that person, might bring on a catastrophe, his acquittal and deliverance would not restore tranquility or remove the grounds of apprehension and alarm.

Under these circumstances, I deem it my duty to call upon the Government of the United States to adopt measures for putting our North-

6. Hawley (1810–1884), a lawyer, public speaker, and editor of the *Buffalo Express*, represented Buffalo in the state assembly in 1840 and 1841. He assisted the prosecution at the trial of McLeod. Hawley was closely associated politically with Seward and the New York Whig leader Thurlow Weed (1797–1882).

7. In November 1840 there were 11,000 British regular troops and 2,500 volunteers.

ern frontier in a perfect condition of defence with as little delay as possible. Major General [Winfield] Scott has submitted to me plans which he informs me have been laid before the President.[8] They contemplate the purchase and fitting up of four Steamboats on Lake Erie—of two on Lake Champlain, and of the completion as a steamer of the large ship of War now on the Stocks at Sacketts Harbor. I beg leave to express my concurrence in these recommendations of General Scott. Extensive as these preparations would be, they are indispensably necessary to secure the frontier against the force actually held by the British Government now for aggression upon our frontier. It seems to me indispensable therefore that such ample measures of defence, should be adopted. I hope moreover that the troops at the several stations on the frontier will be reinforced. I learn that the quantities of ammunition and arms at the stations are very small, and quite insufficient for an exigency of defence. I hope that the Secretary of War [John Canfield Spencer] may think it proper to send ample supplies without delay. I would promptly send such supplies from the arsenals and magazines of this state, if it were not, that in the absence of any proper provision for guarding the stores, they might fall into the hands of agitators and be used for mischievous purposes.

My Secretary, Major [Samuel] Blatchford,[9] who is now at Utica, reports that he finds, a large quantity of gun-powder there belonging to citizens of that place, and lying in a magazine—that measures have been taken to guard the depository, and that the Mayor of Utica[10] very cheerfully entered into the investigation you recommended but as yet no discoveries have been made. I send herewith some extracts from the letters of Mr Stow and Mr Hawley to which reference has been made. I have the honor, to be, With my high respect, Your obedient Servant

William H. Seward

L S . DNA, RG 59 (Misc. Letters). Rec'd September 23, 1841. Endorsed by DW: "Answer that his letter has been rec'd, & will be submitted to the President."

TO WILLIAM HENRY SEWARD

Department of State,
Sir: Washington, 23d September, 1841.

Your letter of the 17th instant[1] respecting the Steam Boats, building

8. See Scott to Secretary of War Bell, September 15, 1841, Seward Papers, University of Rochester. Scott recommended the purchase of a number of steamers to be deployed on the Great Lakes.

9. Blatchford (1820–1893; Columbia 1837) was the son of Seward's friend and political ally, Richard Milford Blatchford (1798–1875; Union

College 1815). Samuel Blatchford later practiced law in New York and was appointed to the U.S. Supreme Court in 1882.

10. Spencer Kellogg (1786–1871) served as mayor of Utica, New York, in 1841.

1. See above, Seward to DW, September 17, 1841.

at Chippewa, was duly received, and inquiry will be made upon that subject. You probably recollect the note from Mr [Henry Stephen] Fox to Mr [John] Forsyth of the 25th of November, 1838,[2] respecting a proposed increase of British naval force on the Lakes; a copy of which, however, I now enclose.

We hear with regret this morning that an attempt has been made to destroy the steam boats at Chippewa,[3] by the discharge of artillery from Navy Island. If we cannot repress these lawless acts, we shall ere long be involved in an inglorious border warfare, of incursion and retaliation, ending perhaps in general hostilities. I am sure we shall have Your Excellency's cordial concurrence on all attempts to bring these offenders to public justice. I have the honor to be, Your Excellency's most obedient servant,   Danl Webster

L S. NRU.

FROM JOSHUA AUSTIN SPENCER

Private
Sir,   Utica 24. Sept. 1841
The time is near at hand when the trial of [Alexander] McLeod is to come on. I have no doubt all sorts of rumors will reach Washington in relation to it. So far as I am able to judge the general belief here is that he had nothing to do with the attack on the Caroline & that he will be acquitted. The public mind in the country is quiet; our Sheriff [David Moulton] has taken pains to put every juror drawn on his guard about being approached on the Subject of the trial.

The attacking party was armed with Guns, Pistols, pikes and cutlasses as is shown by the testimony taken on Commission. The testimony of Col. [Allan] McNab, Thomas Hector, Angus McLeod & Thomas Harris[1] is now returned. It is strong to prove that McLeod had nothing to do with it. Mr. [Hiram] Gardner was at the last advising still in Canada attending to the Execution of other Commissions: Some eight or ten witnesses will attend from Canada to establish the *alibi* in addition to

2. Fox to Forsyth, November 25, 1838, DNA, RG 59 (Notes from Foreign Legations, Britain).

3. DW is probably referring to the account of the incident in the Washington, D.C., *National Intelligencer* of September 23, 1841.

1. Hector, a clerk in the Canadian government, was a member of the raiding party. McLeod, the brother of Alexander McLeod, reportedly did participate in the attack and bore a striking resemblance to the defendant. It may be that the arrest and trial of Alexander McLeod was a case of mistaken identity for his brother. Spencer may mean John Harris, also a member of the boarding party, whose deposition was read at the trial.

the testimony on commission. The proof on this point will be strong and I think *impregnable*.

We understand the Atty. Gen. [Willis Hall] and Dist. Atty. [Jonathan L. Woods] *with many aids*, are making great preparation for the trial. In short I think much evidence will be given to connect him (Mc-L[eod]) with the affair, but it will be from "patriots & refugees" I have to day received letters from Ontario Co. and from Warren, Penna.[2] informing me that desperate villains are coming on as witnesses & giving me their character & history. Mr [Alvin C.] Bradley has written me to day that Mr. [Jonathan L.] Woods the Dist. Atty. keep every thing in darkness. Seth C[otton] Hawley Esq. a Member of Assembly (Gov. [William Henry] Sewards candidate for U.S. Atty.) has been up to Detroit after a Straw deal witness & has just returned. And now gives out, Mr. Bradley says falsely, that he knows nothing & will not attend. The whole conduct of the Atty. Gen. is secret & every effort is making to connect the Prisoner. In this I trust he will fail.

Mr Justice [Samuel] Nelson is too ill to hold the Court. Judge [Philo] Gridley I am happy to say will hold the Circuit. He has no feelings with the Patriots.

I shall know in two or three days much more of the prospects & will then again write you. Other Commissions are expected every mail & Mr. G[ardner] and B[radley] will be here I expect tomorrow. I have strong confidence not free from apprehension. Very truly Yours

J. A. Spencer

ALS. NhHi.

DANIEL FLETCHER WEBSTER TO HENRY STEPHEN FOX

Department of State,

Sir: Washington, 28th Sept. 1841

I am instructed by the President of the United States, in the absence of the Secretary of State,[1] to invite your attention to the accompanying evidence of an outrage said to have been committed on the night of the 19th instant, at the town of Alburg, within the limits of the State of Vermont, on the person of one James W. Grogan,[2] by a party of armed Brit-

---

2. Not found.

1. DW left Washington September 27 to spend several weeks at Marshfield, leaving Fletcher as acting secretary of state.

2. Grogan (b. 1794) was born in the United States but moved to Lower Canada in 1820. He gained notoriety during the Canadian rebellion of 1837 and fled to Vermont. Since May

1841 he had been a resident of Lockport, New York. See Samuel H. Jenison to DW, September 29, 1841, DNA, RG 59 (Misc. Letters), and see below, Sworn Deposition of Grogan, [October 13, 1841]. Jenison (1791–1849), affiliated with the Vermont Anti-Mason party and endorsed by the Whigs, was elected governor in 1836 and served until 1841.

ish soldiers, under the command of their officers. It will appear from these documents that on the night above mentioned, between the hours of two and three o'clock, the dwelling house of William Brown,[3] situated in the town of Alburg, was forcibly entered by a party of armed men, and that, in addition to other acts of violence, the said James W. Grogan, after the infliction upon his person of serious injuries, was seized and carried off, and is said now to be detained in close confinement by the military authorities in Canada.

The President cannot but feel the greatest anxiety as to this most extraordinary transaction. He will not permit himself to doubt but that the British Government will institute an immediate inquiry into all the circumstances attendant upon an act so well calculated to disturb the peaceful relations which now subsist between the Government of Her Britannic Majesty and that of the United States, and that it will immediately upon being informed of the circumstances under which this seizure was made, order the liberation of said Grogan from confinement, and bring to speedy and condign punishment the perpetrators of this violation of the territorial rights of the United States.

I am further instructed by the President, respectfully but urgently, to invite your earliest attention to the subject of this note.

I avail myself of this occasion to offer to you the assurance of my high consideration.   F. Webster Acting Secretary

L C. DNA, RG 59 (Notes to Foreign Legations, Britain). Published in CR, 3:155. Webster was the chief clerk at the State Department. The various enclosures mentioned in this letter are not printed here, but their content is adequately summarized by Fletcher Webster.

FROM WILLIAM HENRY SEWARD

Executive Department
Sir,   Albany October 13th 1841.

I have the honor to inform you that the trial of Alexander McLeod for murder alleged to have been committed in the attack upon the Caroline closed yesterday, and has resulted in the acquittal of the prisoner. I am with very high respect, Your obedient servant,   William H. Seward

A L S . DNA, RG 59 (Misc. Letters). Rec'd October 15, 1841.

SWORN DEPOSITION OF JAMES W. GROGAN

[October 13, 1841]

James W. Grogan of Lockport in the County of Niagara and State of New York of the age of forty-seven years being solemnly sworn to tell the truth and nothing but the truth deposes and says that he was born in Petersburgh in the County of Rensaeller and State of New-York at

3. Grogan's brother-in-law; not otherwise identified.

which place and vicinity he continued to reside untill the year 1815 when he removed to Alburgh in the County of Grand-Isle and State of Vermont where he married and continued to live laboring in the business of farming untill the year 1820. In that year he deposes that he removed to Noyon a Seignory in the Province of Lower Canada a few miles from the Line between the United States and said Province. He there purchased a Lot of land removed his family on to it erected buildings and made other improvements thereon, and continued to reside on said farm and in an adjoining Seignory, untill the Fall of the year 1837 the time of breaking out of the disturbances in Lower Canada at which time he thought it prudent to leave the Province of Canada and cross into Vermont leaving however his family then consisting of a wife and eleven children still living in Canada. He remained in Vermont and other parts of the United States untill the Fall of 1838 making secretly several short visits to his family during the year. In 1838 he returned openly in consequence of an Amnesty promulgated by the Governor of Canada and joined his family. He further deposes and says that in about ten days he was forcibly expelled from the Province by one Lieut. Johnson[1] and several men belonging to a Volunteer Corpse in the service of the Canadian Government. His family soon followed him and ever since he and they have continued to reside in different places in the United States. The Deponent further deposes and says that during the whole time of his residence in Canada he never made any renunciation of citizenship in the United States—never went through with any process of naturalization in said Province or took any oath of allegiance to the Government thereof or to the British Government. This Deponent says that soon after the removal of himself and family into the United States in December 1838 his house and barns were destroyed by fire and as this Deponent is informed and believes by order of an Officer in the service of the Provincial Government.

In the month of May 1841 the Deponent removed to Lockport the place of his present residence. On the 9th day of September last he set out from there to visit St. Albans Franklin County Vermont to attend Court there, having a suit pending in the County Court in which he was a party. The suit grew out of injuries and destruction of property during the disturbances in the Province and the antagonist party was a resident in the Province and an Officer in the Volunteer Militia.[2] The deponent arrived at Alburgh on the 18th day of September and staid over night at the Inn of John M Sowls[3] a few rods only from the Line. This was Saturday night. On Sunday forenoon Deponent saw at said Sowls

1. Not identified.
2. Grogan filed a suit against Nathaniel B. Beardsly for his part in the destruction of Grogan's property in Canada in 1838. Grogan to John Tyler, October 12, 1841, DNA, RG 59 (Misc. Letters).
3. Not identified.

several persons living on the Canadian side of the Line with whom he had previously been acquainted and among the number three soldiers belonging to the Light Dragoons who said they were there in the public service drawing pay from Government, all of which three soldiers the Deponent recognised in the party, which on Sunday evening attacked and kidnapped him as herein after set forth. The Deponent left Sowles on Sunday afternoon to go to the house of William Brown living in Alburgh a Brother in Law of Deponent in proceeding thither he purposely avoided the direct road which for a part of the distance ran on or near the Line from some apprehensions that he might be seized and carried off, and took a circuitous route and reached there about eight oclock in the evening. Brown resides about three miles in a direct course from the Line, as the road runs it is perhaps five miles. The Deponent remained in conversation with said Browns family untill ten or eleven oclock when they & Deponent retired to rest. The house is a one story one with two front rooms and a Kitchen in the rear and two bed rooms adjoining each other. In one of these the Deponent slept, in the other Mr. Brown & his wife.

Soon after 3 oclock, the Deponent being awake, the front door was suddenly burst open and a party of men to the number as near as the Deponent can judge of twelve or fifteen rushed in, one of them carrying a lantern. The two formost were armed with bayonets—the others or most of them were armed with guns & most of them had on their Military badges & dress being the same that the Deponent had often seen worn by the Light Dragoons. The two formost men rushed into or towards Mr. Browns bed room and at this moment Deponent sprang out of bed onto the floor and on being discovered the door being open, they cried out 'there he is'—others cried out 'shoot him' 'blow his brains out' 'put your bayonet into him.'

At this moment two of the soldiers made a rush at the Deponent with their bayonets. Deponent parried the thrusts as well as he could with his hands having no weapons at hand and having no clothes on except his shirt.

A sharp but short contest ensued during which the Deponent was wounded in several places with the bayonet, the severest of which was in the left groin, was violently draged out of the house into the street. Here another portion of the party were stationed. During the struggle in rushing towards the street some had hold of Deponents head others hold of his arms & cries of this sort were uttered 'Damn you why dont you shoot him?' 'Why dont you blow his brains out?'

Here the Deponent fully believing that they intended to murder him on the spot made a desperate effort to free himself from them and at one time very nearly succeeded. He was however overpowered and compelled to submit. In this struggle the Deponent was much bruised and several times wounded with bayonets—was finally forced into a waggon in a perfect state of nudity in a chilly night covered with blood and dirt. The Deponent was once knocked down with the breach of a gun, he was jumped upon by several and choked untill entirely deprived of streangth. He was thrown down in the bottom of the waggon on his back across two muskets & was held down by two men. One sat upon his body & two held his head and a bayonet was placed across his throat. In this condition he was driven at a rapid pace towards Canada. The Deponent begged of them to remove the guns from under him as they caused him great pain & also begged them to get off from him but they paid no heed to either. He then begged them to kill him at once and not thus murder him by piece meal. They drove a distance of about five miles, which brought them into Canada. They then relaxed somewhat and allowed the Deponent to sit up as he was greatly exhausted faint and thirsty. He requested them to give him some water, but they refused saying 'You damed Rebel you will soon be where you will get a plenty of water.' Soon after they started off for Clarenceville a small village about four miles from the Line, being still closely confined and guarded and entirely naked. They arrived at Clarenceville before day light and he was here put into the *guard house* and sentinels placed over him; here again Deponent asked for water and they refused to give him any for some time, but at last brought some warm water. Deponent begged for cold water, but they told him to take that or none. The only bed he had to lie on in the guard room was a Buffalo skin. At about eight oclock in the forenoon he was furnished with a shirt & a pair of cotton pantaloons. While here the soldiers insulted him with much opprobrious language. After receiving some refreshment at about 10 oclock Deponent was put again into the same waggon and conducted by soldiers to Missisqui Bay ten miles from Clarenceville where he was placed in the *guard house.* This post is commanded by Col. Dyer[4] of the British Army, and here he was ironed with hand cuffs, and such with the usual insulting language. He was taken as he supposed before a Magistrate for examination, but no question was asked except what was his name, to which the Deponent replied by giving his name. He was then ordered back to the guard house.

A waggon was then brought and Deponent placed on board & transported <him> under an escort of four Dragoons to Montreal. On the way he received from his friends his clothes from Alburgh & some money. At St. Johns he was placed for the night in the Police station a cold dirty place with nothing to sleep on but an old rug. They refused to supply him with food here, though he had eat nothing after leaving

4. Not identified.

Clarenceville & offered to pay for food. He was compelled to walk from the station to the Railroad cars a distance of about 100 rods, though scarcely able to walk & though he earnestly requested to be conveyed there. He was then conveyed to Montreal & there confined in the guard house a few hours and thence taken to the Jail. Here he was thrust in among felons and rogues of the vilest and most debased description and allowed no other food but bread and water for three or four days. Afterwards he was supplied with other kinds of food by paying for it. The Deponent continued in jail from the 21st of September to the 4th of October and during that time he was furnished with no Copy of any Indictment—no charges of any kind and was not informed when or for what he was to be tried.

On the 4th of October the Sheriff called the Deponent into the office and read an order from Sir Richard [Downes] Jackson[5] the acting Governor of Canada to release him and convey him to the New-York or Vermont Line as he might choose. He was forthwith conducted under the escort of Capt. Comeau[6] and a Police Officer to Alburgh travelling nearly all one night reaching Alburgh at 3 oclock on the morning of the 5th of October. Capt. Comeau and the other officer conducted with perfect civility. The Deponent further says that David Bartlow, Harry Frith, Patric Martin, Stephen Flagg, Robert Hagelton, Seth Phillips, Seargeant Read McVicar and Wood[7] were of the party which seized Deponent all of whom were soldiers in her Majestys service except Phillips & Flagg.

The Deponent further says that no compensation was made him for the unlawful seizure and detention and nothing offered him on reaching Alburgh except that Liberty of which he had been robed. Swanton October 13. 1841   James W Grogan

State of Vermont ⎫
Franklin County ⎭   At Swanton this 13th day of October

A.D. 1841 personally appeared James W Grogan above named to me well known & made solemn oath that the above Deposition contains the truth & nothing but the truth. Before me James Fisk Justice of Peace[8]

Copy. DNA, RG 59 (Misc. Letters). Grogan's deposition was taken by Charles Davis, U.S. attorney for Vermont, and William Barron, a U.S. marshal. Neither Barron nor Davis could be further identified. It was forwarded to Webster on October 15. Davis and Barron to DW, October 15, 1841, DNA, RG 59 (Misc. Letters).

5. Jackson (1777–1845), a professional soldier, served as commander in chief of Canada, 1840–1845, and as acting governor, 1841–1842.

6. Not identified.
7. None identified.
8. Not further identified.

FROM CHARLES DAVIS AND WILLIAM BARRON

Sir,   Montpelier Oct 16. 1841

We addressed you a short communication from St. Albans yesterday
and transmitted therewith James W Grogans Deposition taken at Swanton in our presence.[1] We reached this place this morning and now proceed agreeably to intimations therein to report to your Department our
proceedings more in detail. Having a few days before learned that Grogan
had been released we left Burlington in company on the 12th. inst. hoping to fall in with him before he should have left this part of the
Country.

This we were so fortunate as to do just as he was about to leave for
his home in New York. He readily consented to remain and give us a
full and accurate account of the outrage committed upon him. The
result is contained in the Deposition forwarded. He is an intelligent
man, and we see no reason to doubt the substantial accuracy of his
statement, according as it does in general with various narrations published in Newspapers derived from him; and corroborated as it is in part
by the Depositions of Mr. [William] Brown and his family. We may
venture therefore to refer to it as containing an authentic history of the
transaction.

We endeavored to procure additional information on some points beyond the scope of his personal knowledge, particularly in reference to
the origin of the expedition, and whether the same was countenanced
or authorised by the Canadian Authorities either civil or military. In
this we were not so fortunate as we could have wished. As the evidence
on this point must necessarily for the most part be derived from the
other side of the Line and as we had no means of drawing it thence, we
are unable to speak with any confidence on the subject of the rumors
that have prevailed. It has never been suggested so far as we know that
the officers, in civil authority in the Province were in any manner chargeable with it, and we have nothing beyond hearsay and reports on which
to ground a belief that any Military Officer either participated in or
countenanced it before hand. Still we incline to think the interference
or at least connivance of some one or more commissioned Officers highly
probable. After taking Grogan's Deposition we proceeded immediately to
Alburgh—visited the scene of the outrage—conversed with Mr. Brown
and family—went to different parts of the Town, and onto the Line,
communicating freely with the People there, and apprising them of the
object of our visit and the authority under which we acted.

All appeared to be gratified with the prompt action of this General
Government as well as with that of the Executive of this State [Samuel
H. Jenison] in despaching agents to the scene with directions to investi-

1. See above.

gate the facts. These proceedings were well calculated to allay any symptoms of disorder and to inspire confidence that whatever might be required by the interest and honor of the Country would be promptly attended to by the proper Authorities. The recent Proclamation of the President[2] and various publications which had appeared in the Newspapers had prepared us to expect to find on the Northern border of this State some elements of confusion and disorder which might be readily roused into action upon the occurrence of events of the character of the one in question. In this we were happily disappointed. It was evident that the disorderly state of things which existed at the close of the years 1837 and 1838 no longer existed.

We could not find on inquiry any ground to suppose that secret associations existed here having hostile views towards the neighboring Province; or that Agents or emissaries of secret associations elsewhere were or had been prowling about in this quarter. Grogan was the only person from a distance so far as we could learn whose presence was calculated to excite apprehensions in the minds of the peaceably disposed on either side of the Line; and if his own declarations on oath can be relied on he came here merely to attend to his own private affairs. For these reasons we deemed it unnecessary for us to remain longer in Alburgh or the vicinity, and therefore determined to return to our respective homes, after having drawn up and despached a joint report of our proceedings.

Having mentioned our intention to forward Copies of certain Depositions, taken by directions of his Excellency Govr. Jenison, which he had permitted us to examine at Burlington on our way North, we now would observe that on our arrival here we were informed by him that he had already forwarded them to your Department.[3] We have therefore no further Documents to transmit.

It may not be improper to say further that Govr. Jension has politely shewn to us here a communication which he has just received from Sir Richard [Downes] Jackson, acting Governor of Canada, in reply to a communication made by the former,[4] a Copy of which we have also been permitted to see, couched in the most friendly and satisfactory terms. It is scarsely necessary to say that it explicitly disavowed the acts of those persons, whoever they were, that were concerned in the trans-

2. Tyler issued a proclamation on September 25, 1841, denouncing secret societies and filibusters against Canada. *Messages and Papers*, 4:72–73.

3. See Jenison to DW, September 29, 1841, DNA, RG 59 (Misc. Letters).

4. Jenison to Jackson, September 29, 1841, and Jackson to Jenison, October 6, 1841. The correspondence was submitted to the Vermont legislature on October 20, 1841, and is published in the *Journal of the House of Representatives of the State of Vermont, October Session, 1841* (Montpelier, Vt., 1841), pp. 41 and app., 91–93.

action—promises an immediate investigation into the circumstances, and the prompt discharge of Grogan should it be found that he was seized as alledged in the State of Vermont, and the adoption of the most vigorous measures to bring to punishment any Officers or soldiers in the service of the Government, that may be proved to have taken part in the outrage. We presume this communication and others connected with the subject will in a few days be laid before the Legislature now in session in this place, by Governor [Charles] Paine,[5] and will then be made public.

It only remains for us to add that should future events in the opinion of the Department render our presence on the Frontier necessary, we hold ourselves ready on the receipt of orders to that effect, to repair thither as speedily as possible, determined to exert whatever influence we possess to cause the Laws to be respected and to preserve the peace and tranquility of our border. We have the honor to subscribe ourselves, Sir your obt. servts. Charles Davis, U.S. Atty William Barron Marshal for the District of Vermont

A L S. DNA, RG 59 (Misc. Letters). Rec'd October 22, 1841.

FROM GEORGE C. BATES

Confidential
Sir   Detroit, Octo 20 1841
Your Confidential Communication relative to the movements of the marauders on the Frontier was duly received[1] and my pressing Engagements in our Court (now in session) has prevented an earlier reply. I am *now* and have been since my appointment in daily communication with Gen [Hugh] Brady,[2] and the other officers of the Government, and nothing has or will transpire on the subject without all of the officers both here and in Washington being advised at once. I have a Confidential friend,[3] a Lawyer of respectable standing who is a member of the Patriot association here and *on whom I can rely*. There is no contemplated movement in this quarter as yet; indeed they merely keep up

5. Paine (1779–1853; Harvard 1820), a Whig, was elected governor in 1841 and served until 1843.

1. See Webster's confidential letter of September 25, 1841, enclosed in Secretary of the Treasury to Collectors, October 2, 1841, DNA, RG 56 (General Records of the Department of the Treasury, Letters sent to Collectors of Small Ports).

2. Brady (1768–1851) joined the army in 1792 and fought in the War of 1812. He was assigned in 1835 to the Detroit frontier, where he presided over efforts to curtail the operations of the Patriots. Among his troops may be counted the civilian militia known as the "Brady Guards," which included George C. Bates among its members. *Report of the Pioneer Society of the State of Michigan* (Lansing, 1901), 2:573–579.

3. Not identified.

their organisation without having any definite views for the future. Their society is more respectable in the character of its members than formerly, but is really of no consequence. They have no arms, munitions, drills nor indeed any military organisation, their meetings are occasional and poorly attended. Indeed the ferment seems fast to be aging away, and the little of excitement that remained, has entirely evaporated since [Alexander] McLeods acquittal.[4]

It is possible that when our river is closed they may merely to keep up the bad feeling, cross in small parties at night and burn barracks, and military storehouses, but I am satisfied they have no intention to undertake any concentrated Effort. The laws as you of course know are now wholly insufficient for any cases of this kind and should be promptly amended. But the Government may rest assured that so far as it devolves on their servants at this point both civil and military that its very letter shall be faithfully, honestly and fearlessly executed. I see Gen Brady daily and I shall communicate to him and to the Department, every movement that may be worthy of notice. At present there is not the least cause of anxiety so far as this portion of the frontier is concerned. Respectfully Your Obt Sert   Geo C Bates   U S Dis Atty   Mich

ALS. DNA, RG 59 (Misc. Letters). Rec'd October 27, 1841. Bates (1812–1886; Hobart College 1831) studied law in New York in the office of John Canfield Spencer before moving to Detroit in 1833. He was the Michigan representative to the Whig convention at Harrisburg that nominated William Henry Harrison for the presidency and in 1841 was named U.S. attorney for Michigan.

FROM FRANCIS ORMAND JONATHAN SMITH

Private
Dear Sir—   Portland Novr 20th 1841
    Since I had the honor to write you last on the subject of our Boundary dispute,[1] I have visited different parts of the State, and had extensive personal and epistolary intercourse with the leading men of both parties—and I am persuaded the way is now prepared for a vigorous movement among our people towards the necessary preliminaries of a satisfactory compromise of the dispute.
    I have commenced publishing the outline of them, in a politically

4. For a contrasting view of the strength and intentions of the so-called Patriot societies, see John W. Allen to DW, October 29, 1841, DNA, RG 59 (Misc. Letters). Allen estimated that there were 400 "disorganizers" in the Cleveland, Ohio, area "determined on mischief," and he requested that federal troops be sent to that city. One of Webster's problems as secretary of state was how to respond to such conflicting reports as those of Bates and Allen about the secretive Patriot organizations.

1. See above, Smith to DW, July 2, 1841.

neutral, but extensively circulated religious paper,[2] from which I have so arranged I think, as to secure their reprint in the party newspapers of this State on both sides. And if in this I shall succeed, I feel confident all that was desired, will be accomplished through the Legislature.

Now what is most wanting is, the means of employing a few persons in different parts of the State, in whom I can repose confidence, to devote their time for a month or two next coming, in getting memorials circulated among, and signed by the people, as a basis and inducement for the action of the Legislature. One or two such men in each county, if I could indemnify them for their time and services, would give an effective concentration of the public sense upon points desired for Legislative action. The truth is, divest a subject of *party* interest, and *party* excitement, and it becomes that sort of "every body's business which nobody attends to"—and from that moment it becomes necessary to make it, in some special manner, the business of some, or it will expire from stagnation. If two or three thousand dollars could be rightfully employed in forwarding this matter *at this juncture*, it will accomplish more than armies can do after the subject shall be revived in a belligerent spirit.

Herewith, I send the first article published, already adverted to, & will forward its successor shortly. If you were to consult Gov. [Albion Keith] Parris,[3] of the Comptroller's office, he would cause its republication by the [Washington] Globe, without connecting any name with the request, and the effect might be good here. I have the honor to be with great respect Your Obt Servt.   Francis O.J. Smith

A L S . NhHi. Published in Frederick Merk, *Fruits of Propaganda in the Tyler Administration* (Cambridge, Mass., 1971), pp. 156–157.

TO EDWARD EVERETT

No. 5   Department of State,
Sir: Washington, 20th Nov. 1841.

Although the Department is yet without advice of your arrival in London, I indulge the hope that ere this you will have reached that city, and, having received the archives and other effects of the Legation from Mr. [Thomas] Aspinwall, that you are prepared to enter on the discharge

2. Smith refers to the article published in the Portland, Maine, *Christian Mirror* on November 18, 1841. Smith's article appears under the name "Agricola" and is reprinted in Merk, *Fruits of Propaganda*, pp. 158–172.

3. Parris (1788–1857; Dartmouth 1806), a prominent figure in Maine politics, was governor of Maine from 1822 to 1827 and second comptroller of the U.S. Treasury from 1836 to 1849.

of the duties of your mission. It is not doubted in that event, that you will have given the records of the Legation your early attention, and that you will have perceived, upon a perusal of the recent correspondence between the late Minister of the United States in Great Britain [Andrew Stevenson], and Her Britannic Majesty's Secretary of State for Foreign Affairs [Lord Aberdeen], that among the several subjects which have been discussed between them, those of the most commanding interest and highest importance are, 1st The capture and destruction of the Steamboat "Caroline," at Schlosser, in December, 1837, and the murder of an American citizen by an armed expedition from the Province of Canada, acting under the command of officers in Her Majesty's service, and 2ndly the seizure, search, and detention, by British armed cruisers, of American vessels, principally on the western coast of Africa, under the pretence that such vessels were engaged, or intended to engage, in the African Slave Trade.

There are other points remaining unsettled in the relations between the United States and Great Britain,—especially that respecting the northeastern boundary of the United States,—which are in a course of negotiation between this Department and the British Legation here, but to these it is now only necessary to allude generally.—those of the greatest urgency, weight, and delicacy, under discussion in London, at the present time, are the two first mentioned. Mr. Stevenson's correspondence with this Department reaches down to the 22d ultimo.[1] His last despatches have come to hand too recently to have received as yet full consideration. Instructions will be given you, relative to these important subjects, in due season, and while these instructions are in the course of preparation and transmission, the President directs me to invite your particular examination of the correspondence upon them above referred to. I am, Sir, your obedient servant,   Danl. Webster

LC. DNA, RG 59 (Instructions, Britain).

FROM HENRY STEPHEN FOX

Washington
Sir   November. 26th 1841
With reference to any recent correspondence with the Acting Secretary of State [Daniel Fletcher Webster],[1] upon the subject of the capture and arrest, and subsequent release by order of Her Majesty's Authorities in Canada, of the individual named James Grogan, I am now further

1. No. 134. Stevenson to DW, October 22, 1841, DNA, RG 59 (Despatches, Britain).

1. See above, Daniel Fletcher Webster to Fox, September 28, 1841; see also Fox to Daniel Fletcher Webster, October 21, 1841, DNA, RG 59 (Notes from Foreign Legations, Britain).

enabled to state to you, that Her Majesty's Government in England, upon receiving the first report of the improper arrest and detention of Grogan, and before the arrival of any official communication upon the subject, had immediately transmitted orders to the Acting Governor of Canada [Sir Richard Downes Jackson] for the release of Grogan, and for his restoration to the State of Vermont if the illegality of the arrest should be confirmed.

The Acting Governor of Canada had in the meantime, as you are already informed, anticipated the desire of Her Majesty's Government in this respect, and had further directed an inquiry to be made into the circumstances of Grogan's arrest, with the view of visiting with suitable punishment any persons in Her Majesty's service who should be proved to have been concerned in the affair. The United States Government will perceive that the whole proceeding in this case has been the prompt and voluntary decision of Her Majesty's Government. It has arisen from their own sense of justice, and from a desire to make amends where wrong is proved to have been committed.

I avail myself of this occasion to renew to you the assurance of my distinguished consideration.   H. S. Fox

L S . DNA, RG 59 (Notes from Foreign Legations, Britain). Rec'd November 27, 1841. Published in CR, 3:683–684.

TO HENRY STEPHEN FOX

Department of State,
Sir: Washington, 27th Nov 1841
    Your letter of the 21st ultimo,[1] to the acting Secretary of State [Daniel Fletcher Webster], was duly received at the Department, and I have now the honor to acknowledge, also, the receipt of your letter of the 26th of this month,[2] in which you say "that Her Majesty's Government in England, upon receiving the first report of the improper arrest and detention of [James W.] Grogan, and before the arrival of any official communication upon the subject, had immediately transmitted orders to the Acting Governor of Canada [Sir Richard Downes Jackson] for the release of Grogan, and for his restoration to the State of Vermont if the illegality of the arrest should be confirmed."

I am directed by the President to express his sense of the very proper and prompt manner in which Her Majesty's Government in England, as well as Her Canadian authorities have acted in the case of Grogan; and he trusts that equal regard to justice, and to what is due by one friendly

1. Fox to Daniel Fletcher Webster, October 21, 1841, DNA, RG 59 (Notes   from Foreign Legations, Britain). 2. See above.

nation to another, may distinguish every occasion of intercourse between the two Governments.

I pray you to accept renewed assurances of my distinguished considerations. Danl Webster

LC. DNA, RG 59 (Notes to Foreign Legations, Britain). Extract published in CR, 3:157.

TO HENRY STEPHEN FOX

Department of State
Washington, 29th Nov 1841.

The Undersigned, Secretary of State of the United States, has the honor of calling the attention of Mr. [Henry Stephen] Fox, Her Britannic Majesty's Envoy Extraordinary and Minister Plenipotentiary, to a letter addressed to him by the Undersigned, on the 25th of September last,[1] on the subject of two steam vessels of war which were understood to be built, or purchased, and in the process of equipment, at Chippewa, in Canada; and respectfully to invite as early a reply to that letter as Mr. Fox's information and instructions may enable him to give. It was the object of the Convention of 1817 to prevent, both on the part of the United States and England, the necessity of maintaining expensive naval armaments on the Lakes; to place the Parties on a footing of perfect equality, and to remove causes of jealousy and apprehension, on the borders, on the conclusion of the war, by a mutual agreement to disarm, on both Sides, so far as the waters of the lakes were concerned. It is obvious that a rigid compliance with the terms of the Convention by both Parties, can alone accomplish the purposes intended by it. The convention interdicted the *building*, as well as the equipment, of vessels of war beyond the fixed limit. The United States have not been disposed to make complaint of the temporary deviation from this agreement, by the British Government, in 1838 under what was supposed to be a case of clear and urgent necessity for present self-defence. But it cannot be expected that either Party should acquiesce in the preparation by the other, of naval means beyond the limit fixed in the stipulation, and which are of a nature fitting them for offensive as well as defensive use, upon the ground of a vague and indefinite apprehension of future danger. The Undersigned doubts not that Mr. Fox will see the great importance as well as the great delicacy of this subject. Having thus again called Mr. Fox's attention to it, the Undersigned concludes by observing, that the United States cannot consent to any inequality, in regard to the strictness with which the Convention of 1817 is to be observed by the

1. DW to Fox, September 25, 1841, DNA, RG 59 (Notes to Foreign Lega- tions, Britain).

Parties, whether with respect to the amount of naval force, or the time of its preparation or equipment. The reasons for this are obvious, and must immediately force themselves upon Mr. Fox's consideration.

The Undersigned avails himself of this occasion to renew to Mr. Fox the assurance of his distinguished consideration.   Danl Webster

LC. DNA, RG 59 (Notes to Foreign Legations, Britain). Published in *CR*, 3:157–158.

FROM EDWARD EVERETT

(Private)
My dear Sir,   London 15 Decr 1841.

I received a few days ago at Paris your despatch No. 5 of Nov. 20[1] & your private letter of the same date.[2] I write this by the New York packet ship Oxford, in some hope, that it may reach you before the steam packet of the 4th of January, which is the next steam vessel.

I am greatly indebted to the President, to yourself, and my friends generally, who supported my nomination. I wrote a private letter to the President some time ago;[3] and I have also written to thank Mr [Rufus] Choate.[4] I might say many things on the subject, but I will appropriate the paper to topics now of greater interest, only adding that had my nomination to England been withdrawn & any other substituted, I should have declined it.

I arrived here with my family on the Evg of the 13th. We had rather an unpleasant journey from Paris: the passage from Boulogne to Dover was exceedingly disagreeable, & not free from danger. In fact, I wish the gentlemen in the Senate whose opposition delayed the Confirmation of my appointment no worse punishment, than to have to make a hasty journey by land & water from Naples to London, with a large family, at this season of the year.

I am to be presented to the Queen tomorrow. She directed Lord Aberdeen, immediately on my arrival in town being known to him, to invite me to Windsor, to have an audience for the purpose of presenting my credentials, & afterwards to dine with her Majesty, & sleep at the Castle.

I have just had an audience of Lord Aberdeen relative to this reception, and when that affair was disposed of, his Lordship turned the con-

1. See above, DW to Everett, November 20, 1841.

2. DW to Everett, November 20, 1841, mDW 20688.

3. Everett to Tyler, November 23, 1841, Everett Letterbook (Reel 26), Everett Papers, MHi (Microfilm).

4. Everett to Choate, November 30, 1841, Everett Letterbook (Reel 26), Everett Papers, MHi (Microfilm).

versation on [Alexander] McLeod's affair, by asking what course we intended to adopt, by way of reparation to England, for the injury done her, in subjecting to criminal procedure a British subject, acknowledged by you not to be amenable to such a procedure. He said he had directed Mr [Henry Stephen] Fox, not officially to make any demand on the subject, but to confer with you confidentially in reference to it. He hinted at an amendment of the Constitution, which should prevent the recurrence of such a case. Lord Aberdeen had gone over substantially the same ground, in my former interview with him, three weeks ago. He expressed himself to day pretty strongly on the subject. It was not of course one which I was prepared or authorized to discuss with him. I told him I was very glad, that he had not directed Mr Fox to make any demand in reference to such a matter, for that to call upon a foreign state to alter its Constitution, was a measure of great delicacy. I then observed that the whole affair of the Caroline was one of much delicacy and importance; that I was without any particular instructions in reference to it: but that I was sure the President was disposed to adjust that and all other matters in discussion between the two countries, on conditions consistent with the rights & honor of both. Lord Aberdeen replied to this observation, that he considered the McLeod affair,—that is,—the affair of the trial,—as wholly separate from the destruction of the Caroline. He then spoke of the boundary question, observing that he did not himself precisely know the present state of the question, & on my alluding to the proposed joint convention of exploration, said he promised himself nothing from such an arrangement—that it would be an affair of ten years and,—I think he added,—lead to nothing. I expressed myself the opinion that the controversy turned very much on a point (vizt whether the St Johns' was a river flowing into the Atlantic,) which a survey could not settle. After some observations on both sides relative to the former arbitration, he said he believed it impossible to settle the question, except by compromise. I thought it my duty to caution him against placing too much confidence in the report of Mr [George William] Featherstonhaugh,[5] as it was produced under circumstances, which must detract from the weight of that gentleman's authority.

We then conversed on the subject of an outrage committed on the person of Captn [James] Endicott,[6] the master of the American vessel "Lintin," who for some insult offered, as is alleged, to Mr Bean[7] commanding officer of Her Majesty's ship "Herald" in Macao roads, was, on

5. Featherstonhaugh (1786–1866) conducted a survey of the northeastern frontier for the British in 1839 that contributed little to already existing evidence. Featherstonhaugh lived in America for many years and was a prolific author of geological reports and travel accounts.

6. Not identified.

7. Not identified.

the 24th of last, forcibly taken out of his own ship, carried on board the Herald, and kept there two or three hours.[8] Immediately on receiving the information of this outrage, the Government here expressed its high displeasure and ordered Bean to be dismissed from the service and sent home. He was a valuable officer, who had rendered important services in sounding the river of Canton, previous to the late movements in that quarter; and was left in command of the Herald, in the absence of the Captain. I shall transmit the papers officially to you by the packet of the 4th of January.

I notice what you say in your despatch of the 20th, relative to the affair of the Caroline and the question of search. I shall need your particular instructions, how far the views presented & the tone assumed by Mr [Andrew] Stevenson meet your approbation. I am by no means persuaded, that the settlement of either question has been advanced by him: I shall be pleased to find, that the reverse is not the case. In reference to the question of search, you have of course in your recollection the principles laid down by the Supreme Court of the United States, in the case of the Marianna Flora.[9] You will also be pleased to give me the President's views, as to the degree of urgency to be employed, in reference to the demand for redress, in the case of the Caroline.

You have not caused me to be furnished with the cypher usually transmitted, (I believe) by the department to the foreign ministers. I do not know that there is likely to be use for it, but as occasion may arise, it seems as if I should have it. A copy of it may come to light, among the papers of the legation, which I have not yet had time to explore. My predecessor left no inventory of the various articles belonging to the legation, although he received one from Mr [Aaron] Vail.[10] I shall immediately cause one to be prepared.

I have attended to the affair with Mr [John] Watson[11] of the Brunswick Hotel agreeably to your request.

This letter is written in great haste, and for your private eye. I shall

8. While their ships were anchored near each other in Macao Roads, Endicott allegedly hailed the *Herald* "in a loud tone of provoking insolence." The outraged Bean sent an armed guard that seized Endicott, but even on board the *Herald* the recalcitrant American captain challenged the British naval officer to a fistfight and threatened to "send a Kentucky bullet through him." Everett to DW, December 28, 1841, DNA, RG 59 (Despatches, Britain).

9. 11 Wheaton 1 (1826), a case in which DW appeared as counsel. In his opinion Justice Joseph Story declared that no right of search at sea existed in peacetime.

10. Vail (1796–1878) had a long career in the Department of State, serving in the early 1830s as secretary of the legation and then chargé d'affaires at London. From 1838 to 1840, he was chief clerk of the department, and from 1840 to 1842 he acted as chargé at Madrid.

11. Not identified.

write you fully by the steamer of the 4th of January. Meantime I am as ever faithfully & affectionately yours.

A L . MHi.

TO EDWARD KENT

Private

Dear Sir   Washington Decr. 21st 41

I have this <moment> morn'g recd your private letter of the 15th inst.[1] Its contents are important.

I may say to you the negotiations for a Convention to settle the Boundary Question can hardly be said to have made any positive progress, since last year.

Mr [John] Forsythes counter project, deliv'd in Aug. 1840, recd no answer until just before Ld. Palmerston went out of office, in Aug. 1841. It was then answered, & this answer has reviewed the subject,[2] & other correspondence will ere long take place between the parties. This interest of both parties undoubtedly requires a compromise, & I have no doubt that the position which Maine has assumed is the only obstacle to bringing such compromise about. The English Govt cannot treat with us about a compromise, unless we say we have authority to consummate what we agree to; & although I entertain not the slightest doubt of the just authority of this Govt to settle this question by compromise, as well as in any other way, yet in the present posture of affaires, I suppose it will not be prudent to stir, in the direction of <Maine> compromise without the consent of Maine. I am very glad to learn that it is probable that your land agent will give some accurate idea of the value of the land North of the St Johns.

<It seems to me that the navigation of the St Johns, tho' desirable, is not, after all of any great importance. When the lumber is cut away there wo>

Suppose England should be willing *to pay* for the land north of the River, & leave the question of its navigation to be settled hereafter? Or suppose she should be willing to let our line run from the monument to the mouth of Eel River, & then up the St. Johns, and <then> so through the Lakes?

I should be very glad of your thoughts, on these & on all other points; but incline for the present to think with you, that perhaps the easiest mode of getting the parties together for a compromise may be the creation of a Commission

I hope this may be done this session of Congress. Yrs truly

A L draft. NhHi. Published in Van Tyne, p. 248.

1. Not found.   August 24, 1841.
2. See above, Palmerston to Fox,

TO EDWARD EVERETT

Private

My Dear Sir,   Washington Decr. 28. 1841

I recd your private letter[1] with pleasure, & hope that you will thus address me, by every opportunity. I have not yet shown it to the President,
on account of the suggestions it contains respecting the standing of yr
predecessor, in England [Andrew Stevenson], as I am afraid the Presidents sentiments on that point have not come, as yet, to agree with yours
& mine.

I wish, however, that in your next private letter you would write me,
as you intimated, fully on this subject.

I did not doubt your kind reception by Lord Aberdeen. I had some acquaintance with his Lordship, when in England, was quite pleased with
him, and recd a very kind invitation to visit him at his seat in Scotland,
but my time would not allow. When you see him, I pray you present him
my remembrance & personal regards. His relative Lord Morton,[2] <was>
now of the Queen's Household, is one of the most valued acquaintances
I made in England.

I saw little of Sir Robt Peel. He did not do me the honor of a call.

You are called to your present post, My Dear Sir, at a very important
crisis, & it will require all that you can do, as well as all that we can do
here, to get honorably & peacefully thro all the subjects now pending
between us & England.

On the boundary question, you are well informed. You know that a
negotiation is pending for a joint Commission, with an umpirage. It has
made little progress for a twelve month, but it is intended to hasten it.
Mean time, I believe the good people of Maine would not be unwilling to
see a proper *Conventional* line agreed to. There is much difficulty, however, in starting the proposition. It is my intention to send some confidential person to you in March, (perhaps Mr [Daniel] F[letcher] Webster) that the views of the Queen's Govt may be informally sounded, as
to what would be their notion of a compromise line. But this is not to re-
tard the negotiation of the Convention for a Commission.

Then there is the African Question, & the Caroline question, in regard
to both of which I shall write you as soon as possible; & here is another
of slaves set free at Nassau,[3] which is likely to give us new & great trouble. I know your ability and diligence will enable you soon to master
these questions.

1. See above, Everett to DW, December 15, 1841.

2. George Sholto Douglas, Lord
Morton (1789–1858), was related to
Lord Aberdeen by marriage. The Websters visited Lord Morton during
their trip to England in 1839.

3. The *Creole* case; see DW to
Everett, January 29, 1842, below, and
"The Treaty of Washington."

As to our position here, it is not very enviable. You will have become acquainted with occurences up to the end of the Extra Session. The message at the commencement of the present session has been very well recd by the Country. You will see the Presidents plan of a fiscal agent.[4] This, so far as yet appears, is well thought of by the Country, but our information is only from regions near us. How the Whigs, angry with the proceedings of last session, will [accept] this, is at present not certain. Mr [Henry] Clay's acquiescence or cooperation is not to be calculated upon; but how strenuous will be his efforts of opposition is a matter on which he himself has not yet probably made up his mind. The session will be a very interesting one, as among other subjects that of the revision of the Tariff must come up.

We are House keepers here, in the House formerly occupied by Mr [Thomas] Swann. The boys are both here—Edward [Webster] in Mr [Richard Smith] Coxe's office[5]—& we all desire the kindest regards to your family. Yrs faithfully   Danl Webster

P.S. I wish you would make any suggestions you may think proper, on the subject of a Secretary. I am not satisfied with any name that has occurred, or been suggested, as yet, belonging to a person likely to desire the place. In interim, I doubt not you are satisfied with the services of Col [Thomas] Aspinwall.

A L S . MHi. Extract published in P. R. Frothingham, *Edward Everett, Orator and Statesman* (Boston, 1925), p. 237.

TO DEMAS ADAMS[1]

Private and Confidential   Department of State
Sir,   Dec. 30th 1841
The various rumors, statements, and reports which have been, and still continue to be, received in this city, justify a strong and well grounded suspicion that secret societies, artfully arranged, and systematically organized, do now exist on the northern frontier, avowedly intended to produce a Revolution in Canada. These societies where they meet are distinguished and known by the name of lodges, and of late by the name of Chapters. They extend throughout the whole Upper Province of Can-

4. President Tyler delivered his first Annual Message to Congress, December 7, 1841. In it he revealed a plan for a "board of control" over public funds. *Messages and Papers*, 4:84–87.

5. Coxe (1792–1865; Princeton 1808) was known for his practice in real property law. After his gradua-

tion from Dartmouth in 1841, Edward Webster studied law under Coxe. See Edward Webster to DW, July 21, 1841, mDW 19723.

1. Identical letters were sent to other U.S. officials. See DW to Charles W. Kelso, December 30, 1841, mDW 29276.

ada, and, on the American frontier, from Maine through the whole northern line, with branches south, through Ohio, Tennessee and Kentucky.

In the province of Upper Canada, these chapters meet in small numbers to avoid suspicion, and are said to be provided with arms that are secreted but ready at a minutes notice, to be used when the proper time arrives.

On the American frontier it is believed that the Chapters include many men of apparent respectability of character and wealth; many of them enjoying offices of responsibility, bestowed by the people and some of them Government officers. The names of many members are well known here.

The principle places in which these chapters are held are Syracuse, Auburn, Weed's Port, Rochester, Geneva, Lockport and Buffalo,—west of Buffalo, they are to be found at Dunkirk, Erie, Cleaveland, Sandusky and Detroit.

Magazines containing the usual munitions and appointments of war are believed to be in or about Geneva, Buffalo and in the Lake Erie ports, principally however, at Erie and Cleaveland.

It is believed that in the places above mentioned they have now under their control, at Geneva, or in its neighborhood, several thousand stand of arms, and in the Lake Erie ports a considerable number of cannon of various calibres, some of which were purloined or stolen from the public arsenals in Western New York. They have as they secretly say, several tons of cannon balls, a large quantity of powder, with a supply of pistols, bowie-knives and swords.

It is said that they have two Steamboats and several schooners under their control on Lake Erie, and that they have determined to make an invasion of Canada, on or about the 8th of January next, at or near the mouth of Grand river, on Lake Erie, where they expect to take or destroy the Canadian war steamers Toronto and Minos, which are now laid up for the winter at that place, at which time and place it is understood, the patriots in Canada are expected immediately to join them in such numbers as in their opinion will justify their expectations of a successful rebellion, or, in other words a Revolution.

The time fixed for the expedition is understood, as stated, to be on the approaching 8th day of January, and the port they will probably sail from is believed to be either Cleaveland or Erie, if, indeed, they should undertake the enterprize.

It is certain that their agents have been to Grand river, and acquainted themselves with all the particulars of the situation of the two boats.

This is communicated for your information and you are requested to exercise all diligence and vigilance, to prevent, as far as may be in your power, any and all such infractions of the laws of the United States.

It is hoped that Congress will revive the [Neutrality] Act of 1838; but in the meantime all the provisions of existing laws must be rigidly carried into effect. Yrs respectfully   Danl Webster

L S. OHi. Demas Adams (1792–1857) served as U.S. marshal of Ohio from July 1841 to c. 1857.

FROM EDWARD EVERETT

No. 5   Legation of the United States,
Sir,   London 31st Decr 1841.

At a late hour on the evening of the 26th. I received a note from the Earl of Aberdeen, requesting an interview for the following day, when I met him at the Foreign Office agreeably to the appointment. After one or two general remarks upon the difficulty of bringing about an adjustment of the points of controversy between the Governments, by a continuance of the discussions hitherto carried on, he said that her Majesty's Government had determined to take a decisive step toward that end by sending a special Minister to the United States, with a full power to make a final settlement of all matters in dispute. The special minister was not designed to supersede Mr. [Henry Stephen] Fox; whether to be associated with him or not, I did not collect from his lordship's remark. This step was determined on from a sincere and earnest desire to bring the matters so long in controversy to an amicable settlement; and if, as he did not doubt, the same disposition existed at Washington, he thought this step afforded the most favourable and indeed the only means of carrying it into effect. In the choice of the individual for the mission, Lord Aberdeen added, that he had been mainly influenced by a desire to select a person, who would be peculiarly acceptable in the United States, as well as eminently qualified for the trust, and that he persuaded himself he had found one who, in both respects, was all that could be wished. He then named Lord Ashburton,[1] who had consented to undertake the mission.

Although this communication was of course wholly unexpected to me, I felt no hesitation in expressing the great satisfaction with which I received it. I assured Lord Aberdeen, that the President had nothing more at heart than an honorable adjustment of the matters in discussion be-

1. Alexander Baring, Lord Ashburton, who had first visited the United States in 1795, had many personal and business connections in America. Not only had he invested heavily in land and established many accounts, but he had also married the daughter of William Bingham (1752–1804), U.S. senator from Pennsylvania. After his return to England, Ashburton assumed leadership of the House of Baring and brought it to its zenith in the financial world. Webster represented the interests of the House of Baring in the United States for many years and visited Lord Ashburton in England during his tour of 1839.

tween the two countries,—that I was persuaded a more acceptable selection of a person for the important mission proposed could not have been made,—and that I anticipated the happiest results from this overture.

Lord Aberdeen rejoined that it was more than an *overture*;—that Lord Ashburton would go with full powers to make a definitive arrangement on every point in discussion between the two countries. He was aware of the difficulty of some of them, particularly what had incorrectly been called the right of search, which he deemed the most difficult of all; but he was willing to confide this and all other matters in controversy to Lord Ashburton's discretion. He added that they should have been quite willing to come to a general arrangement here, but they supposed I had not full powers for such a purpose.

This measure being determined on, Lord Aberdeen said he presumed it would be hardly worth while for us to continue the correspondence here, on matters in dispute between the Governments: he of course was quite willing to consider and reply to any statement I might think proper to make on any subject, but pending the negotiations that might take place at Washington, he supposed no benefit could result from a simultaneous discussion here.

I enquired what was to be Lord Ashburton's rank, and Lord Aberdeen answered the usual rank of Minister Plenipotentiary, justly adding that nothing could be added to his weight of character by any higher rank.

I asked him if this communication was to be considered confidential; and he replied that he wished it to be so regarded for a short time, that at present beside obtaining the Queen's consent he had mentioned it only to Sir Robert Peel.

There was an article in the [London] Times to-day containing an annunciation of the mission, evidently made by authority. The article states that the mission was determined on before the receipt of the Message of the President,[2] and that it was not therefore produced by anything contained or omitted in that document. The care with which this statement is made, leads me to suppose that the purpose of sending the mission was communicated to me, at the earliest moment possible after the Queen's command had been taken, in order to anticipate the arrival of the message, which could not be long delayed.

Lord Aberdeen said he was aware the measure would by some persons be called a concession, but that he had determined not to be influenced by such a fear.

We then engaged in some conversation on the African seizures. I told him the sensibility of the people in the United States had been awakened by the gross abuses, which had been committed on American Vessels by Her Majesty's cruizers: that I was sensible there was sometimes exag-

2. In his first Annual Message of December 7, 1841, Tyler discussed Anglo-American relations. *Messages and Papers*, 4:77–78.

geration and misstatement in the accounts of the parties injured smarting under a sense of wrong, but that there was an equally strong motive, on the part of the cruizing officers guilty of the abuse, to palliate their own conduct. I told him that there were cases, in which I could not and did not doubt the most high handed abuses had been committed, far exceeding that which occurred last summer in Macao roads,[3] and which had so promptly been rebuked by Her Majesty's Government; cases, I added, of which, though submitted by Mr. [Andrew] Stevenson as long ago as April last,[4] no notice had yet been taken. Lord Aberdeen assured me with great promptness, that he would give his attention with the utmost cheerfulness to the consideration of any such case, and desired me to give him, on the spot, the names of those I had in my mind. I gave him the names of the "Tigris," the "Sea Mew," and the "Jones," promising to add a fourth on my return home; being the four which formed the subject of a communication from Mr. Stevenson of the 16th of April last, and of which no explanation had yet been given by her Majesty's Government. Lord Aberdeen observed that I was aware it took some time to get an answer to enquiries from the coast of Africa, but that henceforward to Cruizers had been ordered, instead of making periodical returns, to report instantly each case of a vessel detained, searched, or captured, as it occurred. On my return home, I despatched a note to Lord Aberdeen containing the name of the fourth vessel, the "William & Francis," and expressing the opinion that nothing would contribute so much to allay the excitement caused in the United States by these seizures on the Coast of Africa, nor prepare so effectually for a final and satisfactory adjustment of the controversy, as that prompt and ample reparation which, in his note of the 20th. inst.,[5] his Lordship had promised in cases of abuse.

I understood Lord Aberdeen to say that Lord Ashburton would sail for America in the course of January. The Times states that he will sail in a few weeks.

Before leaving Lord Aberdeen, I requested to be furnished with a copy of the treaty concluded between the Five Powers on the 20th. inst.,[6] in advance of its ratification. I made this request, supposing it probable that Lord Ashburton would be instructed to bring this treaty to the President's consideration, and that it would be agreeable to the President to have an

3. This is a reference to the Endicott affair. See above, Everett to DW, December 15, 1841.

4. No. 122. Stevenson to DW, April 19, 1841, DNA, RG 59 (Despatches, Britain). Stevenson enclosed a note he had addressed to Lord Palmerston on April 16, 1841, protesting the

seizures of American vessels off the coast of Africa.

5. Enclosed in No. 4. Everett to DW, December 28, 1841, DNA, RG 59 (Despatches, Britain).

6. Stevenson refers to the Quintuple Treaty of 1841.

opportunity of examining it in advance. Lord Aberdeen readily promised to send me a copy, but it has not yet been received.

The newspapers transmitted by the packet of the 4th of January will acquaint you with the effect produced by the President's message on the public mind. The comments of the leading Journals, making due allowance for National and party prejudice, are upon the whole satisfactory. The tone of the message is regarded as decidedly pacific, and an easier feeling in reference to the relations between the two countries evidently prevails. Even the credit of American Securities has somewhat improved, in consequence of the conviction expressed by the President that they will be ultimately paid; although his distinct disclaimer of any responsibility on the part of the General Government, for the state debts, keeps this improvement within narrow limits.

To prevent delay in obtaining the evidence desired by the Solicitor of the Treasury,[7] I committed the subject to Col. [Thomas] Aspinwall on my return to Paris. He has obtained permission from the Government to copy the document, and I am in hopes of being able to transmit it by the packet of the 4th of January.

The determination of this Government to send a special Minister with full powers to the United States, will supersede the necessity of my being specially instructed on those subjects in controversy, which have hitherto been matters of correspondence here: but I have not thought it necessary on that account to forbear transmitting my despatch No. 4.,[8] which was written before the purpose of sending the minister was made known to me. I have the honor to be, With great respect, Your obedient Servant

Edward Everett

P.S. 3d January 1842

Since the foregoing despatch was written, I have received from Lord Aberdeen a note, (of which a copy is herewith transmitted,) in reply to my memorandum of the 27th of Decr[9] relative to the cases of the "Tigris," the "Sea Mew," "Jones," and "William & Francis." You will be struck with the promptitude evinced by Lord Aberdeen, compared with the delay on the part of Lord Palmerston, who did not refer these same cases to

---

7. The evidence in question is a copy of the document in which Charles II of Britain (1630–1685), who ruled 1660–1685, granted to the Duke of York, James II (1633–1701), part of that territory now constituting Delaware. The request for said deed of March 22, 1683, was made to Tyler by Solicitor of the Treasury Charles Bingham Penrose (1798–1857), solicitor 1841–1845. See Penrose to John Tyler, September 15, 1841, DNA, RG 59 (Misc. Letters).

8. No. 4. Everett to DW, December 28, 1841, DNA, RG 59 (Despatches, Britain), which includes comments on African seizures and the *Caroline*.

9. Everett enclosed a copy of his note to Aberdeen of December 27 and Aberdeen's reply of December 31, 1841, with this letter.

the Admiralty, till more than four months after his attention had been called to them by Mr. Stevenson.

I have also received in confidence from Lord Aberdeen, the promised copy of the Treaty with the Five Powers, for the suppression of the Slave Trade. It was understood by his Lordship, that I was to transmit this document to Washington for the information of the President, but that no public use should be made of it, till the ratifications of the treaty had been exchanged. I forward the treaty as received from Lord Aberdeen, without having retained a copy of it.

L S. DNA, RG 59 (Despatches, Britain). Rec'd January 1842. Extract published in CR, 3:685–687.

TO EDWARD EVERETT

No. 8.   Department of State,
Sir,   Washington, 29th January, 1842.

By the "Britannia," arrived at Boston, I have received your despatch of the 28th December, (N. 4) and your other despatch of the same month (N. 5)[1] with a postscript of the 3d of January.

The necessity of returning an early answer to these communications, (as the "Britannia" is expected to leave Boston the first of February,) obliges me to postpone a reply to those parts of them which are not of considerable and immediate importance.

The President expresses himself gratified with the manner in which the Queen received you, to present your letter of credence, and with the civility and respect which appear to characterise the deportment of Lord Aberdeen, in his intercourse with you; and you will please signify to Lord Aberdeen the President's sincere disposition to bring all matters in discussion between the two Governments to a speedy, as well as an amicable, adjustment.

The President has read Lord Aberdeen's note to you of the 20th December,[2] in reply to Mr. [Andrew] Stevenson's note to Lord Palmerston of the 21st of October;[3] and thinks you were quite right in acknowledging the dispassionate tone of that paper. It is only by the exercise of calm reason, that truth can be arrived at, in questions of a complicated nature; and between States, each of which understands and respects the intelligence and the power of the other, there ought to be no unwillingness to follow its guidance. At the present day, no State is so high as that the principles of its intercourse with other Nations are above question,

1. No. 4. Everett to DW, December 28, 1841, DNA, RG 59 (Despatches, Britain); and Everett to DW, December 31, 1841, above.

2. See above, Everett to DW, December 31, 1841.

3. Stevenson to Palmerston, October 21, 1841, DNA, RG 59 (Despatches, Britain).

or its conduct above scrutiny. On the contrary, the whole civilised world, now vastly better informed on such subjects than in former ages, and alive and sensible to the principles adopted, and the purposes avowed, by the leading States, necessarily constitutes a tribunal, august in character, and formidable in its decisions. And it is before this tribunal, and upon the rules of natural justice, moral propriety, the usages of modern times, and the prescriptions of public law, that Governments which respect themselves, and respect their neighbours, must be prepared to discuss with candor and with dignity, any topics which may have caused differences to spring up between them.

Your despatch of the 31st December announces the important intelligence of a Special Minister from England to the United States, with full power to settle every matter in dispute between the two Governments; and the President directs me to say that he regards this proceeding as originating in an entirely amicable spirit, and that it will be met, on his part, with perfectly corresponding sentiments. The high character of Lord Ashburton is well known to this Government, and it is not doubted that he will enter on the duties assigned him, not only with the advantages of much knowledge and experience in public affairs, but with a true desire to signalize his mission by assisting to place the peace of the two countries on a permanent basis. He will be received with the respect due to his own character, the character of the Government which sends him, and the high importance, to both countries, of the subjects entrusted to his negotiation.

The President approves your conduct in not pursuing in England, the discussion of questions, which are now to become the subjects of negotiation here.

I regret to be obliged to acquaint you with a very serious occurrence which recently took place in a part of one of the Bahama Islands.

It appears that the brig "Creole,"[4] of Richmond, Virginia,—Ensor Master,—bound to New Orleans, sailed from Hampton Roads on the 27th of October last, with a cargo of merchandise, principally tobacco and slaves (about 135 in number); that on the evening of the 7th of November some of the slaves rose upon the crew of the vessel, murdered a passenger named Hewell, who owned some of the negroes, wounded the Captain dangerously, and the first mate and two of the crew severely; that the slaves soon obtained complete possession of the brig, which, under their direction, was taken into the port of Nassau, in the Island of New Providence, where she arrived on the morning of the 9th of the

4. For a detailed account of the *Creole* uprising and related correspondence, see *Senate Documents*, 27th Cong., 2d sess., Serial 396, No. 51. See also Howard Jones, "The Peculiar Institution and National Honor: The Case of the *Creole* Slave Revolt," *Civil War History*, 21 (March 1975): 28–50.

same month; that at the request of the American Consul[5] in that place, the Governor[6] ordered a guard on board to prevent the escape of the mutineers, and with a view to an investigation; that such investigation was accordingly made by two British Magistrates, and that an examination also took place by the Consul, that on the report of the Magistrates, nineteen of the slaves were imprisoned by the local authorities, as having been concerned in the mutiny and murder, and their surrender to the Consul, to be sent to the United States for trial for these crimes, was refused, on the ground that the Governor wished first to communicate with the Government in England on the subject; that through the interference of the colonial authorities, and even before the military guard was removed, the greater number of the remaining slaves was liberated, and encouraged to go beyond the power of the master of the vessel, or the American Consul, by proceedings which neither of them could control. This is the substance of the case, as stated in two protests, one made at Nassau, and one at New Orleans, and the Consuls letters, together with sundry depositions taken by him, copies of which papers are herewith transmitted.[7]

The British Government cannot but see that this case, as presented in these papers, is one calling loudly for redress. The "Creole" was passing from one port of the United States to another, in a voyage perfectly lawful, with merchandise on board, and also with slaves; or persons bound to service, natives of America, and belonging to American citizens, and which are recognised as property by the Constitution of the United States, in those States in which slavery exists. In the course of the voyage some of these slaves rose upon the Master and crew, subdued them, murdered one man, and caused the vessel to be carried into Nassau. The vessel was there taken to a British port, not voluntarily, by those who had the lawful authority over her, but forcibly and violently, against the master's will, and with the consent of nobody but the mutineers and murderers; for there is no evidence that these outrages were committed with the concurrence of any of the slaves, except those actually engaged in them. Under these circumstances it would seem to have been the plain and obvious duty of the authorities at Nassau, a port of a friendly Power, to assist the American Consul in putting an end to the captivity of the master and crew, restoring to them the control of the vessel, and enabling them to resume their voyage, and to take the mutineers and murderers to their own country to answer for their crimes before the proper tribunal. One can not conceive how any other course could justly

5. John F. Bacon, not further identified.

6. Sir Francis Cockburn (1780–1868), a British army officer, was governor of the Bahamas, 1837–1844.

7. The protests, consular letters, and depositions are not in records of the Department of State; they are in *Senate Documents*, Serial 396.

be adopted, or how the duties imposed by that part of the code regulating the intercourse of friendly States, which is generally called the comity of Nations, can otherwise be fulfilled. Here was no violation of British law, attempted or intended, on the part of the Master of the "Creole," nor any infringement of the principles of the law of Nations. The vessel was lawfully engaged in passing from port to port in the United States. By violence and crime she was carried against the Master's will, out of her course, and into the port of a friendly power. All was the result of force. Certainly, ordinary comity and hospitality entitled him to such assistence from the authorities of the place, as should enable him to resume and prosecute his voyage, and bring the offenders to justice. But instead of this, if the facts be as represented in these papers, not only did the authorities give no aid, for any such purpose, but they did actually interfere to set free the slaves, and to enable them to disperse themselves beyond the reach of the Master of the vessel or their owners. A proceeding like this, cannot but cause deep feeling in the United States.[8] It has been my purpose to write you at length upon the subject, in order that you might lay before the Government of Her Majesty, fully and without reserve, the views entertained upon it by that of the United States, and the grounds on which those views are taken. But the early return of the packet precludes the opportunity of going thus into the case in this despatch, and as Lord Ashburton may shortly be expected here, it may be better to enter fully into it with him, if his powers shall be broad enough to embrace it. Some knowledge of the case will have reached England, before his departure, and very probably his Government may have given him instructions. But I request, nevertheless, that you lose no time in calling Lord Aberdeen's attention to it, in a general manner, and giving him a narrative of the transaction, such as may be framed from the papers now communicated, with a distinct declaration that if the facts turn out as stated, this Government thinks it a clear case for indemnification.

You will see that in his letter of the 7th January, 1837,[9] to Mr. Stevenson, respecting the claims for compensation in the cases of the "Comet," "Encomium," and "Enterprize," Lord Palmerston says that "H.M.'s Government is of opinion that the rule by which these claims should be decided is, that those claimants must be considered as entitled to compensation who were lawfully in possession of their slaves within the British territory, and who were disturbed in the legal possession of those slaves by functionaries of the British Government." This admission is broad enough to cover the case of the "Creole," if its circumstances are

8. On January 14, 1842, the Louisiana legislature passed a resolution demanding restitution from the British government; similar resolutions were enacted by the legislatures of Virginia and Mississippi in February and March.

9. Palmerston to Stevenson, January 7, 1837, DNA, RG 59 (Despatches, Britain).

correctly stated. But it does not extend to what we consider the true doctrine, according to the laws and usages of Nations; and therefore cannot be acquiesced in as the exactly correct general rule. It appears to this
Government, that not only is no unfriendly interference by the local
authorities to be allowed, but that aid and succor should be extended in
these as in other cases which may arise affecting the rights and interests
of citizens of friendly States. We know no ground on which it is just to
say that these coloured people had come within, and were within, British
territory, in such sense as that the laws of England affecting and regulating the conditions of persons could properly act upon them. As has
been already said, they were not there voluntarily; no human being belonging to the vessel was within British territories of his own accord,
except the mutineers. There being no importation, nor intent of importation, what right had the British authorities to inquire into the cargo of
the vessel, or the condition of persons on board. These persons might be
slaves for life, they might be slaves for a term of years, under a system
of apprenticeship; they might be bound to service by their own voluntary
act; they might be in confinement for crimes committed, they might be
prisoners of war, or they might be free. How could the British authorities
look into, and decide, any of these questions, or indeed what duty or
power, according to the principles of international intercourse had they
to inquire at all? If, indeed, without unfriendly interference and notwithstanding the fulfilment of all their duties of comity and assistance,
by these authorities, the master of the vessel could not return the persons, nor prevent their escape, then it would be a different question altogether, whether resort could be had to British tribunals, or the power of
the government in any of its branches, to compel their apprehension and
restoration. No one complains that English law shall decide the condition of all persons actually incorporated with British population, unless
there be treaty stipulation, making other provision for special cases. But
in the case of the "Creole" the coloured persons were still on board an
American vessel, that vessel having been forcibly put out of the course
of her voyage by mutiny, the master desiring, still, to resume it, and calling upon the Consul of his Government, resident at the place, and upon
the local authorities to enable him to do so, by freeing him from the imprisonment to which mutiny and murder had subjected him, and furnishing him with such necessary aid and assistance, as are usual in ordinary cases of disaster at sea. These persons, then, cannot be regarded
as being mixed with the British People, or as having changed their character at all, either in regard to country or personal condition. It was no
more than just to consider the vessel as still on her voyage, and entitled
to the succor due to other cases of distress whether arising from accident
or outrage. And that no other view of the subject can be true, is evident
from the very awkward position in which the local authorities have placed

their Government in respect to the mutineers, still held in imprisonment. What is to be done with them? How are they to be punished? The English Government will probably not undertake their trial or punishment, and of what use would it be to send them to the United States, separated from their ship, and at a period so late as that, if they should be sent, before proceedings could be instituted against them, the witnesses might be scattered over half the globe. One of the highest offences known to human laws is thus likely to go altogether unpunished.

In the note of Lord Palmerston to Mr. Stevenson, above referred to, his Lordship said, "that slavery being now abolished throughout the British empire, there can be no well founded claim for compensation in respect of Slaves who, under any circumstances, may come into the British Colonies, any more than there would be with respect to slaves who might be brought into the United Kingdom." I have only to remark upon this, that the Government of the United States sees no ground for any distinction founded on an alteration of British law in the Colonies. We do not consider that the question depends at all on the state of British law. It is not, that in such cases, the active agency of British law is invoked and refused, it is, that unfavorable interference is deprecated, and those good offices and friendly assistances expected, which a Government usu-ally affords to citizens of a friendly Power when instances occur of disaster and distress. All that the United States require, in these cases, they would expect in the ports of England, as well as in those of her colonies. Surely the influence of local law cannot affect the relations of nations, in any such matter as this. Suppose an American vessel with slaves lawfully on board, were to be captured by a British cruiser, as belonging to some belligerent while the United States were at peace. Suppose such prize carried into England, and the neutrality of the vessel fully made out, in the proceedings in Admiralty, and restoration consequently decreed. In such case must not the slaves be restored, exactly in the condition they were when the capture was made? Would any one contend that the fact of their having been carried into England by force, set them free? No alteration of her own local laws can either increase or diminish, or any way affect the duty of the English Government and its colonial authorities in such cases as such duty exists according to the law, the comity, and the usages of Nations. The persons on board the "Creole" could only have been regarded as Americans passing from one part of the United States to another, within the reach of British Authority only for the moment, and this only by force and violence. To seek to give, either to persons or property, thus brought within reach, an English character, or to impart to either English privileges, or to subject either to English burdens or liabilities, cannot, in the opinion of the United States, be justified. Suppose that, by the law of England, all blacks were slaves, and incapable of any other condition; if persons of that colour, free in the

United States, should, in attempting to pass from one port to another in their own country, be thrown by stress of weather, within British jurisdiction, and there detained for an hour or a day, would it be reasonable that the British authority should be made to act upon their condition, and to make them slaves? Or suppose that an article of merchandise, opium for instance, should be declared by the laws of the United States to be a nuisance, a poison, a thing in which no property could lawfully exist, or be asserted; and suppose that an English ship, with such a cargo on board, bound from one English port to another, should be driven by stress of weather, or by mutiny of the crew, into the ports of the United States, would it be held just and reasonable that such cargo should receive its character from American law, and be thrown overboard, and destroyed by the American authorities? It is in vain that any attempt is made to answer these suggestions by appealing to general principles of humanity. This is a point in regard to which Nations must be permitted to act upon different views, if they entertain different views, under their actually existing condition, and yet hold commercial intercourse with one another, or not hold any such intercourse at all. It may be added that all attempts by the Government of one Nation to force the influence of its laws on that of another, for any object whatsoever, generally defeat their own purposes, by producing dissatisfaction, resentment, and exasperation. Better is it, far better in all respects, that each nation should be left, without interference, or annoyance, direct or indirect, to its undoubted right of exercising its own judgment, in regard to all things belonging to its domestic interests and domestic duties.

There are two general considerations of the highest practical importance, to which you will, in the proper manner, invite the attention of Her Majesty's Government.

The first is, that as civilisation has made progress in the world, the intercourse of Nations has become more and more independent of different forms of Government, and different systems of law or religion. It is not now, as it was in ancient times, that every foreigner is considered as, therefore, an enemy; and that as soon as he comes into the country he may be lawfully treated as a slave; nor is the modern intercourse of States carried on mainly or at all, for the purpose of imposing, by one nation on another, new forms of civil Government, new rules of property, or new modes of domestic regulation. The great communities of the world are regarded as wholly independent, each entitled to maintain its own system of law, and government, while all, in their mutual intercourse, are understood to submit to the established rules and principles governing such intercourse. And the perfecting of this system of communication among Nations, requires the strictest application of the doctrine of non-intervention of any with the domestic concerns of others.

The other is, that the United States and England, now by far the two greatest commercial Nations in the world, touch each other both by sea and land, at almost innumerable points, and with systems of jurisprudence essentially alike, yet differing in the forms of their Government, and their laws respecting personal servitude—and that so widely does this last mentioned difference extend its influence, that without the exercise, to the fullest extent, of the doctrine of non-interference, and mutual abstinence from any thing affecting each other's domestic regulations, the peace of the two countries, and therefore the peace of the world, will be always in danger.

The Bahamas (British Possessions) push themselves near to the shores of the United States, and thus lie almost directly in the track of that great part of their coastwise traffic, which doubling the Cape of Florida, connects the cities of the Atlantic with the ports and harbors on the Gulf of Mexico, and the great commercial emporium on the Mississippi. The seas in which these British Possessions are situated, are seas of shallow water, full of reefs and sandbars, subject to violent action of the winds, and to the agitations caused by the Gulf Stream. They must always, therefore, be of dangerous navigation, and accidents must be expected frequently to occur, such as will cause American vessels to be wrecked on British Islands, or compel them to seek shelter in British ports. It is quite essential that the manner in which such vessels, their crews and cargoes, in whatever such cargoes consist, are to be treated in these cases of misfortune and distress, should be clearly and fully known.

You are acquainted with the correspondence which took place a few years ago, between the American and English Governments, respecting the case of the "Enterprise," the "Comet," and the "Encomium." I call your attention to the Journal of the Senate of the United States, containing resolutions unanimously adopted by that body, respecting those cases.[10] These resolutions, I believe, have already been brought to the notice of Her Majesty's Government, but it may be well that both the resolutions themselves, and the debate upon them should be again adverted to. You will find the resolutions of course among the documents regularly transmitted to the Legation, and the debates in the newspapers with which it has also been supplied from this Department.

You will avail yourself of an early opportunity of communicating to Lord Aberdeen, in the manner which you may deem most expedient, the

10. The *Comet* and *Encomium* wrecked in the Bahama Islands in 1831 and 1834. In 1835 a storm forced the *Enterprise* to enter port in Bermuda. In each case British authorities liberated slaves on the ships. The Senate requested that the president communicate correspondence between the governments about the vessels in 1837, 1839, and 1840. *Senate Journal*, 24th Cong., 2d sess., Serial 296, pp. 217–218; and 25th Cong., 3d sess., Serial 337, pp. 182–183. The correspondence is published in *Senate Documents*, 24th Cong., 2d sess., Serial 298, No. 174; and 25th Cong., 3d sess., Serial 340, No. 216.

substance of this despatch; and you will receive further instructions respecting the case of the "Creole," unless it shall become the subject of discussion at Washington.

In all your communications with Her Majesty's Government, you will seek to impress it with a full conviction of the importance to the peace of the two countries of occurences of this kind, and the delicate nature of the questions to which they give rise. I am, Sir, your most obedient servant,   Danl Webster

LC. DNA, RG 59 (Instructions, Britain). Extract published in CR, 3:158–159.

FROM ALBERT FITZ

Sir,   Washington, 21 July 1842.

Having been honoured with Instructions from the Department of State,[1] to proceed to certain of the British West India Islands, for the purpose of ascertaining the strength of the Naval and Military forces there, and the object for which they might be assembled; to examine the fortifications, take plans of them, ascertain the number of guns, describe the disposition of the inhabitants, & when these objects were accomplished, to communicate the result of my observations to your Department, I now beg leave, respectfully, to submit the following

Report.

I first visited the "Bermudas, or Somers' Islands," and from the limited knowledge by us possessed of that region, and the studied secresy maintained by the British Government in relation to it, I spared no pains in obtaining all the information possible. In doing so, I found the utmost caution was necessary, for the Bermudas being of limited extent, an important Naval Depot, and having but a small trade, strangers are looked upon with suspicion and distrust. They are forbidden to approach the Fortifications, and no foreigner is permitted to visit the Dock-yard or Public Works, although he may bear a letter of introduction from citizens of the first respectability, and even from the acquaintances of the Officers commanding.

Within the last eighteen months, three instances have occurred of the arrest of individuals suspected of giving too critical an examination of the works.

These islands contain two commercial Harbours; "Hamilton" in the centre of the group, which from its commodious situation commands nearly all the trade, and "St George" at the East end. The first was formerly incapable of admitting vessels drawing over nine feet of water, but the Government has caused the channel to be deepened at a place

1. Fitz's instructions, which probably were oral, have not been found, but their substance is indicated in this letter.

called "Timlin's Narrows," so that vessels drawing twelve feet, may now enter, and it is proposed to continue the work, until a channel is made of the depth of seventeen feet.

Hamilton Harbour *may* be entered from the Westward, by small vessels, with a southerly or westerly wind; but the navigation is extremely hazardous, and a clear day and smooth water are indispensible, to enable the Pilots to pick their way between the rocks, which surround these islands on the northern and western sides: but the safer and more usual mode, is to enter from the north east, between North Rock and St George.

The great importance of these islands, having been made manifest during the last war between the United States and Great Britain, the British Government, as early as 1816, commenced the construction of a Dockyard at "Ireland Isle," which, from the various alterations and improvements from time to time made, promises to be one of the most impregnable fortresses in the Western hemisphere. By referring to the Map, which I have the honour to submit herewith, and the Plan marked A, in the Appendix,[2] the security of the position, and the difficulty of approaching it, will be perceived. The surrounding rocks rendering the place totally inapproachable in that quarter for Ships, and the strength of the works bidding defiance to smaller vessels. The walls are said to embrace a space of thirty acres; the Dockyard, Public Stores, Barracks, and Magazine, lying within, and being protected by them. Adjacent to the Dockyard, and commanded by its Batteries, is a receiving basin, called the "Camber;" capable of receiving for repairs, a large fleet of vessels of the first class. Upwards of a hundred guns are already mounted upon the walls, and the works are not yet complete. They are to be bomb proof in every department. "Ireland Isle" is nearly two miles in length, and is owned entirely by the Crown. No person disconnected with the public service, is allowed to reside upon it. It contains an extensive Naval Hospital, and a most bountiful supply of all the articles usually required by ships of War. Two steam vessels are constantly kept in commission, for the purpose of towing vessels, and cruising among the islands.

With the exception of a Martello Tower, mounting a twentyfour pounder, on a pivot, at "Whalebone Bay," no other fortification is to be found until you reach the garrisoned town of "St George;" the heights of which are crowned with works of great strength, constructed in accordance with the most approved principles of modern warfare. The Harbour of St George, is the only secure one at present capable of receiving vessels, which draw seventeen feet of water; and, being easy of access, is the port resorted to by vessels in distress. It must be entered, by passing within pistol shot of Fort Conyngham; the oldest and feeblest permanent

2. None of the appendixes or maps   in this volume.
mentioned in the letter are printed

work upon these islands. It mounts twelve twentyfour pounders, but is not bomb proof. For Plan, see Appendix B. This harbour is however, entirely commanded by Forts "Victoria" and "George," hereafter described.

Ships bound to the Dockyard and Hamilton, must pass within range of the guns of Fort Conyngham, and of all the Batteries upon the heights: St George being the key to these waters.

The works consist, first, of "Fort Albert," which is situated about one mile west of "Fort Conyngham." This work is not quite finished, but already mounts seven thirtytwo pounders, is bomb proof, & has a ditch, defended by cross fires of musketry. For plan see appendix C.

About one eighth of a mile westerly from "Fort Albert," upon more elevated ground, stands "Fort Victoria," a complete bomb proof work, of the first class, and great strength; mounting eighteen thirtytwo pounders, and two thirtytwo pound Carronades. For plan see appendix D.

Within a half mile, northerly from Fort "Victoria," is a strong work called Fort "St Katherine," its walls being washed by the sea. It mounts sixteen thirtytwo and sixtyfour pounders, and has a furnace for heating shot. For plan see appendix E.

At a short distance southwesterly from Fort "Victoria," a Star Battery has been commenced, but the work is at present discontinued for the purpose of completing forts, deemed of more importance. For plan see appendix F.

The last work commenced, is upon one of the highest elevations in the islands, and is to be called Fort "George," situated half a mile south west from Fort Victoria. It is to be bomb proof, and will mount four sixtyfour pounders. The hill upon which it stands is of a conical form, and so smoothly graded, that, like the famed hill forts of the Deccan, it is a task of great difficulty to ascend it; and when the Prickly Pear, which is thickly sown upon the glacis, of this Fort, and also of Fort Victoria, has attained its growth, the ascent will be almost impracticable.

The British Government has purchased all the lands in the vicinity of these forts, and labourers are employed in removing buildings and grading the surface, so that no obstructions shall exist in the range of the batteries.

There is a place called "Barrack Hill," overlooking the harbour, on which two twentyfour pounders and twenty brass Field pieces are kept, for the purpose of exercising the troops. There are also quarters for the Artillery, Engineer and Ordnance Officers, and Barracks for four hundred men. Near it, is a large Military Hospital.

On a small islet in the harbour, is a well furnished Ordnance Yard.

In the Parish of Devonshire, at the distance of a mile and a half from Hamilton, stands a very high hill, called "Prospect." This is the only point, from which an uninterrupted view of the sea, upon every side, and consequently of approaching vessels, can be obtained. The Government had been treating for the purchase of this spot, for several months, and during my visit, instructions were received for transferring it to the Crown, for the purpose of erecting extensive Barracks, a Fort and Signal Station, thereon. When this work is accomplished, the five companies of troops heretofore stationed in temporary quarters, in Hamilton, will be transferred there.

At present there are four Signal Stations, viz, Gibbs' Hill, on the south-western extremity, Ireland Isle, on the north western; Mount Langton, the residence of the Governor, near the centre; and Fort Victoria, at the north eastern extremity. Through these, communications are made by Telegraph, to the Governor, to the Admiral's residence, called Clarence Cottage, and to the ships that may be lying at anchor. Every sail that may be descried upon the ocean, is immediately announced from the post nearest the point whence she is discovered, and as she becomes more discernible, the particulars are made known, and repeated from station to station; as the course she is steering, whether passing by, or approaching the land, whether a vessel of war or a merchantman, and her nationality. If she prove to be a foreign vessel of war, the drums beat to quarters, and the drawbridges are raised.

The south side of the islands is the only one susceptible of being landed upon, that remains undefended. This, having no harbour where an enemies fleet might lie, has heretofore been neglected, but the contemplated works on Prospect, will serve to remedy this apparent omission.

Castle Harbour, a large inland sea at the east end, might be rendered capable of sheltering a large fleet, by the removal of some obstructions at its entrance. A proposition has been submitted, either to widen the entrance and fortify its mouth, or else to increase the obstructions, and thus render it inaccessible. The decision of the Government has not yet been made public.

Three delapidated fortresses are now standing at its mouth.

While I was in Bermuda, the Admiral of the West India Squadron was lying there,[3] with a portion of his fleet, consisting of seven vessels, mounting 290 guns, awaiting orders from England, on receipt of which they sailed: two for England, and the remainder for Barbados. This was during the time [Alexander] McLeod's trial was pending, and the report was rife, that they were to sail for the United States, should the intelligence in regard to that individual, prove unsatisfactory. At the same time, a large ship arrived with six hundred tons of shot, shells and ammunition for the forts, and two other vessels, with Government stores, preceded her.

One thousand Convicts, superintended by a company of Sappers, are

3. Vice Admiral Sir Thomas Harvey (1775–1841) was commander of the West India squadron from 1839 until his death.

employed upon the works above described, and another company of Sappers is to be immediately added to the present force.

The present Military force, consists of the Second Battalion of Rifles, and the Twentieth Regiment of Infantry together with a detachment of Artillery, say fifteen hundred men, in a high state of efficiency. The Black and White citizens of the place, are enrolled as Militia; and Col [William] Reid,[4] the Governor, to encourage a military spirit among them, has appointed semimonthly meetings for Target practice; and rewards are bestowed upon the best marksmen.

The inhabitants are well satisfied with their Government, and the large amount of money circulated among them by the Sailors and Soldiers, tends to sustain and increase that spirit. They anticipate great spoils in case of another war with the United States. The opinion is prevalent, that the Americans are very desirous of obtaining possession of these islands, and they are particularly jealous and distrustful of American visitors, and also of Frenchmen, whom they consider as our probable allies. They boast, however, that their isles have remained in obscurity, until their defences have become strong enough to defy the world.

I next visited the island of New Providence. The port of Nassau, being the only harbour possessed by the British Government, between Bermuda and Jamaica, is a very eligible place from which to supply fleets with provisions and assistance, in case of disaster. From its proximity to the American coast, and its command of the Gulf of Mexico, it offers great advantages for the reception of prizes, and the fitting out of Privateers and small vessels of war. The harbour is narrow, running from east to west; it is bounded on the south by the town, and on the north by a narrow rocky key, called Hog Island; it will not safely float vessels drawing over fourteen feet of water. Outside of Hog Island, is the usual riding place for ships of war, making a short visit; and it is used by the Royal Mail Steamers. This, is only deemed safe, in southerly winds, which blow from the land: should the wind blow from any other quarter, ships would be compelled to proceed to Cochian's Anchorage, nine miles southeasterly from Nassau; this is considered a safe and sufficient anchorage in all weathers.

There is a third anchoring place, called Hanover Sound, situated about equidistant from the other two, but it is so difficult of access and egress, to vessels not navigated by steam, that it is seldom resorted to.

Nassau harbour is defended from attack at the eastward, where vessels drawing nine feet [of] water may approach, by "Fort Montagu"; an

4. Reid (1791–1858), of the Royal Engineers, was governor of Bermuda from 1839 to 1846.

inferior work, mounting four eighteen pounders. For plan see appendix marked G.

Its main entrance is defended by "Fort Charlotte," an old work, mounting twentyseven twentyfour pounders, see plan marked H. in the appendix, and also by a water battery of four twentyfour pounders, provided with a furnace for heating shot. See plan I. in appendix.

The town is defended from attack in nearby Fort "Fincastle," situated on the highest point of the hill at the back of the town, and commanding a view of the island. It mounts three twentyfour pounders, and two thirteen inch Howitzers. See plan marked J.

None of these works are bomb proof, nor are they capable of making a long defence. A small force, lying at the anchorage outside of Hog Island, would easily batter them down, and take possession of the place. There is an Ordnance Wharf and Naval Yard, and Barracks for 400 men; and new Barracks for two hundred and fifty more, are now being built.

The military strength of the place consists of five Companies of the Second West India Regiment, and a detachment of Artillery consisting of twenty men. The Bahamas contain about one thousand enrolled militia, white and black, who are required to drill semimonthly.

The disposition and expectations of the inhabitants, resemble those of the Bermudians, with the exception of their not being so jealous of strangers, nor so belligerant towards Americans.

No other port in the Bahamas is occupied by Troops, except Turks' Islands, where a small detachment is stationed as a police guard, for the protection of property, and the preservation of order among the blacks, who work in the salt ponds.

From the Bahamas, I proceeded to the island of Jamaica.

Kingston, its commercial capital, has the only harbour in the island capable of receiving and sheltering a squadron; Port Royal, its entrance or outward harbour, has therefore, long been strongly fortified.

Port Royal contains a large Naval and Military Hospital, extensive Public Stores, and a spacious Dockyard. These are enclosed and defended by Fort "Charles," on the south, and a line of works on either side of it, mounting together 71 guns, of various calibres. For plan, see appendix K.

On the east, by a Redoubt mounting eight twentyfour pounders, and a long line of embankment: see plan L.

And on the north, by a Polygon Battery with ditch, mounting twentyfive twentyfour pounders: see plan M.

At the distance of a mile and a half from Fort Charles, on the opposite side of the Bay, stands the "Apostles' Battery," situated on the side of a mountain: it mounts twelve guns, see plan N.

And about two miles up the bay, at a place where the shallowness of the water, compels vessels to pass within musket shot, stands Fort "Augusta," the strongest fortress in the island. It mounts one hundred guns, and is situated upon a low sandy point: see plan O.

The Ordnance yard, at Kingston, contains a large quantity of ammunition, and six hundred pieces of ordnance. The Arsenal at St Jago de la Vega, or Spanish Town, the seat of Government, is well supplied with small arms.

The city of Kingston, thus admirably defended from attack by sea, is secured against inland invasion, at the south by a neglected work called "Passage Fort"; and on the East, by "Rock Fort," mounting eighteen twentyfour pounders; see plan P. The garrisons of Uppark Camp, Stoney Hill and New Castle; in the mountains, command the passes between the extremities of the Island, and would seem to give to it, all the security of a walled city.

The minor harbours of Port Antonio, Port Morant, Montego Bay, Falmouth and Savanna la Mar, have each small forts, garrisoned by a few Black troops.

There are always one or two ships of war, and war steamers, in commission, at Port Royal. This place is very unhealthy in the summer, and Fort Augusta is so fatal a spot, that it is not considered prudent to keep a garrison in it. A company of Black Artillerists is about to be formed for the purpose of garrisoning these Posts.

The Military strength of the island consists of three Companies of Artillery, a Regiment of Rifles and one of Infantry, and detachments of the Second and Third West India Regiments; in all comprising twentyfive hundred men. The Militia are estimated at Fifteen thousand; white and black: they are drilled semimonthly. The white troops are kept at the Camps in the mountains, for the preservation of their health.

The fortifications of Jamaica, are all of the old school, and by no means impregnable.

At Bridgetown, Barbados, there ar[e] three fortifications, but in an entirely delapidated state: nor could I learn that it was the intention of the Government to rebuild them.

This island is frequently visited by ships of war, and there is always one or more lying at anchor, in Carlisle Bay, but having no harbour, they remain but a short time.

As a military station, however, Barbadoes ranks as the first in the West Indies; the comparative salubrity of its climate, rendering it a desirable depot for the troops destined for service in British Guiana, and the different islands. The Hospitals, Barracks and Parade Ground, are on a very extensive scale, and there are six Signal Stations, for the transmission of intelligence by Telegraph.

The present Military strength of Barbados, consists of a detachment of Artillery, three Regiments of Infantry, and half a Regiment of Black troops. The Militia have not been mustered for four years.

Grenada and Antigua, are the only islands possessed by the English in the little Antilles, containing harbours where ships may lie in safety in stormy weather. These have each a small Navy Yard, defended by ancient fortifications.

All the forts in the British West India Islands, are fast going to decay, and I was informed that in the event of another war, the Government would place more reliance upon fleets, for their protection, than on forts.

So fatal are these stations generally, to the health of white troops, that it is intended to raise two more Regiments at Sierra Leone, for the purpose of garrisoning the various posts, and relieving the white troops, from all active service. There are now, but three W.I. Regiments in commission, and they are distributed in detachments, at St Helena, the coast of Africa, Guiana, the West India Islands and Honduras. Obviously, too small a force, for such extensive possessions.

Bermuda, is evidently considered by the British Government as the key to the United States, and the rendezvous and strong-hold for their fleets. Should a war ever occur, between them and us, *there* would their forces concentrate. It is the only place which they are fortifying, and it is expected that they will continue their labours, until every hill-top, shall be crowned with ordnance.

In my humble endeavours to accomplish the delicate objects of my mission, I have not unfrequently been compelled to resort to stratagem, in order to arrive at a satisfactory conclusion, and great caution and assiduity have been requisite. I have confidence in asserting, that in no instance, has a suspicion been excited of the real purpose of my tour, and that the whole transaction, remains a profound secret. I have the honour to remain, most faithfully and devotedly, Your Obed't Servant.

Albert Fitz.

A L S. DNA, RG 59 (Communications from Special Agents). Fitz (1809–1852), of Boston, had been engaged in the West Indian trade as a supercargo.

The World and Daniel Webster

Throughout the nineteenth century, American foreign policy was directed primarily at Great Britain. The years from 1841 to 1843 were no exception to this rule, for they were dominated by a crisis in Anglo-American relations and the successful resolution of that crisis in the Webster-Ashburton Treaty. But Britain was only one of twenty-four countries in Africa, North and South America, Asia and the Pacific, Europe, and the Middle East with which the United States held diplomatic relations.

In the following section, the editors propose to go beyond the traditional crisis-oriented approach to foreign policy and to provide a representative cross section of the world that Daniel Webster dealt with as secretary of state. The relations of the United States with most nations focused on commercial and claims litigation issues but also involved such matters as the status of American missionaries in the Ottoman Empire. Accordingly, the documents published below incorporate these issues and have been selected to illustrate the overall scope of American foreign policy during Webster's first incumbency at the Department of State. Although such problems as the Danish Sound Dues and American missionaries in Syria may not rank in historical significance with the crisis in Anglo-American relations, they were topics of considerable importance both to the United States and to Secretary of State Webster.

SPAIN

John Quincy Adams aptly characterized Havana as "one of the last inexpungable haunts of African slave-trade pirates" (*Memoirs*, 11:354). In 1839 two Cubans purchased in Havana a number of blacks newly arrived from Africa. The importation of slaves had been forbidden by Spanish law in 1817, but the distinction between legal (*ladinos*, or latinized) and illegal slaves (*bozales*, or those new to the country) was easily evaded in Cuba through the procurement of false documents. The owners, Pedro Montes and Jose Ruiz, left Havana with their human cargo in the ship *Amistad*, but once at sea the Africans under the leadership of Cinqué rose up and captured the vessel. The *bozales* planned to sail the *Amistad* back to Africa, but the ship lacked supplies for a transatlantic voyage, and the blacks on board were inexperienced sailors. They forced Montes to aid them, but by tacking the sails he kept the vessel in American waters. Ultimately, the *Amistad* arrived off the coast of North America, where it was taken into custody by Lieutenant Thomas R. Gedney, a U.S. naval officer, and the *Amistad* blacks were imprisoned.

Through the efforts of abolitionists, the *Amistad* became a cause célèbre with important diplomatic, legal, and political implications. The Spanish government requested a speedy return of the vessel and its cargo, including what was claimed to be slave property, under the terms of the Pinckney Treaty of 1795, and the Van Buren administration wanted to comply with that request. Attorney General Felix Grundy held that the slaves and ship should be returned to their Spanish owners. Gedney and associates, however, filed a claim for salvage on the *Amistad*, and the abolitionists brought criminal charges of illegal enslavement against Montes and Ruiz as part of their overall campaign to obtain the freedom of the Africans. While President Van Buren was holding a vessel in readiness to return the *Amistad* captives to Cuba, the case worked its way through the American court system.

In January 1840 a U.S. district court declared that the blacks of the *Amistad* were not slaves legally imported into Cuba, but free men. On March 9, 1841, after John Quincy Adams had eloquently presented the argument on behalf of the *Amistad* prisoners, the U.S. Supreme Court reaffirmed the lower court decision, awarding salvage rights to American naval officers and declaring the *Amistad* captives free men.

Daniel Webster inherited the *Amistad* issue from John Forsyth and bequeathed it to his successors. On May 29, 1841, the Spanish minister to the United States, Pedro Alcántara de Argaiz, formally demanded indemnification for the vessel, the cargo, and the Africans. He also insisted that Montes and Ruiz be compensated for their incarceration in a New York City jail and that Spain be assured that the *Amistad* proceeding would not serve as a precedent. Advised by Adams that he not "truckle to Spain" (*Memoirs*, 10:469–470), Webster reversed Forsyth's stance and contested the view that the *Amistad* case fell within the terms of the treaty of 1795. The new secretary of state also steadfastly withstood Argaiz's attempts to draw a parallel between the *Amistad* and the *Creole* incidents and to link the *Amistad* case with the payment of claims due the United States by Spain under a convention of 1834.

The unresolved *Amistad* claim continued to be an irritant to Spanish-American relations for many years. Webster had to deal with the issue again during his second term as secretary of state in the 1850s, and the dispute was not terminated until 1861. In that year, Secretary of State William H. Seward rejected the *Amistad* claim as invalid and refused to negotiate any further on the subject.

FROM PEDRO ALCÁNTARA DE ARGAIZ

Washington May 29th 1841

The Undersigned, Envoy Extraordinary and Minister Plenipotentiary of Her Catholic Majesty, has the honour, in compliance with what was agreed on with the Secretary of State in their last conference, to make known to him the conviction of the Undersigned, that the 6th article, as also the [8th,] 9th and 10th, of the treaty of 1795,[1] have not been duly executed, in the affair of the Schooner Amistad, as he conceives that he has proved in his correspondence. The subjects of Her Catholic Majesty have not received the assistance expressed in those (articles) nor have their properties been respected, as is stipulated in the said articles; and this must have been understood by the Attorney General, Mr [Felix] Grundy,[2] as appears by the opinion which he gave in November 1839.[3]

The Government of the Union gave to this affair a course, tortuous, illegal, and contrary to the intention of the contracting Parties.

The Undersigned protested against it in due time,[4] rendering the Government of the United States responsible for the consequences. Knowing however, the embarrassed state of the existing administration, on account of the impossibility on its part, of carrying that treaty into fulfilment, in consequence of the change of circumstances, the Undersigned considers it his duty to demand as he now does,

1—Indemnification for the vessel called *La Amistad*

2—(Indemnification) for her cargo, including the negroes found on board.

3—(Indemnification) for the losses and injuries suffered by (or *inflicted on*) the Spanish subjects Don Pedro Montes, and Don Jose Ruiz during their unjust imprisonment.[5]

1. These provisions of the Treaty of San Lorenzo defined the maritime obligations of Spain and the United States. Article 6 required that each party make effort to protect and defend the vessels of the other; 8 stated that the crews of vessels forced by stress of weather, pirates, or enemies to seek shelter should be treated with humanity; 9 provided that ships and merchandise rescued from pirates should be restored to the owner; 10 afforded the crews of vessels wrecked in the territorial waters of the other country equality of assistance in operations of repair. The translator omitted reference to the eighth article, which was mentioned in the Spanish version. For the text of the treaty, see *Treaties*, 1:318–338.

2. Grundy (1777–1840), who had served in the U.S. Senate since 1829, resigned in 1838 to accept the office of attorney general. The next year Kentucky reelected Grundy, and he resigned his cabinet post to return to the Senate.

3. Grundy advised relegating custody of the ship and the blacks on board to the Spanish minister on the basis of Article 9 of the treaty of 1795. 3 *Opinions of the Attorneys General* 484 (1839).

4. Argaiz to Forsyth, October 3, 1839, DNA, RG 59 (Notes from Foreign Legations, Spain).

5. Montes and Ruiz claimed ownership of the blacks on board the *Amistad*. Montes had purchased four children in the *barracoon* in Cuba, and Ruiz, a suspected slave dealer, bought forty-nine. During the legal proceedings in the United States, Montes and Ruiz were jailed on a complaint brought against them by abolitionists in the name of the

4   The assurance that the course given to this affair, shall never serve as a precedent in analogous cases which may occur.

The Undersigned avails himself of this occasion, to repeat to the Secretary of State, the assurances of his high consideration.   P. A. de Argaiz

Copy. Translation. DNA, RG 59 (Notes from Foreign Legations, Spain). Rec'd May 31, 1841. Published in *Executive Documents*, 27th Cong., 3d sess., Serial 422, No. 191. Argaiz, the Spanish minister to the United States from c. 1838 to 1844, could not be further identified.

TO PEDRO ALCÁNTARA DE ARGAIZ

Department of State,
Washington, 1st Septr, 1841.

The Undersigned has the honor to acknowledge the receipt of the note of M. [Pedro Alcántara] de Argaiz, Envoy Extraordinary and Minister Plenipotentiary of Her Catholic Majesty, of the 29th of May,[1] in which he makes known to the Undersigned his conviction that the sixth, eighth, ninth, and tenth articles of the Treaty of 1795, between the two countries, have not been properly carried into execution in the affair of the schooner "Amistad," as he conceives he has proved in his correspondence, and demands, 1st Indemnification for the vessel called the "Amistad";

2d   Indemnification for the cargo, including the negroes found on board.

3d   Indemnification for the losses and injuries suffered by (or inflicted on) the Spanish Subjects, Don Pedro Montez and Don Jose Ruiz, during their unjust imprisonment; and,

4th   The assurance that the course given to this affair shall never serve as a precedent for any analogous cases that may occur.

This note has been laid before the President, and the Undersigned has been by him instructed to reply as follows.

The President had supposed that after the decision of the Supreme Court of the United States upon this question[2] there would have been no occasion to renew a correspondence upon it between the two Governments, and that M. de Argaiz was aware that the President has no power to review or alter any of the judgments of that court, it being a tribunal

---

Amistad captives. See Christopher Martin, *The Amistad Affair* (New York, 1970), pp. 30–33, 134–135.

1. See above.

2. The U.S. Supreme Court upheld the decision of the federal District Court of Connecticut at New Haven. Justice Joseph Story ruled that the

Amistad captives should not be returned to the Spanish because the Africans were not lawful slaves, but kidnapped contrary to the laws of Spain. Salvage on the vessel, however, was allowed. 15 Peters 518 (1841).

wholly independent of the Executive and one whose decisions must be regarded as final and conclusive upon all questions brought before it. He had hoped too that its decree would have proved satisfactory to M. de Argaiz and the Government of Spain, and that the facts proved and the arguments offered before it, together with the able opinions delivered by its members in rendering the decree would have prevented all disagreement or dissatisfaction with the result to which they arrived. The court was guided in its deliberations as well by the Treaty between the two countries as by the law of nations and of the United States; and it is not for the Executive to question that its decree was in exact conformity with the obligations imposed upon it by that Treaty and those laws. No branch of the Government of the United States, whether Legislative, Executive, or Judiciary can have been influenced by any other motives than those of a sincere desire to perform all the duties, and fulfil all the requirements, exacted of either by the terms of the Treaty between this Government and Spain, with respect to her national character and sovereignty, and a view of preserving and strengthening the friendly relations which have so long and so happily subsisted between them: and the Undersigned hopes that M. de Argaiz himself will eventually join in approbation of the course adopted, convinced, as he must be, of the friendly disposition of all branches of this Government towards his own.

The articles to which M. de Argaiz refers as containing stipulations which have not been carried into effect in the case of the "Amistad" relate to the defence and protection of the persons or property of the subjects or citizens of either country which shall come within the jurisdiction of the other by sea or land.

Of those cited, the ninth article, which provides for the safe keeping and restoration of ships and merchandise rescued from the hands of pirates and robbers, which it declares shall be restored to their true proprietor, after due and sufficient proof shall be made concerning the property thereof, seems the most applicable to the case under consideration.

The Undersigned, after a careful consideration of all the arguments offered by M. de Argaiz, and an examination of the facts which have been made known, is unable to see in what particular this article, or any stipulation contained in it, or either of the others, has been violated or disregarded, or that the course given to this affair has been in any manner contrary to the spirit and intention of any part of the Treaty.

Upon the arrival of the schooner Amistad near our coast, it was with all its cargo, according to the provisions of the ninth article, taken into the custody of the officers of the nearest port. In consequence of a claim preferred for salvage by those who had saved both vessel and cargo, and rescued the subjects of Spain from death, or perhaps imprisonment enduring for life among the savage inhabitants of Africa, the subject of the ownership of the vessel and cargo was brought before the courts.[3] Before those courts also the subjects of Spain submitted their answer to these claims, and their complaints, with how much magnanimity refusing compliance with a just demand for services rendered them at such a time, and in such a situation the Undersigned will not undertake to say. Besides the common articles of merchandise and traffic, there were found on board a number of negroes claimed as the lawful property of Spanish subjects, and said to form part of the cargo; and on these also, as part of the cargo, salvage was claimed by those who had saved them for their owners, if they had any, and their pretended owners from them.

The whole subject then of the ownership of the vessel, and of all the cargo, came properly and legally before the courts, who proceeded, as was their duty under the Treaty, on the presentment of such a case to them, to investigate it carefully, deliberately, and circumspectly. Thus proceeding, the courts, upon the testimony before them, decided, awarding the vessel to its lawful owner, and the cargo to its respective lawful owners, and a certain amount of salvage to those who had been instrumental in saving both. It was found by the courts that the negroes were not the lawful property of any one, and no part of the cargo, and consequently subject to no claim for salvage, but that they were freemen, captured and sold, and held in bondage contrary as well to the laws of Spain as of the United States. And the courts in the just exercise of their power, decided, as they were bound to do, under existing laws and treaties, and upon the facts as they appeared. M. de Argaiz demands indemnification for the vessel and cargo, including the negroes found on board. Were this Government conscious of having inflicted injury upon any, whether a private individual or a powerful nation, indemnification would be readily granted; but the question of the existence of any such injury must be determined by the Government itself. In this case, the Undersigned is of opinion that no injury has been done to any one of the subjects of Spain; but on the contrary, that the Government has gone quite as far in granting them protection and manifesting a favorable disposition towards them as the circumstances under which they came within its notice could demand of it.

What injury has been inflicted on the subjects of Spain, owners of the vessel and cargo, by saving both from complete destruction, or from entire loss to them, and returning both to them, when their legal claims were ascertained?[4] What injury inflicted on those presenting claims to the negroes as slaves, by refusing to allow those claims, proved to be

3. The *Amistad* case first came before the district court at New Haven in January 1840. The hearing is not reported in *Federal Cases*. The most extensive treatment of the trial, drawn from contemporary accounts, is in Christopher Martin, *The Amistad Affair* (New York, 1970), pp. 89–166.

4. Webster errs in saying the ship and cargo were returned to the own-

unfounded, and by all provisions of the code of either country illegal and criminal?

M. de Argaiz will recollect, besides, that in his note of the 26th of November, 1839,[5] he demands these negroes, not as property, but as criminals, or, in his own language, "not as slaves but as assassins." Had they been at any time slaves, they would have become, by their killing and escape from lawful bondage, assassins, and pirates, whose delivery to the Government of Spain is not provided for in any stipulation of the treaty of 1795, and which would have been a matter of comity only, not to be demanded as a right.

The one point involves the other, and a refusal to deliver them certainly is no violation or neglect of any obligation. But the Undersigned does not propose to enter into any argument upon a subject which has already been discussed at length, both before the courts and between the two Governments.

M. de Argaiz demands also indemnification for injuries suffered by, or inflicted on, the Subjects of Spain, in the persons of Messrs. Ruiz and Montez. For any such losses or injuries inflicted on these gentlemen by any one within the jurisdiction of the United States, this Government offers reparation and indemnification through its courts, which stand open to hear their complaints, to ascertain and repair their wrongs, and punish the wrong doers.

The Undersigned therefore is instructed to say that this Government does not perceive with what justice any such demands as M. de Argaiz has presented can be made on it, and confidently expects that all will agree in justifying and approving the course which it has adopted in regard to the affair.

M. de Argaiz demands lastly, "the assurance that the course given to this affair shall never serve as a precedent in any analagous cases which may occur."

While the Undersigned hopes that no misfortune of the kind will ever again take place upon our coasts or elsewhere, and that no circumstances may ever again give rise to such occurrences as those which mark the affair of the "Amistad," from the commencement of her voyage, he assures M. de Argaiz that the Government of the United States will endeavor to discharge itself of all obligations imposed upon it with strict justice, honorably to itself, and respectfully towards those nations with whom it maintains amicable relations.

The Undersigned avails himself of this occasion to offer to M. de Ar-

---

ers. In October 1840 the *Amistad* and its nonhuman cargo were sold to satisfy the salvage claims. R. Earl McClendon, "The *Amistad* Claims: Inconsistencies of Policy," *Political Science Quarterly*, 48 (1933): 390.

5. Argaiz to Forsyth, November 26, 1839, DNA, RG 59 (Notes from Foreign Legations, Spain).

gaiz the assurance of his very high regard and distinguished consideration.   Danl Webster.

L C . DNA, RG 59 (Notes to Foreign Legations, Spain). Published in *Executive Documents*, 27th Cong., 3d sess., Serial 422, No. 191.

FROM PEDRO ALCÁNTARA DE ARGAIZ

Bordentown September 24th 1841—
    The Undersigned, Envoy Extraordinary and Minister Plenipotentiary
of Her Catholic Majesty, has the Honour to acknowledge the receipt of
the note which the Secretary of State of the Federal Government of the
Union, was pleased to address to him, under date of the 1st instant,[1] in
answer to the letter from the Undersigned of the 29th of May last.[2]
    The Secretary of State, before entering upon the discussion of the
points to which the last note from the Undersigned relates, is pleased to
say that the President had supposed, that after the decision of the Supreme Court of the United States upon this question, there would have
been no occasion to renew a correspondence upon it between the two
Governments.
    The Secretary of State, having without doubt carefully read the whole
correspondence which has passed between the Department of State and
the Legation of Her Catholic Majesty upon this subject, since the arrival
of the Schooner Amistad at the port of New London, will have therein
observed, that (this Legation) has ever and constantly, protested against
the jurisdiction of the Courts of the United States; inasmuch as the case
falling under the provisions of the Treaty of 1795, it should be decided
solely and exclusively by the Executive, and not by any other Power. This
the Federal Government of the Union could not but admit, and did in fact
admit, when the Secretary of State's predecessor [John Forsyth] said to
the Undersigned, in his note of the 12th of December 1839[3]—"In connexion with one of the points in the Chevalier [Pedro Alcántara] d'Argaiz's last note, the Undersigned will assure him, that whatever be in the
end, the disposal of the question, it will be in consequence of a decision
emanating from no other source, than the Government of the United
States; and if the agency of the judicial authority shall have been employed in conducting the investigation of the case (it) is because the
judiciary is by the organic Law of the land, a portion, though an independant one, of that Government." Relying upon this, and upon this
promise, the Undersigned quietly awaited the conclusion of the affair;
as did also the Government of Her Catholic Majesty, not doubting that
though the Courts of the United States might go so far as to investigate

1. See above.
2. See above, Argaiz to DW, May
29, 1841.

3. Forsyth to Argaiz, December 12,
1839, DNA, RG 59 (Notes to Foreign
Legations, Spain).

the facts, the final and decisive determination would in any event come from the Executive Power, as had been promised. Under these circumstances the Undersigned does not think that the Government of the Union should be surprised at the continuation of a correspondence, in which, besides the maintenance of a right considered by the Undersigned as indisputable, compliance with a promise is also claimed. If moreover, the President has not the power to destroy or to change in the slightest degree a decision of the Supreme Court of the United States, Her Catholic Majesty's Government cannot agree (*conformarse*—allow–submit to—) that the consequence of this should be in the present case, the open violation of a treaty, which ought to be respected as the Supreme law of the United States.

The Secretary of State says, that, "the Court was guided in its deliberations, as well by the treaty between the two countries, as by the Law of Nations and of the United States; and it is not for the Executive to question, that its decree was in exact conformity with the obligations, imposed upon it, by that treaty and those laws." The Undersigned regrets that there should be between the Secretary of State and himself, so great a difference in the manner of regarding this point; for if the Courts of the Union possess the right of interpreting, considering and deciding, upon treaties contracted between nation and nation, and the Executive Power cannot inquire whether their decrees are or are not conformable with justice, it would be as well to declare, that in order to give to treaties the force of treaties, or at least to render them obligatory, they should be concluded with the Judicial power, or, in better words, that treaties should be made, for them to be afterwards interpreted as the Courts might think proper.

The enlightened Secretary of State will agree with the Undersigned, that one of the things which principally constitute the independence of a country, is the jurisdiction of its Courts; or in other words, that no nation nor its Courts, should assume the faculty of pronouncing judicially upon acts committed within the jurisdiction of another. On this principle, the Undersigned cannot conceive, how the Secretary of State, could for a single moment have supposed, that the Undersigned would have agreed to, and have seen with satisfaction, the decision of a Court of the United States, pronounced upon acts appertaining to Spanish subjects, committed on board of a Spanish vessel, and in the waters of a Spanish territory, within the purview of a treaty and of the Law of Nations.

The Secretary of State, is also pleased to observe, "that the Schooner Amistad, upon her arrival on this coast, was, with all her cargo, according to the provisions of the ninth article, taken into the custody of the officers of the nearest port; and that in consequence of a claim for salvage, the subject of the ownership of the vessel and cargo was brought before the Courts." The Undersigned will not stop to remark upon the magnanimity of a demand for salvage, preferred by officers of a ship of war of the United States; but does the Secretary of State believe that this can justify the intervention of the Courts of the United States in this case, contrary to the opinion given by the Attorney General Mr [Felix] Grundy; and after moreover, the officers themselves had renounced their claim to salvage, as Lieutenant [Thomas R.] Gedney, the Commander of the Washington, himself, declared to the Undersigned?[4]

The Secretary of State also says, that "it was found by the Courts, that the negroes were not the lawful property of anyone." One violation of necessity brought on another, not less unjust; for the Judges of the United States, in order to ascertain whether or not the Africans were the lawful property of Spanish subjects, thought proper to examine the papers found on board of the vessel, which had been given by the authorities of Her Catholic Majesty, in the Island of Cuba; this was a recognition of the right of search, which, besides its not being authorised by any nation, has been combated by writers on public law, and most particularly in the case in question, by the distinguished jurist Mr Grundy, Attorney General of the Union, at the time when the Schooner Amistad arrived on the Anglo American coasts. (See his opinion on this case).

With all these considerations in view, and after having carefully examined the note of the Secretary of State, the Undersigned cannot comprehend upon what that Gentleman founds his assertion, that the Courts of the United States could properly and lawfully take cognisance of this case.

There is however one circumstance which the Undersigned considers well worthy of remark; as the Secretary of State says, that Court decided that the vessel and her cargo belonged to their lawful owners. As the vessel and cargo had been publickly sold, by whose orders or how, neither the Undersigned nor the owner knew, nothing seems to be more just and equitable, than to indemnify promptly, duly and fully, those whose property had been unjustly taken away, in manifest contradiction to the sense and letter of the ninth article of the treaty of 1795; yet when the Undersigned claims the indemnification so justly due, the Secretary of State, makes no reply on this point; limiting himself as may be seen by the twelfth paragraph of his note to the declaration, that "were the Government of the United States conscious of having inflicted injury upon any, whether a private individual or a powerful nation, indemnification would be readily granted.["] The Undersigned conceives that the fact of individuals, subjects of Her Catholic Majesty, having been arbitrarily deprived of their vessel and cargo, should be sufficient to produce the conviction, that indemnification is due to them.

4. Gedney (d. 1857), a career naval officer, had claimed salvage on the Amistad and her cargo but withdrew his claim to the Africans in the face of hostile public opinion.

The Secretary of State asks—"What injury has been inflicted on the subjects of Spain, owners of the vessel and her cargo, by saving both from complete destruction or from entire loss to them, and returning both to them, when their legal claims were ascertained?" In the first place, the Undersigned sees with regret that the Secretary of State is under an erroneous impression; for Her Catholic Majesty's subjects have not received, to this day, either the vessel or her cargo; and how could they have been delivered to them, since they were sold during the absence of those subjects, and without their knowledge? The Undersigned will on his side ask, in what point have the stipulations of the 8th article of the treaty of 1795, been fulfilled towards Her Catholic Majesty's subjects Don Jose Ruiz and Don Pedro Montes? Have they been *treated with humanity*? Has *all favour, protection and help*, been extended to them? Have they *been permitted to remove and depart when and whither they pleased without any let or hindrance*? The unjust imprisonment which they suffered for several months, will serve as an answer to these questions?!

The Undersigned cannot in any way admit the supposition, advanced by the Secretary of State that "even had the negroes been at any time slaves, they would not have become, by their killing and escape from lawful bondage, assassins and pirates; whose delivery to the Government of Spain not having been provided for in any stipulations of the treaty of 1795, it would have been a matter of comity only, not to be demanded as a right." The treaty of 1795 unquestionably does not provide for the delivery of pirates or assassins; but only because, the Contracting Parties could never have imagined, that a case like the present, could have occasioned doubts of any kind, and because the point was so clear, that they did not think it necessary to take it into consideration. Who can forsee the horrible consequences which may result, as well in the islands off Cuba and Porto Rico, as in the Southern States of the Union, should the slaves come to learn—and there will be no want of persons to inform them—that on murdering killing and flying from lawful captivity, whensoever they may be in transportation from one point of the islands to another, and coming to the United States, the delivery of them, on account of their having murdered, killed, or fled, cannot be demanded as a right? The Undersigned leaves to the characteristic penetration of the Secretary of State, (the task of imagining) the severe incalculable evils, which may be occasioned by realizing this supposition.

The Undersigned duly acknowledges the favour of the offer, made by the Secretary of State to the Spanish Subjects Ruiz and Montes, that the Courts of the United States would be open for them to present their complaints, on account of injuries or personal sufferings. To these courts natives as well as foreigners can indifferently have recourse; but Messrs Montes and Ruiz are in a particular position, in which they are placed as well by the treaty of 1795 as by the Law of Nations; and in order to preserve it, they magnanimously suffered a severe imprisonment for months; As they have in consequence placed themselves under the protection of Her Catholic Majesty's Legation, they will through it, as the Undersigned hopes, obtain a happy result from their complaints.

In consideration of all that has been here set forth, the Undersigned takes pleasure in believing, that the Secretary of State will find his demands just, and well founded, and will he doubts not take proper measures for arriving at the happy consummation which he promises to himself. The Undersigned at the same time, thinks it his duty to state, that he has received express orders from his Government, to protest, in the most solemn and formal manner, against all that has been done by the Courts of the United States, in the case of the Schooner Amistad, the fulfilment of this order, being one of the principle objects which the Undersigned proposed to accomplish by this note.

The Undersigned cannot conclude this communication, without conveying to the Secretary of State his acknowledgements, for the expression of his desire to preserve unbroken the old and friendly relations which fortunately and for their mutual prosperity bind Spain to the United States. The Undersigned and his Government cherish the same desires, and with this understanding, he flatters himself that he will shortly receive a proof of the scrupulous exactness with which the Government of the Union fulfills the treaties and stipulations, which unite it with other friendly nations.

The Undersigned avails himself of this opportunity, to repeat to the Secretary of State, the assurances of his high esteem and distinguished consideration. P. A. de Argaiz

Copy. Translation. DNA, RG 59 (Notes from Foreign Legations, Spain). Rec'd September 28, 1841. Published in *Executive Documents*, 27th Cong., 3d sess., Serial 422, No. 191.

FROM HUGH SWINTON LEGARÉ
Private

Office of Attorney General
Dear Sir,   2 March 1842.

I have got a letter from [Pedro Alcántara] d'Argaiz[1] the Spanish Minister who insists on corresponding with me about your business. He begs me to offer to you his most cordial compliments on your very able argument in the case of the Creole,[2] & to express his confidence that it will have convinced *you* that his claims in regard to the Amistad are quite irresistible. He adds that this plea put in by so able an advocate however

1. Not found.
2. See above, DW to Everett, January 29, 1842, in "The Crisis in Anglo-American Relations," pp. 177–185.

unexpected, is not on that account the less aggreeable to him, & will entirely supercede the necessity of his again troubling the Department of State with any communication upon that subject. He trusts, therefore, that he will soon receive an official note from you announcing to him that his cause is gained, & drawing in favour of his constituents upon the Treasury of the U.S. for an indemnity which, he is quite sure, will no longer be withheld. Having done the part of an interpreter let me add that of Yr humble servt & well wisher   H. S. Legaré

A L S . MHi. Legaré (1797–1843; College of South Carolina 1814) studied law in the United States and Europe. President Tyler appointed him attorney general on September 13, 1841, and he served in that capacity until 1843.

TO PEDRO ALCÁNTARA DE ARGAIZ

Department of State,
Washington, 21st June, 1842

The Secretary of State has to acknowledge the receipt of the note of 24th September[1] which M. [Pedro Alcántara] de Argaiz did him the honor to address him.

Viewing that note as intended mainly for a protest against the proceedings of this Government in the case of the Amistad, the Undersigned did not think a reply was desired, or that any advantage would ensue from further prolonging the discussion.

Understanding now from conversation with M. de Argaiz that a reply is expected, the Undersigned proceeds to offer some remarks on the subject of M. de Argaiz's note.

The Undersigned certainly did suppose that the communication to M. de Argaiz of the decision of the Supreme Court would close the correspondence on that subject. The immediate predecessor of the Undersigned [John Forsyth], whose remarks,[2] as quoted by M. de Argaiz, the Undersigned well remembers, meant, and could have meant, nothing more by those remarks than that the decision of the Supreme Court would be the decision of the Government. Mr. Forsyth does not use the word Executive in this connection. He says "Government." "Whatever be in the end the disposal of the question, it will be in consequence of a decision emanating from no other source than the Government of the United States." The Supreme Court is a part of that Government, as Mr. Forsyth remarks, and its decision, in matters lawfully within its jurisdiction, is the final decision of the Government of the United States upon such matters.

M. de Argaiz seems to think that a treaty stipulation cannot be sub-

1. See above, Argaiz to DW, September 24, 1841.
2. See Forsyth to Argaiz, December 12, 1839, DNA, RG 59 (Notes to Foreign Legations, Spain).

jected to the interpretation of the judicial authority; and proceeds to remark that "if the courts of the Union possess the right of interpreting, considering, and deciding upon treaties contracted between nation and nation and the Executive power cannot inquire whether their decrees are or are not conformable with justice, it would be as well to declare that, in order to give to treaties the force of treaties, or at least to render them obligatory, they should be concluded with the judicial power, or, in better words, that treaties should be made for them to be afterwards interpreted as the courts might think proper"; but the Undersigned supposes that nothing is more common, in countries where the Judiciary is an independent branch of the Government, than for questions arising under treaties to be submitted to its decision. Indeed, in all regular Governments questions of private right, arising under treaty stipulations are in their nature judicial questions. With us, a treaty is part of the supreme law of the land: as such, it influences and controls the decisions of all tribunals; and many instances might be quoted of decisions made in the Supreme Court of the United States arising under their several treaties with Spain herself, as well as under treaties between the United States and other nations.[3] Similar instances of judicial decisions on points arising under treaties may be found in the history of France, England, and other Nations. And indeed the Undersigned would take the liberty to remind the Chevalier de Argaiz that this very treaty of 1795 has been made the subject of judicial decision by a Spanish tribunal. The Undersigned would call to the recollection of the Chevalier de Argaiz the case of M[iguel] D[rawing] Hareng, in which the Spanish Colonial Courts decided according to their sense of the intention of the treaty of 1795, and the Intendant confirmed their decree, which was that nothing in that Treaty, exempted Mr Hareng from the payment of certain demands.[4] From this decision this Government was inclined to dissent, but never questioned the right and duty of a Spanish court to consider the intent and effect of a Treaty.

M. de Argaiz states: "The enlightened Secretary of State will agree

3. See, for example, *Moodie* v. *The Phoebe Anne*, 3 Dallas 319 (1796); *Nereida*, 9 Cranch 388 (1815); *The Amiable Isabella*, 6 Wheaton 1 (1821); *Harcourt* v. *Gaillard*, 12 Wheaton 523 (1827); *U.S.* v. *Arredondo*, 6 Peters 691 (1832); *City of New Orleans* v. *Armas*, 9 Peters 224 (1835); *Mitchel* v. *U.S.*, 9 Peters 711 (1835); *Strother* v. *Lucas*, 12 Peters 410 (1838). Wharton *Digest*, vol. 2, No. 133, pp. 31–32.

4. Hareng, a resident of Cuba claiming U.S. citizenship, received an inheritance from his father's Cuban estate, which was taxed by the Spanish colonial courts. Hareng unsuccessfully complained that the tax violated Article 11 of the Treaty of San Lorenzo of 1795, which allowed alien heirs to remove proceeds from estate sales without detraction. Argaiz to Forsyth, December 24, 1840, DNA, RG 59 (Notes from Foreign Legations, Spain).

with the Undersigned, that one of the things which principally constitute the independence of a country, is the jurisdiction of its courts, or, in other words, that no nation, nor its courts, should assume the faculty of pronouncing judicially upon acts committed within the jurisdiction of another. On this principle, the Undersigned cannot conceive how the Secretary of State could for a single moment have supposed, that the Undersigned would have agreed to, and have seen with satisfaction, the decision of a court of the United States pronounced upon acts appertaining to Spanish subjects, committed on board of a Spanish vessel, and in the waters of a Spanish territory, within the purview of a treaty and of the law of nations.

"The Secretary of State is also pleased to observe, 'that the Schooner Amistad, upon her arrival on this coast, was, with all her cargo, according to the provisions of the ninth article, taken into the custody of the officers of the nearest port; and that, in consequence of a claim for salvage, the subject of the ownership of the vessel and cargo was brought before the Courts.' The Undersigned will not stop to remark upon the magnanimity of a demand for salvage preferred by officers of a ship of war of the United States; but does the Secretary of State believe that this can justify the intervention of the courts of the United States in this case, contrary to the opinion given by the Attorney General, Mr. [Felix] Grundy; and after, moreover, the officers themselves had renounced their claim to salvage, as Lieutenant [Thomas R.] Gedney, the commander of the Washington, himself, declared to the Undersigned?

"The Secretary of State also says that 'it was found by the Courts that the negroes were not the lawful property of any one.' One violation of necessity brought on another not less unjust; for the Judges of the United States, in order to ascertain whether or not the Africans were the lawful property of Spanish subjects, thought proper to examine the papers found on board of the vessel, which had been given by the authorities of Her Catholic Majesty, in the Island of Cuba; this was a recognition of the right of search, which, besides its not being authorized by any nation, has been combated by writers on public law, and most particularly, in the case in question, by the distinguished jurist Mr. Grundy, Attorney General of the Union, at the time when the Schooner Amistad arrived on the Anglo American coasts. (See his opinion on this case.)"

The Undersigned will make one more attempt to state the general occurrences of this transaction so plainly as that he cannot be misunderstood, with a hope of convincing M. de Argaiz that nothing has been done by the authorities of the United States, or any of them, not in strict accordance with the principles of public law and the practice of Nations, nothing which can be complained of with justice as an encroachment upon Spanish territories, or visiting and searching Spanish vessels.

The succinct history of the case is the most complete justification which can be made of all that has been done in regard to it in the United States.

Lieutenant Gedney, of the United States brig Washington, on the 27th of June, 1839, discovered the Spanish Schooner Amistad, then at anchor, within half a mile of the shore of the United States. The vessel was then in the possession of certain blacks who had risen upon and killed the Captain. Lieutenant Gedney took possession of and brought in the vessel to the United States; and for this service claimed salvage, upon the common principles of maritime law. The possession of the vessel had become already lost to her owners; and to save her from entire destruction, and to restore her to those owners, was esteemed a meritorious service. The Chevalier de Argaiz must certainly understand that when merchant vessels are met with at sea, so shattered by storms and tempests, or other disasters, or so deprived of their crew as to be unable to prosecute their voyage; in all such cases other vessels falling in with them, and saving them, are entitled to reasonable compensation; and to ascertain the amount of this compensation, the vessel is to be brought in, subjected to judicial proceedings, and justice rendered the claimants and salvors, according to well established rules and principles. Spain herself, in the early ages of commerce, was among the first to establish the principles, and lead in the administration of this part of the maritime law, and these principles now prevail over the whole commercial world; and the highest judicial authority in the United States acting under the influence of the same rules which must have controlled the decision of an English tribunal, a French tribunal, or a Spanish tribunal, has decided that the case was a case for salvage, and has decreed to the salvors a just compensation. The Undersigned is, therefore, quite at a loss to conceive how this transaction can be deemed an encroachment upon the jurisdiction of Spain, or an unlawful visitation and search of Spanish vessels.

At the institution of proceedings in the court, claims were interposed on behalf of Spanish subjects for the vessel and cargo, which were allowed, subject to salvage. Claims were also interposed for the negroes found on board, which were claimed as slaves, and the property of Spanish subjects. On the other hand, the negroes denied that they were slaves and the property of Spanish subjects, or any other persons. It was impossible for the courts to avoid the decisions of the questions thus brought before them; and in deciding them, it was bound to regard the Law of Nations, the laws of Spain, the treaty between Spain and the United States, the laws of the United States, and the evidence produced in the case. Proceeding upon these grounds, after a very patient investigation, and the hearing of elaborate arguments, the court decided that the negroes found on board the Amistad, with one exception,[5] were not slaves,

5. Antonio, the slave of the *Amistad*'s captain, informed the district court

nor the property of any body, but were free persons, and, therefore decreed that they should be set at liberty. All this appears to the Undersigned to be in the common course of such affairs. The questions in which Spanish subjects were interested have been heard and tried before competent tribunals, and one of them has been decided against the Spanish subjects, but this can give no possible ground of complaint on the part of Spain, unless Spain can show that the tribunal has acted corruptly, or has decided wrong in a case in no degree doubtful. Nations are bound to maintain respectable tribunals to which the subjects of States at peace may have recourse for the redress of injuries and the maintenance of their rights. If the character of their tribunals be respectable, impartial, and independent, their decisions are to be regarded as conclusive. The United States have carried the principle of acquiescence in such cases as far as any Nation upon earth; and in respect to the decisions of Spanish tribunals, quite as frequently perhaps as in respect to the tribunals of any other nation.[6] In almost innumerable cases, reclamations sought by citizens of the United States against Spain for alleged captures, seizures, and other wrongs committed by Spanish subjects, the answer has been, that the question had been fairly tried before an impartial Spanish tribunal, having competent jurisdiction, and decided against the claimant; and in the sufficiency of this answer, the Government of the United States has acquiesced. If the tribunal be competent—if it be free from unjust influence—if it be impartial and independent—and, if it has heard the case fully and fairly, its judgment is to stand as decisive of the matter before it.

This principle governs in regard to the decisions of courts of common law, courts of equity, and especially courts of admiralty, where proceedings so often affect the rights and interests of the citizens of foreign States and Governments.

M. de Argaiz complains that the vessel and cargo were sold, and that loss thereby happened to the owners. But all this was inevitable, and no blame attaches on account of it to the tribu[n]al. In cases of an allowance for salvage, if the owner be not present and ready to pay the amount, the property must, necessarily, be sold, that the proceeds be properly apportioned between owner and salvor. This is a daily occurrence in every court of admiralty in the world. Sufficient notice of this intended sale was given in legal form, in order that the claimants might be pres-

---

that he wished to return to Cuba. Later, however, he escaped from custody and was never found.

6. During the Napoleonic Wars, for example, a number of American ships were prized in Spanish courts. Some of these cases were the subject of Article 21 of the treaty of 1795. See *International Arbitrations*, 2: 991–1005, and the chapter on the Spanish claims commission, *Legal Papers*, 2: 175–275.

ent, or might, if they pleased, prevent it by paying the amount awarded for salvage, and receive their property.

The Chevalier de Argaiz complains that Messrs. [Pedro] Montes and [Jose] Ruiz suffered an unjust imprisonment in the United States. The Undersigned cannot but think that such an allegation of injury put forth in behalf of Messrs. Montes and Ruiz, is not a little extraordinary. These persons themselves had held in unjust and cruel confinement certain negroes who, it appeared in trial, were as free as themselves; and these negroes finding themselves within the protection of equal laws, sought redress by a regular appeal to those laws, for the injuries which they had suffered. The pursuit of this redress by the injured parties, it appears, subjected Messrs. Ruiz and Montes to a temporary imprisonment. In the judgment of enlightened men, they will probably be thought to have been very fortunate in escaping severer consequences.

M. de Argaiz's note contains a paragraph of the following tenor:

"The Undersigned cannot in any way admit the supposition advanced by the Secretary of State, that 'even had the negroes been at any time slaves, they would not have become, by their killing and escape from lawful bondage, assassins and pirates, whose delivery to the Government of Spain not having been provided for in any stipulations of the Treaty of 1795, it would have been a matter of comity only, not to be demanded as a right.' The Treaty of 1795 unquestionably does not provide for the delivery of pirates or assassins; but only because the contracting parties could never have imagined that a case like the present could have occasioned doubts of any kind, and because the point was so clear that they did not think it necessary to take it into consideration. Who can foresee the horrible consequences which may result as well in the Islands of Cuba and Porto Rico as in the southern States of the Union, should the slaves come to learn—and there will be no want of persons to inform them—that on murdering, killing, and flying from captivity, whensoever they may be in transportation from one point of the Islands to another, and coming to the United States, the delivery of them, on account of their having murdered, killed, or fled, cannot be demanded as a right? The Undersigned leaves to the characteristic penetration of the Secretary of State (the task of imagining) the severe incalculable evils which may be occasioned by realizing this supposition."

The Undersigned must beg leave to differ entirely from M. de Argaiz in regard to the rule of law for delivering up criminals and fugitives from justice. Although such extradition is sometimes made, yet in the absence of treaty stipulation, it is always matter of comity or courtesy. No Government is understood to be bound by the positive law of nations to deliver up criminals, fugitives from justice, who have sought an asylum within its limits. The Government of the United States has had occasion to hold intercourse on this question with England, France, Russia, Denmark, and Sweden,[7] and it understands it to be the sentiment of all these Governments, as well as the judgment of standard writers on public law, that in the absence of provisions by treaty, the extradition of fugitive offenders is a matter resting in the option and discretion of every Government.

The Undersigned has thus once more gone over the circumstances of this case, and stated the view which the Government of the United States has of it. He sincerely and confidently hopes that the Chevalier de Argaiz will perceive that this Government has violated none of its obligations to Spain, or done injustice, in any manner whatever, to any Spanish subject.

The Undersigned avails himself of this occasion to renew to the Chevalier de Argaiz assurances of his high consideration.

Danl. Webster

L C. DNA, RG 59 (Notes to Foreign Legations, Spain). Published in *Executive Documents*, 27th Cong., 3d sess., Serial 422, No. 109.

FROM PEDRO ALCÁNTARA DE ARGAIZ

[27 June, 1842]

The Undersigned, Envoy Extraordinary, and Minister Plenipotentiary of Her Catholic Majesty, has the honor to acknowledge the receipt of the note addressed to him by Mr Webster, Secretary of State of the Federal Government of the Union, under date of the 21st instant,[1] in answer to his of the 24th of September last.[2]

Before entering fully into the question, however, the Undersigned believes it will not be unimportant to make a cursory observation upon two points contained in his note of the 24th of September last, and to which the Secretary of State refers in his of the 21st instant.

The Undersigned yielding to the imperative voice of his duty which obliges him to pursue this correspondence notwithstanding the decision of the Supreme Court of the United States, cannot but express his surprise that the Secretary of State should regard that decision as opera-

7. Webster probably had in mind discussions with France, Prussia (which DW's copyist may have misread as Russia in this letter), Denmark, and Sweden regarding the *Plattsburg* case and with Britain regarding the *Lee* case. In 1816 the crew of the *Plattsburg* murdered the captain and officers at sea. They scattered in Europe, which led to extradi-tion negotiations with the various governments. In the *Lee* case, the British government demanded that the United States surrender a mutineer. *Ex. Doc.*, 26th Cong., 1st sess., Serial 366, No. 199.

1. See above.

2. See above, Argaiz to DW, September 24, 1841.

tive upon the Government of Her Catholic Majesty. Even should the undersigned have failed to comprehend the precise meaning of the passage cited by him from the note of Mr [John] Forsyth,[3] and should the Secretary of State be accurate in attributing to Mr. Forsyth the idea that the United States, and not a foreign Government would decide this question; still, the Government of Her Catholic Majesty cannot make its claim elsewhere than to the Executive power of the Union, and consequently the determination of the United States can have no force or virtue except as emanating from the Executive power.

The Secretary of State in concluding his note of the 24th instant, seems to admit that the Undersigned had correctly understood the principle maintained by him to be, that these blacks could not be claimed or delivered as slaves, even should they have been held in lawful bondage, if besides being slaves they were also criminals. This is the proposition contained in the note of Mr. Webster of the 1st of September last.[4] Now, however, he confines himself to the principle that free persons charged with offences against foreign governments cannot be delivered by the United States to the Agents of such governments: a question unnecessary and foreign to this case, since here the only persons treated of are the negroes of the Amistad, held in possession as slaves in a Spanish Territory, and into the foundation of whose condition the United States had no jurisdiction to enquire. The Undersigned is very happy to find in the communication addressed by the Secretary to Mr [Edward] Everett, the Minister of the United States at London, upon the case of the Creole,[5] a passage which may be applied directly to the case in question. In establishing the proposition that the blacks found on board the Creole, and the Vessel itself, notwithstanding their physical position, should be considered as held in possession by citizens of the United States, and still pursuing their voyage, Mr Webster says: "And that no other view of the subject can be true, is evident from the very awkward position in which the local authorities have placed their government, in respect to the mutineers still held in imprisonment. What is to be done with them? How are they to be punished? The English government will probably not undertake their trial or punishment; and of what use would it be to send them to the United States, separated from their ship, and at a period so late as that if they should be sent, before proceedings could be instituted against them, the witnesses might be scattered over half the globe. One of the highest offences known to human law is thus likely to go altogether unpunished."

The mere reading of these lines is sufficient to prove to demonstration

3. See Forsyth to Argaiz, December 12, 1839, DNA, RG 59 (Notes to Foreign Legations, Spain).

4. See above, DW to Argaiz, September 1, 1841.

5. See above, DW to Everett, January 29, 1842, in "The Crisis in Anglo-American Relations," pp. 177–185.

that the Secretary of State and the Undersigned agree in principles; the former dissenting only upon the question of their application to the case of the Amistad.

Returning now to the present question, the Undersigned, after a careful perusal of Mr Webster's last note, remarks that his reasoning rests principally upon the ground that, a claim for salvage having been presented, the Courts were obliged to enter into an examination of the papers of the Schooner Amistad; and that being unable to avoid the decision of questions made before them, they pronounced their decree based upon the Law of Nations, the Laws of Spain and of the United States, and the existing Treaty between the two nations. The Undersigned flattered himself so far as to believe that after the reasons set forth in his note of the 24th of September last, there would be no occasion to renew a discussion upon this subject; but since the Secretary of State again dwells upon it, he will enter anew upon the argument, endeavouring to communicate to Mr Webster the conviction under which he himself rests.

The Schooner Amistad, after the frightful occurrences of which she was the theatre, arrived on the 26th of August 1839, off Montauk Point, on Long Island, Montauk Point being three quarters of a mile distant from the Coast, (see the letter of Mr [William S.] Holabird to Mr Forsyth, dated New Haven 5 Novr 1839).[6] The vessel, therefore, was "within the extent of the jurisdiction by sea," of the United States; in establishing which jurisdiction it was proved that she was at the same time upon the high seas. (See the opinion of Judge [Andrew Thompson] Judson delivered in the case of the Amistad, in January 1840, and the opinions of Messieurs Webster and [Joseph] Story cited by him.)[7]

Now, the Sixth Article of the Treaty concluded in 1795 between Spain and the United States is as follows:

"Art. 6. Each party shall endeavour by all means in their power, to protect and defend all vessels and other effects belonging to the citizens or subjects of the other, which shall be within the extent of their jurisdiction by sea or by land; and shall use all their efforts to recover and cause to be restored to the right owners their vessels and effects which may have been taken from them within the extent of their said jurisdiction whether they are at war or not with the power whose subjects have

6. Holabird to Forsyth, November 5, 1839, DNA, RG 59 (Misc. Letters). Holabird (c. 1795–1855) was U.S. district attorney for Connecticut from 1837 to 1841.

7. The district court decision is not reported in *Federal Cases*, but Judson's opinion is printed in the *Hartford* (Conn.) *Courant*, January 16, 1840. Judson cited Webster's arguments in *U.S.* v. *Bevans*, 3 Wheaton 336 (1818) and Story's opinion in the case of the *La Jeune Eugenie*, 2 Mason 90 (1822). Judson (1784–1853), U.S. representative from Connecticut, 1835–1836, resigned his seat in 1836 to accept appointment as district judge of Connecticut, which he held until his death.

taken possession of the said effects." The 9th Article of the same treaty is as follows: "All ships and merchandise, of what nature soever, which shall be rescued out of the hands of any pirates or robbers, on the high seas, shall be brought into some port of either state, and shall be delivered to the custody of the officers of that port, in order to be taken care of, and restored entire to the true proprietor, as soon as due and sufficient proof shall be made concerning the property thereof."

The Brigantine of War Washington, consequently, in succoring the Schooner Amistad, according to the spirit and letter of these articles, did no more than fulfil the obligation which the United States contracted by the signing of that Treaty; and therefore, no such claim for salvage should have been presented; and no court, knowing these stipulations, could or ought to have admitted it; much more, when the claim was made by the commander of a vessel of war of the United States, the Treaty so distinctly prescribing the conduct to have been observed by that officer. Furthermore, although the service rendered to the vessel was morally meritorious, yet if it be considered physically, it is difficult to describe it as either glorious or attended with peril. 1st, Because the Schooner was only three quarters of a mile distant from the coast, and the sea was calm. 2dly Because in the same manner that she had proceeded from the Island of Cuba to the waters of Long Island, she might have continued her navigation, and passed south of the Potomac. And 3dly, Because the criminals who by force, violence, and assassination, had succeeded in possessing themselves of the vessel, were certainly not enemies from whom resistance would be expected, or, congruently, who could give anxiety to the officers of the Washington.

Further: the 9th article of the Treaty directing that property rescued on the high seas shall be *restored entire* to the owners, nothing can be granted for salvage without entirely destroying the sense and the letter of that article, in virtue of which, likewise, the competency of the courts is precluded; to which may be added what Mr Webster very properly says in his despatch to Mr Everett, that the possession and the nationality of the vessel manifested by her papers, are sufficient evidence to repel all foreign jurisdiction.

The Undersigned, then, believes that he has shewn clearly and demonstratively, that as well as the claim for salvage presented by the officers of the Brigantine Washington as the allowance thereof by the Court, are two definite infractions of the 6th & 9th Articles of the Treaty of 1795.

The Schooner Amistad, after having been succored boarded, or captured, was conducted to New London. But from this fact did she cease to be upon the high seas? The Undersigned thinks otherwise, being firmly persuaded that the vessel, morally and legally, continued always under the jurisdiction of Her Catholic Majesty, and consequently, with much greater reason than in the case of the "Creole," may it be said, as ex-

pressed by Mr Webster in his despatch to Mr Everett upon that subject—
"It would seem to have been the plain and obvious duty of the Authorities at Nassau" (at New London) "the port of a friendly power, to assist
the American Consul" (the Spanish Consul) "in putting an end to the
captivity of the Master and crew, restoring to them the control of the
vessel and enabling them to resume their voyage, and to take the mutineers and murderers to their own country, to answer for their crimes
before the proper tribunal. One cannot conceive how any other course
could justly be adopted, or how the duties imposed by" (the Treaty and)
"that part of the code regulating the intercourse of friendly states, which
is generally called the comity of nations, could otherwise be fulfilled.
Here was no violation of British Law" (of American law) "attempted or
intended on the part of the master of the Creole" (of the Amistad) "nor
any infringement of the principles of the law of Nations. The Vessel was
lawfully engaged in passing from port to port of the United States" (of
the Island of Cuba). "By violence and crime she was carried against the
master's will, out of her course, and into the port of a friendly power. All
was the result of force. Certainly, ordinary comity and hospitality entitled them to such assistance from the authorities of the place as should
enable them to resume and prosecute his voyage, and bring the offenders to justice. But, instead of this, if the facts be as represented in these
papers, not only did the authorities give no aid for any such purpose, but
they did actually interfere to set free the slaves, and to enable them to
disperse themselves beyond the reach of the master of the vessel, or their
owners. A proceeding like this cannot but cause deep feeling in the
United States" (in Spain). * * * * * * "There being no importation, nor
intent of importation, what right had the British authorities" (the American authorities) "to enquire into the cargo of the vessel, or the condition
of persons on board? These persons might be slaves for life; they might
be slaves for a term of years, under a system of apprenticeship; they
might be bound to service by their own voluntary act; they might be confined for crimes committed; they might be prisoners of war; or they
might be free" (or they might be *Bozales* or *Ladenos*)[8] "How could the
British Authorities" (the American Authorities) "look into and decide
any of these questions? Or, indeed, what duty or power, according to the
principles of national intercourse, had they to enquire at all"?

The Undersigned likewise believes it necessary to call to mind, that
the principles above cited were not concealed from the Government of

8. The term *bozales*, meaning "inexperienced," referred to slaves imported into Cuba after the Anglo-
Spanish treaty of 1817, which supposedly ended the Spanish slave
trade. *Ladinos*, or "latinized" slaves,
were those imported before 1817. By
Spanish law *ladinos* could be transported within Cuba, but *bozales* could
not. Most officials, however, were
easily convinced to certify any slaves
as *ladinos*.

the Union, that is to say from the Executive power; as is made manifest by various official documents which the Undersigned will take the liberty of citing to Mr Webster.

At the same time that the Secretary of State, Mr Forsyth, received the first note which Her Majesty's Legation addressed to him upon this subject,[9] there came to his hands a letter from Mr Holabird, Attorney of the United States for the District of Connecticut, dated the 9th of September 1839, (and which Mr Webster will find in Document No 185 House of Reps 26 cong. 1st sess.)[10] which is remarkable for the following passage: * * "I would respectfully enquire, Sir, whether there are no treaty stipulations with the Government of Spain that would authorize our government to deliver them" (the negroes) "up to the Spanish Authorities; and if so, whether it could be done before our court sits."

The Undersigned can do no less than invite the attention of the Secretary of State very particularly to the opinion given by Mr [Felix] Grundy; Attorney General of the Union, when the Schr Amistad arrived upon the Anglo-American Coasts; which opinion, after having been adopted by the Cabinet and approved by the President, was by the order of the latter communicated to the Undersigned on the 19th of November 1839, and which is found in Document No 185, page 37.[11] In this paper that eminent Jurisconsult amongst other things says * * "It would scarcely be doubted that, under the law of Nations, property rescued from pirates or robbers by a vessel belonging to a friendly power, and brought into a port of that friendly power, would be restored to the rightful owners, and this without any treaty stipulation. The 9th article of the treaty between Spain and the United States dated 27th October 1795 is as follows: " 'All ships and merchandise of what nature soever which shall be rescued out of the hands of any pirates or robbers on the high seas, shall be brought into some port of either State, and shall be delivered to the custody of the officers of that port, in order to be taken care of, and restored entire to the true proprietor, as soon as due and sufficient proof shall be made concerning the property thereof.' " This makes the case much stronger in favor of the Spanish Claimants. There can be no difference, in reason, whether the vessel be captured on the high seas, or within our own waters or ports; because if captured on the high seas they are to be brought into port; and delivered to the custody of the appropriate public officers; And if captured after having already come into a port, they should be treated in like manner. It therefore seems to me that this case

9. Calderón to Forsyth, September 6, 1839, DNA, RG 59 (Notes from Foreign Legations, Spain). Angel Calderón de la Barca (1790–1861) served as Spanish minister to the United States, 1835–1839, 1844–1855.

10. Holabird to Forsyth, September 9, 1839, *Ex. Doc.*, 26th Cong., 1st sess., Serial 366, No. 185.

11. *Ex. Doc.*, Serial 366, No. 185. For the opinion of the attorney general, see pp. 57–62.

is clearly within the spirit and meaning of the 9th article, and that the vessel and cargo should be restored entire, so far as practicable.

"My opinion further is, that the proper mode of executing this Article of the Treaty in the present case, would be for the President of the United States to issue his order, directed to the Marshal in whose custody the vessel and cargo are, to deliver the same to such persons as may be designated by the Spanish Minister to receive them. The reasons which operate in favor of a delivery to the order of the Spanish Minister are:

"1st   The owners of the vessel and cargo are not all in this Country, and of course a delivery cannot be made to them.

"2d   This has become a subject of discussion between the two governments: and in such a case the restoration should be made to that agent of the Government who is authorized to make, and through whom the demand is made.

"3d   These negroes are charged with an infraction of the Spanish laws: therefore, it is proper that they should be surrendered to the public functionaries of that Government, that, if the laws of Spain have been violated, they may not escape punishment.

"4th   These negroes deny that they are slaves; if they should be delivered to the claimants no opportunity may be afforded for the assertion of their right to freedom. For these reasons, it seems to me that a delivery to the Spanish Minister is the only safe course for this Government to pursue."

In like manner the Undersigned will remind Mr Webster of the note addressed to him by Mr Forsyth on the 6th of January 1840 (Doc. 185 pp. 37 & 38)[12] in which may be read the following remarkable words.

"The President has the more readily been inclined to accede to your request on this particular, on account of one of the leading motives which prompted you to make it; that the negroes, having asserted before the Court of Connecticut that they are not slaves, may have an opportunity of proving the truth of their allegation *before the proper tribunals* of the Island of Cuba, *by whose laws alone*, taken in connexion with the circumstances occurring before the arrival of the negroes in the United States, the question of their condition can be *legally* decided."

Finally, the Undersigned feels bound furthermore to cite the Journal of the Senate of the United States (Doc. 179 pp. 9 & 10, 26 Cong. 2d Sess)[13] which contains resolutions unanimously adopted by that body with regard to the cases of "The Enterprise," "The Encomium" & "The Comet."

12. Forsyth to Argaiz, January 6, 1840, *Ex. Doc.*, Serial 366, No. 185.

13. Argaiz is apparently referring to the Senate resolution on the *Enterprise, Encomium*, and *Comet* (see above, DW to Everett, January 29, 1842, note 10, p. 184) but incorrectly cites published documents on the *Amistad* (*Senate Documents*, 26th Cong., 2d sess., Serial 378, No. 179).

After a careful examination of the reasons set forth as well in this communication as in the residue of the correspondence upon the subject of the Amistad which has passed between Her Majesty's Legation and the Department,—and to which the Undersigned again invites the attention of Mr Webster,—will it still be maintained that the Treaty of 1795 has not been infringed? Will Mr Webster still confidently contend that the Courts of the Union could lawfully proceed in this case? And, finally, can the Government of the United States entertain the smallest doubt with respect to the complete indemnity which is due to the subjects of Her Catholic Majesty, Don José Ruiz, and Don Pedro Montes, for the property of which they have been so unjustly despoiled, and for the sufferings, bodily and mental, which they have undergone during the months of their imprisonment? The Undersigned confidently hopes that the Secretary of State, acknowledging the force and the demonstration resulting from these facts, will at once accede to their just claims.

From the foregoing exposition it is easy to deduce that, over and above the reasons and arguments which Her Majesty's Government through the medium of her legation in the United States has presented in support of this claim (and which in the opinion of the Undersigned have not been overthrown) there results likewise indisputable principles in its favor, emanating from illustrious authorities of the United States, and most especially from Mr Webster the present Secretary of State of the Anglo-American Confederation, in his note to Mr Everett relative to the case of the "Creole."

Before the occurrence of the last mentioned event, the Government of Her Majesty might have entertained the illusion that the Government of the United States in delaying to accede to its just claims had been actuated, perhaps, either by reasons of a political character, and peculiar to the country, or from an erroneous method of considering the question.

At the present day, however, since the doctrines maintained by the United States, through the medium of Mr Webster, are known, there does not and cannot exist the smallest doubt upon this matter. Both Governments possess the same doctrines; Both are altogether agreed upon principles. If therefore, (which is not to be expected or believed,) the Government of the Union should adhere to its refusal, Her Catholic Majesty's Government, much to its regret, will be found to admit the supposition that the friendly sentiments by which it is animated are not reciprocated by the Government of the United States.

The Undersigned deems it also indispensable that he should make known to the Secretary of State that Her Majesty's Government has been pleased to approve the conduct observed by the Undersigned in this case; and very particularly the note of the 29th of May 1841;[14] and that he has

14. See above, Argaiz to DW, May 29, 1841.

received at the same time definite orders from Her Majesty's Government to ask again explicitly and distinctly as he now does, the admission or denial of the four points set forth in the above mentioned note of the 29th of May 1841.

For the purpose of facilitating the Government of the United States in ascertaining the total of the sum claimed, and to convince it how moderate and liberal Her Majesty's subjects have been in their claim of compensation for so many losses and sufferings, the Undersigned has the honor of enclosing herewith copies of authenticated documents[15] whose originals are in his power to ask.

1st   The invoices of the goods, and their prices, which Messrs Ruiz and Montez had on board the Schr Amistad.

2dly   The authenticated proof of the value of the negroes *when purchased in Havana*; and of the damages sustained by Messrs Ruiz and Montez.

3d   The value of the vessel, moderately estimated, after her arrival in the United States, and the value of the negro Antonio.

All which, as the Secretary of State will be pleased to observe, amounts to the sum of $47,405 $\frac{62}{100}$.

If contrary to all the hopes which are entertained; the Government of the United States should refuse to grant this indemnity so justly claimed and due, the Undersigned, in fulfilment of the orders which he has received from Her Majesty's Government, must declare that Spain, considering it offensive to her national dignity, cannot consent that while she discharges with religious scrupulousness the obligations which she has contracted with the United States, they should disregard those which are imposed upon them by the stipulations of the Treaties; and that in consequence of this consideration, the Government of Spain cannot deny to the subjects of Her Majesty the protection which they have the right to require from it. And as it cannot permit the property of those subjects to remain longer abandoned, it will consider the answer of the Secretary of State as conclusive and decisive of the matter. The Undersigned therefore begs that Mr Webster will be pleased to make it as definite as possible.

And finally, as the orders which the Undersigned has received require of him by all means to endeavour to obtain a prompt reply, he will be very happy if it should please Mr Webster to answer him as early as practicable, in order that his note may be seasonably communicated to Her Majesty's government according to its wishes.

The Undersigned, not doubting that the resolution will be in accord-

15. Argaiz refers to several documents dealing with past claim cases   enclosed with this note.

ance with the well founded hopes of Her Majesty's Government, avails himself of this occasion to reiterate to Mr Webster, Secretary of State of the United States, the assurances of his high esteem and distinguished consideration. (signed) P. A. de Argaiz

Copy. Translation. DNA, RG 59 (Notes from Foreign Legations, Spain). Rec'd June 27, 1842. Published in *Executive Documents*, 28th Cong., 1st sess., Serial 442, No. 83.

TO PEDRO ALCÁNTARA DE ARGAIZ

Department of State,
Sir: Washington, 16th Augt., 1842

By a letter received at this Department yesterday, from His Excellency Don Antonio de Larruer, Intendant of Havana,[1] dated on the 23d ultimo,[2] the Department has been informed that the payment due by Spain to the United States on the 1st of this month, under the Treaty of 1834,[3] cannot be made by him until he receives an answer from you as to a pending claim for indemnity, and as to its amount, and the manner of disclaiming or deducting it from this payment. This pending claim, it is to be presumed, is that which you have presented to this Government for alleged wrongs and losses in the case of the Amistad.

I have the President's directions to lose no time in inquiring whether you have been instructed by your Government to signify, in any way, to the Intendant of Havana, that those payments falling due under the late arrangement between the United States and Spain, and intended as a means of enabling Spain more easily to fulfil her solemn Treaty obligations, are to be suspended or abated, or any way affected by the pendency of the claim presented by you in the case of the Amistad. I have the honor to be, with distinguished consideration, your obedient servant.   Danl Webster

L C . DNA, RG 59 (Notes to Foreign Legations, Spain).

TO ANTONIO DE LARRUA

Department of State
Washington Augt. 16th. 1842

I had yesterday the honour to receive your Excellency's letter of the

1. Larrua has not been further identified.

2. Larrua to DW, July 23, 1842, DNA, RG 84 (Records of Foreign Service Posts, Spain).

3. The Convention of 1834 settled claims by Americans against Spain for shipping spoliations during the Latin American revolutions of the 1820s. Spain agreed to a settlement of twelve million rials vellon (about $600,000) bearing an annual interest of 5 percent. See *Treaties*, 3:811–822.

23rd of July,[1] and lose no time in replying to it. Its contents have created surprise. The money due by Spain under the Treaty of 1834, is an acknowledged debt, which her public faith is solemnly bound to discharge. Heretofore, she has not found herself in a condition, at all times, to meet payments in the manner stipulated in the Treaty, as they have successively fallen due. To accommodate Spain, and from a desire to consult her convenience, a mode of payment, not precisely such as the Treaty stipulated, has been assented to, on the part of the United States;[2] and this Government has been officially informed that payment in the mode thus agreed to, would be made at Cuba; and one such payment has been made. Now, at the moment when a second falls due, the President learns from your letter, not without the greatest surprise, that this expected payment can only be made, subject to a deduction for "a claim for indemnification pending." This pending claim, from the reference which you make to the Spanish Minister here [Pedro Alcántara de Argaiz], is supposed to be a claim of indemnity for alleged wrongs or losses in the case of the Amistad. I pray leave to remind your Excellency, that the debt due from Spain, is an acknowledged debt, due by Treaty, and the regular payment of which has been promised and secured by a high and solemn obligation. The claim of indemnity for losses in the case of the Amistad, on the contrary, is not an acknowledged, but a controverted claim; its justice has as yet not been admitted; it is at this moment, a subject of correspondence between the two Governments. And even if it were admitted that there was some foundation for the claim, the amount has never been liquidated or settled. But the whole case is a disputed one. Between this acknowledged debt, on one side, precisely fixed and secured by solemn treaty, and this disputed claim on the other, there is no natural connection; and, I am instructed by the President to say, that this Government can never consent, that any such connection shall be made between them. Whatever claims Spain may make upon it, whether in the Amistad Case, or any other case, it will hear with patience, and discuss with fairness and candor; but it can never consent that the pendency of such claims shall be allowed as a reason for failing to fulfil plain, direct, and positive Treaty engagements.

It will be my duty to transmit a copy of your Excellency's letter, and of this answer, immediately to the American Minister at Madrid [Washington Irving], to be by him communicated to the Spanish Government.

1. See Larrua to DW, July 23, 1842, DNA, RG 84 (Records of Foreign Service Posts, Spain).

2. Instability in Spain caused suspension of interest payments on the treaty settlement after 1836. An agreement, kept secret at the request of Spain, resulted in the resumption of the payments at Havana in 1841. See Aaron Vail to DW, April 4, 1841, DNA, RG 59 (Despatches, Spain). Vail served as chargé d'affaires in Madrid from May 1840 to August 1842.

In the mean time, I have to inform your Excellency that no partial payment of the sum already due, or any payment which admits of any deduction or allowance on any account whatever, will be received. I have the honour to be, with much consideration, Your Excellency's Obdt Servant Danl Webster

L S . Archivo General de Indias, Seville, Spain.

FROM PEDRO ALCÁNTARA DE ARGAIZ

Sir   Bordentown August 19th 1842
   I have the honour to acknowledge the receipt of the note, which you were pleased to address to me, under date of the 16th inst.[1] informing me, that by a communication received in your Department, from His Excellency Don Antonio de Larrua, Intendent of the Island of Cuba, you had learned that the said Intendent cannot make payment of the dividends due on the 1st of the last month, until he shall have received notice from me, relative to a claim pending for indemnification; and you ask me in consequence of orders from the President, whether I have received instructions from my Government, to signify in any way to the Intendent of the Island of Cuba, that the payments due by Spain agreeably to the last arrangement between her and the United States, shall be suspended or abated in consequence of the pending claim respecting the case of the Amistad.
   I have the honour to state to you, in answer to your said note, that, even supposing me to have received instructions from Her Majesty's Government, upon the subject, those (instructions) could not be carried into effect, until I knew the resolution which the Government of the United States might adopt, on the claim which I have pending in the name of Her Majesty, in your Department, and on which I expected an answer on the 15th instant. You Sir, will easily conceive how disagreeable it is to me, to be without the means of giving you fuller explanations. I repeat to you Sir the assurances of my most distinguished consideration. P. A. de Argaiz

Copy. Translation. DNA, RG 59 (Notes from Foreign Legations, Spain). Rec'd August 21, 1842.

TO PEDRO ALCÁNTARA DE ARGAIZ

Department of State,
Washington, 24th Augt., 1842
   The Undersigned has the honor to acknowledge the receipt of the Chevalier [Pedro Alcántara] d'Argaiz's note of the 19th instant.[1]
   As the Chevalier d'Argaiz has not seen fit to give any answer to the

1. See above.   1. See above.

inquiries, proposed to him by the Undersigned, by order of the President, it only remains for the Undersigned to make this matter the subject of a communication to the American Minister in Spain [Washington Irving].

But at the same time, in order that Mr d'Argaiz may be at no loss to understand the sentiments of the American Government in respect to this occurrence, the Undersigned encloses to him copies of the correspondence between His Excellency, the Intendente of Havana [Antonio de Larrua], and this Department.[2]

The Undersigned renews to the Chevalier d'Argaiz the assurances of his distinguished consideration.   Danl Webster

LC. DNA, RG 59 (Notes to Foreign Legations, Spain).

TO WASHINGTON IRVING

Department of State,

No. 5   Washington, Augt. 29, 1842

Sir: You are aware that, under a secret arrangement proposed by the Spanish Government to your predecessor [Aaron Vail], and submitted by him to the President, by whom it was approved, the particulars of which will be found on file among the papers of the Legation at Madrid, a confidential agent was appointed on the part of the United States, to proceed to Havana to receive the amount agreed to be paid there for the benefit of the claimants under the Treaty of 1834.[1] A copy of the instructions given by this Department to that agent, Mr [Tully R.] Wise, at the time of his departure, dated on the 15th February, and of his report of the 7th April, upon his return, embracing his correspondence with the authorities at Havana, is herewith enclosed.[2] By a perusal of these papers you will learn that Mr Wise's agency resulted in his bringing home $60,000, the sum which Spain undertook to advance as the first payment under the arrangement; and the President was gratified in thinking that, in permitting himself to deviate from the Treaty, he had happily acquiesced in the arrangement which Spain herself had offered, whereby a friendly power was accommodated as to a mode of discharging her obligations under the Treaty, and a door was opened for the satisfaction of the just claims of United States' citizens which had been so long deferred.

In consequence of the inconvenience and expense of sending to the Island of Cuba an agent to receive the successive amounts due at stated

2. Presumably Larrua to DW, July 23, 1842, DNA, RG 84 (Records of Foreign Service Posts, Spain), and DW to Larrua, August 16, 1842, above.

1. See Vail to DW, April 4, 1841, DNA, RG 59 (Despatches, Spain).

2. DW to Wise, February 15, 1842, and Wise to DW, April 7, 1842, DNA, RG 84 (Records of Foreign Service Posts, Spain). Wise (1803?–1844) served as the first auditor of the Treasury from June 1842 until his death.

periods under this arrangement, and of an assurance given to Mr. Wise, that such a course would be perfectly acceptable to the Intendant of Havana [Antonio de Larrua], I addressed a letter by direction of the President, to that functionary, dated on the 3d of June,[3] suggesting the expediency of his remitting the amount due on the 14th of this month, without the intervention of an agent. A copy of this letter was transmitted to you in a despatch from this Department, dated the 30th ultimo, and numbered 4.[4] The reply of the Intendente, dated at Havana, on the 23rd ultimo,[5] was received at the Department on the 15th instant, and a copy of it and a translation is herewith enclosed. The reply of the Intendente was submitted to the President, and, by his direction, I immediately addressed a communication to the Intendant, and one to the Chevalier [Pedro Alcántara] d'Argaiz, the Envoy Extraordinary and Minister Plenipotentiary of Spain near this Government, both dated on the 16th instant,[6] copies of which are also transmitted to you with this despatch. To the foregoing papers are added copy of a despatch from this Department to Mr [Lewis] Cass, the Minister of the United States at Paris, dated on the 29th ultimo,[7] on the subject of surrendering the coupons to the Spanish Government, in pursuance of one of the conditions imposed by it when the arrangement was proposed.

The papers referred to in the first part of this despatch are to be found in your files, and those of which copies are now communicated, will put you in possession of all that has passed between the two Governments on the subject to which they relate. The "pending claim" to which allusion is made by the Intendant of Havana, is presumed to be that in the case of the Amistad, and you will perceive that in my note to the Spanish Minister the inquiry is distinctly put whether the Chevalier d'Argaiz has been instructed by his Government to signify, in any way, to the Intendant of Havana, that the payments falling due under the late arrangement between the United States and Spain (an arrangement proposed by Spain, and acceded to by the United States for her accommodation and convenience, and intended to enable her more easily to fulfil her solemn obligations under the Treaty of 1834,) are to be suspended or abated, or in any way affected by the pendency of the claim presented by the Chevalier d'Argaiz in the case of the Amistad.

For full information respecting the case of the Amistad, I transmit herewith a printed document, No. 185, of the House of Representatives, of the 26th Congress, 1st Session,[8] and one of the Senate, No. 179, of the

3. Not found.

4. Not found.

5. See Larrua to DW, July 23, 1842, DNA, RG 84 (Records of Foreign Service Posts, Spain).

6. See above, DW to Larrua and DW to Argaiz, August 16, 1842.

7. No. 66. DW to Cass, July 29, 1842, DNA, RG 84 (Records of Foreign Service Posts, France).

8. *Executive Documents*, 26th Cong., 1st sess., Serial 185, No. 185.

2d Session[9] of the same, to which is added a copy of the correspondence between this Department and the Chevalier d'Argaiz which has passed since the correspondence contained in those documents was communicated to Congress.

On the receipt of this despatch you will take the earliest opportunity of calling upon the Spanish Secretary of State and Foreign Affairs,[10] and stating to him the facts as you will gather them from the various papers herewith transmitted, and you will say distinctly to him that this Government will never consent that any such claim as that proposed by the Chevalier d'Argaiz, whether such as this Government may or may not eventually allow, shall interfere to prevent the payment by Spain of interest on a debt guarantied by solemn treaty, nor that such claim shall be deducted from any such payment, nor, indeed, in any manner be connected with it. The one is a debt liquidated, ascertained, and secured by the most solemn engagements which nations can make—the other is unsettled, disputed, not yet allowed, and guarantied in no manner. That so great an injustice shall be done as to connect these two widely differing claims, this Government hardly believes the Spanish Government intends, or authorizes its representative here, to suggest. I have the honor to be, With great regard, Your obedient servant,   Danl Webster

LC. DNA, RG 59 (Instructions, Spain).

TO PEDRO ALCÁNTARA DE ARGAIZ

Department of State,
Washington, 29th Augt, 1842.

The Undersigned Secretary of State, anxious to give all reasonable satisfaction to the Chevalier [Pedro Alcántara] d'Argaiz, promised him, it is true, to go into the subject again, although he had already addressed him two full notes upon it;[1] and the Undersigned believes it is true also that he signified to the Chevalier d'Argaiz his belief that he could transmit him this third note by the 15th of August. And in fact it did happen that on that day he was engaged upon the preparation of such note at the moment when he received the wholly unexpected communication from the Intendente of Havana [Antonio de Larrua],[2] of which the Chevalier d'Argaiz has now a copy. The receipt of that communication might well cause the Undersigned to pause. He immediately received the President's instructions to make an inquiry of the Chevalier

9. *Senate Documents*, 26th Cong., 2d sess., Serial 378, No. 179.

10. Ildefonso Díez de Ribera, Count Almodóvar (1777–1846) was Spanish foreign minister April–May 1836, March–August 1837, and June 1842–

May 1843.

1. See above, DW to Argaiz, September 1, 1841, and June 21, 1842.

2. Larrua to DW, July 23, 1842, RG 84 (Records of Foreign Service Posts, Spain).

d'Argaiz which the Chevalier d'Argaiz declined to answer.[3] This made it necessary to answer the letter of the Intendente;[4] and the Chevalier d'Argaiz has been made acquainted with that answer;[5] and a despatch upon the subject has been sent also from this Department to the representative of this Government at the Court of Madrid [Washington Irving].[6]

An answer is hoped for from Havana in a few weeks, and from Spain in all due time. But, in the mean time, the Undersigned will consider whether his duty will allow him under the very unexpected and extraordinary occurrences which have arisen, to discuss further the case of the Amistad, until a reply be received to his communication from the Intendente at Havana, or from the American Minister at Madrid. The Chevalier d'Argaiz may be quite assured that this Government can never consent to connect the unacknowledged claim, in the case of the Amistad, with the acknowledged debt due by Spain to the United States, settled and liquidated as it is, and its payment secured by formal and solemn treaty stipulations.

The Undersigned avails himself of this occasion to renew to the Chevalier d'Argaiz the assurance of his distinguished consideration.

Danl Webster

LC. DNA, RG 59 (Notes to Foreign Legations, Spain).

FROM WASHINGTON IRVING

No. 10.   Madrid December 5th 1842
Sir.   Legation of the United States.

Count Almodovar, the first Minister of State, being sufficiently recovered from his Indisposition to attend to business I had an interview with him this morning on the subject of the difficulty which had occurred in respect to the semi-annual payment of interest due 14th August, on the debt owing by Spain to the United States.

On stating the case, the Count assured me that the Spanish Government had never for a moment thought of suffering the claim arising in the case of the Amistad to interfere with the punctual payment of the interest in question; and that he had no doubt the payment had been made long since.

It would appear <from what he said> that <a game of cross purposes has arisen in this matter from some petty arrangement contemplated by> the Chevalier [Pedro Alcántara] D'Argaiz, who expecting a final answer from you on the 15th August relative to the claim for in-

3. See above, DW to Argaiz, August 16, 1842.

4. See above, DW to Larrua, August 16, 1842.

5. See above, DW to Argaiz, August 24, 1842.

6. See above, DW to Irving, August 29, 1842.

demnification in the case of the Amistad and that there would be a payment to be made to the Spanish Claimants resident in Cuba; had written to that effect to the Intendente [Antonio de Larrua] of the Island, advising him to stay his hand in the remittance of the interest, as it might be an accommodation to all parties to pay it into the hands of the indemnified claimants. It was in consequence of this letter that the Intendente wrote you the letter of the 23d July;[1] so that neither he, nor M. Argaiz were acting in consequence of any instructions from the Spanish Government. Such is the explanation given to me of this part of the case.

On receiving the letter from the Chevalier D'Argaiz, The Intendente wrote to the Government at Madrid for instructions. Subsequently however, when he had received your letter,[2] he consulted with the Captain General of the Island of Cuba,[3] and it was determined between them, that the payment of the interest should be made at once without waiting for instructions; and it is presumed by the Count Almodovar that it was so made. The Intendente, however, wrote to the Count, informing him of this determination, and hoping it might be approved by Government. Before that letter reached Madrid, the Government in consequence of the previous letter on the subject, had written to him, ordering him to make the payment without fail or delay; and in no wise to mingle the matter with that of the Amistad.

A few days after sending off this letter, Count Almodovar received a despatch from the Chevalier D'Argaiz, enclosing all the correspondence which he had recently had with the Government of the United States; as this correspondence included your letter to the Chevalier D'Argaiz informing him that you had written on the subject to the Diplomatic representative of the United States at Madrid [Washington Irving];[4] Count Almodovar delayed his reply to the Chevalier until he should receive a communication from me, which he had been continually expecting.

I explained to him the reason of my being so long in making the communication; my instructions having been three months on the road and expressed my great satisfaction at the explanation I had just received, which was entirely in comformity with what had been expected by you, from the honor and good faith of the Spanish Government.

Count Almodovar still seemed nettled that there should have been any doubt of the intentions of the Spanish Government most scrupulously to fulfil its engagements: and expressed some chagrin also that you had not given the answer promised to be furnished to the Chevalier D'Argaiz

1. See Larrua to DW, July 23, 1842, RG 84 (Records of Foreign Service Posts, Spain).

2. See above, DW to Larrua, August 16, 1842.

3. Jeronimo Valdes (1784–1855) fought Peruvian revolutionaries in the 1820s, rose to high rank in the army, and was named captain-general of Cuba in 1841.

4. See above, DW to Argaiz, August 24, 1842.

on the 15 August, to the claims for indemnification in the case of the Amistad; as it kept the claimants out of the property of which they had so long been deprived. He said as the subjects were totally distinct you might have gone on with your correspondence in respect to the Amistad without regard to the question of the payments.

I replied that if he would regard your correspondence attentively, he would find that all the present cross purposes had arisen entirely from the want of a little frankness on the part of the Chevalier D'Argaiz. That you were actually engaged on the promised reply, when you were led, by the letter of the Intendente of Cuba to suppose that the Chevalier D'Argaiz had interposed the pending claim of the Amistad in the way of the regular payment of interest. That exceedingly surprised, you had written to the Chevalier[5] to know whether he had been instructed by his Government to do so; but that he had evaded replying to the enquiry, making a reply dependent on your answer to the Amistad claim.[6] This want of frankness threw a doubt over the matter, which you were exceedingly unwilling to indulge, and obliged you to seek from the Government at Madrid that information which was withheld by its representative at Washington. In the mean time you felt yourself authorised until such information were obtained, to pause in your correspondence respecting a claim which apparently was to be intruded so much out of place.

Before leaving him Count Almodovar requested that I would pass in the form of a note the communication I had been instructed to make, that he might reply in the same manner.

In connection with this subject, permit me to suggest that this Legation be furnished with a Series of the Reports of the Supreme Court: it is quite unnecessary to call your attention to the great advantage of such a collection to all future Ministers of the United States, but I may mention that the Decision of the Supreme Court in the case of the Amistad,[7] which has given rise to this question between the Governments, is to be found, neither among the papers lately transmitted by the Department, nor among those previously existing in the Archives of the Legation.

I have the honor to acknowledge the receipt of Despatch No. 9.[8] from the Department enclosing the Commission of Mr. Robt. B[lair] Campbell,[9] as Consul of the United States for the Port of Havana, and to state that in compliance with its directions I applied on the 29th ulto for the

5. See above, DW to Argaiz, August 16, 1842.

6. See above, Argaiz to DW, August 19, 1842.

7. See above, DW to Argaiz, September 1, 1841, note 2.

8. DW to Irving, October 10, 1842,

DNA, RG 59 (Instructions, Spain).

9. Campbell (d. 1862; South Carolina College 1809) served as U.S. consul at Havana from September 1842 to July 1850. He acted as consul at London from 1854 to 1861.

usual royal Exequatur in his case. I am Sir, very respectfully Your
Obdt Sevt.   Washington Irving

ALS. DNA, RG 59. (Despatches, Spain). Rec'd January 28, 1843.

TO WASHINGTON IRVING

Confidential
No 11.   Department of State
Sir: Washington, 17th Jany. 1843
By my letter to you of the 29th of August last,[1] marked as despatch No 5,
you were informed of the interruption and suspension of the payment
of interest due on the 14th of the same month, under the late agreement
with Spain, of the supposed causes and motives which had led to that
step on the part of the Spanish Minister residing near this Government
[Pedro Alcántara de Argaiz] and the Captain General of Cuba [Jeronimo
Valdes]; and of the ground at once assumed by this Government upon
being made acquainted with a proceeding so unexpected and so ex-
ceptionable. The position taken on that occasion, it appears, has not
been thought tenable, and I have now the satisfaction to state, that on
the 29th ultimo,[2] the Chevalier d'Argaiz formally announced to this Department that he had received from the Treasury of Cuba bills of exchange amounting to $60,000, which he was ready to deliver, and which
have since been delivered, destined for the payment of the 2d instalment
of the interests accruing on the debt of Spain to the United States.
    The communication from the Minister above alluded to, and the de-
livery of the bills, which have not yet come to maturity, were attended
by no explanation whatever, nor has it been thought necessary by the
Government to seek one.
    I have the honor to transmit copy of a private and confidential letter
addressed by this Department on the 14th instant, to Mr. Robert B[lair]
Campbell,[3] Consul of the United States at Havana. It was drawn forth
by information recently communicated to the Department, from a source
so reputable that it could not fail to awaken some concern. The archives
of your Legation will show you that the subject of supposed designs upon
the Island of Cuba by the British Government is by no means new; and
you will also find that the apprehension of such a project has not been
unattended to by the Spanish Government. It was accordingly in view of
what had already past, and what had recently transpired, calculated to
excite anxiety on the part of this Government, in regard to its relations

1. See above, DW to Irving, August 29, 1842.
2. The correct reference is to Argaiz to DW, December 23, 1842, DNA, RG 59 (Notes from Foreign Legations, Spain).
3. See DW to Campbell, January 14, 1843, "Central America and the Caribbean: Cuba," pp. 369–372, below.

with what is to us the most interesting portion of the Spanish Empire, that it was thought expedient to give your predecessor special directions about it, which you will see in the instructions to him from this Department, dated on the 15th July, 1840, and, numbered 2.[4] To these instructions you are now particularly referred, as well as to a confidential despatch, numbered 10, from Mr. [Aaron] Vail, of the 15th January, 1841,[5] detailing what passed in a conference with M. [Joaquin Maria] de Ferrers,[6] at the time Minister of Foreign Affairs at Madrid, from which you will learn the views and the grounds taken by this Government, which it never can relinquish. From the perusal of these documents, you will at once perceive the necessity or propriety of carefully reviewing those instructions, and acting upon them in the mode that you may conceive most judicious for the purpose of again pointing the attention of the Spanish Government to the alleged precariousness of the terms by which Spain is supposed to hold her possessions in this quarter, and to obtain for your Government the best intelligence which is in any way connected with the subject. Whether recent reports are or are not unfounded or exaggerated, it is nevertheless highly desirable that you should sound the Government of Spain, in order that the United States may know its sentiments and purposes with the same certainty and distinctness that those of the United States have been so unreservedly and so repeatedly made known to it. A copy of my letter to the Consul has just been placed by me in the hands of the Chevalier d'Argaiz, the Minister of Spain in Washington.

I transmit a copy of document No 35, just printed by order of the House of Representatives, respecting the Sandwich Islands and China.[7] I am, Sir, respectfully, your obedient servant,   Danl Webster

LC. DNA, RG 59. (Instructions, Spain). Published in *IAA*, 11:29–30.

NETHERLANDS

As the two documents printed below suggest, U.S. relations with the Netherlands were routine during Webster's secretaryship. In the Hatch case, which was resolved satisfactorily, Webster expressed a charac-

4. No. 2. Forsyth to Vail, July 15, 1840, DNA, RG 59 (Instructions, Spain). These instructions directed Vail to offer the Spanish government the alternative of paying off its debt to the United States through Cuban revenue rather than with a direct transfer of funds.

5. No. 10. Vail to Forsyth, January 15, 1841, DNA, RG 59 (Despatches, Spain).

6. Ferrer y Cafranga (1777–1861) served as foreign minister from October 1840 to May 1841.

7. This consists of President Tyler's message of December 31, 1842, on the Hawaiian islands and China, correspondence with Hawaiian agents, and a report on trade between the United States and China. *Executive Documents*, 27th Cong., 3d sess., Serial 420, No. 35.

teristic concern for the protection of American citizens engaged in international commerce. Aside from such random incidents, there was, as chargé d'affaires Christopher Hughes informed Webster, "nothing to write, that could interest you—or the Government—in the slightest degree" (April 25, 1843, below).

TO HARMANUS BLEECKER

Department of State,
Sir: Washington, 3d Septr 1841.

Papers have been communicated to the Department relating to supposed illegal treatment of Captain G. M. Hatch,[1] at Rotterdam, in June last, by authorities at that place. It appears that application was made for your official interference which you refused, and no doubt with propriety, as the case may have appeared to you to be one cognisable by the municipal law of Holland only. If however there should be reason to believe that in the proceedings against the Captain, any rule of the law of nations, or any of the usual courtesies existing between Nations, has been violated, you may address to the Dutch Government such representation or remonstrances as under all the circumstances, may appear to you proper and expedient. It is of much importance that masters and crews of American vessels employed in foreign commerce should always be assured that while they properly observe the laws of the countries which they visit, the eye of their own Government is always upon them, to watch for their safety and the security of their rights.[2] I am, Sir, your obedient servant,   Danl Webster

LC. DNA, RG 59 (Instructions, Netherlands). Bleecker (1779–1849), an Albany lawyer, was a Federalist congressman, 1811–1813. He acted as chargé d'affaires to the Netherlands, 1839–1842.

FROM CHRISTOPHER HUGHES

Private.

My dear Sir,   The Hague; 25th April; 1843.

There is nothing whatever to write to you, worthy to be called a despatch; but it is my duty to say this—and to give you some news of myself;—I fear you may have set me down as negligent & remiss; but,

1. Hatch, captain of an American ship at Rotterdam, has not been further identified.

2. Captain Hatch threw a handspike at a sailor, which resulted in the seaman's death. Bleecker refused the request of other American ship captains to interfere in the Dutch legal process, but he secured the commutation of a five-year sentence. See James Allyn to DW, September 1, 1841, DNA, RG 59 (Misc. Letters); Bleecker to DW, October 18, November 24, December 22, 1841, DNA, RG 59 (Despatches, Netherlands).

really & truly, there is *nothing* to write, that could interest you—or the Government,—in the slightest degree.

The King[1] is in the most perfect health and in the activity & cheerfulness of Youth. His Majesty and all the Royal Family left the Hague, this morning, for their annual visit to Amsterdam; where they will pass a week. This is the great event of the Day; & the only event I have to communicate. It can be of no very great interest, at Washington, to know this; but it is of *such* matters, that my European Diplomatic Colleagues make up the Despatches for their respective Courts; where, they are expected, & read with eagerness.

I was informed, some days since, that a move, or measure, similar to that which took place, a short time ago in London, was in contemplation at Amsterdam—on the part of the Holders of our States Stocks;—and that a Petition, or address, would be sent to me—on their part—such as had been sent to Mr [Edward] Everett.[2]

I just now received a Letter by the morning's mail—of which, the following is a copy.

Copy   Amsterdam 24th April, 1843.

To C. Hughes Esq.
U.S. Charge d'affairs, at the Hague,
Sir,

We take the liberty of apprising you, that a Petition to your goodself, in your official capacity, is in course of signature, here, by holders of Bonds of several states of the American Union.

Had not an indisposition prevented our A. van der Hoop[3] from going to the Hague last week, he would have done himself the honour of waiting upon you, for the purpose of offering to you a copy of the said Petition, with the English Translation. This intention having been frustrated, allow us, for the honour of communicating to you herewith, *officiously, a copy & translation of the Address and of recommending it to your kind perusal.

We have the honour to remain, with great respect. Sir—yr most obedt humble Servts—(Signed): Hope & Co[4]

---

1. William II (1792–1849) ruled 1842–1849.

2. American states owed European banking houses nearly $232 million in January 1843. After the economic crisis of 1837, some states defaulted on payments and others discussed repudiation. The major holders of American securities sent a memorial to Everett in London in February 1843, like the one to Hughes, calling on the states to honor their debts.

3. Not identified.

4. Hope & Company of Amsterdam, along with the Barings and Rothschilds, was a major holder of American securities.

The Petition or address is addressed to me;—it sets forth—respectfully, but firmly, the case & claims of the Bondholders; and says—

"These feelings and these hopes, Sir, we most earnestly entreat, you will be pleased to communicate to the General Government of the Union & to that of the several states. We join our voices to those of the numerous sufferers in an adjacent country, who have also addressed the Representative of the Union, soliciting his good offices in the transmision of their representations & in the furtherance of their wishes. These good offices have not been with-held and We, the Undersigned feel firmly persuaded, that, from you too, Sir, our application will meet with a ready acquiescence."

"Enabled, as you are, Sir, by your station to judge of the impression produced in this country by the events alluded to, & to appreciate the disastrous consequences they have entailed upon so many of our countrymen, we cannot but hope & believe, that you too will not refuse the weight of your influence, on which, we place the utmost reliance, in every proper quarter, & whenever it can be available in promoting our just claims." yr obedt servts &c. &c. &c.

So soon as these papers are received, they shall be sent to Washington. As to "the impression produced, in Holland, by the events alluded to—" it would be difficult to describe the way, in which, the Sufferers & the community in general, speak of *American* faith—& *American* fidelity— in money engagements. *We* may make distinctions between "the Union" & "the States," & with truth, in a *legal* sense. None such are made, or admitted, in Europe. The odium attaches to, & the disgust follows our *National* Name & Fame. Yr obdt servt.   C. Hughes.

* "officiously"—the french idiom—& means good offices; or with friendly intentions. }

ALS. DLC.

RUSSIA

Like U.S. relations with the Netherlands, those with Russia were routine. In 1841, U.S. minister Churchill C. Cambreleng found little worthy of communication from "this remote quarter of Europe" (Cambreleng to DW, March 9, 1841, below), and two years later his successor, Charles S. Todd, similarly reported "no subjects of collision" (Todd to DW, April 4, 1843, below) with the czarist autocracy. Webster's stated goal, as expressed in the instruction to Todd printed below (September 1, 1841), was to maintain the traditional friendship between the two countries. Webster's letter to Todd also provides an example of the standard type of instruction ordinarily given to newly appointed U.S. diplomats.

FROM CHURCHILL CALDOM CAMBRELENG

No. 12

Sir,   St. Petersburg 9 March 1841

I have the honor to transmit herewith a communication from Mr Van [Sassen],[1] the acting consul here in the absence of Mr [Abraham P.] Gibson,[2] transmitting the commercial returns of the last year; and also a despatch from the consulate at Archangel.[3]

Since my appointment to this mission I have received instructions on only one subject of any importance. These were contained in despatch no 2 of the 2 June last[4] and related to a contract between the Hudsons Bay and Russian American Fur Companies, about which I was directed to make inquiry. The information obtained from Sir John Henry Pelly, Deputy Governor of the Hudson Bay Company, you will find in my despatch no 3 of the 21 July last from Paris;[5] which was confirmed by subsequent information received here through Admiral [Adam Ivan] Krustenstern and communicated in my despatch no 8 of the 22 decemr last.[6]

The only important subject which has heretofore occupied the attention of my predecessors, without being terminated, is our proposal to treat with the government on the question of maritime Rights, which you will find very fully discussed in the instructions to Mr [John] Randolph.[7] This subject was afterwards urged upon the attention of the Russian government by Mr [James] Buchanan, as you will see by his correspondence with the Department,[8] but as they declined to negotiate, it was abandoned and has not been reviewed since. If there was no disposition at that time to treat at all, there certainly can be no hope of success in the present state of the relations between Russia and Great

1. Not identified.

2. Gibson, of New York, was appointed consul at Saint Petersburg in 1819.

3. None of the mentioned enclosures are in the RG 59 record.

4. No. 2. Forsyth to Cambreleng, June 2, 1840, DNA, RG 59 (Instructions, Russia).

5. Pelly (1777–1841) had been a governor of the Hudson's Bay Company since 1823 and was a director of the Bank of England from 1839 until his death. The dispatch referred to is No. 3. Cambreleng to Forsyth, July 21, 1840, DNA, RG 59 (Despatches, Russia).

6. Krustenstern (1770–1846) was at that time head of the Russian naval school and had been the first Russian to circumnavigate the globe, 1803–1806. The dispatch referred to is No. 8. Cambreleng to Forsyth, December 22, 1840, DNA, RG 59 (Despatches, Russia).

7. Van Buren to Randolph, June 18, 1830, DNA, RG 59 (Instructions, Russia). Randolph (1773–1833) was officially minister to Russia from May 1830 to July 1831 but spent only one month in Russia before resigning because of ill health.

8. See, for example, Buchanan to Livingston, June 12, 1832, and June 29, 1832, DNA, RG 59 (Despatches, Russia). Buchanan served as the American minister to Russia, 1832–1833.

Britain, and my only motive in noticing the subject is, because I find it among the former instructions to this Legation.

In this remote quarter of Europe we are able to communicate very little intelligence, worthy the attention of the Department, which does not reach Washington from London or Paris quite as soon as it is received here. Indeed almost all political information is derived from one or the other of these sources, which have been for the year past, and must continue to be, the theatres of negotiation between the European Powers.

The course pursued by the french government since the quadruple treaty of July last,[9] is somewhat inexplicable; and as France still perseveres in her heavy military expe[n]ditures for the fortification of Paris and the increase of her army and navy, some doubts are entertained as to the sincerity of the Kings [Louis Philippe] desire to maintain peace. His position is embarrassing. The revolution which placed him upon the Throne, was the work of the Bonapartists, who overthrew the legitimatists. The latter are still hostile to the King, while, from the tone of the Parisian Journals and the popular movements of the French capitol, it would seem that he has lost the confidence and support of the former. As these two parties embrace the great body of the french people, the King is left without support, except in the army, and he may doubt the quiet succession of the Duke of Orleans,[10] without some vigorous effort to render the reigning family popular with the nation. The history of his reign must also give him some cause of alarm. Seventeen changes of ministry in ten years is some evidence of the weakness of the government as it is now organised, and of the necessity of new measures to strengthen the power of the Throne, and to arm it against any internal difficulties which may arise. Whatever may be the secret designs of the King of the French, these extraordinary military preparations and expe[n]ditures have compelled the other continental Powers to increase their armies and to negotiate new loans. Before the spring arrives the French capitol may perhaps be more tranquil under the surveillance of a strong military force, and a better understanding may exist between France and the other European Powers; but in any event these heavy national loans and expe[n]ditures must sensibly affect the commercial interests of Europe and incidentally those of the United States.

The table of the Exports and Imports of this Port for the last year has just been published. The total amount of the Exports is 36.536.813 Silver

9. In the convention of July 15, 1840, Britain, Austria, Prussia, and Russia agreed to coerce a settlement between the pasha of Egypt, Mehemet Ali (1769–1849) who ruled 1805–1848, and the Ottoman sultan, Abdülmejid I (1823–1861), who ruled 1839–1861.

10. Ferdinand Philippe Louis Charles Henri (1810–1842).

Roubles, and the Imports 61,424,980 Silver Roubles. The statistical information relating to commerce of the United States with this Port during the last year, and for many previous years, I have communicated in my former despatches.

The marriage of the Heir Apparent,[11] which it was well understood would take place in April, is now a matter undecided, owing to the long continued indisposition of the Princess of Darmstadt[12] and the great uncertainty, from the character of her disease of her speedy recovery. It is a subject of much annoyance to the Imperial Family.

Allow me to suggest, that the present mode of transmitting the Journal which is received at this Legation from the Department, renders it of very little service, as it seldom reaches here under two months. It is now transmitted by packet, not by the steamers, to London, then to Hamburg and thence to the Custom-House here: in winter by the slow coach and in summer by the steamer to Cronstadt, from whence it reaches the St Petersburg Custom-House in about a week. I receive by the Havre packets a Newyork paper, which by the overland mail, generally reaches me a month earlier than that transmitted by the Department. If the latter were sent through the same channel it would be much more useful. Should the Department make that change, this Legation should be informed of it, as it will be necessary to apply to the Minister of Foreign Affairs for an order to receive it by the mail from France.

My last despatch from the Department bears date the 17 June of last year[13] and I am without anything to attend to. I have had no correspondence with Count [Karl Robert] de Nesselrode worthy of notice—the only notes of any sort of importance relate to an Imposter travelling in this Country under the name of Major Alfred Gordon, late of the United States army, of which I have transmitted copies to the Department.[14]

Permit me through you to present my best respects to the President and to tender him my resignation. I shall of course continue to discharge my duties here until I receive his directions as to whom I shall deliver the archives of this Legation. The time of my departure would also be regulated by any matter of public concern, which might unexpectedly render it necessary to postpone it, under the Presidents instructions and with his approbation. For my personal convenience, I must beg you to do me the favor to communicate to me as early as you can, the Presidents

11. Alexander II (1818–1881) ruled 1855–1881.

12. Marie of Hesse-Darmstadt (1823–1880).

13. Forsyth to Cambreleng, June 17, 1840, DNA, RG 59 (Instructions, Russia).

14. The spurious "Major Gordon" has not been identified. For Cambreleng's note on the matter, see No. 7. Cambreleng to Forsyth, November 25–December 7, 1840, DNA, RG 59 (Despatches, Russia).

decision and instructions; as in this remote region it requires at least three months notice to make the necessary arrangements for returning to America, especially as these must be made in England by anticipation, and as it would be very desireable to avoid a winter passage across the Atlantic. I am with great respect Yr. ob. sr   C C Cambreleng

ALS. DNA, RG 59 (Despatches, Russia). Rec'd April 23, 1841.

TO CHARLES STEWART TODD

Sir: Department of State,
No. 1—Personal Instructions.   Washington, 1st Septr 1841.
The President, with the advice and consent of the Senate, having appointed you Envoy Extraordinary and Minister Plenipotentiary of the United States near His Majesty the Emperor of Russia [Nicholas I], has directed me to inform you of his wish that you should, as soon as your own convenience will permit, proceed to St. Petersburg, and enter upon the discharge of the duties of your mission. The mode of conveyance and route are of course left to your own option.

Your immediate predecessor [Churchill Caldom Cambreleng] on quitting St. Petersburg, deposited with the United States' Consul in that city [Abraham P. Gibson], under instructions from this Department, the archives, documents, &c. &c. of the Legation, for safe keeping. You will accordingly find them in the possession of Mr. Gibson, who will be forthwith advised of your appointment and requested to deliver them over to you on your arrival in the Russian Capital.

You will receive, herewith,

1. Your commission as Envoy Extraordinary and Minister Plenipotentiary of the United States to Russia.
2. A letter of credence to His Majesty the Emperor, with an office copy of the same, which last you will communicate to the Minister of Foreign Affairs [Count de Nesselrode], upon your asking, thro' him, an audience of the Sovereign for the purpose of presenting the original to His Majesty in person.
3. A letter from the President to the Emperor in answer to a communication recently received from His Majesty announcing the marriage of his Son, the hereditary Grand Duke [Alexander II]—a copy of which is also enclosed.
4. A letter of credit on the Bankers of the United States at London, authorizing them to pay your drafts for your salary as it becomes due, and for the contingent expenses of the Legation actually incurred. You will be careful, however, in availing yourself of this authorization, to conform with the established rules of this Department as detailed in the printed personal instructions accompanying

this letter. Your outfit will be paid at this Department as soon as the necessary appropriation is made for that purpose.

5. A set of printed personal instructions prescribed by this Department as rules for the government of all diplomatic Agents abroad.

6. A printed List of Ministers, Consuls, and other diplomatic and Consular Agents of the United States in foreign countries.

7. A printed circular establishing a rule respecting salaries of diplomatic Agents absent from their posts on leave.

8. A circular relative to the form of drafts on the Foreign Intercourse Fund.

9. A Special Passport for yourself and suite.

10. American Archives. First and third volumes. Fourth Series—folio.[1]

11. Gales & Seaton's "Congressional Debates" Vol. IX parts 1, 2—Vol. X.—parts 1, 2, 3, 4—Vol. XI. parts 1, 2,—Vol. XII. parts 1, 2, 3, 4—Vol. XIII.—parts 1, 2—Vol. XIV. parts 1, 2.[2]

Your salary as fixed by law is at the rate of $9000 per annum, with an outfit equal to one year's salary, and a quarter's salary for your return home. By a general rule the compensation of Ministers to foreign courts is made to commence with the date of their commissions, if they quit the United States to proceed on their missions within thirty days from that day; and to cease on their taking leave of the courts to which they are accredited, after the receipt of orders or permission to return. In your case it will accordingly begin on the 27th day of August, 1841.

The instructions of this Department to your predecessors, to which you are referred,—together with the other records and papers belonging to the Legation, will give you an adequate idea of the state of the relations between the United States and Russia. These are at present, and have long been, of the most friendly kind; and in entrusting them to your immediate charge and superintendence, the President indulges a confident hope that no efforts will be spared on your part, to strengthen and confirm the sentiments of mutual good understanding and respect subsisting between the two Governments, and which are not less honorable to the character than advantageous to the interests of the parties.

During your residence at St Petersburg, you may be applied to, from time to time, to interpose in behalf of American citizens, to obtain satisfaction of claims which they may have on the Government of His Imperial Majesty, or the redress of grievances which they may experience in the course of their dealings and transactions. You will in all such cases, where the intervention of the Government may be proper according to the public law, afford such official aid as may appear to you likely

---

1. Peter Force, ed., *American Archives* . . . (6 vols., Washington, D.C., 1837–1853).

2. Volumes 9 through 14 of *Congressional Debates* cover the second session of the 22d Congress through the first session of the 25th Congress, 1832–1837.

to be useful, whether you have special instructions from this Department or not. I am, Sir, your obedient servant,   Danl Webster

LC. DNA, RG 59 (Instructions, Russia). Todd (1791–1871; William and Mary, 1809), a Kentucky Whig, served as minister to Russia, 1841–1846.

FROM CHARLES STEWART TODD

St Petersburg $\frac{23 \text{ March}}{4 \text{ April}}$ 1843.

Sir,

No. 29

I am apprehensive that my communications may be destitute of interest or variety but I am consoled with the reflection that the cause of their barrenness is matter of congratulation. We have no subjects of collision with this Government. The path of duty is plain as well as pleasant. I have only to endeavour to maintain the good feeling long cherished for our Country. I hope I have been successful in this effort, and while I have omitted no suitable occasion, by books, documents or Conversation, to impress a just estimate of our character and resources, it has been my chief aim to conciliate the kind feelings of the Imperial Family, of the Ministers of State, of the influential Noblemen and of the Diplomatic Corps.

Two incidents connected with this subject, partaking somewhat of a public character, may be noticed. The 22nd of February, Washington's birthday occurs, with singular Coincidence according to the Russian style, on the birthday of [William Henry] Harrison. I celebrated both events by a dinner given to some of the Foreign Ministers and Russian Noblemen; and subsequently at the Anniversary dinner 13/26. March of the English Club founded in 1770 and composed of Russians, English and Germans I had the opportunity of conciliating a good feeling by my reply to the Compliment extended to the U. States.

The Affairs of Servia continue to be a source of anxiety to the Imperial Government. I learn from an authority entitled to my confidence that the Emperor [Nicholas I] is dissatisfied with the Course of the Porte; that the subject is rendered more difficult of management from the opinion entertained here that the Members of the Polish Society in Paris are fomenting mutual jealousies in the hope of placing one of their Chiefs at the head of affairs. The Emperor thinks he is in the right and my informant added that in such cases he would not yield and War might be the result. This Communication was made to me in connexion with the hope he expressed that the U. States and England would not suffer the Oregon question[1] to embroil their present happy relations.

1. See below, "The Aftermath and Implementation of the Treaty of Washington: The Oregon Question," pp. 826–850.

I have the honor to enclose a Copy of my note to Count Nesselrode renewing the request as to the case at Kamschatka.[2]

Copy. DNA, RG 59 (Despatches, Russia).

PORTUGAL

Passage of the tariff of September 11, 1841, elicited a protest from the Portuguese government. The Portuguese complained that the *ad valorem* duties imposed upon their wines violated the most-favored-nation clause of the Treaty of Commerce and Navigation of 1840 between the countries. In Webster's response of February 9, 1842, he went beyond the complicated specific issue to deal with the broader question of how to subject treaties to "a reasonable and just construction" (DW to Figanière e Morão, below). The final document in the section is one of the few surviving memorandums of a conversation between Webster and a foreign diplomat.

FROM JOAQUIM CÉSAR DE FIGANIÈRE E MORÃO

Philadelphia 18th November 1841.

The Undersigned, a Member of Her Majesty's Council & Minister Resident of Portugal in the United States of America, by direction of his Government, has the honor to address himself to the Honorable Daniel Webster Secretary of State of the United States, in order to lay before him, for the consideration of the American Government, and its consequent action at the next Session of the Legislative body of the Union, the following observations respecting the Bill concerning Duties and Drawbacks reported to the House of Representatives at the late Session of Congress.[1]

The attention of Her Majesty's Government was called to the Bill in question in consequence of its purporting to lay aside the principle heretofore, & for a long period followed in the United States of imposing Specific duties in Wines and Spirituous liquors on their introduction into this Country and substituting an ad valorem duty which could not be viewed with indifference by the Government of Portugal, in as much as the proposed change, which has since been effected by the subsequent passage of said Bill in both Houses & its approval by the President on the

2. Todd refers to a complaint lodged by supercargo John Dominis of the American brig *Joseph Peabody* concerning the sale of American goods in the port of Kamchatka. Dominis complained that a new regulation that forbade commerce between American ships and Russian merchants until the official community had been supplied had detained him and his ship's company fifteen to twenty days.

1. The Tariff Act of 1842 is in 5 *U.S. Stat.* 548–567. On wines, see esp. pp. 559–560.

11th of September last is, certainly highly detrimental to the consumption of Portuguese Wines in this Country, consequently prejudicial to the Commercial intercourse of the two Nations, which has so shortly ago, and with reciprocal satisfaction, been fixed upon a liberal basis in the Treaty signed at Lisbon on the 26th of August 1840.[2]

When that Treaty was under negotiation and at its termination the duties on wines—the principal export of Portugal—were then and continued to be specifically levied in the United States[;] nor was it at that time intended, to the knowledge of the Queens Government, that the system then followed would so soon, and unexpectedly be changed to the great injury of the Portuguese Staple; moreover, it is argued, the operation of the Act in question infringes if not the letter the Spirit of the said Treaty which violation was surely never contemplated by either the Legislative, or Executive branch of the United States' Government, nevertheless, the fact appears evident when it is taken into consideration that the Wines of Portugal from their nature & peculiar unavoidable circumstances can only reach this Country at a comparatively higher cost than the Wines of other Countries and, of course, be subjected to a higher duty according to the Act of Congress, than the like Wines of those other Countries, & consequently contrary to the provision of the 3d Article of the Treaty of 1840,[3] which would not be the case if the duty were specific as before the passage of the Act.

In order to show the different effects of the two modes of imposing duties on wines, the Undersigned begs to call Mr Webster's attention to the following illustration of them. A pipe of Wine from the Mediterranean, Spain, or any other Country reaches a Port in the United States at a cost let it be supposed, of 30 cents the gallon and a like pipe of Wine from Portugal costing, say, 38 cents the gallon; if the duty be specific, for instance 15 cts, they will both be subjected to the same and neither pay a higher or other duty, than the other, for 15 cts per gallon and no more would be levied upon both pipes, not so, however, according to the Act of the 11th September last, which imposes 20% ad valorem, the Spanish, or other wine will pay only 6 cents per Gallon, while from the like Wine of Portugal will be exacted 760/100 [7.6] cents pr Gallon which *de facto* operates as a discriminating duty against the Portuguese Wines, contrary to the stipulations of the Treaty between the two Countries.

The Undersigned will not on this occasion multiply arguments to prove the injurious effect the Act referred to will have upon the Wines of

2. See *Treaties*, 4:295–325.

3. The section of Article 3 referred to by Figanière provided that Portugal and the United States would not charge each other higher duties than they charged other countries for similar products. The full text of Article 3 is in DW to Figanière e Morão, February 9, 1842, below.

his Country and upon its Commerce generally with the United States, should the present mode of levying the duties upon Wines & spirituous liquors be continued; he flatters himself that the plain statements now offered, together with the verbal observations he very lately had the honor to submit to Mr Webster upon the same subject, will convince him of the fitness of the alteration proposed, in order that the Treaty referred to be not virtually rendered void but available as the two Governments intend for the benefit both of Portugal & the United States.

The Minister of Portugal avails himself of this opportunity to reiterate to the Honorable Secretary of State the assurance of his distinguished consideration & high esteem.   De Figanière e Morão

ALS. DNA, RG 59 (Notes from Foreign Legations, Portugal). Published in *Executive Documents*, 27th Cong., 3d sess., Serial 423, No. 202, pp. 2–3. Figanière e Morão (1798–1866), a career Portuguese diplomat, served as consul at Norfolk and New York before becoming chargé d'affaires to the United States from 1835 to 1838. In 1839 he was transferred to Rio de Janeiro but in 1840 returned to Washington as minister, which post he held until his death.

TO JOAQUIM CÉSAR DE FIGANIÈRE E MORÃO

Department of State,
Washington, 9th Feby., 1842

The Undersigned, Secretary of State of the United States, has the honor to acknowledge Mr [Joaquim César] de Figanière e Morao's note of the 18th November,[1] and has given to it the consideration due to its importance, and to the friendly relations happily subsisting between the two Governments.

The Undersigned regrets that the Government of Portugal should suppose that it has reason to complain in any manner, of a law of the United States as being prejudicial to Portugal, or at variance with the amity and good will subsisting between the two countries, and especially as inconsistent with the treaty obligations of the United States.

The law complained of was enacted on the 11th day of September, 1841, and its main provision was to lay a duty of twenty per cent ad valorem on all such articles as were at that time free, or on which the duty was less than that rate, with certain exceptions. The wines of Portugal not being within the exceptions, and being subject at that time only to a specific duty, may fall under an increased charge, or duty, by the operation of this law.

The third article of the treaty subsisting between the United States and Portugal is in these words:

"No higher or other duties shall be imposed on the importation into the Kingdom and possessions of Portugal, of any article the growth, pro-

1. See above.

duce, or manufacture of the United States of America, and no higher or other duties shall be imposed on the importation into the United States of America of any article the growth, produce, or manufacture of the Kingdom and possessions of Portugal, than such as are or shall be payable on the like article, being the growth, produce, or manufacture of, any other foreign country.

"Nor shall any prohibition be imposed on the importation or exportation of any article the growth, produce, or manufacture of the United States of America, or of the Kingdom and possessions of Portugal to or from the ports of the said Kingdom and possessions of Portugal, or of the said States, which shall not equally extend to all other foreign nations.

"Nor shall any higher or other duties or charges be imposed, in either of the two countries, on the exportation of any articles to the United States of America or to the Kingdom of Portugal, respectively, than such as are payable on the exportation of the like articles to any other foreign country.

"Provided, however, that nothing contained in this article shall be understood or intended to interfere with the stipulation entered into by the United States of America for a special equivalent in regard to French wines, in the convention made by the said States and France, on the fourth day of July, in the year of our Lord one thousand eight hundred and thirty-one,[2] which stipulation will expire, and cease to have effect in the month of February, in the year of our Lord one thousand eight hundred and forty-two."

Mr de Figaniere e Morao thinks that the provision of this article is interfered with by the above mentioned act of Congress. He illustrates his own view of the Subject by putting the case in the following form.

"A pipe of wine from the Mediterranean, or Spain, or any other country, reaches a port in the United States at a cost, let it be supposed, of thirty cents the gallon; and a like pipe of wine from Portugal, costing thirty-eight cents per gallon, if the duty be specific, say fifteen cents— they will both be subject to the same, and neither pay a higher or other duty than the other, for fifteen cents per gallon, and no more would be levied on both pipes. Not so, however, according to the act of the 11th September last, which imposes twenty per cent ad valorem. The Spanish or other wine will pay only six cents per gallon, while from the like wine of Portugal will be exacted $7\frac{60}{100}$ cents per gallon, which, de facto, operates as a discriminating duty against the Portuguese wine, contrary to the stipulations of the treaty between the two countries."

Before proceeding to consider the argument and illustration thus advanced, the Undersigned avails himself of the opportunity of stating to Mr de Figaniere e Morao that the language in the third article of this

2. *Treaties*, 3:641–651.

treaty between the United States and his Government is of the same import with that used in most other treaties of the United States with foreign Powers, and identical with that employed in some of them, and that no complaint has ever been made to this Government by the Governments with whom such treaties have existed, of any injury, injustice, or want of strict compliance with treaty stipulation, on any such ground as has been now taken by the Portuguese Government. It will be at once obvious, therefore, to Mr de Figaniere e Morao that the Government of the United States must take such a view of the question as it can maintain not only in regard to Portugal, but many other Powers also.

The interdict of the treaty is:

"No higher or other duties shall be imposed on the importation into the United States of America, of any article the growth, produce, or manufacture of the Kingdom and possessions of Portugal, than such as are or shall be payable on the like article, being the growth, produce, or manufacture of any other foreign country."

The article on which the duty complained of is laid is wine; and the duty laid on Portuguese wine is exactly the same, in terms, as that laid on the like article (except as excepted in the law,) coming from other countries. In other words, all wines fall under the same duty of 20 per cent *ad valorem*. In terms, therefore, the law is clearly within the treaty.

But Mr de Figaniere e Morao thinks it not in conformity with the spirit and intent of the treaty; because under its operation, a gallon of wine in Portugal may cost more than a gallon of wine in Spain; and therefore 20 per cent on the cost of the gallon of Portuguese wine will be more than 20 per cent on that of the Spanish gallon; and consequently a gallon of Portuguese wine will pay a higher duty than a gallon of Spanish wine. That this may be the result of the operation of the law cannot be denied, and this makes it necessary to inquire what is the true interpretation of this third article of the treaty?

There may sometimes be difficulty without doubt in deciding on the just extent of such a provision, and in applying it in the legislation of States bound to regard it; because in general, articles identically the same, or, in the language of the treaty, alike, or seldom imported from different countries. Yet the provision itself is to be observed, and is to receive a reasonable and just construction. This is the leading rule of interpretation in regard to all treaties and other important compacts. Now it is evident that if Mr de Figaniere e Morao's idea be correct, the Government of the United States could impose no ad valorem duty whatever; because as articles bearing the same general name, and imported from different countries, would of course be of different degrees of value and cost, the country producing those of highest value would always have cause of complaint, if subjected to an *ad valorem* duty. The result would be, that the Government of the United States could not exercise its powers at all in one of the most ordinary modes of taxation. As this consequence would be unreasonable and evidently not within the contemplation of the parties, the reasoning which would conduct us to it must be rejected.

We are to consider then what is the just meaning of the terms, "other or higher duties"; and to inquire by what standard it is to be known and ascertained, whether duties "other and higher" are laid in a given case. Now, to accomplish this, resort must be had to some measure of comparison, simple or mixed, some rule by which the question is to be decided. What is that rule? What is the standard of comparison? Is some one single consideration to fix that standard, or may reference be had to various considerations? Mr de Figaniere e Morao's idea is that the only element of calculation, the only datum to be taken into view, is the quantity of the article; that is to say, he is of opinion that if one gallon pays more duty than another gallon, the duty therefore is higher in the sense of the Treaty. But the Undersigned thinks, with all respect, that this may well be questioned; he thinks costs and value may be regarded as forming parts of the basis of calculation and comparison as well as quantity. It is as reasonable, as seems to him, to understand the Treaty as saying, that merchandise from Portugal shall pay no higher duties than similar merchandise from other countries, according *to its value*, as it is to understand it as saying that it shall pay no higher duties in proportion to its quantity. Cost and value are as reasonable a basis as mere measure, weight, or quantity, in deciding on the comparison of duties. Indeed it appears to the Undersigned that ad valorem duties are likely to be the most unexceptionable of all forms of imposts, so far as stipulations in Treaties like that now under consideration are concerned. Indeed when duties are made specific they are laid on different classes of the same general article at different rates according to their respective degrees of cost or value. Cheap wines are not taxed so high as dearer wines; nor can it be considered as any purpose of the Treaty to abolish such distinctions, so that cost and value ordinarily constitute either the whole or part of the ground upon which rates of duties are fixed. In the case stated by Mr de Figaniere e Morao, the Portuguese wine is assumed as the more costly article. But we may well suppose an opposite case, and a case of specific duties of exactly the same nominal amount, and yet a case in which as it appears to the Undersigned, Portugal might complain with far greater appearance of reason than she now complains of the law of September. There are wines of Portugal, of large consumption, which cost much less than certain wines of France. Let us suppose that a wine of Lisbon cost 50 cents a gallon; and a wine of Bordeaux one dollar; and that each was taxed equally one dollar a gallon in the ports of the United States. Here would be an apparent equality, just such as Mr de Figaniere e Morao now thinks ought to exist. But would there be real equality?

Might not the Portuguese producer say that he did not enjoy substantially the same advantage as his French competitor, inasmuch as his capital and labor, producing an article in greater quantity, but of lower price, were really subjected to a burden twice as great as that which fall on the labor and capital of the French producer? Might he not say, suffer my product, according to its cost and value, to be received into the country upon the same terms, and not other or higher, as the products of other countries? The stipulation contained in the third article of the Treaty between the United States and Portugal, and in other Treaties to which the United States are parties, is just and liberal, and ought to be observed to the fullest practicable extent; but perhaps it may be found that it is necessarily circumscribed within certain limits and subjected to qualifications. And this results from the fact, that in a commercial lease, and according to the common understanding of men, the generic word "article" is subdivisable, and its subdivisions are as well known, and are regarded in as independant and substantive a sense as the generic term itself.

Wine is an article of commerce; but then wine of Oporto, wine of Bordeaux, wine of Madeira, wine of Sicily, are separate articles, so regarded in transactions of commerce; so regarded in the duty laws of various Governments, and especially in those of the United States.

It would therefore not be considered as any infraction of the Treaty with Portugal if Oporto wines were subjected to one duty and Sicily wines to another, because they are, in commercial understanding, different articles. And it may be added, that difference in cost or value may, in many cases, very materially contribute to settle the question of identity or difference between two articles; that is to say in deciding whether two articles are the same, or alike, as the phrase of the Treaty is, reference to the cost of each may be very pertinent and important. For example, the teas of China have heretofore been subject to different rates of duties in the United States, as separate articles, under separate and specific denominations, as Bohea, Congo, Hyson, &c. Now in a disputed case, whether a particular article of that general kind belonged to one or the other of these classes would be an inquiry in the prosecution of which one important element of proof and ground of decision would be the cost of the article; the more especially if the classes bore a considerable resemblance to each other, as is the case with some of them. So, if articles bearing the same general name come from different countries, whether they ought to be regarded as the same article is a question for the solution of which we may look not only to the name, but to their cost and value. And this consideration appears to the Undersigned to show he presumes to say, almost conclusively that if the duty in a given case be *ad valorem* it is of all forms of laying duties that which is most strictly in accordance with the provisions of Treaties, such as that between the United States and Portugal.

The article of the Treaty under consideration was designed as a stipulation that no unfriendly legislation should be resorted to by one party against the other, nor any preference given to the products of other countries with intent to injure or prejudice either party to the Treaty. The Treaty enjoins the Spirit and practice of fair and equal legislation, but neither party supposed itself precluded by its stipulations from the ordinary modes of exercising its own power of making law for raising revenue in its accustomed modes, and if it happen, in any case, that from the operation of laws thus laid with fair intent, and for necessary purposes, inconveniences result to either party, that result must be considered as not intended, but as arising from the nature of the case itself, and therefore as unavoidable.

These are the general views which have presented themselves to the Undersigned in answer to Mr de Figaniere e Morao's note, and he trusts that the Government of Portugal will consider them as satisfactory. Portugal is one of the countries with which the United States, in taking their place in the circle of Nations had early friendly commercial and diplomatic intercourse. Happily nothing has occurred permanently to disturb that intercourse. The two countries have no rivalries, no opposition of interests, no grounds of mutual distrust, and the Undersigned avails himself of this opportunity to express his earnest hope that the harmony now insured by the stipulations of a fair and equal Treaty may long continue, and to signify, at the same time, the high consideration with which he has the honor to regard Mr de Figaniere e Morao.   Danl Webster

LC. DNA, RG 59 (Notes to Foreign Legations, Portugal). Published in *Executive Documents*, 27th Cong., 3d sess., Serial 423, No. 202.

TO JOAQUIM CÉSAR DE FIGANIÈRE E MORÃO, WITH ENCLOSURE

                                           Department of State
Sir: Washington, 14th Jany 1843
In my note to you of the 12th of November last,[1] you were informed that your communications relative to duties on the wines of Portugal, had been from time to time, as they were received, referred to the Treasury Department, and that copies of all your correspondence, on the same subject, which had not before been referred, including your note of the 10th of November,[2] had been that day communicated to the Secretary of

1. DW to Figanière e Morão, November 12, 1842, DNA, RG 59 (Notes to Foreign Legations, Portugal).

2. Figanière e Morão to DW, November 10, 1842, DNA, RG 59 (Notes from Foreign Legations, Portugal).

the Treasury.[3] The whole subject had been considered by that officer, and I have now the honor to submit to you the result of his judgment and decision thereon, which you will find contained in the accompanying copy of his note to me, dated on the 10th instant.[4] I am, Sir, with great consideration, your obedient Servant,   Danl Webster

L C. DNA, RG 59 (Notes to Foreign Legations, Portugal). Published in *Executive Documents*, 27th Cong., 3d sess., Serial 423, No. 202.

ENCLOSURE: FROM WALTER FORWARD

Treasury Department

Sir,   January 10th 1842 (1843.)

I have had the honor to reccive your note of the 12th November last,[1] accompanied by copies of a correspondence between the Department of State and the Minister of Portugal [Joaquim César de Figanière e Morão], in relation to the duties charged in the United States on the wines of Portugal, communicated to this Department for its consideration.

It appears, from the notes of the Minister of Portugal that, previously to the passage of the Tariff act of 30th August last,[2] and while the Revenue law of 11th September 1841[3] was still in force, under which duties ad valorem were levied on all wines imported into the United States, complaint was made, on the part of Portugal, of the effect of that law as violating, if not the letter, the spirit of the Treaty between the United States and Portugal, concluded on the 26th August 1840.[4] The reply of the Department of State to this complaint, under date of the 9th February last,[5] in the opinion of this Department, placed the subject in its true light, and shewed conclusively that the act of 11th September 1841, did no violence to the Treaty with Portugal, either in letter or spirit.

On the passage of the act of 30th August last, in which specific duties are levied on all wines imported into the United States, it appears that renewed remonstrances were made by the Minister of Portugal against alleged infractions of treaty stipulations effected by the provisions of that act.[6] These allegations, it is conceived, are of no greater force than those formerly urged. In adjusting the rates of specific duties, in place

3. Walter Forward (1786–1852) had been an advocate of high tariffs while serving as a congressman from Pennsylvania, 1821–1825. He became secretary of the treasury in September 1841 and served until March 1843.

4. See below.

1. DW to Figanière e Morão, November 12, 1842, DNA, RG 59 (Notes to Foreign Legations, Portugal).

2. The Tariff Act of 1842 imposed varying specific duties, ranging from six to ninety-five cents per gallon on wines and liquors of different nations. 5 *U.S. Stat.* 548–567.

3. See 5 *U.S. Stat.* 463–465.

4. See *Treaties*, 4:295–325.

5. See above, DW to Figanière e Morão, February 9, 1842.

6. Figanière e Morão to DW, November 10, 1842, DNA, RG 59 (Notes from Foreign Legations, Portugal).

of duties ad valorem, on wines, it is assumed and believed that Congress acted with a special reference to the foreign values of the several kinds of this product, and, in good faith intended, and did, in effect, attain as near an approximation to equivalent rates of duty, if charged on such values, as the complicated and uncertain nature of the subject would admit. This being conceded, it must be obvious that the objections presented in the notes of the Minister of Portugal of the 25th August and 10th November last,[7] to the provisions of the act of 30th August 1842, find their satisfactory answer in the note from the Department of State, of 9th February last: for, as "neither of the contracting parties, in making the treaty, could have supposed itself precluded from the ordinary modes of exercising its own power of making laws for raising revenue in its own accustomed modes," the system of specific duties, or that of duties ad valorem might unquestionably be adopted by either government, at its own discretion, without any infractions of treaty stipulations, although some inconvenience might unhappily follow, as an incident, to the commercial interest of one or the other of the contracting parties. In reference to the argument of the Minister of Portugal founded on the occurrence in the treaty of the phrase "like articles," it is thought sufficient by this Department to express its concurrence in the opinion given in the note from the Department of State before referred to, that the wines of different places or different character or designation are, in fact, separate articles, liable, on their several importations, to be charged with different duties by this government, without any violation of our treaty with Portugal.

It may be added, that on an examination of the subject, with reference to the actual effect of the law, and, taking the quantity and value of the various wines imported during 1841 as the basis of calculation, it does not appear that Portugal has any just reason to complain. The enclosed table[8] will shew that while the Madeira Wine of Portugal, under the specific duty of 60 cts per gallon, pays a duty equivalent to 34.41 per cent ad valorem, all the principal wines of other countries, with scarcely a single exception, pay a higher rate ad valorem—some much higher, and several of them double the amount: and that in the few instances in which a lower rate is paid by "other countries," the amount of importations is so small as to be hardly worthy of consideration.

Viewing the question then in every aspect, it must be apparent that the good faith of the government of the United States has been inviolably preserved towards Portugal, as it regarded the existing treaty—and with these views, this Department can perceive no just ground to advise an

7. Figanière e Morão to DW, August 25 and November 10, 1842, DNA, RG 59 (Notes from Foreign Legations, Portugal).

8. The table of "wines imported in 1841" is not included in this publication.

interposition on the part of the President under the provision of law referred to by the Minister of Portugal. I have the honor to be With great respect Sir your obed. Serv.   W. Forward Secy of the Treasury

LS. DNA, RG 59 (Misc. Letters). Published in *Executive Documents*, 27th Cong., 3d sess., Serial 423, No.202.

FROM JOAQUIM CÉSAR DE FIGANIÈRE E MORÃO, WITH ENCLOSURE

Washington D.C. 16th Jany 1843

The Resident Minister of Portugal presents his compliments to the Honbl Secretary of State of the United States, and, having received advice from the Consul in New York[1] of the intended departure, shortly, of a vessel for the port of Lisbon, begs leave to say, he would have been much pleased to have communicated to Her Maj'ys Government, by this opportunity, the termination of the highly important question pending before the American Government; but, not being honored, as yet; with a reply to his Notes of the 25th of August & 10th of November of last year, and addressed to Mr Webster,[2] he regrets his inability to do it, which, however, induces him the more to acquaint his Government with the steps he has taken in relation thereto, and therefore, to forward, by the above vessel, an abstract of the last conversation he held upon the subject in question, with the Honorable Secretary, in the Department of State.[3] But, in so doing, he would be assured his memory was not at fault, when setting down in writing the said conversation. Transcribed from his Journal, he begs leave to enclose the abstract referred to; and, should Mr Webster detect in it any, unintentional, deviation from the true purport of that conversation, Mr de Figanière requests, and expects Mr Webster will do him the favor to mention it.   De Figanière e Morão

Figanière e Morão, January 14, 1843.

ALS. DNA, RG 59 (Notes from Foreign Legations, Portugal). Published in *Executive Documents*, 27th Cong., 3d sess., Serial 423, No. 202. Endorsed: "See note to M. de Figaniere e Morão dated 14 Jan. 1843 which is answer to all that is asked for in this."

ENCLOSURE: MEMORANDUM OF CONVERSATION

30th December 1842—1 O'clock P.M. Called upon the Secretary of State, at the respective Department. After the usual salutations, I observed to Mr Webster, "that my Government blamed me for the delay in bringing the pending negotiation to a close, that he, (Mr. W.) however, was well aware it rested not with me, and I requested anew his particular atten-

1. Noailles Searle, not otherwise identified.
2. Figanière e Morão to DW, August 25 and November 10, 1842,

DNA, RG 59 (Notes from Foreign Legations, Portugal).
3. See below.

tion to this affair: indeed"—I further observed—"while the question lasts, commerce would continue paralized, such has been the result of the Tariff Bill, for, since its passage, I was not aware of the importation of a single gallon of Port wine, and of little, if any, quantity from Madeira." Mr. Webster replied: "Yes, the affair ought to be settled;" then continued saying: "I have already stated to you, that it had been decided, further information should be obtained, and thereupon a Report submitted to the President by the Secretary of the Treasury [Walter Forward]; this Report had as yet not been communicated to the Department of State,[1] altho'," added the Honorable Secretary, "I was under the impression that a previous communication from this Department would have put the matter to rest." Believing that Mr Webster alluded to a note from him dated the 9th February last,[2] I observed, that "if the principle of that communication comes to rule the question, it would have been better for Portugal not to have signed the Treaty; that my Government, to sustain its interpretation in accordance with the intention of the stipulations as communicated to Mr [Washington] Barrow in a note of which the Department had, no doubt, received a copy,[3] might appeal without hesitation to the American Negotiator of that Treaty."[4] Mr Webster observed— "the Treaty will speak for itself"—"In that case," I replied, "you will permit me the remark, that I cannot understand how the Treaty with Portugal can be interpreted differently from those of Prussia and Austria, when those are similar to ours, specially, that of Prussia, which is word for word the same"[5]—"Yes Sir," said Mr. Webster rising from his seat, "be assured your Treaty shall have the same interpretation"—"It is all I request Mr. Webster," said I, "and a speedy termination of the affair"— "Yes Sir," Mr. Webster observed, reseating himself, "I'll write a hasty note to the Secretary of the Treasury, pressing the subject." He did so, sent it off by the messenger,[6] and I took my leave.

AD. DNA, RG 59 (Notes from Foreign Legations, Portugal).

FRANCE

As the document printed below suggests, cultural exchanges are not a

1. See above, Forward to DW, January 10, 1843, enclosed in DW to Figanière e Morão, January 14, 1843.
2. See below, DW to Figanière e Morão, February 9, 1842.
3. Barrow to DW, November 15, 1842, DNA, RG 59 (Despatches, Portugal). Barrow (1817–1866), a Tennessee Whig, served as chargé d'affaires to Portugal, 1841–1844.
4. The treaty of 1840 with Portugal was negotiated by Edward Kavanagh (1795–1844) of Maine, minister to Portugal, 1835–1841, and later one of the Maine commissioners during the Webster-Ashburton negotiations.
5. The Treaty of Commerce of 1829 with Austria is in *Treaties*, 3: 507–521; the commercial treaty of 1828 with Prussia is in *Treaties*, 3: 427–439.
6. Not found.

twentieth-century development. One of Webster's more pleasant responsibilities as secretary of state was to acknowledge "interchanges between Nation and Nation" of knowledge useful to the advancement of science and the humanities.

TO ALPHONSE JOSEPH YVES PAGEOT

Department of State,
Washington 3d Febry 1843.

Sir:

I have the honor to acknowledge the receipt of the letter you addressed to me on the 30th ultimo,[1] announcing the transmission for the Library of Congress, in return for charts and documents received from a branch of this Government, of three boxes of books and charts, which had been placed for that purpose at the disposition of the French Minister of Foreign Affairs[2] by the Chamber of Deputies and Admiral [Guy Victor] Duperré;[3] and informing me that you will take an early occasion soon after their arrival to cause them to be delivered.

Sincerely reciprocating the liberal sentiments which you have been instructed to convey, in the name of the Kings Government, and duly sensible of the friendly manner in which the announcement has been made, I hasten to tender you the proper acknowledgements on the occasion, and to assure you and your government that the Government of the United States regard these interchanges between Nation and Nation of the means of useful knowledge as one of the pleasing proofs of the advancement of the age; in science, humanity, and beneficial intercourse.

I have the honor to offer you the assurance of my distinguished consideration.   Danl Webster

LC. DNA, RG 59 (Notes to Foreign Legations, France). Pageot became chargé to the United States in 1835 but left with the French delegation in January 1836 when relations between the countries ruptured over American spoliation claims. He returned later in 1836, serving as chargé 1836–1837 and 1839–1840 and as minister from 1842 to 1848. Pageot was the son-in-law of Andrew Jackson's friend, Major William Berkeley Lewis (1784–1866).

BELGIUM

Much of the time of a secretary of state, as illustrated in the instruction printed below, was taken up in dealing with long-standing unresolved disputes with other countries. In 1830, during the Belgian rebellion against the Netherlands, the city of Antwerp was bombarded by the

1. Pageot to DW, DNA, RG 59 (Notes from Foreign Legations, France).

2. François Pierre Guillaume Guizot (1787–1874) was French foreign

minister from 1840 to 1848.

3. Duperré (1775–1846) was French minister of marine and colonies, 1834–1836, 1839–1840, 1840–1843.

Dutch. The property of many international traders, stored in the public warehouses, was destroyed. The United States frequently raised the issue of indemnities between 1836 and 1844, but the Belgians denied responsibility (see *International Law Digest*, 6:942–949). Although the Antwerp claims were not resolved during Webster's secretaryship, his instruction to Virgil Maxcy reflects both the strained relations between the United States and Belgium and the attitude of the Whig administration toward revolutions. As usual, Webster relied upon international law in assessing the national obligations that should be honored by "a civilised People."

TO VIRGIL MAXCY

No 12.   Department of State,
Sir: —   Washington, 26th Feby., 1842

I have the honor to inform you that the tender of resignation communicated in your despatch No 40 of the 20th of August last,[1] has been submitted to, and accepted by the President. As the Belgian legislative body, however, does not generally adjourn until the latter part of May, circumstances may arise which might render it desirable that you should remain at Brussels, and the Department therefore leaves it discretionary with you to take leave of the Government on the 1st of May, the period named in your letter of resignation, or, if the public service should require a short delay, to continue at Brussels until the arrival of your successor, who has not yet been appointed.

Your correspondence with the Belgian Government on the subject of the claims of our citizens for indemnification for the loss of property by the destruction of the entrepôt at Antwerp, which has been conducted in accordance with the instruction of your Government,[2] has not been viewed with unconcern, and when taken in connection with the rejection of two successive Treaties, both of which were sought by Belgium, demands grave consideration.[3] The whole subject has been called for in Congress, by two resolutions,[4] copies of which are transmitted for your information.

There is no doubt that the duty or obligation of indemnity, whatever it is, for the losses at Antwerp, falls upon Belgium. The Belgians, as a civilised People, must be considered as at all times under some form of

1. No. 40. Maxcy to DW, August 20, 1841, DNA, RG 59 (Despatches, Belgium).

2. Most of Maxcy's dispatches discuss the claims against Belgium.

3. Two earlier treaties between the United States and Belgium had been accepted by the U.S. Senate in 1833 and 1840 and signed by Presidents Jackson and Van Buren, but they were not ratified by Belgium. *Treaties*, 4:773.

4. Senate Resolutions of July 29, 1841, and February 4, 1842, DNA, RG 59 (Misc. Letters). See also *Executive Journal*, 1837–1841, pp. 51–52.

civil Government; and, however often they may see fit to change this
form, these changes cannot affect their just responsibility to any foreign
State, its citizens or subjects. Succeeding Governments necessarily take
upon themselves, so far at least as foreign nations are concerned, the
obligation of the Governments which preceeded them, whether those
obligations were created by Treaty, or by the general principles of National Law. It is on this ground that the restored Governments of Europe
have made indemnities to foreign States for excesses committed on the
property of citizens or subjects of these States by the Revolutionary Governments. The treaties of indemnity entered into and carried into effect by
the United States, on one side, and France, Spain, and the two Sicilies,[5]
respectively, on the other, are all founded on this universally received
idea. The subjects of foreign States in this respect are on a different footing from domestic subjects. It rests in the discretion of each Government
to decide how far it will indemnify its own citizens for wrongs and injuries inflicted by Revolutions, taking into its consideration both the general principles applicable to such cases, and its own ability. But national
obligations are perpetual, until discharged, and demand at all times a full
and adequate compensation.

The Belgians saw fit to change their Government, which, so far as foreign nations are concerned, they had a right to do. But in doing this they
shook off no national responsibility. The moment the authority of the
King of the Netherlands ceased over the Belgians, that moment every one
of his obligations towards foreign nations, so far as that part of his Kingdom was concerned, devolved on the new Government that succeeded
him.

The American property in the entrepôt at Antwerp was in the custody
of the Government. Its owner, under the circumstances, had no control
over it. A commotion broke out, which shortly ended in the severance of
Belgium from the Kingdom of the Netherlands. The pen of history will
hardly record the transactions of this outbreak as the rise, progress, and
termination of a civil war. Before it had reached that point, the end of
the rising was accomplished, and the division of the countries decided.
Suppose the suppression of the rising had been as sudden as its triumph,
would any one, in such case, say that open and flagrant war, a regular
controversy between hostile and established Governments had existed in
the Netherlands? Certainly, no one would have thought of opposing such
an argument to the responsibility of the actual Government.

In your correspondence you have urged the claim, even supposing
there was an existing civil war, by arguments not yet answered. But if

5. See *Treaties*, 3:641–651
(France, 1831); 711–721 (Two Sicilies, 1832); 811–822 (Spain, 1834).

they should be, or could be, answered, it still remains to be shown that the popular rising which separated Belgium from the Netherlands ever assumed the settled character of civil war. On the contrary, the true view of that transaction is, as it appears to this Government, that the Belgian People, by the force of numbers, and the power of unanimity, changed their Government without war; without more violence than attends other movements which have often recurred, and which, whether successful or unsuccessful, have never been held to create a state of flagrant public hostilities.

Enclosed is a letter of recall.[6] Before closing your mission, you will present the views of this Government again to the attention of that of Belgium, and acquaint it with the dissatisfaction felt by the President in contemplating the present posture of the affairs of the two countries, and with the fact that Congress has called for all information and correspondence touching their present relations. It would be highly gratifying if you should be able, previous to your departure, to obtain such a reply from the Belgian Government as would lead to a well-grounded hope that these relations might promptly be placed upon a more satisfactory basis. I am, Sir, respectfully, your obedient servant, Danl Webster

LC. DNA, RG 59 (Instructions, Belgium). Published in part in *International Law Digest*, 6:945–947. Maxcy (1785–1844; Brown 1804) was the first solicitor of the Treasury, 1830–1837, and chargé d'affaires to Belgium, 1837–1842. Maxcy was killed by the explosion of the gun "Peacemaker" aboard the *Princeton*, February 28, 1844.

DENMARK

Two issues occupied Webster's attention in the United States's relations with Denmark: the sound dues and religious discrimination. Since 1328 Denmark had been collecting fees from vessels passing through the Sound, the main entrance to the Baltic Sea. The right to gather such dues was formally recognized in an agreement at Christianople in 1645, which placed specific duties on some 300 items. A second treaty of 1701 dealt with items not enumerated in the Christianople accord by posting on them a 1 percent tariff based upon the value of the goods at the point of embarkation.

Although the United States recognized the Sound Dues in a treaty with Denmark in 1826, Webster in May 1841 recommended to President Tyler that the administration seek to lower the duties. He pointed out that Americans expended approximately $100,000 a year in sound dues and that they bore the added burden of port fees, since Danish harbors were entered primarily in order to pay the sound dues. Most American

6. The enclosure is not printed in this volume.

commerce passing through the Sound was destined for Russia. Following the lead of the governments of Britain and Sweden-Norway, Webster succeeded in having the dues and port fees revised downward for American vessels and goods in 1842. It was not until 1857, however, that that the Danish sound dues were entirely abolished.

Baptists were persecuted by the Danish government, which upheld the doctrines of the state-supported Lutheran church. Responding to an appeal by the Boston-based Baptist General Convention for Foreign Missions, Webster instructed the U.S. chargé in Copenhagen to assist two representatives sent by the board to intercede with the Danish government on behalf of their European brethren. Webster firmly advised Isaac Rand Jackson to "shield" these representatives "from any oppressive treatment" (April 12, 1842, below).

In retrospect, such issues as the sound dues and the Baptists may seem less historically significant than such landmarks as the Treaty of Washington. At the time, however, as the documents printed below indicate, Webster considered U.S. relations with Denmark as involving questions of great importance.

FROM CALEB CUSHING, WITH ENCLOSURE

Sir: Washington 25 May 1841

I have the honor to submit to you the following details in regard to the Sound Dues & other charges levied on American commerce by the Danish Government at Elsinore.

The *Sound Dues* are charged on the *cargo*, both on going up and coming down the Baltic, according to the rates fixed in the published Government tariff.

In addition to this are the *Sound Port charges* so called, consisting of light money, pass money &c charged on the *ship*.

The United States have very little commerce with Denmark proper; that country taking very little from us, & producing nothing of any magnitude for us to buy.

The cargoes, which pass the Sound in American vessels, are destined for ports within the Baltic, and especially for those of Russia.

At Elsinore, the American ship master, on his arrival in going up, finds commercial brokers established, who undertake the settlement of his Sound Dues & Port charges with the Government. It is not uncommon for the great consignee & shipping houses at St Petersburg to have brokers at Elsinore permanently employed to attend to their business. If, therefore, the American ship master, on his arrival, has cargo conveyed to some one of the great St Petersburg houses, the broker of that house takes care of his Sound Dues & Port charges. Or it may be (as in the case of the bills hereinafter contained)[1] that the American consignor, being permanently engaged in the Baltic trade, has in his regular employment some such broker at Elsinore, to whom his shipmaster is ordered to apply for the despatch of his business there. In either case, the Sound Dues & Port charges are paid through the intervention of a broker, who receives the money from the ship, & pays it over to the Government.

It is customary, further, for the ship to make but one settlement with the broker, and that is in coming down to pass out of the Baltic. That is to say, on going up, the amount due on the upward cargo is ascertained, and advanced to the Danish Government by the broker on the order of the ship; and on coming down, the amount due on the downward cargo is then ascertained, and the payment for both is made to the broker.

This payment the ship master or supercargo makes to the broker in money if he pleases, but more commonly in a bill of exchange drawn upon his owner's correspondent in St Petersburg, or in London, according as he may be ordered.

Annexed hereto & marked (A) is a copy of a bill for Sound Dues charged on cotton on board the Essex, a Massachusetts vessel, on her passage up in May 1840. This cotton paid at the rate of 463 (Danish) specie dollars.[2] It was the invoice of one shipper only, constituting about *one fourths* part of <the whole> an entire cargo for the vessel, which entire cargo would of course pay nearly four times 463 (Danish) specie dollars, say 1800 Danish specie, or 3600 rix banco.

(B) is a copy of the bill of the Sound Dues on the downward cargo of the same vessel, in July 1840, on the same voyage. This cargo paid 164 Danish specie. It was not a full cargo, however; for the vessel would have taken 90 tons of hemp more, in addition to the 60 tons (65 bundles), she actually had. This would give an increase of about 90 (Danish) specie to the bill, making the whole, as for a full cargo, say 254 (Danish) specie Dollars, or 508 rix banco.

(C) & (D) are the bills of Port charges at Elsinore, up & down, on the same vessel & voyage.

Liebman & Mathiason (who sign the bills) were the brokers of the owners of the Essex at Elsinore.

The Essex is an ordinary American freighting vessel, not of the largest size, but such as may be taken for a fair average, or if any thing *within* the truth.

Such a vessel, then, if laden with cotton, would pay on the passage *up* say 1800 specie (Danish) or 3600 rix banco dollars, and coming down

1. The bills are not included in this publication.

2. It is estimated that one Danish specie dollar in 1841 was equal to $1.07 in U.S. currency. Each specie dollar contained the worth of two rixdollars, or forty-eight stivers.

with iron, hemp, & manufactures say 254 specie, or 508 rix banco dollars, making on the whole voyage say 2054 (Danish) specie or 4108 rix banco dollars. All this being tax or duty on the *cargo*, and beside the *Port charge* up & down on the *ship*.

It will be observed that the bills are made out in (*Sp.*) *specie* so much, and (Rbdr) rix banc dollars, just twice the sum of specie. This is in conformity with a provision of the Danish Sound Dues Tariff, by which the Duty is charged in (Danish) specie and may be paid in that, or in currency estimated at a fixed definition of 100 for one, at the option of the payer.

The money called (Danish) specie is better than the Danish crown dollars, 8 specie being equal to 9 crowns. But in fact, the payment is always made in the rix banco currency, the rate of which in London, as charged to the Essex in the settlement of her account with Liebman & Mathiason was 8 r. 3 d. currency to the pound sterling.

I will give one other example, that of a sugar cargo, which composes a large part of the American carrying trade up the Baltic.

The Ark, belonging to the same house as the Essex, carried up the Baltic 2700 boxes of Havana sugar in August 1834. I have now before me the bill of Sound Dues paid on 450 boxes, being just one sixth part of the cargo. It amounts to 776,84 roubles, each rouble being then worth 10½ sterling. So that the whole cargo paid, say 4660 roubles, or £203,17s 6d sterling, in going up.

Carried out in pounds sterling, at the rate of exchange then charged, the (full) upward cargo of the Essex (cotton) would have paid £423 sterling.

For it is to be observed that *cotton* pays double the duty per pound in Sound Dues that raw *sugar* does; the charge on the former being 18 st. per lb, that on the latter but 9 st per lb. Remark, also, in connection with this, that the sugar carried up the Baltic by one vessel is Spanish (Cuban) paying the low duty, while the cotton (paying the high duty) is American.

Carried out in pounds sterling, the Sound dues on the downward cargo of the Essex would be, say £59.

Or, a full cargo of the Essex, up & down, would be £482 sterling charged in Sound Dues alone. I beg pardon if I have extended these explanations too far; and I am very respectfully   C Cushing

ALS. DNA, RG 59 (Misc. Letters). Cushing (1800–1879; Harvard 1817), a wealthy Massachusetts ship owner and merchant, served in Congress as a Whig, 1835–1843. He allied with Tyler and Webster during the cabinet resignation crisis, a decision that led him eventually into the Democratic party. In 1843 Tyler chose Cushing to head the U.S. mission to China (see "Daniel Webster and the Pacific: The China Mission," pp. 877–926, below). Cushing's opposition to the Danish sound dues dated back at least to January 1826, when he argued in the *Boston Monthly Magazine* that the dues were a form of tribute.

ENCLOSURE: [CUSHING TO DW]

Washington 15 April 1841

Enclosed is the discussion of the Sound Duties of which I spoke this morning.[1]

There is a document showing the number of American vessels, on which the Sounds Dues act, & which I have sent for & shall soon receive.

Mr [Henry] Clay's Treaty of 26 April 1826[2] recognises the Sound Dues. I always thought this an unfortunate & questionable act. However, that Treaty being obligatory for 10 years only, & after that variable on a year's notice, the whole subject is now open.

The European movement on this subject at the present time goes beyond the Sound Dues & applies to similar exactions made by Hanover &c on the entrances & canals to some of the German rivers.

It is to be observed that of the goods going up, which pay Sound Dues, the chief part is sugar &c bound for & sold in Russia, & for which the American merchant receives Russian goods for the United States in return. As the Sound Dues are thus a tax on the two cargoes, up & down, Russia and the U.S. have the same interest in putting an end to the exaction.

—Quaere—Has Russia any inducement of state policy to continue the payment?

AL. DNA, RG 59 (Misc. Letters).

FROM MARK HEALEY

Dear Sir,   Boston 26 May 1841

Agreeable to your request,[1] I have made inquiry respecting sound dues paid at Elsinore and find it is not thought of much importance generally with our merchants.—The particulars of these duties you will find stated in the Tariff[2] of which you informed me you had a copy.

The origin of these duties and the reasons why they are still paid by all nations, I presume are to be found in your department.

The most important part of our trade is in Sugar from Cuba to Russia, the duty on a cargo of 3000 boxes will amount to about 2000 dollars. But their quarantine regulations are of much more importance, as they have been sometimes enforced upon very slight grounds, subjecting the ship owner to great expense in unloading and purifying his ship, and

1. With the letter are some unsigned notes on the sound dues, which are not included in this publication.

2. *Treaties*, 3:239–248.

1. No request found.

2. A copy of the Danish tariff showing the rates before and after June 1, 1841, is in *Executive Documents*, 33d Cong., 1st sess., Serial 726, No. 108.

sometimes ships have been detained so long that they have been obliged to Winter in Russia, but this season I learn that the Danish Government have made some new regulations much more favorable—a circular containing this new regulation I will send you enclosed.[3]

I beg again to remind you that there is not any American Consul at St Thomas. It is not a place of much trade with this country, but it is important, as a place of resort for vessels that are disabled, for repairs,—therefore the Consul should be a person well acquainted with Ships and Sailors Yours very respectfully—Mark Healey

ALS. DNA, RG 59 (Misc. Letters). Rec'd May 31, 1841. Healey was associated with the Merchant's National Bank of Boston.

TO ISAAC RAND JACKSON

No 6   Department of State,
Sir:—   Washington, 1st. Septr. 1841.

The Danish Government, by its diplomatic representative near the United States,[1] has officially announced to this Department the result of the discussions between it and Great Britain respecting the sound dues, and, with the announcement, has caused to be communicated a copy of the declaration signed in London on 4th June last by the Danish Minister,[2] at the Court of St. James, and Her Britannic Majesty's Principal Secretary of State for Foreign Affairs [Lord Palmerston], together with a copy of the new tariff. A copy of these documents and of Mr Steen Bille's letter, dated 1st August, presenting explanations of the proceedings, are now enclosed,[3] although it is presumed that you will have come into possession of the former before the arrival of this despatch.

Your predecessor, under date of 26 June, in communicating the same papers,[4] has stated that, on two important articles enumerated in this tariff, viz: on raw sugar and rice in paddy, a duty of two per cent, has been virtually imposed, instead of the one per cent, which is so clearly set forth as the intent and object of the parties. A copy of Mr. Woodside's letter is also transmitted.

3. The enclosure, which is not printed here, is dated March 27, 1841, and is signed by Belfoun, Ellah, Rainals & Co. It is in reference to the quarantine of ships and goods infected by yellow fever.

1. Steen Andersen Billé (1781–1860) was chargé d'affaires to the United States, 1830–1854.

2. Alfred Frederick Blome (1798–1875) was Denmark's minister to Great Britain.

3. In the declaration of June 4, signed by Palmerston and Blome, Denmark agreed to a general reduction in sound duties by accepting a 1 percent tariff on specific valuations for enumerated articles. See Billé to DW, August 1, 1841, DNA, RG 59 (Notes from Foreign Legations, Denmark).

4. Woodside to DW, June 26, 1841, DNA, RG 59 (Despatches, Denmark). Jonathan F. Woodside (1799–1845) of Ohio was chargé d'affaires to Denmark, 1835–1841.

It is expected that you will make yourself thoroughly acquainted with the whole subject of the sound dues, which you are aware is considered of great importance by your Government, and that you will from time to time furnish all the information respecting it which you may be able to obtain. You will however lose no time in bringing the present case to the attention of the Danish Government, and point out the injury likely to be done to the trade of the United States, by the operation of the tariff upon these items which have been specified. If the commerce of our country has already suffered by this exaction, you will demand the immediate restitution, of the overtax, and you will insist, in a firm, though temperate manner, upon a satisfactory guaranty for exemption in future from similar impositions. I am, Sir, respectfully, your obedient servant,

Danl Webster

LC. DNA, RG 59 (Instructions, Denmark). Published in *Executive Documents*, 33d Cong., 1st Sess., Serial 726, No. 108, pp. 2–3.

FROM GUSTAVUS DE NORDIN

Sir,   Washington February 22nd 1842

I have the honour to transmit to you under cover with this, a copy of the Convention recently concluded between the Government of the King my august Sovereign [Charles XIV], and that of His Danish Majesty,[1] for the regulation of the duties to be levied on Swedish and Norwegian vessels passing through the Sound or the (Great and Little) Belts, as also on the cargoes with which those vessels may be laden.[2]

This business—for the completion of which more than three years of negotiations were required—having been thus arranged to the satisfaction of both the parties chiefly concerned the King's Government hastens to communicate the results to those Friendly and Allied powers, which may be interested through their commercial relations, in the navigation of the Baltic. His Majesty takes pleasure in believing that the Government of the United States, will on this occasion appreciate the efforts which the Swedish Government has made, to have the existing treaties with regard to the Sound Duties carried into effect, and to remove the irregularities which had taken root, in the manner of collecting those duties. You will also Sir, not fail to perceive that the Swedish Government has obtained a considerable dimunition (degrévement) with regard to various articles of merchandise which are exported from the United

1. Christian VIII (1786–1848) ruled 1839–1848.

2. The convention of August 23, 1841, between King Charles XIV of Sweden and Norway and King Christian VIII of Denmark, lowered sound dues on Swedish and Norwegian ships, including American goods carried in those vessels.

States, to the countries on the Baltic, and to other articles of which the raw material is derived chiefly from this country.

These results obtained in favour of the general good, and the important advantages offered to navigation, by the new Regulations for passing the custom houses, appear to the King's Government to be of a nature calculated to fix the attention and good wishes of all the maritime powers which may indirectly derive benefits from them, and which by means of the conclusion of the new Convention which will find the greatest difficulties against a similar arrangement between themselves and the Danish Government <lessened> by the conclusion of this Convention. I have the honour to be with the most distinguished consideration—Sir—Your most humble and obedient Servant   Gust. de Nordin

Copy. Translation. DNA, RG 59 (Notes from Foreign Legations, Sweden and Norway). Rec'd February 24, 1842.

TO GUSTAVUS DE NORDIN

Department of State,
Sir:—   Washington, 28th Feby, 1842.

I have the honor to acknowledge the receipt of your note of the 22d instant,[1] and of the copy of the Convention recently concluded between your Government and that of Denmark, for the regulation of the duties to be levied on Swedish and Norwegian vessels passing through the Sound or the Belts, as also on the cargoes with which those vessels may be laden.

In common with all maritime nations navigating the Baltic, the Government of the United States cannot fail to take an interest in the subject of the Sound Dues; and it has been gratified to perceive that on several articles of American production, among others, transported in Swedish or Norwegian vessels, a reduction of duty has been obtained by the Swedish Government, whereby the trade of this country is indirectly benefited. The efforts of your Government in this matter are duly appreciated, and it is hoped may lead the way to conventional arrangements between Denmark and other Powers with a view to securing other commercial stipulations of a beneficial character. I am, Sir, with great consideration your obedient servant,   Danl Webster

LC. DNA, RG 59 (Notes to Foreign Legations, Sweden and Norway).

FROM HEMAN LINCOLN

Washington
Sir,   March 18th,—1842.

I inclose herewith a communication from our Board of Missions[1] to

1. See above.
1. The Baptist Board of Missions,   located in Boston, organized the missionary efforts of Baptist groups. The

which I beg leave most respectfully to ask your *friendly* & *official* attention. I also enclose a copy of the sentence of the Superior Court of Copenhagen in the Kingdom of Denmark upon Peter, & Adolph Frederick Mon-
ster preachers of the Baptist faith, & employed as Missionaries under the
direction of the Board; upon whom notwithstanding they were considered by the Court as *"unimpeachable in their conduct"* a heavy fine has
been imposed, with the costs of Court, after they had suffered all the
hardships of imprisonment for several months. It appears that the conviction of the prisoners was in consequence of the alleged violation of an
arbitrary Law passed in 1745.[2]

The Board in connection with "the American & For Bible Society"[3]
have appointed Rev. Professor Horatio B[alch] Hackett[4] & Rev. Professor
T[homas] J[efferson] Conant[5] as their Representatives at the Court of
Denmark. Both the Gentlemen are men of talents & education as well as
great integrity.

If it is the pleasure of the Department of State to give instructions to
Mr. [Isaac Rand] Jackson Charge D. Affairs, to aid the deputation in endeavoring to procure toleration in religious worship,[6] it will greatly facilitate their efforts in the promotion of human happiness & as they believe the progress of morality & religion. The Board also respectfully request the assistance & cooperation of Mr. [Henry] Wheaton[7] American
Minister at the Prussian Court in Berlin in their efforts in furtherance of
the same object.

I beg leave respectfully to refer the Department to the communications
of the English Deputation which gave the most important facts in the
case. They are contained in the English Bap[tist] Magazine for October
1841 pages 510 & 511 inclusive.[8]

---

enclosure from the board's foreign
secretary contained information
about the Mönster cases.

2. The Mönster brothers, Baptist
ministers of Copenhagen, were jailed
in 1840 and 1841 for violating the
Danish Anabaptist law of 1745.

3. When the American Bible Society withdrew support for Baptist
translations of the Bible, the sect
founded the American and Foreign
Bible Society in 1837 to operate in
conjunction with the Baptist Board
of Missions.

4. Hackett (1806–1875; Amherst
1830), a biblical scholar, taught at
Newton Theological Institute, 1839–
1869, and thereafter at Rochester
Theological Seminary.

5. Conant (1802–1891; Middlebury 1823) studied and taught many
languages. He was ordained a Baptist minister in 1834, and in 1850 he
joined the faculty of Rochester Theological Seminary.

6. See DW to Jackson, April 12,
1842, below.

7. No instruction to Wheaton on
this matter has been found.

8. Baptists in Germany, like those
in Denmark, were jailed for violating
Anabaptist laws. English Baptists
visited Germany and Denmark in
September 1841 with letters of introduction from Foreign Minister Palmerston to petition the governments
for religious toleration. Their letters
are published in *English Baptist*

By an early attention to this subject you will great[ly] oblige our Board as well as Your Obt & very Hb Servant.   Heman Lincoln

ALS. DNA, RG 59 (Misc. Letters). Endorsed: "Answered 12 Apl." Lincoln (1821–1887; Brown 1840) was at that time the treasurer of the Baptist General Convention for Foreign Missions. He became an ordained Baptist minister in 1845 and taught at Newton Theological Institution, 1868–1887.

TO HEMAN LINCOLN

Dear Sir,

Department of State
Washington 12th April 1842.

Your letter of the 4th instant and that to which it refers of the 18th. ult.[1] enclosing a communication in behalf of the Baptist Convention for Foreign Missions have been received.

I request you to assure the Board of Managers that it forms a part of the duty of the Diplomatic Representatives of the United States to extend their protection to American citizens in foreign countries, and it cannot be doubted that upon proper representations no efforts would be spared to protect them in their just rights.

It gives me pleasure to furnish a letter of introduction to Mr. [Isaac Rand] Jackson[2] Chargé d' Affairs of the U.S. at Copenhagen, for the gentlemen, the Rev. Prof. Horatio B. Hartwell[3] and the Rev. T[homas] J[efferson] Conant, whom your Board, in connection with the American and Foreign Bible Society, propose to send to Denmark on a mission. This letter will be found enclosed. I am, dear sir, &c.   Danl Webster

LC. DNA, RG 59 (Domestic Letters).

TO ISAAC RAND JACKSON

Sir:
No. 9.

Department of State,
Washington, 12th April 1842

The bearers of this letter, the Rev. Professor Horatio B[alch] Hartwell [Hackett] and the Rev. Professor T[homas] J[efferson] Conant, are about to visit Denmark under the auspices of the Board of Managers of the Baptist Foreign Missions, in connexion with the American and Foreign Bible Society, and on a Mission to promote the objects of those institutions. They are considered as gentlemen of worth and talents, and as such, and for the good cause they represent, I ask for them any friendly

---

Magazine, 33 (October 1841): 506–511.

1. In the letter of April 4, Lincoln requested a reply to his letter of March 18, 1842, DNA, RG 59 (Misc. Letters).

2. See below.

3. This is presumably a reference to Horatio Balch Hackett. In Lincoln's letter to DW of March 18, 1842, Hackett's name can easily be misread as Hartwell.

attentions you may be able to bestow,[1] and if it should become necessary, your official interventiton to shield them from any oppressive treatment to which they may be subjected in the discharge of their duties. From the high character given of these persons, and the nature of their errand, it is confidently believed that they will not give to the Danish Government any just cause of censure or displeasure. I am, Sir, your obedient servant, Danl Webster

LC. DNA, RG 59 (Instructions, Denmark).

FROM STEEN ANDERSON BILLÉ

Philadelphia June 20th 1842

On the first of August last year the Undersigned, His Danish Majesty's Chargé d'affairs near the Government of the United States, had the honor, by order of his Government, to communicate to the Honorable Daniel Webster, Secretary of State of the United States, the nature and result of the discussions, which for some time past had been carried on in London, relative to the calculation of Sound Dues on Articles not enumerated in the Tariff of Christianople of the year 1645.[1]

He stated at the same time, that it was found convenient and expedient, to settle some other questions of minor importance, relating to the despatch of vessels at the Sound and the fees and other charges payable there independently of the Sound Dues, by an investigation of Commissioners on the spot. These labours have since been brought to a close; and the whole Tariff of Sound and Belt Dues, both specific and ad valorem, the former as fixed by the Tariff of Christianople and the latter as now settled upon the principle of the Treaty of 1701, with all the rules and regulations connected with the subject, have accordingly been embodied in a digest for the general information of all concerned, two printed copies of which, the one in the Danish and the other in the German language, the Undersigned has now the honor, by direction of his Government, to inclose to Mr Webster, to be laid before the President.[2]

His Majesty [Christian VII] flatters himself, that the common interest of all nations, connected with the Baltic Trade, has been duly and impartially attended to in this investigation, so as to secure an unqualified

1. Jackson died at his post on July 27, 1842, shortly before the arrival of Conant and Hackett in Denmark. The Mönsters were released from prison in that same month, and in December the Danish government granted limited rights to Baptists. By the constitution of 1849, full religious toleration was extended in Denmark.

1. The Danish basic tariff schedule was established by treaties with the Netherlands in 1645 and 1701. The same terms were extended to other nations.

2. The enclosure is not included in this publication. Its pertinent terms are developed in the letter.

concurrence and approval at their hands. Though not the work of a regular Congress of nations, which would have been impracticable, if not altogether inapplicable to the case, there has been no secrecy in the matter; on the contrary all suggestions made by other nations, either through their Diplomatic Agents at Copenhagen or by their Consuls, residing at Elsinore, have been cheerfully received and duly considered.

The entire scope and object of the discussions in London were, as stated by the Undersigned in his Note above alluded to, to carry out a general principle in the conversion of an ad valorem duty on nonenumerated Articles, according to the literal rule laid down in the 3d § of the Treaty of 1701, into a specific duty by the means of a fixed valuation as its basis, thereby removing at the same time all complaints in future of arbitrary power in its calculation and exaction. His Majesty having waived all claims to any increase of duty as hitherto compacted, to which said principle might lead in its general application, the whole question turned, as a natural consequence, upon reduction alone, and this reduction being the result of a general principle in its application to all non-enumerated Articles without exception, all discrimination to favor particular interests or particular countries was of course entirely out of the question, while it was the sincere and anxious desire of His Majesty, that equal justice should be done to all.

It is, however, peculiarly gratifying to His Majesty, that most of the Articles, specially enumerated by Mr Webster as those, in which the interests of the United States were particularly involved, and which in his opinion were too heavily charged,[3] have been relieved under the general principle, as belonging to the class of non-enumerated Articles.

By a reference to the Tariff agreed upon, as transmitted to Mr Webster by the former Note of the Undersigned upon this subject, exhibiting the result of the old and new computation in columns opposite to each other, Mr Webster will perceive: 1) that the duty on raw sugar has been reduced from 9 Stivers to 5 Stivers per CWt.[4] 2) that the duty on Coffee has been reduced from 24 Stivers to 6 Stivers per CWt 3) that the duty on Campeachywood has been reduced from 36 Stivers to 8 Stivers per MWt.[5] 4) that the duty on Rice in the husk or Paddy has been reduced from 13⅓ Stivers to 6 Stivers; this reduction is, however, not so apparent from the change of the old unit of a bushel into the new one of four hundred pounds, but will appear by a comparison of the old duty of 1½

3. Billé refers here and subsequently in this letter to DW's report of May 24, 1841, to President Tyler on the sound dues. In the report, Webster complains of duties on various products and objects to such impediments to trade as port charges and the ceremonial lowering of a ship's topsails. *Senate Documents*, 27th Cong., 1st sess., Serial 390, No. 1.

4. CWt, a symbol for hundredweight.

5. MWt, presumably a symbol for thousandweight.

Stivers on the former measure and the new duty of 6 Stivers on the latter weight, taking the weight of a bushel at 45 pounds as a standard, which is the one adopted in the Tariff. 5) that the duty on Cotton yarn has been reduced viz on Twist from 36 Stivers to 15 Stivers per CWt, on sewing yarn from 30 Stivers to 15 Stivers per 50 pounds, and so forth, on cotton stockings from 30 Stivers to 6 Stivers per 50 pairs and on those of smaller size in the same proportion, and that the duty on Cotton Manufactures in general, with the exception of white cotton calicoes as regulated by the Tariff of Christianople, has been reduced to 1 pc ad valorem according to their present actual or invoice value, and 6)—from the general Tariff as now enclosed, that the duty on Segars, Snuff and Tobacco Stems has been reduced in the same way to 1 pc ad valorem according to their present prices.

Hence it will appear that of all the Articles specially enumerated by Mr Webster, the duties on raw Sugar, Coffee and Campeachy wood have in an eminent degree been reduced in a direct way; that the duties on Rice, Cotton and Tobacco, though retained equally with those on all other enumerated Articles in general as regulated by the Tariff of Christianople, the same may nevertheless be said to be favorably affected for the interest of the United States in an indirect way through the reduction of the duty, as above stated, on Paddy and on Cotton Manufactures in general, as well as upon Segars, Snuff and Tobacco Stems, as belonging to the class of non enumerated Articles, leaving only the Article of Rum untouched from the circumstance of the duty on that Article being of the former description; It is, however, not inappropriate to remark, with regard to this latter Article, that the commendable temperance spirit of the age is certainly not in its favor, and as to the Article of Tobacco in particular, the specific duty of the Tariff of Christianople sinks altogether into insignificance compared with the duty imposed upon that Article in most countries as a convenient source of revenue from its minute division in the consumption of the Article and therefore less felt by the community and less affecting the actual importation of that Article for consumption.

The wishes of the United States Government in this respect having thus been met and acted upon to the full extent practicable under a general principle, equally applicable to all nations, having Treaties with Denmark, but accidentally, as it appears, more beneficial to the United States than to many other nations, it is, as above stated, peculiarly gratifying to His Majesty, that the sacrifices made on his part, and immediately carried out through the Customhouse, in the new mode of calculating the ad valorem duties at the Sound, the result of which has been, as shown above, an essential and to His Majesty's Finances most sensible reduction, have had so desirable and prominent a bearing upon the particular interests of the United States, corresponding in a happy manner with the character of the amicable relations, subsisting between the two countries, and which none can appreciate higher than His Majesty does.

Mr Webster having advanced the opinion, or rather presumed it to have been the intention of the framers of the Tariff of Christianople, to fix a duty of about one per centum ad valorem upon the Articles therein enumerated, the Undersigned, without entering upon an argument on specific duties, settled and maintained for centuries as a vested right not to be disturbed, cannot, however, refrain from adverting to the duties on wines therein fixed at the rate of the thirtieth part of their value, as an evidence in point of a different proportion, which moreover will be found to have been repeated and maintained in direct terms in the very Treaty of 1701, relied upon for the one per centum principle.

By a perusal of the Rules and Regulations for the despatch of vessels at the Sound Mr Webster will perceive, that everything has been done, which the intelligence and experience of businessmen of all nations on the spot could suggest for simplifying and facilitating the business to be transacted,—thereby preventing any unnecessary delay, nay! one may even say any delay at all.

A compillation of the entire Tariff, alphabetically arranged, with all the rules and regulations connected with the subject, having been embodied in a concise and clear manner in one single digest, accessible to everybody, no one can be ignorant of his rights or his duties.

No unnecessary formalities are required from the vessels, passing through the Sound; the lowering of Top-sails, as complained of by Mr Webster, has been disposed with, and a display of the national colours of the vessel only required as both proper and expedient. see § 25.

No portcharges or harbour dues, as complained of by Mr Webster, are exacted beyond the light money and customhouse fees, as regulated by the 12th, 13th and 14th §; these latter fees have moreover been reduced in a manner well calculated to give general satisfaction, while on the other hand the allowance of 4 pc on the duty as a remuneration to the Captains has been continued as heretofore. see § 30.

No discrimination is made between direct and indirect trade in the charge of duty on non enumerated Articles with regard to privileged nations, as apprehended by Mr Webster.

The time for the Officers to attend at their respective Offices has been extended and even stretched to the utmost, inasmuch as for receiving the papers and such further explanations as in connection therewith shall be deemed necesary, they are to be at their post every day from the 1st of April to the 31st of October from 4 oClock in the morning to 10 oClock at night and for the remainder of the year from 6 oClock in the morning to 8 oClock at night, with the exception of the month of March, during which time they are to remain one hour longer, and the same rule hold good with regard to the Officers for expediting the papers with the difference of a few hours only. see § 24.

Having delivered his papers and given any additional explanation required, the Captain may at once proceed on his voyage without waiting for a regular clearance, provided his Agent shall give satisfactory security for the payment of the duties, to which the cargo may be liable, against which security, which is a small matter in the routine of business, a clearance in blanco will be granted. see § 27.

All visitation of vessels and their cargoes, belonging to nations having Treaties with Denmark, is entirely dispensed with, inasmuch as full faith and credit will be given to the genuine, bona fide ships papers, certificates and clearances exhibited from the places, where the cargoes have been shipped, and for the case that such papers should not be in due order, applications will be made to the respective Governments, who by Treaties or Conventions may have declared their readiness to take measures for preventing such irregularities in future. see § 28.

The full faith and credit, however, to be given to the ships papers, and the expeditious mode of passing the clearances based thereon, depending in a great measure upon the regularity of these papers and the clearness and distinctness, with which the facts are given, necessary for calculating the duties, beyond a mere general indication of the cargo, viz the particular weights and measures of Articles subject to a specific duty and the value of those that are subject to one ad valorem, it is particularly desirable, that the papers should be made out in such a manner as to secure these advantages, guarding at the same time against fraud on the one side and against overcharge on the other. see § 29.

The Undersigned has accordingly been instructed to recommend this subject to the particular notice of the United States Government for the benefit of their vessels as privileged in the Sound, and where confidence is so largely bestowed for the convenience of trade, it is presumed the United States Government, equally with the Governments of all other nations, will be disposed to countenance and support such indulgences by instructing their Consul at Elsinore[6] to co-operate in case of need with the Board of Customs of the Sound in maintaining inviolate the rules and regulations of the Customs and in preventing fraud upon the revenue from misplaced confidence.

With regard to the light money to be paid in the Sound or the Belts, the Undersigned has the honor of stating, that this duty was originally fixed by a special Treaty on the subject, between Denmark and the United Provinces of the Netherlands of the 12th of Feb 1647, at 2 Specie Dol-

6. Edmund L. Rainals, a resident of Denmark, served as the American consul at Elsinore from 1836 to 1848.

lars for every vessel in ballast and 4 Specie Dollars for every vessel having goods on board, with a visa exclusion, to the continuance and maintenance of the then existing lights, buoys and marks, and that the duty so fixed has never since been increased, though the number of lights, buoys and marks has been more than tripled since that time, and though a reservation was expressly made for additional provisions by negotiation in case any request should be made for the construction of new lights or the placing of new buoys or marks. see the Treaty of the 15th June 1701 § 31.

Denmark has moreover been at a very considerable expence in the construction and maintenance of two floating lights, not contemplated at the time, and by virtue of a Treaty of 1660, concluded at Copenhagen, she has been under the obligation of paying a considerable sum of money annually for the maintenance of lights along the Swedish Coast for the benefit of vessels navigating the Sound, in addition to which His Majesty has lately, at the request of Great Britain, directed a new light house to be constructed on the coast of Jylland, and a third floating light to be placed in a very exposed and dangerous part of the Kattegat not far from the Island of Anholt, and His Majesty has latterly entered into negotiations with Sweden and thereby secured the introduction of various desirable improvements in the Swedish lights, more particularly in that of Falsterbo, in consideration of Denmark raising the annual payment to be made to Sweden from 3500 to 10,000 Specie Dollars.

From a solicitude with His Majesty of securing still further the navigation of the Sound, His Majesty has even gone beyond the wishes indicated in this respect by the maritime nations in general, and deeming the Light of Lindesnes, situated beyond the limits of his dominions on the southern point of Norway, useful to vessels entering or leaving the Kattegat, though not within the scope of the lighthouse system, incumbent on Denmark with regard to the Sound and its adjoining waters as clearly defined by Treaties and the configuration of the coasts, His Majesty has agreed to pay annually to the Norwegian Government 3500 Specie Dollars—a sum abundantly sufficient for the maintenance of said light.

In consideration of all these changes and the very considerable expenses, to which they have led, Great Britain has proposed to increase the light money, as regulated by the special Treaty of 1647, from 2 to 2¼ Specie Dollars for a vessel in ballast, and from 4 to 4½ Specie dollars for a vessel having goods onboard, to which proposition His Majesty has accceded. Under these circumstances no doubt is entertained, but the United States Government will appreciate the improvements above alluded to, and recognize the justice and fairness of the charge, being but small in proportion to the advantages gained, while all other discussions in this matter have been directed to reduction exclusively, and that object attained, as above shown, in a most eminent degree.

The Undersigned cannot dismiss the subject without adverting to the settlement of this whole question as one well calculated to strengthen and perpetuate the bonds of comity and good will, which it has been His Majesty's anxious desire to cultivate and improve with all nations, and with none more than with the United States of America, whose nautical skill and enterprise have made them his neighbours in spite of the expanse of the ocean and the intricacy of the waters separating the two continents of the Globe, and more particularly the northern portions thereof, less favored by nature in climate and therefore more exposed to the inclemency and violence of the weather at certain seasons of the year, to which navigation necessarily must be extended to satisfy the calls of commerce. To encounter, brave and overcome these perils of the sea has been the pride and glory of maritime powers, and a full share of that honor is cheerfully conceded as justly due to the enterprising spirit of the United States, and hence it is a satisfaction to the Undersigned to affirm that their vessels are hailed with unfeigned pleasure and gratification at the shores of his country.

The Undersigned avails himself of this occasion to tender to Mr Webster the assurance of his high and distinguished consideration.

Steen Billé

ALS. DNA, RG 59 (Notes from Foreign Legations, Denmark). Rec'd June 22, 1842. Published in *Executive Documents*, 33d Cong., 1st sess., Serial 726, No. 108.

TO STEEN ANDERSEN BILLÉ

Department of State,
Washington, 27th June, 1842.

The Undersigned, Secretary of State of the United States, has had the honor to receive the note addressed to him on the 20th instant,[1] by Mr. Steen [Andersen] Billé, Chargé d'Affaires of His Majesty the King of Denmark [Christian VII], and the two printed copies of the new tariff of Sound and Belt dues, by which it was accompanied. The observations which Mr. Billé has been pleased to present in this note by direction of his Government, in explanation of the practical effect of the present arrangement, are duly appreciated, and the Undersigned cannot hesitate to concur with him in the opinion that the settlement of this whole question is well calculated to strengthen and perpetuate the bonds of comity and good will between the two countries, an effect as ardently desired by the President as by His Danish Majesty. The representative of the United States at Copenhagen has been fully informed of the satisfaction experienced by the President upon the completion of these commercial regulations, and he has been instructed to take an early opportunity to communicate the expression of it to the Danish Government.

1. See above.

The Undersigned hastens to say to Mr. Billé, that, at his instance, instructions will be promptly transmitted to the Consul of the United States at Elsineur [Edmund L. Rainals], requiring him, in case of need, to cooperate with the Board of Customs of the Sound, in maintaining inviolate the rules and regulations of the customs, and in preventing fraud upon the revenue.

The Undersigned avails himself of this occasion to renew to Mr Billé the assurances of his distinguished consideration.   Danl Webster

LC. DNA, RG 59 (Notes to Foreign Legations, Denmark).

THE MIDDLE EAST AND AFRICA

The Missionaries of Syria

By the 1830s, the Middle East had surpassed the Hawaiian islands as the largest missionary field for Americans. The nonsectarian American Board of Commissioners for Foreign Missions, with headquarters in Boston, concentrated on three missions: to the Nestorians in Persia, to the Armenians in Turkey, and to the Druzes in Syria. Muslim, hence, Ottoman law stipulated the death penalty for apostasy by Sunni Muslims but allowed proselytizing among existing Christian minorities such as the Maronites and heterodox Muslim sects such as the Druzes. By 1840, several schools had been established by the A.B.C.F.M. missionaries for the Druzes in the Mount Lebanon area.

From 1831 until his death on March 3, 1843, Commodore David Porter, an eccentric retired naval officer, represented the United States in the Ottoman Empire. A hero of the War of 1812, Porter has been called the "first American imperialist" because of his abortive effort to annex the island of Nuku Hiva in the Marquesas to the United States during that conflict (see David F. Long, *Nothing Too Daring: A Biography of Commodore David Porter, 1780–1843* [Annapolis, Md., 1970], p. 320). The commodore conducted business from what he dubbed "The Palace," his comfortable home at San Stefano, located some twelve miles from Constantinople. From San Stefano, Porter inundated the Department of State with a constant stream of messy and improperly numbered dispatches, sending approximately 600 (with voluminous enclosures) in twelve years. The commodore was so prolix that in 1841 Secretary Webster bluntly instructed him to write "less frequently," thereby relieving Porter and the department "of much unnecessary toil" (No. 51. DW to Porter, September 22, 1841, DNA, RG 59, Instructions, Turkey).

Porter drew a much sterner rebuke from Webster for his handling of a clash between the American missionaries in Syria and the patriarch of the Maronite church. In 1841 the Maronite patriarch petitioned the sultan to expel the missionaries on the grounds that they were troublemakers trying to excite the inhabitants of the Mount Lebanon area to change their religion and rites, and the Ottoman government asked Porter to facilitate their removal. Porter, in response, adhered strictly to the terms of the Turkish-American Treaty of Commerce and Navigation of May 7, 1830. He observed that the treaty did not give American citizens the right to interfere with the religion of the subjects of the Ottoman Empire and advised the missionaries not to resist expulsion. Porter was unmoved by the demand of those missionaries that they be allowed "the rights common to all American Citizens" (see Eli Smith et al. to Jasper Chasseaud, July 20, 1841, below). After observing that the treaty was "purely of a commercial nature," Porter concluded that there was nothing he could do (Porter to Chasseaud, October 14, 1841, below). As the commodore's lackadaisical attitude suggests, prior to 1842 U.S. diplomats tended to think of American citizens as merchants, not missionaries, and American rights as being primarily commercial, not spiritual. Daniel Webster altered this perception.

In a precedent-setting instruction dated February 2, 1842, written in response to domestic pressure emanating from the A.B.C.F.M., Webster adopted a broader view of the rights of American citizens abroad than had his predecessors. He strongly rebuked Porter and told him to extend to missionaries the same attention and protection granted to merchants. Rufus Anderson, chairman of the Prudential Committee of the A.B.C.F.M., later praised Webster's instruction as "the first formal declaration of our government" that missionaries had a right of protection equal to that of any other American citizen (Anderson, *Memorial Volume of the First Fifty Years of the American Board of Commissioners for Foreign Missions* [4th ed., Boston, 1861], p. 201).

As noted in the previous section, Webster effectively intervened on behalf of the representatives of the Baptist General Convention for Foreign Missions who were sent to Denmark. Webster's Middle Eastern diplomacy also was effective, for the missionaries in Syria were not expelled. Although Europeans had earlier upheld the rights of their missionaries abroad, Webster's representations to the Danish and Ottoman governments mark the first time that the United States extended its official protection to American missionaries serving in foreign lands.

ELI SMITH, WILLIAM MCCLURE THOMSON, SAMUEL WOLCOTT, NATHANIEL ABBOT KEYES, AND LEANDER THOMPSON TO JASPER CHASSEAUD.

Sir,   Beyrout 20. July 1841.

We have the honor to acknowledge the receipt of your note of the 10th, Inclosing copies of a communication from the Minister of Foreign Affairs, of His Sublime Porte to H[is] E[xcellency] the American Ambassador [David Porter], dated Rebia el Auwal 22nd A.H. 1257, touching a complaint of the Maronite Patriarch against ourselves; a Copy of the ambassador's reply to the same, and of his letter to yourself, dated May 16 1841.[1]

In reply to these communications permit us to make the following remarks, which we beg you will submit to H.E. the ambassador.

1   The Petition refered to purports to be from the Maronite Patriarch and *the Inhabitants of Lebanon*. Whereas the Maronites, the only people who acknowledge the Maronite Patriarch for their E[cc]lesiastical head, and who would be likely to petition Government through him, are little more than the moiety of the Inhabitants of Lebanon, while the *Druizes* are so numerous, and their influence has ever been so predominant, that Mount Lebanon is un[i]formly called by the Turks *Druizy Dagh* "the Druize Mountain."[2] That the Druizes have joined in no petition against us, we are certain. With their friendly feelings you are already to some extent acquainted. For further information should it be needed we refer you to the Druizes themselves, their nobility, and the common people, so far as they are acquainted with us.

2.   The Patriarch complains that by opening a number of schools, and by certain attentions, we are exciting the people to change their rites and religion. Whereas we have never opened a school for the Maronites; we have none in their part of the Mountain; even for our own residence when we retire from the summer heat of the city, we have uniformly chosen villages not in the Maronite region, and we have never admitted to our Communion a single Member of the Maronite Church. We have indeed schools for the poor children of Beyrout, which are public, and a few Maronite children may occasionally find their way into them. But these have never been many, we have made no efforts to increase their numbers, and they are always as free to go as they are to come. The teachers moreover, as well as nearly all the scholars, belong to another christian sect, and the only religious school book used, is the bible which all christians acknowledge. How two or three schools of this discription

1. Chasseaud to Thomson et al., July 10, 1841, MH-H. Mehmed Khüsrev Pasha (c. 1765–1855) was Ottoman chief minister, July 1839–May 1841. Yusuf Hubaysh was patriarch of the Maronite church, 1823–1845. A native Syrian Christian sect, the Maronites recognized the pope as the head of the Christian church while maintaining doctrinal and political independence. For the complaint of the Maronite patriarch and Porter's response, see Porter to DW, May 16, 1841, DNA, RG 59 (Despatches, Turkey); Porter to Chasseaud, May 16, 1841, MH-H.

2. The Druzes, an ethnic, religious, and political group from the area around Mount Lebanon, practiced a syncretic religion that incorporated elements from Islamic sects as well as from Judaism and Christianity. Their rites and beliefs were secret. In September 1841 war broke out between the Druzes and the Maronites.

at Beyrout, can possibly disturb the peace of the Maronites at Lebanon, we are at a loss to understand, unless the mere act of teaching poor children to read their Bibles; be in their estimation a just cause of complaint. As we have opportunity and the means we endeavor to instruct the poor and ignorant in useful knowledge, but we are peaceable men, and to make proselytes from other Christian sects, to our own, has never been the object to which we have aimed.

3. His Excellency Zakeria Pacha late Ser Asker of Syria,[3] represented that to prevent our being ill treated, by the inhabitants, it would be necessary to take measures for our removal to other parts. In making such a representation H.E. must certainly have proceeded upon wrong information. We are not aware that any Frank Resident of Beyrout,[4] are less exposed to mob treatment by the inhabitants than ourselves. When a portion of the inhabitants of Lebanon a year ago, rose against the Egyptian Government and beseiged Beyrout, our houses were without the walls and entirely exposed. And yet, while every other Frank, not excepting the Consuls, as well as nearly all the natives fled into the City for protection, we remained in our houses, and not only did we receive no injury in person, or property from the Insurgents, but not even an unkind word, and that though they are mostly Maronites from the heart of the Maronite part of the Mountains. A few months after, during the seize of Beyrout by the Ships of the Sultan and his allies, while even your own house and many others were pillaged, before the surrender of the city, ours remained untouched and we lost not a single article. And now months after Zakeria Pacha's removal from Syria, we are living in all quietness in three different villages of Mount Lebanon, travel up and down it alone, without molestation—and experience nothing but kindness and respect from its inhabitants.

4. There has not to our knowledge occurred any new ground of complaint against us. For more than fifteen years we have resided peaceably in the country and have been pursuing the same course as now. And all the while the officers of the Sultans Government, both before and during the rule of the Pacha of Egypt [Mehemet Ali], have protected us and regarded our rights, as peaceable American Citizens. We have always known indeed that the Patriarch entertains an inveterate enmity against Protestant Christianity. One of his flock who several years ago ventured to declare some of the doctrines and usages of the Maronites contrary to the Bible, he imprisoned, until he died the lingering death of a martyr.[5] Many copies of the Bible printed by the British and Foreign

3. The position of Ser Asker was that of a military governor with great administrative power. Zakeria Pasha was appointed governor of the Mount Lebanon district in January 1841 but was removed by August.

4. The term *Frank* was applied generally to Europeans by Syrians.

5. Assad Shidak, a Maronite Syrian, refused to renounce his conversion and died in prison.

Bible society, which his people had procured to read, he has from time to time caused to be collected and burnt, because they were issued from a Protestant press. Yet why he should now send up this complaint against us, we are unable to conjecture, unless the suggestion of others wiser than ourselves in such matters be true—that he has been encouraged to it by Foreign political intrigues, with which we have nothing to do. And if it be true, that the Patriarch and political partisans, desire to counteract the influence of England, by exciting an odium against her religion, we certainly have a right to ask that they be just in doing it, and not assail us, who have held no agency whatever in these political transactions.

5. Were it true that by "schools" and "attentions" we had led some of the people to change their rites and religion we should have done nothing contrary to the Laws of the country, and for which there do not exist established usages and precedents. Christians have always been allowed the liberty of going from one sect to another without being held amenable therefor to the Turkish tribunals as for a misdemeanor—a liberty fully acknowledged by the legal authorities of the land. And an entire new sect, with a Patriarch at its head, and numerous bishops and clergy, has come into existence within a century, by the proselyting labors of foreign Missionaries, who had no more right by treaty to pursue such labors, than we have. Such is the origin of the Greek Catholic sect of Syria, it being wholly composed of converts from the Greek Church, made by foreign Roman Catholic missionaries. A fetwa[6] from the highest authorities, justified them in this act of dissent, and the Sultan has now no more respectable and faithful christian subjects than they are. And does not the more tolerant and improved Government of the present Sultan, secure to his christian subjects at least an equal liberty of Concience in the choice of the form of Christianity which they shall profess? Or is it protestantism only that is to be excluded, the religion of England, Prussia, Holland, and several other states of Europe, and of the United States of America—a form of Christianity less obnoxious in its rights to Mahommedan feeling than any other—and is a christian subject of the Sultan to be liable to imprisonment and martyrdom by his Patriarch, because he wishes to take the Bible as his guide in matters of religion?

6. It is the Patriarch and not ourselves, that has given just cause of complaint, by acting contrary to the tolerant principles of the Government under which he lives. The Fetwa (a copy of which we subjoin)[7] which declares toleration to the Greek Catholics of Syria, fully proves it

6. A fetwa is the official opinion of an Islamic religious lawyer. French Catholic missionaries had been active in Syria for over a century and as early as 1740 were granted religious privileges.

7. The enclosure is not included in the records of the Department of State.

to be a principle of Mahommedan Law, that christians have the Liberty to go from one sect to the other, including the Franks. It forbids their being forced to obey their Patriarchs and Bishops who would deny them their liberty; and authorizes Mahommedan Magistrates to prevent all interference of Patriarchs and Bishops in such cases. And yet the persecution and death by the Patriarch in his own convent suffered by the Maronite already refered to, and other similar but less aggravated cases, are matters of well known occurrence. In no other part of Syria except in Mount Lebanon could such acts of Clergy oppression have been committed. And it is hoped that under the present improved system of Government, the Patriarch even here, will feel himself obliged to have more regard to the tolerant wishes of the Sultan.

7. Allow us to add in conclusion, that we are not ignorant of, and have ever concienciously regarded, the Laws and usages of the Ottoman Government, and so long as we do this, we believe that the Passports we hold in our hands from the Secretary of State of the Federal Government of the United States, entitles us to the rights common to all American Citizens within the Dominions of the Sultan, rights, which by Treaty, agreeable to those of the Citizens of the most favored nations. These rights, we look to one Ambassador, and after him to our home Government, to secure to us, until it can be legally proved that we have forfeited them. This we trust His Excellency, Commodore Porter will cheerfully do, after being thus informed of the facts of the case. Moreover faithfulness to the relations we sustain to others, requires us to remind you, that a considerable amount of property is involved in this Question. We have been domicilated here for years. Some of our number having come to Beyrout before any other foreigner now here, except perhaps yourself. During this time we had invested a considerable amount of property belonging to those at home, many of whom are among the most respectable men in our country, who furnish us the means of promoting the education and instruction of the poor people around us. This property, should it be illegally sacrificed, would not fail to be inquired after by those whom it concerns.

The above facts, we beg that you will do us the favor carefully to investigate, and so far as you find them supported by truth, report the same to His Excellency the Ambassador. With sentiments of High esteem, we are ever your Most obdt Humble servt   signed / Eli Smith W. Thomson Saml Wolcott N. A. Keyes L. Thompson

Copy. Enclosed with No. 114. Porter to DW, October 16, 1841, DNA, RG 59 (Despatches, Turkey). Rec'd February 1, 1842. Smith (1801–1857; Yale 1821), a scholarly missionary who mastered Arabic, was next sent to Syria by the A.B.C.F.M. in 1826, the year he graduated from Andover Theological Seminary. David H. Finnie has called Smith the "first true American Orientalist." (*Pioneers East: The Early American Experience in the Middle East* [Cambridge, Mass., 1967], p. 196). Thomson (1806–1894; Miami University 1827) attended Princeton Theological Seminary, 1829–1831, and served as a missionary in Syria, 1833–1844, 1850–1857, and 1859–1878. Thomson wrote a classic three-volume account of life in the Middle East, *The Land and the Book* (New York, 1880–1885). Wolcott (1813–1886; Yale 1833) graduated from Andover Theological Seminary in 1837. He was assistant secretary of the A.B.C.F.M., 1837–1839, and a missionary in Beirut, 1839–1843. Keyes (1808–1861; Dartmouth 1835) attended Andover and Lane Theological seminaries. After serving as a missionary in Syria, 1839–1845, he was a minister in the United States. Thompson (1812–1896; Amherst 1835) graduated from Andover Theological Seminary in 1838. He spent four years in Syria, 1840–1844, as a teacher in Beirut. Chasseaud, a British subject and a resident of Syria, was appointed U.S. consul at Beirut in 1835. He was supportive of American missionaries in Syria, and they protested on his behalf when the United States closed the Beirut consulate in 1840. At their urging, the consulate was reopened in August 1842. In 1850 Chasseaud was replaced by an American.

DAVID PORTER TO JASPER CHASSEAUD

                                        U.S. Legation
Sir,   St Steffano October 14, 1841.
I herewith enclose you the copy of my reply to His Excellency the Minister of Foreign Affairs [Mehmed Khüsrev Pasha] of the Sublime Porte [Abdülmejid I], respecting the complaint of the Patriarch of the Maronites of Mount Lebanon [Yusuf Hubaysh] against the American missionaries[1] established there, which I have shown to Mr John P[orter] Brown,[2] the U.S. Dragoman, who says it is an exact copy of what he presented to the Sublime Porte.

Your Letter of the 1. August[3] has been received, enclosing copy of the answer of the American Missionaries in Beyrout[4] to the complaint made by the Sublime Porte, that they had opened a number of schools in the *Druze* mountain of Mount Lebanon, and were by certain attentions exciting the minds of the people to change their rites and religion.

I have communicated the copy of your letter, together with that of their reply to the Sublime Porte, and have to direct that you will take proper measures to ensure to all American Citizens in Syria, the rights

1. The enclosure is not included in the record of No. 114. Porter to DW, October 16, 1841; this is possibly another reference to Porter's note to Chasseaud of May 16, 1841, MH-H.

2. Brown was at that time serving as dragoman at Constantinople. Over the years he acted as dragoman, consul, and secretary of legation. He was instrumental in bringing about the

tour of America by Amin Bey in 1850, the first visit of an Ottoman official to the United States. For the mission of Amin Bey, see *Diplomatic Papers* 2.

3. This letter is also enclosed with No. 114. Porter to DW, October 16, 1841, DNA, RG 59 (Despatches, Turkey).

4. See above.

and privileges secured to them by the Treaty existing between the United States and the Sublime Porte,[5] so long as they do not forfeit them by acting in opposition to the wishes of the Porte.

Our Treaty is purely of a commercial nature, and all the rights are secured by it to American Citizens residing in Turkey. I cannot see that I can do any thing further in the matter. Very Respectfully   Your obt Servt   signed / David Porter

Copy. Enclosed with No. 114. Porter to DW, October 16, 1841, DNA, RG 59 (Despatches, Turkey). Rec'd February 1, 1842.

FROM SAMUEL TURELL ARMSTRONG

Sir   Washington Jan. 31. 1842

As a member of the Prudential Committee of the American Board of Commissioners for Foreign Missions[1] I have to ask your immediate attention to the situation of the Missionaries of this Board in the Ottoman Empire. Commodore [David] Porter has uniformly construed the Treaty, existing between the United States and that Empire, as strictly commercial; and does not extend the customary patronage and protection, which he feels willing to bestow on commercial men, to our missionaries; whereby they are in fact denationalized in the view of foreigners and have to rely on the protection which may be needful for them on the British flag; and have repeatedly expressed their fears lest they should be compelled to cast reproach upon their Country in seeking safety under the folds of a foreign ensign.

I beg not to be understood as reproaching Com. Porter any further than well substantiated fact; tending to prove all I have stated will promote such an end. I have supposed that a letter from the Department requiring him to afford to Missionaries the same aid that is afforded by him to Merchants and the same which British authorities afford to their Missionaries will answer every purpose. While on this subject permit me to say that the unexpected and unexplained abolition of the Consular offices in the Ottoman empire is deemed by all whose opinions we are acquainted with as uncalled for, unwise and tending to degrade our Nation in the eyes of foreigners, and is very embarrassing to those who are in the employment of our Board[2] and I cannot but hope it may be deemed

5. The United States negotiated a commercial treaty with Turkey in 1830. See *Treaties*, 3:541–598.

1. The executive committee of the A.B.C.F.M., of which Armstrong became a member in 1832.

2. Secretary of State John Forsyth closed all the American consulates in the Ottoman Empire in 1840, except those at Constantinople, Smyrna, and Alexandria, because they were not "productive of any public advantage." No. 41. Forsyth to Porter, April 9, 1840, DNA, RG 59 (Instructions, Turkey).

proper to restore those offices without any delay. Very respectfully Your fellow Citizen   Sam. T. Armstrong

A L S . DNA, RG 59 (Misc. Letters). Endorsed: "Com: Porter instructed 2 Feb. 1842. No. 52." Armstrong (1784–1850), a wealthy publisher of religious works, was a Whig representative to the Massachusetts General Court, lieutenant governor, 1833–1835, and governor of Massachusetts in 1835. Defeated in his bid for reelection as governor by Edward Everett, Armstrong was elected mayor of Boston in 1835.

TO DAVID PORTER

No. 52   Department of State
Sir,   Washington, 2nd February, 1842.
    It has been represented to this Department, that the American Missionaries, and other citizens of the United States, not engaged in commercial pursuits, residing and travelling in the Ottoman dominions, do not receive from your Legation that aid and protection to which, as citizens of the United States, they feel themselves entitled; and I have been directed by the President, who is profoundly interested in the matter, to call your immediate attention to the subject, and to instruct you to omit no occasion, where your interference in behalf of such persons, may become necessary or useful, to extend to them all proper succor and attentions, of which they may stand in need, in the same manner that you would to other citizens of the United States, who, as merchants, visit or dwell in Turkey. Enclosed is a letter addressed to me this day, by Ex-Governor [Samuel Turell] Armstrong, of Massachusetts,[1] a gentleman of high character, which will explain to you the nature of the representations that have been made upon this subject, which it appeared due to you, as well as to those interested in the cause it is the object of the representation to shield and to promote, frankly to communicate; and the Department believes that it will only be necessary to invoke your attention to its contents, to insure from you in future to the individuals described what this Government expects from its representatives abroad, in all cases, where citizens of the U. States are concerned.
    It is my opinion that the American Consulates in Syria, which were recently suppressed, might, at this time, be made useful,—an opinion confirmed by circumstances which have occurred since their suppression, and by what Governor Armstrong has stated,—and I have to request that you will communicate your own views, upon the subject, and designate the proper ports in Syria, where, in your judgment, consulates might with advantage be established, as well as the persons whom it would be most expedient to invest with such offices, should the President

1. This is probably a reference to   above.
Armstrong to DW, January 31, 1842,

resolve to re-establish them,[2] I am, Sir, respectfully, Your obedient servant, Danl Webster

LC. DNA, RG 59 (Instructions, Turkey).

TO SAMUEL TURELL ARMSTRONG

My Dear Sir

Washington
Feb. 14. '42

I am obliged & honored by your communication recd this morning, & accept with pleasure a membership, at the Board of Foreign missions.[1]

It is possibly that our information from the East may sometimes be useful to this Board, & I should be quite gratified if you would communicate with me, in the freest manner, in relation to any thing, in which it may be supposed I can render service to the cause. Yrs with entire regard, Danl Webster

ALS. MHi.

FROM DAVID PORTER

No. 125

U.S. Legation

Sir,

St Steffano July 16th 1842.

I have just had the honor to receive your communication of the 2d of February last,[1] enclosing copy of one from the Ex-Governor of Massachusetts [Samuel Turell Armstrong],[2] in which he represents to the Department of State that, American Missionaries and other Citizens of the United States, not engaged in Commercial pursuits, residing and travelling in the Ottoman Dominions, do not receive from this Legation, the aid and protection, to which as Citizens of the United States, they feel themselves entitled.

I beg leave to call your particular attention to my communication of the 16th of May last,[3] wherein I transmitted Copies of a correspondence with the Sublime Porte [Abdülmejid I], on the subject of its complaint against the interference of the American Missionaries, at and in the vicinity of Mount Lebanon, with the rites and religion of the Maronites, and other inhabitants of Mount Lebanon, subjects of the Sublime Porte, which I hoped would have proven satisfactory, but regret to find that the complaints then anticipated, have reached the Department.

2. Chasseaud was reinstated as U.S. consul at Beirut when that consulate was reopened in August. See No. 53. DW to Porter, August 12, 1842, DNA, RG 59 (Instructions, Turkey).

1. By virtue of a donation from Armstrong, DW was made an honorary member of the A.B.C.F.M. See Certificate of Membership, February 10, 1842, mDW 21530.

1. See above, DW to Porter, February 2, 1842.

2. See above, Armstrong to DW, January 31, 1842.

3. See No. 94. Porter to DW, May 16, 1841, DNA, RG 59 (Despatches, Turkey).

Permit me to observe sir, that in no instance whatever have I refused to extend to American Citizens, residing or travelling within the Turkish Dominions, such aid and protection as they have a right to expect from their Minister, and I exceedingly regret to find that representations have been made to the contrary. My patronage and protection, from the period of my arrival in this country, have at all times been extended to Citizens of the United States, either collectively or individually, without distinction, so long as they abstained from an interference with the religious rites of the subjects of the Sublime Porte, and demeaned themselves in such manner, as to avoid complaints on the part of the Government against them. Our Treaty does not extend to our citizens any right to interfere with the religion of the subjects of the Sublime Porte, and on the receipt of the representation of the Minister of Foreign Affairs [Mehmed Khüsrev Pasha],[4] against the American Missionaries, it only remained for me to express my regret that causes of complaint had arisen, and instruct the U.S. Consular Agent at Beyrout [Jasper Chasseaud] to investigate and report to me on the subject.[5] He was also directed to take proper measures to secure to all of our citizens in Syria, the protection extended to them by the Treaty existing between the U.S. and Turkey, so long as they do not forfeit it by acting in opposition to the expressed wishes of the Porte.

Immediately after the suppression of the Consulates in Turkey, which was done in opposition to my wishes, I forwarded to Mr Chasseaud, the Ex-Consul at Beyrout, an appointment of U.S. Consular Agent for that place, and as no complaints of want of consular protection has since reached me from that quarter, I presume that that Agency, has been found sufficient; if however the Government should see proper to appoint a full Consul at Beyrout, I should earnestly recommend that the post should be filled by an American Citizen, with a competent salary, and authority to appoint Agents at the principal towns throughout Syria.[6]

I also enclose you herewith an original certificate from Mr John P[orter] Brown,[7] who is well acquainted with all the circumstances of the case above refered to. I have the honor to be With great respect Your obt servt   David Porter

LS. DNA, RG 59 (Despatches, Turkey). Rec'd September 21, 1841.

4. Enclosed with Porter's dispatch No. 94 to DW of May 16, 1841, DNA, RG 59 (Despatches, Turkey).

5. See above, Porter to Chasseaud, October 14, 1841.

6. Prior to 1855, U.S. consuls and consular agents were usually local merchants and often were foreign nationals like Chasseaud. They received no salary but collected fees for performing their consular duties. In 1855 Congress stipulated that those representing the United States abroad as consuls had to be American citizens and were to be paid regular salaries.

7. The statement by Brown, which endorses Porter's actions, reviews the conflict between the Maronite patriarch and the missionaries.

The J. L. Day Agency and Liberia

The United States's foreign policy toward Africa in the antebellum period focused on the problem of the slave trade. American merchants, however, also carried on a legitimate commerce with various parts of Africa in such goods as camwood and palm oil, and the United States had a special relationship with Liberia. Founded by the American Colonization Society in 1822 as a homeland for free blacks from the United States, Liberia also offered a place to which those Africans liberated from slave traders by the U.S. Navy could be transported. In 1819 Congress had provided for an American agency on the coast of Africa to receive the recaptured Africans, and by the 1840s agents such as James L. Day were appointed in cooperation with the American Colonization Society. An estimated 15,000 American freemen and 5,000 recaptured Africans eventually were taken to Liberia, which became a republic in 1847.

In addition to Liberia and such routine matters as shipwrecked seamen, U.S. relations with Africa occasionally involved outrages such as the *Mary Carver* incident. As the correspondence published below suggests, such instances of murder and plunder on the west coast of Africa were dealt with through what might be called "gunboat diplomacy."

TO JAMES LAWRENCE DAY

Department of State

Sir,   Washington January 10th 1842

The President having appointed you "Agent on the coast of Africa for receiving the negroes, mulattoes, or persons of color delivered from on board vessels seized in the prosecution of the slave-trade by U.S. armed vessels," I herewith enclose your commission.[1] You will be pleased to inform this Department of the result of it, and should it be accepted the name of the State or Country in which you were born. I am, sir, &c

Daniel Webster

Note. Commission sent through the colonization office.

LC. DNA, RG 59 (Domestic Letters). Day (d. 1854; Princeton 1838), of New Jersey, graduated from the University of Pennsylvania medical school in 1840 and accepted the position of physician to the colony of freed slaves in Liberia. Day returned to the United States in 1844 and established a medical practice in Wilkes-Barre, Pennsylvania.

FROM JAMES LAWRENCE DAY

Honoured Sir   Monrovia Sep. 17 1842

By the earliest opportunity I acknowledge the receipt of your letter of

1. The enclosure is not included in the RG 59 record.

10[t]h Jany last[1] enclosing my commission as "Agent on the west coast of Africa &c." Thro' some neglect on the part of the persons into whose hands it passed, it did not reach me till 21st August.

But having early seen a notice of the appointment in the National Gazetter[2]—I opened a correspondence with the Secretary of the Navy[3]—on the subject of the capture of the Sch: Mary Carver & the murder of the captain, and crew, by the natives about 300 miles from this.[4] Please inform me if communications should be to *your* department. The former Agent T[homas] Buchanan[5] Esqr corresponded with the Secretary of the *Navy.*

I would be glad to be informed whether under the commission which is a special one I will be expected to perform any of the duties of a consular or *commercial* agent. It sometimes happens that American sailors are discharged or wrecked on the coast. The question whether I should be warranted in taking care of them & sending them home seems almost superfluous. And I would not ask it did I not know the former agent had some difficulty in getting allowed some expenses he was at on account of a crew of wrecked mariners belonging to the ship <Jupiter> Emperor of Philadelphia.

The American Barque Rhoderick Dhu of Providence Rhode Island is now in our port. The captain R[ichard] Syms captured one of the ringleaders in the massacre of the Mary Carver's crew—who boarded him when off Breaby.[6]

While he was endeavouring to induce the cap. to go on shore & purchase his share of the plunder—the latter was planning to secure the villains in irons, which he effected.

The prisoner was left at cape coast castle in the care of Gov. [George] McLean.[7]

Comr [William] Ramsay sailed from here on the 29[t]h Ultimo for the Leeward coast and will probably go as far as the [Cape Coast] castle and take the prisoner on Board the Vandalia.[8]

1. See above.

2. Not found, but probably a reference to the Philadelphia *Pennsylvania Inquirer and National Gazette.*

3. Abel Parker Upshur (1791–1844; Princeton, Yale) served as secretary of the navy, 1841–1843.

4. On the *Mary Carver*, see below.

5. Buchanan (d. 1841) arrived in Africa in 1836 and became governor of Liberia in 1839. He died in Africa.

6. While trading at Béréby, Sims seized an African who offered to sell him some sails and rope from the *Mary Carver*. The prisoner admitted his complicity with two Africans employed by Sims. Day to DW, October 8, 1842, DNA, RG 59 (Misc. Letters).

7. MacLean (d. 1847), a British army captain, arrived on the Gold Coast in 1828. He represented a group of London merchants at Cape Coast. In 1843 the British government assumed control of the Gold Coast, and MacLean officially became the royal governor, although he had been acting in this capacity prior to his appointment.

8. The U.S.S. *Vandalia*, commanded by Ramsay (d. 1866), was a

Your agent is a native of Morris County in the state of New Jersey. With sentiments of high esteem I am your obedient Servant

J. Lawrence Day

ALS. DNA, RG 59 (Misc. Letters). Rec'd December 10, 1842.

JEREMIAH FARRIS TO JOHN QUINCY ADAMS

Plymouth Mass.

Dear Sir   March 27. 1843.

The Schooner Mary Carver, belonging to the late Nathaniel Carver[1] (deceased) of this town, was chartered to Messrs Q.D. Farwell[2] and others in April 1841 for a trading voyage on the Coast of Africa.

On the 20th of April 1842, at Beribay [Béréby], a trading village on the West Coast of Africa, the natives induced Capt. [Ebenezer] Farwell[3] (brother of the above) to come on shore to see some camwood which they proposed to sell him. On reaching the shore he was treacherously seized, tied to a tree, pelted with stones, beaten with pestles and clubs and otherwise brutally tortured.

While the scene was enacted on shore, the schooner was boarded by part of the tribe and her entire crew murdered. They then returned, informed the Captain of the proceedings with the additional information that they would complete the massacre by killing him also. They then attached a stone to his person by suspending it from his neck, put him into a canoe, put off from the shore, and deliberately threw him overboard, when he sank to rise no more. Capt Farwell begged his life at their hands, on account of his absent wife and child, but they had no care for the entreaties. The Schooner was afterwards beached, plundered and stripped.

My purpose in communicating with you on the subject is to learn that if it was represented to the Government at Washington, it would avail anything, if they would take any measures for redress, and if any could be obtained, if it would be well to do so; or whether in the event that a treaty should be hereafter made between the United States and that Government,[4] it would be advisable to place the documents in possession of the Government at the present time.

---

twenty-gun schooner. The prisoner escaped. John B. Russwurm to Matthew C. Perry, July 10, 1843, *Senate Documents*, 28th Cong., 2d sess., Serial 458, No. 150, p. 41.

    1. Carver (b. 1791).
    2. Not identified.
    3. Not identified.
    4. Perhaps a reference to the government of the Fishmen tribe of the

Ivory Coast, responsible for the murder of the crew of the *Mary Carver*, but more probably to the government of France, since the Ivory Coast had become a French protectorate in 1842. A covenant on the surrender of criminals was made between the United States and France on November 9, 1843. See *Treaties*, 4:515–518.

I shall esteem it a great favour to have your views upon the subject, with such information and direction as you be pleased to communicate. I have the honor to be Very respectfully Your Obedient Servant

Jeremiah Farris

Copy. DNA, RG 59 (Misc. Letters). Farris (1810–c. 1883) was the son-in-law of the owner of the *Mary Carver*.

DANIEL FLETCHER WEBSTER TO JOHN QUINCY ADAMS

Department of State
Sir,   Washington April 3d 1843.

I have the honor to return the letter addressed to you by Mr Jermiah Farris on the 27th ult.[1] which you left at the Department yesterday.

A copy of this letter has been taken and will be transmitted to the Secretary of the Navy [Abel Parker Upshur],[2] with a request that he will give orders to one of the Government ships on that station to inquire into the facts, demand reparation as far as may be, if found due, for the losses suffered, the punishment of those concerned in the outrage, and in the event of both or either of these demands being refused, to inflict such punishment on the guilty as may serve to prevent future enormities of the kind.[3] I have the honor &c.   Fletcher Webster, Actg Secy

LC. DNA, RG 59 (Domestic Letters).

FROM THE OFFICE OF THE AMERICAN COLONIZATION SOCIETY

Washington, March 18, 1843.
Sir:

In reply to your inquiries this morning, I have the honor herewith to transmit the report just submitted to Congress by Mr [John Pendleton] Kennedy, of the Committee on Commerce, with the memorial (to which it refers) of the late colonization convention, together with a speech of the late Francis S[cott] Key, esq., on the nature and extent of protection and aid justly expected for the colonists of Liberia from the General Government.[1]

1. See above.

2. See Daniel Fletcher Webster to Upshur, April 5, 1843, DNA, RG 59 (Domestic Letters).

3. In December 1843 Matthew Calbraith Perry (1794–1858), commander of the Africa squadron, held a parlay at Cape Palmas with the Africans he believed responsible for the plunder of the *Mary Carver*. During the talks a fight broke out and two Africans were killed. Perry burned several villages in retaliation for the *Carver* incident and induced tribal leaders to sign compacts to protect American property. *Senate Documents*, 28th Cong., 2d sess., Serial 458, No. 150, pp. 38–50.

1. The report, with its voluminous appendix, is in *House Reports*, 27th Cong., 3d sess., Serial 428, No. 283. See the memorial, pp. 7–16, and Key's speech, pp. 51–66. Kennedy (1795–1870; Baltimore College

The constitution of the American Colonization Society declares "that the society shall act, to effect its object, in co-operation with the General Government, and such of the States as may adopt regulations upon the subject;" and the meeting that adopted this constitution appointed a committee "to present a respectful memorial to Congress, requesting them to adopt such measures as may be thought most desirable for securing a territory in Africa, or elsewhere, suitable for the colonization of the free people of color."[2] In the opening of their memorial, this committee declare that they are delegated by a highly respectable association of their fellow-citizens, recently organized at the seat of Government, to solicit Congress to aid with the power, the protection, and the resources of the country, the great beneficial object of their institution—an object deemed worthy of the earnest attention, and of the strenuous and persevering exertions, as well of every patriot, in whatever condition of life, as of every enlightened, philanthropic, and practical statesman." You are aware, sir, that in consequence of this and subsequent memorials from the society to Congress, the slave-trade was made piracy by our laws, that the President of the United States was requested to enter into negotiations with foreign powers, to secure the denunciation and punishment of this traffic, as piracy, by all civilized nations; that he was authorized to take charge of any Africans captured by our arms from vessels unlawfully engaged in this trade on the ocean, or when about to land such persons in the United States; that Mr. [James] Monroe, (then President,) believing that the humane provisions of this law could be most economically and effectually fulfilled by placing such Africans within the limits and under the protection of such colony as might be founded by the efforts of the society, determined to act in co-operation with it in regard to the station to be chosen; that the first agent sent out with emigrants by the society, should be the agent also of the Government; and that arms, lumber, and other supplies to this first expedition, were furnished at the expense of the Government; that the first purchase of territory in Liberia was effected by the aid of Captain [Robert Field] Stockton,[3] one of our naval officers; that very important assistance has repeatedly from that time been given by our ships of war on the African coast; and that, as doubts had been expressed by the legal officers of the Government in regard to the interpretation of the act of Congress of the 3d of March,

---

1812), a lawyer and literary figure, was elected to Congress in 1840 and 1842. He opposed Tyler's policies and was defeated for reelection in 1844. Key (1779–1843; St. John's College 1796) was active in the affairs of the American Colonization Society.

2. The constitution of the Coloniza-tion Society and the memorial of January 14, 1817, are found in *House Reports*, Serial 428, No. 283, pp. 208–210, 921–923.

3. In 1821 U.S. naval officer Stockton (1795–1866) purchased land at Cape Mesurado that later became the nucleus of Liberia.

1819, a memorial was addressed to Congress, at its last session, praying that some appropriation, free from doubt and restriction, might be placed at the disposal of the Executive, for the support of any such recaptured Africans as, through the operations of the recent treaty, might be sent to the agency for the same in Liberia; and the sum of five thousand was appropriated for this purpose.[4]

I beg leave further to submit the following extracts from instructions given by the Navy Department to commanders of United States vessels, in relation to the colony of Liberia:

To Captain [Robert Trail] Spence,[5] June 11, 1822.

"When you arrive on the coast of Africa, you will proceed off Cape Messurado, and visit the colony established near this place, and afford all the aid and support in your power to Dr. Eli Ayres,[6] the agent of this Government and the colonists."

To the same.

"By recent accounts received from Cape Messurado, on the coast of Africa, it appears that the American settlement there has been attacked by the natives, and the safety of the people endangered. Their situation is, therefore, such as requires immediate relief and protection. I wish you to remain near them until you shall be relieved, or receive further instructions from this department, and afford to the settlement and to the agent of the Government all the aid and protection in your power."

To the same, April 8, 1823.

"For the greater security of the settlements made at Messurado, be pleased to station at that place, so long as you shall continue on the coast of Africa, or while the settlement is endangered by the natives, as many marines as can conveniently be spared from the United States ship Cyane under your command."[7]

"It is," said the late Chief Justice [John] Marshall, in a letter dated December 14, 1831, "of great importance to retain the countenance and protection of the General Government. Some of our cruisers stationed

4. 3 U.S. Stat. 532–534.

5. Spence (d. 1826), from Portsmouth, New Hampshire, entered the navy in 1800 and was promoted to captain in 1815. Spence commanded the twenty-four-gun corvette, Cyane.

6. Ayres, a Baltimore physician, arrived in Africa as agent of the Colonization Society in 1821 and, with Stockton, purchased Cape Mesurado for the society. Ayres brought colonists to Cape Mesurado in 1822 but removed with a number of them to Sierra Leone within the year. He was later active in the United States on behalf of the Maryland Colonization Society.

7. The instructions and a report from Spence are in House Reports, Serial 428, No. 283.

on the coast of Africa could at the same time interrupt the slave-trade—a horrid traffic, detested by all good men—*and would protect the vessels and commerce of the colony from the pirates that infest those seas. The power of the Government to afford this aid is not, I believe, contested.*"[8]

I will only add, what is stated in my former letter,[9] (a copy of which accompanies this,) that while it is vitally important to secure to the government of Liberia incontestable jurisdiction from Cape Mount to Cape Palmas; and that while the enlargement of these settlements, and their multiplication, will prove most powerful auxiliaries to the overthrow of the slave-trade, and the growth of peaceful and useful commerce—the true objects contemplated by the United States and Great Britain, in one article of the recent treaty—I feel assured that no endeavors on your part, sir, will be wanting to preserve their rights and secure their prosperity. I have the honor to be, sir, with the greatest respect, your most obedient servant, R. R. Gurley.

Text from *Executive Documents*, 28th Cong., 1st sess., Serial 442, No. 162, pp. 15–17. Original not found. Ralph R. Gurley (1797–1872; Yale 1818) became an agent for the American Colonization Society in 1822. He edited the organization magazine, the *African Repository*, for twenty-five years and visited Liberia three times between 1824 and 1867.

TO EDWARD EVERETT

No. 35.   Department of State,
Sir,   Washington, 24 March, 1843.
    I send you, in addition to the papers transmitted with my letter of the 5th of January last,[1] several notes recently addressed to me by the Secretary of the American Colonization Society [Ralph R. Gurley], together with the printed documents &c., accompanying them. Mr Gurley's first communication is dated on the 13th and the other two on the 16th instant.[2] Taken in connection with those previously forwarded to the Legation, they show that the wishes of the Colonists in regard to the territorial extent of their settlement are quite reasonable,—the settlement trending southeasterly from Cape Mount to Cape Palmas, a distance of about three hundred miles only,—and these notes, too, explain the nature of the relations existing between Liberia and the United States. Founded principally with a view to the melioration of the condition of an interesting portion of the great human family, this colony has conciliated, more and more, the good will,—and has from time to time received the aid and

8. Marshall's letter to Gurley is in *House Reports*, Serial 428, No. 283.
    9. Gurley to DW, December 22, 1842, DNA, RG 59 (Misc. Letters).
    1. With his letter to Everett of January 5, 1843, DW had forwarded

letters received from the American Colonization Society dated December 22, 1842, and March 10, 1843, DNA, RG 59 (Instructions, Britain).
    2. Not found.

support,—of this Government. Without having passed any laws for their regulation, the American Government takes a deep interest in the welfare of the People of Liberia, and is disposed to extend to them a just degree of countenance and protection. I am, Sir, with great respect, your obdt. servt.   Danl Webster

LC. DNA, RG 59 (Instructions, Britain).

The "Barbary Powers"

By the 1840s the phrase "Barbary pirates" was no longer a cause for alarm, but the United States's relations with the greatly weakened North African kingdoms of Morocco, Tripoli, and Tunis remained anomalous in more than one way. Contrary to normal diplomatic usage, the United States was represented in those states by salaried consuls who performed diplomatic functions. For some reason, these consulates in the so-called Barbary States seemed to attract a disproportionate number of colorful and erratic individuals such as Thomas N. Carr, Samuel D. Heap, and William B. Hodgson, and their behavior occasionally puzzled secretaries of state such as Daniel Webster. After working much of his life to obtain a consular post, Hodgson abruptly resigned shortly after replacing Heap at Tunis, and Carr became embroiled in a strange dispute with the emperor of Morocco after being relieved as U.S. consul at Tangier. Finally, although the tribute system had been ended, the United States still adhered to the archaic custom of giving presents and gratuities to high officials of the Barbary kingdoms—a practice that Webster undertook to abolish.

TO WILLIAM BROWN HODGSON

No 1   Department of State,
Sir: Washington, 22d Septr, 1841.
   The President having appointed you Consul of the United States to Tunis, in the place of Mr Samuel D[avies] Heap, on whom the office of Principal Dragoman to the Ottoman Porte has been conferred,[1] your commission and a credential letter addressed to the Bey of Tunis [Ahmad Bey], are herewith communicated. In presenting the letter of credence, which you will do in the usual manner, as soon as practicable after your arrival at Tunis, you will take the occasion to inform His Highness of the friendly disposition of the President, and of his earnest desire to cultivate and maintain the relations of amity and peace now happily prevailing between the United States and his Regency.
   A despatch to your predecessor, containing his commission as Dragoman, is herewith committed to your care to be handed to him by you, on

   1. See above, Heap to DW, Novem-   pp. 22–23.
ber 17, 1841, "Dividing the Spoils,"

reaching Tunis. Mr Heap will deliver to you the books, papers, and property of the Consulate (of which you will prepare and transmit hither an exact inventory.) and no doubt furnish you with any assistance you may need in entering upon the discharge of the duties of the Consulate, with which a long residence at Tunis, as Consul, has rendered him familiar.

The commercial intercourse between Tunis and the United States is inconsiderable and the principal objects of your mission will therefore be to cultivate and preserve the friendly relations of the two Governments, and to render to the citizens and commerce of the United States, occasionally resorting to Tunis, all the aid to which they may be entitled, and which may be in your power. It will be expected of you, likewise, to make yourself acquainted with the political state of the country in which you reside, and its relations with other States, and more particularly with those prevailing, or likely to arise, in reference to Algiers,[2] and to communicate what you learn on these subjects to this Department. And indeed any statistical, geographical, or other interesting information, with respect to Tunis, which you may acquire, will be very acceptable to your Government. The leisure you will enjoy will afford you ample time for prosecuting the study of the Oriental languages, and for making researches into the antiquities with which the interesting region whither you are sent, abounds.

As soon as you shall have executed and transmitted to this Department a satisfactory official bond, which ought not to be delayed, you will be expected to lose no time in repairing to the post assigned you, and to keep this Department advised of your movements.

Your salary, at the rate of two thousand dollars per annum, will commence on the 21st instant, which is the date of your commission, and a letter of credit upon the Bankers of the United States at London, authorizing and requesting them to pay it upon your drafts, as it becomes due, is herewith transmitted to you: and they are requested moreover, to pay your drafts for the contingent expenses of the Consulate, not to exceed the sum of eight hundred dollars a year, to be expended in occasional presents and gratuities, to the officers of the Regency, according to the established usage of the place. These expenses will, as usual, be supported by vouchers in all cases where it is practicable to obtain them, this sum being deemed abundantly sufficient for all necessary purposes. On the subject of the allowance for contingent expenses, your predecessor was instructed by this Department, in a despatch dated 28th June, 1836.[3] The act of Congress of the 1st May, 1810,[4] will require your par-

2. France had established a protectorate over Algiers in 1830, and there was concern in the Department of State that France would do the same in Tunis. The French did colonize Tunis, but not until 1881.

3. John Forsyth to Heap, June 28, 1836, DNA, RG 59 (Instructions, Barbary Powers).

ticular attention and observance. By the 4th section of that act, the Consuls of the United States on the Barbary coast are restricted to an expenditure not exceeding three thousand dollars in any one year for presents or gratuities. As is stated above, this sum has been further limited by the President to an annual expenditure of eight hundred dollars. The sum of three thousand dollars will be allowed to enable you to procure the articles which are to be distributed as presents upon your introduction to the Bey,—either in this country, or on your way to Tunis, as may be found most advisable—two thousand dollars of which are to be expended in this country, and the remainder in such articles abroad as have been usually procured on former occasions. It may be well to signify to you that it is the intention of the Department hereafter to omit these presents altogether, being disposed, so far as the United States have commercial intercourse with the Barbary Powers, to carry on those relations as nearly as may be according to the manner adopted in our intercourse with the European States.

I transmit a printed copy of the personal instructions, (with a supplement,) prescribed by this Department for the government of the diplomatic agents of the United States in foreign countries, and your attention is particularly called to those portions of them (marked) which will be found applicable as directions for your official conduct, and which you will therefore consider as forming a part of these instructions. I am, Sir, your obedient Servant,   Danl Webster.

L C . DNA, RG 59 (Instructions, Barbary Powers).

FROM WILLIAM BROWN HODGSON

Consulate of the U. States

Sir,   Tunis, Feby. 16. 1842

Immediately after my arrival here, I conferred with my predecessor [Samuel Davies Heap], upon the subject of a Consular present which I had been authorized to make, on occasion of my presentation to the Bey [Ahmad Bey] according to established usage in Barbary. He informed me, that this usage had been abolished, since the Treaty of France with this Regency, concluded in 1830,[1]—after the conquest of Algiers.

The fourth article of that Treaty provides, that, whether at the installation of a new Consul, or the renewal of a Treaty by Foreign Powers, no presents shall be required by the local authorities, and that, that usage shall henceforth be abolished, and shall not be reestablished.

Such then being the rule of intercourse established between Christian powers and the Mussulman Regencies of Barbary, both the dignity and

4. 2 U.S. Stat. 608–610.
1. Jules De Clercq, ed., Recueil des

traités de la France (20 vols., Paris, 1880–1900), 3:578–581.

the interests of the United States require, that no innovation of that rule be made. It is in accordance too, with that part of your instructions, Sir, to myself, which declares, that it is the intention of the Department "hereafter to omit those presents."[2]

The fact of my having any presents in charge, is only known to my predecessor. He approves, distinctly, of the specimens of American art and manufacture, which I was instructed to procure, and he is of opinion, that a proper distribution of a small portion of those objects among influential persons, cannot but have a favorable influence, in exhibiting the power and resources of the United States. Hence he suggested the presentation to the Bey, of the newly invented American fire-arms, to which I alluded in my dispatch of yesterday:[3] and which have greatly excited the admiration of His Highness.

I hope, Sir, that this suggestion, prompted by the interests of my country, will be approved by yourself.

I shall hold the articles of presents which I have, subject to your future instructions,[4] whether to be sold on account of the Government, or to be sent back to Boston, where they were purchased. These instructions I now very respectfully request. I have the honor to be, Sir, With great respect yr very obt Sert   Wm. B. Hodgson

ALS. DNA, RG 59 (Consular Despatches, Tunis). Rec'd June 10, 1842.

TO JOHN F. MULLOWNY
No 1.   Department of State,
Sir: Washington, 16th March, 1842

The President, by and with the advice and consent of the Senate, having appointed you Consul of the United States for the Empire of Morocco, in the place of Mr Thomas N[elson] Carr,[1] your commission and a letter of credence to the Emperor[2] are herewith communicated, which will be presented by you in the usual manner. You will take the occasion to inform His Majesty of the friendly disposition of the President, and of his earnest desire to maintain and strengthen the amicable relations which now so happily subsist between the United States and his Empire.

2. See above.

3. Hodgson to DW, February 15, 1842, DNA, RG 59 (Consular Despatches, Tunis).

4. DW did not send the requested instructions, perhaps because Hodgson left Tunis in May and formally resigned his post on July 3, 1842. Before leaving Tunis, Hodgson distributed a few of the presents in order to create goodwill for the United States but returned most of them for resale to the account of the U.S. government.

1. Carr, of New York City, was consul at Tangier, 1838–1842. Carr returned to New York in 1843 but resumed duties as consul at Tangier from 1845 to 1848.

2. Abd al-Rahman (1778–1859), emperor of Morocco, 1822–1859.

On the 29th December last, a despatch from the Department, (duplicate of which was afterwards sent, and a copy whereof is now enclosed for your information,) to your predecessor,[3] which apprized him of the contemplated change in the Consulate, desired him, in the event of his leaving Tangier before the arrival of a successor, to place the property and archives of the Consulate in the hands of Mr [Edward William Auriol] Hay,[4] H[is] B[ritish] M[ajesty]'s Consul, or, in case of his absence, with some person on whom the Government could rely for their safe keeping. These will be delivered to you by the person to whom they may have been entrusted, and you will tender suitable acknowledgments on the occasion. One of your earliest duties will be to inform this Department of the condition in which the property is found, and to furnish a complete inventory of the books, papers, and effects of the Consulate which may come into your hands.

The instructions given from time to time to those who have exercised the Consular function at Tangier, embrace the principal objects of your mission, and will serve as a general guide, to which will be added special instructions as occasion may require them.

Your salary, at the rate of two thousand dollars per annum, will commence on the 11th instant, the date of your commission, and a letter of credit upon the Bankers of the United States at London, authorizing and requesting them to pay it upon your drafts, as it becomes due, is herewith transmitted to you. The Bankers will be requested, moreover, to pay your drafts for the contingent expenses of the Consulate, not to exceed the sum of eight hundred dollars per annum, to be expended in occasional presents and gratuities, to the officers of the Empire, according to the established usage of the place. These expenses will, as usual, be supported by vouchers in all practicable cases, this sum being deemed amply sufficient for all necessary purposes.

It has been customary hitherto to furnish Consuls of the United States appointed to the Barbary Powers a large sum of money, for the purpose of procuring presents for the Emperor and for various officers of his Empire. In the instructions given to Mr [William Brown] Hodgson,[5] lately appointed Consul for the Regency of Tunis, it was signified to him that it was the intention of this Department to omit these presents in future; and, in pursuance of this purpose, in which I am strengthened by your own assurances of belief that these presents may be dispensed with in Morocco, without giving offence, no such allowance will now be made, the Department being disposed, so far as the United States have commercial intercourse with the Barbary Powers, to carry on those relations,

3. DW to Carr, December 29, 1841, DNA, RG 59 (Instructions, Barbary Powers).

4. Hay (1785–1845), British consul-general in Morocco, 1829–1845.

5. See above, DW to Hodgson, September 22, 1841.

as nearly as may be, according to the manner adopted in our intercourse with the European States.

As soon as you shall have executed and transmitted to this Department a satisfactory official bond, which ought not to be delayed, you will be expected to lose no time in repairing to the post assigned you, and to keep the Department advised of your movements.

Enclosed is a printed copy of the personal instructions (with a supplement.) prescribed by the Department for the government of the Diplomatic Agents of the United States in foreign countries, which you will consider as a part of these instructions. I am, Sir, respectfully, your obedient Servant   Danl Webster

LC. DNA, RG 59 (Instructions, Barbary Powers). Mullowny was born in Philadelphia but apparently grew up in Tangier, where his father, a retired navy officer, was the U.S. consul. The younger Mullowny learned the language and customs of the place and acted as vice consul at Tangier for many years before his appointment as consul. He served in that capacity from 1842 to 1845.

FROM THOMAS NELSON CARR, WITH ENCLOSURE

No 30   Consulate of the U States
Sir: Tangier March 26th 1842

I hasten to place before the Department of State the accompanying particulars of an outrage committed on my person by the Authorities of the town on the morning of the 25th inst, when about to embark for Gibraltar on my return to the U. States agreeably to your orders.

The contents of the annexed papers bearing upon this subject are as follows.

No. 1. Copy of a letter to the Sultan [Abd al-Rahman] apprising him of my recall and his answer therto.[1]

No. 2 Copy of a letter to the Sultan upon the subject of the outrage.[2]

No. 3. Copy of a Circular addressed to the Consul of the month,[3] notifying through him, the members of the several missions that I had resumed my duties, for the time being, as Consul of the U. States.

1. Carr to Abd al-Rahman, March 1, 1842, and Abd al-Rahman to Carr, March 24, 1842; not included in this publication.

2. See below.

3. Not included in this publication. In 1820, after an epidemic of the plague struck Tangier, the consular agents of the Christian powers organized a health board. They found that by acting in concert they had greater influence on the Moroccan government, and the consuls decided to perpetuate their organization after the plague subsided. Leadership of the consular board rotated on a monthly basis. Mullowny believed that association with the board entangled the United States in controversies that did not involve American national interests, and he refused to participate in the consular corps. See Mullowny to James Buchanan, October 1, 1845, DNA, RG 59 (Consular Despatches, Tangier).

No. 4 Copy of a Circular to the Corps by the President of the month on the recent outrage, with these remarks upon the same.[4]
No. 5 Deposition of the Interpreter.[5] In haste Your ob. Sert

Thomas N Carr

ALS. DNA, RG 59 (Consular Despatches, Tangier). Rec'd May 12, 1842.

ENCLOSURE: THOMAS NELSON CARR TO ABD AL-RAHMAN

U States Consulate
Tangier March 25th 1842

I had the great satisfaction to receive Your Majesty's letter of the 4th Safar [1258], in answer to mine and addressed to Your Majesty, communicating the orders of my Goverment for my recall,[1] and its intention to appoint to the office as successor a gentleman who might daily be expected to arrive. The flattering terms in which Your Majesty was pleased to express your approval of my conduct, while Consul in Your Kingdom, led me to suppose that I was leaving Your Majesty's Kingdom on the best possible terms, but in this opinion I was to be disappointed.

The following brief detail of circumstances which have this day transpired I take the liberty to place before Your Majesty.

After presenting in person Your Majesty's letter, this morning, to the examination of Hadj Mohammed Midjbood, the Lt Governor of the town, to the first Administrator, and others of Your Agents in Tangier, who expressed themselves highly gratified at the testimonials I had borne to their uniform kind treatment to me, I was informed that all arrangements would be immediately made & orders were given, in my presence, to allow me to embark.

Shortly after this interview I proceeded to the marina in company with several members of the Consular Corps when I was stopped by the Capt of the Port who refused me privilege to leave the place, saying he had no orders, to that effect, from the Governor.[2]

After my reply that I was acting from instructions from my Government, and my remonstrance against such treatment, I attempted to proceed when I was violently seized by the throat by a guard who had received his orders for this outrage from the Capt. of the Port. After disengaging myself from this Moor the Capt of the Port next seized upon my

4. Hay to the consular corps, March 25, 1842, not included in this publication.

5. Depositions of Peter Boyn, March 26, 1842, not included in this publication.

1. Abd al-Rahman to Carr, March 24, 1842, and Carr to Abd al-Rahman, March 11, 1842, enclosures in Carr to DW, March 26, 1842, above. Safar is the second month of the Islamic calendar.

2. Buselham Ben Ali.

person, & thus by violent means, have I been prevented leaving your Majesty's Empire agreeably to instructions from my Government.

Such an outrage, I am supported in saying, has but seldom been committed on any Agent of any Christian power accredited to Your Majesty, and it is with a belief that it has not been ordered by Your Majesty that these details have been thus entered upon.

Notwithstanding <Acting upon> this conviction, the Authorities of the town have treacherously studied to insult me and the Government which I represent & I now call upon Your Majesty for full & ample redress for the injuries I have sustained, and in making this demand I have every confidence that I will be supported in it to the fullest extent by that government which has been thus shamefully treated in the person of its representative.   (signed) T.N.C.

Copy. DNA, RG 59 (Consular Despatches, Tangier).

TO JOHN F. MULLOWNY
No 3

Department of State,
Sir: Washington, 3d Augt. 1842.

I have received, and hasten to reply to, your despatch No 3, dated at Gibraltar, on the 15th ultimo,[1] by which it seems that you are placed in a situation which precludes you from repairing to your post and entering upon the duties of the Consulate at Tangier.

The Department does not fully understand the circumstances which induced your predecessor to strike the flag of the United States, nor upon what grounds Commodore [Charles W.] Morgan has felt authorized to interfere in the manner he appears to have done, and to propose to send a messenger to the Emperor of Morocco [Abd al-Rahman].[2] You will, upon the receipt of this despatch, proceed to Tangier on board of the vessel which is directed to receive you, (unless the circumstances referred to above be of a kind to render such a step improper,) from whence you

1. The correct reference is to No. 3. Mullowny to DW, June 15, 1842, DNA, RG 59 (Consular Despatches, Tangier).

2. Following the altercation at the marina, Carr demanded redress from the Moroccan government. When the emperor defended the conduct of the lieutenant governor, Carr, on his own authority, closed the Tangier consulate until the insult was "fully atoned for." No. 2. Carr to DW, April 13, 1842, DNA, RG 59 (Consular Despatches, Tangier). Morgan (d. 1853), the commander of the Mediterranean station, sent one of his officers on an embassy to the emperor and refused to transport Mullowny from Gibraltar to his post until the dispute was settled. See No. 4. Carr to DW, May 30, 1842; No. 3. Mullowny to DW, June 15, 1842; and No. 5. Carr to DW, July 25, 1842, all in DNA, RG 59 (Consular Despatches, Tangier).

will immediately transmit your credence to the Emperor, and if necessary address a communication to the proper authorities, asking an explanation of the existing difficulties, for the purpose of being sent to your Government. You will also furnish, as promptly as possible, a full account of the transaction which led to these difficulties, that your Government may know what course ought to be pursued in regard to the matter, which, as now represented to the Department by Mr [Thomas Nelson] Carr would seem to imply that a wanton and outrageous insult had been offered to the United States in the person of their representative, an act of barbarity which it is difficult to believe possible. On this subject the Department will expect from you full information, and the adoption, on your part, of the most discreet conduct in the attempt you may think it expedient to make to settle the present difficulty; in the execution of which task your good sense and knowledge of the people among whom you are to reside, are relied upon.

A communication on this subject has been made to the Navy Department, copy of which, and of the reply of the Secretary of the Navy [Abel Parker Upshur] will be herewith enclosed.[3] I am, Sir, respectfully, Your obedient Servant,   Danl Webster

LC. DNA, RG 59 (Instructions, Barbary Powers).

FROM JOHN F. MULLOWNY

No. 5.

Sir   Gibraltar 25 December 1842
In obedience to your instructions[1] I have the honor to report to you—
If Mr [Thomas Nelson] Carr had informed the Bashaw of Tangier,[2] that he had been recalled by his Government, and that the same had been reported by him, to the Emperor [Abd al-Rahman], he would have departed from Tangier without the least difficulty. When he arrived at his post, he wrote to inform the Bashaw (Sillowy) that he had been appointed Consul General and Diplomatic Agent, by the President of the United States, to the Empire of Morocco, and in doing so, he did no more than conform with an old established custom, to inform the Bashaw that he was about to reside within the district over which he commanded, this custom is founded upon courtesy, and observed towards the Bashaw by the Consuls, more particularly upon their departure, as it is fresh in the memories of many, when a Bashaw of Tangier was beheaded,

3. DW wrote Secretary Upshur about the Moroccan difficulties on August 1. Upshur's reply of August 3 advised Webster that Morgan would be sent orders to accept Mullowny's decisions. DNA, RG 59 (Misc. Letters).
1. See above.
2. Not identified.

for permitting a Spanish Consul to depart, without observing the ceremony, of exchanging with the Emperor the customary letters of farewell, (as they are called in Arabic) and thus it was, why the Bashaw was anxious to know, whether Mr Carr had the Emperors letter, he ordered the Lieutenant Governor of Tangier [Hadj Mohammed Midjbood] to detain him, when he found he was about to depart, without informing him whether he had exchanged with the Emperor these letters, which order the Lieutenant Governor, did not receive, until the morning Mr Carr was to have embarked, and until after he had read the Emperors letter, and Mr Carr had taken farewell of him.

When Mr Carr arrived upon the beach, in company with Mr [Johann Fredrik Sebastian] Ausenstolpe[3] (Swedish Vice Consul) and others of the Consular Corps, the Captain of the Port informed him that he had orders not to permit him to embark, to which he paid no attention but proceeded on towards the boat, to get on board, when a soldier from the Custom House guard, on the beach, called out, "are there no men amongst us? shall we allow the Christian to embark, against the orders of our Lord and Master" and at the same time intercepted Mr Carr, seized hold of him, and stopped him, upon which he attempted to draw the sword from his cane, to attack the soldier, but was prevented from doing so by Mr Ausenstolpe.

Here there are no signs of a wilful insult intended towards Mr Carr, he brought it upon himself, after being duly warned, and when the above facts were made known to the Lieutenant Governor, the man who took the order to the Captain of the Port, (to detain Mr Carr) and the soldier who stopped him, were both punished, the latter after undergoing the bastinado, was thrown into prison. When the Captain of the Port informed Mr Carr that he had orders not to permit him to embark, it would have been more dignified to have returned to the Consulate, and to have made a formal complaint to the Emperor, without making it appear, that he must have had a scuffle on the beach, (as would appear from his letter) which, the Emperor knew, could never have happened without provocation.

To Mr Carr's letter the Emperor made the following reply

In the name of the Merciful God &c To the servant who enjoys our exalted protection and honor, Thomas Nelson Carr, late Consul for the American Nation, in the protected Tangier, which premised—

Your letter has reached our presence, exalted by God, and we understand its contents, and what you state of that, which happened to you from the officers, in command of the Port, preventing you from embark-

3. Ausenstolpe (1801–1882) entered the consular service of Sweden-Norway in 1827 as secretary to the consul at Tripoli, thereafter serving at Tangier, Algiers, and Lisbon. His translation of the Koran into Swedish was published in 1843.

ing, because we had not sent them our exalted orders to that effect, But they were in the right! it is an known rule, because they cannot let any person leave by sea, without our permission, and we had omitted to write them, to allow you to embark, but now we have written to them, and have ordered them to settle it, (your going away) according to your pleasure, accompanied with what is good and cheerful.

In this letter the Emperor sustains the Bashaw (for giving orders to detain Mr Carr), and takes the blame upon himself, where he says, "and we had omitted to write them, to allow you to embark," But which he never considers it, at all necessary to do, for he never instructs his officers to allow a Consul to depart, the Emperor's letter, is the Consuls passport, and it is his duty, to show it as such, to the proper authorities. Mr Carr could not have been ignorant of this fact, and to have avoided the late difficulty, he ought to have observed the usual ceremony of courtesy, towards the Bashaw, at his departure, the same as he did when he arrived.

Upon receipt of the Emperor's letter, Mr Carr struck the Flag Staff, and immediately departed from Tangier, here I will make but one remark. If the ten Consuls stationed at Tangier, were in the habit of striking their Flag Staves, upon ever[y] pretext similar to this, one or more of them would be continually struck.

Some time after Mr Carr's departure from Tangier, Commodore [Charles W.] Morgan arrived, and took charge of the affair, and it was not long ere he exposed to the Emperor, and Bashaw, that he was quite ignorant of their manners and customs, and as the Moors will prevaricate, even when inclined to be sincere, the Emperor and Bashaw did not fail to exercise these talents in that way, towards Commodore Morgan, I will make no remarks, to the Department, as to Commodore Morgan's proceedings, further than that, he could not have made a more extravagant demand, than he did, when he proposed to conclude, and to add, five or six conventional Articles to the present Treaty.[4] The Emperor would never have put his seal to them, unless absolutely compelled to do so, he looked upon them in the same light he would upon concluding a Treaty, and at signing a Treaty he expects a present, moreover, he expected further authority for negotiating for the same, than Commodore Morgan had produced. I will assure the Department, the Emperor is not inclined to involve himself in a difficulty, with any Christian power at this time, by offering, or permitting any of his officers, to offer, a direct insult to any one of the Consuls stationed at Tangier. The Consuls have acceded to the Custom, to notify the Bashaw, (if residing at a distance) in a complimentary letter, their intentions to depart from the Empire, and quit the district over which he commands, and I submit to the De-

4. The treaty of peace of September 16, 1836, is in *Treaties*, 4:33–69.

partment, whether it were necessary to conclude several conventional articles to the effect, that in future the United States Consul, should forego this ceremony, and submit to it no longer.

I beg to refer you to Commodore Morgan's correspondence,[5] (which no doubt he has transmitted to the Navy Department,) for a perusal of the Emperor, and Bashaw's communications to him. As he did not intimate to Mr [Johan Mathias] Ehrenhoff,[6] (Swedish Consul General, late in charge of the United States Consulate) that his correspondence were to be recorded in the Consulate, I have not called upon that Gentleman for the documents in his possession, as he has only such as he has been able to procure, from the French Vice Consul,[7] to whom Commodore Morgan confided the duty of making his Arabic translations. I have the honor to remain Your most obedient Humble Servt   Jno. F. Mullowny

ALS. DNA, RG 59 (Consular Despatches, Tangiers). Rec'd March 16, 1843.

SOUTH AMERICA

Britain, not the United States, was the dominant foreign power in South America in the nineteenth century. With European diplomats and businessmen assuming the leading role in the capitals of South America, U.S. foreign policy for that region revolved around promoting trade, trying to resolve the seemingly endless claims disputes that grew out of inter-American commercial activity, and protecting the lives and property of citizens of the United States residing in that unsettled part of the world.

As Webster's instruction of December 14, 1841, to John S. Pendleton (printed below) indicates, claims litigation placed a considerable strain on the United States's relations with Chile. The outstanding cases were those of the *Macedonian* and the *Warrior*. In 1818, the *Macedonian* concluded a successful voyage from Boston by selling its cargo in Chile for $145,000, only to have the specie seized by Lord Cochrane, the British officer then in command of the Chilean navy. The second *Macedonian* claim dates to 1821, when that hapless vessel returned to Chile. This time Chilean troops confiscated approximately $70,000 in specie. The *Warrior* case dates to 1820, when Lord Cochrane commandeered the ship and impressed six members of the crew. Increasingly heated American representations made little progress until 1840. In July of that year, Richard Pollard, the U.S. chargé d'affaires, negotiated an informal arrangement of the first *Macedonian* claim with Joaquín Tocornal, the Chilean foreign minister. The American claimants would receive $104,000 plus 5 percent interest. In December, Pollard resolved the *Warrior* case

5. See *Executive Documents*, 27th Cong., 3d sess., Serial 419, No. 22.

6. Ehrenhoff (1777–1854).
7. Not identified.

at $15,000, also with 5 percent interest. The Chilean government, however, adamantly refused to acknowledge the validity of the second *Macedonian* claim, which was not disposed of until 1863. With the king of Belgium acting as arbiter, the American claimants were belatedly awarded $42,240 plus interest. For the history of these complicated litigations, see *International Arbitrations*, 2:1449–1484; *Treaties*, 4:287–293, 325–328; and *Senate Documents*, 35th Cong., 1st sess., Serial 930, No. 58.

Webster's instruction of July 1, 1841, to Allen A. Hall, the newly appointed chargé to Venezuela, also focuses on long-standing claims cases, in particular on that of the *Morris*. The *Morris* case dates to 1825, at which time Colombia, Ecuador, and Venezuela were all part of what was called Greater Colombia. When the three entities became separate states in 1829–1830, they agreed to share responsibility for claims against Greater Colombia. A commission was established at Bogotá to apportion that responsibility. Attempts by the United States to resolve such cases as that of the *Morris* through the commission at Bogotá met with little success. In the instruction to Hall, Secretary Webster tried a new approach. He told Hall to negotiate directly with the government of Venezuela, thereby bypassing the commission. Webster's approach proved successful, and in 1844 Hall reported to Secretary of State John C. Calhoun that Venezuela had agreed to pay $18,000 as its share of the settlement in the case of the *Morris* (March 2, 1844, DNA, RG 59, Despatches, Venezuela). In that same year, New Granada accepted responsibility for approximately $27,000, and in 1850 Ecuador promised to pay $14,000, thereby liquidating the *Morris* dispute (see *Treaties*, 4:523–528 [Venezuela], 663–669 [New Granada], and 5:665–669 [Ecuador]).

In Chile and Venezuela the outstanding claims cases were maritime in nature. In Peru the most important dispute was over the alleged mistreatment of an American national resident in that country, Samuel Franklin Tracy of Middletown, Connecticut. Tracy, who had lived in Lima since 1828, was arrested on March 16, 1839, because of his delay in obeying an order to leave Peru. The order had grown out of Tracy's association with the recently deposed General Andrés Santa Cruz, and though jailed only briefly, Tracy's movements were restricted to the city of Callao for nearly nine months. On April 20, 1839, moreover, a quicksilver mining company located in the Huancavelica mineral district in southern Peru in which Tracy held a one-tenth interest (two shares out of twenty) was dissolved by a decree of the Peruvian government. The mine was then sold to another company that was associated with the new president of Peru, Augustin Gamarra.

Tracy filed a bloated claim of $104,559 for the loss of his property and false imprisonment. For the two shares of stock that had been worth about $10,000 when issued in 1837, he asked $60,000. The rest of the money was to compensate Tracy for personal injuries. As Webster's instruction to James C. Pickett of November 16, 1842 (printed below), demonstrates, the secretary of state was aware that Tracy had exaggerated his claim. Webster assumed that the U.S. government had a basic responsibility to protect the lives and property of American citizens residing and doing business in foreign countries, but he also took into consideration the lawfulness and the propriety of their behavior. Webster's instruction to Pickett also illustrates the importance of time and distance in the conduct of American foreign policy in the 1840s. Since it took three to four months to receive a communication from Lima, Webster allowed Pickett considerable discretion in dealing with the government of Peru. Tracy's claim was still pending when Webster became secretary of state for the second time. Finally, in 1852, acting under further instructions from Webster, John Randolph Clay, the U.S. chargé d'affaires to Peru, concluded a settlement granting Tracy $26,560 (see *Treaties*, 6:59–73).

The George Johnson claim against Uruguay also concerned personal injuries. Johnson's complaint, however, seemed more legitimate and his demand for compensation more modest than that of Tracy, and Webster's responses to the two cases were quite dissimilar. An illiterate black American citizen residing in Uruguay, Johnson was forcibly drafted into the military service of that country, and he was brutally mistreated. Perhaps angered by the reported statement of an army officer to Johnson that the protection of the U.S. government was *"good* for *nothing,"* (Declaration of Johnson, January 29, 1841, enclosed in Hamilton to Vidal, January 30, 1841, below) Webster wanted to employ the U.S. Navy against Montevideo. The president had to remind his secretary of state, a recognized authority on the Constitution of 1787, that only Congress could authorize the use of military force against what Tyler called a "civilized" foreign nation. Unfortunately, an exhaustive search has not uncovered Webster's original draft instruction to Commodore Charles Morris, but the important documents printed below offer a rare glimpse at a militantly nationalistic Daniel Webster bent on upholding the rights of an American citizen and the honor of the U.S. government.

The final set of documents on South America concerns Daniel Webster and Frederic Tudor, one of the more colorful entrepreneurs in American history. Known as the "Ice King," Tudor devoted his life to promoting the use and sale of New England ice around the world. He began exporting ice to tropical climes in 1805, but it was not until the 1820s that his efforts began to show a profit. In the meantime, he endured ridicule and even occasional imprisonment for debt.

In the summer of 1841, Tudor proposed to the Brazilian government an arrangement for the importation of ice at about two cents a pound. He asked that Brazil remit all duties on ice and part of those on return cargoes. When the Brazilian government did not respond favorably,

Tudor turned to Webster for help. Responding in character, Webster instructed the U.S. minister to Brazil to employ his "zealous personal efforts" on behalf of the "Ice King."

Chile

FROM RICHARD POLLARD

No. 95.   Santiago, de Chile,

Sir: November 25, 1841.

Some few days ago letters were received here and in Valparaiso informing that a new Chargé d'Affaires had been appointed by the United States Government for Chile.[1] This news was very unexpected to me; because, President Van Buren who had given me permission to return home requested at the same time that I would remain to make a final adjustment of the claims.[2] I had assumed that I would do so, therefore, I did not think the Government would appoint any other Chargé d'Affaires for this Country until my return to the United States. By thorough examination, I am well acquainted with each subject of the claims and hoped and had a prospect of soon making a conclusive and advantageous settlement of them. But as it has been blazoned forth here that I have been *recalled*, the Chilean government will no doubt be disposed to delay treating further with me on the subject of them, thinking that they will be able to get better terms from my successor than they could from me in their liquidations and payments.

I have finally settled the claim of the *Warrior*. A copy of the note of the Minister accompanying the law in the case, with a translation, I forward with this, marked A.[3] A copy of my answer to the same, marked B, also is with this despatch.[4]

On the 22nd instant I addressed a note to the Chilean Minister upon the subject of the 25th article of the treaty between our Country and this. A copy is herewith, marked, C.[5] As yet he has given me no answer to that note.

1. Pollard's letter of recall is dated July 16, 1841. See No. 24. DW to Pollard, DNA, RG 59 (Instructions, Chile).

2. No. 19. John Forsyth to Pollard, July 8, 1840, DNA, RG 59 (Instructions, Chile).

3. The enclosure is not included in this publication. The Chilean congress authorized satisfaction of a claim for $15,000 to be paid in seven parts with 5 percent interest from September 30, 1839 (Yrarrázaval to Pollard, November 12, 1841). Ramon Luis Yrarrázaval Alcalde (1809–1856) was Chilean minister of interior and foreign relations, 1841–1844. He became minister to Rome in 1845 and later minister to Peru, where he died.

4. Pollard to Yrarrázaval, November 30, 1841; not included in this publication.

5. The enclosure is not included in this publication. Article 25 of the treaty of 1833 specified that the representatives of the two countries would enjoy "favors, immunities, and

I shall leave here directly the new Chargé d'Affaires arrives, which I suppose will be within a few days, and will take with me and pay into the Department the money I have received on account the *Warrior*.

On the first instant I received your despatch No. 23;[6] and at the same time your letter announcing the decease of General [William Henry] Harrison, late President of the United States.[7] I have the honor to be respectfully Yo. obt. Servt.   Rich Pollard

ALS. DNA, RG 59 (Despatches, Chile). Rec'd April 13, 1842. Extract published in *IAA*, 5:175. Pollard (1790–1851; William and Mary 1811), a lawyer from Virginia, served as U.S. chargé d'affaires to Chile from June 28, 1834, to May 12, 1842.

TO JOHN STROTHER PENDLETON

No. 3.   Department of State,
Sir: Washington, 14th December, 1841.

You have received your commission and have taken the oath prescribed by the Constitution. Herewith will be communicated to you.

1. A sealed letter accrediting you to the Minister for Foreign Affairs of Chile and an open copy of the same.
2. A Full Power authorizing you to negotiate and conclude a Convention upon the subject of claims.
3. A special passport.
4. Printed Personal Instructions and the Supplement thereto.
5. Circular relative to draughts of diplomatic agents.
6. Circular relative to the salaries of diplomatic agents absent from their posts.

You have been informed as to the way in which you will receive your salary.

For the contingent expenses of the Legation, which must not exceed five hundred dollars a year without special authority, you will also draw on this Department.

If Mr [Richard] Pollard should have left Chile prior to your arrival there, you will no doubt find the archives of the Legation in the possession of Mr Hobson,[1] who is acting as our Consul at Valparaiso. As soon

exemptions" equal to those of other nations. Pollard had complained that he had to pay postage on his mail, whereas the British consul received mail free. *Treaties*, 3:671–709.

6. Not found.

7. Not found, but probably identical to DW's announcement to the cabinet of April 4, 1841. DNA, RG 59 (Domestic Letters).

1. Three Hobson brothers—

George, William, and Joseph—resided in Chile. George was named U.S. consul at Valparaiso in 1834 but resigned in August 1840. Chargé d'affaires Richard Pollard chose William as acting consul. When William left the post in 1841, Pollard named Joseph as acting consul. Whether DW distinguished the various Hobsons is questionable.

as may be practicable, you will make yourself familiar with the correspondence of the department with your predecessors and their correspondence with the Chilean government, all of which, it is presumed, are in the archives of the mission. The instructions to Mr Pollard appear to be so ample upon the points at issue between the two governments, that nothing more is deemed necessary at present than to direct you to govern yourself by them so far as they may be applicable.[2] You will notice that the expectations raised by an adjustment made by Mr Pollard and Mr [Joaquín] Tocornal,[3] the late Minister for Foreign Affairs of Chile, of claims in the cases of the Macedonian and Warrior, are, according to our most recent intelligence from Santiago, dated the 7th of July, last, in danger of being disappointed.[4] That adjustment, though in some respects informal, was supposed to be binding upon the honor, at least, of that government, and conclusive in regard to the principles of public law, the proof of American property, the amount to be paid and the terms of payment. Nothing seemed to be wanting finally to dispose of the business but an appropriation by the Chilean Legislature, to which body it was understood the Executive intended to submit the arrangement with a request for the means necessary to carry it into effect. Since the date of the adjustment, however, a change of administration has taken place in that country and the new Executive[5] has declined making the application to the legislature referred to, upon the ground that there exists in Lima evidence that the property seized in the case of the Macedonian belonged to subjects of Spain and not to citizens of the United States. This fresh motive for evasion and delay on their part has been met in a proper spirit by Mr Pollard and the President directs that if you should find the affair still open, you will in respectful but significant language remonstrate against its further procrastination. For even supposing that the money belonged to Spaniards, which it did not, the Chilean Admiral[6] had no right to seize or the Chilean Government to use it. Indeed the President is much dissatisfied with the reason assigned for again

2. No. 14. John Forsyth to Pollard, December 23, 1836; No. 18. Forsyth to Pollard, November 26, 1839; and No. 20. Forsyth to Pollard, September 8, 1840, all in DNA, RG 59 (Instructions, Chile).

3. Tocornal Jimenez (1788–1865) was active in the formation of the national government and presided over the Chilean constitutional convention of 1833. In 1837 he assumed overall control of the government. Tocornal ran unsuccessfully for president in 1841 but was afterward named superintendent of the mint.

4. No. 91. Pollard to DW, July 7, 1841, DNA, RG 59 (Despatches, Chile).

5. Manuel Bulnes Prieto (1799–1866) was president of Chile, 1841–1851.

6. Lord Thomas Cochrane (1775–1860) was a daring and able English naval officer, but was often in trouble for his behavior. He was dismissed from the Royal Navy in 1814. He commanded the Chilean navy, 1818–1822, and thereafter the navies of Brazil and Greece. He was reinstated in the British navy in 1842.

postponing the business after so great a lapse of time and such full discussion and considers it as by no means showing a friendly disposition towards this country. Consequently, unless indication of a better spirit shall be offered, by the Government of Chile, and measures adopted without further unjustifiable delay to carry into effect the arrangement between Mr Pollard and Mr Tocornal, the President will feel constrained, though very reluctantly, to deem further negotiation useless, and to take that course towards Chile which the dignity of this Government and its duty to its citizens will require. The whole subject will be laid before the Congress of the United States with a view to such measures of redress as they may deem the circumstances to authorize.[7]

Although the President hopes that there may be no occasion for you to make a communication to the Chilean Government of the tenor adverted to, he is solicitous that, if it should be unavoidable, while conveying a proper impression of the sense of wrong felt by this government at the course persisted in by that of Chile and of its determination to seek amends therefor, you will endeavor to be as conciliatory as circumstances will allow, bearing in mind that the public men of that country are understood to be of a very sensitive temperament and, it is believed, would be far more apt to grant a demand when made in civil language than when preferred in a different manner. But while you will observe respect and courtesy in all your communications, you will give the Chilean government to understand that the President is in earnest and that he expects an immediate compliance with the arrangement entered into with Mr Pollard.[8]

The full power with which you are provided authorizes you to conclude a Convention upon the subject of the claims of our citizens against that Government generally. If, therefore, the Chilean Government should prefer a formal Convention and circumstances should, in your judgment, render that course preferable to the one adopted by Mr Pollard, you will accordingly conclude one, but unless it should be restricted to the cases adjusted by that gentleman, and substantially embrace the terms of that adjustment, you will not sign it without a reference to this department for such further instructions as may then be deemed proper.

The commercial relations between the United States and Chile are regulated by the Treaty concluded at Santiago on the 1st of September,

7. Pendleton and Ramon Luis Yrarrázaval did not conclude a convention but kept the informal arrangements reached by their predecessors, which were submitted to the Chilean congress for approval. See [No. 5]. Pendleton to DW, December 4, 1842, and No. 7. Pendleton to DW, December 15, 1842, DNA, RG 59 (Despatches, Chile).

8. Pendleton disregarded the cautionary aspects of DW's instruction, and his protests became so offensive to the Chilean government that he had to return to the United States in 1844.

1833.[9] One of your principal duties will be to take care that the rights of your countrymen under it and under the public law are respected by the Chilean authorities. In performing this duty, however, you will discriminate between the complaints which may be submitted to you and will not apply to the Chilean Executive for redress when the aggrieved party might, with more propriety, seek it through the medium of the judicial tribunals of that country. I am, Sir, your obedient Servant,

Daniel Webster

LC. DNA, RG 59 (Instructions, Chile). Pendleton (1802–1868) served in the Virginia House of Delegates before his appointment as chargé d'affaires to Chile in August 1841. He returned to the United States in June 1844.

Venezuela

TO ALLEN A. HALL

No. 2   Department of State,
Sir: Washington, 1st July, 1841.

The instructions to your predecessor and his correspondence with this department and with the Venezuelan government, all which, it is presumed, will be found in the archives of the Legation, will acquaint you with the unsettled business of your mission up to the period of Mr [John G.A.] Williamson's decease.[1]

There are a few unadjusted claims of citizens of the United States upon the government of the late Republic of Colombia, which were rejected by the Commissioners of the three States which composed that Republic, appointed for the purpose of disposing of business of that character. The accompanying extracts from instructions to Mr [James] Semple, our Chargé d'Affaires at Bogotá[2] and from his correspondence with this department, with the Government of New Granada and with the commissioners, will apprize you of the names and nature of those demands, of the grounds of the application for redress in each case and of those upon which the claims were rejected by the Commissioners.[3]

9. *Treaties*, 4:671–709.

1. Williamson, chargé d'affaires to Venezuela since 1835, died in that country in August 1840.

2. The instruction to Semple of January 9, 1838, DNA, RG 59 (Instructions, Colombia), contains summaries of the claims presented to the commission. The record also contains additional instructions Semple received during his term as chargé. Semple (1798–1866) practiced law and politics in Illinois before his appointment as chargé d'affaires to

Colombia in 1837. He returned to the United States in 1842 and served in the U.S. Senate, 1843–1847. After leaving public life, Semple entered the real estate business.

3. The commissioners decided they had no authority to rehear cases from the Colombian courts. Semple to John Forsyth, September 10, 1838, DNA, RG 59 (Despatches, Colombia). For Semple's correspondence with the Colombian government and the commissioners, see the despatches, *passim*.

According to the treaty between the three States apportioning their respective liabilities for the debts of Colombia, the share of Venezuela is twenty eight and a half per cent. You will accordingly avail yourself of the earliest proper opportunity after you shall have been received by the Venezuelan Government to notify it that, notwithstanding the course taken by the Board of Commissioners above referred to, it is far from the intention of this government to relinquish the prosecution of those claims, that as the Colombian States have always been considered jointly and severally answerable for them and have been officially informed to that effect, it is expected that the Venezuelan Government will take the subject into its early consideration with a view to that measure of redress which is believed by us to be due: that although this Government cannot deem itself bound by any Compact between foreign governments affecting its rights and interests to which it is not a party and consequently might hold any one of those three States accountable for the whole amount of the demands in question, yet that we are willing in this instance to waive that right and to exonerate them from any further liability on that head upon the condition that they indemnify the sufferers in proportion to the accountability of the States assumed in the Convention referred to. Perhaps it would be advisable for you to present the claims singly, beginning with the case of the brig Morris.[4] As the condemnation of this vessel took place in Venezuela and, as it is believed, the proceeds of the sale resulted to the sole benefit of citizens of that State, it would appear to be peculiarly incumbent on the existing Venezuelan government to make amends to our citizens who were thereby aggrieved. A copy of such papers relating to the case as remain in the department will be communicated to you herewith and Mr Semple will be instructed to cause a transcript to be made of such other documents necessary to substantiate it and the other cases as may be in the archives of the Legation at Bogotá, and to be transmitted to you at Caracas.

A full power, authorizing you to negotiate upon the subject of claims and to conclude a Convention, is one of the accompanying papers.[5] When claims upon foreign governments are comparatively few in number and inconsiderable in amount, they have in several instances been settled by an informal arrangement between our diplomatic agent and the Minister for Foreign Affairs. This is the course which you are recommended to take with those entrusted to your charge. If, however, the Venezuelan government should prefer a Convention upon the subject according to all the forms prescribed by the Constitutions of the two countries, the

4. The *Morris*, which sailed from Cuba for Gibraltar in 1825 with a cargo of Spanish and American goods, was captured in the Strait of Gibraltar by a Colombian privateer and sailed to Puerto Cabello in Venezuela. The prize court acquitted the vessel, but during an appeal the ship and its cargo were sold.

5. Not included in this publication.

power adverted to will enable you and you are hereby instructed to conclude one. The accompanying copy of a Convention between the United States and Texas upon a similar subject, will serve as a form for that purpose.[6] It is not, however, deemed expedient that you should conclude either a General Convention or an arrangement with respect to any particular case, with a reference to this department as to the sum or sums which you might accept. Positive instructions on this point cannot be given before hand, but must be influenced by intelligence from you.

One of your principal duties will be to take care that the provisions of the existing treaty are faithfully observed by the Venezuelan authorities.[7] In doing this, however, you will discriminate between the complaints which may be made to you by our citizens frequenting that country and abstain from any application to the Venezuelan Executive[8] for redress, when there is a good reason to believe that it might be obtained through the medium of the judicial tribunals or that the laws of Venezuela have not been respected by the complaining party.

It is presumed you are aware that the people among whom you are to sojourn are remarkable for peculiarities and prejudices which it will be necessary for you to consult in both your personal and official conduct if you would make yourself acceptable and your mission useful and successful. You will studiously avoid identifying yourself with either of the political parties into which that country may be divided. You may give advice freely when it is asked by public men in relation to public affairs, but you will of course see the propriety of not obtruding it spontaneously and when you express your opinions, it would be best for you to do it discreetly in regard to time, place and circumstances. I am, Sir, your obedient servant,   Daniel Webster

LC. DNA, RG 59 (Instructions, Venezuela). Extract published in *IAA*, 12:466–467. Hall (d. 1867), a Nashville newspaper publisher who supported the Whigs, remained chargé d'affaires to Venezuela until 1844. He was assistant secretary of the Treasury, 1849–1850, and again a newspaper publisher before returning to diplomatic service as minister to Bolivia, 1863–1867.

Peru

FROM JAMES CHAMBERLAYNE PICKETT
No. 52.   Legation of the U. States
Sir: Lima, Novr 27th 1841
    A notion seems to prevail to some extent, among my fellow citizens

6. The United States and Texas concluded a claims convention on April 11, 1838. See *Treaties*, 4:125–131.
    7. The treaty of January 20, 1836, establishing diplomatic relations between the United States and Venezuela, is in *Treaties*, 4:3–32.
    8. Jose Antonio Páez (1790–1873).

residing in Peru, that their Government is bound to guaranty all their contracts and speculations, to which the Peruvian Government may be a party. I entertain a different opinion, which is, that the Government of the United States will not interfere with their contracts, made either with the Gov't. here or with individuals. There may be, however, exceptions to this rule: For instance,—if a citizen of the U.S. obtains a grant of land from the Peruvian Government, for agricultural or mining purposes and is afterwards arbitrarily dispossessed, will his Government support him in a claim for indemnification?

This is an important question in the case of Samuel F. Tracy,[1] who claims compensation, to a large amount, of the Peruvian Gov't. on account of the seizure, in 1839, of a Quicksilver mine, of which he and several natives were grantees. See my 12th despatch.[2]

Enclosed is a copy of a letter to the U.S. Consul at Arequipa,[3] in which I express my opinion about contracts.

Enclosed also, are copies of letters to Captains [French] Forrest & [Charles] Gauntt, commanding the "St. Louis" and "Dale."[4] Capt. Gauntt acted very properly, I think, in declining to give to Gen. [Andrés] Santa-Cruz,[5] a passage to Bolivia, war having been declared against him, by Peru. To do so, would have been, it appears to me, a violation of neutrality; yet some of the officers of the Squadron say they would have given him a passage;—the consequence of doing which would have been, certainly, a serious disturbance of our relations with Peru and the non-ratification of the Convention stipulating for the payment of three hundred thousand dollars, to our citizens, on account of their claims:[6]

1. Not further identified.

2. Pickett to John Forsyth, May 25, 1840, DNA, RG 59 (Despatches, Peru).

3. Pickett to William F. Taylor, September 4, 1841; not printed here.

4. Pickett to Forrest, October 20, 1841; Pickett to Gauntt, November 20, 1841; not printed here. Forrest (1796–1866), commander of the twenty-gun sloop Saint Louis, and Gauntt (d. 1855) both entered the navy in 1811 and were promoted to the rank of commander in 1837. Although referred to in this letter as captains, neither held that rank at the time.

5. Santa Cruz (1792?–1865), elected president of Bolivia in 1829, created a Peru-Bolivian Confederation by force in 1835–1836 by de-feating Peruvian leader Augustin Gamarra (d. 1841). He himself was defeated by a coalition of Peruvian and Chilean forces in 1839 but was proclaimed president of Bolivia in 1841. When Peruvian president Gamarra invaded Bolivia in 1841, the Confederation forces were routed and Santa Cruz was driven from power. In November 1841, Santa Cruz secured passage from Guayaquil, Ecuador, to Europe on a British ship. Thereafter, he lived at Versailles, where he served as minister from Bolivia, until his death.

6. Although the claims convention was signed at Lima on March 17, 1841, because of delays and conditions effected by Peru, the treaty was not ratified until 1846, and not proclaimed until 1847.

And besides this,—but for the weakness of the Government here, there would have followed, in all probability, a declaration of war against us, the expulsion of the citizens of the U.S. from the country and the confiscation of their property.

I will take the liberty of suggesting, that the most explicit and positive instructions should be given to the commanders of our ships of war, in the Pacific, not to interfere, in the slightest manner, in the feuds of the countries on this coast. Instructions to this effect are always given, I believe, to every commander of the Squadron, and they ought to be very peremptory, particularly, as the commanders do not consult the diplomatic agents, about their movements and operations, although their doing so, would not be at all detrimental, in my opinion, to the public interest.

A new source of wealth, or rather, the value of it, has been recently discovered in Peru. It is a production, called in the Indian language, *huano*, and is generally supposed to be the excrement of marine birds, and a chemical analysis and other circumstances favor this opinion; yet some believe it to be of mineral and volcanic origin. It is found in great abundance, in some small islands, a few degrees to the south of Lima, and has been used in agriculture, for manure, from time immemorial. It was so used by the Indians, before the Conquest. Its fertilizing properties are said to be unequalled, and they are certainly very great.[7]

Huano sells in England at ninety dollars the ton, giving a net profit, of at least, fifty. The existing quantity is estimated, vaguely, at forty millions of tons and the annual consumption of it in Peru, at three thousand.

The Peruvian Government, with characteristic recklessness and improvidence, had granted a monopoly of the exportation of *huano*, to an individual, for the term of five years, receiving for the privilege, the sum of sixty thousand dollars only. The grant, however, after being in force between one and two years, has been, this day annulled, on the ground, ostensibly, of fraud and concealment on the part of the grantee, but really, because it was a short-sighted and impolitic measure.[8]

---

7. Webster took no notice of Pickett's reference to guano in 1842, but by 1852 the fertilizer had become so important to American agriculture that Webster risked war with Peru in an attempt to gain control of the guano-rich Lobos Islands. See Kenneth E. Shewmaker, " 'Untaught Diplomacy' : Daniel Webster and the Lobos Islands Controversy," *Diplomatic History*, 1 (Fall 1977): 321–340, and *Diplomatic Papers*, 2.

8. In 1840 Francisco Quiroz (b. 1798), a Peruvian entrepreneur and president of the Lima Chamber of Commerce, obtained a six-year license to export guano. When returning ships brought news of the high prices guano commanded on the London market, however, the Peruvian government canceled the license and made the guano islands state property. Quiroz received a new export contract for one year, but the Peruvian government claimed higher profits. See Jonathan V. Levin, *The*

This resource, if properly managed, will enable Peru to pay all her debts and to rëestablish her credit, without prejudice to the agricultural interests of the country. I have the honor to be, with great respect, Your Obt. Servant   J. C. Pickett

P.S. I enclose a newspaper containing a commercial regulation that may be of use to those who trade from the United States to Peru.[9]

ALS. DNA, RG 59 (Despatches, Peru). Rec'd April 18, 1842. Pickett (1793–1872) was appointed secretary of the legation in Colombia in 1829. He returned to the United States in 1835 but in 1838 became chargé d'affaires to the Peru-Bolivian Confederation and a diplomatic agent to Ecuador. Pickett returned to the United States in 1844.

TO JAMES CHAMBERLAYNE PICKETT

No. 13.   Department of State,
Sir: Washington, 16th November, 1842.

Your despatches to No. 67, inclusive, have been received.[1] The attention of the department to the claims of Mr Samuel F. Tracy having of late been urgently invoked,[2] your remarks upon that subject have been taken into consideration.

If, as is believed to have been the case, Mr Tracy was deprived of his interest in the quicksilver mines of Huancavelica illegally and by violence, no doubt is entertained of the obligation of the Peruvian Government to make good the loss which he thereby sustained, and that the measure of indemnification to him should be the value of his interest at the time it was confiscated. As little can it be questioned that citizens of the United States in foreign countries are entitled by the law of nations to protection in all employments permitted to them by the municipal laws of those countries.

In regard to the particulars of Mr Tracy's account it may be said that the correctness of the charges for losses on sales depends upon the degree in which those sales were compulsory at the time they were made. So far as the circumstances of the case may be learned from the papers in the department, the sales could not have been avoided. The demand for this charge, however, and for its amount, whether more or less than that claimed, is left to your discretion, for being upon the spot, you have the best means of forming a just opinion upon the subject. The charge for imprisonment and maltreatment seems to be fair, but that for losses on his business need not be insisted upon, as it is supposed to be entirely

Export Economies: Their Pattern of Development in Historical Perspective (Cambridge, Mass., 1960), pp. 49–54.

9. Not found in the RG 59 record.

1. No. 67. August 8, 1842, DNA, RG 59 (Despatches, Peru).

2. See Alexander L. Botts to DW, November 23, 1842, DNA, RG 59 (Misc. Letters).

speculative, and, in general, the department does not encourage a presentation to foreign governments of claims of that character.

The Convention negotiated by yourself upon the subject of other claims against the Peruvian government is still pending in the Senate but will probably be acted upon early in the approaching session of that body.[3] How far it may be necessary or prudent to delay pressing that government for an adjustment of the claims not provided for by the Convention until that shall have been ratified, will also be for you to consider.

Your course in claiming damages for Mr Tracy, will likewise be influenced by your opinion as to whether or not the grievances of which he complains were occasioned by any improper interference on his part in the local politics of Peru, for while this government is sensible of its duty to protect citizens of the United States abroad in all their lawful pursuits, those citizens must understand that it is expected of them carefully to abstain from obtrusive meddling with party politics and from giving any just cause of offence to the existing authorities.

The Treaty with Ecuador, also negotiated by you, having been duly proclaimed on the part of this government, copies thereof are herewith transmitted.[4] I am, Sir, your obedient servant,   Daniel Webster

LC. DNA, RG 59 (Instructions, Peru).

Montevideo

ROBERT M. HAMILTON TO FRANCISCO RAMÓN ANTONIO
VIDAL, WITH ENCLOSURE

Consulate of the United States
Monte Video January 30: 1841.

The Undersigned, Consul of the United States of North America, has the honor to enclose herewith, for the consideration of His Excellency the Minister for foreign Affairs, a copy of the declaration of George Johnson, a native citizen of the United States, who during the last four months has been subjected to cruelties inflicted upon his person by sundry Military officers under this Government, unprecedented in civilized Countries;[1]

The Undersigned most respectfully takes leave to refer His Excy, the

3. See above, note 6.

4. The Treaty of Peace, Friendship, Navigation, and Commerce with Ecuador was signed in June 1839, consented to and ratified in 1840, and proclaimed on September 23, 1842. *Treaties*, 4:207–240.

1. See below. Johnson, a black American about thirty-three years old, was born in Delaware but had lived in Uruguay for fifteen years. Charles Morris to DW, April 5, 1842, DNA, RG 59 (Consular Despatches, Uruguay).

Minister to the aforementioned document, for the particulars of the case, and to solicit from His Excy, such information as he may be enabled to procure, to account for the extraordinary severity which has been practised upon his Countryman, & to enable the undersigned to obtain justice & redress, as the case may require. The Undersigned avails himself of this occasion, to offer to His Excy the Minister, the assurances of his distinguished consideration, & deep respect. R. M. Hamilton Consul of the United States, of North America

Copy. Enclosed in Hamilton to DW, May 15, 1841, DNA, RG 59 (Consular Despatches, Montevideo). Hamilton, a native of Baltimore, was appointed U.S. consul at Montevideo in 1838. After his return to the United States, Hamilton requested additional compensation because he had performed diplomatic duties in Uruguay, but the government denied his petitions. See *Senate Reports*, 33d Cong., 1st sess., Serial 707, No. 336; *Senate Reports*, 33d Cong., 2d sess., Serial 775, No. 525; *House Reports*, 34th Cong., 1st sess., Serial 870, No. 292. Vidal (1797–1851), a wealthy businessman, was foreign minister of Uruguay, 1839–1843.

ENCLOSURE: DECLARATION OF GEORGE JOHNSON

Consulate of the United States
Monte Video
Montevideo 29 Jany. 1841

Personally appeared this day before me the Undersigned, Consul of the United States of North America, to the Oriental Republic of the Uruguay, George Johnson, a native citizen of the United States, who being duly sworn on the Holy Evangelists of Almighty God; did say, and declare,

That in the month of October 1840, he was residing at the village of San Salvador, and that he was the owner of a boat with which he gained his subsistence, and that while in the act of making some purchases at a store in the same village on the 21st of October last, a party consisting of two officers, and about twenty men, rode up to the door, and after dismounting, demanded of the declarent to state who he was, when he replied that he was a foreigner, that they then ordered him to mount his own horse, and follow them, that foreigners had to serve as well as others in the Army, which order he was obliged to comply with, until they all arrived at Colonia on the 23d same month and where he was kept a prisoner under a guard for three days, and nights, on the fourth day he was conducted by the same party to a place called "Colla," where he remained two days under guard, & that the said party then departed from that place, leaving the declarent under the charge of the police in that village, two days after an officer & three men took him to "San Jose" & from thence to a division of the Army consisting of about Five hundred men, that were encamped within a half a league of the latter place, the commanding officer taking him in charge, and without asking him, the

Declarent any questions, at about eight o clock at night he was fastened by his extremities to four posts driven in the ground, calculated to stretch his limbs in opposite directions to their fullest extent, and that he was kept in that painful position until daylight, when he was released until the following night, and that the same torture was again inflicted, which rendered him motionless and created the most excrutiating pain, and that the tightness of the fastenings upon his wrists, and ancles, caused them to swell very much, and augment his sufferings, the morning following he was released, and sent to Canelones, under the guard of an officer and three men, where he remained one night only, after which he was brought to the city of Monte Video, and delivered to the Chief of Police, who immediately incarcerated him in the Common prison, and that after having been one month & fifteen days in the said prison, he was taken out & informed by the Chief of Police or his Representative, that he had to serve twelve months in the Army of this Republic, from that date, being the 25th of November 1840, or on board some of the National vessels of War, and that he the Declarent replied that if he was forced to serve against his will, he would prefer the latter service, and that no reasons were assigned for such arbitrary proceedings on the part of his oppressors, and that he was then conducted to the Government Buildings, commonly called the Fort, and taken into one of the offices, which he understood to be that of the Minister of War, and that he was interrogated by one of the assistants or clerks in the said office, as to his name, and to what nation he belonged, all of which questions he answered, informing the enquirer that he was a native of the United States of North America, and that in this Country he was known by the name of George Smith, and that he gave the name of his Father & Mother as Smith to answer for the name of Johnson their true name, the latter being difficult to pronounce in the Spanish language, all of which was written down in his presence by the interrogater that he was then ordered to the Fort of San José & there detained two days & nights, after which he was made to put on military clothing & was sent to Rat Island in this Harbor, where he was compelled to perform military services for fifteen days, when he made his escape in a Boat during the night of the 10th of December last, and that on the 17th of same month he made himself known to this Consulate as an American Citizen, and received an American protection, and the Declarent furthermore states that on the 19th same month when in the vicinity of the English Burial ground going to his lodging house, he was forcibly seized by an officer and four men with concealed Arms who after pinioning his arms with cords, made him march towards the city, and on nearing a house in which there was a light, he requested the officer who proved to be the Adjutant of the Fort San José, to read his American protection, which he had received from this Consulate; that the said officer did read the protection, and observed that it was *good* for *nothing*, and that he was taken to the Fort of San José, and was immediately imprisoned, and that after a confinement of two days, and nights, he was taken into the yard by order of the aforementioned Adjutant, and tied down to a gun carriage, after which he was informed by the said officer, that he should receive *Three hundred lashes*, for insolence to him when he took him prisoner, and that the same number of lashes were inflicted upon his bare body, after which he was again imprisoned, until the next day, when he implored for permission to go to the Hospital, that his lacerated body might be dressed, and healed, the request being granted, he was conducted to that Establishment by a corporal & two soldiers, & that his wounds were examined & dressed by the Surgeon, and that he remained in the Hospital twenty three days under the care of the attendants, after which he was again taken back to the Fort San José, and made to work during the day, and was confined three nights with one of his legs in the stocks. The Declarent furthermore states that he has been compelled to perform military services for nearly four months without receiving any remuneration, and he likewise declares, that he has not voluntarily entered the service of this Republic, or placed his name or mark upon any written or printed document whatever, and that he has never been accused by his Persecutors of having committed any criminal act, save that of alledged insolence to the aforementioned adjutant, who he represents as an inexperienced lad of eighteen or twenty years of age, And the Declarent in conclusion furthermore states that the Commanding officer of the Fort San José, gave him permission this day to take a walk in the city, and that he availed himself of the opportunity to make known his recent sufferings & grievances to the Consul of his Country & that he was ordered by the said officer to return to the Fort, and not to run away. And furthermore the Declarent saith not.

(Signed)   X [George Johnson's mark]

Witness   (signed) C. W. Parsons, Jnr.

In Testimony whereof I hereunto set my hand, and affix the seal of this Consulate of the city of Monte Video this Twenty ninth day of January in the year of our Lord One thousand Eight hundred and forty one.

R. M. Hamilton Consul of the United States of North America

ADS. DNA, RG 59 (Consular Despatches, Montevideo). Published in *Executive Documents*, 27th Cong., 2d sess., Serial 405, No. 267; misdated 1842.

TO JOHN TYLER

Department of State
Washington Aug. 3rd 1841

The Secretary of State has the honor to submit to the President the enclosed letter from Robert M Hamilton Esqr, U.S. Consul at Montevideo, with the documents accompanying it,[1] relative to the cruelties inflicted upon, and the losses sustained by George Johnson, a Citizen of the United States, in consequence of the forcible detention to which he was subjected by the Military Authorities of the Uruguay Republic, and respectfully to suggest whether, it would not be advisable to direct Commodore [Charles] Morris,[2] on his arrival at Brazil, to send a Vessel round to Montevideo, under the command of a prudent officer, with instructions, (to be furnished from this Department) to enquire into the facts of this case. We have no Diplomatic Representative in Montevideo,[3] nor has the Government of that Country any such Agent here. For other & general reasons it appears to me it might be well for a Vessel of War of the United States, to make her appearance in those waters, and this particular outrage, if the narrative be true, calls for strict enquiry. Danl Webster

LS. DNA, RG 59 (Consular Instructions, Montevideo).

DANIEL FLETCHER WEBSTER TO CHARLES MORRIS

Department of State,
Washington, September 30, 1841.

Sir:

I am instructed by the President to enclose to you the accompanying copy of a communication made to this Department by the consul of the United States at Montevideo [Robert M. Hamilton], in the Republic of Uruguay.[1]

You will perceive that the communication contains a statement by George Johnson, who represents himself to be an American citizen, of a series of outrages and cruelties inflicted upon him by the military authorities of that republic, of a most atrocious nature, and which, if actually committed in the manner stated by him, call for an ample reparation to him, and the exemplary punishment of the offenders.

The safety of our citizens visiting or residing in that republic, or in any other portion of South America, where society is in so unsettled a condition, demands on the part of their Government, a constant watchfulness; and nothing but the enforcement of such prompt redress, in every case of

1. See above, Hamilton to Vidal, January 30, 1841, and enclosure.

2. Morris (d. 1856), commander of the U.S. South Atlantic squadron, which was usually stationed off the coast of Brazil. The South Atlantic squadron had been established in 1821.

3. Consuls such as Hamilton ordinarily did not possess the authority to perform diplomatic functions. Moreover, naval officers such as Morris, rather than civilians, often were chosen by the U.S. government to deal with distant countries, especially those perceived to be backward or uncivilized. Naval officers could coordinate diplomacy with force, a combination generally regarded as a prerequisite for dealing with unruly states. See Charles Oscar Paullin, *Diplomatic Negotiations of American Naval Officers, 1778–1883* (Baltimore, 1912).

1. See above, Hamilton to Vidal, January 30, 1841, and enclosure.

a violation of their rights, either of person or property, as shall impress upon those authorities and people a sense of the care which the Government of the United States has over their citizens wherever they may be, and of its determination and ability to afford them protection whenever necessary, is likely to secure them from repeated violence and insult.

The departure of the squadron under your command for the coast of Brazil, gives a favorable opportunity for making known to the authorities of Uruguay the determination of this Government, and of showing to it and other neighboring States that it possesses the means of righting all wrongs which may be committed on its citizens.

You will, therefore, immediately after arriving at your station, either proceed yourself, or despatch one of the ships under your command, in charge of a prudent officer, to Montevideo.

On arrival there, communications must at once be had with the consul of the United States. It will be ascertained, in the first place, whether the individual (Johnson) who makes the complaint is a citizen of the United States, and entitled to the protection of this Government; and, secondly, whether, by any law of that republic, a citizen of another country, voluntarily resident there, can be called upon for any such services as are stated to have been required of him; and, lastly, whether, if so, unnecessary and cruel means have not been resorted to to compel an acquiescence with such requisitions.

If he prove to be a citizen, and not subject by law to any such requirements, he should be called upon to make a personal statement of his grievances, under oath, before the consul of the United States; and if, upon his statement, and after a careful examination of the facts, to assist in ascertaining which the advice of the consul will be commanded, it shall appear that such wrongs as are represented have been done to this citizen, a reparation of them will [be] demanded and a punishment of the guilty insisted on, and such remonstrances made as may be best calculated to obtain compliance with these demands.

If the Government of that country proceed to investigate the affair, and give to you satisfactory assurances of their disposition to render justice to the individual, and their intention to do so without unreasonable delay, you can leave the settlement of the affair in the hands of the consul, having previously agreed with the Government what shall be the nature and extent of the reparation to be made, in case the facts shall prove to be as represented.

If, on the other hand, you receive no assurances of their intention to give satisfaction, or if you perceive in their conduct a purpose of avoiding the demand by pretexts or delays, or any other means of evasion, you will attempt to induce their serious attention to the affair by giving them notice that if, after a reasonable time, the case has not been investigated, and the Government not prepared to give satisfaction, you have orders to inform it, explicitly, that, on making your report to your Government, instructions may be expected from it to enforce proper and just reparation.

If, however, it should appear that there is some law by which such services as were required of Johnson are imposed on citizens of other countries resident there, you will endeavor to ascertain how far it is applicable to his case, what is the nature of the services, how far Johnson complied with the law, whether more was not demanded of him than the law authorized, and, also, whether severe punishment, cruelty, and torture, were not resorted to in order to force him to comply.

If this latter suggestion prove correct, you will demand that proper punishment be inflicted on those who exercised these cruelties, and it is hoped that the authorities of Uruguay will not hesitate to manifest a proper reprobation of such atrocities, by the punishment of all concerned in them.

If you receive the proper assurances of their intention to do so, you can desist from further proceedings, having in the first place secured, as far as possible, the individual (Johnson) from all danger of a repetition of such acts; and you will take occasion to declare to the authorities of Uruguay, that this Government will never submit to any unjust or illegal proceedings against any one of its citizens, however humble, and more especially will it use, on all occasions, whatever means may be necessary to secure ample atonement for the perpetration of any cruelties.

The period during which you will stay in the neighborhood of Montevideo will of course be regulated by the circumstances of the case.

You will lose no time in reporting to this Department your proceedings under these instructions.

The President trusts that no extreme measures may be necessary, but that the Government of Uruguay will at once proceed to give such satisfaction in the case as its own character requires of it, and as the Government justly demands and will insist upon. I have the honor to be your obedient servant,   Fletcher Webster, Acting Secretary

Text from *Executive Documents*, 27th Cong., 2d sess., Serial 405, No. 267. Original not found.

FROM JOHN TYLER

Dr Sir: Washington Oct. 14. 1841
I have deemed it proper to call the attention of the Cabinet to the instructions prepared by you for Com. [Charles] Morriss, in relation to the case of [George] Johnson at Montevideo.[1] They concur in suggesting to

1. DW's original instructions to Commodore Morris have not been found, but the present letter indicates that DW intended military action against Uruguay if the United States did not obtain satisfaction in the Johnson matter.

you the propriety of so modifying the instructions as to direct the Commodore to ascertain the facts, and, if need be, to report to the govt after having made a demand for redress. The idea is that <an attack> a movement on Montevideo, if redress was refused, either in the form of a Blockade or otherwise would be equivalent to a declaration of war agst a civilized Nation which is exclusively intrusted to Congress. What say you? Is the objection well founded? Please answer at your earliest leizure as Morriss will probably be ordered out in a few days. If you concur, you can modify the instructions which will be forwarded.

Mr [Charles Anderson] Wickliffe arrived <last> the evening before the last, and thus the Cabinet is again full.[2] I repeat what I said in my last,[3] that you will find in them able co-workers. The stock authorized by Congress drags heavily.[4] What think you of appointing an agent to Holland? <and> write [Walter] Forward your views.[5] The subject has been much spoken of in Cabinet meeting. We must take care to keep the govt in motion—for unless the recent elections shall have taught the clique more wisdom than they have heretofore displayed, we shall have to encounter a violent opposition this winter.[6]

I shall probably leave in a few days for Virginia. Be assured of my sincere regard   John Tyler

ALS. DLC. Published in *Tylers*, 2:127; misdated October 13, 1841.

TO DANIEL FLETCHER WEBSTER

Dear Fletcher   Oct. 31. 1841
    As Commodore [Charles] Morris may not go to Montevideo himself, but

2. On the resignation of the cabinet appointed by President Harrison, see above, DW to Ketchum, September 10, 1841, "the Crisis in Anglo-American Relations," p. 118. Wickliffe, a Kentucky lawyer and politician, became Tyler's new postmaster general. The other new members of Tyler's cabinet were John Canfield Spencer, secretary of war; Walter Forward, secretary of the Treasury; Hugh Swinton Legaré, attorney general; and Abel Parker Upshur, secretary of the navy. See also *Correspondence*, 5:148–162.

3. Tyler to DW, October 11, 1841, mDW 20535. See *Correspondence*, 5: 166–168.

4. Congress, on July 21, 1841, authorized the president to raise twelve million dollars by selling Treasury notes. 5 *U.S. Stat.* 438.

5. No special agent was appointed, but Tyler sent his friend Duff Green to Europe as a bearer of dispatches and unofficial representative. See Duff Green, *Facts and Suggestions, Biographical, Historical, Financial, and Political Addressed to the People of the United States* (New York, 1866), p. 141. Forward, a well-known Pennsylvania trial lawyer, was active in the formation of the Whig party. Named first comptroller of the currency by Harrison, he served as Tyler's secretary of the Treasury from 1841 to 1843. In November 1849 Forward became U.S. chargé d'affaires to Denmark, serving at that post for two years.

6. The Whigs suffered losses in state elections in the fall of 1841, for which Tyler blamed the Clay faction.

despatch an inferior officer, who may not possess all his prudence, and as the President inclines to think it better to limit the instructions, for the present to inquiry, & remonstrance, & demand of reparation, I have altered the Instructions accordingly, & now forward them. Please read them to the President, if he shall be in Washington; if not, despatch them, under you own signature.[1] Yrs   D. W.

ALS. NhHi.

FROM CHARLES MORRIS, WITH ENCLOSURE

U.S. Ship Delaware
Sir   Rio de Janeiro 21st April 1842
   Since my communication of the 5th instant[1] by the US Sloop Warrior, I have received from Mr [Robert M.] Hamilton, the enclosed copy of a letter from him to the Minister of Foreign Affairs [Francisco Ramón Antonio Vidal] at Monte Video,[2] which appears to close his correspondence with the Government of Uruguay in the case of George Johnson. With much Respect I have the honour to be Sir yr obt srvt
        C Morris Commanding US Squadron on the Brazil Station.

ALS. DNA, RG 59 (Consular Despatches, Montevideo). Rec'd June 14, 1842. Published in *Executive Documents*, 27th Cong., 2d sess., Serial 405, No. 267.

ENCLOSURE: ROBERT M. HAMILTON TO FRANCISCO RAMÓN ANTONIO VIDAL

Consulate of the United States
Montevideo 12th March 1842
   The Undersigned, Consul of the United States, has had the honor to receive from His Excy the Minister of Foreign Affairs [Francisco Ramón Antonio Vidal], his notes of the 25th ultimo & 9th Inst in relation to the claim of George Johnson[1] a citizen of the United States, amounting to Two thousand Six hundred and fifty Spanish Dollars, the justness of which, His Excy, on the part of the Government has been pleased to acknowledge and to issue the necessary orders for the payment of the same, referring the undersigned to the Department of Finance "as to the forms and terms in which the payment was to be made in conformity with the exigencies of the state, and the interests of the said George Johnson," in consequence of which, the undersigned did himself the honor of waiting on His Excy the Minister of Finance[2] on the 10th Inst., and arranged with

For some election results, see *Niles' National Register*, October 16, 1841.
   1. See Daniel Fletcher Webster to Morris, September 30, 1841, above.
   1. An extract of Morris's letter to DW has been published in *Executive Documents*, Serial 405, No. 267. No copy of the entire letter has been found.
   2. See below.
   1. Vidal to Hamilton, February 25 and March 9, 1842, DNA, RG 59 (Consular Despatches, Montevideo).
   2. Francisco Joaquin Muñoz (1791–1851).

that Functionary as to the mode of payment, to the satisfaction of all parties concerned, and he now takes leave to congratulate His Excy the Minister of Foreign Affairs, upon the happy termination of so unpleasant an affair, and he most sincerely trusts, that nothing may occur, to disturb in the slightest degree, the friendly relations which have so long, and happily subsisted, between this Government, and that of the United States.

The undersigned begs leave, to reiterate to his Excy the Minister the assurances of his distinguished consideration and respect.

(Signed) Consul of the United States of N.A.

Copy. DNA, RG 59 (Consular Despatches, Montevideo). Published in *Executive Documents*, 27th Cong., 2d sess., Serial 405, No. 267.

TO CHARLES MORRIS

Department of State,
Sir: Washington, June 15, 1842

Your letters of the 5th and 21st of April, 1842, have been received, with their enclosures.[1] They have been read by the President, and it gives me much pleasure to communicate to you, that the course adopted by you, and the arrangements made with the Republic of Uruguay, (in relation to the cruelties inflicted upon the person of George Johnson, a citizen of the United States, by the military authorities of that republic,) meet with his entire approbation.

As all the demands made by the consul were readily acceded to, it is deemed proper that no further communication be had with the authorities of Uruguay upon the subjects contained in the letter to you from this Department of the 30th of September, 1841,[2] and about which you ask instructions. What has already been done in this case, by the authorities, is viewed by the President as affording ample satisfaction for the injuries complained of; and I have now only to express his hopes that nothing may occur to disturb the friendly relations which have happily subsisted so long between this Government and the Republic of Uruguay. I am, Sir, your obedient servant,   Daniel Webster

Text from *Executive Documents*, 27th Cong., 2d sess., Serial 405, No. 267. Original not found.

Brazil

FROM FREDERIC TUDOR

Sir   Boston March 26th 1842

About year since Mr Stephen Higginson[1] of this town was employed as

1. For Morris's letter of April 21, 1842, and enclosures, see above. An extract of his letter to DW of April 5, 1842, is printed in *Executive Documents*, Serial 405, No. 267.

2. See above, Daniel Fletcher Webster to Morris, September 30, 1841.

1. Probably an obscure scion

my agent to present a memorial to the Govrnt of Brazil, asking certain bounties: or rather the remission of exactions: in aid of the introduction of Ice into that country.

This was asked as a private grant & was either not accorded or hung up for further consideration. I had proposed to introduce the article on a permanent foundation & at a price so that it might be used as a necessary of life & not as a luxury. To endure from years end to years end, as it has been made to do in the East Indies:[2] & that the low price to their community should compensate for the remission of the exactions, which went to defeat the introduction of the article at any price whatever.

Mr Higginson being obliged to leave the business in the unsettled state which I have represented, informed me the matter was taken up by our minister at that court[3] & sent to your department here to know if it would raise its voice on the occasion.[4]

As it is a matter of indifference to me whether an act on this subject of the Government of Brazil be a privilege to me: or a grand remission to all; I beg leave to bring the subject before the eye of my own Government: believing as I do the success of my own memorial: or any other which should produce the necessary remission of exactions, could not do otherwise than give a new extension to this branch of trade: which as it is encreasing: may be considered of some moment in spreading the commerce of the country.

Should the department incline to move at all, in this matter, I will more fully exhibit the difficulties in the case, which operate to prevent the introduction of Ice into Brazil: upon the plan which has been elsewhere successful. I have the honour to be very respectfully yr obd sert

Frederic Tudor

ALS. DNA, RG 59 (Misc. Letters). Rec'd March 29, 1842. Tudor (1783–1864).

TO FREDERIC TUDOR

Department of State

Sir,   Washington 13th April 1842.

Your letter of the 26th ult.[1] was duly received. Our Minister at Rio de Janeiro [William Hunter] had previously communicated with the Department upon the subject of your scheme to supply that city with ice.[2] There

(1808–1870) of the prominent merchant family of Boston.

2. In 1833 Tudor shipped 180 tons of ice to Calcutta, thereby establishing a flourishing trade with the East Indies.

3. William Hunter (1774–1849; Rhode Island College 1791), the U.S. chargé d'affaires and minister at Rio de Janeiro from 1834 to 1843, was a

lawyer and former U.S. senator from Rhode Island.

4. See Hunter to DW, October 26, 1841, DNA, RG 59 (Despatches, Brazil).

1. See above.

2. See Hunter to DW, October 26, 1841, DNA, RG 59 (Despatches, Brazil).

cannot it seems to me, be any doubt that the Brazilian Government would be consulting its own interests if it were to grant you the privileges and exemptions which you desire in relation to the matter but it would not be expedient for this government officially to negotiate for them as a right or as a favor. If however, you should think that the personal good offices of our Minister at Rio would be useful in forwarding your object, I will cheerfully instruct him to employ them in your behalf, and to that end, the more particular account of the difficulties in the case which you offer, would be acceptable. I am &c.   Danl Webster

LC. DNA, RG 59 (Domestic Letters).

TO WILLIAM HUNTER

No. 6   Department of State
Sir: Washington 2nd May, 1842.
    I transmit a copy of two letters which have been addressed to this department by Mr Frederic Tudor, of Boston, relative to the importation of ice at Rio de Janeiro, for which, as you are aware, he is desirous of obtaining certain immunities.[1] His original memorial to the Brazilian government, which accompanied your despatch No. 134, is now returned, a transcript having been taken for the use of the department.[2]
    It is in many respects desirable that Mr Tudor should succeed in his object, and with that view you will afford him all the personal, unofficial aid which you can. Of course it would not be proper for you to enter into a formal correspondence with the Minister for Foreign Affairs[3] upon the subject and it must not be understood that your agency in the business is meant to be public, that the grant, if made, would be considered by this government as such a favor as Brazil could expect from us, or as a right in any way due to Mr Tudor.
    The inducements which that government has so far to modify its fiscal regulations as to gratify his wishes, seem to be obvious and are well explained in his memorial. That document clearly shows that it is not at all probable Rio de Janeiro could enjoy a constant supply of ice upon terms which would be more advantageous to the Imperial or municipal authorities or to the inhabitants of that City, than those which he offers.
    It may be the general policy of the Brazilian government to discourage exemptions like that sought in this instance, and the municipal laws of that Empire as well as its treaties with foreign States may, tacitly at least, forbid them. If, however, Brazil should have reserved to herself any

1. See Tudor to DW, March 26, 1842, and Tudor to DW, April 18, 1842, DNA, RG 59 (Misc. Letters).
2. No. 134. Hunter to DW, October 26, 1841, DNA, RG 59 (Despatches, Brazil). Tudor's memorial of June 28, 1841, is enclosed.
3. Aureliano de Souza de Oliveira Coutinho, not further identified.

power to make them, circumstances certainly render the present a case in which the exercise of that power would be proper and expedient.

It is understood that Mr Tudor would be willing to forego as to Rio de Janeiro, for the present at least, some of the advantages with which his enterprize is attended and encouraged at Havana, Jamaica and Calcutta.[4] His main object is to furnish that City with the article in such quantities and at such prices as to render it essential to the comfort of the great body of the citizens in easy circumstances. All that he deems indispensable for this is that the import and other charges both upon the ice and the vessels which take it, should be discontinued. Aware of the jealous vigilance and intricate precautions in force there to check frauds upon the revenue, he is willing to enter into all stipulations which may be required and that his vessels and their officers should undergo all examinations which may be necessary to guard against an abuse of the privilege.

It is presumed that, from your long residence at Rio de Janeiro you must be acquainted with the means necessary to accomplish this object (if it be practicable) and with the persons by and through whom it would be best to operate for that purpose. Your zealous personal efforts will accordingly be given, animated as I have no doubt they will be by the consciousness that, if successful, they will have contributed to the prosperity of one of your worthy fellow citizens and to the beneficial employment of a considerable amount of the tonnage of the United States.

I also transmit a communication to you from Mr G[eorge] H[enry] Snelling[5] of Boston upon the subject of this letter. This gentleman is a friend of Mr Tudor and has visited this City with authority from him to attend to the business. I am, Sir, your obedient servant, Danl Webster

L S . DNA, RG 84 (Records of Foreign Service Posts, Brazil).

CENTRAL AMERICA AND THE CARIBBEAN

As in South America, Britain was the dominant foreign power in Central America during the first half of the nineteenth century. Prior to the Clayton-Bulwer Treaty of 1850, the United States did not attempt to contest British supremacy in either Central or South America. There was, however, a difference in the American perception of these geographic regions. U.S. interests in South America were almost entirely commercial in nature; Central America, however, was viewed as potentially important strategically because it was the area where an interoceanic communication might be constructed. The actual commercial and diplomatic

4. At these places Tudor received bounties on cargoes of ice.

5. Snelling (1801–1892; Harvard 1819) was a Boston lawyer. The communication from Snelling is not included in RG 84.

presence of the United States in Central America was insignificant in comparison with that of England, but the Murphy mission of 1841–1842 suggests that the Tyler administration was interested in following developments in the region.

William S. Murphy's designation as special agent of the United States to the Central American Confederation originated in President Tyler's desire to provide a patronage appointment to this Whig politician from Ohio. The primary object of the mission was to obtain political information about an area of which the U.S. government knew so little that Murphy was accredited to a Central American Confederation that had disbanded in 1839.

Murphy was successful in the sense that he provided the Department of State with basic information about Central America. As might have been expected, he found British businessmen and diplomats firmly in control of the region and urged that the United States challenge that dominance by negotiating treaties of commerce with such countries as Guatemala. Webster thanked Murphy for his report but did not adopt his recommendations; it was not until 1848 that the United States sent another agent to Central America.

Webster pursued an equally unenterprising and cautious policy toward the so-called State of the Isthmus. When the provinces of Panama and Veraqua declared independence from New Granada in November 1840 and renamed themselves the "State of the Isthmus," they sent William Radcliff to Washington to seek diplomatic recognition. In addition to being the representative of the self-proclaimed country, Radcliff was a New York entrepreneur who had been promoting the construction of an interoceanic canal since the 1830s. In exchange for recognition of the new nation, Radcliff offered the United States attractive canal rights and commercial advantages. Despite the possible gains to be made from a quick move, Webster adhered to traditional policy and declined to establish diplomatic relations with the new state until it had demonstrated the stability necessary to maintain its sovereignty. Webster's legalistic caution proved wise, for word soon arrived that the State of the Isthmus and New Granada had settled their differences and reunited. Webster's conservative approach to the recognition of the State of the Isthmus, however, did not signify indifference to the ancient dream of linking the Atlantic and Pacific oceans. In an instruction to William Matthews Blackford dated May 20, 1842 (printed below), the newly appointed chargé d'affaires to New Granada was directed to diligently protect the interests of the United States in any interoceanic canal or railroad project. Webster, moreover, was supportive when a young engineer named Matthias Oliver Davidson proposed to undertake a survey of possible canal routes in Central America. Although nothing came of Davidson's project, Webster's letter to him of December 14, 1842 (printed below), reflects a concern about the subject. Nevertheless, Webster did not go so far as to advocate, as both Murphy and Radcliff did, an active American foreign policy toward Central America. Rather, he pursued the modest goal of trying to prevent a foreign power from acquiring exclusive rights over an interoceanic communication.

In marked contrast to its mild interest in Central America, the Tyler administration stood ready, if necessary, to confront Great Britain over Cuba. Not only was the Spanish colony important to the United States economically and strategically, but also southerners such as President Tyler were fearful that a revolt in Cuba could lead to slave rebellions in the American South. Alarmed by rumors that abolitionist-minded British officials in Cuba were conspiring to foment a revolution dedicated to the establishment of a black republic, Tyler asked Webster to have the U.S. consul at Havana report on the situation (see Tyler to [DW], December 16, 1841, below).

Webster complied with Tyler's request in the instruction to Consul Robert Blair Campbell of January 14, 1843 (printed below). In that remarkable document, Webster strongly reiterated the no-transfer policy. First applied to Cuba in 1823, the policy was that the United States would oppose the transfer of the island from Spain to any other European power. Webster even went so far as to state that the Tyler administration was prepared to use military force to prevent the establishment of a British protectorate over Cuba. With considerable ire, John Quincy Adams characterized Webster's letter to Campbell as "full of the most combustible matter, putrid with slavery and the slave trade" (*Memoirs*, 11: 350–351).

The rumors turned out to be, as Webster had suspected, "greatly exaggerated" (DW to Washington Irving, March 14, 1843, below), and the instruction of January 14, 1843, probably reflected Tyler's rather than Webster's apprehensions. The directive to Campbell, nevertheless, is revealing. In addition to embodying the traditional policy of the United States toward Cuba, it also suggests the growing concern of southerners about a possible revolutionary upheaval in an island located only ninety miles off the coast of Florida.

The Central American States

FROM JOHN TYLER

My Dear Sir;   [c. July 1841]
  Genl [William Sumter] Murphy of Ohio[1] is poor and his family in dis-

1. Murphy (1796?–1844), a general in the Ohio state militia and a lawyer, had been a Democrat but supported Harrison in 1840. After his mission to Central America, Murphy was named chargé d'affaires to the Republic of Texas. The Senate rejected Murphy's appointment to Tex-

tress—urgent—He is zealous and has been. No man did so much in Ohio, as I had reason to know when there. Is there any place in S. America to which we could send him, or Guatemala might suit. Do me the kindness to [answer] this by tomorrow.

I thank you for the opportunity to peruse Mr [Thomas] Aspinwall's letter.[2] Sir Ro[bert] Peel will do, but Lord Aberdeen and Lord Stanley are not so well.[3] Yrs truly   J. Tyler

ALS. TxSjM.

TO WILLIAM SUMTER MURPHY

Sir:

Department of State,
Washington, 28th July, 1841

The United States had with the Republic of Central America before its disorganization relations of an interesting character.[1] Lying, as that country does, within the tropics, its productions are mostly peculiar to that region and are exchanged with mutual advantage to the parties, for the products and manufactures of the United States. Whilst our citizens have had frequent and grievous causes of complaint against the authorities of other Republics of this hemisphere formerly under the dominion of Spain, those of them who have resorted to Central America for purposes of business or curiosity, have been comparatively unmolested in their pursuits. Consequently, although there has been an interchange of diplomatic agents between the two governments, the business of those functionaries has for the most part been confined to the adjustment of the rules of commercial intercourse between the countries. This was first accomplished by the treaty signed in this City on the 5th of December, 1825.[2] As the commercial articles of that compact were to expire by

---

as in 1844, along with the treaty of annexation signed that year.

2. Aspinwall was the United States consul in London, but the letter referred to has not been found. It was probably written immediately after the Melbourne government had lost a vote of confidence on June 4.

3. Andrew Stevenson, the American minister to Great Britain, had written to Webster on May 18 that a Tory government might be "confidently anticipated." Such a government, under Sir Robert Peel, might be expected to include both Aberdeen and Stanley. When Peel actually became prime minister in September, George Gordon, Lord Aberdeen, was named foreign minister and Edward George Geoffrey Smith, Lord Stanley (1799–1869), became colonial secretary. See No. 124. Stevenson to DW, May 18, 1841, DNA, RG 59 (Despatches, Britain). Stevenson's No. 124 was received at the Department of State on June 4.

1. The five Central American provinces of Spain—Guatemala, San Salvador, Honduras, Nicaragua, and Costa Rica—proclaimed their independence in 1821 and formed a republic in 1823 with its capital in Guatemala City. Political, sectional, and class differences broke up the federation by 1839.

2. See *Treaties*, 3: 209–238.

their own limitation within twelve years from the date of the exchange of the ratifications, the expiration would have taken place on the 2nd of August, 1838. In anticipation of that event, however, in the course of the summer of that year, a special messenger was sent with powers and instructions for Mr [Charles Gerrit] DeWitt, our then Chargé d'Affaires at Guatemala, to negotiate with that government a renewal of the treaty.[3] His overture for that purpose was accepted and a new treaty was signed by him and the Minister for Foreign Affairs of Central America on the 14th of July, 1838.[4] The time limited for the exchange of the ratifications was eight months. Mr DeWitt, who had previously received permission to visit the United States on leave of absence[5] was, in the instructions adverted to, directed to stay in Central America until the treaty should not only be concluded, but ratified by that government. He nevertheless disregarded this order and returned to this country without the ratification of that government to the treaty, but why he took this course was never explained by him, as he died before he received a letter from the department which required the necessary explanations upon the subject.[6]

As the period specified for the exchange of the ratifications would have elapsed before the exchange could have been effected, the President did not think proper to submit the treaty to the Senate.[7] That time was accordingly suffered to expire and the instrument failed to go into operation.

As Mr DeWitt left his post with the understanding and doubtless with the intention that he was to return to Central America, he did not take formal leave of that government prior to his departure. In the letter to Mr DeWitt above referred to, demanding explanations upon the subject of the treaty, he was directed to go back to Guatemala within a limited time, to take final and formal leave of that government and to bring with him to the United States the archives and books of the Legation. His sudden decease frustrated these instructions.

Subsequently, in the summer of 1839, Mr John L[loyd] Stephens was

3. No. 35. John Forsyth to DeWitt, March 28, 1838, DNA, RG 59 (Instructions, Central American States). DeWitt (1789–1839), a lawyer and editor of the Kingston, New York, *Ulster Sentinel*, and a veteran of the 21st Congress, was appointed chargé d'affaires to Central America in January 1833. He returned to the United States in February 1839 and died in April in New York.

4. Colonel M. Alvarez, the minister for foreign affairs of Central America,

could not be further identified. No. 56. DeWitt to Forsyth, July 24, 1838, DNA, RG 59 (Despatches, Central America).

5. No. 33. Forsyth to DeWitt, October 3, 1837, DNA, RG 59 (Instructions, Central American States).

6. No. 3. Forsyth to DeWitt, April 14, 1838, DNA, RG 59 (Instructions, Central American States).

7. *Messages and Papers*, 3:533–534.

sent as a special and confidential agent to Central America for the purposes of announcing to its government, the determination of the President to discontinue our mission there, of explaining the motives which
had led to this determination, of sounding the Central American Executive as to its disposition to apply for authority to extend the time for
exchanging the ratifications of the treaty to one year from the period
when the authority might be granted, provided the treaty itself should
be approved by all the requiste branches of that government; of making
a proposition to that effect accordingly and of bringing to the United
States the public property appertaining to our Legation at Guatemala.[8]
Mr Stephens proceeded on his mission, but as he found on his arrival in
that country a civil war raging and the government virtually dissolved,
he deemed it inexpedient to present his credentials or to comply with
any other part of his instructions than that which related to the books
and papers of the Legation.[9] There is, however, reason to believe that
since his return home a Confederation of some kind and to some extent,
if not comprising all the Provinces of which the Central American Confederation was composed, has been formed in that country. Both the
uncertainty and the probability of this make it highly desirable in the
opinion of the President that this government should be in possession of
authentic information in relation to it and to the present condition and
future prospects of that country generally. The only means of obtaining
such information in regard to countries where the United States have no
regularly accredited diplomatic agent and from which so little is to be
learned through the usual channels of public information, is through an
agency with the title and of the character of that with which Mr Stephens
was charged. The President has therefore determined to employ you in
this service. You will, accordingly, with as little delay as circumstances
will admit, set out on your journey to the City of Guatemala or whatever
other place may, on your arrival in Central America be the seat of the
Government of that Confederation or of a Confederacy of a plurality
of the States which formerly composed that Confederation. To facilitate
your journey, you are herewith furnished with a special passport in your
official capacity which will, it is believed, ensure you all necessary protection. You are also herewith provided with an official letter to the Minister for Foreign Affairs of Central America and with a copy of it for your
own perusal, accrediting you as the special and confidential agent of the

8. Vail to Stephens, August 13,
1839, DNA, RG 59 (Instructions, Central American States). Stephens
(1805–1852; Columbia 1822), later
a renowned traveler and author, recounted his Central American mission in a four-volume work on the
region. He was later active in the
promotion of a transatlantic steam-
ship line and a Panamanian railroad
company.

9. No. 1. Stephens to Forsyth, December 25, 1838, DNA, RG 59 (Despatches, Central America).

United States and apprizing him of the purpose of your agency.[10] You will, as soon as convenient after your arrival, ask of him an audience, at which you will hand him the letter referred to. It is not considered that any formal explanations in regard to the discontinuance of our mission in that country will be necessary or will be expected at this period, as the events which have happened there since the departure of Mr DeWitt are of themselves and are no doubt viewed by them as sufficient to account for our course in that respect.

Besides, therefore, collecting the information above referred to, which you may either transmit to the department from time to time during your absence or embody in a report on your return, if you should find any organized government with the title of the "Federation of Central America", you will endeavor to effect with it the arrangement in regard to the treaty concluded by Mr DeWitt, which Mr Stephens failed to accomplish. For although navigation and trade between the United States and some countries may be regulated with advantage to us by reciprocal legislation only, treaties for that purpose are thought to be particularly necessary and desirable with the mutable governments of the Spanish American States. These, besides defining with precision the rights and duties of the parties, secure the enjoyment of the one and a claim to the other for a term of years in all the territory over which the parties exercised jurisdiction at the time of the conclusion of the treaty.

As it is believed that according to the Constitution of the Central American Government the sanction of both branches of the Legislature is requisite before a treaty with a Foreign Power can be ratified by the Executive, it will be proper for you to suggest, in an interview with the Minister for Foreign Affairs, that the authority to exchange the ratifications at any time within a year from the period when the authority may be granted, should proceed from the same source and might be conveyed by either a joint resolution or separate resolutions of their Congress. The President will apply for similar authority to the Senate of the United States, but although there can be no doubt that it would be given by that body without hesitation, he would rather not make the application until he shall learn the result of your proceedings and those of the Government of Central America in relation to the affair.

You will also suggest that if the Executive of that country shall receive the authority referred to, it would be advisable that the treaty should be ratified without delay and that a person should be empowered on their part to exchange the ratifications in this City within the period mentioned.

Your compensation will be at the rate of eight dollars a day for the time you shall actually have been employed in the performance of the

10. This enclosure is not included in RG 59 record.

duties of your agency. The expense of your journey from your place of residence in the United States to your port of embarkation, of your passage to and from a Central American port and of your journey thence to the seat of Government and back will also be allowed you. Of this you will keep a regular account which, in all cases admitting of it, is to be supported by proper vouchers. An advance of fifteen hundred dollars will be made to you at this department on account of your compensation and travelling expenses. With this sum you will stand charged until, on your return, you render an account by which the debit therefor may be cancelled. It is supposed to be more than sufficient to defray the necessary expenses of your journey. Should it, however, prove otherwise, you are authorized to draw upon this department for such further sum as you may require, not exceeding the amount due you at the date of your draught.

If circumstances should justify you in making to the Government of Central America the propositions referred to above, you are authorized to remain in that country three months if necessary for the purpose of waiting for the answers of that government to them.

If you find the States composing the former Confederation of Central America at war among themselves or in a state of hopeless disunion, there will be no occasion for prolonging your stay and you will therefore return. If any Confederation exist of some but not all those States and this Confederation appear to possess the character of a regular and settled government, you will give this department full information on that subject, to the end that it may be considered whether, abandoning the former treaty, it may not be expedient to treat with such new government.

The object of your appointment is simply to obtain political information, with a view to renewing our former pacific relations with that country. It will hardly be necessary, therefore, for you to extend your route further than to the Capital. Any thing of interest falling within your notice relative to the commerce of the country, its amount and direction, and the nature of the exchanges, you will please to communicate, keeping in mind, nevertheless, what has been already declared to be the main object of your employment. I am, Sir, your obedient servant,

Daniel Webster

LC. DNA, RG 59 (Instructions, Central American States). Published in *IAA*, 3:25–28.

FROM WILLIAM SUMTER MURPHY

Sir.   Guatemala 4th Feby 1842

I arrived in this city on the morning of the 25th December 1841, very sick of a fever taken on the road. I was waited on by several gentlemen,

residents of the city, for I heard on the way that my arrival was anticipated, and that some excitement prevailed touching the supposed objects of my mission. This report was confermed to me by these gentlemen, but they could give no reason for the excitement, or tel how it
arose: only that it prevailed with the Catholic Priesthood, and what they
termed the British party in the city. Deeming it my duty to arrest, if possible, the progress of evil surmises, which might eventuate in ill feeling,
I immediately addressed the Sect of State, of the State of Guatemala,[1] the
following note.

City of Guatemala December 25th 1841

To His Excellency
Don Juan Jose Flores
Sect of State &c &c
Sir. A decent respect for the religious Rites and Ceremonies attendant
upon the present Festival, induces me to forbear any other communication to your Excellency at present, than merely to announce my arrival in this city, as ["]The Special & Confidential Agent of the United
States to the Central American Confederation," and to inform your
Excellency that as soon as a proper regard to Religious exercises will
permit, I shall do myself the Honor to make known to your Excellency,
the object of my mission, in a manner most agreeable to your Excellency. I have the Honor to be your obt Servt.

W. S. Murphy Spl & Confd Agent of the United States &c &c

Translation of the Answer to the foregoing.

(Note)

(Here I may be permitted to remark, that I have had so many interruptions by sickness, traveling &c &c I have reason to fear, that my progress
in the Spanish Tongue, has been hardly equal to its literal translation.
Yet I am sure, I have given the substantial meaning of every sentence.
For the sake of certainty however, I transmit herewith, the originals, that
the Department may have any errors corrected, if any of consequence
have occured in my Translations)

Guatemala Decemb 25th 1841.

To W. S. Murphy
Sir Your Exl Esteemed letter has reached my hands, in which your
arrival in this city is announced to me, as Special Confidential Agent
of the United States of North America, and that the respect due to
the Religious Rites and Festivities of the Day induces your Exl not to
address any other class of Communications.
    In reply I have the Honor to manifest to your Exl that it is a great
pleasure to me (complasant) that the Republic of the United States,

1. Juan José Flores, not otherwise
identified, but not the famous Ecua-
dorian military leader of the same
name.

has sent a Special Confd Agent near my Government, and it is equally agreeable to me, that for that Charge they have selected your Excl. I have the Honor to offer myself to Your Exl as your Exl obt Servt

Juan Jose Flores   Sect of State &c

I had the satisfaction to learn, in a few days after the interchange of these notes, that the desired effect had been produced, and that the current of popular feeling, was running in a better channel.

I also ascertained that the Government of the "Central American Confederation," to which I was accredited did not exist—and that there was not, in these states, a single officer representing that confederation. That it had been, long ago, abolished, and was now, no where, acknowledged to any extent whatever. I was further informed that the States formerly composing that Confederation, were now governed by their own Executive Legislative and Judicial authorities, and under the same Constitutions severally existing, during, the Confederation. That after the entire overthrow of the authorities of the Confederation, the States organised, in some way or other, a sort of League offensive and defensive, for general and united concert of action, for the mutual support of each other, in all matters of a general nature, or which related to foreign countries. But the gentlemen who gave me this information, being merchants & men of business, were not able to give me any particular information of the manner of the formation of that League or the extent to which its operations were limited. In this situation, I was at some loss to know how to act within the letter of my Instructions, and at the same time obtain for the information of the Department of State, the most correct and authoritative information, not only of the nature and extent of this League, but also of the general & particular political conditions and Relative situation of these states, in regard to each other. I wished also to ascertain for the information of the Department of State, the views and feelings of the Governments of these states, towards the U. States, as well as their wishes in relation to the renewal of the Treaty which had expired, & which had been sought to be renewed.

In this difficulty, I hope I have not done wrong, in opening the following Correspondence with the Government of Guatemala, as the only means left me, of obtaining the information, which my Instructions required me to obtain.

Guatemala 3d Janry. 1842

To His Excellency
Don Juan Jose Flores.
Sect of State &c &c
Sir.

Acknowledging the receipt of your note of the 25th Ult. I have the Honor of representing to your Excellency that the Government of the

United States, entertaining the kindest feelings towards the States of central America, and seeking the reestablishment of the commercial relations once so happily existing between, the two countries, appointed the Undersigned, Its Special & Confidential Agent to the "Central American Confederation" supposing that Confederation to exist, or to be acknowledged to some extent, by the Central American States. Finding no officer whatever representing the Government of that Confederation in this city, which was once the acknowledged [location] of its Executive & Legislative Authority, I propose to present my Credentials to your Excellency proforma, as leading to an interchange of correspondence touching the interruption of our commercial relations, and the means of their reestablishment. For this purpose it is proper that I should ask of your Excellency the Honor of a personal interview, at such time & place, as your Excellency consulting your own convenience may appoint. I have the Honor to be your obt Servt

W. S. Murphy   Spl & Confd Agent of the U States &c &c

(Translation of the answer to the Foregoing.)

Guata 4th Janry. 1842

To H Ex W.S. Murphy,
Spl & Confd. Agent &c

Sir. By the very polite note of your Excel of yesterdays date, I have been informed that your Exl not finding in this city any of the authorities which ought to represent the Federation of Central America, and with the object of commencing the duties with which you are charged, you have been pleased to propose presenting to me "proforma" the credentials of the character with which Your Exl is invested, and manifesting at the same time a desire for a personal interview. Your Exl will please to verify both these on any day your Excellency may think proper, as I am disposed to receive the Honor yr Exl is inclined to do me with the greatest pleasure, in the Room of the Department of Government, at 4. o'clock in the afternoon, on any subsequent day of business.

I have the Honor to inform your Exl in conclusion, that I await your Excellns answer naming the day you may designate, in order that I may be at the Beaureau in due anticipation of your Exl arrival. I have the Honor to offer myself anew to your Ex as Your obt servt

Juan Jose Flores   Sect of State &c &c

Guatemala 7th Janry. 1842.

To His Excellency
Don Juan Jose Flores
Sect of State &c &c

I have the honor to acknowledge the receipt of your note of the 4th

Inst designating the Room of the Department of Government as the place of our interview, and politely submitting to me the selection of the day.

In reply, I have the Honor to designate Tuesday next (11th Inst) as the day of our interview, and solicit your Excellency (in consequence of the feeble state of my health) to fix the hour at 11. o'clock in the forenoon, instead of 4. o'clock in the afternoon of that day. I am your obt sevt   W. S. Murphy   Spl & Confd Agent of U.S.

Translation of the Reply to the foregoing.

Guata 8th Janry 1842

To W. S. Murphy
Spl & Confd Agent of the U states of &c &c
   Sir. I have the Honor to advise your Exl of having recd Your Exls very esteemed note of yesterday, informing me that Tuesday next is the day your Exl has thought proper to designate, for the interview your Exl has proposed to me, on which day I shall have the honor to receive your Exl at 11. o'clock in the morning[.]
   With the most respectful deference, I have the Honor to subscribe myself your Exl obt servant.   Juan Jose Flores Sect of State &c &c

11th January 1842.

I had an interview today with the Sect. of State, pursuant to the appointment, in the preceding correspondence. I handed his Excellency the office copy of the Letter from the Sect of State, of the U. States, to the Minister of Foreign Affairs, of the ["]Central American Confederation" [Colonel M. Alvarez][2]—which he received, and having read it, He expressed his satisfaction, at my arrival, and also his great pleasure at the course I had pursued in presenting the Letter to him. He expressed himself as having been hurt at the course Mr [John Lloyd] Stephens pursued, on a similar occasion, and seemed to intimate that the Government felt hurt at his not communicating the object of his visit. He was very ardent in his protestations of regard for the U States, and said he was very much gratified that they desired a renewal of the Treaty relations which once existed between the Two countries. He said he would place the letter before the President & Executive Council,[3] and give me the earliest information of their action. &c. It was not, until the 20th January, that I recd the following note from the Sect of State, though it bears date on the 19th.

2. This letter is not included in the RG 59 record.
3. The president of the Guatemalan Executive Council, 1841–1842, was José Venancio Lopez (1791–1863).

(Translation)

D.U.L. (that is, "Religion,
Union, Liberty")
Guatemala 19th Janry 1842

To His Exl W. S. Murphy
Spl & Confd Agent of the U States &c &c
Sir.

I have the Honor to inform your Excellency that the Councillors charged with the Supreme Executive Power of the State of Guatemala, one of the States which formed the Federation of Central America, has seen the credentials <with> which your Exl did me the Honor to present at the interview on the 11th Inst. Although this Government, has no knowledge of the mission with which Mr. John L. Stephens came charged in the year 1839, he not having exhibitied his credentials to this Government, stil it takes great pleasure on hearing, that the Government of the United States, desires to continue the relations of Amity between that and this Republic, and is much disposed to listen to all the propositions which for that purpose your Exl may be pleased to make, in the understanding that in the course of these relations, this Government is authorised to act only in behalf of the State of Guatemala, and under this intelligence, Your Exl will be pleased to open your official Correspondence, which you have announced to me.

In communicating to your Excellency the above I have the honor of protesting my respect and the very particular Consideration with which I subscribe myself Your Exl most obt Servt.

Juan Jose Flores Sect of State &c &c

(The following note accompanied this letter)

The Secretary of Relations of the Supreme Government of the State of Guatemala, desires to have the Honor of making His Exl W. S. Murphy a visit at his Lodgings, and hopes he will do him the favor to name to him the day & hour he may do so

–Reply–

Guatemala 21st Janry 1842

To His Excellency
Don Juan Jose Flores
Sect of State &c &c
Sir.

I have the honor to acknowledge the receipt of your Esteemed favor of the 19th Inst. signifying the pleasure of the Government of the State of Guatemala to receive such communications as I may have to make, touching the object of my mission to Central America.

It is unnecessary to repeat to your Excellency the assurance already given, of the desire ever manifested by the Government of the United States, to cultivate the most friendly relations with these States. Nor is it deemed necessary to repeat that it is the object of my mission, to obtain such information as will enable the Government of the United States, to consider how and in what manner the reestablishment of the Commercial Relations, formerly existing between the two Countries, can be best effected.

It is important, in the first place to know whither the Government of the State of Guatemala desires for Itself, a renewal of these Treaty Relations with the United States; for if it does not, there can be no propriety in seeking any further, or other, information from your Excellency on the subject.

Your Excellency does indeed represent to the Undersigned, that the Government of the State of Guatemala is pleased to learn, that the Government of the United States desires to continue the relations of Amity between the two countries. But as to the desire of your Government to renew, or reestablish the Treaty Relations, which formerly existed, between these States and those of the United States, your Excellency has given the undersigned no intimation.

Your Excellency will please therefore to signify the views and wishes of your Government on this point, preliminary to every other question which can arise.

I am Glad of the occasion of renewing to your Excellency the assurance of my respect.   W. S. Murphy Spl & Confd Agent U.S.

(I enclosed in the foregoing, the following note, in reply to the note enclosed to me.)

"Mr Murphy is highly gratifyd to learn, that his Excellency the Sect. of Relations, of the Supr Govnt of the State of Guatemala will honor him with a visit.

Sensible of the Honor intended him Mr Murphy will receive his Excellency tomorrow at 4. O'clock. P.M.["]

21st Janry 1842.

22nd January 1842. Pursuant to the above appointment, the Secretary of State dined with me. After dinner he introduced the subject of our former communications, and apoligized for the delay which had occured between his note of the 19th and our first interview, saying that the Supreme Council could not be sooner assembled. That the President and all the Council were highly gratified at the prospect of renewing the Treaty Relations between our respective Countries, and desired him, so to inform me, and that if his note of the 19th Inst did not fully convey that idea to me, it was an error, or oversight in him. And that in his reply to mine of the 21st Inst, (which he said he had received), he should fully make known the views and wishes of his Government to me, that I might transmit it to my Government. That the Council were also unanimously inclined to the opinion, that all the other states entertained the same feeling & wishes, and would readily join in a Treaty with the United States. Indeed he said, there was no doubt of the fact. That they would Ceeze with alacrity—the first occasion to do so. His Excellency proposed, that the 5 States now in League or alliance, Viz, Guatemala, San Salvador, Nicaragua, Honduras and Costa Ryca, should all join in the appointment of one, or more commissioners, authorised to meet such Envoy as the United States might appoint, at Guatemala, as the most central point, to negociate a Treaty, or alter the former one, so as to meet the new state of things here. That each State should ratify it by their several Legislative assemblies, and unite in their appointment of an agent to exchange the Ratifications at Washington City. He seemed to consider, that the former Treaty concluded with Mr [Charles Gerrit] Dewit, could hardly be made to answer the present condition of things here. I could only say to all this, that I would faithfully communicate all the facts to my Government, for its consideration and future action. He said he wished me to do so soon, for he said all good citizens here, looked up to the U States as a model, and that he had no doubt but it would be a great advantage towards the stability & peace of the country to have a Treaty with the U States.

His Excellency informed me that the President of the State had expressed a desire to see me, and wished him to invite me to call on him at the Government Rooms, whenever it suited my convenience, giving him notice of my call. I offered to call the next day, to which the Sect replyd that he would wait on me here, and accompany me to the Rooms.

It was so arranged, & we parted.

January 23d 1842.

Interview with the President. On the 23d Janry. The Sect. of State called on me according to his engagement, and we walked together to the Government Rooms, where we found the President seated with most of the officers of State around him. After the customary salutations were over, the President expressed the great pleasure he felt in common with his fellow citizens, at the arrival of an Agent from the United States; and that it was particularly gratifying to hear, that the U States, wished to renew the Treaty relations which once existed between them, and Central America, and that he particularly desired me to assure my Government, that he had no doubt, that all the States would be as glad to hear it as Guatemala was. And that if the United States sent any agent with authority to make a Treaty he would find no obstacles in the way of its speedy accomplishment. He seemed to say that the Treaty negociated with Mr Dewit, could hardly be made to suit the present condition of things in regard to these States, but did not give any particular reason. He approved of the mode of negociating, and Ratifying a Treaty, which had been suggested by the Sect of State.

I could only say to him what I had said to the Sect of State, that I would truly communicate his views to my Government.

He then added, that these States were about to unite, or had united in the appointment of an Envoy to England, for the purpose of seeking redress for the aggressions committed by the Superintendent at Belize, on the Sovereignty & Territory of the State of Nicaragua, and he also handed me a printed Document on the subject of that aggression, which he requested me to transmit, in my first Despatch to my Government. It is herewith accordingly transmitted, marked No 1.[4] There was much other conversation, to the same purport, after which we separated, with no little ceremony.

On the 1st Feby. I received the following note from the Sect. of State, in answer to mine of the 21st January.

Guatemala 1st February 1842

To His Exl W. S. Murphy
Spl & Confd Agent &c

Sir: The Consular President of the State of Guatemala, being assured of the desire by which the Government of the United States is animated, to cultivate Amity with the Republic of Central America, according to the Exposition which your Exl has been pleased to make to him at the interview of the 23rd ulto,—which was heard with much pleasure reiterates his sentiments of Gratitude to the government of the United States for its benevolence towards the States of Central America, and in his name, I have the Honor to inform your Exl that this Government is much disposed to continue the relations of amity between the two countries, and to ("celebrate") or (ratify) Treaties, that may contribute to tighten the bonds of friendship and stimulate commerce between Central & North America, either by renewing the former Treaty, ratified in Washington, on the 5th December 1825, by Sr. Anto[nio] Jons [Jose] Canas,[5] or by making a new Treaty, with the understanding, that in any case, the Treaty must be subject to the ratification of the Legislative body.

As at present there exists no General Government, to represent the

4. In August 1841 Alexander Macdonald, the British superintendent at Belize, extended his protection to the territorial claims of the Mosquito Indians in Nicaragua. Enclosure No. 1 is a pamphlet containing correspondence on the incident. For a complete account, see Mario Rodríguez, A *Palmerstonian Diplomat in Central America, Frederick Chatfield, Esq.* (Tucson, Ariz., 1964), pp. 239–246.

5. Cañas (d. 1844) had been minister to the United States from the Central American Confederation and was the chief executive of El Salvador, 1838–1840.

whole Republic the councillor, charged with the Executive authority of this State, has ardent hopes that each of the other states which composed the Federation of Central America, may continue for its own part the relations of Amity and Commerce with the U. States, and conceiving that they will all be found disposed to enter into new Treaties for that purpose, He offers to address to their Governments, the necessary invitations, in order, that they may do so, Informing them at the same time of the nature of the Mission with which Your Exl comes charged, Believing that they will adopt the measure of sending commissioners sufficiently authorised for that purpose. In addressing this Letter to your Exl I have also the Honor to reiterate the sentiments of esteem for the Person of your Exl and the Distinguished Consd with which I subt myself &c   *Juan Jose Flores.* &c

(Note. I know this letter is badly translated. The expressions in the original are curious, and hard to express in our Language with brevity. But I send the Original for "greater certainty.")

Two sessions ago, the Legislature of this State appointed a committee to frame a new constitution of Government for the State. I learn that the Committee have completed their Labours, and the Frame of a new Constitution is ready to be submitted to the Legislative assembly which will meet in this City on the 12th day of this month. I shall not be able to see, or obtain a copy, for your information until it is presented to the Legislature, But I learn through a private confidential channel, that it is a purely republican Document, and in one of its clauses, looks to the re-establishment of the Federal Government at some future day. This is all I can learn in regard to it.

This State is divided into two great political Parties—Natives, against English, or the English & other Foreign Merchants in opposition to the Native Inhabitants of the Country, Genl [Rafael] Carrera[6] is at the head of the Native Party, & commands them in the shape of an armed force, holding under the State Government the Commission of Brigd Genl & Commander in Chief of the Army of the State. The "British Party," have in a great measure the *secret* controul of the Councils of the State, but as Genl Carrera is also a member of the Governors, or Presidents Cabinet of Councillors, he is enabled to deter them from any open action against him. The attention of the British Party is therefore now, directed to the Legislature, which is about to set. And I am informed that several English agents are here already, pretending to represent the "British Agricultural & Colonization Society," in endeavouring to obtain from the Legislature, a renewal of old grants of large tracts of Lands on the Dulce

6. Carrera (1814–1865), a mestizo, organized a revolt against the Guatemalan government in 1837. As head of the Guatemalan army, Carrera dominated the government until his death.

& other Rivers, and also new grants including the Sea Ports of the State. I enclose you a Map—No 2—Laying down two of these grants, with such other information noted thereon as I have been able to obtain.[7]

My Humble duty, is confined to obtaining and forwarding political information. I shall not therefore presume to encumber the despatch, with any reflections of my own, upon these most Extraordinary grants. The real object, in obtaining these grants, is to give to the Government of Great Britain a fit occasion, as well as a probable claim, to colonize & settle the main Ports and Rivers of the State, and for the protection of Her Colonies, She finds it eventually necessary to erect Forts, Garrison Towns and actually take Possession of the Country.

Genl Carrera is a Soldier and a Patriot but he is an illiterate man, wholly unacquainted with the "Hooks & Crooks and Convolutions Wild" of matters of State, much less, with the wiley cunning of British Diplomacy in regard to matters of this Kind.

I am informed, that 2. years ago the British Government offered to enter into a Treaty with this State, and such of the other States as chose to unite in the Treaty, for the purpose of accurately defining the limits of the Sovereignty & Jurisdiction of the parties as well as for the better regulation of commercial intercourse, &c &c[.] But, the Government of Guatemala being then at war with San Salvador, and otherwise in great confusion, the proposition was rejected, unless the British Government would first withdraw its claims to all the Territory of Guatemala, & confine itself strictly to the limits of the Belize, as marked out by the Treaty with Spain of 1783. & the Convention of 1786[8]—which the Govt of Great Britain refused to listen to; wherefore the subject was entirely abandoned.

It will be seen by the enclosed Document No 3. that as late as the 10th Novb 1841, His Excellency the Superintendant at Belize, made an effort on behalf of the British Government, to draw the State of Honduras into a Treaty with Her B. Majesty upon the subject of the limits of the Mosquito Kingdom in particular. But he has recd a masterly reproof from the authorities of Honduras, in their reply to this insidious attempt to entrap them.[9]

7. In 1834 the Guatemalan government made a land grant of fourteen million acres to the Eastern Coast of Central America Commercial and Agricultural Company of London. Another grant of one million acres was given to a British subject in Guatemala. The map is included in the RG 59 record.

8. See Francis Gardiner Davenport and Charles Oscar Paullin, eds., *Euro-* *pean Treaties Bearing on the History of the United States and Its Dependencies, 1716–1815* (4 vols., Washington, D.C., 1937), 4:159, 162.

9. Enclosure No. 3. is a copy of the newspaper *Correo Seminario del Salvador* of January 26, 1842, with correspondence between the British superintendent at Belize and Francisco Ferrer (1794–1851), the president of Honduras. The superintendent's let-

Commerce of Guatemala.

The commerce of this State, is almost exclusively carried on, by the Merchants at Belize—in connection with those of the City of Guatemala. Six or Seven Importing Houses in Belize, connected with the 5 or 6 in this City, and all in connection with Houses in London, import through Belize, about one, or one & a half millions of British manufactures annually. Some years more & some less, but an average of this amount. These goods are landed & pay duty at Belize. Whenever they are reshipped, in small vessels, drawing not more than 3 feet, (for larger vessels could not enter the mouth of the Dulce) water, to Isabel, the freight varying from 50 cents to 1$ per 1000 lbs. or 25 to 30 cts pr bbl. Thence after paying duty again, they are packed on mules to Guatemala, where the country merchants from all parts of the State resort to lay in their stocks of goods.

Payments are made partly in money & partly in Indigo, Cochinneal, Sassaparilla, Cocoa, Hides, Ox Horns &c &c[.] These are exported by the Importing Merchants, at a vast profit. Drafts or Bills of Exchange are not at all in use. If a Merchant or Citizen Farmer owes a debt, he sends the Gold or Silver to his Creditor, or it is sent for, or else he pays in these products, which constitute the principal payments made either by Farmers, or Country Merchants.

American Gold, will not pass here at all. I have, with me now upwards of 800$ in American Gold, which I brought from New York, but after I left the vessel at Belize it would not buy anything. I have had therefore to resort to private drafts, on my own personal credit, for a subsistence. Not feeling at liberty to Draw on the Department of State, when I had public money in my hands, and not knowing, but that Mrs [Lucinda Sterret] Murphy[10] may have drawn all I could of right draw for under my instructions. At Belize, the Exchange on London is from one, to two pr ct. below that at New York, or was when I was there.

In fact, the whole Interior of this State, is flooded with British fabrics, through Belize, and the Interior of San Salvador[,] Nicaragua & Honduras, is supplied from the same source through the river and Port of St Johns and the Lake Nicaragua. American manufactures have been shut out of these States, by the vigilant action of British Merchants, protected & urged on, by the British Government, guarding the transit of their goods to all these Ports, & protecting them in all their trade, with her cannon & small arms. From the Belize to the Boco del Toro, She is the Terror of the whole coast. And the officers of the State Governments attempting to exact duties of British Vessels & British goods, in the Sea

ter of November 10, 1841, proposed a boundary treaty between Honduras and the Mosquito kingdom. The Honduran reply of December 31 stated that the tribes of the coast did not constitute a nation.

10. Not otherwise identified.

Ports along this line of Coast, are incessantly complaining of the violations of their Custom House regulations, and the disregard of all their laws in relation to duties, by the British traders & captains. Violations committed with impunity, amounting to smuggling, because protection is extended to the violators by the British forces, always at Hand to offer their protection. Such complaints are universal, & so numerous that I could not recount them in the limits I must observe for this despatch.

The Port of St Johns, opening into the Lake Nicaragua, & leading into the States of San Salvador and Nicaragua, offers the finest field for the sale of American Manufactures. These States, I am informed are in a better state of improvement, the Population more compact, the soil under better cultivation, the Roads more level & transportation quicker & cheaper. There is a good waggon Road from the Port of Grenada on Lake Nicaragua, to the City of Leon, and by tracing the roads laid down on the map herewith enclosed, you will see at once, what an extensive field is here open to the enterprize of our commercial men. It is true, for want of a proper Treaty, to protect them, they may in many instances be liable to imposition & Extortion, but a Treaty can soon be made, if the Department considers it proper to do so, under the existing state of things—a state of things most likely to continue for a number of years however, & long enough at least, for England to take exclusive possession there, as well as at this place, of all the valuable trade & commerce of the country.

The Indigo, Cochinneal, Sassaparilla, Cocoa, Hides &c &c of San Salvador, Nicaragua & Honduras, a great part of which now flows through Guatemala to Belize, will with proper competition, and inducement fall into the channel of the St Johns. The information I have received here, from Merchants & Traders well acquainted with St. Johns River, its Trade & facilities of Commerce, leaves no doubt of this fact, in my mind. Indeed, I most firmly believe, that it would prove, a most singular advantage to the commerce & manufactures of the U States, if we had a Treaty of Commerce & navigation with Honduras, Nicaragua and San Salvador alone. These States, would be proud of the oportunity to enter into Treaty relations at once. And their effects, would be soon felt, to be of a most happy character. The mountain regions which separate the most productive ports of Central America from the ports on the Dulce, can never be so overcrowded, and subjected to such a ready & cheap commercial intercourse; as to enter successfully into compition with the Port of St Johns, for the commerce of the interior of these States. If I could lay down these mountains on the map, you would readily agree with me, that of all the Ports of Central America on the Atlantic, the St Johns offers to the U. States the greatest & most singular commercial advantages. And that no time ought to be lost in treating with the States of Nicaragua[,] Honduras[,] Costa Ryca & San Salvador, at least.

The additional distance by sea to this Port, is of very little moment, when we reflect, that it opens into so vast a region of fine cultivated country, and is in reality, the only key, to the Pacific ocean, which can ever effectually unlock, the vast mountain barriers, that have hitherto, seperated the commerce of the two seas.

Here, at the Port, and on the River St. Johns, and on Lake Nicaragua, the United States should at once plant their flag of commerce, and Guard it well with the provisions of a lasting Treaty with the neighbouring states; and there is no doubt, but that the result will prove of vast, nay of incalculable benifit, to the present and to future generations.

Delay to do this for a few more years, and British Commerce & British manufactures, will wear a channel too broad & too deep and run in a flood too strong, for the infant effort of our country to cross, wade in, or oppose. You will pardon me for stepping out of the strict line of my duty, but I was led away at the momment, by the interest of the subject.

You will find the map marked not only with commercial roads but also, in various places with the several productions most common, & abundantly produced in the regions so marked. This I did on the information of several gentleman who looked over the map for that purpose & pointed out those regions so marked.

They all agree in saying, that if the attention of Importing and Exporting Merchants, was turned to that quarter, in a few years the products of the greatest & most valuable part, of the interior of these States, would flow into the Channel of the St. Johns.

That the only reason why it has not been done before, is that Belize was so Handy to Havana & Jamaica and that the channel of commercial intercourse being through Belize at the first, has continued to run through that port, more from custom, and from the principal capitalists being there and in connection with the Houses in London engaged in the Central American Trade. But they also say, that they have heard many of the best informed of the Belize Merchants remark, that one day, or other, the principal Exports from Central America, will go out from the River St Johns & Lake Nicaragua.

From the tenor of my instructions I did not feel at Liberty to incur the expense of travelling to San Salvador & Nicaragua, and therefore I have sought & obtained the best information here, of those States, which was in my power to obtain. I am informed by gentlemen whose business calls them frequently to Leon & San Salvador, that the States of Nicaragua & San Salvador are decidedly more attached to, and more friendly towards the People & Government of the United States, than the State of Guatemala—That the Citizens of those states are generally better informed, & more civilized, better agriculturalists; and that the country generally is farther advanced in all the arts, in commerce & refinement. They attribute the better feeling prevalent there towards the U. States, to the fact, that, there is no British party there—That the English are generally disliked, and their Government abhored. If such is the case, and I see no reason to doubt it, does it not present a proper occasion for the United States, by a Treaty with those States; to secure to themselves a "share in the great Enterprize of uniting the Atlantic & Pacific Oceans, by a navigable Canal, or Rail Road," through the State of Nicaragua? That this Enterprize will one day or other be undertaken and accomplished, there can be no doubt. And the nation, or people, having the greatest share in it, and controul over it, will, & must, inevitably reap advantages, exclusive of all other Nations, or People, incalculable in extent, & duration. Looking to our possessions on the Pacific & the Columbia River, in connection with such a work, how vast are the consequences, that obtrude resistless, upon the mind! So far as the action of the Legislative assembly, which convenes here on the 12th Inst, may present any matter worthy of notice, I shall communicate it to the Department.

Neither timorous of responsibility on the one hand, nor courting it on the other; but anxious only to fulfil to the Letter and in the Spirit thereof all the Instructions given by the Depart, it has been a matter of anxious enquiry with me, whether I ought now to return home, or await your further instructions. The Political condition of these States seems to have been in some measure anticipated by the Department in that Clause of my instructions which, says,

"If you find the States composing the former Confederations of Central America, at war among themselves, or in a state of hopeless dissention, there will be no reason for prolonging your stay, and you will therefore return. If any Confederation exists of some but not all of those States, and this Confederation appear to possess the character of a regular & setled Government, you will give this Department full information on that subject, to the end that it may be considered, whether abandoning the former Treaty it may not be expedient, to propose to treat with such new Government."[11] I find 1st The Federal Government abolished—2nd Neither war nor dissention among the States—on the contrary peace and Harmony amongst them—Each apparently settled down into a new League or confederacy acting <independent?> on all occasions, relating to other Countries, in concert & confederacy—Each Having its seperate State Government, in full power & authority—and this State of things most likely to continue for a long period of time—I find England, through her Colonial Government, offering to enter into Treaty relations with these States in their present condition—And lastly I find the States willing & anxious to renew their Treaty relations with the U States. Applying this State of things to that clause of my instructions just quoted above, I feel it my duty to remain here, & wait the further orders of the Depart-

11. See above.

ment. If I err in this decision, it arises from an over anxiety to serve the country, & fulfil your instructions; For certainly, in consulting my own feelings & wishes alone, my Health & life, and the Happiness of my family, I should have come to a very different Conclusion.

If the Department should conclude to recal me, I pray that it may be done at a period so early, as to enable me to receive the order of recal at least by the 1st May—as after that time, the rainy seasons set in, and the rivers & streams between this and the Atlantic Seaports will prevent all intercourse, & completely hem me in, until late in September, or October following.

I dislike apoligies. I never could make a good one, But the Chills & Fevers with which I have been afflicted, every other day, ever since my recovery from the Fever, have greatly retarded my Labours, as well as injured my work. I have laboured under great disadvantages—But my health is fast improving. You will pardon, or overlook the many errors in this report. With great respect, I have the Honour to be your obt servt. W. S. Murphy Spl & Confd Agent of the U.S. &c &c

ALS. DNA, RG 59 (Despatches, Central America). Rec'd March 22, 1842. Extract published in *IAA*, 3:165–178.

The "State of the Isthmus"

FROM WILLIAM RADCLIFF

Sir   Washington. December 31st 1841

I have the honor to state to you, for the information of the President, that I have been appointed by the Government of the Isthmus, recently established, its confidential agent near that of the United States; "for the purpose of initiating the international relations which the position of both countries demands and the relations of commerce they are called on to cultivate", in proof of which appointment I beg leave to refer to the document herewith Enclosed, marked A.[1]

As a communication has already been made by the Government of the Isthmus to that of the United States; announcing its separation from New Grenada and erection into an independent State;[2] I beg to refer thereto relative to that fact and the main objects of the Government of the Isthmus; but pursuant to my instructions as its agent, I beg to submit a more special statement of the affairs of the Isthmus; the causes of its separation from N. Grenada; its organization and condition; and its aims and prospects.

1. Mariano Arosemena to Radcliff, August 24, 1841; not included in this publication.

2. Tomás Herrera to Martin Van Buren, December 5, 1840, and Arosemena to DW, July 23, 1841, DNA, RG 59 (Notes from Foreign Legations, Colombia).

In performing this duty, I have to give a sketch of certain facts and occurrences which preceded and led to the present state of affairs of the Isthmus.

Prior to the emancipation of the Spanish Colonies on this Continent, the territory of the Isthmus (then called Darien, in part) composed of the two ancient provinces of Panama and Veragua now erected into a new State, was governed by Spain separately from its other Colonies and wholly disconnected with them. In the year 1821, when other provinces and districts had already declared their independence of Spain and the Republic of Colombia had been formed under the auspices of [Simon] Bolivar,[3] the said provinces of Panama and Veragua declared their independence also; and by invitation from Bolivar united themselves voluntarily to Colombia, as a Department thereof. To that important step were they induced by the hope and expectation of long enjoying the security and advantage of composing part of a great State, well organized, and under an efficient Head; capable of maintaining their Independence of Spain, and affording all the benefits of good Government. But in a few years, violent contentions arose and prevailed throughout Colombia; caused chiefly by the disjointed situation of its component districts and want of congeniality among their inhabitants; the operation of which had been previously counteracted by the necessity of union for achieving their independence of Spain; and that great State became at length dissolved by general consent, except the consent of the Isthmus, and reorganized into three Republics, according to natural boundaries and ancient divisions, called New Grenada, Venezuela, and Ecuador.[4]

In that dissolution and reorganization, the people of the Isthmus took no part; were not consulted; gave no assent to dissolve or to reorganize;—but according to the arrangements made by other Colombians, they were assigned to become a portion or Department of New Grenada; to which State the territory of the Isthmus lies nearer, but from physical circumstances was no more connected with, than with the other two. The people of the Isthmus were compelled however to acquiesce in those arrangements, and try the experiment of a connection with N. Grenada as then constituted; but reserved the privilege of separating therefrom whenever their own welfare and happiness should require it;—hoping that the time would soon arrive when the interest of other nations would become identified with their own in requiring for them an independent existence and co-operating for its establishment.

Altho the right of separation at pleasure was perhaps not expressly reserved and admitted, it was nevertheless understood at the time by all concerned to be a just and necessary consequence of preceding and pass-

3. Bolivar (1783–1830).
4. For a general history of these events and relations with the United States, see E. Taylor Parks, *Colombia and the United States, 1765–1934* (Durham, N.C., 1935), pp. 19–194.

ing events and circumstances. The inference was afforded and the right established by the dissolution and reorganization of Colombia; when the question of secession of a part from the whole under certain circumstances was raised and discussed and settled, as between the component parts thereof, and acquiesced in by all. On that occasion, N. Grenada, the central and largest portion of Colombia and seat of Government, yeilded peaceably to the claim of the other portions of Colombia for separation, and erected itself into a separate and independent State according to admitted boundaries, under its present name. Consequently the Isthmus must have derived therefrom, exclusive of any covenants to the same effect, a similar right to separate itself from N. Grenada and become also an independent State whenever its welfare and happiness should demand it.

But even without that precedent, and the admissions implied in the conduct of all concerned, it is held by the Government of the Isthmus that a separation was perfectly justifiable at the time it took place on other grounds; viz

1st   By reason of the civil war then raging throughout the greater part of N. Grenada (still continuing) and apparently interminable without a dissolution of the State and reorganization under a different form. That war cut off the people of the Isthmus from all communication with Bogota, the seat of the Government, and with the whole State; left them isolated, unprotected, defenceless, without rule or a shadow of authority exercised over them, and obliged to resort to some substitute or suffer the evils of anarchy and confusion. In that predicament the people were driven by necessity to reassume their individual rights and create a new Government for themselves. They did so deliberately, and adopted unanimously their present form of Government. The social tie, thus broken, not through any fault of their own, but through the weakness, instability, or maladministration of the Government of New Grenada, cannot be renewed and made obligatory without the consent of both parties.

2nd   By reason of certain physical and political causes operating so injuriously to the people of the Isthmus while connected with N Grenada prior to the civil war as to preclude all the benefits derivable from good Government and all improvement of their condition in any respect. The experience of many years had proved that mortifying and distressing result. While all the world had been going rapidly ahead, the Isthmus made no advance at all; notwithstanding the great field and powerful motives for improvement there existing. This had been owing partly to the inertness and indifference or neglect of the ruling power at Bogota, and there was no prospect of change in that respect;—but it resulted also in a great measure from the peculiar geographical position of the Isthmus in reference to the main territory of New Grenada, which is of such a nature as to be worth describing.

The Isthmus is situated at the northwestern extremity or angle of South America in a corner of N Grenada, and projects therefrom westerly in a winding irregular form; about 350 miles long, and about 60 miles on an average wide, (in someplaces about 35) enlarging towards the west; bounded by the Atlantic Ocean on the north, the Pacific Ocean on the south; Central America on the West and the lofty Andes on the East which separate it from N Grenada; containing about 20,000 square miles of surface; well watered and wooded; and very fertile; sparsely populated except along the Pacific, but capable of sustaining a very large population in proportion to extent;—and comprising within its bounds the most eligible route for a navigable communication between the Atlantic and Pacific Oceans that nature has afforded between North and South America; as well as the only route now used, or capable of being used, for personal and commercial intercourse between those Oceans and the countries on different sides of this Continent; except that by way of Cape Horn.

By reason of these physical circumstances, the people of the Isthmus could have no communication with any part of New Grenada, except by water; and in order to reach Bogota the Capital and seat of Government they were obliged to embark either upon the Atlantic or Pacific, and if upon the former, (by far the best route and most used) to sail or beat up against the Trade wind to Carthagena, about 270 miles; then go by land about 60 miles to the river Magdalena; then up that river in boats about 500 miles; and then by land to Bogota about 60 or 70 miles; making in all about 900 Miles; requiring probably 50 or 60 days—or if upon the Pacific, to sail to Buena Ventura about 340 miles; and thence to go by land circuitously across two of the loftiest ridges of the Andes, almost impassable and seldom travelled, about 500 miles to Bogota, making in all about 800 Miles and requiring probably less time than the other; but still, less used.

Thus the intercourse between the Isthmus and the seat of Government was extremely difficult, tedious, and precarious; and to such a degree that a communication between the Isthmus and the United States or even Europe would have been far less so. In consequence, the Government of New Grenada could know but little of the wants, desires, and objects of the Isthmus; and took but little interest in its welfare;—neglected to legislate for its benefit;—to provide for the improvement of its local advantages, or bettering its condition in any respect; but took care to exercise the power of collecting imposts from its trade, and from the transit over it's territory. It is then evident that the Isthmus could not be well governed in connection with or as a portion of N. Grenada, but must endure intolerable evils and privations while under that misrule:—from which results also the right it has exercised of separating itself from N Grenada and becoming an independent State, even if the other grounds stated were insufficient to justify the act. Modern doctrine and practice among the new States on this Continent has confirmed the right of separation for such cause. They have frequently combined and separated, dissolved and reorganized, from mere policy or expediency, and without violence;—of which the conduct of Colombia, including N Grenada and the Isthmus, was a notable example;—and that example alone might be relied on by the Isthmus for the Justification of its conduct.

Having thus stated the various facts and reasons which, it is conceived, Justify the Isthmus in separating itself from N Grenada and erecting itself into an Independent State, I beg to observe, that a justification thereof is not offered on the ground of any obligation incurred; but merely from respect to the Government of the United States, and a desire to gain its good opinion and friendship. It was proper and necessary for the Govt of the Isthmus to judge for itself in regard to the course it should pursue relative to N Grenada; and confiding in its rectitude, to meet all the consequences, whether that course was approved by other Governments or not; but if able to convince them, and especially that of the United States, by a candid statement of facts and reasons, of the rectitude of that course, it will afford the Government of the Isthmus a high gratification[.]

With regard to the organization and condition of the Isthmus, which being made known in part by the communications referred to from the Govt thereof to this Govt, under date of the 3d and 23d July last,[5] requires but little more on my part than a repetition thereof, I have to state as follows; viz That in November 1840, an assembly of Deputies chosen by the people of Panama and Veragua declared their independence of N Grenada;—that a convention was then chosen to frame a Constitution, and administer the Government until adopted;—that a Constitution was actually adopted on the 8th of June last (a copy of which was sent to this Govt)[6] and went into operation according to its provisions;—that in pursuance thereof, His Excy Thomas Herrera[7] was appointed President, and Carlos de Ycaza,[8] Vice President of the State (stiled "The State of the Isthmus") and a Legislative Body was also chosen; who respectively entered upon the duties of their stations;—that on the 8th July the President addressed a note to the President of N Grenada,[9] stating the

5. Arosemena to DW, July 3 and 23, 1841, DNA, RG 59 (Notes from Foreign Legations, Colombia).

6. Enclosed in Arosemena to DW, July 3, 1841, DNA, RG 59 (Notes from Foreign Legations, Colombia).

7. Tomás Herrera (1804–1854), an army officer, was administrator of Panama when the province declared its independence from New Granada. When Panama rejoined New Granada in December 1841, Herrera was for a time exiled but returned as governor, 1845–1849.

8. Not identified.

9. The letter of July 8, 1841, is not included in the RG 59 record.

causes of the separation of the Isthmus from that State (a copy of which was sent to this Government) and soon after communicated to each of the Govts of G Britain, France, and the United States;—that the Isthmus had become independent and desired to interchange with them the relations of friendship and commerce;—that the Legislature of the Isthmus has been steadily occupied in enacting laws and regulations for the country providing for it's wants and developing it's resources;—that it has already turned it's attention to the means of improving the passage between the two Oceans; to the encouragement of Steam navigation to and from its opposite sides;—and to the protection and extension of commerce in general;—thus dispensing the benefits of good government to a grateful and rising people, elated with the bright prospects now dawning upon them.

Under these circumstances, the Government of the Isthmus respectfully presents itself as a candidate for admission into the community of civilized nations; to be received and treated as a member thereof according to the law of nations; and it claims that recognition with deference on the simple ground of its actual independence, and having a civil government in successful operation capable of performing the duties and fulfilling the obligations of an Independent Power.

It is of course a primary object of the Government of the Isthmus to be recognized by that of the United States in the usual manner as an Independent State;—to hold diplomatic intercourse with it, and to cultivate the relation of commerce between the two Countries. Such recognition is expected from the United States more readily than from other Governments, in consequence of their general practice towards new States on this Continent; of their proximity to the Isthmus; and of their own interest at stake upon its future condition. It is presumed there will be little or no hesitation on the subject,—upon the ground merely, as stated, of its being independent in fact, and having civil Government in successful operation, capable of performing the duties fulfilling the obligations of an independent Power.

Such was the conduct, it is believed, of the United States in regard to Texas; and such also, long before in regard to the States erected out of the Colonies of Spain, when separating therefrom and assuming independence; and in regard to the three portions of Colombia, when formed into new States, the only question was, whether each had become independent in fact, and had in operation a civil Government capable of acting its part towards other Governments? But as to Texas in particular, the example set by this Government is more striking and conclusive in favor of the recognition of the Isthmus; because the independence of Texas was denied and opposed by Mexico, and a war was then waging and still is, between the two countries on that very point. Consequently it seems to be required by common consistency and impartiality, that this Government should recognize the independence of the Isthmus under all the circumstances of the case without hesitation or delay.

As a further consideration bearing on the subject, it may be proper to advert more particularly to the physical circumstances of the Isthmus, before mentioned, and the results likely to flow therefrom. It comprehends within its bounds a route or passage between the Atlantic and Pacific Oceans; which is the only one used, or capable of being used, for personal and commercial intercourse between the countries on different sides of this Continent, except that by way of Cape Horn; and which is also capable of being improved, by the construction of a Ship Canal, so as to become the most important channel of water communication on Earth;—the greatest thoroughfare for trade and intercourse among mankind. The control of such a route is perhaps one of the highest prerogatives that a nation or Government can enjoy, and it may be exercised with immense effect on the interests of other nations, either for good or for evil. The Government of the Isthmus, having the sole control of that route, is naturally desirous of improving it's advantages for the benefit of it's citizens as far as reason and equity would allow, but is willing to limit the exercize of it's control within proper bounds by treaty stipulations, if other nations would undertake the contemplated improvements for the use and benefit of the World. It desires also to make treaty arrangements with other Governments, whereby the State of the Isthmus shall be considered as always a neutral territory; exempt from compromittal in the wars of other Countries, and as a place of peace and security for all the inhabitants of the Globe who shall wish to pass over it, or send across it their property. This desirable end may probably be secured if proper measures be taken in due time on the part of the United States; and it much behooves this and other Governments to have it well attended to.

Independent of this general arrangement for future benefit in conjunction with others, it would be an object of importance for this Government to secure by treaty stipulations, as soon as may be in its power, the right of way or passage across the Isthmus, in the present or any other state of the passage, on reasonable terms; for the purposes of trade and intercourse with the countries beyond it; and especially with our own territory on the Pacific, the Oregon Territory. The importance of having a communication therewith by way of the Isthmus is daily increasing and demands early attention. And in connection with that object, it would be important too, to secure proper privileges for Steam navigation by citizens of the United States, to and from each side of the Isthmus, and for the transit of public mails across it; similar to what the British have recently done. They have, by an agent of the Royal Mail Steam-packet Company, applied to the new Government of the Isthmus and obtained all the privileges and advantages that could reasonably be asked for the benefit of their Steamers employed on both Oceans and entering their ports on each side, and for the transit of mails, passengers and effects across the Isthmus. The same are equally desirable to the United States, and could no doubt be obtained by using the proper means.

There are other considerations of some weight bearing on the subject, which may be reserved for verbal explanations or future communications. Suffice it only to add; that in the present situation of the Isthmus other Governments may attempt to gain important advantages for themselves, inconsistent [with] the interest of the United States; which requires early attention and counteraction;—or that some powerful Government, or great company or association of individuals, may separately obtain the privilege of constructing a Ship Canal across the Isthmus for their own benefit with the right of control thereof, ever after, or for a long period of years;—which would be incompatible with the interests of the United States and other countries, and requires also to be anticipated and counteracted.

Having stated, very imperfectly, all I deem necessary or useful, in my capacity as agent for the Government of the Isthmus for the consideration of the President of the United States, I have only to express my hopes of its leading to some beneficial results for both the Countries concerned. I have the honor to be Sir—with the highest respect and esteem Yr obt. H. Sevt.   Wm Radcliff

ALS. DNA, RG 59 (Notes from Misc. Foreign States, Panama). Published in *IAA*, 5:574–581. Radcliff, of New York, was U.S. consul and acting chargé d'affaires at Lima, Peru, 1827–1829. He had promoted the idea of an isthmian canal as early as 1826. In a pamphlet entitled *Considerations on . . . a Ship-Canal across the Isthmus . . .* (Washington, D.C., 1836), he called for the construction of an interoceanic canal, and when the provinces of Panama and Veragua declared their independence from the state of New Granada in November 1840 as the State of the Isthmus, Radcliff became their agent in the United States.

TO WILLIAM RADCLIFF

Department of State

Sir: Washington, 28th January, 1842.

Your interesting communication of the 31st of December, last,[1] setting forth the causes which have led the States of Panama and Veragua to declare their independence of the Republic of New Granada and to form for themselves a separate government under the title "of the State of the Isthmus," was laid before the President, who has directed me to acquaint you in reply, that it has been read with the respectful consideration due to the source from which it emanated and with a just sensibility in regard to the invitation which it offers. But although the President does not

1. See above.

doubt that the facts mentioned in it are substantially correct, the short-ness of the time which has elapsed since the declaration of independence referred to was made, the duty of this government to avoid doing any thing which might give just cause of offence to the Republic of New Granada, with which it has hitherto maintained pacific and friendly re-lations, and that wise yet generous caution which have heretofore marked its steps in similar cases, all admonish that there is no occasion in this instance to deviate from the usual course by acknowledging the State of the Isthmus upon information less authentic and satisfactory than in other cases. Measures will consequently be taken without delay to in-quire as to the ability of the States of Panama and Veragua to maintain their independence under their new form of government and to assume the obligations and discharge the duties of an independent power. If the result of such inquiry should be favorable, the application which has been made through you will, it is presumed, be disposed of accordingly. The document which accompanied your note is now returned, a copy of it having been taken. I have the honor to be, Sir, Your obedient Servant,

Daniel Webster

LC. DNA, RG 59 (Instructions, Special Missions). Published in *IAA*, 5:352–353.

FROM WILLIAM RADCLIFF

Sir   Washington February 19th 1842
I had the honor to state to you on the 12th instant,[1] that I had just received a letter from the Secretary of State of the Isthmus [Mariano Arosemena], dated the 6th of last month, by an arrival from Chagre[s] at New York; setting forth that an arrangement by treaty had been en-tered into, on the 31st of December last, between the Isthmus and New Grenada, at the instance of the latter; whereby their connection with each other was to be renewed on terms specified in the accompanying dispatches sent me by the same conveyance; to which I was referred for minute information respecting the same and other matters; but which dispatches had not yet come to my hands, tho daily expected.

Having waited this long for those dispatches, in vain; and caused in-quiry to be made at New York of the owner, master, and passengers of the vessel, by which the letter was brought, without learning what had become of the packet of dispatches for me; except it's having been com-mitted, together with some newspapers, to the care of a passenger who left the vessel at Carthagena and may have retained them all through mistake; I deem it my duty to state without more delay the cause of my not explaining the late acts of the Isthmus, as due to this Government

1. Radcliff to DW, February 12,   Misc. Foreign States, Panama).
1842, DNA, RG 59 (Notes from

on the occasion;—being precluded by the want of information;—and to suggest however the probable cause of the late arrangement between the Isthmus and New Grenada, whatever it's terms and conditions may be, together with it's future bearings.

The civil war which has raged in New Grenada for a year or two past had it's origin in a former essential difference of opinion among it's leading citizens respecting the form of their Government;—some preferring a federal Government, like that of the United States; and others a consolidated Government, like that adopted by Mexico, when a similar difference of opinion prevailed. When the Constitution of Colombia was framed by the Convention elected for the purpose, the consolidated form was after a long and warm debate preferred and adopted; but it continued in force only about ten years, when Colombia became dissolved, and reorganized into three States, New Grenada, Venezuela, and Ecuador. Each of those States then adopted the same consolidated form; but not without much discordance of opinion; especially in New Grenada, whose extensive territory, disjointed Departments, and difficult inter communications seemed to require the federal form of Government; and that more strongly in regard to the Isthmus, on account of its peculiar situation. The consequence to New Grenada has been, that after a feeble and unsuccessful administration of [the] Government for some years, owing partly to its form, and partly to other causes, the body of the people became extremely discontented and a general insubordination prevailed. Partial insurrections first broke out, and finally a general civil war took place upon the ground, as professed generally, of a change being indispensably necessary from the consolidated to a federal form of Government. In that plan the people of the Isthmus fully concurred, and that with more reason than any other Department, on account of their peculiar geographical position, their want of intercourse with the seat of Government and State at large, and the consequent misrule under which they had long laboured. But the result of the war has not been in favor of any change in the form of Government, as far as yet known, especially in reference to the Isthmus; unless by the late arrangement a new system, similar to that of a federal form, or some exceptions in favor of the Isthmus, should have been agreed to. It is quite probable that the Government of New Grenada, from its sending Commissioners to the Isthmus for the purpose of bringing about a reunion, has made concessions and consented to the leading objects of the Isthmus. That however is only presumed; but will soon be known and then be communicated; supposing it still desirable for this Government to be kept informed of whatever transpires in future respecting the Isthmus.

While thus submitting the explanations I concieve due from me as agent for the Isthmus, it strikes me as not improper, and perhaps not quite useless, to avail myself of the occasion respectfully to present for the consideration of the President, some ideas and views of my own, as a citizen of the United States, relative to the Isthmus as affecting this country and others; and [I] hope to be excused for the liberty I take on the ground of attachment to the interests of my own Country.

It appears to my mind very evident and certain, that a free, safe, and convenient passage across the Isthmus from one ocean to the other, both for public and individual purposes, is of great importance to the Government and citizens of the United States, and is destined rapidly to grow; and become ere long of infinitely higher importance to this country and many others. Consequently it must comport with the duty of our Government to consider well all that relates to the right and utility of such a passage; and to anticipate by early attention and action the views and objects that may be promoted or affected by it. The territory through which it extends being under foreign dominion subjects it's use of course to the rulers thereof; and whether it be the Government of New Grenada, or the local Government of the Isthmus, the privilege of using it must be obtained from one or the other with it's own consent. Hitherto it has been subject to the mere will and pleasure of Spain for centuries until the year 1821; and subsequently of Colombia, and New Grenada, successively. No treaty stipulations have ever been made respecting it. Hereafter it will be subject either to New Granada or to the local Government of the Isthmus; depending on the terms of their late reunion; and its use upon any terms will depend on the future will and pleasure, or caprice, or cupidity of one of them, unless otherwise regulated by some treaty stipulations they may be induced to enter into. It is therefore an object of importance to acquire through negotiation the right or privilege desired, and secure by treaty as permanently as possible that which is now dispensed as a favor, revocable at pleasure. The right or privilege wanted is that of entering and using the ports of the Isthmus with our vessels and cargoes for the purposes of trade there or beyond with other countries; and of using the Isthmus as a highway or passage from one ocean to the other for the purposes of intercourse personal and commercial with other countries on each side the Continent; free and clear from all restrictions and impositions whatever except the necessary charges of transportation; together with the permission of improving at our own expense the passage or mode of crossing the Isthmus to some extent or other whenever convenient. The benefits resulting to our Government therefrom would be, a free, safe and easy communication, subject to no interruption whatever, with it's Ministers and Agents residing in the Countries along the western side of America; and also with it's important territory of Oregon; and also with it's squadron usually employed in the Pacific for the protection of our commerce; all which would become vastly more important when steam communication with the Pacific shall be established as now contemplated:—and the benefits resulting therefrom to the Citizens of the United States in general would be a free, safe, rapid, & uninterrupted intercourse, personal and commercial, with all the countries bordering on the Pacific and numerous islands therein, and eastern Asia also; together with a large augmentation of the exchanges usually effected with them, and a considerable advance on the profits of whaling business;—all which would be much more enhanced also by the introduction of Steam navigation to and from the Isthmus on each side, and a proper passage across. These are indeed highly important objects to the United States at large, and will no doubt engage the attention of the General Government without delay.

But I beg leave to refer also very briefly to another object of yet higher importance, which may result in time from the course of measures indicated, or be simultaneously promoted in some degree by corresponding steps. I allude to the grand and unequalled object of opening a navigable communication for Ships of the largest size between the Atlantic and Pacific Oceans through the Isthmus, at or near the present route of crossing it, or wherever else a better route may be found. The attainment of this end is undoubtedly within the scope of reasonable human exertions;—far within it's value, and perhaps trifling in proportion to the benefits it would afford the world at large. But it is of a nature so generally beneficent, and diffuse in its consequences;—so interesting to many different nations, and inviting to a concert of action; that it ought upon every ground of expedience, policy, and equity, to be undertaken and accomplished through the united means and exertions of different nations and appropriated for the use and benefit of the world at large on reasonable terms.

Believing this idea to be entertained and cherished by the leading minds of the world at the present day, and to be gaining on the public mind of this country, including the most distinguished and influential, I beg leave to say, respectfully and with deference, that the period has arrived for our Government to take the subject into serious consideration; and [take] the lead in initiating the measures preliminary to the undertaking.

Some of these measures would be;—to negotiate with the Government controlling the Isthmus for the privilege of constructing the work, and with other Governments respecting a co-operation;—to ascertain by means of scientific examinations the best route for the work, and probable cost thereof;—and to treat with all concerned in the results, for the guaranty of the Independence of the Isthmus as a separate State, and of its permanent neutrality, in case the work be accomplished. I have the honor to be Sir with the highest respect & esteem Your Obedient Servant
Wm Radcliff

ALS. DNA, RG 59 (Notes from Misc. Foreign States, Panama). Published in *IAA*, 5:583–587.

Interoceanic Communications

DANIEL FLETCHER WEBSTER TO WILLIAM MATTHEWS BLACKFORD

No. 2.   Department of State,
Sir: Washington, 20th May, 1842.

You have received your commission as Chargé d'Affaires of the United States to the Republic of New Granada.[1] I now transmit the following papers which will be useful or necessary in the transaction of the business of your mission.[2]

1. A sealed letter accrediting you to the Minister for Foreign Affairs of New Granada and an open copy of the same.

2. A full power, authorizing you to negotiate and conclude a treaty of commerce and navigation with that Republic.

3. A special passport.

4. Printed personal instructions and the supplement thereto with which you will make yourself familiar and will strictly observe.

5. A list of the diplomatic agents and Consuls of the United States abroad.

6. A copy of the principal letters of instruction which have from time to time been addressed by this department to your predecessor [James Semple].

His despatches to the department and his correspondence with the Minister for Foreign Affairs of that Republic[3] with which the records and files of the Legation will, it is presumed, enable you to acquaint yourself, will show the pending business of the mission. This may be described in general terms as of a threefold character. 1. The commercial relations between the two countries.[4] 2. The unadjusted claims of our citizens upon the late Republic of Colombia. 3. Similar claims upon the Government of New Granada.[5]

The anarchy and civil war which had until very recently prevailed for some time in that country, interrupted Mr Semple's negotiations upon these subjects. There is reason to believe, however, that order and quiet are restored there and it is hoped that they may be permanent enough to

1. No. 1. DW to Blackford, February 16, 1842, DNA, RG 59 (Instructions, Colombia).

2. The enclosures are not in the RG 59 record.

3. There were a number of foreign ministers during this turbulent period in Colombian history. The bulk of Semple's correspondence took place with Pedro Alacantara Herran (1804–1872), Miguel Chiari, and Mariano Ospina (1806–1875), who took of-

fice in 1838, 1840, and 1842, respectively.

4. The commercial treaty of 1824 between the United States and Colombia expired in 1837. Semple proposed a new treaty to the Colombian government, but no agreement was settled when he left the country.

5. On American claims against Colombia and New Granada, see the headnote "South America," above, pp. 301–304.

allow you to attend continuously to the affairs which have now devolved upon you, and to prosecute them to a successful result. Still, it is apprehended that an auspicious period for negotiating upon the subject of our commerce with that country may not present itself at least immediately upon your arrival at Bogotá. The full power, therefore, with which you are provided, it is intended you shall use only when a favorable conjuncture for that purpose may arise, and when the Department shall be in possession of sufficient information to form an opinion as to the terms which it may be expedient to offer that government. Consequently, you will communicate the best intelligence which may be within your reach respecting the disposition of the Government of New Granada on this point, and any facts which may tend to show the propriety of modifying the terms which your predecessors were authorized to offer. Such further instructions as may then be thought necessary will be transmitted to you.

The projects for facilitating the communication between the Atlantic and Pacific oceans by means of a canal or railroad across the Isthmus of Panama, are connected with this topic. The states of Panama and Veragua, which comprise that Isthmus, were for some time separated from the other States of New Granada, and in the course of last year applied to this Government to be acknowledged as an independent power with the title of the State of the Isthmus.[6] The application, though not granted, was respectfully received and considered, and a special agent on the part of this government was about to proceed to that quarter for the purpose of inquiring into the ability of the people of the Isthmus to maintain their independence,[7] when intelligence arrived that Panama and Veragua had reünited themselves to New Granada.[8] A treaty of commerce with this Republic, placing our citizens on a footing of equality with other foreigners within its confines, might serve to prevent a grant by the New Granadian Government to any other foreign government, company or individuals of a special privilege in regard to the communication above referred to or, if such privilege should be accorded, might give us a right to claim the same, or indemnification if it should be refused. It is of great importance to the United States that the rail-road or canal referred to should be constructed, and that we should have the free use of it upon the same terms as the citizens or subjects of other commercial nations.

6. See above, Radcliff to DW, December 31, 1841.

7. See DW to Joseph Holt Ingraham, February 11, 1842, DNA, RG 59 (Domestic Letters). Ingraham (1809–1860) was a teacher and a prolific author of popular literature. Ingraham said he attended Bowdoin College, but the school records do not substantiate that claim. Writing to DW on June 15, 1841, Ingraham requested some connection with a foreign service post (DNA, RG 59, Letters of Application and Recommendation, 1837–1845), but his mission was canceled when New Granada and the State of the Isthmus reunited in December 1841.

8. See above.

You will consequently be diligent in your inquiries in relation to this matter.

The causes alluded to above as having constrained Mr Semple to suspend the prosecution of the claims, will, it is presumed, by no means have increased the disposition of that government to recognize and pay them. You will nevertheless avail yourself of the first proper opportunity to apprize the Minister for Foreign Affairs that it is far from the intention of this government to abandon these claims, that we have every reason to expect their speedy recognition, at least, and that any indulgence in regard to their payment to which a consideration of the circumstances of that country might otherwise lead, will not be deemed obligatory upon the United States if New Granada shall persist in refusing to acknowledge the debts. The case of the Brig Morris, especially, is one that ought to be promptly settled. You will have a copy made of the protest and such other of the papers in this case as may be necessary to substantiate it, and transmit the same to Mr Allen A Hall, the Chargé d'Affaires of the United States at Caracas, in order that he may, pursuant to instructions from this Department, demand of the Government of Venezuela, its share of the reparation due.[9]

Agreeably to a general rule, the salary of a diplomatic agent begins with the date of his commission, provided he sets out for his post within a month from that date or assigns satisfactory reasons for further delay. Your salary accordingly began on the tenth of February, last, and will cease when you take leave of the Minister for Foreign Affairs of New Granada to return home. For your salary as it may become due and for the contingent expenses of the Legation, which must not exceed eight hundred dollars a year without special authority, you will draw on this Department.

If Mr Semple should have left Bogotá when you reach there, you will probably find the archives of the Legation in the possession of Mr [Joseph] Gooding,[10] a citizen of the United States residing in that capital, with whom Mr Semple was directed, in that event, to lodge them. I am, Sir, your obedient servant,   Fletcher Webster, Acting Secretary

LC. DNA, RG 59 (Instructions, Colombia). Extract published in *IAA*, 5:353–355. Blackford (1801–1864), of Virginia, was trained in the law but became editor and publisher of the Fredericksburg, Virginia, *Political Arena*. After serving as chargé d'affaires in Colombia from 1842 to 1844, he returned to the United States and became associated with the Lynchburg *Virginian*. During the Civil War Blackford was a financial agent for the Confederacy.

9. See above, DW to Hall, July 1, 1841, "South America: Venezuela," pp. 308–310.

10. The Gooding family had been in Colombia since about 1829. In 1855 Joseph Gooding received concessions for construction of a road and canal across the isthmus.

FROM HIRAM KETCHUM

Dear Sir: New York, Decr 10th 1842
    A young gentleman by the name of *Mat[t]hias [Oliver] Davidson*,[1] an
Engineer, is about visiting Havana for the benefit of his health. He is a
brother of the late Lucritia Davidson a young poetess who died at an early
age, and whose poetical effusions have been collected by Washington
Irving, who has accompanied their publication with a biography of Miss
Davidson.[2] Mr Davidson has been employed as an Engineer on the Croton Water Works, also on the Erie & Long Island Rail Roads, and pro-
duces favorable testimonials from those under whom he has served;
copies of these testimonials [I] have before me, and they are at your service if required; Mr Davidson, while at the South, wishes to take advantage of any professional advantage that may fall in his way, and he has
a great desire to explore the line of the Ship Canal between the Atlantic
and Pacific Ocean. In order to aid him in this enterprise, he desires some
sort of sanction from your department; [he] does not seek employment
from the Government for which he expects compensation, but he would
like to have authority, or a request from the State Department to make
enquiries in respect [to] this enterprize. I suppose a letter from you addressed to him, requesting him, if convenient, to make such enquiries,
and communicate the results of them to you, would be what he desires. If
you would forward me such a letter for him, I would be obliged. Enclosed
is the letter from his brother,[3] a young member of the bar here, which
makes known more fully, than I have explained, the object of Mr Davidson[.] Yours most respectfully

                                                            Hiram Ketchum

ALS. DNA, RG 59 (Misc. Letters).

TO MATTHIAS OLIVER DAVIDSON
                                            Department of State
Sir,   Washington 14th December, 1842
    It has been intimated to this Department that you are about to proceed
to South America, that you have a desire to gratify your curiosity in re-

1. Davidson (1819–1871).

2. Lucretia Maria Davidson (1808–
1825) was a well-known child poet.
Ketchum, however, confuses a collection of the poems of Lucretia M.
Davidson, made by her mother, with
a collection of the poems of Lucretia's
sister, Margaret Miller Davidson
(1823–1838), gathered by Irving. See
[Lucretia M. Davidson], *Poetical Re-

*mains of the Late Lucretia Maria Da-
vidson* (Philadelphia, 1841), and
Washington Irving, *Biography and
Poetical Remains of the Late Margaret Miller Davidson* (Philadelphia,
1841).

3. Morris Miller Davidson (1810–
1854) to Ketchum, December 5,
1842; not included in this publication.

gard to the practicability of a ship canal across the Isthmus of Darien, and that it might be agreeable to you to have some facilities of a public character and to know whether the results of any examinations which you might make would be acceptable to the Department. I accordingly transmit for your use an open Circular letter[1] addressed to the Diplomatic agents and Consuls of the United States in that quarter, and a carrier's passport, and have to state that any information which you may gather in regard to the object above referred to would be thankfully received by the department, but that as no pecuniary provision having reference to it has been made by Congress, the department cannot make you any pecuniary compensation. I am &c   Danl Webster

LC. DNA, RG 59 (Domestic Letters).

Cuba

FROM AARON VAIL
No. 53.
Confidential   Legation of the United States
Sir.   Madrid 30th November 1841.

Some alarm has spread itself in the Spanish West India Islands by the announcement of pending british intervention in bringing about the sudden emancipation of a large portion of the slave population of those Islands.[1] The same announcement, re-produced by the public periodical press of Europe,[2] is beginning to occupy a considerable share of public attention; and this Government, though not laboring under positive fears, has not been without bestowing serious reflections on the subject. I was, a few days ago, invited by the Minister of Foreign Affairs,[3] to an interview on our relations, generally, with the Island of Cuba, which I found, however, to have for its special object the discussion of that portion of said relations which connects itself more particularly with the territorial nationality of the Colony. Mr. Gonzalez began by alluding to the alarm above referred to which he understood from communications recently received had found an echo in the southern portions of the United States. Presuming from this that we would not see without solicitude any pros-

---

1. The circular is not in the RG 59 record.

1. Rumors of British intervention in freeing Cuban slaves arose from a proposal made in December 1840 by Sir Arthur Ingram Aston (1798–1859), the British minister in Madrid, to investigate cases of blacks brought to Cuba after the supposed elimination of the slave trade in 1820. *British and Foreign State Papers, 1841–*

1842 (116 vols., London, 1812–1925), 30:762.

2. See, e.g., the discussion of Aston's proposal in the *British and Foreign Anti-Slavery Reporter*, October 20, 1841.

3. The foreign minister and head of the Spanish government from May 21, 1841, to June 17, 1842, was Antonio González y González (1792–1870).

pect of such an intervention as that which appeared to be apprehended, he inquired whether I could inform him of the views of my Government in that respect.

Our views regarding the Island of Cuba ought not to be a secret to this Government; for they have frequently been communicated to persons at the head of it; and, even since my arrival here, I have had occasion to lay before the last ministry[4] those views as set forth in my instructions.[5] But as those communications were necessarily confidential, and, in all cases, I believe, made verbally, every change of ministry calls for a repetition of them; and hence the occasion again presented for laying them before the Minister, having found out that he was utterly ignorant of them.

I explained to him the importance of our connexion with the Island; first in a commercial point of view, as involving interests of the greatest magnitude, especially with the prospect we are unwilling to abandon of ultimately seeing our intercourse placed upon a more liberal footing than the present. 2nd As connected with the geographical position of the Island, and our aversion to the establishment, so near our shores and in seas so frequented by our trade, of a private naval and military power; and, lastly, with reference to the existence of similar domestic institutions in the Island and the contiguous parts of our territory, and the danger to those institutions of the doctrines professed on the subject and sought to be enforced by Great Britain. As that part of my instructions which relates to the matter had been drawn up with the specific object of such communications I thought I could do no better than draw at the fountain head; and consequently read the entire paragraph to Mr Gonzalez. With its contents he expressed himself highly gratified; but particularly with the closing declaration of our determination in the event of any attempt to wrest from Spain the territorial possession of the Colony.

I called his particular attention to the views of the American Cabinet as to the means Spain[,] herself, possessed of averting the danger, or, at least, of doing away every pretext for it, by a scrupulous fulfilment of her engagements to Great Britain, whether arising from pecuniary liabilities or from her Treaty obligations for the suppression of the African slave trade.[6] Mr Gonzalez answered that not a shadow of any such pretext at present existed, either in reality or in the imagination of the British Gov-

4. The government between September 1840 and May 1841 was headed by Baldomero Espareto, the duke of Vitoria (1792–1870). The foreign minister was Joaquín María Ferrer y Cafranga (1777–1861).

5. John Forsyth to Vail, July 15, 1840, DNA, RG 59 (Instructions, Special Missions).

6. The Spanish government borrowed heavily from British, Dutch, and French bankers after the Napoleonic Wars. Spain agreed in treaties signed September 17, 1817, and June 28, 1835, to abolish the slave trade. See British and Foreign State Papers, 1816–1817 (London, 1838), 4:33–42; British and Foreign State Papers, 1834–1835 (London, 1852), 23:343–374.

ernment. That with reference to the first class of liabilities, the only demands recently urged by Great Britain had been satisfied by the payment
to her, on account of the debt for war subsidies, of the sum of sixty thousand pounds sterling which was to have been passed to the credit of Spain
as the price of certain Islands on the coast of Africa, had the cession of
those Islands been consummated; and that, for the balance of that debt,
which is still very large, England was not now disposed to press its settlement. With regard to the fulfilment of the Treaty obligations for the suppression of the African slave trade, the British Government had been
satisfied on that head also by assurances given to it of the determination
of Spain to carry out the purposes of the Treaty by all means within the
reach of Government, to which effect strict orders had been given to the
Colonial authorities to use all possible means of repression; and to remove the pretext for the introduction of African slaves by the adoption of
all measures calculated to foster the natural increase and the preservation of the native slave population. Independently of these motives for
allaying all fears that might arise from supposed designs of Great Britain
Spain had confidence in her own means of preserving her colonial possessions. Cuba possesses vast military and respectable naval resources:
the population is partial to, and content under, Spanish domination, is,
withal, susceptible of efficient military organization for many purposes of
defence, and animated by a spirit of loyalty that might be depended on.

The immediate cause of the apprehension prevailing in the colonies
grows out of the belief entertained there that England had actually demanded of Spain the immediate emancipation of all the blacks who have
been introduced in the Islands since the Treaties for the suppression of
of the slave trade have been in operation. With all the evidences before
the world of the boldness of British policy in the matter, I thought it difficult to credit the report; but to obviate all doubts, and believing that the
information would not be uninteresting at Washington, I took advantage
of a more recent interview with Mr Gonzalez to ascertain how much truth
there might be in the rumor. Mr Gonzalez answered me, confidentially,
that, of the secret wishes of Great Britain he could not undertake to
speak; but that what had probably given rise to the report of her alleged
demand was the fact of an application having, within the year, actually
been put in by the British Minister at this Court for a return to be prepared by the authorities of Cuba, of the number of blacks now existing in
the Island, who had been introduced since the conclusion of the Treaties
for the suppression of the African slave trade. He added that orders had
been given by the last ministry for the preparation of such returns; but he
wound up by an emphatic and energetic declaration that such returns
should never be furnished to Great Britain. That, the present Government
were willing that the Treaties referred to should receive a full and bona
fide execution, and had taken efficient measures for the entire cessation

of the importation of African slaves; but that, as they considered that the British right under the Treaty to interfere in the matter had ceased with the landing of the slaves and could not follow them within the limits of spanish jurisdiction, the Government had determined to withhold the information requested by the British Minister—a proceeding sufficiently indicative of the spirit in which Spain would be prepared to receive such a proposition as that the supposition of which has excited the fears of the Spanish Colonists. Mr Gonzalez took the occasion of some allusion to the mischief caused by the intemperate zeal of British Abolitionists to say that the late change in the administration of Government in England[7] had brought about a material alteration in the policy hitherto pursued by that country in relation to slavery in the Spanish dominions. He had received late evidences of the existence, of a more moderate and conciliatory spirit in answers, specifically, from Lord Aberdeen to complaints of the conduct of the British Consul at Havana,[8] who had been compelled to abandon the very objectionable course before pursued by him; and also in assurances that the imperious tone assumed by that, and other British Agents and countenanced or overlooked by the late administration in Great Britain, would, in no case, be tolerated by the existing Ministry. I have the honor, Sir, to be with great respect, Your Obt. Servant   A. Vail

ALS. DNA, RG 59 (Despatches, Spain). Rec'd February 18, 1841. Published in *IAA*, 11:326.

FROM JOHN TYLER, WITH ENCLOSURE

Dr Sir;   Dec. 16. 1841

The enclosed letter[1] claims attention. Has our new consul [Robert Blair Campbell] yet gone to Cuba—if not he ought to be ordered forthwith to repair to his post—with special instructions to report from time to time the condition of things. Truly Yrs   J. Tyler

ALS. DNA, RG 59 (Consular Despatches, Havana). Enclosed in William Butler to John Tyler, December 15, 1841.

ENCLOSURE: WADDY THOMPSON TO WILLIAM BUTLER

My Dear Sir,   Marion Alabama Nov. 24. 1841

On my way to this place I met with (on the stage) a very intelligent

7. Prime Minister Melbourne resigned in August 1841, and Sir Robert Peel formed a new government the following month.

8. David Turnbull, a dedicated abolitionist, became British consul at Havana in November 1840. Spanish officials repeatedly requested his recall, but the British government refused to comply. See *British and Foreign State Papers, 1841–1842*, 30: 762–876.

1. See below.

and accomplished spaniard who was on his way to Cuba—charged with a most important commission—important to Cuba and not less so to the slave holding states. He communicated to me the object of his mission and exhibited to me the evidences of it. His name was Miguel De Sylve.[1] The spanish Government have received the most satisfactory evidence that there is a deeply laid scheme of insurrection in Cuba—stimulated and fomented by the Brittish Government through the agency of the Brittish Consul [David Turnbull] and emissaries from Jamaica. This gentleman is charged with the suppression of it. I saw his papers & authority. He informs me that the French Government which is in close alliance with one of the parties in spain is hostile to the movement and has ordered a portion of her navy to that region to watch these movements and give aid if need be. I have long been satisfied that Great Brittain is anxious to extirpate slavery in the West Indies and everywhere else—not from motives of philanthropy but from others purely commercial[.] She has lost her market for her manufactures on the continent of Europe & is loosing it on this. Her last recourse for the maintenance of her purely artificial & factitious [indus]trial system is to build up in the West Indies both a market for her manufactures and the supply of her raw materials. The first step towards this is to crush slave labor—The great rival in the production of the latter. I can think of no movement more vitally interesting to us of the south—Little less so indeed than to the people of Cuba—for if this movement succeeds with our immediate neighborhood of Cuba & immense commerce with that Island it would be in vain to attempt to keep out the contagion. If you think proper you can communicate the contents of this to the President & to Mr Webster—which step or whether any should be taken I do not pretend to indicate but it may be well that they should know what is going on. The information which has reached the spanish Government may not be true—but you may be assured that it is so regarded by them and that the gentleman whom I met Senor De Sylve is charged with the commission I have mentioned.

I will write to you from Mobile on other matters. Please hand the enclosed to Mr. Clagget[.][2] Yrs truly   W Thompson

ALS. DNA, RG 59 (Consular Despatches, Havana). Enclosed in William Butler to John Tyler, December 15, 1841. Thompson (1798–1868; South Carolina College 1814), who served in the U.S. House of Representatives from 1835 to 1841, was a strong opponent of antislavery petitions and an advocate of the recognition and annexation of Texas. In 1842 he was appointed minister to Mexico, where he served until 1844. Butler (1790–1850; South Carolina College 1810), formerly a naval surgeon, was a Whig representative in Congress, 1841–1843.

1. Not identified.   2. Not identified.

TO ROBERT BLAIR CAMPBELL

Private and Confidential.   Department of State,
Sir: Washington, 14th Jany, 1843.

A communication, from a highly respectable source has just been received at this Department, which purports to contain information of so serious a nature, in regard to the present condition of the Island of Cuba, that the President has come to the conclusion that it is expedient to lose no time in ascertaining, if practicable, how far the real facts of the case may correspond with the representations. The name of the individual from whom these accounts have come, is, for good reasons, withheld.[1] It is sufficient to say that they come from the Island, and have been transmitted from thence by a person of high standing, whose statements, as we are told by those who know the source, are believed to be entitled to as much consideration as those of any individual in Cuba. Acting under this belief, and influenced by the consideration that this Government has frequently received intimations from various quarters in regard to Cuba, which give a color of probability to the statements which have thus been recently received, the President has instructed me to make this communication to you, to call your attention to the matter, and to desire you to transmit all the information you possess or can obtain in regard to it.

The necessity of absolute secrecy in every thing that relates to the inquiries you are directed to make, and in the transmission of their result to your Government, has obliged us to send to Havana a special messenger,[2] who will take charge of and deliver to you in person this letter, and who will be directed to remain with you for some short time to afford you opportunity to prepare a reply, and to impart all the intelligence which may be within your reach. It is proper, however, to apprize you that it is highly desirable that there should be as little detention as possible, as the President is exceedingly anxious to be well informed upon the subject at the earliest practicable moment. The messenger is unacquainted with the contents of this letter; and it is not necessary or desirable that the subject of this correspondence should be in any way made known to him. The amount of the information which has been received is this:

The writer represents himself as bound in honor not to reveal what he has made known to his correspondent in the United States to the local authorities of Cuba for reasons which can only be guessed at. His state-

---

1. Domingo del Monte (1804–1853) was a Cuban planter and writer. See Philip S. Foner, *A History of Cuba and Its Relations with the United States* (2 vols., New York, 1962), 1:208–209, 224–225.

2. Thomas Cookendorfer, not otherwise identified. DW to Cookendorfer, January 14, 1843, DNA, RG 59 (Instructions, Special Missions).

ments, confirmed as they appear to be in some particulars by various recent occurrences of a public character, with which you cannot but be familiar, are considered as entitled at least to serious attention, and to call for immediate examination and inquiry.

It is represented that the situation of Cuba is at this moment in the highest degree dangerous and critical, and that Great Britain has resolved upon its ruin; that Spain does not, or will not, see this intention, and that the authorities of the Island are utterly incompetent to meet the crisis; that although according to the treaty of 1817, the slave trade ought not to have been carried on by any subject of Spain, it has, nevertheless, been continued in full vigor up to the year 1841, notwithstanding the incessant remonstrances of the British Government, which was better informed, it is said, from month to month, of every thing that took place in the Island, than the Captain General[3] himself.

It is alleged, that the British Ministry and Abolition Societies finding themselves foiled or eluded by the Colonial and the home Governments have, therefore resolved,—not, perhaps, without secretly congratulating themselves upon the obstinacy of Spain, upon accomplishing their object in a different method, by the total and immediate ruin of the Island. Their agents are said to be now there, in great numbers, offering independence to the Creoles, on condition that they will unite with the colored people in effecting a general emancipation of the slaves, and in converting the Government into a *black Military Republic*, under British protection. The British Abolitionists reckon on the naval force of their Government stationed at Jamaica, and elsewhere; and are said to have offered two large steam ships of war, and to have proposed to the Venezuelian General, [Santiago] Marino,[4] who resides at Kingston, Jamaica, to take the command of an invading army. This is to be seconded, as is suggested, by an insurrection of the slaves and free men of color, supported by the white Creoles. If this scheme should succeed, the influence of Britain in this quarter, it is remarked, will be unlimited. With 600,000 blacks in Cuba, and 800,000 in her West India Islands, she will, it is said, strike a death blow at the existence of slavery in the United States. Intrenched at Havana and San Antonio, ports as impregnable as the rock of Gibraltar, she will be able to close the two entrances to the Gulf of Mexico, and even to prevent the free passage of the commerce of the United States over the Bahama banks, and through the Florida channel.

The local authorities are believed not to be entirely ignorant of the perils which environ them, but are regarded as so torpid as not to be competent to understand the extent and imminency of those perils, nor the policy by which Great Britain is guided. The wealthy planters are de-

3. Miguel Tacón y Rosique (1775–1855) was the captain-general of Cuba from 1834 to 1841. He was re- placed by Jeronimo Valdes.
4. Marino (1788–1854).

scribed as equally blind to the great danger in which they stand of losing their property. They go on, it is said, as usual, buying negroes, clamoring for the continuation of the trade, and denouncing, as seditious persons, and friends of Great Britain, the few who resist the importation of slaves, and encourage the immigration of free whites. The writer points to the census of the population of the Island, taken by authority, and just published, of which he encloses a copy; and, from the proportion between the different colors, he infers the probability that the white creoles will be able to preserve their rights in the future *Ethiopico-Cuban Republic*; and as to the Spaniards, he presumes that they will leave the Island at once.

The writer very naturally supposes that the United States must feel a deep solicitude upon a subject which so nearly concerns their own interests and tranquillity. He seems anxious that public opinion in this Country should be formed upon it and properly directed, and does not hesitate to express the opinion *that the mass of the white population of Cuba, in easy circumstances, including the Spaniards, prefer, and will always prefer, the flag of the United States to that of England.*

In thus communicating to you the substance of the statements of this writer, you will distinctly understand that your Government neither adopts nor rejects his speculations. It is with his statement of supposed facts that it concerns itself; and it is expected that you will examine and report upon them with scrupulous care, and with as much promptness as strict secrecy and discretion will permit: and the whole of the statements is now imparted to you, not to limit, but to guide and direct the inquiries you are called upon to make in so delicate a matter. It is quite obvious, that any attempt, on the part of England, to employ force in Cuba, for any purpose, would bring on a war, involving, possibly, all Europe as well as the United States; and as she can hardly fail to see this, and probably does not desire it, there may be reason to doubt the accuracy of the information we have received, to the extent to which it proceeds. But many causes of excitement and alarm exist; and the great magnitude of the subject makes it the duty of the Government of the United States to disregard no intimations of such intended proceedings which bear the least aspect of probability.

The Spanish Government has long been in possession of the policy and wishes of this Government in regard to Cuba, which have never changed, and has been repeatedly told that the United States never would permit the occupation of that Island by British agents or forces, upon any pretext whatsoever; and that in the event of any attempt to wrest it from her, she might securely rely upon the whole naval, and military resources of this Country to aid her in preserving or recovering it.

A copy of this letter will be immediately transmitted to the American Minister at Madrid [Washington Irving], that he may make such use of the information it contains, as circumstances may appear to require. I am, Sir, respectfully, Your obedient Servant, Danl Webster

LC. DNA, RG 59 (Instructions, Special Missions). Published in *Executive Documents*, 32d Cong., 1st sess., Serial 648, No. 121.

TO WASHINGTON IRVING

No. 13. Department of State,
Sir: Washington, 14th March, 1843

I have the honor to inform you that, on the 22d ultimo, the President communicated to Congress the latest correspondence between this Department and the Spanish Minister [Pedro Alcántara de Argaiz], respecting the Amistad case.[1] A copy of the document containing it is herewith transmitted.

A reply[2] to the confidential letter from this Department, of 11th January,[3] to the Consul at Havana [Robert Blair Campbell], (copy of which was sent to you in my despatch No 11.)[4] has been received. From the reply, it would seem that, as far as the Consul knew, or could obtain intelligence upon the subject, from the authorities of the Island, and from other sources, the information which had been received here is, as was supposed, greatly exaggerated. Enough, however, of danger and alarm still exists in that quarter to render caution and vigilance, on the part of this Government, indispensably necessary.

I transmit the commissions of Franklin Gage,[5] of Maine, and John Hartman,[6] of Philadelphia, the former appointed Consul for the port of Cardenas, and the other for the port of Baracoa, in Cuba—on the receipt of which, you will apply to the Spanish Government for exequaturs, and forward them, when obtained, with the commissions, to their respective consulates. They have been directed to supply you with the means of defraying the expenses that may be incurred. I am, Sir, respectfully, Your obedient servant, Danl Webster

LC. DNA, RG 59 (Instructions, Spain). Extract published in *Executive Documents*, 32d Cong., 1st sess., Serial 648, No. 121.

1. Tyler submitted correspondence between the Spanish minister Argaiz and the Department of State on the *Amistad* on February 27, 1843. *Ex. Doc.*, 27th Cong., 3d sess., Serial 422, No. 191. See also "The World and DW: Spain," above, pp. 193–230.

2. Campbell's response of February 9, 1843, is not in the RG 59 record. John Quincy Adams saw the letter at the Department of State and recorded in his diary that Campbell "discredited entirely the secret informer's tale." See *Memoirs*, 11:354.

3. DW means to refer to his letter to Campbell, January 14, 1843, above.

4. See above, DW to Irving, January 17, 1843, "Spain," pp. 229–230.

5. Gage (d. 1851; Bowdoin 1827) was a physician living at Cárdenas, Cuba.

6. Not further identified.

Mexico, Texas, and the United States

The relations of Mexico, Texas, and the United States were triangular. Although there were important bilateral issues such as the claims held by American citizens against Mexico and the treatment of Indian nations living along the Texas–United States frontier, the foreign policies of the three countries centered on the question of whether Texas was an independent state or a Mexican province in revolt. The United States had recognized the Republic of Texas in 1837, and Britain and France had done so in 1840, but Mexico continued to carry on a halfhearted military conflict against Texas and to regard Texans as disloyal citizens. In historical perspective, the period of Webster's secretaryship was part of a larger drift toward war between the United States and Mexico over such unresolvable issues as Texan sovereignty.

From the Mexican point of view, the primary grievance was the support given Texas by the U.S. government and its citizens. Most Texans had emigrated from the United States—a fact that was reflected in the composition of the Santa Fé expedition. The intensity of Mexican emotions found expression in an unusual circular to the diplomatic corps issued by the foreign minister of Mexico on May 31, 1842. José María de Bocanegra accused the United States of blatantly violating solemn treaty commitments and international law by failing to restrain its nationals from aiding Texans in such ventures as the Santa Fé expedition, and he asserted that Mexico would maintain "the justice of her cause . . . by doing all that is imperiously required, for her honour and dignity" (*IAA*, 8:491–492).

Emotions in the United States were also inflamed. After their surrender to Mexican forces in the fall of 1841, the approximately 350 members of the Santa Fé expedition, about 200 of whom were U.S. citizens, underwent many hardships and indignities. Several were executed during the arduous winter march of 2,000 miles to Mexico City. Once at their destination, some were confined in such institutions as a lepers' prison, and others were compelled to work in chains on the public roads. Reports of the treatment of the prisoners led to mass meetings demanding retribution in New Orleans and other American cities, and the Department of State was inundated with an avalanche of appeals from friends, relatives, congressmen, and state legislatures to take measures to secure the release of the captives. In an instruction to Waddy Thompson, the American minister to Mexico, dated April 5, 1842, Webster wrote that the indignities and privations to which the Americans and Texans had been subjected "were horrible, and, if they were not well authenticated, it would have been incredible" (see below). Through skillful diplomacy, the liberation of the American and Texan captives was secured in the summer of 1842, but feelings remained strong in both the United States and Mexico, and the problem of which Bocanegra had complained persisted.

Hardly had the cases of the Santa Fé prisoners been resolved, when another large group of Texan-Americans found themselves in the custody of Mexico. In retaliation for Mexican forays against Texas, President Sam Houston ordered a raid against Mexico on October 3, 1842. The force under General Alexander Somervell captured Laredo and Guerrero, but when Somervell ordered the expedition's return to Texas, most of the men disobeyed and continued into Mexico under the leadership of the veteran Texas cavalry commander, William S. Fisher. On December 25, the Texans, their ranks further depleted by the return to Texas of their more prudent comrades, attacked the town of Mier. After a hard-fought battle, the Texans surrendered and were ordered to Mexico City. For Daniel Webster, the Mier action meant another negotiation to secure the release of such prisoners as George Bibb Crittenden, the son of Senator John Jordan Crittenden of Kentucky.

Incursions by Texans and Americans into Mexico were more than a source of embarrassment for the United States; they also thwarted the attainment of foreign policy goals such as the mediation of Mexican-Texan differences and the acquisition of California. In response to a request by the government of Texas, Webster on June 22 instructed Thompson to present an offer by the United States to mediate an end to the war between Mexico and Texas. Shortly thereafter, on June 27, Webster also authorized Thompson to try to acquire from Mexico the port of San Francisco in exchange for American claims against Mexico. The initiative for this proposal came from Thompson, who in his first dispatch from Mexico (Thompson to DW, April 29, 1842, below), had characterized California as "the richest, the most beautiful and the healthiest country in the world" and had optimistically concluded that the government of General Antonio López de Santa Anna would exchange the province for American monetary claims against Mexico. Webster narrowed the objective to San Francisco and its environs, and the important instruction of June 27 suggests much about Webster's port-oriented expansionist philosophy. Since the Monroe-Adams administration, the United States had sought a "window" on the Pacific to promote its economic self-interest, and both Tyler and Webster were commercial expansionists. Unlike Tyler, Webster had no desire to annex slaveholding Texas to the United States, but, as Norman A. Graebner has written, he did possess "enormous enthusiasm for spacious ports of call for his Yan-kee constituents" and wanted a Boston or New York City on the Pacific (*Empire on the Pacific: A Study in American Continental Expansion* [New York, 1955], pp. 131, 220).

The untimely seizure of Monterey, the capital of Upper California, on October 19, 1842, by Commodore Thomas ap Catesby Jones ended any slim possibility that the United States might acquire part of California by negotiation or mediate an end to the Mexican-Texan conflict. Indeed, that ostensibly quixotic move can be understood only in the context of the already strained relations between the United States and Mexico. Jones was not the only one who took seriously rumors that war had broken out between the two countries. James C. Pickett, the U.S. chargé d'affaires to Peru, credited the reports, and in July 1842 President Tyler told the Texan chargé to the United States, James Reily, that he did not see "how a war between the United States and Mexico could be avoided" (George P. Garrison, ed., *Diplomatic Correspondence of the Republic of Texas* [3 vols., Washington, D.C., 1908–1911], 1:567). The tense state of Mexican-Texan-American relations led even John Quincy Adams to the conclusion that "Jones's movement on California" was part "of one great system, looking to a war of conquest and plunder from Mexico" (*Memoirs*, 11: 346).

Although there was no plot to seize California from Mexico, as Adams imagined there might be, there is a legitimate question about whether the United States was truly impartial in its attitude toward Mexico and Texas. Adams assessed Thompson's dispatches as "insolent, insulting, and contemptuous" of Mexico, and he found "far too much of the same spirit in the notes of our Secretary of State" (*Memoirs*, 11:353–354). Whether this was the case depends in part on how one reads the docu-ments printed below, but there is much evidence that tends to support Adams's view. The stated goal of the mediation effort was the indepen-dence of Texas; Jones was recalled but not reprimanded for his seizure of Monterey; Webster repeatedly showed Texan diplomats confidential state papers, such as his instructions to Thompson; and, at their request, he remonstrated in January 1843 against the "predatory" manner in which Mexico had allegedly carried on its war against Texas (DW to Thompson, January 31, 1843, below). President Tyler made no secret of his desire to annex the "lone star" republic to the United States, and as early as March 29, 1842, Reily had concluded that Texas had "the friend-ship of the Government of the United States, and the deep sympathy of the people" (Garrison, ed., *Diplomatic Correspondence*, 1:548). Although there was never an imminent danger of war between the United States and Mexico during Webster's secretaryship, the documents printed below suggest that it was not beyond the realm of possibility.

TO JOSEPH EVE

No. 1.   Department of State,
Sir: Washington, 14th June, 1841.

The only important subjects in the relations of the two countries respecting which a difference of opinion has existed between this government and that of Texas, are the boundary from the mouth of the Sabine to the Red River and the proper construction of the 33d article of the treaty between the United States and Mexico in regard to Indians on the frontiers.[1] The first, after having been partially adjusted by the Convention concluded in this City on the 25th of April, 1838, will, it is expected, be brought to a final close in the course of this summer by the joint Commission appointed under that Convention which, according to recent intelligence from the Commissioner on the part of the United States, was about to proceed with the demarcation of the meridian from the intersection of the western bank of the Sabine with the 32nd parallel of north latitude, north to the Red River.[2]

The papers in the files of the Legation and those herewith communicated will acquaint you with the views of the two governments relative to the other subject adverted to.[3]

But although these are the only pending differences between the United States and Texas, there are other topics in the relations between the two countries of which it is proper you should upon this occasion be apprized. The treaty between the United States and Mexico, which has been held to be binding upon Texas in all its parts, contains a stipulation that either party may put an end to the commercial articles upon giving a years' notice to the other.[4] The letter of Mr [Nathaniel] Amory, the representative of Texas here to me, of the 19th ult:[5] which is one of

1. Article 33 of the Treaty of Amity, Commerce, and Navigation of 1831 between the United States and Mexico bound the nations to maintain peaceful relations with the Indians along their border, to restrain hostile Indians from incursions, and to help restore captives taken across the border by Indians. See *Treaties*, 3:599–640, esp. 622–623.

2. In the treaty of April 25, 1838, Texas and the United States each agreed to appoint a commissioner to determine the boundary from the Sabine to the Red River. The U.S. commissioner was John Holmes Overton of Louisiana. The Texas commissioner was Memucan Hunt (1807–1856), the former Texan minister to

the United States. The line was completed on June 24, 1841. See *Treaties*, 4:133–143.

3. Texans believed that Indians from the United States regularly committed depredations in their territory and wished the United States to station troops within Texas. The United States declined the responsibility. There are no enclosures in either the RG 59 letterbox or in RG 84, Archives of the Texas Legation.

4. Article 34 of the 1831 treaty.

5. Amory to DW, May 19, 1841, DNA, RG 59 (Notes from Foreign Legations, Texas); not included in this publication. Amory (1777–1842), from Boston, was chief clerk in the Texas State Department, 1838–1839,

the accompanying papers, gives formal notice of the determination of the Texan government to take that course. The commerce between the two countries will consequently be subject to their respective laws, only, after the 19th of May, next, and until a new and separate treaty shall be negotiated and concluded between the two governments.

It has been stated in the newspapers that pursuant to some late arrangements between Texas and France, the former has agreed to admit French wines imported in French vessels, free of duty.[6] The department has no official information of the fact or any knowledge of the equivalents which the French government may have bestowed for the privilege adverted to. You will consequently lose no time after you shall have been received by that government, in collecting and transmitting to the department all attainable information on those points; for if the alleged discrimination in favor of France should have been granted unconditionally, it would be the right and duty of this government to claim the same privilege upon the same terms.

Your general duty will be to see that the rights of your countrymen under the treaty and the law of nations are respected by the Texan authorities. In doing this, however, you will be careful not to apply to the Executive for the redress of complaints when there is reason to believe that the aggrieved party might obtain the same object by means of the judicial tribunals. I am, Sir, your obedient servant,   Daniel Webster

LC. DNA, RG 59 (Instructions, Texas). Published in *IAA*, 12:27–28. Eve (1784–1843), a Whig politician from Kentucky, was named chargé d'affaires to Texas on April 15, 1841. He was recalled on June 10, 1843, but died in Galveston before he could return.

FROM JOHN TYLER

My Dr Sir;   [c. December 1841]
    I enclose a letter from [Balie] Peyton and [Henry Alexander] Wise as to the Santa fe expedition.[1] My mind strongly inclines to adopt the sug-

and secretary of the Texas legation at Washington, 1839–1842.

6. On February 14, 1840, Texas president Mirabeau Buonaparte Lamar (1798–1859) issued a proclamation abolishing duties on French wines imported into Texas. Lamar's proclamation was revoked on December 21, 1842.

1. Peyton to Wise, December 24, 1841, DNA, RG 59 (Misc. Letters); not included in this publication. Pey-ton (1803–1878; Gallatin College, Tennessee), a U.S. congressman from Tennessee from 1833 to 1837, moved to New Orleans in 1837 and was appointed U.S. district attorney for Louisiana. From 1849 to 1853 Peyton was U.S. minister to Chile. Wise (1806–1876; Washington College, Pennsylvania, 1825), of Virginia, served in Congress from 1833 to 1844. From 1844 to 1847 Wise was U.S. minister to Brazil.

gestion of sending [Leslie] Combes.[2] A failure then could not be visited on our heads. I send these letters this morning so that you may think of it until you come over. Yrs Truly   J Tyler

ALS. DLC.

LESLIE COMBS TO JOHN TYLER

Private.

Dear Sir: New Orleans 19 Dcbr 41
   I have desired Genl [Winfield] Scott to lay before you my letter invoking the immediate & efficient aid of the Government of the U.S. on behalf of my son *Franklin Combs* now held in captivity in Mexico,[1] if indeed he has not been already murdered or allowed to perish by neglect, suffering & disease.

   On my return from Texas to this place some 20 days hence I shall expect to receive information of the action of the Government, & *be prepared to act accordingly*—I write this private letter to you to make suggestions, for your own consideration & which might, if followed out, result in most momentous advantages to the U.S. & cover you & your administration with lasting glory. Genl [Antonio López de] Santa Anna[2] promised Genl [Samuel] Houston[3] to acknowledge Texan Independence, if set free, & he should once again be in power. Well he was liberated & is in power—dictatorial power & the Texans hope & some believe he will perform his promise.[4] *He will do no such thing—He dare not do it*—The prejudice of the Mexican people, of all colours, agt Texas—the religious bigotry of the Catholics—governed by the Priests—The evil of *setting an example* which Yucatan & Tabasco are now claiming to have followed out[5]—which New Mexico & Upper California will soon demand, to say

2. Combs (1793–1881), of Kentucky, was a lawyer and state judge. He served several terms in the Kentucky House of Representatives between 1827 and 1859. Combs supported the Texas Revolution in 1836 by equipping a troop at his own expense.

1. See Combs to Scott and John Jordan Crittenden, December 19, 1841, DNA, RG 59 (Misc. Letters). Franklin Combs (1824–1844) was seventeen years old and apparently in poor health when he went on the expedition.

2. Santa Anna (1794–1876) was four times ruler of Mexico from 1833 to 1855. He assumed command of

the forces against the Texas Revolution and was taken prisoner by General Sam Houston after the Battle of San Jacinto in April 1836.

3. Houston (1793–1863) had been a U.S. congressman, 1823–1827, and governor of Tennessee, 1827–1829, before leading the Texan army in the revolution. Houston became president of Texas in 1836 and was reelected in 1841. He later served as U.S. senator from Texas for fourteen years after 1846 and was governor of Texas from 1859 to 1861.

4. Santa Anna was reelected president of Mexico in October 1841.

5. Separatists in the southeastern coastal provinces of Yucatán and Ta-

nothing of other Provinces—all forbid him to do it; & yet I have no doubt he would be happy to be well rid of the difficulty & of Texas at the same time. Besides what are the true limits of the *Republic* of Texas? Certainly not those of the antient Province of that name, for she claims the Rio del Norte[6] as her present western boundary, including parts of Coahuila & other Mexican provinces; & that boundary she will have, coute qui coute.[7] It is a natural limit for a great Nation as Texas will one day be, & nothing short of it will do. But Santa Anna cannot thus dismember Mexico to aggrandize a rebelious province.

The U. S. once claimed this Rio del Norte as *her* true boundary, but Mr [John Quincy] Adams settled it otherwise.[8] Might not Santa Anna's pulse be felt—his palm gently touched—as to a *sale to the U.S.* up to this limit? this ancient land mark—more natural for Mexico & the U. S. than the little Sabine—For allow me to inform you that most of the commerce of the richest part of Texas must pass to & fro, thro the US. Red River into the Miss[issipp]i.

What the U. S. would do with it when obtained, will be another question. My opinion is that the interest of the whole union—especially the North & the South, requires that the prospective new States of Iowa & Wisconsin shall have some Southern counterpoise, or the North will become too heavy & the Union break in two. Look at the map & think well of this— not as a *Southron*, but as an *American* who loves the Union, & looks on its dissolution with the most serious apprehensions as to its effects upon our free institutions.

It does not require a skilful diplomatist to manage this very delicate question, but a plain, prudent, sensible Man, who would feel his way cautiously & secure his country from danger in all time to come.

I will not trouble you with any further remarks on this question. Your own reflections, when you have looked at the map & considered what I have already said, will no doubt furnish you with most conclusive reasons in favour of the suggested course. It might not do for our *regular* Minister[9] to touch this subject—In truth he is not the man to be intrusted with such an operation.

My mind has been so occupied with my own affairs since I read your

basco declared independence in 1839 and 1840.

6. The Rio Grande was called the Rio Bravo del Norte by Mexico.

7. "Cost what it may."

8. Although many Americans believed the Rio Grande marked the western limit of the Louisiana Purchase of 1803, in the Transcontinental Treaty of February 22, 1819, Secretary of State John Quincy Adams accepted the Sabine River as the boundary between the United States and Spanish territory. See *Treaties,* 3:3–64.

9. The U.S. chargé d'affaires and minister to Mexico from January 5, 1836, to April 21, 1842, was Powhatan Ellis (1790–1863; Dickinson College 1810) of Mississippi, previously a state and federal judge and U.S. senator.

Message[10] that I have formed no opinion as to your currency <sugges-tions> projet. If enacted into a law it shall, as far as I am concerned, have a fair trial & I hope your fond anticipations may be more than rea-lised. I am no system-worshipper, no more than I am a man-worshipper. I am for the country & its prosperity, let who will rule it. Respy Yr M O.S.

Leslie Combs

P.S. I have not breathed these thoughts to any other human beings—not retained a copy of this letter. They are for your *Private* ear—to be adopt-ed or not as you think best[.]

ALS. DNA, RG 59 (Misc. Letters). This is the first of many letters about the Santa Fé prisoners. Most of these letters can be found in the miscellaneous file of the Department of State. On June 20, 1841, about 350 men with several wagons of trading goods left Brushy Creek, Texas, just north of Austin, on an expedition to Santa Fé, in Mexican territory. The stated purpose of the party was to open commercial relations with Santa Fé, but they also planned to en-courage that important trading center to join the Republic of Texas. Without proper provisions or guides, the members of the ill-fated party nearly died of thirst and starvation. After splitting into two groups, they were captured by Mexican soldiers in September and October 1841. Of the several accounts of the Santa Fé expedition, the most important is by one of the participants, George Wilkins Kendall's two-volume *Narrative of the Texan Santa Fé Expedi-tion* (New York, 1844). The identifications of the Santa Fé prisoners named in the following documents are taken primarily from Noel M. Loomis's syn-thesis of the literature, *The Texan-Santa Fé Prisoners* (Norman, Okla., 1958).

TO POWHATAN ELLIS

No. 36.   Department of State,
Sir: Washington, 3d January, 1842.
    The friends of Mr Franklin Combs, son of General Leslie Combs of Kentucky, have applied for the interposition of this government in behalf of that young gentleman,[1] who accompanied the late Texan expedition to Santa Fé in Mexico and is supposed to have been captured and, if alive, to be held in bondage in that country with the other survivors of the expedition. It has been represented to this department that young Combs has never been a citizen of Texas, that he did not repair to that country with any intention of relinquishing his allegiance to this govern-ment or of remaining in Texas, but that he went thither in the autumn of 1840 upon private business of his father and for the benefit which he was assured his feeble health would derive from the mild winter climate of that region. He was, however, detained there by both causes until about the time when the expedition referred to set out. This he deter-mined to accompany merely for the object of confirming his health and

10. Tyler's first Annual Message of   *pers*, 4:74–89.
December 7, 1841. *Messages and Pa-*   1. See above.

gratifying a curiosity both liberal and natural in regard to the unknown lands through which the course of the expedition lay.

As there is no reason to doubt the correctness of this information, you will accordingly make the necessary representations to the Mexican government upon the subject with a view to avert from young Combs if he should be alive, the dangers to which he may be or may have been exposed. You will state that from the respectability of his family and for other reasons there can be no ground for the belief that he would have accompanied the expedition for any other objects than those mentioned and that if he had been aware that the views of the Texan government in despatching it had been hostile or predatory rather than friendly and commercial, as they were understood to have been at the time, he would not have gone in its company. If to this it be objected that the expedition was military in its array and must therefore be presumed to have had warlike designs against the Mexican authorities, it may be answered that the avowed motive of the members of the expedition in bearing arms was to ward off the attacks of hostile Indians and especially of the Comanches who, it is well known, roam in great force along and across the track which was to have been pursued. This objection would apply with much less if with any force to young Combs, as he was no soldier and had never been one and if found with arms, there could in his case be no better ground for the opinion that they were to have been used for purposes of attack and not for those of defence, than if he had accompanied one of the caravans from Missouri to Santa Fé, [by] means of which, as is well known, an extensive trade is carried on between this country and Mexico to the mutual advantage of the parties.

Although young Combs is the only American citizen who accompanied the expedition for whom the interposition of this government has been asked, it is understood that there was another who as little deserves to be subjected to any penal proceedings on the part of the Mexican government. This is Mr George W[ilkins] Kendall of New Orleans.[2]

You will press this case with the utmost earnestness on the Mexican government, as the government of the United States feels itself bound to interfere and to signify its confident expectation that the lives of American citizens will not be sacrificed who have not intentionally done any thing of a public character against Mexico. Even if the conduct of young Combs was indiscreet and ill-judged, yet this government cannot suppose that the government of Mexico would treat him as an armed combatant, found among its enemies. You will take pains to impress the

2. Kendall (1807–1867) was founder and editor of the New Orleans *Daily Picayune*. After his release from Mexican custody Kendall returned to New Orleans and published the two-volume *Narrative of the Texan Santa Fé Expedition* (New York, 1844). Kendall later reported the Mexican War and published a book about it.

Mexican authorities with the feelings which would be excited in this country, if any harsh proceeding should be adopted towards this youth.

You will avail yourself of the opportunity of making to that government the communication, to suggest that, while this government is well disposed to maintain with strict fidelity amicable relations with the Mexican Republic and will not attempt to screen from merited punishment any of our citizens who may be guilty of an infraction of the laws intended to preserve those relations, yet that summary, sanguinary or undue punishment of either Texans or citizens of the United States in Mexico, inevitably tends to excite and foment in this country an acerbity of feeling against Mexico, which will be much more apt to defeat the supposed objects of those punishments than if the offenders were to have a fair trial and, if then convicted, were to be punished in some proportion to their offences. You will, however, make this suggestion in a conciliatory tone, without allowing it to be supposed that this government has any intention to dictate the policy to be adopted by that of the Mexican Republic, upon this or any other subject; but, supposing their disposition towards the United States to be amicable, our wish is merely to point out a way by which, it seems to us, that reciprocal disposition as well as the integrity of the Mexican territory may be more effectually maintained. Accustomed, ourselves, to regular judicial proceedings, fair and full trials and mild punishments, the opposites of these, if exercised by other governments, always serve to check the growth of amity and good will. The interest which we feel for Combs, whose case has been particularly presented to us, and for Mr Kendall also, will lead to the despatching of this communication in the way most likely to carry it soon to your hands. Any reasonable expenses which may be necessary to defray the charge of a special messenger from the Mexican capital to the place of captivity of young Combs and his American associates, or for any other proper purposes necessary for their safety and liberation, will be borne by this government and will be defrayed by you, and for them you will draw on this department, specifying in your draughts their purpose and sending with them such vouchers as you may be able to procure. I am, Sir, your obedient servant,   Daniel Webster

P.S. Since the above was written, application has been made in behalf of Mr J[ohn] C. Howard,[3] a youth of 19 years of age who was also with the expedition and who, we are informed, was not a citizen of Texas. You will likewise inquire into his case and do for him any thing else which you can do with propriety.

LC. DNA, RG 59 (Instructions, Mexico). Published in *IAA*, 8:101–103.

3. Howard (c. 1823–1885) later   1861.
served as a U.S. Army officer, 1847–

TO POWHATAN ELLIS

No. 38.   Department of State,
Sir: Washington, 6th January, 1842.

I addressed you on the 3d instant on behalf of Franklin Combs and Mr [George Wilkins] Kendall,[1] captured by the Mexican army with the Texan expedition, near Santa Fé. The object of this is only to say, what perhaps you would not have failed to understand, that if it should be found that other American citizens were made captives, under like circumstances, and with similar claims to immunity and release, you will exert the same interference in their behalf. I am, with regard, Your obedient servant,   Daniel Webster

LC. DNA, RG 59 (Instructions, Mexico).

TO BALIE PEYTON

Private
Dear Sir,   Washington, January 6th, 1842.

Your letter to the President of the 21st. of December[1] has been read by him, with great interest and anxiety, although it was not the first communication upon the subject.[2] Letters had been previously received from Genl [Leslie] Combs, and information communicated from other quarters, upon which immediate steps were taken. A special Messenger has been despatched from this Department with an instruction to our Minister at Mexico [Powhatan Ellis], of which I enclose a copy.[3] The President will interfere for the life and safety of young [Franklin] Combs to the full extent of his duty. You must be aware of the delicacy of the question, at least as it presents itself to us, without more knowledge of the facts. It is hardly to be doubted that the expedition to Santa Fé from Texas was a military expedition, and therefore one in which citizens of the United States could not engage without violating the laws, and forfeiting the protection of their own Government. We presume, however, upon the representations made here, that Combs was not a part of the expedition; that he had engaged in nothing hostile to Mexico, and that his object was health, and the gratification of a proper desire for information by travel. On this ground the Government interferes in his behalf.

1. See above.
1. Not found.
2. See above, Combs to Tyler, December 19, 1841.
3. See above, DW to Ellis, January 3, 1842. The special messenger, Duncan L. McRae, arrived in New Orleans January 19 and left the same day for Mexico. McRae to DW, January 19, 1842, DNA, RG 59 (Misc. Letters).

The President wishes the most effectual means taken consistent with justice and propriety to secure his safety. Your suggestion of dispatching Genl Combs himself to Mexico has been maturely considered, but upon the whole it has been thought that such a course would not be expedient, on account of the relationship. But on receipt of this if you should be of opinion that the object in view would be promoted by sending a private agent from New Orleans to co-operate with the American Minister in Mexico, the President is willing that such agent, to be selected by you should be immediately dispatched, and his necessary expenses will be defrayed by this Department. He cannot receive any public character, as we have a minister on the spot, but the President's great desire to do all that can be done leads him to say, that if you think a private agency might be useful, he wishes it to be instituted, and that you would select such person as you deem the fittest for such duty, other than General Combs.[4] He the more readily submits this part of the case to your discretion, as before this communication shall reach New Orleans, you may very probably be in posession of much more information than has as yet reached us; and there are likely to be many citizens of New Orleans who are acquainted at Mexico.

As this agent will have no public character, he can only act under direction of the American Minister, to whom he will report himself, on his arrival; and the main advantage to be expected from such agency is this, that a person of respectability and address, well acquainted with Mexico, its manners and language, and perhaps with its present authorities, and acquainted, also, with the character, family and connexions of Combs, [George Wilkins] Kendall and other American citizens who may be in like condition, may by unofficial means and personal efforts co-operate usefully with Mr. Ellis. If you think it allowable, on the whole, that such agent be employed, you will give a copy of this letter as his instructions.

The Collector of New Orleans[5] will have instructions to convey Mr [Duncan L.] McRae to the fittest port in Mexico, by the Revenue Cutter, or other most prompt mode; and if you should think it useful that such private agent as is above mentioned should proceed to Mexico, he may use the same conveyance. You will see by the enclosed that although not applied to by his friends, Mr Kendall's case has not been overlooked and it is the President's wish, that if any other American citizen, innocently in company with the Expedition, should have fallen into the hands of the Mexicans, an equal interference may be made in his behalf. I am, with great regard, yours,   Daniel Webster

LC. DNA, RG 59 (Domestic Letters).

4. Peyton selected Henry E. Lawrence of New Orleans.

5. Thomas Gibbs Morgan (1779–1861).

FROM LESLIE COMBS

Sir: New Orleans 22 Jany 42

Since writing you two days since[1] I have been assured that Mr [Balie] Peytons objection to confering his appointment upon my agent *now* in Mexico, arose from no indisposition to oblige me; but because the individual had been once a citizen of Mexico & then of Texas—and was unknown to him. These very facts & his being a *Jew* recommended him to me as a safe person to send on such a mission. He looks like a Spaniard & can pass himself for one, or for a German or Italian, against whom there are no jealous feelings in Mexico.

Among other evidences of respectability, Genl [Edmund Pendleton] *Gaines*[2] & Genl [Samuel] *Houston* have dined together at his table, when he was in better circumstances.

Mr. Peyton, I understand, would not have sent [Henry E.] Lawrence if he could have found a suitable person.

I still feel very unhappy and aggrieved at the course which has been pursued, for if I have merited nothing at the hands of Mr [John] Tyler, I certainly have done nothing to place myself under the *law* of proscription by his administration.

I feel it to be due to Mr Peyton, to write this additional note, to relieve him from any supposed censure, in my former letter. I have not spoken to him about it.

I would rather *endure wrong* than inflict it, upon another. Very Respy Yr M.O.S.   Leslie Combs

DNA, RG 59 (Misc. Letters). Rec'd February 2, 1842.

FROM LESLIE COMBS

                                              New Orleans
Sir,   9 Febry 1842

I recd, on yesterday a note from our Minister in Mexico [Powhatan Ellis] informing me of my sons release on the 24th Jany.[1] (Some days previous to the arrival of your Special Messenger with his despatches)

I also recd a letter from my son informing me of his having been put in irons *after* the demand made for him by Mr Ellis & in that condition forced to labour in the streets with the other prisoners. He was taken *in chains*, before the President, Dictator, ([Antonio López de] Santa Anna)

1. In his letter of January 20, Combs protested Peyton's choice of Henry E. Lawrence as special agent in preference to his own candidate (who has not been identified). DNA, RG 59 (Misc. Letters).

2. Gaines (1777–1849).
1. Ellis reported the release of Franklin Combs in a dispatch to DW of January 27, 1842, DNA, RG 59 (Despatches, Mexico).

& after a brief course of interrogation & answer his chains were ordered to be stricken off & himself conveyed in same state to the residence of the American Minister.

I also consider it my duty to put in the files of your department the enclosed letters confirmatory of the delicate state of my sons health— the object of his visit to Santa Fe & the cruel & inhuman conduct observed towards him & other captives by the Mexican authorities. The first marked A. is from Chihuahua, dated 25 Octr 1841.[2] The 2d marked B. is from the city of Mexico dated 8 Jany 1842 & both recd on yesterday.[3]

My own private agent arrived in Mexico on the 12th Jany.

I shall take the earliest opportunity to impress to Mr Ellis my sense of gratitude for his prompt & humane interposition on behalf of my son.

I trust that the mild climate & gentle treatment, will soon so far restore his shattered constitution as to enable him to return home. Very respty Yr M. O S.   Leslie Combs

P.S. The letters of Mr [Francis Asbury] Lumsden published in the Picayune of yesterday confirm the within statements & I ask leave to annex a printed comment on the same taken from the N. Orleans Bee of this date.[4]

L S. DNA, RG 59 (Misc. Letters). Rec'd February 21, 1842.

FROM FRANKLIN COMBS

Sir   New Orleans 16 Feb., 1842.

I arrived here day before yesterday and shall leave to day for Kentucky; before doing so, I consider it my duty to enclose this hasty statement of facts connected with my late captivity in Mexico,[1] with the earnest hope that our Government will not only demand the remaining Americans citi-

2. The letter of October 25, 1841, from one William S. Messervy (not included in this publication), advised the elder Combs that his son was in good health but expressed fear for the safety of young Combs and the other prisoners. Messervy loaned the prisoners money for necessities. See Combs to DW, March 2, 1843, DNA, RG 59 (Misc. Letters).

3. The letter of January 8, 1842, from James A. Swett (not included in this publication) discussed the treatment of the prisoners and described the health of Franklin Combs as "feeble."

4. Lumsden (d. 1860), the partner of George Wilkins Kendall in the New Orleans *Daily Picayune*, described the circumstances of the Santa Fé prisoners in two letters from Mexico City. The *New Orleans Bee* editorial of February 9 stated that the treatment of Combs demanded revenge.

1. Although the enclosure has not been found, Franklin Combs's statement was published in the *New Orleans Bee* on February 16, 1842 and in *Niles' National Register* on March 5, 1842.

zen's who have received such inhumane treatment but do all that can be done to save the lives and restore to liberty the gallant but unfortunate Texian's. Most of them are citizen's of the "United States" and have numerous friends and relatives among us.

Their suffering's have already been almost beyond human endurance, and when Genl [Hugh] McLeod and the survivors of his command are thrown into the same dungeon, they must inevitably perish.[2]

I feel very grateful to the President for his prompt measures for my relief, althoug I was released from Prison before his Messenger arrived. I met him in "Perote."[3] Very Respt Y.O.S.   Franklin Combs

P.S. See New Orleans Bee sent by this mail, of 16th Inst., FC.

ALS. DNA, RG 59 (Misc. Letters). Rec'd February 26, 1842.

FROM ALEXANDER LOWRY HOLLIDAY

                                    Hollidaysburgh Huntington Co Penna
Dear Sir   February 16th. 1842

I am under the necessity of asking [a] favor of You, My Brother John[1] has been taken *Prisoner* by the Mexicans. He went with the Company that went to Santa Fee. I was uncertain wether he had went or not, until a few days ago. I see his name among the list of *Prisoners*, he is a favorite Brother and also a favorite amoung his Relatives, which is very large and extends from one end of this State to the Other.

I am advised by several of my Friends to write to You and ask Your interferance on his behalf. Some persons are affraid that as my Brother has been in Texas for some time, and may have lost his Residence in the United States [that] therefore it is out of Your power to do any thing for him. I wish You would give me some advise as to what would be best for me to do, or what rule of procedure would most likely lead to his Release from those Brutal Savages the Mexicans[.] Oh it is horrible to think of having a Brother treated and tortured as he has been by those Savages, and it is still more [so] to Contemplate that the end of their Suffering is not [near].

I have always been an admirer and a Devout friend of Yours—and if

2. The McLeod party of the Santa Fé expedition surrendered to Mexican troops on October 5, 1841. McLeod (c. 1815–1862; U.S. Military Academy 1835), originally of Georgia, resigned from the U.S. Army in 1836 and moved to Texas. He died in Confederate service during the Civil War.

3. A Mexican village near Jalapa in Veracruz province.

1. John Holliday (1811–1842), a commissary officer with the expedition, had lived in Texas many years and fought in the Texas Revolution. He was released in August but died of yellow fever on the voyage home.

You will interfere for the Release of My Brother—You Shall Never be forgotten. I am with due Respect Yours &c   A. L. Holliday

P.S. I would be pleased to here from You Shortly   A.L.H.

ALS. DNA, RG 59 (Misc. Letters). Rec'd February 21, 1842. Holliday (1814–1903) was a Pennsylvania merchant.

TO JOHN M. LEITCH, W. M. YOUNG, ET AL.

Department of State,

Gentlemen: Washington, 16th February, 1842.

I have the honor to inform you that the President has referred to this Department the memorial addressed to him by you in behalf of Thomas S. Lubbock,[1] one of the persons captured with the late Texan expedition to Santa Fé, and has given directions for every thing to be done that can be done with propriety for the safety of that young man. Instructions upon the subject will accordingly be at once despatched to our Minister at Mexico [Powhatan Ellis].[2] I have the honor to be, Gentlemen, Your obedient servant,   Danl Webster

LS. MoSHi. Leitch and Young are not identified.

FROM POWHATAN ELLIS

No. 55   Legation of the US of America
Sir: Mexico 17th February 1842

I have the honor to inform you that I addressed a note on the 31st of January to his Excellency José Maria de Bocanegra, Minister of Foreign Relations and Government, advising him that I had transmitted to my Government copies of his communications of the 27th January, in regard to the violation of the flag of the US, in the port of Sisal, and the alleged attempt which was designed upon two American schooners that were about to arrive in Vera Cruz, for the supposed use of this Government.[1] Upon the representations of the Mexican Government on this subject I felt it to be a courtesy due to it, to transmit to you the facts contained in

1. Not found. Lubbock (1817–1862), originally from Charleston, South Carolina, moved to Texas in 1835 and was an officer with the Santa Fé expedition. Lubbock escaped from the Mexicans and made his way back to Texas.

2. See DW to Ellis, February 26, 1842, below.

1. Bocanegra (1787–1862), a lawyer and justice of the Mexican Supreme Court, was Mexican foreign minister from 1841 to 1844. He in-

formed Ellis on January 27, 1842, that Texans compelled two Mexican citizens to leave the American vessel *Louisa* and detained them two days aboard the Texan brig *Austin*. In a separate communication of the same day, Bocanegra expressed concern that two ships purchased by Mexico would be seized by "enemies of the Republic" in transit from New Orleans to Veracruz. See Ellis to DW, January 27, 1842, DNA, RG 59 (Despatches, Mexico).

its notes. In a letter received from the Vice Consul of the U.S. at Vera Cruz,[2] he informed me that when the Captain of the Louisa was asked whether he had any complaint to make, to this Legation, of the conduct of the publick armed Vessels of Texas, in consequence of the outrage alluded to by Mr de Bocanegra, he replied—that he had not. From this circumstance I am induced to believe there is some mistake in relation to the occurrence alluded to. (See Document No. 1.[)][3]

Long prior to the arrival of Messrs [Duncan K.] McRae and [Henry E.] Lawrence who reached this City on the 2nd of February, as bearers of Despatches, the subject of the Santa Fé Expedition, and the Texan prisoners, had already greatly engaged my attention; I had used all proper exertions to obtain correct information in regard to the circumstances and state of those men, from the time of their capture, and it seems, from the best information I can get, that they were induced by the false representations of one of their own party to surrender their arms,[4] upon an assurance by the authorities of New Mexico, that they would be permitted to return to Texas without further molestation. Shortly after their surrender they were seized and bound, and after the expiration of a brief period, not precisely known to me, were marched as prisoners to this Capital. From the representations of Messers [Thomas] Falconer[5] and [George F. X.] Van Ness,[6] two of the prisoners who have been released,

2. L. S. Hargous, an American merchant residing in Veracruz, was named U.S. vice consul there in January 1842. Hargous, according to Waddy Thompson, gave the American prisoners in Mexico between ten and fifteen thousand dollars. [No. 53]. Ellis to DW, January 22, 1842, DNA, RG 59 (Despatches, Mexico); Waddy Thompson, *Recollections of Mexico* (New York, 1846), pp. 10–11.

3. See Ellis to Bocanegra, January 31, 1842, enclosed in [No. 53]. Ellis to DW, January 22, 1842, DNA, RG 59 (Despatches, Mexico). The documents enclosed with the dispatch are not numbered.

4. John S. Sutton (d. 1862) and William G. Cooke (c. 1808–1847) led one of the two groups into which the Santa Fé expedition was divided. Members of the expedition charged that William P. Lewis, one of the officers, persuaded the Sutton and Cooke party to give up their weapons in exchange for trading privileges at

Santa Fé. He was not held prisoner with the others and apparently obtained trading concessions from the Mexicans. Lewis had lived in Mexico for some time before joining the expedition. Cooke was a noted frontiersman who reputedly saved Santa Anna's life at San Jacinto in 1836. Sutton later fought at Mier and in the Confederate Army during the Civil War.

5. Falconer (1805–1882), an English lawyer who apparently accompanied the expedition as a tourist, was released on February 1, 1842. An account by him appeared in the *New Orleans Bee*, March 11, 1842 (reprinted in *Niles' National Register*, April 2, 1842). For the collected writings of Falconer on the expedition, see F. W. Hodge, ed., *Letters and Notes on the Texan Santa Fé Expedition, 1841–1842* (New York, 1930).

6. Van Ness (c. 1823–1855) went to San Antonio, Texas, in 1838. He was an official representative of the

it appears that they were treated with great cruelty; that three were killed on the route, and two died from exhaustion and suffering.

The first division of these prisoners arrived here in the latter part of Decr 1841,[7] and the men are confined in the convent of Santiago, chained, and forced to work, daily, on the publick roads. The second division reached San Cristobal, about four leagues hence, in the last week of January,[8] and it was immediately discovered that they were afflicted with small pox. The sick, however, were soon separated from the healthy, and were brought to the hospital of San Lazaro in this place, whilst the others were marched on the road to Perote. In addition to their sufferings from fatigue and disease, they were destitute of clothing and all other personal comforts and necessaries. It is, however, due to the subaltern officers who had charge of these unfortunate men in this capital, & at San Cristobal, to state, that they have treated them with as much lenity and kindness as they could consistently with their duty. On the arrival of the first division here, the Foreigners, consisting chiefly of Americans and Englishmen, subscribed liberally both in money and clothing, and thus relieved the pressing wants of that body of men during the coldest part of our winter. (See Doc No 2)[9]

As soon as I possessed myself of all the facts in regard to the connexion of young Franklin Coombs with the Santa Fé Expedition—his arrest —and imprisonment, I was satisfied that he had not accompanied the Texans as a military character, and had not conducted himself in such a manner as to forfeit his right to the protection of our Government. I therefore, immediately represented all the facts to the Minister of Foreign Relations, and demanded his liberation as a Citizen of the United States. I am pleased to have it in my power to inform you, that the Most Excellent the Pro[vision]al Presidt, General, [Antonio López de] Santa Anna, examined personally into the facts of Mr. Coombs's case, and after having satisfied himself that he had not violated any existing Law of the Republick, ordered him to be, forthwith, discharged, and sent him, accompanied by one of his aid de camps, to this Legation, in his private carriage. The fact of his release I had made known to you in my last despatch,[10] and I now have the honor to transmit you all the documents in regard to his case. (See Doct No 3).[11]

Texan government on the expedition. Van Ness was released February 1, 1842, but again became a prisoner when Mexican forces captured San Antonio in September 1842.

7. The Sutton-Cooke group.

8. The McLeod party.

9. The document is not in the RG 59 record. According to Kendall, the prisoners were given food, money, and clothing several times along the march.

10. Ellis to DW, January 27, 1842, DNA, RG 59 (Despatches, Mexico).

11. Ellis enclosed six documents pertaining to Combs; they are not included in this publication. These are Ellis to José Maria Tornel y Mendivil, January 5, 1842; Statement of

Mr George Van Ness has, also, been released by the order of His Excellency The President; tho' his liberation was chiefly effected through the kind agency of General [José Maria] Tornel [y Mendivil], Minister of War and Marine, who had known his father and family during his residence in the U.S. as Minister from Mexico.[12] I had not applied for his release, nor had Mr Van Ness requested that I should do so, and the freedom of this young Gentleman is, consequently, owing to the voluntary and generous act of the Government. (See Doct No. 4).[13]

Previous to the arrival of Mr. McRae with your instructions, I had demanded the liberation of Mr [George Wilkins] Kendall, as a citizen of the United States, who had associated himself with the Santa Fé Expedition in no other way than as a private tourist, travelling as a Citizen of the U.S. desiring to see the Country, and protected by a Mexican passport, granted by the Consul at New Orleans. Upon this demand for the release of Mr Kendall, a correspondence took place between myself and the Minister of Foreign Relations, in reference to the true attitude in which Mr Kendall stood to that Expedition. I regret to inform you that Mr Kendall is still a prisoner, and I am wholly, unable to say when his case will be finally decided, although I have detained my messenger five days in order to receive an answer from Mr. de Bocanegra (See Doct No. 5).[14]

In regard to the other prisoners who claim the protection of the United States, to wit: I[saac] S. Towers, John Thompkins, D[avid] Snively, H[enry] R[idley] Buchanan, LB Sheldon, L. C. Blake, Allensworth Adams,

---

physicians examining Combs, January 9, 1842; Ellis to Bocanegra, January 10, 1842; Tornel to Ellis, January 13, 1842; the record of an interview between Ellis and Tornel, January 17, 1842; Bocanegra to Ellis, January 18, 1842. Tornel y Mendivil (1789–1853), minister of war and marine, served as Mexico's minister to the United States from February 8, 1830, to March 8, 1831.

12. Van Ness was the son of Cornelius Peter Van Ness (1782–1852), a former chief justice of Vermont and U.S. minister to Spain from 1829 to 1836, and the nephew of John Peter Van Ness (1770–1846; Columbia 1789), a U.S. representative from New York, 1801–1803, and mayor of Washington, D.C., 1830–1834.

13. Tornel to Ellis, February 4, 1842; General Gabriel Valencia to Ellis, February 5, 1842; Ellis to Tornel, February 7, 1842; Ellis to Valencia, February 11, 1842; not included in this publication.

14. Kendall maintained that the Mexican consul in New Orleans had issued him a passport for tourist travel in Mexico, which was confiscated when presented to officials in Santa Fé. Mexican authorities at this time believed Kendall was an agent of the Texan government. See Ellis to Bocanegra, February 2 and 5, 1842; the record of a conversation between Ellis and Bocanegra, February 7, 1842; Bocanegra to Ellis, February 9, 1842; a statement by George Van Ness of February 11, 1842, that he witnessed Kendall present his passport in Santa Fé; Bocanegra to Ellis, February 13, 1842; Ellis to Bocanegra, February 14, 1842. All of the above are enclosed in Ellis to DW, February 17, 1842.

J[ames] C. Boyd, Berryman O. Stout, T[heoderick] A. Sully, Jno C. Howard, J[ohn] B. Houghtailing, T[homas] S[tebbins] Torrey, AB. Sutton, and
C[harles] S. Longcope, from the communications addressed to me by the
first named nine individuals you will see that they claim the intervention
of the United States, as citizens thereof, but acknowledge that they accompanied the Expedition mostly as traders.[15] How far this circumstance
will go to relieve them from responsibility to the Laws of this country,
when it is known such trading is illegal will be for the Govt. of the US.
to determine.

These men, it is alleged, by this Government, were found associated
with the invaders of the Mexican territory, and captured with arms in
their hands. Will this allegation be sufficient to authorize the Mexican
authorities to detain those who claim to be citizens of the US. without
the fact being established, by this Government, of their hostile intentions
in entering Mexico under the circumstances attending this Expedition?
It appears to me that the fact of the guilt of the accused party should be
proved by those who make the charge. It will be perceived that by the
law of the 15th Febry 1840,[16] which is the only law on the subject made
known to this Legation, all strangers, entering this country by Texas,
are to be, immediately, sent out of it. This is the only punishment exacted, and the natural consequence, seems to me, that these men, if they
had no hostile intentions, which can be *proved* on them by Mexico, and
not only *charged* by inferences drawn from the supposed character of
the Santa Fé Expedition, are entitled to the full benefit and immunity of
the decree alluded to.

15. Towers to Ellis, December 12,
1841; Towers (d. 1842), a physician
originally from New York, had lived
in Texas since 1838. He was briefly
a member of the Texas House of Representatives, from November 1838
to January 1839. Towers was killed
at the Battle of Mier. Thompkins to
Ellis, January 29, 1842. Thompkins
was a saddler from Illinois. Snively
to Ellis and McLeod to Ellis, January
31, 1842. Snively, from Ohio, claimed
he accompanied the expedition as a
merchant. Buchanan to Ellis, January 31, 1842. Buchanan, from Tennessee, accompanied the expedition
as a merchant. Sheldon to Ellis, February 3, 1842. Sheldon claimed his
residence as Mississippi. Blake to
Ellis, February 5, 1842. Blake was
also of Mississippi. Adams to Ellis,
February 6, 1842. Adams was from
Kentucky. Boyd to Ellis, February
15, 1842. Boyd died of smallpox July
27, 1842, at Veracruz. Stout to Ellis,
February 6, 1842. Stout went to
Texas from Kentucky in 1839. Sully
was reportedly a merchant of Florida
and San Antonio. Houghtailing was
a merchant from New York. Torrey
(1819–1843) came to Texas from
Connecticut in 1840. The Torrey
family operated a number of trading
houses in Texas. Sutton and Longcope were from New York. All of
the documents mentioned above are
enclosed in Ellis to DW, February
17, 1842.

16. See Juan de Canedo to Ellis,
February 15, 1840, advising Ellis of
the edict, enclosed in No. 55. Ellis
to DW, February 17, 1841, DNA, RG
59 (Despatches, Mexico).

It will be seen that this ground has been taken by me in my correspondence with the Minr. of Forn. Relations, in the case of Mr Kendall; but as his case is founded on an exception to the general principle herein stated, I thought it to be my duty to urge his case upon the notice of the Govt. previous to the receipt of your instructions of the 3d January.[17] If I should, hereafter, receive additional testimony as to the peaceful character, pursuits and intentions of these men, I shall take such steps as I may deem judicious under your general instructions. In the mean time I shall be pleased to receive such advice from the Department of State as our Government may think proper for my guidance.

Under existing circumstances I have thought it proper to abstain from carrying out your instructions as to the speedy trial of the Texans. From the present absence of proof of the amicable views of the Santa Fé Expedition, and the feeling that might prevail against the prisoners in any tribunal before which they may be hastily arraigned, it has struck me that it would be more judicious to allow the minds of the authorities to become somewhat tranquillized, before they are brought to a trial which, under present excitement, might probably terminate in the conviction and death of these unfortunate men.

If this despatch is ordered to be published, it may be discreet to except the above paragraph, lest it might come to the notice of the Mexican Government, and prove injurious to the parties interested.

Although I have ordered Mr. McRae to Vera Cruz to await the receipt of this despatch for the Department, yet I shall take the earliest opportunity to advise you by the ordinary mode of conveyance should any thing further of interest subsequently occur.

I acknowledge the receipt of your Despatches nos 36, 37, & 38,[18] and have the honor to enclose files of the Cosmopolita Diario and Siglo Diez y Nueve.[19] I have the honor to be, Sir, with great respect Your most obedient Servant   Powhatan Ellis

P.S. Mr. Duncan K. McRae is charged with these despatches and ordered to proceed forthwith to the seat of Government.   P. Ellis

ALS. DNA, RG 59 (Despatches, Mexico). Extract published in *Senate Documents*, 27th Cong., 2d sess., Serial 398, No. 325, pp. 19–21.

TO POWHATAN ELLIS

No. 45.   Department of State,
Sir: Washington, 26th February, 1842.
    Your despatches to No. 53,[1] inclusive, have been received.

17. See above, DW to Ellis, January 3, 1842.

18. DW to Ellis, January 3, 1842, above; Nos. 37 and 38. January 4 and 6, 1842, DNA, RG 59 (Instructions, Mexico).

19. Not included in the RG 59 record. Journals and newspapers were usually separated from dispatches.

1. [No. 53]. Ellis to DW, January

Since the date of the last letter to you from this department,[2] the interposition of this government has been requested in behalf of Warren D. Haughton, of Massachusetts, Ratcliff Hudson, Albert Goodwin, Geo Barnard, Jr and Mr. Kimball of Connecticut, Charles C. Willis of New York; John Holliday of Pennsylvania, John D. McAlister of Tennessee and Thomas S. Lubbock of South Carolina,[3] all whom are represented to have gone with the Texan expedition to Santa Fé.

If upon proper inquiry, you shall be satisfied that all or any of these persons were citizens of the United States who accompanied the expedition for the sole purpose of enjoying its protection whilst exploring the wilderness through which its course principally lay, and had no hostile designs against Mexico, you will officially demand their release, as they cannot justly be considered as prisoners of war. If, however, they were engaged in the service of the Republic of Texas, whether technically citizens of that Republic or not, the right of Mexico to detain them as prisoners of war cannot be disputed, nor can this government insist upon their liberation. Still, with all proper regard to the rights of Mexico and to the cardinal policy of this government in such instances, it would be impossible for us to view with indifference any dereliction on the part of that government from its duty as a humane belligerent with respect to any persons, whether natives of the United States or not, whom such a calamity had cast within its power. You will consequently, if there should be occasion for it, expostulate orally with the Minister for Foreign Affairs [José María de Bocanegra] upon this subject. You will say that, considering the state of open hostilities which has existed and still exists between the Mexican Republic and Texas, each of those governments will be held bound by the rest of the civilized world, and especially by those nations who have recognized one or both of them, to observe, in their warfare upon one another and in their treatment of prisoners, the

22, 1842, DNA, RG 59 (Despatches, Mexico).

2. No. 44. DW to Ellis, February 9, 1842, DNA, RG 59 (Instructions, Mexico).

3. On Houghton, see W. H. Foster to DW, February 10, 1842, and Timothy W. Hammond to DW, February 11 and 14, 1842, DNA, RG 59 (Misc. Letters). Houghton was a captain with the expedition. On Hudson, Goodwin, Barnard, and Kimball, see Austin Kilbourn to DW, February 12, 1842, DNA, RG 59 (Misc. Letters). Hudson, a captain with the expedition, had lived in Texas for some time. Barnard (1818–1883) came to Texas in 1838 and later became a successful Texas merchant. Goodwin and Kimball have not been identified. On Willis, see H. M. Willis to Rufus Choate, February 8, 1842, DNA, RG 59 (Misc. Letters). Willis was a musician who enlisted in the expedition. On Holliday, see above, Alexander Lowry Holliday to DW, February 16, 1842. On McAlister, see Humphrey Marshall to DW, February 8, 1842, and Meredith P. Gentry to DW, February 26, 1842, DNA, RG 59 (Misc. Letters). McAlister was killed on October 24, 1841, by a Mexican captain when he fell behind on the journey to Mexico City.

rules prescribed by Public Law. If, as is understood, the terms of the capitulation of the Santa Fé expedition were violated by the Mexican officers, if, without probable cause to fear that they would escape, the prisoners have been manacled and have been employed in menial and ignominious services, the Mexican government must, if tried by the rules of Public Law, applicable to such cases, be deemed to have overstepped the line of its right and its duty as a belligerent, and would be thought to have exposed itself to the just reproach of nations. Prisoners of war are to be considered as unfortunate and not as criminal, and are to be treated accordingly. Although the question of detention or liberation is one affecting the interest of the captor alone, and therefore one with which no other government ought to interfere in any way, yet the right to detain by no means implies the right to dispose of the prisoners at the pleasure of the captor. That right involves certain duties, among them, that of providing the prisoners with the necessaries of life and abstaining from the infliction of any punishment upon them which they may not have merited by an offence against the laws of the country since they were taken. If the Mexican government should have allowed and shall continue to allow the Texan prisoners to suffer for want of the necessaries of life, it will next be the duty of the Texan government to provide for their subsistence. If, however, this should not have been done by the time this letter reaches Mexico, the President is willing that you should advance funds for the purchase of necessaries for the persons mentioned above, if found not to have been engaged in Texan service, and for such others, of like character in whose behalf you have been specially instructed, until funds for that purpose may be supplied by their friends. The object of this is that innocent citizens of the United States be not left to suffer for want of the absolute necessaries of life during the period which may elapse before their friends can succor them. I am, Sir, your obedient servant,   Daniel Webster

Lc. DNA, RG 59 (Instructions, Mexico). Published in *Senate Documents*, 27th Cong., 2d sess., Serial 398, No. 325, pp. 6–7.

FROM JOHN CARROLL LEGRAND, WITH ENCLOSURE

Department of State,
Sir,   Annapolis, MD. March 21st. 1842.
    In compliance with the request of the General Assembly of Maryland, I have the honor to transmit the enclosed copy of its resolves,[1] touching a matter therein mentioned, and am, Most Respectfully, Your obedient servant,   Jno. C. LeGrand

Copy. DNA, RG 59 (Misc. Letters). Rec'd March 28, 1842. LeGrand (1814–1861), a lawyer, was secretary of state of Maryland.

    1. See below.

ENCLOSURE: RESOLUTION RELATING TO JOHN T. HOWARD,
A PRISONER IN MEXICO[1]

Whereas, it is represented to this General Assembly, that an expedition of traders from Texas to Mexico was captured and made prisoners at Santa Fe, and are now held in captivity by the Government of Mexico; and whereas, it is further represented, that John T. Howard, a citizen of Maryland, and other citizens of other States, accompanied said expedition, and it is the duty of the Government of the United States, to extend its citizens under all circumstances, such relief and protection as it is within its competency to grant, therefore—

Resolved by the General Assembly of Maryland, That his Excellency, the President of the United States, be requested to use such means as the Constitution of the United States, and the public law of nations may authorise, for amelioriating the condition of the persons captured as aforesaid, and expecially for the purpose of protecting and demanding such citizens of the United States, as may have accompanied said expedition.

Resolved, That His Excellency, the Governor,[2] be requested to cause a copy of the foregoing preamble and resolution to be forwarded to the President of the United States, and also to each of our Senators and Representatives in Congress.

Copy. DNA, RG 59 (Misc. Letters). Resolutions similar to this were passed by the legislatures of Kentucky and Louisiana.

FROM THADDEUS RICHMOND KENDALL, WILLIAM RIX, AND
CATHERINE KENDALL RIX

Sumterville, Alabama
Sir   March 22 1842

The persons who address you this letter, are the brothers and sister of George Wilkins Kendall, now a prisoner in Mexico. The reason we did not apply for the interference of our Government in behalf of our Friend on the earliest news of his captivity is, that we were at sea at the time, and consequently ignorant of his condition. About the time we heard of his seizure, we heard also that our Government had of its own accord, taken steps that we believed would be effectual in gaining his release. For the last four weeks the mails have been completely shut out from us by high waters, and to day, for the first time we have learned of the utter failure of all the efforts that have been made in his favor and the most miserable condition of him and his companions. We trust you will par-

1. The resolution should refer to John C. Howard.
2. Francis Thomas (1799–1876; Saint John's College) served as governor of Maryland from 1841 to 1844.

don us for addressing you a private letter, on a subject, that has already had the immediate, and we had gratefully trusted, the effectual exertion of your public authority. You have probably seen in the public prints, the miserable details of the sufferings of our brother. We address you thus personally, hoping more effectually, to enlist your feelings, and great personal influence in his favor. Mr K[endall] was born and educated in New Hampshire and a more noble and honest soul could not claim your aid. We have heard his mother[1] proudly name you as one with whom in her youth she was acquainted. We now appeal to you for aid and advice. Our brother is suffering unheard of cruelties; at the hands of a people claiming to be civilized, and at the time they are entertaining our Minister [Powhatan Ellis] at their Court. The circumstances of Mr. K[endall's] visit to Mexico are these, He is extensively engaged in publishing a daily paper in New Orleans, during the business season of the year, his labors are of the most arduous, and wearing kind, and he has made it a practice to recreate, during the hot months by traveling. He has usually visited his Father,[2] and Mother, who reside in Burlington Vt. Last Spring he found his health a good deal impaired, and by *advice of his physician*, he determined to go to Santa Fe. His original intention was to go by St Louis. He was detered from this, by a courteous invitation from the Texas commissioners to accompany their expedition as a guest. He at once determined to do so and in company with Mr [Franklin] Combs and Mr [Thomas] Falkoner, the latter of the London press[,] He departed. It is worthy of note that they started under precisely the same circumstances with this exception, Mr K[endall] provided himself with a *passport*. Mr F[alconer] did not. The miserable upshot of the Expedition is well known, and yet by some strange partiality we find Mr. Combs liberated because, if we are rightly informed, *he is the son of a General* and Mr F[alconer], because he is a *Brittish Subject* while our brother broken down by disease the consequence of cruelties which we think should claim the attention of enlightened Governments, if practised towards the citizens of other Governments, is reduced to Slavery and driven out to work the highway. Under these circumstances we ask your aid and advice. Your station, as well as your knowledge of matters of this nature will enable you to inform us what we may hope for him. Respectfully, your obt. servants

Thaddeas R. Kendall   Wm Rix   Catherine Kendall Rix

A L S by Kendall; signed also by the Rixes. DNA, RG 59 (Misc. Letters). Rec'd April 11, 1842. Thaddeus (d. 1882), the brother of George W. Kendall, was a lawyer and merchant in Mobile, Alabama. His sister, Catherine, was married to William Rix (1811–1892), also a Mobile merchant.

1. Abigail Wilkins Kendall (1773–1853).   2. Thaddeus Kendall (1772–1843).

TO EDWARD EVERETT

Private   Washington Mar: 30. 1842
My Dear Sir   10. P.M.

I have only time to say that your despatches, to the 3rd,[1] were recd
this Evening, & have been glanced at, but not read. Lord Ashburton as
yet is not heard from; but he is not out of time, according to other passages recently made from your side to ours.[2]

Mr [Matthew St. Clair] Clark[e]'s house is taken for him,[3] and is quite
in readiness.

We have more excitement here at this moment from the new attempt
of Mexico to reduce Texas.[4] The want of all due preparation on the part
of Texas renders it possible that the Mexican troops may overrun the
Country; but I have no belief they can hold it. There is also a good deal
of feeling in the U.S. about the manner in which certain citizens of ours,
who say they [are] non combatant followers of the Texan expedition to
Santa Fé have been treated by the Mexican authorities. I hope, however,
we may be able to keep the peace.

Congress is doing nothing, at least, no good thing, Endless Debate, &
personal quarrel are the order of the day. The foreign relations of the
Country are ticklish enough; but our domestic condition is terrible. We
are now enjoying the rich fruits of the Compromise Act of Mar: 1833.[5]
Almost the only symptom of returning sense among us is found in the
very general idea now prevalent that there is no course left but to lay
duties in the old way, discriminating & specific, abandoning all notions
of universal *horizontalization* in such things.

Mrs. [Caroline Le Roy] W[ebster] desires her best regards; & I am
obliged to place this at once into the hands of Charles Brown[6] or lose
this chance by the Boston Boat. Yrs   D Webster

ALS. MHi. Published in *W & S*, 16:366–367.

1. These were not official dispatches. See Everett to DW, March
3, 1842, "The Aftermath and Implementation of the Treaty of Washington: The Cass-Webster Debate," pp.
713–714, below. See also Everett's
other letters of March 3, mDW 21772
and mDW 21773.

2. Ashburton arrived in the United
States on April 4, 1842.

3. Clarke (c. 1791–1852) was
clerk of the U.S. House of Representatives from 1822 to 1833 and from
1841 to 1843.

4. Mexican forces invaded Texas
in March 1842. Texas and Mexico
were at war until an armistice was
declared on June 15, 1843.

5. DW's sarcastic comment was in
reference to the Compromise Tariff,
which was signed on March 2, 1833.
The tariff, which provided for the
reduction of duties on various goods,
was vehemently opposed by the New
England states.

6. Brown, a former slave whose
freedom had been purchased by DW,
was employed by DW for many years
as a servant.

FROM ROBERT PERKINS LETCHER, WITH ENCLOSURE

My dear Sir   Frankfort K 2nd April 1842.

The enclosed letter[1] will explain the object of this note. The writer is a very worthy old gentleman and exceedingly devoted to his sons. I have given him every assurance that you will take great pleasure in exerting yourself to release the captives.

I must beg the favor of you my dear Sir, to write the old gentleman a short letter in reply, as I know it would comfort him very much. With great regard your friend   R P Letcher

P.S.

For Christ's sake, and for the country's sake dont let the Land Bill be repealed.[2] All we require, upon God's earth to make us a happy & prosperous people is a good Tariff and a good Nat currency, and he who secures these two great treasures will be hailed as a benefactor for ages to come. May God in his infinite wisdom, *infuse* one single ounce of common practical sense into the head of the president! Enough—I did not mean to trouble you with politics. Yours. RPL.

Copy. NhHi. Letcher, a Whig, served in Congress from 1822 to 1835. He was governor of Kentucky from 1840 to 1844.

ENCLOSURE: WILLIAM ADAMS TO ROBERT PERKINS LETCHER

D Govr   Mt. Vernon Ky Aprl 1. 1842

From information I can rely upon my two sons, Allensworth and John[1] are of the Santa-Fee prisoners. They left Kentucky with stock for Alibamma and after seling out went to Texas on a tradeing expedition. They did not intend to settle there as they have advised me by letter of their intention to return. I am sattisfied they are not citizens of Texas.

Will you do an old friend the favor to corrispond with Mr Webster in their behalf, and git him to open a corrispendence with our Minister at Mexico [Powhatan Ellis], and if they are there to use his exertions to have them released. At all events to let them know that I am advised of their situation and am doing all in my power for them. Be so good as to say to Mr Webster to request our Minister to asertain certainly if they are there (or have perished on the trip) and to write me (directly) to this place. As you are acquainted with Judge [Powhatan] Ellis and Genl [Waddy] Thompson (should he have superseded the Judge) I would thank you to write to them forthwith and make the like request. It would

1. See below.
2. The Land Distribution and Preemption Act of September 4, 1841, was repealed August 30, 1842, ac-

cording to the terms of the tariff act of that year. See 5 *U.S. Stat.* 453–458, 548–567.
1. Not otherwise identified.

be gratifying to me to know that either of those gentlemen had visited my sons in prison. Yr Obt Sevt   William Adams

ALS. NhHi. Adams not identified.

TO WADDY THOMPSON

No. 2.   Department of State,
Sir: Washington, 5th April, 1842.

I have to address you upon the subject of those citizens of the United States who were captured with the Texan expedition to Santa Fé and who, as is believed, were not parties to that expedition so far as it was military and hostile to Mexico, if in fact a hostile invasion of Mexico was among its purposes, but accompanied it only as traders, tourists, travellers, men of letters, or in other characters and capacities, showing them to be non-combatants, but who, nevertheless, were taken and held as prisoners, compelled to undergo incredible hardships in a winter's march of two thousand miles and, at its end, subjected to almost every conceivable degree of indignity and suffering.

By the law and practice of civilized nations, enemies' subjects taken in arms may be made prisoners of war, but every person found in the train of an army is not to be considered as, therefore, a belligerent or an enemy. In all wars and in all countries multitudes of persons follow the march of armies for the purpose of traffic or from motives of curiosity or the influence of other causes, who neither expect to be nor reasonably can be considered belligerents. Whoever in the Texan expedition to Santa Fé was commissioned or enrolled for the military service of Texas, or being armed, was in the pay of that government and engaged in an expedition hostile to Mexico, may be considered as her enemy and might lawfully, therefore, be detained as a prisoner of war. This is not to be doubted, and by the general practice of modern nations it is true, that the fact of having been found in arms with others admitted to be armed for belligerent purposes, raises a presumption of hostile character. In many cases and especially in regard to European wars in modern times, it might be difficult to repel the force of this presumption. It is still, however but a presumption, because it is nevertheless true that a man may be found in arms with no hostile intentions. He may have assumed arms for other purposes and may assert a pacific character with which the fact of his being more or less armed, would be entirely consistent. In former and less civilized ages, cases of this sort existed without number in European society. When the peace of communities was less firmly established by efficient laws, and when, therefore, men often travelled armed for their own defence, or when individuals being armed according to the fashion of the age, yet often journied under the protection of military escorts, or bodies of soldiers, the possession of arms was no evidence of hostile character, circumstances of the times sufficiently explaining such appearances consistently with pacific intentions. And circumstances of the country may repel the presumption of hostility as well as circumstances of the times or the manners of a particular age. The Texan expedition to Santa Fé, in traversing the vast plains between the place from which it set out, and that point, was to pass through a region which no one thinks of entering and crossing without arms, for whatever purpose or with whatever intent he may undertake such enterprize. If he be a hunter, he is armed; if a trader, he is armed; and usually traders go in considerable bodies, that they may be the better able to defend themselves against the roaming savage tribes so constantly met with in those extensive plains. It is not uncommon, indeed, that, for their better defence, companies of traders retain the service of men at arms, who maintain military order and array along the line of their march. When such bodies are met with in countries usually traversed by them, no inference arises from the circumstance of their being armed, of any intention on their part of using such arms for any purpose but that of defence. If tourists or persons wearing any other similar but equally pacific character, set forth on such a journey, they are still armed; armed for subsistence as well as for defence. The fact, therefore, of being found in such a country with arms, does not prove a belligerent or hostile character, since nobody, however peaceable, is found there without arms. If, therefore, individuals armed only according to the custom of the country, but having no hostile purposes of their own and free from all military authority or employment, fall in with or follow the march of troops proceeding towards a point of attack, these individuals are not *combatants* and not subject to be taken and treated as prisoners.

These considerations may be applied to those citizens of the United States for whose release from imprisonment the interposition of this government has been requested. One of those citizens is George Wilkins Kendall.

Mr Kendall is a man of letters, a highly respectable citizen of New Orleans, and was the editor of a literary publication carried on at that place. He was fond of travel at those seasons of the year when most persons who are able leave the city, and having, in previous tours, made himself acquainted with all parts of his own country, and learning, early in the spring of 1841, that a *trading* expedition would start from Texas to Santa Fé about the first of May, he resolved on joining it as a pleasure excursion of a novel and interesting character. His departure and his intentions were publickly announced in the paper with which he was concerned, at the time of his setting forth. His object was declared to be "to take a personal glance over this broad expanse of country, and thus spending the summer, to return, either by Missouri or by the way of lower Mexico, by the usual time when citizens return to New

Orleans for the fall business."[1] The expedition, though having a military equipment, was represented to him as entirely commercial in its character, its object being, as was asserted, to turn the rich Chihuahua trade into the Texan channel. Mr Kendall was no soldier, no revolutionary adventurer, but a man of respectable connexions engaged in prosperous business and fond of the enjoyments of intellectual and social life. It is hardly possible that such a gentleman should have left such a condition to form part of a military expedition, subjecting himself to all its hazards and all its results, in an attempt to subjugate by force of arms a Mexican province five hundred or a thousand miles from his home and his connexions.

Before leaving New Orleans, he obtained a passport from the Mexican Vice Consul in that City. This fact, although it appears to have been denied, is proved by testimony of Mr [Thomas] Falconer and Mr [George F. X.] Van Ness.[2] They can hardly be mistaken, but further evidence on this point may probably be in your possession before you receive this despatch. He armed himself before leaving home as any other person of however pacific character would arm himself for such a tour. Such was Mr Kendall's character, such his objects and such the circumstances under which he joined the ill fated expedition.

Several other prisoners appear from the circumstances to have been as little engaged in any hostile design as Mr Kendall.

John Thompkins is represented to be a citizen of the United States from Greene County, Illinois, where his family, consisting of a wife and five children, still reside. He is a saddler by trade, but left the United States with merchandize for Texas just in time to join the expedition to Santa Fé. His health was delicate, and his object was to improve it to dispose of his merchandize for defraying his expenses and to return to the place of his abode by the way of St. Louis.

David Snively is a man somewhat advanced in life who belongs to the State of Ohio, where he has a wife and several children. He went with the expedition as a trader and had a considerable amount of merchandize with him.

H[enry] R[idley] Buchanan, of Tennessee, went also as a trader and

1. New Orleans *Daily Picayune*, May 18, 1841.

2. Kendall said he obtained a Mexican passport from the Mexican vice consul in New Orleans, Salvador Prats, on May 15, 1841. In a letter to Ellis dated February 10, 1842, Falconer and Van Ness testified that they had seen Kendall's passport, which they said had been taken from him. See Kendall, *Narrative of the Texan Santa Fé Expedition* (New York, 1844), p. 11, and the statement of Falconer and Van Ness enclosed in Ellis to DW, February 17, 1842, DNA, RG 59 (Despatches, Mexico).

took with him property of value which was taken from him. He had arrived in Texas only a month before the expedition set out, and accompanied it with his own pack mules and a servant.

L. B. Sheldon is a member of the Mississippi bar, who accompanied the expedition as a traveller only. He had with him a small amount in merchandize, by the sale of which he expected to defray his travelling expenses. He had gone to Texas in March, 1841, on business which he presumed would not detain him longer than two months, but he subsequently resolved to join the expedition for the purpose above mentioned.

Two persons of the name of Howard[3] were among the captives, natives of or residents in this City or its neighborhood. They are represented as traders who had with them merchandize to the amount of eight or ten thousand dollars.

Thomas S[tebbins] Torry, of Hartford, in Connecticut, is believed to have gone to Texas in December, 1840; and being a trader, joined the expedition as an escort for protection against the Indians or other free booters. He did not intend to return to Texas, but to trade at Santa Fé and between that place and St Louis.

The circumstances of others who have applied for the interposition of this government, are less precisely known. Whatever evidence may be in this department or shall be received hereafter respecting them, will be forwarded to you.

A demand for Mr Kendall's release from confinement, as well as that of others under equally innocent circumstances, has been made by the Minister of the United States at Mexico [Powhatan Ellis] and you will see the correspondence between that Minister and the Mexican Secretary of State [José María de Bocanegra].[4] The correspondence, as you will observe, is principally confined to the case of Mr Kendall.

The Mexican Secretary[5] objects to his release from confinement because he was united with the invading enemies of that country, in whose company he was taken and under whose protection he was journeying, and because the entrance of foreigners into Mexico by the Texan frontier, being prohibited by a Mexican law, even when such foreigners might

3. The reference is to John C. Howard and his brother, George Thomas Howard (1814–1866). The latter was a veteran of the Texas Revolution and many Indian campaigns. George Howard escaped Mexican custody on April 14, 1842. He later served in the Texas Volunteer Cavalry during the Mexican War.

4. See above, Ellis to DW, February 17, 1842; see also No. 57. Ellis to DW, February 26, 1842, DNA, RG 59 (Despatches, Mexico).

5. In this and the ensuing paragraphs, Webster is responding to Bocanegra to Ellis, February 13, 1842 (enclosed in No. 55. Ellis to DW, February 17, 1842, above), and Bocanegra to Ellis, February 18 and 26, 1842 (enclosed in No. 57. Ellis to DW, February 26, 1842), DNA, RG 59 (Despatches, Mexico).

be travelling alone, the prohibition ought to be more strict and severe in the case of their entering by the side of soldiers coming to invade the country. Because, also, Mr Kendall was an agent of the Texans or at least a member of the expedition to New Mexico; in proof of which, a passage in the following words is quoted from the New Orleans Picayune of the 21st of December, last. "A captain Lewis was one of the Commissioners, and the other was Mr. Kendall, Editor of the Picayune."

The Secretary proceeds to assert that those who join invaders ought to be involved in their fate in respect to such warlike measures as it may be necessary to take to repel such invaders, and that in affairs of this nature, all the presumptions are against him who associates himself with an enemy in whose company he is made a prisoner, whatever his intentions may have been. That if Mr Kendall was ignorant of the Mexican law, referred to, it is well known not to be allowable to plead ignorance of any law which had properly been made public. But supposing that he was ignorant of the law, the circumstances of his case, he argues were such that its text could not be literally followed, for the penalty mentioned was intended to apply to one or two persons only and those without hostile accompaniments, who might present themselves on the frontier, and that the law did not deprive the Mexican government of the right of self preservation, a right derived from the law of nature and nations. The Secretary then alludes to documents in the possession of his government which he says place Mr Kendall's conduct in a more serious light; but those documents are neither produced nor described. The Secretary claims that the paragraph quoted from the newspaper was the ground of the proceeding of his government, but says that, proceeding as the paragraph did; from Mr Kendall's partners in business, it might be considered as impartial and served to strengthen the presumptions against him. He denies that it is the duty of his government to allow Mr Kendall the benefit of the context of the article from which the paragraph supposed to inculpate him had been quoted, although the extract may be used against him. He endeavors to prove himself correct in calling Mr Kendall a Commissioner of the Texans, and proceeds to define what he understands a Commissioner to be.

If Mr Kendall had a passport, that, he admits, would be prima facie evidence in his favor, and if it should be ascertained that he had an unconditional passport which had been destroyed by an officer in the Mexican army, he should be set at liberty; and that measures had been taken to ascertain these facts.

These reasons appear to be unfounded in fact, or if true, to furnish no sufficient ground for regarding Mr Kendall as a belligerent enemy or for declining to comply with the demand made by this government in his behalf. In the first place it is said he was united with the invading enemies of the country, in whose company he was taken and under whose protection he was journeying. That he travelled with the Texans is true, but, as has been already said, that fact alone does not constitute him a combatant. It may furnish, in the first instance, a presumption that he was so, but such a presumption may be repelled and is fully repelled by the circumstances of the case. There would be no meaning in that well settled principle of the law of nations which exempts men of letters and other classes of non combatants from the liability of being made prisoners of war if it were an answer to any claim for such exemption that the person making it was united with a military force, or journeying under its protection. As to the assertion that it is against the law of Mexico for foreigners to pass into it, across the line of Texas, it is with no little surprize that the Mexican Secretary of State is found to assign this reason for making Mr Kendall a prisoner. The direction of that law only is to prohibit the travellers' entrance or to send him back, if he does enter. It has no penalty of chains, dungeons, or condemnation to the public works. And the Mexican Secretary himself sufficiently shows that this law has no application to the case, because he says it was intended only for the case of one, two, or a few individuals.

Having quoted this law, and then finding that in its just import it furnished no authority for the treatment, which these citizens of the United States had received, the Mexican Secretary appears to treat the subject as if this law had been set up to assist their claim for liberation, while in truth all that Mr Ellis did, in this respect, was to say that if that law governed the case, then no penalty, no punishment and no treatment of the prisoners could be justified but such as had been prescribed by that law, and thereupon the Secretary adroitly denies that the law applies to the case at all. In this he is no doubt quite right. As to the assertion that Mr Kendall was an agent of the Texans, or a member, properly speaking, of the expedition, and the reference, in proof of this assertion, to the article in the newspaper with which he was connected, all this was founded in misconstruction, as you will see, of the true import of the article itself, even if a newspaper paragraph were fit to be regarded in such a case. In the article Mr Kendall had been called an 'Avant Courier,' merely to signify that he went forward, in approaching Santa Fé, in advance of the rest of the party. If others went forward for other purposes, he might still, in pursuance of his own objects, go with them. But Mr Kendall not being responsible for this article or shown to have any knowledge of it, it cannot be of the least force against him, whatever may be its import.

The Secretary says, finally, that being found in company with an enemy raises a presumption against the party, but the Secretary does not say that this presumption may not be rebutted. Why, indeed, does he call it a presumption, unless he means that it is a thing calling for explanation and which may be explained. It is explained, fully and completely. Mr Kendall, as we think, brings himself clearly within the exemption of the law of nations as practiced in modern times, and to insist on presumptions and to give them the force of conclusive proofs, in defiance of all repelling proofs, is to render that law, in its application to cases of this kind, null and void. If it be admitted that *prima facie*, the presumption is against Mr Kendall, has he not repelled it? He has made an effort to do so, but instead of meeting this effort by argument and the proofs which support it by opposite proofs, the Secretary appears to content himself with stating and repeating, that such is the legal presumption; thus wholly avoiding the true point of the case. This government thinks that the facts stated and proved show Mr Kendall to have been no party to the military expedition of Texas; to have had no hostile intention against Mexico, to have entered her territory for no purpose of assisting to make war on her citizens, dismember her provinces or overturn her government.

It does not satisfactorily appear from any correspondence or information now in this Department, in what light Mexico looks upon those persons made prisoners at Santa Fé, whom she has a right to consider as engaged in the service of Texas and therefore as her enemies. We must presume that she means to regard them as prisoners of war. There is a possibility, however, that a different mode of considering them may be adopted and that they may be thought to be amenable to the municipal laws of Mexico. Any proceeding founded on this idea would undoubtedly be attended with most serious consequences. It is now several years since the independence of Texas, as a separate government, has been acknowledged by the United States, and she has since been recognized in that character by several of the most considerable powers of Europe. The war between her and Mexico, which has continued so long and with such success; that for a long time there has been no hostile foot in Texas, is a public war, and as such it has been and will be regarded by this government. It is not now an outbreak of rebellion, a fresh insurrection, the parties to which may be treated as rebels. The contest, supposed indeed to have been substantially ended, has at least advanced far beyond that point. It is a public war, and persons captured in the course of it who are to be detained at all, are to be detained as prisoners of war and not otherwise.

It is true that the independence of Texas has not been recognized by Mexico. It is equally true that the independence of Mexico has only recently been recognized by Spain,[6] but the United States having acknowledged both the independence of Mexico before Spain acknowledged it and the independence of Texas although Mexico has not yet acknowledged it, stands in the same relation towards both those governments,

6. Spain did not recognize the independence of Mexico until 1836; the United States granted diplomatic recognition to Mexico in 1822.

and is as much bound to protect its citizens in a proper intercourse with Texas against injuries by the government of Mexico, as it would have been to protect such citizens in a like intercourse with Mexico against injuries by Spain. The period which has elapsed since Texas threw off the authority of Mexico, is nearly as long as the whole duration of the revolutionary war of the United States. No effort for the re-subjugation of Texas has been made by Mexico from the time of the battle of San Jacinto on the 21st day of April, 1836, until the commencement of the present year, and during all this period Texas has maintained an independent government, carried on commerce and made treaties with nations in both hemispheres, and kept aloof all attempts at invading her territory. If under these circumstances any citizen of the United States in whose behalf this government has a right on any account or to any extent to interfere should, on a charge of having been found with an armed Texan force acting in hostility to Mexico, be brought to trial and punished as for a violation of the municipal laws of Mexico or as being her subjects engaged in rebellion, after his release has been demanded by this government, consequences of the most serious character would certainly ensue. You will therefore not fail, should any indication render it necessary, to point out distinctly to the government of Mexico the dangers, should the war between her and Texas continue, of considering it, so far as citizens of the United States may be concerned, in any other light than that of a public, national war, in the events and progress of which, prisoners may be made on both sides, and to whose condition the law and usages of nations respecting prisoners of war are justly applicable.

And this makes it proper that I should draw your particular attention to the manner in which the persons taken near Santa Fé have been treated, as we are informed.

Mr Kendall and other persons with him, having been carried to Santa Fé from the place of capture, were there deprived of their arms. To this there can be no objection if we consider them as prisoners of war, because prisoners of war may be lawfully disarmed by the captor; but they were also despoiled, not only of every article of value about their persons, but of their clothing, also, their coats, their hats, their shoes, things indispensable to the long march before them. If these facts be not disproved, they constitute an outrage by the local authorities of Mexico, for which there can be no apology. The privations and indignities to which they were subjected during their march of two thousand miles to the City of Mexico at the most inclement season of the year, were horrible, and if they were not well authenticated, it would have been incredible that they should have been inflicted in this age and in a country calling itself christian and civilized. During many days they had no food, and on others only two ears of corn were distributed to each man. To sustain life, therefore, they were compelled to sell on the way the few remnants of clothing which their captors had left them; but by seeking thus to appease their hunger, they increased the misery which they already endured from exposure to the cold. Most dreadful of all, however, several of them, disabled by sic[k]ness and suffering from keeping up with the others, were deliberately shot without any pro[vo]cation.[7] Those who survived to their journey's end, were many of them afflicted with loathsome disease, and those whose health was not broken down, have been treated, not as the Public Law requires, but in a manner harsh and vindictive, and with a degree of severity equal at least to that usually inflicted by the municipal codes of most civilized and Christian states upon the basest felons. Indeed they appear to have been ranked with these, being thrust into the same dungeon with Mexican malefactors, chained to them in pairs, and when allowed to see the light and breathe the air of heaven, required, as a compensation therefor, to labor beneath the lash of a task-master upon roads and public works of that country.

The government of the United States has no inclination to interfere in the war between Mexico and Texas for the benefit or protection of individuals any further than its clear duties require. But if citizens of the United States who have not renounced nor intended to renounce their allegiance to their own government, nor have entered into the military service of any other government, have nevertheless been found so connected with armed enemies of Mexico, as that they may be lawfully captured and detained as prisoners of war, it is still the duty of this government to take so far a concern in their welfare as to see that, as prisoners of war, they are treated according to the usage of modern times and civilized states. Indeed, although the rights or the safety of none of our citizens were concerned, yet if in a war waged between two neighboring states, the killing, enslaving or cruelly treating of prisoners should be indulged, the United States would feel it to be their duty, as well as their right to remonstrate and to interpose against such a departure from the principles of humanity and civilization. Those principles are common principles, essential alike to the welfare of all nations, and in the preservation of which all nations have, therefore, rights and interests. But their duty to interfere becomes imperative in cases affecting their own citizens. It is therefore that the government of the United States protests against the hardships and cruelties to which the Santa Fé prisoners have been subjected. It protests against this treatment in the name of humanity and the law of nations; in the name of all Christian States, in the name of civilization and the spirit of the age, in the name of all Republics, in the name of Liberty herself, enfeebled and dishonored by all cruelty and all

7. In addition to John McAlister, those executed on the 2,000-mile march to Mexico City were a merchant named Amos A. Golpin and a man named Edward Griffith.

excess; in the name and for the honor of this whole hemisphere. It pro-tests emphatically and earnestly against practices belonging only to bar-barous people in barbarous times.

By the well established rules of national law, prisoners of war are not to be treated harshly unless personally guilty towards him who has them in his power, for he should remember that they are men and unfortunate. When an enemy is conquered and submits, a great soul forgets all resent-ment and is filled with compassion for him. This is the humane language of the law of nations and this is the sentiment of high honor among men. The law of war forbids the wounding, killing, impressment into the troops of the country, the enslaving or the otherwise maltreating of pris-oners of war, unless they have been guilty of some grave crime, and from the obligation of this law, no civilized state can discharge itself.

Every nation on being received at her own request into the circle of civilized governments, must understand that she not only attains rights of sovereignty and the dignity of national character, but that she binds herself also to the strict and faithful observance of all those principles, laws and usages which have obtained currency among civilized States and which have for their object the mitigation of the miseries of war. No community can be allowed to enjoy the benefit of national character in modern times without submitting to all the duties which that character imposes. A Christian people, who exercise sovereign power, who make treaties, maintain diplomatic relations with other States and who should yet refuse to conduct its military operations according to the usages uni-versally observed by such States, would present a character singularly inconsistent and anomolous. This government will not hastily suppose that the Mexican Republic will assume such a character.

There is yet another very important element arising out of the facts of this case. It is asserted and believed that the surrender of some of the persons connected with the expedition was made upon specific terms which were immediately violated by the local Mexican authorities. If there is one rule of the law of war more clear and peremptory than an-other it is, that compacts between enemies, such as truces and capitula-tions, shall be faithfully adhered to, and their non-observance is de-nounced as being manifestly at variance with the true interest and duty, not only of the immediate parties, but of all mankind. Consequently if the surrender of the expedition or, any part of it was conditional, the benefit of those conditions must be insisted upon in favor of Mr Kendall. According to the statement of Messrs Falconer and Van Ness, Mr Ken-dall proceeded two hundred miles in advance of the main body and was taken, with his companions, while they were displaying a flag of truce; and the persons who took them gave assurances that they should not be held as prisoners of war. Here then was a special immunity, promised but afterwards notoriously withheld, as we are bound to believe in the present state of our information upon the subject. If, therefore, this government were not entitled to demand, Mr Kendall's release on the grounds of his having been a non-combatant and a neutral, it might require the government of Mexico to take care that the stipulation of its authorized agents to this effect be scrupulously fulfilled and that on this account those to whom the promise was made should be immediately released, according to that promise.

In conclusion, I am directed by the President of the United States now to instruct you, that on the receipt of this despatch, you inquire carefully and minutely into the circumstances of all those persons who, having been taken near Santa Fé and having claimed the interposition of this government, are still held as prisoners in Mexico, and you will then demand of the Mexican government the release of such of them as appear to have been innocent traders, travellers, men of letters, or for any other reasons justly esteemed non-combatants, being citizens of the United States. To this end it may be proper to direct the Consul[8] to proceed to the places where any of them may be confined, and to take their statements, under oath, as also the statements of other persons to whom they may respectively refer. If the Mexican government deny facts upon which any of the persons claim their release and desire time for further investigation of their respective cases or any of them, proper and suitable time must be allowed, but if any of the persons described in the next preceding paragraph and for whose release you shall have made a demand, shall still be detained for the purpose of further inquiry or otherwise, you will then explicitly demand of the Mexican government that they be treated thence forward with all the lenity which in the most favorable cases belongs to the rights of prisoners of war, that they be not confined in loathsome dungeons, with malefactors and persons diseased, that they be not chained or subjected to ignominy or to any particular rigor in their detention, that they be not obliged to labor on the public works or put to any other hardship. You will state to the Mexican Government that the government of the United States entertains a conviction that these persons ought to be set at liberty, without delay; that it will feel great dissatisfaction if it shall still learn that Mr Kendall, whose case has already been made the subject of an express demand, and others of equal claims to liberation, be not set at liberty at the time when you receive this despatch, but that if the government of Mexico insists upon detaining any of them for further inquiry, it is due to the government of the United States, to its desire to preserve peace and harmony with Mexico and to justice and humanity, that, while detained, these persons should enjoy to the fullest extent, the rights of prisoners of war, and that it expects that a demand, so just and reasonable, a demand respectfully made by

8. William D. Jones, a Cincinnati merchant, was U.S. consul in Mexico City, 1836–1843.

one friendly state to another, will meet with immediate compliance. Having made this demand, you will wait for an answer, and if within ten days you shall not receive assurances that all the persons above mentioned who may still be detained, will be thenceforward treated in the manner which has now been insisted upon, you will hold no further official intercourse with the government until you shall receive further directions from your own government. You will therefore communicate with this Department, detaining for that purpose the messenger who carries this. In your communication, you will state as fully and as accurately as possible, the circumstances of each man's case, as they may appear by all the evidence which at that time may be possessed by the Legation.

In making your demand for the better treatment of the prisoners, you will take especial care not to abandon or weaken the claim for their release, nothing more being intended in that respect than that proper time should be allowed to the Government of Mexico to make such further inquiries as may be necessary.

Your predecessor [Powhatan Ellis] has already been directed, that if any of the persons suffer for the want of the common necessaries of life, he should provide for such wants until otherwise supplied, a direction which you also will observe. I am, Sir, your obedient servant,

Daniel Webster

LC. DNA, RG 59 (Instructions, Mexico). Published in *Senate Documents*, 27th Cong., 2d sess., Serial 398, No. 325, pp. 8–17.

TO WILLIAM ADAMS

Dear Sir   Washington, April 13. 1842.

Govr [Robert Perkins] Letcher has communicated to me your letter to him of the 1st of April,[1] respecting your two sons, supposed to be in Mexico, among the Prisoners taken on the Texan Expedition to Santa Fé. I assure you no pains shall be spared, to make an interference for them, if their objects were as pacific as you represent.

A letter to the American Minister at Mexico [Waddy Thompson], in their behalf will be despatched today,[2] from this Department.

It is not wonderful, my Dear Sir, that as a father you feel anxious for the fate of these young men. I cannot think that any serious harm will ultimately happen to them. At any rate you may rely on this Govt, & this Department, to make every just effort for their release, & return to their friends. I am, with respect &c

AL draft. NhHi. Published in *PC*, 2:118–119.

1. See above, Adams to Letcher, April 1, 1842, enclosed in Letcher to DW, April 2, 1842.

2. DW had already instructed Powhatan Ellis regarding the Adams brothers. See No. 46. DW to Ellis, March 10, 1842, DNA, RG 59 (Instructions, Mexico).

TO JOSEPH EVE

No. 11.   Department of State,
Sir: Washington, 20th April, 1842.

I transmit a copy of a communication to the Department of War from a delegate of the Choctaw nation of Indians, complaining of certain proceedings of inhabitants of that part of Texas contiguous to the lands allotted to his nation in the United States.[1] You will make representation upon this subject to the Texan government,[2] and suggest the expediency of their impressing upon their citizens and officers whose abodes are adjacent to settlements of Indians of the United States, the necessity of abstaining from broils with that race and from giving it any just cause of provocation. Unless this government shall be satisfied that the government of Texas, does all that lies within its power in that respect, it cannot consider itself answerable for any excesses which those savages may perpetrate. I am, Sir, your obedient servant,   Daniel Webster

LC. DNA, RG 59 (Instructions, Texas).

FROM POWHATAN ELLIS

No. 60.   Legation of the US of A.
Sir,   Mexico 28th April 1842

I had the honor to inform you in my despatch dated the 26th of February[1] that this Government had resolved not to release the American Citizens claimed by this Legation. At that time I considered the negotiations upon that subject closed, and immediately despatched Mr [Henry E.] Lawrence to Washington to advise you, thereof, with a view to await your ultimate instructions. Since that time a favorable opportunity presented itself to renew the negotiation without yielding the ground upon which the matter rested, and it has resulted in the liberation of George Wilkins Kendall, David Snively, John C. Howard, T[heoderick] A. Sully, H[enry] R[idley] Buchanan, J[ohn] B Houghtailing and Thos: S Torrey.

1. Peter Perkins Pitchlynn (1806–1881; Choctaw Academy and University of Nashville 1827–1828) to John C. Spencer, March 25, 1842, enclosed in Spencer to DW, March 28, 1842, DNA, RG 59 (Misc. Letters). Pitchlynn, the delegate of the Choctaw Nation in Washington, complained of repeated incursions by Texans into "Choctaw country" during which they murdered Choctaws and stole Negro slaves belonging to them. He called upon the U.S. government to uphold Article 5 of the treaty of September 27, 1830, which obligated the United States "to protect the Choctaws from domestic strife and from foreign enemies." For the treaty of 1830, see Charles J. Kappler, ed., Indian Affairs: Laws and Treaties (5 vols., Washington, D.C., 1904–1941), 2:310–319.

2. The response of the Texan government to Eve's representation is enclosed in Eve to DW, June 11, 1842, DNA, RG 59 (Despatches, Texas).

1. No. 57. Ellis to DW, February 26, 1842, DNA, RG 59 (Despatches, Mexico).

On the 18th. of March I received a letter from Thomas Pratt, one of the prisoners confined in the Accordada stating that William Rosier, was in a bad state of health, and requesting me to intercede with the Government to have him placed where he could receive prompt medical attention.[2] I instructed Mr [Brantz] Mayer,[3] the Secretary of this Legation, to call on General [José Maria] Tornel the Minister of War and Marine, and request that the suffering man might be transferred to the Hospital of San Andres. It was done without hesitation. In this interview General Tornel remarked to Mr Mayer that he thought the question of the liberation of the citizens of the United States could be settled—that he was authorized by the President to arrange the whole matter, and that I should take Mr Kendall with me on my return to the United States. I stated to Mr Mayer that I never would consent to ask his liberation as a matter of favor, inasmuch as I had, in the name of our Government demanded it as a right; but, anxious for his release, I requested the Secretary to call again on General Tornel and to ask an interview, which was given. Nothing satisfactory resulted from my conversation with the Minister; but, he said he would request the *President of the Republick* [Antonio López de Santa Anna] to grant me an interview. Not hearing from General Tornel, after a delay of several days, I addressed an official note to the Minister of Foreign Relations [José María de Bocanegra] on the [11th] of [April][4] desiring an audience of the President, which, took place on the 14th of April, and terminated in the promise of General Santa Anna to liberate those persons claimed as our Citizens. His action upon the subject was suspended in consequence of the publick armed vessels, of the U S. at Vera Cruz,[5] and the blockade of the Mexican ports in the Gulf by the Texan squadron.[6] General Thompson reached this City on the 16th. of April and on the Monday following I applied for an audience of leave which took place on the 21st. instant. I made the usual address on such

2. Not found, but see the letter from Pratt to Ellis, dated February 1842, enclosed in Ellis's dispatch No. 59. April 9, 1842, DNA, RG 59 (Despatches, Mexico). Pratt has not been otherwise identified. Rosier, of Carrollton, Mississippi, went to Texas sometime in 1841 and was taken prisoner by the Mexicans. He apparently was not a member of the Santa Fé expedition. See John Henderson to DW, April 11, 1842, DNA, RG 59 (Misc. Letters). The Acordada was a prison located in Mexico City.

3. Mayer (1809–1879), a lawyer and author of Baltimore, was secretary to the U.S. legation in Mexico from 1841 to 1844.

4. Ellis's note of April 11 and a record of his interview are among the enclosures with the dispatch. None of the enclosures are included in this publication.

5. In his interview of April 14 (of which a record is enclosed in the dispatch), Ellis told Santa Anna that American vessels off Mexico were "only in the ordinary course of their cruise in the Gulph."

6. Texas declared a blockade of the east coast of Mexico on March 26, 1842. The ineffective effort was abandoned on September 12.

occasions (a copy of which I send you) and the President in reply to my remarks liberated the prisoners whom I have already named. Genl. [Waddy] Thompson was then presented by the Minister of Foreign Relations, and received by the Most Excellent the Provl. President. Since he has taken charge of the Legation I am happy to inform you that he has obtained the release of three more of our Citizens—viz: Messrs. A[llensworth] Adams—[John] W Tompkins and LB. Sheldon, and, I doubt not, he will on all occasions make a vigilant and able Representative of our Government.

(See Document No. 1.)

In all my interviews with the Minister of For. Relations as well as with the President, I expressed the desire of the United States to cultivate and maintain the most friendly relations with this Country. The expression of these sentiments has been always cordially reciprocated; and I was *especially* desired by President Santa Anna to make known his wishes on this subject to the President of the United States.

As there has been great excitement in the United States, and odious comparisons drawn between the relative influence of the American and English Legations here, I trust it may not be considered indelicate to state that Mr. [Thomas] Falconer was delivered to the Representative of his Government on the occasion of that Gentleman presenting to the President a letter from his Sovereign announcing the birth of the Prince of Wales. These acts of courtesy are usual on such occasions. The other Englishman was discharged on the ground that he was a relative of the British Minister, without, as I understand, any application being made for that purpose.[7] Besides this I am aware of the fact, and deem it just and proper to record it here, that no British subjects liberty was asked or *demanded*, except the two named above, until after the promised release of our own citizens.

To day, I learn, that the English, French, and Prussian Ministers[8] have received orders for the liberation of the subjects of their respective nations, who were in all respects situated like our citizens released a week since. There is a rumor in the city that the President will, in the course of the summer discharge all the Texan prisoners on their *parole*. Such an act of Justice would reflect the highest honor on General Santa Anna, and do more to elevate his character in the estimation of foreign nations, and

7. According to Franklin Combs's account of his captivity, published in the *New Orleans Bee*, February 16, 1842 (and reprinted in *Niles' National Register*, March 5), English subjects were released while Americans remained imprisoned. The "other Englishman" has not been identified. Richard Pakenham (1797–1868) was the British minister to Mexico from March 12, 1835, to December 14, 1843.

8. Minister from France, Aleye de Cyprey, from Prussia, Baron de Gerolt.

to subdue popular excitement *against him*, than any other move I can possibly conceive.

I regret the many publications which have appeared in the Gazettes in various parts of the United States calculated to prejudice the minds and feelings of all persons as to the course I have taken in my negotiations without a full knowledge of the history of my efforts to procure the liberty of our unfortunate countrymen who were made captives on the ill fated Santa Fé Expedition. The publications referred to, so far as they relate injuriously to me, are not founded on facts, for I have, at all times, been most anxious to fulfill my instructions. It is most probable the writers had a greater desire to strike at a mark much higher than the person who now addresses you, or, we might not have been forced to read the strictures in the Press so discreditable to our country and to those who wrote them.[9]

I shall draw on you for twenty five hundred dollars to defray the expences of our citizens to return home. This sum may be less or more than necessary to effect the object in view, but I cannot, now, know the amount. I trust the course I take will be satisfactory to the Department. So far as I can procure vouchers they shall be obtained.

The Archives of the Legation have been handed to General Thompson, together with your Communications relative to Genl [Hugh] McLeod.[10] Those documents were not received by me until two days before the arrival of Genl Thompson.

The usual exequatur to enable Mr [Edward] Porter[11] to act as US. Consul at Tobasco has been granted by this Government. That for Mr [John H.] Peebles[12] is still witheld.

Before I conclude this my last despatch I will remark that Mr Mayer, the Secretary of this Legation has in all the late difficult negotiations with this Government afforded me the most efficient and cordial cooperation. I should do injustice to my own feelings if I did not thus publickly manifest to you and the President of the United States, the high sense I entertain of his worth and merits as a publick officer, and beg to commend him to the favorable consideration of our Government. I have the honor to be with great respect and esteem Your obedient Servant

Powhatan Ellis

ALS. DNA, RG 59 (Despatches, Mexico). Rec'd May 30. Extract published in *Senate Documents*, 27th Cong., 2d sess., Serial 398, No. 325, pp. 84–86.

9. For an analysis of the criticism that Ellis had not been vigorous enough in trying to obtain the release of the Santa Fé prisoners, see Edwin L. Cobb, "Powhatan Ellis of Mississippi: A Reappraisal," *Journal of Mississippi History*, 30 (May 1968): 91–110. Cobb concludes that the accusation was unfair.

10. Not found.

11. Porter, of Virginia, was U.S. consul at Tabasco from January 25, 1842, to March 14, 1857.

12. Peebles, of Pennsylvania, was U.S. consul at Campeche from October 6, 1841, to September 2, 1842.

FROM WADDY THOMPSON

No. 1.   Legation of the US of America
Sir,   Mexico 29th April 1842.

In the note which I had the honor to address You from New Orleans[1] I informed you that I should not wait any longer for the Ship which had been promised to me by the Secretary of the Navy [Abel Parker Upshur], and that I had determined to take the Revenue Cutter Woodbury, and proceed at once to this place. I was the more prompted to this course from an anxiety, as general as I felt it was flattering to me, on the part of the friends of the American Citizens who were prisoners in Mexico, that I should be at my post. I left New Orleans on the 2nd and arrived in this City on Saturday the 16th instant. On Sunday morning I visited Mr George W[ilkins] Kendall, who was confined in the Convent of San Lazaro,[2] and on the next day I made a similar visit to the other American Citizens who were confined with the Texan prisoners in the Convent of St. Iago. I found their condition and treatment as good as is usual with prisoners of War, except that they were chained and subjected to labor on the publick streets. These things I regarded as a violation of the well established usages of civilized war, and without excuse or apology. Prisoners of War are not regarded by civilized nations as fit subjects of vengeance. By the ameliorated code of our times it is the peculiar characteristick of fair and generous warfare to lighten, by kindness and humanity, the afflictions of a vanquished enemy to which all are subjected by those casualties from which there is no protection either in a just cause, in valor or in talents. I was induced to make these visits both by the dictates of my feelings and by a sense of duty. There was no one in Mexico whom I was so anxious to see as my Countrymen in distress, and none whom I felt it to be so much my duty to see and hear from their own mouths statements of their respective cases, so as to be the better able to make the strongest application for their liberation. I had two very striking proofs of the propriety of this course. A most important, and, in my judgment, the most important fact in the case of Mr Kendall had never been alluded to in the correspondence of my predecessor with the Mexican Government; to wit: that when he was captured he had in his possession, and there were taken from him by the Mexican officers, letters from Texan officers inviting him to join the Santa Fé Expedition, and his letters in reply containing unqualified refusal to do so; and, also, a letter afterwards addressed to him by the acting Secy of State of Texas[3] invit-

1. Thompson to DW, March 31, 1842, DNA, RG 59 (Despatches, Mexico).

2. At the time, San Lazaro served as a lepers' prison as well as a place of confinement for Kendall and a few other Americans.

3. Anson Jones (1798–1858; Jefferson College of Medicine 1827) was secretary of state of Texas from De-

ing him to join the Expedition as a guest until he passed through the Indian country, and that on his arrival at Santa Fé he could leave the party, and a copy of this letter assenting to this proposal. Although these letters had been destroyed their existance and contents were susceptible of proof, and would have placed in so clear a light the pacific intentions of Mr Kendall that his release could not, for a moment have been refused.

The other fact was that I found confined and in chains in the Convent of St Iago three other American Citizens Messrs. [L. B.] Sheldon, [Allensworth] Adams and [John W.] Tompkins, whose cases were in every particular identical with those of the six American traders, who have been released; yet their cases had never been presented to the Mexican Government. I am happy to add that on my making the application contained in my note No 1 to the Mexican Minister of Foreign Affairs [José María de Bocanegra],[4] they have also been released in the most prompt and handsome manner. I am very free to say, however, that independent of the reasons above alluded to I should most certainly have visited these men at the earliest possible moment and, if I could have done nothing else, I would have afforded them the consolation of a visit from the Official Representative of their Country, and the personal assurance that both that representative and Country felt the liveliest Sympathy in their sufferings. I was not deterred from this course by any apprehension that I should thereby offend the Mexican authorities. I believe that such a suspicion would have been unjust to them. But if I had known that it would have been otherwise, my course would have been the same, whilst I should have had too much respect for those authorities and myself to have given any just cause for offence, I could not have shrunk from the exercise of an unquestionable right and the discharge of a duty as unquestionable by any such considerations. I have not found from my experience that any thing was ever gained by such concessions, still less was I restrained by any notion that I was thereby compromitting my official dignity; but that, on the contrary, both my own, and the dignity of my country were more consulted by my visiting my countrymen who were in all respects my equals save in official position; and who were unjustly imprisoned and in chains.

On Monday the 18th I addressed to Mr de Bocanegra the Minister of For. Reln & Govt. the note No. 2 asking an audience of the president of the Mexican Republick [Antonio López de Santa Anna]. The wife of President Santa Anna, who is spoken of by all as a lady of extraordinary worth, was then dangerously ill, and he was in a state of the deepest affliction. He, nevertheless, conceded me an audience on the 21st. see No.

---

cember 13, 1841, to December 9, 1844, and president of Texas from then until February 19, 1846.

4. Thompson to Bocanegra, April 25, 1842. None of the enclosures mentioned in the dispatch are printed here; they are published in Serial 398, pp. 97–104.

3 I regard this as an evidence of his friendly disposition to our Country. Such I believe his feelings to be partly resulting, no doubt, from the marked kindness, which, under very peculiar and exciting circumstances he received from our people and Government; but, still more, because a man of unquestionable ability as he is, he knows the importance to his country of amicable relations with Ours. I delivered to him in Spanish, at my presentation, the short complimentary address which I send you, and was received with marked kindness both by the President and his Cabinet. I find them all gentlemen of polished and kind manners. With Mr de Bocanegra the Minister of For Relations I have been particularly pleased. He is a Gentleman of unsullied and high character, frank and sincere. The promptness with which he has granted the release of the three other prisoners to whom I have alluded, was altogether manly and handsome. You will be informed by Mr [Powhatan] Ellis that on his audience of leave, Prest. Santa Anna announced his determination to release the Americans who had been demanded.[5] I am not called upon to express an opinion either as to the propriety of renewing the request for the liberation of the American prisoners after a demand in the name of our Government nor of the terms in which that request is couched; but I did feel sensibly that this release which had first been asked and afterwards demanded by our Government and refused should have been conceded solely as a personal boon to Mr Ellis, and so expressed, with great particularity. But the note of Mr de Bocanegra of the 23d, No 4 in which the act is stated to have been "solely on account of the close friendship existing between the United States and Mexico," and the liberation of the other three Americans to which I have alluded, has removed much of the unpleasant feeling which was thus produced.—See my reply No 8.—[6]

On my arrival in Mexico, I was informed, and afterwards learned from Mr Ellis that on the 14th of April, two days before my arrival in this city, and when I was hourly expected he had an interview with President Santa Anna, and had been promised the release of the American prisoners. Mr Ellis at the same time told me that he had no hope of the fulfilment of this promise. It was natural that Mr Ellis should desire that these prisoners should be released to him, and not to me, and as I thought that the Mexican Authorities would prefer that the matter should take this course, I was disposed to aid Mr Ellis in his negotiations by every means in my power—the liberation of the prisoners being the primary object.

On Tuesday the 19th. I was not a little surprized to learn that Mr Kendall had been removed from the hospital of San Lazaro, to the Convent

5. See above.

6. In the reply, dated April 27, Thompson expressed gratification for the release of the prisoners and assured the foreign minister that the United States did not extend its protection to U.S. citizens who made war on Mexico.

of St. Iago, and for the first time put in chains. I immediately went to the office of Mr Ellis and proposed that he should write a note to the Minister of Foreign Relations upon the subject, or that we should address him a joint note. He declined doing so saying that he had seen the Minister, the day before, and that he did not think any good would result. I told him that I thought the subsequent placing of Mr Kendall in chains justified and demanded it, and immediately addressed to Mr de Bocanegra the Note No 5.[7] I did not regard it as in any degree abandoning the ground of demand upon which the matter stood to tender this additional evidence upon which that demand was made; but, on the contrary that it was due to the prisoners and respectful to the Mexican Government to do so. In closing the remarks which I have felt it to be my duty to make on this delicate and exciting subject, I beg not to be understood as reflecting on my predecssor Mr Ellis; I am altogether satisfied that he has done all that he deemed proper in the matter, and sincerely desired the release of the Americans who were in Confinement. Immediately after my presentation I addressed to Mr de Bocanegra the note No 6[8]—asking an interview with him. I was satisfied that more could be accomplished in that way than by a formal correspondence. I received from him in reply the Note No 7[9] and called accordingly at his office at the appointed hour, and presented to him the testimony in the cases of Sheldon, Adams and Tompkins, whose claims had been omitted in the list presented by Mr Ellis, and at his request addressed him the note No 1. The cases of these men were acted on with unusual promptness and the orders were given the next day for their release of which I was informed by the Note of Mr Bocanegra No 9 to which I replied immediately by my note No 10.[10]

I received from Mr De Bocanegra, on the 25th. the note No [blank in manuscript] dated on the 23d. and I have the honor to send you my reply No [blank in manuscript].[11]

I take leave to suggest to you the propriety of retaining Mr [L. S.] Hargous as Consul at Vera Cruz. I know no similar station, where a man of firmness and honesty, as well as, good feelings, is so much needed—and I speak the opinion of every American in Mexico when I say that in all these qualities Mr Hargous has no superior. I take leave also to suggest the propriety of making Mr [John] Black[12] the consul at this place—Con-

7. Enclosure, Thompson to Bocanegra, April 19, 1842, not printed here.

8. Enclosure, Thompson to Bocanegra, April 22, 1842, not printed here.

9. Enclosure, Bocanegra to Thompson, April 23, 1842, not printed here.

10. Enclosures, Bocanegra to Thompson, April 26, 1842; Thompson to Bocanegra, April 29, 1842, thanking the foreign minister for the release of the prisoners; neither printed here.

11. Apparently a reference to his enclosure No. 7 and his reply of April 27, which is enclosure No. 8.

12. Black was U.S. consul at Mexico City from March 3, 1843, to October 22, 1861.

sul General. He is in every way a worthy man, and I think such an office with a small salary is required here. On the Western Coast of Mexico where we have an extensive commerce and many Americans reside, we have no Consul North of Mazatlan. Permit me to suggest the appointment of one at Monterey and to recommend [blank in manuscript] for that office. The most outrageous violations of the rights of American Citizens are of frequent occurrence there and our people have been forced to look to the aid of the British Consul,[13] which, I am glad to learn has always been extended to them. No where is the sympathy of language and of race more strongly felt than between the Americans and English in Mexico.

In connexion with this subject there is one of so much importance to our Country and its future destinies, commercial and political, that I regret that I shall have to allude to it with no more time than I shall have to present my views in relation to it.

I believe that this Government would cede to us Texas and the Californias and I am thoroughly satisfied that it is all we shall ever get for the claims of our Merchants on this country. As to Texas I regard it as of but little value compared with California—the richest, the most beautiful and the healthiest country in the world. Our Atlantic border secures us a Commercial ascendency there; with the acquisition of Upper California we should have the same ascendency on the Pacific. The harbor of St. Francisco is capacious enough to receive the navies of all the world, and the neighbourhood furnishes live oak enough to build all the Ships of those navies. Besides this there is the harbor of St Iago [San Diego?], Monterey and others. The mouth of the Columbia River is our only harbor on this coast, and that is, literally, no harbor, as the loss of the Peacock, and other ships, proves.[14] The possession of these harbors would secure the only places of refuge & rest for our numerous fishing vessels, and would no doubt by internal communications with the Arkansas, and other Western Streams secure the trade of India & the whole Pacific Ocean. In addition to which California is destined to be the granary of the Pacific. It is a country in which Slavery is not necessary, and, therefore, if that is made an objection, let there be another compromise. France and England both have had their eyes upon it; The latter has yet. She has already control of the Sandwich Islands, of the Society Islands,

13. Thompson refers to Eustace Barron, the British vice consul at Tepic, on the Gulf of Mexico. Barron was the business associate of James Alexander Forbes, who became the first British vice consul at Monterrey in December 1842.

14. On July 18, 1841, the *Peacock*, a ship in Commander Charles Wilkes's (1798–1877) U.S. Navy Exploring Expedition, grounded on the Columbia River sandbar. The vessel was destroyed by the incoming tide.

New Zealand &c. &c., and thro' the agency of that Embryo East India monopoly, the Hudsons Bay Co. she will ere long have a monopoly of the commerce of the Pacific; and not an American flag will float on its coasts. I am profoundly satisfied that in its bearing upon all the interests of our country, agricultural, political, manufacturing, commercial and fishing the importance of the acquisition of California can not be overestimated. If I could mingle any selfish feelings with interests to my country so vast, I would desire no higher honor than to be an instrument in securing it.

I have been too short a time in this country to venture more than a Conjecture as to its internal politicks. Every single election which has been held and they are nearly all over, has gone against President Santa Anna. The period for the assembling of Congress is the 1st. of June, but I do not think that any one expects that the Congress will meet: It seems to be taken for granted that the Election will be annulled, or, in some other way that the President will retain the absolute power he now exercises. He has a large army amounting to sixty thousand, which will remain faithful to him as long as he pays them. How that is to be done much longer with the peculations of all his subordinate chiefs I do not see. The Mexicans are an ignorant, proud, but I think kind people. I have not seen any people with whom politeness and kindness are more sure to secure a return. They must not be judged by the sanguinary scenes enacted in Texas. No quarter is the law of Spanish civil war, and all the wars of Mexico have been civil wars which are charictaristically sanguinary.

The American and Texan prisoners say that with a very few exceptions the treatment they have received from Mexican officers has been altogether kind. The sympathy of this city is entirely with the prisoners. There is, as it is most natural there should be, a pretty strong prejudice against our country men on account of the Texas war. I think this feeling may be removed, & I shall make all proper exertions to do so, for it is our interest to be on good terms with them, as it is in the interest of all nations, surely, to be with all others. The true course of policy with them is to exhibit our sword—but not to draw it.

I would suggest to you the propriety of not being too prompt to recognize Yucatan.[15] It will do no good, and will certainly offend the feelings of the Mexicans that we should always be the first to take by the hand her insurgent provinces. If the Texan Govt. enforces its blockade, I trust you will cause the Revenue Cutter Woodbury to run between New Orleans and Vera Cruz[;] at all events let it return once, and I shall so request of the Collector of N.O. if he finds it convenient to do so.

15. Yucatán declared independence from Mexico in June 1840. By the terms of a treaty signed December 15, 1843, Yucatán recognized the Mexican government but retained its autonomy.

I have reason to believe that in a short time all the Texan prisoners will be relieved on parole. If they are released can the Revenue Cutter be employed in transporting them[?]

I have this moment read your instructions to Mr Ellis of the 26th Feby.[16] as to certain persons who accompanied the Santa Fé Expedition. I do not think they are any of them entitled to American protection, and I cannot abuse it, or, the confidence of this Govt. by interposing in their behalf. But I repeat that I have a very confident belief that they will all be released in a short time. In that event they will be turned loose on the city, without any means [of] support; to what extent, if any, am I to aid them?

The road from this to Vera Cruz is so infested with robbers, and the mails are so uncertain, that I did not think it safe to risk my despatches by that conveyance, and brought with me to this City Lieut. [John] Faunce[17] of the Woodbury. His Expences have amounted to the sum of Two hundred and seventy five dollars which I have paid him; for which, together with four hundred and seventy five dollars for clothing & necessary expences of the three americans who have been released I have drawn upon you. I hope this will meet your approval.

If the business of the Legation permits and it meets your approbation I shall make an excursion, in the summer to California. I have the honor to be my Dear Sir with great respect Yr ob ser   Waddy Thompson

LS. DNA, RG 59 (Despatches, Mexico). Rec'd May 30. Published in *Senate Documents*, 27th Cong., 2d sess., Serial 398, No. 325, pp. 94–97. The document printed by the Senate does not contain Thompson's lengthy recommendation for the acquisition of California, because it was silently deleted by the Tyler administration before the dispatch was submitted to the Senate.

WADDY THOMPSON TO JOHN TYLER

My Dear Sir.   Mexico May 9. 1842

Since my despatch to Mr. Webster[1] I have had an interview with Gen. [Antonio López de] Santa Anna and although I did not broach to him directly the subject of our correspondence[2] I have but little doubt that I shall be able to accomplish your wishes and to add also the acquisition of upper California. This latter I believe will be by far the most important event that has occurred in our country. Do me the favor to read my despatch to Mr Webster in which my views of the matter are briefly sketched —I should be most happy to illustrate your administration and my own name by an acquisition of such lasting benefit to my country—upon this

16. See above, DW to Ellis, February 26, 1842.

17. Faunce (1807–1891) was a career officer in the U.S. Revenue- Marine.

1. See above.

2. Not found.

subject I beg your special instructions both as to moving on the matter and the extent to which I am to go in the negotiation and the amount to be paid. The acquisition of Upper California will reconcile the northern people as they have Large fishing & commercial interests in the Pacific and we have literally no port there. Be pleased also to have me pretty strongly instructed on the subject of our claims or leave the responsibility to me. Procrastination the policy of all weak governments is peculiarly so with this and they are very poor and will never pay us one farthing unless pretty strong measures are taken.

If contrary to my expectations they should be able to pay the awards they will desire to pay it in this city. The cost of transportation to the co[a]st will be 8 or 10 pr cent shall I receive it here. With the Highest Respect faithfully & Truly yr friend   Waddy Thompson

I have a confident hope of being able to procure the release of all the Texan prisoners very soon

ALS. DNA, RG 59 (Despatches, Mexico). Published in *IAA*, 8:485.

FROM JOSE MARÍA DE BOCANEGRA

National Palace
Mexico, May 31, 1842.

It was only a few days ago that the undersigned Minister of Foreign Relations and Government of the Mexican Republic had the honor to address the Honorable Secretary of State of the United States of America to protest formally to the Government of that Republic, in the name of His Excellency the provisional President [Antonio López de Santa Anna], against the continued hostilities and aggressions of Citizens of those States against Mexican territory;[1] and when he might expect as a result a pleasing change in the state of affairs, he sees himself obliged, by the continuation of these acts, again to call the attention of the Secretary of State to the undeniable tolerance which has been observed and continues to be observed toward the enemies of a Nation sincerely friendly and bound by the solemn pacts of the Treaty[2] which unites the two Republics.

In that note, after informing the Secretary of the prudence with which the Government of Mexico has tried, from the beginning of the revolution of Texas, to conduct its relations with the United States, in order to avoid a rupture between two peoples which, by their importance and other grave considerations appear destined to determine the policy and fortune of the vast and rich American continent, the Undersigned was under the impression that the Washington Government would not pro-

1. See Bocanegra to DW, May 12, 1842, DNA, RG 59 (Notes from Foreign Legations, Mexico).

2. The Treaty of Amity, Commerce, and Navigation of April 5, 1831.

tect openly, secretly or in any manner whatever, the scandalous usurpation of an acknowledged part of National territory. But it regrets to find, by acts patent to all the world, that the same Government of the United States, and the subaltern and local authorities, observe a conduct openly contrary to the most sacred principles of the law of nations, and to the solemn pacts of friendship which exist between the two Nations; sufficient proof of this being found in the fact that the most clamorous public meetings are permitted to be held at various points in those States: arms are recruited, a growing number of volunteers are engaging themselves in the enterprize, and preparation is made to contribute aid when and where possible to the Texans, and to the invasion of a neighboring and friendly Republic.

Such conduct is incomprehensible to the Mexican Government, and frank in its procedure, at the same time animated by the sincere desire that the relations which are today happily maintained between the Republic and the United States may not suffer the slightest alteration, it considers it its duty to repeat in every form its previous protest against such tolerance, whose continuation it will consider as a positive act of hostility against this Republic, which will be guided in its conduct by justice, interest and National dignity.

The undersigned hopes that the Secretary will be good enough to reply with the promptitude required by the importance of this matter, and seizes with pleasure the opportunity to renew to him assurances of the distinguished consideration with which he subscribes himself His very obedient servant,   J. M. de Bocanegra

Copy. Translation. DNA, RG 59 (Notes from Foreign Legations, Mexico). Published in *IAA*, 8:489–490. Rec'd 9 July 1842.

FROM JAMES REILY

> Legation of Texas. Washington
> June 11th. 1842

Private & confidential

The undersigned Charge d. Affaires from the Republic of Texas has the honor to invite the attention of Mr Webster Secretary of State of the United States to the justice & propriety of the intervention of the Government of the United States between Texas & Mexico. In the fall of 1835 the revolution of Texas commenced, and on the 2nd. of March 1836 the declaration of Independence was published to the world and on the 17th of the same month a constitution was adopted guaranteeing to all, political and religious liberty. The battle of San Jacinto was fought on the twenty first day of April 1836, which resulted in the defeat of the Mexican army and the Capture of President Antonio Lopez de Santa Anna, who was generously released after signing the articles of treaty herewith submitted,[1] sent at his own request to this capitol, and by your government despatched home in a public vessel. The numerous Mexican prisoners were treated with great kindness by their captors & numbers of them have since become citizens of Texas and are permitted to exercise all the rights of free citizenship. Since the defeat and capture of Santa Anna, Mexico satisfied of its impossibility, has made no attempt to reconquer Texas, who on the other hand altho victorious & daily increasing in strength and resources has several times sought peace with her, & until at last excited by recent outrages within her territory and a renewed declaration of Genl Santa Anna again to prosecute the war, evinced no intention of molesting or disturbing the safety or quiet of her antagonist. So honest and sincere has been the disposition of the Texan government to cultivate & preserve pacific relations with Mexico that frequent and rich carravans of Mexican traders from the interior of the Mexican territory have again & again been permitted to enter in & depart from our towns undisturbed. In the spring & summer of 1839 when Genl [Antonio] Canales[2] and others under the name of Federalists attempted to revolutionize the Northern provinces of Mexico and establish the Republic of the Rio Grande & had induced men & soldiers with the public arms of the Texan Government to go to their aid, an officer of the Texas army, Col B[enjamin] F. Johnson assistant adjutant General[3] was immediately despatched to take from our volunteers the public arms. Acting under the instructions of the Texan Government in prosecution of this duty he crossed the Rio Grande—performed the task assigned, dismissed as deserters the officers & men of our army who had joined the Federalists, and yet on his return home, he with his party at Comargo was basely betrayed and inhumanly murdered by Officers of the Central Army. Mexican emissaries have been continually sent among the Indian tribes on the North East to excite them to the slaughter of our frontier settlers—from the West several citizens in the discharge of their peaceable avocations have been carried off and either slain or imprisoned in Mexican forts & all our attempts at reconciliation treated with disdain. Texas altho insulted—injured and having every justification to wage a war of invasion kept for a long time from striking any blow against an enemy too cowardly to follow with action her many & loud menaces & too ungenerous and bigoted to entertain the consideration of propositions for peace. Events however have transpired which render it impossible for Texas to remain longer inactive. In March last a military detachment under Genl

1. Not printed here. On May 14, 1836, Santa Anna signed two treaties, one declaring hostilities terminated and the other pledging his support for an independent Texas with a boundary at the Rio Grande. Both agreements were repudiated by the Mexican congress.

2. Canales (1800?–1852?) was a lawyer, military leader, and politician.

3. Not otherwise identified.

[Rafael] Vasquez entered her limits, not for the purpose of bold & manly warfare, but for the mean & contemptible design of plundering the defenceless town of San Antonio, and President Santa Anna, in his letter to Genl [James] Hamilton of Feb 20th 1842, proclaims his intention of again appealing to arms & devoting Texas to all the horrors of war, disregardless of his solemn promises to the contrary as contained in his treaty of May 14th 1836.[4] These demonstrations of continued and unceasing hostility from a defeated enemy leave Texas, no alternative but to anticipate the foe & make the theatre of war beyond the Rio Grande. She never will again consent to await the coming of her merciless and unprincipled antagonist into her own bosom & expose her people—her altars & her helpless women & children to the fires of their savage ferocity. Her resolution is taken & forces are now concentrating to carry the war into Mexico. Nothing but peace can either curb or stay the onward march of our columns of indignant soldiers. For six years Texas has endured repeated injuries & insult—the murder & imprisonment of her citizens & although annoyed every spring by rumors of intended invasion kept quiet, satisfied to leave the question of her independence where the battle of San Jacinto placed it. Urged and incited by the highest considerations of safety—patriotism and national honor the people of Texas, will no longer be checked. In a short time the line of march will be taken up, and such is the enthusiasm infused through out the nation by the expectation of war that every citizen is now acting & laboring with a view of being soon permitted within the Mexican limits of striking for the peace and independence of his country. To save the effusion of blood & prevent the great mass of woe & suffering which must inevitably attend upon such a war, as the Representative of Texas, I would solic[i]t the intervention of the United States, between the two belligerents. This interference is due to herself as the great and leading power upon this continent & having for her neighbors the two contending powers and in friendly intercourse with both. She owes it to the cause of humanity, and Texas might with great propriety claim her powerful mediation upon the ground of having been influenced in her revolution by the hopes of gaining for citizens institutions similar to those of the American Union. Peace and acknowledgement of independence is due to Texas from the inability of Mexico ever to reconquer the country having failed in all her attempts

4. On January 13, 1842, the Texan financial and diplomatic agent James Hamilton (1786–1857) sent a confidential letter to Santa Anna proposing a treaty of peace and the payment of a five-million-dollar indemnity to Mexico by Texas. Santa Anna replied on February 18, not 20, as Reily stated, that the proposed indemnity had aroused his "profound disgust." On March 5, 1842, a force of 700 men under Vasquez occupied San Antonio for two days and plundered the city. The correspondence between Hamilton and Santa Anna is published in *Niles' National Register*, March 26, 1842.

at subjugation & having suffered *six years* to elapse without any demonstration of an actual renewal of hostilities. Texas has been recognized by the United States & the greatest powers of Europe, and has evinced her ability to sustain the administration of a constitutional government. If the United States should refuse to yield her powerful mediation between the two countries, or should fail in the attempt to bring about the recognition of our independence, or a truce of arms for several years, then no alternative is left Texas but to wage a fierce & bloody war. As the Representative of Texas I would most respectfully ask from Mr Webster, able as he is to appreciate the unfortunate condition of people forced to war, and having rendered himself illustrious by ever being found on the side of justice—humanity and constitutional freedom to obtain the mediation of the United States Government between Texas & Mexico, and that she propose to Mexico, 1st The recognition of the Independence of Texas, with the acknowledgement of her limits as defined in the Act of Congress of December 19th 1836.[5] If this is refused then 2ndly The recognition of Texan independence leaving the questions of limits to be settled by future negotiation, stipulating for a cessation of all hostilities until that question is settled. Failing in these then 3dly An armistice or cessation of all hostilities for five years or longer, & which hostilities are not to be renewed with out notice being given by the party intending to renew them of at least twelve months of such intended renewal, & the notice of renewal being made officially through the Government of the United States. With sentiments of highest respect—Yours   James Reily

ALS. DNA, RG 59 (Notes from Foreign Legations, Texas). Published in *IAA*, 12:235–238. Reily (d. 1863) moved to Texas from Kentucky in 1836. He was chargé d'affaires to the United States from December 27, 1841, to August 1, 1842.

FROM JAMES BUCHANAN AND OTHER MEMBERS OF THE PENNSYLVANIA DELEGATION IN CONGRESS

Hall of Representatives
Washington City

Sir: 16 June 1842

The Undersigned, Members of Congress from Pennsylvania, are induced to ask the interposition of your kind offices, in behalf of one of their countrymen, now suffering imprisonment in a foreign Land.

It has been communicated to the Undersigned, from sources which they consider entitled to implicit credit, that John Holliday, a Native of Pennsylvania, of highly respectable kindred and connections in that

5. The act of the Texas Congress defining the republic's boundary from the Sabine River to, and thence up, the Rio Grande to the forty-second parallel is in *Laws of the Republic of Texas*, 1:133–134.

commonwealth, and the descendant of revolutionary ancestry, is now confined as a Prisoner in the Castle of Peroté in Mexico, under circumstances of peculiar hardship. It is represented that Mr. Holliday was captured with a number of other Americans by a Mexican armed force, during the late Santa Fé expedition and that although some, if not all of his fellow prisoners, have been liberated, this young gentleman is still confined in *irons*, in a Mexican Fortress, and treated not as a prisoner of war, but as a common felon on the plea that he is a citizen of Texas. Of the truth of this allegation the Undersigned cannot judge, but if upon investigation it should be discovered that Mr. Holliday is not entitled to protection of this government, nor to a demand for his surrender as a citizen of the United States it is respectfully suggested whether his release may not be procured, as an act of courtesy, through the friendly interference of our minister to Mexico. Success in this effort is earnestly desired by many of the people of Pennsylvania whose sympathies have been awakened by the sufferings of a distressed family. Ver resp Y. &c

B[enjamin] A[lden] Bidlack	James Buchanan
Geo M[ay] Keim	Daniel Sturgeon
C[harles] J[ared] Ingersoll	A[lbert] G[allatin] Marchand
Jno Edwards	J[oseph] R[eed] Ingersoll
W[illiam] W[allace] Irwin	George W[ashington] Toland
James Irvin	Th[omas] M[cKean] T[hompson] McKennan
J[ames] M[cPherson] Russell	Joseph Fornance
A[mos] Gustine	Peter Newhard
W[illiam] Simonton	A[rnold] Plumer
	Jeremiah Brown
	William Jack
	H[enry] W[hite] Beeson

ʟs. DNA, RG 59 (Misc. Letters). Rec'd June 18, 1842.

FROM WADDY THOMPSON

Legation of the US of A

Sir,   Mexico 20th June 1842

I have the happiness to inform you that the Texan prisoners were all liberated on the 13th instant. I regard this act of President [Antonio López de] Santa Anna as one of generosity and magnanimity in every way honorable to him, and I feel that it is only an act of justice to the Mexican people to say that their conduct to the prisoners when they were released was kind and generous in the extreme. The prisoners were released on the parade ground, and when the fact was announced it was received with acclamations by the Mexican Soldiers. As the Texans passed through the immense crowd that was assembled they were most cordially and kindly greeted. When it is remembered that these men had invaded the territory of Mexico as enemies such conduct, and such feelings on the part of the Mexicans are eminently honorable to them.

As my position in relation to this matter has been one of peculiar delicacy and difficulty, I deem it proper to give you a full account of all that I have done towards this result. I have felt very sensibly the difficulty of meeting, on the one hand, the claims of humanity, and discharging the duties of the Representative of a Neutral Nation, and, on the other of not seeming to espouse the cause of Texas.

About the same time that I had the honor to receive your Despatch of the 26 of February[1] in which I was instructed to remonstrate respectfully against any cruel and improper treatment of the Texan prisoners, I received from those who were confined at Perote the Communication No. 1.[2] I called the next day at the office of Genl. [José Maria] Tornel Minister of War and Marine, and as the best means of communicating to him the just and humane views of our Government, both towards this Govt. and that of Texas, and the arguments in support of the course our country had taken in the matter, I exhibited to him those instructions as well as the communication alluded to above. He replied that the affair should be attended to, but that Mr Webster was mistaken in supposing that these prisoners were entitled to the rights of prisoners of war. I answered that you were not; that they were prisoners of war according to the well established principles and usages of all civilized nations; and that his Government had recognized these principles by professing so to regard the prisoners. He asked me, in reply, whether if two hundred Mexicans should invade Louisiana, and, hoist the banner of abolition, we should so regard them. I answered that we would not; but that if they conquered the country, established and organized a Government, without any effort, on the part of our country, for six years, to reconquer the territory, that we should. In short, that I trusted the Governments which had recognized Texas would require of Mexico, that just, and humane treatment of these prisoners to which they were entitled, and, that for one of those Governments I was authorized to speak.

He went on to speak in a tone, manifestly vindictive, to our country, and observed, that when the Mexicans were made prisoners at San Jacinto there was no interposition in their behalf. I replied that our Government had not then recognized Texas, and that we had scarcely heard of the capture of Genl Santa Anna and his command when we also heard that they had been restored to liberty; and that I thought the very marked kindness and distinction with which General Santa Anna had been

1. See above, DW to Ellis, February 26, 1842.

2. The communication from the prisoners, dated April 26, 1842, described the harshness of their conditions and requested assistance. None of the enclosures mentioned in Thompson's dispatch are included in this publication.

treated by our Government made such remarks from him (Genl Tornel) peculiarly improper; besides which, following as it did, upon the massacre of Colonel [James Walker] Fanning's command, and that of the Alamo[3] that any thing short of retaliation in kind was not only no just cause of complaint but was mercy.

In the course of the conversation Genl Tornel said that our conduct to Mexico, a weak power, was very different to that to England which could, at any moment, throw fifty thousand soldiers into our country. I felt called on to repel this insulting language with the warmth and in the terms it merited. I told him that such language was unbecoming his offi·cial station, and the respect which was due to mine, and that it was both untrue and ungrateful; that no Government on earth had received so many evidences of kindness and forbearance from ours as that of Mexico, and, amongst other proofs, I stated that the spoliations on our Commerce by Mexico since her revolution had been greater than those of all the other nations of Christendom united; and that, at a period when for spoliations, less in amount, and of a character infinitely less aggravated, we had threatened France, one of the greatest powers of the Earth, with war, we had used only negotiation and kindness towards Mexico:[4] that I would not be driven by his unjust insinuations, into anything like gasconade, but that the past history of our country certainly evidenced no fear of collision with England: that whilst a war with that country would be deeply regretted by every man in the United States from ten thousand considerations of interest, kindred and friendship, yet if the honor of our country demanded it, no man living doubted what would be our course; and that I did not hesitate to say that the same causes which now existed with Mexico would have caused a war with England, not from any greater friendship for Mexico, but because in a war with England some laurels might be won.

He replied, in explaination, that he had no doubt of the justice and conscienciousness of our Government, and that it was only to a portion of our people that he alluded; and added that he had the greatest confi-

3. In the siege of the Alamo from February 24 to March 6, 1836, 187 Texans and Americans were killed. Fannin (1804–1836), vice Fanning, surrendered his forces to the Mexicans on March 20, after the Battle of Goliad. On March 27, 342 of the men were shot by order of Santa Anna.

4. When the French government failed to pay the first installment of a twenty-five-million-franc indemnity owed the United States, President Andrew Jackson threatened, in his Annual Message of December 1, 1834, to seize French property in reprisal. Before the end of the affair, diplomatic relations were broken; they were restored in May 1836 only through the mediation of the British government. (On the French controversy, see International Arbitrations, 5:4463–4468). At about the same time, however, in his Annual Message of December 5, 1836, Jackson urged forbearance regarding American claims on Mexico. See Messages and Papers, 3:238.

dence in Mr [John] Tyler and yourself and the Whig party; but that he did not like the "loco focos;" (his own words)—and that General [Andrew] Jackson was at the bottom of the Texan movement. I replied that I was glad to hear the expression of his confidence in Mr Tyler and yourself; but that he was mistaken if he supposed any disparagement of the party to which he alluded would be agreeable to me; that, at home I was a Whig, here I was the Representative of my whole country, and that I should despise myself if, whilst acting in that character in a foreign land, I could remember party distinctions or know any party feeling: that the character of the illustrious citizen, to whom he had alluded, was dear to every American, and that I denied, in the broadest terms, his charge upon him: that he may have desired to purchase Texas, but he was incapable, whilst filling the Chief Magistracy, of a friendly nation, of stimulating the Revolution in Texas; and, that his official conduct had proved this, for, at the moment when our aid would have been most effectual for Texas, and when we had just the same cause of war with Mexico as with France, whilst he was urging the strongest measures against the latter power, in an official message to Congress he had recommended forbearance to this country, from motives in the highest degree honorable to him and justly entitling him to the respect of all Mexicans.

I availed myself of this interview (the last I ever intend to have with General Tornel) to ask an explaination of Mr [George Wilkins] Kendall's being removed from San Lazaro to another prison and put in chains, after a positive promise for his release. He replied that it was done out of kindness to Mr Kendall, as he heard that he was sick, and he wished him removed to a more comfortable place. I answered that it was a somewhat odd way of exhibiting kindness by putting chains upon his legs. He replied that this was done without his knowledge. I answered that it had continued forty eight hours after he did know it, and that I regarded it as a gross indignity both to my country, and to one of its most respectable citizens. He replied sarcastically, "Yes—the Editor of the Picayune—"Yes, Sir, said I, and that was the true reason for the act, and not a mistake, as you have said."

I have reason to believe that Genl Tornel was favorably disposed to the release of the prisoners, and has contributed to that result; and should therefore have refrained from communicating these particulars to you, if I had felt at liberty to have done so. The result of this interview with General Tornel was a promise on his part that the truth of the facts stated in the communication to me from Perote should be enquired into. I received, a few days afterwards the note No. 2 from Mr [José María] de Bocanegra the Minister of For. Rels: and Govt. with the enclosures Nos 3 & 4 & 5.[5] I had heard from various sources upon which I relied, and

5. In No. 2, dated May 19, Bocanegra acknowledged receipt of several communications from the prisoners. No. 3, dated May 8, from Mex-

still do, that the prisoners at Perote and Puebla, particularly at the latter place were treated with extreme severity, and I was therefore not a little surprized at the communication from Genl [Hugh] McLeod No. 5. It rendered it impossible that I could interfere further in the matter. You will see, that although Genl McLeod says that his prisoners were well treated, he does not deny that they were made to labor and in chains, as is stated in the communication which they made to me nor is it denied that those at Puebla, in addition to this, were confined with, and chained to the worst Mexican malefactors. I state these facts with no view to disparage either General McLeod or the Mexican Government; but to justify myself for an interference which the letter of Genl McLeod would seem to represent as both causeless and officious. It is due to the Mexican Govt. to say that the prisoners at this place, since my arrival here, have been well treated, and that I therefore believe, that if it has been otherwise at Perote or Puebla it has been without the knowledge or approval of the Government.

Two or three days after this interview with Genl Tornel I received the note from Mr. De Bocanegra No. 6.[6] and waited upon the President at the hour appointed. I was received by him in a manner altogether frank and cordial; but nothing occurred worthy of being reported to you.

Immediately after my arrival here I received a great number of applications from the prisoners of the Santa Fé Expedition asking my official interposition, but not more than seven or eight seemed to me to justify such an act on my part. I determined, however, to present them all to the Mexican Government that it might take whatever course it thought proper; and, accordingly handed all the papers to General Tornel at the interview to which I have alluded. A day or two afterwards he told Mr. [Brantz] Mayer, that in some of the cases which he had examined he thought the applicants were entitled to their liberation, yet as the matter did not belong to his department but to that of Mr. De Bocanegra he returned all the documents. I immediately sent them to Mr. De Bocanegra with the Note No. 7.[7] I was not disposed by any act of apparent impatience or discourtesy to hazard the liberation of all the prisoners, (which I had reason to expect) and, more particularly, as there were so few

ican medical authorities, described various illnesses and injuries of the prisoners, including an accidental stabbing with a bayonet. No. 4, from Tornel to Bocanegra, dated May 13, denied any ill treatment of the prisoners. In No. 5, from Hugh McLeod to Thompson, May 8, the Texan commander denied that his men had been harshly treated.

6. In the note of May 7 Bocanegra invited Thompson to a conference with Santa Anna the next day.

7. In the note dated May 6, 1842, Thompson enclosed documents pertaining to some of the prisoners and remarked that most of the members of the expedition took part for commercial, rather than military, reasons.

whose cases which entitled them to a discharge, some of these, even, being of a doubtful character.

Still as Genl. Tornel had admitted that some of them were entitled to their freedom, after waiting a fortnight I requested Mr. Mayer to call at the office of Mr. De Bocanegra and request an early decision. Mr Mayer was then informed by the Minister of For. Relations that the papers had been delivered by him to Genl Tornel, and that the matter had been referred to him. In the course of a day or two, I received the Note No. 8. to which my note No. 9., in reply, was immediately sent.[8] Here the matter rested for several days, and, receiving no communication on the subject, I requested Mr Mayer to call on Mr Bocanegra and ask that the papers should be returned to me that I might select such as justified a formal demand, and that, I should expect an answer the next day at farthest. Late on the evening of the next day I received the note No 10.[9]

I had on the 11th. of May handed to Mr de Bocanegra the letter to President Santa Ana, No 11[10] with a request that, if he deemed it expedient, he should deliver it. But after the publication of the Circular to the Diplomatick Corps,[11] and the communication to yourself,[12] I regarded my relations with this Government as strictly formal, and I, therefore, directed Mr Mayer to request that if the letter had not been delivered that it should not be, and that if it had, I desired to withdraw it; as no action had been taken upon it. I was, therefore, surprized to find that Mr. de Bocanegra, had misunderstood an application to withdraw that letter as a request to deliver it; but as I was informed by the note of Mr de Bocanegra that the President had, "on the same day that it was delivered, determined on the subject" to which it related, and it was intimated that it was upon that letter that he had acted and as I had other assurances that the determination was to liberate the prisoners, I saw no sufficient reason again to ask the withdrawal of the letter, especially, as it had been written two weeks before the offensive papers to which I have re-

8. In No. 8, of May 28, Foreign Minister Bocanegra informed Thompson that the cases of the prisoners were under consideration. In his reply, No. 9, dated May 28, Thompson maintained that the delays in the cases were unreasonable.

9. The note, dated June 4, informed Thompson that his confidential note of May 11 (see note 14, below) had been delivered to Santa Anna.

10. Thompson's confidential note urged the release of the Santa Fé prisoners and offered the "friendly in-

terposition" of the United States in the difficulties between Mexico and Texas.

11. On May 31, 1842, Bocanegra addressed a circular to the diplomatic corps in Mexico City complaining about the participation of American citizens in disputes between Mexico and Texas. The circular is enclosed in Thompson's dispatch No. 2. June 6, 1842, DNA, RG 59 (Despatches, Mexico.)

12. See above, Bocanegra to DW, May 31, 1842.

ferred. I state these facts thus minutely, least it might be supposed that after the publication of those documents I had approached the Mexican Government in a manner which would have been improper under the circumstances.

I had received from the Texan Commissioners Col [William G.] Cooke and Dr [Richard Fox] Brenham[13] the terms of their capitulation, and if it had become necessary, I should, under your instructions, have demanded that those terms should be complied with. But I deemed it most prudent to wait a reasonable time with the hope that the prisoners would be liberated. I was not disposed to wound the pride of Mexico by such a step unless it became absolutely necessary, and as it might &, probably, would have frustrated the result which had taken place. I, however, informally, communicated to Mr de Bocanegra, that it might become necessary for me to do so.

In closing the account of my agency in this matter, allow me, to say, that I shall be most happy, if in addition to the gratification I have felt at seeing these unfortunate men set at liberty—my conduct shall meet with the approbation of my Government.

I received on the 11th. day of May the Note No. 12 from Mr De Bocanegra,[14] I went immediately to his office, and found that a very great sen-sation had been caused by the rumour of our fleet being off Vera Cruz. I assured him that it was untrue. He was entirely confident that it was true. The next day, however, brought intelligence which removed all ap-prehensions on the subject. Nos. 13 and No. 14 are a note to me and my reply on the subject of the Texan Blockade.[15] No 15 is my answer to en-quiries recently made of me on the same subject by the American Consul at Tampico.[16]

Mr. [Richard] Packenham informed me a few days since that in a con-versation with President Sta Anna on the subject of the complaints of this Govt. against the U:S: that he had said to the President that he thought our Government had done all that was to be expected or that was in its power, to preserve our neutrality in the war between Mexico and Texas, and that the President replied "Well—let them issue proclama-tions, or make some explanations that will satisfy our people."

13. Cooke (1808–1847), from Houston, Texas, and Brenham (c. 1810–1843), a Texas landowner, were civil commissioners with the Santa Fé expedition.

14. The note of May 11 reported the rumor that the U.S. fleet would soon appear off the coast of Veracruz and requested an explanation.

15. In his note No. 13 of May 2, Bocanegra inquired about the atti-tude of the United States toward the Texan blockade of Mexico proclaimed March 26, 1842. In his reply (No. 14) of May 3, Thompson informed the foreign minister that the United States would honor the blockade if it became effective and if it was in ac-cordance with the law of nations.

16. The American consul at Tam-pico from 1842 to 1870 was Franklin Chase of Maine.

I said to you, on a former occasion that I was satisfied the Circular and communication to you were only gasconade and intended for Mexico.[17] Whoever is at the head of this Govt. holds his power so insecurely that the Foreign Relations, even, of the country are conducted mainly with a view to domestick politicks. I have not changed the opinion I heretofore expressed to you & before the liberation of the Texan prisoners that this movement of apparent menace and fierceness was intended to satisfy the Mexicans with that act; and, upon calculation that the release of the prisoners would soften the reply that you might make. So perfectly impotent would this people be in a war with us—(indeed; it would not be a war, but a massacre—) that forbearance to them is the course which is prescribed by a just regard for our own National character. Much is to be pardoned to the petulance of conscious weakness. But there is a limit to this indulgence, and I do not see how our Government is to submit to making further explanations under the direct menace of "positive hostilities." It was in view of this difficulty that I determined to answer the circular to the *Diplomatick Corps.* I sent a copy of that reply to the Minister of For: Relations, accompanied by my note No. 16.[18] If I may be pardoned for making a suggestion to you, I would advise that the tone of your reply, at the same time that it should be pacific, should be very high. I am now satisfied that I was in error in saying that the feelings of any of these people are friendly to us. The feeling is universally and strongly otherwise, and whilst they do not, for a moment, suppose that we have any fears of a collision, they calculate largely on our forbearance. These suggestions may be of use to you in the instructions you may give me on the subject of our claims on this Government.

I have no doubt that it was supposed that the prospect of a war with the U:S: would reconcile the Mexican people to the absolute and despotick power which Prest. Santa Anna now wields.

It is impossible to predict with any degree of certainty what is to be the future course of events here. Their political Revolutions are all conducted with such profound secrecy that the roar of cannon is the first announcement of a revolt. I can, perceive, however, no signs of a commotion. The Constituent Congress is now in session, and some compromise will probably be adopted as to the constitution which it is assembled to form. Santa Anna, besides being supported by a large army, is an able man, in my judgment, not only the ablest man in his country, but the *first* man whom these Southern Republicks have produced. He certainly understands the character of his countrymen, and I really believe he is

17. See Thompson to DW, June 2, 1842, DNA, RG 59 (Despatches, Mexico).

18. No. 16 is a cover note sent with Thompson's reply to Bocanegra's circular. Thompson had already sent a copy of the reply to DW in his dispatch of June 6, 1842, DNA, RG 59 (Despatches, Mexico).

disposed to give them such a government as he thinks best suited to them.

I have drawn on you for $3000. $2.500 of which was given to the Texan Commissioners, and $[blank in manuscript] to Mr [J. L.] Dorsey[19] under your instructions. Mr Packenham—the British Envoy—contributed at the same rate for the transportation of such of the prisoners as were natives of Great Britain. I have charged in my account, also, the sum of $[blank in the manuscript] which I have advanced to such of the prisoners as I thought had claims upon me under your instructions. I have advanced a much larger sum of my own. It is impossible for me to furnish vouchers, as the money was advanced in small sums when I had no means of obtaining them. If there is any difficulty about this, let these charges be disallowed, as I do not intend to make any charge which can admit of a discussion.

If you find it Expedient to send an agent, in the fall, to Yucatan, I should like to go there.

I deem it proper (for particular reasons) to say to you that I am entirely satisfied with the Secretary of this Legation Mr Mayer. He is a young gentleman of good talents and amiable qualities.

I think it proper to add upon the subject of the money advanced for the transportation of such of the Texan prisoners as were natives of the U:S:, that they were left without a dollar, and must have perished of hunger if I had not supplied their wants—as those at Puebla—actually did suffer for some days after their liberation. The British and Prussian Ministers made similar advances for their own countrymen and I found a precedent in the history of my own Govt. The Americans who were made prisoners by Spain, in the wars of the S: American Republicks, were upon their liberation in 1820 sent home at the charge of our Govt. If, however, it is deemed inadmissable, let it be placed to my account.

About the time that the Texans were released I heard that Commodore [Jesse] Wilkinson was at Vera Cruz, and as I saw no prospect of any other means of sending them home, upon the authority of the precedent above referred to, and as I regarded it as falling within the scope of our duties to a friendly Govt. I addressed to him the note No.—17.[20] I do not know whether he has received it, but deemed it my duty to communicate the facts to you.

I have just received the Documents Nos 18 and 19[21]—from the Department of Foreign Affairs.

19. Dorsey, a State Department courier, otherwise unidentified.

20. The note, dated June 13, asked Wilkinson to transport released prisoners from Veracruz to Galveston. Wilkinson (d. 1861) commanded the West Indies station.

21. No. 18 from Bocanegra, dated June 20, transmitted No. 19, a circular from Tornel complaining about interference by foreigners in Mexican internal affairs, especially in Yucatán.

I send you a copy of a letter from Mr [L. S.] Hargous (No. 20.)[22] by which you will perceive the justice of the suggestion made in my first despatch in regard to the retention of this valuable and indefatigable officer in the Consulate at Vera Cruz. I cannot but regard his removal as a loss which will be seriously felt by all our countrymen in Mexico, and, sincerely hope that all the expences he may incur for the released prisoners will be promptly allowed.

I also enclose you a copy of a letter from Mr De Bocanegra under date of the 13 June—No. 21[23]—and files of three of the newspapers published in this City. I have the honor to be with the greatest respect, Your obedt. Servant.   Waddy Thompson

L S. DNA, RG 59 (Despatches, Mexico). Extract published in *IAA*, 8 : 496–502.

TO WADDY THOMPSON

No. 9.   Department of State,
Sir :   Washington, 22nd June, 1842.

The Government of the United States sees with pain a prospect of the immediate resumption of active military operations between Texas and the Mexican Republic. While it claims no right to interfere in the pending controversy between those countries, it cannot, under existing circumstances, be indifferent to a renewal of hostilities between them. Nearly seven years have now elapsed since Texas has maintained its independence, unmolested by invading troops. In that time she has contracted treaties with other powers in both hemispheres and has been making progress in the arts of peace. Events have detached her from Mexico and existing circumstances cannot fail to indicate to all intelligent observers that her ultimate reannexation is among the things most to be doubted. It is notorious that the language, the laws and the habits of the people of the two countries, are dissimilar, that in these and in other respects differences exist so wide, as not to promise happiness to a union between the population of the two States. Texas was heretofore the remotest north-eastern province of Mexico, its distance from the Mexican capital is very great, and the character and population of the intervening country are such that Mexico could hardly hope to exercise over Texas an efficient authority. Without Texas, Mexico would still be not only one of the largest sovereignties of the world, but would possess a territory which,

22. The letter from Hargous of June 15 informed Thompson that Wilkinson had already sailed and requested money to support the released prisoners at Veracruz.

23. In the note Bocanegra informed Thompson that the released prisoners could remain in Mexico. The newspapers are not in the RG 59 record.

for its position and other great natural advantages, would be difficult to be surpassed. Her jurisdiction would still extend over a vast space, embracing, even on the same latitude, in consequence of the different degrees of elevation belonging to its different parts, almost every climate and every production of the habited Globe, while with ports on both oceans, she offers facilities of commerce to the whole world. On the other hand Texas is sufficiently large for a respectable community. Her limits are defined and peace, with an opportunity of improving her resources are much more important to her than any chances of territorial acquisition. The government of the United States feels a strong interest in the welfare of both countries. Both are our neighbours, they are among the newly organized governments, the regenerated systems of this hemisphere. For their own prosperity, as well as for the convenience and advantage of neighboring States, they require repose, security and vigorous application to the arts of peace. Under these circumstances the President directs that if you should receive from the Mexican Government any intimation of its desire for the interposition or mediation of this government for the purpose of bringing about peace between Texas and Mexico, you will state that such interposition or mediation will be cheerfully granted. So long, however, as either of those parties shall be resolved to remain at war with the other, and unless both of them shall request the mediation of the United States, the President would not be inclined to interfere. The opinion of this government upon the subject was expressed in a letter from Mr. [John] Forsyth to Mr. [Richard G.] Dunlap,[1] late representative of Texas here, and in the letter of General [Andrew] Jackson to General [Antonio López de] Santa Anna, therein referred to,[2] a copy of both of which is now transmitted.

Although policy and duty dictate this reserve on our part, it is not to be disguised that the immediate and permanent interests of the United States call loudly for the cessation of hostilities between Texas and Mexico. So long as the war continues, our extensive commerce and navigation in the Gulph of Mexico are liable to vexations and interruptions from one or the other belligerent, our citizens who may desire to trade with or to travel to Mexico across the Texan frontier may be driven back or be seized and their property confiscated, if for no other cause, from the difficulty if not impossibility for the Mexican local authorities to distinguish between them and Texans.

1. Forsyth to Dunlap, July 17, 1839, DNA, RG 59 (Notes to Foreign Legations, Texas); not included in this publication. Dunlap (d. June 24, 1841) was a member of the Tennessee legislature, 1829–1831, before emigrating to Texas in 1837. He was the Texan minister to the United States from March 13, 1839, to April 20, 1840.

2. Jackson's letter to Santa Anna of September 4, 1836, not included in

It is proper to advert to another consideration, which has no small weight in the President's mind. It is the danger, should the war between Mexico and Texas be renewed and prosecuted by the use of considerable military forces, that citizens of the United States would be inclined to take part, either on the one side or the other, to such an extent as might possibly compromit the neutrality and peace of this country, or at least create jealousy and dissatisfaction. Nothing is more probable than that the renewal of the war between Mexico and Texas, and the known fact of the invasion of the latter country by the former, with a large force— would be an occasion for crowds of persons to enter Texas and take their share on the chances of the war. This is a topic upon which you cannot, perhaps, very well speak fully and at length, to the Mexican government, but a remote and delicate intimation of the probability of such occurrences might be made and ought to produce in the counsels of that government great caution and deliberation. The more general ground, which I have already stated, may be exhibited without reserve; that is the President's clear and strong conviction that the war is not only useless, but hopeless, without attainable object, injurious to both parties and likely to be, in its continuance, annoying and vexatious to other commercial nations. The President consequently relies upon your address to bring about the object desired, which he hopes may be accomplished within the limits which have been assigned. I am, Sir, your obedient servant,

Daniel Webster.

L C. DNA, RG 59 (Instructions, Mexico). Published in *IAA*, 8:108–110.

TO JOSEPH EVE

No. 14.   Department of State,
Sir: Washington, 23d June, 1842.

I transmit a copy of a letter and of its enclosures which have been addressed by this department to Mr. [Waddy] Thompson[1] our Minister at Mexico. That communication will make you acquainted with the views of the President relative to the war between Texas and Mexico and with the condition upon which Mr. Thompson has been authorized to offer the mediation of this government for the purpose of putting an end to that war. You will make known to the Secretary of State of Texas [Anson Jones] the substance of the despatch to Mr. Thompson and express, in the name of your government, that it may be deemed to comport with the interests of the Texan government to suspend any offensive military

---

this publication, is in John Spencer Bassett, ed., *Correspondence of Andrew Jackson* (7 vols., Washington,   D.C., 1926–1935), 5:425–426.
1. See above.

operations which may be in contemplation against the Mexican Republic, until it shall learn the result of the negotiation which Mr. Thompson has been instructed to undertake. I am, Sir, your obedient servant,

Daniel Webster.

LC. DNA, RG 59 (Instructions, Texas). Published in *IAA,* 12:38.

TO WADDY THOMPSON

Private   Washington
Dear Sir,   June 27. 1842
    <What was contained> That part of your Despatch, No. 1,[1] <& your private letter to> which <related> relates to California, & your private letter to the President of the 9th. of May[2] have been considered. There is no doubt that the acquisition of so good a port on the Pacific as St. Francisco is a subject <which> well deserving of consideration. It would be useful to the numerous Whaling Ships & trading vessels of the United States, which <find our> navigate the Pacific, & along the Western coast of America. It <might> would in time probably become a place of considerable trade, having a good Country around it, but colonization & settlement could not be expected to advance, in that region, with the same spirit and celerity, as have been experienced on the Northern Atlantic Coast. <In the acquisition of additional> In seeking acquisitions, to be governed as Territories, & lying at a great distance from the United States, we <mu> ought to be governed by much prudence & caution; & a still higher degree of these qualities should be exercised, when large Territorial acquisitions are looked for, with a view to annexation. Nevertheless, the benefits of the possession of a good Harbour on the pacific is so obvious, that to that extent, at least, the President strongly inclines to favor the idea of treating with Mexico.
    <Our d> The claims of Citizens of the United States agt. the Mexican Government are large. The amount of those already awarded, as you will see by another communication by this conveyance, is <a> upwards of two millions of dollars[3] <& a half>; another large amt. failed of being awarded, as is supposed, only because the Umpire did not feel authorized to act upon them, after the expiration of the time limited for the duration of the Commission. There are still other classes of claims, of various descriptions, but amounting in the whole to a large aggregate. <P> You are at liberty to sound the Mexican Govt. upon the subject of a cession of

1. See above, Thompson to DW, April 29, 1842.
2. See above, Thompson to Tyler, May 9, 1842.
3. Presumably William L. Marcy and John Rowan to DW, May 26, 1841, DNA, RG 59 (Misc. Letters).

Territory upon the Pacific, in satisfaction of these claims, or some of them. Although it is desirable that you should <keep> preserve the <Har> Port & Harbor of St. Francisco as the prominent object to be attained, yet, if a cession should be made, St Francisco would naturally accompany the Port. It may be useful, however for divers reasons, that the length & convenience of the Port itself should, at least for the present, be spoken of, as what is chiefly desired by the United States. I do not think that England has any present purpose of obtaining that important place, or would interpose any obstacles to the acquisition of it by the United States. <How> What may be the wishes of France, in this respect, I cannot say. You will please proceed in this matter very cautiously, & quite informally; seeking rather to lead the Mexican Secretary to talk on the subject, than to lead directly to it, yourself. You will be particularly careful <to> not to suffer the Mexican Govt. to suppose that it is an object upon which we have set our hearts, or for the sake of which we should be willing to make large remuneration. The cession must be spoken of, rather as a convenience to Mexico, or a mode of discharging her debts. By no means give countenance to any extravagant expectations. Avoid all premature commitments, content yourself with sounding the Government, endeavor to hear, more than you say, to learn more than you communicate; & apprise us promptly & regularly, of all that may occur on the subject.

Your project of visiting California this season can hardly be realized, as it is likely your presence will be required at your post.[4] I am, Dear Sir, with much true regard, Yrs.

A L draft. NhHi. Published in Van Tyne, pp. 269–270.

FROM JOHN TYLER

D Sir   [June 28, 1842]

I return the Mexican despatch.[1] It is an impudent paper and deserves to be handled with severity. This is the first intimation of complaint and yet how threatening. Yrs   J. Tyler

A L S. DLC. Published in *Tylers*, 2:258. Rec'd June 28, 1842.

4. Thompson indicated in his despatch of April 29, 1842 (see above), that he planned an excursion to California during the summer.

1. In his letter to DW of May 12, 1842, José María de Bocanegra, the Mexican foreign minister, protested the "injuries and inflictions" Mexico had received from Americans. He stated that the failure of the United States to restrain its citizens from aiding Texas violated treaty obligations and international law. DNA, RG 59 (Notes from Foreign Legations, Mexico). For Webster's response to Bocanegra's charges, see DW to Thompson, July 8, 1842, below.

TO WILLIAM MCKENDREE GWIN AND JACOB THOMPSON

Department of State
Gentlemen,   Washington 5th. July 1842
    I have the honor to acknowledge the receipt of your letter of the 2d
inst,[1] requesting that steps might be taken by the Executive for the purpose of obtaining the release of Joseph T. Hatch,[2] a citizen of the United
States who accompanied the late Texan expedititon to Santa Fé, and
who is supposed to be confined in the city of Puebla in Mexico. The most
ample instructions have been given to our Minister accredited to that
government [Waddy Thompson], upon the subject of the citizens of the
United States captured with that expedition and it is understood that all
of them have been liberated whose liberation has been demanded pursuant to those instructions. General Thompson expresses an opinion in his
last despatch that all the others will shortly be released.[3] That Government has, however, been required to treat those whom it has a right to
detain as prisoners of war, and may choose so to detain, according to the
most lenient principles of the modern law of nations. I cordially sympa-
thise in the distress of the family and friends of young Hatch and will
send a copy of your letter to General Thompson with an instruction to
him to inquire into the case.[4] If he could be furnished with proof that
Mr Hatch accompanied the expedition as a non combatant and a neutral,
it would be useful. I have the honor &c.   Danl Webster

LC. DNA, RG 59 (Domestic Letters). Both Gwin (1805–1885; Transylvania
University 1828) and Thompson (1810–1885; University of North Carolina
1831) were at that time serving as congressmen from Mississippi. Gwin served
in the House from 1841 to 1843, and Thompson served from 1839 to 1851.

TO WADDY THOMPSON

No. 10.   Department of State,
Sir: Washington, 8th July, 1842.
    On the 29th of last month a communication was received at this De-
partment from Mr. [José María] de Bocanegra[1] Secretary of State and
foreign relations of the Government of Mexico, having been forwarded
through the agency of Mr. [Joaquín] Velazquez de Leon, at New York,

1. Gwin and Thompson to DW,
July 2, 1842, DNA, RG 59 (Misc. Letters).

2. Hatch, eighteen years old, was
released on June 13, 1842.

3. In his dispatch of April 29, 1842
(see above), Thompson said he expected the release of the prisoners.
Subsequently, in his June 20 dis-

patch (see above), he reported that
all the prisoners were released on
June 13.

4. See No. 12. DW to Thompson,
July 14, 1842, DNA, RG 59 (Instructions, Mexico).

1. Bocanegra to DW, May 12, 1842,
DNA, RG 59 (Notes from Foreign Legations, Mexico).

who informed the department by a letter accompanying that of Mr. de Bocanegra, that he had been appointed Chargé d'Affaires of the Mexican Republic to this Government, although he had not yet presented his credentials.[2] Mr. de Bocanegra's letter is addressed to the Secretary of State of the United States, and bears date the 12th of May. A copy together with a copy of the communication from Mr. Velazquez de Leon transmitting it and of the answer to Mr. Velazquez de Leon, from this Department,[3] you will receive herewith. Upon the receipt of this despatch, you will immediately address a note to Mr. de Bocanegra, in which you will say, that

The Secretary of State of the United States has received a letter addressed to him by Mr. de Bocanegra under date of the 12th of May, and transmitted to the Department of State at Washington, through the agency of Mr Velazquez de Leon, at New York who informs the Government of the United States that he has been appointed Charge d'Affaires of the Mexican Republic, although he has not presented his letter of credence.

The Government of the United States sees, with regret, the adoption on this occasion, of a form of communication quite unusual in diplomatic intercourse, and for which no necessity is known. An Envoy Extraordinary and Minister Plenipotentiary of the United States, fully accredited to the Government of Mexico, was at that moment in its capital, in the actual discharge of his functions, and ready to receive, on behalf of his government, any communication which it might be the pleasure of the President of the Mexican Republic [Antonio López de Santa Anna] to make to it, and it is not improper here to add, that it has been matter of regret with the Government of the United States, that while, being animated with a sincere desire at all times to cultivate the most amicable relations with Mexico, it has not failed to maintain, near that government, a mission of the highest rank known to its usages, Mexico for a long time has had no representative near the Government of the United States.[4]

2. Velazquez de Leon to DW, June 24, 1842, DNA, RG 59 (Notes from Foreign Legations, Mexico); not included in this publication. Velazquez de Leon (1803–1882) served as minister of trade promotion under Santa Anna from 1853 to 1855.

3. DW to Velazquez de Leon, June 29, 1842, DNA, RG 59 (Notes to Foreign Legations, Mexico), declining regular diplomatic intercourse until Velazquez de Leon presented his credentials (not included in this publi-

cation).

4. Under customary nineteenth-century diplomatic practice, foreign ministers communicated not directly with one another but through the agency of diplomats accredited to their respective capitals. On May 12, 1842, there was no accredited Mexican diplomat in Washington. When their minister, Francisco Pizarro Martinez, died in Washington on February 9, 1840, the Mexican government did not replace him with a diplomat

But the manner of the communication from Mr. de Bocanegra, however novel and extraordinary, is less important than its contents and
character, which surprise the Government of the United States by a loud
complaint of the violation of its neutral duties. Mr. de Bocanegra, speaking, as he says, by the express order of the President of the Mexican Republic, declares that the amicable relations between the two countries
might have been lamentably disturbed, since the year 1835, when the
revolution of Texas broke out, had not Mexico given so many evidences
of its forbearance, and made so many and so great sacrifices for the
sake of peace, in order that the world might not see with pain and amaze-
ment two nations which appear destined to establish the policy and interests of the American continent, divided and ravaged by the evils of war.

This language implies that such has been the conduct of the United
States, towards Mexico, that war must have ensued before the present
time, had not Mexico made great sacrifices to avoid such a result, a
charge which the Government of the United States utterly denies and
repels. It is wholly ignorant of any sacrifices made by Mexico, in order
to preserve peace, or of any occasion calling on its government to manifest uncommon forbearance. On the contrary, the government of the
United States cannot but be of opinion that if the history of occurrences
between the two governments, the state of things at this moment existing
between them be regarded, both the one and the other will demonstrate
that it is the conduct of the Government of the United States which has
been marked, in an especial manner, by moderation and forbearance. Injuries and wrongs have been sustained by citizens of the United States,
not inflicted by individual Mexicans, but by the authorities of the government, for which injuries and wrongs, numerous as they are and outrageous as is the character of some of them, and acknowledged as they
are by Mexico herself, redress has been sought only by mild and peaceable means and no indemnity asked but such as the strictest justice imperatively demanded. A desire not to disturb the peace and harmony of
the countries has led the government of the United States to be content
with the lowest measure of remuneration. Mexico herself must admit that
in all these transactions, the conduct of the United States towards her
has been signalized, not by the infliction of injuries but by the manifestation of a friendly feeling and a conciliatory spirit.

The Government of the United States will not be unjust in its sentiments towards Mexico, it will not impute to its Government any desire to
disturb the peace, it acquits it of any design to spread the ravages of war,

---

of equal rank but instead allowed
the post to be held temporarily by
José Miguel Arroyo (1810–1875) as
a chargé d'affaires *ad interim*. The
position at Washington was eventually filled by Juan Nepomuceno Almonte (1803–1869), who acted as
minister from October 27, 1842, to
the break in Mexican-American diplomatic relations on March 6, 1845.

over the two countries, and it leaves it to Mexico herself to avow her own motives for her pacific policy, if she have any other motive than those of expediency and justice, provided, however, that such avowal of her motives carry with it no imputation or reflection upon the good faith and honor of the United States.

The revolution in Texas and the events connected with it and springing out of it, are Mr de Bocanegra's principal topic, and it is in relation to these that his complaint is founded. His Government, he says, flatters itself that the Government of the United States has not promoted the insurrection in Texas, favored the usurpation of its territory or supplied the rebels with vessels, ammunition and money. If Mr. de Bocanegra intends this as a frank admission of the honest and cautious neutrality of the Government of the United States, in the contest between Mexico and Texas, he does that Government justice, and no more than justice, but if the language be intended to intimate an opposite and a reproachful meaning, that meaning is only the more offensive for being insinuated rather than distinctly avowed. Mr. de Bocanegra would seem to represent, that from 1835 to the present time, citizens of the United States if not their government, have been aiding rebels in Texas in arms against the lawful authority of Mexico. This is not a little extraordinary. Mexico may have chosen to consider and may still chuse to consider Texas as having been at all times since 1835, and as still continuing, a rebellious province, but the world has been obliged to take a very different view of the matter. From the time of the battle of San Jacinto in April, 1836, to the present moment, Texas has exhibited the same external signs of national independence as Mexico herself, and with quite as much stability of Government. Practically free and independent, acknowledged as a political sovereignty by the principal Powers of the world, no hostile foot finding rest within her territory, for six or seven years and Mexico herself refraining, for all that period from any further attempt to reestablish her own authority over that territory, it cannot but be surprising to find Mr. de Bocanegra complaining that, for that whole period, citizens of the United States or its government have been favoring the rebels of Texas and supplying them with vessels, ammunition and money, as if the war for the reduction of the province of Texas had been constantly prosecuted by Mexico and her success prevented by these influences from abroad!

The general facts appertaining to the settlement of Texas and the revolution in its government, cannot but be well known to Mr. de Bocanegra. By the Treaty of the 22nd of February, 1819, between the United States and Spain, the Sabine was adopted as the line of boundary between the two powers. Up to that period, no considerable colonization had been effected in Texas, but the territory between the Sabine and the Rio Grande being confirmed to Spain, by the Treaty, applications were made to that power for grants of land, and such grants or permissions of settlement, were in fact made by the Spanish authorities, in favor of citizens of the United States, proposing to emigrate to Texas, in numerous families, before the declaration of independence by Mexico.[5] And these early grants were confirmed, as is well known, by successive acts of the Mexican Government after its separation from Spain. In January, 1823, a national colonization law was passed, holding out strong inducements to all persons who should incline to undertake the settlement of uncultivated lands,[6] and although the Mexican law prohibited for a time citizens of foreign countries from settling, as colonists, in territories immediately adjoining such foreign countries, yet even this restriction was afterwards repealed or suspended. So that in fact, Mexico, from the commencement of her political existence, held out the most liberal inducements to emigrate into her territories, with full knowledge that these inducements were likely to act and expecting they would act with the greatest effect, upon citizens of the United States, especially of the Southern States, whose agricultural pursuits naturally rendered the rich lands of Texas, so well suited to their accustomed occupation, objects of desire to them. The early colonists of Texas from the United States introduced by Moses and Stephen [Fuller] Austin[7] under these inducements and invitations, were persons of most respectable character, and their undertaking was attended with very severe hardships, occasioned in no small degree by the successive changes in the government of Mexico. They nevertheless persevered and accomplished a settlement. And under the encouragements and allurements thus held out by Mexico, other emigrants followed and many thousand colonists from the United States and elsewhere, had settled in Texas within ten years from the date of Mexican Independence. Having some reason to complain, as they thought, of the Government over them, and especially of the aggressions of the Mexican military stationed in Texas, they sought relief by applying to the Supreme Government for the separation of Texas from Coahuila and for a local government for Texas itself. Not having succeeded in this object, in the process of time, in the progress of events, they saw fit to attempt an entire separation from Mexico, to set up a Government of their own and to establish a political sovereignty. War ensued, and the battle of San Jacinto, fought on the 21st of April, 1836, achieved their

5. On February 24, 1821, troops led by Agustín de Iturbide (1783–1824) proclaimed Mexico an independent constitutional monarchy.

6. The Imperial Colonization Law of January 3, 1823, offered inducements of land grants and suspended taxes to encourage emigration to Texas. The terms of the law are in Walter Prescott Webb, ed., *The Handbook of Texas* (2 vols., Austin, Tex., 1952), 2:183–184.

7. In January 1821 Moses Austin (1761–1821), a Missouri lead miner, acquired a grant to settle 300 families in Texas, but he died on June 10. His son, Stephen F. Austin (1793–1836), took over the grant.

Independence. The war was from that time at an end; and in March following the independence of Texas was formally acknowledged by the government of the United States.[8]

In the events leading to the actual result of these hostilities, the United States had no agency and took no part. Its government had from the first abstained from giving aid or succor to either party. It knew its neutral obligations and firmly endeavored to fulfil them all. It acknowledged the independence of Texas, only when that independence was an apparent and ascertained fact; and its example in this particular, has been followed by several of the most considerable powers of Europe.

It has sometimes been stated as if for the purpose of giving more reason to the complaints of Mexico, that of the military force which acted against Mexico with efficiency and success in 1836, a large portion consisted of volunteers then fresh from the United States. But this is a great error. It is well ascertained that of those who bore arms in the Texan ranks in the battle of San Jacinto, three fourths at least were colonists, invited into Texas by the grants and the colonization laws of Mexico, and called to the field by the exigencies of the time in 1836, from their farms and other objects of private pursuit.

Mr de Bocanegra's complaint is two fold; first, that citizens of the United States have supplied the rebels in Texas with ammunition, arms, vessels, money and recruits, have publicly raised forces in their cities and fitted out vessels in their ports, loaded them with munitions of war and marched to commit hostilities against a friendly nation, under the eye and with the knowledge of the public authorities. In all this Mr. de Bocanegra appears to forget that while the United States are at peace with Mexico, they are also at peace with Texas; that both stand on the same footing of friendly nations, that since 1837 the United States have regarded Texas as an Independent sovereignty, as much as Mexico; and that trade and commerce with citizens of a government at war with Mexico cannot, on that account, be regarded as an intercourse by which assistance and succor are given to Mexican rebels. The whole current of Mr. de Bocanegra's remarks runs in the same direction, as if the Independence of Texas had not been acknowledged. It has been acknowledged, it was acknowledged in 1837 against the remonstrance and protest of Mexico; and most of the acts of any importance of which Mr. de Bocanegra complains, flow necessarily from that recognition. He speaks of Texas as still being an integral part of the territory of the Mexican Republic; but he cannot but understand that the United States do not so regard it. The real complaint of Mexico, therefore, is in substance neither more nor less than a complaint against the recognition of Texan Independence. It may be thought rather late to repeat that complaint, and not quite just

8. See John Forsyth to William H. Wharton and Memucan Hunt, March 13, 1837, DNA, RG 59 (Notes to Foreign Legations, Texas).

to confine it to the United States, to the exemption of England, France and Belgium, unless the United States having been the first to acknowledge the independence of Mexico herself, are to be blamed for setting an example for the recognition of that of Texas. But it is still true, that Mr. de Bocanegra's specification of his grounds of complaint and remonstrance, is mainly confined to such transactions and occurrences as are the natural consequence of the political relations existing between Texas and the United States. Acknowledging Texas to be an independent Nation, the government of the United States of course allows and encourages lawful trade and commerce between the two countries. If articles contraband of war be found mingled with this commerce while Mexico and Texas are belligerent States, Mexico has the right to intercept the transit of such articles to her enemy. This is the common right of all belligerents and belongs to Mexico in the same extent as to other nations. But Mr. de Bocanegra is quite well aware that it is not the practice of nations to undertake to prohibit their own subjects, by previous laws, from trafficking in articles contraband of war. Such trade is carried on at the risk of those engaged in it, under the liabilities and penalties prescribed by the Law of Nations or by particular treaties. If it be true, therefore, that citizens of the United States have been engaged in a commerce by which Texas, an enemy of Mexico, has been supplied with arms and munitions of war, the Government of the United States, nevertheless, was not bound to prevent it without a manifest departure from the principles of neutrality, and is in no way answerable for the consequences. The treaty of the 5th of April, 1831, between the United States and Mexico itself shows, most clearly, how little foundation there is for the complaint of trading with Texas, if Texas is to be regarded as a public enemy of Mexico. The 16th article declares 'It shall likewise be lawful for the aforesaid citizens respectively to sail with their vessels and merchandize before mentioned and to trade with the same liberty and security from the places, ports and havens of those who are enemies of both or either party, without any opposition or disturbance whatsoever, not only directly from the places of the enemy, before mentioned, to neutral places, but also from one place belonging to an enemy to another place belonging to an enemy, whether they be under the jurisdiction of the same Government or under several.'[9]

The 18th article enumerates those commodities which shall be regarded as contraband of war;[10] but neither that article nor any other imposes on neither nation any duty of preventing, by previous regulation, commerce in such articles. Such commerce is left to its ordinary fate, according to the law of nations. It is only therefore by insisting, as Mr de Bocanegra does insist, that Texas is still a part of Mexico, that he can maintain any complaint. Let it be repeated, therefore, that if the things

9. *Treaties*, 3:609–611.   10. *Treaties*, 3:611–612.

against which he remonstrates be wrong, they have their source in the original wrong of the acknowledgement of Texan Independence. But that acknowledgement is not likely to be retracted.

There can be no doubt at all that for the last six years, the trade in articles contraband of war, between the United States and Mexico, has been greater than between the United States and Texas. It is probably greater at the present moment. Why has not Texas a right to complain of this? For no reason, certainly, but because the permission to trade, or the actual trading by the citizens of a government in articles contraband of war, is not a breach of neutrality.

Mr de Bocanegra professes himself unable to comprehend how those persons of whom he complains have been able to evade the punishment decreed against them by the laws of the United States; but he does not appear to have a clear idea of the principles or provisions of those laws. The duties of neutral nations in time of war are prescribed by the law of nations, which is imperative and binding upon all governments; and nations not unfrequently establish municipal regulations for the better government of the conduct of their subjects or citizens. This has been done by the United States, in order to maintain with greater certainty, strict and impartial neutrality pending war between other countries. And whenever a violation of neutral duties as they exist by the law of nations, or any breach of its own laws has been brought to the notice of the Government, attention has always been paid to it.

At an early period of the Texan Revolution strict orders were given by the President of the United States to all officers in the South and South western frontier, to take care that the laws should be observed;[11] and the attention of the government of the United States has not been called to any specific violation of them since the manifestation on the part of Mexico of an intention to renew hostilities with Texas. And all officers of the government remain charged with the strict and faithful execution of these laws. On a recent occasion complaint was made by the representatives of Texas, that an armament was fitted out in the United States for the service of Mexico against Texas. Two vessels of war, it was alleged, built or purchased in the United States for the use of the government of Mexico and well understood as intended to be employed against Texas, were equipped and ready to sail from the waters of New York. The case was carefully inquired into, official examination was made and legal counsel invoked. It appeared to be a case of great doubt, but Mexico was allowed the benefit of that doubt, and the vessels left the United States with the whole or a part of their armament actually on board.[12] The same

11. See President Jackson's comments on Texas in *Messages and Papers*, 3:151, and the instructions to federal officials in *Executive Docu-*

ments, 25th Cong., 2d sess., Serial 323, No. 74.

12. On January 8, 1842, Nathaniel Amory, the Texan chargé d'affaires

administration of even handed justice, the same impartial execution of the laws towards all parties, will continue to be observed. If forces have been raised in the United States or vessels fitted out in their ports, for Texan service, contrary to law, no instance of which has as yet come to the knowledge of the government, prompt attention will be paid to the first case, and to all cases which may be made known to it. As to advances, loans or donations of money or goods, made by individuals to the government of Texas or its citizens, Mr. de Bocanegra hardly needs to be informed that there is nothing unlawful in this, so long as Texas is at peace with the United States; and that these are things which no government undertakes to restrain. Other citizens are equally at liberty, should they be so inclined, to show their good will towards Mexico, by the same means. Still less can the government of the United States be called upon to interfere with opinions uttered in the public assemblages of a free people, accustomed to the independent expression of their sentiments resulting in no violation of the laws of their country, or of its duties as a neutral State. Towards the United States, Mexico and Texas stand in the same relation, as independent States at war. Of the character of that war, mankind will form their own opinions, and in the United States at least the utterance of those opinions cannot be suppressed.

The second part of Mr de Bocanegra's complaint is thus stated: "No sooner does the Mexican government, in the exercise of its rights which it cannot and does not desire to renounce, prepare means to recover a possession usurped from it, than the whole population of the United States, especially in the Southern States, is in commotion, and in the most public manner, a large portion of them is directed upon Texas." And how does Mr de Bocanegra suppose that the Government of the United States can prevent, or is bound to undertake to prevent, the people from thus going to Texas? This is emigration, the same emigration, though not under the same circumstances, which Mexico invited to Texas before the revolution. These persons, so far as is known to the government of the United States, repair to Texas, not as citizens of the United States, but as ceasing to be such citizens, and as changing at the same time their allegiance and their domicile. Should they return, after having entered into the service of a foreign State, still claiming to be citizens of the United States, it will be for the authorities of the United States government to determine how far they have violated the municipal laws of the country, and what penalties they have incurred. The Government of the United

in Washington, sent a dispatch to his secretary of state, Anson Jones, reporting a conversation with DW regarding the outfitting of two vessels at New York for Mexican service. The ships were briefly detained but were released when their American owners posted bond ensuring their neutrality. See George P. Garrison, ed., *Diplomatic Correspondence of the Republic of Texas* (3 vols., Washington, D.C., 1908–1911), 1:518–533.

States does not maintain and never has maintained the doctrine of the perpetuity of natural allegiance. And surely Mexico maintains no such doctrine, because her actually existing government, like that of the United States, is founded in the principle that men may throw off the obligations of that allegiance to which they are born. The government of the United States, from its origin, has maintained legal provisions for the naturalization of such subjects of foreign States as may choose to come hither and make their home in the country; and, renouncing their former allegiance, and complying with certain stated requisitions to take upon themselves the character of citizens of this government. Mexico herself has laws granting equal facilities to the naturalization of foreigners. On the other hand the United States have not passed any law restraining their own citizens, native or naturalized, from leaving the country and forming political relations elsewhere. Nor do other governments, in modern times, attempt any such thing. It is true that there are governments which assert the principle of perpetual allegiance; yet, even in cases where this is not rather a matter of theory than practice, the duties of the supposed continuing allegiance are left to be demanded of the subject himself, when within the reach of the power of his former government, and as exigencies may arise, and are not attempted to be enforced by the imposition of previous restraint, preventing men from leaving their country.

Upon this subject of the emigration of individuals from neutral to belligerent States, in regard to which Mr. de Bocanegra appears so indignant, we must be allowed to bring Mexico into her own presence, to compare her with herself and respectfully invite her to judge the matter by her own principles and her own conduct. In her great struggle against Spain for her own independence, did she not open her arms wide to receive all who would come to her, from any part of the world? And did not multitudes flock to her new raised standard of liberty, from the United States, from England, Ireland, France and Italy, many of whom distinguished themselves in her service both by sea and land? She does not appear to have supposed that the governments of these persons, thus coming to unite their fate with hers, were, by allowing the emigration, even pending a civil war, furnishing just cause of offence to Spain. Even in her military operations against Texas, Mexico employed many foreign emigrants, and it may be thought remarkable that in those very operations, not long before the battle of San Jacinto, a native citizen of the United States held high command in her service and performed feats of no mean significance in Texas.[13] Of that toleration, therefore, as she calls it and which she now so warmly denounces, Mexico in that hour of her emergency, embraced the benefits eagerly and to the full extent of

13. Ellis Peter Bean (1783–1846), an adventurer from Tennessee, went to Texas in 1800. He rose to the rank of colonel in the Mexican army.

her power. May we not ask, then, how she can reconcile her present complaints, with her own practice, as well as how she accounts for so long and unbroken a silence upon a subject on which her remonstrance is now so loud?

Spain chose to regard Mexico only in the light of a rebellious province for near twenty years after she had asserted her own independence. Does Mexico now admit that for all that period notwithstanding her practical emancipation from Spanish power, it was unlawful for the subjects and citizens of other governments to carry on with her the ordinary business of commerce or to accept her tempting offers to emigration? Certainly such is not her opinion. Might it not be asked, then, even if the United States had not already and long ago acknowledged the independence of Texas, how long they should be expected to wait for the accomplishment of the object now existing only in purpose and intention, of the resubjugation of that territory by Mexico? How long, let it be asked, in the judgment of Mexico herself, is the fact of actual independence to be held of no avail against an avowed purpose of future re-conquest?

Mr. de Bocanegra is pleased to say, that if war actually existed between the two countries, proceedings more hostile on the part of the United States could not have taken place, than have taken place, nor the insurgents of Texas obtained more effectual coöperation than they have obtained. This opinion, however hazardous to the discernment and just estimate of things, of those who avow it, is yet abstract and theoretical, and so far harmless. The efficiency of American hostility to Mexico has never been tried: the Government has no desire to try it. It would not disturb the peace for the sake of showing how erroneously Mr. de Bocanegra has reasoned, while, on the other hand, it trusts that a just hope may be entertained that Mexico will not inconsiderately and needlessly hasten into an experiment, by which the truth or fallacy of his sentiments may be brought to an actual ascertainment.

Mr. de Bocanegra declares, in conclusion, that his government finds itself under the necessity of protesting solemnly against the aggressions which the citizens of the United States are reiterating upon the Mexican territory; and of declaring, in a positive manner, that it will consider as a violation of the Treaty of Amity, the toleration of that course of conduct which he alleges inflicts on the Mexican Republic the injuries and inconveniences of war. The President exceedingly regrets both the sentiment and the manner of this declaration. But it can admit of but one answer. The Mexican Government appears to require that which could not be granted in whatever language or whatever tone, requested. The government of the United States is a government of law. The Chief Executive Magistrate as well as functionaries in every other Department, is restrained and guided by the constitution and the laws of the land. Neither the constitution nor the law of the land, nor principles known to the usages of modern states, authorize him to interdict lawful trade between the United States and Texas, or to prevent, or attempt to prevent, individuals from leaving the United States for Texas or any other foreign country. If such individuals enter into the service of Texas or any other foreign state, the government of the United States no longer holds over them the shield of its protection. They must stand or fall in their newly assumed character and according to the fortunes which may betide it. But the Government of the United States cannot be called upon to prevent their emigration, and it must be added, that the constitution, public treaties and the laws oblige the President to regard Texas as an Independent State and its territory as no part of the territory of Mexico. Every provision of law, every principle of neutral obligation will be sedulously enforced, in relation to Mexico as in relation to other Powers; and to the same extent and with the same integrity of purpose. All this belongs to the constitutional power and duty of the government and it will all be fulfilled. But the continuance of amity with Mexico cannot be purchased at any higher rate. If the peace of the two countries is to be disturbed, the responsibility will devolve on Mexico. She must be answerable for consequences. The United States, let it be again repeated, desire peace. It would be with infinite pain that they should find themselves in hostile relations with any of the new governments on this continent. But their Government is regulated, limited, full of the spirit of liberty but surrounded, nevertheless, with just restraints; and greatly and fervently as it desires peace with all States, and especially with its more immediate neighbours, yet no fear of a different state of things can be allowed to interrupt its course of equal and exact justice to all nations, nor to jostle it out of the constitutional orbit in which it revolves. I am, Sir, your obedient servant,   Daniel Webster

LC. DNA, RG 59 (Instructions, Mexico). Published in *IAA*, 8:110–120.

FROM JAMES CHAMBERLAYNE PICKETT

No. 69.   Legation of the U. States,
Sir: Lima, Septr 6th 1842.
    Here we think it not improbable, that the United States and Mexico are now at war, believing the Circular of the Mexican Government and the Minister's [José María de Bocanegra] letter to you, of the 31st of May last,[1] calculated to produce such a result.
    We are rather of opinion too, that Mexico has ceded California to Great Britain and that the latter is about to take possession. Admiral [Richard]

1. The circular of May 31, 1842, from Bocanegra to the foreign diplomatic corps in Mexico City is enclosed in Waddy Thompson's dispatch No.

2. June 6, 1842, DNA, RG 59 (Despatches, Mexico). See Bocanegra to DW, May 31, 1842, above.

Thomas[2] sailed yesterday, in the British frigate "Dublin,"—destination unknown, and a corvette left Callao, a few days ago, in the same manner. British vessels of war on this coast, are never sent to sea so mysteriously, on ordinary occasions.

Commodore [Thomas ap Catesby] Jones[3] proceeds immediately, to California, in the "United States," accompanied by the "Cyane" and "Dale."

Lima continues to be tranquil, since the late revolution. [Francisco] Vidal, [Juan Crisotomo] Torrico's[4] antagonist who had advanced from Cuzco, with his army, is said to have retreated, and it is thought at present, that the chances are in favor of Torrico. It is not of much importance I suppose, which succceeds. I have the honor to be, with great respect, Your Obt. Servant.   J. C. Pickett

ALS. DNA, RG 59 (Despatches, Peru). Rec'd December 7.

GEORGE WHITFIELD TERRELL TO JOSEPH EVE

Department of State Texas
Sir   Washington 15th October 1842

I am instructed by his Excellency, the President [Samuel Houston], to submit for your consideration and action, a subject of general concern to civilized nations, but of peculiar interest to Texas, (viz) the character of the war at present waged by Mexico against this country. The President is led to believe, from the nature of the facts involved, that this step will be deemed not only admissible, but entirely proper.

The civilized and Christian world are interested in the unimpaired preservation of those principles and rules of international intercourse, both in peace and war, which have received the impress of wisdom and humanity, and been strengthened through a long course of time by the practice and approval of the most powerful and enlightened of modern states.

To these rules, in their application to the pending difficulties between this Republic and Mexico, your attention is respectfully invited.

When ever a people, separate and sovereign, in their political character, are admitted into the great community of Nations, they incur responsibilities, and contract obligations which are reciprocal in their character, and mutually binding upon all the members of this community, the extent and force of which depend upon that code of ethics which prescribes the reciprocal duties and obligations of each sovereign member;

2. Thomas (1777–1857) commanded the British fleet in the Pacific, 1841–1844.

3. Jones (1790–1858) commanded the U.S. squadron in the Pacific.

4. Torrico (1808–1875) acted as president of Peru from August 16 to November 17, 1842, when he was overthrown by Vidal (1800–1863). Vidal was deposed on March 15, 1843.

Hence arises the right to control the mode of warfare pursued by one nation towards another, and the corresponding duty of providing against the perpetration of acts at variance with the laws of humanity and the settled usages of civilized nations.

In view of the character of hostilities at present waged by Mexico against Texas, and of those principles which have been in the opinion of this government, so frequently and so flagrantly violated by our enemy, the hope is confidently indulged by the President that the direct interference of nations mutually friendly will be exerted to arrest a species of warfare unbecoming the age in which we live and disgraceful to any people professing to be civilized.

The course of conduct uniformly observed by the government and people of Texas towards our enemy, stands in palpable contrast with their manifold enormities and wanton aggressions, and will, it is confidently expected furnish abundant ground for the exercise of the right of interference now invooked.

It has now been nearly seven years since the declaration and establishment of the independence of this Republic. During the whole of this time Mexico, although uniformly asserting the ability and the determination to resubjugate this country, has never made a formidable effort to do so. Her principal war has consisted of silly taunts, and idle threats, of braggadocio bulletans, and gasconading proclamations.

All her boasting threats of invasion have resulted in nothing more than the fitting out and sending into the most exposed portions of our territory, petty marauding parties, for the purpose of pilliging and harrassing the weak and isolated settlements on our western border.

Since march last, no less than three incursions of that character have been made, none of which have continued longer than eight days. The first party was composed of artillery, infantry, rancheros and indian warriers, in all about seven hundred, their attack was made upon the defenceless town of San Antonio.

The second consisting of about six hundred, attacked a party of about two hundred emigrants at Hipantillan. They were repulsed with loss, and retreated out of the country.

The last under general [Adrian] Woll of about thirteen hundred, attacked and took San Antonio, a second time, by surprise, during the session of the District court.[1]

1. On March 5, 1842, Mexican commander Rafael Vásquez had occupied San Antonio. He withdrew on March 7, after plundering the town. At the Battle of Lipantitlán, on the Nueces River, on July 7, 1842, Texans had held off a Mexican assault. Woll (1795–1875), a French adventurer in the Mexican army who rose to the rank of major general, captured San Antonio on September 10, 1842. Learning that the Texan forces were being strengthened, he withdrew on September 20.

His force was composed of regulars rancheros and Indians. The Indians employed by the Mexicans, are fragments of bands originally from the United States, but now located within the limits of Texas.

This government has always refused to employ the services of Indians when tendered against Mexico, and has sought by every possible means to mitigate rather than increase the calamities of war. Persisting in this effort, the President has recourse to the present measure, with a hope to subserve the cause of humanity. Should this effort fail, the government must resort to retaliating measures, growing out of our peculiar situation, which are to be deprecated by every Christian and generous feeling. The rulers of nations are responsible for their preservation; And as a last resort must adopt a just retaliation upon their enemies.

What is most to be deplored in a war of this character is, that the unoffending and defenceless become victims of the most relentless cruelty. War in its most generous and noble aspect, is accompanied by great calamities.

Nations are not benefitted by it, and it must be productive of great individual suffering. But when individuals and nations, are exasperated by repeated wrongs, even cruelty itself may be rendered tolerable, when it is used as retaliation for injuries long endured.

The massacrees and cruelties which have been inflicted upon Texas since the commencement of her revolution, have been responded to by a generous forbearance. But that forbearance cannot be expected longer to exist.

The object of Mexico in her course cannot be misunderstood; By incursions of the character complained of, the spirits of our husbandmen and farmers are depressed—a cry of invasion is kept up, and the excitement incident to war prevents emigration and embarrasses our revenue by deterring men of enterprise and capital from making importations of goods into our country. This for a time may avail her something; but the aggregate of human suffering will be but a poor recompense for the advantages she may gain. The origin genius and character of the people of Texas, are guaranties for her ultimate success. Nations that contribute to her advancement will command her gratitude.

Never since 1836 has Mexico attempted any thing of the character of a general invasion of the country. or conducted the war upon any plan calculated to test the superiority of the two nations upon the field of battle, and bring war to a close by the arbitrament of arms.

These hostile demonstrations thus far, have consisted exclusively in the clandestine approach of small bands of rancheros from the valley of the Rio grande for the purposes of plunder and theft—but sometimes associated with fragments of the Mexican Army, composed for the most part of convict soldiery, fitted for nothing either honorable in enterprise or magnanimous in conduct. The people of Texas being for the most part agriculturalists and engaged in the tillage of the soil, the consequences of this predatory warfare have been to them extremely vexatious and harrassing, without in any degree hastening the adjustment of the difficulties existing between the parties.

Entirely different is the general character of the Mexican population. They are literally a nation of herdsmen, subsisting in a great measure from the proceeds of their flocks and herds, they can move about from place to place, and make their homes wherever inclination or convenience may prompt, without detriment.

Hitherto the conduct and disposition of the government and people of Texas, have been diametrically opposed to those manifested by Mexico. While the one has been depredating upon the property and dwellings of our exposed and defenceless frontier—murdering the inhabitants in cold blood, or forcing them away into a loathsome and too often fatal captivity.

Inciting the numerous tribes of hostile Indians who reside along our northern border, to plunder our exposed settlements, stimulating them to the most cruel and barbarous massacrees and inhuman butcheries, even of our defenceless women and children, and to commit every excess of savage warfare.

The other, animated by the hope of avoiding a further resort to arms and their attendant calamities, for injuries received, returned forbearance. The President has sought to abstain from the effusion of blood, and with that aim has uniformly restrained the impetuosity, and calmed the excitement of his country men, so often aroused, by course of conduct, which violates every right both private and national, and a cruelty and depravity which would disgrace the darkest ages of Feudal barbarism.

The popular impulse might have been turned upon the enemy upon their own soil. The result might have proved that a free people burning with vengeance long restrained, could levy a heavy retribution.

Such being the character of hostile operations against Texas on the part of our enemy, which being plainly violative of every principle of civilized or honorable warfare and at the same time so little calculated to achieve the professed object of the war, the reconquest of Texas. The President confidently hopes the government of the United States will feel not only justified, but even called upon to interpose its high authority to arrest this course of proceeding, and to require of Mexico either the recognition of the independence, or to make war upon her according to the rules established and universally recognized by civilized nations. If Mexico believes herself able to resubjugate this country, her right to make the effort to do so is not denied; on the contrary if she chooses to invade our territory with that purpose, the President, in the name of the people of all Texas, will bid her welcome.

It is not against a war with Mexico that Texas would protest: This she deprecates not. She is willing at any time to stake her existence as a nation upon the issue of a war conducted upon Christian principles. It is alone against the unholy—inhuman and fruitless character it has assumed and still maintains, which violates every rule of honorable warfare, every precept of religion, and sets at defiance even the common sentiments of humanity, against which she protests, and invokes, the interposition of those powerful nations which have recognized her independence. The government of this Republic has already given an earnest of its disposition to consult the wishes of other nations, when those wishes do not conflict with the general interests and convenience of the country.

Fully appreciating the friendly sentiments of those powers which have acknowledged the independence of Texas, and relying much upon their ability and influence in securing an early and permanent adjustment of our difficulties with Mexico[.]

The President in compliance with the desire of those nations expressed through their representatives to this government, revoked the late proclamation of blockade against Mexico, and thus removed every cause of embarrassment to those nations in their intercourse with our enemy.

Having thus yielded the opportunity of retaliating upon our enemy the many injuries received at their hands, the President feels less reluctance in making this representation and invooking the interposition of those nations to put an end to a mode of warfare at once disgraceful to the age, so evil in its consequences to civil society so revolting to every precept of the Christian religion, and shocking to every sentiment of humanity.

The undersigned avails himself of the opportunity of renewing to judge Eve, assurances of high consideration with which he is his obedient servant   (signed) G. W. Terrell atty general and acting secretary of state

Copy. Enclosed with No. 30. Eve to DW, November 1, 1842, DNA, RG 59 (Despatches, Texas). Rec'd November 15. Published in *IAA*, 12:249–253. Terrell (1803–1846), originally from Tennessee, was the attorney general of Texas and acting secretary of state.

FROM WADDY THOMPSON, WITH ENCLOSURE

                              Legation of the United States of America—
Sir.   Mexico December 28: 1842.

I have the honor to send you herewith a copy of a communication from the Minister of Foreign Affairs of this Government [José María de Bocanegra] No. 1:[1] on the subject of the recent events in California and my

1. Bocanegra to Thompson, December 19, 1842, not included in this publication. Bocanegra denounced Commodore Jones's "invasion" of Mexican territory as a massive violation of international law and the conduct of civilized nations. He demanded "reparation and satisfaction . . . which correspond to the magnitude of the offense."

reply No. 2:[2]—all the documents connected with these transactions which were published in the news papers here by the authority of the Government, do not accompany the note of Mr. de Bocanegra. I send you two news papers, containing them;[3] you will see that some of them are of a most offensive character, <and> I thought it my duty to notice them as they had been published by the Government. You will perceive that whilst I have disclaimed the acts of Commodore [Thomas ap Catesby] Jones I have availed myself of other topics to show that the wrong has not all been on our side. It would have done no good you may be assured to have assumed any lower tone. For the Mexican Government are disposed to make the most of this unfortunate affair and I should not be surprized if they were to attempt to have it considered as a payment of all our claims.

I wrote you when I first came that I had no idea that [Antonio López de] Santa Anna would sanction the Constitution which might be adopted by the Congress and that he would have every thing his own way—the result has proven that my conjectures were right. The Congress has been dispersed by the military and a new one called—the members who are to constitute it selected by the President. In the mean time the only Constitution which the Country has is what is called the plan of Tacubaya, which was dictated by the Army under the command of Santa Anna in September 1841—under the 7th. Article of this plan the most absolute and unlimited power Executive, Military and Legislative is exercised by Santa Anna—even to the naming of a substitute as President whilst he is on a visit to his Estate. I send you a copy of this plan of Tacubaya.[4] I have the honor to be with the greatest Respect Your Obt. Servant,

Waddy Thompson

L S . DNA, RG 59 (Despatches, Mexico). Rec'd January 24, 1843. Published in *Executive Documents*, 27th Cong., 3d sess., Serial 422, No. 166, p. 9.

ENCLOSURE: WADDY THOMPSON TO JOSE MARÍA DE BOCANEGRA

Legation of the United States of America—
Mexico December 27th. 1842.

The Undersigned Envoy Extraordinary and Minister Plenipotentiary of the United States of America, had the honor to receive on the 24th the note of His Excellency José Maria de Bocanegra Minister of Foreign Relations and Government of the Republic of Mexico bearing date the 19th. Instant, with its accompanying papers in relation to the invasion of the Town of Monterrey in Upper California by Commodore [Thomas ap Catesby] Jones of the United States Navy.

2. See below.
3. Not included in the RG 59 record.
4. Not included in this publication.

The surprize and regret of your Excellency at these occurrences cannot have exceeded what has been experienced by the Undersigned—who takes great pleasure in assuring your Excellency, that, these acts of the American Commodore were wholly unauthorized by any orders from his government, and that the fullest disclaimer to that effect will be promptly made by the government of the Undersigned with whatever other reparation may be due to the honor of Mexico and which is not incompatible with that of the United States. It must be altogether apparent to your Excellency from the communications which have passed between Commodore Jones and the Mexican officers in California that he has acted solely on his own responsibility, and without any orders from his Government either positive or provisional—and under an impression (in which the Undersigned rejoices that he was mistaken) that a state of war actually existed between the two countries.

The recent course which has been pursued by the Undersigned on another subject must have furnished to your Excellency stronger evidence than mere professions that the feelings of the Government of the United States towards Mexico, are any thing but hostile, and the Undersigned would have been gratified if the disclaimer made by your Excellency of a belief that the conduct of Commodore Jones had been authorized by his Government had not been accompanied by very strong insinuations that he had not acted without such authority. Such a course on the part of the Government of the United States would have deserved all the epithets which your Excellency has applied to it, and it ought not therefore to have been insinuated even, but upon the strongest evidence. The Undersigned knew as well when the intelligence of the events in California first reached this City as he does now, that, Commodore Jones had acted without orders from his Government. That Government is a Republic in fact, as well as in name, and it is therefore impossible that the invasion of the Territory of a friendly power could have been ordered without the authority of an act of Congress. To have done so would not only have been a deep wrong to Mexico but a flagrant violation of the Constitution of the United States, and he also knew, that if it had been considered necessary to invade the Territory of Mexico, that it could only have been done after due warning and that the attack would have been made upon a much stronger point and with a much stronger force.

One of the Officers of the Pacific Squadron has however recently arrived in this City with despatches from Commodore Jones to the Undersigned, and to his Government at Washington. The Undersigned herewith communicates to your Excellency a letter which he has received from Commodore Jones[1] in which he sets forth the reasons upon which he acted. This paper is communicated to your Excellency as the most con-

1. In a note dated October 22, 1842, Jones explained that he concluded the United States and Mexico were at war after seeing newspaper

clusive evidence that he has acted without the orders of his Government. The Undersigned would not be understood as justifying the conduct of the American Commodore, on the contrary he freely admits that he has assumed upon insufficient evidence that a state of War was existing between Mexico and the United States. If such had been the case Mexico would have had no cause of complaint. That the danger of such a state of things was imminent was not the opinion of Commodore Jones alone.

It will be remembered that, at the time of the publication of the note of your Excellency to Mr. Webster as well as the circular addressed to the Diplomatic Corps[2] (a most extraordinary proceeding and only to be understood as an appeal by Mexico to the great community of Nations, and an exposition of the causes which justified her in disturbing the peace of the world), that there were many difficult and important questions pending between the United States and the greatest power of the world—questions which in the opinion of many did not admit the possibility of an amicable adjustment—and whilst the Undersigned will not say that the prospect of a war between the United States and that great power prompted the publication of those very harsh and menacing papers, nor that the settlement of those questions in a manner eminently honorable and equally advantegeous to both countries, has influenced the subsequent course of Mexico, yet it is not to be denied, that, a war between England and the United States would not have diminished the probabilities of a collision between the latter and Mexico, and as furnishing additional ground for the opinion on which Commodore Jones acted, and although the Government of the United States is not disposed to remember these things in unkindness the Undersigned cannot forbear to say that it would better have comported with the professions of sincere friendship which Mexico makes to the United States if any other time had been selected for the publication of those papers.

The Undersigned is gratified to know that nothing has occurred in California which does not admit of an amicable adjustment, by that full reparation which he is quite sure that his government will take great pleasure in making. The Acts of Commodore Jones having been unauthorized by his Government, are therefore only to be regarded as the inconsiderate conduct of an individual officer, and whilst tendering this explanation to your Excellency, the Undersigned begs leave to suggest that your Excellency will scarcely approve of the conduct of the Mexican General [José Manuel] Micheltorena, of the coarse and abusive epithets which he applies to the countrymen of the Undersigned, nor of the tone

accounts containing "highly belligerent" Mexican declarations. See *Ex. Doc.*, Serial 422, No. 166, p. 15.

2. Bocanegra's note to DW of May 12, 1842, DNA, RG 59 (Notes from Foreign Legations, Mexico), and the circular to the diplomatic corps of May 31, 1842, are enclosed in Thompson's dispatch of June 6, 1842, DNA, RG 59 (Despatches, Mexico).

of rudeness and gasconade of his note of the 26th. of October,[3] which the Undersigned has regretted to see published by the Mexican Government without rebuke.

It is surely no dishonor to Mexican Arms that the fortress of Monterrey, was surrendered to so superior a force, and still less so as the Mexican General states, (and it must have been believed by his Government or else it would not have been published with its sanction) that the bare annunciation of his approach at the head of an inferior force, although at the distance of four hundred miles so terrified the American Commodore that from *fear* he took down the flag of his country, which he had never lowered before, and sheathed a sword which he had more than once flashed in the face of a very powerful enemy, an enemy in every way worthy of that sword. The bravest words were certainly used by the Mexican General, subject to some subtraction however from the fact that they were used (if used at all) five days after the castle had been restored, when the American Commodore had discovered and acknowledged his error, and was anxious to atone for it, and when of course his hands were tied.

The Undersigned feels called upon to say that he has the strongest reasons to believe that the note purporting to have been addressed by General Micheltorena to Commodore Jones of the 26th. of October, and numbered 16, as published by the authority of the Mexican Government in the papers of this City and for this reason alone noticed by the Undersigned—was never sent—no doubt from inadvertence or perhaps because after it was written the impropriety of such a letter under the circumstances occurred to General Micheltorena and he declined sending it, but has by a similar inadvertence included it amongst the communications which actually passed between himself and the American Commodore.

As to the matter of pecuniary reparations, the Undersigned has received the most positive assurances that no violation of private property of any sort was committed by his countrymen whilst in possession of Monterrey, and as to any damages which may have been sustained by the Government of Mexico the fullest reparation will be made. Those damages it seems have already been estimated by the Mexican General at fifteen thousand dollars, five hundred suits of clothes and a full band of musical instruments,[4] for injuries suffered in a very rapid march which the Undersigned is informed was never made nor even com-

3. In the letter, Micheltorena (1802–1853), the military governor of California, informed Jones that he was coming to meet him with "lead and cannon" when he learned the navy commander had withdrawn.

See *Ex. Doc.*, Serial 422, No. 166, p. 34.

4. The claims for damages are in *Ex. Doc.*, Serial 422, No. 166, pp. 36–37.

menced. But whatever those damages may have been they will be fully paid, and the Undersigned rejoices that a principle so just will have been settled, so that if hereafter which the Undersigned will not anticipate, the claims of Justice or of national honor shall force either of the Countries to make war upon the other, or to blockade its ports the principle will have been settled that the party in fault shall pay the cost.

The Undersigned avails himself of the occasion to renew to His Excellency José Maria de Bocanegra Minister of Foreign Relations and Government the assurance of his most distinguished consideration

(signed) Waddy Thompson.

Copy. DNA, RG 59 (Despatches, Mexico). Extract published in *Executive Documents*, 27th Cong., 3d sess., Serial 422, No. 166, pp. 12–14.

Mexico, Texas and the United States: The Mier Prisoners

Hardly had the cases of the Santa Fé prisoners been resolved when another large group of Texan-Americans found themselves in the custody of Mexico. In retaliation for Mexican attacks on Texas, President Sam Houston ordered a raid against Mexico on October 3, 1842. The force under General Alexander Somervell (1796–1854) captured Laredo and Guerrero. When Somervell ordered the expedition's return to Texas, however, most of the men disobeyed and continued into Mexico under the leadership of the veteran Texas cavalry commander, William S. Fisher.

On December 25, 1842, the Texans, their ranks further depleted by the return to Texas of their more prudent comrades, attacked the town of Mier. After a lengthy and bloody battle, the Texans surrendered and were ordered to Mexico City. In the letter of January 11, 1843, Thomas Jefferson Green, one of the Mier Expedition leaders, informed President Tyler of their struggle, in which they fought with "unparaleled bravery," and requested the assistance of the U.S. government in obtaining their release (see below).

On February 11, 1843, the prisoners, en route to Mexico City, escaped from their Mexican captors. All but three were recaptured, and as punishment seventeen were selected by lot for execution. During the summer of 1843 the Texans performed manual labor around Mexico City. From time to time a few escaped, a few were released, and some died. The last were freed by President Santa Anna in 1844. As for Green, he escaped sometime in 1843 and made his way back to Texas. Subsequent letters published in this section examine the efforts of Webster and Tyler to mitigate the plight of the Mier prisoners.

THOMAS JEFFERSON GREEN TO JOHN TYLER

Sir,   Matamoras Jany. 11th 1843.

The fortunes of war has made myself and your friend and townsman

Genl W[illia]m S. Fisher,[1] with 348 brave Texians, prisoners of war to Genl. Pedro De Ampudia,[2] commanding the Mexican forces on this frontier. We engaged him on the evening of the 25th Decr. in the city of Mier, and fought nineteen hours with unparaleled bravery, but the multitude prevailed over our bravery. We 260 and they 2500 men—our loss in killed and wounded less than 40 theirs said to be double our aggregate numbers.

Enclosed I send you the written articles of capitulation[3] at which time we had the verbal promise of the Genls. influence that we should be kept upon this frontier until the exchange of prisoners; but today we are informed we are to take up our line of March for the city of Mexico.

This for men who deserve a better fate is a gloomy prospect indied as we in Texas are not in the habit of keeping their prisoners they allways keeping ours. Consequently Texas at present has none to exchange while they hold 320 of ours.

We have not a moment [of] time to solicit your mediation in our behalf and we desire that you place it upon this ground.

In 1836 the Texian government released President [Antonio López de] Santa Anna['s] Genl. [Martín Perfecto de] Cos[4] with 70 officers and 700 men with condition. In—1842 the Mexican government released 250 Santa Fe prisoners leaving [them] still in our debt upon that score 500 men. I have been informed that the Mexican government last year promised [our] government and also that of England & France that the war should be hereafter [waged upon] terms of civilized warfare. If this promise be adhered to that government will surely upon your request release an eaquel number. Of this fact of our releasing 400 of their prisoners in 1836 your old friend Dr. [Branch Tanner] Archer[5] will inform you as also Genl. [Juan Nepomuceno] Almonte, the Mexican Minister near your government who was one of the released prisoners.

Of the 320 Texian prisoners which Mexico now holds comprizes many of the best men & best talents of our young country; and she is vitally concerned in their release among others the gallant young [George Bibb] Crittenden,[6] son, of Senator [John Jordan] C[rittenden] of Kentucky.

1. Fisher (d. 1845) was a veteran Texas cavalry commander.

2. Ampudia (1803–1868) had fought the Texans at the Alamo and San Jacinto.

3. Not included in this publication.

4. Cós was twice captured and released by Texan forces, in December 1835 after the siege of Bexar and again in April 1836 after the Battle of San Jacinto.

5. Archer (1790–1856), a physician, had served two terms in the Virginia House of Delegates before emigrating to Texas in 1831. He served as secretary of war under President Lamar.

6. Crittenden (1812–1880; U.S. Military Academy 1832), the eldest son of John Jordan Crittenden, was released in 1843 primarily due to the efforts of former president Andrew Jackson, who had befriended Santa Anna in 1836.

Should it please your Excellency to use your influence in our behalf it will be of vital importance to us that your Minister Genl. [Waddy] Thompson, be informed of it with all posible despatch, in which case let me beg you to send my brother Colo. C.P. Green, of Mecklenburg Va[7] special messenger, affording him an oppertunity of benefiting me much as well as Fisher, and others.

I must beg you to excuse this hasty & badly written letter as it is now late at night and I have much to do before marching. With sentiments of the highest regard I am your Excellencys Most obt. huml. sert.

Thos. J. Green

ALS. DNA, RG 59 (Misc. Letters). Rec'd March 15, 1843. Green (1802–1863), of the Texas army, was a leader of the Mier Expedition.

TO WADDY THOMPSON

No. 25.   Department of State,
Sir: Washington, 17th January, 1843.

Your despatches to No. [blank in manuscript] inclusive, and your private letter of the 15th ult.[1] have been received. Although the department is without official intelligence of the seizure of Monterey by Commodore [Thomas ap Catesby] Jones, in command of the United States squadron in the Pacific, it is deemed proper that no time should be lost in acquainting the Mexican Government that the transaction was entirely unauthorized. If, therefore, the account of that event should prove to be authentic, you will take occasion to inform the Mexican Minister for Foreign Affairs [José María de Bocanegra], orally, that Commodore Jones had no warrant from this government for the proceeding and that the President exceedingly regrets its occurrence. I am, Sir, your obedient servant,

Daniel Webster

LC. DNA, RG 59 (Instructions, Mexico).

FROM JUAN NEPOMUCENO ALMONTE

Mexican Legation
Washington January 24th 1843.

The Undersigned, Envoy Extraordinary and Minister Plenipotentiary of the Mexican Republic, near the Government of the United States of America, has the honour to acknowledge the receipt of the note, which the Honourable Daniel Webster—Secretary of State was pleased to address to him, on the 21st instant,[1] enclosing a copy of the Instructions

7. Green, not otherwise identified.

1. Thompson's letter of December 15, 1842, DNA, RG 59 (Despatches, Mexico), advises DW of the seizure

of Monterey by Jones.

1. DW to Almonte, January 21, 1843, DNA, RG 59 (Notes to Foreign Legations, Mexico).

addressed by him, on the 17th instant, to Mr Waddy Thompson[2] the American Minister at Mexico, respecting the capture of Monterey in Upper California by Commodore [Thomas ap Catesby] Jones.

The Undersigned expected no less from the sense of justice of the Honourable Mr Webster's Government; he however regrets to observe that in the instructions given to the aforesaid Mr Waddy Thompson Minister of the United States at Mexico, while it is denied that the proceedings of Commodore Jones were authorised, the declaration is omitted, that he will be exemplarily punished for the extraordinary act of excess (*inaudito atentado*) committed by him, in violating the faith of treaties, and abusing the hospitality with which the peaceful inhabitants of Monterey were preparing to receive him. The Undersigned will nevertheless without loss of time, communicate to his Government the note from the Honourable Mr Webster, and the accompanying copy of the instructions; but he will in the mean time inform the Secretary of State that he has just received communications and instructions from His Excellency the Minister of Foreign Relations of Mexico [José María de Bocanegra], wherein he is directed to press for the immediate satisfaction and indemnification which His Government expects to receive from this Republic.

The Honourable Mr Webster will have already been informed of the tenour of the communication addressed to Mr Waddy Thompson, on the 19th of December last, by the Mexican Government;[3] and the Undersigned doubts not, from the good faith of the Government of the United States, that, in reparation of the scandalous infraction of the Treaty of Friendship Commerce and Navigation, existing between the two Republics, committed by one of its officers, who has invoked its name, the said officer will be exemplarily punished, as a warning to other chiefs who incited by his example might, be disposed to commit excesses of equal enormity, if they could be pardoned by their own Government. The delinquency of Commodore Jones, is so serious, so obvious and so notorious, that it would be superfluous to particularise its enormities.

The Undersigned trusts that the Government of the United States will repair the losses, and injuries inflicted by the said Commodore Jones, as well on the inhabitants of Monterey, as on the Mexican Republic. This is an act of rigorous justice, which Mexico has a right to expect and which it is confident of obtaining, if as she believes, and as the Honourable Mr Webster assures, her Government is a Government of Law.

The Undersigned, being desirous for the removal of every obstacle to the intimacy of the relations of friendship and good understanding, which should subsist between two friendly nations, bound by solemn treaties, and, anticipating a happy result to their communications with

2. See above.

3. Bocanegra to Thompson, December 19, 1842, enclosed in Thompson

to DW, December 28, 1842, DNA, RG 59 (Despatches, Mexico).

each other, as he has no grounds for believing the contrary, requests the Honourable Mr Webster Secretary of State, to have the kindness to submit the contents of this note to His Excellency the President, and to communicate to him the resolution of His Excellency, as soon as possible; in order that he may avail himself of the departure of a messenger, whom the Undersigned proposes to despatch to Mexico, and who will quit this City on the 27th instant.

The Undersigned embraces the opportunity here afforded, to repeat to the Honourable Daniel Webster Secretary of State, the assurances of his distinguished consideration.   J. N. Almonte

Copy. Translation. DNA, RG 59 (Notes from Foreign Legations, Mexico). Published in *Executive Documents*, 27th Cong., 3d sess., Serial 422, No. 166, pp. 3–5.

FROM ISAAC VAN ZANDT

Legation of Texas
Washington City

Sir   January 24th. 1843

The undersigned chargé d'affaires of the Republic of Texas has been instructed to communicate to Mr. Webster Secretary of State of the United States the following information, with the desires of the Government of Texas in relation to the same to which Mr. Webster's attention is respectfully invited.

Her Majesty the Queen of Great Britain having agreed by the terms of a convention concluded at London on the 14th of November 1840[1] between her Majesty's Government and the Republic of Texas to tender her good offices of mediation for the purpose of effecting an amicable adjustment of the difficulties now pending between Texas and Mexico, accordingly instructed her Minister in Mexico [Richard Pakenham] to present the same to the Mexican Government. In pursuance of these instructions the mediation of Great Britain was proposed to and rejected by the Government of Mexico. Texas, still animated by a desire to avoid a further collision and resort to arms, sought to obtain a triple mediation of the three great powers, the United States, France and England, with a hope, that, under their auspices a proper settlement of the difficulties alluded to might be secured. To this arrangement the Governments of the United States and France gave their assent with alacrity, while the Government of Great Britain, though expressing an ardent desire to do all in its power, by its good offices of mediation "leans to the opinion that it would be better on all accounts that each party should act separately, but similarly in point of tone and argument, in urging the Mexican Government to re-

1. See *British and Foreign State Papers, 1840–1841* (116 vols., Lon-   don, 1812–1925), 29:84–85.

consider the subject dispassionately and impartially and to lose no time in coming to an accommodation with Texas, on the basis of a recognition of her independence."[2] This suggestion of the British Government has been communicated by Lord Cowley[3] (the English embassador at Paris) to the French Government, which has approved of the same and forwarded the necessary instructions upon the subject to her Minister in Mexico. It is therefore the desire of my Government, in order that there may be a concert of action, that, the Government of the United States will as early as possible (should the same meet with its concurrence) forward the necessary instructions to the American Minister in Mexico [Waddy Thompson], that he may act advisedly upon the subject.

Should the proposed mediation be rejected by Mexico, and she in her madness still cherish the delusive phantom of "the re-subjugation of Texas," then the responsibility of the consequences which must inevitably result, will rest upon her head. Texas will have washed her hands from the blood of those who perish in the fatal strife, having sought by every honorable means to avoid the calamities of war and the miseries and destruction of human life which must follow—An appeal to arms must then determine the contest—if forced to this resort, Texas, conscious of the correctness of her motives and the justice of her cause, will, relying upon the God of battles, take the issue and abide the result.

Actuated by an overruling necessity, and the paramount principles of self preservation, my Government has sanctioned the partial invasion of the Mexican territory, that we might remove the ravages and horrors of war (which the Mexican Government designed to inflict us) from our own country to that of our Enemy. Our object is not to extend our limits—to make conquests of any portion of the territory of Mexico or to inflict upon her citizens the cruelties and inhuman treatment which has characterized her warfare against us. But in battling for peace, even upon our enemies soil, while they shall feel the force of freedom's arm when nerved to the conflict by repeated wrongs and injuries, our acts shall still be governed by a nobleness of principle and a magnanimity of conduct worthy the age in which we live, and becoming the descendants of that race from whom we claim our origin.

2. Following Mexico's rejection of a British mediation proposal on June 8, 1841, Ashbel Smith (1805–1886; Yale 1824), the Texan chargé to Britain and France, proposed a triple mediation by Britain, France, and the United States. Aberdeen rejected the suggestion purportedly because of the poor relations existing between Mexico and the United States. See the letter from Charles Elliot (1801–1875), the British chargé in Texas, to President Houston of December 7, 1842, in George P. Garrison, ed., *Diplomatic Correspondence of the Republic of Texas* (3 vols., Washington, D.C., 1908–1911), 1:637–638.

3. Henry Wellesley, Lord Cowley (1773–1847), was England's ambassador to France, 1841–1846.

I avail myself of this occasion to offer to Mr. Webster renewed assurances of my distinguished consideration.   Isaac Van Zandt

ALS. DNA, RG 59 (Notes from Foreign Legations, Texas). Rec'd January 27. Published in *IAA*, 12:265–267. Van Zandt (1813–1847), a lawyer, moved to Texas from Mississippi in 1838. He became chargé d'affaires to the United States in 1842.

TO JUAN NEPOMUCENO ALMONTE

Department of State,
Washington, 30th January, 1843.

The Undersigned, Secretary of State of the United States, has had the honor to receive the note of the 24th instant of General [Juan Nepomuceno] Almonté,[1] Envoy Extraordinary and Minister Plenipotentiary of the Mexican Republic.

General Almonte has already been made acquainted with the instruction addressed from this Department on the 17th instant to the Minister of the United States at Mexico [Waddy Thompson],[2] respecting the transaction at Monterey in Upper California, in which Commodore [Thomas ap Catesby] Jones was concerned, but General Almonte now expresses his regret that he sees in that instruction, no declaration that Commodore Jones will be exemplarily punished for the extraordinary act of excess committed by him, in violation of the faith of treaties and in abuse of the hospitality with which the peacable inhabitants of Monterery were prepared to receive him.

The Undersigned has the honor to inform General Almonte that before the receipt of his note, the President had given directions for the adoption of such a course of proceeding towards Commodore Jones as in his opinion was due to the circumstances of the case,[3] to the preservation of the principle and practice of absolute and entire abstinence, on the part of military power, from all aggression in time of peace, and especially due to the friendly relations at the present time happily subsisting between the United States and Mexico. But General Almonte and his government must see that Commodore Jones intended no indignity to the Government of Mexico nor any thing unlawful towards her citizens. Unfortunately he supposed, as he asserts, that a state of war actually existed at the time between the two countries. If this supposition had been

1. See above, Almonte to DW, January 24, 1843.
2. See above, DW to Thompson, January 17, 1843.
3. Jones was replaced as commander of the Pacific squadron by Commodore Alexander James Dallas (1791–1844); he was, however, never punished or officially censured. Instead, he was placed in command of the *Ohio* and later, during the Mexican War, was once again made commander of the Pacific squadron.

well founded, all that he did would have been justifiable, so that whatever of imprudence or impropriety he may be chargeable with, there is nothing to show that he intended any affront to the honor of the Mexican Government or to violate the relations of peace.

General Almonte is aware of some of the circumstances in which this belief of the actual existence of a state of hostilities probably might have had its origin. It is not deemed necessary now to advert to those circumstances, nor is it at present known to the Government of the United States what other causes may have existed to strengthen this belief or to make it general along the western shore of this continent. In the clearly manifest absence of all illegal and improper intent, some allowance may be properly extended towards acts of indiscretion, in a quarter so very remote and in which correct information of distant events is not soon or easily, obtained.

If in this transaction citizens of Mexico have received any injury in their persons or property, the Government of the United States will undoubtedly feel itself bound to make ample reparation, and the representations of General Almonte on that subject will receive the most respectful and immediate consideration. Happily no lives were lost nor is it understood that any considerable injury was suffered by any one.

The Undersigned is directed by the President to assure General Almonte and his government, that the government of the United States will at all times be among the last to authorize or justify any aggression on the territory of a nation with whom it is at peace, or any indignity to its government. Sensibly alive to any indignity if offered to itself, it is equally resolved to give no such cause of offence to its neighbors. And the Undersigned is directed to assure General Almonte and his government of the pain and the surprise which the President experienced on receiving information of this transaction. Under these assurances the President hopes that it may pass away without leaving in the mind of the Government of Mexico any other feeling than that in which the government of the United States entirely partakes, a feeling of deep regret at what has happened and a conviction that no such unfortunate and unauthorized occurrence ought in any degree to impair the amicable relations subsisting between the two countries, so evidently to the advantage of both.

The Undersigned has been made acquainted with the communication addressed by the Mexican Secretary of State [José María de] Bocanegra to the Minister of the United States at Mexico and with the answer of the latter gentleman to that communication.[4]

4. Presumably Bocanegra to Thompson, December 19, 1842, on the Jones affair, and Thompson's reply of December 27, 1842, both enclosed in Thompson's dispatch of December 28, 1842, DNA, RG 59 (Despatches, Mexico).

The Undersigned avails himself of this occcasion to offer General Almonte renewed assurances of his most distinguished consideration.

Daniel Webster

LC. DNA, RG 59 (Notes to Foreign Legations, Mexico). Published in *Executive Documents*, 27th Cong., 3d sess., Serial 422, No. 166, pp. 5–6.

TO WADDY THOMPSON

Private.

My dear Sir: Washington, 30th January, 1843.

Your several private letters have duly reached me. In regard to the desire which you express that a new Secretary of Legation may be appointed,[1] I have to say that your dissatisfaction with Mr. [Brantz] Mayer is expressed in too general terms for us either to recall him from his present post or to transfer him to any other Legation. If you were more explicit in your objections, we should better know what to do. Your reasons for desiring him to be recalled from Mexico may be such as to show that he is not fit for employment any where. It is necessary, as the President thinks, that you should state your objections.

Our accounts from Yucatan are not so favorable to the cause of the Campeacheans as you represent yours to be, but even if they were more so and it was likely that they would be triumphant, the expediency of sending thither an agent of any kind, to represent this government, would be a subject for grave and deliberate consideration.[2] In the mean time our existing relations with Mexico are so important, delicate and complicated, that you are likely to have your hands full where you are. There is one subject, however, upon which you are silent and which silence you do not explain. 1003 1416 914 1402 1264.[3] Have you held no

1. Probably a reference to Thompson's letter to President Tyler of November 30, 1842, DNA, RG 59 (Despatches, Mexico), in which Thompson, without explanation, asked for a "different secretary." Thompson in a subsequent letter referred to Mayer as vain, impertinent, and faithless (Thompson to DW, January, n.d., 1843, DNA, RG 59, Despatches, Mexico). Thompson apparently was angry in part because Mayer had written directly to DW regarding a proposed arrangement for unsettled Mexican claims.

2. Thompson's sources and reports regarding Yucatán have not been found. Yucatán declared its independence in June 1840. A reconciliation was achieved on December 15, 1843, in which Yucatán recognized the central government but retained autonomy over its internal affairs.

3. The cipher is WEO28, adopted by the Department of State in 1803 and used by American ministers in Mexico City until 1867. In this letter the code translates: 1003 / Cal, 1416 / if, 914 / orn, 1402 / ia, 1264 /. On the code, see Ralph E. Weber, *United States Diplomatic Codes and Ciphers, 1775–1938* (Chicago, 1979), pp. 151–157, and esp. the key, pp. 478–489.

conversations respecting it with high functionaries at Mexico? Or have you not found a good opportunity? This matter is exciting great interest in this country, and the ice must be broke, some how, whether any thing should come of it or not. I refer you to my former letters[4] and have to request that you will follow the suggestions therein contained, and without any commitment whatever, sound the feeling of the Mexican Government; and that this be done without loss of time. I remain, My dear Sir, with much regard, Your obedient servant, Danl Webster

ls. NhD.

FROM WADDY THOMPSON

My Dear Sir   Mexico Jany 30 1843

It is wholly out of the question to do any thing as to California and after recent events there it would be imprudent to allude to it in any way. Perhaps when this government fails to pay the awards as it doubtless will after striking out the 10 pr cent penalty clause the most important of all[1]—that they may have to give us San Francisco in payment. I wrote you when I first came here that England wanted California.[2] I beleive that I have expressed no single conjecture to you as to matters here which <I> has not been verified by the result at the same time that I am pained to say that very few of my suggestions have been concurred in by you. I *know* that England has designs on California and has actually made a *Treaty* with Mexico securing to Brittish Creditors the right to the lands there in payment of their debts[3]—and that England will interpose this treaty in the way of a cession of California and that in ten years she will own the country.

As to the treaty allow me to say and I do so in no pride of opinion

4. See above, DW to Thompson, June 27, 1842.

1. Thompson concluded, on November 5, 1842, a draft convention for the payment of awards made by the Mexican claims commission, which included a 10 percent penalty on late installments (see Thompson to DW, November 8, 1842, DNA, RG 59, Despatches, Mexico). DW refused to include the penalty in the agreement because he did not wish the Mexican government to think the United States feared nonpayment. DW to Thompson, December 30, 1842, DNA, RG 59 (Instructions, Mexico). The convention is in *Trea-ties*, 4:479–498.

2. See above, Thompson to DW, April 29, 1842.

3. On June 1, 1839, the Mexican congress passed a law that allowed British creditors to exchange their holdings for Mexican lands. Richard Pakenham, the British minister in Mexico, urged his government to establish by this means an English colony in California, but the British signed no treaty and the Foreign Office disapproved Pakenham's scheme. See Ephraim Douglass Adams, *British Interests and Activities in Texas, 1838–1846* (Baltimore, 1910), pp. 237–240.

that it was a great mistake to strike out the ten per cent penalty clause— I should have inserted in the new convention a declaration that the payment of this additional interest was not to be understood as implying any extension of the indulgence in the event of a failure to pay punctually. I cannot now be responsible for the Treaty. I had been instructed in my last despatch to open a negotiation,[4] per the undecided clauses which I had done and could without any difficulty have concluded an arrangement of them. But your last despatch countermanded these orders[5] and I anticipate delay and difficulty. You will see that I have inserted a clause in this convention providing for a new convention[6] which although it imposes no obligation on either of the governments which did not exist before I thought it important should be inserted. I thought that at the same time that the best possible arrangement was made for the award claimants that if I could use their claims so as to secure the claims of <those who> the others I had a right to do so. In other words the awards were the trumps of a weaker hand. If there is any object in having a minister resident at a foreign court It is that from a knowledge of the situation temper &c of the people he may be able to have a clearer view of the policy of his country than it is possible for the cabinet at home to have— and I would add in all respect and sincere friendship that if I have in any way forfeited the confidence and good feelings which induced you to desire my appointment it is neither desirable to me nor will it be profitable to the country for me to remain.

I beg leave to add one word on another subject. On the last night of the session [William Campbell] Preston obtained an appropriation of $6000 expressly intended if not so expressed to cover the advances which I had made—so you considered it yourself.[7] But when I drew for the ballance of this appropriation I am informed that it had already been paid on account of the seven Americans sent home by Mr. [Powhatan] Ellis. These expenses of Mr Ellis had been expressly authorized by you—and I presume had already been paid when this appropriation was made—or if not you had asked no appropriation for that object—implying that it had been paid or that you felt that you had power as well as funds to pay it. Why then is it credited to this appropriation which was notoriously made for another object. I do trust that you will issue an order to the proper officer to have justice done me in this matter very sincerely yr friend &c   Waddy Thompson

ALS. DLC. Endorsed: "Private-File."

4. No. 20. Daniel Fletcher Webster to Thompson, October 13, 1842, DNA, RG 59 (Instructions, Mexico).

5. No. 23. DW to Thompson, December 30, 1842, DNA, RG 59 (Instructions, Mexico).

6. Article 6.

7. *Senate Journal*, 27th Cong., 2d sess., Serial 394, pp. 654–655; *House Journal*, 27th Cong., 2d sess., Serial 400, p. 1480.

TO WADDY THOMPSON

No. 26.   Department of State,
Sir: Washington, 31st January, 1843.

I transmit a copy of two notes addressed to this department by the Chargé d'Affaires of Texas [Isaac Van Zandt]. The first, dated the 14th ult.[1] requests the interposition of this government for the purpose of inducing that of the Mexican Republic to abstain from carrying on the war against Texas by means of predatory incursions, in which the proclamations and promises of the Mexican commanders are flagrantly violated, non-combatants seized and detained as prisoners of war, and private property used or destroyed. This department entirely concurs in the opinion of Mr Van Zandt that practices such as these are not justifiable or sanctioned, by the modern law of nations. You will take occasion to converse with the Mexican Secretary [José María de Bocanegra], in a friendly manner, and represent to him how greatly it would contribute to the advantage as well as the honor of Mexico, to abstain altogether from predatory incursions and other similar modes of warfare. Mexico has an undoubted right to re-subjugate Texas, if she can, so far as other States are concerned, by the common and lawful means of war. But other States are interested and especially the United States, a near neighbor to both parties, are interested not only in the restoration of peace between them, but also in the manner in which the war shall be conducted, if it shall continue. These suggestions may suffice for what you are requested to say, amicably and kindly, to the Mexican Secretary at present. But I may add, for your information, that it is in the contemplation of this government to remonstrate in a more formal manner with Mexico, at a period not far distant, unless she shall consent to make peace with Texas, or shall show the disposition and ability to prosecute the war with respectable forces.

The second note of Mr Van Zandt is dated the 24th instant[2] and relates to the mediation of the United States for the purpose of effecting a recognition by Mexico of the independence of Texas. You will not cease in your endeavors for this purpose, but it is not expected that you will deviate from the instructions which have heretofore been given to you upon the subject. I am, Sir your obedient servant,   Daniel Webster

LC. DNA, RG 59 (Instructions, Mexico). Published in IAA, 8:128–129.

TO WADDY THOMPSON

No. 28.   Department of State,
Sir: Washington, 7th February, 1843.

In the instruction to you No 26 of the 31st ult.,[1] you were directed to

1. Van Zandt to DW, December 14,   2. See above, Van Zandt to DW,
1842, DNA, RG 59 (Notes from For-   January 24, 1843.
eign Legations, Texas).   1. See above.

take occasion to converse with the Mexican Secretary of State [José María de Bocanegra] upon the character of the war waged by Mexico against Texas. You will avail yourself of a similar occcasion to acquaint him in the same way that this government intends to take steps for the purpose of remonstrating with the Texan government upon the subject of marauding incursions into Mexico, whether, with a view to retaliation or otherwise. The duty of the United States as a neighbor to both those countries and as an impartial friend to both, demands that no proper efforts should be omitted by us to induce them, so long as they continue in a state of war with on[e] another, to carry that war on openly, honorably, and according to the rules recognized by all civilized and Christian states in modern times. We owe this duty to them; we owe it to the interest and character of this continent, we owe it to the cause of civilization and human improvement, and we shall discharge it with impartiality and with firmness. I am, Sir, your obedient servant, Daniel Webster

Lc. DNA, RG 59 (Instructions, Mexico). Published in *IAA*, 8:129–130.

FROM JUAN NEPOMUCENO ALMONTE

Mexican Legation—

Washington February 7th 1843—

The Undersigned, Envoy Extraordinary and Minister Plenipotentiary of the Mexican Republic, had the honor to receive the note which the Hon. Daniel Webster, Secretary of State of the United States was pleased to address to him on the 30th ultimo,[1] in answer to that from the Undersigned, dated, the 24th ultimo,[2] respecting the act of violence committed by Commodore [Thomas ap Catesby] Jones in Upper California.

To the Undersigned, it would have been highly satisfactory, to find, expressed in the Hon: Mr Webster's note, those principles of justice which should characterize an enlightened Government, and especially a Government constituted like that of the United States, the sole aim of which is (to secure the supremacy of) the Law.

The Undersigned however observes with regret, that while in the said note, Mr Webster's Government, acknowladges the enormity of the act of violence committed by Commodore Jones, it is merely said in general terms, that the President *has given directions for the adoption of such a course of proceeding towards that officer as in his* (the Presidents) *opinion was due to the circumstances of the case, to the preservation of the principle and practice of absolute and entire abstinence on the part of the military power from all aggression in time of peace; and especially to the friendly relations at present happily subsisting between the United States and Mexico.* The paragraph above quoted, by the Undersigned,

1. See above, DW to Almonte, January 30, 1843.   2. See above, Almonte to DW, January 24, 1843.

does certainly indicate an intention to adopt some course of proceedings towards Commodore Jones: but what is this course to be? It is not made known: and the Honorable Mr Webster must know, that the Mexican Government cannot remain satisfied with that answer. Would it not have been more plain and simple to say at once, that an order had been sent to recal Commodore Jones, and that he would undergo that punishment which the Mexican Government has asked, and has a right to expect? Such language would not have left the slightest doubt as to the course of conduct, which the Government of the United States proposes to pursue, in the case now under consideration; and the Undersigned would have been freed from the painful task of again addressing the Honorable Mr Webster, on an occurrence so disagreeable, and which has so deeply affected the honor of his nation.

In order however to avoid all doubt in a matter so delicate, the Undersigned believes it to be his duty, to demand in the name of his Government, from the Honorable Mr Webster, an explanation of the true meaning of the paragraph relating to the subject, from his above mentioned Note. Without doubt, it cannot be other than that already indicated by the Undersigned; and as it should not be at all inconvenient to the Hon: Secretary of State to give such an explanation; it would serve immediately to dispel the doubts, to which the want of it, must necessarily have given rise, and to prevent the consequences attendant on such a state of uncertainty. This explanation becomes so much the more necessary, from the circumstance, that so long as the Mexican Authorities are not assured, that Commodore Jones has been recalled to be punished as he should be, the naval forces of the United States, now on the coast of Mexico, cannot be regarded by them with any confidence; and the alarm which has been necessarily spread through the whole territory of the Republic, in consequence of the unfortunate occurrence at Monterey, will be prolonged in a manner most pernicious to the interests of both countries.

The Undersigned would be very happy to be able to regard the conduct of the said Commodore, with the same indulgence, with which it is regarded by the Honorable Secretary of State; but he certainly cannot comprehend how, one can be persuaded, that Jones did not intend to violate the relations of peace subsisting between Mexico and the United States, when it is known that this officer took possession of the town of Monterey by force, and when he abandoned it only because he knew that General [José Manuel] Micheltorena was marching with a considerable body of troops, to attack him. Nor could there have been any other cause for this change of conduct in the Commodore, in the short period of twenty four hours; since, for although he says that [he] had received news which convinced him that the two countries were at peace, we know not how he received this information. It is therefore natural to suppose, that the

Mexican troops, and no other cause, induced him to desist from an enterprise, of the fortunate result of which, he probably founded his expectation, on the erroneous supposition, that the inhabitants were discontented, and the country entirely defenceless. His intentions were not, therefore, so innocent as it might be wished, that they should be believed to have been; his proclamation to the inhabitants of California, in which he assures them, that *the flag of the United States would protect for ever*, not only them, but *generations to come*, and the title of *Commander in chief of the Naval and Military expedition for the occupation of the Californias*, with which he signs his official communications, leave no doubt whatever respecting his views.[3] More yet remains to be said on this subject. Was Commodore Jones ignorant that a Treaty of friendship, commerce and navigation between his Government, and that of Mexico, had subsisted for ten years, and that by the terms of the 34th article of that treaty,[4] neither he—Commodore Jones—nor his Government, could commit any act of retaliation, until after justice had been demanded, and that demand had been refused? Did the circumstance that the Commodore was distant three or four thousand leagues from Washington, prevent him from knowing that he was to comply with a solemn compact? Is an officer to consider himself at liberty, to act according to his own discretion, and to make a jest of public treaties, concluded between his Government and foreign nations, from the moment when he quits the Potomac? Does Commodore Jones esteem the peace of Nations so lightly, that on the strength of a mere rumor, of some printed paper, in which war with his country is spoken of, he should consider himself authorized to act in arms against a friendly nation? For the same reason, the Undersigned cannot conceive how such proceedings can find an apology in the enlightened judgment of the Honorable Secretary of State; and from the well known sense of justice of that gentleman, he hopes that, on examining the question more thoroughly, he will see that the said Commodore has committed an outrage of such a nature, as to admit of no apology, and that clemency should not be exercised in cases of that nature.

The Undersigned indeed regrets most deeply, that he is obliged to differ from the opinion of the Honorable Secretary of State, with regard to the case of Commodore Jones: he would however be wanting in his duty, if he should fail to declare the high estimation, which he places, on the assurances received from this Government, that the Mexicans who have sustained any losses, in consequence of the occurrence at Monterey, shall be fully indemnified. Such conduct reflects the highest credit, on the honor and good name of the Government of the United States; and the Undersigned availing himself this excellent disposition, will have the

3. Jones's proclamation of October 19, 1842, is in *Ex. Doc.*, Serial 422, No. 166, pp. 31–32.

4. For Article 34 of the 1831 treaty, see *Treaties*, 3:624–626.

honor in due time, to present to it the statement of the losses and damages sustained on the part of Mexico in the occurrences above mentioned.

The Undersigned in the meantime however, trusts that the Honorable Mr. Webster will be pleased to give him the explanation above mentioned, as soon as possible; and that the United States will adopt with respect to the chiefs or commanders of its naval and land forces, such measures as may serve to inspire Mexico with perfect confidence in future, and may contribute to maintain and consolidate the peace now happily subsisting between the two nations.

The Undersigned embraces this opportunity, to renew to the Honorable Daniel Webster, Secretary of State, the assurances of his most distinguished considerations.   (Signed) J. N. Almonte

Copy. Translation. DNA, RG 59 (Notes from Foreign Legations, Mexico). Rec'd February 7, 1843. Published in *Executive Documents*, 27th Cong., 3d sess., Serial 422, No. 166, pp. 6–8.

FROM JOHN TYLER

Dr Sir: Feb. 9—[1843]

I concur with you in dislike of Gen. [Juan Nepomuceno] Almonte's letter.[1] If we disavow the act and declare that the officer acted without orders—to call upon us to *punish* implies a doubt of our veracity. The national offence is atton'd for by a disavowal. To demand more, is stepping rather beyond the mark. Your suggestion as to the response to be given by sending the intended communication to Congress,[2] to Genl. Almonte—meets my approval.

Can you have your part of the documents ready to be sent in tomorrow? Yrs   J. Tyler.

ALS. DLC. Published in *Tylers*, 2:267. Endorsed: "Private-File."

FROM JOHN JORDAN CRITTENDEN

                                                                        Senate Chamber—
My Dear Sir,   Feby: 24th 1843

It has been my intention, in person, to make to you my acknowledgments for the manner in which you have acted in the affair of my son [George Bibb Crittenden], now a prisoner to the Mexicans.[1] Apprehending that during the remaining brief & busy period of the session, it may

1. See above.
2. See *Executive Documents*, 27th Cong., 3d sess., Serial 422, No. 166. On March 3, DW responded to Almonte's note of February 7 by informing him that Commodore Jones had been recalled from the command of the Pacific squadron (DNA, RG 59, Notes to Foreign Legations, Mexico).

1. See above, Green to Tyler, January 11, 1843.

not be in my power to wait on you personally, I beg you to accept this as an assurance that I am very sensible of the kindness of your conduct in behalf of my son.

Rumours reported in the papers of this morning that Genl [Waddy] Thompson, our minister to Mexico is now on his return home, have occasioned me some uneasiness, and I venture to inquire of you whether there is any foundation for these rumours, or any apprehension to be entertained that he will have left the City of Mexico before the receipt of those letters concerning my son that were lately despatched to him through your Department.[2] Very respectfully yr's &c   J. J. Crittenden.

ALS. NjMoHP. Endorsed: "Private-File."

TO H. L. TURNEY, A. V. BROWN, CAVE JOHNSON, JOSEPH L. WILLIAMS, C. H. WILLIAMS, THOMAS J. CAMPBELL, R. L. CARUTHERS, MILTON BROWN, M. P. GENTRY, W. B. CAMPBELL, AND H. M. WATTERSON

Department of State
Gentlemen,   Washington 25th February 1843

I have the honor to acknowledge the receipt of your letter of the 23d instant,[1] relative to Col. Thomas [Jefferson] Green, son of Judge [Nathan] Green[2] of Tennessee, who was recently taken prisoner by the Mexicans at Mier, and is now in captivity in Mexico. In reply I have the honor to acquaint you that the information contained in your letter and received at this department from other quarters has interested me much in the fate of Colonel Green. The Executive cannot officially demand his release, but I have written a private letter to General [Waddy] Thompson, the Minister of the United States at Mexico, requesting him to use his best endeavors in a private way towards effecting the liberation of the Colonel, or a mitigation of the rigors of his captivity.[3] I have the honor &c   Danl Webster

LC. DNA, RG 59 (Domestic Letters). The addressees are all members of the U.S. House of Representatives from Tennessee.

TO JOHN JORDAN CRITTENDEN

My Dear Sir,   Washington Feb 28th 1843
By some accident I did not receive your note of Feb. 24th. till this

2. See DW's private letter to Thompson of February 7, 1843, mDW 24295.

1. Turney et al. to DW, February 23, 1843, DNA, RG 59 (Misc. Letters).

2. Green (1792–1866), a member of the Tennessee Supreme Court, 1831–1852, and chief justice from 1836.

3. Not found.

morning,[1] altho' I believe it was brought to the Department some days since.

In the matter referred to, I have only performed a duty to the prompt & effective discharge of which I confess I was stimulated by my regard for you & yours.

We have letters from Gen [Waddy] Thompson to the last of last month. He says nothing of coming home. I have no doubt the letters dispatched from this place at the suggestion of your friends overtook Mr [George S.] Curson[2] at N. Orleans. He obtained a Steam Boat, to proceed to.

Will you drop me a line just to say what day you & Mr [John Turney] Morehead[3] expect to leave Washington. Yrs truly.   Danl Webster.

Copy. DLC.

FROM LESLIE COMBS, WITH ENCLOSURE

Dr Sir,   Lexington March 2/43
Your letter to Mr [John Jordan] Crittenden of the 3rd Feby[1] in reference to my claims agt the Government for expenses incurred in releasing my son [Franklin Combs] from captivity in Mexico & sustaining him while in bondage, has been sent to me & in pursuance of one of its suggestions I have caused him to make aff[idavi]t of the principal facts,[2] necessary to entitle me to receive payment of one item—$192—leaving the others for future action if I think proper.

I beg to assure you that I would not have made this demand for remuneration, however just it may be, but that my affairs require all my means to keep them straight.

I have signed my name on the back of the affidavit, over which a re-[cei]pt can be written, when the amt is enclosed as I hope it soon will be.[3]
Respy Yr M.O.S.   Leslie Combs.

ALS. DNA, RG 59 (Misc. Letters). Rec'd March 9, 1843.

1. See above, Crittenden to DW, February 24, 1843.
2. Curson, apparently an acquaintance of Daniel Fletcher Webster and a fellow speculator in Peru, Illinois, lands. Curson's commission as a special messenger is dated July 14, 1842 (DNA, RG 59, Instructions, Mexico). See also DW's private instructions of February 7, 1843, to Curson regarding Crittenden, in PC, 2:166–167.
3. Morehead (1797–1854) served as a Whig senator from Kentucky, 1841–1847.
1. Not found.

2. Not included in this publication.
3. On May 24, 1843, Acting Secretary of State Hugh Swinton Legaré of South Carolina informed Combs that all of the funds appropriated by Congress for reimbursement of expenses incurred in aiding the Santa Fé prisoners had been placed at the disposal of Powhatan Ellis and Waddy Thompson. He advised Combs to correspond directly with Thompson on the subject. Legaré to Combs, May 24, 1843, DNA, RG 59 (Domestic Letters).

ENCLOSURE: ORDER FOR PAYMENT TO LESLIE COMBS

$192.   Chihuahua Octr 31st. 1841

At sight please pay to the order of William S. Messervy One hundred and Ninety-two dollars (being for money advanced to relieve my necessities when a prisoner in Chihuahua (Mexico)) & oblige your Son.

                                                        Franklin S Combs

L s by Franklin S. Combs. DNA, RG 59 (Misc. Letters).

FROM WADDY THOMPSON

Private   Mexico
My Dear Sir   March 18th. 1843
I take the sincerest pleasure in informing you that [George Bibb] Crittenden is safe and that I have received an order for his liberation and that he will return in the vessel which takes this. He was left at Matamoras. I send you a copy of [Antonio López de] Santa Annas letter releasing to me Crittenden and three others for whom I had asked (not in my official character).[1] It is a handsome thing & handsomely done. Some of the prisoners taken at Mier have arrived here and all concur in saying that they have been treated with the most extraordinary kindness such you may be assured is the <natural> general character of the Mexicans. I have received two very positive assurances that the order for shooting those engaged in the revolt has been countermanded[;][2] I hope in some degree through my exertions. You will see that Santa Anna in his letter to me speaks of their arrival in this city. I cannot express to you the happiness which it affords me to be able to communicate this information to you. Very sincerely Yr friend   W Thompson

AL S. DLC.

1. Santa Anna's letter to Thompson, which is dated March 15, 1843, is enclosed in Thompson's dispatch No. 15 to DW of March 14, 1843, DNA, RG 59 (Despatches, Mexico).
2. On February 11, 1843, the Mier prisoners escaped from Mexican custody. Almost all were recaptured and, in retaliation, ordered shot. The order was countermanded, but seventeen of the men—drawn by lot—were executed on March 25, 1843.

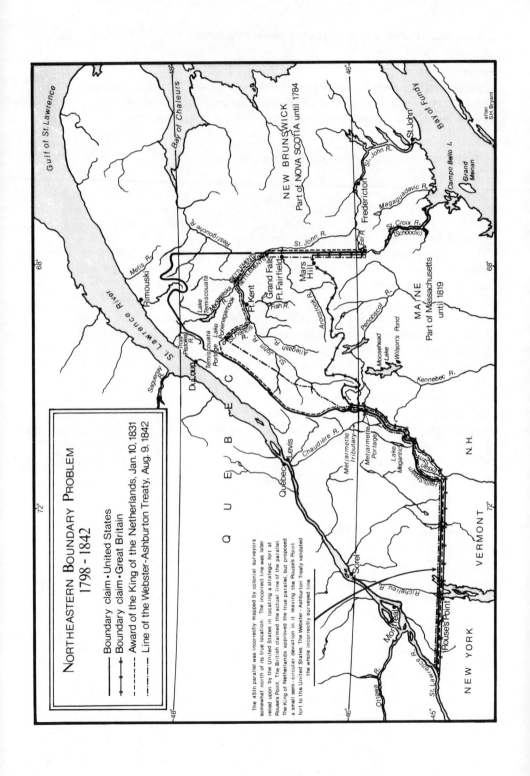

NORTHEASTERN BOUNDARY PROBLEM
1798 - 1842

———— Boundary claim • United States
——•——• Boundary claim • Great Britain
— — — — Award of the King of the Netherlands, Jan. 10, 1831
—••—••— Line of the Webster-Ashburton Treaty, Aug. 9, 1842

The 45th parallel was incorrectly mapped by colonial surveyors
somewhat north of its true location. The incorrect line was later
relied upon by the United States in locating a strategic fort at
Rouse's Point. The British claimed the actual line of the parallel.
The King of Netherlands approved the true parallel, but proposed
a small semi-circular deviation in it leaving the Rouse's Point
fort to the United States. The Webster - Ashburton Treaty validated
the whole incorrectly surveyed line

The Treaty of Washington

Lord Ashburton came to the United States as a self-described "messenger of peace" (see Ashburton to DW, January 2, 1842, below) on April 4, 1842. At about the time of the British special envoy's arrival, Webster confidently told Philip Hone, a New York Whig businessman, that he expected "to settle *all* the differences with England before the first of September" (Allan Nevins, ed., *The Diary of Philip Hone, 1828–1851* [2 vols., New York, 1927], 2:594–595). Webster made the deadline, for the Treaty of Washington was signed on August 9 and approved by the U.S. Senate on August 20, but he did not fully achieve the goal. Although the treaty established the northeastern boundary and also that on the northwestern frontier up to the Lake of the Woods, calmed the visit and search controversy with the joint cruising convention, and incorporated an important article on the extradition of fugitives from justice, it did not resolve all the differences between the two countries. In supplemental correspondence that accompanied the treaty, the still-conflicting positions of the two sides on the *Caroline, Creole*, and impressment controversies were set forth.

Ashburton's statement about the *Caroline* of July 28, 1842, that "what is perhaps most to be regretted is that some explanation and apology for this occurrence was not immediately made" in 1837 (see below) was more an explanation than an apology. Nevertheless, it was interpreted by the United States as a sort of apology, and the exchange of letters on the subject had the merit of allowing the dispute to be forgotten. The *Creole* case was not settled until 1855, when a British-American claims commission awarded $110,330 to the owners of the slaves. In their exchange of notes in 1842 (see DW to Ashburton, August 1, 1842, and Ashburton to DW, August 6, 1842, below), Webster and Ashburton firmly reiterated the respective positions of their governments on the *Creole*, but they succeeded in reducing the issue to a matter of routine diplomatic discussion. Since the secretary of state was caught between the Scylla of a proslavery president from Virginia and the Charybdis of abolitionists from his own state of Massachusetts (see Samuel J. May and Edward Moreton to DW, March 29, 1842, and Tyler to DW, August 7, 1842, below), this was no small achievement. Although Webster's impressment letter of August 8, 1842 (see below), solved nothing, it constituted a classic exposition of the historic American stand on impressment. It also countered the moves of Anglophobes such as Lewis Cass (see Cass to

DW, February 15, 1842, below) and facilitated American acceptance of the treaty by appealing to national pride. Moreover, while the British government did not recognize until 1870 the right of its subjects to change their citizenship, impressment never again became a real problem in Anglo-American relations. Finally, despite Lord Aberdeen's conviction that the absence of an agreement on the boundaries of the Oregon Territory could "greatly impair the value" of the treaty "as a general arrangement of the controversies between the two countries" (see Everett to DW, October 17, 1842, below), the Oregon issue was postponed. Unlike the *Caroline* and *Creole* issues, the Oregon question eventually became a threat to peace between the United States and Great Britain and remained so until it was settled in the Oregon Partition Treaty of June 15, 1846.

Although Webster had not resolved all the differences with Britain, the Treaty of Washington settled boundary disputes as old as the Republic itself and ended a five-year-long crisis in Anglo-American relations. Both Ashburton and Webster looked upon the northeastern boundary question as the centerpiece of their negotiation, and it certainly was one of the most complex diplomatic disputes in American history. It involved not only, as Jared Sparks wrote, a "maze of conflicting opinions and contradictory arguments" about where the cartographical line should be drawn ("The Treaty of Washington," *North American Review*, 56 [April 1843] 460) but also complex constitutional and political problems. Maine politicians had a well-deserved reputation for intransigent opposition to a negotiation for a line by compromise, and some of them even questioned whether the federal government had the authority to cede territory claimed by one of its member states. States, however, Webster observed, could not "be parties to a treaty with a foreign power" nor could foreign nations deal "with a State, upon a question of boundary, or any other question" (DW to Reuel Williams, May 14, 1842, below). Webster's "grand stroke," as he later called it (see DW to Sparks, March 11, 1843, "The Aftermath and Implementation of the Treaty of Washington: The 'Battle of the Maps,' " pp. 785–787, below), was to secure the consent of Maine and Massachusetts to send commissioners to Washington to participate in a limited way in the negotiation. Webster's ingenious ploy circumvented both the constitutional and political dilemmas, but it almost destroyed the negotiation itself. As the documents printed below suggest, the presence of the Maine commissioners injected a contentious spirit into the discussions that drove both Ashburton and Webster to the point of despair (see, for example, Ashburton to DW, July 1, 1842, below). The agents of Maine were able and tough quasi-diplomats who asked much and relinquished little. At one critical juncture, they threatened to go home rather than yield territory on the south bank of the Saint John River, which explains why the United States today has title to the southern Madawaska. In the end, with the aid of two maps of dubious validity and $12,000 from the president's secret service fund, Webster managed to conclude an agreement that satisfied the interests and honor of all the parties, but it was not easy.

Webster's task had been complicated by the continuing shenanigans of the Patriot Hunters. The rumors of preparations for an invasion of Canada reported by George C. Bates (see Bates to DW, June 10 and June 25, 1842, below) were part of a deliberate effort to disrupt Ashburton's mission. Fearing that a successful negotiation would thwart their attempt to provoke a war with Britain, the Patriots even tried to reenact the McLeod affair by having John Sheridan Hogan boast of his role in the destruction of the *Caroline*. Hogan twice succeeded in getting himself arrested by local authorities in Lockport and Rochester, New York, but was released both times. Ironically, Hogan apparently was unable to prove himself guilty. (On the attempts of the Patriots to disrupt the Webster-Ashburton negotiations, see Oscar A. Kinchen, *The Rise and Fall of the Patriot Hunters* [New York, 1956], pp. 117–123.) Although the U.S. government had infiltrated several Patriot organizations with spies, Webster did not know that Hogan was part of a conspiracy (see Lot Clark to DW, March 2, 1842; Joshua A. Spencer to DW, April 8, 1842; and DW to Joseph Story, April 9, 1842, below). The Treaty of Washington, and especially its extradition provision, contributed to the dissolution of the Patriot Hunters' lodges. These Patriot secret societies began to disband after the signing of the treaty in August 1842.

Perhaps the most surprising aspect of the Treaty of Washington was its overwhelming approval by the U.S. Senate and its generally favorable reception in Maine. Despite the opposition of such Maine politicians as Senator Reuel Williams, most of the people and newspapers of the state seem to have responded positively to the agreement (see Kent to Kavanagh, August 16, 1842; and Otis to DW, January 17, 1843, below). As for the vote in the Senate, even Webster had not expected the resounding 39 to 9 margin. He credited Senator William Cabell Rives, the chairman of the Committee on Foreign Relations, with "much of our success" (DW to Rives, [August 21, 1842], below) in gaining the unqualified consent of the Senate. Webster himself contributed mightily to both the senatorial and public approbation of the treaty. Not only was he the silent partner in Francis O. J. Smith's propaganda campaign in Maine, but he also conducted one of his own in Washington. Because of his longstanding friendship with Joseph Gales and William Winston Seaton, the publishers of the Washington, D.C., *National Intelligencer*, Webster enjoyed the liberty of placing unsigned editorials in the columns of one of the nation's most respected and influential newspapers. He used that privilege to good advantage in promoting acceptance of the Treaty of Washington (see, for example, "The Treaty of Washington," August 22, 1842, below). The theme of Webster's anonymous editorials was that the alternative to a compromise settlement was the certain prospect of a disastrous war with Great Britain. As Richard N. Current has pointed out, by the time President Tyler transmitted the treaty to the Senate, those who read newspapers "were quite generally prepared to believe that Webster had disposed of the whole series of troublesome questions and had done so in a way highly favorable to the United States" ("Webster's Propaganda and the Ashburton Treaty," *Mississippi Valley Historical Review*, 34 [September 1947]: 193). Given the facts that John Tyler had become a president without a party and that Webster himself had become suspect among Whigs because of his association with the unpopular administration, the Senate vote and the favorable reception of the treaty by the general public constituted an impressive political triumph. Whatever one thinks of the merits of the treaty itself, Webster excelled as a propagandist.

The documents published in this section include some of Webster's most important state papers, such as that on impressment and the tightly reasoned *Caroline* letter that set forth the precedent-setting doctrine of self-defense (see DW to Ashburton, August 6, 1842, below). Also noteworthy are the documents attesting to Webster's careful attention to detail and heavy reliance on others for advice and information. As Webster put it in a note to Supreme Court justice Joseph Story, "I am in the midst of things; and have need not only for all my own wits, but of the assistance of friends, competent to give efficient aid" (DW to Story, April 9, 1842, below). A significant aspect of the Webster-Ashburton negotiation overlooked by scholars is the extent to which the secretary of state drew upon the knowledge of contemporary authorities on various geographic, legal, and strategic issues in fashioning the arguments and compromises that produced the rapprochement with Great Britain (for example, see DW to Bell and Paine, April 30, 1842; DW to Coffin, May 28, 1842; Renwick to DW, June 11, 1842; DW to Spencer, August 10, 1842; and Abert to Spencer, August 15, 1842, below). Finally, the documents suggest that Webster was a pragmatic realist who distinguished between what nation-states could and should do. Because of this mentality and with the help of eminent contemporary authorities, Webster devised what Attorney General Hugh S. Legaré characterized as a "chefd'oeuvre" of diplomacy (Legaré to DW, July 29, 1842, below).

FROM LORD ASHBURTON

Private   The Grange
My Dear Sir,   2nd Jan'y 1842.
    You will hear by this opportunity, and probably not without some surprise that I have undertaken to cross the Atlantic at this stormy season

of the year as a special messenger of peace & I would not make my sudden appearance at Washington in this my new character of a diplomatist, without sending you a few lines to say that I am coming.[1] My advanced period of life, not unaccompanied by some of its infirmities, has for some time imposed upon me the duty of retirement, and I felt myself justified in declining to form part of an administration just formed by my political friends with whom I have been in habits of confidence and intimacy on public matters.[2] Under these circumstances, it is not without some reluctance that I have suffered myself to be persuaded that I am a person likely to be of service in the important task of settling the difference which seems to stand in the way of that which all men of sense and honesty have most at heart, a good and cordial state of peace and good will between our great countries. In short I am making preparations for my early departure.

A Frigate is preparing for me at Portsmouth. I hope to start before the month is out, and by the end of February or early in March to make my appearance at your seat of Government.[3]

I confine myself for the present simply to the communication of this fact. I hardly need add that I should not have yielded to the pressing solicitations of my friends but for the very strong impressions of the importance of the service, and that the confidence and full powers of my government afforded the best chance of performing it, meeting as I am sure I shall with a corresponding disposition with the existing enlightened Government of America.

The principal aim and object of that part of my life devoted to public objects during the 35 years that I have had a seat in one or the other House of Parliament has been to impress on others the necessity of, and to promote my self peace and harmony between our countries; and although the prevailing good sense of both forbid my entertaining any serious apprehensions on the subject. I am one of those who have always watched with anxiety at all times any threatening circumstances, any clouds which however small may through the neglect of some or the malevolence of others end in a storm the disastrous consequences of which defy exaggeration.

I shall be most happy, my dear Sir, to cooperate with you in this good work. Since my appointment was made the Presidents speech has

1. See Everett to DW, December 31, 1841, "The Crisis in Anglo-American Relations," pp. 173–177, above, and DW to Everett, January 29, 1842, below.

2. Sir Robert Peel formed a Tory government on September 1, 1841. Ashburton had served as minister of trade and master of the mint in Peel's first ministry, December 1834–April 1835.

3. Ashburton sailed on the English frigate *Warspite* in February 1842. He arrived at Annapolis April 4 and was presented to President Tyler on April 6.

reached us,[4] and although it gives us a longer catalogue of differences than I could wish I flatter myself that many if not all will vanish on a candid explanation and discussion, and I am strongly confirmed in that hope by the plain and cordial expressions by which they are accompanied. The material interest of the two countries call loudly for peace and friendship, but what to my mind is of infinitely greater importance I believe the moral improvement and the progressive civilization of the world depend upon it.

But I will not begin my first attempt at Diplomacy with over abundant professions of which I hope I shall shortly prove the sincerity. Lady Ashburton[5] will not be able to accompany me. She would much wish once more to visit her native country but her health and domestic duties make this impossible. I am, my dear Sir, with great truth. Yours sincerely ever

Ashburton.

Copy. NhHi. Published in Van Tyne, pp. 252–254.

FROM EDWARD EVERETT

Confidential
My dear Sir,   London 3 Jan. 1842
(My public despatch will give you the important intelligence of Lord Ashburton's appointment on a special mission to America.[1] In addition to what is reported in the despatch, Lord Aberdeen mentioned particularly, that his known friendly relations with you were among the chief inducements to select Lord Ashburton. No intimation was made by Lord Aberdeen as to the principles on which Lord Ashburton would be authorized to settle any of the points; but he stated repeatedly that he would have full powers to make a final settlement of every thing.

With respect to the right of search in the African seas, is it out of the question for the United States to come into the agreement with the Five Powers?[2] There surely can be nothing derogatory to our honor, in making common cause with them in this way? How would our interests suffer? Having once failed to ratify a treaty with England for this object,[3] there might be a punctilio on the score of consistency. Could not this be obvi-

4. Tyler's Annual Message, delivered December 7, 1841, is in *Messages and Papers*, 4:74–89.
5. Ann Louisa Bingham, Lady Ashburton (1782–1848), was the daughter of wealthy Philadelphia banker and U.S. senator William Bingham.
1. See above, Everett to DW, December 31, 1841, "The Crisis in Anglo-American Relations," pp. 173–177.

2. The Quintuple Treaty of December 20, 1841.
3. The United States and Britain signed a convention on March 13, 1824, allowing mutual search in cases of suspected slave traders. The U.S. Senate consented to the treaty but made amendments that the British refused to accept. *ASP: FR*, 5:315–343, 359–368.

ated by an invitation from the five powers? Such an invitation, if deemed advisable, could no doubt be obtained here, through the agency, in the first instance, of the French Ambassador & Russian minister.[4]

On observing to Mr Duff Green yesterday, that this question of search was a very difficult one, he said he did not think so; that there was nothing in it. I did not however gather what his views were.

Will it not be possible to get 2/3 of the Senate, laying aside party, to agree to some proper arrangement with Lord Ashburton, on all the points in dispute? If Mr [John Caldwell] Calhoun,[5] Mr [Henry] Clay and yourself would confer on this subject, it would be greatly for the benefit of the country. Unless party can be laid aside on this occasion, a friendly settlement is out of the question, & war is inevitable; for if this overture on the part of England fails, where shall we [be] left? I ought to add, however, that this alternative was not suggested to me by any thing, which has fallen from Lord A[berdeen]. It is too evident to need suggestion.)

Col. [Thomas] Aspinwall has or will make a charge of thirty five pounds office rent for the time which elapsed from Mr [Andrew] Stevenson's departure till my arrival with my family, seven weeks and three days. He engaged the house which Mr Stevenson occupied from the time he left, thinking I should arrive by that time. In point of fact I did not receive any reliable information of my appointment till the 16th of Octr. at Naples & Mr. S[tevenson] left London the 23d. The house was engaged by Col. Aspinwall for my accommodation; but as things turned out nobody was accommodated by the Legation. It was greatly for the public convenience and public decorum not to have the "local habitation" of the American mission wholly extinguished; to have the office & archives undisturbed; & a proper place of resort for those wanting passports; and the expense of separate premises and two removals would, I am sure, have exceeded £35. The government allows £80 a year office rent, so that the charge of £35 for seven weeks & three days is but about £25 extra. If the government allow this charge, I shall still be a loser directly to the amount of sixty pounds, by continuing the lease of the house; and consequentially to the amount of at least one hundred pounds more, for I cannot expect to pass from one house to another, without a loss of six weeks or two months' rent; and the house I am now in is to be pulled down in March.

If Mr [Stephen] Pleasanton[6] needs any explanation of this item in Col. A[spinwall]'s acc'ts I wish you would afford it. I am as ever, Dear Sir, most truly yours

P.S. I wrote you a private letter of the 15th Decr. to go by the sailing pack-

4. Louis de Sainte-Aulaire (1778–1849); Philippe Ivanovitch Brunnow (1797–1875).

5. Calhoun (1782–1850; Yale 1804).

6. Pleasanton (d. 1855) served for fifty years as an auditor at the Treasury Department.

et ship Oxford, in which I mentioned that your request relative to Mr [John] Watson had been complied with.[7]

AL. MHi.

FROM LADY ASHBURTON

My dear Mr Webster   Bath House—Jany 12 [1842]

I take great credit to myself for the discretion which has hitherto checked my impulse to write to you, at the risk of appearing unmindful of the very gratifying proofs for your recollection I have received on various occasions; for in truth I had little to tell you beyond the gossip of London society at a moment when I knew your time & attention were absorbed by the most important affairs. I cannot however now resist troubling you with a few lines to say how fully we concur in your discription of Mr [Edward] Everett,[1] who is in every respect calculated to sustain the high opinion *now* entertained of American Statesmen, & to conciliate the regard of all those who have the advantage of knowing him. I should have made his acquaintance as a countrywoman, but I can now boldly urge my claim to his consideration as an acknowledged friend of yours, a privilege I am so apt to boast of, that it is gratifying to my vanity to have it confirmed by you. Mr Everett's brief visit to the Grange was not made under the most cheering circumstances, for my *heroic patriotism* has been sadly depressed by the prospect of a long suspension of our domestic happiness, to say nothing of the great anxiety we all suffer about Lord Ashburtons health, which I fear will be sorely tried in a tedious voyage at this inclement season. These honors were thrust upon him as the person most zealous in the cause of America, & most sanguine as to the possibility of settling the long pending differences between the two countries. God grant that his best hopes may be realised & that I may see him return with a treaty of peace in his pocket. It will go far to compensate us both for the sacrifices we are about to make. At all events pray treat him kindly, & meet his advances with the same friendly feeling he carries towards you, for to borrow your own significant phrase "if you dont like him we can send you nothing better."

He will embark in the Warspite about the 25 of this month, & I hope he will have no difficulty in finding a suitable House at Washington. Mr [Joshua] Bates has promised to write to secure one.[2] Had the season been more propitious I should much have liked to accompany him, & to have seen the vast improvements which have taken place in my native coun-

7. See above, Everett to DW, December 15, 1841, "The Crisis in Anglo-American Relations," pp. 166–169.

1. Not found.
2. Bates to DW, January 3, 1842, extant in Curtis, 2:95–96.

try during an absence of forty years. Adieu my dear Mr Webster & pray believe me to be your truly obliged   A L Ashburton

ALS. NhHi. Published in Van Tyne, pp. 254–255.

FROM EDWARD EVERETT

Private.

My dear Sir,   London 21 Jan. 1842.

Lord Ashburton called upon me yesterday, and informed me that he should probably sail on the 31st of the month. He takes passage in the Warspite, which is called the best frigate in the Navy, and as such is now under orders to convoy the King of Prussia [Frederick William IV] to this country.[1] He said it would depend on the winds which might prevail, whether the vessel would make a port at New York or Annapolis, and enquired of me whether it would make any difference at which port he disembarked, in reference to the privilege of landing his baggage. I did not hesitate, at a venture, to answer in the negative; & I take the liberty to request that you will have particular orders sent both to New York and to Annapolis to allow all the baggage & effects of Lord Ashburton and his suite to be landed free of duty & *free of search*. Free of duty they are entitled to be by the law of Nations; but that privilege loses some part of its value here, by the practice of breaking the packages and examining the contents which here prevails, producing inconvenient delay, risk of injury & loss to articles of small bulk & considerable value, & offensive exposure of one's private concerns in a public office; & all without a shadow of benefit. The only case, in which such a search is needed, would be where there was strong ground of suspicion, that a foreign Minister was attempting to defraud the customs, by introducing articles for others, or for sale. This is a possible case, but to any extent an unlikely one. If attempted only [on] a small scale, breaking the packages is no check; if attempted on a large scale, it would detect itself, & the search might then, in the individual case, be reasonably instituted. I suppose that in our service it is not practiced; & at all events I hope if there is no objection which does not occur to me, that it will not be in the present instance.

Lord Ashburton asked if I had received any instructions relative to "the Creole," which of course I answered in the negative.[2] He deeply regretted the occurrence, & thought it would be a source of greater difficulty than any other; adding that Great Britain could never make compensation for the liberated slaves. He asked if there was any provision for the extradi-

1. The king of Prussia, Frederick William IV, arrived in England on January 22, 1842, to participate in the christening of the Prince of Wales, Edward Albert (1841–1910), born on November 9, 1841.

2. See above, DW to Everett, January 29, 1842, "The Crisis in Anglo-American Relations," pp. 177–185.

tion of criminals between the two Countries, & on my saying there was not, he enquired if there could Constitutionally be such provision. This I answered in the affirmative, adding that by Jay's treaty such provision was made in the case of murder and forgery;[3] and that I thought no objection would exist to the renewal of such a provision, not to extend however to treason or any other political crime. I understood Lord A[shburton] to intimate, that he should be authorized to agree to a stipulation expressly limiting the right of Search in the African Seas to the suppression of the Slave Trade, if the United States would be willing to come into the agreement of the Five Powers on such a condition.[4] If this stipulation could be so expressed, or, by notes exchanged between you & Lord A[shburton], so interpreted as to amount to an express renunciation of impressing seamen; and if it were accompanied with another stipulation that vessels transporting slaves coastwise from one part of the United States to the other were not to be interfered with, would not the chief objections to our joining in the General Agreement of the other Powers of Christendom be removed?

I had an interview the other day with the Russian Minister the Baron [Philippe Ivanovitch] Brunnow, who has since my arrival here treated me with much kindness, and on more than one occasion expressed the wish of the Emperor [Nicholas I], without interfering in the affairs of other States, to do any thing in his power to promote a good understanding between the United States & Great Britain. He said that my predecessor [Andrew Stevenson] was under the impression that the Emperor of Russia was not sorry to see differences between the United States and Great Britain, as such differences might act as a check upon the latter: but such a feeling & policy were entirely unknown to the Emperor. Baron Brunnow hoped that we should settle our differences with Great Britain, without the intervention of any third power; he was glad that the mediation of France was not invoked last year, as it was thought it was about to be: he did not wish his own Emperor's intervention invited, but wanted the two parties to settle their affairs themselves. He then said that he had seen Sir Robert Peel that day, and that from the conversation between them, he felt warranted in saying that this Government would agree to any stipulation which might be necessary to remove the difficulty relative to impressment, as connected with a concession of the right of search.

3. Article 27 of the Jay Treaty of November 19, 1794, had provided for the extradition of forgers and murderers; the treaty expired in 1807. *Treaties*, 2:245–274, esp. p. 263.

4. The Quintuple Treaty of December 20, 1841, between Great Britain, France, Austria, Prussia, and Russia, extended previous anti–slave trade conventions by allowing reciprocal rights of search among the signatories. The French Chamber of Deputies refused its assent, but the other powers ratified the convention on February 19, 1842, in London. See *British and Foreign State Papers, 1841–1842* (116 vols., London, 1812–1825), 30: 269–298.

He then remarked on the fact that at any rate impressment was not to be feared in time of peace, & that in time of war the right of search existed as a belligerent right by the law of nations. He said that if it were the wish of the United States Government, that an invitation should proceed from the Five Powers to that Government, to join their Convention for the suppression of the Slave Trade, such an invitation, he was sure, might easily be procured: adding that, of course, the U.S. Government would not intimate a wish for such an invitation, unless morally sure of accepting it.

Baron Brunnow, in a former conversation, told me he had reason to be confident that this government would agree to a conventional line of Boundary on the North East, and I think he added to take the line of the King of the Netherlands [William I],[5] paying to the U.S. a pecuniary indemnity for the territory north of the St. John's. You are well aware that President Jackson, Mr [John] Forsyth, & other persons of the highest political standing, were in favour of taking the line of the King of the Netherlands: Mr Forsyth told me that General [Andrew] Jackson thought he ought at once to have issued his proclamation declaring the award of the King of the Netherlands final,[6] and that he always afterwards regretted he had not; and that the only occasion in his life, on which he allowed himself to be overruled, was one where he ought to have been particularly tenacious.

29th January.

An article appeared in the Morning Post of the 25th inst,[7] to which I would ask your attention. It was evidently intended to prepare the public to receive the information, that the Government had determined to give up the mutineers in the Creole. Such I am warranted in saying *was* the disposition of the Government, nor can I confidently affirm, that it does not still exist. It has been, however, strongly doubted whether there is any power to give up criminals of any kind to the United States Government. When such extradition in the cases of murder and forgery was provided for by Jay's treaty, a law was passed to carry this provision into effect;[8] and it was expressly enacted in the law, that the powers granted should expire with the treaty. It is most true that a contrary practice has prevailed, & that a murderer was given up within the last year at Liverpool.[9]

---

5. William I (1772–1843) ruled 1815–1840.

6. In his Annual Message of December 6, 1831, Jackson announced he would submit the opinion of the king of the Netherlands to the Senate. On June 23, 1832, the Senate advised the president to open new negotiations. *Messages and Papers*, 2:544–558; *Senate Journal*, 22d Cong., 1st sess., Serial 211, pp. 529–531.

7. The London *Morning Post* article, not included in the RG 59 record, is an account of the mutiny by the officers and crew of the *Creole*.

8. 37 Geo. 3, c. 97.

9. The case was that of a seaman

No written opinion however is found in the case, and it is said to have been done without due consideration. Such is the representation made to me on the subject by Lord Brougham, on two occasions on which he has called upon me. I know that the point has been referred to the law officers of the Crown, but how it has been decided I know not.

Great sensation has been excited both here and at Paris by the all but unanimous adoption in the French Chambers of an amendment to the address, the purport of which is considered as a censure on the treaty of the 20th Decr. between the Five Powers.[10] The ministry, to prevent a worse amendment, agreed to take that which finally prevailed; but this agreement is regarded as compulsory, & Lord Brougham told me to-day that it was feared by the ministry in Paris that they might be driven to leave the treaty unratified. Lord Brougham thinks that this result is the effect of the bitterness felt in France at the conclusion of the treaty of 1841 without the co-operation of France; for though in point of form the treaty between the Five Powers signed on the 20th Decr. was concluded by the present ministry, it was all but concluded under Lord Melbourne. It is supposed M. [François Pierre Guillaume] Guizot would not or did not dare to conclude it with Lord Melbournes ministry, toward which great irritation was felt in France by most persons, & those who did not feel it were obliged to respect it.

It is probable that the appearance of the correspondence between Mr. Stevenson & Lord Palmerston[11] contributed to the feeling manifested in the chambers. General [Lewis] Cass conversed frequently with M. Guizot on the subject and attributed the refusal of the United States to enter into the treaty to the old British claim of impressment. M. Guizot availed himself adroitly of this idea to meet the objection which might be founded on our non-concurrence. "The Americans, (he said) had a ground of opposition to a mutual right of search which did not apply to France: were he an American, he would not grant it!"

31st Jany.

I had another interview to-day with Lord Ashburton at my house. He fears the French Ministry may not be able to ratify the Treaty of the 20th Decr., in the face of the vote of the chambers; and seemed to entertain little hope, under the discouraging circumstance of the non-ratification

---

charged with murder committed on board an American ship in the British port. See No. 128. Stevenson to DW, July 3, 1841, DNA, RG 59 (Despatches, Britain).

10. In response to the annual address of the king, the assembly passed a declaration authored by François Gilbert Jacques Lefebvre (1773–

1856), obliging the French government to protect the "commercial interests and the independence of our flag from any attempt at violation." See the London *Times*, January 26 and 28, 1842.

11. *Executive Documents*, 26th Cong., 2d sess., Serial 386, No. 115.

of France, that America would come into the Treaty. "I think she would come in," (said I,) "if you would renounce impressment." "Do you mean," (he replied,) *in toto*, or only in time of peace?" "The United States" (I said) "could never accept a renunciation merely in time of peace, because this would be a tacit admission of the practice in time of War." I made this remark by way of experiment. His Lordship immediately replied, "For myself, I would gladly renounce it." I caught at this observation, & observed, with some earnestness, "Why will not her Majesty's Government at once disclaim the practice of impressment *in toto*? In peace they do not need it, for the public service in England is preferred to the merchant service; and as to reserving it for a time of war, it is simply a reservation of an American War, in addition to any other, in which Great Britain might be engaged. I was wholly incapable of saying any thing which could wear the appearance of *threat*: I knew that was the last tone to be taken with a government like the British; but that I could say with all truth, that the first case of impressment from an American Ship would be the signal of an American War." Lord A. said "he did not doubt it; that he was well persuaded no attempt would be made to exercise the right again; and that he himself thought it was the part of wisdom to give up with a good grace, what you could not enforce." "Particularly," I added, "when by so doing you can effect other great points." He said there would be difficulties in coming to a practical arrangement, particularly, as to the case of neutral vessels in a British port. Great Britain never would give up the right of retaining men, who, within her own waters, should desert a ship of war and enter a neutral ship. I told him no neutral could expect to harbor British deserters within a British Jurisdiction. He said there would not be time, during the four or five days that he should stay here to mature a project; but added, "*I have no doubt you will be able to accomplish it.*" This seemed to me a very important remark. I know from other quarters, that there is, of late years, a great change in the public mind as to Impressment; and I should be gratified, if the President thought it expedient, to be authorized to sound the British Government on the subject. It would be a most fortunate incident, if we could come to an arrangement on this subject, & as it would remove almost all the difficulties relating to the question of visitation, would go far to restore harmony between the two countries.

The law officers of the Crown have decided against the power to deliver up the 19 slaves guilty of murder in the Creole. They are unanimous. Sir William Follett held out longest, and though he still maintains that there was an undoubted original power, as part of the prerogative, to surrender a foreigner charged with felony, on a proper demand, yet that this power has been so much weakened by treaty stipulations and legal enactments, that it would be unsafe to exercise it, in the absence of such legal and treaty provisions. They also think that the nineteen cannot be tried in any British court.[12] Lord A[shburton] did not disguise from himself the unpleasant aspect given to the affair of the Creole by these conclusions.

As it is scarcely doubtful, (in the present aspect of the matter) that if a demand be made by the Government of the United States for the extradition of the slaves in the Creole, such demand will be refused, I submit to you the expediency of informing me by the next steamer, in what way the President would wish the refusal to be met, both as respects the 19 engaged in the insurrection, & the others: I mean, of course, provided you shall have previously instructed me to make the demand. The grounds of the refusal will be an allegation of a want of power to deliver up the 19, accompanied probably with a copy of the opinion of the Crown lawyers: and in the case of the 105 not concerned in the rising, the grounds for refusing to deliver them up or make compensation for them, will probably be substantially the same as those, which were alleged in the case of "The Enterprize" two or three years ago. I am As ever, Dear Sir, Most truly Yours,   Edward Everett

Mr [Samuel] Rogers and Mr [Henry] Hallam[13] desire their best remembrance.

L s. MHi.

TO EDWARD EVERETT

Private.

My dear Sir,   Washington, January 29. 1842.

Your two despatches and your private letter by the Brittania were duly received.[1] The despatches were read in Cabinet Council, and I showed your private letter to the President. Everything done by you thus far, is approved. The Special Mission was a surprise to us; but the Country receives it very well. For my own part, no selection of a Minister could be more agreeable to me than, that of Lord Ashburton; as I entertain towards him sentiments of great kindness and regard. You are at liberty to signify this, so far as may be proper, to Lord Aberdeen.

I infer, on the whole, that the mission will be single. Mr. [Henry Stephen] Fox, doubtless, will be expected to assist, with counsel and advice; but I rather suppose that the authority and official signatures will be sole.

12. The opinion of January 29, 1842, signed by Advocate General Sir John Dodson (1780–1858), Attorney General Sir Frederick Pollock (1783–1870), and Sir William Follett (1798–1845), is in FO 83/2350 (PRO).

13. Rogers (1763–1855) was an English poet and patron of arts; Hallam (1777–1859) was an English barrister and author.

1. No. 4. Everett to DW, December 28, 1841, DNA, RG 59 (Despatches, Britain); see above, Everett to DW, January 3, 1842, and Everett to DW, December 31, 1841, "The Crisis in Anglo-American Relations," pp. 173–177.

It gives me promise of work enough, overwhelmed as I already am, by affairs growing out of the very unhappy state of things among us, and out of the calls and proceedings of Congress. But my health is good—never better—and if I can so far repress anxiety as to be able *to sleep*, I hope to get through.

I write you to-day quite a hurried despatch, the greater part of which relates to a new Nassau case; of which, you will probably have heard. You will notice that Mr. [John Caldwell] Calhoun made a call for information on this case, three weeks ago;[2] and although I had not time for great preparation, I felt obliged to write.[3] You will make the substance known to Lord Aberdeen, by relating it to him, or in any other way. He will at once see what excitement these occurrences occur in the South, and I doubt not will take proper steps to prevent their recurrence. The Colonial authorities should be directed not to interfere, in such cases, to set slaves at liberty, nor to withhold assistance from any vessel, brought in by mutiny, or driven in by stress of weather.

At present, I entertain more fears on this subject, than on that of the African seizures.

The other subjects mentioned in your communications will be attended to, as soon as possible.

Mrs. [Caroline Le Roy] Webster joins me in kind remembrances to your family. Yours truly,   Danl Webster

LS. MHi. Published in *PC*, 2:113–114.

TO JOSHUA BATES

Washington

My Dr Sir   Jan: 29. '42

I thank you for yr letter by the Britania.[1] Ld Ashburton's mission is quite acceptable here. Nothing could be more agreeable to me, personally, if there is to be a mission, than that Ld Ashburton would be appointed to it. We look for him, abt <Feb> March 1st. I took good note of what you said in your letter about a house. I have already taken the necessary preliminary steps. There will, I think, be no great difficulty on that point.[2]

I am worked quite too hard, & tremble <before> at the idea of the

2. Calhoun called for the papers on the *Creole* on January 10, 1842. *Senate Journal*, 27th Cong., 2d sess., Serial 394, p. 78.

3. See DW's official instruction to Everett, January 29, 1842, "The Crisis in Anglo-American Relations," pp.

177-185.

1. Bates to DW, January 3, 1842, extant in Curtis, 2:95–96.

2. DW arranged for Ashburton to rent the home of Matthew St. Claire Clarke on Lafayette Square.

new duties likely to be imposed by Ld Ashburton's mission. But if I can keep my health I hope to get through.

Give our kind regards to Mrs [Lucretia Sturgis] Bates. We talk of you often, & always with grateful regard.[3] Write me a note, long or short, every packet; because one private note generally gives more useful information than two public despatches. I hope Mr [Edward] Everett gets on well among you. His letters to me are well written, & sensible.

I hope to hear from you by the Oct Steamer, as well as by Lord Ashburton. Yrs always truly,   Danl Webster

ALS. NhD.

TO REUEL WILLIAMS

Private & Confidential
Dear Sir,   Washington Feb. 2d 1842

Recalling the conversation which passed in the Department between Mr [George] Evans & yourself, & me, & also the short interview which I had with you at the Presidents, I now beg leave to address you, on <that> the important subject of those conversations.

Lord Ashburton may be expected in this Country by the first of March, fully empowered & instructed to discuss & settle, definitely every subject in controversy between the United States & England. At the head of this list stands the dispute concerning our North Eastern Boundary, & I suppose this will be entered upon, immediately upon his arrival.

You are aware that a negotiation had been going on between Mr [John] Forsyth & Mr [Henry Stephen] Fox, for many months, before the late change of administration. In the progress of this negotiation, the parties had arrived at an agreement for a joint Commission, with an ultimate reference to arbitration, appointed by <Europea> the sovereigns, or Heads, of other Governments, in case a necessity for such arbitration should arise. On several matters of detail the parties differed, & appear to have been interchanging their respective views & opinions, projects & counter projects, without coming to a <final &> *full* (final) arrangement, down to Aug 1840.[1] Various causes, not now necessary to be explained, have prevented (arrested the progress of the negotiation at that time, & no efficient progress has since been made in it.) any <more> further considerable progress, since that period.

It seems to (have been) be understood on both sides, that <in pursuance of the Treaty of Ghent>, one arbitration having failed, it was the duty of the two parties to proceed to institute another, according to the (spirit of) the Treaty of Ghent, and other Treaties; and (I suppose, that)

3. Lucretia Sturgis married Bates in 1813.
   1. See above, Palmerston to Fox,

August 24, 1841, "The Crisis in Anglo-American Relations," pp. 102–107.

unless some new course be adopted the pending negotiation will be immediately pursued to its conclusion.

But I think it highly probable that Lord Ashburton will come prepared to agree to a *conventional* line of boundary, on such <conditions>, terms & conditions, & with such compensation<s>, as may be thought just & equitable. It is the conviction of the high probability of this, (although we have no authentic information to that effect) that leads the President to desire that the attention of the Government of Maine should be immediately & seriously turned to this subject, with a view of considering whether it <be not disposed> <will not to a certain> might not be useful for that Govt to make itself, to a certain extent, & in a certain form, party to the discussions & conclusions, which may be had between the Govt of the United States & that of England. The Treaty for a conventional line, if one should be agreed upon, must of course be between the United States & England, & could <not> be submitted for <the> ratification <or consent of the Legislature> only to the Senate of the United States. But agents or Commissioners of Maine might represent her interests & wishes, in the negotation, with an understanding that no exchange of Territory, or other proceeding to make a new line by agreement, would be adopted without their express assent. These Commissioners would of course correspond with their own Government, and as they would be possessed of the fullest local information, & well acquainted with the interests, sentiments, & wishes of the People of Maine, <this mode of proceeding would seem> an arrangement entered into with their consent, if happily such an arrangement could be made, would be likely to give satisfaction.

I pray you to have the goodness to confer on this subject with Govr [John] Fairfield, & other Gentlemen, & learn their opinions. You will see that time presses, as I suppose the Legislature of Maine will adjourn in a month. It was deemed of so much importance that this subject should be brought under consideration in Maine, that, with the President's approbation, I have concluded to write to some Gentleman of High character in Maine, inviting his attendance here, immediately, to confer upon the means proper to be adopted, & should probably have addressed myself to Chief Justice [Nathan] Weston.[2] But as you are now on the spot, it has been thought better to communicate with you, in the first instance. If you & other Gentlemen should be of opinion that it wd be useful <is necessary> that a suitable person should come here, at once, to confer with the President, & this Department, more freely & fully than may be done by correspondence, <I trust> we should be very glad to see him; & though I have great respect for Judge Weston, founded on long acquaint-

2. Weston (1782–1872; Dartmouth 1803) was appointed to the Maine Supreme Court in 1820. He became chief justice in 1834 and retired in 1841.

ance, yet if his engagements will not allow him to visit us, any other Gentleman will be agreeable whom Govr Fairfield & yourself may select.

It is our purpose, to put the question, in the fairest manner, <of> to Maine, whether she will <agree> consent to be satisfied with a conventional line, & all its terms & conditions, which Commissioners of her own appointment shall have approved. And it is but candid to say, that for many reasons, some of which are obvious to all, <that> no negotiation for such a line will be opened, or entered upon, without an express previous consent on the part of Maine, to acquiesce <with> in any line, with all its terms, conditions, & compensations, which shall <be> have been thus previously <been> approved. I hope the Government of Maine will think favorably of what I have now suggested; since it is my opinion, that in all probability, five or six years will elapse before the line of the Treaty of 1783 can be ascertained, run, & marked, by proceedings under a Convention for a joint-commission, & an ultimate arbitration. It will be our duty, however, to press the conclusion of such Convention as soon as practicable, unless the Government of Maine <[then?]> should think it compatible with the honor & interest of the State to concur in measures for an earlier settlement of the whole question.

<I am> Allow me to hope for an early acknowledgement of the receipt of this communication.

AL draft. NhHi. Published in Van Tyne, pp. 256–258. Williams (1783–1862), a lawyer, was a Democrat in the U.S. Senate from 1837 to 1843. Williams, who had served on the Maine boundary commission of 1832, was a staunch defender of the state's territorial rights. He became a vociferous opponent of the treaty of 1842.

FROM REUEL WILLIAMS

Private & confidential
Dear Sir   Augusta Feb 12 1842

Since writing to you some days ago[1] I have endeavored to ascertain what may be expected from the Legislature of Maine in reference to the boundary question.

The point of honor, and consistency on the part of the Legislature, are in the way of arriving at what might be satisfactory to both countries.

Maine is confident of the justice & validity of her claim as advanced & insisted upon by her, & has no wish to change the Treaty line. Still I believe she would release to Great Britain such portion of the territory in controversy as the convenience of the latter may require, on an offer of other territory in exchange, or other suitable equivalent.

In her view, Great Britain has interposed an unwarrantable claim to a

1. Williams to DW, February 9, 1842, mDW 21521.

portion of her territory, & has taken & now holds part of it by military force.[2]

To open the way to a friendly adjustment of the question, it would seem that Great Britain should first withdraw all military occupation of the territory in controversy & then a proposition from her for an exchange of territory and equivalents would be met & carried out by Maine in a friendly spirit.

Aware of the difficulties urged by the government of Great Britain as standing in the way of her proposing a conventional line & equivalents to a party not authorised to agree to & establish such a line,[3] the members of the Legislature, as well as the Governor of Maine [John Fairfield], as far as I can ascertain, would agree to any course which can be honorably adopted to afford the parties an opportunity of understanding the objects and views of each other, & of arriving at a settlement of the long pending question of boundary, if possible, without resort to arbitration, indicated by the last, as well as the present administration, as the only remaining course to be adopted.

If the information possessed by the general Government would enable you to propose to the Governor of Maine, or the Legislature, a specific line of boundary; yielding to Maine territory, privileges of navigation or other benefits equivalent to the territory which might be yielded to Great Britain, in lieu of the line described in the Treaty of 1783, it would be well received, & acted upon by the Legislature as the General Government might justly expect from one of its members.

If that cannot be done, then I think that an appeal to Maine as indicated in your letter,[4] would receive grave consideration & be acted upon with a strong desire to adopt the measure, if it shall be deemed consistent with the honor and just pretensions of the state.

Suggestions are made by some that altho' Great Britain has heretofore proposed to treat for a conventional line, *it is not known* that Lord Ashburton will be so instructed, and that if Maine should authorise Commissioners to consider & agree upon a conventional line & its terms, & then learn that no such line or terms were to be *proposed by England*, Maine would then be placed where no American could wish to see her placed.

While I have thus given you the views of the dominant party of Maine, as fairly & fully as I can, it should not be forgotten that much will depend upon the course of the Whigs. Neither party, as such, will be inclined to encounter the united efforts of the other upon this great question. If the Whigs shall, as I think they will, sustain a reasonable proposition from the general government for authority to settle the question upon just

2. See above, Kent to Tyler, May 25, 1841, "The Crisis in Anglo-American Relations," pp. 81–85.

3. See above, Palmerston to Fox, August 24, 1841, "The Crisis in Anglo-American Relations," pp. 102–107.

4. See above.

grounds & with proper limitations it seems to me that the object may be attained; but I speak from appearances & not from authority. The Legis·lature propose to adjourn about the first of March. I am very respecfully Your obt servt   R Williams.

ALS. NhHi. Published in Van Tyne, pp. 258–260.

FROM LEWIS CASS, WITH ENCLOSURE

No. 141.   Legation of the United States
Sir,   Paris, 15th February 1842.

I have not heretofore considered it necessary to write you officially respecting the state of affairs here, having relation to the question of the right of search depending between the American and British Governments. But tho' no direct diplomatic action seemed advisable, till recently, I did not the less observe the progress of events, nor neglect by proper conversations and explanations with those who from their position influenced them, to convey a just notion of the subject in its relation, not only to the United States, but to all other maritime powers, who do not seek the supremacy of the seas. And I have the satisfaction to believe, that my exertions were not wholly useless, either with respect to public opinion or to public measures. I have kept you informed in my private communications[1] of the progress of affairs as well as of my own course of unofficial action, and I have transmitted also such of the French journals, as seemed, in addition to the other information, best calculated to convey to you a correct idea of the state of affairs here and of public feeling.

But I have just taken a step, which renders necessary, a full and free report of the condition of things here, and of the reasons, which have led me to adopt this measure. My letter of the 13th inst to the Minister of Foreign Affairs [François Pierre Guillaume Guizot],[2] a copy of which I enclose, will make known to you my general sentiments concerning the relation in which we are placed with the French Government, by the signature of the Quintuple Treaty for the suppression of the slave trade and by the declarations of Lord Palmerston and Lord Aberdeen, concerning the measures which they claim to be indispensable to its execution.[3] I need add nothing upon this subject.

I hesitated, at first, respecting the true course to be adopted. That it was proper to bring officially [to] the notice of the French Government

1. See above, Cass to DW, March 5 and 15, 1841, "The Crisis in Anglo-American Relations," pp. 37–38, 44–45; see also Cass to DW, [January 24, 1842], mDW 21375, and February 13, 1842, mDW 21552.
2. See below.

3. See Palmerston to Andrew Stevenson, August 27, 1841, enclosed in Stevenson to DW, September 18, 1841; and Aberdeen to Stevenson, October 13, 1841, enclosed in Stevenson to DW, October 22, 1841; all in DNA, RG 59 (Despatches, Britain).

the declaration of that of Great Britain, that the conclusion of these Treaties created an obligation and conferred a right to violate the flag of the
United States, I did not entertain a doubt. What was true of the duty of
one of the parties was true of the duty of each of them. Either, therefore,
the claim of Great Britain was well founded, and in that event the Government of France was about to contract new obligations which might
bring it into collision with the United States, a result I was certain it did
not contemplate; or the claim was unjust, and in that event, the Treaty
was about to be made the pretext of a direct attack upon our rights and
honor, by one of the parties, assuming to be governed by the obligations
it had contracted, towards the other associated powers; a state of things,
which gave us a right to call upon them to disavow such pretensions, and
either to withdraw from an arrangement, which was becoming so menacing to us, or to declare by a solemn act that it was not susceptible of such
a construction, and should not, with their consent, be employed for such
a purpose. My first impression was to present a formal protest against the
ratification of the Treaty. But considering that I had no instructions to
take so decided a measure, and that it would be more respectful to the
French Government, of whose friendly disposition to the United States, I
have had numerous evidences, and probably quite as useful to state generally the bearing of the whole matter upon the United States, without
claiming any specific action, I finally determined to take this course, and
the letter to Mr Guizot is the consequence.

I shall now proceed to make some remarks upon this general subject,
which may not be useless in the consideration which the Government will
necessarily give to it. For some years the English journals have with
much art turned the public attention of Europe from the great question
of maritime right and of the freedom of the seas, involved in our discussions with Great Britain connected with the measures to be adopted for
the suppression of the slave trade, and directed it to that infamous traffic,
sometimes asserting and sometimes insinuating, that our opposition to
the co-operation their Government proposed, originated in the miserable
notion of profit; the profit to be derived from the most wretched of all
commerce. But thanks to the progress of truth, our cause is now well
understood upon the Continent of Europe; and as in all sudden re-actions,
where injustice has been unwillingly done, the public sentiment here and
elsewhere is setting strongly in our favor. The question has not again
been presented in either of the Chambers, but the indications in the Journals, and in all societies are too clear to be misunderstood.

Circumstances have placed us in a position, which if firmly maintained will be equally honorable to ourselves, and useful to all other powers interested in the freedom of the seas. Depend upon it, we have
reached one of those epochs in the progress of a Nation, to which history
looks back, if not as decisive of its destiny, at all events as influencing it,

and as controlling its character and its conduct for a long series of years. England has advanced a pretension, which we can never submit to without dishonour. And in its enunciation she has spared our pride as little as our rights. On the 27. August 1841, she avows the determination and claims the right to search our ships; and this interpolation into the laws of nations is advanced with a coolness, which might well surprize us if any thing could surprize us in the march of human ambition. The pretension is not put forth as a debateable point to be discussed between the two Governments and to be settled in a mutual spirit of amity. But Lord Palmerston distinctly tells us, that the exemption of the vessels of the United States from search *is a doctrine to which the British Government never can nor will subscribe.* And he adds, with a rare comity indeed, that he hopes, "the day is not far distant when the Government of the United States will cease to confound two things which are in their nature entirely different; *will look to things and not to words*["] and becoming wiser from the lessons thus taught will suffer the British cruizers to search their vessels at all times and in all places and content themselves with calling it a visit! For myself I see no mutual concession, by which the parties may be brought together. A contested territory may be divided and a claim for pecuniary injury may be reduced and satisfied. But we cannot divide a great principle, one of the attributes of our independence, nor reduce the sphere of its operation. We can only demand its inviolability, with its just consequences. Under these circumstances, the first question is, if we shall yield; and that being answered in the negative, as I am satisfied, it will be by the universal feeling of the Country, the rest is, will England yield. It is our safer course to believe that she will not, and looking to her line of policy that too is our most rational course. Wherever she has planted her foot, whether on marsh, moor or mountain, under the polar circles, or under the tropics, I will not say never, that word does not belong to the deeds of man, but rarely has she voluntarily withdrawn it. Whenever she has asserted a pretension, she has adhered to it, thro' evil report and thro' good report, in prosperity and in adversity with an iron will and with a firm hand, of which the history of the world furnishes perhaps no equal example since the proudest days of the Roman Empire. In this consistency of purpose, and in the excess even of patriotism, which ministers to it, there is something noble and imposing; and I am among the last to deny the beautiful traits of the English character, or the benefits which England has rendered to the world by her example and her efforts. But she is not the less dangerous in her schemes of ambition from these redeeming considerations; and the time has come, when we must look her designs in the face, and determine to resist or to yield. War is a great evil, but there are evils greater than war, and among these is national degradation. This we have never yet experienced, and I trust we never shall. If Lord Ashburton goes out with such modified propositions, upon the various questions now pending between the two Governments, as you can honorably accept, the result will be a subject of lasting gratification to our Country. And more particularly, if, as I trust, before entering into any discussions, he is prepared to give such explanations, as will show, that we have misunderstood the intentions of the British Government, respecting this claim of a right to change the law of nations, in order to accommodate it to their Treaty stipulations, and its practical consequence, a claim to enter and search our vessels at all times and in all places. This preliminary proceeding would be worthy of the gravity of the circumstances and equally honorable to both Governments. It seems to me it is due to us. I allude to it in this connexion because the subject now necessarily presents itself to the French Government, and because I feel confident, that they are not prepared to support the pretensions of Great Britain.

We have already given one memorable example of moderation to the world, in the rejection of an unanimous application from a neighbouring people for admission into our confederacy.[4] And this too, of a Territory among the most fertile and valuable upon the face of the earth, and destined to become our rival in the production of some of our richest staple articles. When accused of ambition, we may point to this proof of self-denial, and challenge an equal instance of its exercise. It is a fact, worth volumes of professions of disinterestedness and of disclaimers of all desire of self aggrandizement.

It is not to be disguised, that the Quintuple Treaty for the suppression of the slave trade was intended to act upon the United States by its moral force. As to France and England, their co-operation in the necessary measures for the abolition of that traffic was already secured by the Treaties of 1831 & 1833;[5] and as to Prussia, Russia and Austria, I suppose neither of them ever had or ever will have a vessel engaged in that commerce. But, it was hoped, certainly by one of the parties, that this great combination would either induce the United States to follow their example, and submit themselves to the measures indicated or that it would lead to the establishment of some new principles of maritime law without them. But the subject is now so well understood, that we have little to fear from this great combination so long sought and so highly applauded. Its moral force as the "Journal des Debats" justly observes is gone.[6] The discussion

4. Texas proposed annexation to the United States in 1837 but was rebuffed. See Memucan Hunt to John Forsyth, August 4, 1837, DNA, RG 59 (Notes from Foreign Legations, Texas), and Forsyth to Hunt, August 25, 1837, DNA, RG 59 (Notes to Foreign Legations, Texas).

5. France and Great Britain signed

conventions allowing mutual search in restricted waters on November 30, 1831, and on March 22, 1833. See Jules De Clercq, ed., Recueil des traités de la France (20 vols., Paris, 1880–1900), 4:157–159, 226–233.

6. The Paris newspaper Journal des Débats Politiques et Littéraires published an editorial on February 4,

in the Chamber of Deputies and the almost unanimous condemnation of the Treaty will have indicated to you the true state of feeling here. And you will not fail to appreciate the importance of the emphatic declaration of Mr. Guizot during the debates, that the *Americans* were right and that France in the same circumstances would do the same thing. The value of this testimonial to the justice of our cause, made by such a statesman in the face of Europe can hardly be overrated.

Our true policy is to discourage all great Combinations, having for their object the regulation of maritime principles and police. European Confederations, for the regulation of European questions, do not come within the sphere of our policy, as they touch neither our rights nor our interests. But when these Powers extend their care and their jurisdiction over the ocean, I think the time has arrived for us to make ourselves heard. No Nation is more interested than we are in the freedom of commerce, and we do not advance a single pretension, which can give just cause of umbrage to any other Country. If indeed a general Congress of Nations could be assembled, where all might be represented, the weak as well as the strong, then we might fairly take our place there and recognize its decisions as obligatory. But this is a measure so doubtful in itself as well as in its consequences, that it is our interest, as it is in the interest of all people, who do not conceal any projects of aggrandizement in a professed desire to meliorate the maritime code of Nations, to adhere to that code as they find it. This adherence to the established state of things is certainly not inconsistent with any arrangement, which two Nations may be disposed to make, for a single purpose, and for a limited time, to which they may be impelled by considerations of general benevolence. Certainly, if Great Britain and the United States, choose to restrain their citizens from any traffic, condemned by moral considerations and to regulate their joint action upon the subject, they may do so without subjecting themselves to any imputations of interested or ambitious motives. Each must judge for itself whether such a combined movement is in accordance with its policy or with the nature of its institutions. Both may agree to keep squadrons upon the coast of Africa to suppress the slave trade and upon the coast of China to suppress the opium trade; branches of commerce, destructive of human life and happiness; the latter of which has the advantage of being prohibited by the Government of China, and the disadvantage, if we can credit but a small part of the statements of that Government of being far more injurious in its operation than the former. But these mutual agreements, dictated by the most charitable motives, would act merely upon the citizens of the respective Countries; executing them without overrawing others by their imposing

---

1842, criticizing England's efforts to achieve supremacy on the seas by introducing the right of visit in maritime law.

forces and without leading to the establishment of any new principle of Maritime Law.

Nothing can explain to us more clearly the danger of these great combinations, if it does not reveal the object of one or more of the parties in their establishment, than the principle, so frankly developed by Lord Aberdeen, that this "happy concurrence" creates new duties and obligations, before whose *justice and necessity*, the Law of Nations gives way, and to which the interests and independence of Nations are sacrificed. I was therefore much pleased to read in the message of the President of the United States to Congress, at the commencement of the present session,[7] his emphatic declaration, that the United States would not submit to any such pretension. The great Powers of Europe, strong or weak, must understand, if necessary, that our Country in taking her place in the family of Nations, took it with the same rights, as the greatest of them, and there will maintain it, unmoved by any Confederation, which may be formed, and wholly without the sphere of its operations.

The Quintuple Treaty has not yet been ratified by France, nor will it be, I think, without some essential alterations. It is understood that the English Government are much dissatisfied at this determination. The Queen's speech, however, at the opening of the Session,[8] and Sir Robert Peel's remarks last week in answer to a question of Lord Palmerston,[9] seem to take for granted the French ratification. But certainly, when the British Premier made those remarks, he knew the discussion in the Chamber of Deputies and the state of public opinion here, and he ought to have known, that a Constitutional Ministry would hesitate before they would incur the responsibility of such an act.

I observe that Lord Palmerston in the remarks prefatory to his question, dwells upon the *disinterestedness* of his country and of the other parties to this Treaty. This is the old topic of eulogy for England, as its reverse is intended to be of reproach for us. But its day has gone by. Europe fully understands the subject, and in public as in private life, it is not the most disinterested who are always avowing the purity of their intentions. One would think there were objects of misery enough at home to occupy the attention of any English statesman, without that excess of philanthropy which would tilt a spear at every Nation and light up the flames of a general war in order to accomplish its own charitable views in its own exclusive way, almost at the end of the world. It brings forcibly to recollection one of the vagaries of [Jean Jacques] Rousseau, that there are people, who love those who are placed at the extremeties of the earth, in order to excuse themselves for not loving their own neighbors.[10]

7. Tyler's message of December 7, 1841, is in *Messages and Papers*, 4: 74–89.

8. *Hansard's*, 60:1–3.

9. *Hansard's*, 60:145–147.

10. See Allan Bloom, ed. and trans., *Emile: Or On Education* (New York, 1979), p. 39.

In all that precedes, I believe, there is not a word, which, if need be, would not be [received] by every American citizen in Paris. We are here in the midst of stirring circumstances, and can form a safe judgement of the dangers which menace us. If England pushes her purpose into action, we shall have a severe struggle to encounter, and the sooner and the more vigorously we prepare for it the better. If she does not, we shall gain by our exhibition of firmness, and the very state of preparation may lead her to recede. But permit me to press upon you the necessity of instant and extensive arrangements for offensive and defensive war. All other questions, personal, local, and political should give way before this paramount duty. England has fearful means of aggression. No man can yet tell the effect, which the use of steam is to produce upon great warlike operations, and with her accustomed sagacity, she has accumulated a large force of steam vessels. A hostile squadron might at any time carry out to the United States, the first news of war. And it would not be a war like the last one, conducted in many cases by incompetent officers and feebly prosecuted. But she would put forth her utmost strength and she would be felt and ought to be met at every assailable point. I cannot but hope, that the excellent suggestions of the Secretaries of War [John Canfield Spencer] and of the Navy [Abel Parker Upshur] respecting National defence may find general support.[11]

You may naturally think that this is not a very diplomatic despatch. It is not so certainly, so far as diplomacy consists in mystery either of thought or expression. I have felt strongly and I have attempted to speak plainly. I do not belong to the school of that well known French statesman, who said, that language was given to conceal thoughts.[12] If necessary I must claim your indulgence for my candor in consideration of my motives. I see the difficult position of my country and most anxious am I, that it should be seen and appreciated at home. That done, I have no fear for the result. If the sentiments I have expressed are not those of the Government and People of my Country, then I have lived a stirring life, and mixed with my countrymen in every situation, without having learned the American character.

You will perceive, that in my letter to Mr Guizot, I have taken upon myself the responsibility of my interposition. Your course is perfectly free to avow or to disavow my conduct. The President will decide as the public interest requires. I do not shut my eyes to the gravity of the cir-

11. The annual reports of Secretary of War Spencer of December 1, 1841, and of Secretary of the Navy Upshur of December 4, 1841, are in *Senate Documents*, 27th Cong., 2d sess., Serial 395, No. 1, pp. 59–75 and pp. 367–389.

12. In the dialogue between the capon and the poularde, by Voltaire, née François Marie Arouet (1694–1778), the capon remarks that men "n'emploient les paroles que pour déguiser leurs pensées." *Dialogues satiriques & philosophiques* (Paris, 1890), p. 18.

cumstances in which I am placed. In the unforeseen emergency, which presented itself, I have pursued the course, that appeared to me to be dictated by the honor and interest of our Country, and I have the satisfaction to believe, that my measures will not be wholly without beneficial results. It is now for the Government to judge what is its own duty, and to determine whether my conduct shall be approved or disapproved. I am, Sir, very respectfully Your obedient servant, (Signed) Lew Cass

Copy. DNA, RG 59 (Despatches, France). Rec'd April 1842.

ENCLOSURE: LEWIS CASS TO FRANÇOIS PIERRE GUILLAUME GUIZOT

Legation of the United States,
Sir,   Paris, 13th February, 1842.
    The recent signature of a treaty, having for its object the suppression of the African slave trade, by five of the powers of Europe, and to which France is a party, is a fact of such general notoriety that it may be assumed as the basis of any diplomatic representations which the subject may fairly require.

    The United States, being no parties to this Treaty, have no right to enquire into the circumstances which have led to it, nor into the measures it proposes to adopt, except so far as they have reason to believe that their interests may be involved in the course of its execution. Their own desire to put a stop to this traffic is every where known, as well as the early and continued efforts they have adopted to prevent their citizens from prosecuting it. They have been invited by the government of England to become a party to a treaty, which should regulate the action of the combined governments upon this subject. But for reasons satisfactory to themselves, and I believe satisfactory to the world, they have declined this united action, and have chosen to pursue their own measures, and to act upon their own citizens only, without subjecting these to any kind of foreign jurisdiction.

    In a communication from Lord Palmerston, Her Britannic Majesty's Principal Secretary of State for Foreign Affairs, to Mr. [Andrew] Stevenson, the American Minister at London, dated 27th. August 1841,[1] Lord Palmerston claims a right for the British cruizers, and avows the intention of the government to exercise it, to search American vessels at sea in time of peace, with a view to ascertain their national character. He adds that "this examination of papers of merchant-men, suspected of being engaged in the slave trade, even tho' they hoist an United States' flag, is a proceeding, which it is absolutely necessary that British cruizers employed in the suppression of the slave trade should continue to practise" &c. &c.

    1. Palmerston to Stevenson, August 27, 1841, enclosed in No. 132. Stevenson to DW, September 18, 1841, DNA, RG 59 (Despatches, Britain).

In a communication from the successor of Lord Palmerston, Lord Aberdeen, to Mr Stevenson, dated 13th October 1841,[2] the views and determination announced in the first are confirmed, and Lord Aberdeen thus states the ground upon which rests this pretension to search American vessels in time of peace. "But the undersigned must observe that the present happy concurrence of the States of Christendom in this great object (the suppression of the slave trade) not merely justifies but renders indispensable the right now claimed and exercised by the British government;" that is to say, the right of entering and examining American vessels to ascertain their true nationality.

It is no part of my duty to offer any comments upon these pretensions nor upon the reasons advanced to support them. And if it were I shou'd find the duty far better performed for me, than I could perform it for myself, in the annual message of the President of the United States to Congress of 7. December 1841.[3] In that document will be found the views of the American government upon this subject, and it is there emphatically declared that, "However desirous the United States may be for the suppression of the slave trade, they cannot consent to interpolations into the maritime code at the mere will and pleasure of other governments. We deny the right of any such interpolation to any one, or all the nations of the earth, without our consent. We claim to have a voice in all amendments or alterations of that code; and when we are given to understand, as in this instance, by a foreign government, that its treaties with other nations cannot be executed without the establishment and enforcement of new principles of maritime police, to be applied without our consent, we must employ a language neither of equivocal import, or susceptible of misconstruction."

You will perceive, Sir, by these extracts that the British Government has advanced a pretension which it asserts to be indispensable to the execution of its treaties for the suppression of the slave trade, and to which the President of the United States has declared that the American government will not submit. This claim of search, it will be observed, has relation to the isolated Treaties for the abolition of this traffic, which existed at the date of the communications of Lord Palmerston and Lord Aberdeen.[4] It is now known, that the combined treaty upon this subject is more extensive in its operations, more minute in some of the details of its execution, and longer in the duration of its obligations, than the sep-

---

2. Aberdeen to Stevenson, October 13, 1841, enclosed in No. 134. Stevenson to DW, October 22, 1841, DNA, RG 59 (Despatches, Britain).

3. *Messages and Papers*, 4:74–89.

4. This refers to the anti–slave trade treaties between France and Great Britain of November 30, 1831, and March 22, 1833, in Clive Parry, ed., *Consolidated Treaty Series* (165 vols., New York, 1969–   ), 82:272–275; 83:260–275.

arate treaties with France which preceeded it. Of course measures which were not only "justifiable but indispensable" for the execution of the latter will find an equal justice and necessity in the obligations of the former.

With this previous declaration made by one of the parties to this quintuple treaty concerning its operations the United States cannot shut their eyes to their true position. The moral effect, which such a union of five great powers, two of which are eminently maritime, and three of which have perhaps never had a vessel engaged in that traffic, is calculated to produce upon the United States, and upon other nations who like them may be indisposed to these combined movements, though it may be regretted, yet furnishes no just cause of complaint. But the subject assumes another aspect when they are told by one of the parties that their vessels are to be forcibly entered and examined in order to carry into effect these stipulations. Certainly the American government does not believe, that the high powers, contracting parties to this treaty have any wish to compel the United States by force to adopt their measures to the provisions of this treaty or to adopt its stipulations. They have too much confidence in their sense of justice to fear any such result; and they will see with pleasure the prompt disavowal made by yourself, Sir, in the name of your country, at the tribune of the Chamber of Deputies of any intentions of this nature.[5] But were it otherwise, and were it possible they might be deceived in their confident expectations, that would not alter one tittle their course of action. Their duty would be the same, and the same would be their determination to fulfil it. They would prepare themselves with apprehension indeed, but without dismay, with regret but with firmness for one of those desperate struggles which have sometimes occurred in the history of the world, but where a just cause, and the favor of Providence have given strength to comparative weakness and broken down the pride of power.

But I have already said the United States do not fear, that any such united attempt will be made upon their independence. What however they may reasonably fear, and what they do fear, is, that in the execution of this treaty, measures will be taken which they must resist. How far the acts of one of the parties putting its construction upon its own duties and upon the obligations of its co-contractors may involve these in the consequences either of compliance or of refusal, I do not presume to judge. But I may express the hope, that the government of His Majesty before ratifying the treaty will examine maturely the pretensions asserted by one of the parties, and see how these can be reconciled not only with the

5. Reported in the Paris *Journal des Débats Politiques et Littéraires,*   January 25, 1842.

honor and interest of the United States, but with the received principles
of the great Maritime Code of Nations. I may make this appeal with the
more confidence from the relations subsisting between France and the
United States. From a community of interest in the liberty of the seas;
from a community of opinion respecting the principles which guard it;
and from a community in danger should it ever be menaced by the ambition of any maritime power.

It appears to me, Sir, that in asking the attention of His Majesty's Government to the subject of the quintuple treaty, with a view to its reconsideration, I am requesting nothing on the part of the United States
inconsistent with the duties of France to other powers. If during the
course of the discussions upon this treaty, preparatory to the arrange·
ment of its provisions, England has asserted the pretension she now asserts, as a necessary consequence of its obligations, I cannot be wrong in
presuming, that France would not have signed it without guarding
against this impending difficulty. The views of England have become
known, since the signature of the treaty; but fortunately before its ratification. And this change of circumstances may well justify the French
government in interposing such a remedy, as it may think is demanded
by the grave interests involved in this question.

As to the treaties of 1831 and 1833 between France and Great Britain,
for the suppression of the slave trade, I do not consider it my duty to
advert to their stipulations. Their obligations upon the contracting parties, whatever these may be, are now complete; and it is for my government alone to determine what measures the United States ought to take
to avert the consequences with which they are threatened by the construction, which one of the parties has given to these instruments.

I have the honor to transmit, herewith, a copy of the message of the
President of the United States to Congress in December last and of the
annual documents which accompanied it.[6] Among the latter will be
found the correspondence between the British Secretaries of State and
Mr Stevenson upon the subject herein referred to. From these you will
learn the respective views of the American and British Governments.

It is proper for me to add that this communication has been made without an instructions from the United States. I have considered this case
as one of those in which an American representative to a foreign power
should act without awaiting the orders of his Government. I have presumed in the views I have submitted to you, that I express the feelings of
the American government and people. If in this I have deceived myself
the responsibility will be mine. My government will not be committed
and can adopt its course without reference to my interposition. As soon
as I can receive despatches from the United States in answer to my com-

6. See *Senate Documents*, 27th Cong., 2d sess., Serial 395, No. 1.

munication I shall be enabled to declare to you either that my views are those of the President or that my mission is terminated. I avail myself &c.

(signed) Lew Cass

Copy. DNA, RG 59 (Despatches, France). Published in William T. Young, *Sketch of the Life and Public Services of General Lewis Cass . . .* (Detroit, 1852), pp. 166–170.

FROM JARED SPARKS

Private

Dear Sir,   Cambridge, Feby, 15th 1842

I have deliberated for some time on the propriety of communicating to you the substance of this letter, but at length, believing it important that you should possess a knowledge of all the facts respecting the subject to which it alludes, I have concluded to waive the scruples that have hitherto operated on my mind.

While pursuing my researches among the voluminous papers relating to the American Revolution in the *Archives des Affaires Etrangères* in Paris,[1] I found in one of the bound volumes an original letter from Dr. [Benjamin] Franklin[2] to Count [Charles Gravier] de Vergennes,[3] of which the following is an exact transcript.

"Passy, 6 Dec. 1782

Sir,

I have the honor of returning herewith the map your Excellency sent me yesterday. I have marked with a strong red line, according to your desire, the limits of the United States as settled in the preliminaries between the British & American plenipotentiaries. With great respect, I am, &c.   B. Franklin."

This letter was written six days after the preliminaries were signed,[4] and if we could procure the identical map, mentioned by Franklin, it would seem to afford conclusive evidence as to the meaning affixed by the commissioners to the language of the Treaty on the subject of the boundaries. You may well suppose, that I lost no time in making inquiry for the map, not doubting that it would confirm all my previous opinions respecting the validity of our claim. In the geographical department of

1. Sparks spent the time from August 1840 through January 1841 doing research in the archives of London and Paris for a projected history of the American Revolution.

2. Franklin (1706–1790) went to France as a commissioner in 1776. He became the U.S. representative at Paris in September 1778 and was named one of the peace commissioners on June 8, 1781.

3. Vergennes (1717–1787) served as the French foreign minister from 1774 to 1787.

4. The boundary is discussed in Article 2 of the preliminary peace settlement of November 30, 1782. *Treaties,* 2:96–107.

the Archives are sixty thousand maps & charts, but so well arranged, with catalogues & indexes, that any one of them may be easily found. After a little research in the American division, with the aid of the keeper, I came upon a map of North America by [Jean-Baptiste Bourguignon] D'Anville, dated 1746,[5] in size about eighteen inches square, on which was drawn a *strong red-line* throughout the entire boundary of the United States, answering precisely to Franklin's description. The line is bold & distinct in every part, made with red ink, and apparently drawn with a hair pencil, or a pen with a blunt point. There is no other coloring on any part of the map.

Imagine my surprise on discovering, that this line runs wholly south of the St. John's, and between the head waters of that river and those of the Penobscot & Kennebec. In short, it is exactly the line now contended for by Great Britain, except that it concedes more than is claimed. The north line, after departing from the source of the St. Croix, instead of proceeding to Mars Hill, stops far short of that point, and turns off to the west, so as to leave on the British side all the streams which flow into the St. John's between the source of the St. Croix & Mars Hill. It is evident, that the line, from the St. Croix to the Canadian highlands, is inte[n]ded to exclude *all the waters* running into the St. John's.

There is no positive proof, that this map is actually the one marked by Franklin, yet, upon any other supposition, it would be difficult to explain the circumstances of its agreeing so perfectly with his description, and of its being preserved in the place where it would naturally be deposited by Count de Vergennes. I also found another map in the Archives, on which the same boundary was traced in a dotted red line with a pen; apparently copied from the other.

I enclose herewith a map of Maine, on which I have drawn a strong black line corresponding with the red one above mentioned.[6]

I also enclose the copy of a paper, which is curious as showing the views of some of the members of Congress, towards the close of the war, respecting the boundaries. It is a transcript from the original in the handwriting of Gouverneur Morris.[7] The paper seems to have been designed as an additional instruction to the Commissioners, and was probably written in the year 1781. There is no notice of it in the journals, and, from its contents, no one can wonder that it was not adopted. In the

5. D'Anville (1697–1782) was a famed French cartographer.

6. Jared Sparks's map of Maine, not printed here, is reproduced in Howard Jones, *To the Webster-Ashburton Treaty: A Study in Anglo-American Relations, 1783–1843* (Chapel Hill, N.C., 1977), p. 105.

7. Not printed here. In the undated transcript, Morris (1752–1816; King's College 1768), who was a member of the Continental Congress from 1778 to 1779, wrote that since the eastern boundary of Maine "has never yet been ascertained, we conceive it to be open to negotiation; but not so as to be carried westward farther than the river of Kennebeck."

minds of some at that time, it may be presumed, the necessity of a peace was so great, that it was thought the question of boundaries ought not to be an obstacle. Morris drafted the first instructions on the subject of boundaries, as contained in the Secret Journals for August 14th 1779.[8]

In the British offices I have read, with special care, all the correspondence of the British Commissioners with the ministry during the negotiation of the French & American treaties,[9] which contains minute details of the conversations on every point that came under discussion. Much is of course said about the north eastern boundary. The commissioner for the American treaty first took his stand at the Kennebec, but soon retired to the Penobscot, where he maintained an obstinate defence for some time, when he retreated very reluctantly to the St. Croix. In all these discussions, however, not much light is thrown upon the difficulty now at issue. The inferences from the whole are clearly in our favor, but there is little positive or direct testimony; for the obvious reason, perhaps, that the commissioners were talking of a line which had never been surveyed, and of angles & highlands which had neither been fixed nor ascertained by observation.

In April, 1790, Dr. Franklin sent to Mr. [Thomas] Jefferson, then secretary of State, that part of [John] Mitchell's map containing the eastern boundary as marked by himself. He died a few days afterward. Is that map now in the Department of State? If so, it cannot fail to contain important matter.

The whole weight of the controversy raised at the treaty of Ghent,[10] and since continued, rests on the single question of the north line crossing or not crossing the St. John's. Upon this point there could not possibly be any doubt in the minds of the commissioners whatever obscurity there may have been in regard to the actual position of the line in other parts; and it certainly is strange, that neither Mr. [John] Jay nor Mr. John Adams,[11] who lived several years after the controversy began to be agi-

8. Worthington Chauncey Ford, ed., *Journals of the Continental Congress, 1774–1789* (34 vols., Washington, D.C., 1904–1937), 14:955–966.

9. Richard Oswald (1705–1784), a London merchant, was the British commissioner dealing with the Americans. Oswald signed the preliminary treaty of November 30, 1782, but was replaced by David Hartley (1732–1813), a member of Parliament, before the definitive treaty of September 3, 1783, was signed. The British commissioners for negotiations with France were Thomas Grenville (1755–1846) and Alleyne Fitzherbert (1753–

1839). The treaties with the United States are in *Treaties*, 2:96–107 and 151–157. The preliminary and conclusive treaties between Britain and France are in Frances Gardiner Davenport and Charles Oscar Paullin, eds., *European Treaties Bearing on the History of the United States and Its Dependencies, 1716–1815* (4 vols., Washington, D.C., 1937), 4:147–149, 152–154.

10. *Treaties*, 2:574–584.

11. Jay (1745–1829; King's College 1764) and Adams (1735–1826; Harvard 1755) were American peace commissioners in association with

tated, should not have expressed and left on record, some decided opinion. This forbearance, on their part, to say the least, is suspicious.

One thing, however, is clear. The British arguments, as far as they have been carried, are equally defective in consistency & proof. Their appeals to history & ancient records leave us, at last, in a wilderness of conjecture. Confirmations, drawn from these sources, are much more favorable to the American claim than to the English; and yet, whoever reads all that has been written on the subject by both parties will find himself a good deal more perplexed and unsettled, as to the real intentions of the commissioners, than he would be by endeavoring to understand, without comment, the simple words of the treaty. The British construction, proved by maps issued under authority, and acquiesced in by Parliament while the treaty was under discussion, and while Mr. [Richard] Oswald was living, is our strongest argument, and one which has neither been answered nor weakened by the labored statements on the other side.

But I did not intend to proffer opinions when I began this letter. I only meant to communicate a scrap of information, which is curious, if not valuable. I trust you will excuse the liberty I have taken, and accept the assurance of the sincere respect & regard of your most obt St

Jared Sparks

ALS. DNA, RG 59 (Misc. Letters). Rec'd February 21, 1842. Published in Herbert B. Adams, *The Life and Writings of Jared Sparks* (2 vols., Boston, 1893), 2:394–399. Sparks (1789–1866; Harvard, 1815), a professor of history at Harvard from 1839 to 1849, was a prolific editor. His works included a twelve-volume edition of *The Diplomatic Correspondence of the American Revolution* (Boston, 1829–1830).

FROM PELEG SPRAGUE

Private

Dear Sir   Boston Feb 17 1842.

I have received two communications from a distinguished and influential member of the Whig party in Maine relative to the North Eastern boundary question.[1] He says that there are many of both political parties who are now disposed to listen to a proposition for a compromise—but that the State must continue to maintain her present position and insist on her strict rights, until a proposal shall be made to her. I infer from his letters and other information that leading political gentlemen of both parties are unwilling to commit themselves by expressing their views of a compromise in a manner which may be brought before the public and expose them to attack from rivals and opponents. In this posture of affairs

Franklin and Henry Laurens (1724–   1. Not found.
1792).

I have been requested to become a medium of communication between them and yourself—and as, from my present position—aloof from the politics of the day—and my former associations—and some knowledge of the matter in controversy, it is suggested that my agency may be useful[.] I have not thought myself at liberty to refuse.

The Land Agent of Maine Elijah H. [L.] Hamlen [Hamlin] Esqr in his report to the present Legislature has recommended that they should assent to "the settlement of a new boundary line upon reciprocal terms"—and he suggests that we should cede to Great Britian—"The territory north of the St. John above the grand falls or that portion of it lying North and East of the British mail line of communication between the Provinces—["] for "an equivalent in the cession of contiguous territory, the navigation of the St. John and such other recompense as shall be considered equitable and just."[2] These suggestions I am informed have been published in all the Maine news papers[3] without comment—and I am assured that they meet with general approbation.

They are cautiously expressed as to the equivalent as must naturally be expected—but the silent acquiescence with which they are received is of no little importance as evidence that the public mind is prepared upon some considerations to relinquish the strict right to the treaty line—thus leaving the only question to be the terms on which the new boundary shall be established.

Mr. Hamlin in a former part of his report says that it is important to Maine to possess some right in the navigation of the St. John's river, and that she should own the narrow strip of land on the West side of the St. John's river, which embraces the mouths of certain rivers.

My communications from Maine refer to the Land Agents report as a basis of negotiation without presenting any more definite terms. From the information which I possess I believe that many of the leading politicians in the Legislature and the public mind generally in Maine are more disposed to an adjustment of this controversy now than at any time heretofore.

I trust that I need not apologise for making this communication. Nothing but the importance of the subject has induced me to yield to the request of our friends in Maine at a time when I am so much pressed by official labors in consequence of the Bankrupt Law. With profound respect I am yours—   Peleg Sprague

LS. NhHi. Sprague (1793–1880; Harvard 1812), a Kennebec, Maine, lawyer, was a state representative, 1821–1822, a U.S. representative, 1825–1829, and a U.S. senator, 1829–1835. After resigning from the Senate, he opened a law

2. *Report of the Land Agent of the State of Maine, December 31, 1841* (Augusta, Me., 1841), pp. 22–23.

3. See, for example, the Portland *Advertiser*, January 11, 1842.

practice in Boston and served as U.S. district judge for Massachusetts from 1841 to 1865.

TO REUEL WILLIAMS

private & confidential
My dear Sir   Washington Feb 18 1842
Your letter of 12 was recd yesterday.[1] The disposition which appears to animate Govr [John] Fairfield & the other Gentlemen with whom you conferred is such as to give hope, I think, of favorable results. Nothing is more earnestly desired by the President than to terminate the boundary controversy in a manner honorable, satisfactory & useful to Maine & to the whole country.

You remark that it is suggested by some "that altho Great Britain has heretofore proposed to treat for a conventional line, it is not known that Lord Ashburton will be so instructed, & that if Maine should authorise commissioners to consider & agree upon a conventional line & its terms, & then learn that no such line or terms were to be proposed by England Maine would then be placed where no American could wish to see her placed." I have no further information to give respecting Lord Ashburtons instructions. All we know is that Lord Aberdeen informed Mr [Edward] Everett that Lord Ashburton would be clothed with full powers[2] to discuss & definitely settle all questions pending between the two governments.

I have no doubt whatever that his instructions will give him the fullest authority to agree on a conventional line. But if Governor Fairfield & other Gentlemen think that more positive assurance on that point is necessary before any step be taken by Maine, then of course nothing can be done before the Ministers arrival. It may be proper to take this view of the subject & it would not become me to make any objection altho for my own part I should have preferred that a different view might have been taken.

I regret that Gov Fairfield & his friends should be of opinion that any points of honor & consistency on the part of the Legislature are in the way of arriving at what might be satisfactory to both countries. It is true that Maine is confident of the justice & validity of her claim & certainly I think this is a well founded confidence. But it is equally true that England has evinced, on her side, no less confidence. Maine thinks that England has interposed an unwarrantable claim to a portion of her Territory & the Govt of the U.S. thinks that Maine in this opinion is entirely right, but England on the other side asserts that the U.S. & Maine have

1. See above, Williams to DW, February 12, 1842.
2. See above, Everett to DW, December 31, 1841, "The Crisis in Anglo-American Relations," pp. 173–177.

interposed an unwarrantable claim to a portion of her territory & these conflicting opinions & assertions of right must be in some way settled & adjusted. It is true that England occupies or protects a part of the disputed territory by an armed force; but it is equally true that the U. S. occupy & protect another part by an armed force also—and this last force was placed in position at the request of the Governor of Maine. Indeed if I remember correctly Maine asserted in the year 1839 that the question of possession should remain as it then stood, that is that Great Britain should hold one part, Maine not acknowledging her right, & that Maine should hold another part, England not acknowledging her right.[3]

The spirit & general principle of this understanding between Maine & the Govt of New Brunswick has governed the conduct of the Govt of U.S. in all subsequent measures respecting the possession of the disputed territory, the principal alteration, that of substituting U. S. troops for the force of Maine, having been adopted, as I have already said, at the request of Maine. I make this remark, my dear Sir, with no other view than that of expressing the hope, that on more reflection & upon full consideration of all the circumstances, the Government of Maine may not find any obstacle, founded on considerations of honor & consistency, from concurring in the manner suggested in my letter,[4] in a proceeding having in view the establishment of a conventional line, if the British Minister should in fact bring with him proper authority for such a purpose. I am &c

Copy. DLC. ALS draft published in Van Tyne, pp. 260–261.

FROM TILGHMAN MAYFIELD TUCKER

[February 26, 1842]

RESOULUTIONS OF THE LEGISLATURE OF THE STATE OF MISSIS-
SIPPI IN REFERENCE TO THE RIGHT OF SEARCH, AND THE CASE
OF THE AMERICAN BRIG CREOLE.[1]

WHEREAS, the right of search has never been yielded to Great Britain by any treaty stipulations, but hath constantly been denied and resisted; and whereas, many signal examples of aggression upon the immunities of our free flag have of late especially directed the attention of the country to the claim and exercise of a right of search by the British Government, a pretension so justly odious to a liberty-loving people; and where-

3. General Winfield Scott's proposal of March 21, 1839, and Fairfield's acceptance of March 25, 1839, are in the manuscript correspondence relating to the boundary, part 4, at the Maine State Library in Augusta.

4. See above, DW to Williams, February 2, 1842.

1. *Laws of the State of Mississippi* . . . (Jackson, Miss., 1842), pp. 249–252.

as, the minister of Great Britain has recently disclaimed the right in express terms, while he insidiously, and under false pretences, insists upon its exercise;[2] and that would enforce a power usurped by his Government to detain and examine vessels bearing our banner: and whereas, within a few months past, the American brig Creole, on her outward passage to New Orleans, transporting a cargo of slaves, the property of citizens of the United States, shipped thither from Virginia, was, by the insurrectionory crimes of some of these slaves, seized, and the crew forcibly compelled to navigate the said brig into a port of a British West India Island: and whereas, it is evident that the hope of freedom held out by the doctrine of universal emancipation, now apparently so acceptable to the rulers and ruled of Great Britain, certainly stirred up these rebellious slaves to mutiny and murder, and sped their flight to British soil; and whereas, the criminals have not been yielded up to the American consul nor the other slaves to any rightful claimants, but these last have been recognized as passengers and freemen, having free ingress and egress to and from the possessions of the British crown; and whereas, this Creole case particularly affects the property institutions of the south: therefore,

1. *Be it resolved by the Legislature of the State of Mississippi,* That it is the deliberate opinion of the State that the right of search cannot be conceded to Great Britain without a manifest servile submission, unworthy a free nation. That its exercise cannot be permitted, without as well a sacrifice of national independence as a prostration of that personal liberty guaranteed by the Constitution to every citizen of the Republic. And, therefore, our Government should require a complete and entire abandonment of such claim by the British authorities, henceforth and forever.

2. *Resolved,* That any attempt to detain and search our vessels, by British cruisers, should be held and esteemed an unjustifiable outrage on the part of the Queen's Government; and that any such outrage which may have occurred since Lord Aberdeen's note to our envoy at the Court of St. James, of date October thirteenth, eighteen hundred and forty-one, (if any) may well be deemed, by our Government, just cause of war.

3. *Resolved,* That the Legislature of the State, in view of the late murderous insurrection of the slaves on board the Creole, their reception in a British port, the absolute connivance at their crimes, manifest in the protection extended to them by the British authorities, most solemnly declare their firm conviction that if the conduct of those authorities be submitted to, compounded for by the payment of money, or in any other manner, or atoned for in any mode except by the surrender of the actual

---

2. The reference is to Foreign Minister Aberdeen's note of October 13, 1841, disclaiming a right of search but maintaining a right to visit in order to examine a ship's papers.

Aberdeen to Andrew Stevenson, October 13, 1841, enclosed in No. 132. Stevenson to DW, October 22, 1841, DNA, RG 59 (Despatches, Britain).

criminals to the Federal Government, and the delivery of the other identical slaves to their rightful owner or owners, or his or their agents, the slaveholding States would have most just cause to apprehend that the American flag is powerless to protect American property: that the Federal Government is not sufficiently energetic in the maintenance and preservation of their peculiar rights, and that these rights, therefore, are in imminent danger.

4. *Resolved,* That the restitution of the slave property, spoken of in the preceding resolve, and the surrender of the criminals ought to be imperatively demanded of the British authorities; that such demand should be enforced at all hazards, and that it should never be suffered to slumber, nor, for a moment, be relinquished.

5. *Resolved,* That his Excellency, the Governor [Tilghman Mayfield Tucker], be requested to transmit a copy of the foregoing preamble and resolutions to each of our Senators and Representatives in Congress.

ROBERT W[hyte] ROBERTS,[3]

Speaker of the House of Representatives.

J[esse] SPEIGHT,[4]

President of the Senate.

Approved February 26, 1842.

T. M. Tucker

I, LEWIS G. GALLAWAY, Secretary of State of the State of Mississippi,[5] do hereby certify that the foregoing resolutions of the Legislature of the State of Mississippi, in reference to the right of search, and the case of the American brig Creole, approved February 26, 1842, is a just and true copy of the original act filed in my office.

Given under my hand and seal [of] office, this the 15th day of March, 1842.

LEWIS G. GALLAWAY, Secretary of State.

Printed Document. DNA, RG 59 (Misc. Letters). Rec'd April 25, 1842. Endorsed: "With the respects of T. M. Tucker." Tucker (1802–1859), a lawyer and plantation owner, was governor of Mississippi, 1841–1843. He had earlier served in the Mississippi state house and senate from 1831 to 1841. Tucker represented Mississippi in the U.S. Congress as a Democrat, 1843–1845.

3. Roberts (1784–1865), a lawyer and a county judge, was a member of the state legislature from 1838 to 1844. He served in the U.S. Congress as a Democrat, 1843–1847.

4. Speight (1795–1847) represented North Carolina in the U.S. Congress from 1829 to 1837, before moving to Mississippi. Speight was a member, and president of, the Mississippi state senate, 1841–1844. He was a member of the U.S. Senate from 1845 until his death on May 1, 1847.

5. Not further identified.

FROM LOT CLARK

Dear Sir   Lockport N.Y. March 1st 1842

I have but a moment to inform you that a citizen of Hamilton in U[pper] Canada by the name of [John Sheridan] Hogan[1] (I forget his Christian name) is now under arrest and before one of our magistrates on a charge of being in the expedition that captured & burned the Caroline.

As there were no specific facts sworn to, that identified him in the affair, I had hoped that we should be able to induce the magistrate to discharge him; & thus rid the country of a most unpleasant affair.

The examination has been adjourned until morning. Since that time I have ascertained that a witness will be brought in the morning to swear positively to his acknowledgement that he was engaged in the expedition & that his name was the third on the list.

A Writ of Habeas Corpus is being made out to remove the examination before the First Judge of the County Court[2] who is a lawyer [&] a man of enlightened views. But what can he do under the *unfortunate* decision of our supreme court,[3] if Hogan is identified in the affair, he must commit him for trial; and I greatly fear that this result cannot be avoided.

Hogan is a young man about 26 years [old] of good address, is intelligent & seems not much agitated. He was secretary during the trouble in Canada to Sir Allen McNabb [MacNab], & says he was active at that time, was in Buffalo to obtain information at the time of cutting out the Caroline from that port.

I shall do all in my power to prevent his detention, as will nearly all of our more respectable Citizens, nevertheless I have but li[ttle] hope of success.

There is no excitement here, & there would be no difficulty if our state authorities had not put us in a false position.

I have told Hogan if the magistrate, or the Judge should order him committed I would [bail] him if his friends in Canada would indemnify [me]. I would do it without but for the fact that he is [a] stranger, & I know nothing of him.

His impression is that the Canada Authorities will do nothing further by way of bailing him than to demand his release.

I give you this early information of the facts as far as they have progressed, & will keep you advised as they progress.

1. Hogan (1815–1859) was born in Ireland and arrived about 1827 in Canada, where he became a journalist. He was murdered by bandits in 1859.

2. Elias Ransom (1795–1863) was the first judge of the Niagara County Court, 1841–1846.

3. The New York State supreme court had denied a writ of habeas corpus in the McLeod case in July 1841. See above, Spencer to DW, July 12, 1841, "The Crisis in Anglo-American Relations," p. 98.

The feeling of a very great majority here is as it should be on this subject; but it is I fear to be unavailing for the present. Mo Respectfully Your Obt St   Lot Clark

P.S. I have but little doubt they will in the end prove Hogan to have been in the Caroline expedition, & I do not believe *he* can prove an Alibi &c.

ALS. DNA, RG 59 (Misc. Letters). Rec'd March 8, 1842. Clark (1788–1862), a Lockport attorney and businessman, had been a Niagara County district attorney, 1822–1823 and 1828–1836, and a Whig congressman, 1823–1825.

FROM LOT CLARK

10 0. PM

Dear Sir,   Lockport Mar. 2, 1842.

I told you in my letter written last evening[1] that [John Sheridan] Hogan would be brought before the first Judge of the Co. Court [Elias Ransom] this morning on Habeas Corpus. It has been done & the Judge has just discharged him because of the insufficiency of the warrant. No examination has been had of course.

He may be arrested again before he reaches the Canada lines, tho I am in hopes he will not. Public opinion has set in very much against the arrest. It is not believed by those who would be most likely to disturb him, that he was in the expedition.

If he should be taken again, I think they will know enough to hold him to trial.

You will readily see how important it is that there should be legislation by Congress authorising the removal of such cases to the U. S. Court. When such a law passes we shall have quiet & not before. Your obt st

Lot Clark.

ALS. DNA, RG 59 (Misc. Letters). Rec'd March 9, 1842.

TO JARED SPARKS

Private   Department of State,
My Dear Sir: Washington, 4th March 1842.

I have received, and thank you for, your confidential letter of the 15th ultimo,[1] with its enclosures. I happened to make a discovery too much like this, three years ago, of the particulars of which I will give you information on another occasion.[2] Very truly yours,   Danl Webster

LS. MH-H.

1. See above.
1. See above, Sparks to DW, February 15, 1842.
2. In 1838 DW purchased a 1775

edition of John Mitchell's map, which had belonged to the Revolutionary general Friedrich Wilhelm Augustin von Steuben (1730–1794). The docu-

TO WALTER FORWARD

Department of State
Sir,   Washington 14th March 1842
    The British frigate Warspite, having on board His Excellency the Right
Hon. Lord Ashburton, Envoy Extraordinary and Minister Plenipotentiary
from the Court of Great Britain to the Government of the United States, is
expected to arrive very shortly either at New York, Annapolis or Norfolk.
    I have therefore to request, by the President's direction, that you will
give immediate instructions to the Collectors of these ports, respectively,
that on his Lordship's arrival at either of them, the most prompt attention be paid to the immediate landing of his baggage and effects, and
those of his suite, without the charge of duties of course, and also without search or examination, and that such information and aid be given
him as may enable him to transmit such baggage and effects in the most
convenient and speedy manner to this city. I have the honor
                                                                Danl Webster

LC. DNA, RG 59 (Domestic Letters).

TO JOSEPH STORY

Private
Dear Sir: Washington Mar: 17 [1842]
    You will have read the debate in the House of Lords on the Creole sub-
ject, and see that the learned Lords who spoke on that occasion have
quite missed the point.[1] We have not considered as fugitives from justice
either the slaves who were concerned in the mutiny, or those who were
not, and therefore have made no demand for the delivery up of either. I
look upon it that the British Government should have delivered the mutineers to the American Consul [John F. Bacon] to be sent home. I did not
choose to demand it, because I did not wish by making such a demand to
weaken our claim for compensation for the rest of the slaves. I now desire

ment was marked, possibly by John
Jay, with a line along the northeastern boundary that corresponded to
the British claim. DW sold the map
to Charles Stewart Daveis (1788–
1865; Bowdoin 1807), an agent of
Maine in Washington. Sometime in
1842, DW repurchased the Steuben
map from Daveis for the Department
of State, and Jared Sparks used this
map in his confidential mission to
Maine in May to persuade the state's
political leaders to accept participation in a negotiation for a compro-

mise line. See John W. Mulligan to
DW, July 13, 1838, mDW 55415;
and DW's notes on charges made by
Charles Jared Ingersoll, [April 1846],
mDW 26869.
    1. On February 14, 1842, several
peers discussed the *Creole* case, all
agreeing that in the absence of a
treaty or municipal legislation the
British government lacked legal authority to deliver the escaped slaves
to the United States. *Hansard's*, 60:
317–327.

to make a strong case against England on the subject of procuring indemnification for the pirates and murderers. I want to know

First, whether the law of nations does not make a difference between the case of ordinary fugitives from justice, and the case of persons committing offences on the high seas.

Second, What cases you recollect of sending home persons of the last description for trial, and particularly what you remember of the case of the Plattsburg.[2] Yrs truly   Danl Webster

L S. MHi. Published in *W & S*, 16:363–364.

FROM JOSEPH STORY

Dear Sir,   Cambridge March 26. 1842.

Accidental circumstances have prevented me from before answering your letter of the 17th. instant.[1] I now do it with great pleasure.

The first part of your Inquiry is whether the Law of Nations does not make a difference between the case of ordinary fugitives from justice and the case of persons committing offences upon the high seas. I am not aware that any such distinction has ever been made theoretically, or even practically, except so far as Piracy (which I will presently consider) may be supposed to constitute an exception. Offences committed on the high seas are exclusively cognisable by the Courts of the Nations, to which the ships, on board of which they have been committed, belong. Such ships are treated as being subject to the municipal laws of their own country, and to none others. No other nation has any right, or duty to take cognisance of, or to punish such offences. And on this account, as the offences are merely municipal, no distinction has been taken between fugitives from justice, violating municipal laws, on the ocean, and those violating those laws on land. This subject was a good deal considered in the case of the U.S. v Palmer (3 Wheat: R. 610) and U.S: v. Klintock (5 Wheat: R. 144) and U.S: v Furlong (5 Wheat: R. 184.).[2]

But wherever the Crew of a Ship of any nation have usurped the com-

2. The *Plattsburg*, of Baltimore, sailed for Trieste in July 1816 with a cargo of coffee and 42,000 Spanish dollars. Midway across the Atlantic, the crew murdered the captain, first mate, and supercargo and sailed the ship to Norway. When their free spending attracted the attention of authorities, the mutineers scattered, but five were arrested in Sweden and Denmark and extradited to the United States. In an unreported case, *U.S. v. Williams*, the five were tried in the U.S. Circuit Court before Justice Story and District Judge John Davis (1761–1847; Harvard 1781) in December 1818, and four of them were convicted and hanged. See *Executive Documents*, 26th Cong., 1st sess., Serial 366, No. 199.

1. See above.

2. *U.S.* v. *Palmer*, 3 Wheaton 610 (1818); *U.S.* v. *Klintock*, 5 Wheaton 144 (1820); *U.S.* v. *Furlong*, 5 Wheaton 184 (1820).

mand thereof, and assumed the character of pirates, there, the general rule has been that *all* nations may take cognizance of, and punish their subsequent piratical acts; for the ship has then lost her national character. This was expressly held in U.S: v Klintock (5 Wheat: R. 610.) U.S. v Smith (5 Wheat. R. 154) and U.S. v Furlong & als. (5 Wheat. R. 144.) and US. v Holmes (5 Wheat: R. 412).[3] It has, therefore, become a common practice for all nations to take cognizance of and to punish piratical offences, although committed on board of Ships, which originally belonged to another foreign nation, the ship having by force or usurpation lost her national character.

But although every nation is deemed thus at liberty to punish piracy, whenever the pirates are brought within its own dominions, it is by no means uncommon for a nation, under such circumstances, to remit the offenders for trial to the Country, to which the ship belonged. This, however, has always been understood to be a matter of comity and discretion, and not of national duty. Several cases have occured in the Circuit Court, in my circuit, where this has taken place. Thus in the case of U. States v: Tully;[4] the Prisoners were arrested in St. Luccia, and sent to the U. States and were there tried and convicted. The case of US. v: Ross[5] was a case where a South American Govt. (I forget which one) sent home the offendors for trial. But the most striking case was that of U.S. v: Gibert 2d Sumner R. 20&c[6] where the British Government ordered the Spanish Pirates, who plundered the Brig Mexican, of Salem, to be sent to Boston for trial and they were accordingly sent and tried and convicted. The offenders were originally arrested by British Officers in Africa, and were sent to England, and then were by order of the British, sent here, and a British officer as a witness accompanied them (see 2 Sumn. R. 24. *note*). This was understood at the time to be, not a matter of duty, but a matter of discretion and comity.

Your second question is, as to what cases I recollect as to sending persons of the last description (that is, offenders on the high seas) home for trial, and particularly what I remember of the case of the Plattsburg.

I have already stated several cases in my circuit; and I believe more have occurred; and in cases of municipal offenses, I have a strong impression that American Seamen <were> have been often sent home who have committed crimes of a malignant character; such as murder, revolt, and manslaughter. But I cannot recall the particular cases. A search in the Clerk's office of the Circuit Court in Boston would, I doubt not, pre-

---

3. *U.S.* v. *Smith*, 5 Wheaton 153 (1820); *U.S.* v. *Holmes*, 5 Wheaton 412 (1820).

4. *U.S.* v. *Tully et al.*, 1 Gallison 247 (1812).

5. *U.S.* v. *Ross*, 1 Gallison 624 (1813).

6. *U.S.* v. *Gibert et al.*, 2 Sumner 19 (1834).

sent many such. I doubt not, that many cases have occurred in other Districts, especially in New York. In respect to the case of the Plattsburg, I suppose, that you refer to that case, as it came before the Supreme Court; and is reported in 10th Wheaton R. 133.[7] You will there find all the facts stated at large. If there be any other case of the Plattsburg involving other facts; it has not as yet occured to my memory.

The real question, however, in the Creole Case is not a question as to the delivering up of fugitives from Justice as of property, and property coming by the vis major and involuntarily into a foreign port. Suppose the case had been one of shipwreck, and the Cargo had been ordinary goods, no one could well doubt that in the present state of civilization every nation would feel itself bound by the general doctrines of comity and humanity and justice to protect and restore such property, and to give a right of reclaiming it from wrong doers. The question then is reduced to this, whether there is a sound distinction between that case, and the case of Slaves, who are property and held as property by their owners, in America, and are by the vis major, or by shipwreck found in a foreign port. It is certainly true, that no nation held itself bound to recognise the state or the rights of slavery, which are recognised and allowed by any other Country. And if slaves come *voluntarily* into a Country with the consent of their masters, they are deemed free. The only point, left of my argument seems to be whether the like privilege applies, where they are in such Country by the vis major, or by shipwreck. I have always inclined to think that <a nation> this must be deemed [a] matter of comity, which a nation was at liberty to concede or refuse, and not a right of another nation to claim or enforce as strictly arising under the Law of nations. Could an action be maintainable in a Court of Justice to enforce a right to slave property in New England or any other non slaveholding state in a case not covered by the Constitution, or by a Treaty! The argument, ab inconvenienti, may be addressed with great force to Great Britain on this subject; but it strikes me to furnish a ground for mutual Treaty Stipulations as to slave property and the slave trade, fit to be pressed in negotiations, <but> although difficult to support as a positive public right independant of Treaty. See the Armistad, 15 Peters. A. and the Penna Slave Case[8] in Supreme Court last term. Believe me most truly Your's

Joseph Story

Copy. NhHi. Published in Van Tyne, pp. 263–266.

7. DW had inquired in his letter of March 17, 1842, about the *Plattsburg* piracy case, *U.S.* v. *Williams* (CCDMass), but Story responded with a reference to the Supreme Court *Plattsburg* case of 1825 involving a slave vessel captured by the U.S. Navy off the African coast.

8. *U.S.* v. *The Amistad*, 15 *Peters* 518 (1841); *Prigg* v. *Pennsylvania*, 16 *Peters* 539 (1842).

FROM SAMUEL JOSEPH MAY AND EDWARD MORETON

South Scituate, Masstts.

Sir.   March 29. 1842.

At a large meeting of Abolitionists and other friends of freedom and humanity, gathered in this place from all parts of Plymouth County, on Friday, March 25th., the following Resolutions were, after a serious and animated debate, passed unanimously—the audience rising from their seats, the more emphatically to express their assent. It was afterwards ordered that a copy of them, signed by the President and Secretary of the meeting, be immediately transmitted to you, Sir, with the request that you would, at your earliest convenience communicate the same to the President of the United States and his cabinet.

Resolved, that if we are justly called upon to eulogize [George] Washington, and the patriots of the Revolution, for encountering a seven years war to preserve their rights, much more are we bound to applaud the courage and heroism of Madison Washington, and his comrades on board "the Creole," in asserting their liberty and throwing off an oppression, "one hour of which," to use the language of [Thomas] Jefferson, "was fraught with more misery than ages of that, which our Fathers rose in rebellion to oppose."[1]

Whereas the President of these United States and his Cabinet, by their letter of Instructions to the American Minister at the Court of St James [Edward Everett], respecting the Creole,[2] have committed this country to a war with England, inasmuch as they have, in that despatch, taken a position, from which there seems to be no room for our Government to retreat, but with disgrace in the eyes of the nations, a position however, in which Great Britain, without the abandonment of her well known policy cannot acquiesce, on every consideration of justice and moral right ought not to acquiesce, and from a regard to her own honor surely will not acquiesce,

Resolved, that, under God, nothing but the thunder of the popular voice will save the freemen of this Union from that [egregious] inconsistency, and flagrant crime of fighting against Liberty, for the perpetual reign of tyrants over helpless slaves.

Therefore, we do, hereby, call upon our fellow citizens of the Old Colony, of Massachusetts, and of all the free states to declare, in one accord with us, that if the horrid conflict does ensue, our Government must ex-

1. Jefferson had expressed this sentiment to Jean Nicholas Demeunier, an editor of the *Encyclopedie Methodique*, in a letter of June 26, 1786. See Julian P. Boyd et al., eds., *The Papers of Thomas Jefferson* (19 vols. to date, Princeton, N.J., 1950–), 10: 63.

2. See above, DW to Everett, January 29, 1842, "The Crisis in Anglo-American Relations," pp. 177–185.

pect no aid, no countenance from this quarter, but may be assured that we of the North, shall do all that we may, by moral means, to discourage and paralyze those who would go to enforce the wrong. We will not ourselves fight, and we will do all we can to dissuade others from fighting for the protection of slavery, or of the Slave Trade, either foreign or domestic. Samuel J. May Prest. of the meeting. Edward Moreton Secy.

ALS by May, signed also by Moreton. DLC. Endorsed: "S. J. May, *Private.*" May (1797–1871; Harvard 1817) was a Unitarian minister and leader of the Massachusetts Anti-Slavery Society. Moreton, the secretary of the meeting that passed these resolutions, is not otherwise identified.

FROM JOSHUA AUSTIN SPENCER

Sir,   Utica 2, April 1842
With this is sent a no. of the Utica daily gazette[1] containing an account of the second arrest of [John Sheridan] *Hogan.* I know nothing more on the subject than the article contains.

Your Department shall be kept advised of this matter. I have the honor to be Sir, Your very obt. servt   J. A. Spencer

ALS. DNA, RG 59 (Misc. Letters). Rec'd April 6, 1842.

TO LEWIS CASS

No. 62.   Department of State,
Sir,   Washington, 5th April, 1842.
By the arrival of the steam packet at Boston on the 27th day of last month, I had the honor to receive your several despatches down to the 26th of February.[1] That vessel had been so long delayed on her passage to America, that after the receipt here of the communications brought by her, there was not time to prepare answers in season to reach Boston before the time fixed for her departure on her return. The most I was able to do was to write a short note to Mr. [Edward] Everett,[2] to signify that the mail from London had come safe to hand.

The President has been closely attentive to recent occurrences in Europe, connected with the treaty of the Five Powers, of which we received a copy soon after its signature in December. He has witnessed with especial interest, the sentiments to which that treaty appears to have given

1. The *Utica* (N.Y.) *Daily Gazette* of April 2, 1842, recounting the second arrest of Hogan in that city, suggested that he might become "a second McLeod" and called upon the people to "prepare to fight the McLeod controversy over again."

1. Cass's last dispatch of February, No. 143 (received at the State Department in April), is dated February 25.

2. See above, DW to Everett, March 30, 1842, "Mexico, Texas, and the United States," p. 398.

rise in France, as manifested by the Debates in the Chambers and the publications of the Parisian press; and he is now officially informed of the course which you felt it to be your duty to take, by the receipt of a copy of the letter addressed by you to Mr. [François Pierre Guillaume] Guizot, on the 13th of February.[3]

When the President entered upon the duties of his present office, in April of last year, a correspondence, as you know, had been long pending, and was still pending, in London, between the Minister of the United States [Andrew Stevenson] and Her Britannic Majesty's Secretary of State for Foreign Affairs [Lord Palmerston], respecting certain seizures and detentions of American vessels, on the coast of Africa, by armed British cruisers, and generally respecting the visitation and search of American vessels by such cruisers in those seas. A general approbation of Mr. Stevenson's notes to the British Minister in regard to this subject was soon after communicated to that gentleman by the President's order, from this Department. The state of things in England in the early part of last summer, did not appear to favor a very active continuance or prosecution of this correspondence; and as Mr. Stevenson had already received permission to return home, no new instructions were addressed to him.

Circumstances occurred, as you are aware, which delayed Mr. Everett's arrival at the post assigned to him, as Minister to London, and in the meantime, in the latter part of August, the correspondence between Lord Palmerston and Mr. Stevenson was, somewhat unexpectedly, resumed afresh, not only on the subject of the African Seizures, but on other subjects.

Mr. Everett arrived in London only in the latter part of November, and in fact was not presented to the Queen until the 16th day of December. While we were waiting to hear of his appearance at his post, the session of Congress was fast approaching; and under these circumstances the President felt it to be his duty to announce, publicly and solemnly, the principles by which the Government would be conducted in regard to the visitation and search of ships at sea.[4] As one of the most considerable commercial and maritime States of the world, as interested in whatever may in any degree endanger or threaten the common independence of nations upon the seas, it was fit that this Government should avow the sentiments which it has heretofore always maintained, and from which it cannot, under any circumstances, depart. You are quite too well acquainted with the language of the message on which your letter is bottomed, to need its recital here. It expresses what we consider the true

3. See above, Cass to Guizot, February 13, 1842, enclosed in Cass to DW, February 15, 1842.

4. In his first Annual Message, December 7, 1841, President Tyler stated that the United States "can not consent to interpolations into the maritime code at the mere will and pleasure of other governments." *Messages and Papers*, 4:77.

American doctrine, and that which will therefore govern us in all future negotiations on the subject.

While instructions for Mr. Everett were in the course of preparation, signifying to him in what manner it might be practicable to preserve the peace of the country, consistently with the principles of the Message, and yet so as to enable the Government to fulfil all its duties, and meet its own wishes, and the wishes of the People of the United States in regard to the suppression of the African Slave Trade, it was announced that the English Government had appointed Lord Ashburton as a Special Minister to this country, fully authorized to treat of, and definitely settle, all matters in difference between the two countries. Of course no instructions were forwarded to Mr. Everett, respecting any of those matters. You perceive, then, that up to the present moment, we rest upon the sentiments of the Message. Beyond the fair scope and purport of that document, we are not committed, on the one hand, nor on the other. We reserve to ourselves the undiminished right to receive or to offer propositions on the delicate subjects embraced in the treaty of the Five Powers, to negotiate thereupon as we may be advised, never departing from our principles, but desirous, while we carefully maintain all our rights, to the fullest extent, of fulfilling our duties also, as one of the maritime States of the world.

The President considers your letter to Mr. Guizot to have been founded, as it purports, upon the Message delivered by him at the opening of the present session of Congress; as intended to give assurance to the French Government that the principles of that message would be adhered to; and that the Government of the United States would regret to see other Nations, especially France, an old ally of the United States, and a distinguished champion of the liberty of the seas, agree to any arrangement between other States which might, in its influences, produce effects unfavorable to this country; and to which arrangement therefore, this country itself might not be able to accede.

The President directs me to say that he approves your letter, and warmly commends the motives which animated you in presenting it. The whole subject is now before us here, or will be shortly, as Lord Ashburton arrived last evening, and without intending to intimate, at present, what modes of settling this point of difference with England will be proposed, you may receive two propositions as certain:

1st. That in the absence of treaty stipulations, the United States will maintain the immunity of merchant vessels on the sea, to the fullest extent which the law of Nations authorizes.

2ndly. That if the Government of the United States, animated by a sincere desire to put an end to the African Slave Trade shall be induced to enter into treaty stipulations, for that purpose, with any foreign Power, those stipulations shall be such as shall be strictly limited to their true and single object such as shall not be embarrassing to innocent commerce, and such especially as shall neither imply any inequality, nor can tend in any way to establish such inequality, in their practical operations.

You are requested to communicate these sentiments to Mr. Guizot, at the same time that you signify to him the President's approbation of your letter; and are requested to add an expression of the sincere pleasure which it gives the President to see the constant sensibility of the French Government to the maintenance of the great principles of national equality upon the ocean. Fully sympathizing with [that] Government in abhorrence of the African Slave Trade, he appreciates the high motives and the comprehensive views of the true permanent interests of mankind, which induces it to act with great caution in giving its sanction to a measure susceptible of interpretations, or of modes of execution which might be in opposition to the independence of Nations, and the freedom of the seas. I am, Sir, your obedient servant   Danl Webster

LC. DNA, RG 59 (Instructions, France). Published in *Senate Documents*, 27th Cong., 3d sess., Serial 416, No. 223, pp. 2–4.

FROM JOSHUA AUSTIN SPENCER

Sir,   Utica 8, April 1842

Before this reaches Washington you will doubtless have seen in the papers that [John Sheridan] Hogan is discharged for want of sufficient testimony.[1] This is indeed a wonder. I think it must have been for the want of sufficient *credible* testimony.

Lord Ashburton having arrived it is to be hoped that the whole ground of the Caroline affair will be embraced in a treaty of settlement. Unless it is, and it is stipulated that no prosecution shall be instituted against any one connected with the attack, we shall have no repose on the frontier. Very respectfully &c.   J. A. Spencer

ALS. DNA, RG 59 (Misc. Letters). Rec'd April 13, 1842.

TO JOSEPH STORY

Private & Confidential   Washington
My Dear Sir,   April 9. 1842

I am truly obliged to you for your very satisfactory letter of the 25. of March.[1] The rules of law stated in it are unquestionably stated with great correctness. Lord A[shburton] has shown me, *confidentially* the report of the law officers of the Crown, ([John] Dodson, [Jonathan Frederick] Pollock, & [William Webb] Follett) on the case of the Creole. Their opinions do not differ from any thing stated in your letter.

1. See, for example, the Albany *Daily Argus*, April 7, 1842.

1. The letter from Story to DW is March 26, 1842, above.

I am in the midst of things; and have need not only for all my own wits, but of the assistance of friends, competent to give efficient aid.

You can do more for me, than all the rest of the world; because you can give me the lights I most want; & if you furnish them I shall be confident they will be true lights. I shall trouble you greatly, the next three months. For the present, I have to ask that you send me a draft of two Articles.

1st. A stipulation, prescribing the manner in which vessels of one party, driven by stress of weather, or carried by violence, agt. the will of her master & owners, into the possessions of the other, shall be treated. I think you may put in something to this effect, viz, "shall be suffered to refit, repair damage, <& if the master or owner be> & proceed on her voyage, without inquiring into the condition or character of things or persons on board; & to receive all such documents or certificates as may be necessary, in order to enable her to prosecute her voyage.

2. A proper article for the *Extradition* of Criminals. This should be comprehensive enough to embrace the Canada cases as well as others.

I can say nothing, except that I am at work. This second [John Sheridan] Hogan Case is horribly unfortunate.

I hope I may hear from you, at your earliest convenience. Yrs

D. Webster

Dr Sir

The "Plattsburg" case, which I mentioned was the case of Mr [Isaac] McKims[2] Schooner. The pirates were tried before you & han[ge]d— Danes Sweeds, &c. The proceedings of the Govt in that case show the different practices of nations, *on extradition.* You will find all collected in Doc: 199. H. of R. 26. Con. 1st Session. Report from Sec. State, May 9. 1840.[3]

ALS. MHi. Published in *W & S,* 16:367–368.

TO FRANCIS ORMAND JONATHAN SMITH

Private   Washington
My Dear Sir   April 10. 42

I yesterday addressed an important official letter to the Govr. of Maine [John Fairfield].[1] He will undoubtedly make its general contents known,

2. McKim (1775–1838), a Baltimore merchant with extensive shipping interests, was a member of the Maryland senate, 1821–1823, and served in Congress, 1823–1825 and 1833–1838.

3. *Executive Documents,* 26th Cong., 1st sess., Serial 366, No. 199.
1. DW's official letter to Governors Fairfield of Maine and Davis of Massachusetts is dated April 11, 1842 (below).

& I am informed will be very likely to consult Mr [John] Anderson[2] & other Portland friends. It is a moment, likely to produce important results, & I must therefore pray your attention to the subject, about which I have written the Govr—that is to say, the Boundary question. I verily believe the time has come for a vigorous effort for ending that controversy.[3] I, am, Dr Sir yrs   Danl Webster

ALS. NHi. Published in Frederick Merk, *Fruits of Propaganda in the Tyler Administration* (Cambridge, Mass., 1971), pp. 174–175.

TO JOHN FAIRFIELD AND JOHN DAVIS

Department of State
To His Excellency   Washington 11th April 1842.
Your Excellency is aware that previous to March 1841, a negotiation had been going on for some time, between the Secretary of State of the United States [John Forsyth], under the direction of the President and the British Minister accredited to this Government [Henry Stephen Fox], having for its object the creation of a joint Commission for settling the controversy respecting the northeastern boundary of the United States, with a provision for an ultimate reference to arbitraters to be appointed by some of the sovereigns of Europe, in case an arbitration should become necessary. On the leading features of a Convention for this purpose the two Governments were agreed, but, in several matters of detail the parties differed, and appear to have been interchanging their respective views and opinions, projects and counterprojects, without coming to a final arrangement down to August 1840. Various causes, not now necessary to be explained, arrested the progress of the negotiation at that time, and no considerable advance has since been made in it.

It seems to have been understood, on both sides that one arbitration having failed, it was the duty of the two Parties to proceed to institute another, according to the spirit of the treaty of Ghent, and other treaties: and the President has felt it to be his duty, unless some new course should be proposed to cause the negotiation to be resumed, and pressed to its conclusion. But I have now to inform your Excellency that Lord Ashburton, a Minister Plenipotentiary and special has arrived at the seat of the Government of the United States charged with full powers from his sovereign to negotiate and settle the different matters in discus-

2. Anderson (1792–1853; Bowdoin 1813), a lawyer of Portland, Maine, represented the state in Congress from 1825 to 1833. From 1833 to 1836 he was mayor of Portland, and from 1837 to 1841, collector of the port. In 1842 he was again mayor of Portland.

3. For the reply, see Smith to DW, April 16, 1842, *Correspondence* 5: 200.

sion between the two Governments. I have further to state to you, that he has officially announced to this Department that in regard to the boundary question he has authority to treat for a conventional line, or line by agreement, on such terms and conditions, and with such mutual considerations and equivalents as may be thought just and equitable and that he is ready to enter upon a negotiation, for such conventional line, so soon as this Government shall say that it is authorized and ready, on its part, to commence such negotiation.

Under these circumstances the President has felt it to be his duty to call the serious attention of the Governments of Maine and Massachusetts to the subject and to submit to these Governments the propriety of their co-operation, to a certain extent and in a certain form, in an endeavor to terminate a controversy already of so long duration; and which seems very likely to be still considerably further protracted before the desired end of a final adjustment shall be attained, unless a shorter course of arriving at that end be adopted, than such as has heretofore been pursued, and as the two Governments are still pursuing.

Yet without the concurrence of the two states whose rights are more immediately concerned, both having an interest in the soil, and one of them in the jurisdiction and Government, the duty of this Government will be to adopt no new course, but in compliance with treaty stipulations, and in furtherance of what has already been done to hasten the pending negotiations as fast as possible.

But the President thinks it a highly desirable object to prevent the delays necessarily incident to any settlement of the question by these means. Such delays are great and unavoidable. It has been found that an exploration and examination of the several lines constitute a work of three years. The existing commission for making such exploration under the authority of the United States has been occupied two summers,[1] and a very considerable portion of the work remains still to be done. If a joint commission should be appointed, and should go through the same work, and the Commissioners should disagree as is very possible, and an arbitration on that account become indispensible, the arbitrators might find it necessary to make an exploration and survey themselves, or cause the same to be done by others, of their own appointment. If to these causes operating to postpone the final decision, be added the time necessary to appoint arbitrators, and for their preparation to leave Europe for the service, and the various retarding incidents always attending such operations, seven or eight years constitute, perhaps, the shortest period within which we can look for a final result. In the mean time, great ex-

1. On July 20, 1840, Congress appropriated $25,000 for the exploration and survey of the northeastern boundary. An additional appropriation of $75,000 was voted February 27, 1841. 5 U.S. Stat. 402, 413–414.

penses have been incurred, and further expenses cannot be avoided. It is well known that the controversy has brought heavy charges upon Maine herself, to the remuneration or proper settlement of which she cannot be expected to be indifferent. The exploration by the Government of the United States has already cost a hundred thousand dollars, and the charge of another summer's work is in prospect. These facts may be sufficient to form a probable estimate of the whole expence likely to be incurred, before the controversy can be settled by arbitration; and our experience admonishes us, that even another arbitration might possibly fail.

The opinion of this Government upon the justice and validity of the American claim has been expressed at so many times, and in so many forms, that a repetition of that opinion is not necessary. But the subject is a subject in dispute. The Government has agreed to make it matter of reference and arbitration; and it must fulfil that agreement, unless another mode for settling the controversy should be resorted to, with the hope of producing speedier decision. The President proposes, then, that the Governments of Maine and Massachusetts should, severally, appoint a Commission or Commissioners empowered to confer with the authorities of this Government upon a Conventional line, or line by agreement, with its terms, conditions, considerations and equivalents, with an understanding that no such line will be agreed upon without the assent of such commissioners.

This mode of proceeding, or some other which shall express assent before hand, seems indispensable, if any negotiation for a Conventional line is to be had, since if happily, a treaty should be the result of the negotiation, it can only be submitted to the Senate of the United States for ratification.

It is a subject of deep and sincere regret to the President that the British Plenipotentiary did not arrive in the country, and make known his powers, in time to have made this communication before the annual session of the Legislature of the two States had been brought to a close.[2] He perceives and laments the inconvenience which may be experienced from reassembling those Legislatures. But the British mission is a special one; it does not supersede the resident mission of the British Government at Washington, and its stay in the United States is not expected to be long. In addition to these considerations it is to be suggested that more than four months of the session of Congress have already passed, and it is highly desirable, if any treaty for a conventional line should be agreed on, it should be concluded before the session shall terminate, not only because of the necessity of the ratification of the Sen-

2. The legislature of Massachusetts adjourned March 4, 1842; that of Maine, March 18, 1842.

ate, but also because it is not impossible that measures may be thought adviseable or become important, which can only be accomplished by the authority of both Houses.

These considerations, in addition to the importance of the subject, and a firm conviction in the mind of the President that the interests of both Countries, as well as the interests of the two states more immediately concerned require a prompt effort to bring this dispute to an end, constrain him to express an earnest hope that your Excellency will convene the legislature of Maine/Massachusetts, and submit the subject to its grave and candid deliberations. I am &c   Danl Webster

LC. DNA, RG 59 (Domestic Letters). Published in *Senate Documents*, 27th Cong., 3d sess., Serial 413, No. 1, pp. 64–66.

FROM JOSEPH STORY

My dear Sir,   Cambridge April 19. 1842.

I have been very busy with cases in Bankruptcy and other matters or I should have answered your last letter[1] before this time. I now send a sketch of *three* Articles[2] <by> of a Treaty upon three of the critical points, to which you have directed my attention—(1) fugitives from Justice; (2) vessels with slaves going into British ports by stress of weather &c, (3) Acts done under Government <crews> orders, like [Alexander] McLeod's case &c.

As to the first I have taken the 17th Article of Jay's Treaty of 1794,[3] as my main guide, as far as it goes. But it stops short of pointing <of> out how the surrender is to be accomplished, (as I think it should be) through the judicial power, which gave <me> rise to the senseless popular clamour in Johnathan Robinson's case.[4] I have added the proper provision.

As to the second, I have drawn it up with considerable fulness, and directness meaning to meet the difficulty in language calm and yet clear; with the proper grounds as to the right of examination <with> into the character of the persons on board, whether properly held as slaves or not; to prevent public odium and clamour. As to the third, I can only say, that considering the importance to our national peace and Security, it is more properly a matter for treaty stipulation, than for an act of Congress. I hope therefore it may be adopted. The first part of the

1. See above, DW to Story, April 9, 1842.

2. Not found.

3. Extradition is discussed in Article 27 of the treaty of 1794.

4. In 1799 Thomas Nash, alias Jonathan Robbins, committed murder on board the British warship *Hermione* and fled to the United States, where he claimed rights of citizenship. The U.S. government returned Nash to British authorities in accordance with the Jay Treaty. See *International Law Digest*, 4:270, 281.

<claim> clause is *vital* to its just operation by excluding the Judicial action where the act is clearly authorized by the Sovereign. This will cut up the difficulty by the root.

If I had more time I would probably have given more finish to the phraseology; but you can easily <command> amend and alter it. I am sure the provisions are in *substance* right and will reach the evils.

In the article about fugitives from *Justice* I have put in the crimes only, which most usually occur, and will be likely to call for the inter-position of the Government for extradition. If you think it too broad, you can strike out any part of the enumeration, you may think best. I have purposely excluded political offences, as involving <many> very de-bateable matters not to say also, that they might hazard the ratification by our Senate from popular clamour.

I am most anxious to have all our difficulties with Great Britain set-tled for I love peace, and I wish well to G. B. as well as to my own Coun-try; and I have not the slightest doubt, that all matters may, if met in the right Spirit be settled honourably for the interests and permanent peace of both Countries. I will therefore, hold myself ready at all times to aid your efforts, whenever you may think I can be of any real use in accomplishing so desirable an end.

In my judgment we ought to accede to the Treaty of the five Powers as to the search of Slave vessels and to suppress the Slave Trade. That Treaty is exceedingly well drawn, and most carefully weighed. We might do so by a single article, merely referring, as to the modus operandi, to the provisions of that Treaty, and agreeing to have them regulate our article as far as they are applicable.

I confess that I despair of Congress; and I believe this is becoming a very pervading feeling among all our intelligent men. If we are to be saved at all, it must be by different counsels; and by the Executive tak-ing, as to our foreign affairs, a bold and firm ground, but conciliatory.

I regret, that our Ministers, [Lewis] Cass, and [Henry] Wheaton, should intermeddle with these matters uncalled for. They have a ten-dency to embarrass our negotiations; and I am surprized that they should write without orders, and thus inflame, if not misdirect the pub-lic mind. I have seen Cass's pamphlet,[5] but not Wheaton's.[6] Cass's pam-phlet is calculated to do much mischief *here* as well as in *France*. Be-lieve me most truly Your's   Joseph Story

Copy. NhHi. Published in Van Tyne, pp. 267–268.

5. Lewis Cass, *The Right of Search: An Examination of the Ques-tion, now in discussion, between the American and British Governments, concerning the Right of Search. By an American* (Paris, 1842).

6. Henry Wheaton, *Enquiry into the Validity of the British Claim to a Right of Visitation and Search of American Vessels suspected to be engaged in the African Slave Trade* (London, 1842).

TO LEWIS CASS

Private.

My dear Sir: Washington, 25 April, 1842.

I have your private letter of 12 March.[1] Its contents are interesting, as I perceive the lively concern still manifested towards what we may do here, respecting the right of visit and of search. We keep ourselves as cool as possible on this subject, not intending to surrender any point of national interest, or national honor; and yet resolved to fulfil all our duties respecting the abolition of the African slave trade. We have come to no understanding, as yet, with Lord Ashburton, upon any of the questions in difference between the two countries, although we have conversed freely in regard to them all. He manifests a good spirit, and assures us of the amicable temper of his government. There are serious difficulties, however, on some of the questions. You will have learned that the ground assumed by us in the "Creole" case, was wholly misunderstood in Europe at the time you wrote me on that subject.[2] The points debated in the English House of Lords, you will have seen, were quite beside the real question. We know not how the facts of the "Creole" case may eventually turn out, but the general principle stated in my letter to Mr. [Edward] Everett,[3] we shall never relinquish. The boundary question is one of the most troublesome. I am most anxious to terminate that by a just compromise, lest state claims interfere, and the matter thus become complicated. I will try to send you by this conveyance a letter addressed by me to the Governors of Massachusetts [John Davis] and Maine [John Fairfield] respectively.[4] The Governor of the former state feels himself authorized to appoint commissioners, and the Governor of the latter will assemble the Legislature. Your's with very true regard,   Danl Webster

LS. MiU-C. Published in Curtis, 2:186.

TO EDWARD EVERETT

Private.

My dear Sir: Washington, 25 April, 1842.

Lord Ashburton has been received here with much kindness, by the Government and the public. His personal demeanor makes friends, and we all think he has come with an honest and sincere intent of removing

1. Cass to DW, March 12, 1842, mDW 21868. In this letter, Cass denounced the Quintuple Treaty and the "vile hypocrisy" of the British.

2. Cass to DW, February 20, 1842, DNA, RG 59 (Despatches, France).

3. See above, DW to Everett, January 29, 1842, "The Crisis in Anglo-American Relations," pp. 177–185.

4. See above, DW to Fairfield and Davis, April 11, 1842.

all causes of jealousy, disquietude, or difference between the two countries; and certainly do not suppose a better selection could have been made. On most of the points in difference, I verily believe we could come to a satisfactory adjustment; but I confess my fears stick deep in the boundary business. There are several reasons for this, some of which I will shortly state.

First, it is impossible to make the People of the United States believe there is any serious doubt about the intention of the treaty, or serious difficulty in executing that intention.

The common argument here, when stated in its shortest form, stands upon these propositions:

1. The northwest angle of Nova Scotia is the thing to be found.
2. That angle is to be ascertained by running a line due north from the source of the St. Croix river, till that line reaches the highlands, and then along the *said* highlands—which said highlands divide the rivers entering into the St. Lawrence from those which fall into the Atlantic.
3. Suppose it a matter of doubt whether the St. John's and the Restigouche fall into the Atlantic, then the rule of just interpretation is, that if one element in the description be uncertain, it is to be explained by others which are certain.
4. And it is certain, that, by the treaty, our Eastern boundary is to be a north and south line.
5. And it is equally certain that this line is to run north till it reaches highlands, from whose northern watershed the rivers flow into the Saint Lawrence.
6. These two things being, one mathematically, and the other physically, certain, control the uncertainty, in the other element of description.
7. The British argument, assuming that the Bay of Fundy, and more especially the Bay of Chaleurs, are not the Atlantic Ocean, within the meaning of the treaty, insists that the rivers flowing into these bays, are not therefore, in the sense of the treaty, rivers falling into the Atlantic; and, therefore, the highlands to which we claim have not that southern or eastern watershed, which the treaty calls for; and as it is agreed nevertheless that we must somewhere find highlands, and go to them, whose northern waters run into the St. Lawrence, the conclusion is, that the different parts of the description in the treaty do not cohere, and that therefore the treaty cannot be executed.
8. Our answer to this is two-fold.
   1st What may be doubtful in itself may be made certain by other things which are certain; and in as much as the treaty does certainly demand a due north line, and does certainly demand highlands from whose northern sides the rivers flow into the St. Lawrence, these two

certain things make it clear that the parties to the treaty considered the rivers flowing from the south or east of the *said* highlands to be rivers falling into the Atlantic.

2. But, secondly, if all the parts of the description in the treaty do not cohere, it by no means follows that all must be set aside. If there be certainly enough in some parts of a description to enable us to arrive at a just knowledge of the thing, other parts, not comformable, may and must be rejected.

It is true that in matters of bargain, where mutual considerations are stated, if those on one side be found impracticable, those on the other ought not in justice to stand. But the reason for this by no means applies to cases of mere description. In all cases of the purchase and sale of lands, it is a rule universally received, that one part of the description may be corrected and controlled by other parts: and if, in this case, the line is to run due north, and is to run to highlands which from their northern slopes send rivers into the St. Lawrence, then it is irresistibly clear that the northwest angle of Nova Scotia can be found, and that the treaty, therefore, may be executed. With this view of the real merits of the question, the idea of concession and compromise is not very palatable, although considerate men think it is high time the question was settled. But concession and compromise become more difficult from the interference of state claims. There are certain equivalents, connected with boundaries in other parts of the frontier, which might be available, but then they do not affect Maine. The object must be to find equivalents *in Maine*; and this is not easy, unless a liberal spirit pervade the British Government.

No doubt the great object of England is to retain her old and convenient communication between her two Provinces. I deem this reasonable, and am prepared to recommend it. I am prepared to allow England to hold the Madawasca Settlements, on both sides the St. Johns, coming, in this respect, on our side of the line recommended by the King of the Netherlands [William I]; but this upon equivalents, vizt

1. The right of conveying lumber and produce from all the tributaries of the St. Johns down that river to its mouth, with no other tax or toll than shall attach to British timber. I can conceive no objection to this, as I suppose the result would favor all the objects of the present wise policy of England.

2. That from some point on the north and south line, not a great way north of the monument, the line of division should turn at right angles due east to the river, and then run up the river; thus giving us the narrow part of that little strip of land lying on the west of the St. Johns, and east of the north and south line. There is not, I suppose any great value in this. There are few settlers on it, and a majority of them, as I learn, would as willingly belong to us, as to England. But its great value

in the negotiation would be that it would be a clear concession; it would be a grant of something plainly belonging to England; and this would enable us to press upon Maine the propriety of conceding to England whatever a large and liberal view of her necessity may require, in regard to a communication between her own Provinces.

I can think of nothing so likely as these two arrangements, to bring us together and give us all peace and good feeling.

The great body of the intelligent people of the United States desire, I have no doubt a firm and settled peace. But there are here, as in some European States, agitators, uneasy and restless spirits, who desire change, disturbance, and a new state of things. But a still more powerful class among us is made up of men of some consideration also, although they hardly desire war, yet as little desire a permanent and settled peace. They rejoice in instances of collision, in all incidents which ruffle the waters, and in whatever makes probable war a subject of speculation and conversation. I quite regret to say that our public councils are not always free from feelings of this kind, and these feelings easily spread and kindle under the fanning of patriotic professions, and an apparent readiness to offer conflicts to the greatest power in the world.

You will appreciate properly the weight of these considerations, and see the difficulties which lie in our path; difficulties which I nevertheless am most anxious to overcome, as I fervently desire the continuance and confirmation of national peace.

The present Ministry receives a bequest of troubles from its predecessors. China, India, American questions,[1] &c. &c. I certainly wish the Queen's government well through all these difficulties. I hope Lord Aberdeen will duly estimate the importance of settling matters with us in such a manner as to perpetuate good feeling between the two countries; and that he will regard such a result as an achievement worthy to distinguish his management of Her Majesty's Foreign Affairs. Be pleased to make to His Lordship the tender of my personal regards. I am, D. Sir, always yr's.   Danl Webster

L S. MHi. Published in *PC*, 2:121–123.

TO JOSEPH STORY

Washington
My Dear Sir   April 25 1842

I thank you, cordially, for your letter[1] & its accompaniments. They are of great use to me, and come in exact season.

1. In addition to problems with the United States, England fought a war in Afghanistan, 1839–1842, and the Opium War of 1841–1842 with China.
   1. See above, Story to DW, April 19, 1842.

I hope to be in Boston the 2nd or 3rd of May. If you shall not be detained too long in Portland, I hope to see you before I return. I need a whole morning with you. Things look well, in some respects, but in others I see great difficulties. Much will depend on Congress's passing the two Bills before them in season.[2] Lord Ashburton is quite well disposed, & altogether master of the subjects, committed to his care. I know not how we shall come out. Yrs   D. Webster

ALS. MHi. Published in *W & S*, 16:369.

TO EDWARD EVERETT

My Dear Sir:
Private.   Washington, 26th April, 1842.
    General [Lewis] Cass and Mr [Henry] Wheaton have nearly overwhelmed us with their letters and pamphlets, on the subject of visit and search.[1] I must say, between ourselves, that General Cass' pamphlet, however distinguished for ardent American feeling, is, nevertheless, as a piece of law logic, quite inconclusive. I think, as it might be said of other compositions on the same subject, that it contains passages which yield all that is contended for on the other side. Quite a breeze seems to have been excited in Paris and on the Continent, generally, in regard to the Quintuple Treaty, and the probability of our accession to it. Here, we are calm, and intend to fulfil our duties, without entering into any of these questions. Our position, in respect to these maritime questions, is peculiar. Hitherto, we have been on the side of the neutral, and the minor naval powers; powers always most forward in contending for the freedom of the seas, in the utmost latitude of that freedom. But we are in the process of change. We are no longer a minor commercial power, nor do we know that we have any particular exemption from war, if war should again break out. We see no necessity, then, of being in haste to do that which our political men sometimes call "defining our position." To avoid all this, and to escape the necessity of mingling ourselves, at present, in the discussions now so rife in Europe, I have proposed to Lord Ashburton to come to an agreement that England and the United

2. One of the measures to which DW referred was the bill for "further remedial justice in the courts of the U.S.," the McLeod bill, which became law August 29, 1842 (see 5 *U.S. Stat.* 539–540 and "The Aftermath and Implementation of the Treaty of Washington: The Law of August 29, 1842," pp. 705–709, below). The other was probably the

bill introduced January 19, 1842, to renew the Neutrality Law of March 10, 1838. The bill passed the Senate on March 18, 1842, but was tabled in the House on August 31. *Senate Journal*, 27th Cong., 2d sess., Serial 394, pp. 98, 231; *House Journal*, 27th Cong., 2d sess., Serial 400, p. 1476.

    1. See above, Story to DW, April 19, 1842, notes 5 and 6.

States shall maintain, for a limited time, each an independent squadron on the coast of Africa, comprising such a number of vessels and of such force as may be agreed on, with instructions to their Commanders respectively to act in concert, so far as may be necessary, in order that no slave ship, under whatever flag she may sail, shall be free from *visitation and search*. This is our project. Lord Ashburton, so far, appears to think well of it, and probably will write to Lord Aberdeen in regard to it,[2] by this conveyance. I should like to know your opinion of it; but have most particularly to request, that you will keep it to yourself, except so far as Lord Aberdeen may wish to speak of it, with you. I do not desire that this purpose should be known across the channel, at present. I have thought it a more manly and elevated proceeding, on our part, to make provision, in this way, to execute our laws, than to ask another Power to do that for us, and to that end to make visits of American vessels, or vessels appearing to be such, necessary. An arrangement of this kind, will, I think, be acceptable here, and I trust will prove effectual. If it should so prove, we shall not only have fulfilled our duty, as created by the Treaty of Ghent, towards England, but shall also have accomplished an object greatly desired by the Government and People of this country. Yrs always truly   Danl Webster

LS. MHi. Published in *PC*, 2:124–125.

LORD ASHBURTON TO LORD ABERDEEN

Private.

Dear Ld Aberdeen,   Washington 26 April 1842

By this opportunity, the Great Western, you will receive two very long letters from me.[1] The one on the subject of the Maine Boundary, the other on all the other various subjects which I am occupied with settling here. I fear you will find them heavy reading, they have proved to me not less heavy writing, but I am not aware that I could have made my case clear in fewer words. My object has been to make you acquainted with the exact position in which I stand, and I hope you will think that position favorable, as far as it goes. I certainly think so myself. My difficulties are not with the President or his Chief Minister. The dispositions of both are favorable, but in the singular state of parties here, which makes them powerless, I am not always sure of being much advanced when I have agreed with them. The inclosed private letter from Old [Albert] Gallatin will explain this anomalous state of things.[2] I should add

2. Ashburton to Aberdeen, April 25, 1842, FO 5/379 (PRO).

1. See Ashburton's official dispatches Nos. 2 and 3 of April 25, 1842, FO 5/379 (PRO).

2. See Gallatin to Ashburton, April 20, 1842, in Henry Adams, ed., *Writings of Albert Gallatin* (3 vols., Philadelphia, 1879), 2:596–597. Gallatin advised Ashburton that

however for your satisfaction that I think we stand well with the Legislature and tolerably so with the great public. I do not therefore at all despair of success, though I am well aware of the chances & accidents which may baffle all calculation.

I rather flatter myself that you will be pleased with what we are doing with respect to Slavery, but with the success of this are more or less connected the collateral subjects of Extradition and of security for the navigation of the Bahama Channel. To these points and also to the proposed plan for joint Cruizing on the coast of Africa I must beg your early attention. I say early, because the people here must be taken while they are in the mood, because Congress can not be expected to sit beyond the end of June, because there is an evident disposition to make a sweep of all differences at the same time, and lastly because your humble servant feels that he is not good for any prolonged residence. Though we are not yet through April the thermometer is at 80 and my nerves begin to give me warning.

But there is one point upon which I must earnestly press for as immediate an answer as can be made. I allude to the Maine boundary. My powers by your last letter place the whole of this negotiation in jeopardy.[3] I have discussed this so amply that I will not here trouble you with repetitions, further than to say that although I have from present appearances no right to say that your wishes are unattainable I have less to predict the contrary, and if you had read to me your present instructions before I left London I should have ventured under such circumstances to give an opinion that it was inexpedient to send this Mission. The failure in this the main point makes likely a failure in all others and a General failure, I need hardly tell you, leaves our relations with this ungovernable people in a much worse state than if no solemn attempt at settlement had ever been made. Whatever Mr. [George William] Featherstonhaugh may lead those who listen to him to think, the universal opinion here is that an equivalent for the arbitrators boundary is the utmost we can or do expect. The powers from Maine & Massachusetts may be here towards the end of May and this vexed affair must be settled off hand if it is ever to be settled. You may rely upon my doing what I can but if my ultimatum is to stand where it does I can not be answerable for consequences. You will see what I have said upon the possible intervention of a money payment. Of this there seems at present little

President Tyler did not have the support of either the Whigs or the Democrats.

3. In his original instructions of February 8, 1842 (No. 2), Aberdeen gave the special minister great latitude in arranging a northeastern boundary settlement. On March 31, 1842, however, Aberdeen issued revised instructions (No. 6), which stated that some improvement over the award of the king of the Netherlands was "essential." See FO 5/378 (PRO).

appearance but I do not feel sure that when those Maine deputies arrive they may not be otherwise advised,—on this point I must "voir venir." The case of the navigation of the St Johns may offer means of compensation; to this and to the suggested exchange as explained by the map excuse my calling your early attention and my repeating that an almost immediate answer is desirable. You will see by examining the military opinions that they are in many respects contradictory more especially those of Sir G[eorge] Murray & Sir J[ames] Kempt.[4] I can not doubt that the road by the St Johns is the important thing to be considered, and that this is best done by securing the strip connected with the Madawaska settlement. I hope I do not write too bluntly to my masters on this subject in my new quality of a diplomatic servant, but I am strongly impressed with the danger of letting the soldiers have their own way in this matter.

The publication of your letter to [Edward] Everett about *Search* has done great good.[5] When I pressed this upon Webster & asked why it was not made here, I found he wanted to bring this with the whole question together before the Senate, he added "the publication would leave you & me nothing to settle." [Lewis] Cass's conceited letters & writings make little impression here though his public character enables him to do mischief at Paris.[6] He is working to stir up the anti English feeling in France & America, and is making what the Americans term "political Capital" for the Presidential Election. He would be recalled but for the fear of making a martyr of him. While I am busy here he can not be safer than where he is. You will find inclosed his last private letter to Webster & also one more interesting from [Henry] Wheaton[7] a man of real sense & talent. They will give you the gossip in Paris about your quintuple treaty rather amusingly. Pray destroy them as they were communicated to me in confidence. The ministers here are desirous that nothing should be communicated to Paris as to what we are about & the same recommen-

4. British military experts agreed on the necessity of a line of communications from Halifax to Quebec but differed over the routes. Murray (1772–1846) favored a southern route along the Saint John River and thence to Quebec. Kempt (1764–1854) preferred a more northern route along the Bay of Chaleur.

5. Aberdeen to Everett, December 20, 1841, enclosed in No. 4. Everett to DW, December 28, 1841, DNA, RG 59 (Despatches, Britain). In the letter, published in the London *Times* of March 30, 1842, Aberdeen disclaimed any right to search an American ship but maintained a right of visit to determine a vessel's true nationality. The letter also praised the Quintuple Treaty as a "Holy Alliance" against slavery.

6. Cass's pamphlet on the right of search was published in Paris in January 1842. See Cass to Guizot, February 13, 1842, enclosed in Cass to DW, February 15, 1842, above.

7. See Cass to DW, March 12, 1842, mDW 21829, and Wheaton to DW, February 15, 1842, mDW 21590.

dation is given to Everett. I hope you all cherish properly that truly good man. Ever my dear Sir faithfully your servt.   A.

The decision of the case of the Tigris comes very à propos, it was one of great scandal and wholly indefensible. There came at the same time some account of a very courteous execution of the right of visiting under the new instructions.[8]

The new Tariff also is popular from north to south.[9] I would recommend your being a little cautious as to the *mode* of yielding the point long ago contested by America as to the Duty on Rice said to have been kept up by us contrary to treaty. If possible the change should be made prospective, by way of solving a *doubt* not determining a *right*. You will otherwise have a heavy claim on you for arrears. Webster estimated them at £80000. It is clear that the Dealers or speculators calculated on Existing duties such as were actually collected without knowing much about Treaties. They have therefore no equitable ground for claim.[10]

ALS. Uk.

TO CHARLES H. BELL AND JOHN S. PAINE

Department of State
Gentlemen   Washington April 30th 1842
    Your experience in the service on the coast of Africa has probably enabled you to give information to the Government on some points con-

8. The American ship *Tigris* was searched and prized as a suspected slaver by a British navy officer on October 7, 1840. After the case was dismissed by the U.S. Circuit Court of Massachusetts (23 *Federal Cases* 1220–1222), Aberdeen invited the owner to submit a statement of damages. Ashburton refers to an account in the Washington, D.C., *National Intelligencer* of April 26, 1842, in which the captain of the *Tigris* declared that he had lately been treated with "civility and consideration" by British officers in African waters. In February 1841, British cruisers on the coast of Africa were instructed not to interfere with American vessels, even if they were suspected of being slavers.

9. Ashburton refers to Sir Robert Peel's proposed reductions in the British tariff presented to the House of Commons on March 11, 1842. His speech appeared in the *National Intelligencer* on April 21, 1842.

10. By the terms of Article 2 of the commercial convention of July 3, 1815 (*Treaties*, 2:595–600, esp. pp. 596–597), Britain and the United States granted each other most-favored-nation status for their products. A British law passed in 1836, however, caused British custom agents to charge higher duties for American rough rice than for African rice. After many protests, Foreign Minister Aberdeen agreed, in a letter to Andrew Stevenson of October 20, 1841, to charge equal duties in the future. See *Executive Documents*, 27th Cong., 2d sess., Serial 401, No. 2, and 28th Cong., 1st sess., Serial 444, No. 278.

nected with the slave trade on that coast, in respect to which it is desirable that the most accurate knowledge attainable should be possessed. These particulars are:

1. The extent of the Western coast of Africa, along which the slave trade is supposed to be carried on, with the rivers, creeks, inlets, bays, harbors or parts of the coast to which it is understood slave ships most frequently resort.

2. The space or belt along the shore within which Cruizers may be usefully employed, for the purpose of detecting vessels engaged in the traffic.

3. The general course of proceeding of a slave ship, after leaving Brazil or the West Indies, on a voyage to the coast of Africa for slaves, including her manner of approach to the shore, her previous bargain or arrangement for the purchase of slaves; the time of her usual stay on or near the coast, and the means by which she has communication with persons on land.

4. The nature of the stations or barracoons in which slaves are collected on shore to be sold to the traders; whether usually on rivers, creeks, or inlets, or on or near the open shore.

5. The usual articles of equipment and preparation, and the manner of fitting up by which a vessel is known to be a slaver, though not caught with slaves on board.

6. The utility of employing vessels of different nations to cruize together, so that one or the other might have a right to visit and search every vessel which might be met with under suspicious circumstances, either as belonging to the country of the vessel visiting and searching, or to some other country, which has, by Treaty, conceded such right of visitation and search.

7. To what places slaves from slave ships could be most conveniently taken.

8. Finally, what number of vessels and of what size and description, it would be necessary to employ on the Western Coast of Africa, in order to put an entire end to the traffick in slaves; and for what number of years it would probably be necessary to maintain such force to accomplish that purpose.

You will please to add such observations as the state of your knowledge may allow, relative to the slave trade on the Eastern Coast of Africa. I have the honor to be &c   Danl Webster.

LC. DNA, RG 59 (Domestic Letters). Published in *Executive Documents*, 27th Cong., 3d sess., Serial 418, No. 2, pp. 108–109. Bell (1798–1875) and Paine (d. 1859) were career U.S. Navy officers who had served in African waters. In March 1840 Paine made an unauthorized agreement with the senior British naval officer in African waters, William Tucker, that allowed a mutual search of English and American vessels suspected of engaging in the slave trade. Secretary of the Navy James Kirke Paulding (1779–1860), however, disapproved the agreement.

TO REUEL WILLIAMS

> Washington.
> Saturday Eve'
> May 7th 1842.

My Dear Sir,

I have perused the draft of a Resolution, which you were kind enough to place in my hands this morning.[1]

I should be very sorry that you should recommend to Govr [John] Fairfield, or to the Legislature, a Resolution with any restriction whatever. If you propose one restriction, others will propose others; and the Legislature will at once enter upon the discussion of terms, and nobody can tell in what such a discussion might end.

Besides, if the British Minister [Lord Ashburton] should find that we are limited and restricted by terms and restrictions previously imposed by Maine, he might, very probably, decline to enter upon the negotiation at all, as he might think, that, under such circumstances, the condition of the parties would not be equal. The English Government, judging from its previous communications, will think it has gone very far, in agreeing to treat upon the terms stated in my letter to the Governor of Maine;[2] that is, upon terms which prevent the Government of the United States from agreeing to any line of compromise, without the previous assent of the Commissioners of Maine. To tie up our hands further, by Legislative restrictions imposed on those very Commissioners, would appear to place us under so much embarassment, that I should hardly hope that a negotiation for a line by agreement would be undertaken.

It is quite obvious, that if Maine imposes restrictions, Massachusetts may impose restrictions also: and it is not only possible, but from all I know highly probable, that the limitations proposed by the two States would not only be different, but contradictory. Be assured, My Dear Sir, we shall not be likely to accomplish any thing, by way of compromise, in any other way than by sending from both States, as Commissioners, wise and prudent men, possessing, in full measure, the public confidence, and left perfectly free to act according to their discretion. Nor can I per-

---

1. Not found, but its purport is indicated in the text. The Maine legislature passed, and the governor approved on May 26, a resolution agreeing to the appointment of four commissioners to represent the state in the boundary negotiations. Although the commissioners were authorized to approve a conventional line, they had to be unanimous in their approval. *Acts and Resolves Passed by the Twenty-Second Legislature of the State of Maine, 1842* (Augusta, Me., 1842), pp. 110–111.

2. See above, DW to Fairfield and Davis, April 11, 1842.

ceive any danger in this. These Gentlemen will be well informed of the sentiments of the people of the States; they will be in daily intercourse with all their respective Delegations here; and will be able to communicate with the Governors, and other Gentlemen at home, on every occurrence, or the rising of any question, which may appear to make such communication desirable.

As to the particular proviso, attached to your Resolution, I should think its adoption highly inexpedient. I can conceive that it may be an object of great importance to England, and for which she would yield an equivalent of much value to Maine, to establish the line in such manner as to embrace the Madawasca settlement, on both sides the river, within her Territories.

Allow me to say, in conclusion that as yet the British Minister has made no proposition whatever, about a line by compromise. He is not authorised so to do, till we say to him that we are ready to treat fully and freely, and to enter upon the whole subject of the line, and all its conditions and equivalents. I pray you, My Dear Sir, to urge upon your friends in Maine, the great importance of giving a fair and free trial, to this attempt for settling, in a satisfactory manner, a controversy, of such long standing, and which has caused so much trouble and expense. Yours very truly   Danl Webster

LS. DLC.

FROM JOHN TYLER

Sir: May 8, 1842.

I return the despatches from Mr [Edward] Everett.[1] Mr. [Daniel] Jenifers private letter[2] contains an account of mere ceremonials in which you would take but little interest. Would it be possible to induce G. B. to abandon the claim to impress seamen in time of war from American ships. It would add lustre to your negociation. Truly yrs   J. Tyler

ALS. DLC. Published in *Tylers*, 2:224.

FROM CHARLES H. BELL AND JOHN S. PAINE

Sir,

Washington City
May 10th 1842.

In accordance with the wishes expressed in your communication of

1. These are probably one, or more, of Everett's Nos. 7, 8, 9, and 10 of March 1, March 23, March 26, and April 4, 1842, respectively, which were received at the State Department in April. DNA, RG 59 (Despatches, Britain).

2. Not found, but see Jenifer to DW, March 9, 1842, DNA, RG 59 (Despatches, Austria), describing his reception by Austrian officials. Jenifer (1791–1855), who represented Maryland in Congress from 1831–1833 and 1835–1841, was U.S. minister to Austria from August 27, 1841, to July 7, 1845.

the 30th ultimo,[1] we have the honor to submit the following statement.

In reply to the first particular, viz "The extent of the Western Coast of Africa along which the slave trade is supposed to be carried on, with the rivers, creeks, inlets, bays, harbours or ports of the coast to which it is understood slave ships most frequently resort."

The slave trade from Western Africa to America is carried on wholly between Senegal Lat: 16° N. Longitude 16½° W. and Cape Frio in Lat: 18° S. Long. 12° E. a space (following the windings of the coast at the distance of three or four miles) or more than 3600 miles.

There are scattered along the coast five English, four French, five American, six Portuguese, six or eight Dutch and four or five Danish settlements; besides many which have been abandoned by their respective Governments.

These settlements are generally isolated; many of them only a fortress without any town, while a few are clusters of villages & farms.

The British, French, and particularly the American settlements exercise an important influence in suppressing the slave trade.

The influence of the Danes and Dutch is not material.

The Portuguese influence is supposed to favor the continuance of the trade, except the counter influence of the British, thro' treaty stipulations.[2]

North of the Portuguese cluster of settlements of which Bissao is the capital, and south of Benguela (also Portuguese) there is believed to be no probability of a revival of the slave trade to any extent.

This leaves about 3000 miles of Coast to which the trade (principally with Cuba, Porto Rico & Brazil) is limited.

There are hundreds of trading places on the Coast, calling themselves "factories," and each claiming the protection of some civilized power. Some of these were the sites of abandoned colonies, others have been established by trading companies or individuals.

The actual jurisdiction of a tribe on the coast seldom exceeds ten miles, though these small tribes are sometimes more or less perfectly associated for a greater distance.

Of these factories and tribes, a few have never been directly engaged in the slave trade, and are opposed to it; but the great preponderance is of the slave trading interest.

To enumerate the rivers and inlets of this Coast, would not convey a just idea of the slave country or practices; as the embarcation often takes place from the beach where there is no inlet—but we will state a few of the most noted.

1. See above, DW to Bell and Paine, April 30, 1842.

2. In 1815, Britain and Portugal concluded a treaty for the suppression of the slave trade. See *British and Foreign State Papers* (116 vols., London, 1812–1925), 2:348–355.

Commencing at Cape Roxo in Lat: 12° 30′ N and running down the coast as far as the river Mellacoree in Lat. 9° N. the slave trade is more or less carried on, but (in consequence of the vigilance of cruisers) not to the same extent it was a few years ago.

Another portion of the coast from the limits of the Sierra Leone colony to Cape Mount, (a space including the mouths of six or more rivers) the slave trade is extensively prosecuted. Here commences the jurisdiction of the American Colonization Society, which extends to Grand Bassa—there are several slave stations between Grand Bassa and Cape Palmas—from thence eastwardly to Cape Coast Castle, situated near the meridian of Greenwich, we believe there are no slave stations—but eastward of this, and in the bights of Benin and Biafra, along the whole coast (which includes the mouths of the great rivers Benin or Formosa, Nun, old & new Calabar, Bonny, Camerons, Gaboon and Congo) with few exceptions, down to Benguela in Lat 13° south, the slave trade is carried on to a very great extent.

2d "The space or belt along the shore, within which cruisers may be usefully employed, for the purpose of detecting vessels engaged in the traffic."

Men of War should always cruise as near the shore as the safety of the vessel will admit, in order to take advantage of the land and sea breezes. Twenty or thirty miles from the coast there are continual calms, where vessels are subject to vexatious delays—besides which ships engaged in the slave trade, keep close in with the land in order to reach their places of destination.

3d "The general course of proceeding of a slave ship after leaving Brazil or the West Indies on a voyage to the coast of Africa for slaves, including her manner of approach to the shore; her previous bargain or arrangement for the purchase of slaves; the time of her usual stay on or near the coast, and the means by which she has communication with persons on land."

Vessels bound from the coast of Brazil or the West Indies to the coast of Africa, are obliged, in consequence of the trade winds, to run north as far as the Latitude of thirty or thirty five, to get into the variable winds—thence to the eastward, until they reach the longitude of Cape Verd Islands; then steer to the southward to their port of destination—and, if bound as far to the eastward as the Gulf of Guinea, usually make the land near Cape Mount or Cape Palmas. Vessels from Brazil bound to the southern part of the coast of Africa, run south as far as the Latitude of 35° S and make up their Easting on the southern variables.

Slave vessels are generally owned or chartered by those persons who have an interest in the slave establishments on the Coast of Africa, where the slaves are collected and confined in Baracoons, or slave prisons ready for transhipment the moment the vessel arrives. They are therefore detained but a short time after arriving at their place of destination. Instances have come to my notice of vessels arriving at a slave station in the evening, landing their cargo, taking on board all their slaves, and sailing with the land breeze the following morning.

It is not unusual however, for vessels unconnected with any particular slave establishment, to make their purchases after arrival. If any delay is likely to occur, an agent is landed, and the vessel stands to sea, and remains absent, for as long a time as may be thought necessary to complete their arrangements. The slavers communicate with the shore, either with their own boats, or boats and canoes belonging to the stations, assisted by the Kroomen[3] in the employ of those on shore.

4th "The nature of the stations or *Baracoons* in which slaves are collected on shore to be sold to the traders whether usually on rivers, creeks or inlets, or on or near the open shore."

The slave stations are variously situated—some near the mouth, others a considerable distance up the rivers, and many directly on the sea shore. The baracoons are thached buildings, made sufficiently strong to secure the slaves; and enough of them to contain, in some instances, several thousand. The slaves are collected by the negro chiefs in the vicinity and sold to the persons in charge of the stations, where they are kept confined until an opportunity offers to ship them off.

Materials of all kinds necessary to convert a common trader into a slave ship are kept on hand; and the change can be completed in a few hours. A number of Kroomen are employed, and boats and canoes ready for immediate service.

The slave stations are generally fortified with cannon and muskets not only to guard against a rising of the slaves but to protect them from sudden attacks of the natives in the vicinity, and to command their respect.

5th "The usual articles of equipment and preparation and the manner of fitting up, by which a vessel is known to be a slaver, though not caught with slaves on board."

Vessels engaged in the slave trade are either fitted up with a slave deck, or have the materials on board prepared to put one up in a few hours—their hatches, instead of being close[d], as is usual in merchantmen, have gratings—they are supplied with boilers sufficiently large to cook rice or farhina for the number of slaves they expect to receive—an extra number of water casks, many more than are sufficient for a common crew—also a number of shackles to secure their slaves—most of these articles however are concealed; and every thing is done to disguise the Vessel.

3. "Kroomen" refers to members of a West African ethnic group, the Kroo or Kru, who were skilled seamen.

It is not unusual for them to have several sets of papers, two or more persons representing themselves, as Captains or Masters of the Vessel, and flags of all nations, every device is resorted to, to deceive, should they encounter a Cruiser.

Some are armed with only a few muskets, others have a number of heavy guns according to the size of the Vessel; and they range from sixty to Four hundred tons burden with Crews from ten to upwards of one hundred men.

6th "The utility of employing Vessels of different nations to cruize together, so that one or the other might have a right to visit and search every vessel which might be met with under suspicious circumstances, either as belonging to the Country of the Vessel visiting or searching, or to some other country which has, by Treaty, conceded such right of visitation and search."

We are of opinion that a squadron should be kept on the Coast of Africa to co-operate with the British, or other nations, interested in stopping the slave trade; and that the most efficient mode would be, for Vessels to cruise in couples, one of each nation.

7. "To what places slaves taken from slave ships on the coast could be most conveniently taken."

If captured under the American flag, send them to Cape Mesurrda, Liberia; or if convenient, to such other of the American settlements as the agent of the United States there, may wish.

8. "Finally, what number of vessels and of what size and description, it would be necessary to employ on the western coast of Africa, in order to put an entire end to the traffic in slaves: and for what number of years it would probably be necessary to maintain such force to accomplish that purpose," adding "such observations as the state of your knowledge may allow, relative to the slave trade on the Eastern Coast of Africa."

As our personal knowledge of the coast extends to only that part of it comprised between Cape Verd and Cape Palmas, it is difficult to state the exact force required for this service. Not less however than the following we think necessary.

One first class sloop of war.

One steamer from 200 to 300 tons burden.

Two (eight or ten gun) Brigs or schooners.

Ten schooners of about one hundred tons, each with four guns.

One store ship of, from 250, to 350 tons, all the vessels to have one tenth less than their compliments of men, to be filled up with Kroomen on their arrival on the coast.

A steamer (to be fitted up if possible to burn either wood or coal as circumstances require) will be essentially necessary.

That part of the coast of Africa from which slaves are exported, is subject to light winds and calms. A steamer propelled at the rate of six miles an hour, could easily overtake the fastest sailing vessels, and would be a great auxillary in ascending rivers and towing boats, in order to attack slave stations. Less duty is performed by sailing cruisers on this coast than on any other we are acquainted with, from the reasons just stated: and the importance of steam vessels is much increased by this difficulty.

We cannot state confidently how long such force would be necessary, but we are of opinion that in three years the trade would be so far destroyed, as to enable the United States to withdraw a greater part, while a small force of observation would be necessary, until the natives had become accustomed to other occupations, and lost all hope of again engaging in the traffic.

In connection with this subject we beg leave to remark, that the American fair trader, is sometimes obstructed in the most vexatious manner by armed British merchantmen, sustained by British cruisers. This arises from the practice which exists with the commanders of single cruisers, the agents of trading companies, the masters of merchantmen and others, making agreements, treaties, or as the expression there is "books," securing to themselves the exclusive trade with the tribe or district. A late instance of this unreasonable and probably unauthorized, spirit of monopoly, has come to our notice near Cape Mount, where the native chief was induced to believe that he could not make a treaty with the American colonists, because he had made one with the commander of a British cruiser.

The same commander, it is asserted, has also threatened the Governor of the Colony at Monrovia, that he will make reprisals on the commerce of the colony for exercising the usual jurisdiction at Bassa Cove, only two or three miles from their towns of Bassa and Edina.

Our knowledge of the commanders of British Cruisers authorizes us to say, that their conduct is not usually thus unfriendly; but many instances show the propriety of the guarding the interests of the fair dealer, who is generally opposed to the slave trade.

Respecting these treaties or agreements with the tribes, we think that only the commanders of squadrons, or Governors of Colonies should be permitted to make them—and with those over whom their Government cannot reasonably claim jurisdiction, treaties should not be made to the exclusion of other mercantile powers trading on the coast, as has sometimes been done; and all treaties should contain a prohibition of the slave trade.

Commanders of squadrons and Governors of Colonies should be authorized and directed to seize every opportunity, and make use of all honorable means of inducing the native tribes, and particularly the Emperor of Ashantee, the Empress or Potentate at Loango,[4] and other powerful nations, to enter into agreements to put a stop, as far as their influence extends, to the traffic—to seize and send home for trial all foreigners found on the coast engaged in the slave trade, whether belonging to vessels or residing on the coast, (for should these persons be permitted to remain, even after their slave stations are destroyed, they will erect others at points probably less assailable,) and should be enjoined to extend their protection to fair traders, though not of their own nation.

Commanders of Squadrons and Governors should be authorized and directed to destroy all slave factories, within the reach of the force employed; and to proclaim to the tribes in the vicinity, that they must not be renewed, on pain of having their villages also destroyed.

We have little knowledge of the details respecting the slave trade on the Eastern Coast of Africa. No instance has come to our knowledge of the use of the American flag there. From the best information we can obtain, it seems that a large trade is carried on by Portuguese colonies, the Arab Chiefs, and Negro tribes. Their greatest markets are the Mahomatan countries bordering on the Red Sea and Persian Gulf, the Portuguese East India Colonies—Bombay and perhaps other British possessions in the East Indies. This part of the trade is probably in the hands of the Arabian vessels. Many are also shipped to Brazil; and some perhaps find their way to Cuba and Porto Rico.

In concluding this subject we beg leave to remark, that the field of operations to carry on the slave trade is so extensive, the profits so great, and the obstacles in the path so many, so various, so difficult, that every means should be used by civilized nations, and particularly by the United States and Great Britain to effect the object; and we do not believe that any material good can result without an earnest and cordial co-operation. We have the honor to be With high respect Your Obedt Servants,

Chas H. Bell   Jno. S. Paine

L s. DNA, RG 59 (Misc. Letters). Published in *Executive Documents*, 27th Cong., 3d sess., Serial 418, No. 2, pp. 109–113.

TO JARED SPARKS

Boston, May 14, 1842

My Dear Sir Saturday Eve'

I arrived in this City today, & have a great desire to see you this Evening, for the purpose of engaging you, if so I may do, to proceed to *Augusta*, Maine, on Monday, on a confidential errand.[1] I send out a Car-

---

4. Kwaku Dua I (1834–1867) was emperor of the Ashantee. The potentate of Loango is not identified.

1. See DW to Sparks, [May 16, 1842], and Sparks to DW, May 19, 1842, below.

riage, to bring you in, & it will take you back. You will find me, if you can make it convenient to come, at Mr [James William] Paige's,[2] Summer Street. Yrs truly   Danl Webster

ALS. MH-H. Published in *W & S*, 16:371.

TO REUEL WILLIAMS

Private
Dear Sir: Boston, May 14th 1842.

The manner in which Maine and Massachusetts are desired to take part in the proposed attempt to settle the boundary question by a conventional line, will appear in my official letter to Governor [John] Fairfield and Governor [John] Davis.[1] The subject has received a great deal of attention, since Lord Ashburton's mission was announced, and the course adopted is that which the President, and those with whom he has advised, esteemed, not only the best, but the only one, which could be resorted to, with propriety, and with any prospect of success. If objection be made to it, such objection is likely to be founded on the following suggestions, vizt

1. That the Legislature of Maine ought to be called upon to say, in advance, what line of boundary would be acceptable to her, and with what conditions or equivalents.

2. Or, secondly, if no such declaration be previously made by Maine, then, that any line which should be agreed upon by the Government of the United States and that of Great Britain, ought, with all its conditions and equivalents, to be submitted to the final approval or disapproval of her Legislature.

Both these suggestions have been maturely and carefully considered, with an anxious desire to give to the whole proceeding a direction most satisfactory to the State; but the result is, that each of these modes has been thought to be inadmissable.

As to the first, it is liable to several objections. England proposes to negotiate, to treat, to confer, to receive and exchange propositions, on the subject of a compromise line; and her Minister declares himself authorized to act freely and without restraint; to hear any proposition from the other side, and to offer on his own side any proposition which he may think fair, reasonable, and useful. But if the Government of the United States is to approach the discussion with unalterable conditions already fixed and laid down, the British Minister would be likely to insist that the condition of the parties was unequal; that there could, in fact, be no

2. Paige (1792–1868), a half brother of DW's first wife, Grace Fletcher Webster (1781–1828), was a wealthy merchant of Boston.

1. See above, DW to Fairfield and Davis, April 11, 1842.

free conference, no untrammelled discussion, terms being already pre-scribed; that the transaction would, in effect, cease to be a negotiation, and become a mere question of compliance or non-compliance, with cer-tain conditions already laid down, and from which there could be no de-parture; and that while the Government of the United States was under restraints of this kind, he might say he should decline to open the nego-tiation at all. The English Government is very likely to think that it has gone very far in agreeing to treat upon the terms stated in my letter to the Governor; that is, upon terms which prevent the Government of the United States from agreeing upon any line of compromise, without the previous assent of Maine, through her commissioners. If our hands be still further tied up, by limitations and restrictions imposed on the power of those very commissioners, it may present a case in which not only the British Government, but the Government of the United States may well doubt whether it be worth while to make any attempt to establish a line by agreement; so that the whole negotiation might fail at its very first step.

But if this preliminary objection could be got over, the practical diffi-culties which present themselves to proceeding under previous limita-tions and restrictions, appear to be insuperable. In the first place it is to be remembered, that if Maine may make fixed conditions in advance, so may Massachusetts also; and as the interests of the two States is somewhat different, their conditions might well be expected to be differ-ent. And, indeed, there is reason to believe that, in point of fact, if the two States, without consultation with each other, and with the Govern-ment of the United States, were now severally to prescribe conditions, those conditions would be found to be, not only different, but contradic-tory. It is only by full and free communications between their respective agents, and with the authorities of the Government of the United States, by comparison of sentiments, and by a calm and dispassionate considera-tion of all interests and all opinions, that the States themselves are likely to be brought to agree upon the same terms.

In the next place, it is to be borne in mind that the negotiation is to proceed upon the idea of mutual concessions and equivalents; and how can the Legislature of Maine declare what may be proper to be conceded, and what could not be conceded, until it knows what equivalent is offered?

It is impossible to foresee all the propositions, modifications, and sug-gestions which may be made, in the progress of the business; and if the Commissioners of Maine should be bound down by unalterable restric-tions on their powers, they might very probably find themselves unable to obtain advantages of the highest importance to the State.

As to the other general suggestion, that the treaty, or convention, ought to be submitted to the final approval or disapproval of Maine, all must see that such a course could not be followed. The States cannot be parties to a treaty with a foreign power; nor can any foreign power negotiate with a State, upon a question of boundary, or any other question. This results from the nature of the powers, conferred, respectively, on the General and on the State Governments; and from the time when a negotiation for a line by compromise was first suggested, it has been seen and understood that the treaty for such line, if made at all, could only be made by and between the Government of the United States, and that of Great Britain. As early as 1834, the British Government required, as a preliminary to any attempt to negotiate a conventional line, that it should be satisfied, that the Federal Government was possessed of the necessary powers to carry into effect any arrangement upon which the two parties might agree;[2] and the Government of the United States could not have doubted the propriety of this, whether suggested by England or not.

On the whole, therefore, I fervently hope that the Legislature of Maine will be satisfied that the mode of proceeding stated in my letter, is the right mode; and that there is little probability of arriving at the result so properly desired, in any other manner, than by appointing on the part of both the States concerned, wise and prudent men, as Commissioners, possessing in full measure, the confidence of their respective States, and left perfectly free to act according to their discretion. Nor can I see any danger in this. These gentlemen will be well informed of the sentiments of the people of the States; they will be in daily intercourse with their delegations in Congress; and will be able, also, to communicate with the Governor and other gentlemen at home, on every occurrence, or the springing up of any question which may appear to make such communication desirable.

A fear has been entertained—I hope not extensively—that the Government might be willing to surrender interests of Maine, for equivalents to be found elsewhere. Certainly no such purpose ever was, or ever will be, entertained by me for a moment; and full assurance, in this respect, is given to the State by the declaration that no treaty will be signed for a line by convention, till it be assented to with all its terms, conditions, and equivalents, by her own Commissioners. They will take care that if any thing be yielded which Maine claims, the equivalent received for it will be such as shall enure to the benefit of Maine herself.

The British Minister has, as yet, made no proposition whatever, respecting a settlement of this question by a line of compromise; nor will he make any, until the Government of the United States assures him that

2. See the two notes from British Minister Charles Richard Vaughan to Secretary of State Louis McLane of February 10, 1834, DNA, RG 59 (Notes from Foreign Legations, Britain). McLane (1785–1861; Newark College) served as secretary of state, 1833–1834.

it is ready to treat, fully and freely, and to enter upon the whole subject
of such a line, with its conditions and equivalents, with ample power to
carry into effect what may be agreed on.

I pray you, my dear Sir, to press upon your friends the great importance of giving a fair and free trial to this attempt for settling, in a satisfactory manner, a controversy so inconvenient and injurious to all parties, of such long standing, and which has already caused so much
trouble and expense. I am, with true regard, Your obedient servant,
(signed)   Danl Webster.

Copy. DLC.

TO EDWARD EVERETT

Private.
My dear Sir: Boston, May 16th 1842.
I left Washington on the 12th and came to this city partly on business
connected with the boundary question, and partly on other accounts.
Your despatch by the "Caledonia" had been received,[1] and there seemed
nothing to require immediate answer. The King of Hanover, I fear, will
hardly find us willing to extend further the principle of unrestricted
trade.[2] We are already suffering too much from our liberality, in regard
to that subject, in other instances. The whole subject of reciprocal treaties must soon receive the careful consideration of the Government;
meanwhile, inquiries, resolutions, and calls for information, in regard
to it, abound in Congress.[3] At the moment of leaving Washington, I had
an opportunity of running over a copy of Lord Aberdeen's letter to you,
in answer to your's on the "Creole" case.[4] I confess I was a good deal disappointed at its contents. Its general character seems to be controversial,
and it does not fall in happily with what is attempted to be carried on
here. There are, also, misapprehensions which quite surprise me. How is
it possible for Lord Aberdeen to understand your letter as demanding the

1. Everett's dispatch No. 11 of
April 15, 1842, was received at the
State Department on May 7. DNA,
RG 59 (Despatches, Britain). The
Caledonia left Liverpool on April 19
and arrived in Boston on May 5.

2. Ernest Augustus (1771–1851)
ruled as King of Hanover from 1837
to 1851. In his dispatch of April 15
Everett reported that the Hanoverian
minister to Britain had proposed an
extension of an 1840 commercial
convention. The convention is in
Treaties, 4:257–274.

3. See the discussion in the Senate on April 14, 1842, of a resolution
submitted by New Hampshire senator Levi Woodbury calling for inquiry into reciprocity arrangements
with other countries. *Cong. Globe*,
27th Cong., 2d sess., pt. 1, p. 420.

4. Aberdeen's response of April 18
to Everett's *Creole* note of March 1
was mailed by Everett on May 2 and
was not received in Washington until
May 21. Webster presumably saw a
copy delivered to the British legation
by the *Caledonia*.

surrender of fugitives from justice? Or how is it possible that he could imagine that any thing said in the debates in the House of Lords, upon which he lays such stress, had any thing to do with any point raised by us? But far worse than all misapprehension and mistake, is the light in which Lord Aberdeen seems inclined to regard the mutineers and murderers, who carried the "Creole" into Nassau. I may do his Lordship injustice, as the paper was hardly in my hands five minutes; but he appeared to me to look upon these persons as very innocent individuals, who had chosen to come into Her Majesty's dominions, with a ship, the possession and control of which they had very rightfully obtained. This appears to me to be at least the tendency and the result of his remarks. As these persons had done nothing unlawful, the ship, of course, was their's; and if suit had been brought against them for it, in Her Majesty's Courts, Lord Aberdeen's reasoning would appear to furnish them with a competent defence! You will have seen what passed in the court at Nassau, when the Consul of the United States made an attempt to bring the mutineers and murderers to trial, as pirates. We have never said, nor supposed, they could be tried in the British Courts as pirates; but the Chief Justice of the Bahama Islands completely justifies these persons for all they had done, and goes far out of his way to express doctrines and sentiments, which appear to us to be absolutely ferocious.[5] If such sentiments are to pervade the British tribunals, and to find favor at home, consequences of the most grave character must certainly ensue. I really hope and trust, that I misunderstand Lord Aberdeen's language; but as to that of the Chief Justice, it is as little capable of being misunderstood as it is of being justified, or excused. I shall probably receive a copy of this paper by the "Acadia," and will examine it more closely.

I find Lord Ashburton just and reasonable in all his general opinions and sentiments. Nothing specific is agreed upon, as yet. He waits to hear from his Government, and I wait to see what the Legislature of Maine will do. It assembles on the 18th. I must confess I have great fears of the tenacity of Maine, and the tenacity of the British Government, on points not important to either. If the matter were in the <high> sole discretion of Lord Ashburton and myself, I am persuaded we should find little difficulty.

I hope to be back to Washington in ten days. Your's truly

Danl Webster

L S. MHi. Published in Curtis, 2:99–100.

5. When the American consul, Timothy Darling, brought piracy charges against the *Creole* mutineers, the chief justice declared that the slaves "had a natural and inalienable right to regain their freedom in the manner they did." See Darling's letter of April 16, 1842, enclosed in DW to Ashburton, May 4, 1842, FO 5/379 (PRO).

TO JARED SPARKS

[May 16, 1842]

My Dear Sir   Monday, 1 0 clock

I thank you for your letter.[1] Herewith I send a confidential letter to Govr [John] Fairfield.[2] I have spoken to him of the absolute necessity of secrecy; & you will therefore tell him all you know, relying, as I do, on his discretion & caution.

I wish you a pleasant journey. Yrs truly   Danl Webster

ALS. MH-H. Published in *W & S*, 16:371. Endorsed: "May 16, 1842."

FROM EDWARD EVERETT

Private.

Dear Sir,   London 19 May 1842.

I now transmit to you a copy of my note to Lord Aberdeen of the 17th instant,[1] on the subject of the boundary. It is strictly confined to topics which were mentioned in the conversation between us on the 13th. I[n] that conversation, Lord Aberdeen spoke of the argument from the instructions of 1779 as decisive against us, and as far more powerful than any other argument in favor of the British construction.

At the drawing-room to-day, held in honor of the Queen's birth day,[2] Lord Aberdeen admitted that the facts alleged in my note, if correctly stated, furnished a satisfactory answer to that argument. He then said he presumed I did not propose that we should engage in a formal discussion of the Boundary. I said no, but that I was anxious, before he wrote to Lord Ashburton by the Great Western, that he should have those points presented to his own mind, which had been touched upon in our conversation.

He then said he was afraid there would be great difficulty in giving up the strip west of the St. John's. It was a new demand, & they were not prepared for it; still however it should be considered. He added that

1. See Sparks to DW, May 16, 1842, mDW 22471, in which Sparks agreed to undertake a mission to Governor Fairfield and commented on a recent article in the *Westminster Review* about the boundary.

2. DW's letter to Fairfield of May 16, 1842, explaining Sparks's confidential mission, is extant in Herbert B. Adams, ed., *Life and Writings of Jared Sparks* (2 vols., Boston, 1893), 2:401.

1. In the note Everett responded to a suggestion by Aberdeen that since the peace negotiators at Paris had not agreed on a boundary along the Saint John River, as proposed in the American instructions of 1779, it could be assumed that the United States had received no territory north of the river in the settlement. Everett replied that it was likely that the United States was meant to receive some territory north of the Saint John in a compromise of the line. Everett to Aberdeen, May 17, 1842 (MHi).

2. Victoria celebrated her birthday on May 24.

though he would not, in the slightest degree, commit himself about the navigation of the St. Johns, it was plain that without it, the possession of any part of the disputed territory would be far less valuable; and for this reason the opening of the river furnished an obvious basis of compromise. Still there were great objections. I asked him what they were; and he replied, a general reluctance to admit us into their rivers, and a fear that it would give us a monopoly of the timber trade. I told him I thought the benefit would be shared by the two countries.

He said he would admit that he was now satisfied of one thing which he never could believe before, vizt that we are sincere in thinking we are in the right. He said that Mr [Humphrey St. John] Mildmay[3] had written, that no one who was not in the country, could conceive the intense unanimity which prevails on this subject.

I pressed Lord Aberdeen about a new search for the original map. I fancied he rather evaded that point: he said he believed they had found an old map. The manner in which he spoke convinced me this was not the map in question; but probably one supposed to be favorable to their claim. I said perhaps it was that of which Mr Devonshire had caused a re-impression to be made a few years ago, and which was of no value, as it was an old French map, constructed near a century and a half since, for the purpose of pushing Acadia as far as possible to the Westward.[4] I ten, that no one who was not in the country, could conceive the intense happened to know that a good deal of importance had, two or three years ago, been attached to this map.

Lord Aberdeen said, but we have got beyond these considerations & must settle the question on other grounds. He added, it seems to be the general opinion that the Boundary question is the only one that is very difficult to settle.

It may be proper to observe that the description of New Brunswick by [Charles] Morris, in 1788, from which I have cited a very valuable passage, is found anonymously in the third Volume of Massachusetts His-

3. Mildmay (1794–1853), the husband of Ashburton's eldest daughter, Anne Eugenia (d. 1839), accompanied the mission as a secretary.

4. Everett might be referring to William George Spencer Cavendish, the sixth duke of Devonshire (1790–1858), a bibliophile and collector. He also apparently thought Aberdeen was referring to a map by Vincenzo Coronelli (1650–1718) published in Paris in 1689 and referred to in the 1840 boundary report by George William Featherstonhaugh and Richard

Zachariah Mudge (1790–1854), a career British army engineer. Actually Aberdeen's comments were in reference to an impression of a first-edition Mitchell map found in the British archives after Ashburton's departure for the United States. The map was later shown to Everett. See Everett to DW, March 31, 1843, "The Aftermath and Implementation of the Treaty of Washington: The 'Battle of the Maps,'" pp. 787–793, below; see also *Treaties*, 3:346–347, 4:407.

torical Collections. I get at the author, by comparing Waits State papers Vol. X, styled confidential, page 11 at top, and page 35 at bottom.[5] I suppose it would hardly be evidence in a court of law, but as an historical authority there can be no doubt.

I am not sure that the original map by [John] Mitchell, used by our negotiators at Paris, & sent by them to their Government is lost. I recollect once enquiring about it, but I could not sufficiently recal the result, to express myself more distinctly than I have done. The tracing of the line as we claim it, would not much help us if it could be found; but the absence of any line like that claimed by the British would be respectable negative evidence. I am, Dear Sir, as ever, faithfully yours,

Edward Everett.

LS. MHi.

FROM JARED SPARKS

Private
My dear Sir,   Augusta, Maine, May 19. 1842
I arrived here yesterday, and have had two interviews with Governor [John] Fairfield. I stated to him as fully and as clearly as I could, the particulars which you desired me to communicate. He saw at once their bearing, and seemed to view them as worthy of deep consideration; and I think he was gratified with the measure you had adopted to place them before him. He spoke frankly of the whole subject, expressing his conviction strongly, that now is the time to settle the dispute, and that the preliminaries of the negotiation ought to be placed on such a footing as to remove all the obstacles to a fair adjustment. He regards the opportunity now presented as a most favorable one, & says we have little to hope from another arbitration in Europe, if we cannot agree upon reasonable & honorable terms offered to us at home. He would have the Commissioners go without instructions, and with full powers. From the tenor of all his remarks, I cannot doubt his sincere desire, by all the means he can use, to promote the negotiation and bring it to a speedy issue.

I have conversed with several of the leading members of both branches of the legislature. There is certainly a good spirit abroad, and more free from the influence of party biasses than could have been expected. A committee of one member from each county and nine senators has been sitting yesterday and to day. They voted unanimously to send Commis-

5. Morris was the British surveyor general of Nova Scotia in 1788. See *Collections of the Massachusetts Historical Society*, 3, 1st series (1794): 99–101, and *State Papers and Publick Documents of the United States* (10 vols., 2d ed., Boston, 1817), 10: 11, 35.

sioners, and, with three dissenting voices, to send them without instructions. But I find there are some apprehensions as to the turn which things may take in the debates. There is a small party for instructions, another small party, who profess to distrust the powers of the legislature, and who would have a convention expressly chosen, by the people, and I have heard of some members, who are opposed to any kind of action. These remnants combined may become formidable. Yet the votes of the Committee would seem to indicate a better result. Mr [Peleg] Sprague will doubtless inform you more largely on these points.[1]

I have heard much said incidentally about equivalents. They will accept no money from the British government, not a farthing. It would be derogatory to the dignity of the State. Upon this there is but one opinion. Some kind of privelege in the navigation of the St. John's will be insisted on. They talk of Islands at the mouth of the St Croix, particularly Campobello, & the Grand Menan, which they say ought to have belonged to the United States by the treaty of peace, & in this they are probably right. In short I have heard nothing extravagant, or apparently unreasonable concerning equivalents. They expect the United States to pay all the charges they have incurred in defending the territory.

It has been proposed to send four commissioners, two of each political party. Of course nothing has been decided on this subject, but I think they will certainly send an equal number of each party.

Since writing the above I have called to take leave of the Governor. He spoke cautiously as to the probable action of the legislature. He requested me to present his respects to you, and to assure you that he heartily concurs in your views as to the manner of meeting the advances of the British Government, that he shall aid them as far as may be in his power, and that he hopes you "will have the pleasure and the honor of completing the negotiation."

I expect to be at home by saturday night. I am, dear Sir, respectfully & truly your most obt servt   Jared Sparks.

LC. MH-H. Published in Curtis, 2:100–102.

TO DANIEL FLETCHER WEBSTER

Marshfield
Saturday Morning
May 21. '42
½ past 4

My Dear Son

I have a note from you, last evening,[1] & am glad all are well at The Department. I am recruiting, in health & strength very fast, & find it

1. See Sprague to DW, May 18, 1842, mDW 22484, and May 20, 1842, mDW 22506; see also below.
1. Not found.

most delightful to be here. Julia & her husband[2] are with me. The weather has been cold, & we had a frost last night. The grass is white on the lawn, this moment.

I fear injury to the fruit.

Marshfield never looked so well. [Seth] Peterson & I have talked over politics. He says, the fault is in Congress; that Mr [John] Tyler is not to blame, for being President & that they ought to take right hold, man-fashion, & do up the public business.

I am going out this morning to wet a line. My chief concern is about your mother's [Caroline Le Roy Webster] health. Julia wrote her, last night, & I shall write tomorrow.

Show her this. I wish most earnestly she were here. She wd soon be well. You mention that she <had> has had recourse to the physicians.

I shall be hasting back—if I do not hear of her being better soon.

Pray show these letters[3] to the President—they prove that Maine is doing well. I have attended to that business, thoroughly. Yrs   D. W.

I care nothing for such fellows as Garret Davis[4]

ALS. NhHi. Published in *PC*, 2:128.

FROM JOHN OTIS

Dear Sir,   Hallowell May 26. 1842—

The resolve,[1] with a slight amendment referring to the preamble, reported by the committee, & which was a copy of the one drafted by you,

2. Julia Webster (1818–1848) had married Samuel Appleton Appleton (1811–1861) in 1839.

3. Possibly Sparks to DW, May 19, 1842, above; Peleg Sprague to DW, May 18, 1842, mDW 22484, advising DW that a committee of the Maine legislature had agreed to appoint four boundary commissioners; and Peleg Sprague to DW, May 20, 1842, mDW 22506, informing DW that the commissioners would not be encumbered by restrictions.

4. DW, on April 5, 1842, had requested Secretary of War John Canfield Spencer to dismiss a clerk in the Pension Office who had charged DW with accepting a bribe. Davis (1801–1872), a Whig congressman from Kentucky, called for an inquiry into the removal on May 16, 1842. *Cong. Globe*, 27th Cong., 2d sess., p.

503; DW to Spencer, April 5, 1842, *Correspondence* 5:199.

1. The Maine legislature resolved on May 25, 1842, to select four commissioners to confer with the U.S. government on the boundary negotiations. The preamble restated Maine's claim to territory according to the terms of the treaty of 1783 and declared that the government of the United States lacked authority to conclude a treaty without the state's consent. DW was probably responsible for the portion of the preamble describing the boundary as a "vexed question," amenable to a settlement by a conventional line. *Acts and Resolves Passed by the Twenty-Second Legislature of the State of Maine, 1842* (Augusta, Me., 1842), pp. 110–111.

passed the House of Representatives yesterday, with only Eleven votes in the negative, in a full house. You will recollect that it passed the Senate by a vote of 30 to 1. On the vote in the Senate, after adopting the amendment of the House, it was unanimous. Last evening a meeting of each party was held separate, & a nomination of four commissioners was made, & today they were elected with few scattering votes. The Commissioners are Edward Kavanaugh of Damariscotta Mills, Edward Kent of Bangor, William P[itt] Prebble[2] of Portland, & John Otis of Hallowell. Mr Kavanaugh will leave today for his home, to be prepared to leave at any time you will write him, & signify to either of us that we may inform the others, when it will be desirable for us to be at Washington. If not otherwise determined by your wishes, Mr K[avanaugh] & myself proposed to write to Judge Prebble & Gov. Kent to meet us at Boston at the Tremont House, Wednesday, the 8th day of June. An earlier day may be appointed, if you think it desirable. I shall write to Mr. [Peleg] Sprague, as soon, as the time is fixed upon, & shall ask him to invite the Massachusetts Com[missioner]s[3] to meet us there—if we do not communicate with them directly.

The *appointment* of commissioners is certainly popular—the result of their doings will be watched with much interest. With Great Respect, I am, Your friend & obt. Svt.   John Otis

ALS. DLC. Otis (1801–1856; Bowdoin 1823) was at that time a Hallowell lawyer and member of the state legislature. He served in Congress as a Whig, 1849–1851.

TO GEORGE W. COFFIN

Sir,   Boston May 28. 1842
For the better performance of official duties, I am desirous of obtaining information on certain points, connected with the public lands of Massachusetts & Maine, which information your public situation has probably made you able to communicate.

The inquiries which I wish to propose are;
1st   What quantity of unsold land still belongs to the two States, as nearly as may be known, assuming the true Boundary between Maine & the British Provinces to be such as the United States as-

2. Preble (1783–1857; Harvard 1806), a lawyer and judge, had participated in the presentation of the American case in the course of the arbitration of the northeastern boundary by the Netherlands but opposed accepting the resulting award of 1831.

3. Charles Allen (1797–1869), a lawyer and for many years a member of the Massachusetts legislature; Abbott Lawrence (1792–1855), a prominent Boston merchant; and John Mills, a Springfield lawyer and Democrat, had all served on the Massachusetts-Connecticut boundary commission of 1826. Allen and Lawrence were Whigs.

sert, beyond the St. Johns; & taking the British claim, on the South of St Johns, in each of two ways, towit,

1st according to the alledged line of Highlands, running from Mars Hill;

2. According to the award of the King of Holland [William I].

II.   What is the average price at which the public lands in Maine have sold, per acre, for the last five or ten years; & how far North have lands been sold.

III.   What is the estimated value of the lands, North of the St Johns, per acre; or what its value, compared with that of lands South of St John's.

IV.   Does the value of these lands <essentially> much depend on the timber, which may be standing upon them; and are the lands north of the St John's timbered, or <not> how well timbered, in comparison with those on the South?

V.   <What> Of the well timbered lands <in Maine, both within & without the disputed territory>, what portion lies on the waters of the St Johns; & what would, in your opinion be the value of the right of transporting this timber down that River to the Sea, without import or toll.

VI.   Is the land lying on the streams which run into the St Johns from the South such, as that it is likely to be valuable for cultivation, when the timber is removed; and what produce is it likely to afford?

VII.   Will the land to the north of the St Johns, or any considerable part of it, ever be valuable for cultivation?

You will be pleased to consider this communication as confidential; and I shall be obliged to you to be as full and particular as possible, on each branch of this inquiry, & also in regard to every thing else, touching the importance & value of these lands, stating as well the result of your own observation, as that of other evidence in your possession.[1]

AL draft. MHi. Coffin was the state land agent of Massachusetts.

1. On June 3, Coffin and Levi Bradley, the land agent for Maine, made a joint response to DW's inquiry. They answered DW's questions, respectively, by estimating the unsold public land to be about 6.4 million acres; the average price at which the land had sold since 1831 at $1.10 per acre; the value of the land north of the Saint John as equal to that south of the river; the land south of the Netherlands award as valuable for both cultivation and timber and that north of the line mainly for timber; the right of transporting timber free of charge down the Saint John to be "of great value"; the lands bordering the streams running into the Saint John to be valuable for cultivation; and the land north of the Saint John to be of little value for cultivation. In the letter, Elijah L. Hamlin, the land agent for Maine in 1838 and 1841, expressed his complete agreement with the estimates of Coffin and Bradley. See

LORD ASHBURTON TO LORD ABERDEEN

Private

Dear Ld Aberdeen.   Washington 29 May 1842

You will see that I have not made much progress here since you last heard from me,[1] but there was no possibility of making any. Webster is away—the Legislature of Maine was deliberating—and I was, and still am, waiting your instructions on important points; without which I should equally have been unable to move even if all other parties had been prepared. Webster will now be here in three or four days—the Maine Delegation in about a week and about that time I may expect your answer. We shall then, I trust, get seriously & actively to work. In the meantime our position continues favorable. The reductions of the estimates for the army and navy[2] founded on expectations of peace, as explained in my public letter, have given no small alarm & offence to the President, and I found him in conversation expressing doubts whether all parties would be so likely to agree as was at first supposed. His own paper here at the same time endeavoured to alarm the public with some mysterious half warlike articles, of which you will find enclosed a short specimen.[3] The artifice is generally seen through & will I think fail, but if the Cabinet had foreseen consequences they would certainly have moved more slowly towards pacification until they had lowered their estimates. This manouvre has been ill managed in Webster's absence, and as the Maine negotiation would, if trifled with, be easily made to fail altogether I am not apprehensive that he will run any such risk. My expectation is that after all the bluster about not selling their Country, the Maine people will very soon come to want money, but I shall put myself on the defensive and take care that the demand come from them. Without this solvent the equivalent for the Arbitrator's line is the utmost attainable terms. I thought so at first and I am now assured of it.

The President is weak & vacillating though essentially an honest man, but I see some persons collecting about him here of rather ominous character, [Andrew] Stephenson, the late Minister in England [Benjamin]

Coffin and Bradley to DW, June 3, 1842, DNA, RG 76 (Records of the Boundary and Claims Commissions and Arbitrations and Miscellaneous Documents Relating to the Northeast Boundary, 1827–1842).

1. Ashburton sent two dispatches, numbered 6 and 7, on May 12, 1842. FO 5/379 (PRO).

2. The House and Senate debated substantial reductions in the 1842 appropriations for the army (H.R. 75) and navy (H.R. 76) throughout the second session of the Twenty-seventh Congress. Ashburton reported these developments to Aberdeen in his No. 7. For a guide to the history of the bills, see *House Journal*, 27th Cong., 2d sess., Serial 400, p. 1494, and *Senate Journal*, 27th Cong., 2d sess., Serial 394, p. xxi.

3. Ashburton enclosed a clipping from the Washington, D.C., *Daily Madisonian* of May 25, 1842, deploring the proposed reductions in the army and navy budgets.

Rush, both ill disposed towards us. The former calls himself the President's personal friend, and my suspicion is that he is in league with old [Lewis] Cass in Paris who is as busy as he can be in endeavouring to keep up hostile feelings on every point between the two countries. I am told he is coming here himself, perceiving probably that his correspondence with Webster[4] does not produce the fruits he expected, and in the meantime Stephensons suggestions combined with the disappointment about the estimates are perhaps producing some effect on the President, but I trust to Websters presence for setting this all right. Excuse my wandering for a moment from my own affairs to Paris where the state of things must be so much better known to you than to me, but the mischievous projects there evidently connect themselves with what is passing here.

At Paris the great scheme for mischief seems adjourned till the death of the king [Louis Philippe].[5] I apprehend that [Louis Adolphe] Thiers[6] & his party have induced the successor to think that his throne is to be secured by a war with us if he can make it with any chance of success, and hence the very angry feelings every where maintained. I have no doubt that Cass & Stephenson are in concert with them to secure coopertion in America. My second son[7] who lives in Paris more than I could wish, writes to me & states facts confirmatory of this opinion, which is also further confirmed by what I see about me here. This storm will soon or late and probably soon, break over our heads, but if you can keep the great powers united and keep French intrigue down in Spain, the defensive attitude may deter even the most rash. But I hold the conciliation of this country to be a most important part of your case. I believe the moment favorable for that conciliation and it is this opinion which induces me to wish to see this negotiation carried something beyond a mere duly formal settlement of questions in dispute, but converted into the means of establishing that better feeling which may prevent the present proneness to future misunderstandings. These are the considerations which lead me to press upon you subjects rather beyond my instructions— slave trade prevention—extradition—Impressment—Bahama Channel &c. If I were master I would make a settlement of all these questions, and get up a sound cordial feeling, but I know not what you may think

4. See below, "The Aftermath and Implementation of the Treaty of Washington: The Cass-Webster Controversy," pp. 710–775.

5. By 1842 the sixty-nine-year-old monarch and his chief minister, François Guizot, were committed to peace in Europe. The king's son, and chosen successor, Ferdinand Louis Charles, the duc d'Orléans, was con-

sidered less pacific toward England.

6. Thiers (1797–1877), historian and statesman, served as minister of foreign affairs in 1836 and 1840.

7. Francis Baring (1800–1889), who became the third baron Ashburton in 1864, had married the daughter of the duc de Bassano, one of Napoleon's ministers.

of my projects. I rather expect to receive little encouragement from you excepting in the matter of the coast of Africa, on which subject I have little doubt of your wishes. I would further discharge my duty by cautioning you not to mistake or undervalue the *power* of this Country. You will be told that it is a mass of ungovernable & unmanageable anarchy, and so it is in many respects. To a common observer it might be a matter of doubt how this confederation can hold together another year. Bankrupt finances—Bad administration & jobbing in every department —A loose ill connected mass of conflicting interest, in short apparently nothing for the eye of confidence to rest upon. Yet with all these disadvantages I believe that the energies & power of the country would be found to be immense in the case of war and that the jarring elements would unite for that purpose. This is [Henry Stephen] Foxs opinion, who as you know, is no admirer of any thing here, but I should make my letter too long for your reading if I pursue the subject & I shall therefore conclude by adding my humble advice that you humour the wild Beast, and my humble opinion that it may easily be done. Ever my Dear Ld Aberdeen Your truly devoted   Ashburton

ALS. Uk.

TO JARED SPARKS

Private
My Dear Sir,   Boston June 1. 1842
    I have recd the Papers & Books, entrusted to your care, & your two letters.[1] I am quite convinced your mission was of importance. I shall soon write you on the subject of your *compensation*.[2] Yrs truly
                                                                        Danl Webster

ALS. MH-H.

WILLIAM HENRY SEWARD TO JOHN TYLER

State of New York   Executive Department.
Sir,   Albany June 4th 1842
    Laws were heretofore passed in this state and in the Canadian provinces authorizing the mutual surrendering of fugitives from justice.[1] I

1. See Sparks to DW, May 19, 1842, above, and May 25, 1842, mDW 22541, in which Sparks advises DW that the books and papers he took to Maine were left at James W. Paige's house in Boston.
2. Drawing the money from the president's secret fund for the con-

duct of foreign relations, which had been established by Congress in 1810, DW paid Sparks $250 for his travel expenses and for his map.
1. In 1822 New York passed an act authorizing the governor to surrender accused criminals. The government of Canada passed a similar law

formed an opinion on examining the subject, that the power in such cases where a foreign state was concerned, was a national one, and did not reside in the State governments. The decision of the Supreme Court of the United States in the case which went from Vermont,[2] if it did not establish that constitutional principle, at least rendered doubtful the right of the state, so that the power could no longer be safely exercised. Nevertheless, the Canadian authorities in pursuance of the provincial laws and as an act of courtesy, have, until recently, surrendered fugitives. On the 21st of May last I applied to His Excellency Sir Charles Bagot, Governor General of British North America to surrender a fugitive from this state, and I learn from his reply that doubts have arisen on the part of the Imperial Government whether this power can be legally exercised by the colonial authorities,[3] and he has therefore received instructions not to surrender fugitives without special permission.

The evils resulting from suffering criminals to obtain refuge in border states are so manifest that they need not be described. These evils in this state are much aggravated by the increased facilities of ha[ven]. The subject is of such great importance that it seems proper to submit it for your consideration. I beg leave to suggest whether it would not be expedient to give it a place among the subjects of negotiation between the United States and Great Britain; and I beg leave to add, that if for any cause it shall be thought inexpedient to establish general regulations— the obvious interest of the parties might induce a consent that this state and the adjoining provinces should enter into an agreement which would be limited to the demanding and surrendering of fugitives passing over Northern and Eastern frontiers, and to be so guarded as to exclude political cases.

I have the honor to submit herewith a copy of the communications which have passed between this State and His Excellency Sir Charles Bagot relating to the subject.[4] I remain with very high respect, Your most obedient servant.   William H. Seward

L S . DNA, RG 59 (Misc. Letters). Rec'd June 9, 1842.

---

in 1833. When William H. Seward became governor in 1839, he concluded that extradition was an exclusively national function. See John Bassett Moore, *A Treatise on Extradition and Interstate Rendition* (2 vols., Boston, 1891), 1:59–60, 624–626.

2. *Holmes* v. *Jennison*, 14 Peters 540 (1840).

3. Not printed here. On May 21,

1842, Seward had written the governor-general of Canada, Sir Charles Bagot (1781–1843), requesting the surrender of an escaped felon. Bagot refused in his reply of May 27, 1842.

4. Seward to Bagot, May 21, 1842, and Bagot to Seward, May 27, 1842, can be found with Seward's letter to Tyler in DNA, RG 59 (Misc. Letters).

FROM GEORGE C. BATES

(Confidential)   United States District Attys
Sir   Office Detroit June 10th 1842

I have learned to day that a person by the name of Ketchum,[1] has within a few days surrendered himself to the authorities in Canada, and that information was received through him by the officers on the other side that a new Patriot movement was about to be made on this Frontier; that a large force (5,000 men) was drilling at or near Maumee, that a war schooner was being built on the St Clair, and that the Steam Boat Milwaukee under the veteran Capt [Chesley] Blake,[2] and the Sandusky, Capt Floyd,[3] had been engaged from the 24 of June to the 24 of August to carry on the "war." This Mr Ketchum has been sent down to Quebec a kind of prisoner of war. And the probability is that these Exaggerated stories have been ere this received by you, in the imposing form of a communication through the British minister [Henry Stephen Fox]. It is also said that another man who does not give his name has also, gone to London and confirms these statements, and remains as a Hostage, until his assertions are proven to be true, by the result. To day word has been brought over, of other communications made by different spies to the Commanding officer at Sandwich[4]—involving Oliver Newbury[5] and some of our most respectable Citizens in this most foolish crusade. I have conferred with Gen [George M.] Brooke[6] now in command here during the absence of Gen [Hugh] Brady and with Col [Edward] Brooks our Collector;[7] and a confidential agent will leave in the morning boat for Maumee to look for the Army of five Thousand men, said to be drilling at that point. And another will go to Harsons Island in the St. Clair to find the war schooner which British rumor says is being built there. I have in company with Gen Brooks crossed the River this afternoon, and have had a long conference with Col Young, in command at Sandwich. After a careful examination of all the facts and rumors I believe the whole thing to be a mere trick of these desperate people who will keep up the Excitement on the Frontier by any means, and for any

1. Probably William Ketchum, the son of a Canadian tannery owner, who fled to the United States after the collapse of the rebellion in 1838.
2. Blake (d. 1855) was a well-known Great Lakes steamboat captain.
3. Not identified.
4. Colonel Plomer Young, not otherwise identified.
5. Newbury, a Detroit business-

man, could not be further identified.
6. Brooke (d. 1851) was the commanding officer of the Detroit barracks from June 1842 to August 1845.
7. Brooks, referred to as colonel because he had commanded the Detroit City Guards, was collector of customs at Detroit from 1841 to 1845.

purpose. The officers in Canada seem to believe them & that an actual movement is about to be made, and to prevent any alarm on your part I deem it my duty to state the above facts, and to assure you that we are all on the watch along this line. That the Patriot organisation is kept up, the posting of signs, and lodges and secret meetings continue, I have no doubt. But I am equally certain that no men are or have been drilling at Maumee or else where, for an invasion of Canada, that all the stories about Steam Boats, cannon, arms &c. are the merest nonsense that these idle vagabonds can circulate. Still we have felt it our duty to leave nothing undone, that prudence could dictate to satisfy the Canadian officers that they were deceived, and that our Government was in good faith endeavoring to enforce its laws.

Should any thing transpire worth reporting to you, I shall at once advise you, in the mean time let me assure you, that if under your auspices the great points of contention which have so long remained open between us and Great Britain shall be finally removed, that the present and future generations on both sides [of] the Atlantic will owe you a debt of gratitude never to be repaid, and that the Peaceful feelings revived by your care, between these two great nations, will never be disturbed or endangered by the miserable machinations, and silly stories of the self Styled ["]Patriots." With Respect I have the honor to be Your Obt. Sevt.   Geo. C. Bates

ALS. DNA, RG 59 (Misc. Letters).

FROM JAMES RENWICK

Private   Columbia College New York
Sir,   11th June 1842

I ought to state that I missed Mr [Abbott] Lawrence. He set out from New York the same afternoon that I saw him in company with the commissioners of Maine.

I have to communicate another fact in respect to the value of the land in the disputed territory. Gov. [Edward] Kent stated in reply, I think to questions of Mr Lawrence: that, the State of Maine, selling only to actual settlers, charged 50 cts per acre. Of this one fourth was paid in cash, the remaining three fourths in notes, which might be paid by work upon the ground. This refers to the valley of the Aroostook which is the best land in the territory. I am Sir With much respect Yr Most Obdt Servt

Jas Renwick

ALS. NhHi. Renwick (1792–1863; Columbia 1807) was a professor of engineering at Columbia. He had been appointed one of the commissioners to explore and survey the northeastern boundary in 1840 and was chairman of the commission in 1842. At DW's request, Renwick provided the secretary of state with detailed geographical information about the territory in dispute.

Although DW's confidential letters to Renwick have not been found, the nature of their correspondence can be discerned from Renwick's frequent reports. See Renwick to DW, January 8, March 4, April 2, July 3, 9, 10, 25, August 11, 20, and November 12, 1842, in DNA, RG 76 (Records of the Boundary and Claims Commissions and Arbitrations and Miscellaneous Documents Relating to the Northeast Boundary, 1827–1842).

FROM LORD ASHBURTON

Sir   Washington 13th June 1842

On considering the most effectual mode of proceeding to arrive at an amicable and satisfactory termination of the long continued controversy respecting the North Eastern Boundary between the British Colony of New Brunswick and the State of Maine, I believe that I may confidently conclude from what has passed in the preliminary conferences which I have had the honour of holding with you, that we concur in the opinion that no advantage would be gained by reverting to the interminable discussion on the general grounds on which each party considers their claims respectively to rest. In the course of the many years that this discussion has lasted every argument on either side is apparently exhausted, and that without any approach to an agreement. The present attempt therefore of a settlement must rest for its success, not on the renewal of a controversy, but on proceeding on the presumption that, all means of reciprocal conviction having failed, as also the experiment of calling in the aid of a friendly arbiter and umpire, there remains only the alternative of a compromise for the solution of this otherwise apparently insurmountable difficulty; unless indeed it were determined to try a second arbitration attended by its delay, trouble, and expence, in defiance of past experience as to the probability of any more satisfactory result.

It is undoubtedly true that, should our present attempt unfortunately fail, there might remain no other alternative but a second reference; yet when I consider all the difficulty and uncertainty attending it, I trust that all parties interested will come to the conclusion that the very intricate details connected with the case must be better known and judged by our two Governments than any diligence can make them to be by any third party, and that a sincere candid disposition to give reciprocally fair weight to the arguments on either side is likely to lead us to a more satisfactory settlement than an engagement to abide by the uncertain award of a less competent tribunal. The very friendly and cordial reception given by you, Sir, as well as by all the authorities of your government to the assurance that my mission here by my Sovereign has been determined by an unfeigned desire to settle this and all other questions of difference between us in principles of conciliation and justice, forbid me to anticipate the possibility of the failure of our endeavours applied with sincerity to this purpose.

With this view of the case, therefore, although not unprepared to enter into the general argument, I abstain from so doing from the conviction that an amicable settlement of this vexed question, so generally desired, will be thereby best promoted.

But at the same time some opinions have been industriously emitted throughout this controversy, and in some instances by persons in authority, of a description so much calculated to mislead the public mind, that I think it may be of service to offer a few observations.

I do not of course complain of the earnest adherence of partisans on either side of the general arguments on which their case is supposed to rest, but a position has been taken, and facts have been repeatedly stated, which I am sure the authorities of the federal Government will be abundantly able to contradict, but which have evidently given rise to much public misapprehension. It is maintained that the whole of this controversy about the Boundary began in 1814,[1] that up to that period the line as claimed by Maine was undisputed by Great Britain, and that the claim was avowedly founded in motives of interest, to obtain the means of conveniently connecting the British provinces. I confine these remarks to the refuting this imputation; and I should indeed not have entered upon controversy even on this, if it did not appear to me to involve in some degree a question of national sincerity and good faith.

The assertion is founded on the discussions which preceded the Treaty of Peace, signed at Ghent in 1814. It is perfectly true that a proposal was submitted by the British Plenipotentiaries for the revision of the boundary line on the North Eastern frontier, and that it was founded on the position that it was desired to secure the communication between the Provinces, the precise delimitation of which was at that time imperfectly known. The American Plenipotentiaries in their first communication from Ghent to the Secretary of State admit that the British Ministers expressly disclaimed any intention of acquiring an increase of territory, and that they proposed the revision for the purpose of preventing uncertainty and dispute,[2] a purpose sufficiently justified by subsequent events.

1. Maine officials had long contended that the British had considered the northeastern boundary question a subject of minor importance until the Ghent negotiations of 1814. See the report dated February 16, 1828, of a committee of the Maine senate and house in *ASP: FR*, 6:893–913, esp. p. 901. In 1840 Albert Gallatin maintained that the British first made a "pretension to the contested territory" at Ghent. See his *Right of the United States of America to the North-Eastern Boundary . . .* (New York, 1840), p. 114.

2. American Commissioners to James Monroe, August 12, 1814, *ASP: FR*, 3:705. The American commissioners were John Quincy Adams; James Ashton Bayard (1767–1815; Princeton 1784), a Federalist senator from Delaware; Henry Clay, the Speaker of the House of Representatives; Albert Gallatin; Jonathan Russell (1771–1832; Rhode Island College 1791), of Rhode Island, who

Again in their note of the 4 Septr 1814,[3] the British Ministers remind those from America that the boundary had never been ascertained, and that the line *claimed by America*, which interrupted the communication between Halifax and Quebec, never could have been in the contemplation of the parties to the Treaty of Peace of 1783. The same view of the case will be found to pervade all the communications between the Plenipotentiaries of the two Countries at Ghent. There was no attempt to press any cession of territory on the ground of policy or expedience, but although the precise geography of the Country was then imperfectly known, it was notorious at the time that different opinions existed as to the boundary likely to result from continuing the north line from the head of the river St Croix. This appears to have been so clearly known and admitted by the American Plenipotentiaries that they, in submitting to the conference the Project of a Treaty, offer a preamble to their 4th article in these words—"Whereas neither *that part of* the Highlands lying due north from the source of the river St Croix and designated in the former Treaty of Peace between the two Powers as the northwest angle of Nova Scotia, nor the north-westernmost head of the Connecticut river, has yet been ascertained &c &c."[4] It should here be observed that these are the words proposed not by the British, but by the American negotiators, and that they were finally adopted by both in the fifth article of the Treaty.[5]

To close my observations upon what passed on this subject at Ghent I would draw your attention to the letter of Mr [Albert] Gallatin, one of the American Plenipotentiaries, to Mr Secretary [James] Monroe, of the 25th Decr 1814.[6] He offers the following conjecture as to what might probably be the arguments of Great Britain against the line set up by America. "They hope that the river which empties into the Bay des Chaleurs, in the Gulf of St Lawrence, has its source so far west as to intervene between the head waters of the River St John's and those of the streams emptying into the River St Lawrence, so that the line north from the source of the River St Croix will first strike the heights of land which divide the waters emptying into the Atlantic ocean (River St John's) from those emptying into the *Gulf* of St Lawrence (River des Chaleurs),

---

from January 18, 1814, to October 22, 1818, was U.S. minister to Sweden and Norway.

3. British Commissioners to American Commissioners, September 4, 1814, *ASP: FR*, 3:714. The British peace commissioners were Lord James Gambier (1756–1833), an admiral in the Royal Navy; Henry Goulburn (1784–1856), who had been a member of Parliament and

under secretary for the Home Department and for war and the colonies; William Adams (1772–1851), an expert in maritime law.

4. The project of November 10, 1814, is in *ASP: FR*, 3:735–740. The quotation is on p. 735.

5. *Treaties*, 2:577–578.

6. Gallatin to Monroe, December 25, 1814, *ASP: FR*, 4:810–811.

and afterwards the heights of land which divide the waters emptying into the *Gulf* of St. Lawrence (River des Chaleurs), from those emptying into the River St Lawrence; but that the said line never can, in the words of the treaty, strike any spot of land actually dividing the waters emptying into the Atlantic ocean from those which fall into the River St Lawrence."

So obvious an argument in opposition to the line claimed by America could not escape the known sagacity of Mr Gallatin: I state it not for the purpose of discussing its merit, but to show that, at Ghent, not only the fact was well known that this boundary was a matter in dispute, but that the arguments respecting it had then been weighed by the gentleman so eminent in its subsequent discussion. Indeed the fact that the American ministers made this disputed question a matter for reference by a Treaty, afterwards ratified by the President and Senate, must to every candid mind be sufficient proof that it was generally considered to be involved in sufficient doubt to entitle it to such a mode of solution. It cannot possibly be supposed that the President and Senate would have admitted by Treaty doubts respecting this boundary, if they had been heard of for the first time through the pretensions of the British Plenipotentiaries at Ghent.

If the argument or assertions which I am now noticing, and to which I studiously confine myself, had not come from authority, I should owe some apology for these observations. The history of this unfortunate controversy is too well known to you, Sir, and stands but too voluminously recorded in your department, to make them necessary for your own information.

The repeated discussions between the two Countries, and the repeated projects for settlement which have occupied every successive administration of the United States, sufficiently prove how unfounded is the assertion that doubts and difficulties respecting this boundary had their first origin in the year 1814. It is true that down to that time, and indeed to a later period, the local features of the Country were little known, and the different arguments had in consequence not assumed any definite form; but sufficient was known to both parties to satisfy them of the impossibility of tracing strictly the boundary prescribed by the Treaty of Peace of 1783.

I would refer in proof of this simply to American authorities, and those of the very first order.

In the year 1802, Mr [James] Madison, at that time Secretary of State for the United States, in his instructions to Mr Rufus King,[7] observed that the difficulty in fixing the northwest angle of Nova Scotia "arises from a reference in the Treaty of 1783, to highlands, which it is now

7. Madison to King, June 8, 1802, *ASP: FR*, 2:585.

found have no definite existence" and he suggests the appointment of a commission, to be jointly appointed, "to determine on a point most proper to be *substituted* for the description in article II of the Treaty of 1783."

Again Mr President Jefferson, in a message to Congress, on the 17th Octr 1803,[8] stated that " a further knowledge of the ground in the northeastern and north western angles of the United States has evinced that the boundaries established by the Treaty of Paris, between the British territories and ours, on those points were too imperfectly described to be susceptible of execution."

These opinions of two most distinguished American statesmen gave rise to a convention of boundary, made in London by Mr Rufus King and Lord Hawkesbury,[9] which, from other circumstances which it is not necessary to refer to, was not ratified by the Senate.

I might further refer you on this subject to the report of Judge [James] Sullivan, who acted as Commissioner of the United States for settling the controversy with Great Britain respecting the true river St Croix, who says "The boundary between Nova Scotia and Canada was described by the King's proclamation in the same mode of expression as that used in the treaty of peace. Commissioners who were appointed to settle that line have traversed the Country in vain to find the highlands designated as the boundary."[10]

With these known facts, how can it possibly be maintained that doubts about the boundary arose for the first time in the year 1814?

I need not pursue this subject further. Indeed it would have been useless to treat of it at all with any person having before him the records of the diplomatic history of the two Countries for the last half a century. My object in adverting to it, is to correct an error arising, I am ready to believe, not from any intention to misrepresent, but from want of information, and which seemed to be sufficiently circulated to make some refutation useful towards promoting the desired friendly and equitable settlement of this question.

8. *Messages and Papers*, 1:347.

9. In the convention of May 12, 1803, the British foreign secretary, Robert Banks Jenkinson, Lord Hawkesbury (1770–1828), and U.S. minister Rufus King agreed to a plan for the settlement of a North American boundary line. The Senate, however, refused on February 9, 1804, to consent to Article 5, which described a portion of the northwestern boundary as the shortest line from the northwestern point of the Lake of the Woods to the source of the Mississippi River. *ASP: FR*, 2: 584–585, 591.

10. Sullivan (1744–1808) had been a lawyer in Biddeford, Maine, before his appointment to the Superior Court of Massachusetts in 1776. In 1782 he left the court to become a member of the Continental Congress. Sullivan was selected in 1796 to present the American case before the Saint Croix boundary commission, appointed in accordance with Article 5 of the Jay Treaty. Sullivan's report of May 20, 1802, is in *ASP: FR*, 2:586–587.

We believe the position maintained by us on the subject of this boundary to be founded in justice and equity; and we deny that we have been determined in our pretensions by policy and expedience. I might perhaps fairly admit that those last mentioned considerations have prompted in some measure our perseverance in maintaining them. The territory in controversy is, for that portion of it at least which is likely to come to Great Britain by any amicable settlement, as worthless for any purposes of habitation or cultivation as probably any tract of equal size on the habitable globe, and if it were not for the obvious circumstance of its connecting the British North American provinces, I believe I might venture to say that, whatever might have been the merits of our case, we should long since have given up the controversy and willingly have made the sacrifice to the wishes of a country with which it is so much our interest, as it is our desire, to maintain the most perfect harmony and good will.

I trust that this sentiment must be manifest in my unreserved communication with you on this and all other subjects connected with my mission. If I have failed in this respect I shall have ill obeyed the instructions of my government and the earnest dictates of my personal inclination. Permit me, Sir, to avail myself of this my first opportunity of formally addressing you, to assure you unfeignedly of my most distinguished consideration.   Ashburton

LS. DNA, RG 59 (Notes from Foreign Legations, Britain). Published in *Senate Documents*, 27th Cong., 3d sess., Serial 413, No. 1, pp. 34–37.

TO EDWARD EVERETT

Private.
My dear Sir: Washington 14 June 1842.
I know not that I have much to say by this conveyance. Your private communications by the "Caledonia" were duly received. I need hardly say that I *feel* every thing contained in that letter which you marked as *particularly* confidential. One of its topics will be alluded to, and the evil corrected.[1]

Your letter to Lord Aberdeen on the boundary question is quite judicious.[2] You place the argument *de rebus externis* handsomely and strongly. Nevertheless I must tell you, in particular confidence, that I hope you will *forbear to press the search after maps in England or elsewhere!* Our strength is on the letter of the treaty.

1. See Everett's private letter to Webster of May 19, 1842, above, and a confidential letter of May 20, 1842, in which Everett complains about the conduct of Lewis Cass and Duff Green, in *Correspondence* 5:209–211.
2. Everett to Aberdeen, May 17, 1842, DNA, RG 59 (Despatches, Britain).

The Commissioners presented themselves yesterday, and I have had a conversation with them today. They appear disposed to accomplish the object of their appointment. Mr [William Pitt] Preble's appointment excited some fear as he may be supposed to have old wounds.[3] But so far he manifests no improper temper or feeling. Lord Ashburton is looking daily for his final instructions. On their arrival we can decide in twenty four hours whether there will be a settlement of the difficulty.[4] There must be mutual cessions. We must have more or less of the strip lying west of the St. John's. The importance of this, in order to uphold the character of the proposed treaty *as an exchange of equivalents*, is incalculable: Its importance to England nothing: And so far as we can learn the inhabitants from a little above Woodstock to the river, are as willing to be on one side as the other. I pray you to state this matter pointedly and urgently to Lord Aberdeen; for I greatly fear that unless Lord Ashburton is left at liberty in this particular there is danger of his returning to England *re infecta*. Let me repeat that the great object is to show mutual concession, and granting of what may be regarded *in the light of equivalents*. The absolute value of the thing is not the point of interest. Yrs. faithfully always   Danl Webster

L S. MHi. Published in Curtis, 2:102–103.

TO LORD ASHBURTON

Department of State
Washington 17th June, 1842.

Lord Ashburton having been charged by the Queen's Government with full powers to negotiate and settle all matters in discussion between the United States and England, and having, on his arrival at Washington, announced that in relation to the question of the Northeastern Boundary of the United States he was authorized to treat for a conventional line, or line by agreement, on such terms and conditions, and with such mutual considerations and equivalents as might be thought just and equitable; and that he was ready to enter upon a negotiation for such conventional line, so soon as this Government should say that it was authorized, and ready on its part to commence such negotiation, the Undersigned Secretary of State of the United States has now the honor to acquaint his

3. Preble had a well-deserved reputation as an opponent of compromise. In 1831 he authored a pamphlet in which he argued that the the federal government had no constitutional right to cede the territory of a state "without the consent of the State interested." See *The Decision of the King of the Netherlands Considered in Reference to the Rights of the United States, and of the State of Maine* (Portland, Me., 1831), pp. 12–13.

4. Ashburton's final instructions on the northeastern boundary were sent on May 26, 1842. FO 5/378 (PRO).

Lordship, by direction of the President, that the Undersigned is ready, on behalf of the Government of the United States and duly authorized to proceed to the consideration of such conventional line, or line by agreement; and will be happy to have an interview, on that subject, at his Lordship's convenience.

The Undersigned avails himself of this occasion to tender to Lord Ashburton assurances of his distinguished consideration.

Danl Webster.

LC. DNA, RG 59 (Notes to Foreign Legations, Britain).

FROM LORD ASHBURTON

Sir   Washington 21st June 1842

The letter you did me the honour of addressing me the 17th instant[1] informed me that you were now prepared and authorised to enter with me into discussion of that portion of the differences between our two countries which relates to the North-Eastern boundary; and we had the following day our first formal conference for this purpose, with a view to consider, in the first instance, the best mode of proceeding to arrive at what is so much desired by all parties, an amicable and at the same time equitable settlement of a controversy, which, with the best intentions, the authorities of the two countries for nearly half a century have in vain endeavoured to effect.

The result of this conference has been that I have been invited by you to state generally my view of this case and of the expectations of my government; and although I am aware that in the ordinary practice of diplomatic intercourse I should expose myself to some disadvantage by so doing, I nevertheless do not hesitate to comply, promising only that the following observations are to be considered merely as memoranda for discussion, and not as formal propositions to have any binding effect, should our negotiation have the unfortunate fate of the many which have preceded it, of ending in disappointment.

I believe you are sufficiently aware of the circumstances which induced me personally to undertake this mission. If the part which during a long life I have taken in public affairs is marked by any particular character, it has been by an earnest persevering desire to maintain peace and to promote harmony between our two countries. My exertions were unavailingly employed to prevent the last unfortunate war, and have since been unremitting in watching any passing clouds which might at any time forebode its renewal. On the accession to power of the present ministers, in England, perceiving the same wise and honourable spirit to prevail with them, I could not resist the temptation and the hope of

1. See above.

being of some service to my country and to our common race, at a time of life when no other cause could have had sufficient interest to draw me from a retirement better suited to my age and to my inclinations.

I trust, Sir, that you will have perceived, in the course of my hitherto informal communications with you, that I approach my duties generally without any of those devices and manoeuvres which are supposed, I believe ignorantly, to be the useful tools of ordinary diplomacy. With a person of your penetration they would avail as little as they would with the intelligent public of the two great enlightened countries of whose interests we are treating. I know no other mode of acting than open plain dealing, and I therefore disregard willingly all the disadvantage of complying with the invitation given me to be the first to speak on this question of the Eastern Boundary. It is already agreed that we abstain from a continued discussion of the arguments by which the lines of the two countries are reciprocally maintained, and I have so well observed this rule that I have not even communicated to you a volume of additional controversial matter which I brought with me,[2] and much of which would, if controversy were our object, be of no inconsiderable weight and importance. It would be in the event only of the failure of this negotiation, which I will not anticipate, that we should be again driven into the labyrinth from which it is our purpose to escape, and that failing to interpret strictly the words of the Treaty, we should be obliged to search again into contemporaneous occurrences and opinions for principles of construction which might shed light on the actual intentions of the parties.

Our success must on the contrary depend on the reciprocal admission or presumption that the Royal Arbiter was so far right when he came to the conclusion which others had come to before him, that the Treaty of 1783 was not executable according to its strict expression, and that the case was therefore one for agreement by compromise. The only point upon which I thought it my duty to enter upon any thing like controversy is that referred to in my letter of the 13th instant;[3] and I did so to rescue my government and myself from an imputation of unworthy motives and the charge that they had set up a claim, which they knew to be unfounded, from mere considerations of policy or convenience. The assertions of persons in my position on subjects connected with their diplomatic duties are naturally received by the world with some caution, but I trust you will believe me when I assure you that I should not be the person to come here on any such errand. I do not pretend, nor have I

2. Ashburton refers to a 1785 map by William Faden (1750–1836), which showed the territory as far south and west as the Saint John River to be British territory. See Preble et al. to DW, June 29, 1842, below.

3. See above, Ashburton to DW, June 13, 1842.

ever thought, the claim of Great Britain with respect to this Boundary, any more than the claim of America, to be unattended with difficulties. Those claims have been considered by impartial men of high authority and unquestioned ability to be equally so attended; and therefore it is that this is a question for a compromise; and it is this compromise which it has become our duty to endeavour to accomplish. I will only here add the most solemn assurance, which I would not lightly make, that after a long and careful consideration of all the arguments and inferences, direct and circumstantial, bearing on the whole of this truly difficult question, it is my settled conviction that it was the intentions of the parties to the treaty of Peace of 1783, however imperfectly those intentions may have been executed, to leave to Great Britain, by their description of Boundaries, the whole of the waters of the River St John.

The length of these preliminary observations requires perhaps some apology, but I now proceed to comply with your application to me to state the principles and conditions, on which it appears to me that this compromise, which it is agreed we should attempt, should be founded.

A new Boundary is in fact to be traced between the State of Maine and the Province of New Brunswick. In doing this, reference must be had to the extent and value of the territory in dispute, but as a general principle, we cannot do better than keep in mind the intention of the framers of the first Treaty of peace in 1783, as expressed in the preamble to the provisional articles in the following words: "Whereas reciprocal advantages and mutual convenience are found by experience to form the only permanent foundation of Peace and Friendship between States &c."[4] I have on a former occasion explained the reasons which have induced the British Government to maintain their rights in this controversy beyond any apparent value in the object in dispute, to be the establishing a good boundary between our two Countries, so as to prevent collision and dispute, and an unobstructed communication and connection of our Colonies with each other.[5] Further, it is desired to retain under the jurisdiction of each government respectively such inhabitants as have for a length of time been so living, and to whom a transfer of allegiance might be painful or distressing.

These are shortly the objects we have in view and which we must now see to reconcile to a practical division of the territory in dispute. Great Britain has no wish of aggrandizement for any general purpose of increased dominion, as you must be satisfied by the liberality with which I have professed myself ready to treat questions of boundaries in other quarters where no considerations of particular convenience or fitness occur.[6] I might further prove this by calling your attention to the fact

4. *Treaties*, 2:96.
5. See above, Ashburton to DW, June 13, 1842.

6. In the survey of 1818 authorized by the Treaty of Ghent, it was discovered that the true line of the

that of the land likely to come to us by any practicable settlement, nine tenth parts of it are, from its position and quality, wholly worthless. It can support no population, it grows even little timber of value, and can be of no service but as a boundary, though from its desert nature an useful boundary, for two distinct governments.

In considering on the map a division of the territory in question this remarkable circumstance must be kept in mind, that a division of acres by their number would be a very unequal division of their value. The southern portion of this territory, the valley of the Aroostook, is represented to be one of the most beautiful, and most fertile tracts of land in this part of the continent; capable of the highest state of cultivation, and covered with fine timber; while the northern portion, with the exception of that small part comprized within the Madawaska settlement, is of the miserable description I have stated. It would be no exaggeration to say, that one acre on the Aroostook would be of much more value than ten acres north of the St John. There would be therefore no equality in making a division of acre for acre.

But although I remind you of this circumstance, I do not call on you to act upon it. On the contrary I am willing that you should have the advantage of this settlement both in the quantity and the quality of this land. All I wish is to call this fact in proof of my assertion, that the object of Great Britain was simply to claim that, which was essential to her and would form a convenient boundary, and to leave all the more material advantages of this bargain to the State of Maine.

I now come to the more immediate application of these principles to a definite line of boundary, and looking at the map with reference to the sole object of Great Britain as already described, the line of the St Johns from where the north line from the St Croix strikes it up to some one of its sources, seems evidently to suit both parties, with the exception which I shall presently mention. This line throws the waste and barren tract to Great Britain, and the rich and valuable lands to Maine, but it makes a good boundary, one which avoids collision and probable dispute, and for the reasons stated we should be satisfied with it, if it were not for the peculiar circumstances of a settlement formed on both sides of the St John's, from the mouth of the Madawaska up to that of the Fish river.[7]

---

forty-fifth parallel was actually about three-quarters of a mile south of the existing boundary line. During the War of 1812 the United States had erected a fort north of the true parallel, at Rouses Point. In the course of the negotiations Ashburton agreed to modify the border around the fort, which the United States considered the key to control of Lake Cham-

plain, in order to include it in U.S. territory.

7. The Acadians, descendants of the earliest French settlers in Canada, had suffered a number of persecutions and exiles at the hands of the British. In 1783 they were removed from their settlements around Fredericton in favor of Loyalists from America. Thereafter a number

The history and circumstances of this settlement are well known to you. It was originally formed from the French establishments in Acadia, and has been uninterruptedly under French or British dominion and never under any other laws. The inhabitants have professed great apprehensions of being surrendered by Great Britain, and have lately sent an earnest petition to the Queen, deprecating that being done. Further this settlement forms one united community all connected together, and living some on one and some on the other side of the River, which forms a sort of High road between them. It seems self evident that no more inconvenient line of boundary could well be drawn, than one which divides in two an existing municipality; inconvenient as well to the inhabitants themselves, as to the authorities under which they are to live. There would be evident hardship, I might say cruelty, in separating this now happy and contented village, to say nothing of the bickerings and probable collisions likely to arise from taking in this spot the precise line of the river which would under other circumstances satisfy us. Indeed I should consider that such a separation of these industrious settlers, by placing them under separate laws and governments, a most harsh proceeding, and that we should thereby abandon the great object we should have in view, of the happiness and convenience of the people, and the fixing a boundary the least likely to occasion future strife.

I dwell on this circumstance at some length in justification of the necessity I am under of departing to this inconsiderable extent from the marked line of the river St John's. What line should be taken to cover this difficulty I shall have to consider with you, but I cannot in any case abandon the obvious interests of these people. It will be seen by an inspection of the map that it is not possible to meet this difficulty by making over to Maine the northern portion of this settlement, as that would be giving up by Great Britain the immediately adjoining communications with Canada, which it is her principal object to preserve.

These observations dispose of those parts of this question, which immediately concern the State of Maine, but it may be well at the same time to state my views respecting the adjoining boundary of the States of New Hampshire, Vermont, and New York, because they made part of the reference to the King of the Netherlands [William I], and were indeed the only part of the subject in dispute upon which a distinct decision was given.

The question here at issue between the two Countries was as to the correct determination of the parallel of latitude and the true source of the Connecticut river. Upon both these points decisions were pronounced in favour of Great Britain, and I might add that the case of America, as matter of right, was but feebly and doubtingly supported by her own

---

of Acadian settlements were established along the Madawaska.

authorities. I am nevertheless disposed to surrender the whole of this case, if we should succeed in settling as proposed the boundary of Maine. There is a point or two in this line of boundary where I may have to consider, with the assistance of the surveyors acquainted with the localities, the convenience of the resident settlers, as also what line may best suit the immediate country at the head of the Connecticut River, but substantially the government of America shall be satisfied, and this point be yielded to them.

This concession, considered with reference to the value of the land ceded, which is generally reported to be fertile, and contains a position at Rouse's point much coveted in the course of the controversy, would under ordinary circumstances be considered of considerable importance. The concession will however be made by Great Britain without reluctance, not only to mark the liberal and conciliatory spirit by which it is desired to distinguish these negotiations, but because the case is in some respects analogous to that of the Madawaska settlement before considered. It is believed that the settlers on the narrow strip, which would be transferred to Great Britain by rectifying the 45th parallel of Latitude, which was formerly incorrectly laid down, are principally from the United States, and that their opinions and habits incline them to give a preference to that form of Government, under which, before the discovery of the error in question, they supposed themselves to be living. It cannot be desired by Her Majesty to acquire any addition of territory under such circumstances, whatever may be the weight of her rights, but it will be observed that the same argument applies almost exactly to the Madawaska settlement, and justifies the reservation I am there obliged to make. In these days the convenience and happiness of the people to be governed will ever be the chief guide in transactions of this description between such governments as those of Great Britain and the United States.

Before quitting this subject I would observe, that it is rumoured that Major [James Duncan] Graham, in his late survey in Maine, reports some deviation from the true north of the line from the head of the St Croix towards the St John's.[8] I would here also propose to abide by the old line long established, and from which the deviation by Major Graham is, I am told, inconsiderable, without at all doubting the accuracy and good faith of that very distinguished officer.

8. Graham (c. 1799–1856; U.S. Military Academy 1817), a lieutenant colonel in the corps of topographical engineers, was one of the boundary commissioners appointed by Congress in 1840 (see above, DW to Fairfield and Davis, April 11, 1842, note 1). The reports of the commissioners are in *Executive Documents*, 26th Cong., 2d sess., Serial 384, No. 102; *Senate Documents*, 27th Cong., 2d sess., Serial 396, No. 97; *Ex. Doc.*, 27th Cong., 3d sess., Serial 420, No. 31.

In stating the important concessions I am prepared to make on a final settlement of these boundaries, I am sensible that concessions to one state of this Union are not always to be made available for the satisfaction of any other; but you are aware that I am treating with the United States and that for a long line of important boundaries, and that I could not presume to enter on the question how this settlement might operate on, or be in any way compensated to, the different states of the Confederacy. I should however add my unfeigned belief that what I have proposed will appear reasonable, with reference to the interests of the State of Maine considered singly. That the proposition taken as a whole will be satisfactory to the country at large I can entertain no doubt.

I abstain from noticing here the boundaries further west which I am prepared to consider and to settle, because they seem to form part of a case which it will be more convenient to treat separately.

In the course of these discussions much anxiety has been expressed that Maine should be assured of some means of communication by the St John's, more especially for the conveyance of her Lumber. This subject I am very willing to consider, being sensible of the great importance of it to that State, and that the friendly and peaceful relations between neighbouring countries cannot be better secured than by reciprocally providing for all their wants and interests. Lumber must for many years be the principal produce of the extensive valley of the Aroostook and of the southern borders of the St John's, and it is evident that this article of trade being worth anything must mainly depend upon its having access to the sea through that river. It is further evident that there can be no such access under any arrangement, otherwise than by the consent of the Province of New Brunswick. It is my wish to seek an early opportunity of considering with some person well acquainted with the commerce of that country, what can be done to give it the greatest possible freedom and extent, without trenching too much on the fiscal regulations of the two Countries. But in the mean time in order to meet at once the urgent wants and wishes of Maine in this respect, I would engage that, on the final settlement of these differences, all lumber and produce of the forest of the tributary waters of the St John's shall be received freely without duty, and dealt with in every respect like the same articles of New Brunswick. I can not now say positively whether I may be able to go further, but this seems to me what is principally required. Suggestions have at times been thrown out of making the Port and River of St John's free to the two Countries, but I think you will be sensible that this could not be done without some reciprocity for the trade of St John's in ports of the United States, and that in endeavouring to regulate this we should be embarking in an intricate question much and often discussed between the two Countries. It cannot also fail to occur to you that joint rights in the same harbours and waters must be a fruitful source of dissension, and that it behoves us to be careful not to sow the seeds of future differences in the settlement of those of our own day.

I have now stated, as I was desired to do, my views of the terms on which it appears to me that this settlement may be made. It must be sufficiently evident that I have not treated the subject in the ordinary form of a bargain, where the party making the proposal leaves himself something to give up. The case would not admit of this, even if I could bring myself so to act. It would have been useless for me to ask what I know could not be yielded, and I can unfeignedly say that even if your vigilance did not forbid me to expect to gain any undue advantage over you, I should have no wish to do so. The Treaty we have to make will be subjected to the scrutiny of a jealous and criticizing public, and it would ill answer its main purpose of producing and perpetuating harmony and good will, if its provisions were not considered by good and reasonable men to make a just and equitable settlement of this long continued controversy.

Permit me, Sir, to conclude with the assurance of my distinguished consideration.   Ashburton

L S . DNA, RG 59 (Notes from Foreign Legations, Britain). Rec'd June 22, 1842. Published in *Senate Documents*, 27th Cong., 3d sess., Serial 413, No. 1, pp. 39–44.

FROM GEORGE C. BATES

United States Dis Attys Office

Sir   Detroit June 25 1842

Since the date of my last communication,[1] the individual employed by me has returned from his mission, and has laid before me more accurate information. Some ten days since a convention was held at Vienna ten miles south of Monroe. [Henry S.] Handy,[2] a well known leader and about one Hundred persons were there. The settlement is mostly French and a Lodge was organised, among them by a Col Le fevre[3] formerly of Montreal or that vicinity. Handy addressed them, stating that they had some sixty pieces of artillery, about the same number of tens of shell & shot, 7000 stands small arms, concealed along the Lakes, that no action would take place until *after Harvest*. He also informed them that a brother in Law of a Col Beugrand,[4] *then present*, with three others had a large contract on the Ohio Canal about 30 miles above Maumee, that they could

1. See above, Bates to DW, June 10, 1842.

2. Handy had been a leading Patriot Hunters officer since 1838. In that year, he organized the so-called

Secret Order of the Sons of Liberty on the Michigan frontier.

3. Not identified.

4. Not identified.

and would employ some 7000 men in finishing it, as they were required to complete it by the 1 of Octo. That none but Patriots would be employed but all who wanted labor could find it there with good pay until the time arrived. He also stated that all donations of horses provisions &c. were forwarded there, and were to be redelivered or paid for by these contractors when the proper time arrived. He also stated that their enrolment amounted to 250,000 in different parts of the Union, that their organisation was perfect, that they had friends in Washington who were spies on Government and gave them notice from time to time of all that passed, that they were well advised that no neutrality Bill could ever again be forced through Congress. After the convention adjourned Handy, Beugrand, Le fevre, and my friend, returned in the night to Detroit, by private conveyance, and during the ride, they recapitulated fully all these facts with more minute details. Handy, [Donald] McLeod,[5] [Lucius Versus] Bi[e]rce,[6] and Lefevre and Beugrand remained here several days, holding d[aily] councils and midnight meetings, to all of which my informant was admitted. In all cases when a man is taken into the lodge, who is out of employment he is at once sent to the canal to work, and as every thing is excessively dull here, they of course continue to pick up many who are glad to find employ on any terms. Our agent was finally commissioned by Handy as confidential bearer of despatches and has now gone to Cleavland, and from there he will go to the Maumee to ascertain with his own eyes how far these statements are true. McLeod has gone to Milwaukie to look for recruits there. Handy has gone below again, to look into affairs on the Niagara Frontier. Such are the [statements] made to me, many of which are unquestionably true but still I do *not believe* that any movement will actually occur. I cannot believe that any men can so foolishly and madly rush on to certain destruction. It is however my duty to state, that another agent of mine (a man in whose opinion I have *great confidence*[)] thinks that they really and in earnest intend to try the experiment. He also states that they speak with great bitterness of our Collector [Edward Brooks] and myself and threaten us with every kind of vengeance. E[lijah] J. Roberts,[7] the Adjutant General

5. McLeod (1779–1879), a native of Scotland, served in the British navy and army before emigrating in 1816 to Canada, where he became an advocate of reform.

6. Bierce (1801–1876), a lawyer and politician from Akron, Ohio, became an active supporter of the Canadian rebellion. In 1838, a Patriot army under his command captured and briefly held the town of Windsor in Upper Canada. He was arrested for violating U.S. neutrality law, but the judge, an old friend, dismissed the case. Bierce was elected mayor of Akron six times from 1839 to 1868 and served in the state senate, 1862–1863.

7. Roberts, a Detroit newspaperman and a member of the Michigan legislature, was generally reputed to be a member of the Patriots.

of our State is acting Adjutant General in their service. He meets with them frequently and all commissions are signed by him. His friends say that when the time for movement comes that [Edward] Theller[,][8] Handy, McLeod and that Class are to be suspended, and new and more respect·able officers selected. My informant is an Englishman who is well known to officers in Canada,[9] and who earnestly believes all the statements made to me, but I am wholly incredulous. I can but think it is all but a mere device of these vagabonds to keep up public excitement and to live on the donations and charities of their deluded followers. Still I deem it my duty to lay the whole matter before you, and to solicit advice as to the course to be pursued. The Patriots imagine that the Law of 1838 repealed the law of 1818, and that having expired by its own limitation, there is now no neutrality Law. We have taken no pains to undeceive them on the subject. The story of [Oliver] Newbury's connection with them is a most foul slander on as true a friend of yours and Government as lives. So too with old [Chesley] Blake. No vessel is building on the St Clair, and the steamboats engaged by them are of the smallest and poorest class; their plan is to land on the Lake shore in as strong a body as possible and remain in the uninhabited part of the country, until they are attacked, and have tried their fortunes, in an engagement, where if successful, they mean to raise their flag, around which they foolishly suppose the inhabitants will rally. We shall be advised of all their movements, and whenever they are armed and ready to embark, then arrest their leaders, and seise their arms munitions &c. All the officers at this point are united and we keep up daily communications with the other side so that nothing can possibly be left undone to prevent, the disgrace which their conduct will bring on themselves and their cause. In conclusion I state it as my firm conviction, that the plans will end as they have done on former occasions, and that you have no *real cause* to anticipate any trouble or further annoyance, on the subject. With sentiments of respect, I remain Your Obt Sevt.   Geo C Bates.

P.S. I keep no copies of these letters lest they should fall into improper hands. Is there any danger of spies on your Department, who could in any way obtain access to them in Washington?   G C B

ALS. DNA, RG 59 (Misc. Letters). Rec'd July 4, 1842.

8. Theller (1804–1859) was born in Ireland but moved to Canada and then to the United States when a young man. In 1838 he was captured while leading a naval assault on Canada. He escaped from prison and returned to Detroit, where he was indicted for violation of U.S. neutrality law and later acquitted.

9. Possibly William Jones Kent, an English spy who became a member of a Patriot organization at Brownhelm, Ohio.

TO EDWARD EVERETT

Confidential & particular
My Dear Sir   June 28. 1842.

I hardly know what to say to you of the state of our affairs here, except that it is bad enough, & at present not growing better. You are happy to be away. You see the Newspapers, & in them all sorts of rumors of changes.[1] I have no reason to believe that any present change in the Presidents Councils is likely to take place, but no one knows what an hour may bring forth. The truth is, the friends of Mr [Henry] Clay, some of them, seek to embarrass the President, in all things, to the extent of their power. This causes resentment in him; & between their factious spirits & his resentment of what he regards as intended insult, no one can tell what may happen to the public interests. You will receive with this a letter marked "private," but parts of which I am willing should get to the knowledge of Lord Aberdeen.[2] *The truth is, Lord Ashburton is not left free*; if he were, we should place the peace of the two countries on an immovable basis. In half a century, so good an opportunity will not, in all probability, occur again.

As it is, it will be as much as we can do to patch up things, so as to "command the peace of the present."

I cannot decide on a Secretary for you, but intend not to delay the matter much longer.[3] Your private letters are very valuable. Having written fully about our own affairs, if you have ever a leisure a moment, talk a little about English persons & things. Yours always faithfully   D.W.

ALS. MH.

FROM WILLIAM PITT PREBLE, EDWARD KAVANAGH, EDWARD KENT, AND JOHN OTIS

Sir,   Washington June 29. 1842
The Undersigned Commissioners of Maine have given to the Letter of

1. In the course of the negotiations with Ashburton, DW constantly had to wind his way through the maze of Washington politics. Warfare between President Tyler and the Clay Whigs, underway since William Henry Harrison's death, intensified in the spring and summer of 1842. The Washington, D.C., *Daily Madisonian*, Tyler's official paper, reported on May 7, 1842, the existence of a conspiracy by "ultra Whig members of Congress" to force the president to resign. By June 28, political society buzzed with unsubstantiated rumors, reported in the Washington, D.C., *National Intelligencer* of that date, that cabinet resignations or removals were about to occur.

2. In an accompanying private letter dated June 28, Webster discussed the importance of the negotiations with Ashburton and his concern that they might fail to resolve the issues between the countries. See mDW 22763.

3. Everett had complained to DW about his need for adequate secretarial help. See Everett to DW, March 30, 1842, mDW 22023.

Lord Ashburton, addressed to you, under date of the 21st inst,[1] and by you communicated to them, all the consideration, which the importance of the subject, of which it treats, the views it expresses, and the proposition it submits to you, demand.

There are passages in his Lordships communication, the exact extent of the meaning of which the undersigned are not quite sure that they fully understand.

In speaking of the inhabitants on the south side of the St John, in the Madawasca settlement, he says "I cannot in any case abandon the obvious interest of these people." Again in speaking of the proposition submitted by him, he remarks "I have not treated the subject in the ordinary form of a bargain, where the party making the proposal leaves himself something to give up. The case would not admit of this, even if I could bring myself so to act."

If his Lordship's meaning is that the proposed boundary by agreement, or conventional line, between the State of Maine and the Province of New Brunswick, must at all events be established on the South side of the St John, extending from the due North line to Fish river, and at a distance back from the river, so as to include the Madawasca settlement, and that the adoption of such a line is a sine qua non now on the part of the British Government, the Commissioners on the part of the State of Maine feel it their duty as distinctly to say, that any attempt at an amicable adjustment of the controversy, respecting the Northeastern boundary on that basis, with the consent of Maine would be entirely fruitless.

The people of Maine have a deep settled conviction, and the fullest confidence, in the justice of their claim, to its utmost extent; yet being appealed to, as a constituent member of the American Union, and called upon as such to yield something, in a spirit of patriotism for the common good, and to listen in a spirit of peace, of accommodation and good neighbourhood to propositions for an amicable settlement of the existing controversy, they have cheerfully and promptly responded to the appeal. Her Governor and Legislature in good faith immediately adopted the measures necessary on her part, with a view to relinquish to Great Britain, such portion of Territory and jurisdiction, as might be needed by her for her accommodation, on such terms, and for such equivalents as might be mutually satisfactory. Beyond this nothing more was supposed to be expected or desired. During the negotiations at Ghent, the British Commissioners, in a communication to the American Commissioners, dated Oct. 8. 1814,[2] distinctly avow, that the British Government never required [that] all that portion of Massachusets, intervening between the Province of New Brunswick and Quebec, should be ceded to Great Britain, but only that "*small portion* of unsettled country, which intercepts the communi-

1. See above, Ashburton to DW, June 21, 1842.   2. *ASP: FR*, 3:721–723.

cation between Halifax and Quebec." So, his Lordship in his communication admits that, "the reasons which have induced the British Government to maintain their rights '(claim)' in this controversy" are, "the establishing a good boundary between our two countries, so as to prevent collisions and dispute, and an unobstructed communication and connection of our colonies, with each other." Again, looking, as he says, on the map for such a boundary "with reference to the sole object of Great Brittain, as already described the line of the St Johns from where the North line from the St Croix strikes it, up to some one of its sources, seems evidently to suit both parties," &c. Indeed the portion of Territory which Great Britain needs for her accommodation is so perfectly obvious, that no material difference of opinion, it is believed, has ever been expressed on the subject. It is that portion, which lies north of the St John, and East of the Madawasca rivers, with a strip of convenient width on the west side of the latter river, and of the Lake from which it issues.

Sent here then under this state of things, and with these views by the Legislature of Maine, in a spirit of peace and conciliation, her commissioners were surprized, and pained to be repelled, as it were, in the outset, by such a proposition as his Lordship has submitted to you. On carefully analyzing it, it will be seen, that in addition to all the territory needed by Great Britain for her accommodation, as stated and admitted by her own authorities and agents, it requires that Maine should further yield a valuable territory of more than fifty miles in extent, lying along the South side of the St John, extending from the due North line westerly to Fish River, and so back from the river St John, as it is understood, to the Eagle lakes, and probably to the little Madawasca and Aroostook. Speaking of this branch of his proposition, his Lordship treats it merely as "departing to this inconsiderable extent from the marked line of the river St John." His Lordship does not state how much further up the river he contemplates going. His language implies, that the distance to Fish river, although over fifty miles, is only an inconsiderable part of the whole extent contemplated. This part of the proposition then, would seem to imply a relinquishment also on the part of Maine, of a large portion of her territory North of the St John and west of the Madawasca rivers. In this view of the case it is due to the Governor and Legislature and people of Maine to say, that they had not expected such a proposition. If they had, nothing is hazarded in saying no Commissioners would have been sent here to receive and consider it. And in this state of things, it becomes a bounden duty on the part of the Undersigned to say to you, that if the yielding and relinquishing on the part of the State of Maine, of any portion of Territory, however small, on the South side of the St John be with her Britannic Majestys Government a sine qua non to an amicable settlement of the boundary of Maine, the mission of the Commissioners of Maine is ended. They came not to throw obstacles in the way to the successful accomplishment of the great work you have on hand—that of consolidating an honorable peace between two great nations, but on the contrary, they came prepared to yield much, to sacrifice much on the part of Maine, to the peace of the Union, and the interest of her sister States. If the hopes of the people of Maine and of the United States are to be disappointed, it is believed the fault lies not at the door of the Governor, or Legislature of Maine, or of her Commissioners.

At the date of the earliest maps of that Country, the river now called the Madawasca, had not acquired a distinctive name, and consequently the source of that river was regarded as one of the sources, if not the principal source, of the St John. On looking at the Map, it will at once be seen, that the general course of the St John and Madawasca, from the mouth of the former to the source of the latter, are one and the same. As connected with this fact, we find that, at least, five different Maps published in London in the years 1765, 1769, 1771, 1774, 1775,[3] place the Northwest angle of Nova Scotia on the highlands, at the source of that branch of the St John, then without distinctive appellation, but now known as the Madawasca. One of these five is specially quoted in the report of the Committee of Congress of the 16 August 1782,[4] so often referred to in this controversy. In no map of a date prior to the Treaty of 1783, it is believed, is the Northwest angle of Nova Scotia placed on the highlands, at the source of any branch whatever, of the St John, but the Madawasca. Hence the proposition of the American Commissioners in 1782, in discussing the subject of the boundaries of the United States, to begin at the Northwest Angle of Nova Scotia, on the highlands, at the source of the St John.[5] Respect for the distinguished men who negociated the treaty of peace of 1783 would induce the Undersigned to renew the proposition, so far as regards adopting the Madawasca, as a boundary, were it not that being prepared to yield all that is needed for the accommodation of Great Britain, they are aware that a strip on the West side of that river, is nec-

3. Of nineteen maps mentioned in Albert Gallatin's 1840 memoir on the northeastern boundary, five best match the description given here by the Maine commissioners. These are Palairet's Map of North America, 1765; Kitchen's British Dominions in North America of 1769, prepared for John Knox's *History of the War in America*; Bell's North America, improved from D'Anville, 1771; Dunn's British Empire in North America, 1774; Bowen and Gibson's North America, 1775. See Albert Gallatin, *The Right of the United States of America to the North-Eastern Boundary . . .* (New York, 1840), pp. 76–77.

4. Worthington Chauncey Ford, ed., *Journals of the Continental Congress, 1774–1789* (34 vols., Washington, D.C., 1904–1937), 23:481–524. The report refers to a map by Bowen, p. 509.

5. See the agreement of October 8, 1782, between the American and British commissioners in Francis Wharton, ed., *Revolutionary Diplomatic Correspondence of the United States* (6 vols., Washington, D.C., 1889), 5: 805–808.

essary to that object. The particular map quoted in the Report above mentioned, is that of Eman[ue]l Bowen, Geographer to the King [George II],[6] published in 1775, in which the Penobscot and a line drawn from one of its sources, crossing the St John, to the source of that branch now called the Madawasca, are distinctly laid down, as the western boundary of Nova Scotia. So in all the maps which place the Northwest Angle of Nova Scotia on the highlands, at the source of the St John, those highlands and that source are on the North side of the Malloostook, which is now known to be the main branch of the St John. The inference or assumption then, that it was not the intention of the Commissioners, who negociated the Treaty of peace, that any portion of the valley or waters of the St John should be included within the limits of the United States, because the American negociators of that Treaty proposed the Northwest Angle of Nova-Scotia on the highlands, at the source of the St John, as the place of beginning, in establishing the boundaries of the United States, is, it is believed, wholly unwarranted. The fact, on the contrary, as it seems to the undersigned, disproves any such intention or supposition, on the part of the American Commissioners.

The British Commissaries Messrs [William] Mildmay and [Ruvigny] De Cosne in their reply of the 23rd January 1753 to the French Commissaries, say "We have sufficiently proved, first, that Acadia (Nova Scotia) has had an inland limit from the earliest times, and secondly that that limit has ever been the River St Lawrence."[7] At that time then, the British Government contended, that the Northwest angle of Nova Scotia was formed by the River St Lawrence, as one line, and a line drawn North from the St Croix to the St Lawrence as the other—and this is in conformity with the position assigned to it on [John] Mitchels map and some others. By the grant to Sir William Alexander,[8] the Northwest angle of Nova Scotia was also placed at the River St Lawrence, although, its precise locality on that river is not determined, by the language of the grant. The French Commissaries on their part contended, that the limits of Canada extended on the South side of the Saint Lawrence, so as to embrace the territory watered by the rivers that empty themselves into

6. Bowen (d. 1767) was a London map engraver from about 1720 until his death. Bowen was the official map engraver of King George II (1683–1760), who ruled 1727–1760.

7. Mildmay (d. 1771) and Cosné (not further identified) represented Britain on the Anglo-French commission established in accordance with the provisional peace of Aix-la-Chapelle of 1748. The note of January 23, 1753, is in the Mildmay Letter-books at MiU-C. The French commissaries were Roland-Michel Barin, Comte de la Galissoniere (1693–1756), a French naval officer and earlier governor-general of New France, and the French statesman Etienne de Silhouette (1709–1767).

8. Alexander (c. 1567–1640) was granted jurisdiction over Nova Scotia on September 10, 1621. An extract of the grant is in *ASP: FR*, 6:913–914.

the river St Lawrence, "les pays dont les eaux vont se rendre dans le fleuve Saint-Laurent." The Commissions granted to the Governor of Canada and all the public documents issued by the authority of the French Government fully sustain their position.

There is no ground, say they, for entertaining a doubt that all the Commissions granted by the King, for the Government of Canada, were conceived in the same terms. In the Splendid Universal Atlas published at Paris by [Gilles Robert] De Vaugondy and Son in 1757,[9] there is a map dated 1755, and referred to expressly by the author, who was Geographer to the King, as illustrating the dispute between France and Great Britain, in regard to the boundaries of their respective territories. On this map, the dividing ridge or highlands is placed where the U. States have ever contended it is only to be found; and what is deserving of notice is, that the Northwest angle of Nova-Scotia is there placed on these highlands, at the head of the lake there called Melaousta; the line separating Nova Scotia from New England being drawn through the centre of that lake, to the source of the St Croix. The disputes above referred to having led to a war between France and Great Britain—France finally ceded to Great Britain, in Feby 1763, Canada, and abandoned all claim to Nova Scotia and the whole territory in controversy between the two powers. On the 7th Oct. 1763, His Britannic Majesty issued his proclamation[10] defining the Southern boundary of Canada, or the Province of Quebec, and establishing it where the French Government had always contended it was. Immediately afterward he also defined and established the western limit of Nova Scotia, alleging by way of justification of certain pretensions, which had been put forward in opposition in Massachusetts, in regard to the Penobscot as a boundary, that although he might have removed the line as far west as the Penobscot, yet he would limit himself at the St Croix. Accordingly the western boundary of Nova Scotia, was in November 1763, defined and established as follows "by a line" &c "across the entrance of the Bay of Fundy, to the mouth of the River St Croix, by the said river to its source, and by a line drawn due North from thence to the southern boundary of our Province of Quebec."[11] The Northwest angle of Nova Scotia was by these two documents, established in November 1763, and defined to be, the angle formed by the line last described, and the line which "passes along the highlands, which divide the rivers that empty

9. Vaugondy (1686–1766) became the royal geographer in 1730. His son, Didier Robert de Vaugondy (1723–1786), succeeded him as geographer in 1760.

10. *Annual Register 1763*, vol. 6, *State Papers* (London, 1796), pp. 208–213. George III (1738–1820)

ruled from 1760 to 1820.

11. The proclamation of November 21, 1763, is the same as a commission issued to Governor Montague Wilmot (d. 1766). See *International Arbitrations*, 1:51. A draft of the commission is in *ASP: FR*, 6:916–917.

themselves into the said river St Lawrence, from those which fall into the Sea, and also along the North coast of the Bay des Chaleurs." We now see wherefore it was, that the distinguished men who negotiated the Treaty of peace, were so particular in describing the precise position and giving so exact a definition of the Northwest angle of Nova Scotia, mentioned in the treaty. They distinc[t]ly and explicitly state that motive to be, that "all disputes which might arise in future, on the subject of the boundaries of the United States, may be prevented."[12] Their starting bounds, or point of departure, is the Northwest angle of Nova Scotia. Here the question presents itself, what northwest angle? They describe it: not that Northwest Angle which in several maps is laid down on the highlands, at the Madawasca source of the St John; not that Northwest angle, on the southern bank of the River St Lawrence laid down on Mitchels map, and so strenuously contended for by the British Government and British Commissaries, in their dispute with France; not that Northwest angle on the River St Lawrence described in the Charter or grant by King James to Sir William Alexander, but the Northwest Angle of Nova Scotia, defined and established in Novr 1763, "to wit; that angle which is formed by a line, drawn due North from the source of St Croix River, to the highlands" &c and further, that there might be no ground, for reviving the old pretension, in regard to the Penobscot, or any other Western river being intended as the St Croix, the river St Croix intended in the Treaty, is declared to have its mouth in the Bay of Fundy, Nor, is there any pretence of any doubt or question having been raised, until long after the Treaty of peace, as to what highlands were intended in the proclamation of 1763, as constituting the southern boundary of Quebec. So far from it, the Parliament of Great Britain in 1774 passed the Quebec act,[13] which was one of the greivances, complained of by the colonies, and which confirmed the boundaries, so far as the <present> matter under consideration is concerned, defined and established by that proclamation. Of these two public acts, the American Commissioners were not ignorant, nor misinformed. They are both expressly referred to, and mentioned in the report of Aug. 16. 1782, already mentioned. To find these highlands, the state[s]-man and jurist, who has no other object in view than to expound the Treaty, according to its terms and provisions, uninfluenced by any secret bias, or preconceived theory, will, it is believed, begin, not at the mouth or source of the St Croix, but on the bank of the River St Lawrence, at a point North of the source of the river St Croix, and following the due north line so called, southward, he will find no difficulty in discovering the line of the "*versants*" from which issue the rivers that empty themselves into the river St Lawrence. The whole and exclusive object and in-

12. The quotation is from Article 2 of the definitive treaty of peace signed September 3, 1783. See *Treaties*, 2:152.

13. *British Statutes at Large*, 13 and 14 Geo. III c. 83, pp. 549–554.

tent of the proclamation of 1763 so far as relates to this matter of boundary in that section of country, was not in any way to affect or alter the limits of jurisdiction over the territory lying south of that line of *"versants"* but only to cut off from Nova Scotia and Massachusetts that portion of territory which was watered by the rivers which empty themselves into the river St Lawrence. Accordingly the due north line or boundary between Nova Scotia and Massachusetts is described as extending "from the source of the St Croix to the southern boundary of our Province of Quebec."

The Commissioners of Maine do not consider themselves as sent here to argue the question of right in regard to the conflicting claims to the disputed territory, nor to listen to an argument in opposition to the claim of Maine. Their mission contemplated a far different and more conciliatory object. They have however felt themselves compelled in justice to Maine to reply to two positions assumed by Lord Ashburton the soundness of which with great deference and respect for his Lordship they cannot admit—first that "it was the intention of the parties to the treaty of peace of 1783 to leave to Great Britain by their description of boundaries the whole waters of the river St John"—secondly "that the treaty of 1783 was not executable according to its strict expression." His Lordship also speaks of "a volume of additional controversial matter which he has not communicated but which he has brought with him and much of which would be of no inconsiderable weight and importance, if controversy were our object." Among the matter referred to in that volume the undersigned believe they have reason to conjecture will be found a map entitled "North America with the New Discoveries" by William Faden Geographer to the King published in the Year 1785. That map a copy of which is now before the undersigned, communicated by you[,] extends the British Possessions so as to include the waters of the St John and dispenses with the due North line of the Treaty altogether. The Map referred to is a small one, of small pretensions. It is however somewhat remarkable that the same William Faden published in 1783 a map prepared with great care entitled "The United States of North America with the British and Spanish Territories according to the Treaty" in which he lays down the boundary of Quebec according to the act of 1774 and the boundary of the United States in precise accordance with the American claim. He was not at that time Geographer to the King. It is well known that difficulties very soon after the treaty of peace began to spring up between the United States and Great Britain which became more and more exasperated until the conclusion of the treaty negotiated by Mr [John] Jay. During that period the Boundaries of the United States became more restricted on more British maps than the one published by Mr Faden. How far the new light let in upon him by the feeling of the times and his new position enlightened the mind of Mr Faden in making his new discoveries it is neither our duty nor our disposition to discuss. Mr Faden and others were only imitating in this particular what had been done some thirty years before during the controversy between France and Great Britain—and again in the subsequent one between the Crown and Massachusetts—when the officers of the Crown were endeavouring to reclaim the territory east of the Penobscot.[14]

As they have been assured that Lord Ashburton is restrained by his instructions from yielding the island of Grand Manan, or any of the islands in Passamaquoddy bay, or even any portion of the narrow strip of territory which lies between the due North line from the source of the St Croix, and the St John river above Eel river so called, as an equivalent for any portion of the territory claimed by Maine as within her boundaries, her commissioners on their part feel themselves constrained to say that the portion of territory within the limits of Maine as claimed by her which they are prepared in a spirit of peace and good neighbourhood to yield for the accommodation of Great Britain must be restrained and confined to such portion only and in such reasonable extent as is necessary to secure to Great Britain "an unobstructed communication and connection of her colonies with each other." It appears by his communication to you that his Lordship proposes to yield the disputed territory claimed by New Hampshire at the sources of the Connecticut river, the strip of disputed territory at the head of Vermont in the possession of that State north of the Forty fifth parallel of latitude and the strip of disputed territory, embracing Rouse's point, on Lake Champlain north of the same parallel, in the possession of the State of New York, notwithstanding these have been decided by the Arbiter to belong of right to Great Britain. Now the undersigned are fully aware of the importance of having all these difficulties in regard to boundaries amicably adjusted and that it is highly desirable to the United States to have them so adjusted and to the particular states interested to be confirmed and quieted in their respective limits and possessions. But it cannot have escaped your attention that all this is proposed to be done partly at the expense of Massachusetts, but principally at the expense of Maine. The only thing in the nature of an equivalent offered to Maine and Massachusetts relates to a concession by Great Britain of the right of transporting the produce of the forests without duty down the St John. It is not the intention of the undersigned to depreciate or underrate the value of such a concession; but it is con-

14. During the American Revolution, a number of Loyalists established a garrison at the mouth of the Penobscot River. In an effort to build a Loyalist enclave, some British officials unsuccessfully attempted to renew a 1764 plan to separate Maine and Massachusetts along the Penobscot. See Henry S. Burrage, *Maine in the Northeastern Boundary Controversy* (Portland, Maine, 1919), pp. 13, 20–22.

tended that it is a privilege as desirable to New Brunswick as it is to Maine and Massachusetts. It is to the territory of Maine watered by the St John and its tributary streams that the City of St John must look for the principal material to sustain her external commerce—for her means to pay for the supplies she receives from the mother country. The unobstructed navigation of the St John for the transportation of the products of the forests free of toll or duty of any kind whatever would be a concession mutually advantageous to Maine and Massachusetts on the one part and to Great Britain and New Brunswick on the other, but being mutually advantageous it ought not perhaps to be treated exactly in the character of an equivalent. Yielding however to the force of the considerations which have been referred to, considerations which affect materially the interests of Maine and Massachusetts as members of the Union and assuming it for granted and as a condition that the United States themselves will furnish to the *two* States such an equivalent as in justice and equity they ought to do the Undersigned with the assent and concurrence of the Commissioners of Massachusetts propose the following as a conventional line or line by agreement between the United States and the State of Maine on the one part and Great Britain and the territories of her Britannic Majesty on the other viz—Beginning at the middle of the main channel of the River St John, where the due North line from the source of the River St Croix crosses the St John; thence, westerly by the middle of the main channel of the St John, to a point three miles westerly of the mouth of the river Madawasca; thence, by a straight line, to the outlet of Long Lake; thence westerly, by a direct line to the point where the River St Francis empties itself into Lake Pohengamook; thence continuing in the same direct line, to the highlands which divide the waters emptying themselves into the River Du Loup from those which empty themselves into the river St Francis.

In proposing this line the following reasons have presented themselves to the Undersigned for adopting it as a conventional line or line by agreement in preference to any other

1st It yields to Great Britain all she needs to secure to her "an unobstructed communication and connection of her colonies with each other" —and connected with the unobstructed and free navigation of the St John seems to meet the legitimate wants of all parties.

2nd The most natural boundary from the due North line to the highlands of the treaty would be the St John and the Madawasca to its source as first proposed by the American Commissioners, who negotiated the peace of 1783. But as that boundary taken in its whole extent would cut off the communication between the British Colonies at the grand portage the line here proposed removes that difficulty. At or near the point where the proposed line leaves the St John, which from the due north line from the St Croix pursues a northwesterly course upward the river suddenly turns and trends for a distance of about five miles nearly south, and thence for its whole course upward to its source trends southerly of West. To pursue the line of the St John further west than the point indicated, which is about three miles above the mouth of the Madawasca, would be to adopt an angular line projecting itself into the American territory. The outlet of Long Lake is proposed as a natural and permanent bound which cannot be mistaken. And for the same reason the inlet of Lake Pohenagamook is also proposed; and the line being continued to the highlands removes all possible ground of misapprehension and controversy.

3rd As Great Britain has restrained her Minister Plenipotentiary from granting any territorial equivalent to be incorporated into the territorial limits of Maine any further concession of territory on the part of Maine could hardly it is apprehended be expected from her.

In making the proposition above submitted on their part in connection with a concession on the part of Great Britain of the unobstructed navigation of the St John and all its branches and tributaries which in any part flow from the Territory of the United States for the transportation of the lumber and products of the forest free of toll or duty the undersigned had supposed it quite possible that they had misapprehended the meaning intended to be conveyed by the expression of Lord Ashburton where he speaks of "some one of the sources of the St John." But they have now just learned informally that the expression was used by him advisedly meaning thereby some one of the sources of that river situated in the vicinity of the sources of the Penobscot and Chaudiere. His proposition therefore extends to a yielding on the part of Maine of the whole territory on the North side of the St John from the due North line to its source; and this too without any territorial equivalent to Maine. With this explanation the language of Lord Ashburton in calling the Southern border of the St John from the due North line to the mouth of Fish river an "inconsiderable extent" is more readily understood. To this part of the proposition, there is only one reply. Whatever may be the solicitude of the undersigned that the difficulties which have arisen in regard to the boundaries of Maine may be amicably and definitively arranged, the proposition, as now explained and understood, cannot be acceded to.

In making the offer they have submitted, the undersigned are sensible their proposition involves a sacrifice of no inconsiderable portion of the just claims and expectations of Maine. It is made in the spirit of peace, of conciliation. It is made to satisfy her sister states that Maine is not pertinacious or unreasonable but is desirous of peace and ready to make large sacrifices for the general good.

Before closing this communication the undersigned feel it their duty to say something by way of explanation of their views in regard to the

French settlers at Madawasca. In any treaty which may be made with Great Britain affecting these people the grants which have been made to them by New Brunswick may and ought to be confirmed to them in fee simple with such provision in regard to the possessory rights acquired by other actual settlers there as may be just and equitable and also the right may be reserved to the settlers on both banks of the river to elect, within some reasonable period, and determine, of which government the individuals, signifying their election, will remain or become citizens or subjects. If then they should have any preference, they will have it in their power on mature consideration and reflection to decide for themselves and act accordingly. The hard lot and sufferings of these people and of their fathers give them a claim to our sympathies. The atrocious cruelties practiced upon their ancestors are matters of history. The appalling details of them are among their traditions. The fathers and the mothers have taught them to their children. When fleeing from their oppressors in 1785 they settled down in the wilderness at Madawasca they believed and understood themselves to be within the limits and jurisdiction of the United States, a people of whom France had been the friend and ally in the war which had just terminated in their independence, and who was still the friend and ally of France in peace. Their history since that period has lost little of its interest. Too few in number—too weak in resources—too remote to expect or receive aid they have submitted to whatever master assumed authority over them. With a knowledge of their history and the wrongs they and their ancestors have suffered it will be difficult for the people of Maine to bring themselves into the belief that these people are opposed to living under the mild and gentle sway of our free institutions. It will be equally difficult for the people of Maine to satisfy themselves that it is only from a lively and disinterested sympathy for these poor Frenchmen that the Government of Great Britain is so solicitous to retain possession of the South bank of the St John extending from the due north line more than fifty miles up to Fish river. On the best consideration they have been able to give to this subject the undersigned can see nothing in the condition or circumstances of these settlers which would justify them in abandoning the very obvious and only natural boundary, to adopt one that must be altogether arbitrary.

The undersigned avail themselves of this occasion to tender to Mr Webster Secretary of State assurances of their distinguished consideration and respect.

Wm P Preble   Edward Kavanagh   Edward Kent   John Otis

ls. DNA, RG 76 (Records of the Boundary and Claims Commissions and Arbitrations and Miscellaneous Documents Relating to the Northeast Boundary, 1827–1842). Published in *Senate Documents*, 27th Cong., 3d sess., Serial 413, No. 1, pp. 72–80.

FROM LORD ASHBURTON

private
My Dear Mr Webster   1 July 1842
  I must throw myself on your compassion to contrive some how or other
to get me released. I contrive to crawl about in these heats by day & pass
my nights in a sleepless fever. In short I shall positively not outlive this
affair if it is to be much prolonged. I had hoped that these Gentlemen from
the North East would be equally averse to this roasting. Could you not
press them to come to the point and say whether we can or can not agree?
I do not see why I should be kept waiting while Maine & Massachusetts
settle their accounts with the General Government.
  I am rather apprehensive that there is an inclination *somewhere* to
keep this negotiation in suspense on grounds unconnected with the mere
difficulties of the case itself. Pray save me from these profound politicians, for my nerves will not stand so much cunning wisdom. Ever My
Dear Sir Yours sincerely   A.

I shall not venture upon a walk through the sun unless I hear that you
have something to tell me.
You promised me the Oregon report[1] if you have it pray send it me.

ALS. DLC. Published in Curtis, 2:113.

FROM LORD ASHBURTON
Private   [c. July 2, 1842]
  I return you My Dear Sir your letter of the Maine Commissioners in
which it is easy enough to perceive the Masters hand.[1]
  These gentlemen take their departure always from the presumption
that the whole Territory belongs to them and that they are benevolently
giving us a certain portion. I do not well see how a Secretary of State of
the U.S. can repeat such sentiments as his own, but you will best judge
in what shape this paper had best reach me.
  I have had this morning a long conversation with Mr [Edward] Kava-

1. Ashburton refers to a report on
Oregon made in June 1842 by Lieutenant Charles Wilkes, head of the
U.S. Exploring Expedition of 1838–
1842. Public accounts of the report
invigorated American interest in the
territory and probably helped prevent further negotiations by DW and
Ashburton on Oregon. The report to
Secretary of the Navy Abel P. Upshur,
which advocated U.S. military occupation of the Oregon country as far

north as the Fraser River, was not
published until July 15, 1911, when
it appeared in the *Congressional Record*, 62d Cong., 1st sess., pt. 3, pp.
2977–2983.
  1. See above, Preble et al. to DW,
June 29, 1842. The remark concerning the "Masters hand" probably refers to William Pitt Preble, considered
the most difficult of the commissioners.

nagh & I should like to communicate to you what passed: If you are at home this evening I will call on you. I found him a sensible liberal man.

We both agreed that we should do no good in continuing the negotiation with long controversial memorials & that we must get by some shorter cut to ascertain whether we can agree. I can not say that I quite despair but my confidence of doing any thing is a good deal shaken. I have personally no objection to any communication with these Gentlemen which you approve.

I like much your Cruising convention. The question will come when & where the Instructions shall be prepared. Yours Sincerely   A.

ALS. DLC. Published in Curtis, 2:113.

TO LORD ASHBURTON

Department of State,
My Lord: Washington, 8 July, 1842.

Your notes of the 13th and the 21st of June,[1] were duly received.

In the first of these, you correctly say that, in our conferences on the boundary question, we have both been of opinion that no advantage would be gained by resorting, at this time, to the discussion at length of the grounds on which each party considers its claim of right to rest. At the same time you deem it expedient, nevertheless, to offer some observations calculated, in your judgment, to repel a supposed allegation or suggestion, that this controversy only began in 1814; that up to that period the American claim was undisputed, and that the English claim, as now set forth, is founded merely in motives of interest. Nothing is more natural than that your Lordship should desire to repel an imputation which would impeach the sincerity and good faith of your Government, and all the weight which justice and candor require is given to your Lordship's observations in this respect. It is not my purpose, nor do I conceive it pertinent to the occasion, to go into any consideration of the facts and reasonings presented by you, to show the good faith and sincerity of England in the claim asserted by her. Any such discussion would be a departure from the question of right, now subsisting between the two Governments, and would be, more especially, unfit for an occasion in which the parties are approaching each other in a friendly spirit, with the hope of terminating the controversy by agreement. Following your Lordship's example, however, I must be permitted to say, that few questions have ever arisen under this Government, in regard to which a stronger or more general conviction was felt that the country was in the right, than this question of the Northeastern Boundary. To say nothing of the sentiments of the Governments, and People of the States more directly interested, whose opinions may be supposed capable of bias, both Houses of Con-

1. Ashburton to DW, June 13 and 21, 1842, above.

gress, after full and repeated consideration, have affirmed the validity of the American claim,[2] by a unanimity experienced on very few other subjects; and the general judgment of the whole People seems to be the same way. Abstaining from all historical facts, all contemporaneous expositions, and all external arguments and circumstances, I will venture to present to your Lordship a very condensed view of the reasons which produce in this country a conviction that a boundary line may be ascertained, run, and delineated, with precision, under and according to the words of the Stipulation in the Treaty of 1783; that no doubt can be raised by any part of that Stipulation which other parts of it do not remove or explain, and that a line so run would include all that the United States claim. This view is presented by a series of short propositions.

1. The northwest angle of Nova Scotia is the thing to be sought for and found.

2. That angle is to be ascertained by running a line due north from the source of the St. Croix river till that line reaches the highlands, and where such north line intersects the highlands there is the angle; and thence the line is to run along the *said* highlands, which *said* highlands divide those rivers which empty themselves into the river St. Lawrence from those that fall into the Atlantic ocean. The angle required, therefore, is an angle made by the intersection of a due north line with highlands, from one slope of which the rivers empty themselves into the river St. Lawrence, and from the other into the Atlantic Ocean.

3. Supposing it to be a matter of doubt whether the St. John and the Restigouche are rivers falling into the Atlantic Ocean, in the sense of the Treaty, then the rule of just interpretation is, that if one element or one part in the description be uncertain, it is to be explained by others which are certain, if there be such others. Now, there is no doubt as to the rivers which fall into the St. Lawrence. They are certain, and to their sources the north line is to run, since at their sources the highlands required by the Treaty do certainly exist. And, departing for a moment from the rule just prescribed to myself, I will remind your Lordship that the joint commissioners and agents of the two Governments in 1817, in giving the surveyors instructions for finding these highlands, directed them, in terms, to proceed upon a due north line "till they should arrive at some one of the streams connected with the river St. Lawrence," and then to explore the highlands from that point to the northwesternmost head of Connecticut river.[3] It is indisputable that a line run according to these instructions,

2. The Senate unanimously passed on July 4, 1838, a set of resolutions affirming the validity of the American claim to the "full extent of all the territory in dispute." The House unani- mously concurred on July 7. See the *Cong. Globe*, 25th Cong., 2d sess., pp. 496–497, 502.

3. DW refers to the instructions approved on June 9, 1817, for the

thus given by the commissioners and agents of both Governments, would give to the United States all that they have at any time claimed.

4. It is certain that by the Treaty the eastern boundary of the United States, from the head of the St. Croix, is to be a due north and south line; and it is equally certain that this line is to run north till it reaches highlands from whose northern watershed the rivers flow into the river St. Lawrence.

5. These two things being, one mathematically and the other physically, certain in themselves, and capable of being precisely marked and delineated, explain or control the uncertainty, if there be uncertainty, in the other part or element of the description.

6. The British argument, assuming that the Bay of Fundy, and more especially the Bay of Chaleurs, are not the Atlantic Ocean, within the meaning of the Treaty, insists that the rivers flowing into these bays are not, therefore, in the sense of the Treaty, rivers falling into the Atlantic, and therefore the highlands to which the United States claim have not that southern or eastern watershed which the Treaty calls for; and as it is agreed, nevertheless, that we must somewhere find highlands, and go to them, whose northern waters run into the St. Lawrence, the conclusion is, that the different parts of the description in the Treaty do not cohere, and that therefore the Treaty cannot be executed.

7. Our answer to this, as is obvious from what has already been said, is twofold:

First. What may be doubtful in itself may be made certain by other things which are certain; and inasmuch as the Treaty does certainly demand a due north line, and does certainly demand the extension of that line to highlands from whose northern sides the rivers flow into the river St. Lawrence, thence two clear requirements make it plain that the parties to the Treaty considered, in fact, the rivers flowing from the south or east of the *said* highlands to be rivers falling into the Atlantic Ocean, because they have placed St. Lawrence rivers and the Atlantic rivers in contradistinction to each other, as rivers running in opposite directions, but with their sources in the same highlands. Rivers fed from these highland fountains, running north or northwest, are rivers emptying themselves into the St. Lawrence, and rivers arising from the same fountains, and running in an opposite direction, seem to be as clearly meant to be desig-

---

survey undertaken in accordance with the terms of Article 5 of the Treaty of Ghent. The British officials were commissioner Thomas Barclay (1753–1830; King's College 1772), principal agent Ward Chipman (1754–1824), and surveyor Joseph Bouchette (1774–1841). The American officials were commissioner Cornelius Peter Van Ness, agent William C. Bradley, and surveyor John Johnson (1771–1842). On the instructions, see *International Arbitrations*, 1:74.

nated by the character of Atlantic rivers. And, as strongly corroborating this view of the subject, allow me to call your Lordship's attention to two facts:

1. The coast of the Atlantic Ocean, from Penobscot river northeasterly, and the western shore of the Bay of Fundy, which is but a continuation of the coast, and is in a line with it, is very nearly parallel to the course of the river St. Lawrence through the same latitudes. This is obvious from the map.

2. The rivers which, from their sources in the same ridge flow respectively into the St. Lawrence and into the Bay of Fundy, and even into the Bay of Chaleurs, run with remarkable uniformity in directions almost exactly opposite, as if hastening away from a common origin to their different destinations, by the shortest course. The only considerable exception to this is the northern sweep of the upper part of the St. John; but the smaller streams, flowing into this part of that river from the west, still strictly obey the general rule.

Now, if, from a certain general line on the face of the country, or as delineated on the map, rivers are found flowing away in opposite directions, however strongly it may be asserted that the mountains or eminences are but isolated elevations, it is nevertheless absolutely certain that such a line does, in fact, define a ridge of highlands which turns the waters both ways.

And as the Commissioners in 1783 had the map before them; as they saw the parallelism of the seacoast and the course of the St. Lawrence; as they saw rivers rising from a common line and running, some north or northwest, the others south or southeast; and as they speak of some of these rivers as emptying themselves into the river St. Lawrence, and of the others falling into the Atlantic Ocean; and *as they make no third class*, is there a reasonable doubt in which class they intended to comprehend all the rivers running in a direction from the St. Lawrence, whether falling immediately or only ultimately into the Atlantic Ocean?

If there be nothing incoherent or inconsequential in this chain of remarks, it will satisfy your Lordship, I trust, that it is not without reason that American opinion has settled firmly in the conviction of the rights of the American side of the question; and I forbear from going into the consideration of the mass of other arguments and proofs, for the same reasons which restrain your Lordship from entering into an extended discussion of the question, as well as because your Lordship will have an opportunity of perusing a paper addressed to me by the Commissioners of Maine,[4] which strongly presents the subject on other grounds and in other lights.

I am now to consider your Lordship's note of the 21st June. Before

4. See above, Preble et al. to DW, June 29, 1842.

entering upon this, I have the President's instructions to say that he fully appreciates the motives which induced your Lordship personally to undertake your present mission; that he is quite aware that your public life has been distinguished by efforts to maintain peace and harmony between the two countries; that he quite well recollects that your exertions were employed to prevent the late war, and that he doubts not the sincerity of your declaration, that nothing could have drawn you from your retirement, and induced you to engage in your present undertaking, but the hope of being of service to your country and to our common race. And I have the utmost pleasure, my Lord, in acknowledging the frankness, candor, and plain dealing, which have characterized your official intercourse with this Government; nor am I permitted or inclined to entertain any doubt of your Lordship's entire conviction, as expressed by yourself, as to the merits of this controversy and the difficulties of the case. The question before us is, whether these confident opinions on both sides, of the rightful nature and just strength of our respective claims, will permit us, while a desire to preserve harmony, and a disposition to yield liberally to mutual convenience, so strongly incite us to come together and to unite on a line by agreement.

It appears to be your Lordship's opinion, that the line of the St. John, from the point where the north line from the St. Croix strikes that river, up to some one of its sources, evidently suits both parties, with an exception, however, of that part of the Madawaska settlement which is on the south side of the St. John, which you propose should be included within the British territory. That, as a line by agreement, the St. John, for some distance upwards from its intersection by the line running north from the St. Croix, would be a very convenient boundary for the two parties, is readily admitted; but it is a very important question how far up, and to which of the sources of this river, this line should extend. Above Madawaska, the course of the river turns to the south, and, stretching away towards the sources of the Penobscot, leaves far to the north the line of communication between New Brunswick and Canada. That line departs from the St. John altogether near Madawaska, and keeping principally upon the left or north bank of the Madawaska, and proceeding by way of the Temiscouata lake, reaches the St. Lawrence at the mouth of the river Du Loup.

There are, then, two important subjects for consideration:

First. Whether the United States can agree to cede, relinquish, or cease to claim, any part of the territory west of the north line from the St. Croix, and south of the St. John. And I think it but candid to say, at once, that we see insurmountable objections to admitting the line to come south of the river. Your Lordship's observations upon the propriety of preserving the unity of the Madawaska settlement are in a great measure just, and altogether founded, I doubt not, in entirely good motives. They savor of humanity and a kind regard to the interests and feelings of individuals. But the difficulties seem insuperable. The river, as your Lordship remarks, seems a natural boundary, and in this part of it to run in a convenient direction. It is a line always clear and indisputable. If we depart from it, where shall we find another boundary equally natural, equally clear, and conforming to the same general course[?] A departure from the line of the river, moreover, would open new questions about equivalents, which it would probably be found impracticable to settle. If your Lordship was at liberty, as I understand you not to be, to cede the whole or a part of the territory commonly called the strip, lying east of the north line and west of the St. John, considerations might be found in such a cession, possibly, for some new demarkation west of the north line and south of the river. But, in the present posture of things, I cannot hold out the expectation to your Lordship that any thing south of the river can be yielded.

And perhaps the inconvenience to the settlers on the southern bank, of making the river the boundary, is less considerable than your Lordship supposes. These settlers are scattered along a considerable extent, very likely soon to connect themselves with whomsoever may come to live near them, and though of different origin, and some difference of religion, not likely on the whole, to be greatly dissimilar from other borderers occupying the neighboring territory, their rights of property would, of course, be all preserved, both of inheritance and alienation; and if some of them should choose to retain the social and political relations under which they now are, their removal, for that purpose, to the north bank, drawing after it no loss of property or of means of subsistence, would not be a great hardship. Your Lordship suggests the inconvenience of dividing a municipality by a line of national boundary; and certainly there is force in the observation; but if, departing from the river, we were to establish to the south of it an artificial line upon the land there might be points on such line at which the people would live in numbers on both sides; and a mere mathematical line might thus divide villages, while it divided nations. The experience of the world, and our own experience, shows the propriety of making rivers boundaries, whenever their courses suit the general object, for the same reason that, in other cases to which they are applicable, mountain ranges, or ridges of highlands, are adopted for the same purpose; these last being perhaps still more convenient lines of division than rivers—being equally clear and prominent objects, and the population of neighboring countries bordering on a mountain line of separation being usually thin and inconsiderable on either side. Rivers and inland waters constitute the boundary between the United States and the territories of Her Majesty for some thousands of miles westward from the place where the forty-fifth degree of north latitude intersects the St. Lawrence; and along this line, though occasional irregularities and outbreaks have taken place, always by the agency and instigation of agitators and lawless men, friends of neither country, yet it is clear that no better demarcation of limits could be made. And at the northeast, along the space through which the St. Croix constitutes the line of separation, controversies and conflicts are not heard of; but similarity of language, character, and pursuits, and mutual respect for the rights of each other, preserve the general peace.

Upon the whole, my Lord, feeling that there may be inconvenience, and perhaps a small degree of hardship, I yet cannot admit that there is any cruelty, in separating the Madawaska settlers south of the St. John, so far as political relations are concerned, from their neighbors on the north of that river. In the present state of society and of peace which exists between the two countries, the severance of political relations need not to disturb social and family intercourse; while high considerations, affecting both the present and the future, seem to me to require that, following natural indications, we adhere to the St. John, in this part of its course, as the line of division.

The next question is, how far upwards this boundary ought to be observed, and along which of its branches? This question would be easily settled, if what may be called the main branch of the river, in this part of it, differing from the general character of rivers in this region of country, did not make a sudden turn. But if we consider the main branch of the St. John that which has been recently usually so denominated, your Lordship observes that, near the mouth of the Madawaska, it turns almost at right angles, and pushes its sources towards those of the Penobscot. Contiguity and compactness of territory can hardly be preserved by following a stream which makes not occasional windings, but at once so great a deflection from its previous course. The Madawaska is one of its branches or principal sources, and, as the map shows, is very much a continuance of the line of the principal river, from the Great Falls upward. The natural course would therefore seem to be to continue along this branch.

We understand, and indeed collect, from your Lordship's note, that, with whatever opinion of her right to the disputed territory, England, in asserting it, has principally in view to maintain, on her own soil, her accustomed line of communication between Canada and New Brunswick. We acknowledge the general justice and propriety of this object, and agree at once that, with suitable equivalents, a conventional line ought to be such as to secure it to England. The question, therefore, simply is, what line will secure it?

The common communication between the provinces follows the course of the St. John, from the Great Falls to the mouth of the Madawaska, and then, not turning away to the south with the course of the main stream, identifies itself with that of the Madawaska, going along with it to the

Temiscouata lakes, thence along those lakes, and so across the highlands, to streams running into the St. Lawrence. And this line of communication we are willing to agree shall hereafter be within acknowledged British territory, upon such conditions and considerations as may be assented to. The Madawaska and the forementioned lakes might conveniently constitute the boundary. But I believe it is true that, in some part of the distance above the mouth of the Madawaska, it has been found convenient to establish the course of communication on the south bank of that river. This consideration may be important enough to justify a departure from what would otherwise be desirable, and the running of the line at some distance south of the Madawaska, observing natural monuments where it may be practicable, and thus leaving the whole valley of the Madawaska on the British side.

The United States, therefore, upon the adjustment of proper equivalents, would not object to a line of boundary which should begin at the middle of the main channel of the river St. John, where that river is intersected by a due north line, extended from the source of the St. Croix; thence, proceeding westerly, by the middle of the main channel of that river, to a point three miles westerly of the mouth of the Madawaska; thence, by a straight line, to the outlet of Long Lake; thence, westerly, by a direct line, to the point where the river St. Francis empties itself into the lake called Pohenagamook; thence, continuing in the same direct line, to the highlands which divide the waters falling into the river Du Loup from those which fall into the river St. Francis. Having thus arrived at the highlands, I shall be ready to confer on the correct manner of following them to the northwesternmost head of the Connecticut river.

Such a line as has been now described would secure to England a free intercourse between Canada and New Brunswick; and, with the navigation of the St. John yielded to the United States, would appear to meet the wants of all parties. Your Lordship's proposition in regard to the navigation is received as just, and as constituting, so far as it may go, a natural equivalent. Probably the use of the river for the transportation of the products of the forest, grown on the American side of the line, would be equally advantageous to both parties, and therefore, in granting it, no sacrifice of British interest would be incurred. A conviction of this, together with their confidence in the validity of their own claim, is very likely to lead the two States immediately concerned to consider their relinquishment of the lands north of the line much in the light of a mere cession. It need not be denied, that to secure this privilege, and to have a right to enjoy it free from tax, toll, or other liability or inability, is an object of considerable importance to the people of Maine.

Your Lordship intimates that, as a part of the general arrangement of boundaries, England would be willing to surrender to the United States Rouse's point, and all the territory heretofore supposed to be within the boundaries of New Hampshire, Vermont, and New York, but which a correct ascertainment of the forty-fifth parallel of north latitude shows to be included within the British line. This concession is, no doubt, of some value. If made, its benefits would enure partly to these three States and partly to the United States, and none of it to the particular interests of Maine and Massachusetts. If regarded, therefore, as a part of the equivalent for the manner of adjusting the Northeastern Boundary, these two last mentioned States would, perhaps, expect that the value, if it could be ascertained, should be paid to them. On this point further consideration may be necessary.

If, in other respects, we should be able to agree on a boundary, the points which you refer to, connected with the ascertainment of the head of the Connecticut, will be attended to, and Captain [Andrew] Talcott,[5] who made the exploration in that quarter, will be ready to communicate the result of his observations. I have the honor to be, with distinguished consideration, your obedient servant,   Danl Webster.

L C. DNA, RG 59 (Notes to Foreign Legations, Britain). Published in *Senate Documents*, 27th Cong., 3d sess., Serial 413, No. 1, pp. 44–50.

FROM LORD ASHBURTON

Sir   Washington July 11th, 1842

I lose no time in acknowledging the receipt of the note you did me the honor of addressing me on the 8th instant;[1] and I beg in the first place to say that I am duly sensible of the assurance you give me that the President has been pleased to appreciate the motives which induced my present mission, and much flattered by your recognition of the candor and frankness which have hitherto marked our intercourse.

I had hoped that we had escaped by mutual consent from a return to the endless and fruitless argument on the general question of the rights of our respective governments in the matter of the North Eastern boundary. It seemed to have been decided by so many high and competent authorities that the precise geographical point so long looked for was not to be found that it necessarily followed that any hope of settlement must rest upon an amicable compromise. The arrival here of Commissioners from Maine and Massachusetts and the admitted disposition of the two Governments have given the public a very general expectation that this

5. Talcott (c. 1797–1883; U.S. Military Academy 1818), an army engineer, had been assigned to the fort at Rouses Point in 1818–1819. He resigned from the army in 1836 and served on the northeastern boundary commission with James Renwick and James D. Graham from July 1840 to February 1843. The reports of the commission are in *Executive Documents*, 26th Cong., 2d sess., Serial 384, and 27th Cong., 2d sess., Serial 402.

1. See above.

compromise might at last be effected, and I hope you will excuse my expressing my regret that the note now before me, and the Paper from the gentlemen from Maine addressed to you which accompanied it,[2] should have contained so much of a renewal of the old controversy, and should not have been confined to the simple question whether we could or could not agree to terms of settlement. If the observations contained in my note of the 13th ulto[3] have given rise to these consequences, I much regret it, and I would now pass over all these more than useless discussions and proceed at once to notice the proposals you make, if I were not apprehensive that my so doing might be construed into some want of respect for the parties from whom these observations have proceeded.

I will however endeavour to bring within a narrow compass what I have to say on the subject, and the more so, because with all deference to you, Sir, I may add that there is little in these arguments that is new or that has not been often advanced and refuted during the many past years of controversy.

I should except from this want of novelty the position, to me entirely new, advanced by the Commissioners from Maine, that the north west angle of Nova Scotia, which is, as you express it, "the thing to be sought for and found," was at the head of the Madawaska river; which river, it is maintained by a long argument, supported by authorities and maps, was always considered as the real St. Johns, and this is stated to justify the opinion expressed by the old Congress in 1779 that this north west angle was at the source of the St. John's.

Giving all possible consideration to this apparently new discovery, I cannot say that it appears well founded. Looking at [John] Mitchell's map, the use of which by the negotiators of the Peace of 1783 has been always so much relied upon on the part of America, there is nothing more clearly marked than the great distinct channel of the upper St. John's, and it seems hardly possible that the negotiators or the Congress should have made the supposed mistake. But supposing this hypothesis were well founded, the Temiscouata lake is then now to be this long lost angle of Nova Scotia. What becomes then of the point so long contended for by Maine between the Metis and one of the tributaries of the Ristigouche? These points must be about 50 miles apart. Both can not be true, and if it be maintained as I rather collect it to be from the paper of the Maine Commissioners, that the point at the Metis is the true Boundary, as being the point stricken by the north line, though the other be the true North West angle of Nova Scotia, there is at least an end of the whole argument resting upon this North West angle being, as stated by you, "the thing to be sought for and found."

2. See above, Preble et al. to DW, June 29, 1842.

3. See above, Ashburton to DW, June 13, 1842.

If this new discovery leads us to no other inference we can hardly fail to derive from it the conviction that all the ingenuity applied to unravel this mystery leaves us equally in the dark, and that it is not without reason that it has been decided by so many persons, after careful examination, that this boundary is not susceptible of settlement according to the precise words of the Treaty.

This decision has been come to by Mr. [James] Madison in 1802, by Mr. [Thomas] Jefferson in 1803, by Judge [James] Sullivan about the same time, by the arbiter in 1831, and it has been acted upon by nearly every secretary of state of the United States during the controversy from that time to this; for although in a case in dispute each party during the dispute endeavours to hold his own, I am not aware that any secretary of state, or any President of the United States, has ever treated this subject otherwise than as one attended by that degree of uncertainty, that it could only be solved by an arbiter or by a compromise. I would appeal to your candor, Sir, to say whether at this time, and under these circumstances, it is fair to speak of this disputed territory as belonging indisputably to one party, and to be yielded by way of concession and for equivalents to the other. Any convention I may sign must be for a division of that which is in doubt and dispute. With any arrangements between the State of Maine and the general government I have nothing to do; and if, which God forbid, our endeavours at an amicable compromise should at last fail, I must hold that Great Britain retains her right at least equal to that of the United States, to every part of the territory in dispute, until by a renewed reference, or by the skill of some more fortunate negotiator this difference may be brought to a close.

I have now only to add a few observations upon the arguments contained in your own note.

Some stress is laid upon the fact that the joint Commissioners of the two Governments in 1817 directed the surveyors to run the north line from the St. Croix until it met waters running into the St. Lawrence. The lines to be run were to ascertain the geographical facts of the case. No proceeding could be more proper. The claims of the two parties varied, and it was natural that, in the first instance a line should be run north to the extent claimed by either party. Where that line would reach, and what highlands or streams it might strike was unknown; so much so that Mr. [Albert] Gallatin in his letter from Ghent,[4] mentioned in my note of the 13th ulto, expressed his doubts on this subject. His prediction turned out to be true. The point where the line strikes the Metis was a point not fulfilling the words of the Treaty. It did not divide the waters as desired, unless the Bay of Chaleurs and the Gulf of St. Lawrence are considered

4. Gallatin to James Monroe, December 25, 1814, in *ASP: FR*, 4: 810–811.

to answer the description of the Atlantic ocean. Mr Gallatin was sensible of this, and intimates that if this fact created doubt, the lands about the Ristigouche might be given up, but he forgets that in giving up this territory he gives up his argument, for he maintains in opposition to the British line of Boundary that it does not *continuously and in all its parts* divide the waters as required by the Treaty. The American line was in this respect equally deficient, and it is useless therefore here to consider whether it would have been preferable to the British line, if it had divided the waters of the St. Lawrence from those of the St. John's. To make even a plausible case for the American line, both the St. John's and the Ristigouche must be held to be rivers emptying into the Atlantic ocean. The Royal Arbiter says it would be *hazardous* so to class them. I believe that whatever argument might be made in the case of the St. Johns connected with the distinctions with which it was mentioned in the Treaty, to consider the Ristigouche as flowing into the Atlantic ocean would be more than hazardous, it would be most absurd.

At all events I would submit to you that no inference could be drawn from the Commissioners in 1817 having ordered a north line to be run, the same Commissioners after drawing the line having disagreed as to any conclusions from it.

I am rather surprised that an inspection of the map should lead us to such different views of the course of the rivers and of the coast, as stated by you. I find that the upper St. John's and the Ristigouche, so far from cutting at right angles the parallel lines of the coast and the St. Lawrence as you say, run in their main course nearly parallel with them. I am not aware that the fact is important although it seems connected with your argument.

My inspection of these maps and my examination of the documents lead me to a very strong conviction that the Highlands, contemplated by the negotiators of the Treaty, were the only Highlands then known to them at the head of the Penobscot, Kennebec, and the rivers West of the St. Croix; and that they did not precisely know how the north line from the St. Croix would strike them; and if it were not my wish to shorten this discussion I believe a very good argument might be drawn from the words of the treaty in proof of this. In the negotiations with Mr. [Edward] Livingston and afterwards with Mr. [Louis] McLane, this view seemed to prevail, and, as you are aware, there were proposals to search for these highlands to the west,[5] where alone I believe they will be found to answer

5. Livingston was Andrew Jackson's secretary of state from May 24, 1831, to May 29, 1833. He was succeeded by Louis McLane, who served from May 29, 1833, to June 30, 1834. On the proposals regarding the location of the highlands, see Livingston to Charles Richard Vaughn, April 30 and May 28, 1833, and McLane to Vaughn, June 5, 1833, March 11 and 21, 1834, all in DNA, RG 59 (Notes to Foreign Legations, Britain).

perfectly the description of the Treaty. If this question should unfortunately go to a further reference, I should by no means despair of finding some confirmation of this view of the case.

I shall now, Sir, close what I have to say on the controversial part of this question. I should not have treated of it at all, but from respect to the gentlemen from Maine whose arguments you conveyed to me; and I shall certainly not renew it unless called upon by you to do so. Our immediate business is with the compromise of what is not otherwise to be settled, and argument and controversy, far from assisting to that end, have more generally a tendency to irritate and excite.

Referring then to our more immediate subject of a line by agreement, I deeply regret, on reading your observations and proposals, that we are yet so far asunder. I always thought this part of our duty better performed by conference than by correspondence, unless indeed we had the misfortune not to be able ultimately to agree, in which case it would certainly be necessary that our two countries should see clearly on paper how nearly we had approached to each other, and on whom the blame at last rested of leaving unsettled a question involving such serious consequences. I would still recommend this course of personal discussion and conference, but in the mean time I proceed to notice the proposals and observations contained in your note.

It is sufficiently explained in my plan for a settlement, why I was anxious not to divide in two parts, by any new line of boundary, the Madawaska settlements; and I am sorry to say that the information I have since received, both as to local circumstances and the anxiety of the people themselves tends strongly to confirm my impressions. At the same time you will have seen that I was sensible that some good reason should be assigned why we should not be satisfied with what you justly term the otherwise perfect boundary of the St. John's. In your reply you recognize the difficulties of the case, and do justice to our motives, but you state distinctly, on the part of your Government, that you can consent to no line which should bring us over the St. John's without some equivalent of Territory to be found out of the limits of that part which is in dispute; and you refer more particularly to a certain narrow strip lying between the north line and the river. This strip I have no power to give up; and I beg to add that the refusal of my Government is founded simply on their objection to dispose arbitrarily of the persons and property of Her Majesty's subjects living by preference under her authority, an objection which you are sensible applies with peculiar force to the inhabitants of this part of New Brunswick.

I had hoped that the other equivalents which I had offered, combined with the sense entertained by the Government of the United States of the pressing importance of the case on the ground of humanity, would have been sufficient for the purpose I so anxiously desired; but perceiving from your note, as well as from personal conversation that concession on this point is insisted upon, I might be disposed to consider whether my anxious desire to arrive at a friendly settlement would not justify me in yielding, however reluctantly, if the latter part of your proposals did not, if finally persevered in, forbid all hope of any settlement whatever.

The Boundary you propose, supposing the British Territory not to come over the St. John's, is to run from the north side of that river, three miles above its junction with the Madawaska over an arbitrary line, which my map does not exactly permit me to follow, until it reaches somewhere the St. Francis. I need not examine this line in its precise details, because I am obliged frankly to state that it is inadmissible. I think I might, Sir, fairly appeal to your candid judgment to say, whether this is a proposition of conciliation, whether, after all antecedent discussions on this subject, it could be reasonably expected that, whatever might be the anxiety of my government for a friendly settlement, I could be found with power to accede to such terms. I need not observe to you that this would give to Great Britain less than the award of the arbiter, while at the same time she would be called upon to give up what that arbiter awarded to her, and, if I do not mistake you, the floatage of the lumber of Maine down the St. John's is also expected to be surrendered.

I must beg to say that I am quite at a loss to account for such a proposal. Your own principle of maintaining the great river as the best boundary is abandoned, an arbitrary line is drawn which nobody ever suggested before, and I can only suppose this course to be dictated by that general assumption that, notwithstanding all former admissions and decisions to the contrary, this territory said to be in dispute, in truth belongs to one party, to be doled out as a favour to the other—an assumption which cannot for a moment be admitted, and which you, Sir, with the records of your office before you will hardly maintain.

The position in which this negotiation now stands seems to prove what I have before ventured to advance, that it would have a better chance of success by conference than by correspondence; at all events that we should sooner arrive at ascertaining what we can or can not do. Slow, unnecessarily slow, our progress has hitherto been, and the public seem, somehow or other, to have become informed that there are differences.[6] I hope when we come to discuss them, that they will prove less serious than they are supposed to be; but it is very desirable that doubts and distrusts should be set at rest, and that public credit and the transactions of commerce should suffer the least possible disturbance. For although, should this negotiation unfortunately fail, it will be our duty immediately

6. The Washington, D.C., *National Intelligencer* of July 9, 1842, reported the rumor that a successful settlement was in jeopardy because of the intractability of one of the parties.

to place it in some new course of further reference, it is not to be disguised that such a result must be productive of considerable public anxiety and disappointment.

What I have said with respect to the case of the Madawaska settlements will I trust sufficiently prove my disposition to approach such a discussion with the true spirit of conciliation, and I trust you will permit me to express a hope that it will be met with a corresponding feeling.

Before concluding, I wish to add a few words respecting the line of the St. John's to one of its sources, and the navigation for certain purposes of that river. It may be true that the district between the St. Johns and the Highlands west of the St. Francis, may be of some extent, but your own surveyors will confirm to you that it is of very little value either for cultivation or timber. Is it reasonable that in the division of an object in dispute, its intrinsic value should be wholly disregarded, and its size or extent be alone considered?

I would further suggest for your consideration whether, supposing the division by the King of the Netherlands [William I] to be admitted to satisfy fairly the equity of the case between the parties, what is proposed to be added by Great Britain viz: the strip on the 45th parallel of Latitude, and the use of the navigation of the St. John's, be not an ample compensation for what we ask in return, viz: that barren strip above the upper St. John's, which is wanted for no other purpose than as a boundary, for which purpose it is admitted on all sides to be most convenient.

The right to use the St. John's for floating down the lumber of Maine on the same terms as the river is used by the Queen's subjects, is now treated as a matter of light importance. This is not uncommon when a concession of any kind is about to be yielded, but I beg to remind you that this was not formerly so considered. It has been repeatedly solicited and invariably refused, and no minister of Great Britain has before been permitted to connect this concession with the settlement of the boundary. It is considered by my Government as a very important concession. I am sure that it must be considered by all persons in Maine connected with the lumber trade, as not only valuable but indispensable, and I am compelled to add that I am empowered to allow this privilege only in the event of a settlement of the boundary on satisfactory terms. It is said in the memorandum of the Maine Commissioners that this conceded navigation will be as useful to the town of St. John as to the lumberers of Maine, but it will not escape you that, even if this be so, it is a concession necessary to give any value whatever to so bulky an article as lumber, which being not otherwise disposable would bear any reasonable Toll which the provincial authorities of New Brunswick might think it expedient to levy upon it. Further it should not be forgotten that the Timber, once at the mouth of the St. John's, will have the privilege of reaching the British as well as other markets, and lastly that it is a very different thing to hold a privilege of this important description by right or by mere sufferance, to be granted or withheld at pleasure.

I have to apologize for entering into these details in treating of the great question with which we are occupied, but they seemed called for by observations contained in the paper you send me.

I beg, Sir, you will be assured of my unfeigned and distinguished consideration.   Ashburton

LS. DNA, RG 59 (Notes from Foreign Legations, Britain). Rec'd July 11, 1842. Published in *Senate Documents*, 27th Cong., 3d sess., Serial 413, No. 1, pp. 50–56.

TO WILLIAM PITT PREBLE, EDWARD KAVANAGH, EDWARD KENT, AND JOHN OTIS, WITH ENCLOSURE

DEPARTMENT OF STATE

GENTLEMEN: Washington, July 15, 1842.

You have had an opportunity of reading Lord Ashburton's note to me of the 11th of July.[1] Since that date, I have had full and frequent conferences with him respecting the Eastern boundary, and believe I understand what is practicable to be done on that subject, so far as he is concerned. In these conferences, he has made no positive or binding proposition, thinking, perhaps, it would be more desirable, under present circumstances, that such proposition should proceed from the side of the United States. I have reason to believe, however, that he would agree to a line of boundary between the United States and the British provinces of Canada and New Brunswick, such as is described in a paper accompanying this, (marked B,)[2] and identified by my signature.

In establishing the line between the monument and the St. John, it is thought necessary to adhere to that run and marked by the surveyors of the two Governments in 1817 and 1818. There is no doubt that the line recently run by Major [James Duncan] Graham is more entirely accurate; but, being an *ex parte* line, there would be objections to agreeing to it without examination, and thus another survey would become necessary. Grants and settlements also have been made, in conformity with the former line; and its errors are so inconsiderable, that it is not thought that their correction is a sufficient object to disturb these settlements. Similar considerations have had great weight in adjusting the line in other parts of it.

The territory in dispute between the two countries contains 12,027 square miles—equal to 7,697,280 acres.

By the line described in the accompanying paper, there will be as-

1. See above.   2. See below.

signed to the United States 7,015 square miles—equal to 4,489,600 acres; and to England 5,012 square miles—equal to 3,207,680 acres.

By the award of the King of the Netherlands [William I], there was assigned to the United States 7,908 square miles—5,061,120 acres; to England 4,119 square miles—2,636,160 acres.

The territory proposed to be relinquished to England, south of the line of the King of the Netherlands, is, as you will see, the mountain range, from the upper part of the St. Francis river to the meeting of the two contested lines of boundary, at the Metjarmette portage, in the highlands near the source of the St. John. This mountain tract contains 893 square miles—equal to 571,520 acres. It is supposed to be of no value for cultivation or settlement. On this point, you will see, herewith, a letter from Captain [Andrew] Talcott,[3] who has been occupied two summers in exploring the line of the highlands, and is intimately acquainted with the territory. The line leaves to the United States, between the base of the hills and the left bank of the St. John, and lying along upon the river, a territory of 657,280 acres, embracing, without doubt, all the valuable land south of the St. Francis and west of the St. John. Of the general division of the territory, it is believed it may be safely said, that while the portion remaining with the United States, is, in quantity, seven-twelfths, in value it is at least four-fifths of the whole.

Nor is it supposed that the possession of the mountain region is of any importance, in connexion with the defence of the country or any military operations. It lies below all the accustomed practicable passages for troops into and out of Lower Canada—that is to say, the Chaudiere, Lake Champlain, and the Richelieu and the St. Lawrence. If an army, with its *materiel*, could possibly pass into Canada, over these mountains, it would only find itself on the banks of the St. Lawrence, *below* Quebec; and, on the other hand, it is not conceivable that an invading enemy from Lower Canada would attempt a passage in this direction, leaving the Chaudiere on one hand and the route by Madawaska on the other.

If this line should be agreed to on the part of the United States, I suppose that the British minister would, as an equivalent, stipulate, first, for the use of the river St. John, for the conveyance of the timber growing on any of its branches to tide water, free from discriminating tolls, impositions, or inabilities of any kind, the timber enjoying all the privileges of British colonial timber. All opinions concur, that this privilege of navigation must greatly enhance the value of the territory and the timber growing thereon, and prove exceedingly useful to the people of Maine. Second. That Rouse's point, in Lake Champlain, and the lands heretofore supposed to be within the limits of New Hampshire, Vermont, and New

3. Talcott to DW, July 14, 1842, DNA, RG 76 (Records of the Boundary and Claims Commissions and Arbitrations).

York, but which a correct ascertainment of the 45th parallel of latitude shows to be in Canada, should be surrendered to the United States.

It is probable, also, that the disputed line of boundary in Lake Superior might be so adjusted as to leave a disputed island within the United States.[4]

These cessions on the part of England would enure partly to the benefit of the States of New Hampshire, Vermont, and New York, but principally to the United States. The consideration on the part of England, for making them, would be the manner agreed upon for adjusting the Eastern boundary. The price of the cession, therefore, whatever it might be, would in fairness belong to the two States interested in the manner of that adjustment.

Under the influence of these considerations, I am authorized to say, that if the commissioners of the two States assent to the line as described in the accompanying paper, the United States will undertake to pay to these States the sum of two hundred and fifty thousand dollars, to be divided between them in equal moieties; and, also, to undertake for the settlement and payment of the expenses incurred by those States for the maintenance of the civil posse; and, also, for a survey which it was found necessary to make.

The line suggested, with the compensations and equivalents which have been stated, is now submitted for your consideration. That it is all which might have been hoped for, looking to the strength of the American claim, can hardly be said. But, as the settlement of a controversy of such duration is a matter of high importance, as equivalents of undoubted value are offered, as longer postponement and delay would lead to further inconvenience, and to the incurring of further expenses, and as no better occasion, or perhaps any other occasion, for settling the boundary by agreement, and on the principle of equivalents, is ever likely to present itself, the Government of the United States hopes that the commissioners of the two States will find it to be consistent with their duty, to assent to the line proposed, and to the terms and conditions attending the proposition.

The President has felt the deepest anxiety for an amicable settlement of the question, in a manner honorable to the country, and such as should preserve the rights and interests of the States concerned. From the moment of the announcement of Lord Ashburton's mission, he has sedulously endeavored to pursue a course the most respectful towards the States, and the most useful to their interests, as well as the most becoming to the character and dignity of the Government. He will be happy if the result shall be such as shall satisfy Maine and Massachusetts, as well as the rest of the country. With these sentiments on the part

4. See Ashburton to DW, July 16, 1842, below.

of the President, and with the conviction that no more advantageous arrangement can be made the subject is now referred to the grave deliberation of the commissioners. I have the honor to be, with great respect, your obedient servant, Daniel Webster

Text from *Senate Documents*, 27th Cong., 3d sess., Serial 413, No. 1, pp. 81–83. Original not found. An AL s draft is in DNA, RG 76 (Records of the Boundary and Claims Commissions and Arbitrations and Miscellaneous Documents Relating to the Northeast Boundary, 1827–1842).

ENCLOSURE: B

Beginning at the monument at the source of the river St. Croix as designated by the Commissioners under the fifth article of the treaty of 1794 between the Governments of the United States and Great Britain; thence, north, following the exploring line run and marked by the surveyors of the two Governments in the years 1817 and 1818, under the fifth article of the Treaty of Ghent, to its intersection with the river St. John and to the middle of the channel thereof; thence, up the middle of the main channel of the said river St. John, to the mouth of the river St. Francis; thence, up the middle of the channel of the said river Saint Francis, and of the lakes through which it flows, to the outlet of the Lake Pohenagamook; thence, southwesterly, in a straight line, to a point on the northwest branch of the river St. John, which point shall be ten miles distant from the main branch of the St. John, in a straight line, and in the nearest direction, but if the said point shall be found to be less than seven miles from the nearest point of the summit or crest of the highlands that divide those rivers which empty themselves into the river St. Lawrence from those which fall into the Atlantic Ocean, then the said point shall be made to recede down the said river to a point seven miles in a straight line from the said <dividing highlands> summit or crest; thence, in a straight line, in a course about south, eight degrees west, to the point where the parallel of latitude of 46° 25′ intersects the southwest branch of the Saint John; thence, southerly, by the said branch to the source thereof in the highlands at the Metjarmette Portage; thence, down along the said highlands <around the head waters of Indian Stream, and so on to the highlands which divide that stream on the one hand, and Hall's Stream on the other> to the head of Hall's Stream; thence down the middle of said stream, till the line thus run intersects the old line of boundary surveyed and marked by [Thomas] Valentine and [John] Collins,[1] previously to the year 1774, as the 45° of latitude, and which has been known and understood to be the line of actual division between the

1. Between 1771 and 1774 Valentine, the surveyor general of New York, and Collins (d. 1795), the deputy surveyor of Quebec, ran a line of survey along the forty-fifth parallel. This is the line that was later discovered to be nearly a mile too far north of the true line, thereby placing the

States of New York and Vermont on one side, and the British Province of Canada on the other; and from said point of intersection, west, along the said dividing line, as heretofore known and understood, to the Iroquois or St Lawrence river.

Copy, with emendations by DW. DNA, RG 59 (Records of the Boundary and Claims Commissions and Arbitrations and Miscellaneous Documents Relating to the Northeast Boundary, 1827–1842). Published in *Senate Documents*, 27th Cong., 3d sess., Serial 413, No. 1, pp. 83–84.

FROM LORD ASHBURTON

Sir   Washington 16 July 1842

There is a further question of disputed boundary between Great Britain and the United States, called the North West boundary, about which we have had some conferences; and I now proceed to state the terms which I am ready to agree to for the settlement of this difference. As the principal object in dispute is to be given up by Great Britain, I trust, Sir, that you will here again recognize the spirit of friendly conciliation which has guided my Government in disposing of these questions.

I have already sufficiently discussed with you the boundaries between Her Majesty's provinces and the United States from the monument at the head of the River St. Croix to the monument on the river St. Lawrence near the village of St. Regis.

The Commissioners under the sixth article of the Treaty of Ghent succeeded in continuing this boundary from St. Regis through the St. Lawrence and the great Northern Lakes up to a point in the channel between Lake Huron and Lake Superior.

A further continuation of this boundary from this point through Lake Superior to the Lake of the Woods was confided to the same Commissioners under the 7th article of the Treaty of Ghent; but they were unfortunately unable to agree, and have consequently left this portion of the boundary undetermined.[1] Its final settlement has been much desired by both Governments, and urgently pressed by communications from Mr. Secretary [John] Forsyth to Mr. [Henry Stephen] Fox in 1839 and 1840.[2]

American fort at Rouses Point in Canadian territory.

1. Peter Buell Porter (1773–1844) represented the United States on the northwestern boundary commission that first met on November 18, 1816, and concluded on December 24, 1827. The British representative was Anthony Barclay, the son of Ghent commissioner Thomas Barclay, who represented England on the northeastern boundary commission. On the northwestern commission and the settlement, see *International Arbitrations*, 1:162–195. For the reports of the commissioners and accompanying documents, see *Executive Documents*, 25th Cong., 2d sess., Serial 331, No. 451.

2. See Forsyth to Fox, July 29,

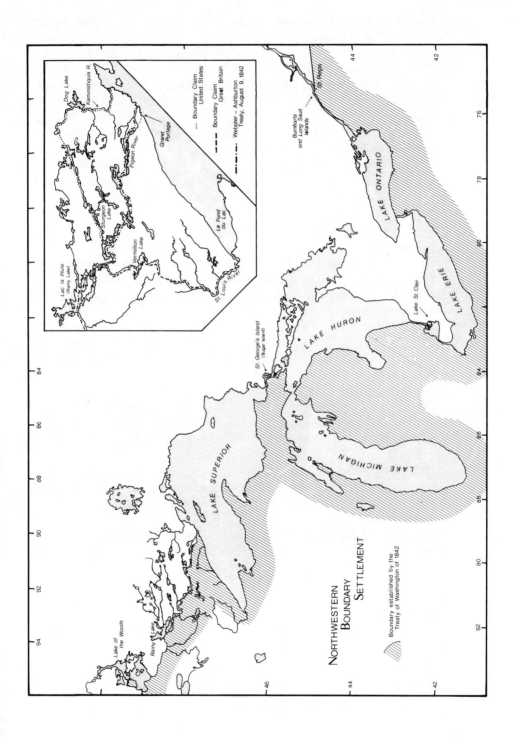

NORTHWESTERN BOUNDARY SETTLEMENT

Boundary established by the Treaty of Washington of 1842

...... Boundary Claim United States
– – – Boundary Claim Great Britain
–··–··– Webster – Ashburton Treaty, August 9, 1842

Lake of the Woods

Rainy Lake

LAKE SUPERIOR

St. George's Island (Sugar Island)

LAKE HURON

LAKE MICHIGAN

Lake St. Clair

LAKE ERIE

LAKE ONTARIO

Burnharts and Long Sault Islands

St. Regis

Lac la Pluie (Rainy Lake)

Dog Lake

Kaministiquia R.

Pigeon River

Sturgeon Lake

Vermillion Lake

Grand Portage

La Fond du Lac

St. Louis River

What I have now to propose can not, I feel assured, be otherwise than satisfactory for this purpose.

The Commissioners who failed in their endeavours to make this settlement, differed on two points.

First, as to the appropriation of an island called St. George's Island, lying in the water communication between Lake Huron and Lake Superior; and

Secondly, as to the boundary through the water communications from Lake Superior to the Lake of the Woods.

The first point I am ready to give up to you, and you are no doubt aware that it is the only object of any real value in this controversy. The island of St. George's is reported to contain 25920 acres of very fertile land, but, the other things connected with these boundaries being satisfactorily arranged, a line shall be drawn so as to throw this Island within the limits of the United States.

In considering the second point, it really appears of little importance to either party how the line be determined through the wild country between Lake Superior and the Lake of the Woods, but it is important that some line should be fixed and known.

The American Commissioner asked for the line from Lake Superior up the River Kamanastiquia to the Lake called Dog Lake, which he supposed to be the same as that called Long Lake in the Treaties, thence through Sturgeon Lake to the Lac La Pluie, to that point where the two lines assumed by the Commissioners again meet.

The British Commissioner, on the other hand, contended for a line from the Southwestern extremity at a point called Le fond du Lac to the middle of the mouth of the Estuary or Lake of St. Louis River, thence up that river through Vermilion river to Lac La Pluie.

Attempts were made to compromise these differences, but they failed, apparently more from neither party being willing to give up the Island of St George's, than from much importance being attached to any other part of the case.

Upon the line from Lake Superior to the Lake of the Woods both Commissioners agreed to abandon their respective claims and to adopt a middle course, for which the American Commissioner admitted that there was some ground of preference. This was from Pigeon River, a point between the Kamanastiquia and the fond du Lac, and although there were differences as to the precise point near the mouth of Pigeon river where the line should begin, neither party seem to have attached much importance to this part of the subject.

I would propose that the line be taken from a point about six miles

1839, DNA, RG 59 (Notes to Foreign Legations, Britain). No communication of 1840 on the northwestern boundary is found in Notes to Foreign Legations.

south of Pigeon river where the grand portage commences on the Lake, and continued along the line of the said Portage alternately by Land and Water to Lac la Pluie: the existing route by land and by water remaining common to both parties. This line has the advantage of being known and attended with no doubt or uncertainty in running it.

In making the important concession on this boundary of the Isle St. George, I must attach a condition to it of accommodation, which experience has proved to be necessary in the navigation of the Great Waters which bound the two Countries; an accommodation which can, I apprehend, be no possible inconvenience to either. This was asked by the British Commissioner in the course of the attempts of compromise above alluded to, but nothing was done because he was not then prepared, as I am now, to yield the property and sovereignty of St. George's Island.

The first of these two cases is at the head of Lake St. Clair, where the river of that name, empties into it from Lake Huron. It is represented that the channel bordering the United States' coast in this part is not only the best for navigation, but with some winds is the only serviceable passage. I do not know that under such circumstances the passage of a British vessel would be refused, but on a final settlement of boundaries, it is desirable to stipulate for what the Commissioners would probably have settled had the facts been known to them.

The other case of nearly the same description occurs on the St. Lawrence some miles above the boundary at St. Regis. In distributing the islands of the River by the Commissioners Burnharts Island and the Long Sault Islands were assigned to America. This part of the river has very formidable rapids, and the only safe passage is on the Southern or American side between those Islands and the main land. We want a clause in our present treaty to say that for a short distance, viz: from the upper end of upper Long Sault Island to the lower end of Burnhart's Island, the several channels of the river shall be used in common by the Boatmen of the two Countries.

I am not aware that these very reasonable demands are likely to meet with any objection; especially where the United States will have surrendered to them all that is essential in the boundary I have now to propose to you. I beg you will be assured, Sir, of my unfeigned and distinguished consideration. Ashburton.

L S. DNA, RG 59 (Notes from Foreign Legations, Britain). Published in *Senate Documents*, 27th Cong., 3d sess., Serial 413, No. 1.

FROM WILLIAM PITT PREBLE, EDWARD KAVANAGH, EDWARD KENT, AND JOHN OTIS

Sir   Washington July 16. 1842.

We learn from the letter addressed to you by Lord Ashburton dated the 11th inst.,[1] and by you communicated to the Commissioners of Maine and Massachusetts, that the line, proposed by us as a conventional line, with the assent and concurrence of the Commissioners of Massachusetts, in our note to you of the 29th ulto,[2] is inadmissible. His Lordship even expresses himself as being "quite at a loss to account for such a proposal," and appeals to your candid judgment to say, "whether this is a proposition of conciliation," and whether it could reasonably be expected that, whatever might be the anxiety of his government for a friendly settlement, he could be found with power to accede to such terms. That public, to which his Lordship more than once alludes in both his letters,[3] will have it in their power to judge which proposition on the whole under all the circumstances of the case, is best entitled to the character of conciliatory, his Lordships or ours. To you, Sir, the Commissioners must be permitted to insist, that they did intend and consider their offer as a proposition of conciliation, however it may appear to Lord Ashburton. It is predicated upon the basis of yielding to Great Britain all she needs, and more than she needs, for the natural, convenient and "unobstructed communication and connexion of her colonies with each other" —a desire on her part to obtain which, is believed to be at the bottom of this controversy, and the necessity of securing which, even his Lordship seems to admit, has been the main reason of her continuing to persist in it. The Royal Arbiter [William I], as his Lordship is pleased to call him, clearly understood this; and governed himself accordingly. He recommended the yielding on the part of the United States of this portion of territory, coupling it at the same time with a yielding on the part of Great Britain, to the United States, of Rouse's point, on Lake Champlain, and the Fort there erected, with its kilometrical radius, and so much of the Territory adjacent, as might be necessary to include it. The existence of such a place and its fortifications had not been even alluded to in the American Statements, nor by the American Agents. The British Agents could not suffer such a fact to pass unnoticed. They studiously informed the Royal Arbiter in their first statement, and took care to advert to it again in their second, that there was "a certain point called *Rouse's point*, where there happened to be an important American Fort, which had been erected not long before at considerable expense, as a defence for that frontier." Thus admonished of the fact, the Royal Arbiter readily availed himself of it, and placed the value and convenience of this supposed important military position and fortification to the account of the United States, as an offset for the territory in Maine, needed for the convenience of Great Britain and for "the unobstructed communication and

1. See above, Ashburton to DW, July 11, 1842.

2. See above, Preble et al. to DW, June 29, 1842.

3. In addition to his note of July 11, see Ashburton's reference to public scrutiny of the negotiations, in his letter to DW of June 21, 1842, above.

connexion of her colonies with each other," supposing without doubt, that in so doing, he was promoting the interest and objects and convenience of both nations.[4] When therefore Lord Ashburton bases his proposition on the supposition that, "the division by the King of the Netherlands satisfied fairly the equity of the case between the parties," and restrains that Monarch's views to an equitable division of the territory in dispute in Maine only, he overlooks, as it appears to us, the fact, that both matters were before His Majesty's mind at one and the same time; and that, as in the one instance he recommended that a certain portion of territory should be yielded by the United States to Great Britain for her accommodation, so in the other he recommended, that a certain other portion of territory belonging of right to Great Britain in his opinion, should be yielded by Great Britain to the United States for their supposed accommodation and security. It is true that Rouse's point had formerly been considered, as of great importance, as a military position; and that the United States had expended very large sums of money in erecting fortifications there. The Royal Arbiter therefore, acting under the influence of the ex parte information so gratuitously furnished him, might well attach to Rouse's point and its fortifications an inflated importance, and taking the whole relations and interests of the parties before him into consideration might regard his recommendation, as satisfying fairly the equity of the case between the parties. But however this may be, it is certain, that what would be an equitable division of the territory in dispute was never submitted to the King of the Netherlands at all by the United States,— that no evidence upon that point was placed before him by the United States,—nor were the United States or their Agent ever heard or consulted on that point by him. Against the adoption of his recommendation in this respect the State of Maine has ever solemnly protested; and the Senate of the United States, who alone had the constitutional power to adopt and ratify it, rejected it with great unanimity. The recommendation of the Royal Arbiter therefore, given under such circumstances, can in no way affect the rights of the parties in interest; and is in fact entitled to no more consideration and respect, than that of any other gentleman of equal intelligence and information under the same circumstances. We feel it our duty therefore to say to you, that the hypothesis, assumed by Lord Ashburton, that the portion of disputed territory, cut off from Maine by the line recommended by the King of the Netherlands, should be yielded to Great Britain without any equivalent whatever, cannot be, and in our opinion ought not for a moment to be, admitted or acquiesced in by the Commissioners of Maine.

Among the objections made by Lord Ashburton to the line proposed by

4. A summary of the statements of the American and British agents and the decision of the king of the Neth- erlands is in *International Arbitrations*, 1:100–136.

us, drawn from the bend of the St John, three miles above the mouth of the Madawaska, to the outlet of Long Lake, one is, that it is an arbitrary line, which nobody ever suggested before; and, that it would give to Great Britain less than the award of the arbiter. All this is true. But the line, proposed by us, is a straight line, like that from the source of the St Croix, drawn from one well known natural monument to another well known natural monument within convenient distances of each other, and about which there could be no mistake or dispute. It yields also all, and more than all, that is needed by Great Britain, for the unobstructed communication and connexion of her colonies with each other; and, as suggested by us in our note of the 29th ult, was proposed, rather than the channel of the Madawaska, solely for that reason and on that account. And what does Great Britain want of more? If the true character of that territory be of the description, *"the miserable description,"* stated by his Lordship in his note of the 21st ult,[5] why should he feel it to be an objection, that the line, proposed by us, would give to Great Britain less, than the award of the arbiter, when it gives her enough to answer all her purposes? Beyond the designated bend of the St John, the course of that river is such, as to make with the St Francis an acute angle, thereby forming between them a wedge of territory inserting itself for its whole length, according to that award, into the territory of the United States. Again, at the mouth of Turtle river, so called, a few miles above the designated bend of the St John, there is a small settlement of Americans holding their lands under grants from Maine and Massachusetts.[6] Again, the river St Francis is one, whose course is exceedingly crooked, having many sharp bends, so that while the distance by the river and lakes from the Grand Portage to the mouth of the St Francis is estimated by the assistant geologist of Massachusetts,[7] who followed it down its whole length, at not less than eighty five miles, the distance from the one point to the other in a straight line is only about forty miles. Moreover, the line recommended by the King of the Netherlands without any knowledge of the topography of the country, is believed to be impracticable, on account of there being in fact no such stream emptying into the lake, as in his recommendation he supposes to exist. And we will add, that however miserable his Lordship may consider the territory there to be, we regard it as of much value, inasmuch as it is well known to be covered with a fine

5. See above, Ashburton to DW, June 21, 1842.

6. Most likely a reference to the American settlements at the mouth of the Mariumpticook (Baker) River, where John Baker (1787–1868) and James Bacon, Maine lumbermen, were each granted 100-acre lots by Maine and Massachusetts in 1825. Baker was arrested by British authorities in September 1827 after he and other Americans of the area proclaimed their settlements to be in U.S. territory. See *ASP: FR,* 6:838–855, 936–945.

7. Not identified.

growth of timber, equal, it is said, to any to be found on the disputed territory.

In connexion with these considerations, we wish to add a few words on the subject of the right to float down our timber on the St John, since his Lordship has made it a special subject of comment. Great changes, as his Lordship well knows, are brought about in a state of things by the mere course of time. The timber of New Brunswick, suitable for the British market has nearly all disappeared. While they had a supply of their own, the right of carrying down our lumber was most strenuously and pertinaciously resisted, as Lord Ashburton himself states. A very large quantity of the most valuable lumber is situated upon the banks of the Alagash above the falls of that river. By first throwing a dam across the Alagash and then with a common pick axe and spade digging a channel across the range of British highlands, our enterprizing lumbermen have found the means of turning the valuable timber of the Alagash down the river Penobscot. More than six million feet of this lumber were sawed in the Mills on the Penobscot the last season. How far the change in the disposition of the British Cabinet, which his Lordship speaks of, has been effected by these and the like considerations, it is not our purpose to enquire—nor do we mean to be understood, as undervaluing this change of policy. Our object has been to show, that Great Britain in making the proposition, is pursuing her own objects, and promoting her own interest; and not making any sacrifice by way of an equivalent for concessions on our part. It will not have escaped your recollection, that the river St John is not a river navigable from the Sea, in the ordinary acceptation of that expression. There is a ledge running across the mouth of that river of such a character, that owing to the very high tides in the Bay of Fundy, there is a fall of about twenty feet out, at low water, and a fall of some four feet in, at high water. It is only about forty five minutes in a tide, that you can pass in or out of the river at all; and even during that short period the passage is a difficult and dangerous one. So, again, there is a fall of about forty feet on the Aroostook before you reach the American territory; and a fall also on the St John itself of eighty feet, before you reach the State of Maine, as you follow up the river. The boasted free navigation of the St John and its tributaries from the disputed territory may well be illustrated by the free navigation of the Potomac to this City from the valley of the Shenandoah. When therefore, as Commissioners of Maine, we consented to accept, as an equivalent from Great Britain for the territory proposed to be yielded to her for her convenience and accommodation, the free navigation of the St John for the floating down of our lumber, we did consider ourselves under all the circumstances of the case, as having proposed all, that a liberal spirit of conciliation could require us to do. And it will not be deemed improper by you, if we here advert to the fact, that we cannot regard the relinquishment by the British Government of any claim heretofore advanced by it to territory within the limits of Maine, as asserted by her, as a consideration or equivalent for the yielding on our part to Great Britain of any other portion of the same territory. On this point the declarations of the Legislature of Maine are explicit; and we are bound to respect them.

By his Lordship's note of the 11th inst, we learn, that he withdraws that part of his proposition, which relates to a cession of territory on the south side of the St John. Even with this restriction of his proposition, the adoption of the St John, as a boundary from the line, drawn due north from the source of the St Croix, at its intersection with the St John to a source of that river in the vicinity of the sources of the Penobscot and Metjarmette, would yield to Great Britain nearly four millions of acres, and more than one half of the whole territory, to which she has ever pretended to set up a claim. Nor is this all. His Lordship further proposes to abide by the exploring line, so called, run and marked in 1817, from the monument at the source of the St. Croix,—a line, which interferes with and cuts off a portion of the grants, made long before by Massachusetts. This line is well known not to be the *true* line,—never was run as such, nor pretended so to be. It takes however from Maine a strip of territory, which is nearly a mile wide, where it crosses the St John, and which diminishes in width, till it reaches the monument. His Lordship's proposition contemplates the adoption and establishment of that exploring line, as the true boundary. It does not fall within our province to consider the value of those shreds and patches, which his Lordship proposed to yield to the United States, as an equivalent. In New Hampshire, he consents to take the true north west source of Connecticut river, instead of the north east source, as being the source intended in the Treaty of 1783. In Vermont he will abide by the old line, which was run marked and solemnly established, nearly seventy years ago. In New York he will abide by the same old line, the effect of rectifying it, being merely to give to New York a small angular strip on the west, and Great Britain a small angular strip on the east. These small tracts and parings, shaved from the States just named, and the right of floating down the St John the products of the forest, as already explained, constitute alone the sum and magnitude of the equivalent offered by his Lordship for the whole territory of Maine on the north side of the St John. Whether such a proposition has preeminent claims over the one we have made, to be regarded as a "proposition of conciliation," we leave to that public, to which his Lordship is pleased so often to refer.

Lord Ashburton has been led into an error, unintentional no doubt on his part, if he supposes, that, in submitting to you, what we apprehend to be the reason, why the precise and peculiar phraseology, used in the treaty of 1783, respecting the north west angle of Nova Scotia, was adopted by the distinguished men, who framed it, our object was, to revive and enter upon a controversy, which for the present at least should be permitted to rest in peace. His Lordship in his letter to you of the 21st ult, had assumed it as a fact, and as the ground, upon which the negotiation for an amicable settlement was to proceed, that the language and phraseology of the Treaty of 1783 was such, "that the Treaty itself was not executable according to its strict expression." We on our part could make no such "admission," nor acquiesce in any such "presumption," nor by our silence even be supposed for a moment to proceed in the negotiation on any such ground or hypothesis. Nor could we suffer to pass without observation the declaration of a settled conviction on the part of the Minister of Great Britain, made under such circumstances and with such bearings, "that it was the intention of the parties to the treaty of 1783 to leave to Great Britain the whole of the waters of the St John." If his Lordship would have avoided the introduction of any remarks, bearing on these points on our part, it seems to us, that he himself should have avoided giving occasion for them. It is not a little remarkable, that the very dispute, which the sagacious men, who framed the treaty, endeavoured by their studied and select phraseology and terms to guard against, should have arisen notwithstanding all their care and precaution.

We have already shown in our letter to you of the 29th ult, that the Members of the Continental Congress and the framers of the Treaty of 1783 well knew of the existence and prescriptions of the proclamation of 1763, and the provisions of the Quebec Act of 1774. They also well knew, that the North west Angle of Nova Scotia and the North east angle of Massachusetts (Maine) were adjacent angles.

They knew, that the jurisdiction of Massachusetts and Nova Scotia extended back from the Atlantic Ocean to the southern boundary of the province of Quebec. And they well knew, that the southern boundary of the province of Quebec, both by the proclamation of 1763 and the Quebec act of 1774 was, the north side of the Bay des Chaleurs and the line of the highlands, lying on the south side of the St Lawrence, in which the rivers, that empty themselves into the river St Lawrence on that side take their rise. When however they came to enquire whereabouts was the line, that separated Massachusetts from Nova Scotia, they were at a loss. Accordingly both in the instructions, drawn up and sanctioned in 1779, and in the report and doings of the Congress in August 1782, it was proposed, that the eastern boundary should be "a line to be settled and adjusted between that part of the State of Massachusetts Bay formerly called the Province of Maine, and the Colony of Nova Scotia according to their respective right." The Committee of Congress in their report of 16 August 1782, after suggesting several vague and unsatisfactory reasons for considering the St Johns as the true boundary, add, "we are obliged to urge probabilities." "But we wish that the north eastern boundary of Massachusetts may be left to future discussion, when *other evidences* may be obtained, which *the war has removed from us.*"

Mr [John] Adams in his answer to an interrogatory, propounded to him 15 Aug 1797,[8] says, speaking of the negotiations at Paris—"Documents from the public offices in England were brought over and laid before us." Again, "the ultimate agreement was, to adhere to the charter of Massachusetts Bay[9] and St Croix river, mentioned in it, which was supposed to be delineated on [John] Mitchell's map." The Charter of Massachusetts Bay, here referred to, originally embraced Nova Scotia also. But Nova Scotia having been erected into a separate Province, the limits and jurisdiction of Massachusetts were curtailed and restricted to the western boundary, and that boundary was the river St Croix. To remove all doubts in regard to the limit or boundary between Nova Scotia and Massachusetts Bay, the King of Great Britain [George III] on the twenty first day of November 1763, established and defined it as follows, viz "To the westward, although our said Province (Nova Scotia) hath anciently extended, and doth of right extend, as far as the river Pentagonet or Penobscot, it shall be bounded by a line drawn from Cape Sable across the entrance of the Bay of Fundy to the mouth of the river St Croix, by the said river to its source, and by a line drawn due north from thence to the southern boundary of our Colony of Quebec"[;] that is to say, to the line of the highlands, from whose northern declivity issue the streams, that form the rivers, which empty themselves into the river St Lawrence on its south side. Instead therefore of leaving the eastern boundary of Massachusetts to future discussion, as proposed provisionally in the instructions of Congress of 1779, and by the Committee in 1782, in order to get "other evidences," the Commissioners at Paris, having the documents before them, and to prevent all disputes, which might in future arise on the subject of boundaries, at once ingrafted into the Treaty the boundary, prescribed by the document of 21 Novr 1763, already quoted, as the boundary between Nova Scotia and the United States. Hence also in connexion with the facts, stated in our communication, in respect to the uncertainty, that had existed, in regard to the true position of the northwest angle of Nova Scotia, the peculiar care and abundant caution, with which they specified and defined, which of all those places or positions, where the northwest angle of Nova Scotia had been supposed to be situated, was the place or position of the northwest angle of Nova Scotia, intended by the framers of the Treaty. We do not assume to say, that any

8. Adams was interviewed by the Saint Croix commissioners at his home in Quincy. The questions and answers are in *International Arbitrations*, 1:18–20.

9. The charter of 1691 uniting Massachusetts Bay and Nova Scotia is in *Charters and General Laws of the Colony and Province of Massachusetts Bay* (Boston, 1814), pp. 18–37.

other and different view of these facts is most absurd, but we will venture to say, with the most entire respect for Lord Ashburton, that in our opinion an argument, drawn from notorious and well authenticated facts, such as these, whether it be an old or a new discovery, is deserving of more careful examination and more consideration, than his Lordship seems to have bestowed upon it.

There is one other view, presented with much confidence, in his Lordship's letters, which we cannot permit to pass unnoticed. We mean the expression of his belief that, "to consider the Ristigouche, as flowing into the Atlantic Ocean, would be more than hazardous, it would be most absurd."

The southern boundary of the colony of Quebec is declared by the proclamation of 1763 to be "a line, which passes along the Highlands which divide the rivers that empty themselves into the said river St Lawrence from those which fall into the sea, and also along the north coast of the Bay des Chaleurs and the coast of the Gulph of St Lawrence" &c. The place of the mouth of the *river* St Lawrence, in contradistinction to the *Gulph* of St Lawrence is a point established beyond all dispute. It is at the west end of the island of Anticosti. The river Ristigouche, which empties itself through the Bay des Chaleurs into the Gulph of St Lawrence is by the proclamation classed and considered as one of "the rivers, which empty themselves into the sea," notwithstanding the Bay des Chaleurs and the Gulph of St Lawrence are both named by their distinctive appellations in the same sentence. In another part of the same instrument the Governors are inhibited from passing any patents for any lands beyond the heads of any of "the rivers, which fall into the *Atlantic Ocean* from the west and north west." And in another clause it is said: Our will and pleasure as aforesaid (is) to reserve all the lands and territories lying to the westward of the sources of "the rivers, which fall into the *sea* from the west and northwest *as aforesaid*," Here the words "Sea," and "Atlantic Ocean," are used indiscriminately, the one being substituted for the other in reference to the rivers, which flow from the west and northwest, the river Ristigouche being one of these rivers. This also is in accordance with the view entertained and expressed in his argument in 1797 by the British agent, who in speaking of the Province of Quebec, says, that by the proclamation of 7th Oct 1763 it is "bounded on the south by the highlands, which divide the rivers, that empty themselves into the river St Lawrence, from those which fall into the sea, or Atlantic Ocean."[10] So in the Commission to Guy Carleton of 27 Decr 1774,[11] the Ristigouche is again classed and considered, as a river falling into the sea; and what is more striking in the same sentence, in which it speaks of the islands of

10. Ward Chipman's argument is quoted in the 1828 report of the Maine legislature, in *ASP: FR*, 6:899.

11. Carleton (1724–1808) was governor of Quebec from 1775 to 1777.

Madelaine, in *the Gulph of St Lawrence*, it speaks of "the river St John, which discharges itself into *the sea* nearly opposite the west end of the island of Anticosti." After the passage of the Quebec Act and prior to the treaty of 1783 the southern boundary of the Province of Quebec was described as being "a line from the Bay of Chaleurs along the highlands, which divide the rivers, that empty themselves into the river St Lawrence from those, which fall into the sea, to a point in forty five degrees of northern Latitude on the eastern bank of the river Connecticut," &c. Again, after the treaty of 1783, the southern boundary of the Province of Quebec is described, as "a line from the Bay of Chaleurs, along the highlands which divide the rivers that empty themselves into the river St Lawrence from those which fall into the Atlantic Ocean to the northwesternmost head of Connecticut river," &c. But the point of beginning being the same, and the point at the Connecticut substantially the same, that point after the Treaty being only placed further north,—and the rivers taking their rise in the northern declivity being described in the same identical words, the inference appears irresistible, that the highlands referred to are one and the same; and that the rivers, taking their rise in the southern declivity and described before the treaty, as falling into the Sea, and after the treaty as falling into the Atlantic Ocean, are one and the same rivers, the words *sea* and *Atlantic Ocean* being used indiscriminately, and the one substituted for the other, as had already been done before in the proclamation of 1763. The only difference in the description of the boundary of the Province of Quebec, and that of the Treaty of 1783 is, that the boundary of the Province of Quebec begins at the Bay of Chaleurs, whereas, that of the Treaty begins at a point farther west. Hence it plainly appears, that under the classification of rivers with reference to these highlands, as made by the Proclamation of 1763, and recognized in the Treaty of 1783, the River Ristigouche was then classed and considered as a river, which falls into the Sea or Atlantic Ocean, in contradistinction to the rivers, which empty themselves into the river St Lawrence. We are therefore wholly unable to perceive wherein consists the great absurdity at the present day in expounding the language of the Treaty of 1783, of considering the river Ristigouche as a river which falls into the Atlantic Ocean, unless it be that by so doing you interfere with the claims and pretensions of Great Britain.

There is one other portion of his Lordships note in which he attributes certain opinions to Mr [James] Sullivan, Mr [James] Madison, Mr [Thomas] Jefferson, Mr [Albert] Gallatin and others, which we would have wished to notice in order to show how much his Lordship has been disposed to make out of a very little; but the further discussion of this subject we have considered as productive of little good and hardly falling within our Province. We have now only to repeat what we as distinctly stated in our note of the 29th ult., that his Lordship's proposition as now modified, namely, that Maine should yield to Great Britain all the territory north of the St John cannot be acceded to on our part. With great respect and consideration, we have the honor to be, Sir, your obedient servants,

Wm. P. Preble   Edward Kavanagh   Edward Kent   John Otis

LS. DNA, RG 59 (Records of the Boundary and Claims Commissions and Arbitrations and Miscellaneous Documents Relating to the Northeast Boundary, 1827–1842). Published in *Senate Documents*, 27th Cong., 3d sess., Serial 413, No. 1, pp. 84–91.

SECRET CONTINGENT FUND ACCOUNT

19 July 1842

To	J[ohn Jordan] Crittenden for expenses of Journey to NY & payment	100[1]
"	F[rancis] O[rmand] J[onathan] Smith for services connected with the N.E. boundary	2000[2]
"	Alex. Powell for <journey connected> & stay on the frontier in 1841 on the subject of the disturbances	1000[3]
	J. McClintock for journey & expenses on the same business	500
"	J Smith for services on the frontier	200
"	J. Birch	100
"	J Andrews on business of the boundary	60
	J[ohn] P[lummer] Healey journey to R. Island contingencies &c. May 1842	100[4]
	A[lbert] Smith in relation to Boundary	200[5]
	—Smith	200
	amounting to $4460	

AD, endorsed by DW. NhHi. Although superficially an intrusion, this document is significant in this place. It shows that even before the negotiations with Ashburton were completed Secretary Webster made note of his disbursements from the Contingent Fund, while they were still fresh in his mind. The accounting, in other words, was not set down in 1846 to comply with the demands of the Vinton Committee, but was a part of the contemporary record. See mDW 26869–26889, 55180–55417; and *Correspondence* 6.

1. Crittenden actually received $1,000. See accounting in the Vinton Report, mDW 55330, 55410.

2. See Smith to Webster, June 7, 1841, above, and August 12, 1842, below; also Merk, *Fruits of Propaganda in the Tyler Administration*, pp. 59–64.

3. DW sent Powell to Utica to infiltrate the Patriot Hunters lodges in that vicinity. Powell's report, dated November 25, 1841, is in *Correspondence*, 5:172–173. McClintock, J.

Smith, and Birch probably were associated with the Powell mission.

4. Healy was sent to Rhode Island on a confidential mission in connection with the Dorr Rebellion (see *Correspondence*, 5:201–214, passim). Although the Contingent Fund was technically to be used only for the prosecution of foreign relations, this application of it seems to have raised no doubts in Webster's mind, or Tyler's.

5. Smith (1793–1867; Brown 1813)

FROM EDWARD KAVANAGH, EDWARD KENT, AND JOHN OTIS,
WITH ENCLOSURE

Washington, 23d. July, 1842.

The Undersigned, three of the Commissioners of Maine, present their respects to Mr Webster, and have the honor to enclose an answer to his communication of the 15th instant,[1] proposing a Conventional line between the State of Maine and the adjoining British Provinces.

They regret that, by some casualty, the paper annexed (marked A) has been much disfigured, and that the departure of Judge [William Pitt] Preble, since its signature,[2] prevents their substituting it by another. They, therefore, append a copy to the original.[3]

Edward Kavanagh   Edward Kent   John Otis

L S. RG 76 (Records of the Boundary and Claims Commissions and Arbitrations and Miscellaneous Documents Relating to the Northeast Boundary, 1827–1842). Rec'd July 23, 1842.

ENCLOSURE: FROM EDWARD KAVANAGH, EDWARD KENT, JOHN OTIS, AND
WILLIAM PITT PREBLE

Sir: Washington, July 22d, 1842.

The Undersigned, Commissioners of the State of Maine on the subject of the North Eastern Boundary, have the honor to acknowledge the receipt of your note addressed to them under date of the 15th. inst,[1] with enclosures therein referred to. The proposition first submitted by the special Minister of Great Britain [Lord Ashburton] on the subject of the boundary having been disagreed to, and the proposition made on the part of the United States with the assent of the Commissioners of Maine and Massachusetts, having been rejected as inadmissible coupled with an expression of surprise, that it should have been made and Lord Ashburton, in the same communication, having intimated a preference for conference rather than correspondence,[2] and having omitted in his note to make any new proposition, except a qualified withdrawal of a part of his former one, we learn from your note, that you "have had full and frequent conferences with him respecting the North Eastern Boundary," and that you "believe you understand what is practicable to be done on that subject, so far as he (Lord Ashburton) is concerned." We also learn

---

was a Democratic member of Congress from Maine.

1. See above, DW to Preble et al., July 15, 1842.

2. Ashburton wrote Lord Aberdeen that as soon as Preble had reluctantly agreed to a compromise line he "went off to his wilds in Maine as sulky as a Bear." Ashburton to Aberdeen, July

28, 1842 (Uk).

3. See below.

1. See above, DW to Preble et al., July 15, 1842.

2. See above, Ashburton to DW, June 21, 1842; Preble et al. to DW, June 29, 1842; DW to Ashburton, July 8, 1842; and Ashburton to DW, July 11, 1842.

that "in these conferences he has made no positive or binding proposition, thinking, perhaps, it would be more desirable, under present circumstances, that such a proposition should proceed from the side of the United States;" but that you have reason to believe, that he would agree to a line of boundary such as is described in the paper accompanying your note, marked B, and also, that you entertain the conviction "that no more advantageous arrangement can be made," and, with this conviction, you refer the subject to the grave deliberation of the Commissioners.

Regarding this as substantially a proposition on the part of the United States, with the knowledge and assent of Great Britain, and as the one most favorable to us which, under any circumstances, the latter Government would either offer or accept, the Undersigned have not failed to bestow upon it the grave deliberation and consideration which its nature and importance, and their own responsible position, demand. If the result of that deliberation should not fully justify the expressed hopes, or meet the expectations and views, of the Government of the United States, we beg you to be assured, that such failure will be the result of their firm convictions of duty to the States they represent, and will not arise from any want of an anxious desire, on their part, to bring the controversy to an amicable, just and honorable termination. In coming to this consideration, they have not been unmindful that the State of Maine, with the firmest conviction of her absolute right to the whole territory drawn into controversy, and sustained, as she has been, by the unanimous concurrence of her Sister-States, and of the Government of the Union, repeatedly expressed and cordially given, and without a wavering doubt as to the perfect practicability of marking the Treaty-line upon the face of the earth, according to her claim, has yet, at all times, manifested a spirit of forbearance and patience under what she could not but deem unfounded pretensions, and unwarrantable delays, and irritating encroachments. In the midst of all the provocations to resistance, and to the assertion and maintenance of her extreme rights, she has never forgotten that she is a Member of the Union; and she has endeavoured to deserve the respect, sympathy and co-operation of her Sister States, by pursuing a course equally removed from pusillanimity and rashness, and by maintaining her difficult position, in a spirit that would forbear much for peace, but would yield nothing through fear. At all times, and under all circumstances, she has been ready and anxious to bring the controversy to a close, upon terms honorable and equitable, and to unite in any proper scheme to effect that object. In this spirit, and with these convictions, Maine instantly and cheerfully acceded to the proposal of the General Government, made through you, to appoint Commissioners.[3]

3. See above, DW to Fairfield and Davis, April 11, 1842. Maine's acceptance, dated May 25, 1842, is in *Executive Documents,* 27th Cong., 3d sess., Serial 418, No. 2, pp. 66–67.

That no obstacle might be interposed to the successful issue of this negotiation, her Legislature gave to her Commissioners ample and unlimited powers which, but for the presumed necessity of the case, her People would be slow to yield to any Functionaries. Her Commissioners, thus appointed and thus empowered, assumed the duties imposed upon them, in the spirit and with the views of the Government and People of Maine. They came to the negotiation with a firm conviction of her rights; but, with a disposition and determination to meet a conciliatory proposition for a Conventional line in a similar spirit, and to yield, for any reasonable equivalent, all that they presumed would be asked, or desired, by the other party. They, with the other Citizens of Maine, were not unapprised of the fact, so often alluded to in our former communications, that England had long been anxious to obtain the undisputed possession of that portion of the territory which would enable her to maintain a direct and uninterrupted communication between her Provinces. So far as they could learn from any source, this was the only professed object she had in view, and the only one which had been regarded as in contemplation. With this understanding, the Undersigned at once decided to yield, upon the most liberal terms, this long-sought convenience, and they indulged the confident expectation, that such a concession would, at once, meet all the wants and wishes of the English Government, and bring the mission to a speedy and satisfactory close. When, therefore, we were met, at the outset, by a proposition which required the cession, on our part, of all the territory north of the St. John River, and enough of the territory on the south to include the Madawaska settlement, extending at least fifty miles up that River, with no other equivalents to us than the limited right to float timber down that River, and to the United States the small tracts adjacent to the forty fifth parallel of Latitude, in other States, we could not but express our regret to be thus, as it were, repelled. But, regarding this rather as the extreme limit of a claim, subject, notwithstanding the strong language of Lord Ashburton, to be restrained and limited, we deemed it proper, in our communication of the 16th. inst,[4] after declining to accede to the proposition, in conjunction with the Commissioners of Massachusetts, to point out and offer a Conventional line of boundary, as therein specified. In fixing on this line, we were mainly anxious to select such a one as should, at once, and preeminently, give to Great Britain all that was necessary for her understood object, and to preserve to Maine the remainder of her territory. To accomplish this object, we departed from the River, to secure the unobstructed use of the accustomed way from Quebec to Halifax. We are not aware that any objection has been made, from any quarter, to this line, as not giving up to Great

4. See above, Preble et al. to DW, July 16, 1842.

Britain all that she needed, or could reasonably ask, for the above purpose. And, although Lord Ashburton did not deem it necessary to "examine the line (proposed) in its precise details," or to look at a Map on
which it could most readily be traced; and, although he has seen fit to
say that he was "quite at a loss to account for such a proposal," yet he
has not intimated that the line suggested fails, in any respect; to meet
the object we had in view, and which we frankly and readily avowed. It
is well known to you, Sir, that we had determined upon no such inflexi-
ble adherence to that exact demarcation as would have prevented us
from changing it, upon any reasonable evidence that it did not, in every
respect, meet the requirements of the above-stated proposition in relation
to a perfect line of communication. But, believing then, as we do now,
that it did thus meet all these requirements; and although it was, as we
feel bound to say, the general and confident expectation of the People of
Maine, that any relinquishment on our part, of jurisdiction and territory
would be, *in part* at least, compensated from that strip of contiguous territory on the west bank of the St. John, yet, when we were solemnly assured that no such cession could be made under his Lordship's instructions, we forebore to press for this reasonable and just exchange, and
contented ourselves with accepting the limited right of navigation of the
River, as the only equivalent from Great Britain for the territory and
jurisdiction we offered to surrender. And, as you will remark, we offerred
not merely a right of way on land for a similar easement on the water,
but the entire and absolute title to the land and jurisdiction of the large
tract North and East of the line specified. It cannot be denied that it preserves to us a frontier in a forest almost impenetrable on the North,
which would defend itself by its own natural character; and that, if any
thing should be deducted from the agricultural value of that portion beyond the Madawaska settlements, on account of its ruggedness and
want of attraction to Settlers, much may justly be added to its value as
a boundary between the two Nations.

The value of this tract to Great Britain, both in a civil and military
point of view, cannot be overlooked. It gives her the much coveted route
for the movement of troops in war, and her mails and Passengers in
peace, and is most particularly important in case of renewed outbreaks
in her North American Colonies. The assumption of jurisdiction in the
Madawaska settlement, and the pertinacity with which it has been maintained, are practical evidence of the value attached to the tract by the
Government of Her Britannic Majesty.

We have alluded to these views of the value and importance of this
territory, not with any design of expressing our regret that we thus offerred it; but, to show that we are fully aware of all these views and circumstances affecting the question, and that we duly appreciate the far-

seeing sagacity and prudence of those British Statesmen who so early attempted to secure it, as a cession, by negotiation, and the suggestion of equivalents.

The answer of Lord Ashburton to your note of the 8th. instant contained a distinct rejection of our offer, with a substantial withdrawal of his claim to any territory south of the River St. John, but not modifying the claim for the relinquishment on the part of Maine and the United States, of all North of that River. Our views, in reference to many of the topics in his Lordship's reply, we have had the honor heretofore to communicate to you, in our note of the 16th. instant; and to that answer we would now refer as forming an important part of this negotiation, and as containing our refusal of the line indicated. We are now called upon to consider the final proposition made by, or through, the Government of the United States, for our consideration and acceptance. The line indicated may be shortly defined, as the line recommended by the King of the Netherlands [William I], and an addition thereto of a strip of land, at the base of the Highlands, running to the source of the South West Branch of the St. John. The examination and consideration of all other lines, which might better meet our views and objects, have been precluded by the declaration, and other plenary evidence we have, that the line specified in your communication is the most advantageous that can be offerred to us; and that no one of less extent, or yielding in fact less to the other party, can be deemed admissible. We are, therefore, brought to the single and simple consideration of the question, whether we can, consistently with our views of our duty to the State we represent, accept the proposition submitted by you.

So far as any claim is interposed, based upon a supposed equity arising from the recommendation of the King of the Netherlands, we have only to refer to our former note for our views on that topic. We have now only to add, that we came to this conference, untrammelled and free, to see if, in a spirit of amity and equity, we could not find and agree upon some new line, which, whilst it yielded all that was needed by one party, might fairly be the motive and groundwork for equivalent territory, or rights, granted to the other; and, that we cannot make any admission, or consent to any proposition, which would not [only] revive, but put vitality and power into that which, up to this time, has never possessed either. We base our whole action on grounds entirely independent of that advice of the Arbiter.

It may, possibly, be intimated in this connection, as it has more than once been heretofore, that the Commissioners of Maine, and the People of that State, are disposed to regard the whole territory as clearly falling within their rightful limits, and are not willing to consider the question as one in doubt and dispute, and, therefore, one to be settled as if each party had nearly, or quite, equal claims. Certainly, Sir, the People and

Government of Maine do not deny that the question has been drawn into dispute. They have had too many, and too recent, painful evidences of that fact, to allow such a doubt, however much at a loss they may be to perceive any just or tenable grounds on which the adversary claim is based. For years, they have borne and forborne, and struggled to maintain their rights, in a peaceable and, yet, unflinching spirit against what appeared to them injustice from abroad, and neglect at home. But, they have yet to learn that the mere fact that an adverse claim is made and persisted in, and maintained by ingenuity and ability for a series of years, increasing in extent and varying its grounds as years roll on, is to be regarded as a reason why courtesy should require, in opposition to the fact, a relinquishment of the plain, explicit and sincere language of perfect conviction, and unwavering confidence; or, that a continued adverse and resisted claim may yet, by mere lapse of time and reiteration, ripen into a right. But, we desire it to be distinctly remembered that, in this attempt to negotiate for a conventional line, Maine has not insisted, or even requested, that any formal or virtual admission of her title to the whole territory should be a condition preliminary to a settlement. We hold, and we claim, the right to express, at all times and in all suitable places, our opinion of the perfect right of Maine to the whole territory; but, we have never assumed it, as a point of honor, that our adversary should acknowledge it. Indeed, we have endeavoured to view the subject rather in reference to a settlement, on even hard terms for us, than to dwell on the strong aspect of the case when we look at the naked question of our right and title under the Treaty. It could hardly be expected, however, that we should silently, and thus virtually, acquiesce in any assumption that our claim was unsustained, and that "the Treaty line was not executable." On this point we expressed ourselves fully in a former note.[5]

In returning to the direct consideration of the last proposition, and the terms and conditions attending it, in justice to ourselves and our State, we feel bound to declare, and we confidently appeal to you, Sir, in confirmation of the declaration, that this negotiation has been conducted, on our part, with no mercenary views, and with no design to extort unreasonable equivalents, or extravagant compensation. The State of Maine has always felt an insuperable repugnance to parting with any portion even of her disputed territory, for mere pecuniary recompense from adverse claimants. She comes here for no mere bargain for the sale of acres, in the spirit or with the arts of trafic. Her Commissioners have been much less anxious to secure benefit and recompense, than to preserve the State from unnecessary curtailment and dismemberment. The proposition we made is evidence of the fact. We have heretofore ex-

5. See above, Preble et al. to DW, July 16, 1842.

pressed some opinions of the mutual character of the benefits to each party from the free navigation of the St. John. Without entering, however, upon the particular consideration of the terms and conditions, which we have not thought it necessary to do, we distinctly state that our great repugnance to the line is based upon the extent of territory required to be yielded. We may, however, in passing, remark that all the pecuniary offers contained in your note, most liberally construed, would scarcely recompense and repay to Maine the amount of money, and interest, which she has actually expended in defending and protecting the territory from wrongs arising and threatened by reason of its condition as disputed ground.

Considering, then, this proposition as involving the surrender of more territory than the avowed objects of England require, as removing our landmarks from the well-known, and well-defined, boundary of the Treaty of 1783, on the crest of the highlands, besides insisting upon the line of the Arbiter in its full extent, we feel bound to say, after the most careful and anxious consideration, that we cannot bring our minds to the conviction that the proposal is such as Maine had a right to expect.

But, we are not unaware of the expectations which have been, and still are, entertained of a favorable issue to this negotiation by the Government and People of this Country, and the great disappointment which would be felt, and expressed, at its failure. Nor are we unmindful of the future, warned, as we have been, by the past, that any attempts to determine the line by arbitration may be either fruitless, or with a result more to be deplored.

We are, now, given to understand that the Executive of the United States, representing the sovereignty of the Union, assents to the proposal, and that this Department of the Government at least is anxious for its acceptance, as, in its view, most expedient for the general good. The Commissioners of Massachusetts have already given their assent,[6] on behalf of that Commonwealth. Thus situated, the Commissioners of Maine, invoking the spirit of attachment and patriotic devotion of their State to the Union, and being willing to yield to the deliberate convictions of her Sister-States as to the path of duty, and to interpose no obstacles to an adjustment which the general judgment of the Nation shall pronounce as honorable and expedient, even if that judgment shall lead to a surrender of a portion of the birth-right of the People of their State, and prized by them because it is their birth-right, have determined to overcome their objections to the proposal, so far as to say, that if, upon mature consideration, the Senate of the United States shall advise, and consent to, the ratification of a Treaty, corresponding in its terms with

6. See Abbott Lawrence, John Mills, and Charles Allen to DW, July 20, 1842, RG 76 (Records of the Boundary and Claims Commissions and Arbitrations).

your proposal, and with the conditions in our Memorendum accompanying this note, marked A,[7] and identified by our signatures, they, by virtue of the power vested in them by the Resolves of the Legislature of Maine, give the assent of that State to such Conventional line, with the terms, conditions and equivalents herein mentioned. We have the honor to be, Sir, with high respect, your obedient Servants

Edward Kavanagh   Edward Kent   John Otis   Wm. P. Preble

L S. DNA, RG 76 (Records of the Boundary and Claims Commissions and Arbitrations and Miscellaneous Documents Relating to the Northeast Boundary, 1827–1842). Rec'd July 23, 1842. Published in *Senate Documents*, 27th Cong., 3d sess., Serial 413, No. 1, pp. 93–99.

TO LORD ASHBURTON

Department of State,

My Lord: Washington, 27th. July, 1842

I have now to propose to your Lordship a line of division embracing the disputed portions of the boundary between the United States and the British provinces of New Brunswick and the Canadas, with its considerations and equivalents, such as conforms, I believe, in substance, to the result of the many conferences and discussions which have taken place between us.

The acknowledged territories of the United States and England join upon each other from the Atlantic Ocean to the eastern foot of the Rocky Mountains, a distance of more than three thousand miles. From the ocean to the source of the St. Croix the line of division has been ascertained and fixed by agreement: from the source of the St. Croix to a point near St. Regis, on the river St. Lawrence, it may be considered as unsettled or controverted; from this last mentioned point, along the St. Lawrence and through the lakes, it is settled, until it reaches the water communication between Lake Huron and Lake Superior. At this point the commissioners, under the seventh article of the Treaty of Ghent, found a subject of disagreement which they could not overcome, in deciding up which branch or channel the line should proceed, till it should reach a point in the middle of St. Mary's river, about one mile above St. George's or Sugar Island.[1]

From the middle of the water communication between the two lakes, at the point last mentioned, the commissioners extended the line through the remaining part of that water communication, and across Lake Superior, to a point north of Ile Royale; but they could not agree in what direction the line should run from this last mentioned point, nor where it should leave Lake Superior, nor how it should be extended to the Rainy

7. Enclosure not printed here.
1. See Ashburton's northwestern boundary proposal in his letter to DW of July 16, 1842, above.

Lake, or Lac la Pluie. From this last mentioned lake, they agreed on the line to the northwesternmost point of the Lake of the Woods, which they found to be in latitude 49 degrees 23 minutes 55 seconds. The line extends, according to existing treaties, due south from this point to the 49th. parallel of north latitude, and by that parallel to the Rocky Mountains.

Not being able to agree upon the whole line, the commissioners, under the seventh article, did not make any joint report to their respective Governments. So far as they agreed on any part of the line, that part has been considered settled; but it may be well to give validity to these portions of the line by a treaty.

To complete the boundary line, therefore, and to remove all doubts and disputes, it is necessary for the two Governments to come to an agreement on three points:

1st. What shall be the line on the northeastern and northern limits of the United States, from the St. Croix to the St. Lawrence. This is by far the most important and difficult of the subjects, and involves the principal questions of equivalents and compensations.

2d. What shall be the course of the boundary from the point where the commissioners, under the sixth article of the Treaty of Ghent, terminated their labors—to wit: a point in the Neebish channel, near Muddy Lake, in the water communication between Lake Huron and Lake Superior, to a point in the middle of St. Mary's river, one mile above Sugar Island. This question is important, as it involves the ownership of that island.

3d. What shall be the line from the point north of Ile Royale, in Lake Superior, to which the Commissioners of the two Governments arrived, by agreement, to the Rainy Lake; and also to confirm those parts of the line to which the said Commissioners agreed.

Besides agreeing upon the line of division through these controverted portions of the boundary, you have suggested also, as the proposed setlement proceeds upon the ground of compromise and equivalents, that boats belonging to Her Majesty's subjects may pass the falls of the Long Saut in the St. Lawrence, on either side of the Long Saut Islands; and that the passages between the islands lying at or near the junction of the river St. Clair, with the lake of that name, shall be severally free and open to the vessels of both countries. There appears no reasonable objection to what is requested in these particulars; and on the part of the United States it is desirable, that their vessels, proceeding in from Lake Erie into the Detroit river, should have the privilege of passing between Bois Blanc, an island belonging to England, and the Canadian shore, the deeper and better channel belonging to that side.

The line, then, now proposed to be agreed to, may be thus described.

Beginning at the monument at the source of the river St. Croix, as designated and agreed to by the Commissioners, under the fifth article of the Treaty of 1794, between the Governments of the United States and Great Britain; thence, north, following the exploring line run and marked by the surveyors of the two Governments in the years 1817 and 1818, under the fifth article of the Treaty of Ghent, to its intersection with the river St. John, and to the middle of the channel thereof; thence, up the middle of the main channel of the said river St. John, to the mouth of the river St. Francis; thence, up the middle of the channel of the said river St. Francis, and of the lakes through which it flowes, to the outlet of the Lake Pohenagamook; thence, southwesterly, in a straight line, to a point on the northwest branch of the river St. John, which point shall be ten miles distant from the main branch of the St. John, in a straight line, and in the nearest direction; but, if the said point shall be found to be less than seven miles from the nearest point of the summit or crest of the highlands that divide those rivers which empty themselves into the river St. Lawrence from those which fall into the river St. John's, then the said point shall be made to recede down the said river to a point seven miles in a straight line, from the said summit or crest; thence, in a straight line, in a course about south, eight degrees west, to the point where the parallel of latitude of 46 degrees 25 minutes north intersects the southwest branch of the St. John's; thence, southerly, by the said branch, to the source thereof in the highlands at the Metjarmette portage; thence, down along the said highlands which divide the waters which empty themselves into the river St. Lawrence, from those which fall into the Atlantic Ocean, to the head of Hall's Stream; thence, down the middle of said stream, till the line thus run intersects the old line of boundary, surveyed and marked by [Thomas] Valentine and [John] Collins previously to the year 1774, as the forty-fifth degree of north latitude, and which has been known and understood to be the line of actual division between the States of New York and Vermont, on one side, and the British province of Canada on the other; and from said point of intersection, west, along the said dividing line, as heretofore known and understood to the Iroquois or St. Lawrence river; and from the place where the joint commissioners terminated their labors, under the sixth article of the Treaty of Ghent, to wit: at a point in the Neebish channel, near Muddy Lake, the line shall run into and along the ship channel between St. Joseph's and St. Tammany Islands, to the division of the channel at or near the head of St. Joseph's Island; thence, turning eastwardly and northwardly, around the lower end of St. George's or Sugar Island, and following the middle of the channel which divides St. George's from St. Joseph's Island; thence, up the east Neebish channel, nearest to George's Island, through the middle of Lake George; thence, west of Jonas Island, into St. Mary's river, to a point in the middle of that river, about one mile above St. George's or Sugar Island, so as to appropriate and assign the said island to the United States; thence, adopting the line traced on the maps by the Commissioners, through the river St. Mary['s] and Lake Superior, to a point north of Ile Royale, in said lake, one hundred yards to the north and east of Ile Chapeau, which last-mentioned island lies near the northeastern point of Ile Royale, where the line marked by the Commissioners terminates; and from the last-mentioned point, south-westerly, through the middle of the sound between Ile Royale and the northwestern main land, to the mouth of Pigeon River, and up said river to and through the north and south Fowl Lakes, to the lakes of the height of land, between Lake Superior and the Lake of the Woods; thence, along the water communication, to Lake Saisaginaga, and through that lake; thence, to and through Cypress Lake, Lac du Bois Blanc, Lac la Croix, Little Vermillion Lake, and Lake Namecan, and through the several smaller lakes, straits, or streams, connecting the lakes here mentioned to that point in Lac la Pluie, or Rainy Lake, at the Chaudiere Falls, from which the Commissioners traced the line, to the most northwestern point of the Lake of the Woods; thence, along the said line to the said most northwestern point, being in latitude 49 degrees 23 minutes 55 seconds north, and in longitude 95 degrees 14 minutes 38 seconds west, from the observatory at Greenwich; thence, according to existing treaties, the line extends due south to its intersection with the forty-ninth parallel of north latitude, and along that parallel to the Rocky Mountains. (It being under-stood that all the water communications, and all the usual portages along the line from Lake Superior to the Lake of the Woods, and also Grand Portage, from the shore of Lake Superior to the Lake of the Woods, and the Grand Portage, from the shore of Lake Superior to the Pigeon River, as now actually used, shall be free and open to the use of the sub-jects and citizens of both countries.)

It is desirable to follow the description and the exact line of the origi-nal treaty as far as practicable. There is reason to think that "Long Lake," mentioned in the Treaty of 1783, was merely the estuary of the Pigeon river, as no lake called "Long Lake," or any other water strictly conform-ing to the idea of a lake, is found in that quarter. This opinion is strength-ened by the fact that the words of the Treaty would seem to imply that the water intended as "Long Lake," was immediately joining Lake Su-perior. In one respect an exact compliance with the words of the Treaty is not practicable. There is no continuous water communication between Lake Superior and the Lake of the Woods, as the Lake of the Woods is known to discharge its waters through the Red River of the north into Hudson's Bay. The dividing height or ridge between the eastern sources of the tributaries of the Lake of the Woods and the western sources of Pigeon River appears, by authentic maps, to be distant about forty miles from the mouth of Pigeon River, on the shore of Lake Superior.

It is not improbable that in the imperfection of knowledge which then existed of those remote countries, and perhaps misled by [John] Mitchell's map, the negotiators of the Treaty of 1783 supposed the Lake of the Woods to discharge its waters into Lake Superior. The broken and difficult nature of the water communication from Lake Superior to the Lake of the Woods renders numerous portages necessary; and it is right that these water communications and these portages should make a common highway, where necessary, for the use of the subjects and citizens of both Governments.

When the proposed line shall be properly described in the Treaty, the grant by England of the right to use the waters of the river St. John's for the purpose of transporting to the mouth of that river all the timber and agricultural products raised in Maine, on the waters of the St. Johns, or any of its tributaries, without subjection to any discriminating toll, duty, or disability, is to be inserted. Provision should also be made for quieting and confirming the titles of all persons having claims to lands on either side of the line, whether such titles be perfect or inchoate only, and to the same extent in which they would have been confirmed by their respective Governments had no change taken place. What has been agreed to, also, in respect to the common use of certain passages in the rivers and lakes, as already stated, must be made matter of regular stipulation.[2]

Your Lordship is also informed, by correspondence which formerly took place between the two Governments, that there is a fund arising from the sale of timber, concerning which fund an understanding was had some years ago. It will be expedient to provide by the Treaty that this arrangement shall be carried into effect.[3]

A proper article will be necessary to provide for the creation of a commission to run and mark some parts of the line between Maine and the British Provinces.[4]

These several objects appear to me to embrace all respecting the boundary line and its equivalents which the Treaty needs to contain as matters of stipulation between the United States and England. I have the honor to be, with high consideration, your Lordship's most obedient servant,   Danl Webster.

LC. DNA, RG 59 (Notes to Foreign Legations, Britain). Published in *Senate Documents*, 27th Cong., 3d sess., Serial 413, No. 1, pp. 58–61.

2. These provisions were incorporated in Articles 1, 2, 3, 4, 6, and 7 of the treaty. *Treaties*, 4:364–369.

3. See Charles R. Vaughn to Louis McLane, February 28, 1834, DNA, RG 59 (Notes from Foreign Legations, Britain), in which the British minister informed the secretary of state that the disputed territory fund would be held in account until the boundary settlement. The arrangements for the fund are in Article 5 of the treaty. *Treaties*, 4:367–368.

4. Article 6 of the treaty. *Treaties*, 4:368.

TO LORD ASHBURTON

My Lord:

Department of State,
Washington, 27th. July, 1842.

In relation to the case of the "Caroline," which we have heretofore made the subject of conference, I have thought it right to place in your hands an extract of a letter from this Department to Mr. [Henry Stephen] Fox, of the 24th. of April, 1841,[1] and an extract from the message of the President of the United States to Congress at the commencement of its present session.[2] These papers you have, no doubt, already seen; but they are, nevertheless, now communicated, as such a communication is considered a ready mode of presenting the view which this Government entertains of the destruction of that vessel.

The act of which the Government of the United States complains is not to be considered as justifiable or unjustifiable, as the question of the lawfulness or unlawfulness of the employment in which the "Caroline" was engaged may be decided the one way or the other. That act is of itself a wrong, and an offence to the sovereignty and the dignity of the United States, being a violation of their soil and territory—a wrong for which, to this day, no atonement, or even apology, has been made by Her Majesty's Government. Your Lordship cannot but be aware that self-respect, the consciousness of independence and national equality, and a sensitiveness to whatever may touch the honor of the country—a sensitiveness which this Government will ever feel and ever cultivate—make this a matter of high importance, and I must be allowed to ask for it your Lordship's grave consideration. I have the honor to be, my Lord, your Lordship's most obedient servant,   Danl. Webster.

LC. DNA, RG 59 (Notes to Foreign Legations, Britain). Published in *Senate Documents*, 27th Cong., 3d sess., Serial 413, No. 1, p. 126.

FROM LORD ASHBURTON

DEAR SIR: [c. July 1842]

I shall be glad to see Mr. [John Caldwell] Calhoun to-morrow morning at the hour he mentions, and I wish I knew any thing very satisfactory

1. See above, DW to Fox, April 24, 1841, "The Crisis in Anglo-American Relations," pp. 58–68.
2. *Messages and Papers*, 4:75–77. In the message of December 7, 1841, President Tyler defined "the real question at issue" in the *Caroline* dispute as whether a foreign government, "except in a case of the most urgent and extreme necessity," had the right to invade the territory of another "either to arrest the persons or destroy the property of those who may have violated the municipal laws of such foreign government or have disregarded their obligations arising under the law of nations." He emphatically denied any such right.

to suggest or propose in the matter of the Creole, which ends in being my greatest difficulty; but I will see what may be done.

I fear that Mr. [Hugh Swinton] Legarè's proposal will not answer.[1] It leaves open the whole of the difficulty on my side. I apprehend we shall make nothing of any article for this purpose, and that what is done must be done by letter.

I have had my interview with the gentlemen of Maine, and I incline to think they will consent to our line. I explained that I was at the end of *my* line, and that they must therefore say yes or no. I also pressed an early answer through you, which I believe you will receive this evening or to-morrow. Your servant, ASHBURTON

Text from Curtis, 2:120. Original not found.

FROM LORD ASHBURTON

Sir.   Washington 28 July 1842

In the course of our conferences on the several subjects of difference which it was the object of my mission to endeavour to settle, the unfortunate case of the Caroline, with its attendant consequences, could not escape our attention; for although it is not of a description to be susceptible of any settlement by a convention or treaty, yet being connected with the highest considerations of national honour and dignity it has given rise at times to deep excitement, so as more than once to endanger the maintenance of peace.

The note you did me the honour of addressing me the 27 inst.[1] reminds me that however disposed your Government might be to be satisfied with the explanations which it has been my duty to offer, the natural anxiety of the public mind requires that these explanations should be more durably recorded in our correspondence, and you send me a copy of your note to Mr. [Henry Stephen] Fox, Her Britannic Majesty's minister here, and an extract from the speech of the President of the United States to Congress, at the opening of the present session, as a ready mode of presenting the view entertained on this subject by the Government of the United States.

It is so far satisfactory to perceive that we are perfectly agreed as to the general principles of international law applicable to this unfortunate case. Respect for the inviolable character of the territory of independent nations is the most essential foundation of civilization. It is useless to strengthen a principle so generally acknowledged by any appeal to authorities on international law, and you may be assured, Sir, that Her

1. See Legaré to DW, July 29, 1842, below, and his proposal of July 20, 1842, in *Opinions of Attorneys General, Executive Documents*, 31st Cong., 2d sess., Serial 603, No. 55, 2: 1533–1538.

1. See above, DW to Ashburton, July 27, 1842.

Majesty's Government set the highest possible value on this principle, and are sensible of their duty to support it by their conduct and example for the maintenanace of peace and order in the world. If a sense of moral responsibility were not a sufficient surety for their observance of this duty towards all nations, it will be readily believed that the most common dictates of interest and policy would lead to it in the case of a long conterminous boundary of some thousand miles with a country of such great and growing power as the United States of America, inhabited by a kindred race, gifted with all its activity and all its susceptibility on points of national honour.

Every consideration therefore leads us to set as highly as your Government can possibly do this paramount obligation of reciprocal respect for the independent territory of each. But however strong this duty may be it is admitted by all writers, by all Jurists, by the occasional practice of all nations, not excepting your own, that a strong overpowering necessity may arise, when this great principle may and must be suspended. It must be so for the shortest possible period, during the continuance of an admitted overruling necessity, and strictly confined within the narrowest limits imposed by that necessity. 'Self' defence is the first law of our nature and it must be recognised by every code which professes to regulate the condition and relations of man. Upon this modification, if I may so call it, of the great general principle, we seem also to be agreed, and on this part of the subject I have done little more than repeat the sentiments, though in less forcible language, admitted and maintained by you in the letter to which you refer me.

Agreeing therefore on the general principle and on the possible exception to which it is liable, the only question between us is whether this occurrence came within the limits fairly to be assigned to such exception, whether, to use your words, there was "that necessity of self defence, instant, overwhelming, leaving no choice of means" which preceded the destruction of the Caroline, while moored to the shore of the United States. Give me leave to say, Sir, with all possible admiration of your very ingenuous discussion of the general principles which are supposed to govern the right and practice of interference by the people of one country in the wars and quarrels of others, that this part of your argument is little applicable to our immediate case. If Great Britain, America, or any other country suffer their people to fit out expeditions to take part in distant quarrels, such conduct may according to the circumstances of each case, be justly matter of complaint, and perhaps these transactions have generally been in late times too much overlooked or connived at. But the case we are considering is of a wholly different description, and may be best determined by answering the following question. Supposing a man standing on ground where you have no legal right to follow him has a weapon long enough to reach you, and is striking you down and endangering your life, How long are you bound to wait for the assistance of the authority having the legal power to relieve you? Or, to bring the facts more immediately home to the case, if cannon are moving and setting up in a battery which can reach you and are actually destroying life and property by their fire, If you have remonstrated for some time without effect, and see no prospect of relief, when begins your right to defend yourself should you have no other means of doing so, than by seizing your assailent on the verge of a neutral territory?

I am unwilling to recall to your recollection the particulars of this case, but I am obliged very shortly to do so, to shew what was at the time the extent of the existing justification, for upon this entirely depends the question whether a gross insult has or has not been offered to the Government and people of the United States.

After some tumultuous proceedings in Upper Canada which were of short duration and were suppressed by the Militia of the Country, the persons criminally concerned in them took refuge in the neighboring state of New York, and with a very large addition to their numbers openly collected, invaded the Canadian territory taking possession of Navy Island.

This invasion took place the 16th of December 1837; a gradual accession of numbers and of military ammunition continued openly, and though under the sanction of no public authority, at least with no public hinderance until the 29th of the same month, when several hundred men were collected, and twelve pieces of ordnance, which could only have been procured from some public store or arsenal, were actually mounted on Navy Island and were used to fire within easy range upon the unoffending inhabitants of the opposite shore. Remonstrances, wholly ineffectual were made; so ineffectual indeed that a Militia regiment, stationed on the neighboring American island, looked on without any attempt at interference, while shots were fired from the American island itself. This important fact stands on the best American authority; being stated in a letter to Mr. [John] Forsyth of the 6th of Feby 1838, of Mr. [Nathaniel S.] Benton, attorney of the United States,[2] the gentleman sent by your Government to enquire into the facts of the case, who adds, very properly, that he makes the statement "with deep regret and mortification."

This force, formed of all the reckless and mischievous people of the border, formidable from their numbers and from their armament, had in their pay and as part of their establishment this steamboat, Caroline, the important means and instrument by which numbers and arms were hourly increasing. I might safely put it to any candid man acquainted with the existing state of things, to say whether the military commander

2. Benton was the U.S. district attorney for northern New York.

in Canada had the remotest reason on the 29th of December to expect to be relieved from this state of suffering by the protective intervention of any American authority. How long could a Government, having the paramount duty of protecting its own people, be reasonably expected to wait for what they had then no reason to expect? What would have been the conduct of American officers—what has been their conduct under circumstances much less aggravated? I would appeal to you, Sir, to say whether the facts which you say would alone justify this act, viz: "a necessity of self defence, instant, overwhelming, leaving no choice of means and no moment for deliberation," were not applicable to this case in as high a degree as they ever were to any case of a similar description in the history of nations.

Nearly five years are now past since this occurrence, there has been time for the public to deliberate upon it calmly, and I believe I may take it to be the opinion of candid and honourable men, that the British officers who executed this transaction and their Government who approved it, intended no slight or disrespect to the sovereign authority of the United States. That they intended no such disrespect, I can most solemnly affirm, and I trust it will be admitted that no inference to the contrary can fairly be drawn even by the most susceptible on points of national honour.

Notwithstanding my wish that the explanations I had to make might not revive in any degree any feelings of irritation, I do not see how I could treat this subject without this short recital of facts, because the proof that no disrespect was intended is mainly to be looked for in the extent of the justification.

There remains only a point or two which I should wish to notice, to remove in some degree the impression which your rather highly coloured description of this transaction is calculated to make. The mode of telling a story often tends to distort facts, and in this case more than in any other it is important to arrive at plain unvarnished truth.

It appears from every account that the expedition was sent to capture the Caroline when she was expected to be found on the British ground of Navy island, and that it was only owing to the orders of the rebel leader being disobeyed, that she was not so found. When the British officer came round the point of the island in the night, he first discovered that the vessel was moored to the other shore. He was not by this deterred from making the capture, and his conduct was approved. But you will perceive that there was here most decidedly the case of justification mentioned in your note that there should be "no moment left for deliberation." I mention this circumstance to shew also that the expedition was not planned with a premeditated purpose of attacking the enemy within the jurisdiction of the United States, but that the necessity of so doing arose from altered circumstances at the moment of execution.

I have only further to notice the highly coloured picture drawn in your note of the facts attending the execution of this service. Some importance is attached to the attack having been made in the night and the vessel having been set on fire and floated down the falls of the river, and it is insinuated rather than asserted that there was carelessness as to the lives of the persons on board. The account given by the distinguished officer who commanded the expedition distinctly refutes or satisfactorily explains these assertions. The time of night was purposely selected as most likely to ensure the execution with the least loss of life, and it is expressly stated that the strength of the current not permitting the vessel to be carried off and it being necessary to destroy her by fire, she was drawn into the stream for the express purpose of preventing injury to persons or property of the inhabitants at Schlosser.

I would willingly have abstained from a return to the facts of this transaction, my duty being to offer those explanations and assurances which may lead to satisfy the public mind and to the cessation of all angry feeling, but it appeared to me that some explanation of parts of the case, apparently misunderstood, might be of service for this purpose.

Although it is believed that a candid and impartial consideration of the whole history of this unfortunate event will lead to the conclusion that there were grounds of justification as strong as were ever presented in such cases, and above all that no slight of the authority of the United States was ever intended, yet it must be admitted that there was in the hurried execution of this necessary service a violation of territory, and I am instructed to assure you that Her Majesty's Government consider this as a most serious fact, and that far from thinking that an event of this kind should be lightly risked, they would unfeignedly deprecate its recurrence. Looking back to what passed at this distance of time, what is perhaps most to be regretted is that some explanation and apology for this occurrence was not immediately made: this with a frank explanation of the necessity of the case might and probably would have prevented much of the exasperation and of the subsequent complaints and recriminations to which it gave rise.

There are possible cases in the relation of nations as of individuals, where necessity which controls all other laws may be pleaded, but it is neither easy nor safe to attempt to define the rights or limits properly assignable to such a plea. This must always be a subject of much delicacy, and should be considered by friendly nations with great candour and forbearance. The intentions of the parties must mainly be looked to, and can it for a moment be supposed that Great Britain would intentionally and wantonly provoke a great and powerful neighbour?

Her Majesty's Government earnestly desire that a reciprocal respect for the independent jurisdiction and authority of neighbouring states may be considered among the first duties of all governments, and I have to repeat the assurance of regret they feel that the event of which I am treating should have disturbed the harmony they so anxiously wish to maintain with the American people and Government.

Connected with these transactions there have also been circumstances of which I believe it is generally admitted that Great Britain has also had just ground to complain. Individuals have been made personally liable for acts done under the avowed authority of their Government; and there are now many brave men exposed to personal consequences for no other cause than having served their country. That this is contrary to every principle of international law it is useless for me to insist. Indeed it has been admitted by every authority of your Government; but, owing to a conflict of laws, difficulties have intervened much to the regret of those authorities in giving practical effect to these principles, and for these difficulties some remedy has been by all desired. It is no business of mine to enter upon the consideration of them, nor have I sufficient information for the purpose, but I trust you will excuse my addressing to you the enquiry, whether the Government of the United States is now in a condition to secure in effect and in practice the principle, which has never been denied in argument, that individuals acting under legitimate authority are not personally responsible for executing the orders of their Government. That the power when it exists will be used on every fit occasion I am well assured, and I am bound to admit that looking through the voluminous correspondence concerning these transactions, there appears no indisposition with any of the authorities of the federal Government under its several administrations to do justice in this respect in as far as their means and powers would allow.

I trust, Sir, I may now be permitted to hope that all feelings of resentment and ill will resulting from these truly unfortunate events may be buried in oblivion, and that they may be succeeded by those of harmony and friendship which it is certainly the interest and I also believe the inclination of all to promote. I beg, Sir, you will be assured of my high and unfeigned consideration   Ashburton

LS. DNA, RG 59 (Notes from Foreign Legations, Britain). Published in *CR*, 3:766–771.

FROM HUGH SWINTON LEGARÉ

Private.

Dear Sir   29 July, 1842.

I called at your office to say that the President had consulted me upon your *Creole* letter.[1] I like it in its present shape, &, if *nothing better can*

1 See DW to Ashburton, August 1, 1842, below. Legaré probably is referring to a draft. The procedure followed was that after discussions with Ashburton, DW drafted letters and sent them to the president for his revisions and approval.

be done, should think the explicit recognition of the law of nations as you there lay it down, as seeming enough for the *nonce*. But this is only *my* opinion—which is in other words, the opinion of the most *moderate* of all men on all such subjects. Others would not concur with me. The President himself with whom I conversed at great length seems dissatisfied & told me [John Caldwell] Calhoun, after conversing with Ld. Ashburton was of opinion that he had power to settle the point & would do so if he were strongly pressed. Of this you are a much better judge than I—perhaps, than he.

At any rate, I think it *very* desirable that something shd. be done to put an end to the *odious* questions that seem but too likely to spring up out of the course of conduct lately adopted & approved in the British colonies.

A declaration of the law of nations as it stands has certainly great advantages to recommend it.

1st. Our rights under it will be independent of treaty i.e. of the will of others.

2d. they will give no new cause of scandal even to fanatics.

3d. it will not expose the present British ministry, who seem more reasonable than the others have been, on this delicate matter, to be weakened by popular clamour Ita *lex scripta* est[2] will be a good plea in bar—there are few mouths it doesn't stop.

But there are others—I take it a majority of So[uthern] Men—who have more faith in "the bee's wax" as Cade[3] calls it—& will make a terrible pother if there be nothing forthcoming under hand & seal.

They may make common cause in Senate with the malcontents on the Boundary question, & fling the whole work into the river—which were a thousand pities.

Will you mark all this—& see what can be done to complete the business & give you the honour due to a chefd'oeuvre. Very faithfully yrs

H. S. Legaré.

ALS. MHi.

FROM LORD ASHBURTON

Private

My Dear Mr Webster,   Sunday 31 July 1842.

Using the words of Walter Scott when he sent one of his novels to his publisher—I send you my Creole D__n her.[1]

I leave her in my original sheets to save time, believing that you can read my scrawl. Pray see if you think I could mend this case with a view

---

2. "Thus the law stands written."
3. Cade is a character in Shakespeare's *Henry IV* and *Henry VI*. The quotation is from *Henry VI*, act 4, scene 2.

1. See Ashburton to DW, August 6, 1842, below.

to conciliation. I have treated it quite fairly for I really believe it would be best settled in London. I also believe something satisfactory may & should be there settled.

Would it be well to leave extradition to be settled at the same time? The questions are more or less connected. I have no objection to either course. I congratulate you on the return of breathing weather. I really believe that if yesterday's sirocco had continued I should not have lived to sign any treaty with you, which is now the great object, as it is likely to be the fifth act of my life. Ever my Dear Sir Yours truly   Ashburton

ALS. NhHi. Published in Van Tyne, pp. 272–273.

TO LORD ASHBURTON

My Lord:

Department of State,
Washington, August 1, 1842.

The President has learned with much regret, that you are not empowered by your Government to enter into a formal stipulation for the better security of vessels of the United States, when meeting with disasters in passing between the United States and the Bahama Islands, and driven, by such disasters, into British ports. This is a subject which is deemed to be of great importance, and which cannot, on the present occasion, be overlooked.

Your Lordship is aware that several cases have occurred within the last few years which have caused much complaint. In some of these cases compensation has been made by the English Government for the interference of the local authorities with American vessels having slaves on board, by which interference these slaves were set free. In other cases, such compensation has been refused.[1] It appears to the President to be for the interest of both countries that the recurrence of similar cases in future should be prevented as far as possible.

Your Lordship has been acquainted with the case of the "Creole," a vessel carried into the port of Nassau last winter by persons who had risen upon the lawful authority of the vessel, and, in the accomplishment of their purpose, had committed murder on a person on board.

The opinions which that occurrence gave occasion for this Government to express, in regard to the rights and duties of friendly and civilized maritime States, placed by Providence near to each other, were well considered, and are entertained with entire confidence. The facts in the particular case of the "Creole" are controverted: positive and officious interference by the colonial authorities to set the slaves free being alleged on one side, and denied on the other.

It is not my present purpose to discuss this difference of opinion as to

1. DW refers to the cases of the *Comet, Encomium, Enterprise,* and *Hermosa.* See above, DW to Everett, January 29, 1842, and *International Law Digest,* 2:350–352.

the evidence in the case as it at present exists, because the rights of individuals having rendered necessary a more thorough and a judicial investigation of facts and circumstances attending the transaction, such investigation is understood to be now in progress, and its result, when known, will render me more able than at this moment to present to the British Government a full and accurate view of the whole case. But it is my purpose, and my duty, to invite your Lordship's attention to the general subject, and your serious consideration of some practical means of giving security to the coasting trade of the United States against unlawful annoyance and interruption along this part of their shore. The Bahama Islands approach the coast of Florida within a few leagues, and, with the coast, form a long and narrow channel, filled with innumerable small islands and banks of sand, and the navigation difficult and dangerous, not only on these accounts, but from the violence of the winds and the variable nature of the currents. Accidents are of course frequent, and necessity often compels vessels of the United States, in attempting to double Cape Florida, to seek shelter in the ports of these islands. Along this passage, the Atlantic States hold intercourse with the States on the Gulf and the Mississippi, and through it the products of the valley of that river (a region of vast extent and boundless fertility.) find a main outlet to the sea, in their destination to the markets of the world.

No particular ground of complaint exists as to the treatment which American vessels usually receive in these ports, unless they happen to have slaves on board; but, in cases of that kind, complaints have been made, as already stated, of officious interference of the colonial authorities with the vessel, for the purpose of changing the condition in which these persons are, by the laws of their own country, and of setting them free.

In the Southern States of this Union slavery exists by the laws of the States and under the guarantee of the Constitution of the United States; and it has existed in them for a period long antecedent to the time when they ceased to be British colonies. In this state of things, it will happen that slaves will be often on board coasting vessels, as hands, as servants attending the families of their owners, or for the purpose of being carried from port to port. For the security of the rights of their citizens, when vessels having persons of this description on board are driven by stress of weather, or carried by unlawful force, into British ports, the United States propose the introduction of no new principle into the law of nations. They require only a faithful and exact observance of the injunctions of that code, as understood and practiced in modern times.

Your Lordship observes that I have spoken only of American vessels driven into British ports by the disasters of the seas, or carried in by unlawful force. I confine my remarks to these cases, because they are the common cases, and because they are the cases which the law of nations most emphatically exempts from interference. The maritime law is full of instances of the application of that great and practical rule, which declares that that which is the clear result of necessity ought to draw after it no penalty and no hazard. If a ship be driven by stress of weather into a prohibited port, or into an open port, with prohibited articles on board, in neither case is any forfeiture incurred. And what may be considered a still stronger case, it has been decided by eminent English authority, and that decision has received general approbation, that if a vessel be driven, by necessity, into a port strictly blockaded, this necessity is good defence, and exempts her from penalty.[2]

A vessel on the high seas, beyond the distance of a marine league from the shore, is regarded as part of the territory of the nation to which she belongs, and subjected exclusively to the jurisdiction of that nation. If, against the will of her master or owner, she be driven or carried nearer to the land, or even into port, those who have, or ought to have, control over her, struggling all the while to keep her upon the high seas, and so within the exclusive jurisdiction of her own Government, what reason or justice is there in creating a distinction between her rights and immunities, in a position thus the result of absolute necessity, and the same rights and immunities before superior power had forced her out of her voluntary course?

But, my Lord, the rule of law, and the comity and practice of nations, go much further than these cases of necessity, and allow even to a merchant vessel coming into any open port of another country voluntarily, for the purposes of lawful trade, to bring with her, and keep over her, to a very considerable extent, the jurisdiction and authority of the laws of her own country, excluding, to this extent, by consequence, the jurisdiction of the local law. A ship, say the publicists, though at anchor in a foreign harbor, preserves its jurisdiction and its laws.[3] It is natural to consider the vessels of a nation as parts of its territory, though at sea, as the State retains its jurisdiction over them; and, according to the commonly received custom, this jurisdiction is preserved over the vessels, even in parts of the sea subject to a foreign dominion.

This is the doctrine of the law of nations, clearly laid down by writers of received authority, and entirely conformable, as it is supposed, with the practices of modern nations.

2. This was a doctrine pronounced by the maritime scholar and admiralty judge William Scott, Lord Stowell (1745–1836). See Coleman Phillipson, ed., *Wheaton's Elements of International Law* (5th ed., London, 1916), p. 772.

3. DW relied on the views of the French Council of State, which had ruled thus in 1806 in two cases involving American ships. However, English, and even American, law had maintained the right of a state to extend jurisdiction over merchant vessels in their ports. See the discussion in Phillipson, ed., *Wheaton's Elements*, pp. 163–165, 168.

If a murder be committed on board of an American vessel, by one of the crew upon another or upon a passenger, or by a passenger on one of the crew or another passenger, while such vessel is lying in a port within the jurisdiction of a foreign State or Sovereignty, the offence is cognizable and punishable by the proper court of the United States, in the same manner as if such offence had been committed on board the vessel on the high seas. The law of England is supposed to be the same.

It is true that the jurisdiction of a nation over a vessel belonging to it, while lying in the port of another, is not necessarily wholly exclusive. We do not so consider or so assert it. For any unlawful acts done by her while thus lying in port, and for all contracts entered into while there, by her master or owners, she and they must doubtless be answerable to the laws of the place. Nor, if her master or crew, while on board in such port, break the peace of the community by the commission of crimes, can exemption be claimed for them. But, nevertheless, the law of nations, as I have stated it, and the statutes of Governments founded on that law, as I have referred to them, show that enlightened nations, in modern times, do clearly hold that the jurisdiction and laws of a nation accompany her ships, not only over the high seas, but into ports and harbors, or wheresoever else they may be water-borne, for the general purpose of governing and regulating the rights, duties, and obligations of those on board thereof, and that, to the extent of the exercise of this jurisdiction, they are considered as parts of the territory of the nation herself.

If a vessel be driven by weather into the ports of another nation, it would hardly be alleged by any one that, by the mere force of such arrival within the waters of the State, the law of that State would so attach to the vessel as to affect existing rights of property beween persons on board, whether arising from contract or otherwise. The local law would not operate to make the goods of one man to become the goods of another man. Nor ought it to affect their personal obligations, or existing relations between themselves, nor was it ever supposed to have such effect, until the delicate and exciting question which has caused these interferences in the British islands arose. The local law in these cases dissolves no obligations or relations lawfully entered into or lawfully existing according to the laws of the ship's country. If it did, intercourse of civilized men between nation and nation must cease. Marriages are frequently celebrated in one country in a manner not lawful or valid in another; but did any body ever doubt that marriages are valid all over the civilized world, if valid in the country in which they took place? Did any ever imagine that local law acted upon such marriages, to annihilate their obligation, if the parties should visit a country in which marriages must be celebrated in another form?

It may be said that, in such instances, personal relations are founded in contract, and therefore to be respected; but that the relation of master and slave is not founded in contract, and therefore is to be respected only by the law of the place which recognises it. Whoever so reasons encounters the authority of the whole body of public law, from Grotius[4] down; because there are numerous instances in which the law itself presumes or implies contracts; and prominent among these instances is the very relation which we are now considering, and which relation is holden by law to draw after it mutuality of obligation.

Is not the relation between a father and his minor children acknowledged, when they go abroad? And on what contract is this founded, but a contract raised by general principles of law, from the relation of the parties?

Your Lordship will please to bear in mind, that, the proposition which I am endeavoring to support is, that by the comity of the law of nations, and the practice of modern times, merchant vessels entering open ports of other nations, for the purpose of trade, are presumed to be allowed to bring with them, and to retain, for their protection and government, the jurisdiction and laws of their own country. All this, I repeat, is presumed to be allowed; because the ports are open, because trade is invited, and because, under these circumstances, such permission or allowance is according to general usage. It is not denied that all this may be refused; and this suggests a distinction, the disregard of which may perhaps account for most of the difficulties arising in cases of this sort; that is to say, the distinction between what a State may do if it pleases, and what it is presumed to do, or not to do, in the absence of any positive declaration of its will. A State might declare that all foreign marriages should be regarded as null and void, within its territory; that a foreign father, arriving with an infant son, should no longer have authority or control over him; that, on the arrival of a foreign vessel in its ports, all shipping articles and all indentures of apprenticeship, between her crew and her owners or masters, should cease to be binding. These, and many other things equally irrational and absurd, a sovereign State has doubtless the power to do. But they are not to be presumed. It is not to be taken for granted, *ab ante*, that it is the will of the sovereign State thus to withdraw itself from the circle of civilized nations. It will be time enough to believe this to be its intention, when it formally announces that intention, by appropriate enactments, edicts, or other declarations. In regard to slavery within the British territories, there is a well-known and clear promulgation of the will of the sovereign authority; that is to say, there is a well-known rule of her law. As to England herself, that law has long existed; and recent acts of Parliament establish the same law for the

4. Huig de Groot (1583–1645), was a Dutch-born authority on international law and author of the classic volumes *De jure praedae* (1604) and *De jure belli ac pacis* (1625).

colonies. The usual mode of stating the rule of English law is, that no sooner does a slave reach the shore of England, than he is free. This is true; but it means no more than that, when a slave comes within the exclusive jurisdiction of England, he ceases to be a slave, because the law of England positively and notoriously prohibits and forbids the existence of such a relation between man and man. But it does not mean that English authorities, with this rule of English law in their hands, may enter where the jurisdiction of another nation is acknowledged to exist, and destroy those rights, obligations, and interests, lawfully existing under the authority of such other nation. No such construction and no such effect, can be rightfully given to the British law. It is true that it is competent to the British Parliament, by express statute provision, to declare that no foreign jurisdiction of any kind should exist, in or over a vessel, after its arrival voluntarily in her ports. And so she might close all her ports to the ships of all nations. A State may also declare, in the absence of treaty stipulations, that foreigners shall not sue in her courts, nor travel in her territories, nor carry away funds or goods received for debts. We need not inquire what would be the condition of a country that should establish such laws, nor in what relation they would leave her towards the States of the civilized world. Her power to make such laws is unquestionable; but, in the absence of direct and positive enactments to that effect, the presumption is that the opposites of these things exist. While her ports are open to foreign trade, it is to be presumed that she expects foreign ships to enter them, bringing with them the jurisdiction of their own Government, and the protection of its laws, to the same extent that her ships, and the ships of other commercial States, carry with them the jurisdiction of their respective Governments into the open ports of the world; just as it is presumed, while the contrary is not avowed, that strangers may travel in a civilized country, in a time of peace, sue in its courts, and bring away their property.

A merchant vessel enters the port of a friendly State, and enjoys while there the protection of her own laws, and is under the jurisdiction of her own Government, not in derogation of the sovereignty of the place, but by the presumed allowance or permission of that sovereignty. This permission or allowance is founded on the comity of nations, like the other cases which have been mentioned; and this comity is part, and a most important and valuable part, of the law of nations, to which all nations are presumed to assent until they make their dissent known. In the silence of any positive rule, affirming or denying or restraining the operation of foreign laws, their tacit adoption is presumed to the usual extent. It is upon this ground that courts of law expound contracts according to the law of the place in which they are made; and instances almost innumerable exist, in which, by the general practice of civilized countries, the laws of one will be recognised and often executed in another. This is the comity of nations; and it is upon this as its solid basis, that the intercourse of civilized States is maintained.

But while that which has now been said is understood to be the voluntary and adopted law of nations, in cases of the voluntary entry of merchant vessels into the ports of other countries, it is nevertheless true that vessels in such ports, only through an overruling necessity, may place their claim for exemption from interference on still higher principles; that is to say, principles held in more sacred regard by the comity, the courtesy, or indeed the common sense of justice of all civilized States.

Even in regard to cases of necessity, however, there are things of an unfriendly and offensive character, which yet it may not be easy to say that a nation might not do. For example, a nation might declare her will to be and make it the law of her dominions; that foreign vessels, cast away on her shores, should be lost to their owners, and subject to the ancient law of wreck. Or a neutral State, while shutting her ports to the armed vessels of belligerents, as she has a right to do, might resolve on seizing and confiscating vessels of that description, which should be driven to take shelter in her harbors by the violence of the storms of the ocean. But laws of this character, however within the absolute competence of Governments, could only be passed, if passed at all, under willingness to meet the last responsibility to which nations are subjected.

The presumption is stronger, therefore, in regard to vessels driven into foreign ports by necessity, and seeking only temporary refuge, than in regard to those which enter them voluntarily, and for purposes of trade, that they will not be interfered with; and that, unless they commit, while in port, some act against the laws of the place, they will be permitted to receive supplies, to repair damages, and to depart unmolested.

If, therefore, vessels of the United States, pursuing lawful voyages from port to port, along their own shore, are driven by stress of weather, or carried by unlawful force, into English ports, the Government of the United States cannot consent that the local authorities in those ports shall take advantage of such misfortunes, and enter them for the purpose of interfering with the condition of persons or things on board, as established by their own laws. If slaves, the property of citizens of the United States, escape into the British territories, it is not expected that they will be restored. In that case the territorial jurisdiction of England will have become exclusive over them, and must decide their condition. But slaves on board of an American vessel, lying in British waters, are not within the exclusive jurisdiction of England, or under the exclusive operation of English law, and this founds the broad distinction between the cases. If persons, guilty of crimes in the United States, seek an asylum in the British dominions, they will not be demanded until provision for such cases be made by treaty: because the giving up of criminals, fugitive from justice, is agreed and understood to be a matter in which every nation regulates its conduct according to its own discretion. It is no breach of comity to refuse such surrender.

On the other hand, vessels of the United States, driven by necessity into British ports, and staying there no longer than such necessity exists, violating no law, nor having intent to violate any law, will claim, and there will be claimed for them, protection and security, freedom from molestation, and from all interference with the character or condition of persons or things on board. In the opinion of the Government of the United States, such vessels, so driven and so detained by necessity in a friendly port, ought to be regarded as still pursuing their original voyage, and turned out of their direct course only by disaster, or by wrongful violence; that they ought to receive all assistance necessary to enable them to resume that direct course; and that interference and molestation by the local authorities, where the whole voyage is lawful, both in act and intent, is ground for just and grave complaint.

Your Lordship's discernment and large experience in affairs cannot fail to suggest to you how important it is to merchants and navigators engaged in the coasting trade of a country so large in extent as the United States, that they should feel secure against all but the ordinary causes of maritime loss. The possessions of the two Governments closely approach each other. This proximity, which ought to make us friends and good neighbors, may, without proper care and regulation, itself prove a ceaseless cause of vexation, irritation, and disquiet.

If your Lordship has no authority to enter into a stipulation by treaty for the prevention of such occurrences hereafter as have already happened, occurrences so likely to disturb that peace between the two countries which it is the object of your Lordship's mission to establish and confirm, you may still be so far acquainted with the sentiments of your Government as to be able to engage that instructions shall be given to the local authorities in the islands, which shall lead them to regulate their conduct in conformity with the rights of citizens of the United States, and the just expectations of their Government, and in such manner as shall, in future, take away all reasonable ground of complaint. It would be with the most profound regret that the President should see that, whilst it is now hoped so many other subjects of difference may be harmoniously adjusted, nothing should be done in regard to this dangerous source of future collisions.

I avail myself of this occasion to renew to your Lordship the assurances of my distinguished consideration.   Danl Webster.

LC. DNA, RG 59 (Notes to Foreign Legations, Britain). Published in *Senate Documents*, 27th Cong., 3d sess., Serial 413, No. 1, pp. 116–122.

FROM LORD ASHBURTON

Sir   Washington August 6. 1842

You may be well assured that I am duly sensible of the great importance of the subject to which you call my attention in the note which
you did me the honour of addressing me the 1st Instant,[1] in which you
inform me that the President had been pleased to express his regret that
I was not empowered by my government to enter into a formal stipulation for the better security of vessels of the United States when meeting
with disasters in passing between the United States and the Bahama islands, and driven by such disasters into British ports.

It is, I believe, unnecessary that I should tell you that the case of the
Creole was known in London a few days only before my departure. No
complaint had at that time been made by Mr Everett. The subject was
not therefore among those which it was the immediate object of my mission to discuss. But at the same time I must admit that from the moment
I was acquainted with the facts of this case, I was sensible of all its importance, and I should not think myself without power to consider of
some adjustment of and remedy for a great acknowledged difficulty, if I
could see my way clearly to any satisfactory course, and if I had not
arrived at the conclusion, after very anxious consideration, that for the
reasons which I will state, this question had better be treated in London
where it will have a much increased chance of settlement on terms likely
to satisfy the interests of the United States.

The immediate case of the Creole would be easily disposed of; but it
involves a class and description of cases which, for the purpose of affording that security you seek for the trade of America through the Bahama
channel, brings into consideration questions of law both national and
international of the highest importance; and to increase the delicacy and
difficulty of the subject, public feeling is sensitively alive to everything
connected with it. These circumstances bring me to the conviction that
although I really believe that much may be done to meet the wishes of
your Government, the means of doing so would be best considered in
London where immediate reference may be had to the highest authorities
on every point of delicacy and difficulty that may arise. Whatever I might
attempt would be more or less under the disadvantage of being fettered
by apprehensions of responsibility, and I might thereby be kept within
limits which my Government at home might disregard. In other words I
believe you would have a better chance in this settlement with them than
with me. I state this after some imperfect endeavours by correspondence
to come at satisfactory explanations. If I were in this instance treating of
ordinary material interests, I should proceed with more confidence, but

1. See above.

anxious as I unfeignedly am that all questions likely to disturb future good understanding between us should be averted, I strongly recommend this question of the security of the Bahama channel being referred for discussion in London.

This opinion is more decidedly confirmed by your very elaborate and important argument on the application of the general principles of the law of nations to these subjects; an argument to which your authority necessarily gives great weight, but in which I would not presume to follow you with my own imperfect means. Great Britain and the United States, covering all the seas of the world with their commerce, have the greatest possible interest in maintaining sound and pure principles of international law, as well as the practice of reciprocal aid and good offices in all their harbours and possessions. With respect to the latter it is satisfactory to know that the disposition of the respective Governments and people leaves little to be desired with the single exception of those very delicate and perplexing questions which have recently arisen from the state of slavery; and even these seem confined, and likely to continue to be confined, to the narrow passage of the Bahama channel. At no other part of the British possessions are American vessels with slaves ever likely to touch, nor are they likely to touch there otherwise than from the pressure of very urgent necessity. The difficulty therefore, as well as the desired remedy, is apparently confined within narrow limits.

Upon the great general principles affecting this case we do not differ. You admit that if slaves, the property of American citizens, escape into British territories, it is not expected that they will be restored, and you may be well assured that there is no wish on our part that they should reach our shores, or that British possessions should be used as decoys for the violators of the laws of a friendly neighbour.

When these slaves do reach us by whatever means, there is no alternative. The present state of British law is in this respect too well known to require repetition, nor need I remind you that it is exactly the same with the laws of every part of the United States, where a state of slavery is not recognised, and that the slave put on shore at Nassau would be dealt with exactly as would a foreign slave landed under any circumstances whatever at Boston.

But what constitutes the being within British dominion; from which these consequences are to follow? Is a vessel passing through the Bahama channel, and forced involuntarily either from storm or mutiny into British waters to be so considered? What power have the authorities of those islands to take cognisance of persons or property in such vessels? These are questions which you, Sir, have discussed at great length and with evident ability. Although you have advanced some propositions which rather surprize and startle me, I do not pretend to judge them but what is very clear is that great principles are involved in a discussion, which it would ill become me lightly to enter upon, and I am confirmed by this consideration in wishing that the subject be referred to where it will be perfectly weighed and examined.

It behoves the authorities of our two Governments well to guard themselves against establishing by their diplomatic intercourse false precedents and principles, and that they do not for the purpose of meeting a passing difficulty, set examples which may hereafter mislead the world.

It is not intended on this occasion to consider in detail the particular instances which have given rise to these discussions; they have already been stated and explained. Our object is rather to look to the means of future prevention of such occurrences. That this may be obtained I have little doubt, although we may not be able immediately to agree on the precise stipulations of a treaty. On the part of Great Britain there are certain great principles too deeply rooted in the consciences and sympathies of the people for any minister to be able to overlook. And any engagement I might make in opposition to them would be instantly disavowed. But at the same time that we maintain our own laws within our own territories we are bound to respect those of our neighbours, and to listen to every possible suggestion of means of averting from them every annoyance and injury. I have great confidence that this may be effectually done in the present instance; but the case to be met and remedied is new and must not be too hastily dealt with. You may however be assured that measures so important for the preservation of friendly intercourse between the two countries shall not be neglected.

In the mean time I can engage that instructions shall be given to the Governors of Her Majesty's Colonies on the southern borders of the United States to execute their own laws with careful attention to the wish of their Government to maintain good neighbourhood; and that there shall be no officious interference with American vessels driven by accident or by violence into those ports. The laws and duties of hospitality shall be executed, and these seem neither to require nor to justify any further inquisition into the state of persons or things on board of vessels so situated, than may be indispensable to enforce the observance of the municipal law of the Colony and the proper regulation of its harbours and waters.

A strict and careful attention to these rules applied in good faith to all transactions as they arise will, I hope and believe, without any abandonment of great general principles, lead to the avoidance of any excitement or agitation on this very sensitive subject of slavery, and consequently of those irritating feelings which may have a tendency to bring into peril all the great interests connected with the maintenance of peace.

I further trust that friendly sentiments, and a conviction of the importance of cherishing them, will on all occasions lead the two countries to consider favourably any further arrangements which may be judged necessary for the reciprocal protection of their interests.

I hope, Sir, that this explanation on this very important subject will be satisfactory to the President, and that he will see in it no diminution of that earnest desire, which you have been pleased to recognise in me, to perform my work of reconciliation and friendship; but that he will rather perceive in my suggestion in this particular instance that it is made with a wellfounded hope of thereby better obtaining the object we have in view.

I beg to renew to you, Sir, the assurances of my high consideration.

Ashburton

LS. DNA, RG 59 (Notes from Foreign Legations, Britain). Published in *Senate Documents*, 27th Cong., 3d sess., Serial 413, No. 1, pp. 122–124.

TO LORD ASHBURTON

Department of State,
Washington, 6th. Augt., 1842.

Your Lordship's note of the 28th of July, in answer to mine of the 27th, respecting the case of the "Caroline," has been received,[1] and laid before the President.

The President sees with pleasure that your Lordship fully admits those great principles of public law, applicable to cases of this kind, which this Government has expressed; and that on your part, as on ours, respect for the inviolable character of the territory of independent States is the most essential foundation of civilization. And while it is admitted, on both sides, that there are exceptions to this rule, he is gratified to find that your Lordship admits that such exceptions must come within the limitations stated and the terms used in a former communication from this Department to the British plenipotentiary here.[2] Undoubtedly it is just, that while it is admitted that exceptions growing out of the great law of self-defence do exist, those exceptions should be confined to cases in which the "necessity of self-defence is instant, overwhelming, and leaving no choice of means, and no moment for deliberation."

Understanding these principles alike, the difference between the two Governments is only whether the facts in the case of the "Caroline" make out a case of such necessity for the purpose of self-defence. Seeing that the transaction is not recent, having happened in the time of one of his predecessors; seeing that your Lordship, in the name of your Government, solemnly declares that no slight or disrespect was intended to the sovereign authority of the United States; seeing that it is acknowledged

1. See above, DW to Ashburton, July 27, 1842, and Ashburton to DW, July 28, 1842.

2. See above, DW to Fox, April 24, 1841, "The Crisis in Anglo-American Relations," pp. 58–68.

that, whether justifiable or not, there was yet a violation of the territory of the United States, and that you are instructed to say that your Government considers that as a most serious occurrence; seeing, finally, that it is now admitted that an explanation and apology for this violation was due at the time, the President is content to receive these acknowledgments and assurances in the conciliatory spirit which marks your Lordship's letter, and will make this subject, as a complaint of violation of territory, the topic of no further discussion between the two Governments.

As to that part of your Lordship's note which relates to other occurrences springing out of the case of the "Caroline," with which occurrences the name of Alexander McLeod has become connected, I have to say that the Government of the United States entirely adhere to the sentiments and opinions expressed in the communications from this Department to Mr. [Henry Stephen] Fox.[3] This Government has admitted, that for an act committed by the command of his sovereign, *jure belli*, an individual cannot be responsible, in the ordinary courts of another State. It would regard it as a high indignity if a citizen of its own, acting under its authority, and by its special command, in such cases, were held to answer in a municipal tribunal, and to undergo punishment, as if the behest of his Government were no defence or protection to him.

But your Lordship is aware that, in regular constitutional Governments, persons arrested on charges of high crimes can only be discharged by some judicial proceeding. It is so in England; it is so in the colonies and provinces of England. The forms of judicial proceeding differ in different countries, being more rapid in some and more dilatory in others; and, it may be added, generally more dilatory, or at least more cautious, in cases affecting life, in Governments of a strictly limited than in those of a more unlimited character. It was a subject of regret that the release of McLeod was so long delayed. A State court, and that not of the highest jurisdiction, decided that, on summary application, embarrassed as it would appear, by technical difficulties, he could not be released by that court. His discharge, shortly afterwards, by a jury, to whom he preferred to submit his case, rendered unnecessary the further prosecution of the legal question. It is for the Congress of the United States, whose attention has been called to the subject, to say what further provision ought to be made to expedite proceedings in such cases; and, in answer to your Lordship's question towards the close of your note, I have to say that the Government of the United States holds itself not only fully disposed, but fully competent, to carry into practice every principle which it avows or acknowledges, and to fulfill every duty and obligation which it owes to foreign Governments, their citizens, or subjects.

3. In addition to DW to Fox, April 24, 1841, see DW to Fox, September 20, 1841, both in "The Crisis in Anglo-American Relations," above, pp. 58–68, 144–145.

I have the honor to be, my Lord, with great consideration, your obedient servant,   Danl Webster.

ᴌs. DNA, RG 59 (Notes to Foreign Legations, Britain). Published in *Senate Documents*, 27th Cong., 3d sess., Serial 413, No. 1, pp. 137–138.

FROM JOHN TYLER

Dear Sir;   Aug. 7. 1842

I have most carefully looked over the extract from Ld. Ashburton's proposed letter on the subject of the Creole,[1] which I now return to enable you more readily to comprehend my suggestions in regard to it. The substitution of a few words in some places and addition in others will make it entirely acceptable.

1. In the 5 line in place of the words "to execute thier own laws" substitute "thier system of police." A vessell driven in by stress of weather has to be dealt with according to the police laws of the port or place—not the general laws of England.

2. In the 8 and 9 lines—the following language is used—"there shall be no officious interference with American vessells driven *by accident* into those ports." Now why shall *officious* interference with vessells driven in *by accident* be alone prohibited—why not if brought in by any controullable occurence? *Officious interference* is an offence against good manners—and is universally reprehended. Does his Lordship mean to say that if the crew of a vessell navigated solely by Whites sieze on the vessell and carry her into Nassau, that *officious interference* will not be restraind? Shall *officiousness* be justified in one case and not in all? I cannot see any the slightest ground in reason for tolerating officious interference in one case and not in all. There is a degree of repugnance manifested as to the employment of proper terms which I know not how to reconcile to a desire for peace. I am obligd to see that if slaves were out of the question that repugnance would not exist. The term *mutiny* would then readily find a place in the extradition article—and after all is England visited by any crime because slavery exists in the U. States, other than the original crime of its introduction? And because it does exist, is *officious interference* only to be restraind in cases af accident, befalling a vessell and driving it into Nassau? I wish his Lordship could be brought to the use of other terms. <England as a nation>

3. In the 11th line the word *ordinary* should be omitted. If it be surplusage it has no business there—if it be restrictive, then it should not be there.

4. In the third line from the bottom the language is, "any further ar-

1. For Ashburton's final *Creole* letter to DW, see above, August 6, 1842. See also the discussion in *Tylers*, 2: 221–224.

rangements which *future* events." The sentence as it now stands, includes the idea that no further arrangements are called for by *past* events—when on the contrary if I understand the letter of his Lordship the Creole case is to be referd for discussion in London. Past events clearly prove the necessity of further regulation. The sentence can readily be modified.

The extradition articles had better be omitted altogether. If a slave kills his master and flees, a Nassau jury or court would declare the act to have been committed in self defence and without malice. The main point is therefore unprovided for. It might be different if the delivery was to follow the demand.

If nothing better can be obtain I am for leaving the matter as it is—but I shall always be ready to listen to your views. Most truly yrs

John Tyler

ALS. DLC. Published in *Tylers*, 2:221–222.

TO LORD ASHBURTON

Department of State,
My Lord: Washington, Augt. 8, 1842.

I have the honor to acknowledge the receipt of your Lordship's note of the 6th. instant, in answer to mine of the 1st.,[1] upon the subject of a stipulation for the better security of American vessels driven by accident or carried by force into the British West India ports.

The President would have been gratified if you had felt yourself at liberty to proceed at once to consider of some proper arrangement, by formal treaty, for this object; but there may be weight in the reasons which you urge for referring such mode of stipulation for consideration in London.

The President places his reliance on those principles of public law which were stated in my note to your Lordship, and which are regarded as equally well-founded and important; and on your Lordship's engagement that instructions shall be given to the Governors of Her Majesty's colonies to execute their own laws with careful attention to the wish of their Government to maintain good neighborhood, and that there shall be no officious interference with American vessels driven by accident or by violence into those ports; that the laws and duties of hospitality shall be executed, and that these seem neither to require nor to justify any further inquisition into the state of persons or things on board of vessels so situated than may be indispensable to enforce the observance of the municipal law of the colony, and the proper regulation of its harbors and waters. He indulges the hope, nevertheless, that, actuated by a just sense of what is due to the mutual interests of the two countries, and the main-

1. See above, DW to Ashburton,   DW, August 6, 1842.
August 1, 1842, and Ashburton to

tenance of a permanent peace between them, Her Majesty's Government will not fail to see the importance of removing, by such further stipulations, by treaty or otherwise, as may be found to be necessary, all cause of complaint connected with this subject. I have the honor to be, with high consideration, your Lordship's obedient servant,   Danl. Webster.

LC. DNA, RG 59 (Notes to Foreign Legations, Britain). Published in *Senate Documents*, 27th Cong., 3d sess., No. 1, pp. 124–125.

TO LORD ASHBURTON

My Lord:

Department of State,
Washington, 8th Augt., 1842.

We have had several conversations on the subject of impressment, but I do not understand that your Lordship has instructions from your Government to negotiate upon it, nor does the Government of the United States see any utility in opening such negotiation, unless the British Government is prepared to renounce the practice in all future wars.

No cause has produced to so great an extent, and for so long a period, disturbing and irritating influences on the political relations of the United States and England, as the impressment of seamen by British cruisers from American merchant vessels.

From the commencement of the French Revolution to the breaking out of the war between the two countries in 1812, hardly a year elapsed without loud complaint and earnest remonstrance. A deep feeling of opposition to the right claimed, and to the practice exercised under it, and not unfrequently exercised without the least regard to what justice and humanity would have dictated, even if the right itself had been admitted, took possession of the public mind of America, and this feeling, it is well known, coöperated most powerfully with other causes, to produce the state of hostilities which ensued.

At different periods, both before and since the war, negotiations have taken place between the two Governments, with the hope of finding some means of quieting these complaints.[1] At some times, the effectual abolition of the practice has been requested and treated of; at other times, its temporary suspension; and, at other times again, the limitation of its exercise, and some security against its enormous abuses.

A common destiny has attended these efforts; they have all failed. The question stands at this moment where it stood fifty years ago. The nearest approach to a settlement was a convention proposed in 1803, and which had come to the point of signature, when it was broken off in consequence of the British Government insisting that the *narrow seas*

1. For a survey of the American and British positions on impressment up to the Webster-Ashburton nego- tiations, see *International Law Digest*, 2:987–999.

should be expressly excepted out of the sphere over which the contemplated stipulations against impressment should extend. The American Minister, Mr [Rufus] King, regarded this exception as quite inadmissible, and chose rather to abandon the negotiation than to acquiesce in the doctrine which it proposed to establish.[2]

England asserts the right of impressing British subjects, in time of war, out of neutral merchant vessels, and of deciding, by her visiting officers, who among the crews of such merchant vessels are British subjects. She asserts this as a legal exercise of the prerogative of the Crown; which prerogative is alleged to be founded on the English law of perpetual and indissoluble allegiance of the subject, and his obligation, under all circumstances, and for his whole life, to render military service to the Crown whenever required.

This statement, made in the words of eminent British jurists, shows, at once, that the English claim is far broader than the basis or platform on which it is raised. The law relied on is English law; the obligations[3] insisted on are obligations existing between the Crown of England and its subjects. This law and these obligations, it is admitted, may be such as England may choose they shall be. But then they must be confined to the parties. Impressment of seamen, out of and beyond English territory, and from on board the ships of other nations, is an interference with the rights of other nations; is further, therefore, than English prerogative can legally extend; and is nothing but an attempt to enforce the peculiar law of England beyond the dominions and jurisdiction of the Crown. The claim asserts an extra territorial authority to the manifest injury and annoyance of the citizens and subjects of other States, on board their own vessels on the high seas.

Every merchant vessel on the seas is rightfully considered as part of the territory of the country to which it belongs. The entry, therefore, into such vessel, being neutral, by a belligerent, is an act of force, and is *prima facie* a wrong, a trespass, which can be justified only when done for some purpose allowed to form a sufficient justification by the law of nations. But a British cruiser enters an American merchant vessel in order to take therefrom supposed British subjects; offering no justification therefore, under the law of nations, but claiming the right under the law of England respecting the King's prerogative. This cannot be defended. English soil, English territory, English jurisdiction, is the appropriate sphere for the operation of English law. The ocean is the sphere of the law of nations; and any merchant vessel on the seas is, by that law, under the protection of the laws of her own nation, and may claim im-

---

2. See King to Madison, July, 1803, ASP: FR, 2:503–504.

3. English courts had long assumed that subjects owed the crown life-long allegiance. The best-known formulation of the doctrine is in *Calvin's case* (1609). For *Calvin's case* see 7 Coke's Reports 1 (1609).

munity, unless in cases in which that law allows her to be entered or visited.

If this notion of perpetual allegiance, and the consequent power of the prerogative, was the law of the world, if it formed part of the conventional code of nations, and was usually practised like the right of visiting neutral ships for the purpose of discovering and seizing enemy's property, then impressment might be defended as a common right, and there would be no remedy for the evil till the national code should be altered. But this is by no means the case. There is no such principle incorporated into the code of nations. The doctrine stands only as English law—not as national law; and English law cannot be of force beyond English dominion. Whatever duties or relations that law creates between the sovereign and his subjects can be enforced and maintained only within the realm, or proper possessions or territory of the sovereign. There may be quite as just a prerogative right to the property of subjects as to their personal services, in any exigency of the State; but no Government thinks of controlling by its own laws property of its subjects situated abroad; much less does any Government think of entering the territory of another Power, for the purpose of seizing such property, and applying it to its own uses—as laws, the prerogatives of the Crown of England, have no obligation on persons or property domiciled or situated abroad.

"When, therefore," says an authority not unknown or unregarded on either side of the Atlantic, "we speak of the right of a State to bind its own native subjects every where, we speak only of its own claim and exercise of Sovereignty over them, when they return within its own territorial jurisdiction, and not of its right to compel or require obedience to such laws, on the part of other nations, within their own territorial sovereignty. On the contrary, every nation has an exclusive right to regulate persons and things within its own territory, according to its sovereign will and public policy."[4]

The good sense of these principles, their remarkable pertinency to the subject now under consideration, and the extraordinary consequences resulting from the British doctrine, are signally manifested by that which we see taking place every day. England acknowledges herself overburdened with population of the poorer classes. Every instance of the emigration of persons of those classes is regarded by her as a benefit. England, therefore, encourages emigration; means are notoriously supplied to emigrants to assist their conveyance from public funds; and the new world, and most especially these United States, receive the many thousands of her subjects thus ejected from the bosom of their native land by the necessities of their condition. They came away from poverty and dis-

4. The quotation is from Joseph Story's *Commentaries on the Conflict of Laws, Foreign and Domestic* . . . (8th ed., Boston, 1883), p. 25. The book was first published in 1834.

tress, in over-crowded cities, to seek employment, comfort, and new homes, in a country of free institutions, possessed by a kindred race, speaking their own language, and having laws and usages in many respects like those to which they have been accustomed; and a country which, upon the whole, is found to possess more attractions for persons of their character and condition than any other on the face of the globe. It is stated that in the quarter of the year ending with June last, more than twenty-six thousand emigrants left the single port of Liverpool, for the United States, being four or five times as many as left the same port within the same period for the British colonies and all other parts of the world. Of these crowds of emigrants, many arrive in our cities in circumstances of great destitution, and the charities of the country, both public and private, are severely taxed to relieve their immediate wants. In time they mingle with the new community in which they find themselves, and seek means of living—some find employment in the cities; others go to the frontiers, to cultivate lands reclaimed from the forest; and a greater or less number of the residue, becoming in time naturalized citizens, enter into the merchant service, under the flag of their adopted country.

Now, my Lord, if war should break out between England and a European Power, can any thing be more unjust, any thing more irreconcilable to the general sentiments of mankind, than that England should seek out these persons, thus encouraged by her, and compelled by their own condition, to leave their native homes, tear them away from their new employments, their new political relations, and their domestic connexions, and force them to undergo the dangers and hardships of military service, for a country which has thus ceased to be their own country? Certainly, certainly, my Lord, there can be but one answer to this question. Is it, not far more reasonable that England should either prevent such emigration of her subjects, or that, if she encourage and promote it, she should leave them, not to the embroilment of a double and contradictory allegiance, but to their own voluntary choice, to form such relations, political or social, as they see fit, in the country where they are to find their bread, and to the laws and institutions of which they are to look for defence and protection?

A question of such serious importance ought now to be put at rest. If the United States give shelter and protection to those whom the policy of England annually casts upon their shores—if, by the benign influence of their Government and institutions, and by the happy condition of the country, those emigrants become raised from poverty to comfort, finding it easy even to become landholders, and being allowed to partake in the enjoyment of all civil rights—if all this may be done (and all this is done, under the countenance and encouragement of England herself,) is it not high time, my Lord, that, yielding that which had its origin in feudal ideas as inconsistent with the present state of society, and especially with the intercourse and relations subsisting between the old world and the new, England should, at length, formally disclaim all right to the services of such persons, and renounce all control over their conduct?

But impressment is subject to objections of a much wider range. If it could be justified in its application to those who are declared to be its only object, it still remains true that, in its exercise, it touches the political rights of other Governments, and endangers the security of their own native subjects and citizens. The sovereignty of the State is concerned in maintaining its exclusive jurisdiction and possession over its merchant ships on the seas, except so far as the law of nations justifies intrusion upon that possession for special purposes; and all experience has shown that no member of a crew, wherever born, is safe against impressment when a ship is visited.

The evils and injuries resulting from the actual practice can hardly be overrated, and have ever proved themselves to be such as should lead to its relinquishment, even if it were founded in any defensible principle. The difficulty of discriminating between English subjects and American citizens has always been found to be great, even when an honest purpose of discrimination has existed. But the Lieutenant of a man-of-war, having necessity for men, is apt to be a summary judge, and his decisions will be quite as significant of his own wants and his own power, as of the truth and justice of the case. An extract from a letter of Mr. King, of the 13th of April, 1797, to the American Secretary of State [James Madison], shows something of the enormous extent of these wrongful seizures:[5]

"Instead of a few, and these in many instances equivocal cases, I have," says he, "since the month of July past, made application for the discharge from British men-of-war of two hundred and seventy-one seamen, who, stating themselves to be Americans, have claimed my interference. Of this number, eighty-six have been ordered by the Admiralty to be discharged, thirty-seven more have been detained as British subjects or as American volunteers, or for want of proof that they are Americans; and to my applications for the discharge of the remaining one hundred and forty-eight I have received no answer—the ships on board of which these seamen were detained having, in many instances, sailed before an examination was made, in consequence of my application.

"It is certain that some of those who have applied to me are not American citizens, but the exceptions are, in my opinion, few, and the evidence, exclusive of certificates, has been such as, in most cases, to satisfy me that the applicants were real Americans, who have been forced

5. King to Madison, April 13, 1797, *ASP: FR*, 2:146.

into the British service, and who, with singular constancy, have generally persevered in refusing pay or bounty, though in some instances they have been in service more than two years."

But the injuries of impressment are by no means confined to its immediate subjects or the individuals on whom it is practiced. Vessels suffer from the weakening of their crews, and voyages are often delayed, and not unfrequently broken up, by subtraction from the number of necessary hands by impressment. And, what is of still greater and more general moment, the fear of impressment has been found to create great difficulty in obtaining sailors for the American merchant service, in times of European war. Seafaring men, otherwise inclined to enter into that service, are, as experience has shown, deterred by the fear of finding themselves ere long in compulsory military service in British ships of war. Many instances have occurred, fully established in proof, in which raw seamen, natives of the United States, fresh from the fields of agriculture, entering for the first time on shipboard, have been impressed before they made the land, placed on the decks of British men-of-war, and compelled to serve for years before they could obtain their release or revisit their country and their homes. Such instances become known, and their effect in discouraging young men from engaging in the merchant service of their country can neither be doubted nor wondered at. More than all, my Lord, the practice of impressment, whenever it has existed, has produced, not conciliation and good feeling, but resentment, exasperation, and animosity, between the two great commercial countries of the world.

In the calm and quiet which have succeeded the late war—a condition so favorable for dispassionate consideration—England herself has evidently seen the harshness of impressment, even when exercised on seamen in her own merchant service, and she has adopted measures calculated, if not to renounce the power or to abolish the practice, yet at least to supersede its necessity by other means of manning the royal navy, more compatible with justice and the rights of individuals, and far more conformable to the spirit and sentiments of the age.

Under these circumstances, the Government of the United States has used the occasion of your Lordship's pacific mission to renew this whole subject, and to bring it to your notice, and that of your Government. It has reflected on the past, pondered the condition of the present, and endeavored to anticipate, so far as might be in its power, the probable future; and I am now to communicate to your Lordship the result of these deliberations.

The American Government, then, is prepared to say that the practice of impressing seamen from American vessels cannot be allowed to take place. That practice is founded on principles which it does not recognise, and is invariably attended by consequences so unjust, so injurious, and of such formidable magnitude, as cannot be submitted to.

In the early disputes between the two Governments on this so long contested topic, the distinguished person to whose hand were first intrusted the seals of this Department declared, that "the simplest rule will be, that the vessel being American shall be evidence that the seamen on board are such."[6]

Fifty years' experience, the utter failure of many negotiations, and a careful reconsideration now had of the whole subject, at a moment when the passions are laid, and no present interest or emergency exists to bias the judgment, have fully convinced this Government that this is not only the simplest and best, but the only rule which can be adopted and observed, consistently with the rights and honor of the United States and the security of their citizens. That rule announces, therefore, what will hereafter be the principle maintained by their Government. In every regularly documented American merchant vessel the crew who navigate it will find their protection in the flag which is over them.

This announcement is not made, my Lord, to revive useless recollections of the past, nor to stir the embers from fires which have been, in a great degree, smothered by many years of peace. Far otherwise. Its purpose is to extinguish those fires effectually, before new incidents arise to fan them into flame. The communication is in the spirit of peace, and for the sake of peace, and springs from a deep and conscientious conviction that high interests of both nations require that this so long contested and controverted subject should now be finally put to rest. I persuade myself, my Lord, that you will do justice to this frank and sincere avowal of motives, and that you will communicate your sentiments, in this respect, to your Government.

This letter closes, my Lord, on my part, our official correspondence, and I gladly use the occasion to offer you the assurance of my high and sincere regard.   Danl. Webster.

LC. DNA, RG 59 (Notes to Foreign Legations, Britain). Published in *Senate Documents*, 27th Cong., 3d sess., Serial 413, No. 1, pp. 139–144.

FROM JOHN TYLER

My Dear Sir;   Aug. 8. 1842

Your note gives me the most sincere pleasure.[1] Let what come that may, the affair settled with England, and we shall have cause for unmix'd joy. Take my best thanks for your zeal and industry in accomplishing

6. Thomas Jefferson to Thomas Pinckney, June 11, 1792, *ASP: FR*, 3:574.

1. Not found; probably a note informing Tyler of the completion of the negotiations.

this important matter. Tomorrow at ten I shall be glad to be surrounded by the Cabinet.

But I would rather have you ponder over the idea of separate conventions for each subject.[2] Many friends think that a single Treaty is best— reserve this if you can for to morrow. Yrs   J. Tyler

P.S. I fear the extradition article, but we will confer to morrow.

ALS. NhHi. Published in Van Tyne, p. 275.

LORD ASHBURTON TO LORD ABERDEEN

Private
My Dear Ld Aberdeen,   Washington 9 Aug 1842.

This has been a busy day with me and not one of the least happy of my life for you will see that my treaties are signed and all my business settled, but I have not much time left beyond what was necessary for unavoidable business. My great plague was the Creole and you will see how I have at last disposed of it. At least a dozen various attempts at explanation were tried and there came only yesterday a querulous foolish letter from the President to Webster[1] which made me fear we might at last stick fast, and if it were not that the general object of the mission is popular in the Country I think this would have been the case. My settlement on this point was at last but sulkily received by him.[2] How it may be considered by you remains to be seen. I have only to beg you will recollect that it was a case attended with no inconsiderable difficulties. The Secretary of State behaved well & liberally throughout, but you will see that he has prepared a voluminous budget[3] for popular impression to go to the Senate. I am not apprehensive about the fate of both Treaty and Convention. The former I think quite safe. The fate of the latter is rather less certain. The President inclined to tack them together to make sure of the latter but I did not like to risk my Boundaries. I shall remain here a few days & move north where I shall linger about ten more before I embark. I remain for the chance of any thing occurring [on] a useless pretence of visiting friends, but I would not have the appearance of waiting for the decision of the Senate. The President has again vetoed the

2. Initially, DW and Ashburton drew up a treaty covering the boundary negotiations and a separate convention concerning the suppression of the slave trade and extradition. At Tyler's instance, the treaty and the convention articles were combined. The boundary settlement became Articles 1–7 of the treaty; the slave trade and extradition convention, Articles 8–11. See *Treaties*, 4:375–377.
1. See above.
2. See above, Ashburton to DW, August 6, 1842.
3. Ashburton apparently used the word *budget* in its original sense, meaning a pouch with its contents, such as a portfolio filled with documents.

Tariff this morning,[4] and parties are in great commotion. I have not been much abroad to have opinions but I incline to think the Congress will yield. I hope My Dear Lord to see you about the end of September. The weather is become temperate but now my work is off my hands I become impatient to see the chalk cliffs of our channel. Yours sincerely

Ashburton

ALS. Uk.

TO JOHN CANFIELD SPENCER

Department of State

Sir,   Washington. August 10, 1842

General [Winfield] Scott has furnished to the President a memorandum of his opinion respecting the value and importance of Rouse's point,[1] as a military post, and the Territory adjoining it and running along by the South side of the actually existing line of Boundary; but to the north of that line, if it should be corrected according to recent surveys.

I have thought it might be useful to obtain, also, the opinions of other eminent military men, on the same subject. If convenient, I should be glad to be furnished with such opinions from persons in your Department the most fit to be consulted.[2] Your obt. servt   Danl. Webster.

LC. DNA, RG 59 (Domestic Letters).

FROM FRANCIS ORMAND JONATHAN SMITH, WITH ENCLOSURE

Private

Dr Sir—   Portland Augt 12. 1842

I suppose we may consider our long disputed boundary as now settled —and the people of Maine feel that great credit is due to your efforts in bringing a forty years dispute to a close. I feel gratified in the result, from a conviction of many years standing that a new mode of approaching the subject, and such a one as you have adopted, would accomplish it, while another forty years of circuitous diplomacy would have availed nothing.

Considering the matter settled, I presume you can feel justified in enabling me to fulfil certain assurances which I made to a few individuals at different points in this state, whose services and influence I had occasion to resort to, in order to adjust the tone and direction of the party

4. See *Messages and Papers*, 4: 183–189.

1. See Scott's Memoranda for the President, July 1, 1842, DNA, RG 76 (Records of the Boundary and Claims Commissions and Arbitrations and Miscellaneous Documents Relating to the Northeast Boundary, 1827–1842). Scott felt that Rouses Point was superior as "a defensive work" to "any other south of it" and important to the protection of Albany.

2. See Abert to Spencer, August 15, 1842, below.

presses, and through them, of public sentiment, to the purpose so desirable of accomplishment under your administration.[1] For my own services, you can also make such allowance from the contingent fund as you may deem proper—merely remarking, that all that was contemplated in my original letter to you of May 1841,[2] on this subject, so far as Maine & the voice of her people are concerned, has been happily realised.

To the individuals alluded to above, three in number, I gave an assurance that in the event of a settlement of the boundary, under your negotiation, they should be allowed a *reasonable* remuneration for their time and incidental expenses—and I should like to be able to remit them $100 or $125 each, if in my power. Nevertheless, I assumed no authority to bind your Department in any official manner on the subject—but the whole rests in my confidential intercourse with them—and I leave it, after stating the fact, wholly at your discretion. I presume the contingent fund will be ample, and your control over it ample, to do whatever you may think just.

I send herewith a bill for a voucher,[3] with entire consent for you to fill the blanks as you may deem proper. And I do it thus seasonably, lest there be ground for the rumor, (as I trust there is not) that you will shortly claim a right to retire from the administration of the State Department.

I beg you to believe that whether you remain in your present, or any other posititon of the public service, my best wishes will attend your efforts and I shall be most happy in any opportunity of my being serviceable to you in this region of our country. I am most truly Your friend & Obt Servt   Francis O. J. Smith

ALS. DNA, RG 59 (Letters to the President requesting Authorization of Disbursements, Bureau of Accounts). Published in Frederick Merk, *Fruits of Propaganda in the Tyler Administration* (Cambridge, Mass., 1971), pp. 176–177.

ENCLOSURE: EXPENSE VOUCHER

1842	State Department of the United States—
August—	To Francis O.J. Smith, D[ebto]r

To services as special agent upon the N.E Boundary
from May 1841— $2000

1. In his testimony of May 25, 1846, before the House select committee investigating Charles Jared Ingersoll's charges of official misconduct against DW, Smith said that DW was never aware of the names of the agents. Nor did Smith reveal their names in 1846. See *House Reports*, 29th Cong., 1st sess., Serial 490, No. 684, pp. 16–17.

2. As nearly as can be determined, Smith's original letter to DW was written not in May but on June 7, 1841. See above, "The Crisis in Anglo-American Relations," pp. 94–96.

3. See below.

To services of assistants and their incidental expenses—   500

Supra Cr[edit]
By cash Paid me, as per my receipt to Hon D. Webster,
of May 1841 $500
    Bal. Recd of D. Webster, Secy of State $
Francis O.J. Smith

ALS. DNA, RG 59 (Letters to the President requesting Authorization of Disbursements, Bureau of Accounts). Published in Frederick Merk, *Fruits of Propaganda in the Tyler Administration* (Cambridge, Mass., 1971), p. 178. Smith left blank the amount to be paid the special agent and his assistants. DW filled in the amounts.

JOHN JAMES ABERT TO JOHN CANFIELD SPENCER

                              Bureau of Topographical Engrs
Sir,   Washington Augst 15th 1842.
    In reply to your letter of the 11th instant[1] I have the honor to submit the following report.
    "Rouses Point as a military Post," involves two highly important considerations.
    First its ability to command the entrance of Lake Champlain and
    Second its influence upon military operations of attack or defence, and upon the quiet of that frontier.
    Although Rouses Point means geographically a projecting point on the western shore of the Lake, yet in a military aspect it is understood to designate the whole site or post, or extent of ground requisite in the combination of the complete defence of the passage into the Lake, extending from the point proper to the old boundary north. A reference to the map hereto annexed[2] will show that this extent embraces about 1300 yards, including the small projection into the Lake about 400 yards south of the boundary called Island Point, and about 900 north of Rouses point. Immediately at the boundary, the Lake is about 1200 yards wide, which width it maintains for a short distance only to the south, about 250 yards, when it suddenly widens, on its eastern shore, into a broad curving bay, averaging about 2000 yards wide. This bay terminates at the point called Woody point on the map, where the distance from Rouses

1. Spencer's letter, which passed on DW's request for information about the value of Rouses Point, was addressed to the head of the Army Corps of Engineers, Colonel Joseph Gilbert Totten. Spencer to Totten, August 11, 1842, RG 77 (Office of the Chief Engineers, Letters Received). Totten (1788–1864; U.S. Military Academy 1805), after serving on the Niagara frontier in the War of 1812, supervised construction of the fort at Rouses Point from 1817 to 1819. Totten became chief engineer of the army in 1838 and held that post until his death.

2. Enclosure not printed here.

point is about 1400 yards. The channel of the Lake passes near its western shore, and nearly parallel to it, and in the whole distance from the boundary to Rouses, it no where exceeds about 800 yards from that shore. At the Island before spoken of its farthest edge is within 500 yards, and at Rouses point, within about 600 yards. This channel is about 350 yards wide, it continues narrow for about 800 yards below Rouses Point, when it gradually expands itself. The whole ship channel is therefore in this distance under the complete controul of the shore and point of land just indicated. From Rouses Point south, the western shore of the Lake curves inland, as far south as about 3,500 yards from Rouses, to a projecting part of the shore, called on the map the "north point of Point au fer." The eastern shore from Woody point to Windmill point continues nearly straight. The distance across the Lake between this last named point and and the north point of Point au fer, is about one mile. From these points south, the Lake widens so rapidly and so extensively, that no ideas, of defending the passage can be entertained in that direction. Between Rouses and the north point of Point au fer [on] the map, the Lake shores are about 2000 yards apart; the channel, which in this space has widened to about 1000 yards, occupying nearly the centre of the passage. From this description of the locality, which will be readily understood by referring to the map, it will I think be admitted that combinations for the defence of the passage must be confined within the limits of the boundary line as traced upon the map, and the north point of point au fer. The question then becomes one of a choice, within this limited locality, of that position, or combination of positions, which will furnish the most effectual and the most complete defence.

Taking one mile as the effective range of a 24 pounder, the point blank range at about 500 yards, it will be seen that any works at Windmill Point and the north point of Point au fer, cannot enter into combination with those at Rouses Point, as the first is about a mile and a half from Rouses Point, and the second about two. The channel also between these two points is so wide, that vessels drawing 18 feet water may pass at a distance of 3/4 of a mile from either, and need not pass nearer than about half a mile of either. These distances show that a fleet in its efforts to force the passage of the Lake, would be for about 2 1/2 miles, under the effective range of the guns from these Forts, but at no time within the point blank range. The works at each point must also be adequate to their own defence in every direction, as no assistance or mutual defence can be extended from one to the other. These remarks I think will show that the defence of the passage from these two points, will require large and costly works, and be in the end imperfect, yet if there be no more favorable positions, necessity will oblige the choice, and the skill of the Engineer will have to be exerted to remedy the defects of the locality.

The next position for the defence of the passage into the Lake is that of Rouses Point, and its combinations. These may be supposed to consist of a formidable battery upon Island Point, also one at Rouses Point, and a small regular work upon the eminence at B. Temporary batteries may also be constructed upon the whole line of the shore from the boundary to Rouses Point, as throughout the whole of this distance, the most remote part of the channel does not exceed 800 yards from the shore, the centre of it not more than 650. Through a space therefore of about 2000 yards, a fleet in an attempt to force the pass, would be exposed in a narrow channel, to the fire from these temporary batteries on the shore at so short a distance, and to the point blank fire of the batteries from Island Point and from Rouses Point, also to the effective range of all these batteries and of the guns from the citadel work, for about three miles. And as from the direction of the channel as well as from its limited breadth, a fleet would be incapable of manoeuvering in it, or of presenting its own batteries except when immediately abreast of the Forts, I can scarcely imagine the rashness which would attempt to force the passage, or any other result than the destruction of the fleet. The site to my understanding is a perfect key, and will enable the Government <to do what it cannot do without it, to> completely to controul the entrance to the Lake. In its single aspect therefore, of its ability to command the entrance of the Lake, the possession of Rouses Point is above all price, as it enables the Government to do effectually and at the least cost that which cannot be so well done without it. There is no point, even outside of the 18 foot channel, in the shoal water of the passage in which a boat would be beyond the effective range of the batteries, and if to the combinations of the points named, should be added that of a battery in the shoal water on the eastern side of the channel or the occupation of Woody Point, it may with the utmost propriety be considered, as a passage which if properly defended cannot be forced by any fleet which can navigate the Lake.

But independent of the greater or less advantages, which one of these sites may be supposed to possess over the other, the posssssion of Rouses Point and vicinity up to the old boundary, restores to the United States, the whole extent of every part of that Territory which it once had, and upon which any system for defending the northern entrance of the Lake admits of being projected.

Immediately after the late war with Great Britain, during which the mastery on Lake Champlain, had been long contested, and which was at last decided by the memorable naval engagements under [Thomas] McDonough,[3] the necessity and economy of controuling the entrance of the Lake by works of the most permanent and effective character were so

3. MacDonough (1783–1825), in command of the American fleet on Lake Champlain during the War of 1812, inflicted a decisive defeat on the British at the Battle of Plattsburgh on September 11, 1814.

obvious <in itself>, and had been made so <palpable> important a consequence of the events of that War, that the War Department directed the most thorough examination of the locality, with the view of selecting sites for the requisite fortifications. The result of this examination, and of an investigation of all facts collected, by a Board of Engineer Officers of which (if I am not mistaken) the present chief of the Corps of Engineers was a member, was in the adoption of the Rouses Point locality, as the most suitable and most efficient position for the purposes to be accomplished.

The same distinguished officer digested the plan of works, to occupy the site, of no inconsiderable magnitude. The construction of them was commenced and had been pressed forward with some activity, when it was ascertained by the joint operations of the commissioners under the Treaty of Ghent, that the parallel of 45, instead of passing some distance north of Rouses Point as had hitherto been understood, and as it had at one time been traced, would intersect the Point itself and probably the projected work there. As this threw all the advantages of that position out of our jurisdiction, the partially completed works at that place were abandoned.

Nothing now remained for our Government in reference to the defence of the entrance of the Lake from the North, but to seek some other position. It was not however until during the disturbed condition of that frontier in 37 & 38, that its action was seriously directed to a second choice.

<In 1838> Additional surveys and examinations <were> <had been> having been made, and Rouses Point being no longer considered within our jurisdiction, the second and only alternative, of the defences combined with the position of Windmill Point, were adopted. This choice however, <should be> was viewed I believe only as a *pisaller*, and inasmuch as no expenditures have yet been made <upon it> in reference to it, if the site of Rouses Point as formerly possessed by the United States, can yet be controulled, there will probably be scarce a doubt of the propriety of adopting its much greater and more decided advantages.

The boundary line from the lake (vicinity of Rouses Point) to the St Laurence at St Regis, passes over the <ridge> region of high lands which separates the waters of the St Laurence from those of Lake Champlain. It rises gradually from the Lake until it attains an elevation of about 1000 feet, at a distance of about 25 to 30 miles from the Lake. On arriving at this vicinity the country is broken and somewhat mountaineous, and that part of the state may be considered as comparatively a wilderness. The best cultivated part of the country and the most thickly inhabited, adjacent to the boundary line, is Clinton and part of Franklin

Counties, which possess a population of about 45,000. The principal road connecting the Lake with the St Laurence near St Regis, passes within the vicinity of the boundary line, and as it would be <principally> chiefly by this road that intercourse between the Lake and the St Laurence in that quarter would have to be maintained, because the mountaineous and wilderness region south of the line offers the most serious obstacles to roads farther south and roads from any points of the interior of the State not in some degree <parallel to this> in the same direction, would lose the advantage of having one extremity resting upon the Lake, under the protection of the only locality which admits of an effective defence of the northern entrance of the Lake.

From an examination of the line of the St Laurence, and of the character of the country on its southern shore, it is hardly probable that any system of attack, or of defence will be involved in the military operations of either party upon that extensive line below the City of Quebec. Operations of this character will therefore of necessity be limited from Quebec and above. Between Quebec and Montreal, such is the character of the river and of its shores, and of access to those shores from the interior of either country, that considerations of attack or defence become still more restricted, and cannot be considered as within the reach of reasonable probability below Montreal. This last City may be considered as the head of the navigation of the river from the Sea, or as the point where the character of the navigation has to be changed to that which suits a rapid river with frequent falls, and the artificial facilities of canals.

Montreal is already the centre of a great navigation from below and from the upper Lakes, by way of the river, and through the interior by the Rideau Canal.[4] Montreal is therefore from its position the great depot and base of military operations and supplies in that quarter, and for all the country above it. It becomes then a position of extreme value in considerations of attack or of defence from either side. The interior passage by the Rideau Canal, renders the defence of the river above Montreal, of itself, an object of minor importance; but with a view of the quiet and security of so important a depot, and of all means of intercourse with the upper country, it is more than probable that, on the supposition of a State of War, our enemy would seize the mountain passes on the N. York boundary line before mentioned, if only with the defensive view of throwing his line of military frontier as far from the St. Laurence as possible. But with views of offensive operations such a course would be highly essential, to cover the flank of his invading line, the opposite flank of which would of necessity have to rest upon the Lake.

4. The Rideau Canal, constructed between 1826 and 1832, and the Rideau River extend from Ottawa city to Lake Ontario, near Kingston.

From the short description previously given of the <country of the> newyork boundary line, it will be conceived that all offensive operations of a serious character must be adjacent to the Lake, which must protect the flank of an invading army, and furnish it with supplies. Consequently, the possession of the Lake, becomes an essential, nay, a necessary concomitant in any system of offensive operations against us. Similar reasoning, applied to offensive operations on our part, give to the command of the Lake a similar preponderance, and renders all views of offensive operations on our part, certainly abortive if the command of the Lake be not possessed by us, and probably successful if it be. The position therefore which secures to us this command, has an influence beyond its simple capability of defending the entrance, in that of its vital influence on any digested system of attack or defence in that quarter. The Lake in the possession of an enemy would threaten our line of communication with the upper Lakes by the way of the North River. It would bring him within about three days march of Troy and Albany, and of our principal Arsenal at Watervleit, against which a sudden and well directed movement, might be successful in the destruction of the Government stores at these places. The ability to inflict such a blow would force us upon the defensive in that quarter; and if successfully inflicted, the gain would be immense, and the sacrifice to the enemy insignificant if it were even that of the whole detachment employed on the duty.

It will not do to suppose an enemy wanting in the intelligence and enterprize requisite to throw us upon the defensive and to place himself, in his most vulnerable quarter, in a state of great security, and no possession would be so important to him in these respects as the possession of that Lake.

A work at Rouses Point would stand upon the very line of operations by either party, and neither would venture to penetrate beyond it without its possession.

The entire Coast of Lake Champlain south of Rouses Point, may be stated at about 400 miles, penetrating <south> within the States of New York and Vermont; possessing an extensive inland trade; its shores and adjacent counties thickly populated, by a hardy race of agriculturists, mechanics and merchants. The quiet of so extensive a region, and the protection of such interests is at any time a matter of great national importance, but in a period of War this quiet and the vast supplies which would in consequence be derived from the Lake, and cannot well be derived to the frontier if this quiet be destroyed or hazarded, give to the position which will ensure it an importance and value not easily to be estimated in money. There is another consideration of great weight which should not be omitted. If the entrance to the Lake be controlled by us, all struggles, and the vast expeditures which they entail for naval ascendancy upon its waters, become unnecessary and are saved.

I have said that it was hardly probable that any system of attack on the part of an enemy, would be based upon the frontier east of the Sorel, because of its wilderness and mountainous character, and of the unimportant objects to be gained after these barriers shall have been passed. The enemy upon this whole line would place himself of choice on the defence, nor would he have much reason to fear offensive operations on our part. To any object worth a movement the barrier of the St Laurence would present an insurmountable obstacle, to those not possessing a maratime superiority, and the possession of this, of itself puts all apprehensions of excursions from an enemy in that quarter at rest. I of course do not refer in these remarks, to those singular enterprizes, combinations of extraordinary energy and genius, such as the winter campaign upon Quebec during our revolutionary struggle.[5] These would be as feasible hereafter as then, and if ever successful, would be aided rather by leaving the frontier as it is; than by indicating their probability and facilitating their progress, by advanced posts.

Nor do I mean by my remarks to allude to probabilities of attack upon the Eastern maratime possessions of either party this side the St Laurence. These depend upon totally different considerations than those <of> belonging to the inland frontier, in reference to which they may be considered as completely independent.

In periods of War, predatory excursions upon this line of inland frontier, will occasionally occur, but would no doubt in time be discontinued from the conviction which patriotism as well as common sense would establish, that they were destitute of all national consequences, and productive only of individual distress and individual injury.

Much of this inland frontier to which I have alluded, has received a thorough military examination, by General [John Ellis] Wool,[6] and by Major J[ames] D[uncan] Graham of the Corps of Topographical Engineers in 1838. For the views and opinions of these officers, allow me to refer you to Senate Document No. 35, 3d Session, 25th Congress. Very respectfully Sir Your Obt Servt   J. J. Abert Col Corps of Engrs

LS. DNA, RG 76 (Records of the Boundary and Claims Commissions and Arbitrations and Miscellaneous Documents Relating to the Northeast Boundary, 1827–1842). Abert (1788–1863; U.S. Military Academy 1811) was the chief officer of the army topographical engineers from 1814 until his retirement in 1861.

5. On September 24, 1775, a thousand men under Benedict Arnold (1741–1801) began a march to Quebec from Fort Western, Maine. After encountering many difficulties in the wilderness, they reached Quebec and futilely attacked the fortress on December 31.

6. Wool (1784–1869).

EDWARD KENT TO EDWARD KAVANAGH

Dear Sir   Bangor Augst 16 1842

I did not reach home until Saturday evening last, having remained in Massachusetts about a week. I found your letter here awaiting my arrival.[1] I was very sorry to find that your old enemy was still troubling you—and I fear you found your whole journey fatiguing & painful. I trust that you have found relief since your return.

I have been highly gratified to find so general and hearty approval of our proceedings by the sober, discreet & honest men of the State. In this community I have scarcely met with a man who is not well satisfied that it was much better to settle as we did than to leave the subject open for future reference or as an open question. Most of our people go farther & say they think we have made an excellent bargain and better than they expected. A few uneasy spirits attempt to find fault or to doubt and cavil and I see "the [Bangor] Democrat" of today is disposed to speculate upon some points and to insinuate doubts & fears.[2] But I am assured and I have no doubt that the great mass of the people are well satisfied and that the final result will be a general acquiescence in the arrangement. The bug bear of miltary advantages on the strip will not frighten any body. The Argus has taken an honorable and fair stand[3] and if the candid, judicious and independent men of all parties stand firm these attempts to create a breeze will be total failures. I think we have cause to congratulate ourselves that so good a spirit prevails in the State and that we are judged so fairly & candidly. I have no fears that injustice will be done to us in the final judgment of the people.

I hardly know what to say in relation to our meeting. I must leave that to your decision. I can attend any time before the middle of September. I think it would be well to be assured of the ratification of the treaty at Washington before making up our report. I think also it would be well for us each to be making minutes of points to be considered and inserted. I wish you would draw up the report.[4] It properly belongs to you to do it and if your health will permit I trust you will do it. I have heard nothing from Gov [John] Fairfield and do not know how he regards the settlement. I see Bro [John] Otis has made a speech on our subject at the Whig

1. Not found.

2. Not found.

3. The Portland *Eastern Argus* supported the treaty in a number of editorials. On August 13, 1842, the *Argus* announced the ratification of the treaty as "Glorious news."

4. The report of the Maine commissioners to Governor Fairfield, written by William Pitt Preble and dated January 4, 1843, concluded that the terms of the treaty "were the most favorable to Maine that could have been secured." See Henry S. Burrage, *Maine in the Northeastern Boundary Controversy* (Portland, Maine, 1919), pp. 358–360.

County Convention.[5] I should have preferred *if any speech was to be made*, that it should have been at some [general] meeting. I have seen the reports to [the] Democratic Convention in Kennebeck[6] but I regard them as the expression on[ly] of a few managers & not the real voice of the people. The great object seems to be to kill Webster. But the country is more anxious for an honorable settlement of the question than for the fate of any politician. Very truly Your friend & obt sevt   Edward Kent

ALS. Diocese of Portland, Maine. Published in William Leo Lucey, S.J., "Some Correspondence of the Maine Commissioners Regarding the Webster-Ashburton Treaty," *New England Quarterly*, 15 (March 1942): 345–346.

TO JOHN PLUMMER HEALY

My Dear Sir   Washington Aug. 17. 1842
    I can say nothing about politics—or what is wise, or unwise. I hope however to run home, very early next month, & before your Convention meets.[1]
    Nothing can be worse than the state of things here. It is quite uncertain whether Congress will do any thing. The Treaty will be acted upon, this week. No doubt it will be assailed, as would any Treaty, and as ratification requires two thirds, it is [its] fate is not absolutely certain. But it is a good treaty, & I do not think it will be killed.
    I used to have an insurance on Marshfield, at Mr Snelling's.[2] Was it transferred to Mr [Joseph] Balch's?[3] My man—Mr [Seth] Weston[4] wants the main barn insured—say for 2000—as it is an expensive barn, & now has $1200 worth, so he says of hay & grain [in] it.
    Indeed I should like the old insurance on the whole property, which I think was $5,000—& something extra, an additional for the Barn. Please get this done, & give a check on Merchants Bank for the premium. I have not drawn upon the little sum you placed there. Yrs truly   D.W.

ALS. MHi. Healy (1810–1882; Dartmouth 1835) read law with DW, 1835–1838, and remained in his office as an associate until 1852. He served in the Massachusetts legislature in 1841, 1849, and 1850, and in the state senate in 1854.

———

5. Otis spoke on the treaty before a convention of Kennebec County Whigs at Augusta on August 10, 1842. See the Portland *Advertiser*, August 13, 1842.
    6. Not found.
    1. Massachusetts Whigs gathered at Faneuil Hall in Boston on September 14, 1842. DW addressed an audience there on September 30. See *W & S*, 3:109–140.

2. Probably a reference to Nathaniel G. Snelling, president of the Massachusetts Fire & Marine Insurance Company.
    3. Balch was president of the Merchants' Insurance Company of Boston.
    4. Weston (1804–1876), a Marshfield carpenter, who was employed by Webster.

TO [GEORGE TICKNOR]

Dear Sir

    The work is done—39—to 9.[1] Yrs   D.W.

[August 20, 1842]
Saturday Eve'
10. oclock

ALS. NhD.

TO WILLIAM CABELL RIVES

My Dear Sir,

[August 21, 1842]
Sunday Morning

    I thank you for your kind note, last Evening,[1] & I am duly sensible how much of our success is due to your able & fortunate efforts. All speak most highly of the manner in which you conducted the discussion.

    On some incidental matters, I would be pleased to see you, as you go to the Senate tomorrow morning. Yrs truly   Danl Webster

ALS. DLC. Rives (1793–1868; William and Mary 1809), of Virginia, the chairman of the Senate Committee on Foreign Relations, guided the Webster-Ashburton Treaty through the Senate.

TO [JOHN TYLER]

My dear sir,

[August 21, 1842]
Sunday Morning

    I thank you for your obliging note.[1] Our success in the Senate was signal, indeed. Mr [William S.] Derrick[2] will call on you, about one, to day, for a necessary signature & will be off for England tomorrow morning. He will be back with the Queens ratification by the time I have done making *chowder* at Marshfield, & we can then have the treaty published & proclaimed. Meantime I suppose the Senate will remove the enjoinder of secrecy from the correspondence on the subject of the "Caroline," the "Creole," & "Impressment";[3] & will see what the public say, on those matters.

    I shall come to see you tomorrow. Yrs truly   Danl Webster. Yr paper will be returned this P.M.

Copy. NhHi. Published in Van Tyne, pp. 276–277, but misdated August 28, 1842.

1. The final vote on the treaty is in *Cong. Globe*, 27th Cong., 3d sess., p. 2. Remarks on the treaty may be found in this volume of the *Globe*, *passim*.

1. Not found.

1. This is probably a reference to Tyler's note of August 21, mDW 23239, informing DW of the ratification of the treaty the previous evening.

2. Derrick (c. 1802–1852), originally from Pennsylvania, was a clerk in the State Department from 1827 until his death.

3. The Senate voted unanimously on August 30, 1842, to remove the injunction of secrecy on the treaty proceedings. See *Cong. Globe*, 27th Cong., 3d sess., p. 2.

EDITORIAL: THE TREATY OF WASHINGTON

Monday, August 22, 1842.

The Treaty with ENGLAND, the first, we believe, ever negotiated with that Power in the United States, was RATIFIED BY THE SENATE on Saturday evening (at about nine o'clock) after a discussion of four days. The proceedings are not made public; but it is generally understood that the vote of ratification was no less strong than THIRTY-NINE *Yeas* against NINE *Nays*.

When we consider the variety of subjects which the Treaty is supposed to embrace, their magnitude, and the obvious and acknowledged difficulty of some of them; and when we consider the state of the country, and the effects of that unhappy party spirit, which, in regard to other important subjects, so much distracts our public councils, this strong and decisive majority, necessarily made up of members of all parties, reflects the highest credit upon those who have conducted the negotiation, and gives the fullest assurance that the National honor has been maintained, and all the great interests affected by the Treaty effectually upheld and promoted.

Most sincerely and cordially do we felicitate the country on this auspicious result; and we may properly congratulate the World on the event, since, if any of the difficulties, now settled, had terminated in war between the United States and England, such a war must have convulsed the globe. We cannot but indulge the hope that this favorable settlement of affairs with England is but the first, in a series of measures and events, tending to restore the country to its former prosperity. Let us hail it as the welcome harbinger of better times!

Up to the last year, the Boundary Question had lingered along, events occurring but too frequently, in the mean time, to create new exasperations, and difficulties springing up in regard to other subjects of interest and sensitiveness. Formal diplomatic correspondence seemed to do nothing towards terminating, or even allaying, these controversies. In this state of things, the new English Ministry resolved to signify at once their sense of the importance of an immediate adjustment, and their respect for the Government of the United States, by sending a Special and Extraordinary Mission. For this work of reconciliation and peace they selected Lord ASHBURTON; and surely a wiser or a better choice could not have been made. Lord ASHBURTON arrived at Washington about five months ago, and was received by the President, and Members of Congress of all parties, and by the citizens of this place, with distinguished respect and civility. To all this kindness he has made full and just return. His general intercourse in our society has been most agreeable; and now that, having accomplished his work, he has left us, probably again never to visit our city, it is but justice to say that he has left among all classes a deep and most favorable impression of his character and deportment. A man advanced in life, fully acquainted for many years with affairs between his own country and ours, always endeavoring in his public conduct to preserve amity between them, he came to this country, not to enter upon a career of showy diplomacy, or to swell the volume, already too large, of unproductive correspondence, but to sit down to existing topics, in a business-like way, to treat them frankly and fairly, to say what he could do, and what he could not, and to remove all obstacles, as far as he could. We fully believe all this to be true of his objects and purposes. As he is reported to have said of himself, he "came not to make difficulties, but to make a Treaty." We have heard the Commissioners of the States of MAINE and MASSACHUSETTS, who had necessarily much intercourse with him, speak, in terms as sincere as complimentary, of the frankness, good faith, kindness, and evenness of temper, which he invariably displayed in all their interviews with him. In a word, every voice speaks well of this "fine old English gentleman." Long may he yet live to enjoy the satisfaction of reflecting on the good he has accomplished!

It is no more than just also to say, that, from the moment of the annunciation of Lord ASHBURTON's mission, the conduct of our Government in this matter has been both wise and judicious. The first object was to settle, if possible, the long-contested Boundary question, by agreement and compromise; a settlement rendered so much more difficult than it would have been by the necessity of consulting the inclinations and wishes of two important States of the Union.

Of the industry and ability with which this important affair has been conducted, we have already expressed our opinion fully and frankly. In addition to which, we ought not to withhold from the Secretary of State the credit due for the comprehensive and business-like manner in which he commenced and prosecuted the whole negotiation. In the conduct of it he discarded all local feeling, and showed that he was governed by a truly national spirit and ambition. Whilst on a great Eastern question he consulted Eastern men and Eastern interests, on matters affecting other portions of the Union he consulted with equal sedulousness those whose feelings and interests were peculiarly involved in them.

Those who have been most opposed to Mr. WEBSTER's remaining in the Cabinet are understood to admit that it was fortunate for the country that he was there at this important juncture. We doubt whether any other citizen would have had it in his power to bring the affair to so happy an issue. Able as he has heretofore shown himself in the Senate, he has proved himself no less wise in counsel, and resolute in action. We say this, upon information upon which we rely, derived as it is from those who have been actors in the negotiation, or made acquainted with its merits.

The treaty itself, which has been ratified by this Government, cannot be published and proclaimed before it has been ratified by both Governments. It is understood, however, that it provides for the settlement, not only of the boundary question, but of other important matters, of which probably we shall be soon able to lay before our readers, though not in official form, all the material points of the adjustment.

Unsigned editorial. Text from the Washington, D.C., *National Intelligencer*, August 23, 1842. DW wrote the draft of this editorial (mDW 23263). Because of his friendship with William Winston Seaton (1785–1866) and Joseph Gales (1786–1860), the publishers of the *National Intelligencer*, DW was able to place his unsigned editorials in the columns of one of the nation's most influential newspapers.

TO JOHN TYLER

MY DEAR SIR,—   August 24, 1842.
I greatly thank you for your kind and obliging letter of this morning.[1]
I showed it to my wife [Caroline Le Roy Webster], now on the eve of her departure for the North, and she immediately sequestered it, saying that she should keep it and treasure it up.
I shall never speak of this negotiation, my dear Sir, which I believe is destined to make some figure in the history of the country, without doing you justice. Your steady support and confidence, your anxious and intelligent attention to what was in progress, and your exceedingly obliging and pleasant intercourse, both with the British minister [Lord Ashburton] and the commissioners of the States, have given every possible facility to my agency in this important transaction. Nor ought I to forget the cordial coöperation of my colleagues in the cabinet, to every one of whom I am indebted for valuable assistance. Believe me, dear Sir, with great sincerity and esteem, yours,   Dan'l Webster.

Text from *PC*, 2:146–147. Original not found.

TO EDWARD EVERETT

Confidential & personal
My Dear Sir   Washington Aug. 25. 1842
Having got through with Lord Ashburton, I have time to write you freely, upon several points of a personal nature, which you have sometimes alluded to.
In the first place, as to the relations between Mr [Henry] Clay's friends & myself, they have been hostile, and are still only in a sort of truce. These Gentlemen, angry at my remaining in the Cabinet after the explo-

1. Not found.

sion of Septr '41, assaulted me in every possible form, in Congress & more especially thro' the press, with a degree of venom & abuse, such as we only used to look for in the globe.[1] This attack began at Louisville, last Decr, & was kept up about three months.[2] Public opinion reacted, upon it, & they were glad to quit. Since that period, they have been more in a coaxing mood; but still there is no confidence & little communication between them & me.

Mr Clay denounces all *conventions*; nominations in his favor are taking place, wherever they can be got up, & individual *pledges* to support him are recd, much after the fashion [of] the Temperance pledges. So much for my relations with Mr Clay.

With Mr [John] Tyler, I have got along very well so far as respects the affairs of my own Department, except that he has felt himself obliged to make some appointments, which were very bad. But his unhappy course on the revenue subject, including his 4 vetos, have really left him without much support.[3] We could have lived thro' the Vetos of last year, because they were connected with an unpopular subject; but the effect of the Vetos of this year has been overwhelming, throughout all the North & West. I foresaw & foretold it all, but could not prevent it. The consequence is likely to be, that the President must hereafter look for support principally to that party which *did not* bring him into power; and it is easy to see that this necessity must lead to changes. My own opinion is, he ought to remodel his Cabinet. That is, if he intends to hold on his present course of administration. You will see that all the Whig presses cry out for my immediate retirement.[4] I understand much of the motive in all this; they wish for freer scope, in their assaults upon this President. I shall not be hurried; but yet I have to say to you that I do not

1. The *Washington Globe* was a partisan Democratic newspaper that had been critical of DW for many years.

2. George Dennison Prentice (1802–1870; Brown 1823), the editor of the *Louisville* (Ky.) *Daily Journal*, a Clay organ, commenced a vituperative personal attack on DW on January 25, 1842. The *Journal* carried a report alleging that DW had assaulted a woman seeking employment at the State Department. The deeply offended DW produced affidavits from State Department employees denying the accusation, and the newspaper later published a retraction of the charges. On the various charges made against DW, see Theodore Frelinghuysen to DW, Feb-

ruary 11, 1842, and Ambrose D. Mann to DW, May 6 and May 25, 1842, in *Correspondence* 5:190, 205–206, 212–213.

3. Tyler's bank vetoes of August 16 and September 9, 1841, and the tariff bill vetoes of June 29 and August 9, 1842, are in *Messages and Papers*, 4:63–68, 68–72, 180–183, 183–189.

4. See, for example, the *Boston Semi-Weekly Atlas* of August 13, 1842, which stated that DW's Whig friends had "firm confidence in his adherence to the principles of the Party—and they are ready to receive him into their arms and their confidence, as soon as he can shake himself clear of the contaminating contact of the Locofoco President Tyler."

expect to stay long where I am. I can bring the President no support, nor can I act with those on whom he is most likely hereafter to rely. Personally we are on the best terms; & certainly I shall neither leave him with abruptness, nor join any party against him, when I do leave him. I talk freely with him, on these subjects, & tho' I think he wd. prefer I should stay, I doubt not he sees how difficult it will be to do so. Then, you will ask, what do I propose to do? Probably, nothing. It has been intimated that the door of the Senate would be readily opened, if I chose to step in. But I have no wish to re-enter upon that career. I presume I could go abroad, & Paris has been mentioned, as it seems not improper to make soon a change in that mission. But my ignorance of the language is a flat ban, as we say in the law, to that proposition. I could go no where but to England; & you are yet hardly warm in your place. Besides, I do not know how I could stand the expense, even for a single year.

There are two or three subjects remaining for negotiation with England. 1. Some formal stipulation for such cases as that of the Creole. 2. The Oregon Boundary.[5] 3. A new arrangement about the W[est] I[ndies] trade.[6] This last is quite important.

I shall leave this City, next week, for a month; & from Marshfield look out upon things, & perhaps come to some decision, as to the future, more definite than any yet formed.

Lord Ashburton has left the best feelings behind him. It is impossible any one should have borne himself better than he has done, in his intercourse with our People. The Treaty is a good one, fair & honorable for both Countries. I believe it will be quite satisfactory here. The 9 votes agt. it are understood to be those of [Reuel] Williams, [James] Buchanan, [Daniel] Sturgeon, Perry Smith, [Arthur Pendleton] Bagbee, [Charles Magill] Conrad, [Thomas Hart] Benton, [Lewis Fields] Lynn, & [William] Allen.[7] I suppose the Treaty & Debates will soon be published. Buchanan appeared, I learn, more wrathful, & more *mean* than any one else. Mr [John Caldwell] Calhoun is understood to have supported the negotiation, in a very handsome manner.

I hope you like our African Cruising arrangement, & the correspondence on impressment.

---

5. See below, "The Aftermath and Implementation of the Treaty of Washington: The Oregon Question," pp. 826–850.

6. DW believed that the West Indies Reciprocity Agreement of 1830 was unfavorable to New England shipping interests. He called for renegotiation of the agreement in his September 30, 1842, speech at Faneuil Hall. See *Works*, 2:122–123 and *Speeches* 2.

7. Sturgeon (1789–1878) was a Democrat from Pennsylvania; Smith (1783–1852), a Democrat from Connecticut; Bagby (1794–1858), a Democrat from Alabama; Conrad (1804–1878), a Whig from Louisiana; Benton (1782–1858), a Democrat from Missouri; Linn (1796–1843), a Democrat from Missouri; Allen (1803–1879), a Democrat from

Mrs [Caroline Le Roy] Webster thanks you for all your kind remembrances, & desires her love to Mrs [Charlotte Brooks] Everett & the daughters.[8] Pray present me to them, in the kindest manner.

P.S. I wish Lord Aberdeen could understand the importance of a *change* in the resident mission here. The truth is, as at present filled, it is worse than useless. I have spoken freely to Lord Ashburton on the subject. Some person of frank & social manners—whose house should be *known* to have an inside to it—& who should hold social & hospitable intercourse with members of Congress, &c., is quite desirable to fill the place. From what I hear of Lord [Charles John] Canning,[9] I should suppose he was quite fit. If our old friend Evelyn Denison[10] was of the right political association, I think he would do exceedingly well. Not that he has great position & decided talent, but he is well-mannered, agreeable, & has always felt good temper towards us; and is of good connexions at home. If a man of rank be sent, it should be one who suits rank, in personal character. Our people might feel rather complimented, by sending a peer; I think that was true, in Lord Ashburton's case; but you know that any ostentation or apparent pride of rank would only give offense to us, simple republicans.[11] Yrs truly always   D Webster

ALS. MHi.

FROM EDWARD EVERETT

Private.

My dear Sir,   London 16 September 1842.

I need not say that the last steamer is the most welcome arrival we have had from America, since I have been here. Although, after the confident tone of your last communication,[1] I could not doubt that the treaty would be ratified, and was even led to hope that a revenue bill would pass, I must own I did not feel certain enough of either event, not to rejoice most heartily at getting the tidings. I shall take advantage of the state of good feeling, which I am sure the news will produce, to press for a general settlement of these vexatious old scores on the coast of Africa, which form the subject of my present correspondence, and see if

---

Ohio. Conrad was the only Whig to vote against the treaty.

8. Anne Gorham Everett (1823–1844) and Charlotte Brooks Everett (1825–1879).

9. Canning (1812–1862) was under secretary for foreign affairs, 1841–1846, and governor of India, 1856–1862.

10. Denison (1800–1873), a member of Parliament, had made DW's

acquaintance during a tour of America in 1824. Denison and DW kept up a correspondence over the years, and the Englishman treated the Websters with graciousness during their visit to England in 1839.

11. The inhospitable Henry Stephen Fox was replaced as minister to the United States by Richard Pakenham on February 21, 1844.

1. Not found.

I cannot clear them all off. Indeed, if I were provided with instructions sufficiently in detail, I should not despair, at so favorable a juncture, of inducing this Government to come to some reasonable adjustment of the Oregon question,—and the West India trade. Lord Aberdeen, some months ago, dropped a remark on the latter point, which I reported to you at the time, which showed a good predisposition on that subject.[2] The good offices of Lord Ashburton might be resorted to, with the best effect for this purpose.

I have had time only to run my eye hastily over the correspondence connected with the treaty. You have never, I think, shewn greater force of argument or controversial skill. It is amusing to see how Lord Ashburton surrenders, without a struggle, the field of argument. It is all first-rate, but the letter on impressment[3] is, I think, the best:—perhaps because the ground is there impregnable, alike in reference to natural equity and public law.

The mode of disposing of the African question is capital. The naval power to be kept in the African seas is not greater than our commerce demands. By cordial co-operation with the cruizers of this Government, the trade may, I believe, be broken up. But you ought to pass a law forbidding the building and equipping ships for the Slave-trade, in order to get rid of the difficulty which presented itself in the trial of the "*Catherine*."[4]

I learn, for the first time, from these papers, the history of Lieutenant [John S.] Paine's agreement with Commodore [William] Tucker. Not a word on the subject is to be found in this office. Mr. [Andrew] Stevenson derived his knowledge even of the existence of the agreement, from Lord Palmerston. It was scandalously abused by the British Cruizers. Under this agreement,—which only authorized them to turn over to cruizers of the United States, the American vessels concerned in the slave-trade which they might detain,—they sent the "*Tigris*," captured on frivolous grounds, to the United States;[5]—the "*Jones*" to Sierra Leone;[6]—and

2. Not found.

3. See above, DW to Ashburton, August 8, 1842.

4. The *Catharine* outfitted for the slave trade in Havana under the protection of the U.S. flag. Off the coast of Africa in 1839 a British cruiser searched the vessel and found that it also carried fraudulent Spanish papers for the return voyage with slaves. The British sent the ship for trial to New York, where the U.S. Circuit Court upheld the seizure. See *U.S.* v. *Catharine*, in 25 *Federal Cases* 332–344.

5. The *Tigris* was detained by a British warship off Angola in October 1840 after a British officer learned that an African youth was held on board. The ship was sent to Boston for trial, but the U.S. attorney concluded the *Tigris* was not outfitted for the slave trade and declined to prosecute. See Henry Stephen Fox to John Forsyth, February 5, 1841, DNA, RG 59 (Notes from Foreign Legations, Britain), and Forsyth to Fox, March 1, 1841, DNA, RG 59 (Notes to Foreign Legations, Britain).

6. The *Jones* was seized in August

after keeping the *"Douglass"* eight days, discharged her, without sending her to any tribunal, where the causes of arrest could be enquired into.[7]

Pray let me know what ground ought to be taken about this agreement. Where it was thus abused, it cannot, of course, be allowed as a justification.

With respect to the *"Jones,"* though there is no reason to suspect her as being foreign property, (the pretext, I suppose, under which she was ordered to Sierra Leone) there are some matters alleged in the depositions of four of her seamen, taken before Col. [Thomas] Aspinwall and forwarded with the original papers in the case to Mr. Stevenson, which seem to require notice;[8] particularly if,—as stated in one of those depositions,—the owners of the *"Jones"* are also the owners of the *"Butterfly,"* which was condemned as a slave-trader at New York.[9]

The *"Douglass"* too, I fear, was some how or other concerned in the slave-trade. The account given of her equipments & destination is far from satisfactory. I am, Dear Sir, as ever, Most faithfully yours,

Edward Everett.

LS. MHi.

FROM EDWARD EVERETT

Private
My dear Sir,   London 17 Octr. 1842.

In my letter of the 1st from Wentworth,[1] I informed you that, before leaving town on the 22d ult. for a short excursion in the country, I agreed with Lord Aberdeen, that, if he should be ready to ratify the treaty before my return, he would let me know it by letter, and I would immediately come back to London. Accordingly on the 10th, being then at Auckland

or September 1840 and sent to Sierra Leone, where the vessel was detained over two years without proceedings. See Stevenson to DW, April 19, 1841, enclosing his protest to Aberdeen of April 16, 1841, and Everett's protest enclosed in No. 22. Everett to DW, September 16, 1842, DNA, RG 59 (Despatches, Britain).

7. The *Douglass*, on a voyage from Havana to Africa, was detained by the British warship *Termagant* from October 21 to 29, 1839. See Everett's review of the case in his note to Aberdeen, November 12, 1842, enclosed in No. 28. Everett to DW, No-

vember 18, 1842, DNA, RG 59 (Despatches, Britain).

8. The affidavits, tending to show that the *Jones* was outfitted for the slave trade, are in DNA, RG 84 (Miscellaneous Record Book of the Consulate-General of the United States in London).

9. The *Butterfly*, with slave equippage on board, was seized by the British navy off the coast of Africa on August 26, 1839. The case came before the U.S. Supreme Court as *U.S. v. Morris*, 14 *Peters* 464 (1840).

1. Everett to DW, October 1, 1842, mDW 23492.

Castle, the seat of the Bishop of Durham,[2] I received a note from Lord Aberdeen, requesting to see me as soon as convenient. I was to have started the next day for the Lakes of Cumberland, but disengaging myself from my appointments in that quarter, I immediately returned to town, & on the 13th, exchanged the ratifications of the treaty at the Foreign Office. Mr [William S.] Derrick, who goes out in the Great Western, will take the British ratification; and by this opportunity also I shall transmit you a despatch,[3] although there is nothing of any great interest to form the subject of one.

After exchanging the ratifications on Thursday last, Lord Aberdeen and myself entered into a general conversation. In reference to the attacks on the treaty by a portion of the liberal press, (especially the Morning Chronicle and the Globe),[4] I remarked to him, that these attacks were fairly offset by those made on the American side of the water. He admitted the justice of this reflection, & expressed a strong wish to be furnished with some of the articles written in the United States against the treaty. In running my eye over the numbers of the Washington Globe, which have appeared the last six weeks,[5] I find matter enough of the kind in question, but mixed with so much ribaldry & containing so little argument, as to be hardly worth showing Lord Aberdeen. If any thing really clever and able against the treaty comes out, (which to be sure is scarcely possible), I wish you would send it to me. If the speeches of Messrs [James] Buchanan, [Thomas Hart] Benton, and [William] Allen in secret session should be published, they will probably be just what is wanted here as an offset to the attacks of the Whig journalists, who are venting Lord Palmerston's pique.[6]

Lord Aberdeen said a great deal on a much more important topic vizt. the non-arrangement of the Oregon question. He deeply regretted its not being included in the treaty: repeated what he had told me before, that Lord Ashburton was fully instructed on the subject, in every conceivable aspect in which the question could be presented; & scarcely knew why it had not been made the subject of an attempt at least at arrangement.

2. Edward Maltby (1770–1859) was bishop of Durham from 1836 to 1856.

3. See Everett's dispatches to DW, No. 25. October 19, 1842, and No. 26. October 20, 1842, DNA, RG 59 (Despatches, Britain).

4. See the articles by Lord Palmerston attacking the treaty, reprinted from the London Morning Chronicle in the Washington, D.C. National Intelligencer, January 26, 28, 31, and February 2, 4, 9, 16, 1843. The London newspapers Globe and Traveler of September 15, 1842, also criticized the treaty.

5. See, for example, the article in the Washington Globe of August 12, 1842, charging that DW had "sacrificed his duty to his country, to advance the strength and glory of England."

6. Benton's and Buchanan's speeches in the secret sessions of August 18 and 19, 1842, are in Cong. Globe, 27th Cong., 3d sess., pp. 1–27, 101–110. No remarks by Allen are recorded.

Lord Aberdeen said he very greatly feared, that strong measures relative to an occupation of an undefined portion of the country might be brought forward & pressed at the next congress, which would kindle very uneasy feelings, & greatly impair the value of the lately concluded treaty, in its influence on the public mind, as a general arrangement of the controversies between the two countries. He dwelt much on this idea. He then said he really wished we would come to an arrangement—if not final—(which would be much the best,) at least to leave things, for some good time, in *statu quo*. I endeavored to draw from him the terms, on which Great Britain would come to an agreement, but on this subject he was of course wary. I found, however, that he had turned his thoughts to some arrangement, by which the United States should agree to come down as far south as the Columbia River, and make that stream their boundary on the north & northwest, in consideration of some extension to the south, to be obtained from Mexico, so as to give us another port in that direction. He did not say that this extension was to be procured for us by Great Britain; though it would seem as if his suggestion could point only to that;—because, if we can obtain the extension directly ourselves from Mexico, it can be no consideration for a concession, on our part, to Great Britain. Lord Aberdeen in pursuing the topic, expressed a strong desire, that I would write to Washington for instructions on this subject, and added the decided opinion, that it could be arranged to the satisfaction of both parties.

The Great Western & the Acadia bring various documents from the department of State particularly the former, but no communication from yourself to me. By the latter we have your great speech in Faneuil-Hall. It is given entire, though not in the best report, in the "Times" of this morning, & spoken of as a document which will well repay perusal. I need not say how much obliged to you I am, for the kind allusion to myself.[7] I rejoice that you have had an opportunity of speaking out, on some of the topics which form the subject of the speech, and shall look forward with great anxiety to the further exposition promised of your views. With respect to the plan for a "Board of Exchequer," I do not know whether it will strengthen the confidence which you avow in that measure, that it was decidedly approved,—when the Report from the Treasury first reached this Country,—by Mr [John] Horseley Palmer.[8] He told me he thought very favorably of it.

7. DW's speech of September 30, 1842, is in *Works*, 2:117–140. DW referred to Everett as a distinguished citizen representing the United States with "much credit to himself and to his country" (p. 127).

8. For DW's remarks in the Faneuil Hall speech on the exchequer plan, see *Works*, 2:134–138. The report from Secretary of the Treasury Walter Forward on the plan is in *Executive Documents*, 27th Cong., 2d sess., Serial 401, No. 20. Palmer (1779–1858) was a director of the Bank of England and currency expert.

I have lately received a letter from General [Lewis] Cass,[9] saying that he has asked his recal, and shall take passage on the 19th of Novr. for the United States. He informs me that he has taken this resolution so suddenly, as to have made but a short time before an agreement for a house, which will involve a heavy pecuniary loss. I do not gather from his letter the cause of his sudden determination to return. If it results from any communication from the Government, you will of course need no information from me. I judge from what Mr [Jonathan] Prescott Hall[10] reports to me of his conversation, that it is in consequence of representations from his friends in America, to the effect, that if he is to be a Presidential Candidate, he must come home, and take the field in person.

Much kind remembrance was had of you in the family of the Archbishop of York,[11] on occasion of our visit the other day at Bishopthorpe. I am as ever, with sincere attachment, faithfully Yours,   E. E.

Genl. Duff Green, who is just from Paris, informs me, that (to use his own words) Genl. Cass goes home "under protest against the treaty"; that is, as he explained it, to come out as a Presidential Candidate on that ground. The candidacy in his—D[uff] G[reen]'s—opinion lies between Mr [John Caldwell] Calhoun and Genl. Cass, on the democratic side. Mr [Martin] Van B[uren] according to him has no chance even in his own state.

ALS. MHi.

FROM JOHN OTIS

Dear Sir,   Hallowell Jany 17, 1843.

I send you the Report of the Comrs. of Maine to the Executive of this state.[1] It was drawn up by Judge [William Pitt] Preble. The report has been committed to a committee, selected in the Senate by ballot. Mr. [Edward] Kavanaugh being President asked to be excused from making the appointment. Whether a majority of the committee *professes* to be adverse to the Treaty or favourable to the settlement, I am not informed.[2] If I could depend upon the *privately* expresssed opinions of members, I

9. Not found.

10. Hall (1796–1862; Yale 1817), a leader of the New York bar, toured Europe in 1842.

11. Edward Vernon Harcourt (1757–1847) was archbishop of York from 1807 until his death.

1. The report of the commissioners of January 4, 1843, is in *Documents Printed by Order of the Legislature of the State of Maine* (Augusta, Me., 1843).

2. The committee report of March 21, 1843, criticized the "tyrannical threats" by DW addressed to the Maine commissioners during the negotiations and presented a set of resolves declaring the treaty unsatisfactory. *Maine Legislative Documents*, Senate Doc. No. 52 (Augusta, Me., 1843).

should be sure of a majority of the Legislature in favor of the Treaty, but so many party influences are brought to bear in such a body that I would not under take to predict the result in advance of their action. I am sure that the great body of the people of the state are well satisfied that the question of boundary is placed beyond the reach of politicians, and of partizan influence.

I understand a resolve was yesterday introduced into the Senate, calling upon the President, or Congress, for information in relation to the "disputed boundary fund."[3] This being a matter in which many individuals, & some of them influential members of the Legislature, have private claims, it comes home to their business more directly than the great public interests. I have had more inquiries about the settlement of this fund than about any other part of the arrangement. I feel particularly desirous that this should be settled in that spirit of liberality which Lord Ashburton assured us it should be. The six months named in the Treaty has not expired since its ratification, & it is probable the account of that fund has not been furnished you, & the call will, therefore, be ineffectual. If a statement of the account has been made, it may be a question whether it would be expedient to make it public before you are satisfied that it includes all you have a right to ask under the arrangement, & the assurance that was given that the settlement should be made in a spirit of liberality. With Great Respect, your friend,   John Otis

ALS. NhD.

3. The resolution, passed January 24, 1843, is in *Resolves of Maine,* 1843 (Augusta, Me., 1843).

The Aftermath and Implementation of the Treaty of Washington

THE LAW OF AUGUST 29, 1842

An important outcome of the Treaty of Washington was what might be called the "McLeod law" of August 29, 1842. Despite the fact that Webster had accepted the British contention that under international law an individual could not be held personally responsible for participation in actions authorized by his government, the trial of Alexander McLeod had contradicted that view and had jeopardized Anglo-American relations. In his first Annual Message of December 7, 1841, President Tyler suggested to Congress "the propriety" of providing for removal from the state to the federal judiciary of cases involving "the faithful observance and execution of our international obligations." He also pointedly observed that James Grogan had been discharged immediately by "the authorities of Upper Canada" (*Messages and Papers*, 4: 75). Shortly thereafter, Lord Aberdeen, perplexed by the ambiguities of American federalism, strongly urged the Tyler administration to seek a constitutional amendment to prevent the recurrence of cases similar to that of McLeod (see Everett to DW, December 15, 1841, "The Crisis in Anglo-American Relations," pp. 166–169, above).

In January 1842, at the request of Senator John Macpherson Berrien, the chairman of the Judiciary Committee, Webster confidentially drafted a bill to transfer such cases as McLeod's from state to federal jurisdiction (see Berrien to DW, January 10, 1842, below). The draft has not been found, but its contents can be inferred from a letter written by Webster to Berrien on January 14 (see DW to Berrien, January 14, 1842, below). John Sheridan Hogan's arrest less than two months later for alleged participation in the *Caroline* raid underscored the need for legislation (see Lot Clark to DW, March 2, 1842, "The Treaty of Washington," p. 523, above), and with that event in mind, on March 8 Tyler reiterated his request that Congress provide for removal from state to federal tribunals of cases involving "national questions" (*Messages and Papers*, 4:103).

Under Senator Berrien's leadership, on August 29, 1842, Congress passed "An Act to Provide further Remedial Justice in the Courts of the United States" (5 *U.S. Stat.* 539–540). The law, which Chancellor James Kent characterized as a "momentous" improvement in the American codes (see Kent to DW, December 21, 1842, below), granted U.S. district court and Supreme Court justices the power to issue writs of habeas corpus to determine whether individuals claiming to be acting under the explicit authority of a foreign nation could be tried in an American court or should be remanded to their own governments. Webster's goal, as stated in the letter to Berrien, was to safeguard "the peace of the Country"; the new statute made a significant contribution to that end.

FROM JOHN MACPHERSON BERRIEN

Washington
Sir   10 Jany '42

I have received your communication of the 6th inst covering a copy of one from the Secretary of War [John Canfield Spencer], and of an extract from a letter to him.[1] I will take an early occasion to present this communication to the Judiciary Committee. In the mean time, as the subject to which it relates, must have been maturely considered by you during the pendency of the prosecution against [Alexander] McCleod, will you allow me to ask if you have thought of any specific provisions, by which the views of the President in relation to the transfer of criminal cases from the State to the Federal tribunals, may be accomplished. The law which regulates it, must I presume provide[:]

1. For the application by the President to the State tribunal, and for the stay or discharge of further proceedings therein, on filing such application.

2. The application of the President, would be founded on evidence furnished by the foreign Government requiring his interposition—but of the sufficiency of that evidence, to render the law effectual, it ought to provide that he and not the State tribunal should be the judge.

3. For the delivery of the accused person to some competent federal officer to be designated in the act—and for investing him with authority and means to secure the safe removal of the accused.

The transfer of civil causes from the state to the Federal tribunals, for the purpose of being tried in the latter, is free from difficulty, because in the cases in which that transfer is authorised, the Federal Courts have jurisdiction. But this would not be true of a criminal prosecution for an offence against the laws of a particular State. The application of

1. See John C. Spencer to DW, January 5, 1842, DNA, RG 59 (Misc. Letters). Spencer enclosed a letter from Seth C. Hawley of December 27, 1841. Hawley observed that members of the *Caroline* raiding party frequently entered the United States and warned that the result could be another "McLeod Case." In March John Sheridan Hogan was arrested for his alleged participation in the raid. See above, Lot Clark to DW, March 1 and March 2, 1842, and Joshua A. Spencer to DW, April 2 and April 8, 1842, "The Treaty of Washington," pp. 522–523, 529, 532.

the President must then be made to operate as a peremptory bar to further proceedings in the State Court—and the transfer be made for the sole purpose of enabling him to comply with the requisition of the foreign Government. Do you trace the authority to pass a law investing the President with such power, to any other source, than that given to Congress in the last clause of the 8th section of the Constitution, taken in connection with the fact that he is the Representative of this Government, in its intercourse with foreign nations?

I shall be obliged by any suggestions you may be disposed to make in reply to this note, and by receiving them as early as may consist with your convenience. I have the honor to be very respectfully Sir Yr Ob. st.

Jn: Macpherson: Berrien

PS. It has occurred to me further to suggest the enquiry whether the writ of Habeas Corpus may not under proper legal provisions be used for the accomplishment of the object in view.

ALS. DNA, RG 59 (Misc. Letters). Rec'd January 10, 1842. Berrien (1781–1856; Princeton 1796), a Whig senator from Georgia, 1824–1829 and 1841–1852, and attorney general of the United States, 1829–1831, was at that time chairman of the Senate Committee on the Judiciary.

TO JOHN MACPHERSON BERRIEN

My Dear Sir   W. 14 January, 1842.

In compliance with your request, I send you the draft of a Bill,[1] such as appears to me calculated to answer the intended purposes. You will of course consider this as a private, & wholly unofficial act, intended merely to facilitate your own labors, if it may have that effect, & not as being proposed, or recommended by the Executive Govt. Neither the President, nor the Atty Genl [Hugh Swinton Legaré] has seen it, nor indeed any other head of Department. The Executive Govt. deems some measure quite necessary, but what that measure ought to be, it leaves entirely to the wisdom of Congress. In making this draft of a Bill, I have conformed as far as practicable to the provisions of previous & existing laws, with the exception, that a provision for proceeding by way of Habeas Corpus is added, as suggested by yourself.

I hope the Bill may be put into such shape, as that the Com[mitt]ee may cordially recommend, & Congress pass it, as I think the object important to the peace of the Country.

The Constitutional authority for such a measure I suppose rests on the truth of these propositions, viz

I. That the Judicial power of the United States extends to all cases coming under the Constitution, Laws, & Treaties thereof.

1. Not found.

II. That questions under the Law of Nations, affecting the relations of the United States with foreign States, or Sovereignties, & connected with the power of war & peace, & which respect asserted rights, or claims of foreign States, or <those> Sovereignties, or those things in regard to which one nation is answerable to another, belong to the proper jurisdiction of the Govt. of the United States, & that cases arising <under> upon those, are cases coming under the Constitution of the United States.

I am, Dear Sir, with regard, Your Ob Serv.   D. W.

A L S draft. NhHi. Published in *PC*, 2:112–113.

FROM JAMES KENT

Dear Sir   New York December 21. 1842

I thank you for your friendly note of the 17th Inst.[1] with the Correspondence between you & Lord Ashburton. That Correspondence I had previously perused, & I was much pleased with the ability, Candor & Precision with which the Negotiation was conducted. Several of the Principles declared in these State Papers were so important, & so well & clearly expressed, that I had already made a note of them in the M.S. Pages of the 1st Vol. of my Comm. to be incorporated in the next Edition.[2]

The [Alexander] McLeod Case is happily terminated. I never had or could entertain any doubt of the enormous Error of the judicial opinions in that Case. The Opinion of [Esek] Cowen I thought was written in very bad Taste, with disgusting Pedantry & waste of Learning. My only difficulty was as to the want of a clear & certain Provision in the judiciary act of 1789[3] to remove the Proceeding into the federal Courts, & that difficulty is now happily removed by the Act of Congress of August 27th 1842. That Act & the 10th article of the Treaty providing for the Surrender of Fugitives, are momentous & most auspicious Improvements in our national & diplomatic Codes.

I thank you for the kind feelings you have done me the Honor & the Goodness to express in respect to my Health & condition. I am indeed in my 80th year but thank God I am wonderfully well & active, & my ardor for reading, & my sensibilities are I think as alive as ever to the charms of Nature, of Literature & Society. I keep aloof from all fashionable Parties except when my daughter (Mrs. [Elizabeth Kent] H[one]) has some small ones at my House, at which Ma and I are obliged to be present,[4] &

1. DW to Kent, December 17, 1842, mDW 23903.

2. *Commentaries on American Law* (5th ed., 4 vols., New York, 1844).

3. 1 *U.S. Stat.* 73–93.

4. Kent married Elizabeth Baily (1768–1851) in 1785. Their daughter, Elizabeth (b. 1796), married Isaac S. Hone, the nephew of New York merchant Philip Hone (1780–1851).

I chat & flatter as much as ever with pretty Ladies. My reading is regular & constant—all the *Reports* of law decisions as fast as I can procure them—all the *Periodicals* foreign & domestic & old *Literature*, & *new Books* are steadily turned over. I have been reading a day or two past at intervals Dr [Thomas] Arnold's[5] History of Rome. He is a great admirer of [Georg Barthold] Niebuhr[6] & his Criticisms are doubtless true and just but dull. I relieve myself by going from some of his allusions to one of the *Muses* or Books of Herodotus, or Livy, or Vertot, & they amuse my old age like enchanting historical Novels. I don't like altogether bald, naked, sterile facts. I like a little of the Poetry of History as well as of life itself in all its modifications. I deal Sufficiently with dry & stern Facts when I study law Cases. I recurred to one of [Edward] Gibbon's[7] Chapters on the Irruption of the Northern Nations into the Roman Provinces, & with what delight and cold admiration! He has Truth favorably stated but adorned with Taste, Style wisdom & surpassing Energy & Eloquence of Language.

I partly ride & partly walk down town daily to my office, & have occasional Opinions to give, but more out of the State than in it, & then hasten up to my attractive Home & office on Union Square facing the lofty Jet d'eau which is constantly playing before my Eyes. The associations with that water are to me delightful. I was born on my Father's Farm in Putnam County in the Eastern part of the Highlands, & *that farm was bounded E. on the Croton River*, where I used to fish & swim in my youthful days. God bless the stream. How would it have astonished my Parents if they had been foretold in 1770 that their eldest Son would live in the midst of the City of New York with that very Croton pouring its pure & living waters through the Shoals & throwing its majestic Columns of water 56 feet into the air![8]

So you see how charmingly I am enabled in my Evening days Ducere solicito jucunda oblivia vito.[9] I am dear Sir Yours very respectfully

James Kent

ALS. DLC. Published in *PC*, 2:160–162. Kent (1763–1847; Yale 1781), a distinguished American jurist, was appointed to the New York Supreme Court in 1798, became chief justice of the court in 1804, and was named chancellor of the New York Court of Chancery in 1814.

5. Arnold (1795–1842).

6. Niebuhr (1776–1831).

7. Gibbon (1737–1794).

8. The Croton aqueduct was completed in June 1842.

9. "To quaff sweet forgetfulness of life's cares," from Horace, *Satires, Epistles, and Ars Poetica*, II, No. 6, line 62 (Trans. H. Ruston Fairclough, London, 1956), 215.

THE CASS-WEBSTER CONTROVERSY

On August 24, 1842, John Quincy Adams called upon the secretary of state to congratulate him on the successful negotiation with Lord Ashburton. During the course of their conversation, according to Adams, Webster "spoke with great severity of the conduct" of Lewis Cass. Cass, he said, had sought "to make great political headway upon a popular gale" with his unauthorized protest against the Quintuple Treaty (*Memoirs*, 11:243). That agreement of December 20, 1841, between Austria, Britain, France, Prussia, and Russia allowed the signatories a mutual right of search in order to suppress the African slave trade. The gale caused by Cass's protest against the Quintuple Treaty soon picked up momentum and turned into a storm. On September 17, Cass requested permission to retire from his post as U.S. minister to France, and on October 3 he composed a second protest. This time Cass directed his ire against his own government.

The most extraordinary aftermath of the Treaty of Washington was what Cass aptly characterized as the "war of words" between himself and Webster over Article 8 of that agreement (Cass to DW, March 7, 1843, below). Commencing with the letter of October 3, the Cass-Webster controversy over the joint-cruising convention is contained in five documents. Webster responded to Cass on November 14, Cass penned a counterresponse on December 11, Webster made a further reply on December 20, and the debate concluded with a fifty-two-page missive by Cass on March 7, 1843. Cass did not know about Webster's letter of December 20, 1842, until sometime after February 24, 1843, when President Tyler submitted the correspondence to the U.S. Senate. Although Cass had conferred with Secretary Webster in Washington in January, nothing had been said about the document that ostensibly had been written on December 20. When Cass eventually received a copy, he noticed that it had been posted at Washington on February 23. Clearly, each man was trying to get in the final word, and Cass did so with his lengthy pamphlet-size letter of March 7, which, along with all the previous correspondence, was published during March 1843 in the *Washington Globe* and the *National Intelligencer*.

As the publication history of the "war of words" suggests, the Cass-Webster controversy was in part political. In 1841, as Cass's biographer puts it, Cass became infected with "a virus commonly known as the presidential bug" (Frank B. Woodford, *Lewis Cass: The Last Jeffersonian* [New Brunswick, New Jersey, 1950], p. 215), and he returned to the United States in late 1842 in order to promote his candidacy for the Democratic nomination for the presidency. More than politics was involved, however, for Cass was an intense Anglophobe. During the War of 1812, he had fought against the British in the Northwest, rising to the

rank of brigadier general, and he tended thereafter to associate patriotism with opposition to Great Britain. As Cass wrote in his letter to Webster of March 7, 1843, one of the "offences" he was least likely to be
found guilty of was favoring the "pretensions of England." He would, he
continued, "meet the first" attempt of the British navy to search an
American vessel "by war" (see below). Cass suspected that the allegedly
philanthropic British crusade to suppress the slave trade was largely a
diabolical pretext to further the ancient British goal of "supremacy upon
the ocean" (Cass to DW, December 11, 1842, below). Like Cass, Webster
by 1841 had been infected with the presidential virus. Indeed, his presidential aspirations date at least to 1834, and possibly as early as 1826–
1827. In contrast with Cass, however, Webster had opposed the War of
1812, was less suspicious of British motives, and had fashioned the
accord with Ashburton in order to avoid war with England.

The historical importance of the Cass-Webster controversy lies less in
the realm of emotions and politics than in differences of interpretation
and of principle. Cass's major objections to the joint-cruising convention were that it constituted a potentially dangerous departure from the
fundamental principle of avoiding "entangling alliances" (Cass to DW,
December 11, 1842, below) and that it did not contain an explicit disavowal by the British of a right to search American vessels during time
of peace, which he described as a "sin of omission" (Cass to DW, March
7, 1843, below). In his strongly worded letter of November 14, 1842,
Webster sweepingly condemned Cass's analysis as a "tissue of mistakes."
Article 8, he stated, did not depart from George Washington's maxims of
nonintervention because "the abolition of the African Slave Trade is an
American subject, as emphatically as it is a European subject" and even
more so in that the United States "took the first great steps in declaring
that trade unlawful" (DW to Cass, November 14, 1842, below). As for
the assertion that the Tyler administration should have made a British
repudiation of the right of search a precondition to the joint-cruising
convention, Webster in his letter of December 20, 1842, dismissed the
idea as inappropriate, unnecessary, and likely to be no more "effectual
than the Chinese method of defending their towns by painting grotesque
and hideous figures on the walls, to fright away assailing foes" (see
below). Cass held his ground on both issues, maintaining that Article 8
was "an improvident arrangement which left us worse than it found us,"
and he rejected the Chinese analogy as a "reductio ad absurdum" (Cass
to DW, March 7, 1843, below).

Neither man convinced the other on either of the two central points
in dispute, but their correspondence nevertheless is revealing and significant. Webster and Cass agreed that what the latter called "the national
interest" (Cass to DW, March 7, 1843, below) should be upheld, and both
were realists in the sense that they believed that power would be the ulti-

mate arbiter of the question of search (see Cass to DW, December 11, 1842, and DW to Cass, December 20, 1842, below). But they differed substantially in their respective interpretations of the basic American foreign policy of isolationism. Webster's views seem to have been derived from Washington's Farewell Address of September 17, 1796; Cass seems to have relied more on Thomas Jefferson's "entangling alliances with none" inaugural message of March 4, 1801. Washington's "Great Rule of Conduct" had allowed for "temporary alliances" for extraordinary situations, whereas Jefferson had been more categorical in advising against political connections with European states (see *Messages and Papers*, 1:213–224, 321–324). To put it another way, Webster looked more toward the past, but Cass looked more toward the future, when American policymakers tended to accept a doctrinaire definition and to ignore Washingon's qualifying phrases.

Historians have paid little attention to the Cass-Webster controversy and have totally overlooked its importance as a debate over basic American foreign policy. This neglect may be due to the vagaries of scholarship, but it also may be related to Cass's miserable handwriting. He began a letter to Webster dated February 20, 1842, with the comment that he would "not inflict upon" the secretary of state a communication in his own hand, perceiving "it would be too great a tax upon your forbearance" (see Cass to DW, February 20, 1842, DNA, RG 59, Despatches, France). Aware of the problems his nearly indecipherable scrawl created for others, Cass usually employed the services of an amanuensis while serving as minister to France. On December 11, 1842, Cass apparently had little concern about taxing Webster's forbearance, for the letter of that date could be entered in a contest for the worst handwriting of the nineteenth century. The clerks at the Department of State who prepared the copy of that letter for publication in *Senate Documents* began by misdating it 1843. Their text of the letter itself contains frequent and serious errors. For example, one sentence in Senate Document No. 223 has Cass stating that "I remark, that England never urged the United States to enter into a conventional arrangement by which joint action of the two Countries in the suppression of the slave trade might be secured" (see *Senate Documents*, 27th Cong., 3d sess., Serial 416, No. 223, p. 40). By misreading "then" for "never," those who prepared the document for publication in 1843 had Cass stating the opposite of what he had in fact written.

Although the Cass-Webster controversy ended inconclusively, with neither side prevailing, it has considerable historical significance. By the 1820s, isolationism, which called for avoiding permanent alliances and keeping to a minimum involvement in the political controversies of Europe, had become a basic dogma of American foreign policy. The only subject open to discussion was the application of the principles of isolationism to particular situations. Such discussions occurred in 1825–1826 over the proposal of President John Quincy Adams to send American delegates to the Congress of American States in Panama and in 1849–1852 over whether the United States should support the liberal revolutions that broke out in Europe in 1848 (for an analysis of the debates of 1825–1826 and 1849–1852, see Richard W. Leopold, *The Growth of American Foreign Policy: A History* [New York, 1962], pp. 22–26). The Cass-Webster correspondence printed below merits close scrutiny because it contains the only important debate over the policy of isolationism carried on between 1825 and mid-century.

FROM EDWARD EVERETT

Confidential

My dear Sir,   London 3 March 1842.

Genl. [Lewis] Cass took it into his head that I was dissatisfied with his publishing a pamphlet on the Right of Search[1] & that I evinced my dissatisfaction by slighting his letters: he is now satisfied that this opinion was groundless; & has transmitted me a copy of a singular letter he wrote you while he was laboring under that impression.[2] It is literally a *response au silence* de M. Everett. The general in his ardor makes the matter rather worse that it was. Five days only elapsed between the receipt of the first of his letters and my answer.[3] In this interval I gave copies of his pamphlet to the two persons who I thought he would most wish to see it, (he omits their names in his letter to you) vizt. Lord Ashburton & Lord Brougham and I distributed the other copies according to his wish. That I did not write him more promptly & more at length was owing solely to my having full as much as I could do, to get ready my letters public & private for the packet. You will probably trace in his extreme susceptibility and in his taking it for granted that in my letters to you I had attributed the preparation of his pamphlet to "strange" motives[4] the operation of his own consciousness that he was open to the imputation. I however (you recollect) did not make it but expressly gave him credit

1. Lewis Cass, *The Right of Search: An Examination of the Question, now in discussion, between the American and British Governments, Concerning the Right of Search. By an American* (Paris, 1842).

2. Not found.

3. Cass's first letter of January 25, 1842, sending Everett a copy of his

pamphlet on search has not been found, but it is referred to in Everett to Cass, February 1, 1842, Everett Letterbook, (Reel 26), Everett Papers, MHi (Microfilm).

4. See Everett to DW, January 31, 1842, mDW 21455, February 2, 1842, mDW 21486, and March 1, 1842, mDW 21738.

for meaning well. I doubted the expediency of an interference of that kind in a matter which Lord Ashburton's mission had placed directly in your hands.

The present packet will take out to you Genl Cass protest against the ratification of the treaty of 20th Decr. by France.[5] He has communicated it to me & I cannot but think this step also, however well meant, as of doubtful expediency. It gives great offence & can do no good. I have no doubt M. [François Pierre Guillaume] Guizot was pleased to have the protest made, as it gave him a new reason for delay till he could ascertain his position. If France does not mean to ratify the treaty it will not be on acct of our protest, & we shall bear the odium of producing a result occasioned by other causes. If France does ratify in spite of the Protest where shall we stand? As the general denounced nothing less than war his protest must either be approved or disavowed. Is it prudent or right to compel you to take either part of the alternatives?

The General informs M. Guizot at the end of his protest that on the arrival of his next despatches from home he shall be able to announce to him the President's approval of his course or the end of his mission. That remark does not need my commentary.

I am at a loss to understand this new zeal of the Genl. against these treaties. The treaties between France & England of 1831 & 1833 were precisely the same except on the extent of the zones for search. I never heard that Genl. [Andrew] Jackson's cabinet of which Genl. Cass was a member considered these treaties as so very menacing to our independence; nor did they draw forth these denunciations of War with England. Peace with England was the cardinal principle of Genl. J[ackson]'s foreign policy. Unfortunately it is not quite so popular a topic to electioneer upon. Gen C[ass] I am told breathes nothing but War & has imparted his belligerent notions to his country men at Paris. I am disposed to leave that matter to the Gv't at home. The Russian minister [Philippe Ivanovitch Brunnow] told me last Ev'g that M. Guizot would ratify the treaty & dissolve the Chambers, adding that Genl. C[ass] was duped by M Guizot

LC. MHi.

TO LEWIS CASS

No. 68.   Department of State,
Sir: Washington, 29th Augt. 1842.

You will see by the enclosed the result of the negotiations lately had in this city between this Department and Lord Ashburton. The treaty has been ratified by the President and Senate.

5. See above, Cass to Guizot, February 13, 1842, enclosed in Cass to   DW, February 15, 1842, "The Treaty of Washington," pp. 509–513.

In communicating to you this treaty, I am directed by the President to draw your particular attention to those articles which relate to the suppression of the African Slave Trade.

After full and anxious consideration of this very delicate subject, the Government of the United States has come to the conclusion which you will see expressed in the President's message to the Senate accompanying the treaty.[1]

Without intending or desiring to influence the policy of other Governments on this important subject this Government has reflected on what was due to its own character and position, as the leading maritime power on the American continent, left free to make such choice of means for the fulfilment of its duties, as it should deem best suited to its dignity. The result of their reflections has been, that it does not concur in measures which, for whatever benevolent purpose they may be adopted, or with whatever care and moderation they may be exercised, have yet a tendency to place the police of the seas in the hands of a single power. It chooses rather to follow its own laws, with its own sanction, and to carry them into execution by its own authority. Disposed to act in the spirit of the most cordial concurrence with other nations for the suppression of the African Slave Trade, that great reproach of our times, it deems it to be right nevertheless that this action, though concurrent, should be independent; and it believes that from this independence it will derive a greater degree of efficiency.

You will perceive, however, that, in the opinion of this Government, cruising against slave dealers on the coast of Africa is not all which is necessary to be done, in order to put an end to the traffic. There are markets for slaves, or the unhappy natives of Africa would not be seized, chained, and carried over the Ocean into slavery. These markets ought to be shut. And in the treaty now communicated to you, the high contracting parties have stipulated "that they will unite in all becoming representations and remonstrances, with any and all powers within whose dominions such markets are allowed to exist; and that they will urge upon all such powers the propriety and duty of closing such markets effectually at once and forever."[2]

You are furnished, then, with the American policy in regard to this interesting subject. First, Independent but cordially concurrent efforts of maritime States to suppress, as far as possible, the trade on the coast by means of competent and well appointed squadrons, to watch the shores and scour the neighboring seas. Secondly, concurrent becoming remonstrance with all Governments who tolerate within their territories,

1. Tyler's message of August 11, 1842, accompanying the Treaty of Washington is in *Messages and Papers*, 4:162–169.

2. DW refers to Article 9 of the Treaty of Washington, which was directed primarily at Brazil and Spain.

markets for the purchase of African negroes. There is much reason to believe, that if other States professing equal hostility to this nefarious traffic, would give their own powerful concurrence and cooperation to these remonstrances, the general effect would be satisfactory, and that the cupidity and crimes of individuals would at length cease to find both their temptation and their reward in the bosom of Christian States, and in the permission of Christian Governments.

It will still remain for each Government to revise, execute, and make more effectual, its own municipal laws, against its subjects or citizens who shall be concerned in, or in any way give aid or countenance to others concerned in this traffic.

You are at liberty to make the contents of this despatch known to the French Government. I have the honor to be, Sir, your obedient servant,

Danl. Webster.

LC. DNA, RG 59 (Instructions, France).

FROM LEWIS CASS

No. 160.   Legation of the United States,
Sir,   Paris, 17th September 1842.

The mail by the steam packet, which left Boston the 1st instant, has just arrived, and has brought intelligence of the ratification of the Treaties recently concluded with Great Britain. All apprehensions, therefore, of any immediate difficulties with that Country are at an end, and I do not see, that any public interest demands my further residence in Europe. I can no longer be useful here, and the state of my private affairs requires my presence at home. Under these circumstances, I beg you to submit to the President my wish for permission to retire from this mission, and to return to the United States without delay. In the hope, that there will be no objection to this measure, I shall proceed to make my arrangements to leave here about the 13th November, so as to embark in the steamer of the 19th November. I cannot delay my departure any longer, as I am anxious to finish my voyage before the winter weather.

I have therefore to pray you to favour me with an answer by the return steam packet, enclosing my letters of recall, and authorizing me to transfer the Legation to the Secretary Mr [Henry] Ledyard, as Chargé d'Affaires,[1] till a Minister can be sent out. He is every way competent to discharge the duties. I am, Sir, respectfully, your obedient servant,

Lew Cass.

LS. DNA, RG 59 (Despatches, France). Rec'd October 8, 1842.

1. For the letter of recall, see Daniel Fletcher Webster to Cass, October 11, 1842, DNA, RG 59 (Instructions, France). Ledyard (1812–1880; Columbia 1830), Cass's son-in-law, was secretary of the legation in Paris from 1839 to 1842 and chargé d'affaires from 1839 to 1845.

FROM LEWIS CASS

No. 161.   Legation of the United States,
Sir,   Paris, 3rd October 1842.

The last packet brought me your letter of August 29th,[1] announcing the conclusion of a Treaty with Great Britain, and accompanied by a copy of it, and of the correspondence between the Ministers charged with the negociations, and directing me to make known to Mr. [François Pierre Guillaume] Guizot the sentiments of the American Government upon that part of the Treaty, which provides for the cooperation of the United States in the efforts making to suppress the African Slave Trade. I thought I should best fulfil your intentions by communicating a copy, in extenso, of your letter. This I accordingly did yesterday. I trust I shall be able, before my departure, to transmit to you the acknowledgment of its receipt by Mr. Guizot.

In executing this duty, I felt too well what was due to my Government and Country, to intimate any regret to a foreign power that some declaration had not preceded the Treaty, or some stipulation accompanied it, by which the extraordinary pretension of Great Britain to search our ships, at all times and in all places, first put forth to the world by Lord Palmerston on the 27th August 1841, and on the 13th October following, again peremptorily claimed as a right by Lord Aberdeen,[2] would have been abrogated, as equally incompatible with the laws of Nations and with the independence of the United States. I confined myself, therefore, to a simple communication of your letter.

But this reserve ceases when I address my own Government, and connected as I feel my official conduct and reputation with this question of the right of search, I am sure I shall find an excuse for what might otherwise be considered presumption, if as one of the last acts of my official career, I submit to you and thr'o you to the President the peculiar circumstances in which I am placed by the conclusion of this Treaty, and by the communication of your letter to Mr. Guizot.

Before proceeding further, however, permit me to remark that no one rejoices more sincerely than I do at the termination of our difficulties with Great Britain, *so far as they are terminated.* That Country and ours have so many moral and material interests, involved in their intercourse, that their respective governments and inhabitants may well feel more than ordinary solicitude for the preservation of peace between these two great Nations. Our past history, however, will be unprofitable, if it do

1. See above, DW to Cass, August 29, 1842.

2. Palmerston to Stevenson, August 27, 1841, enclosed in Stevenson to DW, September 18, 1841, "The Crisis in Anglo-American Relations," pp. 124–134, above; and Aberdeen to Stevenson, October 13, 1841, enclosed in No. 134. Stevenson to DW, October 22, 1841, DNA, RG 59 (Despatches, Britain).

not teach us, that unjust pretensions, affecting our rights and honor are best met by being promptly repelled when first urged, and by being received in a spirit of resistance worthy the character of our people and of the great trust confided to us as the depositaries of the freest system of Government which the world has yet witnessed.

I had the honor in my letter of the 17th ulto[3] to solicit permission to return to the United States. That letter was written the day a copy of the Treaty reached Paris, and the remark which I then made to you, that "I could no longer be useful here," has been confirmed by subsequent reflection and by the receipt of your letter and of the correspondence accompanying it. I feel that I could no longer remain here honorably for myself, or advantageously for our Country. In my letter to you of the 15th February last,[4] transmitting a copy of my protest against the ratification of the Quintuple Treaty, for the suppression of the African Slave Trade, I took the liberty of suggesting the propriety of demanding from Lord Ashburton, previously to entering into any negociation, a distinct renunciation of this claim to search our vessels. I thought then as I do now, that this course was demanded by a just self respect, and would be supported by that great tribunal of public opinion which sustains our Government when right and corrects it when wrong. The pretension, itself, was one of the most flagrant outrages, which could be aimed at an independent Nation, and the mode of its enunciation was as coolly contemptuous as diplomatic ingenuity could suggest. We were told, that to the doctrine that American vessels were free from the search of foreign cruizers in time of peace, "the British Government never could or would subscribe."[5] And we were told too there was reason to expect, that the United States would themselves become converts to the same opinion, and this expectation was founded on the hope that "they would cease to confound two things which are in their nature entirely different, and would look to things and not to words."[6] And the very concluding paragraph of the British correspondence tells us, in effect, that we may take whatever course we please, but that England will adhere to this pretension to board our vessels, when and where her cruizers may find them. A portion of this paragraph is equally significant and unceremonious. "It is for the American Government (says Lord Aberdeen) alone to determine what may be due to a just regard for their national dignity and na-

3. See above.

4. See above, Cass to DW, February 15, 1842, "The Treaty of Washington," pp. 502–513.

5. The quotation is from Palmerston to Stevenson, August 27, 1841, enclosed in Stevenson to DW, September 18, 1841, "The Crisis in Anglo-American Relations," pp. 124–134, above.

6. The quotation is from Palmerston to Stevenson, August 27, 1841, enclosed in Stevenson to DW, September 18, 1842, "The Crisis in Anglo-American Relations," pp. 124–134, above.

tional independence."[7] I doubt if in the wide range of modern diplomacy, a more obnoxious claim has been urged in a more obnoxious manner.

This claim, thus asserted and supported, was promptly met and firmly repelled by the President in his message at the commencement of the last session of Congress; and in your letter to me approving the course I had adopted in relation to the question of the ratification by France of the Quintuple Treaty, you consider the principles of that message as the established policy of the Government.[8] Under these circumstances of the assertion and denial of this new claim of maritime police, the eyes of Europe were upon these two great naval powers, one of which had advanced a pretension, and avowed her determination to enforce it, which might at any moment bring them into collision. So far our national dignity was uncompromitted.

But England then urged the United States to enter into a conventional arrangement, by which we might be pledged to concur, with her in measures for the suppression of the Slave Trade. Till these we had executed our own laws in our own way. But yielding to this application, and departing from our former principle of avoiding European combinations upon subjects not American, we stipulated in a solemn Treaty that we would carry into effect our own laws, and fixed the minimum force, we would employ for that purpose.[9] Certainly a laudable desire to terminate this horrible man-stealing and man selling, may well justify us in going farther, in changing one of the fundamental principles of our policy, in order to effect this object, than we would go to effect any other. It is so much more a question of feeling than of reasoning, that we can hardly be wrong in yielding to that impulse, which leads us to desire to unite our efforts with those of other nations for the protection of the most sacred human rights. But while making so important a concession to the renewed application of England, it seems to me, we might well have said to her, *before we treat upon this matter, there is a preliminary question connected with it, which must be settled. We will do no act, which may by any possibility appear to be a recognition of your claim to search our vessels. That claim has arisen out of this very subject, or at any rate this*

---

7. The quotation is from Aberdeen to Stevenson, October 13, 1841, enclosed in No. 134. Stevenson to DW, October 22, 1841, DNA, RG 59 (Despatches, Britain).

8. See Tyler's first Annual Message, of December 7, 1841, in *Messages and Papers*, 4:74–89, esp. p. 77. DW's letter to Cass approving his conduct is April 5, 1842, "The Treaty of Washington," pp. 529–532, above.

9. Article 8 of the Treaty of Washington provided that each signatory would maintain on the coast of Africa a naval force or squadron of "not less than eighty guns." These squadrons, though independent of one another, were "to act in concert and cooperation, upon mutual consultation," for the suppression of the slave trade.

subject has been the pretext for its assertion, and if we now negociate upon it, and our concurrence is yielded, you must relinquish as solemnly as you have announced this most offensive pretension. If this is not done, by now making a conventional arrangement with you, and leaving you free to take your own course, we shall, in effect, abandon the ground we have assumed, and with it our rights and honour.

In carefully looking at the 7th and 8th articles of the Treaty,[10] providing for our cooperation in the measures for the suppression of this traffic, I do not see, that they change in the slightest degree the preexisting right claimed by Great Britain to arrest and search our vessels. That claim, as advanced both by Lord Palmerston and Lord Aberdeen, rested on the assumption that the Treaties between England and other European powers upon this subject could not be executed without its exercise, and that *the happy concurrence of these powers not only justified this exercise but rendered it indispensible.* By the recent Treaty, we are to keep a squadron upon the coast of Africa. We have kept one there for years,[11] during the whole term indeed of these efforts to put a stop to this most iniquitous commerce. The effect of the Treaty is therefore to render it obligatory upon us by a Convention to do what we have long done voluntarily; to place our municipal laws, in some measure, beyond the reach of Congress; and to increase the strength of the squadron employed on this duty. But if a British cruizer meet a vessel bearing the American flag, where there is no American ship of war to examine her, it is obvious, that it is quite as *indispensible* and *justifiable*, that the cruizer should search this vessel to ascertain her nationality, since the conclusion of the Treaty as it was before. The mutual rights of the parties are in this respect wholly untouched; their pretensions exist in full force; and what they could do prior to this arrangement they may now do; for tho' they have respectively sanctioned the employment of a force to give effect "to the laws, rights and obligations of the two Countries," yet they have not prohibited the use of any other measure, which either party may be disposed to adopt.

It is unnecessary to push these considerations farther, and in carrying them thus far, I have found the task an unpleasant one. Nothing but justice to myself could have induced me to do it. I could not clearly explain my position here, without this recapitulation. My protest of 13th February distinctly asserted that the United States would resist the pretension

10. Cass erred. Article 7 of the Webster-Ashburton Treaty provided for free and open passage of various channels along the northeastern and northwestern boundary. He should have referred to Articles 8 and 9.

11. In order to implement Article 8 of the Treaty of Washington, the African squadron was established in 1843. Prior to that time, the United States had occasionally stationed one or two vessels off the west coast of Africa, but not enough vessels to constitute a squadron or to prevent the widespread abuse of the American flag by slavers.

of England to search our vessels. I avowed at the same time, that this was but my personal declaration, liable to be confirmed or disavowed by my Government. I now find a Treaty has been concluded between Great Britain and the United States, which provides for the cooperation of the latter in efforts to abolish the Slave Trade, but which contains no renunciation by the former of the extraordinary pretension, resulting, as she said, from the exigencies of these very efforts, and which pretension I felt it my duty to denounce to the French Government. In all this I presume to offer no further judgement, than as I am personally affected by the course of the proceedings, and I feel they have placed me in a false position, whence I can escape but by returning home with the least possible delay. I trust, therefore, that the President will have felt no hesitation in granting me the permission which I asked for. I am, Sir, very respectfully, Your obedient servant.   Lew Cass

LS. DNA, RG 59 (Despatches, France). Rec'd November 7, 1842. Published in *Senate Documents*, 27th Cong., 3d sess., Serial 416, No. 223, pp. 34–37.

FROM EDWARD EVERETT

Private

My dear Sir,   London 3 Novr. 1842.

I have nothing of particular interest to communicate to you, in addition to the contents of my despatch.[1] You will find in the Morning Chronicle of yesterday, extracted from Fraser's magazine, a pretty fair specimen of the extravagant lengths of the party press. In this article there is a quotation from "John Bull," given with approbation, to the effect, that "It is certain that L'd Ashburton has discharged the duties of his mission, as the British plenipotentiary, supereminently to the satisfaction of one of the contracting parties. Throughout the whole vast territory of the United States, from the old debateable land of Maine to the mouth of the Mississippi, from the city of Newyork to the remote banks of the Missouri, there is not one single murmur of disapprobation at any one of his proceedings."[2] Would it not do good to have this article from Fraser, or some of the Articles of corresponding purport in the Morning Chronicle, inserted in some of our papers.

I ran over to Paris last week to bring my second daughter [Charlotte Brooks Everett] home; being absent from my post not quite six days. At Paris I saw General [Lewis] Cass, & he read to me his letter to You,[3] disapproving of those articles of the treaty, which relate to the suppression of the slave trade. I mention this without breach of confidence, for the General reads the letter to every one that visits him. He told me that, if

1. No. 27. Everett to DW, November 2, 1842, DNA, RG 59 (Despatches, Britain).

2. See *Fraser's Magazine*, 26 (November 1842): 579–594, esp. p. 582.

3. See above.

he had been in the Senate, he should have voted for the treaty, with a protestando. It is a little curious, that, while he makes it such an objection to the treaty, that it abandons the American ground on the right of Search, & for that reason demands his recal, the ultra liberal French press, which, on this point, might be expected to be as sharp-sighted as the General, considers the selfsame Articles as an abandonment by England of her pretensions, and taunts Mr [François Pierre Guillaume] Guizot for allowing the United States to carry a point of such magnitude, in her negotiations with great Britain, which France had been obliged to give up.

I sent you last summer the famous speech of M. [Louis Adolphe] Thiers on the Regency law.[4] After that speech was made, the King [Louis Philippe] wrote M. Thiers, the same evening, an autograph letter, saying that he should now die content. This I had from the Marquis de la Valette,[5] French Chargé d'Affaires at Turin, (who dined with me the day before yesterday), to whom M. Thiers himself told it. But, as it would be excessively difficult to arrange a ministry which should unite M. Guizot & M. Thiers, an indication like this of M. Thiers' having repossessed himself of the King's confidence, would augur the reverse of stability to M. Guizot's ministry. In fact, I judge from the tone of the French press favorable to M. Guizot, (who came into power now just two years since, vizt. 29 Octr. 1840) that a ministerial crisis is thought very likely to happen, at the next session of the chambers.

As you receive the "Examiner" at the department, I would observe, that the statement relative to the comparative quality of American & English beef & pork ascribed to me, in an extract from a speech made by Sir John [Tyssen] Tyrell,[6] which you will find in the Examiner of 29th Octr. was not, as erroneously reported, made by Sir John on my authority. I never said a word in public on the subject;—and a remark of mine quoted by Sir John on the turnip culture, & given in the same extract from his speech, in the Examiner of the 29th, bears but a faint resemblance to what I really said. I have furnished some of our editors with the means of correcting these errors, should correction be rendered necessary by invidious comments at home.[7]

4. In a speech delivered August 20, 1842, Thiers defended a regency bill designed to ensure the succession of the minority heir to the throne.

5. De la Valette (1806–1881).

6. Tyrell (1795–1877).

7. The London *Examiner* of October 29, 1842, printed a speech by Tyrell in which the Conservative member of Parliament said that Everett had acknowledged in a recent speech "that not the slightest comparison existed between American and English beef or pork." Tyrell also stated that Everett had informed him that it was impossible to grow turnips in the United States. Everett sent letters to the editors of the *North American Review* (November 3), the New York *Commercial Advertiser* (November 3), and the Washington, D.C., *National Intelligencer* (November 3)

With respect to my attendance & speaking at public meetings, I would not have you or the President deem me insensible of the great caution, which ought to be observed;—not only not to be present at any meeting, where my attendance is of doubtful expediency, but not to multiply appearances at meetings whose objects, singly taken, are unobjectionable; and wholly to abstain from any remarks, calculated to be taken in ill part, on either side of the water. With these qualifications ever present to my mind, I have been told, in my letters from America, that good was then supposed to be done by conciliatory remarks made by me, on proper occasions, at public meetings here, and the same opinion is frequently expressed to me, in this Country. Still, however, I decline more frequently than I accept invitations; and the annoyance which I feel, at seeing myself misreported is so great, that I am disposed to practice still greater forbearance in that respect. I enclose you a copy of the correspondence, which has passed between me & Sir John Tyrell[8] on the subject of the extract from his speech in the Examiner of the 29th Octr. I am as ever, dear Sir, with sincere attachment, faithfully Yours,   E. E.

Post script

I write this on a different sheet, because I do not wish my copyist to see it. I have already given you some notion of the way in which Genl. [Duff] Green has constituted himself a sort of special envoy to the English and French governments.[9] He has told me to day, that he has had interviews, (as I was already aware) with Lord Aberdeen, Sir R[obert] Peel, Lord Ripon,[10] & Mr Macgregor,[11] in which he has made overtures to them, on the part of the United States, for a treaty of commerce, on the basis of the reciprocal introduction of articles the growth & manufacture of the two Countries, on favorable terms. And the like to M. Guizot, to whom he was introduced by Genl Cass for this purpose,—a procedure quite in keeping, with some others of the worthy general. Though I was early informed of these unauthorized intrigues of Genl G[reen] with the Government here, I did not think it necessary to take any steps in consequence: Not believing that men of experience would be misled by any representations of unauthorized private individuals. Gen Green, with great coolness, told me that if the President would send out a special agent in the

---

about Tyrell's speech. See Everett Letterbook, (Reel 22), Everett Papers, MHi (Microfilm).

8. See Everett to Tyrell, October 31, 1842; Everett Letterbook, (Reel 22); Tyrell to Everett, November 2, 1842, (Reel 8); and Everett to Tyrell, November 4, 1842, (Reel 26), Everett Papers, MHi (Microfilm).

9. See, for example, Everett to DW, May 20, 1842, mDW 22501.

10. Frederick John Robinson (1782–1859), the first earl of Ripon, was president of the Board of Trade from 1841 to 1843.

11. This is probably a reference to John Macgregor (1797–1857), joint secretary to the Board of Trade from 1839 to 1847.

spring, he had so prepared the way, that the treaty would be easily made. The agent of course to be himself; for he soon added that he was coming out in the spring.

ALS. MHi. Rec'd November 26, 1842.

TO LEWIS CASS

No. 73.   Department of State,
Sir: Washington, Novr 14th 1842.
    I have the honor to acknowledge the receipt of your despatch of the 3d of October,[1] brought by the "Great Western," which arrived at New York on the 6th instant.
    It is probable you will have embarked for the United States before any communication can now reach you; but as it is thought proper that your letter should be answered, and as circumstances may possibly have occurred to delay your departure, this will be transmitted to Paris in the ordinary way.
    Your letter has caused the President considerable concern. Entertaining a lively sense of the respectable and useful manner in which you have discharged, for several years, the duties of an important foreign mission, it occasions him real regret and pain that your last official communication should be of such a character as that he cannot give to it his entire and cordial approbation.
    It appears to be intended as a sort of protest, or remonstrance, in the form of an official despatch, against a transaction of the Government to which you were not a party, in which you had no agency whatever, and for the results of which you were no way answerable. This would seem an unusual and extraordinary proceeding. In common with every other citizen of the Republic, you have an unquestionable right to form opinions upon public transactions, and the conduct of public men. But it will hardly be thought to be among either the duties or privileges of a Minister abroad, to make formal remonstrances and protests against proceedings of the various branches of the Government at home, upon subjects in relation to which he himself has not been charged with any duty, or pa[r]taken any responsibility.
    The negotiation and conclusion of the treaty of Washington were in the hands of the President and Senate. They had acted upon this important subject according to their convictions of duty, and of the public interest; and had ratified the treaty. It was a thing done: and although your opinion might be at variance with that of the President and Senate, it is not perceived that you had any cause of complaint, remonstrance, or

1. See above, Cass to DW, October 3, 1842.

protest, more than any other citizen who might entertain the same opinion.

In your letter of the 17th of September,[2] requesting your recall, you observe, "the mail by the steam packet which left Boston the 18th has just arrived, and has brought intelligence of the ratification of the treaties recently concluded with Great Britain. All apprehensions, therefore, of any immediate difficulties with that country are at an end, and I do not see that any public interest demands my further residence in Europe. I can no longer be useful here, and the state of my private affairs requires my presence at home. Under these circumstances, I beg you to submit to the President my wish for permission to retire from this mission, and to return to the United States without delay."

As you appeared, at that time, not to be acquainted with the provisions of the treaty, it was inferred that your desire to return home proceeded from the conviction, *that inasmuch as all apprehensions of immediate differences with Great Britain were at an end*, you would no longer be useful at Paris. Placing this interpretation on your letter, and believing, as you yourself allege, that your long absence abroad rendered it desirable for you to give some attention to your private affairs in this country, the President lost no time in yielding to your request, and in doing so, signified the sentiments of approbation which he entertained for your conduct abroad. You may then well imagine the great astonishment which the declaration contained in your despatch of the 3rd of October, that you could no longer remain in France honorably to yourself or advantageously to the country; and that the proceedings of this Government had placed you in a false position from which you could escape only by returning home created in his mind.

The President perceives not the slightest foundation for these opinions. He cannot see how your usefulness as Minister to France, should be terminated by the settlement of the difficulties and disputes between the United States and Great Britain. You have been charged with no duties connected with the settlement of these questions, or in any way relating to them beyond the communication to the French Government of the President's approbation of your letter of the 13th of February,[3] written without previous instructions from this Department. This Government is not informed of any other act or proceeding of your's connected with any part of the subject; nor does it know that your official conduct and character have become in any other way connected with the question of the right of search, and that letter having been approved,

2. See above, Cass to DW, September 17, 1842.

3. See above, Cass to Guizot, February 13, 1842, enclosed in Cass to DW, February 15, 1842, and DW to Cass, April 5, 1842, "The Treaty of Washington," pp. 509–513, 529–532.

and the French Government having been so informed, the President is altogether at a loss to understand how you can regard yourself as placed in a false position. If the character or conduct of any one was to be affected, it would only be the character and conduct of the President himself. The government has done nothing, most assuredly, to place you in a false position. Representing your country at a foreign court, you saw a transaction about to take place, between the Government to which you were accredited and another Power, which you thought might have a prejudicial effect on the interest of your own country. Thinking, as it is to be presumed, that the case was too pressing to wait for instructions, you presented a protest against that transaction, and your government approved your proceeding. This is your only official connection with the whole subject. If, after this, the President had sanctioned the negotiation of a treaty, and the Senate had ratified it, containing provisions in the highest degree objectionable, however the government might be discredited, your exemption from all blame and censure would have been complete. Having delivered your letter of the 13th of February to the French Government, and having received the President's approbation of that proceding, it is most manifest that you could be in no degree responsible for what should be done afterwards, and done by others. The President therefore cannot conceive what particular or personal interest of your's was affected by the subsequent negotiation here, or how the treaty, the result of that negotiation, should put an end to your usefulness as a public Minister at the court of France, or any way affect your official character or conduct.

It is impossible not to see, that such a proceeding as you have seen fit to adopt, might produce much inconvenience, and even serious prejudice to the public interests. Your opinion is against the treaty, a treaty concluded and formally ratified, and, to support that opinion, while yet in the service of the Government, you put a construction on its provisions, such as your own government does not put upon them, such as you must be aware, the enlightened public of Europe does not put upon them, and such as England herself has not put upon them as yet, so far as we know.

It may become necessary, hereafter, to publish your letter, in connexion with other correspondence of the mission;[4] and although it is not to be presumed that you looked to such publication, because such a presumption would impute to you a claim to put forth your private opinions upon the conduct of the President and Senate, in a transaction finished and concluded, through the imposing form of a public despatch, yet, if

4. In response to Senate resolutions of December 20, 1842, and February 9, 1843, the correspondence between Cass and DW was published in *Senate Documents*, 27th Cong., 3d sess., Serial 416, No. 223; see also 29th Cong., 1st sess., Serial 477, No. 377.

published, it cannot be foreseen how far England might here after rely on your authority for a construction favorable to her own pretensions, and inconsistent with the interest and honor of the United States. It is certain that you would most sedulously desire to avoid any such attitude. You would be slow to express opinions, in a solemn and official form, favorable to another government, and on the authority of which opinions that other Government might here after found new claims or set up new pretensions. It is for this reason, as well as others, that the President feels so much regret at your desire of placing your construction of the provisions of the treaty, and your objections to those provisions, according to your construction, upon the records of the government.

Before examining the several objections suggested by you, it may be proper to take notice of what you say upon the course of the negotiation. In regard to this, having observed that the national dignity of the United States had not been compromitted down to the time of the President's message to the last session of Congress, you proceed to say, "But England then urged the United States to enter into a conventional arrangement by which we might be pledged to concur with her in measures for the suppression of the Slave Trade. Till then we had executed our own laws in our own way. But yielding to this application, and departing from our former principle of avoiding European combinations upon subjects not American, we stipulated in a solemn treaty that we would carry into effect our own laws, and fixed the minimum force we could employ for that purpose."

The President cannot conceive how you should have been led to adventure upon such a statement as this. It is but a tissue of mistakes. England did not urge the United States to enter into this conventional arrangement. The United States yielded to no application from England. The proposition for abolishing the Slave Trade, as it stands in the treaty, was an American proposition; it originated with the Executive Government of the United States, which cheerfully assumes all its responsibility. It stands upon it as its own mode of fulfilling its duties and accomplishing its objects. Nor have the United States departed in this treaty, in the slightest degree, from their former principles of avoiding European combinations upon subjects not American, because the abolition of the African Slave Trade is an American subject, as emphatically as it is an European subject; and, indeed, more so, inasmuch as the Government of the United States took the first great steps in declaring that trade unlawful, and in attempting its extinction.[5] The abolition of this traffic is an object of the highest interest to the American people, and the American Government; and you seem strangely to have overlooked, altogether, the im-

5. The United States declared the slave trade illegal in 1794. 1 *U.S. Stat.* 347–349. Slave trading was declared piracy in 1820. 3 *U.S. Stat.* 600–601.

portant fact, that nearly thirty years ago, by the treaty of Ghent, the United States bound themselves, by solemn compact with England, to continue "their efforts to promote its entire abolition,"[6] both parties pledging themselves, by that treaty, to use their best endeavors to accomplish so desirable an object.

Again, you speak of an important concession, made to the renewed application of England. But the treaty let it be repeated, makes no concession to England whatever. It complies with no demand, grants no application, conforms to no request. All these statements thus by you made, and which are so exceedingly erroneous, seem calculated to hold up the idea that, in this treaty, your government has been acting a subordinate, or even a complying, part.

The President is not a little startled, that you should make such totally groundless assumptions of fact, and then leave a discreditable inference to be drawn from them. He directs me not only to repel this inference as it ought to be repelled but also to bring to your serious consideration and reflection the propriety of such an assumed narration of facts, as your despatch in this respect puts forth.

Having informed the Department that a copy of the letter of the 24th of August, addressed by me to you,[7] had been delivered to Mr. [François Pierre Guillaume] Guizot, you proceed to say, "in executing this duty, I felt too well what was due to my Government and country, to intimate my regret to a foreign Power that some declaration had not preceded the treaty, or some stipulation accompanied it, by which the extraordinary pretension of Great Britain to search our ships, at all times and in all places, first put forth to the world by Lord Palmerston on the 27th August 1841, and on the 13th October following again peremptorily claimed as a right by Lord Aberdeen, would have been abrogated, as equally incompatible with the laws of Nations and with the independence of the United States. I confined myself, therefore, to a simple communication of your letter." It may be true that the British pretension leads necessarily to consequences as broad and general as your statement. But it is no more than fair to state that pretension in the words of the British Government itself; and then it becomes matter of consideration and argument how broad and extensive it really is. The last statement of this pretension of claim by the British government is contained in Lord Aberdeen's note to Mr. [Andrew] Stevenson of the 13th October, 1841. It is in these words, "the Undersigned readily admits that to visit and search American vessels, in time of peace, when that right of search is not granted by treaty, would be an infraction of public law, and a violation of national dignity

6. Article 10 of the Treaty of Ghent. *Treaties*, 2:581.

7. The remark should refer to the instructions of August 29, 1842, vice August 24. Cass informed DW in his dispatch of October 3, 1842, above, that he had given a copy of the instruction to Guizot.

and independence. But no such right is asserted. We sincerely desire to respect the vessels of the United States; but we may reasonably expect to know what it really is that we respect. Doubtless the flag is *prima-facie* evidence of the nationality of the vessel; and if this evidence were in its nature conclusive and irrefragable, it ought to preclude any further inquiry. But it is sufficiently notorious that the flags of all nations are liable to be assumed by those who have no right or title to bear them. Mr Stevenson himself fully admits the extent to which the American flag has been employed for the purpose of covering this infamous traffic. The Undersigned joins with Mr Stevenson in deeply lamenting the evil; and he agrees with him in thinking that the United States ought not to be considered responsible for this abuse of their flag. But if all inquiry be resisted, even when carried no further than to ascertain the nationality of the vessel, and impunity be claimed for the most lawless and desperate of mankind in the commission of this fraud, the Undersigned greatly fears that it may be regarded as something like an assumption of that responsibility which has been deprecated by Mr Stevenson." . . . . . .

"The Undersigned renounces all pretension on the part of the British Government to visit and search American vessels in time of peace. Nor is it, as American, that such vessels are ever visited; but it has been the invariable practice of the British Navy, and as the Undersigned believes, of all navies in the world, to ascertain by visit the real nationality of merchant vessels met with on the high seas, if there be good reason to apprehend their illegal character." . . . . . "The Undersigned admits, that if the British cruiser should possess a knowledge of the American character of any vessel, his visitation of such vessel would be entirely unjustifiable. He further admits, that so much respect and honor are due to the American flag, that no vessel bearing it ought to be visited by a British cruiser, except under the most grave suspicion and well-founded doubts of the genuineness of its character.

"The Undersigned, although with pain, must add that if such visit should lead to the proof of the American origin of the vessel, and that she was avowedly engaged in the Slave Trade, exhibiting to view the manacles, fetters, and other usual implements of torture, or had even a number of these unfortunate beings on board, no British officer could interfere further. He might give information to the cruisers of the United States, but it could not be in his own power to arrest or impede the prosecution of the voyage and the success of the undertaking.

"It is obvious, therefore, that the utmost caution is necessary in the exercise of this right claimed by Great Britain. While we have recourse to the necessary, and indeed the only means of detecting imposture, the practice will be carefully guarded and limited to cases of strong suspicion. The Undersigned begs to assure Mr Stevenson that the most precise and positive instructions have been issued to Her Majesty's officers on this subject." Such are the words of the British claim or pretension; and it stood in this form at the delivery of the President's message to Congress in December last;[8] a message in which you are pleased to say that the British pretension was promptly met and firmly resisted.

I may now proceed to a more particular examination of the objections which you made to the treaty.

You observe that you think a just self respect required of the Government of the United States to demand of Lord Ashburton a distinct renunciation of the British claim to search our vessels, previous to entering into any negotiation. The Government has thought otherwise: and this appears to be your main objection to the treaty, if indeed, it be not the only one which is clearly and distinctly stated. The government of the United States supposed that, in this respect, it stood in a position in which it had no occasion to demand any thing, or ask for any thing, of England. The British pretension, whatever it was, or however extensive, was well known to the President, at the date of his message to Congress at the opening of the last session. And I must be allowed to remind you how the President treated this subject, in that communication.

"However desirous the United States may be," said he, "for the suppression of the slave trade, they cannot consent to interpolations into the maritime code, at the mere will and pleasure of other governments. We deny the right of any such interpolation to any one, or all the Nations of the earth without our consent. We claim to have a voice in all amendments or alterations of that code, and when we are given to understand, as in this instance, by a foreign Government, that its treaties with other Nations cannot be executed without the establishment and enforcement of new principles of maritime police, to be applied without our consent, we must employ a language neither of equivocal import, nor susceptible of misconstruction. American citizens prosecuting a lawful commerce in the African seas under the flag of their country, are not responsible for the abuse or unlawful use of that flag by others; nor can they rightfully, on account of any such alleged abuses, be interrupted, molested, or detained, while on the ocean, and if thus molested and detained, while pursuing honest voyages in the usual way, and violating no law themselves, they are unquestionably entitled to indemnity."

This declaration of the President stands, not a syllable of it has been, or will be retracted. The principles which it announces, rest on their inherent justice and propriety, on their conformity to public law; and, so far as we are concerned, on the determination and ability of the country to maintain them. To these principles the government is pledged, and that pledge it will be at all times ready to redeem.

8. *Messages and Papers*, 4:74–89.

But what is your own language on this point? You say, "this claim, (the British claim) thus asserted and supported, was promptly met and firmly repelled by the President in his message at the commencement of the last session of Congress; and in your letter to me approving the course I had adopted in relation to the question of the ratification by France of the Quintuple Treaty, you consider the principles of that message as the established policy of the Government." And you add, "so far, our national dignity was uncompromitted." If this be so, what is there which has since occurred, to compromit this dignity? You shall yourself be judge of this; because you say, in a subsequent part of your letter, that "the mutual rights of the Parties are in this respect wholly untouched." If then, the British pretension has been promptly met and firmly repelled by the President's message; if, so far, our national dignity had not been compromitted; and if, as you further say, our rights remain wholly untouched by any subsequent act or proceeding, what ground is there on which to found complaint against the treaty?

But your sentiments, on this point, do not concur with the opinions of your government. That government is of opinion that the sentiments of the message, which you so highly approve, are reaffirmed and corroborated by the treaty, and the correspondence accompanying it. The very object sought to be obtained, in proposing the mode adopted for abolishing the Slave Trade, was, to take away all pretence, whatever, for interrupting lawful commerce by the visitation of American vessels. Allow me to refer you, on this point, to the following passage in the message of the President to the Senate accompanying the treaty:[9]

"In my message at the commencement of the present session of Congress, I endeavored to state the principles which this Government supports respecting the right of search and the immunity of flags. Desirous of maintaining those principles, fully, at the same time that existing obligations should be fulfilled, I have thought it most consistent with the dignity and honor of the country that it should execute its own laws, and perform its own obligations, by its own means and its own power. The examination or visitation of the merchant vessels of one nation, by the cruisers of another, for any purposes, except those known and acknowledged by the law of Nations, under whatever restraints or regulations it may take place, may lead to dangerous results. It is far better, by other means to supersede any supposed necessity, or any motive, for such examination or visit. Interference with a merchant vessel by an armed cruiser, is always a delicate proceeding, apt to touch the point of national honor, as well as to affect the interests of individuals. It has been thought, therefore, expedient, not only in accordance with the stipulations of the treaty of Ghent, but at the same time as removing all pretext on the part

9. *Messages and Papers,* 4:162–169, esp. 167–168.

of others for violating the immunities of the American flag upon the seas, as they exist and are defined by the law of Nations, to enter into the articles now submitted to the Senate.

"The treaty which I now submit to you proposes no alteration, mitigation, or modification of the rules of the law of Nations. It provides simply that each of the two Governments shall maintain on the coast of Africa a sufficient squadron to enforce, separately and respectively, the laws, rights, and obligations of the two countries for the suppression of the Slave Trade."

In the actual posture of things, the President thought that the Government of the United States, standing on its own rights and its own solemn declarations, would only weaken its position by making such a demand as appears to you to have been expedient. We maintain the public law of the world as we receive it, and understand it to be established. We defend our own rights, and our own honor, meeting all aggression at the boundary. Here we may well stop.

You are pleased to observe that "under the circumstances of the assertion of the British claim, in the correspondence of the British Secretaries, and of its denial by the President of the United States, the eyes of Europe were upon these two great naval powers; one of which had advanced a pretension, and avowed her determination to enforce it which might at any moment bring them into collision."

It is certainly true that the attention of Europe has been very much awakened, of late years, to the general subject, and quite alive, also, to whatever might take place, in regard to it, between the United States and Great Britain. And it is highly satisfactory to find, that so far as we can learn, the opinion is universal that the government of the United States has fully sustained its rights and its dignity by the treaty which has been concluded. Europe, we believe, is happy to see that a collision which might have disturbed the peace of the whole civilized world, has been avoided, in a manner which reconciles the performance of a high national duty, and the fulfilment of positive stipulations, to the perfect immunity of flags, and the equality of nations upon the ocean. I must be permitted to add, that from every agent of the government abroad who has been heard from on the subject, with the single exception of your own letter,—(an exception most deeply regretted,)—as well as from every part of Europe where maritime rights have advocates and defenders, we have received nothing but congratulation. And at this moment, if the general sources of information may be trusted, our example has recommended itself, already, to the regard of States the most jealous of British ascendency at sea; and the treaty against which you remonstrate, may soon come to be esteemed by them, as a fit model for imitation.

Towards the close of your despatch you are pleased to say,—"By the recent treaty we are to keep a squadron upon the coast of Africa. We have kept one there for years, during the whole term, indeed, of these efforts to put a stop to this most iniquitous commerce. The effect of the treaty is, therefore, to render it obligatory upon us, by a convention, to do what we have long done involuntarily [voluntarily]; to place our municipal laws in some measure beyond the reach of Congress."

As to the effect of the treaty in placing our municipal laws in some measure beyond the reach of Congress, it is sufficient to say, that all treaties containing obligations necessarily do this. All treaties of commerce do it; and, indeed, there is hardly a treaty existing, to which the United States are party, which does not to some extent, or in some way, restrain the legislative power. Treaties could not be made without producing this effect. But your remark would seem to imply that, in your judgment, there is something derogatory to the character and dignity of the country, in thus stipulating with a foreign Power for a concurrent effort to execute the laws of each. It would be a sufficient refutation of this objection to say, that, if in this arrangement there be any thing derogatory to the character and dignity of one Party, it must be equally derogatory, since the stipulation is perfectly mutual, to the character and dignity of both. But it is derogatory to the character and dignity of neither. The objection seems to proceed still upon the implied ground that the abolition of the Slave Trade is more a duty of Great Britain, or a more leading object with her, than it is or should be with us, as if, in this great effort of civilized nations to do away [with] the most cruel traffic that ever scourged or disgraced the world, we had not as high and honorable, as just and merciful a part to act, as any other nation upon the face of the earth. Let it be forever remembered, that in this great work of humanity and justice, the United States took the lead, themselves. This government declared the Slave trade unlawful; and in this declaration it has been followed by the great Powers of Europe. This Government declared the Slave Trade to be piracy, and in this, too, its example has been followed by other States. This government—this young Government, springing up in this new world within half a century, founded on the broadest principles of civil liberty, and sustained by the moral sense and intelligence of the People, has gone in advance of all other nations in summoning the civilized world to a common effort to put down and destroy a nefarious traffic, reproachful to human nature. It has not deemed that it suffers any derogation from its character or its dignity, if in seeking to fulfil this sacred duty, it act, as far as necessary, on fair and equal terms of concert with other Powers, having in view the same praiseworthy object. Such were its sentiments when it entered into the solemn stipulations of the treaty of Ghent, such were its sentiments when it requested England to concur with us in declaring the slave trade to be piracy, and such are the sentiments which it has manifested on all other proper occasions.

In conclusion, I have to repeat the expression of the President's deep regret at the general tone and character of your letter, and to assure you of the great happiness it would have afforded him, if, concurring with the judgment of the President and Senate,—concurring with what appears to be the general sense of the country,—concurring in all the manifestations of enlightened public opinion in Europe, you had seen nothing in the treaty of the 9th of August, to which you could not give your cordial approbation. I have the honor to be, With respect, Your obedient servant,   Danl Webster.

LC. DNA, RG 59 (Instructions, France). Published in *Senate Documents*, 27th Cong., 3d sess., Serial 416, No. 223, pp. 6–13.

FROM LEWIS CASS

Sir   New York—Dec. 11th 1842

Upon my arrival here yesterday the duplicate of your letter of Nov 11.[1] was delivered to me. I embrace the first moment in my power to acknowledge its receipt.

I am too well aware of what is due from me to the government to renew, or unnecessarily to prolong, the discussion of the subject contained in my letter of Oct 3.[2] In submitting to you the views I entertained I fulfilled a duty, which, in my opinion circumstances imposed upon me. But I should consider myself obnoxious to the censure of improper interference, with which you have not sparingly reproached me, but from which I trust I shall satisfy you I am free, did I seek to make my correspondence with the Department the vehicle for obtruding my sentiments upon the government. Still I am anxious not to be misunderstood, and more especially since you give me to understand that the communications which have passed between us upon this subject, are to be published and thus submitted to the great tribunal of public opinion, which will be called upon to decide respecting the course I have deemed it necessary to adopt, as well as the manner in which I have fulfilled the task. And as you have in several instances, misapprehended my views, and adapted your reasoning to your constructions, rather than to my sentiments, and as I have full confidence in your desire to do me justice, I must beg leave briefly to lay before you such considerations connected with my letter & your comments upon it, as are essential to a correct judgment between us.

And first with respect to the procedure on my part.

You object to my whole course of action in this matter because it appears to you to be "intended as a sort of protest or remonstrance against a transaction of the government" &c.

1. Cass means November 14. See above.

2. See above, Cass to DW, October 3, 1842.

I have been very unhappy in the mode, in which I have expressed myself, if I am justly liable to this charge. My letter is not a protest or remonstrance. It is a simple answer to a despatch, which I had the honor to receive from you. In your letter of August 29[3] you communicated to me the views of the President in relation to the Treaty then recently concluded with England. And you also authorized me to make known these views to the French Government. This I did, both in conversation and in writing. Here was a despatch requiring my action, and which received it in good faith. But I did not coincide with you in opinion, respecting an important bearing of this Treaty. I thought it left us in a worse position than it found us. And so thinking, I deemed it my right, & felt it my duty, to lay before you the impression, which the matter had left upon my mind. I did so, the result is before you. Under these circumstances was I guilty of indiscretion, or of an impertinent interference, still more offensive, which, it seems to me from the tone of your letter is the construction you put upon my action?

This question will perhaps be best answered by another. Is it the duty of a diplomatic agent to receive all the communications of his government and to carry into effect instructions, sub silentio, whatever may be his own sentiments in relation to them? Or is he not bound, as a faithful representative, to communicate freely but respectfully his own views, that these may be considered, & receive their due weight, in that particular case, or other circumstances, involving similar considerations? It seems to me, that the bare enunciation of the principle is all that is necessary for my justification. I am speaking now of the propriety of my action, not of the manner in which it was performed. I may have executed the task well or ill. I may have introduced topics unadvisedly, & urged them indiscreetly. All this I leave without remark. I am only endeavoring here to free myself from the serious charge which you bring against me. If I have misapprehended the duties of an American diplomatic agent upon this subject, I am well satisfied to have withdrawn by a timely resignation from a position in which my own self respect would not permit me to remain. And I may express the conviction that there is no government, certainly none this side of Constantinople, which would not encourage rather than rebuke the free expression of the views of their representatives in Foreign Countries. But independently of this general objection to all action on my part, you present me with another, perhaps still more formidable but which is applicable only to the circumstances of this case. Without repeating in full the view you urge upon this part of the subject, I shall condense the objection into the proposition, that the expression of my sentiments to the government upon this occasion might induce England hereafter "to rely upon my authority for

3. See above, DW to Cass, August 29, 1842.

a construction favorable to her own pretensions & inconsistent with the interest & honor of the United States."

In the first place I would remark that I have written for my own government not for that of England. The publication of my letter which is to produce this result is to be the act of the government and not my act. But if the President should think that the slightest injury to the public interest would ensue from the disclosure of my views, the letter may be buried in the Archives of the Department and thus forgotten & rendered harmless.

But even were immediate publicity to be given to it, I know my own insignificance too well to believe it would produce the slightest influence upon the pretensions or the course of England. The English public & especially the English statesmen are too sagacious to need the suggestions of any foreigner, & too pertinacious in the assertion of their claims to seek his authority for their support. When England in her progress to that supremacy upon the ocean, which has been the steady object of her ambition for centuries, & will continue to be so, abandons a single pretension, after she has once advanced it, then there may be reason to believe she has adopted a system of moderation, which may be strengthened or weakened as the opinion of others is favorable or unfavorable to her. There is no evidence that that time is near. But were it otherwise, does it follow that in all discussions between nations it is the duty of every man to believe, that his own government has attained every object, which the interest or honour of the country requires, or not believing it, to remain silent, and to refrain from all representations, either to the government itself, or to the publick, with a view to the ultimate correction of the error, & to the relief of his country from a false position? I must confess I do not carry my patriotic devotion thus far. I agree, that when nations have appealed from argument to force, and where a war is raging, it is the duty of every citizen to put all other considerations behind him, and avoiding profitless & party discussions upon the past, to join with head, heart & hand to repel the common foe. At such a time I would not speak words of censure even to my countrymen, lest I should be overheard by the enemy. And that this is not with me a barren doctrine, I trust I have given sufficient evidence in perilous times. But I was not prepared for that excess of patriotic zeal, pardon me the expression, for such it appears to me, which would carry this reserve into all the actions of the government as well in peace as in war. I believe that in our recent treaty with England, sufficient precaution was not taken to guard against her claim to search our ships. This belief I entertain in common with many other citizens, in office & out of office, & I as well as they have expressed it. It has been declared in the Senate, in the public journals, in every district of our Country. And I cannot feel that this avowal of our sentiments, in whatever form it is made, whether official or unofficial, justly subjects us to the charge of taking a course, which may hereafter enable other governments to "set up new pretensions."

Permit me now to advert to the serious charge you have made against me, of venturing upon *a statement, which is a tissue of mistakes.* This statement you quote, & it is that part of my letter, in which after showing that to a certain point of time, our national honor had been preserved inviolate, I proceed to show that the subsequent course of events had not been equally fortunate. I remark, that England then urged the United States to enter into a conventional arrangement by which the joint action of the two Countries in the suppression of the slave trade might be secured. You pronounce this statement a mistake, & assert that the proposition came from our government.

That the particular mode, in which the governments should act in concert, as finally arranged in the treaty, was suggested by yourself, I never doubted. And if this is the construction I am to give to your denial of my correctness, there is no difficulty upon the subject. The question between us is untouched. All I said was that England continued to prosecute the matter, that she presented it for negociation, & that, we therefore, consented to its introduction. And if Lord Ashburton did not come out, with instructions from his government to endeavor to effect some arrangement upon this subject, the world has strangely misunderstood one of the great objects of his mission, & I have misunderstood that paragraph in your first note,[4] where you say that Lord Ashburton comes with full powers to negociate & settle all matters in discussion between England & the United States. But the very fact of his coming here, & of his acceding to any stipulations respecting the slave trade is conclusive proof, that his government were desirous to obtain the co-operation of the U.S. I had supposed our government would scarcely take the initiative in this matter & urge it upon that of Great Britain either in Washington or in London. If it did so, I can only express my regret, & confess that I have been led inadvertently into an error.

You then proceed to remark, in continuation of this *tissue of mistakes*, that in entering into this arrangement the United States did not depart from the principle of avoiding European combinations upon a subject not American, because the abolition of the slave trade is equally an American & European subject. This may be so, I may be wrong in the application of the principle. But such an erroneous conclusion scarcely justifies the epithet of an *adventurous statement one of a tissue of mistakes.* But apart from this, I still think that combinations of this kind are among the "entangling alliances" against which the great statesman, whose exposition of our Constitution will go down to posterity with the instrument

4. DW to Cass, April 5, 1842, "The   above.
Treaty of Washington," pp. 529–532,

itself, warned his Countrymen. And the perpetually recurring difficulties which are presenting themselves in the execution of the conventions between France & England upon this subject should be a caution to nations against the introduction of new maritime principles, whose operation & results it is difficult to foresee.

But is the suppression of the African slave trade one of those American objects, in the attainment of which we ought to seek the co-operation of other nations, & regulate our own duties & theirs by treaty stipulations? I do not think so. In the first place, the principle would necessarily lead us to form alliances with every maritime nation. It is not England alone whose flag rides over the seas. Other countries must co-operate, if any co-operation is necessary. And if we have made propositions to England to join us in this effort, I do not see, why we stop there & deprive ourselves of the aid which the action of other nations would afford. I doubt if the people of this country are prepared for such extensive combinations.

But again, while fully agreeing with you in all the odium you cast upon that infamous traffic, it appears to me that any object interesting to humanity, & in which nations may with propriety engage, has the same claim, if not in degree, at least in principle, upon our interference, & calls upon us for a union with other nations to effect it. It may be easily seen, not where such a doctrine would conduct us, that escapes human sagacity, but towards what ruinous consequences it leads.

You conclude this branch of the subject by informing me that you are directed by the President to bring to my "serious consideration & reflection the propriety of such an assumed narration of facts, as your despatch in this respect puts forth."

I shall not say one word to give the President any cause of offence, & if I felt that I was justly obnoxious to this censure, I should admit to the rebuke in silence. He would have a right to make it, & it would be my duty to acquiesce. But I have that confidence in his innate love of justice, that he will receive my explanations, & judge me by my words, & not by unauthorized constructions.

Now in all that I have said in the paragraph to which you allude, & which you have so strongly qualified, you have pointed out but one fact, as erroneous, & that is the assertion, that the introduction of the subject of the slave trade into the treaty was due to the application of England. And whether even this was an error depends upon the construction to be given to your explanation. All else, I repeat it, all else, to the very least idea, is matter of inference. It is my deduction from the circumstances of the case. I may be right or wrong, logically, in the conclusions I have reached, but certainly I am not morally responsible for their correctness, as I should be if I asserted merely naked facts. It is therefore with not a little astonishment I have read & re-read, what I wrote, & the commentary you have been pleased to make upon it. It is neither necessary nor proper, that I should renew the general subject of my letter, & therefore I do not feel it my duty to trouble you with any remarks respecting the views you have presented me of the pretensions of the British Govt. to search our ships. But when you proceed to array me against myself, I must claim the right to vindicate my own consistency. You quote me, & quote me correctly, as saying, that up to the delivery of the annual message of 1841 our national dignity was uncompromitted. You then ask what has since occurred to compromit this dignity, & add emphatically that I shall myself be the judge of this, because in a subsequent part of my despatch I say the mutual right of the parties are wholly unchanged. And you ask, if they are unchanged, what ground there is on which to found a complaint against the treaty. I think that a very brief retrospect will be the best answer I can give to this question, and that it will redeem me from the implied charge of inconsistency.

I never said nor intimated in my despatch to you, nor in any manner whatever, that our govt. had conceded to that of England the right to search our ships. That idea however, pervades your letter, & is very apparent in that part of it, which brings to my observation the possible effect of my views upon the English Govt. But in this you do me, tho' I am sure unintentionally, great injustice. I repeatedly state that the recent treaty leaves the rights of the parties as it found them. My difficulty is not, that we have made a positive concession, but that we have acted unadvisedly in not making the abandonment of this pretension, a previous condition to any conventional arrangement upon the general subject. I had supposed, till I read your letter, that this view was too distinctly expressed in my despatch to admit of any misconstruction. I will condense into a small space what I deem it necessary to say in defence of my consistency.

England claimed the right, in order as she said, to carry into effect certain treaties, she had formed for the suppression of the slave trade, to board & search our vessels upon the high seas, wherever she might find them. Our govt. with energy & promptitude repelled this pretension. Shortly after a Special British Ambassador arrived in our Country, having powers to treat upon this matter of the slave trade. The negociation terminated by an arrangement, which secures the co-operation of the United States in the efforts that England is making upon this subject. But not a word is said upon the serious claim, that subjects to the naval inquisition of a commercial rival our ships, which the enterprise of our merchants is sending to every part of the Globe. And yet this claim arises out of the very subject matter embraced in this treaty. We negociate with England for the suppression of the slave trade, at the very moment her statesmen are telling us, in no measured terms, that to suppress it she will violate our flag, & that she will never give up this pretension.

Now here it appears to me the Govt. should have stopped. The English negociator should have been told, we abhor as much as you do, the traffic in human beings, and we will do all that our peculiar institutions permit to put an end to it. But we will not suffer this matter to be made the pretext for wounding our honor & violating our rights. We will not take a single step, till you renounce this claim. We have denounced it already, & if we should negociate upon the subject matter, without settling this preliminary question, it may seem like an abandonment of the ground we have taken, or an indifference to the consequences.

Had this course been pursued, the sincerity of the British Govt. would have undergone a practical test, from which there would have been no escape. It would not have been necessary to quote the last despatch of Lord Aberdeen to show what he meant in another, or Lord Palmerston in the first. If such a proposition had been made & accepted, our honor would have been vindicated, our rights secured, & a bright example of sincerity & moderation would have been given to the world by a great nation. If it had been rejected, that would have proved that our cooperation in the suppression of the slave trade was a question of minor importance to be sacrificed to the preservation of a pretension intended to introduce an entire change in the maritime police of the world.

Why this very obvious course was not adopted, I am utterly at a loss to conjecture, & that it was not, is precisely the objection to which the whole arrangement is liable. Instead of the high ground we should then have occupied, we now find ourselves seriously discussing the question, whether or not England will enforce this claim. That she will do so, when her interest requires it, I have no more doubt, than I have that she has already given us abundant proofs that the received code of public law is but a feeble barrier, when it stands in the way of power & ambition. Lord Palmerston & Lord Aberdeen both tell us she will.

You refer to that part of my letter in which I observe, that the effect of the new stipulation is to place our municipal laws in some measure beyond the reach of Congress, & remark, that such is often the effect of commercial treaties. It is so, & we can only expect to obtain commercial advantages by stipulations for corresponding advantages, which, while they endure are beyond the reach of ordinary legislation. This is matter of necessity. But this necessity does not exist in the punishment of crimes. We are able to enforce our own laws. And I do not see, that the power to enforce those of England gives us any just compensation for permitting her to interfere in our criminal code, whether the offence is committed upon the land or upon the water. It seems to me, a principle fraught with dangerous consequences, & which a prudent government had better avoid.

There is but one other topic which I consider it necessary to advert to, but that is an important one, & I pray your indulgence, while I briefly allude to it.

You speak of the ratification of the treaty by the President & Senate, & add that it does not appear to you that I had any grounds of complaint because their opinion was at variance with mine. I submit that this is making an issue for me, which I have not made for myself. In no part of my letter will be found the slightest imputation upon the President or Senate for the ratification of this treaty. I could not make such an imputation for the plain reason that I never censured the ratification. I am under the impression that if I had had a vote to give, I should have been found among the majority upon that occasion. This, however, would have been upon the condition, that some declaration should be annexed to the act of ratification, denouncing the pretension to search our ships. I would then have sent the instrument to the British Govt., & placed upon them the responsibility of its final rejection or ratification. And I am sure we should have had the opinion of the world with us under such circumstances.

The rejection of a treaty, duly negociated is a serious question; to be avoided whenever it can be without too great a sacrifice. Though the national faith is not actually committed, still it is more or less engaged. And there were peculiar circumstances, growing out of long standing difficulties, which rendered an amicable arrangement of the various matters in dispute with England a subject of great national interest. But the negociation of a treaty *is* a far different subject. Topics are omitted or introduced at the discretion of the negociators, & they are responsible, to use the language of an eminent & able Senator, for "what it contains & what it omits."[5] This treaty in my opinion omits a most important & necessary stipulation & therefore as it seems to me, its negociation in this particular was unfortunate for the Country.

In conclusion, I beg you to tender to the President my thanks, for the kind appreciation he made of my services in the letter of recall,[6] & to express to him my hope that on a full consideration of the circumstances, he will be satisfied that if my course was not one he can approve, it at all events was such as to relieve me from the charge of an improper interference in a subject not within the sphere of my duties.

I must pray you as an act of justice, to give the same publicity to this letter, that you may give to my letter of Oct. 3d & to your answer. Very respectfully, Sir, I have the honor to be Your Obt Servt   Lew Cass.

ALS. DNA, RG 59 (Despatches, France). Published in *Senate Documents*,

5. See Thomas Hart Benton's remarks in the secret session of the Senate of August 18, 1842, in *Cong. Globe*, 27th Cong., 3d sess., app., p. 2.

6. Daniel Fletcher Webster to Cass, October 11, 1842, DNA, RG 59 (Instructions, France).

27th Cong., 3d sess., Serial 416, No. 223, pp. 37–43, where it is misdated December 11, 1843.

TO LEWIS CASS

Department of State,

Sir   Washington, 20th Decr 1842.

Your letter of the 11th instant[1] has been submitted to the President. He directs me to say, in reply, that he continues to regard your correspondence, of which this letter is part, as being quite irregular from the beginning. You had asked leave to retire from your mission; the leave was granted by the President with kind and friendly remarks upon the manner in which you had discharged its duties.[2] Having asked for this honorable recal which was promptly given, you afterwards addressed to this Department your letter of the 3rd of October,[3] which, however, it may appear to you, the President cannot but consider as a remonstrance, a protest, against the treaty of the 9th of August; in other words, an attack upon his administration, for the negotiation and conclusion of that treaty. He certainly was not prepared for this. It came upon him with no small surprise; and he still feels that you must have been, at the moment, under the influence of temporary impressions which, he cannot but hope, have ere now worn away.

A few remarks upon some of the points of your last letter must now close the correspondence.

In the first place; you object to my having called your letter of October 3rd a "protest or remonstrance" against a transaction of the government, and observe that you must have been unhappy in the mode of expressing yourself, if you are liable to this charge.

What other construction your letter will bear, I cannot perceive. The transaction was *finished*. No letter or remarks of yourself, or any one else, could undo it, if desirable. Your opinions were unsolicited. If given as a citizen, then it was altogether unusual to address them to this Department, in an official despatch; if as a public functionary, the whole subject matter was quite aside from the duties of your particular station. In your letter you did not propose any thing *to be done*, but objected to what had been done. You did not suggest any method of remedying what you were pleased to consider a defect, but stated what you thought to be reasons for fearing its consequences. You declared that there had been, in your opinion, an omission to assert American rights, to which omission you gave the Department to understand that you would never have consented.

1. See above.

2. See Cass to DW, September 17, 1842, above, and Daniel Fletcher Webster to Cass, October 11, 1842,

DNA, RG 59 (Instructions, France).

3. See above, Cass to DW, October 3, 1842.

In all this there is nothing but protest and remonstrance; and though your letter be not formally entitled such, I cannot see that it can be construed, in effect, as any thing else; and must continue to think, therefore, that the terms used are entirely applicable and proper.

In the next place you say, "You give me to understand that the communications which have passed between us on this subject, are to be published, and submitted to the great tribunal of public opinion."

It would have been better if you had quoted my remark with entire correctness. What I said was, not that the communications which have passed between us *are to be* published, or *must* be published, but that "it may become necessary hereafter to publish your letter in connection with other correspondence of the mission, and although it is not to be presumed that you looked to such publication, because such a presumption would impute to you a claim to put forth your private opinions upon the conduct of the President and Senate, in a transaction finished and concluded,—through the imposing form of a public despatch, yet, if published, it cannot be foreseen how far England might hereafter rely on your authority for a construction favorable to her own pretensions and inconsistent with the interest and honor of the United States."

In another part of your letter you observe; "The publication of my letter, which is to produce this result, is to be the act of the Government, and not my act. But if the President should think that the slightest injury to the public interest would ensue from the disclosure of my views, the letter may be buried in the Archives of the Department, and thus forgotten and rendered harmless."

To this I have to remark, in the first place, that instances have occurred, in other times, not unknown to you, in which highly important letters from Ministers of the United States in Europe to their own government, have found their way into the newspapers of Europe when that government itself held it to be inconsistent with the interests of the United States to make such letter public.[4] But it is hardly worth while to pursue a topic like this.

You are pleased to ask, "Is it the duty of a diplomatic agent to receive all the communications of his government and to carry into effect their instructions, *sub silentio*, whatever may be his own sentiments in relation to them? Or is he not bound, as a faithful representative, to communicate freely but respectfully his own views, that these may be considered, and receive their due weight, in that particular case, or in other

4. In 1835, while Cass was secretary of war in the Jackson administration, the president transmitted the official correspondence of the U.S. minister to France, Edward Livingston, to Congress. The publication of the correspondence in Paris newspapers irritated the French and eroded Livingston's effectiveness at the mission. See *Executive Documents*, 23d Cong., 2d sess., Serial 274, No. 174.

circumstances, involving similar considerations? It seems to me, that the bare enunciation of the principle is all that is necessary for my justification. I am speaking now of the propriety of my action, not of the manner in which it was performed. I may have executed the task well or ill. I may have introduced topics unadvisedly and urged them indiscreetly. All this I leave without remark. I am only endeavoring here to free myself from the serious charge which you bring against me. If I have misapprehended the duties of an American diplomatic agent upon this subject, I am well satisfied to have withdrawn by a timely resignation from a position in which my own self respect would not permit me to remain. And I may express the conviction that there is no Government, certainly none this side of Constantinople, which would not encourage rather than rebuke the free expression of the views of their representatives in foreign countries."

I answer, certainly not. In the letter to which you were replying, it was fully stated, that "in common with every other citizen of the Republic, you have an unquestionable right to form opinions upon public transactions, and the conduct of public men. But it will hardly be thought to be among either the duties or the privileges of a minister abroad to make formal remonstrances and protests against proceedings of the various branches of the Government at home upon subjects in relation to which he himself has not been charged with any duty, or pa[r]taken any responsibility."

You have not been requested to bestow your approbation upon the treaty, however gratifying it would have been to the President to see that in that respect, you united with other distinguished public agents abroad. Like all citizens of the Republic, you are quite at liberty to exercise your own judgment upon that as upon other transactions. But neither your observations, nor this concession cover the case. They do not show that, as a public Minister abroad, it is a part of your official functions, in a public despatch, to remonstrate against the conduct of the government at home, in relation to a transaction in which you bore no part, and for which you were no way answerable. The President and Senate must be permitted to judge for themselves in a matter solely within their control. Nor do I know that in complaining of your protest against their proceedings in a case of this kind, any thing has been done to warrant on your part an invidious and unjust reference to Constantinople. If you could show, by the general practice of diplomatic functionaries in the civilized part of the world, and, more especially, if you could show, by any precedent drawn from the conduct of the many distinguished men who have represented the government of the United States abroad, that your letter of the 3rd of October was, in its general object, tone, and character within the usual limits of diplomatic correspondence, you may be quite assured that the President would not have recourse to the code of Turkey in order to find precedents the other way.

You complain that in the letter from this Department, of the 14th of November,[5] a statement contained in yours of the 3rd of October, is called a tissue of mistakes, and you attempt to show the impropriety of this appellation.

Let the point be distinctly stated, and what you say in reply be then considered.

In your letter of October 3rd you remark "that England then urged the United States to enter into a conventional arrangement by which we might be pledged to concur with her in measures for the suppression of the slave trade. Till then, we had executed our own laws in our own way. But yielding to this application, and departing from our former principle of avoiding European combinations upon subjects not American, we stipulated in a solemn treaty that we would carry into effect our own laws, and fixed the minimum force we would employ for that purpose."

The letter of this Department of the 14th November having quoted this passage, proceeds to observe, that "the President cannot conceive how you should have been led to adventure upon such a statement as this. It is but a tissue of mistakes. England did not urge the United States to enter into this conventional arrangement. The United States yielded to no application from England. The proposition for abolishing the slave trade, as it stands in the treaty, was an American proposition, it originated with the Executive government of the United States, which cheerfully assumes all its responsibility. It stands upon it as its own mode of fulfilling its duties and accomplishing its objects. Nor have the United States departed in the slightest degree from their former principles of avoiding European combinations upon subjects not American; because the abolition of the African Slave Trade is an American subject as emphatically as it is an European subject; and indeed more so, inasmuch as the government of the United States took the first great step in declaring that trade unlawful, and in attempting its extinction. The abolition of this traffic is an object of the highest interest to the American people and the American Government, and you seem strangely to have overlooked, altogether, the important fact, that nearly thirty years ago, by the treaty of Ghent, the United States bound themselves by solemn compact with England, to continue their efforts to promote its entire abolition; both parties pledging themselves by that treaty, to use their best endeavors to accomplish so desirable an object."

Now, in answer to this, you observe in your last letter,—"that the particular mode in which the Governments should act in concert as finally arranged in the treaty, was suggested by yourself, I never doubted. And if this is the construction I am to give of your denial of my correctness,

5. See above, DW to Cass, November 14, 1842.

there is no difficulty upon the subject. The question between us is untouched. All I said was, that England continued to prosecute the matter, that she presented it for negotiation, and that we thereupon consented to its introduction. And if Lord Ashburton did not come out with instructions from his government to endeavor to effect some arrangement upon this subject, the world has strangely misunderstood one of the great objects of his mission, and I have misunderstood that paragraph in your first note when you say that Lord Ashburton comes with full powers to negotiate and settle all matters in discussion between England and the United States. But the very fact of his coming here, and of his acceding to any stipulations respecting the slave trade is conclusive proof that his Government were desirous to obtain the coöperation of the United States. I had supposed that our government would scarcely take the initiative in this matter, and urge it upon that of Great Britain, either in Washington or in London. If it did so, I can only express my regret, and confess that I have been led inadvertently into an error."

It would appear from all this, that that which in your first letter, appeared as a direct statement of facts of which you would naturally be presumed to have knowledge sinks at last into inferences and conjectures. But in attempting to escape from some of the mistakes of this tissue, you have fallen into others. "All I said was," you observe, "that England continued to prosecute the matter, that she presented it for negotiation, and that we therefore consented to its introduction." Now the English Minister no more presented this subject for negotiation than the government of the United States presented it. Nor can it be said that the United States consented to its introduction in any other sense than it may be said that the British Minister consented to it. Will you be good enough to review the series of your own assertions on this subject, and see whether they can possibly be regarded merely as a statement of your own inferences? Your only authentic fact is the general one, that the British Minister came clothed with full power to negotiate and settle all matters in discussion. This you say is conclusive proof that his government was desirous to obtain the coöperation of the United States respecting the Slave Trade and then you infer,

That England continued to prosecute this matter, and presented it for negotiation; and that the United States consented to its introduction, and give to this inference the shape of a direct statement of a fact.

You might have made the same remarks, and with the same propriety, in relation to the subject of the "Creole," that of Impressment, the Extradition of fugitive criminals, or any thing else embraced in the treaty or in the correspondence, and then have converted these inferences of your own into so many facts. And it is upon conjectures like these, it is upon such inferences of your own, that you made the direct and formal statement in your letter of the 3rd of October, that "England then urged the

United States to enter into a conventional arrangement by which we might be pledged to concur with her in measures for the suppression of the Slave Trade. Till then we had executed our own laws in our own way. But yielding to this application, and departing from our former principle of avoiding European combinations upon subjects not American, we stipulated in a solemn treaty that we would carry into effect our own laws; and fixed the minimum force we would employ for that purpose."

The President was well warranted, therefore, in requesting your serious reconsideration and review of that statement.

Suppose your letter to go before the public unanswered and uncontradicted—suppose it to mingle itself with the general political history of the country, as an official letter among the archives of the Department of State—would not the general mass of readers understand you as reciting facts, rather than as drawing your own conclusions? As stating history rather than as presenting an argument? It is of an incorrect narrative that the President complains. It is, that in your hotel at Paris, you should undertake to write a history of a very delicate part of a negotiation carried on at Washington, with which you had nothing to do, and of the history of which you had no authentic information; and which history, as you narrate it, reflects not a little on the independence, wisdom, and public spirit, of the Administration.

As of the history of this part of the negotiation you were not well informed, the President cannot but think it would have been more just in you to have refrained from any attempt to give an account of it.

You observe further, "I never mentioned in my despatch to you, nor in any manner whatever, that our Government had conceded to that of England the right to search our ships. That idea, however, pervades your letter, and is very apparent in that part of it which brings to my observation the possible effect of my views upon the English Government. But in this you do me, though I am sure unintentionally, great injustice. I repeatedly state that the recent treaty leaves the rights of the Parties as it found them. My difficulty is, not that we have made a positive concession, but that we have acted unadvisedly in not making the abandonment of this pretension a previous condition to any conventional arrangement upon the general subject.["]

On this part of your letter, I must be allowed to make two remarks.

The first is—inasmuch as the treaty gives no color or pretext whatever, to any right of searching our ships, a declaration against such a right would have been no more suitable to this treaty than a declaration against the right of sacking our towns, in time of peace, or any other outrage.

The rights of merchant vessels of the United States, on the high seas, as understood by this government, have been clearly and fully asserted.

As asserted, they will be maintained; nor would a declaration such as you propose have increased its resolution, or its ability, in this respect. The government of the United States relies on its own power, and on the effective support of the people, to assert, successfully, all the rights of all its citizens, on the sea as well as on the land; and it asks respect for these rights not as a boon or favor from any Nation. The President's message,[6] most certainly, is a clear declaration of what the country understands to be its rights, and his determination to maintain them; not a mere promise to negotiate for these rights, or to endeavor to bring other Powers into an acknowledgement of them, either express or implied. Whereas, if I understand the meaning of this part of your letter, you would have advised that something should have been offered to England which she might have regarded as a benefit, but coupled with such a declaration or condition as that, if she receive the boon, it would have been a recognition by her of a claim which we make as matter of right. The President's view of the proper duty of the government has certainly been quite different. Being convinced that the doctrine asserted by this government is the true doctrine of the law of Nations, and feeling the competency of the government to uphold and enforce it for itself, he has not sought, but on the contrary has sedulously avoided to change this ground, and to place the just rights of this country upon the assent, express or implied of any Power whatever.

The Government thought no skilfully extorted promises necessary in any such cases. It asks no such pledges of any Nation. If its character for ability and readiness to protect and defend its own rights and dignity is not sufficient to preserve them from violation, no interpolation of promise to respect them, ingeniously woven into treaties would be likely to afford such protection. And as our rights and liberties depend for existence upon our power to maintain them, general and vague protests are not likely to be more effectual than the Chinese method of defending their towns by painting grotesque and hideous figures on the walls, to fright away assailing foes.

My other remark on this portion of your letter is this:

Suppose a declaration to the effect that this treaty should not be considered as sacrificing any American rights had been appended, and the treaty thus fortified had been sent to Great Britain as you propose: and suppose that that government, with equal ingenuity had appended an equivalent written declaration that it should not be considered as sacrificing any British right, how much more defined would have been the rights of either Party, or how much clearer the meaning and interpreta-

6. Tyler's message of December 7,   74–89.
1841, is in *Messages and Papers*, 4:

tion of the treaty? Or in other words, what is the value of a protest on one side balanced by an exactly equivalent protest on the other?

No Nation is presumed to sacrifice its rights, or give up what justly belongs to it, unless it expressly stipulates that, for some good reason or adequate consideration, it does make such relinquishment; and an unnecessary asseveration that it does not intend to sacrifice just rights, would seem only calculated to invite aggression. Such proclamations would seem better devised for concealing weakness and apprehension than for manifesting conscious strength and self reliance, or for inspiring respect in others.

Towards the end of your letter you are pleased to observe:

"The rejection of a treaty, duly negotiated, is a serious question, to be avoided whenever it can be without too great a sacrifice. Though the national faith is not actually committed, still it is more or less engaged. And there were peculiar circumstances growing out of long standing difficulties which rendered an amicable arrangement of the various matters in dispute with England a subject of great national interest. But the negotiation of a treaty is a far different subject. Topics are omitted or introduced at the discretion of the negotiators, and they are responsible, to use the language of an eminent and able Senator, for 'what it contains and what it omits.' This treaty, in my opinion, omits a most important and necessary stipulation, and therefore, as it seems to me, its negotiating, in this particular, was unfortunate for the country."

The President directs me to say, in reply to this, that in the treaty of Washington, no topics were omitted, and no topics introduced, at the mere discretion of the negotiator; that the negotiation proceeded, from step to step, and from day to day, under his own immediate supervision and direction; that he himself takes the responsibility for what the treaty contains, and what it omits, and cheerfully leaves the merits of the whole to the judgment of the country.

I now conclude this letter, and close this correspondence, by repeating, once more, the expression of the President's regret, that you should have commenced it by your letter of the 3rd of October.

It is painful to him to have with you any cause of difference. He has a just appreciation of your character, and your public services, at home and abroad. He cannot but persuade himself, that you must be aware, yourself, by this time, that your letter of October was written under erroneous impressions, and that there is no foundation for the opinions, respecting the treaty, which it expresses, and that it would have been far better, on all accounts if no such letter had been written. I have the honor to be, Sir, yr obdt servt.   Danl Webster.

LC. DNA, RG 59 (Instructions, France). Published in *Senate Documents*, 27th Cong., 3d sess., Serial 416, No. 223, pp. 14–20.

FROM JOHN TYLER

Dr Sir   [February 1843]
   Sir Robert Peels speech[1] renders the publication of the correspondence
with [Lewis] Cass more urgent. Every day's delay will injure us. Let the
whole blast be at once over.[2] Yrs   J Tyler

ALS. NhHi. Published in Van Tyne, pp. 285–286.

FROM LEWIS CASS

Sir.   Detroit March 7th 1843.
   I have just received your letter dated December 20th 1842,[1] and post
marked Washington Feby 23rd 1843, which commences by stating that
my letter of the 11th instant, (that is my letter of December 11th 1842)[2]
had been submitted to the President.
   I had no desire to continue the correspondence, which has arisen between us. I had said all I felt called upon to say in my own defence, and
I had determined there to leave the subject. This determination I expressed to you, immediately before I left Washington in January, when
you intimated to me, that you should probably answer my letter of December 11th. I should not have departed from this resolution, had I not
felt it due to my self, that the actual date of the receipt of your letter
should be established. I have reason to suppose, that the correspondence
between us has ere this been submitted to Congress, and that it will thus
come before the Nation. Your late letter has no doubt made part of these
documents, and persons reading it may well suppose it was written the
20th of December last, and received by me while I was yet at Washington.
   The error will, no doubt, be readily explained at the Department, for
I need hardly say I am sure it was unintentional. But in the mean time
it may do me serious injury, for while at the seat of Government, where
this correspondence was well known, I more than once stated, that my
letter of December 11th was unanswered.
   It is essential therefore to me, that it should be known, that this statement was true, and this can now only be done by spreading the correction, as widely as the error has been spread.
   This is my first and principal reason for again writing you, and with-

1. In a speech in the House of
Commons on February 2, 1843, Sir
Robert Peel renewed the British distinction between the visit and the
search of foreign ships. See *Hansard's*, 66:86–98.
   2. The correspondence with Cass
was submitted to the Senate on February 24, 1843, and published in
Senate Documents, 27th Cong., 3d
sess., Serial 416, No. 223.
   1. See above, DW to Cass, December 20, 1842.
   2. See above, Cass to DW, December 11, 1842.

out this reason, I doubt if I should have broken the silence I intended to keep, though there are passages in your letter, that might well have induced me to depart from this resolution. The correspondence has already grown to an unreasonable length, and I am very unwilling to prolong it; but as I am compelled to write from the circumstances adverted to, I shall, without further apology, proceed to examine some of the topics presented in your last letter, and also to call to your observation some very offensive remarks, contained in your despatch of November 14th,[3] and, to my surprise, repeated in the recent one. Before doing this, however, I shall advert to one view presented in the November letter, and which the haste with which my reply was written, prevented me from considering.

Even if I had entertained a desire still further to discuss the questions, which have arisen between us out of the treaty of Washington, the course, which events connected with that treaty, are now taking, would have rendered such a measure wholly unnecessary for any purpose I had originally in view. All I feared and foretold has come to pass. The British pretension to search our ships, instead of having been put to rest, has assumed a more threatening and imposing form, by the recent declaration of the British Government, that they intend to enforce it.[4] As you already know the 17th of last September, the very day I read the treaty in a New York paper, I solicited my recall.[5] I stated to you, I felt that I could not remain abroad, honorably for myself, nor usefully for our Country, and that I considered the omission of a stipulation in that treaty, which settled the African slave trade question, to guard against the right of search or visitation, or by what other name it may please the British Government and Country to express this claim to violate our flag and to board our vessels, as a fatal error; considering particularly, that this pretension had been first put forth and justified in connexion with that traffic. And so viewing the subject, I felt that the course I had taken in France in opposition to the ratification of the quintuple treaty, which was intended to engraft this principle upon the law of Nations, had not been supported by the Government, as I thought it should have been.

In my protest to Mr. [François Pierre Guillaume] Guizot of Feby 13th 1842,[6] I had staked my diplomatic situation and character upon this support.

Your letter of April 5th 1842,[7] conveyed the Presidents approval of my

3. See above, DW to Cass, November 14, 1842.

4. This refers to Peel's speech of February 2, 1843, in *Hansard's*, 66: 86–98.

5. See above, Cass to DW, September 17, 1842.

6. See above, Cass to Guizot, February 13, 1842, enclosed in Cass to DW, February 15, 1842, "The Treaty of Washington," pp. 509–513.

7. See above, DW to Cass, April 5, 1842, "The Treaty of Washington," pp. 529–532.

conduct, and this you consider in your letter of Nov 14 1842, as taking from me all further responsibility.

You say that "having delivered my letter to Mr Guizot, and having read the President's approbation of that proceeding, it is most manifest, that you could in no degree be responsible for what should be done afterwards and done by others." You add as a corollary from this proposition, that "the President therefore cannot conceive what particular or personal interest of yours was affected by the subsequent negociation here, or how the treaty, the result of that negociation, should put an end to your usefulness as a Public Minister, at the Court of France, or in any way affect your official character or conduct."

The answer to this is so obvious, that I cannot but express my surprise, it has escaped your observation. A diplomatic agent, without instructions, takes a responsible step, which he thinks called for by the honor and the interests of his country.

He states, that he acts without the knowledge of his Government, and that if unsupported he must return home. You think, that the approval of his course by his own Government absolves him from all further responsibility, and that, happen what may, his honor and usefulness are unimpaired. My opinion is far different. If his Government approve his course upon paper and abandon in effect the measures he advocates, he cannot represent his country, as his country ought to be represented abroad. And I may safely add, that no man fit to be sent upon a foreign mission, would hesitate a moment as to the course he ought to pursue. He would not entrench himself behind his paper approval, for if he did, he would hear words of reproach, respecting his Government, which no man of honor could submit to. In my case you approved my proceedings; but as I say and believe, you did not guard against this pretension of England to search our ships, which occasioned my interposition; as it should have been guarded against; and thus, in fact, left me unsupported.

It is by this process of feeling and reasoning, that I reached the conclusion you censure, in no measured terms, and I trust you will now see, "how the treaty, the result of that negociation, should put an end to my usefulness as a public minister at the Court of France."

It put an end to it, because I said the American Government would resist the right of search.

The Government said the same thing, but unfortunately went on to make a treaty respecting the slave trade with England, without saying a word about this pretension, at the very time England had announced to the world, that she would search our ships, in order to carry into effect the treaties, she had negociated with other nations upon this very subject matter.

And now I am gravely told, that I might have remained, after this, the representative of my Country, because my official conduct and character were not affected.

I am not considering which of us is right in his view of the proper course of the Government respecting this treaty. I lay that out of the question. I contend, that, in my opinion, I was not sufficiently supported, and this being so, that I ought to have returned.

You contend that my opinion has nothing to do with the matter, that the Government took upon itself the responsibility, and therefore, even if a treaty had afterwards been negociated "contain[in]g provisions in the highest degree objectionable, however the Government might be discredited," the minister was free, and that his "usefulness" could not be thereby affected.

I shall not argue this point with you. It is a question of feeling quite as much as of reasoning, and he who would remain at a Foreign Court under these circumstances, to represent a "discredited" Government has no sentiments in common with me upon the subject. You state in your letter dated December 20th that a declaration, guarding against this claim to search our vessels would have been "no more suitable to this treaty, than a declaration against the right of sacking our towns in time of peace, or any other outrage."

You enlarge upon this proposition, and in fact a considerable portion of your letter is occupied with the defence of the omission of such a declaration. You suppose I had advanced the idea "that something should have been offered to England as a benefit, but coupled with such a declaration or condition, as that if she received the boon, it would have been a recognition by her of a claim which we make as a matter of right."

You add, that the President satisfied of the justice of the American doctrine has "avoided to change this ground, and to place the just right of the Country upon the assent express or implied of any power whatever." "The Government thought no skilfully extorted promises necessary in any such cases" &c. All this, and much more in your letter upon this topic, appear to me very extraordinary. I never made a suggestion of the nature you suppose. I never for a moment presumed the Government would hold out to England a consideration for the disavowal of this pretension. What I really said I will here repeat from my letter to you of February 15th 1842.[8] But before quoting the paragraph, I will make a quotation from what immediately precedes, to show that I had a correct notion of what would be the course of England. The *holy* Chinese war is ended and the British Army has withdrawn to the east of the Indies.[9] The

8. See above, Cass to DW, February 15, 1842, "The Treaty of Washington," pp. 502–509.

9. The British-Chinese war ended with the Treaty of Nanking on August 29, 1842, and in October British

pattern Republic as we are contemptuously called, can now be attended to.

After showing, that this pretension to search our ships, is a claim, to which this country can never submit, I remark, "the next question is, will England yield?" "It is our safer course to believe she will not, and looking to her line of policy, that too is our natural course. Wherever she has planted a foot, whether on Marsh, Moor or Mountain, under the polar circles, as under the tropics, I will not say never, that word does not belong to the deeds, of man, but rarely has she withdrawn it.

Whenever she has asserted a pretension she has adhered to it, through good report and through evil report, in prosperity and in adversity, with an iron will and a firm hand, of which the history of the world affords no equal example since the proudest days of the Roman Empire," &c, "and the time has come when we must look her designs in the face, and determine to resist or to yield. War is a great evil, but there are greater evils than war, and among these is national degradation.

This we have never yet experienced and I trust we never shall."

"If Lord Ashburton goes out with such modified propositions upon the various questions now pending between the two Governments, as you can honorably accept, the result will be a subject of lasting gratification to our Country. And more particularly if as I trust, before entering into any discussions, he is prepared to give such explanations, as will show that we have misunderstood the intentions of the British Government respecting this claim of a right to change the law of Nations, in order to accomodate it to their treaty stipulations, and its practical consequences, a claim to enter and search our vessels at all times and in all places. This preliminary proceeding would be worthy of the gravity of the circumstances and equally honorable to both governments."

Whether in all I said above, respecting the tenacity of England in the prosecution of her claims, new or old, I was justified by the characteristic traits of her history, let me be judged by the late emphatic declaration of the Chief of the British Cabinet [Robert Peel] made to the House of Commons and through them to the world, and which we are significantly told was cheered by both sides of the House; and whether I am right in saying that, I never thought of proposing that a "benefit" should be offered to England for the relinquishment of this pretension, as you allege, let me be judged by my own words.

My letter of December 11th is in accordance with these views. After stating the nature of this claim, I continue, "Now here it appears to me the Government should have stopped. The English negociation should have been told, We abhor as much as you do this traffic in human beings, and we will do all our peculiar institutions permit to put an end to it. But

---

military forces were withdrawn from Kabul, Afghanistan.

we will not suffer this matter to be made the pretext for wounding our honor and violating our rights. We will not take a single step till you have renounced this claim. We have already denounced it, and if we should negociate upon this subject matter, without settling this preliminary question, it would seem like an abandonment of the ground we have taken, or an indifference to the consequences."

This last paragraph touches, in my opinion, the true issue between us of this part of the controversy. You say, that the insertion of a declaration against the right of search "would have been no more suitable to this treaty, than a declaration against the right of sacking our towns in time of peace" &c&c, and hence draw the conclusion that its omission was both honorable and politic. As this sin of omission is the principal charge I make against this treaty, and as it is the one you labor most earnestly to reason away, I must be permitted again briefly to refer to it.

The British Government, in order as they said to execute certain treaties, they had formed for the suppression of the slave trade, claimed the right to board and examine American ships. The American Government denied this pretension, and thus stood the parties before the world. Then comes a British negociator to our shores to settle the subjects in difference between the two countries. Two of these are settled. One is this slave trade question, the very question which gave rise to the monstrous pretension, that is preparing for us so much trouble. And this is distinctly admitted in the Presidents Message which states that "after the boundary the question which seemed to threaten the greatest embarrassment was that connected with the African slave trade."[10]

You negociated upon the subject matter, knowing the construction the British Government had given to its other slave trade treaties, and knowing, what is clear in itself, as stated in my letter of October 3rd 1842,[11] and what Sir Robert Peel has now fully confirmed, that "if a British cruiser meet a vessel bearing the American flag, where there is no American Ship to examine her, it is obvious that it is quite as *indispensable* and *justifiable* that the Cruiser should search this vessel to ascertain her nationality, since the conclusion of the Treaty, as it was before."

The error, therefore, was in negociating upon this very subject <matter>, leaving to the other party to say, we have concluded an arrangement respecting the slave trade with you, since our mutual pretensions concerning the right of search have been made known. You were aware that our claim arose out of that subject <matter>, and as you have not guarded against it, we shall enforce it.

As to the analogy between such a claim and one to sack a town in time of peace, it is a sufficient answer to say that when such a pretension is

10. Cass refers to Tyler's second Annual Message, of December 6, 1842, *Messages and Papers*, 4:194–209, esp. p. 195.

11. See above, Cass to DW, October 3, 1842.

solemnly put forth to the world by England, I shall think any Government deserving the severest reprobation, which would go on and negociate upon a subject matter, connected with the origin of such a claim, without a sufficient security against it. More particularly, if as in this case, the subject matter relates to a question of general benevolence, urged upon us, no doubt by *the most philanthropic motives*, but which no just principle requires us to intermeddle with, at the sacrifice of the first attributes of our Independence.

You make some remarks upon the impropriety of requiring from any nation a solemn renunciation of an unjust pretension, and you proceed to observe, that the President, "has not sought, but, on the contrary, has sedulously avoided to change the ground, and to place the just rights of the Country upon the assent, express or implied, of any power whatever." "The Government thought no skilfully extorted promises necessary in any such cases."

As to the extortion of promises, it is a question of ethics, which has no place here.

As to the propriety of requiring a Nation formally to disavow an unjust pretension, before entering into a negociation with her; or if she will not do so, of then telling her, we shall stand upon our public denial of your claim, and will not negociate with you; it seems to me that such a course is equally honorable and politic. Is not diplomatic history full of these efforts to procure such disavowals, and who before ever expressed a doubt of the policy of these measures? Have we not, time after time, endeavoured to induce England to stipulate, that she would not impress seamen from our ships? And did you not in the course of the late negociation with Lord Ashburton strive to procure the solemn abandonment of this claim?

There is conclusive proof of this in your letter to the British Minister of August 8th 1842,[12] where you say, after having conversed with him, that "the Government of the United States does not see any utility in opening such negociation, unless the *British Government is prepared to renounce the practice in all future wars.*"

You remark also in the same letter, that both before and since the war, negociations have taken place between the two Governments, with the hope of finding some means of quieting these complaints" (of impressment.) You allude also to the convention formed for this purpose by Mr [Rufus] King in 1803, and to the "utter failure of many negociations upon the subject."

Were all these fruitless efforts so long carried on, liable to the objec-

12. See above, DW to Ashburton, August 8, 1842, "The Treaty of Wash- ington," pp. 673–679.

tion you raise, that any Nation, calling upon another to disavow an unjust pretension, weakens its own cause, and "that no interpolation of a promise to respect them (that is our rights and dignity) ingeniously woven into treaties would be likely to afford such protection?["]

Now what becomes of the analogy you seek to establish, and which by a reductio ad absurdum is intended to show that these conventional disavowals of contested pretensions are "skilfully extorted promises" inconsistent with our dignity and interest? What becomes of the claim to sack our towns in time of peace, and of "protests" which you liken to Chinese figures painted on cities to frighten away the enemy?

From the time of Washington to this day almost every administration has sought to procure from the British Government a solemn relinquishment of her claim to impress our seamen, and never before was it discovered that the effort was unworthy and dishonorable.

And during all the period of the long war between England & France, at the close of the last century and at the beginning of this, when the laws of nations and the rights of neutrals were equally contemned, how many attempts were made by our Government, to induce that of Great Britan to abandon her unjust pretensions, and to stipulate that she would no more exercise them? And that too for a "boon." Our public documents are filled with proofs of this. I shall refer to one or two which ever you will deem conclusive.

In a letter from Mr [James] Madison to Messrs [James] Monroe and [William] Pinkney, dated May 20th 1807,[13] our negociators are told that, "without a provision against impressment substantially such as is contemplated in your original instructions, no treaty is to be concluded."

Again in a letter from Mr Madison to Mr Monroe, dated January 5th 1804,[14] the former remarks that "the plan of a convention, contemplated by the President is limited to the cases of impressment of our seaman, of blockades, *of visiting and searching our vessels*, of contraband of war, and of the trade with hostile colonies, with a few other cases, affecting our maritime rights, *embracing however as inducements to Great Britan to do us justice* therein, a provision for the surrender of deserting seaman and soldiers, and for the prevention of contraband supplies to her enemies."

Then follows the plan of a convention for these purposes.

And this *projet* was the work of Mr Madison, directed by Mr [Thomas]

---

13. The instruction from Secretary of State Madison to Monroe and Pinkney, then negotiating in London on impressment, is in *ASP: FR*, 3:166–173. Pinkney (1764–1822) served as U.S. minister to Britain, 1807– 1811.

14. The full text of the instruction is in Gaillard Hunt, ed., *Writings of James Madison* (9 vols., New York, 1900–1910), 7:79–114, esp. p. 80.

Jefferson, and addressed to Mr Monroe. The "rights and dignity" of the United States were as safe in their hands as they will ever be in mortal hands.

And even if I had recommended, as I have not, a "boon" or "favor" or "benefit" to be given to England, in consideration of her relinquishment of this offensive claim, I should not have wanted higher precedents to justify me.

You object to the suggestion, I made, that a declaration should have accompanied the ratification of the treaty, denying the right to search our ships, and you ask, apparently emphatically, if this had been done, and if the British "Government with equal ingenuity had appended an equivalent written declaration that it should not be considered as sacrificing any British right, how much more defined would have been the right of either party, or how much more clear the meaning and interpretation of the treaty?"

I am very unwilling to believe you do not wish to deal sincerely with me in this matter, and I must therefore attribute the strange error you have committed, in the construction of my language, to a hasty perusal of it. Had you read it with due care you would have found, that I spoke not of an *ex parte* declaration, but of a declaration mutually assented to, and which thereby would have become a portion of the treaty. A declaration putting a construction upon the instrument, which would thus have been ratified with a knowledge of it. After meeting your assertion, that the tendency of my letter was to impute blame to the President and Senate for the ratification of the treaty, and showing, that it was not the ratification, but the negociation I censured, I add "I am under the impression if I had had a vote to give, I should have been found among the majority upon that occasion.

This, however, would have been upon the condition, that some declaration should be annexed to the act of ratification, denouncing the pretension to search our ships. I would thus have sent the instrument to the British Government, and placed upon them the responsibility of its final rejection or ratification, and I am sure we should have had the opinion of the world with us under such circumstances." I need add nothing to this branch of the subject. It is clear, that I spoke here of a conditional ratification, depending upon the assent to be given by the other party to the declaration, concerning the claim of search.

There would have been here no room for the diplomatic retort you suggest.

There could have been no counter declaration, for then the whole arrangement would have been void. As I said in my letter of December 11th "Had this course been pursued, the sincerity of the British Government would have undergone a practical test, from which there would have been no escape. It would not have been necessary to quote the last despatch of

Lord Aberdeen to show what he meant in another, or Lord Palmerston in the first. If such a proposition had been made and accepted, our honor would have been vindicated, our rights secured and a bright example of sincerity and moderation would have been given to the world by a great nation. If it had been rejected, that would have proved that our cooperation in the suppression of the slave trade was a question of minor importance, to be sacrificed to the preservation of a pretension, intended to introduce an entire change into the Maritime police of the world.["] "Why this very obvious course was not adopted I am utterly at a loss to conjecture, and that it was not, is precisely the objection to which the whole arrangement is liable. Instead of the high ground, we should then have occupied, we find ourselves seriously discussing the question, whether or not England will enforce this claim."

There was a very unco[u]rteous tone pervading your letter to me of November 14th 1842. A kind of official loftiness, which, however it may suit other meridians, does not belong to an American functionary, writing to an American Citizen.

My answer to that letter was very hastily written. It was prepared, as you will perceive, by the date and by your receipt of it, the very day the Post Master of New York handed me your communication.

I was aware that the subject ought to occupy more time, and that justice was not done to it. But you had intimated, pretty distinctly in your letter, that our correspondence was to be published, and I was apprehensive it might, some how or other, find its way to the public, before I could correct the erroneous impression, which your letter was calculated to produce. Under these circumstances my attention was drawn to the general course of reasoning, rather than to the mode in which this was conveyed. And although there were one or two paragraphs, so plainly unco[u]rteous, that they could not escape my observation, still I passed them by, having little taste for a war of words.

But in your letter, dated December 20th and received February 23rd these offensive expressions are repeated, and the same process is adopted to prove me guilty of misstatement, which is contained in the preceding letter. I met this attempt at that time, without any reference to the language which you used. I shall meet it again, but I shall take leave to precede my defence by reminding you of the comity, which an American Secretary of State owes to his countrymen. You say, "the President is not a little startled, that you should make such totally groundless assumptions of fact, and then leave a discreditable inference to be drawn from them. He directs me, not only to repel this inference, as it ought to be repelled, but also to bring to your serious consideration and reflection the propriety of such an assumed narrative of facts, as your despatch, in this respect, puts forth."

"The President cannot conceive how you should have been led to adventure upon such a statement as this. *It is but a tissue of mistakes*." "All these statements, thus by you made and which are so exceedingly erroneous" &c.

And in your last letter you say that "in attempting to escape from some of the mistakes of this tissue you have fallen into others" &c.

Following your example, it would have been easy to find a retort for these expressions, which would want neither point nor truth. But my own self respect, and still more my respect for that great tribunal of public opinion, which is to judge between us, forbid me from imitating your course upon this occasion. I would remind you, that there is nothing in your official position, nothing in our relative situation, which can justify this lofty assumption of superiority. I doubt if a parallel can be found in diplomatic history since Napolean swayed the destinies of the world.

But the use, which you make of the Presidents name, in this undignified language, is even more to be regretted, than the epithets themselves. That high functionary should not be invoked, when a private Citizen is thus assailed. Under different circumstances, such conduct might be imitated by the other party, and a system of criminations and of recrimination introduced into the correspondence of the Department, equally injurious to the public interest, and incompatible with the public honor. Upon the present occasion, no such result will happen. I have too much respect for the chief Magistracy of my country, and too much regard for the distinguished individual, who occupies that high post, to introduce his name unnecessarily into this discussion.

And notwithstanding you have appealed to him, I shall still consider the language as yours, and not as his. Many others would not be as forbearing. I say the "language," for it is that which I censure. I do not question your right, nor the right of any other person freely to examine and to meet statements and arguments at discretion. But let this be done with the courtesey of a gentleman.

I shall now proceed, as briefly as possible, to examine these charges of *an assumed narrative of facts*, of *groundless assumption, and of a tissue of mistakes*, which you have once and again preferred against me. But first, let us see what is the grave fault you alledge I have committed. I will state it in your own words.

"Before examining the several objections, suggested by you, it may be proper to take notice of what you say, upon the course of the negociation. In regard to this, having observed, that the national dignity of the United States had not been compromitted down to the time of the Presidents Message at the last Session you proceed to say, But England then urged the United States to enter into a conventional arrangement by which we might be pledged to concur with her in measures for the suppression of the slave trade. Till then we had executed our own laws in our own way. But yielding to the application, and departing from our former principle of avoiding European combinations upon subjects not American, we stipulated, in a solemn treaty, that we would carry into effect our own laws, and fixed the minimum force, we would employ for that purpose."

After this quotation you thus continue. "The President cannot conceive how you should have been led to adventure upon such a statement as this. It is but a tissue of mistakes. The United States yielded to no application from England; the proposition for abolishing the slave trade, *as it stands in the treaty*, was an American proposition; it originated with the Executive Government of the United States, which cheerfully assumes all its responsibility. It stands upon its own mode of fulfilling its duties and accomplishing its objects. Nor have the United States departed in this treaty, in the slightest degree, from their former principles of avoiding European Combinations upon subjects not American, because the abolition of the African slave trade is an American subject, as emphatically as it is an European subject, and indeed more so, inasmuch as the Government of the United States took the first great step in declaring that trade unlawful, and in attempting its extinction. The abolition of this traffic is an object of the highest interest to the American people, and the American Government; and you seem strangely to have overlooked the important fact, that nearly thirty years ago, by the treaty of Ghent, the United States bound themselves, by a solemn compact with England, to continue 'their efforts for its entire abolition,' both parties pledging themselves by that treaty to use their best endeavors to accomplish so desirable an object."

"Again you speak of an important concession made to the renewed application of England. But the treaty, let it be repeated, makes no concession whatever to England. It complies with no demand, conforms to no request. All these statements thus by you made, and which are so exceedingly erroneous, seem calculated to hold up the idea, that in this treaty your government has been acting a subordinate or even a complying part." And then follows the grandiloquent passage I have already quoted, commencing in such a solemn style, that the President was "startled" at all these grievous offences of mine.

Thus stands your charge in the letter of November 11th 1842.[15] It is renewed in that of December 20th. In my answer to the first I vindicated myself, and I tho't successfully, against your complaint, and never supposed it would again rise up in judgment against me. I told you, that you had qualified as a tissue of mistakes a paragraph, which contained one statement, as a fact, to wit: that England has urged our Government to enter into a treaty stipulation for putting an end to the slave trade to

15. Cass means to refer to DW's dispatch of November 14, 1842, above.

which we yielded. I told you still further why I, as well as the world supposed, that the application for this stipulation came from England. She had pursued this object steadily for forty years, and she had sent out a special minister charged to negociate upon that, as well as upon other subjects. We had no interest to form a slave trade convention. You refer to the treaty of Ghent, as creating obligations upon this matter, but that treaty makes not the slightest allusion to any further arrangements, and has no more connection with the treaty of Washington than with the convention respecting armed vessels upon the Lakes.

It was complete in itself, and neither required nor looked to any other stipulations between the parties. And we had executed it in good faith.

For these reasons, I supposed, that Lord Ashburton came out to propose to us to enter into another treaty upon this subject. And I thus stated it, as an historical fact. In my answer I further called to your observation, that the rest of the paragraph was matter of inference or deduction, not admitting qualifications, applicable, not to inferences, but to assertions. As I shall, bye and by, have occasion to refer again to this branch of the subject, I shall not pursue it any further at present.

In your last letter you reiterate in substance, what you had previously said, and add that "it would appear from all this, that that, which in your first letter appeared as a direct statement of fact, of which you would naturally be presumed to have had knowledge, sinks at last into inference and conjecture." Now here is a very obvious error, which by the slightest attention to what I said would have been avoided, but I will not qualify the mistake as a *tissue* of any thing.

I did not say, that the statement of facts, to which you refer, was all matter of inference. I said expressly that the statement <of facts> respecting the desire of England—that we should enter into this negociation was put forward as a well known fact, but that "all else, I repeat it, all else, to the very least idea is matter of inference." Let the correctness of this assertion be judged by a reference to the paragraph. You continue "But in attempting to escape from some of the mistakes of this tissue, you have fallen into others."

You then refer to my statement that England continued to prosecute the matter, and that we consented to its introduction. This however, it is very clear, is but the same idea before suggested and combatted in your first letter. You say the English "Minister no more presented the subject for negociation than the Government of the United States presented it."

You then ask me to "review my series of assertions on this subject and see whether they can possibly be regarded merely as a statement of your own inferences."

It would be but a waste of time to repeat what I have already said, that I assumed as a historical fact, believed by every body, that Lord Ashburton came to urge the negociation of this treaty and that upon this point we yielded to the desire of England. When you say this is one of the "inferences," to which I refer, you furnish me with language and statements which are not my own.

But after all, why this strange pertinacity in dwelling upon this point? Why this studied and repeated attempt to prove me guilty of a *tissue of mistakes*, because I believed Lord Ashburton submitted propositions upon this question of the slave trade, and that our Government acceded to them? I have already shown, that this opinion was a natural one and held in common with the Country, and I trust I shall show this still more clearly. But even if not so, how does this change the State of things? Does it prove, that the negociator was more sagacious or the treaty more useful and honorable? The result is the same, and the inquiry is therefore, confined to the process. You will please to recollect, I objected, that we had yielded to the application of England, and made a treaty upon this subject, without guarding against a dishonorable pretension, she had advanced respecting it.

This is the whole charge, which has provoked all this "startling" reproof. To this you answer, as though this answer took away all censure, that the "British Minister no more presented the subject for negociation than the government of the United States presented it." That is, in other words, *that the matter was jointly conducted and terminated.* And is it possible you can believe that this circumstance takes away the grave responsibility of an improvident arrangement which left us worse than it found us?

And what is sincerely to be deplored by every American, which led the President of the United States in his Annual Message to Congress, a document read by the world, to put a construction upon this instrument, which the English Prime Minister has contradicted in the most solemn manner and in no measured terms? The President in his Message of 1841,[16] says that this claim of "visit and enquiry" was "regarded as the right of search, presented only in a new form and expressed in different words," and he adds that he had denounced it as inadmissable by the United States. He then proceeds to speak of the recent treaty, and thus continues, "From this it will be seen that the ground assumed in the Message (to wit: that the United States would never submit to this new fangled claim of "visit and enquiry") has been fully maint[a]ined, at the same time that the stipulations of the treaty of Ghent are to be carried out in good faith by the two countries, and *that all pretence is removed for interference with our commerce for any purpose by a foreign Government.*"

This construction the English Government deny and boldly avow their

16. Cass means to refer to Tyler's second Annual Message, of December 6, 1842. The quotation is in *Messages and Papers*, 4:196.

adherence to the claim to board and examine our vessels. Now where can you find one word in the treaty, which but intimates that this question respecting "visitation" has been ever taken up or touched? Unfortunately no such word is there, nor is there any principle of sound construction, which can supply it[s] place. What I said to you in my letter of October 3rd upon this topic, may perhaps produce more impression now, than it did then. It has been marvellously confirmed. I remarked "In carefully looking at the 7th and 8th articles of the treaty, providing for the suppression of this traffic, I do not see that they change in the slightest degree the preexisting rights, claimed by Great Britan, to search our ships.

That claim, as advanced, both by Lord Palmerston and Lord Aberdeen, rests on the assumption, that the treaties between England and other European powers upon this subject, could not be executed, without its exercise, and that the *happy concurrence of these powers not only justified, but rendered it indispensable*. By the recent treaty we are to keep a squadron on the coast of Africa. We have kept one there for years[;] during the whole time, indeed, of these efforts to put a stop to this most iniquitous commerce.

The effect of the Treaty, therefore is to render it obligatory upon us, by a convention, to do what we have long done voluntarily, to place our municipal laws, in some measure beyond the reach of Congress, and to increase the strength of the squadron employed on this duty."

"But if a British cruiser meet a vessel bearing the American flag, where there is no American Ship of War to examine her, it is obvious that it is quite as *indispensable* and *justifiable*, that the cruiser should search this vessel to ascertain her nationality, since the conclusion of this treaty, as it was before. The mutual rights of the parties are, in this respect, wholly untouched, their pretensions exist in full force, and what they could do, prior to this arrangement, they may do now; for though they have respectively sanctioned the employment of a force to give effect 'to the laws, rights and obligations of the two countries,' yet they have not prohibited the use of any other measures which either party may be disposed to adopt."

What was opinion when I wrote, has now become fact.

In all this I beg not to be misunderstood. I do not wish again to subject myself to the charge, you made against me, of favoring the pretensions of England. That is one of the last offences I desire to commit, or if I know myself, that I am likely to commit.

I think the pretension she advances, to search our vessels, and to call this search a "visitation," is one of the most injurious and unjustifiable claims of modern days.

I would meet the first exercise of it by war. It leads directly to impressment, and subjects our whole Commercial Marine, to the mercy of a jealous rival. It is but another step in her march towards universal domination. I do not believe our Government have acknowledged this claim, or ever thought of acknowledging it. I believe the President and all his Cabinet are too honorable and too patriotic ever to harbor a thought of their surrendering one of our proudest national rights. But, as I said before, it is an act of omission and not of commission, I censure. It is because a treaty has been made, embracing the slave trade, and because no security is found there against the exercise of this pretension, which threatened as the President said in his Message, the greatest embarrassment and was "connected with the African slave trade."

But to return to your charge of my want of good faith in this "tissue of mistakes." In any discussion, concerning the origin and nature of the propositions, which led to the 7th and 8th articles of the treaty of Washington, respecting the slave trade, you have greatly the advantage over any antagonist.

It is a remarkable fact, and without precedent, probably, in modern diplomacy, that not one written word is to be found in the documents relating to this treaty, which passed between the negociators, and which led to this new and important stipulation. I presume these functionaries met often and conversed upon the various topics pending between them, and that then some protocol of their meeting, or some correspondence was prepared, embodying their views.

One would suppose, that this course was necessary, as well for themselves as for the information of their Governments, and I may add, in the case of the American negociator, for the information of the people, equally his Sovereign and the Sovereign of the Government he represented. Was all this omitted, or has it been suppressed? As was said by a Senator from Pennsylvania, in the debate upon the ratification of this Treaty, and said with as much truth as beauty, "The tracks of the Negociators were upon sand, and the returning tide has effaced them forever."[17]

In the question relating to impressment, there is no such reserve. We have a letter on that vital subject from each party.[18]

And yet this correspondence led to nothing, and when it was prepared, it was known, it would lead to nothing. Why it is there, it passes my comprehension to judge. When in conversation with the British Negociator,

17. See the speech by James Buchanan in the secret session of the Senate of August 9, 1842, in *Cong. Globe*, 27th Cong., 3d sess., app., pp. 101–110, esp. p. 103.

18. See above, DW to Ashburton, August 8, 1842, "The Treaty of Washington," pp. 673–679, and Ashburton to DW, August 9, 1842, in *Senate Documents*, 27th Cong., 3d sess., Serial 413, No. 1, pp. 144–145.

you found he was not prepared to make any concession upon this subject, why introduce it at all, and give his Government another opportunity to assert its pretension, and to avow its determination to enforce it? What was gained by this?

You could hardly expect to shed new light upon a question, discussed by Jefferson and Madison; and you could hardly expect, that any declaration of resistance to the practice could be more emphatic than the resistance of the last war, and the numerous remonstrances against the doctrine with which our diplomatic history abounds. An important subject is introduced into the treaty, without any discussion, and another, still more important is discussed without introduction, and with the full knowledge, that it would not be introduced. Allow me again to spread before you the paragraph you quote, and which contains the "tissue of mistakes" which occupies so conspicuous a place in your letter.

"But England then urged the United States to enter into a conventional arrangement, by which we might be pledged to concur with her in the measures for the suppression of the slave trade. Till then we had executed our own laws in our own way. But yielding to this application and departing from our former principle of avoiding European combinations upon subjects not American, we stipulated in a solemn treaty, that we would carry into effect our own laws and fixed the minimum force we would employ for that purpose." This is the whole charge, as you make it. This is the paragraph in reference to which you say, "The President cannot conceive how you should have been led to adventure upon such a statement as this." Now let us analyze this matter, and see if it is as "startling" as you suppose. How many facts are here stated, and of these, how many are denied or doubted?

First. England urged us to make a treaty for the suppression of the Slave trade.

Second. We yielded to this application.

Third. Before then we had executed our own laws in our own way.

Fourth. We departed thereby from an old principle of avoiding European combinations upon subjects not American.

Fifth. We stipulated we would carry into effect our own laws.

Sixth. We fixed the minimum force we would employ for that purpose.

Here is the whole indictment.

Now for the defence.

I suppose I may pass over the second fact. It depends entirely upon the first, and is in truth a part of it. If England urged this Treaty upon us, and we thereupon assented to the negociation of it, we of course yielded to the application. I suppose I may pass over the third fact. No one will dispute its truth. Or if it is denied, let it be shown, when before now our laws were enforced by virtue of treaty stipulations. I suppose I may pass over the fourth. It is a matter of opinion, as I said in my former letter, of inference.

No one can place it in that category of facts, for the truth of which he who advances them is morally responsible.

You say that the suppression of the slave trade is interesting to the United States, and that therefore we have not departed, in the formation of the treaty from the wholesome maxim of non-combination.

I say it is interesting also, but that our duties can be fully performed without any European combination, and that such a mutual arrangement is injurious and violates one of the articles of our political faith. And in proof of the danger of these arrangements, I refer to the "perpetually recurring difficulties which are presenting themselves in the execution of the conventions between France and England upon this subject." I suppose I may pass over the fifth fact, for no one can question, that by the treaty we do stipulate to carry into effect our own laws. The eighth article expressly declares, that the object is to "enforce the laws" &c of each of the two countries. I suppose, also, I may pass over the sixth fact, for the same eighth article provides, that the squadron to be employed in suppressing the slave trade shall "carry in all not less than eighty guns." Here is the minimum. We thus remove five of these condemned facts from the act of accusation.

There remains one to support the charge you have made, and to justify the unqualified language you have employed. And what is this solitary proof of my bad faith? Here it is. I said, that England had urged our government to enter into stipulations for suppressing the slave trade to which we had yielded. I am "startled" myself at the importance you attach to my views of this matter, and to the gravity of the reproof these have led to. I have already remarked, that all the world suppose Lord Ashburton came here with propositions upon this, as well as upon some other subject in dispute, between the two Governments. And at the moment I am writing I find in the papers an extract of a letter from Mr [Edward] Everett to you presented to the House of Representatives by Mr [Caleb] Cushing,[19] which fully confirms my previous impressions. In that letter, Mr Everett says, he was told by Lord Aberdeen on the 27th of December 1841, that Lord Ashburton was going to the United States "with full power to settle any point in discussion, embodying what was called the right of search, which was the most difficult."

And another incident comes opportunely to confirm all this. It is the statement of a Senator, who from his position ought to know the circumstances and who from his high character, is entitled to all credit. Col

19. See above, Everett to DW, December 31, 1841, "The Crisis in Anglo-American Relations," pp. 173–177. Cushing served as a congressman from Massachusetts from 1839 to 1843.

[William Rufus de Vane] King said, in the Senate on the 23rd, ulto speaking of this claim to visit our vessels,[20] "It was intollerable. Here then was a direct point of collision and that was what brought Lord Ashburton to this Country with the view of adjusting this difficulty."

I may express the surprise I felt when I read the following paragraph in your last letter, urged with as much emphasis as though the merits of the treaty and of our whole controversy, twined upon this point.

Truly when such undue importance is given to a topic, so little meriting it, when its discussion occupies seven folio pages of your last letter, and three pages of its predecessor, and when the view you present is most elaborately prepared, I may well presume, that a substantial defence of your various positions is not easily found. This is the paragraph.

"Suppose your letter to go before the public unanswered and uncontradicted; suppose it to mingle itself with the general political history of the Country as an official letter among the archives of the Department of State, would not the general mass of readers understand you as reciting facts, rather than as drawing your own conclusions?"

As stating history, rather than as presenting an Argument? It is of an incorrect narrative, that the President complains. It is that in your Hotel at Parris, you should undertake to write a history of a very delicate part of a negociation carried on at Washington, with which you had nothing to do, & of which you had no authentic information, and which history; as you narrate it, reflects not a little on the independence, wisdom, and public spirit of the Administration."

Strange indeed that this "history" and "narrative" and "delicate part of a negociation" &c-&c-&c are to be charged to a simple suggestion, or assertion if you please, that Lord Ashburton came over to make propositions to the Government respecting the slave trade, which were accepted.

But before quitting this topic I shall appeal to your own authority. You remarked to me in your letter of Nov 14 that "the United States yielded to no application from England. The proposition for abolishing the slave trade *as it stands in the treaty* was an American proposition: it originated with the Executive Government of the United States, which cheerfully assumed its responsibility." You remarked in your letter of December 20th "Now the English Minister no more presented the subject for negociation, than the Government of the United States presented it. Nor can it be said that the United States consented to its introduction in any other sense than it may be said, that the British Minister consented to it." All this is too diplomatic for me. I can neither clearly comprehend what is meant in the last quotation, nor so far as I comprehend it, can I recon-

20. King's remarks are in *Cong. Globe*, 27th Cong., 3d sess., p. 335. King (1786–1853; University of North Carolina 1803) represented Alabama in the Senate from 1819 to 1844 and was president *pro tempore* from 1836 to 1841.

cile it with the other. Whether either fairly contradicts my suggestion, that the introduction of the slave trade stipulation into the treaty was due to the application of England, I leave to those who are more competent to judge your language than I am, to determine. At first it is a guarded proposition that the provision *as it stands in the treaty*, is the work of the American Government, and at last this provision owes its paternity as much to our Government as to the other.

But I may well appeal to your own candour to say if the special pleading in the first quotation meets the issue between us.

I said, we consented to the introduction of the slave trade stipulation into the treaty, upon the application of England, and you do not spare your reproof for this assertion, through ten pages of your letter, because the proposition, *as it stands in the treaty*, was an American proposition.

But if you mean by all this, that Lord Ashburton did not make any proposition to our Government upon this subject, but that you pressed it upon him, as you would seem to intimate, in order to repel the suggestion I made, then I must be permitted to say that there is nothing more extraordinary in all our diplomatic history. I shall not enlarge upon this topic, but merely ask what benefit an American Negociator saw for his Country in this arrangement, connecting us with another nation, and exposing us, both in principle and practice, to consequences, which human sagacity cannot even conjecture? I will ask in the words of the Presidents Message: *what adjustment of a difficulty of great magnitude and importance* in relation to this matter took place, if it was not this very question. What other "embarrassment (still in the words of the Message) was connected with the African slave trade?" Both Lord Palmerston and Lord Aberdeen in 1841, expressly disavowed the right to search American vessels,[21] with a view to prevent their engaging in the slave trade—they both declared and Sir Robert Peel repeated the declaration in his last speech, (I quote the words of the last) "The right of search, connected with American Vessels we entirely disclaim, nay more, if we knew that an American Vessel was furnished with all the materials requisite for the slave trade, &c, Still we should be bound to let that vessel pass on." And that our Government knew their view is distinctly stated by the President in his Message, who says that Lord Aberdeen "expressly disclaimed all right to detain an American ship on the high seas, even if found with a cargo of slaves on board, and restricted the pretension to a mere claim to *visit and enquire*." This claim, the President adds "was regarded as the right of search, presented only in a new form, and ex-

21. See above, Palmerston to Stevenson, August 27, 1841, enclosed in Stevenson to DW, September 18, 1841, "The Crisis in Anglo-American Relations," pp. 124–134, and Aberdeen to Stevenson, October 13, 1841, enclosed in No. 134. Stevenson to DW, October 22, 1841, DNA, RG 59 (Despatches, Britain).

pressed in different words and I therefore feel it my duty to declare in my annual message to Congress that no such concession could be made, and that the United States had both the ability and inclination to enforce their own laws" &c. I repeat then, what other point remained to be *adjusted* upon this general subject, but this very claim of *visitation*, and if this was not adjusted as it is now clear it was not, what "adjustment" did take place? And why was the stipulation introduced into the treaty, as though we could not keep a squadron on the coast of Africa, and execute our own laws, without binding ourselves in a solemn convention with Great Britain to do so? And all this, you intimate, without even a request on her part.

I here close this controversy, and I shall close the correspondence by a few remarks upon the serious position, in which our Country is now placed. It affords me no pleasure to find, that all I foretold respecting the course of the British Government, in relation to this pretension to search our ships has been signally confirmed by the recent declaration of Sir Robert Peel. The accomplishment has soon, too soon, followed the prediction. I said in my letter to you of Feby 15 1842, as I have already stated, that England rarely, if ever, abandoned a pretension, and that in my opinion, she would enforce this. And in my letter to you of December 11. 1842, speaking of the probability that she would carry into effect her doctrine, I said, "That she will do so when her interest requires it, I have no more doubt, than I have, that she has already given abundant proofs that the received code of public law is but a feeble barrier, when it stands in the way of power and ambition. Both Lord Palmerston and Lord Aberdeen tell us she will." *And now a greater than either has said so*, and as the London Times expresses it,[22] he has said it in the most emphatic manner. And what then is our position? Sir Robert Peel has declared, that the British Government never will relinquish this claim to *search* our vessels, calling it a *visitation*, and the London Times, the great exponent of the principles and purposes of the English Government and Aristocracy, said, on the 31st of last December, a month before this declaration, that "England has not abandoned one tittle of her claim (to search our vessels); The treaty does not afford the smallest presumption that she has, and the United States would find, that the right would continue to be unflinchingly, (aye, that is the word) unflinchingly exercised.["] And it adds that this "essential right of the British Navy" would never be relinquished. Sir Robert Peel is a cautious statesman. He does not deal in abstractions. He does not make declarations, in the face of the world to remain inoperative, particularly when such declarations are cheered by both sides of the House in a manner to shew beyond a doubt, that they are responded to by the public feeling of the Country. And the "Times," well informed of the views of the Government a month before these were

22. See the editorial in the London *Times*, December 31, 1842.

communicated to the Nation, would not have said that *the right would be unflinchingly exercised*, if it were to remain a dead letter.

We all know to what this pretension leads, and to what it is intended to lead. That it will virtually subject our whole commercial marine to the English Navy. It is an insult to the common sense of the world, to talk about a difference in their effects, between a search for one purpose and a search for another; and to call a search to ascertain the character of a vessel and to carry her in for condemnation, at the will of a Midshipman perhaps, if he believes, or affects to believe she belongs to one country and claims to belong to another, to that great gulph, always ready to swallow American property, a British Court of Admiralty—to call, I say, such a search a *visitation*, and by this change of names to justify the pretension; all this was reserved for the nineteenth century. For what is a "visitation[?]"

It is not enough, to look at the flag, for any "bunting" as Lord Palmerston calls it, may be hoisted. It is not enough to look at the men, for all marines contain foreigners, as well as natives. It is not enough to look at the papers, for they may be simulated.

It is not enough to look at the log book, for that may be false or forged.

It is not enough to look at the cargo, for that proves nothing. But it is obvious that all these will be looked at to satisfy the inquisitor and his inquisition.

The London Sun said last year, very justly, "If the Americans sanction the examination of their ships, for the mere purpose of ascertaining if a vessel bearing the American flag is *bona fide*, an American vessel, they sanction a rigid examination of the vessel herself."[23] And it is to be borne in mind that the right to examine presupposes the right to send in, if the examination is not satisfactory to the officer, and to condemn if not satisfactory to the judge. What follows let our history from 1793 to 1815 tell.

But this is the least injury sought to be entailed upon us. Heretofore, agreeably to her own doctrine, England could only impress our seaman in time of War, for she claimed the right to board our vessels merely as a belligerent right, which ceased when she was at peace. And she conceded, and so said the Prince Regent[24] in his celebrated declaration of January 9th, 1813, in answer to the manifesto of the American Government,[25]

23. Cass quotes the *London Sun* article at length in his pamphlet *The Right of Search: An Examination of the Question, now in discussion, between the American and British Governments, concerning the Right of Search. By an American* (Paris, 1842), which is reprinted in William T. Young, *Sketch of the Life and Public Services of General Lewis Cass . . .* (Detroit, 1852), pp. 136–166, esp. p. 150.

24. George IV (1762–1830) was Prince Regent 1811–1820 and ruled as king 1820–1830.

25. The statement made in response to the American declaration

that a British Cruiser could not board an American Ship for the purpose of impressment; but that having once entered, under a legal right, then the boarding officer could seize whoever he pleased, to be transferred to a foreign Navy, there to fight against his own Country. Now the British Government has devised a plan, by which our vessels may be boarded in time of peace, and thus the whole seaman of the United States may be placed at the disposition of England in peace and war.

We now understand the full value of impressment and why Lord Ashburton would not relinquish it; and we understand what the London Times means when it says, that ["]this right of visitation, which is to be 'unflinchingly exercised,' is essential to the British Navy."

No pretension in modern times has advanced more rapidly than this. It is but a year or two since Lord Stowell, the well known English Admiralty Judge, solemnly decided that "no nation can exercise a right of *visitation*, (mark that word) and search upon the common and unappropriated part of the Ocean, except upon the belligerent claim."[26] And still later, the Duke of Wellington said in the House of Lords "that if there was one point more to be avoided than another it was that relating to the *visitation* of vessels belonging to the (American) Union."[27] The first time we heard of this pretension, as a serious claim, was from Lord Palmerston on the 27th of August 1841, and the next was from Lord Aberdeen, on the 13th of October following; and it was then put forth as "indispensable and justifiable," in the execution of certain slave trade treaties formed with the "States of Christendom." Now the British Government claim that it has become a settled part of the law of Nations. And our ships are to be searched says Sir Robert Peel to ascertain if a "grievous wrong has not been done to the American flag." This is really one of the most extraordinary assumptions of modern days.

Our flag is to be violated to see if it has been abused! The whole country knows where the "grievous wrong" would be, if this principle were carried into practice.

There are a thousand reasons, founded upon common ancestry, upon language, upon institutions and upon interests why we should earnestly desire peace with the English people. But will their Government permit it! This I doubt. England has great power, and she is not slow to exercise it. She has great pride, and she is not slow to indulge it. We are in the way, both of her ambition and of her interest; and ambition and interest need never march far in search of pretexts for war.

----

of war is in *British and Foreign State Papers 1812–1814* (116 vols., London, 1812–1925), 1 (pt. 2):1508–1520. Madison's war message is in *Messages and Papers*, 1:499–505.

26. Stowell's decision was in 1817, in the case of the *Louis*. See *International Law Digest*, 2:886, 916.

27. The speech by Arthur Wellesley, duke of Wellington (1769–1852), of August 15, 1839, is in *Hansard's*, 50:304–311, esp. p. 310.

It becomes every American to ask if he is prepared to yield this right of search. For myself I think it is better to defend the outworks, than the Citadel.

To fight for the first inch of Territory, rather than for the last. To maintain our honor when attacked, rather than to wait, till we have none to be attacked or maintained, and such I trust and hope will be the unwavering determination of the Government and of the Country.

What I anticipated when I commenced this letter has come to pass. The documents, calld for by Col [Thomas Hart] Benton, have been sent into the Senate,[28] as I perceive by the last papers. Your recent letter will now go out with the others and reach the American people. I have no means of clearing myself from the difficulties you have spread round me but by submitting my views as you have submitted yours, to the decision of the Country. I am now a private citizen. Twice since I became such, you have presented to me, in elaborately prepared documents, your sentiments upon some important topics arising out of the late treaty.

These documents now make part of the political history of the Country.

There are therefore no considerations of duty nor of propriety, to restrain me from appealing to the same great tribunal to judge between us. From endeavoring to redeem myself, from some severe charges, you have made against me. I have been written *at*, but the public have been written *to*. I shall therefore not hesitate to authorize the immediate publication of this letter, being little disposed to leave it to be buried in the Archives of the Department of State.

At the moment of signing my letter, the Presidents Message of February 27th 1843,[29] respecting the Treaty of Washington and the right of search has reached me. I think every American should go with the President in his reprobation of this doctrine. I refer however to the Message to say, that had it been in my possession when the body of this letter was prepared, I should have quoted it instead of quoting the other Messages, because in this, the views are more elaborately prepared, than in those showing that the claim of *visitation* was perfectly comprehended by our Government when this Treaty was negociated, that it was denounced as wholly inadmissable, and that the treaty was supposed to have made "a practical settlement of the question."

One or two reflections force themselves upon my mind, which I shall submit to you even at this late moment.

28. Benton called for the Cass-Webster correspondence on the Quintuple Treaty on February 3, 1843 (*Senate Journal*, 27th Cong., 3d sess., Serial 412, pp. 145–146). The documents, submitted on February 24, are published in *Senate Documents*, 27th Cong., 3d sess., Serial 416, No. 223.

29. See *Messages and Papers*, 4: 229–232.

In the first place this claim to search our vessels, under the pretence of *visiting them*, though connected in its origin, or rather announced as connected, with the African slave trade, is coextensive with the Ocean. The principles upon which it rests, as far as they rest on any, are of universal application.

For wherever a British Cruiser meets a vessel, bearing the American flag, such Cruiser may wish to know if a "grievous wrong" has been committed, and whether she is truly what she appears to be.

Such are the necessary consequences of this doctrine, and such we now ascertain is the extent to which it is to be pushed.

It is distinctly announced by Sir Robert Peel in his late speech that this right of visitation is not necessarily connected with the slave trade, and this is confirmed by the "Times" which says "that this right has obviously no intrinsic or necessary connexion with the slave trade," and "that it is a part of the Marine code of nations."

How then could a conventional arrangement, obliging us to keep a squadron upon the Coast of Africa, guard against its exercise, or "supercede," in the words of the message "any supposed necessity, or any motive for such examination or visit." Again, how could it guard against these effects, even if the operation of the doctrine were limited to search or visitation in slave trade latitudes?

England said to us, We have made a Treaty with France, by which we have a right to search her ships, and to send them in for condemnation, if they are engaged in the slave trade. If we cannot search your ships, we cannot execute this treaty, because a French Vessel by hoisting an American flag, will place herself beyond the reach of our Cruisers. Therefore we shall *visit* your ships.

Now it is manifest, that our squadron upon the coast of Africa will not change, in the slghtest degree, this state of things. A French Vessel may still hoist an American flag and thus protect a cargo of slaves, as far as this protects it, in any part of the great ocean from the African coast to the coast of Brazil. Is this squadron of 80 Guns, or is any vessel of it to be everywhere?

And where it is not, what will prevent any ship from placing an American flag at its mast head?

I am stating, not defending, the British doctrine, and I do not enter here into those obvious considerations, which demonstrate its fallacy and injustice.

This I have attempted elsewhere, but with what success, it does not become me to judge. I *have* attempted to shew that because any of the "States of Christendom" choose to form treaties for the attainment of objects, military, commercial, or *philanthropic*, such mutual arrangements give them no right to change the established laws of nations, and to stop and search our vessels upon the great highway of the world. It is the slave trade today, but it may be the sugar trade tomorrow and the cotton trade the day after. But besides it is obvious, that all the cases put by the British political casuists, in support of this new doctrine, are mere questions of identity, where he who does the deed and boards the vessel, acts, not upon his right, but upon his responsibility, and like the Sheriff, who arrests a person upon a writ, is justified or not according to the result.

But it is clear, that this claim, as asserted, is not at all inconsistent with our new treaty stipulation, that this stipulation does not render unnecessary the exercise of the claim, and therefore that as, it does not expressly, so neither does it by fair implication "make a practical settlement" of the question, nor does the "eighth article" remove "all possible pretext on the ground of mere necessity to visit and detain our ships upon the African coast, because of the alleged abuse of our flag by Slave traders of other Nations." Very respectfully, Sir I have the honor to be Your obedient servant   Lew Cass.

L S. DNA, RG 59 (Despatches, France). Rec'd March 16, 1843. Published in *Senate Documents*, 29th Cong., 1st sess., Serial 477, No. 377, pp. 229–248.

THE "BATTLE OF THE MAPS"

In a letter to Senator William Cabell Rives in 1844, Lord Ashburton referred to what he called the "battle of the maps." The controversy over which of several contemporary maps contained the true boundary as agreed to at Paris in 1783, he continued, "may remain a vexed question to puzzle future historians" (Ashburton to Rives, August 26, 1844, as cited in Howard Jones, *To the Webster-Ashburton Treaty: A Study in Anglo-American Relations, 1783–1843* [Chapel Hill, N.C., 1977], p. 102). Ashburton's words were prophetic, for the map upon which Benjamin Franklin allegedly marked with a bold red line the boundary separating British North America from the United States has never been found, and scholars continue to puzzle over the cartographical issues.

Maps played little role in the actual negotiation between Ashburton and Webster, for the diplomats tried to avoid historical and geographical arguments and sought instead a settlement by conventional line. Both before and after the signing of the Treaty of Washington on August 9, 1842, however, Webster used the Sparks and Steuben maps as propaganda devices. Jared Sparks had taken them along on his confidential trip to Augusta in May 1842 to persuade the officials of Maine to accept a negotiation for a compromise line, and Webster sent the Sparks map to Senator Rives to be employed as he saw fit in the debate over the treaty (see above, "The Treaty of Washington," pp. 556–557). Rives showed the Sparks map to his fellow senators, contending that in any future arbitration of the northeastern boundary dispute it "could not fail . . . to give increased confidence and emphasis to the pretensions of Great Britain"

(*Cong. Globe*, 27th Cong., 3d sess., app., p. 61). The validity of the Sparks document was immediately attacked by several senators. Thomas Hart Benton not only questioned the authenticity of the red line drawn by Sparks but also claimed that if it were accurate, Webster had committed "a fraud upon the British" by not revealing it to Ashburton (*Cong. Globe*, p. 16). It was the publication of the Senate debate that fueled the "battle of the maps," for George William Featherstonhaugh and Lord Palmerston took advantage of the revelation by Rives and the remarks by Benton to launch a full-scale assault on Daniel Webster and the Treaty of Washington.

The opening round of the "battle of the maps" was fired by Featherstonhaugh in February 1843, when he published a pamphlet in London entitled *Observations upon the Treaty of Washington*. Featherstonhaugh, an English geologist, had lived in the United States for many years prior to his appointment by Palmerston as the general agent of the Foreign Office on the northeastern boundary question. In 1839, after heading a British survey of that disputed boundary, he returned to England. It may have been Featherstonhaugh, moreover, who brought the King George map to the foreign minister's attention. Upon learning of the existence of the map, which upheld the American claim, Palmerston had it removed from the British Museum in 1839 and placed it in the files of the Foreign Office. As for Featherstonhaugh, he continued to be employed by the Foreign Office and wrote his *Observations* in 1843.

The pamphlet is a curious one. Featherstonhaugh concluded his ninety-six-page analysis by calling Ashburton's mission a success and praising the treaty as "an enduring monument of the moderation and wisdom of the Councils of Great Britain" (p. 96). He appended, however, an eleven-page "Supplement" to the pamphlet. After the manuscript had gone to press, he explained, he had read in the *Washington Globe* an extract of the speech in which Senator Rives revealed the existence of the Sparks map. "There being no room," Featherstonhaugh wrote, "to doubt its authenticity, we are unavoidably brought to a conviction that whilst the highest functionaries of the American Government were dealing with Lord Ashburton with a seeming integrity, they were, in fact, deceiving him." The Tyler administration, he concluded, had in its possession the cartographical evidence "that the United States never had had the slightest shadow of right to any part of the territory they have been disputing with Great Britain for near fifty years" (pp. 102–103).

Taking his lead from Featherstonhaugh, Palmerston fired another round, privately denouncing Ashburton as a "half Yankee" (see Herbert C. F. Bell, *Lord Palmerston* [2 vols., New York and Toronto, 1936], 1: 333–334) and publicly assailing the treaty in Parliament on March 21, 1843, as "a bad and very disadvantageous bargain for England" (*Hansard's*, 67:1163). On the same day, in what Webster called a manly speech (DW to Everett, April 25, 1843, below), Sir Robert Peel responded to Palmerston. After reviewing the cartographical evidence, Peel argued that all of it was inconclusive because there was no indication that any of the various maps had been officially accepted by the peacemakers in 1783. "Nothing can be more fallacious," he stated, "than founding a claim upon contemporary maps, unless you can also prove that they were adopted by the negotiators." Peel also revealed the existence of the King George map, which had been found by Ashburton in the Foreign Office upon his return to England. By pointing out that Palmerston had not revealed its existence to Webster, Peel dealt a devastating blow to the criticisms of both Palmerston and Featherstonhaugh. He countered further the accusation that Webster had acted perfidiously in not disclosing the Sparks map to Ashburton with the observation that "it is rather hard to expect that the negotiator on the part of the United States should be held bound to disclose to the diplomatist with whom he was in treaty all the weak parts of his case, and I think, therefore, that the reflection cast upon Mr. Webster—a gentleman of worth and honour—are, with respect to this matter, very unjust" (*Hansard's*, 67:1247–1249).

On the other side of the Atlantic, Webster also became embroiled in the "battle of the maps." Like Rives, he had contended only that the Sparks map would have been used by an arbiter as evidence favoring the British position if the northeastern boundary had not been resolved by a conventional line. He did not claim that the Sparks map was that agreed upon by the negotiators at Paris in 1783. In an interesting correspondence with Jared Sparks, Webster found "the contradiction of maps . . . very remarkable" (DW to Sparks, February 15, 1843, below). Sparks, on the other hand, expressed regret at ever having become involved in the controversy over maps and confessed to being mystified on the subject (Sparks to DW, February 8 and February 21, 1843, below).

Webster countered the arguments of Palmerston and Featherstonhaugh in an unsigned editorial in the Washington, D.C., *National Intelligencer*, which focused on the latter's charge that the United States had misled Ashburton by not showing him the Sparks map. Webster responded anonymously that, like lawyers, diplomats were under no obligation to maintain "the plausibility" of the other side's claim (see "The Boundary Maps," February 27, 1843, below). In a letter to Edward Everett of April 25, 1843, Webster bitterly characterized Featherstonhaugh as "shallow, and conceited, with quite a lurch towards mischief." He went on to say that he had read Peel's speech, which was the climax of the "battle of the maps," with considerable gratitude. Webster also stated that, like Peel, he found that no map was conclusive since none could definitely be dated to "*after* the Treaty was agreed to" and as bearing "marked lines, which may not have been lines of proposal, merely" (DW to Everett, April 25, 1843, below). Webster's general view, as set forth in an earlier letter to the vice president of the New-York Historical Society, was that the evidence from the various maps was "not conclusive, either way, for want of proof that any of them was marked, authentically, as shewing the line . . . on which the Commissioners ultimately agreed" (DW to Lawrence, April 24, 1843, below).

The fundamental problem in the still-unresolved "battle of the maps" is that those who negotiated the Peace of Paris in 1783 did not attach an official map to the treaty. As Hunter Miller has written, "unless we know something more about a 'red line' drawn on a copy of Mitchell's Map than that it *is* a red line on such a copy, its historical significance is nil" (*Treaties*, 3:348–349). Perhaps, as Jared Sparks observed in 1843, "little more can be done, than to place the maps in contrast, and leave them to neutralize each other" (Sparks to DW, February 21, 1843, below).

FROM JARED SPARKS

Private

Dear Sir,   Cambridge, Feb. 8th 1843

It has fallen to my task to prepare an article for the N[orth] A[merican] Review on the late treaty.[1] Mr. Gray,[2] who had it in hand, has abandoned it, & the Documents have been sent to me. On so threadbare a subject it will be in vain to say any thing new, & my only endeavor will be to set forth the principal points in as clear and forcible a manner as I can.

The business of the Paris map has taken a different turn from what I ever anticipated, & I doubt if anything would have induced me to furnish the information, if I could have foreseen that my name would have been bandied about in the Senate in the way it has been;[3] especially as it will operate to my disadvantage in the public offices in London, where it was before suspected, although without the least foundation, that I was searching for boundary matters. I still believe, however, that I did my duty, & I am not disposed to murmur at the consequences.

If any hints occur to you, which you may desire to have incorporated

1. The article by Sparks, "The Treaty of Washington," is in *North American Review*, 56 (April 1843): 452–496.

2. Probably Francis Calley Gray, with whom DW had earlier corresponded about the boundary (see above, DW to Gray, May 11, 1841, "The Crisis in Anglo-American Relations," pp. 73–75). The reference also could be to Frederick Turell Gray (1804–1855), the financial agent and publisher of the *North American Review*.

3. During the debate on the Treaty of Washington, Senator William Cabell Rives revealed that Sparks had sent to the Foreign Relations Committee what was believed to be "Franklin's Red-Line map," evidence that cast doubt on the American boundary claim. Thomas Hart Benton, however, declared that "any schoolboy or girl" could have drawn the red line on the map Sparks found. See *Cong. Globe*, 27th Cong., 3d sess., p. 121, and app., p. 61.

into the article on the treaty, I shall be glad to receive them. Such opinions as I have hitherto been able to form are entirely in favor of the Treaty.

You will recollect, that I sent to you by the hands of Mr. Dwight[4] a copy of [William] Faden's map, of 1783,—with printed notes in the margin. If this map can be readily found, I shall be much obliged if you will cause it to be returned to me by mail. I am, Sir, with great respect & regard, your most obt St.   Jared Sparks

ALS. NhD.

FROM EDWARD EVERETT

Private
My dear Sir,   London 10 Feb. 1843.

The principal topic in conversation & the papers the past week, as far as American affairs is concerned, is Mr [Jared] Sparks' map. I send you a pamphlet by Mr [George William] Featherstonehaugh, the supplement to which is the source, from which most persons here derive all they know of the facts of the case, so that their knowledge comes accompanied by his invidious comments.[1] Whether, after all, Mr Sparks' map was so certainly that, which Dr [Benjamin] Franklin marked for the Comte de Vergennes as to justify you in abandoning a claim supported by the letter of the treaty, and, as we think, by the great mass of historical and documentary evidence, including the whole series of English maps from 1755 to 1783, no one stops to enquire; nor whether you did not make precisely the use of it, which prudence & good faith required, that is, to induce a compliance, on the part of Maine & the Senate with a settlement of the question, not widely different from the line of the map, and giving Great Britain all which she had declared to be important. In denouncing the concealment of this map from Lord Ashburton, they forget the extreme & avowed jealousy, which has existed in reference to their own Archives; from which not a line relative to the negotiation of 1783 has been permitted to transpire. I must, however, do Lord Ashburton the justice to say, that he has evinced no feeling on the subject. He said, if he had been apprized of the existence & character of the map, he should have been

4. Probably Sparks's friend Edmund Dwight (1780–1849; Yale 1799), the Boston merchant and manufacturer.

1. Featherstonhaugh's pamphlet, critical of the Webster-Ashburton negotiation, was published in London in 1843. In response to the news about Sparks's red-line map, he added a supplement charging "that whilst the highest functionaries of the American Government were dealing with Lord Ashburton with a seeming integrity, they were, in fact, deceiving him," by concealing the evidence of the map. See Featherstonhaugh's *Observations upon the Treaty of Washington*, p. 102.

obliged to wait for fresh instructions, but should not have been unwilling to adopt the line which was actually agreed upon. Lord Aberdeen also said to me that, he would have agreed to the line of the treaty, even if he had been acquainted with Mr Sparks' map, so desirous was he of a settlement of the question, on what we should have been obliged, in that case, to admit were favorable terms for us. He said, however, that he could not but feel that the incident of the map had produced considerable bitterness in the public mind generally. He did not approve of the manner, in which Featherstonehaugh had brought the subject forward in the supplement to his pamphlet, which Lord A[berdeen] added was not shown to him, as it ought to have been, considering Featherstonehaugh's official connection with the Boundary question. He then passed to the topic of the Oregon territory, repeated his complaint of the manner, in which that subject is mentioned in the message of the president, at the commencement of the Session: and said he presumed of course that Dr [Lewis Fields] Linn's bill would not become a law, as that was War.[2]

The day before yesterday Lord Ashburton showed me a note, which he had received that day from a Mr Hartley offering to communicate to him the private letters and a map of Mr David Hartley, who negotiated the definitive treaty of 1783.[3] Lord Ashburton has promised to let me see them, as soon as they are sent to him. I need not say that if there is any thing bearing upon the question, I shall lose no time in acquainting you with it. Desiring my best remembrance to the President, I remain, Dear Sir, as ever affectionately Yours,   Edward Everett.

Lord Aberdeen, while expressing in strong terms the opinion, that Mr Sparks' map was certainly that marked by Franklin added that "the letter of the treaty was with us," that is, the United States.

ALS. MHi.

TO JARED SPARKS

Private & Confidential   Washington
My Dear Sir,   Feb. 15. 1843.
    I have the pleasure to acknowledge the receipt of your letter of 8th,[1] and am delighted that you are about to take the Treaty in hand. The sub-

2. In his second Annual Message, of December 6, 1842, President Tyler referred to the Oregon country as U.S. territory (*Messages and Papers*, 4: 196). Linn's bill called for fortification and occupation of the Oregon Territory and the extension of U.S. jurisdiction there. The bill passed the Senate on February 3, 1843, but the

House took no action on the measure.
    3. David Hartley signed the definitive treaty of peace with the United States in 1783. The Hartley who approached Lord Ashburton about the negotiator's private letters is not identified.
    1. See above, Sparks to DW, February 8, 1843.

ject could not be placed better. If I have any documents &c. which wd. be useful, they will be much at your service. I will see that all the speeches, &c are sent to you.

I entirely regret any publication was made about the [Benjamin] Franklin map; tho' I do not think much importance justly attaches to it. The Sender could not keep secrets, & Mr. [William Cabell] Rives' thought the matter itself of so much importance, that he must be permitted to use it.[2]

The contradiction of maps, in this case, is very remarkable, & will make a very good point in your article. [John] Mitchells map, (which was before the Commons) & the several maps published in London while the Treaty was under debatement in Parliament, & many others, are all clearly & indisputably in our favor. So is *Robert's*, which he did not alter from his former map, in his Edition of his Atlas, published *after* the Treaty of 1783, & in the preface to which he gives the boundaries, as agreed to in the Treaty.[3]

The Map you saw, & [Jean] Lattree's map,[4] (of which Mr Rives gives an account, originated, no doubt with Dr. Franklin. This map of Lattree's was public, & so was [Guillaume] *Delisles*; which last is mentioned in a postscript to a letter, which I recd from Lord A[shburton] & of which postscript I enclosed a copy.[5]

I incline to the opinion, that Dr. F[ranklin] was in an error; for, otherwise, there must have been an inconceivable blunder, in drawing up the Treaty; because nothing, as appears to me, can be suggested as a plausible reason, for placing the N. W. Angle of Nova Scotia *south* of all the waters which fall into the St Johns. There is an irreconcilable hostility, between the Franklin map, & the plain words of the Treaty. I shall enclose, tomorrow, [William] Faden's map[6] to you.

Please command me, in any thing relating to these matters. Yrs truly

Danl Webster

2. The sender was probably DW himself. On August 10, 1842, DW sent Senate Foreign Relations Committee chairman Rives two packages of "secret papers" (mDW 23143). Rives spoke for the treaty, using Sparks's evidence, on August 17 and 19. See *Cong. Globe*, 27th Cong., 3d sess., app., pp. 59–67.

3. The reference is to Robert's *Universal Atlas*, originally published in 1757.

4. Lattré, a Paris engraver, published a map of the United States in 1784. During the debate on the treaty, Senator Benton introduced the sub-ject of Lattré's map, intending to use it to discredit Sparks's map. Rives, in a devastating rebuttal, observed that the Lattré map confirmed that found by Sparks. See *Cong. Globe*, 27th Cong., 3d sess., p. 111.

5. DeLisle's (1675–1726) map of Canada was first published in 1703. The enclosure has not been found, but the original from Ashburton of August 22, 1842 (mDW 23249), informed DW that "a gentleman" had brought him a copy of DeLisle's map.

6. Faden's map, which supported the American claim, was published in London in 1785. William Faden

[The following remarks are by Jared Sparks:]

The "error" here ascribed to Franklin is by no means so clear. The position of the "North West Angle of Nova Scotia" was utterly undefined & uncertain. The Commissioners might choose for themselves where to fix it. In the first instructions to Mr. [John] Adams for negotiating the Treaty, (Secret Journal, Vol. II. p. 225), the eastern boundary then claimed by the United States is as follows;

"—a line to be drawn from the *North West angle of Nova Scotia* along the highlands which divide those rivers which empty themselves into the river St. Lawrence, from those which fall into the Atlantic Ocean, the North-western-most head of Connecticut river, — east by a line to be drawn along the middle of St. John's river *from its source* to its mouth in the Bay of Fundy."[7]

From this paragraph it is evident, that the members of the old Congress, in the year 1779, supposed the North-west angle of Nova Scotia to be at a point in the highlands north of the *source* of the St. John's river, although the words of the treaty as understood by Mr. Webster, would place this angle several hundred miles east of the point on the same range of highlands. The British say that the North-west angle was on the highlands *south* of the St. John's and there is nothing in the treaty, which positively determines which range of highlands was meant. Hence it does not follow that Franklin's line in regard to this point is erron[eous]. The words of the treaty are so vague, that they admit of either construction. In fact they define nothing.   J. S.

ALS by DW; ANS by Sparks. MH-H. The remarks after DW's signature are by Sparks.

FROM JARED SPARKS

Private

My dear Sir,   Cambridge, Feb. 21. 1843

Allow me so far to avail myself of the permission granted in your letter,[1] as to ask a single question. Mr [Thomas Hart] Benton clamors against the article concerning the navigation of the St. John's,[2] because it does not

---

was the geographer to King George III, and his map bore the inscription "A map of the Boundary of the United States, as agreed to by the treaty of 1783; by Mr. Faden, Geographer to the King." Sparks had a high regard for Faden, calling him "eminent in his profession" and his map "conclusive evidence of the state of opinion on the subject at that time in England, among those who were the most capable of forming a correct judgment." See "The Treaty of Washington," *North American Review* 56 (April 1843): 474.

7. The instructions to Adams are in Francis Wharton, ed., *Revolutionary Diplomatic Correspondence of the United States* (6 vols., Washington, D.C., 1889), 3:300–303.

1. See above.

2. Article 3 of the treaty deals with

grant the *right of way* to Maine, as it does to the British settlers along the mountains. On the first reading of the article, I did not doubt that the privilege was reciprocal, but on a further examination the language seems a little ambiguous. In regard to the inhabitants of Maine, it says, they "shall have free access *into* and through the said river;" and the British inhabitants "shall have free access *to* and through the river." Are these privileges intended to be precisely the same in both cases?[3] Can the people of Maine, on the tributaries of the St. John, take their lumber & produce across the strip of land to the St. John above Eel River, with the same freedom, that the people at the foot of the mountains can across the American territory north of the St. John? I am afraid not; and yet I do not see why they should not have been allowed to do it, since the treaty confines the privilege to the growth of produce on the tributaries of the St. John. What reason can there be for a difference in the two cases? Or does this difference find a place among the equivalents? Or is there no difference?

The conflict of maps is very extraordinary, considering the sources in which these maps originated on both sides. But I can hardly believe that Dr. [Benjamin] Franklin was mistaken, and yet I cannot explain the mystery. I think little more can be done, than to place the maps in contrast, and leave them to neutralize each other. There is no evidence that the [Friedrich Wilhelm Augustin von] Steuben map had been seen by Franklin. The "wording of the treaty," as you are aware, is copied almost literally from the instructions of Congress to the Commissioners. These instructions were written by Gouverneur Morris, who, I am persuaded, had no profound knowledge of this subject. I confess the silence of Mr. [John] Jay & Mr. [John] Adams on this question is an argument more powerful in my mind against us, than all the maps. They lived many years after the treaty of Ghent. They had freely given their opinion in regard to the true St. Croix; and why should they be silent, utterly silent, on this occasion, so important to the country, when their positive declaration could not have failed to carry the point in our favor before any tribunal?

The farther I look into the matter of the new treaty, the more I am convinced, that it is a most important & fortunate acquisition.

I enclose the memorandum,[4] which you requested, and am, Dear Sir, Respectfully & truly yours,   Jared Sparks

P.S. I this moment learn that a pamphlet, written by [George William]

---

navigation privileges on the St. John (*Treaties* 4:366–367). In his speech of August 18, 1842, Benton argued that the treaty did not grant Americans equal access to the river. See *Cong. Globe*, 27th Cong., 3d sess.,

app., p. 7.

3. In response to this question, DW wrote at the bottom of the page in his own hand: "yes—undoubtedly—."

4. The enclosure has not been found.

Featherston[haugh], has come over in the packet, in which he describes a map lately discovered in one of the public offices in London, (supposed to have been used by the commissioners) which accords with the Franklin map. He also parades with the Franklin map in an Appendix. I have not seen the pamphlet. The *Times* also has an article on the subject.[5]

I would not encroach upon your time, but if you can send me a line without delay concerning the St. John navigation article, I shall be much obliged, as the printers will soon be after me.   J. S.

ALS, with notation by DW. CtY.

EDITORIAL: "THE BOUNDARY MAPS"

February 27, 1843.

Though we have no ambition, and make no pretence, to become champions for the present Administration, in regard to its home measures, we feel entirely disposed to stand up for it, in questions between this Government and foreign Powers, where we believe it to be in the right, as we undoubtingly believe it to have been throughout the whole negotiation of the late Treaty with Great Britain.

The London *Times*, in common with other London papers, is very angry at what it civilly calls *a trick*,[1] practised by our Secretary of State, in regard to a *Map* mentioned in Mr. [William Cabell] RIVES's published speech on the Treaty. As we have not been able to lay this speech, or indeed any of the speeches on the Treaty, before our readers, we state, for their information, that we have turned to that speech, in the file of the *Globe*, to find the ground for this coarse and unworthy charge of *trickery* in the "Times;" and truly it appears to us that there is not the slightest foundation for it.

The Representatives of Great Britain and the United States met in this city professedly to make a *compromise*, and settlement by *agreement*.

It was not their purpose to discuss, at length, the rights of the parties, or the merits of their respective titles to the territory in dispute. While this compromise was proceeding, Lord ASHBURTON signified to Mr. WEBSTER that he had brought with him newly discovered papers, which he thought quite explanatory of the Treaty of 1783; but he did not show them, nor particularly describe their nature. A compromise was agreed upon; and, while the Treaty was in the Senate, and under discussion, the Chairman of the Committee on Foreign Affairs (Mr. RIVES) adverted to a Map which had been found in the Foreign Office at Paris, and which

5. The London *Times* on February 6, 1843, stated that after Ashburton's departure for the United States an old map was found in the British public offices marked with a red line that corroborated the British claim. The map was not used in the negotiations because it could not be authenticated.

1. London *Times*, February 4, 1843.

it was supposed might be connected with a letter written by Dr. [Benjamin] FRANKLIN to the Count DE VERGENNES, of the 6th of December, 1783; and that those two documents, if they could be proved to have reference to each other, showed such color for the British claim as might have had influence before an Arbitration. Hereupon Mr. [Thomas Hart] BENTON produced another Parisian Map, supposed to coincide exactly with that found by Mr. [Jared] Sparks, for the purpose of showing, as he said, that the latter discovered nothing new, or which might not have been found in other places.

It is probable that these Maps had no great influence, either way; but it is strange that it should be thought to have been a part of Mr. WEBSTER's duty to furnish Lord ASHBURTON with a doubtful, though plausible, piece of evidence of this kind, to aid and strengthen the British claim. When parties meet to settle a dispute, is it usual for each to state to the other all his grounds for fearing that he might not recover all he claimed, if the dispute should go on? Besides, these maps, letters, &c. were all as accessible to one party as much as to the other. The industry of the English Foreign-Office had, it would seem, found papers not known to this Government. They were not communicated. And if among public archives papers had been found, and placed in the hands of the Government of the United States, what *obligation* was there to communicate them to the English Government?

To have shown the map and letter of Dr. FRANKLIN would not only have been the extreme of folly, but in all likelihood would have produced great mischief. What would Lord ASHBURTON have done? If he had attached importance to the map, he could have made no Treaty, and the whole affair would have remained only the more embroiled. No doubt he is thankful that he knew nothing of it, if, indeed, such be the case. It was a matter, after all, which, if it had been known, would have been vastly more likely to do harm than good—more likely to create new difficulties than to settle old ones.

But our purpose in noticing this subject, was principally to express our own opinion upon the notion of a part of the London press, that Mr. WEBSTER was bound to perform an act so void of sense as to furnish the British Envoy with new grounds for maintaining the plausibility of the British claim.

Unsigned editorial. Text from the Washington, D.C., *National Intelligencer*, February 27, 1843. DW wrote the draft of this editorial (mDW 24421).

TO JARED SPARKS

Dear Sir   Washington Mar: 11. 43

In the pressure of affairs, at the close of the Session, I have not found time to consider the questions suggested by you, touching that part of the Treaty which respects the Navigation of the St. Johns.[1] I apprehend no practical difficulty on that head; because I believe all the considerable People in the Province will be entirely disposed to give every facility to the introduction of American lumber &c, into the River. It may be doubtful, therefore, whether it is worth while to discuss Mr. [George William] Featherstonehaugh's budget of questions. He is a vain & light man. I hope you have read Mr [Rufus] Choate's speech.[2] On the Eastern & Western Boundary questions, he is very able, & has placed them in their true light.

I have been for some time inclined to suggest to you, whether your Review of the Treaty should not be divided into two numbers, or parts; the first embracing all the agreements of boundary, with their various Equivalents; the second, the correspondence on questions of public law, especially *Impressment of Seamen*. I confess I consider this last branch of the subject as full of importance; &, if it should be postponed, should much desire an interview with you, which I shall have the opportunity of holding.

As to the Boundary subject, you understand it well. What is likely to be overlooked, by superficial thinkers, is the value of Rouse's Point. England will never visit us with an army from Canada for the purpose of conquest; but if she had retained Rouses' Point, she would at all times have access to Lake Champlain, & might in two days place a force within two days March of the City of Albany. The defence of the Country, therefore, would require a large military force in that neighborhood.

As to the *conduct* of the negotiation, there is one point in which I wish to speak to you very freely, even at the hazard of a well founded imputation of some vanity. The grand stroke, was to get the *previous* consent of Maine & Massachusetts. Nobody else had attempted this; it had occurred to nobody else; it was a movement of great delicacy, & of very doubtful result. But it was made, with how much skill & judgment in the manner, you must judge; & it succeeded, & to this success the fortunate result of the whole negotiation is to be attributed. I am, Dear sir, with great regard, Yrs   Danl Webster

You notice the great majorities, with which after all the high sounding notes of opposition, the appropriations for the Treaty passed both Houses. There is, probably, no instance of a similar approach to unanimity. In the Senate, 4 votes were found against it; in the House about 40.[3]

1. See above, Sparks to DW, February 21, 1843.

2. In a speech on Linn's Oregon bill in the Senate on February 3, 1843, Choate maintained that DW and Ashburton had properly directed their attention to the northeastern boundary, leaving the "distant desert" of Oregon for later. See *Cong. Globe*, 27th Cong., 3d sess., app., pp. 222–229, esp. p. 224.

3. House Bill No. 697, appropriating $532,727.74 for carrying into effect the treaty, passed the House on

Mar. 14. 1843

P. Script.

As belonging to what I have considered might be the second part of the Review, I should have mentioned the Cruising Articles. Indeed they constitute a most important topic, of themselves.

You have not yet seen my correspondence with Genl. [Lewis] Cass:[4] I will send it as soon as possible.

I am now drawing up a Despatch to Mr [Edward] Everett, in answer to Lord Aberdeens late communication to Mr [Henry Stephen] Fox.[5]

DW.

ALS. MH-H. Published in *W & S*, 16:397–398.

FROM EDWARD EVERETT

(Confidential)

My dear Sir,   London 31 March 1843

If the discovery of Mr [Jared] Sparks' map in Paris was a singular incident, the bringing to light of Mr [Richard] Oswald's at London is much more singular.[1] Lord Aberdeen assured me, that he was not aware of its existence, till after the conclusion of the treaty, and the stir made about [Benjamin] Franklin's map, and Lord Ashburton was equally ignorant of it till his return. It was, however, brought from the British Museum, to

___

February 28, 1843, and the Senate on March 2. *House Journal*, 27th Cong., 3d sess., Serial 413, pp. 496, 528.

4. See above, "The Aftermath and Implementation of the Treaty of Washington: The Cass-Webster Controversy," pp. 710–775.

5. In an instruction to Fox of January 18, 1843, Aberdeen took exception to President Tyler's rejection of any distinction between visit and search (see *British and Foreign State Papers, 1841–1842* [116 vols., London, 1812–1925], 32:443). DW's formal response is in his instruction to Everett of March 28, 1843, "The Aftermath and Implementation of the Treaty of Washington: The 'Visit' and 'Search' Controversy," pp. 807–817, below.

1. In response to Lord Palmerston's harsh criticism that DW had outwitted Ashburton by concealing Sparks's red-line map, Sir Robert Peel delivered a speech in Parliament on

March 21, 1843, in which he revealed the existence of another map. The so-called King George or Oswald map had supposedly been marked by the British negotiator Richard Oswald in 1783 and then deposited in the British Museum in 1829 as part of the library collection of King George III. As drawn on this map, the boundary line favored the American claim. In 1839, the map was transferred at Palmerston's order from the museum to the custody of the Foreign Office, where it remained filed away and forgotten until brought to Peel's attention in 1843. See *Hansard's*, 67:1248–1249; *Treaties*, 4:408–411. Recently, Howard Jones found evidence that Ashburton himself discovered the Oswald map after his return from the United States. See Jones, *To the Webster-Ashburton Treaty: A Study in Anglo-American Relations, 1783–1843* (Chapel Hill, N.C., 1977), p. 109.

the Foreign Office in Lord Palmerston's time, and was known to him and Mr [George William] Featherstonehaugh. In whose custody it has been since the change of Ministry, so that it did not come to Lord Aberdeen's knowledge I was not told; very likely in that of Mr Featherstonehaugh himself, who has been employed till lately as a sort of general agent for the boundary question. Be this as it may, I was truly rejoiced at Lord Aberdeen's voluntary disclaimer of all previous knowledge of it, and so I said to him; for I could not have reconciled with that candor and good faith for which I have always given him credit, his repeated assurance to me last summer, that there was no plan or map in their possession bearing on the question, not previously made known, had he all the time been aware of the existence of this very remarkable map, which I consider a far clearer and stronger evidence in our favor, than anything else of the kind which has ever been adduced. I am perfectly persuaded that it is the Map, on which the boundary established by the treaty of 1783 was marked for the information of King George III by Mr Oswald himself, or some one under his direction. The line marked on this map and called in four different places the "Boundary described by Mr Oswald," is the line admitted by both parties to be the line of the treaty as far as the two parties agree, and it gives to us the portion of the line, on which we differ.

The ground on which it is here maintained that this map so marked cannot be with certainty depended on, as indicating the line of the treaty is this. We know historically that Mr Oswald, being deemed in the progress of the negotiation too yielding, Mr [Henry] Strachey, as under Secretary of State in the confidence of Mr [Thomas] Townsend, was sent out to assist him[2] and that a better line for England was obtained by him than had been agreed to by Mr Oswald. So much is certain, and it has been suggested as possible, that the line on King George the Third's map, called "the Boundary described by Mr Oswald," is that first line.

But it can be reduced to a certainty that such is not the case; that the line on King George's Map is not Mr Oswald's first rejected line, and it can be brought to the very highest degree of probability, that this map contains the line of the treaty as described by Mr Oswald himself.

On the 8th of October 1782 articles of agreement were entered into, between Mr Oswald on the one hand and Dr Franklin and Mr [John] Jay on the other, (Mr [John] Adams had not then arrived from Holland), according to which the boundary on the *East* was to be the St John's from its source to its mouth in the bay of Fundy.[3] Our negotiators were aware

2. Strachey (1736–1810). Townsend (1733–1800) was Home Office secretary in Shelburne's administration. Sir William Petty, Earl of Shelburne (1737–1805) was prime minister, 1782–1783.

3. See Francis Wharton, ed., *Revolutionary Diplomatic Correspondence of the United States* (6 vols., Washington, D.C., 1889), 5:805–808.

that, on the principle of adhering to the old charters, there was no ground, on the part of Massachusetts, to claim the St John's as the boundary; and Mr Oswald appears to have obtained from them a promise to recede westwardly from that river to the true boundary of Massachusetts, according to the old charters, as the same should be afterwards ascertained. In reference to this, the following note was appended to this plan of a treaty vizt,—

"Alteration to be made in the treaty respecting the boundaries of Nova Scotia vizt East, the true line between which and the United States shall be settled by commissioners as soon as may be after the war." By this same *projet* the states were to be bounded *North* by a line drawn from the North west angle of Nova Scotia along the highlands which divide those rivers which empty themselves into the St Lawrence from those which flow into the Atlantic Ocean, to the northernmost head of Connecticut river, thence down along the middle of that river to the 45th degree of North latitude, and thence due west, on the 45th degree to the north westernmost side of the river St Lawrence, thence straight to the south end of Lake Nipissing, and thence straight to the source of the Mississippi."

These articles were sent over to London for the approbation of the King (see Franklin's correspondence IV. p. 49)[4] and after a delay of two or three weeks, it having been thought that Mr Oswald was too yielding, (as has been already observed) Mr Strachey was sent over to obtain more favorable terms, in reference to the boundary and some other points. The Commissioners had "much contestation with him on the boundary and other articles" and a new agreement was come to, which bore date 6th November.[5] By this second set of articles, the *northern* boundary, beginning as before at the north-western angle of Nova Scotia and passing by the highlands to and down the Connecticut river to the 45th degree of north latitude, was to run on that parallel to the Mississippi. The *Eastern* boundary was the same as that which is contained in the treaty actually concluded, with an immaterial difference in the phraseology.

In addition to the proposal, embodied in the second *projet* of a treaty, it appears from the history of the negotiation, that the American Commissioners submitted a third, which Mr Strachey also took to London, which agreed with the second as far as the eastern boundary is concerned, but on the north substituted the line through the centre of the lakes for the forty fifth degree of latitude. Messrs Oswald and Strachey considered and justly that either of these lines was better than that

4. See Franklin to Robert R. Livingston, December 5, 1782, in Jared Sparks, ed., *The Diplomatic Correspondence of the American Revolution* (12 vols., Boston, 1829–1830),

4:49.

5. Wharton, ed., *Revolutionary Diplomatic Correspondence*, 6:96–100.

agreed to by Mr Oswald on the 8th of October, both as respects Canada and Nova Scotia.

After a short stay in London, Mr Strachey returned to Paris bringing the assent of his government to the third proposal, which is the boundary of the treaty as actually concluded.

It appears from the correspondence that the United States Commissioners were brought without difficulty, to recede from the St John's to the St Croix, but that they steadily refused the efforts of Messrs Oswald and Strachey to bring the boundary west of the latter river. Thus then it is certain that the line originally proposed by Mr Oswald, and which is described in the first project of a treaty of 8th October made the St John's the boundary on the East of a line from the south end of Nipissing to the source of the Mississippi the boundary on the North. There is no trace of any other line agreed to by Mr Oswald and afterwards rejected.

The alternative lines as offered by the American Ministers as a second and third proposal giving a more favorable boundary than Mr Oswalds, both as to Nova Scotia and Canada; did so, in reference to Nova Scotia, by bringing the boundary westward from the St John's to the St Croix, (in which respect the two lines agreed) and in substituting on the north either the 45° of N. Latitude or the middle of the lakes. The latter was adopted by England and both were better than the line of the first project accepted by Mr Oswald.

It follows that the line formed in King George the Third's map and there called "the boundary as described by Mr Oswald our negotiator," is *not* the line of October 8th but one of the alternative lines of which the choice was obtained by Mr Strachey and is the line of the present treaty.

This line is the line always claimed by the United States which is thereby shewn to be the true line by the map of Mr Oswald. I humbly conceive that this train of argument is direct and unanswerable.

The above was chiefly written before I had seen Mr Oswald's map, which I have since, by the kindness of Sir Robert Peel and Lord Aberdeen, been permitted to do. It is a copy of [John] Mitchell'[s] in fine preservation. The boundaries between the British and French possessions in America "as fixed by the treaty of Utrecht" are marked upon it in a very full distinct line, at least a tenth of an inch broad, and those words written in several places. In like manner, the line giving our boundary as we have always claimed it, that is, carrying the north western angle of Nova Scotia far to the north of the St John's is drawn very carefully, in a bold red line full a tenth of an inch broad; and in four different places along the line distinctly written "the boundary described by Mr Oswald." What is very noticeable is, that a line narrower, but drawn with care with an instrument, from the lower end of lake Nipissing to the source of the Mississippi, as far as the map permits such a line to run, had once been drawn on the map, and has since been partially erased, though still distinctly visible.

Lord Aberdeen shewed me, at the same time, another map alluded to by Sir Robert Peel, also a copy of Mitchell, which after Lord Ashburton left England was found in the State Paper Office.[6] It is on rollers, and from having long been hung up is much soiled and defaced. It gives the Boundary as claimed by Great Britain. The line is faintly but plainly drawn in red crayon with a black lead pencil mark running by its side. There is nothing written on any part of the map, to shew by whom or when these lines were drawn; but I was informed that professional mapmakers pronounced the lines to be ancient. To me the red crayon line appeared ancient and the lead pencil modern.

Mr [Henry Unwin] Addington,[7] Under Secretary of State, told me yesterday, that since the noise had been made about Franklin's map, several copies of Mitchell's map belonging to individuals had been brought to his office for examination, all containing the line as claimed by England, but no two drawing it the same way.

Nothing, however, has come to light at all comparable to Oswald's in the way of authenticity; and in fact I think that when the historical evidence adduced in the first part of this letter is weighed, the evidence of the map is complete, that Mr Oswald understood the boundary as we claim it.

When I addressed to Lord Aberdeen my note of 17th May 1842,[8] urging in the most emphatic manner a new search in the British archives for the map sent over by the negotiators of the treaty to the Government in London, I did it with the knowledge derived from a confidential source, that such a map had been, and a full belief that it was still, in existence.

It will throw a little light on the candor and fairness of the press, in this connection, when I state that, notwithstanding the unanimity with which they denounced the concealment from Lord Ashburton of Dr Franklin's map, not one London journal, that I have seen, has called the attention of its readers to the handsome vindication of your conduct by Sir Robert Peel, nor to the circumstance that the existence of Oswald's map had been concealed from us.

Before I close this long letter, I will just say, that I regretted that the extract from my despatch of the 3 February was communicated to the

6. See *Hansard's* 67:1247. This so-called Record Office Map is described by Hunter Miller in *Treaties*, 3:346–347. Miller points out that Everett erred in saying that the map shows the boundary in favor of Great Britain.

7. Addington (1790–1870) was permanent under secretary for foreign affairs, 1842–1854.

8. Everett to Aberdeen, May 17, 1842, (Reel 22), Everett Papers, MHi (Microfilm).

two houses. The commentary upon it in the "Times" of the 18th March though certainly neither official or semi-official, contains, I have no doubt, the view (bating the absurd and invidious personalities,) which Sir Robert Peel, had he alluded to the subject again, would have taken of it. But no allusion to the incident was made on either side of the House, in the great debate of the 22nd.[9]

In conversation with Lord Aberdeen, and in reference to the assent which he understands you to have expressed to the doctrines set forth in his letter to me of 20 December 1841, I have told him, that I incline to think there was some mistake on Lord Ashburton's part: that you neither, at the time nor since, had ever led me to think, that you admitted the existence of any right of visitation in time of peace: that I had no doubt you had expressed your satisfaction with the practical solution of the difficulty contained in his letter of 20th December vizt that of making compensation when by mistake they board our vessels; but that I apprehend you to hold that the law of nations is now, what it was when Lord Stowell, in the case of the "Louis," deemed that there was any right of visitation or interruption.[10]

If this is *not* your view of it you are not committed by it; for I have only advanced it as the doctrine I suppose you to entertain.

I remain of the opinion which I ventured to express to you last year, that it would have been good policy to offer to join the Quintuple treaty, if the British would renounce the right to impress men from our ships.[11] If they agreed, we should have carried a *very great* point, and it seems to me should have reconciled our people to coming into the Quintuple treaty: If they did not agree, we should have put them decidedly in the wrong, and placed ourselves on vantage ground in the controversy.

You will observe how the right of visit is treated in the last pages of the article in the Edinburgh Review on Mr [Henry] Wheaton's history of the study of the law of nations, in the number of the Edinburgh for April. The article is by Mr [Nassau William] Senior.[12]

9. An extract of Everett's dispatch of February 3, 1843, was submitted to the Senate on February 24, 1843, and appears in *Senate Documents*, 27th Cong., 3d sess., Serial 416, No. 223, pp. 46–47. In it Everett expressed surprise at an allegation by Peel that he had not responded to Aberdeen's letter of December 20, 1841 (enclosed in No. 4, Everett to DW, December 28, 1841, DNA, RG 59, Despatches, Britain), regarding the search question. The London *Times* of March 18 observed that Everett's "surprise would have been materially lessened if before writing home he had taken the trouble of comprehending what Sir *R. PEEL* said." The debate of March 21–22, 1843, is in *Hansard's*, 67:1162–1285, 1290–1313.

10. See *International Law Digest*, 1:726–727, 2:886, 916.

11. See above, Everett to DW, January 21, 1842, "The Treaty of Washington," pp. 491–496.

12. Senior defended the right of visiting a ship in order to determine

Much as I have written you, by this vessel, I am afraid you will have to read another private letter. The "Great Western" is not yet in. I have nothing from you later than *January 30th.* I am as ever faithfully and affectionately yours,   (signed) E. E. We have nothing further yet about [David] Hartley's Map, in reference to which Mr George Sumner undertook an investigation, thus far without result.[13]

LC. MHi.

TO WILLIAM BEACH LAWRENCE, WITH ENCLOSURE

Dear Sir,   April 22 '43

I have concluded to send you this note, to be submitted to Mr [Albert] Gallatin, & to be published, or not, as he & you may think fit;[1] & if published, to be altered, in any [way] which may appear to you expedient.

I confess I was struck, in finding how very nearly the same words were used by Sir R[obert] P[eel] & myself, & speaking on the point of my withholding the knowledge of the Paris map.[2] You might add a paragraph to this effect, if you thought proper.

Ld Aberdeen assured Mr [Edward] Everett that neither he nor Ld Ashburton knew the existence of the [Richard] Oswald map.[3] But it was known to Lord Palmerstone, & Mr [George William] Featherstonhaugh, as stated in the *note.* Yrs truly   D Webster

ALS. NHi. Lawrence (1800–1881; Columbia 1818) had served as Gallatin's secretary of legation in London. In 1843 Lawrence was vice president of the New-York Historical Society.

ENCLOSURE: TO WILLIAM BEACH LAWRENCE

Note.

In the Debates in the British House of Commons on the 21st of March,[1]

its true nationality. See *Edinburgh Review,* 77 (April 1843): 161–198, esp. pp. 196–197.

13. On Hartley's map, see above, Everett to DW, February 10, 1843. Sumner (1817–1863), the brother of Charles Sumner (1811–1874; Harvard 1830), spent many years in Europe and assisted Everett in seeking information about the Hartley material.

1. See below. DW and Gallatin spoke before the New-York Historical Society on April 15, 1843, about the boundary settlement. Gallatin afterward prepared their remarks for publication, and he included the sub-

stance of DW's note. See Albert Gallatin and Daniel Webster, *A Memoir on the North-Eastern Boundary, in Connexion with Mr. Jay's Map* (New York, 1843), esp. pp. 69–74.

2. See DW's remarks in the *Memoir,* pp. 57–68. British newspapers carrying accounts of Peel's remarks in the parliamentary debate of March 21 were received in New York on April 19. The similarity between Peel's and DW's comments about Sparks's map is pointed out in the *Memoir,* p. 73.

3. See above, Everett to DW, February 10, 1843.

1. See *Hansard's,* 67:1248–1249.

the important fact was disclosed, that the Map used by Mr [Richard] Oswald had been discovered in the British Museum.

The following paragraphs from the speech of Sir Robert Peel prove, not only that the map found in Paris, by Mr. [Jared] Sparks, had already become known to the British Government, but show also that Mr. Oswald's map, exactly corresponding with Mr. [John] Jay's,[2] had been in the possession of Lord Palmerston, and that he did not communicate it to the Government of the United States:

We have authority for stating that Lord Aberdeen has said that he was not personally aware of the existence of this map till after the conclusion of the Treaty, and that Lord Ashburton was equally ignorant of it, till his return to England. It was brought from the British Museum in Lord Palmerston's time, and was known to him. It was known, also to Mr. [George William] Featherstonhaugh, and was very likely in that gentleman's custody, as he was employed, till lately, in England, as a sort of general agent for the Boundary Question. This map is perfectly well authenticated, it agrees, exactly, with Mr. Jay's map, and it proves, as conclusively as any such evidence can prove, the validity of the claim of the United States. Mr. Featherstonhaugh knew of its existence, when he wrote the supplement to his pamphlet, and knew that *it had not been made known to the Government of the United States.*

Copy. NHi.

TO WILLIAM BEACH LAWRENCE

Dear Sir,   Washington April 24th 1843

In one particular I incline to think that I expressed myself too strongly in the *note* which I sent on Saturday.[1] I think I said that the map, which Mr. [George William] Featherstonhaugh had in his hands when he wrote his Supplement was "conclusive" in favor of our claim. It was strong evidence, most strong, certainly; but then as the marks on the map may have been designed, and probably were, to point out Mr. [Richard] Oswald's proposition, and as that proposition was not finally agreed to, a question may still arise, whether the line finally settled was intended, in this part of it, to correspond with Mr. Oswald's. I incline very much to concur with Sir Robert Peel, that the evidence from maps is not conclusive, either way, for want of proof that any one of them was marked, authentically, as shewing the line, and for the purpose of shewing the line, on which the Commissioners ultimately agreed.[2] Yours truly.

                                                        Danl Webster

LS. NHi.

2. For a discussion of the Jay map, see DW to Everett, April 25, 1843, below.

1. See above.
2. See *Hansard's*, 67:1247–1249.

TO EDWARD EVERETT

Private.

My Dear Sir: Washington, April 25th, 1843.

Two or three months ago, Mr P[eter] A[ugustus] Jay[1] of New York, one of the Sons, as you know, of John Jay, died. About the end of last month, it was made known that among his papers was found a copy of [John] Mitchell's map, with evident marks upon it of having belonged to his father, and of having been used in Paris, in 1782. The map was carried to Mr [Albert] Gallatin, who still keeps up great interest for whatever relates to the Boundary Question, and Mr Gallatin thought it of considerable importance; and it was agreed, that he should take an occasion to read a lecture to the New York Historical Society, of which he is President, on the Boundary subject, in which he should explain the bearing of whatever evidence this new found map might furnish.[2] I happened to be in New York, the 6th & 7th of April, and visited Mr Gallatin, and saw the map.

His lecture was then fixed for Saturday the 15th, and I promised to attend. I did attend, heard the lecture, and made a short speech myself. Some account of these things you will see in the papers. Mr Gallatin's lecture, which is interesting, will be printed, by the Society, and my little Speech, corrected from the newspapers, appended.[3] I have some hopes that the publication will be completed, so that some copies may go to you, by this conveyance. If that should happen, please give one to Lord Ashburton, Lord Aberdeen, Sir Robert Peel, &c.

I had hardly reached my post here, from New York, before I learned, by your letters, as well as by the published debates in the House of Commons, that Mr [Richard] Oswald's copy of Mitchell's map was at last found.[4] I have read your account of that matter with interest, and have also perused all the debates, down to what I think Lord Ashburton might fairly enough call Lord Palmerston's "capitulation."

You will see that Mr Jay's Map and Mr Oswald's map are alike. What one proves, the other proves. Neither of them is absolutely conclusive; because neither proves the line found upon it to have been drawn, in any part, *after* the Treaty was agreed to, and for the purpose of setting forth the Boundary, *as* agreed to. On the contrary, it is clear, that the greater part of the line, called Mr Oswald's line, never was agreed to. I concur,

1. Jay (1776–1843; Columbia 1794), the eldest son of John Jay, died on February 20.

2. The Jay map contained the same line as the King George map and bore the notation "Mr. Oswald's Line." Gallatin discussed the map at length in Gallatin and Webster, *A Memoir on the North-Eastern Boundary, in Connexion with Mr. Jay's Map* (New York, 1843), pp. 5–53.

3. DW's speech is in *Memoir*, pp. 57–68.

4. See Everett to DW, March 31, 1843, above, and Everett to DW, April 5, 1843, mDW 24829.

therefore, entirely in the opinion expressed by Sir Robert Peel, that no map, nor all the maps, settle the question; because they bear no marked lines, which may not have been lines of proposal, merely. In other words, none of them shows a line, clearly purporting to be a line, drawn for the purpose of shewing on the map, a boundary which had been agreed on.

Both these last discovered maps are evidence, and important evidence; but in my judgment more weight attaches to the maps published by [John] Bew,[5] under the circumstances of that publication, than to either or both of these.

And now, I hope we have arrived at the end of all investigation of Boundary lines by maps; for I hardly expect any other discoveries will be made. The universal sentiment here, is, and certainly I concur in it with very great cordiality, approaching to personal gratitude, that Sir Robert Peel treated the matter of the Paris map, in a very handsome way. It required of him a degree of manliness and independence, becoming his character, and honorable to his feelings, to rebuke such reproachful charges, as those with which Mr [George William] Featherstonhaugh, that man of two Countries, had caused the leading presses of London to be filled. It was always surprising to me, that the Government of Great Britain ever employed Mr Featherstonhaugh. It did not know him, as well as you and I know him. He is shallow, and conceited, with quite a lurch towards mischief. Yrs truly always   Danl Webster

LS. MHi. Published in Curtis, 2:169–170.

THE EXTRADITION TREATY PROJECTS
WITH FRANCE AND PRUSSIA

Article 10 of the Treaty of Washington, which remained in force until 1935, established the model for extradition conventions between the United States and other countries. It provided that the signatories would "deliver up to justice" individuals properly charged with the nonpolitical crimes of "murder, or assault with intent to commit murder, or Piracy, or arson, or robbery, or Forgery, or the utterance of forged paper" (*Treaties*, 4:369–370). In 1843, both France and Prussia requested the negotiation of agreements similar to that contained in Article 10, and the Tyler administration readily acceded to these overtures.

On April 26, 1843, Webster agreed to enter into a treaty project with the French minister to the United States "embracing stipulations similar in their nature to those embodied in the tenth article" (DW to Pageot,

5. Bew (d. 1793), a London bookseller, published a report on the boundary in 1783. The map published with his report favored the claims later made by the United States.

April 26, 1843, below). The resulting extradition convention was signed by Webster's successor, Abel P. Upshur, on November 9. After its approval by the U.S. Senate on February 1, 1844, ratifications were exchanged and the treaty was proclaimed on April 13.

The treaty project with Prussia did not proceed as smoothly. On March 16, 1843, Webster sent Henry Wheaton, the U.S. minister in Berlin, a draft convention that he had agreed upon with Friedrich Ludwig von Roenne, the Prussian minister to the United States. Wheaton was granted full power to sign the accord in Berlin (No. 39. DW to Wheaton, March 16, 1843, DNA, RG 59, Instructions, German States), which he finally did on January 29, 1845. Although the convention of 1845 was unanimously accepted by the U.S. Senate on June 21, 1848, President James K. Polk declined to ratify it because of a stipulation that seemed to defer to the Prussian doctrine of perpetual allegiance (see *Treaties*, 6:25–27).

In 1851, when Webster was again secretary of state, the Prussians renewed their request for an agreement on extradition. On June 16, 1852, Webster initialed the convention, which after being consented to by the U.S. Senate and ratified by President Franklin Pierce, became the law of the land on June 1, 1853. Thus, Daniel Webster not only established in Article 10 of the Treaty of Washington the model for American extradition treaties but also contributed to the negotiation of similar accords with France and Prussia.

TO WILLIAM HENRY SEWARD, WITH ENCLOSURE

                                        Department of State
Sir   Washington 20th December 1842.
An answer to your letter has been delayed, till the subject to which it refers could receive attention and deliberation.[1]

The Treaty of the 9th of August having become the law of the land, is obligatory on the President and must be carried into execution by him, in all cases, except those, in regard to which, from the nature of things, the authority or aid of the Legislature is indispensable. No act of Congress is deemed necessary, to enable the President to make requisitions for criminals, fugitive from justice, in the proper cases.

The evidence upon which such requisitions will be made, and the manner of issuing them, are stated in the printed paper which I enclose for your information.[2] I have the honor &c.   Danl Webster.

LC. DNA, RG 59 (Domestic Letters).

1. Seward to DW, December 1, 1842, DNA, RG 59 (Misc. Letters). Seward had requested an explanation of the extradition procedures estab-lished by Article 10 of the Treaty of Washington.
   2. See below.

ENCLOSURE:

In causing requisitions to be made on the British authorities under the treaty of 9th August, 1842, for the surrender of criminals, fugitive from justice, it must be made to appear to the President of the United States—

1st That one of the offences enumerated in the treaty has been committed within the jurisdiction of the United States, or some one of the States or Territories.

2d That the person charged with the offence has fled from the United States, and taken refuge in the British Dominions.

Upon the presentment of evidence of these facts, the President will grant a requisition requesting the delivery of the person charged, provided that such evidence of criminality be exhibited before the British authorities as, according to the laws of the place where the person charged shall be found, would justify his apprehension and commitment for trial if a like crime or offence had there been committed. The regular and most proper evidence of the guilt of the fugitive would be a copy, properly certified, of an indictment found against him, by a grand jury, or proof of the issuing of a warrant for his arrest by some competent authority.

If the fugitive be charged with the violation of a law of a State or Territory, his delivery will be required to be made to the authorities of such State or Territory.

If the offence charged be a violation of a law of the United States (such as piracy, murder on board vessels of the United States, or in arsenals and dock-yards, &c.) the delivery will be required to be made to the officers or authorities of the United States.

The expence of the apprehension and delivery to be borne by the party applying for the requisition of the Government, except in cases of crimes against the United States.

DNA, RG 59 (Domestic Letters).

FROM FRIEDRICH LUDWIG VON ROENNE

Dear Sir,   Washington February 23d 1843.

By your kind permission I beg leave to recur to the subject of our conversation of this morning. Since the facilities of communication between this country and Europe have become so great and numerous, it happens more frequently than ever, that persons who have committed crimes in Germany seek refuge in the United States and vice versa. This is more particularly the case with regard to functionaries having charge of public monies, and to merchants who have defrauded their creditors, by which the revenue and the commerce of the two countries are seriously injured. To guard against this evil, as far as the United States and

Great Britain are concerned, the tenth article of the treaty lately concluded between the two countries, contains a provision for the mutual delivery of persons, charged with certain crimes. Would the United States be willing to enter into a similar agreement with Prussia and the States forming the German Custom-Union? If so, it would be desirable to add to the list of crimes mentioned in the 10th article of the treaty above alluded to, the crimes of fabricating or fraudulently altering documents, fabricating and circulating counterfeit money (both coin and paper-money) and fraudulent bankruptcy.

Should the United States be willing to enter into any agreement of the kind, I beg leave to suggest, that it might be well, in order to avoid unnecessary delay, to send full powers to that effect to the United States Minister at Berlin [Henry Wheaton], as I contemplate availing myself this spring of a leave of absence granted to me by my Government, to go to Europe. With sentiments of the highest regard I have the honor to remain, dear Sir, most respectfully your obedt servt   Roenne

ALS. DNA, RG 59 (Notes from Foreign Legations, German States). Rec'd February 24, 1843. Roenne (1798–1865) was the Prussian chargé d'affaires and minister to the United States from June 24, 1834, to December 14, 1844, and again from January 26 to December 22, 1849.

TO FRIEDRICH LUDWIG VON ROENNE

Dear Sir: Washington, 2d March, 1843.

The subject of your informal letter of the 23d of February[1] has been considered.

You suggest the propriety of an arrangement between the United States, on the one side, and Prussia and the States forming the German Customs-Union on the other, for the mutual extradition of criminals, fugitive from justice, similar to that contained in the 10th article of the late treaty between the United States and England.

It seems due to the civilization and principles of order which characterize the present age, that no Christian State should furnish an asylum to malefactors, escaping from the justice of their own country; and the good of communities the more strongly requires that no such immunities for offences should exist in proportion as commerce and intercourse increase between them.

Mutual arrangements between Nations destroying, in the minds of the ill disposed, hopes of such means of escape, may be expected to fulfil, in some degree, the great end and object of criminal legislation and all penal enactments; that is to say the prevention of crimes.

At present, this Government has no such stipulation except with that of Great Britain, whose neighborhood to us, on this continent, as well as

1. See above.

the great degree of intercourse between the two countries rendered a mutual obligation of this nature the more important. But intercourse between the United States, and Prussia, and Germany, already considerable, is rapidly increasing, and the President is inclined to consider quite formally, the subject which you have caused to be brought to his notice.

I will ask of you the favor of a personal conference upon the matter, at your convenience.

We should hear, with most sincere regret, of your purpose of going to Europe, in the Spring, if you had not accompanied the information with the qualification, that you do so only on leave of absence.

I pray you to be assured, my dear Sir, of my high and cordial regard.

Danl Webster.

LC. DNA, RG 59 (Notes to Foreign Legations, German States).

FROM JOHN TYLER

D Sir   March 16 [1843]
I can see no objection to the proposed convention with Prussia but suggest that a provision be introduced expressly guarding agst the possibility *of constructive crime* arising out of political offences—murder &c might be charged as arising in revolution &c &c. Yrs   J Tyler

ALS. DLC.

TO FRIEDRICH LUDWIG VON ROENNE

                                                        Department of State,
Sir,   Washington, 16th March, 1843.
Your "projet" of a convention for the extradition of criminals, fugitive from justice, in certain cases, communicated to this Department with your note of the 9th of March,[1] has been submitted to the President. An amendment suggested by him, and intended only to secure a greater degree of explicitness, has been incorporated into your draft; and, thus amended, the President directs me to say that the "projet" is acceptable to him, and, if it prove so to you, a full power will be sent to Mr. [Henry] Wheaton to sign it,[2] should it meet the approbation of your Government.

1. Roenne to DW, March 9, 1843, DNA, RG 59 (Notes from Foreign Legations, German States). The text of the proposed convention is in *Treaties*, 6:23–24.

2. DW authorized Wheaton on March 16 to negotiate the proposed convention as amended in Berlin (No. 39. DW to Wheaton, March 16, 1843, Instructions, German States), and Roenne signified his approval of what DW had done the following day (Roenne to DW, March 17, 1843, DNA, RG 59, Notes from Foreign Legations, Prussia).

A copy, as amended, is herewith communicated to you. I have the honor to be, with great consideration, your obedient servant,   Danl Webster.

LC. DNA, RG 59 (Notes to Foreign Legations, German States).

FROM JOHN TYLER

Apl 25 1843

The President returns Mr [Alphonse Joseph Yves] Pageots letter and the papers accompanying it.[1] He can percieve no good reason for declining a negociation for the conclusion of a convention of Extradition between France and the U. States. The same can be properly guarded so as to preclude political offences.

AL. DLC.

TO ALPHONSE JOSEPH YVES PAGEOT

Department of State,
Washington 26th April, 1843.

The Undersigned has the honor to acknowledge the receipt of the note addressed to him on the 21st instant[1] by Mr. [Alphonse Joseph Yves] Pageot, Minister Plenipotentiary of His Majesty the king of the French [Louis Philippe] at Washington, proposing on the part of His Majesty's Government, with the view of strengthening the friendly relations between the United States and France, the conclusion of a convention for the surrender of criminals, fugitive from justice, embracing stipulations similar in their nature to those embodied in the tenth article of the late treaty between this Government and that of Her Britannic Majesty.

The communication of Mr. Pageot has been submitted to the President, who, after due consideration of the subject, consents to entertain the proposition offered by Mr. Pageot; and has accordingly directed the Undersigned to signify the willingness of this Government to enter upon the negotiation of a convention of extradition between the United States and France upon the general basis of the tenth article of the recent treaty of Washington, with such modifications as the contracting parties may deem best calculated to be useful to the interests of the citizens and subjects of the two countries, by rendering as efficient as possible the provi-

1. In a note of April 21, 1843, Pageot proposed an extradition agreement similar to Article 10 of the Treaty of Washington. He enclosed copies of earlier conventions France had concluded with Switzerland (1828), Belgium (1834), Sardinia (1838), and Great Britain (February 13, 1843). Pageot to DW, April 21, 1843, DNA, RG 59 (Notes from Foreign Legations, France).

1. Pageot to DW, April 21, 1843, DNA, RG 59 (Notes from Foreign Legations, France).

sions of the instrument by which the objects in view are sought to be attained.

The Undersigned avails himself of the occasion to renew to Mr. Pageot the assurance of his high consideration.   Danl Webster.

LC. DNA, RG 59 (Notes to Foreign Legations, France).

THE "VISIT" AND "SEARCH" CONTROVERSY

In his second Annual Message to Congress on December 6, 1842, President John Tyler lauded the Treaty of Washington as providing "the means of preserving for an indefinite period the amicable relations happily existing between the two Governments." He then proceeded to jeopardize those very relations by carelessly overstating the accomplishment and scope of Article 8 of that accord. After observing that during the Webster-Ashburton negotiations the question of the African slave trade had been second in importance to only the northeastern boundary dispute, Tyler interpreted the joint-cruising convention as removing "all pretense . . . for interference with our commerce for any purpose whatever by a foreign government" (*Messages and Papers*, 4:194–196). These words reignited a controversy, for British officials were outraged by the president's implication that England had abandoned its claim of a right to "visit" American merchant vessels on the high seas in order to determine whether they were slavers illegally flying the flag of the United States (see Everett to DW, February 1, 1843, below). The way in which Tyler "treated the subject of the Right of Search," Lord Aberdeen wrote on February 25, 1843, "was really scandalous" (Louis J. Jennings, ed., *The Croker Papers: The Correspondence and Diaries of the Late Right Honourable John Wilson Croker* [3 vols., London, 1884], 2:399).

The controversy began on August 27, 1841, when Lord Palmerston formulated a distinction between "visit" and "search." He made no claim to exercise the belligerent right of search during peacetime or in the absence of specific treaty stipulations, but he did assert a right to "visit" vessels flying the American flag and suspected of being slavers in order to ascertain their true nationality (Palmerston to Stevenson, August 27, 1841, enclosed in Stevenson to DW, September 18, 1841, "The Crisis in Anglo-American Relations," pp. 124–134, above). The problem was that slave traders were evading British cruisers by resorting in ever-increasing numbers to the use of American colors. Since the British by 1841 had negotiated mutual search treaties with all of the other important maritime nations, only the flag of the United States remained to protect slavers from the systematic British crusade to abolish the traffic in human beings. Because of memories of impressment, concern about possible interference with legitimate commerce, and a growing sensitivity among southerners about the subject of slavery, the United States refused to negotiate a mutual search convention and adhered doggedly to its traditional stance of defending the freedom of the seas. Andrew Stevenson, the U.S. minister to Britain, responded to Palmerston on September 10 by dismissing the distinction between visit and search as "wholly fictitious" (Stevenson to Palmerston, September 10, 1841, enclosed in No. 132. Stevenson to DW, September 18, 1841, DNA, RG 59, Despatches, Britain).

With the change in ministry, it was Lord Aberdeen who answered Stevenson's note of September 10. Although he employed more diplomatic language than did Palmerston, Aberdeen upheld his predecessor's assertion of a right of visit, or, as he rephrased it, a "Right of Enquiry" (Aberdeen to Stevenson, October 13, 1841, enclosed in No. 134. Stevenson to DW, October 22, 1841, DNA, RG 59, Despatches, Britain). In a more elaborate letter to Stevenson's successor, Aberdeen informed Edward Everett that Britain would grant "prompt and ample reparation" to any American vessel that suffered loss or injury because of boardings or detentions growing out of Britain's right to ascertain the nationality of vessels suspected of being engaged in the slave trade. The British maintained only, he said, a right to inspect ships that seemed to be illegally hoisting the American flag. Britain did not claim a right to board genuinely American vessels (Aberdeen to Everett, December 20, 1841, enclosed in No. 3. Everett to DW, November 30, 1841, DNA, RG 59, Despatches, Britain).

During the negotiations that led to the Treaty of Washington, Ashburton and Webster deliberately avoided a discussion of the sensitive visit and search issue. With Britain unwilling to make a concession on impressment and the United States unwilling to grant a right of search during peacetime, President Tyler suggested that each nation establish an independent naval force off the coast of Africa. Although separate and distinct, the two squadrons would cooperate in suppressing the slave trade. Aberdeen preferred a mutual search treaty, but he accepted the joint-cruising solution as the best that could be obtained under the circumstances. Article 8, then, did not resolve the dispute over visit and search. Rather, it deliberately evaded the problem. Thus, it is not surprising that President Tyler's second Annual Message evoked a strong public response from British leaders.

In Parliament on February 2, 1843, Sir Robert Peel asserted that the president of the United States had not provided "a correct account of the negotiations relative to the right of visit." He then reiterated the distinction between visit and search and denied that Britain had abandoned the right of visit in the Treaty of Washington. "The right we claim," he said, "is to know whether a vessel pretending to be American, and hoisting the

American flag, be *bona fide* American." In acceding to Article 8, Peel concluded, Britain had not given up its "claims in the slightest degree" (*Hansard's*, 66:88).

To the secretary of state fell the responsibility of trying to reconcile the conflicting interpretations of a treaty that had been signed just six months earlier. Webster accomplished that difficult task in one of his ablest state papers, an instruction to Everett dated March 28, 1843. After conceding that Aberdeen and Peel were correct in stating that the claim of a right of visit had not been dealt with in Article 8, Webster assessed the joint-cruising convention as rendering unnecessary "both the assertion and the denial" of a right of search. He then restated the American position that international law did not distinguish between visit and search. "If such well known distinction exists," he asked rhetorically, "where are the proofs of it? What writers of authority on the public law, what adjudications in courts of Admiralty, what public treaties recognise it?" Any detention of an American ship by a British cruiser during peacetime, he continued, was "a wrong—a trespass." Webster concluded his masterful analysis of the law of nations by again agreeing with his adversary. The purpose of Article 8 was to circumvent differences over visit and search, thereby enabling the two countries to "act concurrently . . . for the suppression of a traffic which both regard as a reproach upon the civilisation of the age, and at war with every principle of humanity, and every Christian sentiment" (DW to Everett, March 28, 1843, below).

Hugh G. Soulsby, the historian of the visit and search dispute, has characterized Webster's instruction of March 28, 1843, as "a definitive document of utmost importance" and the best statement "of the American case that had been made in the course of the controversy over the right of visit" (*The Right of Search and the Slave Trade in Anglo-American Relations* [Baltimore, 1933], p. 100). Although the British did not finally renounce their pretension to a right of visit until 1858, Webster's logic almost persuaded them to do so in 1843. Everett read Webster's letter to Aberdeen on April 22. Aberdeen said that he "would not pledge himself to a concurrence in every statement" made by the secretary of state, but he expressed satisfaction with the dispassionate tone in which Webster had written. Aberdeen then made a remarkable statement. He told Everett that he agreed with Webster "in denying, that there is any distinction between a right of visit and a right of search" (No. 36. Everett to DW, April 27, 1843, DNA, RG 59, Despatches, Britain).

Aberdeen's concurrence with Webster's view did not terminate the visit and search controversy. To begin with, the joint-cruising convention did not work as well as both sides had hoped. In his instructions of March 30, 1843, to Commodore Matthew C. Perry, Secretary of the Navy Abel P. Upshur was cautious in assessing the obligations of the United States under Article 8. He not only explicitly stated that the "paramount interest" of the United States was the protection of legitimate American commerce with Africa rather than the suppression of the slave trade but also wrote that the United States did not recognize the right of any foreign nation to visit and search American vessels. In short, Upshur interpreted the joint-cruising convention as designed primarily to prevent abuses of the flag of the United States (see below, Upshur to Perry, March 30, 1843). There seems to have been a difference, at least of emphasis, between Webster, on the one hand, and Tyler and Upshur, on the other. The secretary of state stressed the cooperative aspects of Article 8, but the president and the secretary of the Navy paid more attention to the limited nature of the commitments growing out of that treaty stipulation. The situation was equally confused on the British side. Aberdeen apparently agreed with Webster that there was no difference between the rights of visit and search; Peel maintained that the two were "quite distinct" (*Hansard's*, 68:88). As Aberdeen himself recognized, he was at odds with his own prime minister on the subject (see Everett to DW, April 27, 1843, below).

For Webster, the somewhat metaphysical dispute over "visit" and "search" ended inconclusively, for he resigned as secretary of state before he could respond to Everett's dispatch of April 27, 1843. The joint-cruising convention that he negotiated with Ashburton was effective in the sense that interference with ships flying the American flag by British cruisers was rare for many years after 1842. It was ineffective, however, in the sense that it did not contribute significantly to the suppression of the African slave trade. With the inadequately equipped American squadron spending more time protecting legitimate American commerce than cooperating with the British squadron, slave traders continued to abuse the Stars and Stripes. Indeed, the visit and search controversy revived in 1857 when British cruisers again began seizing slavers hoisting the American flag. When Secretary of State Lewis Cass threatened to abrogate the joint-cruising convention, the British backed down. In 1858, they formally abandoned their pretension to a right of visit. It was not until 1862, when Britain and the United States signed a treaty granting a mutual right of search, that the inhuman traffic was finally suppressed.

FROM EDWARD EVERETT

Confidential
My dear Sir,   London 1 Feb. 1843.
    On the 3d of January, I received a note from Lord Aberdeen,[1] requesting me to come & see him at the Foreign Office, at 1/2 past Three P.M. that day. We make up the despatches at Four in the afternoons of the 3d

1. Not found.

of the month, so that I had no opportunity, by the steamer of the next day, to acquaint you with the result of our interview.

He opened the conversation by observing, that he had read those parts of the President's Message, at the beginning of the session, which relate to the N. W. boundary & the Treaty,[2] with disappointment & pain; that what was said on both questions was, as he conceived, calculated, though of course not intended, to convey an erroneous impression as to the facts of the case; that it would be naturally inferred, from the manner in which the topic is mentioned[,] that, after an effort on Lord Ashburton's part, to bring the Government of the United States to accede to some British pretension as to the right of search or visit, he had been obliged to yield, and agree to the arrangement contained in the treaty; whereas, from the first, satisfaction was professed on your part with the manner, in which the claim of G.B. as to the right of visit is stated, in Lord Aberdeen's letter to me of Decr 20, 1841,[3] and no opposition made by Lord Ashburton to the arrangement finally adopted: the allusion to General [Lewis] Cass' protest & the formal approval of it were wholly unexpected, after the reports of Mr [Henry Stephen] Fox of your views on that point,[4] confirmed as they were by Lord Ashburton: that he was obliged to infer that there was a difference of opinion between you & the President on that point: a very embarrassing circumstance, because the Secretary of State, as the organ of the Government, in its intercourse with foreign powers, spoke in the President's name: that there was one passage which amounted to an exhortation to France to withdraw from treaties with England of long standing, which was certainly unfriendly, he might almost say hostile: that from the mode in which the question of the N. W. boundary was mentioned vizt that the President will not "delay to urge on Great Britain the importance of an early settlement," an inference directly the opposite of the fact, as he understood it, would naturally be drawn: Great Britain had from the time she discovered, that (contrary to her wishes & expectations) this question had not been settled by Lord Ashburton, been constantly urging upon the U.S., through me & Mr Fox, to enter into nego-

2. See Tyler's message of December 6, 1842, in *Messages and Papers*, 4:194–209, esp. pp. 195–196. Tyler described Oregon as U.S. territory claimed in part by Britain. On the slave trade issue, he stated that the British "claim to visit and inquire" was simply the principle of search "expressed in different words." He also reiterated his approval of Lewis Cass's correspondence with the French government on the Quintuple Treaty (see above, Cass to Guizot, February 13, 1842, enclosed in Cass to DW, February 15, 1842, "The Treaty of Washington," pp. 509–513).

3. Aberdeen to Everett, December 20, 1841, enclosed in No. 4. Everett to DW, December 28, 1841, DNA, RG 59 (Despatches, Britain).

4. In his dispatch No. 41 of December 12, 1842, Fox noted Tyler's approval of Cass in the Annual Message and added that DW's views were "much at variance" with the president's. FO 115/79 (PRO).

tiation on the subject: he said it was not the practice of the Queen to make a long speech at the opening of parliament; if it were, they should be compelled to advise her Majesty to use a different language from that of the Message on all these points.[5]

He then read me the correspondence between yourself & Mr Fox on this subject, and a despatch of Mr Fox, written after the appearance of the President's message, alluding to the points above indicated,[6] much as Lord Aberdeen himself had done.

I ought to add that Lord Aberdeen's manner, in making the observations of which I have repeated the substance, was mild & respectful, and the expression rather that of regret than offence.

He told me that he did not expect from me any reply to his remarks, neither did he wish them communicated to my government, though he had no objection to my doing it, if I thought proper.

Mr George Sumner (brother to Mr Charles S[umner]) told me, a few Evenings since, that he had been informed by Mr Rowe,[7] appeal clerk of the privy Council, that the British government had intimated to the French government the expediency of expressing its dissatisfaction to the government of the United States, at the manner, in which the President alludes to the subject of the right of search for the suppression of the slave trade, in his Message at the Opening of Congress. I am, as ever, most truly Yours   E.E.

ALS. MHi. Endorsed: "Private-file."

TO EDWARD EVERETT

No. 36.   Department of State,
Sir: Washington, 28th March, 1843.

I transmit to you with this despatch, a message from the President of the United States to Congress communicated on the 27th of February, and accompanied by a report made from this Department to the President, of the substance of a despatch from Lord Aberdeen to Mr [Henry Stephen] Fox, which was by him read to me on the 24th ultimo.[1]

5. Queen Victoria's speech of February 2, 1843, is in *Hansard's*, 66: 1–6. The Treaty of Washington was mentioned only briefly, as confirming "the amicable Relations of the Two Countries."

6. See Fox to DW, November 15, 1842, urging a settlement of the Oregon boundary, and DW to Fox, November 25, 1842, conveying the wish of the United States to open negotiations on the subject. DNA, RG 59

(Notes from Foreign Legations, Britain, and Notes to Foreign Legations, Britain). The dispatch from Fox is probably his No. 4 of January 20, 1842, on Oregon. FO 115/84 (PRO).

7. Not otherwise identified.

1. Tyler's message of February 27, 1843, is in *Messages and Papers*, 4: 229–232. The report from the Department of State is in *Executive Documents*, 27th Cong., 3d sess., Serial 422, No. 192. An extract of

Lord Aberdeen's despatch, as you will perceive was occasioned by a passage in the President's message to Congress, at the opening of its late session. The particular passage is not stated by his Lordship; but no mistake will be committed, it is presumed, in considering it to be that which was quoted by Sir Robert Peel and other gentlemen in the debate in the House of Commons on the answer to the Queen's speech, on the 3d of February.[2]

The President regrets that it should have become necessary to hold a diplomatic correspondence upon the subject of a communication from the head of the Executive Government to the Legislature; drawing after it, as in this case, the further necessity of referring to observations made by persons in high and responsible stations in the debates of public bodies. Such a necessity however, seems to be unavoidably incurred in consequence of Lord Aberdeen's despatch; for although the President's recent message may be regarded as, a clear exposition of his opinions on the subject, yet a just respect for Her Majesty's Government, and a disposition to meet all questions with promptness, as well as with frankness and candor, require that a formal answer should be made to that despatch.

The words in the message at the opening of the session which are complained of, it is supposed are the following: "Although Lord Aberdeen in his correspondence with the American Envoys at London, expressly disclaimed all right to detain an American ship on the high seas, even if found with a cargo of slaves on board, and restricted the British pretension to a mere claim to visit and inquire, yet it could not well be discerned by the Executive of the United States how such visit and inquiry could be made without detention on the voyage, and consequent interruption to the trade. It was regarded as the right of search, presented only in a new form, and expressed in different words; and I therefore felt it to be my duty distinctly to declare, in my annual message to Congress,[3] that no such concession could be made, and that the United States had both the will and the ability to enforce their own laws and to protect their flag from being used for purposes wholly forbidden by those laws, and obnoxious to the moral censure of the world."

This statement would tend, as Lord Aberdeen thinks, to convey the supposition not only that the question of the right of search had been

the letter from Aberdeen to Fox of January 18, 1843, criticizing Tyler's remarks on the visit and search issue in his Annual Message of December 6, 1842, is in *British and Foreign State Papers, 1841–1842* (116 vols., London, 1812–1925), 32:443–444.

2. Peel's speech began on February 2, and the debate extended to the next day. *Hansard's*, 66:86–98.

3. Tyler's first Annual Message, of December 7, 1841, in *Messages and Papers*, 4:77.

disavowed by the British Plenipotentiary at Washington, but that Great Britain had made concessions on that point.

Lord Aberdeen is entirely correct in saying that the claim of a right of search was not discussed during the late negotiation, and that neither was any concession required by this Government, nor any made by that of Her Britannic Majesty.

The eighth and ninth articles of the treaty of Washington, constitute a mutual stipulation for concerted efforts to abolish the African Slave Trade. This stipulation, it may be admitted, has no other effects on the pretensions of either party than this: Great Britain had claimed as a *right* that which this government could not admit to be a *right*, and in the exercise of a just and proper spirit of amity, a mode was resorted to which might render unnecessary both the assertion and the denial of such claim.

There probably are those who think that what Lord Aberdeen calls a right of visit, and which he attempts to distinguish from the right of search, ought to have been expressly acknowledged by the Government of the United States; at the same time, there are those on the other side, who think that the formal surrender of such right of visit should have been demanded by the United States, as a precedent condition to the negotiation for treaty stipulations on the subject of the African Slave Trade. But the treaty neither asserts the claim in terms, nor denies the claim in terms; it neither formally insists upon it nor formally renounces it. Still the whole proceeding shows, that the object of the stipulation was to avoid such differences and disputes as had already arisen, and the serious practical evils and inconveniences which, it cannot be denied, are always liable to result from the practice which Great Britain has asserted to be lawful. These evils and inconveniences had been acknowledged by both governments. They had been such as to cause much irritation, and to threaten to disturb the amicable sentiments which prevailed between them. Both governments were sincerely desirous of abolishing the slave trade; both governments were equally desirous of avoiding occasion of complaint by their respective citizens and subjects, and both governments regarded the 8th and 9th articles as effectual for their avowed purpose; and likely, at the same time, to preserve all friendly relations, and to take away causes of future individual complaints. The treaty of Washington was intended to fulfil the obligations of the treaty of Ghent. It stands by itself, is clear and intelligible. It speaks its own language, and manifests its own purpose. It needs no interpretation, and requires no comment. As a fact, as an important occurrence in national intercourse, it may have important bearings on existing questions, respecting the public law; and individuals, or perhaps governments, may not agree as to what these bearings really are. Great Britain has discussions, if not controversies, with other great European States upon the subject of visit and search.[4] These States will naturally make their own commentary on the treaty of Washington, and draw their own inferences from the fact that such a treaty has been entered into. Its stipulations, in the mean time, are plain, explicit, satisfactory to both Parties, and will be fulfilled on the part of the United States, and it is not doubted on the part of Great Britain also, with the utmost good faith.

Holding this to be the true character of the treaty, I might perhaps excuse myself from entering into the consideration of the grounds of that claim of a right to visit merchant ships, for certain purposes in time of peace, which Lord Aberdeen asserts for the British Government, and declares that it can never surrender. But I deem it right, nevertheless, and no more than justly respectful towards the British Government not to leave the point without remark.

In his recent message to Congress the President, referring to the language of Lord Aberdeen in his note to Mr [Edward] Everett of the 20th of December, 1841, and in his late despatch to Mr Fox, says, "these declarations may well lead us to doubt whether the apparent difference between the two Governments is not rather one of definition than of principle."

Lord Aberdeen in his note to you of the 20th of December, says "the Undersigned again renounces, as he has already done in the most explicit terms, any right on the part of the British Government to search American vessels in time of peace. The right of search, except when specially conceded by treaty, is a purely belligerent right, and can have no existence on the high seas during peace. The Undersigned apprehends, however, that the right of search is not confined to the verification of the nationality of the vessel, but also extends to the object of the voyage, and the nature of the cargo. The sole purpose of the British cruisers is to ascertain whether the vessels they meet are really American or not. The right asserted has, in truth, no resemblance to the right of search, either in principle or practice. It is simply a right to satisfy the Party who has a legitimate interest in knowing the truth that the vessel actually is what her colours announce. This right we concede as freely as we exercise. The British cruisers are not instructed to detain American vessels, under any circumstances whatever; on the contrary, they are ordered to abstain from all interference with them, be they slavers or otherwise. But where reasonable suspicion exists that the American flag has been abused, for the purpose of covering the vessel of another Nation, it would appear scarcely credible, had it not been made manifest by the repeated protest of their representative, that the Government of the United States, which has stigmatised and abolished the trade itself,

4. See, for example, the report on negotiations regarding visit and search with Portugal and with France in *British and Foreign State Papers, 1841–1842* (116 vols., London, 1812–1925), 30:917–920, 31:513–515.

should object to the adoption of such means as are indispensably necessary for ascertaining the truth."

And in his recent despatch to Mr Fox, his Lordship further says, "that the President might be assured that Great Britain would always respect the just claims of the United States. That the British Government made no pretension to interfere in any manner whatever, either by detention, visit, or search, with the vessels of the United States, known or believed to be such; but that it still maintained, and would exercise when necessary, its own right to ascertain the genuineness of any flag which a suspected vessel might bear; that if, in the exercise of this right, either from involuntary error, or in spite of every precaution, loss or injury should be sustained, a prompt reparation would be afforded; but that it should entertain, for a single instant, the notion of abandoning the right itself, would be quite impossible."

This then is the British claim as asserted by Her Majesty's Government.

In his remarks in the speech already referred to, in the House of Commons, the first Minister of the crown said, "there is nothing more distinct than the right of visit is from the right of search. Search is a belligerent right, and not to be exercised in time of peace, except when it has been conceded by treaty. The right of search extends not only to the vessel but to the cargo also. The right of visit is quite distinct from this, though the two are often confounded. The right of search, with respect to American vessels, we entirely and utterly disclaim; nay, more, if we knew that an American vessel were furnished with all the materials requisite for the slave trade; if we knew that the decks were prepared to receive hundreds of human beings, within a space in which life is almost impossible, still we should be bound to let that American vessel pass on. But the right we claim is to know whether a vessel pretending to be American, and hoisting the American flag, be *bona fide* American."

The President's message is regarded as holding opinions in opposition to these.

The British Government then supposes that the right of visit and the right of search are essentially distinct in their nature; and that this difference is well known and generally acknowledged; that the difference between them consists in their different objects and purposes,—one,— the visit,—having for its object, nothing but to ascertain the nationality of the vessel; the other,—the search,—being an inquisition not only into the nationality of the vessel, but the nature and objects of her voyage, and the true ownership of her cargo.

The Government of the United States, on the other hand maintains that there is no such well known and acknowledged, nor indeed any, broad and genuine difference between what has been usually called visit, and what has been usually called search; that the right of visit, to be effectual, must come in the end to include search; and thus to exercise, in peace, an authority which the law of Nations only allows in time of war. If such well known distinction exists, where are the proofs of it? What writers of authority on the public law, what adjudications in courts of Admiralty, what public treaties recognise it? No such recognition has presented itself to the Government of the United States; but, on the contrary, it understands that public writers, courts of law, and solemn treaties have, for two centuries, used the words "visit" and "search" in the same sense.[5] What Great Britain and the United States mean by the "right of search," in its broadest sense, is called by continental writers and jurists by no other name than the "right of search." Visit, therefore, as it has been understood, implies not only a right to inquire into the national character, but to detain the vessel, to stop the progress of the voyage, to examine papers, to decide on their regularity and authenticity, and to make inquisition on board for enemy's property, and into the business which the vessel is engaged in. In other words, it describes the entire right of belligerent visitation and search. Such a right is justly disclaimed by the British Government in time of peace. They, nevertheless, insist on a right which they denominate a right of visit, and by that word describe the claim they assert. Therefore it is proper and due to the importance and delicacy of the questions involved, to take care that, in discussing them, both governments understand the terms which may be used in the same sense. If, indeed, it should be manifest, that the difference between the Parties is only verbal, it might be hoped that no harm would be done; but the Government of the United States thinks itself not justly chargeable with excessive jealousy, or with too great scrupulosity in the use of words, in insisting on its opinion that there is no such distinction as the British Government maintains between visit and search, and that there is no right to visit, in time of peace, except in the execution of revenue laws, or other municipal regulations, in which cases the right is usually exercised near the coast or within the marine league; or where the vessel is justly suspected of violating the law of Nations by piratical aggression: but wherever exercised it is a right of search. Nor can the United States' Government agree that the term "right" is justly applied to such exercise of power as the British Government thinks it indispensable to maintain in certain cases.

5. In his *Law of Nations*, first published in 1773, Emmerich von Vattel discussed the right of search but did not address the issue of visitation (see Book 3, chap. 7, paragraph 114). In the case of the *Louis*, in 1817, Lord Stowell spoke of the "right of visitation and search" without distinguishing between the terms (see *International Law Digest*, 2:886, 916). In a number of treaties between Britain and Continental powers, no difference was indicated between visit and search. See, for example, the anti–slave trade treaties of 1817 between Britain and Spain and Britain and Portugal in *British and Foreign State Papers, 1816–1817* (116 vols., London, 1812–1925), 4: 33–46, 85–95.

The right asserted is a right to ascertain whether a merchant vessel is justly entitled to the protection of the flag which she may happen to have hoisted, such vessel being in circumstances which render her liable to the suspicion—first, that she is not entitled to the protection of the flag; and, secondly, that if not entitled to it, she is either by the law of England as an English vessel, or the provisions of treaties with certain European powers, subject to the supervision and search of British cruisers.

And yet Lord Aberdeen says, "that if, in the exercise of this right, either from involuntary error, or in spite of every precaution, loss or injury should be sustained, a prompt reparation would be afforded."

It is not easy to perceive how these consequences can be admitted justly to flow from the fair exercise of a clear right. If injury be produced by the exercise of a right, it would seem strange that it should be repaired as if it had been the effect of a wrongful act. The general rule of law certainly is, that in the proper and prudent exercise of his own rights, no one is answerable for undesigned injuries. It may be said that the right is a qualified right; that it is a right to do certain acts of force, at the risk of turning out to be wrongdoers, and of being made answerable for all damages. But such an argument would prove every trespass to be matter of right, subject only to just responsibility. If force were allowed to such reasoning, in other cases, it would follow that an individual's right in his own property, was hardly more than a well-founded claim for compensation, if he should be deprived of it. But compensation is that which is rendered for injury, and is not commutation, or forced equivalents for acknowledged rights. It implies, at least in its general interpretation, the commission of some wrongful act.

But without pressing further these inquiries into the accuracy and propriety of definitions, and the uses of words, I proceed to draw your attention to the thing itself, and to consider what these acts are which the British government insists its cruisers have a right to perform, and to what consequences they naturally and necessarily lead. An eminent member of the House of Commons thus states the British claim, and his statement is acquiesced in and adopted by the first Minister of the crown.

["]The claim of this country is for the right of our cruisers to ascertain whether a merchant vessel is justly entitled to the protection of the flag which she may happen to have hoisted, such vessel being in circumstances which rendered her liable to the suspicion—first, that she was not entitled to the protection of the flag; and, secondly, if not entitled to it, she was, either under the law of Nations or the provisions of treaties, subject to the supervision and control of other cruisers."[6]

Now the question is, by what means is this ascertainment to be effected?

6. The statement by Sir Charles Wood (1800–1885), a member of

As we understand the general and settled rules of public law in respect to ships of war sailing under the authority of their government, "to arrest pirates and other public offenders," there is no reason why they may not approach any vessels descried at sea for the purpose of ascertaining their real characters. Such a right of approach seems indispensable for the fair and discreet exercise of their authority; and the use of it cannot be justly deemed indicative of any design to insult or injure those they approach, or to impede them in their lawful commerce. On the other hand, it is as clear that no ship is, under such circumstances, bound to lie by, or wait the approach of any other ship. She is at full liberty to pursue her voyage in her own way, and to use all necessary precautions to avoid any suspected sinister enterprise or hostile attack. Her right to the free use of the ocean is as perfect as that of any other. An entire equality is presumed to exist. She has a right to consult her own safety; but at the same time she must take care not to violate the rights of others. She may use any precautions dictated by the prudence or fears of her officers; either as to delay, or the progress or course of her voyage; but she is not at liberty to inflict injuries upon other innocent parties, simply because of conjectural dangers.

But if the vessel thus approached attempts to avoid the vessel approaching, or does not comply with her commanders order to send him her papers for his inspection, nor consent to be visited or detained, what is next to be done? Is force to be used? And if force be used, may that force be lawfully repelled? These questions lead at once to the elemental principle, the essence of the British claim. Suppose the merchant vessel be, in truth, an American vessel engaged in lawful commerce, and that she does not choose to be detained. Suppose she resists the visit. What is the consequence? In those cases in which the belligerent right of visit exists, resistance to the exercise of that right is regarded as just cause of condemnation, both of vessel and cargo. Is that penalty, or what other penalty, to be incurred by resistance to visit in time of peace? Or suppose that force be met by force, gun returned for gun, and the commander of the cruiser, or some of his seamen be killed; what description of offence will have been committed? It would be said, in behalf of the commander of the cruiser, that he mistook the vessel for a vessel of England, Brazil, or Portugal; but does this mistake of his take away from the American vessel the right of self defence? The writers of authority declare it to be a principle of natural law, that the privilege of self defence exists against an assailant, who mistakes the object of his attack for another whom he had a right to assail.[7]

Parliament from 1832 to 1865, is in *Hansard's*, 66:77.

7. See, for example, Grotius, *De Jure Belli ac Pacis Libri Tres*, trans.

Francis W. Kelsey (2 vols., Oxford and London, 1925), Book 2, chap. 1, sec. 3, and Pufendorf, *De Jure Naturae et Gentium Libri Octo*, trans.

Lord Aberdeen cannot fail to see, therefore, what serious consequences might ensue, if it were to be admitted that this claim to visit, in time of peace, however limited or defined, should be permitted to exist as a strict matter of right; for if it exist as a right it must be followed by corresponding duties and obligations, and the failure to fulfil those duties would naturally draw penal consequences after it, till ere long it would become, in truth, little less, or little other, than the belligerent right of search.

If visit, or visitation, be not accompanied by search, it might well be, in most cases, merely idle. A sight of papers may be demanded, and papers may be produced. But it is known that slave traders carry false papers, and different sets of papers. A search for other papers, then, must be made, where suspicion justifies it, or else the whole proceeding would be nugatory. In suspicious cases, the language and general appearance of the crew, are among the means of ascertaining the national character of the vessel. The cargo on board, also, often indicates the country from which she comes. Her log book, showing the previous course and events of her voyage, her internal fitment and equipment, are all evidences for her, or against her, on her allegation of character. These matters, it is obvious, can only be ascertained by rigorous search.

It may be asked, if a vessel may not be called on to show her papers, why does she carry papers? No doubt she may be called on to show her papers; but the question is, where, when, and by whom? Not in time of peace, on the high seas, where her rights are equal to the rights of any other vessel, and where none has a right to molest her. The use of her papers is, in time of war, to prove her neutrality, when visited by belligerent cruisers; and in both peace and war to show her national character, and the lawfulness of her voyage in those ports of other countries, to which she may proceed for purposes of trade. It appears to the Government of the United States that the view of the whole subject which is the most naturally taken, is also the most legal, and most in analogy with other cases. British cruisers have a right to detain British merchantmen for certain purposes; and they have a right, acquired by treaty, to detain merchant vessels of several other Nations for the same purposes: But they have no right at all to detain an American merchant vessel. This Lord Aberdeen admits in the fullest manner. Any detention of an American vessel by a British cruiser is therefore a wrong—a trespass—although it may be done under the belief that she was a British vessel, or that she belonged to a nation which had conceded the right of such detention to the British cruisers; and the trespass, therefore, an involuntary trespass. If a ship of war, in thick weather, or in the darkness of the night, fire upon and sink a neutral vessel, under the belief that she is an

---

C. H. Oldfather and W. A. Oldfather   Book 2, chap. 5, sec. 5.
(2 vols., Oxford and London, 1934),

enemy's vessel, this is a trespass—a mere wrong—and cannot be said to be an act done under any right, accompanied by responsibility for damages. So, if a civil officer on land have process against one individual, and through mistake arrest another, this arrest is wholly tortious: No one would think of saying that it was done under any lawful exercise of authority, subject only to responsibility; or that it was any thing but a mere trespass, though an unintentional trespass. The municipal law does not undertake to lay down beforehand any rule for the government of such cases. And as little, in the opinion of the Government of the United States, does the public law of the world lay down beforehand any rule for the government of cases of involuntary trespasses, detentions, and injuries at sea; except that in both classes of cases, law and reason make a distinction between injuries committed through mistake, and injuries committed by design; the former being entitled to fair and just compensation, the latter demanding exemplary damages, and sometimes personal punishment. The Government of the United States has frequently made known its opinion, which it now repeats, that the practice of detaining American vessels, subject to just compensation, however guarded by instructions, or however cautiously exercised, necessarily leads to serious inconvenience and injury. The amount of loss cannot be always well ascertained. Compensation, if it be adequate in the amount, may still necessarily be long delayed, and the pendency of such claims always proves troublesome to the Governments of both countries. These detentions, too, frequently irritate individuals—cause warm blood, and produce nothing but ill effects on the amicable relations existing between the countries. We wish, therefore, to put an end to them; and to avoid all occasion for their recurrence.

On the whole, the government of the United States, while it has not conceded a mutual right of visit and search, as has been done by the parties to the Quintuple treaty of December, 1841, does not admit that, by the law and practice of Nations, there is any such thing as a right of visit, distinguished by well known rules and definitions, from the right of search.

It does not admit that visit of American merchant vessels by British cruisers is founded on any right, notwithstanding the cruiser may suppose such vessel to be British, Brazilian, or Portuguese. It cannot but see that the detention and examination of American vessels by British cruisers has already led to consequences, and it fears that if continued, would still lead to further consequences, highly injurious to the lawful commerce of the United States.

At the same time the government of the United States fully admits that its flag can give no immunity to pirates, nor to any other than to regularly documented American vessels; and it was upon this view of the whole case, and with a firm conviction of the truth of these sentiments, that it cheerfully assumed the duties contained in the treaty of Washington; in the hope that thereby causes of difficulty and of difference might be altogether removed, and that the two Powers might be enabled to act concurrently, cordially, and effectually, for the suppression of a traffic which both regard as a reproach upon the civilisation of the age, and at war with every principle of humanity, and every Christian sentiment.

The Government of the United States has no interest, nor is it under the influence of any opinions which should lead it to desire any derogation of the just authority and rights of maritime power. But in the convictions which it entertains, and in the measures which it has adopted, it has been governed solely by a sincere desire to support those principles and those practices which it believes to be conformable to public law, and favorable to the peace and harmony of Nations.

Both Houses of Congress, with a remarkable degree of unanimity, have made express provisions for carrying into effect the 8th article of the treaty.[8] An American squadron will immediately proceed to the coast of Africa. Instructions for its commander are in the course of preparation, and copies will be furnished to the British government; and the President confidently believes that the cordial concurrence of the two Governments, in the mode agreed on, will be more effectual than any efforts yet made for the suppression of the Slave Trade.

You will read this despatch to Lord Aberdeen, and if he desire it, give him a copy. I am, Sir, respectfully, Your obedient servant,

Danl Webster.

LC. DNA, RG 59 (Instructions, Britain). Published in *Senate Documents*, 29th Cong., 1st sess., Serial 477, No. 377, pp. 132–140.

ABEL PARKER UPSHUR TO MATTHEW CALBRAITH PERRY

Navy Department
Sir: March 30th 1843.

You will proceed as soon as possible, with the squadron under your command, to the Coast of Africa.[1] You are charged with the protection of American Commerce in that quarter, and with the suppression of the Slave Trade, so far as the same may be carried on by American Citizens or under the American Flag.

The Commerce of the United States, with the Western Coast of Africa, is rapidly increasing, and becoming every day, more and more valuable. Heretofore it has been conducted under many circumstances of dis-

---

8. The act of March 3, 1843, is in 5 U.S. *Stat.* 623.

1. Perry's West Africa squadron consisted of the flagship *Saratoga*, a twenty-two-gun sloop; the thirty-six-gun sloop *Macedonian*; the sixteen-gun sloop *Decatur*; and the ten-gun brig *Porpoise*.

advantage in consequence of the unprotected condition in which it has been left. In the conduct of your command, you will be careful to ascertain its present condition and its probable future course and extent, and you will afford to it all the aid and support which it may require. The rights of our Citizens engaged in lawful Commerce are under the protection of our flag, and it is the chief purpose, as well as the chief duty, of our Naval power to see that these rights are not improperly abridged, or invaded. To what extent your interposition for this purpose may be required, it is impossible to foresee. The Department relies with full confidence on your judgment and discretion, so to employ the force under your command, as to protect the rights and interests of your own Countrymen, without violating those of any other people; and therefore deems it unnecessary—as indeed, it would be almost impossible—to give you specific instructions upon the subject.

In regard to the other branch of your duties, viz: the suppression of the Slave Trade, the following views and instructions are given for your guidance.

The United States are sincerely desirous wholly to suppress this iniquitous traffic, and with that view have declared it to be piracy. They have recently, by their treaty with England, come under specific Stipulations upon the subject, to which your particular attention is called. I enclose a copy of the treaty, lately concluded between the two Countries, and refer you to the 8th Article of it.[2] The object which the two governments have in view, and the mode in which they propose to accomplish it, will be at once perceived from the plain language of this Article.

I need not, I am sure, impress upon you the importance of strictly observing this Stipulation, and of preserving inviolate the pledged faith of your Country upon this point. Nevertheless, the following suggestions may be found useful, in enabling you to understand, fully and precisely, the views of your own Government, upon this delicate and interesting subject.

This Government does not acknowledge a *right* in any other nation, to visit and detain the vessels of American Citizens, engaged in Commerce. By the general consent of all civilized nations, vessels suspected of acts which are piracy by the law of nations, *may be* so visited, for the purpose of ascertaining their true character. Even in this case, however, there must be *probable cause*, that is, a reasonable ground of suspicion; and the visit must be made in good faith, and must be conducted with, and limited to, the sole purpose above mentioned. Any wrong done in the exercise of this privilege, beyond what its legitimate object *requires*, makes the visiting power a trespasser. It is also to be observed that the piracy of which I speak, is piracy by the laws of nations, and not that

2. *Treaties*, 4:369.

which is made so, by the municipal laws of any particular Country. Of this latter character is the Slave Trade, which is declared to be piracy by Act of Congress.[3] The right therefore, which by the general consent of nations, exists in regard to vessels suspected of being engaged in piracy, does not extend to those suspected of being employed in the Slave Trade. As to them, there is no right of visitation or search, so far as American vessels are concerned, except by our own vessels of war. But the claim of the U. States that their trading vessels shall not be visited for *any* purpose, (except on suspicion of piracy) by the cruisers of other nations, pre-supposes that the vessel visited is *really* American. In *what manner* this fact is to be ascertained, is the only question which presents any difficulty. The flag which the vessel wears, is *prima facie*, although it is not conclusive proof of her nationality; it is a mere emblem, and it loses its true character when it is worn by those who have no right to wear it. Any vessel which displays the American flag, claims to be American, and therefore, may be rightfully boarded and examined by an American cruiser, if there be any circumstance attending her to justify a suspicion that she is not what she professes to be. But this privilege does not extend to cruisers of any other Nation; that is, it cannot be conceded to them as a *right*. The United States certainly do not claim that the mere hoisting of their flag, shall give immunity to those who have no right to wear it. Such a pretension would subject their flag to degradation and dishonor, because it would make it a cover for piracy, and other crimes of similar atrocity; but they *do* claim that their own Citizens who rightfully display it, shall have all the protection which it implies. Whenever therefore, a cruiser of any other nation, shall venture to board a vessel under the flag of the U. States, she will do it upon her responsibility for all consequences. If the vessel so boarded, shall prove to be American, the act will not be justified by you, but the injured party will be left to such redress either in the tribunals of England or by an appeal to his own Country, as the nature of the case may require. If the vessel prove not to be American the U. States have no cause of complaint notwithstanding she has worn their flag.

These principles are believed to be well understood and settled. Indeed, the Article of the treaty to which I have called your attention, was agreed to with the obvious view of preventing all difficulty or disagreement upon this point. The U. States in stipulating to keep a Squadron of not fewer than eighty guns, on the Coast of Africa, meant to give to England and all the world, an assurance of her determination and ability to protect her own flag against abuse, and thus to remove all pretext for any interference with it by other Nations. England accepted this Stipulation as

3. The slave trade was declared piracy, punishable by death, in an act of May 15, 1820. The law was made permanent in an act of January 30, 1823. 3 *U.S. Stat.* 600–601, 721.

satisfactory so far as she was concerned and therefore she has no reason, and I trust, has no wish, to invade the rights of the U. States, in that respect. I advert to the subject here, only to put you in possession of the views of your own Government, for your guidance in forming such arrangements as you may find it convenient to make, for co-operation with British Cruisers. I should consider it highly desirable that a vessel of each Nation, should as far as possible cruise in company with a vessel of the other, so that each may be in a condition to assert the rights and prevent the abuse of the flag of its own Country. In this way, all just grounds of difference or collision will be removed, while this harmonious co-operation of the two powers will go far to insure the full accomplishment of their common object, in the suppression of the Slave Trade.

On approaching the Coast, your first object will be, to make yourself acquainted with the actual condition of the great interests which are entrusted to your protection. With this view, you will communicate as far as you conveniently can, with the several accredited agents of our Government with the Colony of Liberia, and with any and all sources of information on which you may venture to rely. Your operations against the Slave Trade, will, of course, be influenced in a great degree, by this information. Your own observation and experience while heretofore in service upon that Coast,[4] will enable you to direct your enquiries in a proper channel, and has already supplied you with much valuable information. The cunning of the Slave Trader however, is constantly devising new disguises and schemes of deception, by which he may elude dectection and escape the consequences of his crimes. To some of these it may be useful to call your attention.

It is not to be supposed that vessels destined for the Slave Trade, will *exhibit* any of the usual arrangements for that business. They take especial care to put on the appearance of honest traders, and to be always prepared as if engaged in pursuits of lawful commerce. It is their practice to run in to some river or inlet where they have reason to believe that slaves may be obtained, make their bargains with the slave factors, deposit their hand-cuffs, and other things calculated to betray them, and then sail on an ostensible trading voyage to some neighboring port. At the appointed time, they return and as the Slaves are then ready to be shipped, they are taken on board without delay, and the vessel proceeds on her voyage. Thus the Slavers do not carry, within themselves, any positive proof of their guilt, except before they reach the Coast, and after they leave it with Slaves on board. Nevertheless there are a variety of signs and indications, by which their true character may, at all times, be conjectured. Among these are the following.

4. In 1820 Perry had served as executive officer aboard the *Cyane* in African waters, and in 1821 he was given command of the *Shark* for a voyage to Africa.

1st Double sets of papers. It is well known that false papers may be easily obtained, and at very little cost. No vessel engaged in honest commerce requires them.

2d An unusual number of water casks, or tanks: a supply of provisions beyond what the ostensible voyage would require: and any other preparation or arrangement not usual in the trade in which the vessel professes to be engaged.

3d The log book should be particularly examined. It is understood to be a common practice among Slavers, to keep two logs; the one representing the true route, and the other a false one. By exhibiting the false log, they represent themselves as having been in positions which would not expose them to the suspicion of Slave trading; but this fraud may be easily detected by judicious questioning.

4th The shipping list may afford strong presumptive evidence upon the subject. In consequence of the great exposure, hardships and hazards of the Slave-Trade, the wages of sailors engaged in it, are generally much higher than are paid in any regular and lawful trade; and of course, it may reasonably be inferred that a crew Shipped at prices extravagant and unusual are not destined for any usual sea duty.

5th Consular certificates are often forged, and in lieu of the usual consular seal, the impression is made with a American half dollar.

These are a few of the devices to which the Slave Trader resorts. In calling your attention to them, I have in view only to impress you with a deep sense of the artful character of the adversaries, with whom you have to deal, and of the reckless disregard of all truth and honor, as well as of all law and humanity. Nothing but the utmost vigilance and caution, will enable you to detect them. I have no doubt that your own observation and sagacity, will soon discover other contrivances for deceiving, and escaping you, and I have as little doubt that you will apply, promptly and effectually, the requisite means of defeating all such attempts. The service in which you are engaged, requires the greatest prudence and the soundest discretion. It is to be borne in mind that while the U. States, sincerely desire the suppression of the Slave Trade, and design to exert their power, in good faith, for the accomplishment of that object, they do not regard the success of their efforts as their paramount interest nor as their paramount duty. They are not prepared to sacrifice to it any of their rights as an independent Nation, nor will the object in view, justify the exposure of their own people, to injurious and vexatious interruptions, in the prosecution of their lawful pursuits. Great caution is to be observed, upon this point. There is reason to believe that the flag of the U. States has been often used, to cover the traffic in Slaves, and it is supposed that no good citizen of the U. States will complain that a cruizer of his own Country, acting upon well grounded suspicion, visits his vessel in order to ascertain her true character. But he is nevertheless, not to be exposed to unnecessary and vexatious detention; nor to any harsh or un-civil treatment. On this point, I am sure I need not give you instructions. While therefore, the utmost vigilance is to be exacted, to detect Slave traders, great care must be taken, not unnecessarily to interrupt the citizens, whether of our own or other countries, in their lawful pursuits.

Your cruising ground will extend from the Medeira and Canary Islands to the Bight of Biafra, and from the Coast of Africa to the 30th degree of West Longitude. If however, it should be found necessary, in the prosecution of the objects of your cruise, to go beyond these limits, you will not hesitate to do so.

The many disagreeable circumstances which attend a cruise on the Coast of Africa, added to the danger to health from any improper exposure in that climate, have induced me to make the following arrangements for the health and comfort of your crews.

A general rendezvous and depôt for provisions and Stores, will be established at Port Praya; supplies will be sent out at short intervals and in small quantities, to guard against the danger of losing the stores by the influences of the climate. It is desirable that your vessels should be kept as actively employed as possible consistently with the health and comfort of the crew; but occasional reliefs from duty, and reasonable rest and refreshment on shore, will be necessary. With a view to this, it will be well that they leave Port Praya one at a time and after such intervals of time as may seem necessary, running down the Coast to the end of their cruising ground, and returning to Port Praya, either along the Coast, or farther out at sea, as may seem most advisable. To perform this circuit will probably require about sixty days, at the end of which time, fresh supplies will be necessary, and some relaxation to the crews will be proper.

These may be sought either at Port Praya, or at the Madeira or Canary Islands, as may be most advisable. By this arrangement, entire employment will be given to your vessels, and they will be so distributed as to cover the entire space of your cruising ground. The fact that different vessels of war appear, in rapid succession, at the same points, will impress the natives with a high idea of our vigilance and strength and will inspire them with a just fear of offending us, by any outrage committed on our Citizens or their property. Effectual protection & security will thus be afforded to our citizens engaged in lawful commerce in those Countries, while, at the same time, your operations against the Slave Trade will be in no degree interrupted or embarrassed.

I enclose a copy of a letter of instructions to Captain [William] Ramsay relative to the recent outrage upon American Citizens and their property, by the inhabitants of little Beriba.[5] As Captain Ramsay was pre-

5. For information about the *Mary Carver* incident, see "The World and

vented from executing the designs of the Department, you will consider the letter to him, as instructions to you, not only in that particular case, but in all others of like kind, which may come to your knowledge.

As soon as the necessary vessels can be prepared, they will be sent to the African Coast. In the mean time, you will proceed as soon as possible to that Station. The Porpoise, under command of Lieut. [Arthur] Lewis, has already sailed, and will await your arrival at Port Praya.[6] As soon as you shall join her, you will proceed to the execution of the purposes of your cruise.

Before proceeding to sea, you will cause a complete muster roll of the Officers and crew attached to your Ship, to be transmitted to the Department. I am respectfully yours.   A. P. Upshur

Copy. DNA, RG 59 (Misc. Letters).

FROM EDWARD EVERETT

Private

My dear Sir   London 27 April 1843.

On the 22d instant, as I have informed you in my public despatch,[1] I called on Lord Aberdeen & read to him your letter to me of 28th March on the subject of visitation & search.[2] He said it was an excellent document: that he did not know that he should wish to alter a word: that he concurred with you in the proposition, that there is no such distinction as that between a right of search & a right of visit, that he did not agree with Sir Robert Peel on that point;[3] that perhaps he himself had not expressed himself as distinctly as he might on that head in his letter to me of Decr 20th 1841;[4]—that that letter was written *currente calamo*, and he only wondered that it had stood criticism so well; perhaps he might say that with the lapse of time & the progress of the discussion, his ideas had become more definite than they then were. This was on Saturday. The next day Lord Aberdeen sent me a note from the Country, (where he usually goes at the end of the week) requesting to see me on Tuesday,

Daniel Webster: The Middle East and Africa," pp. 283–290, above. On December 13, 1843, Perry avenged the *Mary Carver* outrage by destroying the Fishmen village of Little Berebee on the Ivory Coast.

6. Lewis (d. 1854) failed to take command of the vessel. He was furloughed from active duty on July 19, 1843. The command of the *Porpoise* was given to Lieutenant Henry S. Stellwagen (d. 1866).

1. See No. 36. Everett to DW, April 27, 1843, DNA, RG 59 (Despatches, Britain).

2. See above, DW to Everett, March 28, 1843.

3. See Peel's speech of February 2, 1843, in *Hansard's*, 66:88–91.

4. Aberdeen to Everett, December 20, 1841, enclosed in No. 4. Everett to DW, December 28, 1841, DNA, RG 59 (Despatches, Britain). Aberdeen renounced any right of search but upheld the right to visit foreign ships to ascertain their nationality.

—when I went to the Foreign office. He then said that, on reflecting on the answer to be returned to your despatch which I had read to him on Saturday, he had encountered a difficulty of this kind: that, whereas your despatch purports to be and is a comment upon and answer to his letter to me of 20 Decr 1841, which the President also had spoken of in his Message at the commencement of the Session as containing inadmissible doctrine,[5] yet you had declared yourself, at the time, to Lord Ashburton perfectly satisfied with that letter; that Lord Ashburton had referred to this declaration in the House of Lords and that he himself (Lord Aberdeen) in his despatch to Mr [Henry Stephen] Fox which was read to you had done the same in a distinct manner, and that this despatch was now printed in Extenso, by order of Parliament.[6] He did not see that, in replying to your despatch Nro 36 to me, he could avoid saying something to this effect, that he conceived he had reason to suppose that you had been fully satisfied with the doctrines of his letter to me of 20th Decr 1841. As this rested on your oral communications with Lord Ashburton, he feared (if pressed), that it might place you and him in a position of some embarrassment with each other, which he wished to avoid; that if I could make any suggestion which would go to remove the difficulty it would gratify him; and he was willing to wait a reasonable time, to give me opportunity to receive any explanation from you, which you might wish to make on this head.

I told him that the difficulty did not seem to me serious: that I could not, of course, undertake to offer any explanation as to what you had said orally to Lord Ashburton; that oral statements were always subject to some degree of misapprehension; I assured him that in your most confidential communications to me, you had never alluded to his letter of 20 Decr 1841. in any other terms than those in which you now mention it; that I did not in fact see what there was to be explained, for in the same degree in which he was satisfied with your despatch to me of March 28th 1843, (& he had professed himself entirely so), you had reason to be satisfied with his letter to me of 20th Decr 1841; that if your despatch appeared in some degree a reply to his letter, it was because that letter had received, particularly from Sir Robert Peel, an interpretation, which he himself (Lord Aberdeen) admitted he did not altogether concur in; that he would recollect the President, in his last message,[7] stated that [there]

5. See Tyler's Annual Message of December 6, 1842, in *Messages and Papers*, 4:194–209, esp. pp. 195–196.

6. Speaking in the House of Lords on April 3, 1843, Ashburton said that while in the United States he had received no complaint regarding the policy set down in Aberdeen's note to Everett of December 20, 1841.

Hansard's, 68:316–317. An extract of Aberdeen's note to Fox of January 18, 1843 (which was read by Fox to DW on February 24), is in *British and Foreign State Papers* (116 vols., London, 1812–1925), 32:443–444.

7. Tyler's message of February 27, 1843, is in *Messages and Papers*, 4:229–232.

was no essential difference between the doctrine of the American Government & that of Great Britain as explained by Lord Aberdeen; and that he would perceive, that your despatch was mainly occupied with arguing against the distinction between a Right of Visitation and a Right of Search, as maintained by Sir Robert Peel. These observations did not appear entirely to remove the difficulty alluded to above, in Lord Aberdeen's mind, and I told him I would mention the subject confidentially to you.

On reflecting further upon the matter, however, I am not satified that I should do right to acquiesce in Lord Aberdeen's withholding his answer, —as he proposed,—in order to await any communication you may choose to make. If his object really is as he assured me with every appearance of sincerity, to consult your feelings, he will either so wait, or he will so express himself as to avoid the possibility of giving you dissatisfaction. But I do not think I ought to admit that there is anything that needs explanation; and I determined to see him again and say so explicitly.

Since the foregoing was written, I have seen Lord Aberdeen again. Before I could enter into any explanations, on the subject, he remarked that contrary to the opinion I had expressed to him, your despatch had appeared in the Newspapers,[8] and this he added would make it necessary for him to reply to it without much delay. I told him that before I was aware of its being in the papers, I had determined to say to him that I could not agree to his postponing any notice he might think it necessary to take of your despatch, in order to give time for explanations from you of the kind thus referred to: that I did not conceive that any were necessary; nor did I see how he could, after saying that he could not wish a word in your despatch altered. He said he did not, by using that expression, mean that he entirely concurred with all the statements in the despatch, but that he entirely approved its tone and manner of treating the subject. He repeated, however, in the course of our conversation, that he agreed with you that no distinction could be drawn between the right of visit and the right of search. I told [him] if he agreed to that, I did not perceive what else there could be to differ upon; or why he should suppose that there was an inconsistency between a general assent to the doctrines of his letter to me of 20 Decr 1841 and the writing of your despatch. He said he could not but think so, in consequence of your having expressed a wish to Mr Fox to have a copy of Lord Aberdeen's despatch to him, with the omission of the part, in which allusion was made to the oral statements made by you to Lord Ashburton; of the omission of any reference to this, in the abstract of the despatch submitted by you to the President; and of a like omission in a letter which you had written to

8. Extracts from DW's No. 36, March 28, 1843, appeared in the London *Times* on April 27.

Lord Ashburton upon the general subject.[9] I told him I could not undertake to explain matters of this kind, of which I thought he overrated the significance; but I thought when he came to read your letter carefully, he would find that it was a reply not so much to his of 20 Decr 1841 as to Sir R. Peel's speech.

This is about the whole of what past. You will easily conceive that I felt the delicacy of my position in a conversation of this nature. If I have misstated your views, you are not at all committed by anything I have said. I am, Dear Sir, as ever, most faithfully & affectionately Yours,   E.E.

LC. MHi. Published in Curtis, 2:165.

THE OREGON QUESTION

In 1841, the Oregon country, as it had come to be called, comprised the territory west of the Rocky Mountains and between the 42° latitude in the south and 54° 40′ in the north. It was a vast wilderness, incorporating about forty times the acreage involved in the northeastern boundary dispute. Oregon also contained, as Frederick Merk has written, "the only frontage on the Pacific to which the United States had any undisputed claim prior to the Mexican War" (*History of the Westward Movement* [New York, 1978], p. 309). The coastline between 42°, the transcontinental boundary with Mexican California, and the Columbia River was American territory. Unfortunately for the United States, however, not a single good deep-water port was located in this area. "All the good harbors between the Russian Settlements & California," as Webster wrote in 1842, were contained in the Strait of Juan de Fuca, and that frontage on the ocean was claimed by Great Britain (DW to Edward Everett, November 28, 1842, below).

In their boundary dispute with the United States, the British were willing to accept a line starting at the crest of the Rocky Mountains and running along the forty-ninth parallel to its intersection with the Columbia River. From there, the line of demarcation would follow that river to the sea. The United States insisted on a boundary that ran true to the forty-ninth parallel all the way to the Pacific Ocean. Thus, the region actually in contention was a triangle of territory between the Columbia River and the forty-ninth parallel. Since the only safe and usable harbors were located from the Strait of Juan de Fuca to Puget Sound, the disputed area held great commercial significance.

Unable to agree on a division of the Oregon country, Britain and the

9. No such written communication between DW and Ashburton has been found. During a speech in Parliament on April 7, 1843, Lord Brougham indicated that there were no written notes between DW and Ashburton on the issue of visit and search but that when the subject was raised, DW "cut short all discussion." *Hansard's*, 68:620–621.

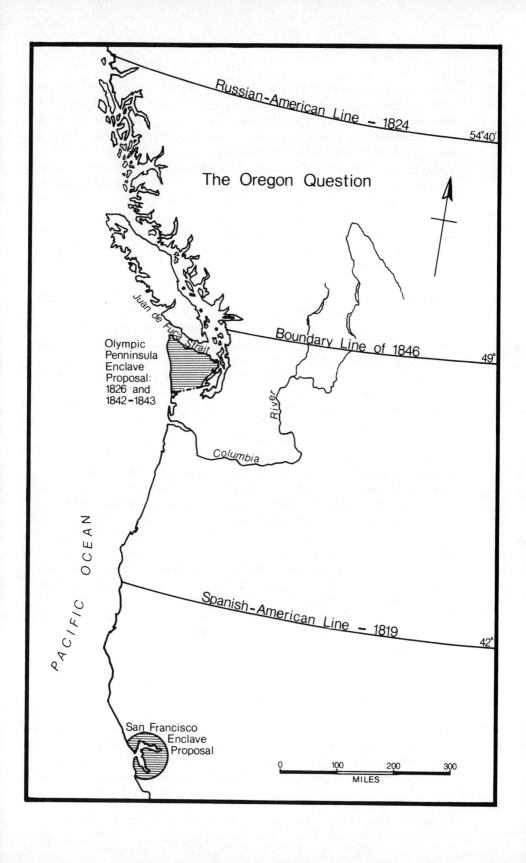

The Oregon Question

Russian-American Line — 1824

54°40'

Boundary Line of 1846

49°

Juan de Fuca Strait

Olympic
Penninsula
Enclave
Proposal:
1826 and
1842–1843

Columbia

River

PACIFIC OCEAN

Spanish-American Line — 1819

42°

San Francisco
Enclave
Proposal

0   100   200   300
MILES

United States negotiated the convention of October 20, 1818. Under its terms, Oregon was declared "free and open" for ten years to the settlers and traders of both countries (*Treaties*, 2:658–662). The next attempt to resolve the Oregon question was undertaken in 1826, when Albert Gallatin was selected by President John Quincy Adams as the American commissioner to treat with Henry Unwin Addington and William Huskisson, the plenipotentiaries chosen by Foreign Secretary George Canning. With Britain insistent on the Columbia River boundary, and the United States, on the forty-ninth parallel, the modest outcome was the convention of August 6, 1827. It extended indefinitely the agreement of 1818, with the added stipulation that either signatory could abrogate the pact by giving the other a twelve-month notice of its intention to do so (*Treaties*, 3:309–314).

During the negotiations that led to the renewal of 1827, Canning authorized a proposal that had an important impact on the subsequent diplomacy. In order to meet the American demand for a deep-water port, Addington offered Gallatin a quadrilateral tract of land adjoining the Strait of Juan de Fuca, comprising what is known today as the Olympic Peninsula. Although rejected in 1826–1827, Canning's proposal was instrumental to the failure of the two parties to resolve the Oregon question in 1842–1843, and it may have served as a precedent for Webster's unusual tripartite plan.

The third attempt to resolve the Oregon boundary dispute was quickly aborted. In April 1842, shortly after his arrival in the United States, Lord Ashburton introduced the subject. Based upon his instructions of February 8, he proposed the line that had been repeatedly declined by the United States in the past—the forty-ninth parallel to the Columbia River, and thence to the sea. Ashburton then informed Webster that such was the limit of his instructions, and he did not renew Canning's enclave offer of 1826. The only authoritative account of Webster's response is contained in a dispatch from Ashburton to Aberdeen dated April 25. After objecting that the line proposed would leave the United States without a harbor on the Pacific, Webster tentatively advanced what came to be known as the tripartite plan. If Mexico could be persuaded to relinquish San Francisco to the United States, Webster suggested, the United States might be inclined to accept the Columbia River boundary. Webster was apparently attempting to break the logjam caused by Ashburton's anachronistic instructions and to acquire America's first Pacific outlet to the trade of East Asia. His project, it seems, would have merely required the British to refrain from any opposition to an American acquisition of San Francisco from Mexico. Although Ashburton stated that Britain "could take no part in any arrangement" with Mexico and that he had "no power to enter upon the subject at all," he told Webster that he did not anticipate any objection to a voluntary cession on the part of Mexico.

Ashburton then referred the problem to his government (No. 2. Ashburton to Aberdeen, April 25, 1842, FO 5/379, PRO). Neither Ashburton nor Webster considered Oregon very important, and this one exchange constituted their only discussion of the question.

Aside from indifference, the key to the failure of Webster and Ashburton to deal with the Oregon question in 1842 lies in the instructions of February 8. The part relating to Oregon was drawn up by Addington. He certainly was knowledgeable about the problem, having served as minister to the United States from 1824 to 1825 and then as a participant in the negotiation of 1826–1827. Addington became permanent under secretary for foreign affairs on January 16, 1842, just in time to help draft Ashburton's instructions. He made no reference to the enclave offer of 1826, he did not supply Ashburton with a copy of the minutes of what had occurred in that year, and he did not even inform Aberdeen of Canning's proposal, which Addington himself had presented to Gallatin. Lord Ashburton apparently remained unaware of Addington's negligence throughout his stay in the United States, and Lord Aberdeen did not learn of the enclave offer until November 1843, when Edward Everett, who had been informed of it by Webster (see DW to Everett, November 28, 1842, below), in turn told the foreign secretary. Although Frederick Merk considers the tripartite plan a "flight from reality," he argues persuasively that the inability of Webster and Ashburton to resolve the Oregon question was preordained by the retrograde instruction of February 8, which had been drawn up by a high-ranking bureaucrat who was unfriendly toward the United States. That instruction, Merk writes, "sent a chain reaction of confusion flowing through the negotiation." It misled both Ashburton and Webster and prompted the secretary of state to advance the "misty and unrealistic intimation" that has puzzled historians to this day (*The Oregon Question: Essays in Anglo-American Diplomacy and Politics* [Cambridge, Mass., 1967], pp. 211–215).

Fatigue, the American climate, and the strained relations between the United States and Mexico also played a role in sidetracking the Oregon question in 1842. As early as April 26, with the thermometer registering eighty degrees, Ashburton warned Aberdeen that he was "not good for any prolonged residence" in the United States (see above, Ashburton to Aberdeen, April 26, 1842, "The Treaty of Washington," pp. 544–547). By August, after enduring nearly four months of the oppressive heat and humidity of Washington and completing the exhausting negotiation of the northeastern boundary dispute, Ashburton was more than ready to return to England (see above, Ashburton to DW, July 31, 1842, "The Treaty of Washington," pp. 657–658). In October, Commodore Thomas ap Catesby Jones seized Monterey, confirming Mexico's indisposition to consider the cession of any territory to the United States (see above, "Mexico, Texas, and the United States," pp. 373–481).

In that same month, Aberdeen, still unaware of his own government's contributions to the deadlock over Oregon, expressed deep regret that the issue had not been resolved in the Treaty of Washington (see above, Everett to DW, October 17, 1842, "The Treaty of Washington," pp. 700–703). On October 18, he instructed Henry S. Fox to propose that negotiations on "the only remaining subject of Territorial Difference" between the two countries be conducted by Everett in London (see below). While the Tyler administration was considering how to respond to Aberdeen's initiative (DW to Everett, November 28, 1842, below), the president sent to Congress his extraordinary second Annual Message of December 6. In addition to renewing the "visit" and "search" controversy, Tyler provoked the British with his remarks about the Pacific Northwest. After referring to Oregon as "the Territory of the United States . . . to a portion of which Great Britain lays claims," he told Congress that he would "not delay to urge" upon the British the importance of an early resolution of the Oregon question (*Messages and Papers*, 4:196). Aberdeen told Everett that it was misleading for the president to insinuate that the United States had taken the lead in urging Britain to settle the Oregon boundary dispute, when in fact the opposite was true (see above, Everett to DW, February 1, 1843, "The Aftermath and Implementation of the Treaty of Washington: The 'Visit' and 'Search' Controversy," pp. 805–807). Privately, Aberdeen characterized Tyler's statements about Oregon as "most uncandid" (Aberdeen to Croker, February 25, 1843, in Louis J. Jennings, ed., *The Croker Papers: The Correspondence and Diaries of the Late Right Honourable John Wilson Croker* [3 vols., London, 1884], 2:399).

In the meantime, on January 29, 1843, Webster transformed his tripartite intimation of 1842 into a plan. If Mexico would sell Upper California to the United States, the United States would accept a division of the Oregon territory along the lines proposed by Canning in 1826. Mexico would use the money paid by the United States to reimburse both American and British claimants, and the United States would acquire two enclaves containing adequate harbors, the one from Britain and the other from Mexico (see DW to Everett, November 28, 1842, and January 29, 1843, below). Webster did not, as many scholars assume, contemplate simply relinquishing the territory north of the Columbia River in exchange for British acquiescence in a Mexican cession that included the port of San Francisco. Having been made aware of the perilous sandbar at the mouth of the Columbia River by the June 1842 report of Lieutenant Charles Wilkes, Webster knew that the Strait of Juan de Fuca contained "all the good harbors" in the disputed area (DW to Everett, November 28, 1842, below). As suggested in the documents printed below, he seems to have had in mind going back to Canning's enclave proposal of 1826, and he wanted to conduct the negotiation himself in London as a special envoy.

By the winter of 1842–1843, Webster was seeking a graceful exit from the Tyler administration. With the president moving toward the annexation of Texas and a political rapprochement with segments of the Democratic party, Webster knew that his days as secretary of state were numbered. Hoping to follow the happy precedent of the Ashburton mission, Webster on February 24 confidentially asked Caleb Cushing to consult with John Quincy Adams to see whether the House Committee on Foreign Affairs would recommend the appropriation of funds for a special commissioner to Britain to resolve the Oregon question (DW to Cushing, February 24, 1843, below). On February 28, Adams moved that a bill under consideration be amended to provide funds "for a special Minister" to Britain, but the motion failed (Adams, *Memoirs*, 11:329–330).

Even if Congress had made provision for a special mission to Britain, it is doubtful that the tripartite plan would have fared well. When Adams discovered in March what Webster had in mind, he denounced the proposal as an abyss of duplicity (Adams, *Memoirs*, 11:344–347). Mexico remained firmly opposed to any territorial bargain with the United States, and Aberdeen, still oblivious to what Addington had wrought, expressed "a decided repugnance" to becoming a party to the tripartite initiative. The foreign secretary also was decidedly lukewarm toward the idea of a special mission (see Everett to DW, February 27, 1843, below).

In the absence of any resolution of the Oregon question, Webster was determined to uphold the interests of the United States. His last important state paper on the subject, a letter to the secretary of the Navy dated March 21, 1843, requested that the commander of the Pacific squadron be instructed "to maintain, by force, if necessary, the rights of American citizens" in Oregon (see DW to Abel P. Upshur, below). Webster considered Oregon itself of little value, characterizing it as "a poor country, in comparison with the U. States, or even with California" (DW to Everett, January 29, 1843, below). With his mercantile outlook, however, he was determined to try to acquire for the United States a harbor on the Pacific to facilitate access to the markets of Asia. As for the tripartite project, it lapsed with Webster's resignation from his cabinet post, never to be revived again.

FROM HENRY STEPHEN FOX, WITH ENCLOSURE

Washington
Sir,   November 15th 1842

With reference to our recent conversation upon the Question of the Oregon or North Western Boundary, when I conveyed to you the desire of Her Majesty's Government that instructions should at an early period be addressed to the United States Minister in London [Edward Everett], empowering him to treat with such Person as may be appointed by Her Majesty on the part of Great Britain, for a final settlement of that Question,

I have now the honor to enclose to you the extract of a Despatch addressed to me upon the subject by the Earl of Aberdeen,[1] in which the wishes of Her Majesty's Government are fully and satisfactorily set forth. I feel persuaded that the great importance of the matter at issue, and the friendly and conciliatory manner of Lord Aberdeens proposal, will induce the President of the United States to bestow thereupon his early and serious attention.

I avail myself of this occasion to renew to you the assurance of my distinguished consideration.   H. S. Fox

L S. DNA, RG 59 (Notes from Foreign Legations, Britain).

ENCLOSURE: LORD ABERDEEN TO HENRY STEPHEN FOX

Extract.   Foreign Office
Sir,   October 18th 1842.
The Ratifications of the Treaty concluded on the 9th of August between Great Britain and the United States, were exchanged by me on the 13th instant with the Minister of the United States accredited to the Court of Her Majesty [Edward Everett].

The more important Question of the Disputed Boundary between Her Majesty's North American Provinces and the United States being thus settled and the feelings which have been mutually produced in the People of Both Countries by this settlement being evidently favorable and indicative of a general desire to continue on the best footing with each other, it has appeared to Her Majesty's Government that Both Parties would act wisely in availing themselves of so auspicious a moment to endeavour to bring to a settlement the only remaining subject of Territorial Difference, which although not so hazardous as that of the North Eastern Boundary is, nevertheless, even at this moment, not without risk to the good understanding between the Two Countries, and may in course of time be attended with the same disruption of danger to their mutual peace as the Question which has recently been adjusted. I speak of the Line of Boundary West of the Rocky Mountains.

You are aware that Lord Ashburton was furnished with specific and detailed instructions, with respect to the treatment of this point of difference between the Two Governments,[1] in the general negotiations with which he was entrusted, and which he has brought to a satisfactory issue.

For reasons which it is not necessary here to state at length, that point, after having been made the subject of Conference with the American Secretary of State, was not further pressed. The main ground alleged by

1. See below.   February 8, 1842, FO 5/378 (PRO).
1. No. 2. Aberdeen to Ashburton,

His Lordship for abstaining from proposing to carry on the discussion with respect to the Question of the North West Boundary was the apprehension, lest, by so doing, the settlement of the far more important matter of the North Eastern Boundary should be impeded, or exposed to the hazard of failure.[2]

This ground of apprehension now no longer exists and Her Majesty's Government, therefore, being anxious to endeavour to remove, so far as depends on them, all cause, however remote of even contingent risk to the good understanding now so happily restored between two Countries which ought never to be at variance with Each other, have determined to propose to the Government of the United States to meet them in an endeavour to adjust by Treaty the unsettled question of Boundary West of the Rocky Mountains.

On the receipt of this despatch, therefore, I have to desire that you will propose to Mr Webster to move the President to furnish the United States Minister at this Court, with such Instructions as will enable him to enter upon the negotiation of this matter with such Person as may be appointed by Her Majesty for that object. And you will assure him, at the same time, that we are prepared to proceed to the consideration of it in a perfect spirit of fairness, and to adjust it on a basis of equitable compromise. I am with great truth and regard, Sir, your most obedient humble servant.

Aberdeen.

Copy. DNA, RG 59 (Notes from Foreign Legations, Britain).

TO HENRY STEPHEN FOX

Department of State,
Sir: Washington, 25th Novr 1842.

I have the honor to acknowledge the receipt of your note of the 15th instant, upon the question of the Oregon or northwestern boundary, with an extract of a despatch recently addressed to you on the same subject by the Earl of Aberdeen,[1] explanatory of the wishes of Her Majesty's Government, both of which I laid before the President a few days afterwards.

He directed me to say that he concurred entirely in the expediency of making the question respecting the Oregon territory a subject of immediate attention and negotiation between the two governments. He had already formed the purpose of expressing this opinion in his message to Congress;[2] and at no distant day a communication will be made to the Minister of the United States in London [Edward Everett].

2. See No. 10. Ashburton to Aberdeen, June 29, 1842, FO 5/379 (PRO).
1. See above.

2. In his second Annual Message, of December 6, 1842, President Tyler stated that the Oregon question had not been dealt with in the Webster-

I pray you to accept the renewed assurance of my distinguished consideration.   Danl Webster.

LC. DNA, RG 59 (Notes to Foreign Legations, Britain).

TO EDWARD EVERETT

Private   Washington
My Dear Sir,   Nov. 28. 1842

I believe I have nothing, which needs to be made the subject of a Public Despatch, by this conveyance. Some topics, however, in your recent private letters,[1] require attention.

1st   The first of these subjects is the Oregon Territory. The President quite agrees with Lord Aberdeen & Sir Robt Peel, that both Governments should avail themselves of the present opportunity to settle, if they can settle, all disputes respecting this Territory. Mr [Henry Stephen] Fox has made us a communication, relative to the subject;[2] but before this was recd the President had prepared a notice of it, to be inserted in his Message to Congress next week. The question is, how, or upon what basis, is a negotiation to be opened? The title is disputed, between the Parties; shall this question of title be referred to a third Power? Or, if a compromise be attempted, in what form or on what principle? A Division of the Territory might naturally be suggested; and at first blush the Columbia River might seem to present itself as a convenient line of Division. But there are great peculiarities about this River. It affords very small accommodations to commerce, in comparison with its size, or volume of water. For nine months in the year, the navigation of its mouth is regarded as impracticable; & for the rest, quite uncertain & inconvenient. If we should consent to be limited by the River, on the North, we shall not have one tolerable harbour on the whole coast. The Straits of St Juan de Fuca, & the inland waters with which they communicate undoubtedly contain all the good harbors between the Russian Settlements & California. You remember, that when the subject was last up, there was a proposition that the U.S. should hold an isolated Territory, embracing some of these inland waters, & to have a passage thro the Straits.[3] But disconnected Terri-

---

Ashburton negotiations when it "became manifest" that any attempt to do so "would lead to a protracted discussion," thereby jeopardizing "other more pressing matters." He would not, he continued, "delay to urge on Great Britain the importance of its earliest settlement." *Messages and Papers,* 4:196.

1. See Everett to DW, October 17,

1842, mDW 23576, in which Everett discussed Oregon, and his note of October 20, 1842, published in *Correspondence* 5:247.

2. See above, Fox to DW, November 15, 1842.

3. In 1826, the British offered the United States an enclave in Oregon bounded on the north by the Juan de Fuca Strait, on the east by a line

tories are inconvenient. England wants a good harbor, in the Sounds connected with the ocean thro these Straits; she may want, also, the privilege of transporting furs, & other commodities down the Rivers. And I suppose it is an object with her to retain the settlement at Vancouver, & the other small settlements farther north, under her jurisdiction, & protection. Does she want any more? I doubt whether she can contemplate any considerable colonization in these regions. I doubt exceedingly whether it be an inviting country to agricultural settlers.

At present, there are not above 700 White persons on the whole Territory, both sides the River, & from California to Lat. 54 North; & about 20,000 Indians. It has been suggested, that the line of boundary might begin, on the sea, or the entrance of the Straits of St Juan de Fuca—follow up those straits, give us a harbor at the southwest corner of these inland waters, & then continue South, striking the River below Vancouver, & then following the River to its intersection with the 49th Lat. North. I describe this without reference to the maps, or without having them before me; but you will understand the general idea.

2. Commercial Intercourse. This divides itself into two heads, Navigation & Commerce.

1. Navigation. It is not to be disguised that great dissatisfaction exists in this Country with the present state of our intercourse with the British Colonies. Both Houses of Congress moved on the subject, at the last session, & very full & striking reports were made in one of them.[4] While our Treaty with England gives us a fair & equal chance in the direct trade between the U.S. & the English possessions in Europe, our navigation is exposed to great inconvenience in all that regards intercourse with the British West Indies.

This is a proper subject for negotiation; & the President would be happy that the two Governments should agree to take it into consideration.

2. Commerce. By this I mean the question of *duties*, about which, as you know Genl [Duff] Green had conversation with Lord Ripon and Mr [John] McGregor.[5] This matter is difficult & delicate. We regard the primary object of duties to be Revenue; & the power of laying duties

---

from Admiralty Inlet to Hood's Inlet, and on the south from Hood's Inlet to Gray's Harbor on the ocean. The American negotiator, Albert Gallatin, rejected the offer. See Gallatin to Clay, December 2, 1826, in *ASP: FR*, 6:655–656.

4. During the second session of the Twenty-seventh Congress, a number of memorials were presented calling for modification or repeal of the commercial regulations with the British colonies as established in the convention of August 6, 1827. See the *Senate Journal* and *House Journal*, 27th Cong., 2d sess., Serial 394, No. 400. The House report of April 14, 1842, is in *House Reports*, 27th Cong., 2d sess., Serial 409, No. 650. For the convention of 1827, see *Treaties*, 4: 315–385.

5. See above, Everett to DW, No-

is one of the express grants to Congress. How far can the Treaty-making power be properly extended, in these cases? We have had but two instances, I think, & both under very particular circumstances, & very much limited; & yet both a good deal complained of. If you have the means at hand, turn to the Debates of 1796, on the Treaty making power, its just nature & extent. See especially Mr [James] Madison's speech, Mr [Jeremiah] Smith's of New Hampshire, and Mr [William Branch] Giles'.[6] Mr Madison's general notion was, that the Treaty making power ought not to be so far extended, as to interfere with subjects, a power over which was expressly granted to Congress by the Constitution. And perhaps this doctrine cannot well be disputed. Any attempt, therefore, to regulate duties, by Treaties, must be very well considered, before it is entered upon.

I believe that the President would not be altogether disinclined to send a Special Mission to England, in the ensuing Spring or Summer, to treat of the foregoing subjects; not, certainly, from any want of confidence in your skill & ability, but as a return of the respect showed to us by Lord Ashburton's mission. This may very much depend on the chance of success; for a Special Mission failing, would leave things worse than it found them. As to intercourse with the Colonies, if something be not soon done by Treaty, there is great probability that Congress will be induced to make it the subject of Legislative enactments.

I believe the President would be gratified, if you should accidentally converse with Lord Aberdeen, on these subjects, & learn, so far as you can, his inclinations. On the commercial part of the case, you may perhaps find occasion to say something to Lord Ripon, or Mr [William Ewart] Gladstone.[7] It will be very well to hold up to Lord Aberdeen the great importance of settling the Oregon business, the probability that Congress may provide for sending a force into that region, &c. &c. And you may very safely assure the Gentlemen connected with the Board of Trade, that we shall be after <by> them, by Acts of Congress, unless they will come to some reasonable relaxation of their present system of Colonial Intercourse.

As Lord Ashburton will probably be in Town by January, you will have

vember 3, 1842, "The Aftermath and Implementation of the Treaty of Washington: The Cass-Webster Controversy," pp. 721–724.

6. The debate, which lasted from March 7 to April 7, 1796, is in *Annals of Congress*, 4th Cong., 1st sess., pp. 426–784. See Madison's remarks, pp. 437 and 774–781; those by Jeremiah

Smith (1759–1842), pp. 593–601; and William Branch Giles (1762–1830; Princeton 1781), pp. 500–514.

7. Gladstone (1809–1898), a member of Parliament from 1833 to 1895, was vice president of the Board of Trade from 1841 until May 1843, when he became president.

opportunity of falling into conversation with him, on this subject, which I hope you will improve.

We shall be considering of instructions to be given to you, if the idea of a special mission, now quite in embryo, should not be matured.

Congress assembles this day week. With what temper remains to be seen. The Whigs, as you know have been every where beaten, and quite deservedly. Their great concern, since Genl. [William Henry] Harrisons death, has been to make a successor to Mr [John] Tyler; & for that succession they will have no one but Mr [Henry] Clay. The result so far, is as disastrous to the Whig cause as was foreseen, by all persons of any sagacity. Blights & mildews afford the same auspices for good crops, as Mr Clay's name does for political & party success. I suppose the Whig Party may be regarded as now broken up. The name may remain, but without entirely new leaders, the members of the party can never again be rallied. A vast portion of the moderate & disinterested, will join in support of the President; & there is reason to think some portion of the other party, composed of persons of like character, will take a similar course. The President will meet Congress with an excellent message, likely I think to be quite well received.[8] But for the dissensions between him & Congress, respecting matters which all now admit were of no importance, his administration would have been highly popular. He has two years yet, in which to show his management of public affairs, & I cannot but think he will gain on the public confidence.

Genl [Lewis] Cass' letter, which you saw, or heard, was duly recd.[9] It will be answered, & of that answer I shall send you a copy, by the next conveyance.

My family is yet at the North, but I look for Mrs [Caroline Le Roy] W[ebster] to join me this week. I had a glorious month of leisure on the sea coast, where Seth Peterson & I settled many a knotty point. I went also to my native hills, for ten days, & frolicked with other young fellows of that region. My health is quite good, & I mean to take political events with a good deal of philosophy.

I pray you make my most kind remembrances to Mrs [Charlotte Brooks] Everett, & your daughters [Anne Gorham Everett and Charlotte Brooks Everett], & believe me, my Dear Sir, Ever mo. truly Yrs

Danl Webster

P.S. I was excessively proud of what you report Mr [Samuel] Rogers to

8. Tyler's message of December 6, 1842, is in *Messages and Papers*, 4: 194–209.

9. See above, Cass to DW, October 3, 1842, and DW's response of November 14, 1842, "The Aftermath and Implementation of the Treaty of Washington: The Cass-Webster Controversy," pp. 717–721, 724–734.

have said, of my Letter on Impressment, as well as by your own friendly sayings on that point.[10] I must confess I never took more pains to make a clear case, & to put it in short compass.

Pray give Mr Rogers, & his Sister, assurances of my most sincere & cordial regard.

ALS. MHi. Published (with silent deletions) in *PC*, 2:153–154.

FROM EDWARD EVERETT

Private

My dear Sir,   London 2 Jan. 1843.

I received your letter marked "Private"[1] by the Steamer of the 1st Decr.

With respect to the Oregon boundary, there is no necessity of my urging the expediency of settling it upon this Government. I have not seen Lord Aberdeen for any purpose, since the result of Lord Ashburton's negociations was known in this Country, that he has not expressed the wish, that this question should be immediately taken up by the two Governments. I think there is some feeling, that Lord Ashburton did not do all he might, to include this subject in his treaty. The purport of Lord Aberdeen's despatch to Mr [Henry Stephen] Fox was communicated to you.[2] Mr Fox wrote back in reply, that you had informed him, that the President concurred in the sentiments expressed by Lord Aberdeen, as to the expediency of a prompt adjustment, & that a communication would be made to me on the subject. Lord Aberdeen and myself were both on a visit to Sir Robert Peel, when the letters by the Steamer of the 1st Decr arrived. Lord Aberdeen got his sooner than I received mine. He took me aside, with an expression of evident satisfaction, and stating what Mr Fox had written to him, said, that he considered this as an intimation, on your part, that I should be instructed to negotiate with him, (as requested in his note to Mr Fox), for the settlement of the Oregon boundary. As my letters had not then reached me, I could say nothing on the subject. The next day they came, and it was not without disappointment, that Lord Aberdeen perceived, that he had some what misapprehended the account of your observations to Mr Fox. On the subject of the terms on which the boundary could be settled, he was more reasonable, than I expected to find him. Lord Ashburton, I believe, was instructed not to allow us to cross the Columbia river to the North; but when I sketched to him your idea, as stated in your letter of the 28th Novr, although he did not

10. See Everett to DW, October 20, 1842, in *Correspondence* 5:247. DW's impressment letter is above, DW to Ashburton, August 8, 1842, "The Treaty of Washington," pp. 673–679.

1. See above.

2. See above, Fox to DW, November 15, 1842, and enclosure, Aberdeen to Fox, October 18, 1842.

say *totidem verbis* that he would agree to that line, he said "I do not think we should have any difficulty in settling it."

I then sounded him as to his willingness to entertain the consideration of a relaxation of the colonial system, in reference to the trade between the U.S. and British West Indies. He did not seem much to like it; said he could give no opinion without knowing what we desired; that they could not be expected to give up gratuitously a system, merely on the ground, that it was found favorable to British tonnage, if that was the case. They would consider, of course, any proposal we might have to make on the subject.

With respect to commerce generally, I found that Genl. [Duff] Green's conversation had left no distinct impression on his mind: he said he recollected only that Genl. G[reen] had said, that if G. Britain would take our *Indian Corn* on a low duty, that the United States would do the same by their manufactures. At this point, we were interrupted. Lord Ripon was also on a visit to Sir R. Peel at the same time, and I broached the topic of a commercial treaty with him. He asked if we could give them any advantages to the exclusion of other nations? I told him, that though there was no constitutional obstacle to its being done, our practice had been to offer the same terms to all nations; and though we might agree to admit their manufactures on low duties, provided that they would take our products in the same way, we should probably think it necessary to grant the same privilege to all other nations willing to accede to the same condition. Mr Fox, it seems, had written to Lord Aberdeen, that the idea of a special mission had been thrown out in the United States, and something was said on that topic, in the conversation above alluded to, between Lord Aberdeen & myself. Lord A[berdeen] said he would talk with Sir Robert Peel about it; but the suggestion did not appear to strike him favorably. He said that if it failed in its objects, it would leave matters worse than it found them. He appeared unwilling to admit the necessity of a special mission, fearful, as it seemed to me, that doing so would detract from the importance of the Treaty just concluded. He intimated that a special mission was an extraordinary step to be resorted to, in critical cases, when the ordinary method of procedure had failed; and seemed reluctant to admit, that such was the existing state of things.

After my return from Drayton Manor, I went, by invitation, to pass Christmas with my wife [Charlotte Brooks Everett] & daughter at Lord Ashburtons. In compliance with your directions, I conferred with him freely on the various topics of your letter. He was a good deal struck with what I said, as to Lord Aberdeen's reception of my proposal, about the Boundary. He said he could have settled it with you, had he been authorized to concede us a strip North of Columbia river, terminating in a port, within the Straits of Juan de Fuca. With respect to the West India trade & a commercial treaty, he said there was a disposition very favorable to entertaining any proposal for more liberal arrangements as to commerce generally. With respect to a special mission, Lord Ashburton viewed it much as Lord Aberdeen had done; with some feeling I thought of personal objection to a measure, which might seem to derogate from the value of his own arrangement. He said, however, that if the United States thought proper to institute such a mission, it would of course be received with all honor and respect. On my return to town, I called on Mr [John] MacGregor at the board of trade. His character is known to you. He is of the most liberal school of political economists. He is for free trade to the fullest extent, & would agree to any relaxation of the Colonial System or the existing restraints on commerce. His views to this degree are, of course, not shared by the present Ministry; but I have no doubt Lord Ashburton is right in saying there is a disposition to entertain favorably all proposals for a more liberal intercourse with us.

Allow me to say, that, while I should by no means despair of obtaining from G.B. a relaxation in reference to the W. India trade, if we could offer them any thing like a *quid pro quo*, perhaps even without any consideration, I should greatly doubt the policy, on the part of the President, yourself, & Mr [Caleb] Cushing, of taking up the subject in the way of legislative measures,[3] *unless the democratic leaders in opposition will join in the responsibility*. The danger of such a policy was fully demonstrated in Mr. [John Quincy] Adams' time.[4] If made a party question, it will go against you. I am by no means sure that the British would regret the interruption of the direct trade with the United States, even in their own bottoms. They would expect to get it down the St Lawrence. Lord Ashburton threw out this suggestion.

Sir Robert Peel said they understood that the Chinese meant to admit us to a participation of the enlarged trade in their ports, but not the French. The Great Seal was yesterday attached to the Chinese treaty.[5]

With respect to the Mission, I think the President sh'd do what he thinks best, with regard to small objections here. It cannot but be honorably received. I need not add, that if, as I trust, you are to be the Minister, nothing would afford me greater pleasure. Pray remember us all most

---

3. Cushing, a member of the House Committee on Foreign Affairs, submitted the report of April 14, 1842, on British trade restrictions referred to in DW's letter to Everett of November 28, above.

4. In his second Annual Message, of December 5, 1826, President Adams recommended economic retaliation against the British because of their restrictions on the colonial trade (*Messages and Papers*, 2:350–364). With Congress hopelessly split over the issue, no legislation was enacted. Adams then resorted to retaliation by proclamation.

5. The Treaty of Nanking, which was signed on August 29, 1842, is in *British and Foreign State Papers, 1841–1842* (London, 116 vols., 1812–1925), 30:389–403.

kindly in your family circle & believe me, as ever, affectionately Yours
Edward Everett.

ALS. MHi.

TO EDWARD EVERETT

Private and Confidential.

My Dear Sir: Washington, Jany 29, 1843.

Your despatch and private letter by the "Caledonia," (Jany 3d) were received yesterday,[1] and I write this hastily, as it must leave Washington to-morrow morning, in order to reach the vessel at Boston before her departure on the 1st of February.

You will have noticed that the business of the Oregon Territory is exciting a good deal of interest in Congress. A bill was introduced into the Senate by Dr [Lewis Fields] Linn, not only for extending criminal jurisdiction over our citizens in that region, (after the example of the English statute,) but also making prospective regulations for granting lands to settlers. This latter part of the measure is opposed, as being inconsistent with existing arrangements between the two Governments. Mr. [John Caldwell] Calhoun, Mr. [John Macpherson] Berrien, Mr [Rufus] Choate, Mr. [George] McDuffie,[2] and others have spoken strongly in opposition to the bill, and Mr [Thomas Hart] Benton, Dr Linn, Mr [Samuel] McRoberts,[3] and other western gentlemen in favor of it. The probability is, it will not pass the Senate.[4] This new outbreak of interest and zeal for Oregon has its origin in motives and objects this side the Rocky Mountains. The truth is, there are lovers of agitation; and when most topics of dispute are settled, those which remain are fallen on with new earnestness and avidity. We feel the importance of settling this question if we can; but we fear embarrassments, and difficulties, not, perhaps, so much from the subject itself, as from the purposes of men, and of parties, connected with it. Mr. Calhoun distinguished himself by his support of the late

1. No. 30. Everett to DW, December 30, 1842, DNA, RG 59 (Despatches, Britain). The private letter is Everett to DW, January 2, 1843, above.

2. McDuffie (1790–1851; University of South Carolina 1813) served as a congressman from South Carolina, 1821–1834, and as senator, 1842–1846.

3. McRoberts (1799–1843; Transylvania University) served as senator from Illinois, 1841–1843.

4. The existing agreement providing for free and open access to the Oregon Territory was signed on October 20, 1818, and renewed on August 6, 1827 (*Treaties*, 2:658–662, 3:309–314). Linn's bill for the occupation and fortification of Oregon passed the Senate on February 3 but was not considered in the House. The congressional debates are in *Cong. Globe*, 27th Cong., 3d sess., pp. 99–100, 238–240; see also app., *passim*.

treaty. You know his position before the country, in regard to the approaching election of President. Mr. Benton, as leader of the [Martin] Van Buren party, or at least of the more violent part of it, is disposed to make war upon every thing which Mr Calhoun supports; and seems much inclined at present to get up an anti-English feeling, whenever and wherever possible. You have read his speech on the treaty,[5] written as it is said, after the adjournment of the Senate. In the spirit of this speech he fell upon Oregon; and the treaty and the Oregon questions are now under discussion together.

I have conversed with the President since he was made acquainted with the contents of your last private letter. We gather from that, that Lord Aberdeen and Lord Ashburton are, on the whole, of opinion, that a special mission would hardly be advisable. But the President still retains a strong impression that such a measure would be useful.

You know what has been said about a cession of California to the United States. England, as we learn from you, as well as from other sources, would rather favor such a transaction, if it might be the means of settling the Oregon business. It has occurred to me, therefore, to consider, whether it might not be possible to make a *tripartite* arrangement.

1. Mexico to cede Upper California to the United States.

2. United States to pay for the cession _____ millions of dollars.

3. Of this sum, _____ millions to be paid to citizens of U.S. having claims on Mexico.

4. The residue to English subjects, having claims, or holding bonds, against Mexico.

5. The line between U.S. and England, in Oregon, to be run pretty much as I mentioned to you.

These are only thoughts, not yet shaped into opinions.

The truth is, if we negotiate about Oregon alone, I hardly know what instructions to give you; because I cannot tell what sort of a treaty two-thirds of the Senate would be sure to agree to. Here is the difficulty. My own opinion of the value of that whole country is by no means as high as that of many others. It is a poor country, in comparison with the U. States, or even with California. And if our most mischievous spirit of party could be laid, I have no doubt a proper adjustment of all disputes respecting the territory might readily be effected. But almost any treaty would be opposed; and "two-thirds" is a great majority, to be expected on any measure, in the present state of things here. If we are to treat on this question, as a distinct and unconnected matter, there would be some advantage in entering on the negotiation here, as during the session of Congress we might be able to ascertain what would be satisfactory to the

5. Benton's speech of August 18, 1842, is in *Cong. Globe*, 27th Cong., 3d sess., app., pp. 1–27, esp. pp. 17–19.

Senate. But I fear that this Department and Mr. Fox would not be likely to make any very rapid progress.

I ought to say, that we do not yet know how far Mexico would listen to the idea of the cession of California. Mr. [Waddy] Thompson has been instructed to sound its Government, on that particular, but we have as yet no answer.[6] I have spoken on the subject to Genl [Juan Nepomuceno] Almonté; but he has, at present, no instructions. The revolutionary state of that Government, its war with Texas, and Yucatan, may prove favorable, or unfavorable, to the cession, according to circumstances, and the interests and objects of those in power at the moment.

We hope to hear from you again before the rising of Congress; and perhaps your next communication will determine the President's mind, on the subject of the extra mission. I believe the gentlemen of the Cabinet are all in favor of the measure, and that Mr Calhoun, and his friends in the Senate, also think well of it. (As to the person who would be sent, I suppose I may say the President would probably nominate me, if I should incline to go; but it is a question I should have great doubts about. If I could see a strong probability of effecting *both* objects—California and Oregon—I should not decline the undertaking.)

You are aware that if Congress should be now called on for an appropriation for the outfit and salary of a Minister, he must be nominated to the *Senate*, at the present session, according to those ideas of the powers of the President, which Southern gentlemen (and the President himself,) have held. This may probably oblige the President to come to a conclusion on the subject, sooner than may be convenient, or might be wished.

If nothing should be heard from you before the 3d of March, either to confirm or to weaken the President's present impression, it is quite probable he may recommend provision for the mission to Congress, and nominate the Minister; and yet not despatch him till more information be received, or further consideration had. If, therefore, you should hear of a nomination, you will not infer that a mission is absolutely decided on.

On receipt of this, I wish you would hold a free and confidential conversation with Lord Aberdeen, on the various points suggested in this private letter. The President has the strongest desire to settle this Oregon dispute, as well as every other difficulty with England. We all fully believe that the English Government is animated by an equally just and friendly spirit. Both Governments, undoubtedly, would rejoice to see this object accomplished soon. The way of accomplishing it, then, becomes a subject for mutual consultation; and you may assure Lord Aberdeen of, what I hope he does not doubt, <are> the perfect sincerity, good faith,

6. See above, DW to Thompson, June 27, 1842, and Thompson to DW, January 30, 1843, "Mexico, Texas, and the United States," pp. 440–441, 472–473.

and spirit of amity, with which we shall receive and reciprocate an inter-change of unofficial opinions, as to the course which the interest of both countries requires should now be adopted.

Your answer to this may be expected by the steamer which shall leave Liverpool on the 4th of March; and on its receipt here the President will make up his mind, if not done before, as to future proceedings.

No gentleman has yet been named as successor to Genl [Lewis] Cass. You will see that the President has recommended to Congress to make provision for some sort of a mission to China.[7] If the provision should be ample, and you were in the country, I think I should advise the President to send you to the Celestial Empire. It would be a mission full of inter-est, and with your powers of application and attainments you would make great additions to your stock of ideas. I have great difficulty in fixing on a proper person.

Be kind enough to make my most friendly regards to your family, and believe me always most truly Your friend and obedt. servt,

Danl Webster

LS. MHi. Published in Curtis, 2:175–177.

TO CALEB CUSHING

Private & Confidential
My Dear Sir;   Feb: 24. 1843
I wish to submit the enclosed three papers to the confidential perusal of Mr [John Quincy] Adams and yourself.[1] The near approach of the close of the session makes it indispensable to decide, soon, on transmit-ting or not, such a message as is roughly exhibited in the draft, one of the three papers enclosed.

Having perused the papers, if Mr. Adams think it advisable, I should be glad the Com[mitt]ee might be consulted on the expediency of the measure, Mr. Adams & yourself stating to them the general circum-stances. The<y> members are so many, I think it would not be advisable to read the letters to them.

We learn, from many sources, the great anxiety of England to settle the Oregon question; & we are encouraged, too, to think, that she is ready to listen to us, on the subject of the Colonial trade.

---

7. On December 30, 1842, Presi-dent Tyler recommended that Con-gress appropriate funds for a mission to China. See *Messages and Papers*, 4:211–214.

1. Not found. In his memoirs, however, John Quincy Adams re-corded that on February 25 Cushing had shown him "a confidential letter with enclosures" urging the House Committee on Foreign Affairs to rec-ommend an appropriation for a spe-cial mission to England. On February 28 the committee voted down the re-quest. See *Memoirs*, 11:327, 329–330.

We expect that such information will be recd next month, or by the middle of April, as will enable the President to come to a conclusion on the subject of a mission, if he should have the power to send one.

It would be quite prejudicial to recommend the measure, & that Congress should not adopt it. Without the hearty concurrence & cooperation, therefore, of the Com[mitt]ee it would probably be better that the attempt should not be made. I must pray you & Mr Adams to regard this as strictly confidential. Yrs truly   Danl Webster

ALS. DLC.

TO EDWARD EVERETT

Private
My Dear Sir   Washington Feb. 25. '43
    Your several communications by the Acadia, were duly recd, dates to the 3. Feby.[1]

In your official Despatch are many matters requiring attention, which it is impossible to answer by the return of that steamer, which leaves Boston the 1st March. We suppose the Great Western may be expected to leave N.Y. for Bristol, on or about the 15. of March, & by that vessel you will hear from us, in relation to all subjects, requiring communication.

Sir Robert Peel's speech has made something of a breeze, in Congress.[2] Mr [Henry Stephen] Fox has also read me a despatch, on the same subject, from Lord Aberdeen.[3] I caused your communication of Feb. 3rd to be immediately published,[4] showing his errors, in certain matters of fact. There are other errors, as we think, in his observations, of which notice will be taken, in some due manner; altho', perhaps, on this subject, the dispute, if it be so called, has come to be only a controversy about words.

1. The Department of State on February 22 and 24 received Everett's dispatches No. 31 of January 28 and an unnumbered dispatch of January 31, 1843. DNA, RG 59 (Despatches, Britain). Everett's No. 31, although bearing the date January 28, contained additional comments dated to February 3 and seems to have been written on that day. DW also received a private letter from Everett dated February 1, 1843 (see above, "The Aftermath and Implementation of the Treaty of Washington: The 'Visit' and 'Search' Controversy," pp. 805–807).

2. Peel's speech of February 2, 1843, is in *Hansard's* 66:86–98. Peel's remarks were discussed in the House on February 22 and 23; see *Cong. Globe*, 27th Cong., 3d sess., pp. 329, 331–336.

3. See above, Aberdeen to Fox, October 18, 1842, enclosed in Fox to DW, November 15, 1842.

4. An extract from Everett's dispatch No. 31, along with the text of the House debate on Peel's speech, appeared in the Washington, D.C., *National Intelligencer*, February 24, 1843.

Sir Robert says there is a well known difference between "Visit" & "Search." What authority has he, for this? I know of none. "Visite" is the French word, & is exactly equivalent to the English word Search. The *"Droite de Visite"* is the phrase by which all the Continental writers, so far as I know, describe that, which in England is called the "right of Search."

Probably I shall address you a despatch on these matters to be read to Lord Aberdeen;[5] but I cannot prepare it for this conveyance.

As to the Special Mission, the President is still strongly inclined to make provision for it, if Congress so see fit; but in the present temper of the two Houses, I exceedingly doubt whether the vote wd be carried. There are a great many people in this Country who want war with England; & many more who desire to keep up agitation. All these would be likely to oppose all extraordinary efforts to settle difficulties. The President seems to think *I* might assist in doing something in England, but I do not feel any confidence, in that respect.

If I knew <*whether*> that you would like our first Oriental Mission, I might think, possibly, of succeeding you, for a year in England.

Mr [Walter] Forward is to leave the Treasury this week. He is likely to be succeeded by Mr [John Canfield] Spencer or Mr [Caleb] Cushing.[6]

Congress has but 5 days more; & I shall be glad when those 5. expire. It is the strangest collection of men which we have had, under that name, since 1789.

Eve'—P.S. I have talked with many persons today. The result leaves the matter of the Special Mission as uncertain as ever. Yours most cordially,   Danl Webster

ALS. MHi.

FROM EDWARD EVERETT

Private.

My dear sir,   London 27 Feb. 1843.

Since my last despatch to you, I have received your public & private communication of the 27th January.[1] I lost no time in seeking an interview with Lord Aberdeen, & held a free conversation with him on the points alluded to in your private letter. With respect to a special mission, Lord Aberdeen appeared to entertain the same feeling as before; and he

5. See above, DW to Everett, March 28, 1843, "The Aftermath and Implementation of the Treaty of Washington: "The 'Visit' and 'Search' Controversy," pp. 807–817.

6. Spencer succeeded Forward as secretary of the Treasury.

1. The letters from DW to Everett are January 29, vice January 27, 1843. See the private letter, printed above. The public letter is No. 27. DNA, RG 59 (Instructions, Britain).

added that on mentioning the subject to Sir Robert Peel at Drayton, Sir R[obert] concurred with him, that a case for a special mission did not seem to exist, and & that if it failed, it would leave the question of the Oregon boundary, in a more difficult position than it now stood. He added, however, that it was an affair for the Government of the United States to decide, and if we thought proper to send a special minister, he would, of course, be received kindly & honorably.

With respect to the plan suggested by you for a *tripartite* arrangement, on the basis of a purchase of California, it did not appear to strike him very favorably. He admitted that he had formerly expressed to me a full willingness, on the part of England, that we should acquire a port on the Pacific, and that he had connected that idea with the adjustment of the Oregon boundary; but he said he did not mean to be understood, that England would wish to be a party to the steps taken for such an acquisition; nor had he supposed that we wished to go farther than to San Francisco. He had, however, no objection whatever to our buying California, if the Mexicans were willing to sell it, which he greatly doubted. He reminded me, with some pleasantry, that I had expressed some uneasiness, a short time since, at a report that a British Squadron was on its way to the coasts of California, while at about the same time we had ourselves invaded it & seized the capital.[2] I told him that this was the unauthorized act of the commander of one of our vessels, proceeding on a report, that war had broken out between us & Mexico. He said he did not doubt it; and repeated that England had no objection to our acquiring California, if the Mexicans would cede it; but he felt a decided repugnance to becoming a party to any pecuniary arrangement like that suggested by you. We then spoke of the terms on which the Oregon boundary could be settled. I repeated to him your plan for a strip of land, terminating in a port within the strait of Juan de Fuca, and he unrolled a large map of N. America, (Arrowsmith's, I believe,) published in 1825, in order to see what sort of a boundary this would give.[3] On this map a boundary was partially indicated in the coloring, substantially along the 49° of North Latitude, West, as well as East, of the Rocky Mountains. Pointing to the small extent of the debateable land, he said he could not and did not believe, that there could be any difficulty in coming to an amicable & reasonable settlement: that they would agree to any thing not positively discreditable; that they could not go on giving up every thing; but that they had no wish or feeling but for an honorable settlement. He then asked whether we should not be willing to make the Columbia river the bound-

2. On the temporary occupation of Monterey by Commodore Thomas ap Catesby Jones, see above, "Mexico, Texas, and the United States," pp. 373–481.

3. Aaron Arrowsmith (1750–1823) was a well-known London cartographer and publisher.

ary, provided it were stipulated that the Port at the Mouth should be as free to us as to them? I answered this question, by asking why *they* could not agree to the converse of this, vizt to run the line on the 49° to the sea, but we to allow them the free navigation of the River and the Port at the Mouth to be free? To this I do not recollect that Lord Aberdeen made any specific answer. He expressed great satisfaction at the assurance that the President & yourself were earnestly desirous of settling the question amicably, & repeated that, this being the case, there could not be much difficulty. On his making a slight allusion to the manner, in which this subject is spoken of in the President's Message at the beginning of the session, I told him that it was Lord Ashburton's opinion, that he could have come to arrangement with you on the subject, had he been authorized to accede to a proposal, like that for a strip of land running up to the Straits of Juan de Fuca.[4] He admitted that Lord Ashburton was not authorized, by his instructions to agree to a boundary North of the river. By this time, it was five oclock in the P.M. and Lord Aberdeen was obliged to go to the House of Lords. On parting he said "We'll have another conversation before the packet sails, & see if we cannot hit upon some plan of settling matters." I have accordingly sent him a note desiring him to name a time for another interview, & I will in another letter, let you know the result of the conversation.

I have seen Messrs [William] Richards & [Timoteo] Haalilio several times.[5] As Sir George Simpson was associated in the commission,[6] Mr Richards thought it better that the first approach to this Government should be obtained through his intervention, rather than mine, and in this I concurred with him. They have had an interview with Lord Aberdeen, who appears (as Mr Richards thinks) to hesitate a little, as to any formal act of recognition. Lord Aberdeen did not consider your letter to the Hawaiian Commissioners of the 19th Decr 1842, as entirely decisive as to the purpose of the government of the United States, to recognize the independent sovreignty of the Islands.[7] I shall, when I see Lord A[berdeen], acquaint him with what has been done, and what is doing in reference to this subject at Washington: but I suppose that if the appropriation asked for should be made, steps will be taken by the President, which will speak for themselves. It seems that as soon as Messrs Halileo

4. See Tyler's message of December 6, 1842, in *Messages and Papers*, 4: 194–209, esp. p. 196. For the remark by Ashburton, see above, Everett to DW, January 2, 1843.

5. Richards (1793–1847; Williams 1819); Haalilio (d. 1844); on the Richards-Haalilio mission, see below, "Daniel Webster and the Pacific: The 'Tyler Doctrine,'" pp. 851–877.

6. Simpson (1792–1860), who administered the Hudson's Bay Company from 1821 to 1856, also acted as an agent for Hawaii in England.

7. See DW to Haalilio and Richards, December 19, 1842, below, "Daniel Webster and the Pacific: The 'Tyler Doctrine,'" pp. 870–871.

& Richards left the Islands for the United States, the British consul[8] started clandestinely for England, leaving behind him an angry and insolent letter of complaint to the government of the Islands; and that he has succeeded in inspiring Lord Aberdeen with a notion, that, though the government of the United States have no intention of acquiring a control over the government of the Sandwich islands directly, the[y] perhaps look forward to the possession of a virtual & substantial influence, through the medium of the American missionaries, which would amount to an exclusive ascendancy, prejudicial to the interests of other countries. This was Mr Richard's opinion of the effect upon Lord Aberdeen's mind of the insinuations of the British consul. Should such prove to be the case,—as I can hardly think,—I shall probably find no difficulty, in removing such a groundless impression. I am, Dear sir, as ever most faithfully Yours   Edward Everett

LC. MHi.

TO ABEL PARKER UPSHUR

Department of State
Sir,   Washington 21st March 1843
    As Commodore [Alexander James] Dallas[1] is about to proceed to the Pacific, to take the command of the American Squadron in that sea, I have to ask of you that you will, in your instructions to him, draw his particular attention to the Territory claimed by the United States beyond the Rocky Mountains and lying along the shore of that ocean. Great Britain, as you know, asserts claim to the same territory, and by a Convention entered into between the two Governments, in 1818,[2] it was stipulated that any country claimed by either party, on the northwest coast of America, westward of the Stony Mountains, should, together with its harbors, bays, and creeks, and the navigation of all rivers within the same, be free and open, for the term of ten years, to the vessels, citizens and subjects of the two powers. And by the Convention of August, 1827,[3] these stipulations were further indefinitely extended and continued in force.
    The respective claims of the parties being not yet settled, and the agreement being still operative, the United States will faithfully fulfil that agreement, on their side, while it is proper that they should take care that no subordinate officer or agent of the British Government violate it on hers. Should an attempt be made by the British or any other

8. Richard Charlton, who was the first British consul in Hawaii, served at that post from 1825 to 1843.

1. Dallas replaced Commodore Thomas ap Catesby Jones as commander of the Pacific squadron after the Monterey affair.

2. The convention of October 20, 1818, is in *Treaties*, 2:658–662.

3. The convention of August 6, 1827, is in *Treaties*, 3:309–314.

nation to take possession of the mouth of the Columbia river, so as to control its trade, the duty would devolve upon Commodore Dallas of making a temperate yet firm representation, addressed to the proper officer, of the impossibility of submitting to such an invasion of the rights of the United States and of demands that no restriction whatever, shall be placed upon American citizens engaged in lawful pursuits in that quarter. If these proceedings, on his part, should not prove effectual in procuring the removal of the cause of complaint, it would be well for the Commodore, distinctly to announce his instructions to maintain by force, if necessary, the rights of American citizens. Whatever claim any other nation may assert to the Columbia river, an equal right on the part of the United States is to be advanced—care being taken not to wave their claim of exclusive jurisdiction, but expressly reserving that question for the American Government.

In the event of any attempt being made to interrupt American vessels trading to the river Columbia, the most prompt and effectual protection should be extended to them: in such mode as the circumstances of the case may appear to require. And if any improper interference with the present state of things in this Territory seem likely to be made by any British or other authority, no time should be lost by Commodore Dallas in signifying to such authority the nature of his instructions and in reporting the fact to this Government.

The Conventions of 1818. and of 1827. above referred to will be found, at length, in the sixth and eighth volume of the United States Laws. pp. 607 and 890. I am &c.   Danl Webster.

LC. DNA, RG 59 (Domestic Letters).

Daniel Webster and the Pacific

THE "TYLER DOCTRINE"

The United States had not yet become a Pacific power in the early 1840s, but the Tyler administration was Pacific-minded. Webster's abortive tripartite plan was designed in part to acquire deep-water ports in California and Oregon for America's enterprising merchants. The so-called Tyler Doctrine of 1842, which established the first coherent U.S. foreign policy toward the Hawaiian islands, also reflected the interest of the Tyler administration in the Pacific region. As with Oregon, the guiding hand in shaping American policy toward Hawaii was that of Secretary of State Daniel Webster.

Prior to the Whig administration of Tyler and Webster, the U.S. government had paid little attention to the remote "Sandwich islands," as they were called. Although a commercial agent had been appointed in 1820, American diplomatic contacts were haphazard and infrequent. In 1826, the ubiquitous naval commander Thomas ap Catesby Jones negotiated a treaty of friendship and commerce with the native chiefs of the islands. Washington was so little interested in Jones's unauthorized agreement that it was not even submitted to the U.S. Senate. Until about 1830, Britain, not the United States, held dominant control over the Hawaiian islands. By the time Webster became secretary of state, however, there had been a remarkable growth of American influence in the islands. That transformation was not due to the actions of the U.S. government. Rather, it was brought about by New England merchants and missionaries.

By 1841, Americans were preeminent in the economic life of the Hawaiian islands. Since the early nineteenth century Hawaii had functioned as an integral part of the profitable China trade. Departing from the ports of New England and New York with such goods as beads, blankets, ginseng, and rum, American merchant vessels sailed around Cape Horn to Honolulu, where they resupplied and took aboard sandalwood. From Honolulu they plied along the coast of the Pacific Northwest, exchanging such items as beads and blankets for furs, especially those of the sea otter. When the ships were filled with cargo, they sailed for Canton, where furs, ginseng, and sandalwood were traded for the silks and teas that brought high prices in Boston and New York City. In addition to being a way station in the China trade, Hawaii had also served since the 1820s as the center for the thriving American whaling industry in the Pacific. By the 1840s, Americans also dominated the import trade with Hawaii and even held the most extensive agricultural enterprises in the islands. James Jackson Jarves (1818–1888), the editor of the Honolulu *Polynesian*, estimated that from 1836 to 1841 American imports to Hawaii were four times as valuable as those coming from England. During the same period, according to Jarves's calculations, 358 American merchant vessels (four-fifths of which were whalers) touched at Honolulu, as compared with 82 ships for the British and 7 for the French (see Jarves, *History of the Sandwich Islands* [2d ed., Boston, 1844], pp. 361–362).

New England missionaries made an even greater impact on the Sandwich islands. The American Board of Commissioners for Foreign Missions, which had its headquarters in Boston, sent its first party of missionaries to Hawaii in 1819–1820. By 1842, the board had sponsored the establishment of seventy-nine mission stations, six schools, and two printing houses in the islands. More than 12,000 Hawaiians had been converted to Protestantism, and more than 15,000 had been educated in the schools, including the children of native chiefs. Hawaiian rulers such as Kamehameha III, moreover, came to rely on the missionaries for advice in commercial and political affairs. William Richards, for example, left the Hawaiian mission in 1838 to become one of the most important counselors to Kamehameha. Because of men such as Richards, Americans had a profound impact on the culture and society of the Hawiian kingdom. By 1842, as Ralph S. Kuykendall has written, American influence and interests in Hawaii were "probably superior to those of all other foreign powers combined" (Kuykendall, "American Interests and American Influence in Hawaii in 1842," *Thirty-Ninth Annual Report of the Hawaiian Historical Society* [Honolulu, 1931], p. 48).

American influence, particularly that of the missionaries, indirectly led to the persecution of Catholics in the Hawaiian islands, which, in turn, helps to explain the origins of the Tyler Doctrine. Beginning in 1829, native Catholics were discriminated against and French priests were expelled from the islands. On December 18, 1837, Kamehameha III issued "An Ordinance Rejecting the Catholic Religion." This sweeping law forbade the teaching of Catholicism and banned priests from entering the islands (for the law of 1837, see Ralph S. Kuykendall, *The Hawaiian Kingdom 1778–1854: Foundation and Transformation* [Honolulu, 1938], pp. 150–151). In July 1839 Captain Cyrille Pierre Théodore Laplace of the frigate *Artémise*, under instructions from his government, signed a treaty with the Hawaiians that granted religious equality to Catholics, provided special commercial privileges for French goods, and established a $20,000 fund as a guarantee of good behavior in the future by the Hawaiian chiefs. Laplace extracted these concessions by blockading Honolulu harbor and threatening to bombard the town. Laplace's gunboat diplomacy exposed the weakness of the Hawaiian kingdom and raised the possibility that it might become the colony of a European power.

The Laplace affair alarmed both the American missionaries and the Hawaiian government. In 1839, the American Board of Commissioners for Foreign Missions began memorializing Congress to provide its stations and educational establishments in Hawaii with protection from aggression by European nations. The letter from Hiram Bingham printed below (Bingham to DW, July 21, 1841) was part of the effort by the board to secure the support of the U.S. government. Bingham, who was with the first group of American missionaries sent to the islands in 1819–1820 and who holds the distinction of having reduced the Hawaiian language to writing, held interviews, with both Tyler and Webster. According to Bingham, Webster stated that missionaries deserved more protection than other Americans residing abroad and promised to lodge at least a nominal protest of the Laplace incident with the French authorities (Bingham to Rufus Anderson, July 23, 1841, as cited in Harold Whitman Bradley, *The American Frontier in Hawaii: The Pioneers, 1789–1843* [Stanford, Calif., 1942], pp. 315–316). There is, however, no record of any protest by Webster, and the Tyler administration continued to adhere to the traditional attitude of indifference toward the fate of the Hawaiian islands.

It was primarily the sustained diplomatic effort of the Hawaiian government to gain international recognition of its independence that finally induced the United States to formulate a foreign policy toward the Sandwich islands. Responding to the implications of the Laplace incident, Kamehameha in 1840 designated Thomas Jefferson Farnham (1804–1848), a lawyer and world traveler from Illinois who allegedly had influence in Washington, as his diplomatic agent with instructions to secure an acknowledgment of Hawaiian sovereignty from Britain, France, and the United States. Although Farnham wrote Webster in 1841 seeking recognition of his official character as an envoy from the king of Hawaii (Farnham to DW, November 25, 1841, DNA, RG 59, Notes from Foreign Legations, Hawaii), he accomplished nothing. There is no record of any response by Webster, and Farnham apparently made no further communication to the Department of State.

The second attempt by the Hawaiian government to gain admission into the family of nations was no more successful than the first. Peter A. Brinsmade arrived in Washington in March 1842 bearing a letter from Kamehameha III to President Tyler. Kamehameha proposed that the United States enter into a convention with Britain and France recognizing the independence of Hawaii "in its monarchial form" and stipulating that disputes between Hawaii and the three powers be resolved in an unusual way. Disagreements between Hawaii and the United States were to be settled by the British and French ministers resident in Washington, those between Hawaii and Britain by the American and French ministers resident in London, and those between Hawaii and France by the American and British ministers resident in Paris (see Kamehameha III to Tyler, November 24, 1841, enclosed in Brinsmade to DW, April 8, 1842, below). On April 8, Brinsmade also provided the secretary of state with detailed information about "the Malta of the North Pacific" (Brinsmade to DW, below). Brinsmade's remarkable letter, which contained a broad geopolitical analysis of the importance of Hawaii to the United States, received no reply from Webster. Nevertheless, that communication and Brinsmade himself embodied American interests and influence in the Sandwich islands. Although Brinsmade was not a missionary, he had studied for the ministry at Andover Theological Seminary and Yale Divinity School and had close relations with the American Board of Commissioners for Foreign Mission's missionaries in Hawaii. He also was a partner in the firm of Ladd & Company, which established the first permanent sugar plantation in the islands in 1835. Moreover, from 1839 to 1846 Brinsmade served as U.S. commercial agent in Honolulu. From Washington, Brinsmade went to London and Paris, where both Lord Aberdeen and François Guizot declined to participate in a tripartite guarantee of Hawaiian independence.

On their third try, the Hawaiians finally elicited a response from the United States. William Richards and Timoteo Haalilio arrived in Washington on December 5, 1842, with instructions to achieve the goals set forth in King Kamehameha's letter of 1841 to President Tyler. Haalilio, described by John Quincy Adams as "a strong, stout-built man, nearly black as an Ethiopian, but with a European face, and wool for hair" (*Memoirs*, 11:274–275), was a native chief and the private secretary to Kamehameha. Between December 7 and December 29 they had seven meetings with the secretary of state, and they also were introduced to the president and the other members of the cabinet.

The Tyler administration's response to Haalilio and Richards was cautious and measured. According to the journal of William Richards, which recounted the conversations in Washington, the Hawaiian envoys were received coolly at their first meeting with Webster on December 7. He professed not to remember much about the Brinsmade mission and suggested that Haalilio and Richards proceed to London and first seek diplomatic recognition from the British (The Journal of William Richards, December 7, 1842, cited in Bradley, *American Frontier in Hawaii*, pp. 407, 441–442). At their second visit with Webster, on December 9, he requested that they put their views in writing, which they did on December 14 (see Haalilio and Richards to DW, December 14, 1842, below). When the third session with the secretary of state on December 23 elicited only a promise to respond to their note of December 14 and to write a letter of introduction to Edward Everett in London (see DW to Everett, December 24, 1842, below), Richards began hinting that if he failed to secure acceptance of Hawaiian independence from the United States, the British government would be asked to establish a protectorate over the islands. Hawaiian prospects for American diplomatic support immediately improved. At his meeting with President Tyler on December 27, Richards repeated his intimation that Britain might be asked to extend its protection over the Sandwich islands. The next day Webster indicated that the United States might recognize Hawaiian sovereignty, and on December 29 he read to Haalilio and Richards the formal response of the Tyler administration to their note of December 14. It was not, Richards recorded in his journal, quite what he wanted (The Journal of William Richards, December 29, 1842, cited in Bradley, *American Frontier in Hawaii*, pp. 443–444).

Although Webster's letter to Haalilio and Richards bearing the date December 19, 1842 (below), is commonly regarded as the first official state paper acknowledging Hawaiian independence, it is an ambiguous document that presents difficulties. To begin with, it may have been backdated or misdated. The Hawaiian envoys did not receive a copy of the letter, which probably should be dated December 29, until December 30. Secondly, as John Quincy Adams astutely observed, in "not very explicit language" Webster evaded "a direct acknowledgement" of Hawaiian sovereignty and declined to negotiate a treaty with Haalilio and Richards (*Memoirs*, 11:283–284). Webster also refused to exchange diplomats with the Hawaiian government and explicitly stated that the United States would continue "to be represented in the islands by a consul or agent." Nevertheless, Webster's letter revealed considerable knowledge on his part of the importance of the Hawaiian islands to the interests of the United States and set forth what came to be known as the Tyler Doctrine.

That doctrine is contained in the president's special message to Congress of December 30. The message seems to have been written by Webster, and it followed closely the ideas and even the words contained in his letter to Haalilio and Richards of December 19. Tyler began by pointing out that the Sandwich islands were closer to North America than to any other continent, that they were especially important to the American whale fishery in the Pacific Ocean, and that American citizens held substantial property investments in the islands. Since the islands were nearer to the United States than to Europe and since "five-sixths" of all the vessels visiting them annually were American, the U.S. government would be dissatisfied "at any attempt by another power . . . to take possession of the islands, colonize them, and subvert the native Government." The president went on to disclaim any intention of acquiring special commercial advantages or "exclusive control over the Hawaiian Government." Rather, the United States was "content with its independent existence" and anxiously desired Hawaiian "security and prosperity." Should any other foreign nation adopt "an opposite policy," the United States, because of the "very large intercourse" of American citizens with the islands, would be justified "in making a decided remonstrance" (*Messages and Papers*, 4:211–212). With these words, President Tyler extended the noncolonization and nonintervention principles of the Monroe Doctrine to the Hawaiian islands and established a foreign policy toward the islands that lasted until the United States annexed them in 1898.

Taken together, Webster's letter of December 19 and Tyler's message of December 30 implicitly defined Hawaii as an American sphere of influence. Neither document, however, granted diplomatic recognition to Hawaii as an independent nation. Although Webster wrote Everett on December 29 that the Tyler administration was taking "the lead, in declaring for the Independence of the Islands" (see below), his instructions of March 15, 1843, to George Brown convey a different story. Brown was specifically told that he was given the title "Commissioner" because it had not yet been "deemed expedient . . . fully to recognize the independence" of Hawaii. Commissioner Brown was to maintain Hawaiian independence from other foreign powers and to "frustrate" any attempts by them to obtain exclusive commercial or political influence in the islands, but he was not given the status ordinarily conferred on diplomats residing in countries regarded by the United States as fully independent and sovereign (DW to Brown, March 15, 1843, below).

The ambiguity of American policy caused problems for Haalilio and Richards in Europe. Although Guizot told them that France would acknowledge Hawaiian independence (see Henry Ledyard to DW, March 23, 1843, below), Aberdeen refused to grant diplomatic recognition because the United States had not done so. The British foreign secretary assessed Webster's letter of December 19 as a virtual denial of Hawaiian sovereignty and possibly a ploy to establish an American protectorate over the islands (see Haalilio and Richards to DW, March 3, 1843, below). Webster responded by disclaiming a "sinister purpose, of any kind, on the part of the United States" toward that "remote but interesting groupe of Islands" (DW to Everett, March 23, 1843, below). On November 28, 1843, Britain and France issued a joint declaration acknowledging Hawaii as an independent state, but the United States did not follow suit until July 6, 1844, when Secretary of State John C. Calhoun specifically assured Haalilio and Richards that Washington fully recognized the independence of the Hawaiian kingdom.

John Quincy Adams attributed the evasiveness in Webster's approach to Hawaii to the fact that Hawaiians were "black" (*Memoirs*, 11:274–

275), and William Richards thought that it grew out of Webster's unwillingness to take any step that might not be politically popular (see Kuykendall, *Hawaiian Kingdom*, p. 193). Neither of these explanations is satisfactory, and Webster's cautiousness can best be understood in terms of the limited goals of the Tyler administration. Responding to the subtle diplomacy of Richards, Webster and Tyler became concerned about the specter of Britain or France establishing a protectorate over the Hawaiian islands. Knowing that the British had annexed New Zealand in 1840–1841 and that the French had seized the Marquesas in 1842, Webster stated the "sole object" of American policy to be the preservation of the independence and neutrality of Hawaii (DW to Everett, March 23, 1843, below). Although he repudiated any colonial ambitions on the part of the United States, Webster wanted to protect the interests of American merchants and missionaries. He had already articulated the principles of supporting American missionaries abroad in the instruction to David Porter of February 2, 1842 (see "The World and Daniel Webster: The Middle East and Africa," pp. 280–281, above), and he was sensitive to the economic importance of the Hawaiian islands to American merchants and whalers (see DW to Haalilio and Richards, December 19, 1842, and DW to Brown, March 15, 1843, below). The Tyler Doctrine was designed to uphold these cultural and economic interests by denying the Hawaiian islands to any European power.

The Tyler Doctrine constitutes one of Webster's most significant diplomatic achievements, for it ended official indifference toward the Hawaiian islands and established a policy that lasted for more than fifty years. With it, Webster fashioned a flexible but coherent foreign policy that asserted that the United States would support Hawaiian independence because of the preponderance of American influence and interests there. The Tyler Doctrine extended some of the principles of the Monroe Doctrine of 1823 to the Pacific, and it anticipated those of the Open Door Notes of 1899–1900. Like the Open Door Notes, the Tyler Doctrine called for maintaining the territorial integrity of a weak nation threatened by European colonialism, and it similarly repudiated any special privileges for the United States while asking for equality of commercial access. The new foreign policy originated by Daniel Webster drew upon the principles of the past, and it paved the way for those of the future.

FROM HIRAM BINGHAM

Sir,   Washington July 21. 1841

I know your time is valuable, and have been unwilling to occupy it improperly. You kindly encouraged me to expect another interview. I feel it necessary to leave the city to day. My honored patrons will expect of me some account of my visit here; I feel anxious to have my fellow missionaries assured of protection. If you can allow me a few moments interview to inquire whether you have considered the subject, & whether the general expectation of the public at least of our Board and its numerous friends will probably be answered by the notice this government will take of the proceedings of Capt [Cyrille Pierre Théodore] Laplace,[1] I shall feel greatly obliged. Very respectfully your Huml Sert   H. Bingham

P.S. Should I not be able to gain an interview of a few minutes, on account of my patrons, will it be possible for you to give me a line, to the care of Genl [Nathan] Towson[2] of this city? To day, or at a more convenient season? and thus greatly oblige, your humble sert   H. B.

ALS. DNA, RG 59 (Misc. Letters). Rec'd July 21, 1841. Bingham (1789–1869; Middlebury College 1816) graduated from Andover Theological Seminary in 1819 and sailed for Hawaii on October 23, 1819. He was the leading missionary in Hawaii from 1820 until he returned to the United States in August 1840. Bingham visited Washington in July 1841 and spoke with President Tyler and DW.

FROM PETER ALLAN BRINSMADE, WITH ENCLOSURE

Washington City
Sir   April 8th 1842
    Previously to my leaving the Sandwich Islands about three months since, the King [Kamehameha III] placed in my hands a communication addressed to the President of the United States[1] desiring me to deliver it in person if practicable. He apprized me of the purport of the communication, and stated to me in some detail the views which determined him in making it, and the objects which he hoped to realize. I feel it due to him to submit to the Department the explanations he made to me, and due to the Government to state my own views, derived from a residency of nearly ten years in that Country, of the bearing of his proposals upon American Commerce and other interests connected with that Archipelago.
    The King in proposing that the independence of his Government shall be acknowledged in the form suggested, does not mean to imply that it has ever been a dependancy upon any foreign power: He feels that his independent Sovereignty has been in *fact* recognized by the foreign Gov-

1. In December 1837, King Kamehameha III (1813–1854), who ruled Hawaii from 1825 to 1854, issued an ordinance against the teaching or practice of the Catholic religion. The French government ordered Captain Laplace (1793–1875) to obtain reparations. Laplace sailed into Honolulu on July 9, 1839, and issued an ultimatum calling for an apology, resti-tution of Catholic privileges, and a $20,000 indemnity, to which the Hawaiians agreed. Laplace also obtained a treaty granting the French commercial privileges and extraterritorial rights.
    2. Towson (1784–1854), a hero of the War of 1812, was a distant relative of Bingham by marriage.
    1. See below.

ernments with whose authority he has been brought in contact by the commercial intercourse of their subjects or citizens so far as the *responsibilities* of an independent Sovereign have been [involved] but, that his independence has been accorded to him in *form* only. So far as the *privileges* and *immunities* of a Sovereign have been involved, he has been treated with as one under obligations to comply with exactions required for the protection and furtherance of foreign interests, but not as one authorized to require reciprocities favourable to his own Government and people. He feels that in his relations to foreign powers, he has rather been employed as an instrument to subserve their interests, than respected as a Ruler of his own people and the protector of their welfare— that he has been regarded more as a subject of foreign than as the minister of domestic justice, and therefore that his foreign relations on their present footing are more the occasion of embarrassment and humiliation than of encouragement and support.

His proposition is that he may be now formally placed before the world upon the dignity of his rights as well as upon the obligations of his duty. That his rights may not be wantonly and with impunity invaded, under any future circumstances of error and prejudice, or of political expediency, by the authority of either of the Governments to which he addresses his proposals, his chief security would be in their treaty stipulations to that effect—each to the other. He feels such a security to be indispensible to him particularly in a prospective view; for he is perfectly aware of the [adverse] claims of the United States and Great Britain to the territory of the North West Coast and is fully alive to the exposure in which his Islands would be placed in the event of that territory passing under the jurisdiction of the United States to the exclusion of that of the British Government. He is sufficiently informed that the Sandwich Islands constitute the Malta of the North Pacific, and knows full well that the independence or neutrality of their Government could not be protected from the ambition that grasps at the maratime supremacy of the world, but by the shield of an obligation for which adequate power would demand respect.

He has now entered upon a promising experiment of organizing and administering a Government through the medium of Constitutional law applicable to his own people and to the interests of all imigrants to the Country and to the commercial enterprizes connected with its markets. I beg leave to refer you to the volume sent herewith and to the translation of the Constitution adopted by the Government.[2] The translation of the

2. Not included in the RG 59 record. A copy of the constitution of October 8, 1840, is in *British and Foreign State Papers, 1841–1842* (116 vols., London, 1812–1925), 31:1256– 1263. Although continuing the monarchy, the constitution of 1840 also established a representative body and a supreme court and guaranteed freedom of religion.

laws was not completed when I left, but when completed will be forwarded to the Department. The whole I believe to be truly the production of native minds, and will I think be judged creditable to them, when it is considered that twenty years ago their language was an unwritten one and that then the nation was, in the darkest sense, without intelligence morality or Government. All the governmental measures that have been originated and put in operation for the last few years have had the direct tendency and object to elevate and improve the natives, by encouraging among all classes the arts and usages of a Civilized State. Domestic and Social order pervail to an extent never before known in the Country, and known in the instance of but few so recently in a perfectly barbarous condition. Industry is stimulated and directed to a profitable development of the natural wealth of the Country. The wants of the people are rapidly becoming Civilized, and the means of supplying such wants are keeping pace with the demand.

The attention of the Government has been strongly turned to the systematic education of the youth and children of the Country. Ample provision is made by law for the support of common schools, giving to every child in the nation the opportunity of receiving at least elementary instruction in the various departments of useful knowledge. All the young children of the Rulers, are at a boarding school in a very intelligent American family where they are making rapid proficiency in a course of thorough education in the English language.[3] Among them are the adopted and acknowledged successor to the present King and the declared future Governors of each of the Islands in the group.

The soil and climate are adapted to the production of every variety of tropical vegetation to an indefinite extent, and throughout the group, general attention is being turned to the cultivation of Sugar Coffee Indigo Silk Wheat &c and liberal encouragements are offered by the Government to foreign enterprise and capital with which the native population can unite their industry to turn into the channels of commerce their almost inexhaustible resources. Under the influence of these changes in the habits and pursuits of the people many of the causes of the former rapid descents of the population have been arrested, and an increase is now clearly perceptible.

But of all the many promising indications of permanence and advancement in the character and purposes of the Government and of the improvement of the people in Civilization, wealth and happiness, I know of none more favourable than the attitudes in which the King now places himself before the three most powerful and elevated Governments on the globe, looking to them for countenance and protection. That he honestly proposes in his relations to foreign Governments or their subjects,

3. Children of the Hawaiian royal families were educated in the school run by Amos Starr Cooke (1810–1871; Yale 1834), a missionary.

to do right, I am firmly persuaded—indeed I doubt if there be a sovereign on earth whose moral sense has a stronger control over his public acts, or who has a stronger purpose to do right on principle.

The honesty of his intentions in that respect could not well have been indicated more clearly than is done where in his proposals to the Governments of the United States, England and France, he expresses his desire that every act of his in his relations to those Governments by which either might be aggrieved, may be passed upon by an umpire of their own. He seems aware that in his limited experience in civil Government and equally limited knowledge of international law, he is liable to commit errors, and he wishes to secure in future, a forbearance that has seldom been shown him, till he can fairly be heard. His proposition for an umpirage suggests a most happy expedient for the adjustment of all difficulties that might otherwise threaten the peace of his people or the harmony of his foreign relations.

In wishing to be released from the obligations of his engagements with the Commanders of War Ships, he aims principally to remove an otherwise insuperable obstacle to raising a revenue for the support of his government by duties on imports. His engagements to Capt [Cyrille Pierre Théodore] Laplace, [primarily] in favour of the French, but by virtue of previous engagements equally favourable to all other nations, limit him to five Per. Cent, ad valorum duty, which would scarcely more than pay the expense of collecting. It is probable however, that, were the Country to be placed under the auspices that would be opened upon it, in the event of his present proposals being favourably entertained, its available resources would soon be so abundant as to authorize much heavier importations than are at present warranted, and consequently an ample revenue be realized by a ten or fifteen Pr. Cent. duty. Revenue by duty on imports would manifestly be the most impartial mode of taxation upon such a people, as each would pay in proportion to his consumption, and the consumption of each would be in proportion to his resources; and the tax would also [lie] equally upon the foreign settlers in the Country and upon the natives. I believe that the French King has expressed a willingness to revise that and other objectionable features of the "treaty" with Capt Laplace and probably would annul it altogether, as the constitution of the Government guarantees toleration in all matters of religious faith and observance.

The advantages to American interests that would be a consequence of the proposed treaty are numerous and obvious. American residents in the Country would be particularly benefitted by the security and permanent value to their property which would be afforded by such a guarantee of the stability and independence of the Government. Their interests are identified with the interests of the Country. Indeed every thing existing at present in the Country that looks like permanent improvements in

Government and Civilization, has grown up in connexion with their enterprise and Capital. Very considerable investments have been made in dwellings, warehouses, mechanic's shops, and wharves, and large amounts are employed in the cultivation and manufacture of agricultural productions. I suppose that the whole amount of American capital invested in permanent forms and employed in the commercial mercantile and agricultural operations of our Citizens resident in the Islands, is not less that one and a half millions of dollars. The inducements portended in the past success of adventurers in that direction, and by the facilities offered by the Government to men of good character and influence, and by the surpassing salubrity of the climate, will doubtless draw into the Country many more of our New England families whose attention and energies must be applied to the only existing sources of wealth. The results of such an application have not been and would not be limited to the immediate interests of those exerting it; for as the wealth of the country lies in its soil and the capabilities of its people, just in proportion to the development of that wealth, would a market be opened for foreign merchandise. The operations of one establishment alone, for the cultivation and manufacture of Sugar, created during the last year a market for more than forty thousand dollars of American goods; and one press for the manufactory of paint oil from the candle nut which went into operation in June last had opened within six months a sale for several thousands more. There is every probability that similar enterprises of our Citizens would increase and extend almost indefinitely should the Government not pass into other hands; and I see not why, that in the progress of a few years, a market may not be located for millions of American produce. But should the policy of a British Collonial establishment be brought upon the Country American enterprise there would of course wither and die.

The importance of the independence and neutrality contemplated in the proposals of the King, to our commercial interests touching at these Islands, is incalculable. I beg leave to refer you to a statement in the [Honolulu] "Polynesian" sent herewith of Sept 12th 1840,[4] showing statistics of the estimated business at the port of Honolulu alone for a few years previously. An equally large, perhaps larger, number of American whale ships touched at Lahaina during the same time. The imports and exports of the last year were about 100% greater than of any year embraced in that statement. My views of the probable future increase will be inferred from the prospects I have already presented.

Ships employed in the Whale fishery could find no other ports for procuring refreshments and supplies in proceeding to and returning from their cruising ground off the coast of Japan; and to be shut out of the

4. Not included in the RG 59 record.

ports of that Archipelago as they are from New Holland and New Zealand would so far as can at present be seen break up their operations on that ground. The convenience of that branch of commerce in the North Pacific seems to require serious consideration and will not, I trust, fail to have a due prominence in the deliberations which will dispose of the proposals submitted by His Hawaiian Majesty.

The geographical position of the Sandwich Islands gives them an importance of daily increasing interests, particularly so in their relation to the Western Coast of North America; and to their importance in that relation our Government cannot be too actively alive. The results of the explorations and surveys made in the interior and on the shores of the Oregon Territory by the Commander [Charles Wilkes] and Officers of the Exploring Expedition will probably in a few weeks be laid before the Government, and I believe will show the expediency, to say nothing of the [practicability] of asserting and maintaining our claim to the whole territory to 54° 40'. All the gentlemen of the Expedition concur in the opinion that the occupancy of the shores of Pugetts Sound and of the waters dividing Vancouvers Island from the continent must originate a very active commerce. They represent that whole country to be, for its facilities for ship building and the lumber trade, to the Pacific Coast of vastly greater importance than the State of Maine is to the Atlantic Coast. The interior is described as a rich country for grain and grazing, and Vancouvers Island is said to be a bed of coal. Whenever that coast shall be settled under the auspices of our Government, its prosperity must be materially modified by the character and policy of the Government that shall exist at the Sandwich Islands.

Political changes are almost certain to occur soon in the territory of California. That interesting region of Country with its extensive line of coast, cannot remain long under the miserable misrule of Mexico. There are more of Saxon brains and blood in the population scattered along its shores than Mexican Authority can long control, and whatever may be the future political relations of that Country to our own, the sympathies of its people will probably be with ours and its commerce in the Pacific, at least equally affected by the policy that shall have the predominance in that Ocean.

The locality of the Hawaiian Govnt, [drawing] additional importance from their lying in the track of a large proportion of the Commerce of the Pacific in the courses through which it has thus far been conducted, and further, unless the onward movement of the world shall be arrested and men everywhere stand still, they lie in the track of communication that will soon connect the whole Continent of America with that of Asia. The time cannot be distant when the obstacles dividing the Atlantic and Pacific Oceans will be surmounted, and there can be but little doubt, that the Eastern Coast of China and the Coast of Japan will ere long be opened to the active and pressing commerce of the world. Whenever those events and the consequent changes in the course of a large proportion of the commerce of the world shall have occurred, the ports of the Sandwich Islands, ought, for the common welfare, and for American interests particularly, to be under a Government neutral in its relations and power.

It would seem scarcely probable or possible that a more favourable time or fit occasion to confirm and assure permanency to such a Government, will occur. I have not entertained a doubt that the proposals now before the Executive would be favourably regarded by the Government of this Country. It is perfectly obvious that the interests of France in the neutrality proposed are, in some most important respects, in harmony with those of the United States, and it is possible if not probable that the magnanimity of England would accord to the Hawaiian Govt. the rights which it asks to have confirmed.

It has occurred to me as possible that the refusal of France to unite with England in her favorite measures for a maratime supremacy, might oppose the success of any overtures of France to England looking like an alliance of any sort, but if not, I have thought that France might be induced to move in a proposition to England and the United States for a convention in accordance with the wishes of the Hawaiian King. She owes some reparation to him, to the United States, to her own national character and to the moral sentiment of the world, for the severities inflicted by the anomalous proceedings of Capt Laplace and might the more readily fall into this measure to discharge the obligation. But whether if France were to lend, or appear to lend, as the measure, a favourable result would be more likely to be realized, than if a correspondence leading to the proposed convention were to be instituted by the Government of the United States, I am unable to judge.

I have in my charge communications to the Queen of England and the King of France [Louis Philippe], of the same tenor of that addressed to the President of the United States, which, unless other disposition of them shall be suggested to me, I shall immediately commit to the British and French Legations in this City so that they may go forward under cover of their despatches to their respective Governments. In the course of a few weeks, it is my purpose to proceed to Europe and shall visit London and Paris. If the interests of the United States, present and prospective, render a convention for the objects proposed desirable, and if it be a matter of indifference so far as those interests are concerned whether the convention shall take place and [date] at Washington London or Paris, and consequently powers and instructions to the American Ministers at London and Paris requisite for negotiation at either place shall be authorized by the President, I may perhaps be of some service by the information I might furnish to those Diplomatists and by the wider influence I might originate through gentlemen whose acquaintance I enjoy or may make. If I can in any way serve the interests of my fellow Citizens residing at the Islands, or the more extended interests of the Country which have necessarily passed under my observation and engaged my attention in the Pacific, I shall be happy to be advised by the Department. With the highest considerations I have the honor to be Sir Yr. Mo. Obt Sevt. P. A. Brinsmade

ALS. DNA, RG 59 (Consular Despatches, Honolulu). Rec'd April 13, 1842. Brinsmade (1804–1859; Bowdoin 1826) first went to Hawaii in 1833 as a merchant. He was U.S. consul in Honolulu from 1839 to 1846. In November 1841 Brinsmade became the agent of the Hawaiian government in its effort to obtain recognition of Hawaiian independence by the United States, Great Britain, and France.

ENCLOSURE: KAMEHAMEHA III TO JOHN TYLER

Done at own residence at Lahaina, Maui, on the 24th day of Nov. 1841 To John Tyler, President of the United States of America.

The government of the Hawaiian Islands, urged by the necessity imposed upon it by their location, and their consequent connection with the great commercial Nations, and desirous of servicing the highest welfare of its own subjects, and at the same time of rendering a service to those subjects of foreign realms who do business in this archipelago, presents to the Sovereigns of the great Nations hereafter mentioned, and especially to the President of the United States of America, the following propositions,

1. That the government of the United States of America enter into convention with the governments of Great Britain and France, mutually acknowledging and guaranteeing the independance of the Hawaiian government in its monarchial form under its present sovereign and his heirs according to the constitution already adopted.

2. That the three high contracting Powers allow to the Hawaiian government, all the rights[,] privileges and immunities conceded by the acknowledged laws of Nations to a free and independant State.

3. That for the purpose of permanently securing justice, peace, and amity, the contracting parties agree to the following manner of adjusting any difficulties or misunderstanding which may unhappily arise between the Hawaiian government and any subject or subjects of either of the three nations herein mentioned, that is to say,

Should any misunderstanding unhappily arise between the Hawaiian government, and the government of the United States of America, or any of its citizens, then the British and French Ministers resident at Washington shall constitute a reference to decide all questions of dispute, and their decision shall be final.

Should any misunderstanding unhappily arise between the Hawaiian government and the government of Great Britain or any of her subjects, then the Ministers from the United States of America and from France, resident at London shall constitute a reference to decide all questions of dispute, and their decision shall be final.

Should any misunderstanding unhappily arise between the Hawaiian government and the government of France, or any of her subjects, then the Ministers of the United States of America and of Great Britain, resident in Paris, shall constitute a reference to decide all questions of dispute, and their decision shall be final.

4. That all articles of agreement or promises made by his Hawaiian Majesty to any commanders or officers of Ships of War shall be considered as null and void, while he at the same time, pledges to the citizens of every nation resident in his Kingdom, all the protection, rights[,] privileges and immunities, which the citizens of one nation have a right to expect from the government of another, at peace with their own.

The above is submitted to the President of the United States of America, as the same also will be to the governments of Great Britain and France, with the full conviction and confidence that the adoption would no less subserve the interests of the three great nations than it will the interests of the Hawaiian Islands. In true Faith   Kamehameha III

Copy. Translation. DNA, RG 59 (Notes from Foreign Legations, Hawaii). Similar letters were also addressed to the governments of Great Britain and France.

FROM TIMOTEO HAALILIO AND WILLIAM RICHARDS

Sir   Washington, Decr 14 1842

The undersigned having been duly commissioned by his Majesty Kamehameha III, King of all the Hawaiian Islands, to represent his Government, and promote its interests in the United States, wish to call the attention of your Government to the existing relations beween the two Countries.

In the year 1826, articles of Agreement in the form of a Treaty, were entered into between His Majesty's Government and Thos. Ap Catesby Jones, Commanding the U. States Sloop of War Peacock.[1] His Majesty has never received any notice of that Treaty's being ratified nor intimation that it was approved by the Government of the United States. His Majesty has nevertheless during the last Sixteen years governed himself by the regulations of that Treaty in all his intercourse with Citizens of the United States.

1. See *Treaties*, 3:269–281. Although the United States never ratified the treaty of commerce and navigation of December 23, 1826, Hunter Miller regards it as "clearly an international act" (p. 274) in the sense that it was observed and treated as such by both signatories.

Subsequently to the above, similar forms of agreement have been entered into between His Majesty and Officers commanding Vessels of War of different nations of Europe, but, so far as is known to the undersigned, those agreements have never received the sanction of their several Governments. These facts, viewed in connection with their attendant circumstances, have led his Majesty to feel considerable embarrassment in managing his foreign relations, and has awakened the very strong desire that his Kingdom should be *formally* acknowledged by the civilized nations of the world, as a Sovereign and Independent State.

His Majesty considers that this acknowledgement has already been tacitly, but virtually made both in the United States and in Europe, by the appointment of Consuls and, Commercial Agents to reside in his dominions, and, by the formal manner in which the Commanders of National Vessels have transacted business with him, many of whom have professedly acted under the express instructions of their several Governments. But he is nevertheless of opinion, that, the time has now arrived when both the interests and the honor of his Kingdom demand a more formal acknowledgement than has hitherto been made by any foreign Government.

It is His Majesty's request, that, the Government of the United States will take into consideration the nature, the extent, and, the rapidity of those changes which have taken place in his dominions during the last few years; changes which he has the happiness to believe, are honorable both to his Government, and, to the people over whom it rules. Twenty three years ago the Nation had no written language, and, no character in which to write it. The language had never been systematized nor reduced to any kind of form. The people had no acquaintance with Christianity, nor with the valuable institutions or usages of civilized life. The nation had no fixed form or regulations of Government, except as they were dictated by those who were in authority or might by any means acquire power. The right of property was not acknowledged, and, was therefore but partially enjoyed,—there were no Courts of Justice, and the wills of chieftains was absolute,—the property of foreigners had no protection, except, in the kind disposition of individuals. But, under the fostering influence, patronage & care of His Majesty, and, that of his predecessors, the language has been reduced to visible and systematized form, and, is now written by a large and respectable proportion of the people. Schools have been established throughout his dominions, and, are supported principally by the government, and there are but few among the younger people who are unable to read. They have now in their own language, a library embracing a considerable variety of books, on a variety of subjects, including the Holy Scriptures, works on Natural History, Civil History, Church History, Geography, Political Economy, Mathematics, Statute Law, besides a number of Elementary books.

A regular Monarchial Government has been organized of a limited and representative character, a translation of the Constitution of which, we herewith transmit. A code of Laws, both civil and criminal has been enacted and published.[2] The Legislature holds an annual meeting for the purpose of adding to, and amending this code. Courts of Justice have been established, and regular trials by jury required in all important cases. Foreigners of different nations have testified their confidence in these Courts, by bringing suits in cases where many thousands of dollars worth of property was involved, and, that too in cases, when with but a very short delay, they could have been carried before the Courts of other Countries.

It has moreover been the uniform practice of Consuls, and Commercial Agents, resident in His Majesty's dominions, and, also of all Commanders of National Vessels visiting those dominions, to demand all that protection, both of person and property which is demanded of sovereign and independent States, and, this his Majesty believes has been duly & efficiently extended.

While therefore all is demanded of his government, and all is rendered by it, which is demanded of, or rendered by the Government of Sovereign and independent States, he feels, that he has a right to expect his state to be acknowledged as such, and, thus be formally received into the general compact of Sovereign nations.

In the request, which his Majesty hereby makes to the Government of the United States, he has of course for his direct object the promotion of the interests of his own Kingdom, but, he is also very fully convinced, that, the important interests of all the great commercial nations will also be materially subserved by his dominions remaining as they have hitherto been, independent. Their position is such, that they constitute the great centre of the whale fishery for most of the world. They are on the principal line of communication between the Western Continent of America and the Eastern Continent of Asia, and, such are the prevailing winds in that ocean, that all vessels requiring repairs, or supplies, either of Provisions or of water, naturally, touch at those islands, whether the vessels sail from Columbia river on the North, or, from the far distant parts of Mexico, Central America and Peru upon the South. And, it should be further added, that, there is no other place in all that part of the Pacific Ocean, where repairs of Vessels can be made to so good an advantage or, supplies be obtained in such abundance, and, on so favorable terms.

His Majesty wishes also to remind the Government of the United

2. In 1842 Richards authored a *Translation of the Constitution and* *Laws of the Hawaiian Islands*, which was published at Lahainaluna.

States, that the amount of property belonging to their citizens, which is either landed at, or enters the various harbors and roadsteads of his dominions and, is consequently, more or less dependent on the protection of his Government, cannot be less than from five to seven millions of dollars annually. This property lies in some ninety or a hundred whaling ships, and their cargoes and in some twelve or fifteen merchant vessels, besides also a considerable amount of other property belonging to American Citizens on shore. At some seasons there have been not less than three or four millions of dollars worth of American property and some 1400 American Citizens at the same time at the various parts of the Islands requiring, consequently in some degree the protection of his Majesty, and, he has the happiness of believing, that, efficient and satisfactory aid has always been extended to those who have required it. In evidence corroborative of many of the facts herein stated, the undersigned do not hesitate to refer to documentary evidence which they believe must be among the papers in your department of State, recently furnished by Commanders of National Vessels, but, more especially by the U. States Commercial Agent resident at Honolulu [Peter Allan Brinsmade].

His Majesty is also desirous that there should be a definite arrangement for the settlement of any <further> future difficulties which may unhappily arise, and, which, between sovereign & independant nations would ordinarily be the subject of diplomatic correspondence.

To carry into effect these desirable objects, the undersigned are authorized by his Majesty Kamehameha III to enter into negociation with the authorities of the States, by Convention, Treaty, or otherwise, whenever the latter shall acknowledge the Sovereignty of the former, and, as evidence that the undersigned are thus authorized, they are prepared to present official papers from his Majesty, whenever the way is open for them to be received.

The undersigned will further state, that they are directed to proceed from the U. States to Europe for the purpose of obtaining from some of the principle Governments there, the same acknowledgements which it is the object of this letter to obtain from the Government of the U. States. Accept Sir the assurances of the High Consideration with which the undersigned have the honor to be Your Obedient Servants

Timoteo Haalilio   William Richards

LS. DNA, RG 59 (Notes from Foreign Legations, Hawaii). Rec'd December 18, 1842. Published in *Executive Documents*, 27th Cong., 3d sess., Serial 420, No. 35, pp. 4–6. Haalilio was the private secretary and financial advisor of King Kamehameha III. In July 1842 Haalilio sailed with William Richards on a mission to win recognition of Hawaiian independence from the governments of the United States, Great Britain, and France. He died on the voyage home in

1844. Richards went to Hawaii as a missionary in 1822 and in 1838 became influential as advisor to the king and other chiefs.

TO TIMOTEO HAALILIO AND WILLIAM RICHARDS

Gentlemen: Washington, December 19th 1842

I have received the letter which you did me the honor to address to me under date of the 14th instant,[1] stating that you had been commissioned to represent in the United States the Government of the Hawaiian Islands, inviting the attention of this Government to the relations between the two countries and intimating a desire for a recognition of the Hawaiian government by that of the United States.

Your communication has been laid before the President and by him considered.

The advantages of your country to navigators in the Pacific, and in particular to the numerous vessels and vast tonnage of the United States frequenting that sea are fully estimated; and just acknowledgements are due to the government and inhabitants of the Islands for their numerous acts of hospitality to the citizens of the United States.

The United States have regarded the existing authorities in the Sandwich Islands as a Government suited to the condition of the people and resting on their own choice; and the President is of opinion that the interests of all the Commercial nations require that this Government should not be interfered with by foreign powers. Of the vessels which visit the Islands, it is known that a great majority belong to the United States. The United States, therefore, are more interested in the fate of the Islands and of their government, than any other Nation can be; and this consideration induces the President to be quite willing to declare as the sense of the government of the United States that the government of the Sandwich Islands ought to be respected; that no power ought either to take possession of the Islands as a conquest or for the purpose of colonization; and that no power ought to seek for any undue control over the existing Government, or any exclusive privileges or preferences in matters of commerce.

Entertaining these sentiments, the President does not see any present necessity for the negotiation of a formal Treaty, or the appointment or reception of diplomatic characters. A Consul or agent from this Government will continue to reside in the Islands. He will receive particular instructions to pay just and careful attention to any claims or complaints which may be brought against the Government or people of the Islands by citizens of the United States; and he will be also instructed to receive any complaint which may be made by that Government for acts of indi-

1. See above.

viduals, citizens of the United States, on account of which the interference of this Government may be requested; and to transmit such complaint to this Department.

It is not improbable that this correspondence may be made the subject of a communication to Congress;[2] and it will be officially made known to the Governments of the principal Commercial powers of Europe. I have the honor to be, Gentlemen, Your obt servt   Danl Webster

ʟs. H-Ar. Published in *Executive Documents*, 27th Cong., 3d sess., Serial 420, No. 35, pp. 6–7.

TO EDWARD EVERETT

Private   Department of State,
Sir: Washington, 24th December, 1842.
This will be presented to you by Messrs Timoteo Haalilio and William Richards, who are commissioned by the government of the Hawaiian Islands to obtain an acknowledgement by other governments of the independence of those Islands. I will thank you to forward their object in any way you can, with propriety, during their sojourn in England. I am, Sir, your obedient servant,   Danl Webster

ʟs. MHi.

TO EDWARD EVERETT

Private & Confidential
My Dear Sir,   Washington Decr. 29. 42
We have your various communications, to the 3rd inst.[1] There are, I believe, one or two matters, which ought to be made subjects of remark in a public despatch; but the truth is, I am overdone with work, & must postpone some things.

Your remarks about New-Zealand, & the Sandwich Islands were luckily timed.[2] It so happens, that agents, from the latter, are now here. A correspondence between them & my Dept will be sent to Congress tomorrow. We take the lead, in declaring for the Independence of the Islands. We think, also, of recommending to Congress to make provision for a *Commission* to China.

Mr. [Thomas Hart] Benton has published what *purports* to be his Speech on the Treaty, in secret session in the Senate.[3] It is a huge mass

2. See *Ex. Doc.*, Serial 420, No. 35.

1. Everett's private letter of December 3, 1842, is published in *Correspondence* 5:253–255.

2. In a letter to DW dated November 30, 1842, mDW 23813, Everett expressed his belief that if the United States acquiesced in the British claim of sovereignty over New Zealand, the British would soon claim Hawaii and the Society Islands. He recommended a tripartite guarantee of Hawaiian independence and neutrality by Britain, France, and the United States.

of trash. You will herewith receive two or three copies, & one directed for Lord Ashburton. It is quite discreditable, I fear to the character of the Country. Together with certain other persons, he is attempting to make a great rally agt. the Admin on the Treaty subject. I do not think he will succeed. You will see Mr. [William Cabell] Rives' Speech.⁴ I have never said any thing to you about Mr [Jared] *Sparks'* discoveries; & am sorry Mr. Rives had reason, as he thought, to bring the matter out. It is a delicate, tho' a very important, affair. You may readily suppose this was of no little importance, in obtaining the consent of Maine, *ab ante*, to any line which her commissioners might agree to. Mr. Sparks made a visit to Augusta, while the Legislature was in session. The Treaty becomes, every day, more & more popular, & commendations & congratulations pour in upon us, on all sides. I begin to think it was rather a lucky hit. I understand that Chancellor [James] Kent & Judge [Joseph] Story have pinned me on their sleeves, by adding my letters to the text of their commentaries on public law; and the good old Mr [Peter Stephen] Duponceau⁵ is quite in ecstasies. I confess I am proud of the letter on Impressment, especially since you told me what Mr. [Samuel] Rogers said of it, & what you thought yourself.⁶ It is the best, of my letters.

I doubt whether Congress will do any thing, this session. There is a subdued feeling among the [Henry] Clay Whigs, but I see no disposition to go ahead, with positive measures. Our good old Commonwealth is stranded, upon *ultraism*. The chances are rather in favor of Mr. [Marcus] Morton's being Gov. If Mr [John] Davis had run, *without carrying weight*, he would have come in, by 10.000.⁷

Pray send me any thing interesting, in the way of books. I want some good light reading. Novels, Geography, Biography,—any thing not too scientific, & out of the limits of law & politics.

We all desire our love to your wife [Charlotte Brooks Everett] & daughters [Anne Gorham Everett and Charlotte Brooks Everett]. Always remember me to Mr Rogers, [Henry] Hallam, Sir Robt [Harry] Ingliss, Lord Lyndhurst, Lord Brougham, &c. &c. Do you know the good old Earl of Lonsdale?—or the Earl of Devon? or Sir Thomas Dyke Ackland?⁸ Yrs truly   D. Webster

ALS. MHi.

3. See Benton's speech on the Treaty of Washington in *Cong. Globe*, 27th Cong., 3d sess., app., pp. 1–27.

4. *Cong. Globe*, 27th Cong., 3d sess., app., pp. 59–67. On the map controversy, see "The Aftermath and Implementation of the Treaty of Washington: The 'Battle of the Maps,'" pp. 775–796.

5. Duponceau (1760–1844) was

the president of the American Philosophical Society.

6. See above, Everett to DW, September 16, 1842, "The Treaty of Washington," pp. 698–700.

7. Morton (1784–1864; Brown 1804), a Democrat, was elected governor over Davis by the Massachusetts senate in 1842.

8. Inglis (1786–1855), vice Ingliss,

FROM TIMOTEO HAALILIO AND WILLIAM RICHARDS

Sir   London March 3d 1843

Since our arrival in this city we have had some intercourse with Lord Aberdeen on the same subject upon which we had the honor of addressing you during our late visit in Washington and of receiving your reply bearing date of December 19th 1842.[1]

His Lordship questioned us as to what has been done and said by the government of the U.S.A. on the subject, and we answered his inquiries freely. In the same open manner we deem it proper to communicate to the government of the U.S.A. the views of Lord Aberdeen on the subject.

His Lordship remarked that the letter which we had the honor to receive from you did not acknowledge the Independence of the Islands, but virtually denied it, in as much as it contained a refusal to enter into treaty.

He moreover implied a suspicion that the government of the U.S.A. was endeavoring, while it could not hold Colonies in form to do so in fact by executing an influence over the Sandwich Island government in favor of American interests to the injury of British.

This suspicion he grounded on certain complaints made against the Sandwich Island government, by the British Consul [Richard Charlton], that the government is actually partial to the Americans.

His lordship expressed the opinion that the British government would not concede the Independence of the Islands, and one reason which he mentioned why it would not do it was the fact, that the Americans, (who have far greater Interests at the Islands than the British), have not done it.

As we have thought it possible that a knowledge of these facts would induce the government to make communications to its Minister on the subject, we deemed it expedient and proper to communicate them. With distinguished consideration We have the honor to be, Your Obedt Sevts

Timoteo Haalilio   William Richards

L s. DNA, RG 59 (Notes from Foreign Legations, Hawaii). Rec'd April 17, 1843.

TO GEORGE BROWN

No. 1.   Department of State.
Sir: Washington, 15th March, 1843.

The accompanying Message of the President to Congress of the 30th

---

was a Tory politician; John Singleton Copley, Lord Lyndhurst (1772–1863), was the lord chancellor, 1841–1846; William Lowther, the earl of Lonsdale (1757–1844); William Reginald Courtenay, the earl of

Devon (1807–1888), was a member of Parliament, 1841–1849; Acland (1787–1871), vice Ackland, was a member of Parliament from North Devon, 1835–1857.

1. See above, Haalilio and Rich-

of December, last, transmitting a correspondence between this Department and certain agents of the Sandwich Islands then in this City,[1] will acquaint you with the view which he entertains of the relations between the United States and those Islands and with the objects and motives of this government for cultivating and strengthening those relations. Congress having complied with his suggestion by providing for a Commissioner to reside at the Islands,[2] you have been chosen for that purpose. A commission appointing you to the office will be found among the papers which you will receive herewith, and a letter from this Department addressed to that Minister of the King of the Islands [Kamehameha III] who may be charged with their foreign relations, accrediting you in your official character. The title selected for your mission has reference, in part, to its purposes. It is not deemed expedient at this juncture fully to recognize the independence of the Islands or the right of their government to that equality of treatment and consideration which is due and usually allowed to those governments to which we send and from which we receive diplomatic agents of the ordinary ranks. By this, however, it is not meant to intimate that the Islands so far as regards all other powers, are not entirely independent; on the contrary, this is a fact respecting which no doubt is felt, and the hope that through the agency of the Commissioner that independence might be preserved, has probably—in a great degree led to the compliance by Congress with the recommendation of the President. It is obvious from circumstances connected with their position, that the interests of the United States require that no other power should possess or colonize the Sandwich Islands or exercise over their government an influence which would lead to partial or exclusive favors in matters of navigation or trade. One of your principal duties, therefore, will be to watch the movements of such agents of other governments as may visit the Islands. You will endeavor to obtain the earliest intelligence respecting the objects of those visits, and if you should think that, if accomplished, they would be detrimental to the interests of the United States, you will make such representations to the authorities of the Islands as in your judgment would be most likely to frustrate them. You will also endeavor to impress upon those authorities the necessity of abstaining from giving just cause of complaint to the governments of those powers whose policy is to increase their possessions and multiply their colonies abroad. This duty can best be performed by the prompt and impartial administration of justice according to the laws and customs of the Islands, in such cases of difference as may occur between their

ards to DW, December 14, 1842, and DW's reply of December 19, 1842.

1. The correspondence with Haalilio and Richards and the president's message is in *Executive Documents*, 27th Cong., 3d sess., Serial 420, No. 35.

2. See *House Reports*, 27th Cong., 3d sess., Serial 426, No. 93.

officers and citizens and the officers, citizens or subjects of other governments. You will give the government of the Sandwich Islands distinctly to understand that the Government of the United States in all its proceedings and in setting on foot your mission, has not in any degree been actuated by a desire or intention to secure itself exclusive privileges in matters of navigation or trade or to prevent any or all other commercial nations from an equal participation with ourselves in the benefits of an intercourse with those Islands. We seek no control over their government, nor any undue influence whatever. Our only wish is that the integrity and independence of the Hawaiian territory may be scrupulously maintained and that its government should be entirely impartial towards foreigners of every nation. In making resolute and stern resistance, therefore, to any claim of favor or exclusive privilege, by other powers, you will at all times, frankly disavow any desire that favors or exclusive privileges should be granted to the United States, their ships, commerce or citizens.

You will transmit to the Department full and exact information respecting the trade of the United States and of other nations with the Islands. Any suggestions which may occur to you having in view of any improvement of the commerce of the United States with the Islands will be acceptable. Your attention is particularly requested to the nature of the fiscal regulations in force there, to their effects upon foreign commerce generally, and to the policy of the government in regard to this subject. If those regulations should be frequently changed or if there should be cause to apprehend the imposition of discriminating duties upon our navigation and trade, the expediency of negotiating a treaty with that government which would determine for a series of years the reciprocal rights and duties of the parties in regard to those subjects, will be taken into consideration.

After you shall have resided long enough at the Sandwich Islands to have made yourself familiar with the state of public affairs there and shall have communicated to the department the results of your observations, you may make a visit to the Society Islands for the purpose of examining and reporting upon their condition and prospects. It is advisable, however, that your absence from your post should not be prolonged beyond the period absolutely necessary for that purpose.

It is understood that you will proceed to the Pacific by the way of Chagres and Panama. This government has it in contemplation to establish a post between those places for the conveyance of letters to and from the United States. The details of the project have not been definitively decided upon for want of as full information as is desirable in regard to the means and methods of transportation across the Isthmus. You will consequently avail yourself of such opportunities as you may enjoy, to collect information of the character referred to and communicate the same to the Department from either Chagres or Panama. You will also endeavor to ascertain whether there is a proper person residing at Chagres to whom the appointment of Consul of the United States would be acceptable and who would also be a suitable person to employ as a mail agent. Congress has appropriated one thousand dollars to defray the expenses of transmitting the mails, including the pay of agents; and if a person should be appointed Consul and mail agent at Chagres, he might of course expect to receive a due share of that fund.

The books and documents with which the diplomatic agents of the United States are usually provided, and a special passport are likewise herewith communicated to you.

Congress has appropriated three thousand dollars for your compensation, and you will also be allowed at the rate of five hundred dollars a year for the contingent expenses of your mission of the character mentioned in the printed personal instructions which have been communicated to you. For your compensation as it may become due and for the contingent expenses, you will draw on this Department. I am, Sir, your obedient servant,   Daniel Webster.

LC. DNA, RG 59 (Instructions, Special Missions). Brown, from Beverly, Massachusetts, was appointed commissioner to Hawaii on March 3, 1843. He resigned from the post on May 20, 1845, and sailed from Hawaii aboard the brig *William Neilson*, which was lost at sea.

TO EDWARD EVERETT

No. 34.   Department of State,
Sir: Washington, 23d March, 1843.

The course adopted by this Government in regard to the Sandwich Islands has for its sole object the preservation of the independence of those Islands, and the maintenance by their Government of an entire impartiality in their intercourse with foreign States. The United States desire to exercise no undue influence or control, over the government of the Islands, nor to obtain from it any grant of exclusive privileges whatever. This was solemnly declared in the President's message to Congress;[1] and it is declared, also, in the instructions given to Mr. [George] Brown, of which you will receive herewith a copy.[2]

The President would exceedingly regret, that suspicion of a sinister purpose, of any kind, on the part of the United States, should prevent England and France from adopting the same pacific, just, and conservative course towards the government and people of this remote but interesting groupe of Islands. I am, Sir, &c. &c. &c.   Danl Webster.

LC. DNA, RG 59 (Instructions, Britain).

1. Tyler's message of December 30, 1842, is in *Messages and Papers*, 4: 211–214.
2. See above.

FROM HENRY LEDYARD

No. 7.   Legation of the United States
Sir,   Paris, 23rd March 1843.

I have thought that it might be interesting to you to know the result of the interview between Messrs [Timoteo] Haalilio and [William] Richards the Agents of the Sandwich Islands with Mr [François Pierre Guillaume] Guizot. These gentlemen arrived here a few days since from London and immediately obtained an audience of the Minister of Foreign Affairs. They had prepared a memorandum of the objects of their visit, among which were the acknowledgment of the independence of these Islands by the French Government, certain modifications in the Treaty imposed upon the King [Kamehameha III] by Capt [Cyrille Pierre Théodore] Laplace and the removal of the French Consul.[1] Mr. Guizot received them with great kindness and, after perusing the memorandum, gave them to understand that France would recognize their independence, and that the article of the Treaty having reference to the introduction of spirituous liquors into the Islands should be abrogated; the other points he reserved for future consideration.

I have the honor to enclose a copy of part of a map showing the boundary between Maine and the English provinces.[2] The original I found at the Foreign Office and is entitled "Map of the United States of North America according to the Treaty. by Wm Faden, 1783." This is probably the Map referred to by the Maine Commissioners (in their letter to you of 29th June 1842)[3] in which the boundary is laid down in accordance with the American claim.

25th March.   Since writing the above I have seen the Report of the debate in the House of Commons on the Treaty on the 21st inst, in which Sir Robert Peel refers to this Map by Faden.[4]

The Levant mail has just arrived and brings the account of Commodore [David] Porter's death at Constantinople on the 3rd inst. Mr [John Porter] Brown had assumed the charge of the Legation. I am, Sir, very respectfully your obedient servant   Henry Ledyard.

ALS. DNA, RG 59 (Despatches, France). Rec'd April 21, 1843.

THE CHINA MISSION

Prior to 1842, the U.S. government paid little attention to the Chinese empire. Since the famous voyage of the *Empress of China* in 1784–

1. The French consul at Honolulu was Jules Dudoit, a merchant, appointed in July 1837. He was not removed until 1848.

2. Map not printed here.

3. See above, Preble et al. to DW,

June 29, 1842, "The Treaty of Washington," pp. 592–603.

4. Peel's remarks of February 28, 1843, are in *Hansard's*, 67:1218–1267, esp. p. 1248.

1785, Americans had been engaged in the China trade. In 1830, more-over, American religious activities had begun in China with the arrival of Elijah C. Bridgman (1801–1861; Amherst 1826) of the American Board of Commissioners for Foreign Missions. But merchants such as Thomas Handasyd Perkins, who established a trading house in Canton in 1803, and religious leaders such as Bridgman and Peter Parker, who became the first Protestant medical missionary in China in 1834, were not supported by the U.S. government. Although there was an American consul at Canton, merchants and missionaries were left almost entirely on their own.

In 1842–1843, the Tyler administration initiated the first U.S. foreign policy toward China. In the same message of December 30, 1842, in which he set forth the Tyler Doctrine, the president asked Congress to authorize funds to send a commissioner to China to protect American citizens and commerce and, if appropriate, "to address himself to the high functionaries of the Empire, or through them to the Emperor himself" (*Messages and Papers*, 4:211–214). On March 3, 1843, Congress provided $40,000 for a diplomatic mission to China, and on May 8 Secretary of State Daniel Webster drew up the historic instructions to Caleb Cushing, who headed the mission that led to America's first bilateral agreement with China, the Treaty of Wanghia of July 3, 1844.

The formulation of an American foreign policy toward China can be explained primarily as a response to the Anglo-Chinese war of 1839–1842. Because of the uncertainties generated by the so-called Opium War, American merchants and missionaries appealed to the U.S. government to stabilize relations with China. On May 29, 1839, and on January 9, 1840, American traders in Canton sent memorials to Congress requesting that a commercial agent be sent to China to negotiate a treaty. Congress, in turn, passed resolutions in January and December 1840 seeking information from the executive branch about the status of American citizens and commerce in China. On April 9, 1840, moreover, a memorial from the merchants of Boston and Salem asked that a naval force be dispatched to Chinese waters to protect American interests. The Van Buren administration ordered Commodore Lawrence Kearny (1789–1868) to proceed to China. In 1842, Kearny obtained a vague assurance from Chinese authorities that Americans would not be discriminated against in matters of foreign trade, but that noncommittal statement did not place Chinese-American relations on a treaty basis.

In the meantime, the voice of a prominent American missionary was added to that of the merchants. In 1840, while the Opium War was still in progress, Peter Parker left China for the United States. Parker, who had acquired an international reputation as an outstanding humanitarian, was lionized upon his arrival in the United States. In January 1841 he preached a sermon before Congress. He also held an interview with

President Martin Van Buren and Secretary of State John Forsyth. They referred him to President-elect Harrison and Secretary-designate Webster. On January 22, Parker met with Webster, who asked the missionary to put his ideas on paper. On January 30, Parker wrote the letter that is printed below. The thrust of Parker's argument was that the United States should send a minister *"direct and without delay"* to the court of the Chinese emperor.

In March 1841 Daniel Webster became secretary of state and Peter Parker married Harriet Colby Webster (1818–1896). Although Harriet was not actually related to Daniel Webster, both he and Fletcher referred to her as a "cousin." Daniel Webster, moreover, felt, as he wrote in 1840, a "great concern for her" (DW to Mrs. John Agg, April 2, [1840], mDW 16602). The decision to pursue an active policy toward China may have been influenced by the secretary of state's affection for Harriet Webster Parker, but this is only a speculation. Probably more important was Peter Parker himself, for he constituted a virtual one-man lobby for an American diplomatic mission to China.

On September 16, 1841, Parker held another interview with Webster, and on the same day he met with Tyler. Parker later told John Quincy Adams that the president had said that he "had his eye fixed upon China, and would avail himself of any favorable opportunity to commence a negotiation with the Celestial Empire" (*Memoirs*, 11:166–167). Since that occasion did not occur until more than a year later, the influence of Parker on American policy toward China is difficult to assess. Perhaps, as Parker's biographer has written, the missionary's visits to Tyler and Webster "added a timely, extra push toward the ultimate creation of a diplomatic mission to the Orient" (Edward V. Gulick, *Peter Parker and the Opening of China* [Cambridge, Mass., 1973], p. 108). Parker returned to China in June 1842 with his young wife, who became the first Western woman to reside in China on a relatively permanent basis. In 1844, Parker, along with Bridgman, served as secretary and interpreter for Caleb Cushing.

With the Anglo-Chinese conflict still in progress in 1841, the time had "not yet come," as Adams put it, for a diplomatic mission to China (*Memoirs*, 10:445). Britain's victory in the Opium War as reflected in the Treaty of Nanking of August 29, 1842, however, rendered the sending of a commissioner to China both necessary and timely. The Nanking accord was one of the most important international agreements of the nineteenth century. From the Chinese point of view, it was the first of a series of unequal treaties with Western nations. Prior to 1842, Canton had been the only port at which the Chinese allowed trade with foreigners. By the terms of the Treaty of Nanking, China agreed to open four new ports, abolish the co-hong, establish regular commercial duties, cede Hong Kong, and pay an indemnity of $21 million. In effect, the Chinese had been compelled to end their tribute system and to accept the European conception of international relations. The extent to which the United States would share in the benefits gained by the British, however, was an open question (see Everett to DW, November 29, 1842, below). Desiring above all to secure American access to the China market on terms as favorable as those gained by Britain, President Tyler sent to Congress his special message of December 30, 1842.

That message, which was authored by Webster, pointed out that the Treaty of Nanking provided "neither for the admission or the exclusion of the ships" of nations other than England. An important object of the China mission would be to determine whether American vessels could gain equal access to the treaty ports. The primary rationale for sending a commissioner to China was that "the commercial interests of the United States connected with China" required "at the present moment a degree of attention and vigilance." In the long run, moreover, the Nanking accord promised to erode the Chinese "spirit of nonintercourse" and to open to normal relations an empire containing 300,000,000 subjects (*Messages and Papers*, 4:211–214).

Although the message of December 30 speculated about the trade potential of the future, it also contained a realistic appraisal of the existing China market. In the short run, Chinese habits and traditions and the "cheapness" of Chinese labor would probably discourage "any great and sudden demand" for Western goods (*Messages and Papers*, 4:213–214). This description of the obstacles to trade with China seems to have been based upon the perceptive analysis contained in Edward Everett's dispatch to Webster of November 29, which the Department of State received on December 26 (see below).

The congressional response to the message of December 30 reflected the unstable politics of the day. By late 1842, Tyler's position had deteriorated to the point that he had become a rarity in American history—a president without a party. Tyler's sour comment to Webster, that if Congress did not make a liberal appropriation, the commissioner to China could be sent in "any little cock-boat," must be understood in the context of the politics of 1842–1843 (Tyler to DW, January–February 1843, below). The U.S. Senate did not take final action on the China mission until March 3, 1843, the very last day of the third session of the Twenty-seventh Congress. The appropriation bill, moreover, was amended to require that the commissioner could not be appointed without the approval of the Senate, which explains why the nomination of Edward Everett to head the mission was rushed to that body at literally the eleventh hour. Senator Thomas Hart Benton of Missouri, furthermore, availed himself of the opportunity to launch a vituperative attack on the Tyler administration.

Benton's speech of March 3 contained most of the criticisms that have been leveled against the China mission since 1843. The senator objected to the proposal on many grounds. It was, he said, unnecessary, too expensive, and politically inspired. Since American trade with the Chinese empire had prospered for fifty years and continued to grow, there was no need to send a commissioner to China at "unparalleled" cost to negotiate a treaty. The intention in nominating Everett, Benton continued, was to "enable a gentleman, who loves to travel in Europe and Asia, to extend his travels to the Celestial Empire at the expense of the United States, and to write a book." Behind Everett, he also insinuated, lurked Webster, who wanted the post of minister to Britain. Instead of being designed "for any public purpose," the China mission was "wholly personal and individual, and invented to one person for vacating his place for the benefit of another." "I repeat it," Benton exclaimed, "this mission is not created for the country, but invented for a man; and he is now waiting to take it, and to go and bump his head nineteen times against the ground, in order to purchase the privilege of standing up before his Celestial Majesty" (*Cong. Globe*, 27th Cong., 3d sess., pp. 391–392).

Even many of those who voted for the China mission believed that it had been concocted to provide the secretary of state with a graceful exit from the Tyler administration. John Quincy Adams, for example, viewed the proposal as a substitute for the abortive special mission to England and "the back door by which Webster skilfully secures to himself a safe retreat from the Tyler Cabinet" (*Memoirs*, 11:335). The controversial issue of whether the China initiative was in part a political intrigue by Tyler and Webster is dealt with extensively in the correspondence published below. Webster consistently denied the widespread rumor that he was trying to replace Everett in London. On March 10, 1843, in the same letter in which he informed Everett of his appointment as commissioner to China, Webster stated that there was "not one chance in a thousand" that he would take the post of minister to Britain even if it were vacant (see below). In a subsequent communication, the secretary of state explained that representing the United States abroad as an ordinary diplomat would not add to his stature and would be taking a step down from the high office that he had attained (DW to Everett, March 29, 1843, below). The correspondence between Webster and Everett also suggests that although the idea of heading a special mission to England had been attractive to the secretary of state, he had little inclination to replace his friend at the Court of St. James. In any event, after some equivocation, Everett declined the appointment as commissioner to China (see Everett to DW, April 3 and 18, 1843, below).

Tyler and Webster then turned to Caleb Cushing, who had been rejected three times as secretary of the Treasury by the Senate on the same day, March 3, 1843. On May 8, Cushing received a recess appointment as U.S. commissioner to China. Fletcher Webster had been designated secretary to the China mission earlier, on April 24. Cushing was a good second choice, and he turned out to be an able diplomat, but his selection smacked of the politics of revenge and Fletcher Webster's of nepotism. Everett's initial appointment was important for a different reason.

Everett's selection was more an indication of the great value the Tyler administration attached to the China mission than it was a demonstration of political opportunism. He was independently chosen by both Tyler and Webster because they believed that he was the best man for a significant assignment. Even Adams felt that Everett was the ideal choice (see *Memoirs*, 11:336–337). In a revealing letter to Thomas B. Curtis, Webster wrote that he considered the China mission to be more significant than any that had "ever proceeded from this Country, & more important than any other, likely to succeed it, in our days." Everett, he continued, "is the man for it, & I am anxious he should accept it" (DW to Curtis, March 12, 1843, below). The subsequent actions of Tyler and Webster indicate that they placed the highest priority on the China mission.

One of the most fascinating documents published below is the list of books and gifts for the China mission. The document, drawn up on April 11, 1843, contains extensive annotations by Tyler and Webster. The attention they gave to the items to be sent to China reflects their intense interest in the China mission, and the list also is a revealing commentary on American cultural values in the 1840s. The gifts to be presented to the Chinese included "a *Globe*, that the Celestials may see they are not the 'Central Kingdom,'" and the emphasis was on American technology and military armaments. Thus, for example, the Chinese were to receive a model steam engine, Colt revolvers, and Kentucky rifles (see below).

As the list of books and gifts suggests, the Tyler administration devoted considerable time and attention to the China mission. Webster, in particular, worked very hard to make the effort a success. On March 17, he wrote Thomas L. Smith of the Treasury Department requesting detailed information about American trade with China (see below). Three days later, Webster issued a circular asking "intelligent persons" acquainted with China to provide the Department of State with advice about how to cultivate friendly relations with that nation and how to open and enlarge "commercial intercourse between the two countries" (March 20, 1843, below). As had previously been the case with regard to the Treaty of Washington, the secretary of state was trying to base American foreign policy on the best intelligence that was available to him.

Even before Webster issued the circular of March 20, 1843, he was receiving unsolicited advice from interested citizens (see Edward Carrington to DW, March 2, 1843, below). The circular itself elicited half a dozen responses, all of them from entrepreneurs interested in the China trade. The carefully considered replies of these merchants not only were helpful to Webster in drawing up the instructions for Caleb Cushing but also constitute important sources of historical information about the China trade and the attitudes of Americans toward the Chinese empire. Thomas H. Perkins, for example, explained the co-hong system, and Edwin M. Lewis provided a catalogue of the "kinds of petty tyranny and exaction" to which foreign businessmen were subjected in China (see Perkins to DW, April 3, 1843, and Lewis to DW, April 20, 1843, below). The most influential response to the circular was that of John Murray Forbes, who was designated by the Boston merchants engaged in the China trade to be their spokesman (see Sarah Forbes Hughes, ed., *Letters and Recollections of John Murray Forbes* [2 vols., Boston and New York, 1899], 1:115). Much of his advice, such as being attentive to etiquette and military technology, was accepted by Tyler and Webster (see Forbes et al. to DW, April 29, 1843, below).

In addition to the documents published in this volume, the files of the Department of State contain three other responses to Webster's circular. William Wilson & Son, the only house in Baltimore engaged in the China trade, told Webster that the sole issue was the securement of commercial rights comparable to those attained by the British in the Treaty of Nanking. The New York establishment of William Edgar Howland and William Henry Aspinwall (1807–1875) recommended that a large fleet be sent along with the commissioner in order to gain the respect of the Chinese. Nathaniel L. Griswold (c. 1795–1847) and George Griswold (c. 1800–1859), also merchants of New York, similarly urged that the China mission be accompanied by a "respectable" naval force to impress the Chinese with American power. They stated, moreover, that the United States should accept no commercial arrangement less advantageous than that granted to any other nation (see Wilson & Son to DW, March 31, 1843; Howland and Aspinwall to DW, April 5, 1843; N. L. and G. Griswold to DW, May 13, 1843; all in DNA, RG 59, Misc. Letters). The primary concern of those who responded to the circular of March 20, as expressed in the words of Forbes, was that American trade should be admitted to the China market "upon the same footing with the most favored nation" and that it would be "impolitic to accept anything less" (Forbes et al. to DW, April 29, 1843, below).

The opinions and suggestions of those who responded to the circular had a discernible impact on the instructions of May 8, 1843, which Webster prepared with unusual care. He emphasized that the mission was "entirely pacific" in its nature and that the primary goal was to "secure the entry of American ships and cargoes" into the treaty ports "on terms as favorable as those which are enjoyed by English merchants." Cushing was directed to try to see the emperor in person, but this was a secondary objective subordinate to the first, and he was given the option of abandoning what would have been an unprecedented trip to Peking if it endangered securing most-favored-nation status in the China market (DW to Cushing, May 8, 1843, below).

Webster was quite explicit as to the manner in which Cushing was to conduct the negotiation for a treaty of friendship and commerce. Employing the utmost tact, he was to view himself as a "messenger of peace." He was to be respectful toward Chinese officials, but he was to do nothing that, like the "*Kotou*" (kowtow), implied inferiority on the part of Americans. In avoiding even the appearance of being a "tribute bearer," he was to tell the Chinese that the U.S. government "is always controlled by a sense of religion and of honor." The Chinese were to be made aware of the power of the United States. In so informing them, Cushing was to recount how Americans, "sword in hand," had won their independence from Britain "after a seven years' war." Finally, he was to emphasize that American friendship with China depended upon the negotiation of a commercial agreement containing terms as favorable as those granted the British in the Treaty of Nanking.

The instruction of May 8, 1843, established the first coherent American foreign policy toward China and led in 1844 to the Treaty of Wanghia, which provided the United States with the great advantage of most-favored-nation treatment. Taken together with the Tyler Doctrine of 1842, the instruction of 1843 entitles Webster to be known as the pioneer in fashioning an American foreign policy toward the Pacific and East Asia. The Tyler administration perceived Hawaii and China to be part of the same general problem, that of defining American interests in the Pacific region. In contrast to the Tyler Doctrine, Webster did not state as an objective the upholding of Chinese independence, but he did similarly call for equality of commercial access to the market of a foreign country that was in danger of coming under the domination of one of the great powers of Europe. The major difference between Hawaii and China was that the United States did not hold the preponderant influence in the Chinese empire that it did in the Sandwich islands. Webster's judicious shaping of policy goals took this important distinction into consideration.

The instruction to Cushing, like the Tyler Doctrine, so accurately reflected the nature of American interests that it constituted the basis of American foreign policy for half a century. It was, moreover, the cornerstone for the Open Door doctrine of 1899–1900. The historic instruction of May 8, 1843, was also Webster's last official act. On the same day that he initialed the directive to Cushing, he signed his letter of resignation as secretary of state.

FROM PETER PARKER

Sir,   Washington Jany 30th 1841.

The desinterestedness of my motive and the vast importance of the object, were my apology for seeking the audience with which you were pleased to favor me and my worthy friend Rev: L[eonard] Bacon a few days since.[1] The readiness with which you entered into the subject, and your own request that I would express in writing, for yourself and others whom it may concern, the facts and suggestion then Submitted, relative to the *crisis* that exists between China and this Country,[2] are my excuse for briefly addressing you on this occasion.

Here allow me to premise, it is not a subject that has been taken up precipitately But one that has been a subject of consideration and unqualified approbation with Gentlemen of intelligence, who contemplate it entirely disconnected with personal ends. Indeed such is the nature of the case that there seems a peculiar propriety in its being submitted to the consideration of the American Government as a concern that affects the whole Nation, rather than any particular section of it. Were the merchants of our Commercial cities to be most forward in presenting it, it might be Suspected that private interest<s> was the motive that prompted them, and the Subject would not Stand as at present upon its own basis.

The suggestion Submitted with all defference to the Consideration of the Executive Department of the American Government, is the expediency of improving the present unprecedented Crisis in the relation of this Government and China, to Send a *Minister Plenipotentiary, direct and without delay to the Court of Taou Kwang.*[3]

Several considerations urge the propriety of such an Envoy.

1. Whatever course the British Government may have taken, and be the result of their negotiations or coercive measures, as they may, on the arrival of your Minister, such will be the unsettled relations between China and America, as to demand the attention of this Government.

2. The second consideration, tho' *first* it may be in importance, is that an American Minister, possessing the requisite qualifications of *age—ability* and *rank* may be most timely and acceptable both to the Chinese and English as a *Mediator* in the adjustment of the difficulties of these

1. Parker and his friend Bacon met with DW on January 22, 1841. Bacon (1802–1881; Yale 1820) was minister of the First Church of New Haven from 1825 to 1866.

2. Parker regarded the Opium War between China and Britain as a general crisis. He believed that the continuation of the war would strengthen groups in China who favored seclusion from the West. See Edward V. Gulick, *Peter Parker and the Opening of China* (Cambridge, Mass., 1973), pp. 98–99.

3. Tao Kuang, or Dao Guang (1782–1850), became emperor in 1821 and ruled until his death.

two nations, and the restoration of the foreign Commerce upon terms advantageous & honorable to all.

The mediation of America was a Subject of frequent Conversation with Chinese of intelligence and not new to officers of Govern't also previous to my leaving that Country. The mediation of William IV in the recent dispute between France and America, was known to the Imperial Commissioner Lin,[4] and as he is in the practice of Communicating directly to the Emperor every item of important foreign intelligence, it is probable that His Majesty is made acquainted with this fact. It is a Subject the Chinese appreciate, they well understand the meaning of "chung-keen-jen" [chung chieh jen] or middle man and regard this a rational way of adjusting public difficulties. Not to Speak too confidently, there is a strong presumption that the Chinese will be happy to avail themselves of such a mediation for[:]

3. After all the affected disregard the Chinese have manifested for foreign Commerce, Imperial Edicts often representing the revenue derived from it as comparable to the "feathers down," there is abundant evidence to the contrary. I believe the desire is *Strong* and *extensive* to continue the foreign trade. The representation of a late Governor of the two Provinces of Canton and Kwang se, was to the point in this respect. In a memorial to the Emperor, the revenue from foreign Commerce so often Spoken of as the "feathers down" he contended, is untrue: for in a great measure the Soldiery of these two Provinces is Sustained by it, and upon it, in part at least, depends the Support of the Imperial Household. This sentiment is sustained also by the Hongmerchants[5] and others. But for the Spongy texture of the Imperial officers the value of this revenue would be still more apparent to His Majesty. The revenue is greater in *fact* than in *name*.

The office of Superintendent of Customs,[6] in which this Imperial officer and his attendants are able to defraud the Government is "farmed out" at an exorbitant Sum, So that what in other Countries is paid in

4. Lin Tse-hsü, or Lin Ze-xu (1785–1850), a talented administrator, was named commissioner for Kwangtung in 1839 and was ordered to eradicate the opium trade. The Opium War between Britain and China began after Lin had 20,000 chests of British-owned opium burned. On the British mediation in 1836 of a claims dispute between France and the United States, see *International Arbitrations*, 5:4467. William IV (1765–1837), ruled from 1830 to 1837.

5. The hong merchants, or cohong, were a group of about a dozen Chinese who held a monopoly on trade with foreigners at Canton.

6. This was one of the most lucrative posts in China. The Hoppo, or superintendent of customs at Canton, was appointed by Peking for a three-year period. He collected custom duties through the hong merchants.

fixed Salaries, is obtained here by fraud. For example, in the importation of American domestics, these are landed by so much duty on a bale. As these pass the Custom house four bales are included in one and having passed the hoops are removed, and instead of one bale there are four: the Stipulated duty is paid on one to the Emperor, and that on the remaining three goes to His Excellency the *Hoppo* and his Servants.

4. The Chinese only wish for a method of pacification and restoration of Commerce, by which the Government shall not *"lose face"* or credit, at the Same time it effects the cessation of the *Opium* traffic. By Imperial Edict the British trade is "cut off *for ever*":[7] and without Some pretext that Shall appear plausible to the people the Emperor cannot without lowering himself in their estimation revoke his Decree. Through an impartial Mediator such explanations, and apologies, where apologies are due, might be made on either hand, as <I> should obviate this difficulty, and may be the means in an overruling Providence of preventing a deplorable Sacrifice of property and life.

5. There is Serious ground of apprehension that if the subject is not *Seasonably* attended to that all *foreign intercourse will be cut off*, and China will act after the policy of Japan. Even now this is the wish of one of the two great factions into which the Chinese Government is divided as is apparent by the whole tenor of the measures recently adopted by *Lin Tsih Seu* [Lin Tse hsü]. The foreign residences in Canton have been enclosed by a row of pallisades in the river forming a Semicircle and extending Some distance above and below them. The area in front is enclosed by a high fence, and gates extend across the Streets, so that in five minutes at any time, the foreigners may be made prisoners in their own houses. *Privileges* of going abroad upon the river, and in the Suburbs and neighboring villages for air and exercise formerly enjoyed are now prohibited. Tho' the Commerce is desired and thousands and tens of thousands of silk manufactories, and tea cultivators, depend upon it, yet as the least of two evils, the government may with one decisive Stroke cut off *all* foreign intercourse. This plan has been suggested by one Memorialist—Tsang-Wang-Yen (Chinese Repository vol: 8, p. 560).[8] It is urged if all are treated alike none can Complain<s> of partiallity. The trade once prohibited, it will be more difficult to restore, than it is now to preserve it by timely attention. The importance of the Chinese Commerce to this Country as a source of Comfort and healthy gratifications requires no Comment, and the *moral* benefits to the Chinese, which are suspended

7. The imperial edict of March 18, 1839, ending the opium trade is in *Executive Documents*, 26th Cong., 1st sess., Serial 365, No. 119, pp. 14–17.

8. Tseng Wang-yen, or Zeng Wang-yan, the mayor of Peking, proposed total cessation of all foreign trade. See *The Chinese Repository*, 8 (March 1840): 560–567.

upon this issue, are such as a free, enlightened & Christian nation like ours can best appreciate. It should not be forgotten that a trade of about $12.000.000. per annum is also worth preserving and protecting.

6. The American Nation probably stands higher in the confidence of the Chinese than any other nation. American merchants have had but a limited traffic in the prohibited article—whlist [whilst] some, as well known to that Government have taken a decided Stand against it, and have exerted their influence to expose the evil and to rouse the moral Sense of Western nations against it. America is known not to be a colonizing Nation and *A person of the highest diplomatic tact Should be selected for the undertaking.* A man who is qualified to execute a Similar Mission to any of the Continental Powers of Europe, might not be the individual for this occasion. If among those who have presided over this Nation, one could be selected, besides his experience and skill in public affairs, the mere circumstance, that he has been Chief Magistrate, or an "Emperor" of the United States of America as the Chinese would regard him, —would go far to secure for him *respect* and *access* to the "*Celestial Court.*"

The Emperor of China now in his 70th year[9] would feel a Strong Sympathy and regard for one approaching his own advanced age, and of *Similar Rank*—who had come over so many tens of thousands of Lees [li][10] to the "inner land." And the person of this description, like the Hon. Member of Congress who has so far interested himself in China as to call for information respecting it might shrink from the undertaking at so advanced an age yet would it not be an *enviable climax* to a long life of devotedness to one's Country, to effect an honorable treaty with such an Empire,[11] to save, as is quite possible, a vast effusion of blood; and to achieve an object which will be a blessing to *the Universal World*—To benefit a nation, an Empire, to do good to a generation, and especially to generations of unborn millions are noblest of noble objects, are adapted to the capacities of the most desinterested and *noble* minds, and are worthy the Enterprize of the *American Government*. With sentiments of long cherished admiration and esteem, I am most respectfully, Your obdt Svt.   Peter Parker.

A great object is gained by calling your attention to this subject, without carrying it out in all its details.   P. P.

LS. CtY-M. Published in George B. Stevens and W. Fisher Markwick, *The Life,*

9. In 1841, the emperor was in his fifty-ninth, not his seventieth, year.

10. Li is a Chinese measure of distance equal to about a third of a mile.

11. Parker hoped former president John Quincy Adams would be sent as minister to China. Adams called for information about contacts between China and the United States in the House on December 16, 1840. See *Ex. Doc.*, 26th Cong., 2d sess., Serial 383, No. 71, pp. 1–83.

Letters, and Journals of the Rev. and Hon. Peter Parker, M.D. (Boston and Chicago, 1896), pp. 184–188. Parker (1804–1888; Yale 1831) received his medical degree from Yale and was ordained a Presbyterian minister in 1834. In June 1834 he sailed for China, where he established a medical clinic.

FROM EDWARD EVERETT

Nro. 29.

Sir, London 29 November 1842.

I received, a short time since, from Messrs [Robert] Brookhouse & [William] Hunt of Salem,—the owners of the *"Tigris"* and *"Sea Mew,"* a letter, complaining of the delay which had taken place on the part of this Government, in making the promised compensation for the losses suffered by those gentlemen, in consequence of the capture and detention of their vessels in the African seas.[1] Being myself of opinion that their complaint was founded in reason, I deemed the reception of their letter a fit occasion for addressing Lord Aberdeen again on the subject. I accordingly prepared and transmitted a note, reminding him of his promise and of the delay which had taken place in its fulfilment,[2] and sending him a copy of the letter of Messrs Brookhouse and Hunt. The difficulty, as had been intimated to me by Lord Aberdeen himself, a few weeks since, in an informal conversation on the subject, is not in his department, but in the Treasury, from which it is always extremely difficult to obtain the final liquidation and payment of a claim of this kind. I have made as distinct an allusion, as seemed to me expedient, to the cause of the delay. My note to Lord Aberdeen received a very early reply,[3] from which it appears that he has addressed another communication to the Treasury, probably accompanied with a copy of my note to himself on this subject. The promptitude of his answer induces me to hope, that he will have presented the subject to the Treasury in such a light, as will bring that department to prompt action on the claim. A copy of the correspondence accompanies this despatch.

I also transmit a copy of a correspondence with the Foreign office, on

1. Brookhouse (d. 1864) and Hunt were the proprietors of one of the largest American firms trading with West Africa in the 1840s. On the *Tigris*, see above, Everett to DW, September 16, 1842, "The Treaty of Washington," pp. 698–700. The *Sea Mew* was detained off Africa by a British ship on October 27, 1840. After it was determined that the *Sea Mew* was engaged in legitimate trade. the British agreed to pay compensation. See No. 15, Everett to DW, June 17, 1842, DNA, RG 59 (Despatches, Britain), which encloses Aberdeen's promise of compensation, dated June 16, 1842. Brookhouse and Hunt sent a letter to Everett about August 5, 1842, inquiring about their claim. See Everett to Aberdeen, August 5, 1842, Everett Letterbook, (Reel 21), Everett Papers, MHi (Microfilm).

2. Everett to Aberdeen, November 22, 1842, enclosed; not printed here.

3. Aberdeen to Everett, November 23, 1842, enclosed; not printed here.

the subject of a medal to be presented to Captain [John] Collins of the "*Roscius*," for saving the lives of the crew of the "*Scotia*" in 1839.[4] I am not acquainted with the manner, in which our Government has been accustomed to make its acknowledgements, for similar acts of humanity towards citizens of the United States. Is there anything which prevents its being done in the same way? If this is deemed unadvisable, some other official acknowledgment ought to take place. You will recollect, that, on the 25th Augt 1841; Eleven persons of the ship's company of the American vessel "*Mary Anne*," were rescued from drowning, by the Captain of the English brig "*Rover*," as set forth in my Despatch of 28th Decemr last.[5]

I had hoped to be able with this despatch, to transmit the copy of a note to Lord Aberdeen, on the subject of the complaints of our merchants, against the colonial Authorities in New Zealand.[6] I find, however, that this matter is rather more complicated, than I at first supposed; and I may perhaps be under the necessity of applying to you for further instructions. If it is possible to present the subject to the British Government in a proper form, without the delay required for further communication with Washington, I shall not fail to do so.

I enclose with this despatch a copy of a letter from Mr [Joseph] Balestier, Consul of the United States at Singapore, dated the 20th September last, and containing a copy of Sir Henry Pottinger's circular to the British subjects in China, announcing the brilliant success of the Chinese campaign.[7] The same mail from India brought the tidings of the reoccupation of Ghuzni and Caubril by the British armies, and the recovery of all the prisoners but one. This important intelligence, it is scarcely necessary to add, has been received with unbounded satisfaction, by the Government and the people of this country. The termination of the wars in India and China, on honorable and advantageous terms, takes from the finances of this country an increasing burden they were little able to

4. Aberdeen to Everett, November 22, 1842, enclosed; not printed here. Collins (c. 1795–1857), a packet operator, saved the crew of the *Scotia*, which foundered at sea on December 5, 1839.

5. See No. 4. Everett to DW, December 28, 1841, DNA, RG 59 (Despatches, Britain).

6. Britain declared sovereignty over New Zealand on May 21, 1840. American merchants there complained because British officials confiscated lands that had been settled by Americans before the British had declared their authority and because the British imposed higher duties on American goods imported into New Zealand. Everett enclosed to DW a draft of his unsent letter to Aberdeen, dated November 1842; not printed here.

7. Balestier, from Massachusetts, was U.S. consul at Singapore from July 14, 1836, to January 21, 1852. His letter of September 20, 1842, and Pottinger's circular of August 26, 1842, are enclosed; not printed here. Pottinger (1789–1856) was the British minister to China.

bear; and under every other aspect, presents subjects of congratulation. In India it relieves the Ministry from the painful necessity of carrying on a war, commenced by their predecessors, disapproved by themselves, but from which there was considered to be no escape till the prisoners were recovered, and the disasters of the last campaign retrieved by some brilliant success. Some uncertainty existed as to the course which would be pursued when those objects should be attained; but this uncertainty is dispelled by a proclamation of Lord Ellenborough contained in the papers of the 28th, in which, it is announced that the British Armies are to be withdrawn from Affghanistan, and the Sutlej as the North Western boundary of the Indian Empire. Nor is this annunciation made without pretty intelligible reflections on the mistaken policy, which dictated the original invasion of this region under Lord Auckland's Government.[8] It is shocking to reflect on the waste of treasure and of life occasioned by a conquest, which, after a lapse of two years, it is deemed a piece of good fortune to be able, without descredit, to abandon.

The result of the campaign in China is still more satisfactory.[9] I am well informed that the possible consequences of the war in that country were regarded by this Government with great anxiety. There was well grounded reason for the fear, that the progress of that war should teach the Chinese how to fight, as it had already shown that they did not lack courage. When we reflect on the climate, (identical with our own under the same parallels and other local circumstances,) and consider that the seat of war was in a low alluvial country, south of the thirty fifth degree of north latitude, the perils of a midsummer's campaign, to regiments some of them fresh from England, may be well understood. From these and all the other dangers and burdens of the war, the Government and the country are unexpectedly and honorably extricated.

Sanguine expectations are entertained of great benefits to result to the Commerce of England, from an extended market for her fabrics in

8. In January 1842 some 3,000 British troops were ambushed and killed during their retreat from Kabul. Those who survived and a number of other civilians from Kabul were made prisoners. Kabul was reconquered by the British on September 15, 1842, and the prisoners were rescued. The proclamation by Edward Law, Lord Ellenborough (1790–1871), the governor-general of India from 1841 to 1844, is in the London *Times*, November 28, 1842. George Eden, Lord Auckland (1784–1849), was gov-ernor-general of India from 1835 to 1841.

9. The Opium War in China was concluded by the Treaty of Nanking of August 29, 1842, negotiated by Sir Henry Pottinger. The treaty opened five Chinese ports to foreign trade, ceded Hong Kong to Britain, and stipulated that China would pay a war indemnity. See *British and Foreign State Papers, 1841–1842* (116 vols., London, 1812–1925), 30:389–402.

China. I am inclined to think these expectations premature. The demand for Foreign fabrics in China, has thus far been a limited one, with no indications of a tendency toward rapid expansion. The extremely dense population of the country,—the consequent cheapness of labor,—the difficulty which in all old countries attends extensive changes of the habits of the people,—a difficulty supposed to be as great in China as in any other part of the world,—will present serious obstacles to any sudden process of substituting foreign for domestic fabrics.

How far the other civilized nations of the world will partake the benefit which may accrue to England from the recent events in China, cannot yet be foreseen. It will be difficult for England permanently to maintain a monopoly of any important privileges, even were it for the interest of the Chinese (which it would not be,) that such monopoly should exist. The liberal press of London, in its comments on the course which things will probably take, assumes it is certain, that other nations are to come in, for a share of the advantages of an increased intercourse with China. Lord Palmerston, in a conversation which I happened to hold with him a few evenings since, expressed the same sentiment. He informed me also, that the terms of Sir H. Pottinger's arrangement, were in precise conformity with the instructions of the late ministry. No provision, you observe, is made for the establishment of permanent diplomatic relations between the two countries. This omission was not accidental. Lord Palmerston observed that, having no ulterior political objects, it was not the wish of the late ministry to embarrass the settlement of the present controversy by a demand for the admission of an ambassador; & Lord Fitzgerald,[10] (president of the Board of Control under the present Ministry,) who took part in the conversation alluded to, concurred in the soundness of that view. I remarked, that I supposed this would be matter to be decided by circumstances, as they might hereafter arise, and to this observation Lord Fitzgerald assented.

I confess I think it will be difficult, if a greatly extended intercourse with China is to take place, to dispense with a representative of the British Government, fully accredited to that of China and resident at its capital. Experience has shewn the impossibility of transacting business of importance and delicacy with the provincial governors. The Character of the Chinese despotism, which makes it impossible to transmit with safety any unfavorable intelligence to the central government, with the Universal corruption of the subordinate functionaries, points to the necessity of a diplomatic establishment at Pekin. It is supposed that till the entrance of the British forces into the Yang-tse-Kiang[11] at the com-

10. William Vesey-Fitzgerald, Lord Fitzgerald (1783–1843), served as president of the Board of Control from October 1841 to May 1843.

11. On July 15, 1840, the British blockaded the mouth of the Yangtze River, the most important commercial waterway of China at that time.

mencement of the present campaign, the Emperor had never been truly informed as to the origin & progress of the war, or the near approach of a crisis.

Although next to nothing is known of the interior political condition of the Chinese Empire, the recency of its conquest by the present dominant race has always led me to suppose, that there might be a very extensive disaffection on the part of the people toward the Government, which, if skilfully encouraged and made use of by a foreign power, might prove the means of an entire subversion of the Tartar dynasty. This view of the subject has, I understand, been confirmed by many circumstances which have occured in the present campaign: —and the private letters received by the Government, went so far as to express the apprehension, that an insurrection might break out, before the conclusion of an arrangement with the Imperial authorities; —an event which would, of course, have been productive of embarrassment and delay.

I have lately received from Mr [John] MacGregor, the intelligent assistant Secretary of the Board of Trade, a duplicate copy of the fifth part of his Report on the commercial regulations of foreign countries, containing the Tarriffs of the German Zoll-verein or Customs' Union, and of some of the other German states. In the introduction will be found a very lucid and instructive account of the history and organization of the Customs' Union. Not being sure whether this fifth part was among those, which I received from Mr McGregor and transmitted to the Department last summer, I have thought it advisable to forward this copy to Washington. Changes have been made in the duties on some articles, at the recent meeting of the deputies of the Zoll-verein, but as this subject is peculiarly within Mr [Henry] Wheaton's province, it is wholly unnecessary that I should enlarge upon it.[12]

Having received information from a respectable American merchant now in London that preparations are making in this country, on a large scale, to smuggle British fabrics into the United States, I have thought it my duty, under my general instructions, to call the attention of our consuls to the subject. I have accordingly addressed a circular letter to the Consuls at this port, at Liverpool, Bristol, Leeds, and Glasgow, a copy of which is herewith enclosed. I also enclosed a copy of a reply to this circular received from the Consul at Hull.[13]

A demand was recently made upon me for the payment of the crown

12. MacGregor wrote a report on the "Commercial Tariffs and Regulations of the Several States of Europe and America." The report is not included in the RG 59 record. For Wheaton's remarks on the meeting of the Customs Union, see No. 206.

Wheaton to DW, November 16, 1842, DNA, RG 59 (Despatches, German States).

13. The enclosed circular is dated November 26, 1842, and the reply from the consulate at Hull is dated November 29, 1842.

taxes on the house in which I reside, and where the office of the Legation is kept. This demand was apparently made through inadvertence or ignorance of duty, on the part of the Collector, & was immediately abandoned by the surveyor. I enclose you a copy of the letters which were exchanged on the subject.

Since the foregoing was written, I have received, by the Patrick Henry, a parcel from the United States, containing despatches, letters and papers, for the continental legations and for our Consul at this port [Thomas Aspinwall], a letter for the Messrs Rothschilds, with your despatch Nro 25, transmitting the Commissions of Messrs [Charles H.] Delavan and [James] McHenry, appointed Consuls of the United States at Sydney, Nova Scotia, and Londonderry,[14] and the letter of Mr Fletcher Webster of the 31st October, enclosing a communication on the subject of casts of the Elgin marbles, addressed to the Honorable John C[anfield] Spencer;[15] all of which will receive due attention. I am, Sir, With much respect, Your obedient servant,   Edward Everett.

LS. DNA, RG 59 (Despatches, Britain). Rec'd December 26, 1842.

FROM JOHN TYLER

D Sir   [January–February 1843]
    If Congress makes a liberal appropriation[,] such as becomes the subject I propose to send to China, the Pennsylvania. If they make a small affair of it any little cock-boat will do.[1] Yrs   J. Tyler

ALS. DLC. Published in *Tylers*, 2:263.

FROM EDWARD CARRINGTON

Private
Sir,   Providence 2 March 1843
    I notice that it is proposed to send an Ambassador to China, to look after and protect our Commerce in that quarter; participating to a small

14. No. 25. Daniel Fletcher Webster to Everett, November 2, 1842, DNA, RG 59 (Instructions, Britain). Delavan, from New York, was U.S. consul at Sydney, Nova Scotia, from from October 21, 1842, to January 30, 1843. McHenry, from Philadelphia, was consul at Londonderry from December 18, 1842, to September 18, 1845. The letter sent for the Rothschilds has not been found.

15. Daniel Fletcher Webster to Everett, October 31, 1842, DNA, RG 59 (Instructions, Britain).

1. In response to President Tyler's message of December 30, 1842 (*Messages and Papers*, 4:211–214), Congress on March 3, 1843, appropriated $40,000 for the China mission. See *Cong. Globe*, 27th Cong., 3d sess., pp. 323, 391–392. The *Pennsylvania*, a 120-gun ship of the line, was not sent on the mission. Four ships accompanied Caleb Cushing: the steam frigate *Missouri*, frigate *Brandywine*, sloop *St. Louis*, and brig *Perry*.

degree in the trade with that Country and having resided a number of years at Canton, as Consul for the United States, have had an opportunity to learn something of the character of that People.

There is no nation who is more sensitive on points of et<t>equette, rank and distenction, than the Emperor [Tao Kuang/Dao Guang] and State officers of the "Celestial Empire". The occupation of Merchant, however respectable, is not regarded as entitled to *rank*, in Communications with the officers of the Goverment. Houqua, the very wealthy and talented Merchant at Canton, and head of the "Co-Hong" (a Company of Merchants), a "Brevet Mandarin["] of the *"Blue Button,"* so long as he follows Merchandising, this Brevet distinction avails him nothing.[1]

It appears to me, in selecting a person for this mission, it would be *un*advisable to send other than an able Statesman, who holds or has held important office under our Goverment, certainly *not* a person, who had been known at Canton as a mere "Merchant" or trader. Such an one, would carry but little importance of Character with the Chinese.

It might be advisable, for the Ambassador to attach to his Suite, some one or two intelligent Merchants, well acquainted with the trade between the two Countries and who have had experience in China, of which there are many now at Canton, and in this Country, who have resided there, and recently returned.

I apprehend there will be great difficulty in obtaining a competent Interpreter. The Chinese "Linguists" at Canton, cannot be called interpreters, they neither read, write or speak English. They speak a "jargon["] of English and Chinese, words in general use in buying and selling of Merchandise, and act as linguist in passing goods thro' the Custom House, to and from the Shipping—but they know nothing of any foreign language, and are not conversant in the Court language, at Pekin.

The British have a Mr [John Robert] Morrison, Mr [Robert] Thom and Mr [Karl Friedrich August] Gutzlaff as their Interpreters,[2] the two first, are British Subjects. I believe we have no American, that is acquainted with the Chinese language.

The most favorable places to find an intepreter, would be Batavia, Prince of Wales Island (straits of Malacca where there is a College for Instructing the Chinese and English languages,)[3] & at Singapore and

1. Howqua, Wu Ping-chien, or Wu Bing-jian (1796–1843), the merchant prince of Canton, was worth an estimated 26 million Spanish dollars. Members of the Chinese ruling class in the Manchu dynasty were ranked in nine groups, identified by colored buttons on the top of their hats. Blue buttons identified those in the third and fourth ranks of society.

2. Morrison (1814–1843) was born at Macao and succeeded his father as interpreter for the British at Canton. Thom (1807–1846), who came to China in 1834 and learned Chinese, became British consul at Ningpo in 1844. Gutzlaff (d. 1851), a German, also worked for the British as an interpreter.

3. The Anglo-Chinese College at

Macao—heretofore, it has been almost impossible to obtain the aid of a Chinese at Canton, to write any representation or act in any manner, on behalf of a foreigner, when thought necessary to make a representation to the local goverment of Canton—the objection arises on the part of the Chinese, from a *fear* of the officers of the Goverment charging them with exciting foreigners to importune the Goverment; but even if the Chinese were willing to engage as Interpreters, there is no one Competent to do so.

The Ratified English and Chinese Treaty, was dispatched from London 5th Jany and it is probable it will again reach England with the Ratification of the Emperor, by the [1st] August,[4] and it will then be known, if any exclusive commercial privileges are Secured to the English, at the new opened ports. It must I think be sometime before there can be much trade carried on at these new ports, and when commenced, attended with many perplexities thrown in the way by the Chinese officers. I have the honor to be very respectfully Yr obt Servant   Ed Carrington

ALS. DNA, RG 59 (Misc. Letters). Carrington (c. 1775–1843), a merchant of Providence, Rhode Island, was U.S. consul at Canton from 1805 to 1813.

TO EDWARD EVERETT

Private

My dear Sir: Washington, 10th March, 1843.

In an official despatch of this date, I communicate to you, your appointment as Commissioner to China.[1] It was not expected that any appointment would have been made so soon. The bill as it passed the House under the recommendation of Mr. [John Quincy] Adams, gave the President an authority, to be exercised whenever he should think proper. While it was in the Senate, and at the very last hour of the session, an amendment was made, requiring the assent of the Senate to the appointment of a Commissioner. An immediate nomination, therefore became necessary, your name was sent in, and the nomination confirmed with very general satisfaction—I believe, indeed, without any opposition.[2]

The appointment gives, I think, universal pleasure. The President is

---

Malacca, was established in 1820 by Dr. Robert Morrison (1782–1834).

4. The Treaty of Nanking of August 29, 1842, *British and Foreign State Papers, 1841–1842* (116 vols., London, 1812–1925), 30:389–402.

1. No. 30. DW to Everett, March 10, 1843, DNA, RG 59 (Instructions, Britain).

2. The bill providing for the China mission passed the House on February 20 and the Senate on March 3, 1843. *Cong. Globe*, 27th Cong., 3d sess., pp. 323, 391–392. Everett's nomination was approved by the Senate on March 3, 1843, by a vote of 24 to 10. See *Journal of the Executive Proceedings of the Senate* (Washington, D.C., 1887), 6:190–191.

sincerely desirous that you should accept the appointment, because he thinks you eminently fitted to fulfil its duties. You see it said in the newspapers, that the object in nominating you to China, is to make way for your humble servant to go to London. I will tell you the whole truth about this, without reserve.

I believe that the President thinks that there might be some advantages from an undertaking by me, to settle remaining difficulties with England. I suppose this led him to entertain the idea, now abandoned, (at least for the present,) of an extra mission. But in the present state of things I have no wish to go to England—not the slightest. To succeed you in England for the mere purpose of carrying on, for a year or two, the general business of the mission, is what I could not think of. I do not mean, only, that I would not be the occasion of transferring you elsewhere, for any such purpose; but I mean that if the place were vacant, I would not accept an appointment to fill it, unless I saw that something might be done, beyond the ordinary routine of duties. At present I see little or no prospect of accomplishing any great objects.

Embarrassed as the Administration is here, and difficult as are the questions with which it has to deal, I find my hopes of success faint. Besides, I do not know who is to fill this place (which I suppose I shall soon vacate,) and therefore cannot anticipate the instructions which I might receive. The President is most anxious to signalize his administration by an adjustment of the remaining difficulties with England, and by the making of a beneficial commercial arrangement. If, for that purpose, a negotiation could be carried on here, I would give the President all the aid in my power, whether in or out of office, in carrying it forward. But without seeing, clearly, how I was to get through, and arrive at a satisfactory result, I could not consent to cross the water. I wish you, therefore, to feel, that so far as I am concerned, your appointment to China had not its origin, in a desire that your present place should be vacated. If it were vacant now, or should be vacated by you, there is not one chance in a thousand that I should fill it.

In a former communication, if not in more than one, I hinted to you that we had thought of you for China.[3]

We are now in hourly expectation of the arrival of the "Great Western,["] from Liverpool (11th February) and coming by way of Madeira; and the packet from Liverpool of the 4th ultimo, may be looked for in eight or nine days. In writing to me by one or the other of these conveyances, you may possibly have said something about China. If I should find you speaking upon the subject of the mission as if it were entirely out of the case for you to think of it, perhaps the President would be

3. See DW to Everett, January 29, 1843, "The Aftermath and Implementation of the Treaty of Washington: The Oregon Question," pp. 841–844, above, and DW to Everett, January 30, 1843, mDW 24193.

authorized to consider such declaration as a *declining*. Your language must, however, be very strong, before he would give it that construction.

You will observe that while the act of Congress imposes a limit on your annual compensation, it does not affect the Presidents direction in regard to an outfit. The President is not only desirous, but anxious, that you should undertake the mission, as he knows nobody so well qualified, and he is disposed to be as liberal in his allowances as the law and his public duty will allow. The extent of consequent expenditures cannot be foreseen, nor the duration of the mission known. If it should be longer than was contemplated, or the contingencies prove greater, and necessarily so great as not to be capable of being paid out of the specific appropriation, aided as far as might be proper, by the fund for general contingencies of foreign intercourse, Congress will soon be in session again, and no doubt would readily make all further necessary appropriations.

It is not intended to dazzle the Emperor [Tao Kuang/Dao Guang] by show, nor soothe him by presents; still the mission should be respectable, and the Commissioner should have the means proper and necessary to carry forward the undertaking.

March 14.—The "Great Western["] arrived at New York on the 12th and we ought to have received whatever she brought for us last evening; but nothing came. As her route was to be circuitous, perhaps nothing was sent by her; but I incline to think some accident happened to delay the bag at New York. As the vessel sails on her return <voyage> on the 16th any thing for Europe must be mailed here today. I shall remain in the Department till the receipt of the mail this evening (8 o'clock,) and if any thing comes from you, will acknowledge it, and contrive to get my letter to New York, in season, by express or otherwise.

I see that a debate has been had in the Lords, on the Treaty, right of search, &c. and that a discussion on the same topics was expected to occur in the Commons on the 23rd.[4] It has been my purpose to send to you, by this conveyance, a despatch in reply to that read to me by Mr. [Henry Stephen] Fox from Lord Aberdeen. The paper is drawn; but I am now inclined to wait till I have an opportunity of reading the debates of which I have spoken.[5] The Liverpool packet now out ten days, may be expected in six or seven more, and will be likely to bring us the "tart reply, the learning, and the logic, and the wit."

4. Lord Brougham raised the visit and search issue in the House of Lords on February 7 and 16, 1843. See *Hansard's*, 66:214–219, 695. The debates in the Commons, which took place on March 21 and 22, 1843, are in *Hansard's*, 67:1162–1285, 1290–1313.

5. Aberdeen to Fox, January 18, 1843, extract in *British and Foreign State Papers, 1841–1842* (116 vols., London, 1812–1925), 32:443–444. DW's response to Aberdeen's dispatch is above, DW to Everett, March 28, 1843, "The Aftermath and Implementation of the Treaty of Washington: The 'Visit' and 'Search' Controversy," pp. 807–817.

Mr. Adams came to see me yesterday. He feels the greatest anxiety that you should undertake the China mission, which he regards as a most important affair.[6] I think Fletcher Webster will go out as Secretary. I might have mentioned when speaking of your compensation, that if you return to the United States before departing to China, you will of course have your return allowance.

Fletcher Webster thinks it would be more agreeable to go by the Mediterranean, and the overland route. That might be done; and a vessel of war, sent a sufficient length of time in advance might take you up at Aden or Bombay. In all these things your wishes would be much consulted.

P.S. Tuesday Eve' Mar. 14. 8 o clock. I have just recd your Despatch, by the G[reat] W[estern] & private letter; both principally relating to the Debates in Parliament, on the Treaty, and the *map*.[7] The latter subject appears to have obtained a preposterous importance.

I shall examine Lord Brougham's Speech, & if necessary take notice of it in my Despatch to you, by next conveyance. Make our best regards to your family, & believe me always truly Yrs   Danl Webster

L S, with postscript in DW's hand. MHi. Published in Curtis, 2:178–180.

TO THOMAS BUCKMINSTER CURTIS

Private

My Dear Sir;   Washington Mar. 12. 43

I thank you for your letter of the 10th.[1] It is true, that Mr [Edward] Everetts nomination to China, as any other nomination at the moment must have been, was the result of present necessity. The meddlers in the Senate had mended, or marred, Mr [John Quincy] Adams' bill,[2] so, that it required an immediate nomination. But from the moment the President's message was sent to Congress, recommending the Mission,[3] I have had Mr Everett in my eye; & gave him a hint to that effect, a month ago.[4]

6. See Adams, *Memoirs*, 11:336–337. Adams expressed his approval of Everett's appointment and described the China mission as one of "transcendent importance."

7. See Everett to DW, February 10, 1843, "The Aftermath and Implementation of the Treaty of Washington: The 'Battle of the Maps,'" pp. 779–780, above, and Everett's dispatch No. 32 of the same date, DNA, RG 59 (Despatches, Britain).

1. Not found.

2. Adams's bill provided for the China mission. *Cong. Globe*, 27th *Cong.*, 3d sess., pp. 323, 391–392.

3. Tyler's message of December 30, 1842, is in *Messages and Papers*, 4:211–214.

4. See above, DW to Everett, January 29, 1843, "The Aftermath and Implementation of the Treaty of Washington: The Oregon Question," pp. 841–844, and DW to Everett, January 30, 1843, mDW 24193.

The President, also, without a suggestion of Mr Everett's name from me, wrote me a note, inviting my consideration of him;[5] which note I sent to Mr Everett. I consider it a more important mission than ever proceeded from this Country, & more important than any other, likely to succeed it, in our days. Mr Everett is the man for it, & I am anxious he should accept it.

I am sorry Mr [Nathan] Hale publishes such trash, as I see in his paper of friday, from the Baltimore Patriot, respecting my *objects* in recommending Mr Everett.[6] Mr. Hale, or whoever conducts his paper, seems to have fallen under the influence of a positively unfriendly spirit. Why need he circulate imputations, else, upon the motives of his friends? Indeed, since I have been in my present situation, the "Daily" has been silent, & sullen, except when it could complain; not withstanding some little kindness, on my part, to its connexions. I will say to you, My Dear Sir, in confidence & privately, what I will not condescend to tell the Newspapers, that I have not the slightest wish to go to England, nor any expectation of being sent thither. I regard the English Mission, or any other Mission, as subordinate to the situation, which I now hold. If I were to remain in the public service, I should prefer to remain where I am. The only reluctance I had in recommending Mr Everett, was the difficulty, I felt, in filling his place in London.

For myself, nothing could induce me to go abroad, at my age, & without fortune, but a much clearer prospect of accomplishing great good, than I am now able to see. My expectation is, truly, to be, very shortly, in the midst of the circles of private life.

The rejection of Mr [Caleb] Cushing was scandalous;[7] yet it is a peice of the policy which the ultra Whigs are pursuing; or rather of the follies which they are committing, for there is no *policy* in the matter; all is anger, spleen, & violence. This letter is intended as private; but you may show it to C[harles] P[elham] C[urtis]. Yrs truly   D.W.

Mr Cushing is by far the ablest man in the late H. of R. except Mr Adams. He is thoroughly acquainted with all our N.E. interests, & has always supported them with zeal & ability. He was always ready, & al-

5. See Tyler to DW, January 30, 1843, mDW 24222.

6. Hale (1784–1863), who married Edward Everett's sister, Sarah Preston Everett, was the editor of the Boston *Daily Advertiser*. On March 10, 1843, the *Advertiser* carried an article that was attributed to the Washington correspondent of the Baltimore *Patriot*. According to the article, those senators who voted against Everett's confirmation as commissioner to China "had no objection to Mr. Everett." Rather, they suspected "that the design was to pave the way for sending Mr. Webster to England" and were registering a protest against that devious plan.

7. The Senate on March 3, 1843, three times rejected Tyler's nomination of Cushing for secretary of the Treasury. See *Journal of the Executive Proceedings of the Senate* (Washington, D.C., 1887), 6:186–190.

most the only one that was so—to stand up for N. England, her principles, her character, & her men. And yet *Whig* Senators from Vermont, R. Island, & Cont. *rejected* him.[8] I do think it the most discreditable, as well as the strangest proceeding, which has occurred for years. If his constituents have any spirit, they ought to send him back, if he will come, by acclamation.

ALS. MHi. Curtis (1795–1872), a wealthy Boston merchant and banker, was the brother of Charles Pelham Curtis (1792–1864; Harvard 1811).

TO THOMAS L. SMITH

Department of State

Sir,   Washington March 17th 1842 [1843]

This Department is desirous of preparing for the use of the China Mission the most full and particular account of the Trade between the United States and that Empire. The annual commercial volume published under your direction will of course be furnished,[1] but if it be in your power to supply any information more in detail, or which may give additional particulars, I will be obliged to you to communicate the same to this Department.[2] I am &c.   Danl Webster.

LC. DNA, RG 59 (Domestic Letters). Smith (d. 1871), of Virginia, was the register of the Treasury from 1829 to 1845 and the first auditor of the Treasury from 1849 until his death.

CIRCULAR

DEPARTMENT OF STATE.

SIR: WASHINGTON, March 20, 1843.

You will have learned that, under the authority of an act of Congress,

8. Among those voting against Cushing were Vermont senators Samuel Chandler Crofts (1768–1853; Harvard 1790) and Samuel Shethar Phelps (1793–1855; Yale 1811); Rhode Island's William Sprague (1799–1856) and James Fowler Simmons (1795–1864); and Connecticut's Jabez Williams Huntington (1788–1847; Yale 1806).

1. The register of the Treasury annually prepared a report on the commerce and navigation of the United States. See, for example, the report for the year ending September 30, 1842, in *Executive Documents*, 27th Cong., 3d sess., Serial 425, No. 220.

2. Smith transmitted DW's request for information to the collectors of customs in Baltimore, Boston, New York City, Philadelphia, and Salem. In their responses, these officials listed the principal houses in their ports that were involved in the China trade. See N. F. Williams (collector of customs of Baltimore) to DW, March 18, 1843; Charles Freichel (deputy collector of customs of Philadelphia) to DW, March 20, 1843; Levi Lincoln (collector of customs of Boston) to DW, March 22, 1843; John B. Knight (deputy collector of customs of Salem) to DW, March 22, 1843; and J. S. Hone (assistant collector of customs of New York) to DW, March 24, 1843; all in DNA, RG 59 (Misc. Letters).

a public mission is about to proceed from the United States to China,[1] for the purpose of cultivating friendly relations with that Empire, and of opening and enlarging, as far as practicable, commercial intercourse between the two countries.

For its own information, and the use of the mission, the Government desires to avail itself of opinions and suggestions of intelligent persons, who have had personal acquaintance with that country, or have been concerned extensively in the trade between it and the United States.

The general objects of the mission sufficiently indicate the points to which these suggestions may refer.

Any communication from you on the subject would be gratefully received by this Department. Very respectfully, Your obedient servant,

(signed) Danl Webster.

Printed Copy. DNA, RG 59 (Misc. Letters).

TO EDWARD EVERETT

Personal and Confidential
My Dear Sir;   Mar. 29. 1843

Our friend, & your relative, Mr [Nathan] Hale is in a strangely sour humour. Ever since I came into this Department, he has been, at best, cold, & not infrequently almost hostile. He seems to have taken it into his head, that my principal object in life, is to thwart *you*. He has no doubt, that your nomination to China had no other origin, than a desire, on my part, to succeed you, in England. He thinks I am constantly full of plots, for your overthrow. And other persons, whose case is not quite so stark, I am sorry to learn, speak of your nomination to China as *atrocious*—or an *insult*. These things, I confess, provoke me a little; but as I know you to be guiltless of them, they do [not] weaken my regard & affection for you, in any degree.

I have told you, & now repeat, that nothing would tempt me to go abroad, but the strong probability of accomplishing some great & immediate good. When a special mission was talked of, I did not wish to be charged with it. On the contrary, I strongly urged the President, if such a measure should be adopted, to join a Southern man, with you. The matter was suggested to Mr [John Caldwell] Calhoun, & his feelings sounded; but he altogether declined.

I am not so foolish as to imagine, that I can do more in England, for the good of the Country, than you can. I know that you stand there, entirely well, enjoying the respect of all classes, & all persons; & I could not stand better. Besides, I am willing to confess, that having filled the situation which I now hold, I do not wish to be despatched on any mission. Mr

1. The act of March 3, 1843, appropriating the funds for the mission   is in 5 *U.S. Stats.* 624.

[George] Canning did not add to his reputation by going abroad, having been Secretary of State, altho' he went *as an Embassador*.[1] Do not suppose, therefore, My Dear Sir, for a single moment, that your going to China will oblige me, by leaving your <pleasan> present place open for me.

Mr Hale, in the abundance of his regard for you, however oddly manifested, will have it that you just squeezed thro the Senate. The truth is, there were 10 votes agt you, & 30—or 40 for you.[2]

I cannot now go into an account of our present political condition. In the most entire confidence, I have to say, that I do not expect to remain at this table two months. Who will succeed me, I know not. I intend to prepare the Instructions for the China Commission; & probably shall do little more. I am, Dr Sir, on whatever quarter of the globe you are, truly yrs   Danl Webster

ALS. MHi.

FROM THOMAS HANDASYD PERKINS

Sir,   Boston Apr. 3. 1843

I have received, the Circular from the Department[1] over which you preside, asking information of "persons who have had personal acquaintance with China, or have been extensively concerned in the Trade to that Country" in relation to the Commercial interests of this Country in its trade with China & I belong it is true, to the Category desagnated in your letter, tho' my *personal* communication is of more than half a Century since, and *all intercourse* has subsided ten years or more. You are aware that since the Trade of Europe with China, has been confined to Canton, all the trade between Foreigners and the Celestial Empire, is presumed *in the eye of the law*, to be done by certain Persons appointed by the Emperor, denominated *Hong Merchants*, and the board is denominated, the *Cohong*—this body is held responsible to Foreigners for the Debts of each individual. A Duty has been exacted by this board, upon all imports and exports, and which is called the *Consoo fund* out of which, sums due from any member of the Cohong, to Foreigners are to be refunded. This is all well; but the fact is, that they take what time they please, to pay the demand. In one instance during the establishment of my late House under the Term of Perkins & Co, one of the Co Hong was in their debt,

1. Canning, who was British foreign secretary from 1807 to 1809, became ambassador to Portugal in 1814. No U.S. diplomat held the rank of ambassador until 1893.

2. The vote in the Senate confirming Everett's nomination as commissioner to China was 24 to 10. *Journal of the Executive Proceedings of the Senate* (Washington, D.C., 1887), 6:190–191.

1. See above, Circular, March 20, 1843.

between two and three hundred thousand Dollars, and it was ten years before the whole amount was paid, *and without interest*—so that if the interest of the Country which is 12 Per C' and sometimes higher, was compounded, at the end of each year, *you receive nothing*—from which there was no appeal—nor was there any Court to which a foreigner could appeal, for enforcing a debt due from a person, not of the Co Hong, as no such person was authorized by Government to trade with Strangers, the foreign trade being confined by Govt to the board before mentioned. I presume that by the arrangement made by Sir H[enry] Pottinger this matter will be altered[2]—indeed report says the Co Hong is to be done away, and which will make it necessary for the security of those trading with China, that there should be an authority to which an appeal would lay.

I think it may be said to be true that the lower and midling classes of the Chinese are knavish, at least in their dealings with foreigners, tho' it may be otherway in their intercourse with each other. I have known Chinese <in> whose upright diportment might be as much depended upon as upon any Merchant on our exchange. The establishment of a Tribunal, which remedy the evil above stated will I presume be provided by the arrangement between G. Britain and China; and I have no doubt that all that is acceeded to the demands of Sir Henry, will be granted to us. It is my opinion that we stand even better with the Chinese, than the English, and that there will be a disposition to favour the U. States to quite as great extent as shall be extended to any other Country.

I think it a good precaution, thus early to send a person of high standing to China, to represent the Commercial interests of our Merchants at the Imperial Court, and should the Person named by the President accept the appointment I conceive that we cannot be better represented—my fear is that he will not consent to be so long absent as such a Mission would require. I think it was wise not to appoint a person engaged in commerce to the Situation, to which Mr [Edward] Everett has been named. I presume that a Consul or Commercial Agent will be found to be necessary at each Port opened for trade.[3]

Altho' from what has appeared in the public papers, <that> the British Negotiator, appears to stipulate only for his own Government, still [it] is not to be presumed that it is, *to the exclusion of other Nations*, and that we of course shall be received on the same terms with the English. I am Sir Your Obed' Servant   T. H. Perkins

ALS. DNA, RG 59 (Misc. Letters). Rec'd April 5, 1843. Perkins (1764–1854), a prominent Boston merchant shipper, specialized in the China trade.

2. The Treaty of Nanking of August 29, 1842, abolished the co-hong and provided for a schedule of custom duties.

3. The Treaty of Nanking opened five ports for trade: Canton, Amoy, Foochow, Ningpo, and Shanghai.

FROM EDWARD EVERETT

Private

My dear Sir,   London 3 April 1843.

I received yesterday (Sunday) the letter bags by the "Great Western" with your despatches Nrs 30. 31. and 32 and your private letter of the 10–14th March,[1] acquainting me with my appointment as Commissioner to China. You appear to be a little disappointed, at not having heard anything from me on this subject by the "Great Western," on her outward passage. It was however first mentioned by you to me, in your letter of Jan. 29,[2] in which you said "If the provision should be ample, and you were in the Country, I think I should advise the President to send you to the Celestial Empire." The chief part of your letter had reference to a special mission to this Court, and the objects to be obtained by it. This letter did not, of course reach me till after the "Great Western" had sailed, which was the 11th February. The following day January 30th, you wrote me a note for the purpose of transmitting one from the President on the Chinese Mission; but the President's note was not enclosed by you.[3] This came by a sailing vessel and reached me two or three weeks ago. This is all you have written me on the subject. Your letter of 29 January led me to think that the special Mission would certainly be recommended to Congress and a nomination made at the Session just closed; and Mr [Henry Stephen] Fox's information to Lord Aberdeen named the day when the message would be sent. After receiving your letter of the 29th Jan. and your note of the 30th my first opportunity of writing was by the steamer of the 4th of March. You had anticipated that I should not have it in my power to write anything, which would reach you before the close of the session, and accordingly prepared me to expect, that a special minister might be appointed; but that whether he were dispatched or not might, in some measure, depend on what I should write. I accordingly threw all the light on the subject of the special Mission, which I was able to do, from the purport of my conferences with Lord Aberdeen.[4] Of China I said nothing, both because whatever I might say would come too late to affect the question of a nomination; and because I did not regard my nomination as likely to take place. A letter of Col. [Robert Charles] Winthrop's of the middle of February, which

1. DW to Everett No. 30. March 10, 1843; No. 31. March 13, 1843; and No. 32. March 14, 1843; all in DNA, RG 59 (Instructions, Britain). DW's private letter to Everett, March 10, 1843, is printed above.

2. See above, DW to Everett, January 29, 1843, "The Aftermath and Implementation of the Treaty of Washington: The Oregon Question," pp. 841–844.

3. See DW to Everett, January 30, 1843, mDW 24193.

4. See above, Everett to DW, February 27, 1843, "The Aftermath and Implementation of the Treaty of Washington: The Oregon Question," pp. 846–849.

reached me by a sailing vessel about the middle of March, first made me think it somewhat more probable.[5]

And now that the intelligence has reached me of my appointment, I am at the greatest loss what to say. I cannot possibly come to a decision without a further time for reflection. Your letters have not been 24 hours in my hands and the "Great Western" brought not a line from Boston, to aid us in making up our minds. The first impression is that of breaking up the establishment here, at the time when the cost and inconvenience of settling one's self have just been met, and we begin to feel a little at home;—leaving a Country like England and going to one which my wife [Charlotte Brooks Everett] and children, if I take them with me, cannot enter;—going with an appointment, liberal for an ordinary American Mission, but strongly contrasting with those of the European embassies, which from time to time have been sent to that Country;—without even a diplomatic title and rank, recognized by the Law of Nations, and necessary perhaps to secure to me its immunities;—with faint probability of being myself allowed to go to the seat of the Chinese Government except on conditions to which I could not submit. In addition to this, the last news from Canton is such, as to make it less likely than before, that the Chinese will be favorably disposed to open the door more widely to foreigners, than they have been compelled to do by force. You will have seen the letter of Sir Henry Pottinger to the Merchants at Canton, on occasion of the burning of the British Factories, and shewing a state of things and of Chinese feeling, unpropitious to any immediate extension of foreign intercourse.[6] Whether to take my family into the latitude of Macao (within the tropics) or leave them; if I leave them, where, are questions which greatly add to my embarrassment.

Were I a young man,—at the bottom of the class,—without a family,— there is much in the appointment to rouse my ambition and excite my faculties. But I shall be past 49 when you get this letter and I have a wife and five children of ages to stand in the greatest need of a father's care.

These are the feelings which have crowded upon me. They are first impressions; they may give way to other views. Reflection may convince me, that here, as on other trying occasions of my life, it is my *duty* to allow myself to be borne along upon the tide, on which Providence seems to

5. Winthrop to Everett, February 12, 1843, (Reel 8B), Everett Papers, MHi (Microfilm). Winthrop (1809–1894; Harvard 1828) served as U.S. representative from Massachusetts, 1840–1850, and as U.S. senator, 1850–1851.

6. On December 7, 1842, Chinese rioters attacked foreign trading factories in Canton. Pottinger's correspondence with the merchants on the disturbances is in *British and Foreign State Papers, 1841–1842* (116 vols., London, 1812–1925), 30: 125–135.

launch me. If I can come to that conclusion, I shall be at peace. But I must turn the subject over in my mind,—confer calmly with my family,—get more information than I possess as to the light in which this Government would regard a Mission from the United States to China— in short *think it over*; without which I cannot decide.

The little delay this will occasion, I take for granted, will put you and the President to no inconvenience, as you give me to understand, that the appointment would not have been so soon made, but for the necessity of acting before the adjournment of Congress. You intimate indeed, if I understand your expression, that unless I positively decline by this steamer, I shall be considered as accepting. I think, however, on reflection, that you will be of opinion, that I am entitled to more than a single day's delay. But if a categorical answer is required by this vessel, it must be respectfully to decline the appointment.

I shall write the President a word of acknowledgement of his obliging letter of the 14th March[7] and of this new proof of his confidence; but I shall not have time, nor am I otherwise able, to enter more fully into the subject;—on which by the steamer of the 19th, I hope to be able to write decidedly to you and to him. I remain, as ever, faithfully yours,

(signed) Edward Everett.

LC. MHi.

LIST OF ARTICLES FOR THE LEGATION TO CHINA

[April 11, 1843]

1st   Laws of the U. States and other customary books furnished from the State Department. [Notation by Tyler: "State"; by DW: "done"]

2nd   A Set of the best Charts, or most recent and correct Atlas; and if possible, a *Globe*, that the Celestials may see they are not the "Central Kingdom." [Notation by Tyler: "State"; by DW: "done"]

3rd   A pair six shooting pistols, small size. A pair of do., large size. [Notation by Tyler: "War"; by DW: "done & more too"]

Six shooting rifle—good American (commonly called Kentucky) Rifle. Some of the handsome arms, manufactured in the U. States. (These can probably be furnished from the War and Navy Dept's.) [Notation by DW: "get" and "Navy"]

4th   Model of War Steamer, armed and rigged. Either Hunter's or Stockton's—or after the old style, like the Missouri [Notation by DW: "State for enquiry" and "full model of engine"]

7. Tyler to Everett, March 14, 1843,   (Microfilm).
(Reel 8B), Everett Papers, MHi

5th   Model of Steam Excavator [Notation by DW: "not done"]
6th   Model of Locomotive Steam Engine; [Notation by DW: *"not done"*] and—plan of a Rail Road [Notation by DW: "not done"]
7th   A Daguerreotype apparatus. Some one attached to the Mission should learn the use of this. It can, perhaps, be best purchased in France, but could with difficulty be forwarded thence to China. [Notation by Tyler: "State"]
8th   Some approved elementary works on Fortification, Gunnery, Shipbuilding, Military and Naval Strategy—Geology, and Chemistry, and Encyclopaedia Americana. [Notation by Tyler: "State"; by DW: "done & more too"]
9th   Telescope, or Spy Glass. Barometer and Thermometer. [Notation by Tyler: "Navy"]
10th   Some of the useful articles made of India Rubber. [Notation by Tyler: "State"]
The usual articles of manufacture, both American and English, are abundant in China.
History of the U. States
Naval actions of late war.
History of the Revolution or
Marshals life of Washington.[1] [The last three entries are in Tyler's hand and contain the notation: "State."]

Books &c for the China Mission

Box 1.	12 vols
Waites State papers[2]	12 vols
Diplomatic correspondence	19 — "
&c Code	2 — "
Am Almanac	1 — "
Blue Books	1 — "
Commercial Regulations	3 — "
Am. Archives	3 — "
Secret Journals	4 — "
Journal of Fed. Convention	1 — "
Box 2. State papers (Gales & Seaton)	21 — "
Box 3. Laws U.S. & Pamphlets	9 — "
Congressional Debates	31 — "
N.E. Boundary	1 — "
Box 4. 6th Census	4 — "
1/2 Rm Envelope	

1. John Marshall, *The Life of George Washington* (Philadelphia, 1804–1807).
2. Thomas B. Wait and Sons, ed., *State Papers and Publick Documents of the United States . . .* (2d ed., Boston, 1817).

Box 5.   Documents 2d 26th & 1st 27th Cong
          Senate Docs 2d 27th
Box 6.   40 vols Rees Encyclopedia from F. Taylor[3]
Box 7.   7 vols do & other Book from F. Taylor
1 Box contains 1 Flag & Staff
                1 Gilt Eagle
                2 Seals
                1 Shield & Arms
1 Box   1 Case Pistols
1   "   Degarreotype apparatus
1   "   Press for Seals

Ordnance Stores

2 Percussion Muskets complete
1 Musket wiper
1 Screw driver
1 Ball screw
1 Spring vice
2 Hull's Carbines with Swivel bars & spring rods complete
1 Hull's Carbine ball mould
1 Spring vice
1 do wiper
1 do Screw driver
2—6 inch Allens & Thurbers revolving pistols with cases complete
2—4 inch Allens & Thurbers revolving pistols with cases complete
2—5 inch Colts repeating pistols complete
2 Colts Carbines complete
2   "   Powder flasks
2   "   Bullet pouches
2   "   Carbine screw drivers
2   "   Ball moulds
2   "   Percussion primers
1—   Jenks long carbine with bayonet & appendages complete
1   Jenks short Carbine & appendages complete
2   Kentucky rifles complete
2   Cavalry Sabres
2   Infantry officers swords
2   Artillery Swords
2   Cavalry sabre belts & plates
2   Infantry officers swords, belts & plates
2   Artillery   do   do
2   do sword belts

3. Abraham Rees, *The Cyclopedia*   1805–1825).
(rev. ed., 41 vols., Philadelphia,

1	Jenks rifle with appendages complete
2	Musket cartridge Boxes
2	do—do Box plates attached
2	do— do Belts
2	do— do Belt plates
2	do—Bayonet seatband, with frogs
2	do Waist belts
2	do Belt plates
2	do Gun swings
2	do Brushes & picks
500	Musket percussion caps
5000	Percussion Caps for small arms
200	Cannon percussion primers
1	Cannon lock & wire complete
3	Tin Boxes.

1 Box.	McCartneys embassy	3 vols & 1 large Atlas[4]
	Ellis' Journal	1 "[5]
	Barrons travels	1 "[6]
	4 Rms letter paper	
	5 do Cap do	6 Blk lines

2 grs Blotting

Copy. DNA, RG 59 (Misc. Letters). Endorsed by John Tyler: "Mr F[letcher] Webster will attend to this. The model of the steam ship would require too much time to complete if not on hand. He will please see the Secretaries of War & Navy. J. Tyler Apl. 11. 1843."

FROM EDWARD EVERETT

Private

My dear Sir,   London 18 April 1843

Since I wrote to you on the 3d inst.,[1] I have your private letter of the 25th February.[2] In giving you my reasons for not accepting the mission to China, I can do no more than refer you to my letter to the President of this date.[3] There are other very important considerations & difficulties,

4. Probably a reference to Aeneas Anderson's book, *A Narrative of the British Embassy to China* (New York, 1795), which was written while he was in the service of George Macartney, the British ambassador extraordinary and plenipotentiary to Peking, 1792–1794.

5. Possibly William Ellis, *A Journal of a Tour Around Hawaii, the Largest of the Sandwich Islands* (Boston, 1825).

6. Not identified.

1. See above, Everett to DW, April 3, 1843.

2. DW to Everett, February 25, 1843, mDW 24407, in which DW again raised the subject of the China mission.

3. Everett to Tyler, April 18, 1843, Everett Letterbook, (Reel 22), Everett Papers, MHi (Microfilm).

which in time might possibly be removed, though certainly not under a twelve month, & perhaps not at all. But as the domestic reasons I have stated are of themselves decisive, I have not felt it advisable to adduce others, arising from the nature of the service.

Immediately after receiving information of my appointment, I sought a conference with Lord Aberdeen on the subject of an American mission to China. He disclaimed all jealousy, and convinced me that he felt none. He did not, however, appear to think that any good would come of an attempt to send a mission to Peking. Their embassies, he said, had done no good. It had been left to Sir Henry Pottinger's discretion to exchange the ratifications at Canton or go to Peking: he is not to press for the latter course, if the Chinese object. England,—Lord Aberdeen assured me, had no eye to exclusive privileges, in their recent transactions with the Chinese. On the contrary, the British Negotiator last summer counselled them as a matter of policy, to open the new ports to the trade of the world.

There is an expression in my letter to you of the 3d inst. which I wish to explain, vizt that if "I were at the bottom of the class," the mission to China would arouse my ambition. The context of the paragraph will show, that I had mainly in view that freedom from family ties, which belongs to younger men. I certainly cannot consider a diplomatic mission to the Emperor of China [Tao Kuang/Dao Guang] as otherwise than a very honorable appointment. But with reference to the rank of a Commissioner to China, unless accredited as an Embassador or Minister, although entrusted even with the highest powers of peace and war at the outports, I may observe, that when Captain [Charles] Eliot was recalled by the late government, he was made Consul General to Texas. It is true he was superseded, on account of dissatisfaction with his administration, but he was not recalled in disgrace; & Sir Robert Peel, shortly before he left England for Texas, paid a high compliment, in the House of Commons, to his ability & integrity.[4]

There is but one other topic, on which it is necessary for me to say a single word, vizt that of your succeeding me in this place. I hope I have said all that I could with propriety on that point, in my letter to the President. Had you given me to understand, that my vacating my office here would be certainly or very probably followed by your accepting it, and that this arrangement was desired by the President & yourself, I should, in declining the mission to China, have tendered to the President an unconditional resignation of my place here. But as you state in your private

4. Elliot, vice Eliot, was the British representative in Canton from 1837 until recalled in January 1841 for his handling of the opium controversy. Peel defended Elliot in the House of Commons on May 24, 1842. See *Hansard's*, 63:686–687.

letter to me,[5] that, if my place at this Court were vacant now or should be vacated by me, there is not one chance in a thousand that you should fill it; in fact, as there is no appropriation for an outfit, I have thought that the course I have taken would best suit the President's convenience.

I will only repeat, from the close of my letter of the 16th September last,[6] that I hope if any change is proposed affecting me, I shall not be kept unnecessarily in suspense. No man can command the spirits necessary for the successful discharge of laborious & responsible duties, in a position so precarious & uncertain as that which I have filled for more than six months. I remain, Dear Sir, as ever, with sincere attachment, faithfully Yours,   Edward Everett.

ALS. MHi.

FROM EDWIN M. LEWIS

Sir   Philadelphia April 20th 1843

In reply to the Circular of 20th March[1] from your department, requesting information and suggestions for the use of the Public Mission about to proceed from the United States to China. We beg leave to offer the following remarks on such points as appear to us to be the most prominent, at same time would state that our personal acquaintance with China, commenced in 1831, when our Senior partner[2] went thither as Supercargo, since which time we have been engaged in the trade; one or other of 4 Brothers of our family having gone out in same capacity, and the 5th Brother, Theodore C. Lewis[3] is now on his way thither as Supercargo of Ship Talbot.

The entire system adopted by the Chinese in their intercourse with Foreigners is one which was devised when the trade was in its infancy, and is of course entirely unsuited to the extensive transactions now carried on in Canton, and subjects foreign commerce to all kinds of petty tyranny and exaction. Under their tariff of duties and manner of collecting them, there has grown up a System of corruption and fraud, unparralleled for its method and extent, all classes of their government officers, from the lowest tidewaiter to the Viceroy himself, participating.

Every Vessel entering the port of Canton is obliged to pay a number of very burdensome and vexatious fees, and also to get a Hong Merchant to go security for the good behaviour of her consignes and crew. These Hong Merchants are the only Chinese who are legally allowed to trade

5. See above, DW to Everett, March 10, 1843.

6. Everett to DW, September 16, 1842, mDW 23429.

1. See above, Circular, March 20, 1843.

2. Not identified.

3. Not identified.

with foreigners, they however for a small commission permit others to trade in their name. This Hong monopoly has we understand been abolished—if not, it should be.

The Linguist's fee of $216. on every Vessel is paid to permit a Chinese Linguist to transact our Custom House business, and should be abolished and the duties be collected as we shall suggest hereinafter. The House Compradore's fee of $119. on every vessel permits a chinese Compradore or House Steward to purchase our provisions & fuel. This office should be abolished. We may as well state here that the Man[darins] exact a fee from every chinaman who has any transactions with foreigners.

The most onerous charge is that called "Rumshaw & Measurement" and constitute the Port Charges. Each vessel is visited soon after her arrival by a superior Mandarin who superintends the measurement of the ship, Chinese fashion. The measurement is the port charge; the Rumshaw, being the [payment?] to the Mandarin and his subordinates, this last charge is 1600 taels or $2223.—[for?] every Vessel, the measurement charge amounts to $1500 to $2000 on every Vessel. These charges are very excessive and should be reformed; they are also very [un]equal as vessels carrying 600 tons of goods pay nearly as much as those carrying 110 tons. We would suggest that a regular tonnage duty be substituted. Should the Custom House business be transacted as we shall hereinafter suggest, the Rumshaw at least should cease.

The Pilots should be stationed at Hong Kong as well as at Macao, as all [ships] arriving from the Eastward or during the continuance of the North East Monsoons are at present detained at least two days in sending to Macao for their Pilot.

The subject of a regular Tariff of Import and Export Duties is the most important to which the attention of the Commission will be directed, and covers a very wide field. The present duties, such as they are, are most of all excessive and unequal, having been imposed upwards of a century ago ([as] we understand) and have continued undiminished though in many cases increased. They were first levied when Merchandises bore far different relative values to what they now do. We should recommend the Commission to contact the resident Merchants and any Supercargoes who may be in China and take their opinions as its guide, referring at same time to the alterations demanded or obtained by other nations.

The Chinese do not understand the principles of the debenture system, [to the] contrary they consider all goods arriving in their waters, as subject to the same duties as if landed and consumed in their Country; this regulation of theirs is very oppressive in cases where merchandise is sold to be [sent to] another part of the world, not landed in China, but merely transhipped from one vessel into another. This should be reformed and a debenture system introduced. Another subject of complaint is the imposition of arbitrary and temporary duties, such as those levied to pay the expenses of a war or of a famine, or to pay the debts of a defaulting Hong merchant. These together with sudden stoppages of the Trade should be prohibited; in the latter case the innocent always far outnumber the offenders,—sometimes the trade has been stopped for weeks for the *accidental* offence of one man, and some 20 Vessels in port with valuable cargoes, and at heavy expenses.

Our government should always have a respectable squadron in the Chinese waters, both for protection and to create a suitable regard for our flag and our Merchants. The trade to China from the United States has averaged since 1818 Six and a half Millions of dollars annually of exports from Canton, and employed an annual average of 13.000 tons of Shipping. We think this trade should receive the especial countenance and protection of government, as it opens a large and encreasing market for our domestic manufactures, particularly Brown Cotton goods, in which we both excel and can undersell the British.

Our government should always have a Consul at Canton, as that Port will undoubtedly be the great entrepot for all vessels going hence—this Consul should be appointed for terms of not less than five years, nothing being more disliked by the Chinese than changes—give them sufficient time to learn the character and intentions of our Consul and all will go well, and his influence will be extended and permanent. The Salary of this Consul should be at least $8000 per annum, and we would recommend $10.000. The reason for this large Salary is the very great expense of living (House rent, fuel and provisions) in Canton. Besides which a residence in that country is an honorable exile, almost in solitude, society being so very limited. A salary we think best; as the fees of office as now directed by law, have been found insufficient to renew the silk flag in its wearing out. The Invoices in each vessel are few in number, but generally large in amount. This Consul should be prohibited from transacting any business of a commercial character, as no men in the world are more jealous of each other than the small number of residents, supercargoes, and consignors engaged in this trade; and rather than have a business man appointed Consul, we scruple not to say, that all concerned would rather let things go on as heretofore, than submit their invoices outwards and homeward to the inspection of an interested rival. Besides, many articles of Imports and Exports must be kept secret, otherwise the best concocted plans would be frustrated and prove ruinous—this feature must be apparent when you consider the length of time (12 or 14 months) necessary to perform a voyage to China and back. A single cargo sometimes costs half a million of dollars.

The Consul should have extraordinary powers, and the Commission should make an arrangement with the Chinese government, to enable the Consul to collect from the American Merchants all duties, port charges &c and pay [them] over to the Custom House officers. By so doing many, if not all of the [vexatious] delays and expenses would be avoided; and smuggling prevented.

The punishment of Criminals should not be left to the sanguinary code of China, but all American delinquents should be delivered into the custody of the Commander of our Squadron, who in conjunction with the Consul should have [power] to examine witnesses, take depositions &c, which together with the accused should be sent to the United States in a government vessel and the case tried by the Supreme Court, a certified Copy of whose decision should be sent to the Chinese Authorities to satisfy them that justice had been done according to our laws.

Shipwrecked sailors should receive the attention of the Mandaring, have their necessities relieved and be forwarded in safety to the Consul, who should [pay?] all expenses.

Foreigners are restricted in <China> Canton to a very small space of ground; and until very recently, Ladies were forbidden to go there. We would suggest that either a small district of the adjoining country be appropriated for their use or else that a circular road be constructed and the use of horses and vehicles permitted. Residents and others should be permitted to take their families to Canton. Respectfully &c Your obedient svts   Edwin M. Lewis & Co.

ALS. DNA, RG 59 (Misc. Letters). Rec'd April 23, 1843. Edwin M. Lewis, a China merchant, could not be further identified. The Lewis family of Philadelphia had been actively engaged in the China trade since 1831.

TO EDWARD EVERETT

Private & entirely Confidential
My Dear Sir   April 23. 1843
    Your Despatch of the 28th of March, & your private letters of the 31st of that month & the 3rd of April, all by the Britania, came safe to hand.[1] I do not wonder that you see objection, to going to China, & that you require time to think of the matter. It will never cease to be subject of regret with me, that the Senate hurried us into a nomination, before we had time to consult you. I perceive it is rather the wish of your mind not to go, & I suggested to the President yesterday, that I thought it might be as well to decide, at once, in favor of nominating somebody else. But he said, in reply, that from your letter to him, he inferred that you had no

1. See No. 34. Everett to DW, March 28, 1843, DNA, RG 59 (Despatches, Britain). See Everett to DW, March 31, 1843, "The Aftermath and Implementation of the Treaty of Washington: The 'Battle of the Maps,'" pp. 787–793, above, and Everett to DW, April 3, 1843, above.

decided feeling about it, & really wished for time. Of course, nothing will be done, until we hear farther from you. F[letcher] Webster will go out as Secretary, & is already making preparation.

Before you receive this, I shall be at Marshfield, in private life. This, you have already been led to anticipate. It would not be true, to say that I leave the Depart without regret. I like its duties, & think I see some things ahead, in which I might be useful. But in the present posture of things, my connexion with the Administration would, I fear, soon get to be awkward. If you go to China, the President is likely to wish to send me to London; but I cannot go. I could stay but something more than a year, as changes abroad are very likely to correspond with changes at home; & it would require half that time to inform myself of the regular business of the mission. I sometimes feel as if I wished, that Lord Aberdeen & Sir Robert Peel had thought more favorably of a special mission. With more of countenance from that side, the measure might have found favor here; & in my opinion this is the moment for something more than an ordinary effort to settle the Oregon dispute, & the commercial questions. I do not suppose that any individual could do this much better than yourself, & have no confidence that I could do it as well. But I am, after all, a good deal inclined to think, that a Special Mission is a measure more likely to bring something to pass, immediately, than the effects of a stationary & ordinary legation. I hope, however, that my successor will give you immediate instruction on these subjects, if you remain where you are. Who that successor may be, I do not know. It is probable Mr [Hugh Swinton] Legaré may take charge of the Dept for the present—perhaps for some months, as Acting Secretary.

P.S. April 28.

If the President were not a candidate for the Presidency, he & I should get along very well together. But he is such candidate, & is evidently seeking support from the loco foco party. He will be disappointed. They will certainly cheat him. But he cannot be convinced of this truth. They are now hanging round him from Boston, ([Daniel D.] Brodhead, [Isaac O.] Barnes, [Robert] Rantoul [Jr.] &c)[2] promising him the support of the Democratic Party, if he will remove the Collector, Atty, Naval Officer &c, & give the places to them. All this is very likely to be done, when I am

2. Brodhead, a merchant and Boston bank director, was associated with the Democratic newspaper, the Boston *Statesman*. Tyler named Barnes U.S. marshal for Massachusetts during the congressional recess of 1844, and Barnes was confirmed by the Senate on January 15, 1845.

Rantoul (1805–1852; Harvard 1826), a lawyer, was named collector for the port of Boston during the recess of 1843 but was rejected by the Senate on March 14, 1844. Rantoul was then named U.S. district attorney for Massachusetts.

gone. I am afraid the *future* of this administration does not promise much of glory. Yrs   D. W.

ALS. MHi.

FROM JOHN MURRAY FORBES ET AL.

Sir,   Boston April 29th 1843

Having received a circular from the Department of State, asking suggestions regarding the proposed Mission to China,[1] we avail of the opportunity thus afforded us, to offer such opinions as the present state of our information will warrant, & should further accounts from that quarter change our views, we shall communicate them at a future time.

Firstly. The Chinese having conceived the idea that we have but few ships of war, owing to their never having seen more than two at a time & always one of these a small vessel, we recommend sending the Commissioner out accompanied by a respectable fleet, say not less than three or four square rigged vessels & a schooner of 100 to 150 tons, of light draft of water, to act as a tender or despatch vessel.

The latter should be unencumbered with a large number of guns & crew & should be a fast sailer.

Such a vessel would be of great use in entering on a new navigation, to sound channels & procure supplies and information; Or perhaps economy would be promoted by giving the Commodore authority to charter a Schooner in China, which could undoubtedly be done at from $600 to $1000 pr. month for the time actually in service, & by this means an experienced pilot for the N. E. coast of China [would] be secured in the master of the Schooner.

Secondly. No presents should be sent, *as such*, lest the Chinese should call them tribute, as was done when two English Embassies so signally failed,[2] but in order to cement the good feeling between the two Governments it would be well that the Mission should be provided with scientific drawings & models of Steamboats, Railroads, Cannon & perhaps of Fortifications; these to be produced only if a fit opportunity offered after the first objects of the Mission had been accomplished by its honorable reception; If there could be attached to the Squadron an Engineer who understands both civil & warlike Engineering & a practical mechanic who is thoroughly skilled in the latest mode of casting & especially of *boreing* cannon they might under some circumstances be of the greatest service to the objects of the Mission.

The Chinese look upon us as friends but they have a great fear of en-

1. See above, Circular, March 20, 1843.

2. In August 1793 an English embassy arrived in Peking with hopes of establishing a residency, but the Chinese refused the overture. In 1815 another British embassy went to Peking, but after one day the Chinese asked them to leave.

croachment by other foreign nations [and] if we could in a quiet way, without infringing upon the courtesies due to Great Britain, contribute anything to [their] means of defence against further aggression, it would open the eyes of the Emperor [Tao Kuang/Dao Guang] to the value of an Alliance with us, more than the prospect of increasing their trade an hundred fold.

Thirdly. As to the best time of the year for sailing of the Expedition; The most *pleasant* season [for] the passage is to leave between the 1st February & 15th June, but merchant ships full of cargo go out, at the most un[favorable] season of the year in four months & a well appointed ship of war ought to do *at least as well*.

We think it by all means advisable that the Mission should touch at Macao for information, but any official communication with the Provincial authorities should be studiously avoided unless some *strong* necessity for it arises as they are generally corrupt & disposed to take advantage of Foreigners.

The Commissioner could there determine understandingly what course to pursue: it is *possible* that it might be expedient for the Mission to land at Canton & go by the inland route to Pekin, but it is more likely that the mouth of the Peiho river would be selected by the Commissioner; in the first named case it would probably be advisable that the Fleet should proceed as far North as the Season of the year would permit to be done without risk.

After 1st September it is said to be unsafe for large vessels to remain in the anchorages of the Gulf of Pee-chi-lee & from 1st November to 1st April very strong northerly winds and currents prevail in the China Sea, which make the passage from Canton up the coast difficult for dull sailing vessels, but the passage is constantly made by trading vessels; In fact it depends upon the energy of the Officer selected to command the Expedition & upon the stringency of the orders given him regarding despatch, whether the passage from here to Canton shall be made at the *worst* Season in 120 days, or *double that time*, & whether the passage thence to the northern ports in China shall be delayed till the Fair Monsoon sets in, or shall be made in 20 to 30 days at *any* season.

It is not to be denied that our merchant ships usually go quicker from place to place than ships of war but if the public service requires despatch we do not doubt that Officers can be found who *will make* our fast sailing ships-of-war do as well as our cargo ships, or better. Other things being equal the best season for the Mission to arrive at Macao would be 1st March as it could then after getting all needful information & taking on board the Linguists, reach the mouth of Peiho at the beginning of the pleasant season.

Fourthly. When the time is fixed for the departure of the Mission it would be well to write by the [first] sailing merchantmen which constantly offer, to the Consul at Canton[3] directing him to inform the provincial authorities of its appointment & that it will proceed to the mouth of the Peiho, as was done by the former English Embassy. This will give time to communicate with the Court [at] Pekin & if any serious objection is made to this route to the Capitol, the Commissioner might deem it advisable to take some other.

Fifthly. It is of the very first importance that provision should be made for the employment of at least two competent Foreign Linguists, as the Chinese Linguists cannot be depended upon to translate the simplest communication; To secure this object it would be well to authorize the Consul to engage several persons, subject entirely to the confirmation of the Commissioner on his arrival.

Dr. [Peter] Parker, now there, might be induced to [serve] & his celebrity among the Chinese as a Surgeon added [to] some experience in the Chinese language would [render] him a *great accession* to the Mission.

Sixthly. Regarding the time when it is desired that the Mission should reach Canton, we could form a better opinion if we knew whether the English intend to send an Envoy to Pekin or to seek for the present no further direct intercourse with the Court of Pekin than that which resulted in the late Treaty. In the first case there are obvious advantages in allowing them to take the lead.

We have to deal with a peculiar people, where a precedent established by the Court becomes in practice the law of the Land.

However well-disposed they may be towards us, it is to be feared, if it lies with us to send the first Embassy to their Court that they will, if only for the sake of establishing a precedent, contest every inch of ground, & endeavour to get the advantage of us in settling points of etiquette, which tho' apparently unimportant may if yielded lead to much mischief hereafter.

On the other hand if they have to deal with the English first, & endeavour to play this game, a threat of an appeal to arms will soon bring them to reason & on whatever terms they receive the British Embassy, both their pride & policy will induce them to accord the same to us.

We should say then that the sooner our Mission can reach the Court *after* a successful British or other European Embassy has arrived there the better.

Let us follow them if possible before their relations are so permanently fixed with the Court of Pekin as to encourage them to use their influence *secretly* to have obstacles thrown in our way.

3. The U.S. consul at Canton from April 1843 to September 1855 was Paul Siemen Forbes (1808–1886) of Massachusetts.

If the English do not intend to send an Embassy or if from any cause it devolves upon our Mission to precede theirs, we think that *infinite caution is required at every step.*

It would be a great error to suppose that if we fail in our negotiations we shall be no worse off than if the attempt had never been made.

The Chinese want no political intercourse with Foreign Nations & they will only permit it either thro' fear of armed compulsion, or through a politic desire to offer to us *voluntarily* what has been *forced* upon them by others.

If they find that we recede from any position once taken they learn our weakness & will take advantage of it to the utmost.

All experience in Chinese affairs shows that no Foreign Nation ever yet gained any disputed point by peaceful negotiations.

To all representations of the expediency or mutual benefit, or the justice of any change in ex[ternal] relations they made one unanswerable reply, "We neither want your trade nor your alliance; if you choose to come here & conform to 'old custom' you are graciously permitted to do so; if you do not like our ways you can go home."

So far from gaining anything by repeated attempts to negotiate, the English have uniformly brought on them[selves] impositions & restrictions, until the contempt which the Chinese had acquired for Foreigners betrayed them into ill treatment of the British Superintendent Capt. [Charles] Elliott, which gave an excuse for the late successful armed negotiation.

We now share their newly acquired respect for the power of Foreign Nations; & we have reason to believe that without any Mission we shall share all t[he] practical commercial advantages granted to any Nation.

These solid advantages we must hazard if we involve ourselves in any discussion with the Chinese; for [we] assume that our Government is not prepared to *enforce* the reception of an Envoy, the formation of a Commercial treaty or even the admission of our Commerce upon equal terms with the English. What then is to be done?

We can only say that the opportunity now seems more favorable, than any before offered for sending an Embassy, that the chances are much in favour of its honorable reception, & of our securing *by treaty*, what we should otherwise only enjoy by sufferance; equality with other Nations in the China trade; but if the Chinese will not freely grant what we ask let us not get involved in a contest of diplomacy with them: Let our Envoy feel his way carefully & take up no position from which there is any reasonable chance of his being driven, for if he once begins to yield, there will be no end to his retreat until the condition of our trade is made worse than it ever was.

Let him constantly remember that he is in point of fact no stronger than those who have so often been defeated & that the English will be very ready if any discussion does arise to say to the Chinese, "Make your own terms with these Americans, their government is so different from ours that there is no probability of their going to War."

If our Envoy does not see his way clear to *succeed* let him *do nothing*, let him await the proper time to act & if his patience fail, let him be authorized to return home leaving some member of his Mission; as Chargé to wait for an opening, for we repeat our firm conviction that he can only do mischief by attempting to gain any point by negotiation which the Chinese are not ready to grant out of compliment to our neutrality in the late war, out of policy, or finally out of an unfounded fear of our enforcing our demands by arms.

Seventhly. As to the objects which we should attempt to gain by treaty.;

All we could ask would be, to admit our trade upon the same footing with the most favored nation & we think it would be impolitic to accept anything less.

Rather than do so the Mission should withdraw without making any treaty; but we have hardly a doubt that this much will be readily granted.

Finally. If consistent with the usages of the Department we think time would be gained by having the Secretary of Legation sail as early as possible for China, so as to be there a considerable time in advance of the Mission for the purpose of getting acquanted with Chinese affairs, making the necessary arrangements with Linguists, & collecting such information for the Commissioner as would enable him to act promptly on his arrival.

It would undoubtedly be best for the Secretary to hold no communication with the authorities of Canton.

If in the foregoing remarks we have committed the error of extending the expression of our opinions to points, where the Government only want facts we must trust for our excuse to the latitude apparently allowed by the Circular to which we are replying. We are Sir very respectfully Your obedt Servants   J[ohn] M[urray] Forbes,   Sam[uel] Cabot, R[obert] B[ennett] Forbes,   Tho[mas] H[andasyd] Perkins,   Wm Appleton,   N[athan] Appleton,   John L[owell] Gardner

LS. DNA, RG 59 (Misc. Letters). Forbes (1813–1898) went on a trading voyage to China at the age of fifteen and remained there seven years. During his time there he made a fortune. The letter is also signed by Samuel Cabot (1784–1863), a partner in the firm of Thomas Handasyd Perkins, and by Perkins himself; Robert Bennett Forbes (1804–1889), the China merchant and sea captain; William Appleton (1786–1862), a merchant and later a congressman from Suffolk, Massachusetts; Nathan Appleton (1779–1861), the textile manufacturer and congressman from Boston; and John Lowell Gardner (1804–1884), East Indian merchant and railroad magnate.

TO CALEB CUSHING

No. 1.   Department of State,
Sir,   Washington, May 8, 1843.

You have been appointed by the President Commissioner to China, and Envoy Extraordinary and Minister Plenipotentiary of the United States to the Court of that Empire. The ordinary general or circular letter of instructions will be placed in your hands, and another letter stating the composition or organization of the Mission, your own allowances, the allowance of the Secretary, and other matters connected with the expenditures about to be incurred under the authority of Congress.[1]

It now remains for this Department to say something of the political objects of the Mission, and the manner in which it is hoped these objects may be accomplished. It is less necessary, than it might otherwise be, to enter into a detailed statement of the considerations which have led to the institution of the Mission, not only as you will be furnished with a copy of the President's communication to Congress, recommending provision to be made for the measure,[2] but also as your connexion with Congress has necessarily brought those considerations to your notice and contemplation.

Occurrences happening in China within the last two years have resulted in events which are likely to be of much importance as well to the United States as to the rest of the civilized world. Of their still more important consequences to China herself, it is not necessary here to speak. The hostilities which have been carried on between that Empire and England, have resulted, among other consequences, in opening four important ports to English commerce, viz: Amoy, Ning-po, Shang-hai, and Fow-chow-fow.

These ports belong to some of the richest, most productive, and most populous provinces of the Empire; and are likely to become very important marts of commerce. A leading object of the Mission in which you are now to be engaged, is to secure the entry of American ships and cargoes into these ports, on terms as favorable as those which are enjoyed by English merchants. It is not necessary to dwell, here, on the great and well known amount of imports of the productions of China into the United States. These imports, especially in the great article of tea, are not likely to be diminished. Heretofore they have been paid for in the precious metals, or, more recently, by bills drawn on London. At one time, indeed, American paper, of certain descriptions was found to be an available remittance. Latterly a considerable trade has sprung up in the export of certain American manufactures to China. To augment these

1. See No. 2. DW to Cushing, May 8, 1843, DNA, RG 59 (Instructions, China).

2. See *Messages and Papers*, 4: 211–214.

exports, by obtaining the most favorable commercial facilities, and cultivating, to the greatest extent practicable, friendly commercial intercourse with China, in all its accessible ports, is matter of moment to the commercial and manufacturing, as well as the agricultural and mining, interests of the United States. It cannot be foreseen how rapidly, or how slowly, a people of such peculiar habits as the Chinese, and apparently so tenaciously attached to their habits, may adopt the sentiments, ideas, and customs of other nations. But if prejudiced and strongly wedded to their own usages, the Chinese are still understood to be ingenious, acute, and inquisitive. Experience, thus far, if it does not strongly animate and encourage efforts to introduce some of the arts and the products of other countries into China, is not, nevertheless, of a character, and such as should entirely repress those efforts. You will be furnished with accounts, as accurate as can be obtained, of the history and present state of the export trade of the United States to China.

As your Mission has in view only friendly and commercial objects, objects, it is supposed, equally useful to both countries, the natural jealousy of the Chinese, and their repulsive feeling towards foreigners, it is hoped may be in some degree removed or mitigated by prudence and address on your part. Your constant aim must be to produce a full conviction on the minds of the Government and the people that your Mission is entirely pacific; that you come with no purposes of hostility or annoyance; that you are a messenger of peace, sent from the greatest Power in America to the greatest Empire in Asia, to offer respect and good will, and to establish the means of friendly intercourse. It will be expedient, on all occasions, to cultivate the friendly dispositions of the Government and people, by manifesting a proper respect for their institutions and manners, and avoiding, as far as possible, the giving of offence, either to their pride or their prejudices. You will use the earliest, and all succeeding occasions, to signify that the Government which sends you has no disposition to encourage, and will not encourage, any violation of the commercial regulations of China, by citizens of the United States. You will state, in the fullest manner, the acknowledgment of this Government, that the commercial regulations of the Empire, having become fairly and fully known, ought to be respected by all ships, and all persons, visiting its ports; and if citizens of the United States, under these circumstances, are found violating well known laws of trade, their Government will not interfere to protect them from the consequences of their own illegal conduct. You will, at the same time, assert and maintain, on all occasions, the equality and independence of your own country. The Chinese are apt to speak of persons coming into the Empire from other nations as tribute bearers to the Emperor [Tao Kuang/Dao Guang]. This idea has been fostered perhaps by the costly parade embassies of England. All ideas of this kind, respecting your Mission, must, should they arise, be immediately met by a declaration, not made ostentatiously, or in a manner reproachful towards others, that you are no tribute bearer; that your Government pays tribute to none; and expects tribute from none; and that even as to presents, your Government neither makes nor accepts presents. You will signify to all Chinese authorities, and others, that it is deemed to be quite below the dignity of the Emperor of China, and the President of the United States of America to be concerning themselves with such unimportant matters as presents from one to the other; that the intercourse between the heads of two such Governments should be made to embrace only great political questions, the tender of mutual regard, and the establishment of useful relations.

It is of course desirable that you should be able to reach Pekin, and the Court and person of the Emperor, if practicable. You will accordingly at all times signify this as being your purpose and the object of your Mission; and perhaps it may be well to advance as near to the Capital as shall be found practicable, without waiting to announce your arrival in the country. The purpose of seeing the Emperor in person must be persisted in as long as may be becoming and proper. You will inform the officers of the Government that you have a letter of friendship from the President of the United States to the Emperor, signed by the President's own hand,[3] which you cannot deliver except to the Emperor himself, or some high officer of the Court in his presence. You will say, also, that you have a commission conferring on you the highest rank among representatives of your Government; and that this, also, can only be exhibited to the Emperor, or his chief officer. You may expect to encounter, of course, if you get to Pekin, the old question of the *Kotou.*

In regard to the mode of managing this matter, much must be left to your discretion, as circumstances may occur. All pains should be taken to avoid the giving of offence, or the wounding of the national pride; but, at the same time, you will be careful to do nothing which may seem, even to the Chinese themselves, to imply any inferiority on the part of your Government, or any thing less than perfect independence of all Nations. You will say that the Government of the United States is always controlled by a sense of religion and of honor; that Nations differ in their religious opinions and observances; that you cannot do any thing which the religion of your own country, or its sentiments of honor, forbid; that you have the most profound respect for His Majesty the Emperor; that you are ready to make to him all manifestations of homage which are consistent with your own sense; and that you are sure His Majesty is too just to desire you to violate your own duty; that you should deem yourself quite unworthy to appear before His Majesty as peace bearer from

3. The letter from Tyler to the emperor, dated July 13, 1843, is in *Senate Documents*, Serial 457, No. 138, p. 8.

a great and powerful Nation, if you should do any thing against religion or against honor, as understood by the Government and people in the country you come from. Taking care thus in no way to allow the Government or people of China to consider you as tribute bearer from your Government, or as acknowledging its inferiority, in any respect, to that of China, or any other Nation, you will bear in mind, at the same time, what is due to your own personal dignity and the character which you bear. You will represent to the Chinese authorities, nevertheless, that you are directed to pay to His Majesty the Emperor the same marks of respect and homage as are paid by your Government to His Majesty the Emperor of Russia [Nicholas I], or any other of the great Powers of the world.

A letter, signed by the President, as above intimated, and addressed to the Emperor, will be placed in your hands. As has been already stated, you will say that this letter can only be delivered to the Emperor, or to some one of the great officers of State, in his presence. Nevertheless, if this cannot be done, and the Emperor should still manifest a desire to receive the letter, you may consider the propriety of sending it to him, upon an assurance that a friendly answer to it shall be sent, signed by the hand of the Emperor himself.

It will be no part of your duty to enter into controversies which may exist between China and any European State; nor will you, in your communications, fail to abstain altogether from any sentiment, or any expression, which might give to other Governments just cause of offence. It will be quite proper, however, that you should, in a proper manner, always keep before the eyes of the Chinese the high character, importance, and power of the United States. You may speak of the extent of their territory, their great commerce spread over all seas, their powerful navy, every where giving protection to that commerce, and the numerous schools and institutions established in them, to teach men knowledge and wisdom. It cannot be wrong for you to make known, where not known, that the United States, once a country subject to England, threw off that subjection, years ago, asserted its independence, sword in hand, established that independence, after a seven years' war, and now meets England upon equal terms upon the ocean and upon the land. The remoteness of the United States from China, and still more the fact that they have no colonial possessions in her neighborhood, will naturally lead to the indulgence of a less suspicious and more friendly feeling, than may have been entertained towards England, even before the late war between England and China. It cannot be doubted that the immense power of England in India must be regarded by the Chinese Government with dissatisfaction, if not with some degree of alarm. You will take care to show strongly how free the Chinese Government may well be from all jealousy arising from such causes towards the United States. Finally, you will signify, in decided terms, and a positive manner, that the Government of the United States would find it impossible to remain on terms of friendship and regard with the Emperor, if greater privileges, or commercial facilities, should be allowed to the subject of any other Government, than should be granted to citizens of the United States.

It is hoped and trusted that you will succeed in making a treaty such as has been concluded between England and China; and if one containing fuller and more regular stipulations could be entered into, it would be conducting Chinese intercourse one step further towards the principles which regulate the public relations of the European and American States. I am, Sir, very respectfully, Your obedient servant,   Danl Webster.

LC. DNA, RG 59 (Instructions, China). Published in *Senate Documents*, 28th Cong., 2d sess., Serial 457, No. 138, pp. 1–5.

Resignation

Daniel Webster had decided to resign as secretary of state by March 1, 1843 (see DW to Hiram Ketchum, March 1, 1843, below). On March 29, he wrote Edward Everett that he intended to prepare the guidelines for the China mission and then to leave the Department of State (see above, DW to Everett, March 29, 1843, "Daniel Webster and the Pacific: The China Mission," pp. 902–903). That is precisely what he did; on the same day that he signed the instruction to Caleb Cushing, he filed his formal letter of resignation.

Webster enjoyed being secretary of state, and he did not leave that office without regret. He liked the "large and comprehensive" duties of the first executive position that he had ever held. Webster had also found the secretaryship to be intellectually stimulating. "Every day" had provided "new acquisitions of knowledge" (DW to Ketchum, March 1, 1843, below). He felt, moreover, that there were further contributions that he could make to American foreign policy as secretary of state, such as ensuring the effective implementation of the joint-cruising convention for the suppression of the African slave trade (see DW to Everett, April 27, 1843, below).

Why, then, did Webster resign? There were several reasons. Tyler had become anathema to most of Webster's Whig friends, and even his wife had "imbibed a mortal aversion" to his remaining in the Tyler cabinet (DW to Ketchum, March 1, 1843, below). Webster might have withstood the advice of friends and the feelings of Caroline Le Roy Webster, but in the winter of 1842–1843 President Tyler began moving toward two objectives that the secretary of state could not support. The first was the annexation of Texas, and the second was Tyler's nomination for the presidency by the Democratic party.

Tyler began to lay definite plans to bring Texas into the Union in December 1842. Since Webster opposed the annexation of that slaveholding republic, the president needed to ease him out of the cabinet. The proposed special mission to Britain to resolve the Oregon question was designed to provide Webster with a graceful exit. It would have allowed him to avoid a humiliating resignation and to gain a prestigious assignment, but in February 1843 the House Committee on Foreign Affairs refused to recommend the appropriation of the necessary funds. By March, as Isaac Van Zandt, the Texan chargé d'affaires to the United States, wrote, Webster was very much in the way of plans to annex Texas (Van Zandt to Anson Jones, March 15, 1843, in *Tylers*, 3:129).

Tyler's quest for the presidency in his own right was of equal importance in explaining Webster's decision to resign. By April, the president was actively pursuing the rapprochement with loco foco Democrats that would culminate in a third-party movement in 1843–1844. These political maneuverings placed Webster in what he characterized as an increasingly "awkward" position (see above, DW to Everett, April 23, 1843, "Daniel Webster and the Pacific: The China Mission," pp. 915–917).

Despite their policy and political differences, Tyler and Webster parted without rancor. The secretary of state's letter of resignation was gracious, as was the president's response, in which he thanked Webster for "the zeal and ability" with which he had discharged his duties (see DW to Tyler and Tyler to DW, May 8, 1843, below). In the years after 1843, Tyler and Webster continued to disagree over issues. Webster, for example, publicly opposed the annexation of Texas. Nevertheless, their personal friendship remained intact until Webster's death in 1852. According to the president's son, Tyler often remarked that "of all the gentlemen that filled his cabinet at different times, not one" had been "more agreeable" than Daniel Webster (*Tylers*, 2:264).

As for Webster, his stated ambition had been to leave office with the country in "as good condition" as he had found it (see DW to Thomas B. Curtis, April 29, 1843, below). In light of the Treaty of Washington alone, it can be said that he had achieved that goal. Webster felt that his greatest accomplishment as secretary of state had been to preserve "the peace of the world" by resolving the outstanding issues between Britain and the United States (DW to Everett, April 27, 1843, below). In addition, he formulated the precedent-setting doctrine of self-defense, extended the official protection of the U.S. government to American missionaries serving in foreign lands, secured the release of the Santa Fé prisoners, contributed to the "McLeod law," drafted the Tyler Doctrine, and authored the instructions for the China mission.

Despite his many achievements in foreign policy, Webster left office with his political influence shattered. By staying in the Tyler cabinet as long as he had, Webster had defied Henry Clay and the Whig majority. The price of apostasy would be a long uphill struggle to regain status in the Whig party. Indeed, Webster was so pessimistic about his political prospects in 1843 that he did not expect to return to public life (see DW to Ketchum, March 1, 1843, below). He was not much of a prophet. Not only did he return to public life, but in 1850 Daniel Webster also again became secretary of state.

TO HIRAM KETCHUM

Private, & Strictly Confidential   Mar. 1. 1843
My Dear Sir,   8. A.M.

I shall leave the Department of State; but in coming to this conclusion, I have acted against my own clear judgment; & the consciousness of this gives me some uneasiness. I believe, that by remaining in my present situation, I could do more for my own reputation, & for the good of the Country, than I can ever hope to do in any other. But I yield, to the judgment of friends, whom I know to be sincere, & who may be right, & to the importunity of my Wife [Caroline Le Roy Webster], who has imbibed a mortal aversion to my remaining in the Cabinet.

The number of days or weeks, which may elapse before I can wind up some pending business, I do not feel able at present to say; but the thing itself is decided.

When I leave this table, I shall do it with regret, because the duties of the office are agreeable. They fall in with the general course of my studies and attainments, so far as I have any attainments, are of a large & comprehensive nature, & lead, every day, to new acquisitions of knowledge.

Nor shall I leave this office, with any expectation, on the whole, of ever returning to public life. There are but few situations which I could take, & I am so far advanced in years, & such is the State of the Country, & its political parties, that it does not seem to me to be likely that that, which I could take, will come in my way.

This is entirely for yourself; I conclude it, with thanking you heartily for your true friendship, & constant support, thro some troubled & trying scenes; & may Heaven preserve & bless you, & yours!   Danl Webster

ALS. NhD.

TO EDWARD EVERETT

Private.
My Dear Sir: April 27th, 1843.

I send you a copy of the Intelligencer of March 25th, and a copy also of that paper of yesterday, for the purpose of drawing your attention to an Editorial Article in each, for which I am responsible.[1] X in yesterday's paper is Horace Everett.[2] Disappointment, or some other cause has, led him to rank himself with the *disaffected*. Whatever *I* do, he is sure to find

1. In the unsigned editorial of March 25, DW discussed the slave trade convention of 1824 between the United States and Britain. The similarly unsigned commentary in the Washington, D.C., *National Intelligencer* of April 26, entitled "Re-

marks by the Editors," sarcastically criticized the notion that the U.S. government should make representations in behalf of American vessels actually engaged in the illegal slave trade.

fault with; and though we used to think him a person of some talent, he is always wrong, growing vain and conceited, in his old age, without growing wiser.

I took a good deal of pains, to procure a solemn declaration to be made by the President, in his message to the Senate, to the effect that this Government could not and would not interfere, in behalf of American vessels, found engaged in the Slave trade.[3] I deem this to be of the very first importance. It will check designs of Slave dealings, in their bud. I already see consequences of magnitude resulting from it. It is now understood, that in every application for interference, made at this Department, for alleged detention by British Cruisers, the case will be strictly inquired into, and closely sifted; and if just suspicion be awakened, not only will no interference be made, but the case itself will be referred to the prosecuting officers of the Government. I wish Lord Aberdeen and Sir Robert Peel may be assured of this.

I feel great confidence, that the two Governments may escape all future collision, or disputes, about the right of search, and this is a most desirable object with me. I am well aware, that misled by circumstances, American vessels may sometimes be mistaken for English, or Spanish, or Portuguese. But, in general, serious consequences in such cases may be avoided, if parties conduct themselves with moderation and prudence. I trust that my last public despatch to you,[4] the Instructions given to our African Squadron,[5] the President's Message to the Senate, already referred to, and such use as you may properly make of this private letter,—will satisfy the British Government of the sincere desire felt by us to accomplish the object, common to both Governments, without prejudice or danger to the just rights of either.

Nothing gives me more satisfaction, in leaving this Department, than the humble trust, that the questions, which have existed between the two Countries, and which have been subjects of discussion, since I came into office, will be found to have been settled, in a manner honorable to both, likely to promote harmony and good will between them, and to preserve the peace of the world. Your's always cordially,   Danl Webster

LS. MHi. Published in Curtis, 2:165–166.

2. In the *Intelligencer* of April 26, Vermont congressman Horace Everett (1779–1851; Brown 1797) denounced the idea of allowing British cruisers any jurisdiction over American shipping. Everett served in the U.S. House of Representatives from 1829 to 1843.

3. See Tyler's message of January 9, 1843, in *Messages and Papers*, 4:215–220, esp. p. 218.

4. See above, DW to Everett, March 28, 1843, "The Aftermath and Implementation of the Treaty of Washington: The 'Visit' and 'Search' Controversy," pp. 807–817.

5. See above, Upshur to Perry, March 30, 1843, "The Aftermath and Implementation of the Treaty of Washington: The 'Visit' and 'Search' Controversy," pp. 817–823.

TO THOMAS BUCKMINSTER CURTIS

Washington

My Dear Sir   April 29 '43

I am under much obligation to your friend, Mr G[eorge] T[icknor] Curtis, for the kind article which he has taken the pains to prepare for the press,[1] & which you send me.

Too partial in his Estimate of my ability to serve the public, he is still no more than just to the motives which influenced my conduct, in a moment rather critical, to my reputation, & to the preservation of the regard of friends.

The result has been fortunate, I must say, beyond my expectation. Candor, good sense, & honest patriotism, appear to be resuming their just influence, sooner than I looked for.

I expect, My Dear Sir, to be among you, with my green bag under my arm, in next month.

If I leave the public service, & the honor of the Country, in as good condition as I found them, my ambition ought to be satisfied. Yrs truly

Danl Webster

ALS. NhD.

TO JOHN TYLER

My Dear Sir;   May 8, 1843.

I have caused a formal resignation of my office, as Secretary of State, to be filed in the Department.[1]

In ceasing to hold any connexion with the Government, I remember with pleasure the friendly feelings and personal kindness which have subsisted between yourself and me, during the time that I have borne a part in your counsels. And I must be permitted to add, that while entertaining the best wishes for your personal welfare, there is, at the same time, no one who more sincerely or ardently desires the prosperity, success, and honor of your Administration. Yours very truly,

(signed) Danl Webster

Copy. DLC. Published in Curtis, 2:211. Endorsed by DW: "Copy of letter of resignation, & answer May 8. 1843." Tyler's answer is published below.

FROM JOHN TYLER

My Dear Sir: Washington, May 8th, 1843.

I have received your note of this day,[1] informing me of your formal resignation of the office of Secretary of State.

1. Not found. Curtis (1812–1894; Harvard 1832) was a member of the Massachusetts House of Representatives from 1840 to 1843.
1. See mDW 55569–55572.
1. See above.

It only remains for me to reciprocate, as I truly do, the warm sentiments of regard which you have expressed towards me, and to return you
my thanks for the zeal and ability with which you have discharged the
various and complicated duties which have devolved upon you. I do not
mean to flatter you in saying, that, in conducting the most delicate and
important negotiations, you have manifested powers of intellect of the
highest order, and in all things a true American heart.

Take with you, my dear Sir, into your retirement, my best wishes for
your health, happiness, and long life. (Signed) John Tyler.

Copy. DLC. Published in Curtis, 2:211–212.

Index

Individuals identified in the *Dictionary of American Biography* are denoted by an asterisk immediately following the name, those in the *Biographical Directory of the American Congress* by a dagger. Identifications in the present volume are indicated by page numbers set in boldface type.

Abd al-Rahman, 295, 297, 298; letter from T. N. Carr, 296–297
Abdülmejid I, sultan of Ottoman Empire, **235n**, 278, 281
Aberdeen, George Hamilton-Gordon, Lord, xix, 33, **94n**, 22, 123–124, 163, 166–167, 170, 329, 367, 468, 484, 488, 489, 705, 718–719, 728, 740, 784, 767, 854, 889, 890, 911, 916; *Creole* case 560, 561; sees Edward Everett, 173–177; on McLeod affair, 167; maps, Northeast boundary, 787, 788, 790, 792, 793, 794; Northeast boundary, 562–563, 780; Northwest boundary, 701–702, 806–807, 830, 831, 832–833, 838–839, 843; on right of search, 520n, 546, 717, 728–730, 769, 772, 802, 803, 804, 808–809, 810, 813–815, 823–825, 845–846; letters from Ashburton, 544–547, 569–571, 680–681; letter to H. S. Fox, 832–833
Abert, John James:* letter to J. C. Spencer, 683–**689**
Acadia, 585–586n, 586
Acordada prison (Mexico City), 413
Acre, Syria, 38n
"Act to Provide Further Remedial Justice in the Courts of the United States." *See* Law of August 29, 1842
Adams, Allensworth, 391, 392n, 399, 414, 417, 419
Adams, Demas: letter to, 171–**173**
Adams, John,*† **515–516**, 634, 782, 783
Adams, John (Santa Fé prisoner), 399

Adams, John Quincy,*† xvii, xxv–xxvi, 7, **12**, 23n, 193, 372n, 375, 576n, 710, 713, 830, 831, 854, 855, 856, 879; *Amistad* case, 12, 194; on China mission, 881, 882, 896, 899; Texas boundaries, 379; opinion of DW, xv, 328; letter from J. Farris, 285–286; letter from D. F. Webster, 286
Adams, William (father of Allensworth and John): letter to R. P. Letcher, 399–400; letter from DW, 411
Adams, William (maritime law expert), **577n**
Addington, Henry Unwin, **791**, 828, 829, 831
Africa: joint cruising, 699, 710. *See also* Slave trade
African seizures, 108, 163, 174–175, 530
Ahmad Bey (Tunis), **23n**, 290, 292, 293
Alamo, siege of, 430
Alagash River, 631
Alburg[h], Vt., 152, 153, 154, 158, 159
Alexander II, czar of Russia, **236**
Alexander, Sir William, **596**, 598
Algiers, 291, 292
Alhambra, The (Washington Irving), 7
Allen, Charles,† **567n**
Allen, William, 697, 701
Allenburgh, Canada, 148
Almodovar, Ildefónso Diez de Ribera, Count, **225n**, 226, 227–228
Almonte, Juan Nepomuceno, **444n**,

LIBRARY OF CONGRESS CATALOGING IN PUBLICATION DATA (REVISED)

Webster, Daniel, 1782–1852.
  The papers of Daniel Webster.

  Series 3: Kenneth E. Shewmaker, editor.
  Includes indexes.
  Contents: ser. 1 Correspondence: v. 1, 1798–1824.
v. 2, 1825–1829. v. 3, 1830–1834. v. 4, 1835–
1839. —   — ser. 3 Diplomatic papers: v. 1. 1841–
1843.
    1. United States—Politics and government—1783–1865—
Sources. 2. Webster, Daniel, 1782–1852. I. Wiltse,
Charles Maurice, 1907–   . II. Moser, Harold D.
III. Shewmaker, Kenneth E., 1936–   . IV. Dartmouth
College. V. Title.
E337.8.W373   973.5′092′4 [B]   73-92705
ISBN 0-87451-245-X (ser. 3, v. 1)